Directory of Unpublished
Experimental Mental Measures

VOLUME 8

BERT A. GOLDMAN

DAVID F. MITCHELL

...

Series Editors: Bert A. Goldman and David F. Mitchell

American Psychological Association, Washington, DC

Published by
American Psychological Association
750 First Street, NE
Washington, DC 20002
www.apa.org

To order
APA Order Department
P.O. Box 92984
Washington, DC 20090-2984
Tel: (800) 374-2721, Direct: (202) 336-5510
Fax: (202) 336-5502, TDD/TTY: (202) 336-6123
Online: www.apa.org/books/
Email: order@apa.org

In the U.K., Europe, Africa, and the Middle East, copies may be ordered from
American Psychological Association
3 Henrietta Street
Covent Garden, London
WC2E 8LU England

Typeset in Bodoni and Futura by EPS Group, Inc., Easton, MD

Printer: Automated Graphic Systems, White Plains, MD
Technical/Production Editor: Rosemary Moulton
Cover designer: Minker Design, Bethesda, MD

ISBN: 155798-951-6

Printed in the United States of America
First Edition

Contents

Preface v

CHAPTER 1: Achievement 3

CHAPTER 2: Adjustment—Educational 12

CHAPTER 3: Adjustment—Psychological 31

CHAPTER 4: Adjustment—Social 99

CHAPTER 5: Adjustment—Vocational 149

CHAPTER 6: Aptitude 184

CHAPTER 7: Attitudes 185

CHAPTER 8: Behavior 222

CHAPTER 9: Communication 274

CHAPTER 10: Concept Meaning 282

CHAPTER 11: Creativity 283

CHAPTER 12: Development... 285

CHAPTER 13: Family... 289

CHAPTER 14: Institutional Information 334

CHAPTER 15: Motivation.. 373

CHAPTER 16: Perception.. 396

CHAPTER 17: Personality 476

CHAPTER 18: Preference.. 503

CHAPTER 19: Problem Solving and Reasoning 514

CHAPTER 20: Status... 522

CHAPTER 21: Trait Measurement................................... 523

CHAPTER 22: Values.. 535

CHAPTER 23: Vocational Evaluation 550

CHAPTER 24: Vocational Interest................................... 574

Author Index... 592

Subject Index 606

About the Editors 669

...

Preface

Purpose: This *Directory of Unpublished Experimental Mental Measures* Vol. 8, marks the latest in a series of publications designed to fill a need for reference tools in behavioral and social sciences research. The authors believe there is an ongoing need for a directory such as this to enable researchers to determine what types of noncommercial experimental test instruments are currently in use. This reference provides researchers with ready access to information about recently developed or recently used experimental measurement scales. The instruments are not evaluated, but the information given about each test should make it possible for researchers to make a preliminary judgment of its usefulness. It does not provide all necessary information for researchers contemplating the use of a particular instrument. It does describe basic test properties and in most cases identifies additional sources from which technical information concerning an instrument can be obtained.

Development: Thirty-six relevant professional journals available to the authors were examined. The following list includes those journals that, in the judgment of the authors, contained instruments of value to researchers in education, psychology, and sociology. Foreign journals were not surveyed for use in this directory. Measures published only in dissertations were excluded as a matter of expediency and because the microfilm abstracts generally contain minimal information.

American Journal of Sociology
Brain and Language
Career Development Quarterly
Child Development
Child Study Journal
Educational and Psychological Measurement
Educational Research Quarterly
Gifted Child Quarterly
Journal of Applied Psychology
Journal of College Student Development
Journal of Consulting and Clinical Psychology
Journal of Counseling Psychology
Journal of Creative Behavior
Journal of Educational Psychology
Journal of Educational Research
Journal of Experimental Education
Journal of General Psychology
Journal of Marriage and the Family
Journal of Occupational Psychology
Journal of Personality Assessment
Journal of Psychopathology and Behavioral Assessment
Journal of Research and Development in Education

Journal of Research in Personality
Journal of School Psychology
Journal of Social Psychology
Journal of Vocational Behavior
Measurement and Evaluation in Counseling and Development
Perceptual and Motor Skills
Personnel Psychology
Psychological Reports
Research in Higher Education
School Counselor (since October 1997, *Professional School Counselor*)
Social Psychology Quarterly
Sociology of Education
Vocational Guidance Quarterly

Volume 8 lists tests described in the 1996–2000 issues of the previously cited journals. An attempt was made to omit commercially published standardized tests; task-type activities such as memory word lists used in serial-learning research; and achievement tests developed for a single, isolated course of study. Readers should not assume that the instruments described herein form a representative sample of the universe of unpublished experimental mental measures.

Organization: Following is a brief description of each of the 24 categories under which the authors grouped the measures of Volume 8.

Achievement: Measures learning and/or comprehension in specific areas. Also includes tests of memory and tests of spatial ability.

Adjustment—Educational: Measures academic satisfaction. Also includes tests of school anxiety and teacher–student relationships.

Adjustment—Psychological: Evaluates conditions and levels of adjustment along the psychological dimension including, for example, tests of mood, fear of death, anxiety, and depression.

Adjustment—Social: Evaluates aspects of interactions with others. Also includes tests of alienation, conformity, need for social approval, social desirability, interpersonal attraction and sensitivity, acculturation, and racial and ethnic identity.

Adjustment—Vocational: Identifies burnout, vocational maturity, job-related stress, job frustration, job satisfaction, and so forth.

Aptitude: Predicts success in given activities.

Attitudes: Measures reaction to and beliefs about a variety of experiences and objects.

Behavior: Measures general and specific types of activities such as classroom behavior, leader behavior, alcohol, eating and drug-use behavior, and abusive and violent behavior.

Communication: Evaluates information exchange. Also includes tests of self-dsclosure, leader–member exchange, and feedback.

Concept Meaning: Measures one's understanding of words and other concepts. Also includes tests of conceptual structure and style and information processing.

Creativity: Measures ability to reorganize data or information into unique configurations. Also includes tests of divergent thinking.

Development: Measures emerging characteristics, primarily for preschool ages. Also includes tests of cognitive and moral development.

Family: Measures intrafamily relations. Also includes tests of marital satisfaction, nurturance, and parental interest.

Institutional Information: Evaluates institutions and their functioning,

community and involvement satisfaction, and organizational climate.
Also includes job characteristics and distributive and procedural justice.

Motivation: Measures goal strength. Also includes measures of curiosity
and need to achieve.

Perception: Determines how one sees self and other objects. Includes tests
dealing with empathy, imagery, locus of control, self-concept, self-
esteem, and time. Also includes role conflict.

Personality: Measures general personal attributes. Also includes biographical information, defense mechanisms, and temperament.

Preference: Identifies choices. Also includes tests of object preference,
taste preference, and sex-role preference.

Problem Solving and Reasoning: Measures general ability to reason
through a number of alternative solutions, to generate such solutions
to problems, and so forth.

Status: Identifies a hierarchy of acceptability.

Trait Measurement: Identify and evaluates unitary traits. Also includes
tests of anger, authoritarianism, blame, cheating, and narcissism.

Values: Measures worth one ascribes to an object or activity. Includes
tests of moral, philosophical, political, and religious values.

Vocational Evaluation: Evaluates a person for a specific position. Also
includes client–therapist working alliance and mentoring.

Vocational Interest: Measures interest in specific occupations and voca-
tions as well as interest in general categories of activity. Also includes
organizational commitment and career commitment.

The choice of the category under which each test was grouped was
determined by the purpose of the test and/or its apparent content. The
authors attempted to include basic facts for each test. Three facts are
always listed: test name, purpose, and source. In addition, at least four
of the following facts (starred in the list below) had to be present in the
source for the test to be listed in the *Directory*: number of items, time
required, format, reliability, validity, or related research. Readers should
note that, if no information was given for any one of the starred facts,
the heading was not included in the entry. For example, if no information
about validity was given in the source, validity was not listed in the test
entry.

Test Name

The name of the test listed in the directory was usually given by the author
of the paper in which it was found. When a test name was not given in
the source, one was created for it by the authors of the *Directory*.

Purpose

The general purpose of each scale was usually stated in the source or was
suggested by its name. When available, additional detail about the test's
purpose is given.

Description

Number of items: The number of items in a scale as stated in the source.

Time required: Few scales are administered under a time constraint.
When they are, the time requirements are specified here.

Format: The description of the format of the scales varied widely in the
source. The authors of the *Directory* have presented the essential char-

acteristics of the format such as general type (Likert, true–false, checklist, and semantic differential). Less common formats are briefly described in additional detail as needed.

Statistics

Reliability: When available, reliabilities and the *N*s on which they were based are reported. Commonly reported reliabilities are alpha, split-half, item–total, and KR-20.

Validity: When available, validity data were reported. The authors of the *Directory* have also included correlations with other tests and group difference information that help define the characteristic being measured by the test.

Source

Author

Title

Journal (includes date of publication, volume, and page number)

Related Research

The purpose of this section is to provide additional information about the test. In some cases the original source of the test is given. If an existing test was revised for use with a special population, the original version may be cited. In other cases, a publication that offered additional technical information is listed.

Readers should note that the numbers within the Index refer to test numbers, not page numbers.

As a convenience to readers, the authors have incorporated the indexes from the seven previous volumes in this Index and in doing so have converted all page numbers in Volume 1 to test numbers. Thus, numbers 1 through 339 refer to tests in Volume 1, numbers 340 through 1034 refer to tests in Volume 2, numbers 1035 through 1595 refer to tests in Volume 3, numbers 1596 through 2369 refer to tests in Volume 4, numbers 2370 through 3665 refer to tests in Volume 5, numbers 3666 through 5363 refer to tests in Volume 6, and numbers 5364 through 7441 refer to tests in Volume 7. Numbers 7442 to 10209 refer to tests in Volume 8.

The authors thank Julia Capone for supervising the typing of much of the manuscript. Also thanks to Sonja Beach and Suzanne Williams for typing segments of the manuscript. Special appreciation is expressed to Richard Allen for doing the complex and time-consuming final sorting and processing of the entries included in this volume. Their efforts made it possible to finish the manuscript on schedule. A portion of the cost of preparing this manuscript was supported by a grant from the School of Education Department of Curriculum and Instruction at the University of North Carolina at Greensboro. Further, the authors wish to thank the American Psychological Association for continuing the publication of the *Directories*.

Bert Arthur Goldman
David F. Mitchell

Directory of Unpublished

Experimental Mental Measures

VOLUME 8

CHAPTER 1
Achievement

7442

Test Name: AIDS AWARENESS QUESTIONNAIRE

Purpose: To measure awareness and knowledge of AIDS.

Number of Items: 39

Format: True/false format. All items are presented.

Reliability: Alpha was .70. Split-half reliability was .72.

Author: Peltzer, K., et al.

Article: AIDS awareness of secondary school pupils in the northern province of South Africa.

Journal: *Psychological Reports*, December 1998, *83*(3) Part 1, 955–958.

Related Research: MacLachlan, M., et al. (1997). AIDS education for youth active learning: A school based approach from Malawi. *International Journal of Educational Development, 17*, 41–50.

7443

Test Name: AUTHOR RECOGNITION TEST

Purpose: To measure amount of reading people do.

Number of Items: 25

Format: Included nonauthors as foils.

Reliability: Coefficient alpha was .80.

Validity: Correlation with other variables ranged from .34 to .75.

Author: Lee, S.-Y., et al.

Article: The Author Recognition Test and Vocabulary Knowledge: A replication.

Journal: *Perceptual and Motor Skills*, December 1997, *85*(3, Part 2), 1428–1430.

Related Research: West, R., et al. (1993). Reading in the real world and its correlates. *Reading Research Quarterly, 28*, 35–50.

7444

Test Name: CHAPMAN-COOK SPEED OF READING TEST

Purpose: To assess comprehension and speed of reading.

Number of Items: 25

Time Required: 2.5 minutes

Format: There is one disconcordant word in each of 25 paragraphs, which are to be found by the respondent.

Reliability: Test-retest (2 weeks) reliabilities ranged from .63 to .82.

Validity: Correlations with other variables ranged from .23 to .60.

Author: Holtzer, R., et al.

Article: Chapman-Cook Speed of Reading Test: Performance of college students.

Journal: *Perceptual and Motor Skills*, April 1998, *86*(2), 687–690.

Related Research: Chapman, J., & Cook, S. (1923). A principle of the single variable in a speed of reading cross-out test. *Journal of Educational Research, 8*, 389–396.

7445

Test Name: CHILDREN'S AUTHOR CHECKLIST

Purpose: To enable parents to identify authors of children's books from a list of authors and foils.

Number of Items: 60

Format: Parents check those book authors believed to be those of children's books. All items are presented.

Reliability: Spearman-Brown coefficient was .88.

Validity: Correlations with other variables ranged from −.23 to .73.

Author: Senechal, M., et al.

Article: Knowledge of storybooks as a predictor of young children's vocabulary.

Journal: *Journal of Educational Psychology*, September 1996, *88*(3), 520–536.

7446

Test Name: CHILDREN'S COGNITIVE ABILITY SCALES

Purpose: To obtain parent ratings of their children's cognitive abilities in terms of fluid and crystallized intelligence.

Number of Items: 20

Format: Four-point scales are anchored by 0 (not at all) and 3 (very much). All items are presented.

Reliability: Alphas ranged from .60 to .89 across subscales.

Validity: Correlations with other variables ranged from −.23 to .83.

Author: Waschbusch, D. A., et al.

Article: Are parents accurate reporters of their child's cognitive abilities?

Journal: *Journal of Psychopathology and Behavioral Assessment*, March 2000, *22*(1), 61–77.

7447

Test Name: CHILDREN'S TITLE CHECKLIST

Purpose: To enable parents to identify children's books from a list of books and foils.

Number of Items: 61

Format: Parents check those book titles believed to be children's books. All items are presented.

Reliability: Spearman-Brown coefficient was .86.

Validity: Correlations with other variables ranged from −.34 to .73.

Author: Senechal, M., et al.

Article: Knowledge of storybooks as a predictor of young children's vocabulary.

Journal: *Educational Psychology*, September 1996, *88*(3), 520–536.

7448

Test Name: COGNITIVE ABILITY TEST

Purpose: To measure cognitive ability.

Number of Items: 30

Format: Includes verbal, quantitative, and reasoning skills.

Reliability: Coefficient alpha was .87.

Validity: Correlation with self-reported high school grades was .10 and with educational level achieved, the correlation was .26. Correlations with additional variables ranged from −.12 to .32.

Author: Weekley, J. A., and Jones, C.

Article: Video-based situational testing.

Journal: *Personnel Psychology*, Spring 1997, *50*(1), 25–49.

7449

Test Name: EARTH SCIENCE ACHIEVEMENT TEST

Purpose: To measure earth science achievement.

Number of Items: 26

Format: Items involved knowledge, comprehension, and application. Responses are multiple-choice. Sample items are presented.

Reliability: Coefficient alpha was .82.

Author: Chang, C. Y., and Mao, S. L.

Article: Comparison of Taiwan science students' outcomes with inquiry-group versus traditional instruction.

Journal: *Journal of Educational Research*, July/August 1999, *92*(6), 340–346.

Related Research: Mao, S. L., & Chang, C. Y. (1997). *The effects of instructional strategies on ninth-grade students' skills of data interpretation and concept formation*. Unpublished report. National Science Council No. NSC 86-2511-S-003-024.

7450

Test Name: ESSENTIAL ELEMENTS OF ELEMENTARY SCHOOL MATHEMATICS TEST —REVISED

Purpose: To measure meaningful knowledge of mathematical content.

Number of Items: 25

Format: Multiple-choice format. Sample items are presented.

Reliability: Coefficient alpha was .86.

Author: Quinn, R. J.

Article: Effects of mathematics methods courses on the mathematical attitudes and content knowledge of preservice teachers.

Journal: *Journal of Educational Research*, November/December 1997, *91*(2), 108–113.

Related Research: White, M. A. (1986). Preservice teachers' achievement in the essential elements of elementary school mathematics: The development of an evaluation instrument (Doctoral dissertation, University of Houston, 1986). *Dissertation Abstracts International*, 47, 2068A.

7451

Test Name: EVERYDAY SPATIAL ACTIVITIES TEST

Purpose: To identify various types of spatial abilities for college students.

Number of Items: 20

Reliability: Test-retest (2 weeks) reliability was .83.

Validity: Correlations with external criterion measures of spatial abilities were .35 and .32.

Author: Groth-Marnat, G., and Teal, M.

Article: Block design as a measure of everyday spatial ability: A study of ecological validity.

Journal: *Perceptual and Motor Skills*, April 2000, *90*(2), 522–526.

Related Research: Lunnenborg, P. W., & Lunnenborg, C. A. (1986). Everyday spatial activities for studying differential spatial experience and vocational behavior. *Journal of Vocational Behavior, 28*, 135–141.

7452

Test Name: FIGURAL INTERSECTION TEST

Purpose: To measure M-power (the number of separate schemes that a subject can simultaneously activate).

Number of Items: 36

Format: The subject's task is to find the area of intersection and mark it with a dot.

Reliability: Split-half reliability was .87.

Author: Niaz, M., and Caraucan, E.

Article: 'Learning-to-learn': A neo-Piagetian interpretation of the potential for learning.

Journal: *Perceptual and Motor Skills*, June 1998, *86*(3) Part 2, 1291–1298.

Related Research: Pascal-Leone, J., & Burtis, P. J. (1974). *FIT: Figural Intersection Test, a group measure of M-capacity.* (Unpublished manuscript, York University, North York, Ontario).

7453

Test Name: HIV KNOWLEDGE QUESTIONNAIRE

Purpose: To assess knowledge of HIV transmission and prevention.

Number of Items: 45

Reliability: Alpha was .45. Stability coefficients ranged from .91 (2-weeks) to .90 (12-weeks).

Validity: A single factor was obtained with diverse samples.

Author: Carey, M. P., et al.

Article: Enhancing motivation to reduce the risk of HIV infection for economically disadvantaged urban women.

Journal: *Journal of Consulting and Clinical Psychology*, August 1997, *65*(4), 531–541.

Related Research: Cary, M. P., et al. (1997). The HIV Knowledge Questionnaire's development and evaluation of a reliable, valid, and practical self-administered questionnaire. *AIDS and Behavior, 1*, 61–74.

7454

Test Name: HIV/AIDS AND THE LAW SCALE

Purpose: To assess knowledge of the law regulating issues related to HIV and AIDS.

Number of Items: 10

Format: True/false format. All items are presented.

Reliability: Cronbach alpha was .74. Test-retest reliability was .83.

Validity: Correlation with knowledge of AIDS/HIV was .41

Author: Paniagua, F. A.

Article: Knowledge of laws regulating issues related to HIV and AIDS: Development of the HIV/AIDS and the law scale.

Journal: *Psychological Reports*, June 1999, *84*(3) Part 2, 1345–1353.

7455

Test Name: HIV/AIDS KNOWLEDGE INVENTORY

Purpose: To assess HIV/AIDS knowledge.

Number of Items: 25

Format: True/false format.

Reliability: Alpha coefficients ranged from .57 to .63.

Author: Guth, L. J., et al.

Article: Student attitudes toward AIDS and homosexuality: The effects of a speaker with HIV.

Journal: *Journal of College Student Development*, September/October 2000, *41*(5), 503–512.

Related Research: Carney, J., et al. (1994). The relationship between attitudes toward persons who are gay and persons with AIDS, and HIV and AIDS knowledge. *Journal of Counseling and Development, 72*, 646–650.

7456

Test Name: HIV/AIDS KNOWLEDGE SCALE FOR TEACHERS

Purpose: To measure knowledge of HIV/AIDS.

Number of Items: 58

Format: Eighteen item responses are anchored by 1 (true) and 3 (not true). Seventeen item responses are anchored by 1 (very likely) and 5 (do not know). Twenty-five responses are anchored by 1 (strongly agree) and 5 (strongly disagree).

Reliability: Cronbach alphas varied from .65 to .69 across subscales.

Author: Peltzer, K.

Article: Knowledge and attitudes about HIV/AIDS of a sample of school teachers in South Africa.

Journal: *Psychological Reports*, December 2000, *87*(3), Part 2, 1065–1066.

Related Research: Koch, P. B., & Singer, M. D. (1998) HIV/AIDS Knowledge and Attitudes Scales for Teachers. In C. M. Davis et al. (Eds.), *Handbook of sexuality-related measures* (pp. 317–320). London: Sage.

7457

Test Name: HIV/AIDS RISK KNOWLEDGE SCALE

Purpose: To measure HIV/AIDS knowledge.

Number of Items: 40

Format: True/false format.

Reliability: Cronbach alpha was .74.

Author: Paniagua, F. A., et al.

Article: Knowledge of laws regulating issues related to HIV/AIDS: Development of the HIV/AIDS and the law scale.

Journal: *Psychological Reports*, June 1999, *84*(3) Part 2, 1345–1353.

Related Research: Paniagua, F. A., et al. (1997). The assessment of HIV/AIDS knowledge, attitudes, self-efficacy, and susceptibility among psychiatrically hospitalized adolescents. *Journal of HIV/AIDS Prevention and Education for Adolescents and Children, 1,* 65–104.

7458

Test Name: KIDNEY DISEASE QUESTIONNAIRE

Purpose: To measure knowledge of kidney disease and its treatment.

Number of Items: 30

Format: Multiple-choice format.

Reliability: Alpha was .85.

Validity: Correlations with other variables ranged from −.51 to .32.

Author: Katz, R. C., et al.

Article: Knowledge of disease and dietary compliance in patients with end-stage renal disease.

Journal: *Psychological Reports*, February 1998, *82*(1), 331–336.

Related Research: Devins, G., et al. (1990). The Kidney Disease Questionnaire: A test for measuring patient knowledge about end-stage renal disease. *Journal of Clinical Epidemiology, 3,* 297–307.

7459

Test Name: KNOWLEDGE OF AIDS SCALE

Purpose: To measure knowledge of AIDS.

Number of Items: 22

Format: Yes-no-unsure response categories.

Reliability: Alpha was .77. Spearman-Brown coefficient was .66. Other coefficients ranged from .63 to .82.

Author: Nicholas, L., et al.

Article: Reliability of a knowledge of AIDS scale: A replication.

Journal: *Psychological Reports*, October 1996, *79*(2), 529–530.

Related Research: Zimet, G. D. (1992). Reliability of AIDS knowledge scales: Conceptual issues. *AIDS Education and Prevention, 4,* 334–338.

7460

Test Name: KQ SCALE

Purpose: To measure knowledge of the seriousness of skin cancer,

risk factors for skin cancer, and knowledge of sunscreen use.

Number of Items: 26

Format: True-false format.

Reliability: Alpha was .78.

Author: Rodriguez, J. R.

Article: Promoting healthier behaviors, attitudes and beliefs toward sun exposure in parents of young children.

Journal: *Journal of Consulting and Clinical Psychology*, December 1996, *64*(6), 1431–1436.

Related Research: Katz, R. C., & Jernigan, S. (1991). Brief report: An empirically derived educational program for detecting and preventing skin cancer. *Journal of Behavioral Medicine, 14,* 421–428.

7461

Test Name: MASTERY ORIENTATION SCALE

Purpose: To enable parents to evaluate their child's mastery orientation.

Number of Items: 5

Format: Responses are made on a 5-point scale ranging from 1 (not at all) to 5 (a lot). All items are presented.

Reliability: Coefficient alpha was .67.

Validity: Correlations with other variables ranged from .04 to .38.

Author: Watkins, T. J.

Article: Teacher communications, child achievement, and parent traits in parent involvement models.

Journal: *Journal of Educational Research*, September/October 1997, *91*(1), 3–14.

Related Research: Ames, C., & Archer, J. (1988). Achievement goals in the classroom: Students' learning strategies and motivation process. *Journal of Educational Psychology*, *80*, 260–267.

7462

Test Name: MENTAL ROTATION TEST

Purpose: To measure three-dimensional spatial visualization.

Number of Items: 20

Time Required: 5 minutes for each of two sections.

Format: A standard figure is matched with two identified but rotated figures.

Reliability: Test-retest (1 year) reliability was .80 (*n* = 109).

Author: Achter, J. A., et al.

Article: Multipotentiality among the intellectually gifted: "It was never there and already it's vanishing."

Journal: *Journal of Counseling Psychology*, January 1996, *43*(1), 65–76.

Related Research: Vandenburg, S. G., & Kuse, A. R. (1978). Mental rotation: A group test of three-dimensional spatial visualization. *Perceptual Motor Skills, 47,* 599–604.

7463

Test Name: MULTIPLICATION AND DIVISION OF EXPONENTS DIAGNOSTIC TEST

Purpose: To diagnose students' difficulties in the multiplication and division of exponents.

Number of Items: 38

Format: Includes two parallel sub-tests of 19 items each.

Reliability: Coefficient alpha was .96.

Validity: Correlation with semester mathematics grade was .71.

Author: Birenbaum, M., et al.

Article: On agreement of diagnostic classifications from parallel sub-tests: Score reliability at the micro level.

Journal: *Educational and Psychological Measurement,* August 1997, *57*(4), 559–568.

Related Research: Nasser, F. (1989). *Effects of sex, test anxiety and item sequence on performance of a dispute test in exponents* (in Hebrew). Unpublished M.A. thesis, School of Education, Tel Aviv University.

7464

Test Name: PARENT STORYBOOK TITLE RECOGNITION CHECKLIST

Purpose: To determine the books parents may have encountered while engaging in activities to enhance their children's literacy experiences.

Number of Items: 20

Format: A checklist consisting of book titles interspersed with foils. All items are presented.

Reliability: Spearman-Brown split-half reliability was .82.

Validity: Correlations with other variables ranged from .03 to .62.

Author: Frijters, J. C., et al.

Article: Direct and mediated influences of home literacy and literacy interest on prereaders' oral vocabulary and early written language skill.

Journal: *Journal of Educational Psychology*, September 2000, *92*(3), 466–477.

Related Research: Stanovich, K. E., & West, R. F. (1989).

Exposure to print and orthographic processing. *Reading Research Quarterly, 24,* 402–433.

7465

Test Name: PERFORMANCE ORIENTATION SCALE

Purpose: To enable parents to evaluate their child's performance orientation.

Number of Items: 6

Format: Responses are made on a 5-point scale ranging from 1 (not at all) to 5 (a lot). All items are presented.

Reliability: Coefficient alpha was .78.

Validity: Correlations with other variables ranged from −.28 to .41.

Author: Watkins, T. J.

Article: Teacher communications, child achievement, and parent traits in parent involvement models.

Journal: *Journal of Educational Research*, September/October 1997, *91*(1), 3–14.

Related Research: Ames, C., & Archer, J. (1988). Achievement goals in the classroom: Students' learning strategies and motivation process. *Journal of Educational Psychology, 80,* 260–267.

7466

Test Name: PRACTICAL INTELLECTUAL ASSESSMENT QUESTIONNAIRE

Purpose: To assess practical skills.

Number of Items: 20

Format: Includes skills in social competence, skills lay people perceive as representative of everyday intelligence, and skills designed to tap problem-solving strategies.

Reliability: Alpha coefficients ranged from .70 to .83.

Author: Heng, M. A.

Article: Scrutinizing common sense: The role of practical intelligence in intellectual giftedness.

Journal: *Gifted Child Quarterly,* Summer 2000, *44*(3), 171–182.

Related Research: Berg, C. A. (1987). *Children's knowledge of effective strategies in the solution of everyday problems.* Unpublished doctoral dissertation, Yale University, CT.

7467

Test Name: PROSPECTIVE MEMORY AIDS QUESTIONNAIRE

Purpose: To assess how often individuals use memory aids in the effort to remember to do something in the future.

Number of Items: 18

Format: Respondents report the number of times they used each aid in the past week. All items are presented.

Reliability: Test-retest reliabilities (one month) ranged from .44 to .78 across types of memory aids.

Author: Long, T. E., et al.

Article: Women as middle-aged individuals report using more prospective memory aids.

Journal: *Psychological Reports,* December 1999, *85*(3, Part 2), 1139–1153.

Related Research: Gilewski, M. J., et al. (1990). The memory functioning questionnaire for assessment of memory complaints in adulthood and old age.

Psychology and Aging, 5, 482–490.

7468

Test Name: PURDUE SPATIAL VISUALIZATION TEST: ROTATIONS—MODIFIED

Purpose: To measure teachers' ability to visualize mentally rotations of objects in space.

Number of Items: 20

Time Required: 8 minutes

Reliability: Coefficient alpha was .77. Split-half reliability was .89.

Author: Hassan, M. M., and Abed, A. S.

Article: Differences in spatial visualization as a function of scores on hemisphericity of mathematics teachers.

Journal: *Perceptual and Motor Skills,* April 1999, *88*(2), 387–390.

Related Research: Battista, M. T. (1990). Spatial visualization and gender differences in high school geometry, *Journal for Research in Mathematics Education, 21,* 47–60.

7469

Test Name: SCALE FOR RATING STUDENTS' PARTICIPATION IN THE LOCAL GIFTED EDUCATION PROGRAM

Purpose: To enable gifted teachers to assess the performance of students in the gifted program.

Number of Items: 10

Format: Responses are made on a 0 to 5 scale.

Reliability: Coefficient alpha was .94.

Author: Hunsaker, S. L., et al.

Article: An analysis of teacher nominations and student performance in gifted programs.

Journal: *Gifted Child Quarterly,* Spring 1997, *41*(2), 19–24.

Related Research: Renzulli, J. S., & Westberg, K. (1991). *Scale for rating students' participation in the local gifted education program.* Storrs, CT: University of Connecticut.

7470

Test Name: STERNBERG TRIARC ABILITIES TEST

Purpose: To assess analytical, creative, and practical abilities in the verbal, quantitative, figural, and essay domains.

Number of Items: 36 plus 3 essay items.

Format: Includes 12 subtests: Analytical-Verbal, Analytic-Quantitative, Analytical-Figural, Practical-Verbal, Practical-Quantitative, Practical-Figural, Creative-Verbal, Creative-Quantitative, Creative-Figural, Analytical-Essay, Creative-Essay, and Practical-Essay.

Validity: Correlations with achievement ranged from .30 to .46.

Author: Sternberg, R. L.

Article: A triarchic approach to the understanding and assessment of intelligence in multicultural populations.

Journal: *Journal of School Psychology,* Summer 1999, *37*(2), 145–159.

Related Research: Sternberg, R. L. (1993). *Sternberg Triarchic Test.* Unpublished test.

7471

Test Name: STUDY SKILLS MEASURE

Purpose: To measure study skills.

Number of Items: 21

Format: Includes 3 factors: Study Habits, Study Self-Efficacy, and Firefighter Self-Efficacy. Responses are made on a 7-point agree-disagree scale. Examples are presented.

Reliability: Alpha coefficients ranged from .70 to .87.

Validity: Correlation with other variables ranged from −.49 to .47.

Author: Ryan, A. M., et al.

Article: Test preparation programs in selection contexts: Self-selection and program effectiveness.

Journal: *Personnel Psychology*, Autumn 1998, *51*(3), 599–621.

7472

Test Name: SUICIDE KNOWLEDGE SCALES

Purpose: To assess the knowledge of school counselors about what to do if a student threatens suicide, risk factors associated with suicide attempts, and appropriate school responses to suicide completion.

Number of Items: 35

Format: Checklist format. All items are presented.

Reliability: Test-retest reliabilities ranged from .73 to .85. KR-20 reliabilities ranged from .85 to .89.

Author: King, K. A., et al.

Article: Preventing adolescent suicide: Do high school counselors know the risk?

Journal: *Professional School*

Counseling, April 2000, *3*(4), 255–263.

Related Research: Popenhagen, M. P., et al. (1998). Adolescent suicide: Detection, intervention, and prevention. *Professional School Counseling, 1*, 30–36.

7473

Test Name: TEST OF READING PERFORMANCE (GREEK)

Purpose: To assess letter knowledge, phoneme blending, word identification, morphology knowledge, syntactic knowledge, and passage comprehension.

Number of Items: 483

Reliability: Cronbach alpha was .83 for the full scale.

Validity: Correlations between measured variables ranged from −.10 to .63. Several validity tests are presented.

Author: Sideridis, G. D., and Padeliadu, S.

Article: An examination of the psychometric properties of the Test of Reading Performance using structural equation modeling.

Journal: *Psychological Reports*, June 2000, *86*(3, Part 1), 789–802.

7474

Test Name: VANDENBERG MENTAL ROTATION TEST

Purpose: To measure mental rotation.

Number of Items: 20

Time Required: 5 minutes for each of two sections.

Format: Includes 2 sections: Participants are to match

correctly two out of four choices to a standard.

Reliability: Alpha coefficients were .85 and .87.

Author: Li, C., et al.

Article: Writing Chinese characters and success on Mental Rotation Test.

Journal: *Perceptual and Motor Skills*, June 1999, *88*(3) Part 2, 1261–1270.

Related Research: Vanderberg, S. G., & Kuse, A. R. (1978). Mental rotations, a group test of three-dimensional spatial visualization. *Perceptual and Motor Skills, 48*, 599–604.

7475

Test Name: VISIONING ABILITY SCALE

Purpose: To assess the ability to create mental imagery.

Number of Items: 12

Format: Five-point scales are anchored by 1 (strongly disagree) and 5 (strongly agree). All items are presented.

Reliability: Test-retest reliability was .80. Cronbach alphas ranged from .86 to .87 across samples.

Validity: Correlations with other variables ranged from .03 to .41.

Author: Thoms, P., and Blasko, D.

Article: Preliminary validation of a visioning ability scale.

Journal: *Psychological Reports*, August 1999, *85*(1), 105–113.

7476

Test Name: VISUALIZATION TESTS

Purpose: To measure visualization skills

Format: Includes 4 tests: Cube, Clock, F, and Subtraction. Many of the materials are presented.

Reliability: Test-retest reliabilities ranged from .78 to .90.

Validity: Correlations with visual and nonvisual strategies ranged from −.36 to .73.

Author: Abbate, C. S., and Nuovo, S. F.

Article: Attentional memory and visualization strategies in mental additions.

Journal: *Perceptual and Motor Skills*, December 1998, *87*(3) Part 1, 955–962.

Related Research: Brooks, L. R. (1968). Spatial and verbal components of the act of recall. *Canadian Journal of Psychology*, *16*, 342–361.

Parrott, C. A. (1986). Visual imagery training: Stimulating utilization of imaginal process. *Journal of Mental Imagery*, *10*, 47–64. Paivio, A. (1971). *Imagery and verbal processes*. New York: Holt, Rinehart, and Winston.

7477

Test Name: VIVIDNESS OF HAPTIC MOVEMENT IMAGERY QUESTIONNAIRE

Purpose: To measure the capacity to imagine the sensations of movement.

Number of Items: 24

Format: Responses are made on a 5-point scale ranging from 1 (perfectly clear and as vivid as the real situation) to 5 (no image at all, you only know that you

are thinking of the skill). Directions are presented.

Reliability: Coefficient alpha was .90.

Author: Campos, A., et al.

Article: Vividness of visual and haptic imagery of movement.

Journal: *Perceptual and Motor Skills*, August 1998, *87*(1), 271–274.

Related Research: Isaac, A., et al. (1986). An instrument for assessing imagery of movement: The Vividness of Movement Imagery Questionnaire (VMIQ). *Journal of Mental Imagery*, *10*, 23–30.

7478

Test Name: VIVIDNESS OF VISUAL IMAGERY FOR FACES

Purpose: To measure vividness of visual imagery for faces.

Number of Items: 10

Reliability: Split-half corrected reliability coefficients ranged from .64 to .89.

Validity: Correlation with other variables were .14 (face recognition memory performance) and .40 (control of visual imagery for faces).

Author: McKelvie, S. J.

Article: Split-half reliability of two facial imagery questionnaires.

Journal: *Perceptual and Motor Skills*, December 1998, *87*(3) Part 1, 953–954.

Related Research: McKelvie, S. J. (1993). Vividness of visual imagery for faces as a predictor of facial recognition memory performance: A revised view. *Perceptual and Motor Skills*, *76*, 1083–1088.

7479

Test Name: VIVIDNESS OF VISUAL IMAGERY QUESTIONNAIRE

Purpose: To enable respondents to imagine visual images and to rate the vividness of the image formed.

Number of Items: 16

Format: Responses are made on a 5-point scale ranging from 1 (no image at all, you only know that you are thinking of the object) to 5 (perfectly clear and as vivid as normal vision).

Reliability: Coefficient alpha was .83. Test-retest (2 months) was .67.

Author: Wolmer, L., et al.

Article: Image control from childhood to adolescence.

Journal: *Perceptual and Motor Skills*, October 1999, *89*(2), 471–485.

Related Research: Isaacs, A. R., & Marks, D. F. (1994). Individual differences in mental imagery experience: Developmental changes in specialization. *British Journal of Psychology*, *85*, 479–500.

7480

Test Name: VOCABULARY RECOGNITION TEST

Purpose: To provide a measure of vocabulary knowledge.

Number of Items: 39

Format: Subjects simply indicated whether they knew the words without defining them. Foils of nonwords were included.

Reliability: Coefficient alpha was .84.

Validity: Correlations with the Author Recognition Test ranged from .50 to .75.

Author: Lee, S.-Y., et al.

Article: The Author Recognition Test and vocabulary knowledge: A replication.

Journal: *Perceptual and Motor Skills*, December 1997, *85*(3, Part II), 1428–1430.

Related Research: Anderson, R., & Freebody, P. (1981). Vocabulary knowledge. In J. Guthrie (Ed.), *Comprehension and teaching: Research reviews* (pp. 77–117). Newark, DE: International Reading Association.

7481

Test Name: WATER ORIENTATION AND SWIMMING SKILL INVENTORY

Purpose: To assess water orientation and preliminary swimming skills.

Number of Items: 23

Format: Responses are made on a 5-point scale ranging from 0 (skill not applicable) to 5 (subject fully completes skill independently). All items are presented.

Reliability: Coefficient alpha on first 15 items was .94.

Author: Hutzler, Y., et al.

Article: Effects of a movement

and swimming program on water orientation skills and self-concept of kindergarten children with cerebral palsy.

Journal: *Perceptual and Motor Skills*, February 1998, *86*(1), 111–118.

Related Research: Killian, K. J., et al. (1984). Measuring water orientation and beginner swim skills of autistic individuals. *Adapted Physical Activity Quarterly*, *1*, 287–295.

7482

Test Name: WELLINGHAM-JONES HANDWRITING TEST

Purpose: To measure physical and psychological changes in handwriting.

Number of Items: 7

Format: Responses are made on a 5-point scale.

Reliability: Alpha coefficients ranged from .55 to .78.

Author: Wellingham-Jones, P., and Fearn, W.

Article: Handwriting in assessing treatment for substance abuse.

Journal: *Perceptual and Motor Skills*, April 1998, *86*(2), 577–578.

Related Research: Wellingham-Jones, P. (1993). Handwriting

assessment in substance abuse treatment. *AHAF Journal*, *26*(6), 1–4.

7483

Test Name: WORD CATEGORY SEQUENCING TEST

Purpose: To determine word-category recall.

Number of Items: 40

Format: Includes 5 sets of 8 words each. The 5 word categories are: nouns, verbs, adjectives, adverbs, and prepositions. All items are included.

Reliability: Interjudge and test-retest agreements ranged from 87.5% to 90.3%.

Validity: Correlations with the Porch Index of Communicative Ability ranged from .39 to .79.

Author: Sommers, R. K.

Article: Some relationships between skills in word-category recall and factors in adult aphasia.

Journal: *Perceptual and Motor Skills*, August 1998, *87*(1), 187–198.

Related Research: Sommers, R. K. (1987). *Word-Category Sequencing Test.* Unpublished test. Kent, OH: Kent State University.

CHAPTER 2
Adjustment—Educational

7484

Test Name: ACADEMIC EXAMINATIONS COPING STRATEGIES SCALE

Purpose: To assess coping strategies for academic examinations.

Number of Items: 18

Format: Includes 4 categories: Self-Encouragement, Indirect Preparation, Cognitive Avoidance, and Problem Orientation. Responses are made on a 4-point scale ranging from 1 (never) to 4 (often).

Reliability: Alpha coefficients ranged from .45 to .71.

Author: Lai, J. C. L., and Wan, W.

Article: Dispositional optimism and coping with academic examinations.

Journal: *Perceptual and Motor Skills*, August 1996, *83*(1), 23–27.

Related Research: Hong, Y. Y., & Lam, D. J. (1992). Appraisal, coping, and guilt as correlates of test anxiety. In K. Hagtvet (Ed.), *Advances in test anxiety research* (Vol. 7, pp. 227–287). Amsterdam: Swets and Zeitlinger.

7485

Test Name: ACHIEVEMENT ANXIETY TEST

Purpose: To measure facilitating and debilitating test anxiety.

Format: Includes 2 scales: Facilitating and Debilitating Test Anxiety.

Reliability: Test-retest (10 weeks) reliability coefficients were in the middle .80s. Test-retest (8 months) reliability coefficients were in the middle .70s.

Validity: Correlation with other variables ranged from .37 to .69.

Author: Kazelskis, R., et al.

Article: Mathematics anxiety and test anxiety: Separate constructs?

Journal: *Journal of Experimental Education*, Winter 2000, *68*(2), 137–146.

Related Research: Alpert, R., & Haber, R. N. (1960). Anxiety in academic achievement situations. *Journal of Abnormal and Social Psychology, 61,* 207–215.

7486

Test Name: CAMPUS CONNECTEDNESS SCALE

Purpose: To measure a student's sense of belonging on campus.

Number of Items: 14

Format: Scales range from 1 (strongly disagree) to 6 (strongly agree).

Reliability: Coefficient alpha was .92.

Author: Lee, R. M., and Davis, C., III.

Article: Cultural orientation, past multicultural experience, and a sense of belonging on campus for Asian American college students.

Journal: *Journal of College Student Development*, January/February 2000, *41*(1), 110–115.

Related Research: Lee, R. M., et al. (1999). *A contextual measure of belongingness: The Campus Connectedness Scale.* Unpublished manuscript.

7487

Test Name: CHEMISTRY LABORATORY ANXIETY INSTRUMENT

Purpose: To measure anxiety of students in college chemistry laboratories.

Number of Items: 20

Format: Includes 5 dimensions: Working with Chemicals, Using Equipment and Procedure, Collecting Data, Working with Other Students, and Having Adequate Time. Responses are made on a 5-point scale ranging from 1 (strongly disagree) to 5 (strongly agree). All items are presented.

Reliability: Reliabilities ranged from .73 to .88.

Author: Bowen, C. W.

Article: Development and score validation of chemistry laboratory anxiety instrument (CLAI) for college chemistry students.

Journal: *Educational and Psychological Measurement*, February 1999, *59*(1), 171–185.

Related Research: Abraham, M. A., et al. (1997). The nature and state of general chemistry laboratory courses offered by colleges and universities in the United States. *Journal of Chemical Education, 74,* 591–594.

7488

Test Name: CHILD RATING SCALE

Purpose: To measure adjustment to schools as rule compliance/acting out, anxiety/withdrawal, peer social skills, and school interest.

Number of Items: 24

Format: Three-point scales range from 1 (usually no) to 3 (usually yes). Sample items are presented.

Reliability: Median alpha was .65.

Validity: Correlation with other variables ranged from −.42 to .63.

Author: Hagborg, W. J.

Article: The Child Rating Scale and its use with middle school students.

Journal: *Psychological Reports*, October 2000, *87*(2), 381–388.

Related Research: Primary Mental Health Project. (1995). *Screening and evaluation measures and forms guidelines*. Rochester, NY: Primary Mental Health Project.

7489

Test Name: CHILD RATING SCALE

Purpose: To measure children's self-reported school adjustment.

Number of Items: 25

Format: Responses are made on a 3-point scale: 1 (usually no), 2 (sometimes), and 3 (usually yes). Includes 4 factors: Rule Compliance, Anxiety/Withdrawal, School Interest, and Peer Social Skills. Examples are presented.

Reliability: Alpha coefficients ranged from .82 to .87.

Author: Fagen, D. B., et al.

Article: Relationships between

parent-child relational variables and child test variables in highly stressed urban families.

Journal: *Child Study Journal*, 1996, *26*(2), 87–108.

Related Research: Hightower, A. D., et al (1987). The Child Rating Scale: The development and psychometric refinement of a socioemotional self-rating scale for young children. *School Psychology Review*, *16*, 239–255.

7490

Test Name: CLASS INTEREST QUESTIONNAIRE

Purpose: To measure student's interest in the class.

Number of Items: 13

Format: Includes two sections: Interest in Psychology and Enjoyments of Lectures. Responses are made on a 7-point scale ranging from 1 (strongly disagree) to 7 (strongly agree). All items are presented.

Validity: Correlations with other variables ranged from −.26 to .42.

Author: Harackiewicz, J. M., et al.

Article: Short-term and long-term consequences of achievement goals: Predicting interest and performance over time.

Journal: *Journal of Educational Psychology*, June 2000, *92*(2), 316–330.

Related Research: Harackiewicz, J. M., et al. (1997). Predictors and consequences of achievement goals in the college classroom: Maintaining interest and making the grade. *Journal of Personality and Social Psychology*, *73*, 1284–1295.

7491

Test Name: COLLEGE ADJUSTMENT INVENTORY

Purpose: To assess achievement, conscientiousness and resiliency of college students.

Number of Items: 24

Format: Six-point Likert scales ranged from "strongly disagree" to "strongly agree."

Reliability: Alpha coefficients ranged from .75 to .85 across subscales.

Validity: Correlations with other variables ranged from −.07 to .35.

Author: Tross, S. A., et al.

Article: Not just the usual cast of characters: Using personality to predict college performance and retention.

Journal: *Journal of College Student Development*, May/June 2000, *41*(3), 323–334.

Related Research: Osher, L. W., et al. (1995). *The College Adjustment Inventory*. Technical Report. Success Programs, Georgia Institute of Technology, Atlanta, GA.

7492

Test Name: COLLEGE DISTRESS INVENTORY

Purpose: To measure the mental health of college students.

Number of Items: 44

Format: Six-point scales range from "never" to "always." Sample items are presented.

Reliability: Alpha coefficients ranged from .83 to .93.

Author: Solberg, V. S., et al.

Article: The Adaptive Success Identity Plan (ASIP): A career intervention for college students.

Journal: *Career Development Quarterly*, September 1998, *47*(1), 48–95.

Related Research: Ryan, N. E., et al. (1994). Racial/ethnic, gender and within group differences in college distress. In V. S. Solberg (Chair), *Recommendations for designing culturally relevant college persistence programming*. Symposium conducted at the 102nd Annual Convention of the American Psychological Association, Los Angeles.

7493

Test Name: COLLEGE ENVIRONMENTAL STRESS INDEX—MODIFIED

Purpose: To assess the financial, academic, familial and personal stress of Latino college students.

Number of Items: 39

Format: Five-point Likert format.

Reliability: Coefficient alpha was .81.

Validity: Correlations with other variables ranged from −.23 to .22.

Author: Gloria, A. M., et al.

Article: African American students' persistence at a predominately white university: Influences of social support, university comfort and self-beliefs.

Journal: *Journal of College Student Development*, May/June 1999, *40*(3), 257–268.

Related Research: Munoz, D. G. (1986). Identifying areas of stress for Chicano undergraduates. In M. A. Olivas (Ed.), *Latino college students* (pp. 131–156). New York: Teachers College Press.

7494

Test Name: COLLEGE STRESS INVENTORY

Purpose: To measure stress of college-specific tasks.

Number of Items: 21

Format: Scales range from 1 (never) to 5 (always). Sample items are presented.

Reliability: Coefficient alpha was .89.

Author: Solberg, V. S., et al.

Article: The Adaptive Success Identity Plan (ASIP): A career intervention for college students.

Journal: *Career Development Quarterly*, September 1998, *47*(1), 48–95.

Related Research: Solberg, V. S., et al. (1993). Development of the College Stress Inventory for use with Hispanic populations: A confirmatory analytic approach. *Hispanic Journal of Behavioral Sciences, 15*, 490–497.

7495

Test Name: COLLEGE STUDENT SOCIAL SUPPORT SCALE

Purpose: To measure social support in terms of availability, helpfulness and reception.

Number of Items: Less than 45, but not specified.

Format: Five-point Likert format.

Reliability: Alpha coefficients ranged from .78 to .93 across subscales.

Author: McGrath, P. B., et al.

Article: Introduction of the College Student Social Support Scale: Factor structure and reliability assessment.

Journal: *Journal of College Student Development*, July/August 2000, *41*(4), 415–426.

Related Research: Procidano, M. E., & Heller, K. (1983). Measures of perceived social support from friends and family: Three validation studies. *American Journal of Community Psychology, 11*, 1–24.

7496

Test Name: COLLEGE STUDENTS' PERCEIVED ACADEMIC STRESS SCALE

Purpose: To measure college students' perception of academic stress intensity.

Number of Items: 6

Format: Responses are made on a 7-point scale ranging from 1 (not at all stressful) to 7 (extremely successful). Examples are presented.

Reliability: Alpha coefficients were .78 and .84.

Validity: Correlations with other variables ranged from −.62 to .51.

Author: Nonis, S. A., et al.

Article: Influence of perceived control over time on college students' stress and stress-related outcomes.

Journal: *Research in Higher Education*, October 1998, *39*(5), 587–605.

Related Research: Rocha-Singh, I. A. (1994). Perceived stress among graduate students: Development and validation of the graduate stress inventory. *Educational and Psychological Measurement, 54*, 714–729.

7497

Test Name: COMPUTER ANXIETY SCALE

Purpose: To measure computer anxiety.

Number of Items: 19

Format: Five-point Likert format.

Reliability: Chronbach's alpha was .88.

Validity: Correlations with other variables ranged from −.61 to −.20.

Author: Bozionelos, N.

Article: Psychology and computer use: XLV. Cognitive spontaneity as a correlate of computer anxiety and attitudes toward computer use.

Journal: *Psychological Reports*, April 1997, *80*(2), 395–402.

Related Research: Heinssen, R. K., et al. (1987). Assessing computer anxiety: Development and validation of the Computer Anxiety Rating Scale. *Computers in Human Behavior*, *3*, 49–59.

7498

Test Name: CULTURAL CONGRUITY SCALE

Purpose: To assess congruence between students' personal values and those of the university.

Number of Items: 13

Reliability: Alpha coefficients ranged from .81 to .89.

Validity: Correlations with other variables ranged from −.34 to .46.

Author: Gloria, A. M., et al.

Article: African American students' persistence at a predominately white university: Influences of social support, university comfort and self-beliefs.

Journal: *Journal of College Student Development*, May/June 1999, *40*(3), 257–268.

Related Research: Gloria, A. M., et al. (1996). The validation of the University Environment Scale and the College Congruity Scale.

Hispanic Journal of Behavioral Science, *18*, 533–549.

7499

Test Name: DESIRE FOR CONTROL ON EXAMINATION SCALE

Purpose: To measure the desire for control on examinations.

Number of Items: 13

Format: Responses are made on a 5-point scale ranging from 1 (never applies to me) to 5 (always applies to me). All items are presented.

Reliability: Alpha coefficients were .80 and .78.

Validity: Correlations with other variables ranged from .00 to .34.

Author: Wise, S. L., et al.

Article: The development and validation of a scale measuring desire for control on examination.

Journal: *Educational and Psychological Measurement*, August 1996, *56*(4), 710–718.

7500

Test Name: EDUCATIONAL ETHOS SCALE

Purpose: To assess satisfaction with faculty, instruction and other elements of campus life.

Number of Items: 7

Format: Scales range from 5 (very satisfied) to 1 (very dissatisfied). All items are presented.

Reliability: Coefficient alpha was .85.

Validity: Correlations with other variables ranged from .00 to .41.

Author: Bradley, J. S., and Graham, S. W.

Article: The effect of educational ethos and campus involvement on

self-reported college outcomes for traditional and nontraditional undergraduates.

Journal: *Journal of College Student Development*, September/October 2000, *41*(5), 488–502.

7501

Test Name: ENJOYMENT-INTEREST SUBSCALE

Purpose: To measure pupils' enjoyment-interest in their school physical education program.

Number of Items: 5

Format: Responses are made on a 5-point scale.

Reliability: Coefficient alpha was .76.

Validity: Correlations with other variables ranged from .06 to .47.

Author: Spray, C. M.

Article: Predicting participation in noncompulsory physical education: Do goal perspectives matter?

Journal: *Perceptual and Motor Skills*, June 2000, *90*(3) Part 2, 1207–1215.

Related Research: McAuley, E., et al. (1989). Psychometric properties of the Intrinsic Motivation Inventory in a competitive sport setting: A confirmatory factor analysis. *Research Quarterly for Exercise and Sports*, *60*, 48–58.

7502

Test Name: EXAM STATE ANXIETY

Purpose: To measure test anxiety.

Number of Items: 4

Format: Scales range from 1 (strongly disagree) to 5 (strongly agree). Sample items are presented.

Reliability: Coefficient alphas ranged from .88 to .93.

Validity: Correlations with other variables ranged from −.18 to .58.

Author: Chen, G., et al.

Article: Examination of relationships among trait-like individual differences, state-like individual differences, and learning performance.

Journal: *Journal of Applied Psychology,* December 2000, 85(6), 835–847.

Related Research: Riskind, J. H., & Maddux, J. E. (1993). Loomingness, helplessness, and fearfulness: An integration of harm-looming and self-efficacy models of fear. *Journal of Social and Clinical Psychology, 12,* 73–89.

7503

Test Name: FOREIGN LANGUAGE CLASSROOM ANXIETY SCALE

Purpose: To assess the degree of anxiety felt by students during foreign language class.

Number of Items: 33

Format: Likert-type questionnaire

Reliability: Alpha coefficients were .93 and .94. Test-retest (8 weeks) reliability coefficient was .93.

Validity: Correlations with other variables ranged from −.46 to .16

Author: Onwuegbuzie, A. J., et al.

Article: Cognitive, affective, personality, and demographic predictors of foreign-language achievement.

Journal: *Journal of Educational Research,* September/October 2000, 94(1), 3–15.

Related Research: Horowitz,

E. K., et al (1986). Foreign language classroom anxiety. *Modern Language Journal, 70,* 125–130.

7504

Test Name: FRESHMAN TRANSITION QUESTIONNAIRE

Purpose: To measure adjustment among foreign students in Japan.

Number of Items: 31

Format: Four-point response scales.

Reliability: Alphas ranged from .90 to .91.

Author: Jon, Y. H., and Fukuda, H.

Article: Comparison of differences in the association of social support and adjustment between Chinese and Japanese students in Japan: A research note.

Journal: *Psychological Reports,* August 1996, 79(1), 107–112.

Related Research: Uehara, A. (1988). [Cross-cultural adjustment for foreign students.] In Faculty of Education, Hiroshima University (Ed.) [*Theoretical and practical studies on language acquisition and cross-cultured adjustment*] (pp. 111–124). Hiroshima: Faculty of Education, Hiroshima University. [In Japanese].

7505

Test Name: FRIEDBEN TEST ANXIETY SCALE

Purpose: To measure adolescent test anxiety.

Number of Items: 23

Format: Includes 3 subscales: Social Derogation, Cognitive Obstruction, and Tenseness. All items are presented.

Reliability: Alpha coefficients ranged from .81 to .91.

Validity: Correlation with other variables ranged from .52 to .84.

Author: Friedman, I. A., and Bendas-Jacob, O.

Article: Measuring perceived test anxiety on adolescents: A self-report scale.

Journal: *Educational and Psychological Measurement,* December, 1997, 47(6), 1035–1046.

7506

Test Name: GENERAL, ACADEMIC, AND SOCIAL HASSLES SCALE FOR STUDENTS

Purpose: To assess college student hassles experienced during the past month.

Number of Items: 84

Format: Includes 3 areas: General Hassles, Academic Hassles, and Social Hassles. Responses indicate frequency. Examples are presented.

Reliability: Reliabilities exceeded .90.

Author: Dunkley, D. M., et al.

Article: The relation between perfectionism and distress: Hassles, coping and perceived social support as mediators and moderators.

Journal: *Journal of Counseling Psychology,* October 2000, 47(4), 437–453.

Related Research: Blankenstein, K. R., & Flett, G. L. (1993). *Development of the General Hassles Scale for Students.* Unpublished manuscript.

7507

Test Name: GIBB EXPERIMENTAL TEST OF TESTWISENESS

Purpose: To test the cue-use component of testwiseness.

Number of Items: 70

Format: Multiple-choice format. Includes 7 subskills: Alliterative cues, Length cues, Grammar cues, and Giveaway cues.

Reliability: KR-20 reliability coefficient was .72. Test-retest (2 weeks) reliability was .64.

Author: Harmon, M. G., et al.

Article: Confirmatory factor analysis of the Gibb Experimental Test of Testwiseness.

Journal: April 1996, *56*(2), 276–286.

Related Research: Gibb, B. (1964). *Testwiseness as secondary cue response* (doctoral dissertation, Stanford University), Ann Arbor, MI: University Microfilms (No. 64-7643).

7508

Test Name: HIGH SCHOOL SOCIAL AND ACADEMIC INTEGRATION SCALE

Purpose: To measure peer relationships, parental influence, non-classroom teacher interaction, school importance, teachers and intellectual growth, personal academic satisfaction and faculty and peer concern.

Number of Items: 36

Format: Scales range from 1 (strongly disagree) to 5 (strongly agree).

Reliability: Alpha coefficients ranged from .55 to .79.

Author: Corbin, S. S., et al.

Article: Principal components of a scale measuring social and academic integration in high school.

Journal: *Educational Research Quarterly*, June 1997, *20*(4), 37–49.

Related Research: Pascarella, E. T., & Terenzini, P. T. (1980). Predicting freshman persistence and voluntary dropout decisions from a theoretic model. *Journal of Higher Education*, *51*, 60–75.

7509

Test Name: HOPE SCALE

Purpose: To measure students' hope about achieving their goals.

Number of Items: 12

Format: Responses are made on a 4-point Likert-type scale ranging from 1 (agree) to 4 (disagree). Sample items are presented.

Reliability: Alpha coefficients ranged from .74 to .84, Test-retest (3 weeks) reliability was .85, test-retest (8 weeks) reliability was .73.

Validity: Correlations with other variables ranged from −.57 to .51.

Author: Jackson, C. C., and Neville, H. A.

Article: Influence of social identity attitudes on African American college students' vocational identity and hope.

Journal: *Journal of Vocational Behavior*, August 1998, *53*(1), 97–113.

Related Research: Snyder, C. R., et al. (1991). The will and the ways: Development and validation of an individual-differences measure of hope. *Journal of Personality and Social Psychology*, *60*, 570–585.

7510

Test Name: IDENTIFICATION WITH SCHOOL QUESTIONNAIRE

Purpose: To assess school identification.

Number of Items: 16

Format: Responses are made on a 6-point agree-disagree response scale.

Reliability: Coefficient alpha was .82.

Author: Voelkl, K. E., and Frone, M. R.

Article: Predictors of substance use at school among high school students.

Journal: *Journal of Educational Psychology*, September 2000, *92*(3), 583–592.

Related Research: Voelkl, K. E. (1996). Measuring students' identification with school. *Educational and Psychological Measurement*, *56*, 760–770.

7511

Test Name: IDENTIFICATION WITH THE UNIVERSITY SCALE

Purpose: To measure identification with the university one attends.

Number of Items: 16

Format: Scales range from 1 (strongly disagree) to 7 (strongly agree). Sample items are presented.

Reliability: Internal consistency was .84.

Authors: Zea, M. C., et al.

Article: Predicting intention to remain in college among ethnic minority and nonminority students.

Journal: *Journal of Social*

Psychology, April 1997, *137*(2), 149–160.

Related Research: Luthanen, R., & Crocker, J. (1992). A collective self-esteem scale: Self-evaluation of one's social identity. *Personality and Social Psychology Bulletin, 18*, 302–318.

7512

Test Name: INSTITUTIONAL COMMITMENT SCALE

Purpose: To determine the confidence students have in their institutional choice, and their perceptions of institutional fit and quality.

Number of Items: 4

Format: Responses are made on a 5-point Likert scale ranging from "strongly agree" to "strongly disagree."

Reliability: Coefficient alpha was .78.

Validity: Correlations with other variables ranged from −.38 to .42.

Author: Sandler, M. E.

Article: Career decision-making self-efficacy, perceived stress, and an integrated model of student persistence: A structural model of finances, attitudes, behavior, and career development.

Journal: *Research in Higher Education*, October 2000, *41*(5), 537–580.

Related Research: Pascarella, E., & Terenzini, P. (1979). Interaction effects in Spady's and Tinto's conceptual models of college dropouts. *Sociology of Education, 52*, 197–210.

7513

Test Name: INTELLECTUAL ACHIEVEMENT RESPONSIBILITY QUESTIONNAIRE

Purpose: To measure students' beliefs about responsibility for educational achievement outcomes.

Number of Items: 34

Format: A forced-choice scale.

Validity: Correlation with the Hopelessness Scale for Children was −.29.

Author: Wehmeyer, M. L., and Palmer, S. B.

Article: Factor structure and construct validity of scores on the Hopelessness Scale for Children with students with cognitive disabilities.

Journal: *Educational and Psychological Measurement*, August 1998, *58*(4), 661–667.

Related Research: Crandall, V. C., et al. (1965). Children's beliefs in their own control of reinforcements in intellectual-academics achievement situations. *Child Development, 33*, 643–661.

7514

Test Name: INTENTION OF SEEKING COUNSELING INVENTORY

Purpose: To indicate the likelihood that a college student will seek counseling.

Number of Items: 17

Format: Includes 3 factors: Psychological and Interpersonal Concerns, Academic Concerns, and Drug Use Concerns. Responses are made on a 6-point scale ranging from 1 (very unlikely) to 6 (very likely).

Reliability: Alpha coefficients ranged from .71 to .90.

Validity: Correlations with other variables ranged from −.01 to .35.

Author: Cepeda-Benito, A., and Short, P.

Article: Self-concealment, avoidance of psychological services, and perceived likelihood of seeking professional help.

Journal: *Journal of Counseling Psychology*, January 1998, *45*(1), 58–64.

Related Research: Cash, T. F., et al. (1975). When counselors are heard but not seen: Initial impact of physical attractiveness. *Journal of Counseling Psychology, 22*, 273–279.

7515

Test Name: INVOLVEMENT SCALE

Purpose: To identify parental school involvement.

Number of Items: 3

Format: Responses are made on a 3-point scale ranging from 1 (never) to 3 (frequently).

Reliability: Coefficient alpha was .81.

Author: Griffith, J.

Article: Relation of parental involvement, empowerment, and school traits to student academic performance.

Journal: *Journal of Educational Research*, September/October 1996, *90*(1), 33–41.

Related Research: Reynolds, A. J. (1992). Comparing measures of parental involvement and their effects on academic achievement. *Early Childhood Research Quarterly, 7*(3), 441–462.

7516

Test Name: LEP/ESL NEEDS SCALE

Purpose: To assess needs of ESL students.

Number of Items: 9

Format: Scales range from 1 (much needed) to 4 (not needed at all). All items are presented.

Reliability: Coefficient alpha was .73 (student) and .79 (teacher).

Author: Lopes, S. A.

Article: What is still needed in English as a Second Language K-12 teaching?

Journal: *Educational Research Quarterly,* June 2000, *23*(4), 52–69.

Related Research: Long, M. H., & Richards, J. C. (Eds.). (1987). *Methodology in TESOL: A book of readings.* Massachusetts: Heinle & Heinle.

7517

Test Name: LIFE EVENTS SURVEY FOR COLLEGIATE ATHLETES

Purpose: To assess the impact of stressors.

Number of Items: 69

Format: Scales range from −4 (extremely negative) to 4 (extremely positive). Sample items are presented.

Reliability: Test-retest reliabilities ranged from .76 to .84.

Validity: Correlations with another athlete stress scale ranged from .22 to .52.

Author: Petrie, T. A., and Stoever, S.

Article: Academic and nonacademic predictors of female student athletes' academic performances.

Journal: *Journal of College Student Development,* November/December 1997, *38*(6), 599–608.

Related Research: Petrie, T. A.

(1992). Psychosocial antecedents of athletic injury: The effects of life stress and social support on women collegiate gymnasts. *Behavioral Medicine, 18,* 127–138.

7518

Test Name: LONELINESS AND SOCIAL DISSATISFACTION QUESTIONAIRE

Purpose: To measure children's affective experience in school.

Number of Items: 27

Format: Responses are either "yes," "no," or "sometimes." Examples are presented.

Reliability: Coefficient alpha was .75.

Author: Birch, S. H., and Ladd, G. W.

Article: The teacher-child relationship and children's early school adjustment.

Journal: *Journal of School Psychology,* Spring 1997, *35*(1), 61–79.

Related Research: Cassidy, J., & Asher, S. R. (1992). Loneliness and peer relations in young children. *Child Development, 63,* 350–365.

7519

Test Name: LONELINESS SCALE

Purpose: To examine feelings of loneliness at school.

Number of Items: 16

Format: Responses are made on a 5-point scale ranging from 1 (that's not true at all for me) to 5 (that's always true for me).

Reliability: Coefficient alpha was .86.

Validity: Correlations with other variables ranged from −.42 to .47.

Author: Juvonen, J., et al.

Article: Peer harassment, psychological adjustment, and school functioning in early adolescence.

Journal: *Journal of Educational Psychology,* June 2000, *92*(2), 349–359.

Related Research: Asher, S. R., & Wheeler, V. A. (1985). Children's loneliness: A comparison of rejected and neglected peer status. *Journal of Counseling & Clinical Psychology, 53,* 500–505.

7520

Test Name: MATERNAL SCHOOL INVOLVEMENT SCALE

Purpose: To indicate maternal school involvement.

Number of Items: 15

Format: Responses are either 0 (mother never involved) or 1 (mother had been involved).

Reliability: Coefficient alpha was .86.

Validity: Correlation's with other variables ranged from −.18 to .27.

Author: Brody, G. H., and Flor, D. L.

Article: Maternal resources, parenting practices, and child competence in rural, single-parent African American families.

Journal: *Child Development,* June 1998, *69*(3), 803–816.

Related Research: Brody, G. H., et al. (1995). Linking family processes and academic competence among rural African American youths. *Journal of Marriage and the Family, 57,* 567–579.

7521

Test Name: MATHEMATICS ANXIETY INDEXES

Purpose: To measure dread, anxiety, and dislike of mathematics.

Number of Items: 7

Format: Five-point scales are anchored by 1 (not at all in agreement) and 5 (completely in agreement). All items are presented.

Reliability: Alphas ranged from .60 to .76 across subscales.

Validity: Correlations with other variables ranged from −.47 to .11.

Author: Abu-Hilal, M. M.

Article: A structural model for predicting mathematics achievement: Its relation with anxiety and self-concept in mathematics.

Journal: *Psychological Reports*, June 2000, *86*(3, Part 1), 835–847.

Related Research: Ahmad, S. S. (1988). Psychological, personal, and cognitive correlates of math anxiety among Gulf college students. *The Arab Journal of Humanities*, 3, 136–177.

7522

Test Name: MATHEMATICS ANXIETY QUESTIONNAIRE

Purpose: To assess one's negative affect reactions to mathematics and worry about performance in mathematics.

Number of Items: 11

Format: Includes two scales: Negative Affective Reactions Scale and the Worry Scale.

Reliability: Alpha coefficients were .76 and .82. Split-half reliability was .89.

Validity: Correlations with other variables ranged from .44 to .59.

Author: Kazelskis, R., et al.

Article: Mathematics anxiety and test anxiety: Separate constructs?

Journal: *Journal of Experimental Education*, Winter 2000, *68*(2), 137–146.

Related Research: Wigfield, A., & Meece, J. L. (1988). Math anxiety in elementary and secondary school students. *Journal of Educational Psychology*, *80*(2), 210–216.

7523

Test Name: MATHEMATICS ANXIETY SCALE

Purpose: To measure math anxiety.

Number of Items: 10

Format: Five-point scales.

Reliability: Split-half reliability was .92.

Validity: Correlations with other math anxiety scales ranged from .68 to .78.

Author: Lussier, G.

Article: Sex and mathematical background as predictors of anxiety and self-efficacy in mathematics.

Journal: *Psychological Reports*, December 1996, *79*(3) Part 1, 827–833.

Related Research: Betz, N. E. (1978). Prevalence, distribution, and correlates of mathematics anxiety in college students. *Journal of Counseling Psychology*, 25, 441–448.

7524

Test Name: MATHEMATICS ANXIETY SCALE

Purpose: To measure mathematics anxiety.

Number of Items: 12

Format: Responses are made on a 5-point Likert-type scale ranging from "strongly agree" to "strongly disagree."

Reliability: Split-half reliability was .89.

Author: Kazelskis, R.

Article: Some dimensions of mathematics anxiety: A factor analysis across instruments.

Journal: *Educational and Psychological Measurement*, August 1998, *58*(4), 623–633.

Related Research: Fennema, E., & Sherman, J. A. (1976). Fennema-Sherman Mathematics Attitude Scale: Instruments designed to measure attitudes toward the learning of mathematics by females and males. *JAS Catalog of Selected Documents in Psychology*, 6, 31.

7525

Test Name: MULTIDIMENSIONAL STUDENTS' LIFE SATISFACTION SCALE— SCHOOL SUBSCALE

Purpose: To assess overall satisfaction with school experiences.

Number of Items: 8

Format: Responses are made in a 6-point scale ranging from 1 (strongly agree) to 6 (strongly disagree). An example is presented.

Reliability: Internal consistency was estimated at .84. Test-retest (4 weeks) reliability was .70.

Validity: Correlated .68 with the Quality of School Life Scale.

Author: Huebner, E. S., and McCullough, G.

Article: Correlates of school satisfaction among adolescents.

Journal: *Journal of Educational Research*, May/June 2000, *93*(5), 331–335.

Related Research: Huebner, E. S. (1994). Preliminary development and validation of a multidimensional life satisfaction scale for children. *Psychological Assessment, 6*, 149–158.

7526

Test Name: PARENT CONCERNS ABOUT THEIR CHILDREN'S SCHOOL PROGRAM QUESTIONNAIRE

Purpose: To identify parent concern about their children's school program.

Number of Items: 22

Format: Includes 4 factors: Concerns about involvement, concerns about program effectiveness, need for change, and lack of knowledge. Responses are made on a 7-point scale ranging from "not at all true about me at this time" to "very true about me at this time." All items are presented.

Reliability: Alpha coefficients ranged from .75 to .81.

Author: Daniel, L. G., and King, D. A.

Article: Impact of inclusion education on academic achievement, student behavior and self-esteem, and parental attitudes.

Journal: *Journal of Educational Research*, November/December 1997, *91*(2), 67–80.

Related Research: Hall, G. E., et al. (1977). *Measuring stages of concern about the innovation: A manual for use of the SOC questionnaire*. Austin, TX: Research and Development

Center for Teacher Education, University of Texas at Austin.

7527

Test Name: PARENT INVOLVEMENT SCALE

Purpose: To identify parents' involvement with their child's schooling.

Number of Items: 7

Format: Responses are made on 5-point scales. All items are presented.

Reliability: Coefficient alpha was .86.

Validity: Correlations with other variables ranged from −.40 to .41.

Author: Watkins, T. J.

Article: Teacher communications, child achievement, and parent traits in parent involvement models.

Journal: *Journal of Educational Research*, September/October 1997, *91*(1), 3–14.

Related Research: Ames, C., et al. (1993, April). *Effects of parent involvement strategies on parents' perceptions and the development of children's motivation*. Paper presented at the annual meeting of the American Educational Research Association, Atlanta.

7528

Test Name: PARENTAL INVOLVEMENT INITIATED BY TEACHER SCALE

Purpose: To identify how often teachers attempt to involve parents in their children's work.

Number of Items: 8

Format: Responses are made on a 5-point scale ranging from 1 (never) to 5 (almost every day).

Reliability: Coefficient alpha was .83.

Validity: Correlations with other variables ranged from −.32 to .39.

Author: Shumow, L., et al.

Article: School divorce, family characteristics, and home-school relations: Contributors to school achievement.

Journal: *Journal of Educational Psychology*, September 1996, *88*(3), 451–460.

7529

Test Name: PARENTAL INVOLVEMENT SCALES

Purpose: To measure parent-school communication and parents' participation in school.

Number of Items: 11

Format: Frequency scales range from 1 to 6. A Yes/No format is used on four items. All items are described.

Reliability: Alpha coefficients ranged from .74 to .82 across subscales.

Author: Carbonaro, W. J.

Article: A little help from my friends' parents: Intergenerational closure and educational outcomes.

Journal: *Sociology of Education*, October 1999, *71*(4), 295–313.

Related Research: Ho, E. S. C., & Willms, D. (1996). Effects of parental involvement on eighth-grade achievement. *Sociology of Education, 69*, 126–141.

7530

Test Name: PEER VICTIMIZATION SCALE

Purpose: To measure peer victimization.

Number of Items: 4

Format: Responses are made on a 3-point scale ranging from 1 (no or never) to 3 (a lot). Includes 4 types of peer aggression.

Reliability: Alpha coefficients were .70 and .74.

Validity: Correlations with other variables ranged from −.03 to −.20.

Author: Ladd, G. W., et al.

Article: Classroom peer acceptance, friendship, and victimization: Distinct relational systems that contribute uniquely to children's school adjustment?

Journal: *Child Development*, December 1997, *68*(6), 1181–1197.

Related Research: Kochenderfer, B. J., & Ladd, G. W. (1997). Victimized children's responses to peers' aggression: Behaviors associated with reduced versus continued victimization. *Development and Psychopathology*, *9*, 59–73.

7531

Test Name: PERCEIVED ACADEMIC PERFORMANCE SCALE

Purpose: To measure students' perceived academic performance.

Number of Items: 2

Format: Responses are made on a 7-point scale ranging from 1 (very poor) to 7 (very good). All items are presented.

Reliability: Coefficient alpha was .89.

Validity: Correlations with other variables ranged from −.18 to .61.

Author: Nonis, S. A., et al.

Article: Influence of perceived control over time on college

students' stress and stress-related outcomes.

Journal: *Research in Higher Education*, October 1998, *39*(5), 587–605.

Related Research: Macan, T. H., et al. (1990). College students' time management: Correlations with academic performance and stress, *Journal of Educational Psychology*, *82*(4), 760–768.

7532

Test Name: PERCEIVED PEER AND TEACHER EXPECTATIONS MEASURE

Purpose: To measure students' perceptions of what peers and teachers expect of them.

Number of Items: 3

Format: Responses are made on a 6-point scale ranging from "strongly disagree" to "strongly agree." All items are presented.

Reliability: Coefficient alpha was .75.

Validity: Correlations with other variables ranged from −.15 to .42.

Author: Dai, D. Y.

Article: To be or not to be (challenged), that is the question: Task and ego orientation among high-ability, high-achieving adolescents.

Journal: *Journal of Experimental Education*, Summer 2000, *68*(4), 311–330.

Related Research: Dai, D. Y., & Feldhusen, J. F. (1996). Goal orientations of gifted students. *Gifted and Talented International*, *11*, 84–88.

7533

Test Name: PERSISTENCE/ VOLUNTARY DROPOUT DECISIONS SCALE

Purpose: To assess persistence decisions of college students.

Number of Items: 30

Format: Scales range from 1 (strongly disagree) to 5 (strongly agree). Sample items are presented.

Reliability: Coefficient alpha was .86.

Validity: Correlations with other variables ranged from −.50 to .22.

Author: Gloria, A. M., et al.

Article: African American students' persistence at a predominately white university: Influences of social support, university comfort and self-beliefs.

Journal: *Journal of College Student Development*, May/June 1999, *40*(3), 257–268.

Related Research: Pascarella, E. T., & Terenzini, P. T. (1980). Predicting freshman persistence and voluntary dropout decisions from a theoretical model. *Journal of Higher Education*, *51*, 60–75.

7534

Test Name: PERSONAL CONTACT SCALE

Purpose: To assess the personal contacts and degree of involvement of students in campus life.

Number of Items: 7

Format: Scales range from 1 (strongly disagree) to 5 (strongly agree). All items are presented.

Reliability: Alpha coefficients ranged from .71 to .81 across two subscales.

Validity: Correlations with other variables ranged from −.29 to −.07.

Author: Mohr, J. J., et al.

Article: So close, yet so far: Predictors of attrition in college seniors.

Journal: *Journal of College Student Development*, July/August 1998, *39*(4), 343–354.

7535

Test Name: PIANTA STUDENT-TEACHER RELATIONSHIP SCALE

Purpose: To enable teachers to report teacher-child relationships.

Number of Items: 30

Format: Includes 3 subscales. Responses are made on a 5-point scale. Examples are presented.

Reliability: Alpha coefficients for two subscales were .75 and .81.

Author: Howes, C., et al.

Article: Stability and continuity of child-caregiver and child–peer relationships.

Journal: *Child Development*, April 1998, *69*(2), 418–426.

Related Research: Pianta, R. (1994). Patterns of relationships between children and kindergarten teachers. *Journal of School Psychology*, *32*, 15–31.

7536

Test Name: PRACTICAL PROBLEM QUESTIONNAIRE

Purpose: To measure students' perceptions of their strategies for effectively dealing with practical problems in and out of school settings.

Number of Items: 25

Format: Includes strategies for dealing effectively with problems in and out of school.

Reliability: Alpha coefficients ranged from .63 to .84.

Author: Heng, M. A.

Article: Scrutinizing common sense: The role of practical intelligence in intellectual giftedness.

Journal: *Gifted Child Quarterly*, Summer 2000, *44*(3), 171–182.

Related Research: Berg, C. A. (1987). *Children's knowledge of effective strategies in the solution of everyday problems.* Unpublished doctoral dissertation, Yale University, CT.

7537

Test Name: PROCRASTINATION ASSESSMENT SCALE

Purpose: To assess academic procrastination.

Number of Items: 38

Format: Includes 3 parts: frequency, problems, and reasons. Responses are made on 5-point scales.

Reliability: Alpha coefficients ranged from .70 to .80. Test-retest reliabilities (6 weeks) ranged from .65 to .74.

Author: Ferrari, J. R., et al.

Article: The antecedents and consequences of academic excuse-making: Examining individual differences in procrastination.

Journal: *Research in Higher Education*, April 1998, *39*(2), 199–215.

Related Research: Soloman, L. J., & Rothblum, E. D. (1984). Academic procrastination: Frequency and cognitive behavioral correlates. *Journal of Counseling Psychology*, *31*, 503–509.

7538

Test Name: PROCRASTINATION INVENTORY-REVISED

Purpose: To measure college student procrastination.

Number of Items: 42

Format: Includes 11 subscales: Low Frustration Tolerance, Perfectionism, Rebellion, Difficulty Making Decisions, Need for Approval, Unable to Take Help, Procrastination as a Work Style, Fear of Finishing Graduate School, Self-Denigration, Insufficient Reinforcement/Lack of Structure, and Task Aversiveness. Responses are made on a 5-point scale ranging from 1 (not at all true of me) to 5 (definitely true of me).

Reliability: Reliability coefficients ranged from .34 to .86.

Author: Johnson, E. M., et al.

Article: Psychometric characterization of the revised Procrastination Inventory.

Journal: *Research in Higher Education*, April 2000, *41*(2), 269–279.

Related Research: Muszynski, S. Y., & Akamatsu, T. J. (1991). Delay in completion of doctoral dissertations in clinical psychology. *Professional Psychology: Research and Practice*, *22*, 119–123.

7539

Test Name: REVISED MATHEMATICS ANXIETY RATING SCALE

Purpose: To measure mathematics anxiety.

Number of Items: 25

Format: Includes 3 dimensions: Math Test Anxiety, Numerical Anxiety, and Math Course Anxiety.

Reliability: Alpha coefficients ranged from .84 to .96. Test-retest (2 weeks) reliability was .86.

Validity: Correlations with other variables ranged from .36 to .80.

Author: Kazelskis, R., et al.

Article: Mathematics anxiety and test anxiety: Separate constructs?

Journal: *Journal of Experimental Education*, Winter 2000, *68*(2), 137–146.

Related Research: Richardson, F. C., & Suinn, R. M. (1972). The Mathematics Anxiety Rating Scale: Psychometric data. *Journal of Counseling Psychology, 19*, 551–554.

7540

Test Name: ROOMMATE RELATIONSHIP INVENTORY

Purpose: To measure perceptions of roommate relationships.

Number of Items: 24

Format: Scales range from 1 (strongly disagree) to 5 (strongly agree).

Reliability: Coefficient alpha was .95.

Validity: Correlation with a measure of roommate rapport was .91.

Author: Phelps, R. E., et al.

Article: Roommate satisfaction and ethnic pride in same-race and mixed-race university roommate pairs.

Journal: *Journal of College Student Development*, July/August 1996, *37*(4), 377–388.

Related Research: Winston, R. B., Jr., & Yaranovich, M. F. (1994). Quality of roommate relationships: Development of the Roommate Relationship Inventory. *Journal of College and University Student Housing, 24*, 6–11.

Phelps, R. E. (1998). Roommate satisfaction and ethnic identity in mixed-race and white university

roommate dyads. *Journal of College Student Development, 39,* 194–203.

7541

Test Name: SCHOLASTIC COMPETENCE SUBSCALE

Purpose: To describe children's confidence in school work.

Number of Items: 6

Format: The children indicate whether each statement is either "really true" or "sort of true." The statements divide the children into two groups and the children are asked if they are more like the first or the second group.

Reliability: Coefficient alpha was .77.

Author: Rhodes, J. E., et al.

Article: Agents of change: Pathways through which mentoring relationships influence adolescents' academic adjustment.

Journal: *Child Development*, November/December 2000, *71*(6), 1662–1671.

Related Research: Harter, S. (1986). Cognitive-developmental processes in the integration of concepts about emotions and the self [special issue: Developmental perspectives or social-cognitive theories]. *Social Cognition, 4,* 119–151.

7542

Test Name: SCHOOL ADJUSTMENT SCALE

Purpose: To assess adjustment to school.

Number of Items: 20

Format: All items are presented.

Reliability: Alpha coefficients

ranged from .60 to .88 across subscales.

Validity: Correlations with other variables ranged from −.60 to .37.

Author: Tarter, R. E., et al.

Article: The Drug-Use Screening Inventory: School adjustment correlates of substance abuse.

Journal: *Measurement and Evaluation in Counseling and Development*, April 1996, *29*(1), 25–34.

Related Research: Tarter, R., & Hegedus, A. (1992). The Drug Use Screening Inventory: Its application in the evaluation and treatment of alcohol and drug abuse. *Alcohol, Health and Research World, 15,* 65–75.

7543

Test Name: SCHOOL CONNECTION SCALE

Purpose: To measure youths' feelings of connection to a particular school context.

Number of Items: 16

Format: Four-point scales are anchored by "strongly agree" and "strongly disagree." All items are presented.

Reliability: Cronbach alpha was .86 (total scale) and ranged from .51 to .85 across subscales.

Validity: Correlations with other variables ranged from −.32 to .09.

Author: Brown, R. A., et al.

Article: The School Connection Scale: A factor analysis.

Journal: *Psychological Reports*, December 2000, *87*(3, Part 1), 851–858.

7544

Test Name: SCHOOL LIKING AND AVOIDANCE QUESTIONNAIRE

Purpose: To measure school liking and avoidance.

Number of Items: 14

Format: Includes two factors: School Liking and School Avoidance. Responses are made on a 3-point scale ranging from 3 (Yes) through 2 (Sometimes) to 1 (No). Examples are presented.

Reliability: Alpha coefficients ranged from .87 to .76.

Validity: Correlations with other variables ranged from −.39 to .29.

Author: Ladd, G. W., et al.

Article: Classroom peer acceptance, friendship, and victimization: Distinct relational systems that contribute uniquely to children's school adjustment?

Journal: *Child Development*, December 1997, *68*(6), 1181–1197.

Related Research: Ladd, G. W., et al. (1996). Friendship quality as a predictor of young children's early school adjustment. *Child Development*, *67*, 1103–1118.

7545

Test Name: SCHOOL PERFORMANCE RATING SCALE

Purpose: To assess the academic performance of children diagnosed with attention deficit hyperactivity disorder.

Number of Items: 16

Format: Includes task completion, classroom and test scores, academic achievement, and classroom skills. All items are included.

Validity: Correlations with the ADD-H comprehensive Teachers' Rating Scale ranged from −.45 to .91.

Author: Raggio, D. J., and Pierce, J.

Article: Use of the School Performance Rating Scale with children treated for attention deficit hyperactivity disorder.

Journal: *Perceptual and Motor Skills*, June 1999, *88*(3) Part 1, 957–960.

Related Research: Ullman, R. K., & Sleator, E. K. (1985). Attention deficit disorder children with and without hyperactivity: Which behaviors are helped by stimulants? *Clinical Pediatrics*, *24*, 547–551.

7546

Test Name: SCHOOL SATISFACTION SCALE

Purpose: To assess attitudes about school.

Number of Items: 9

Format: Scales range from 1 (strongly disagree) to 6 (strongly agree).

Reliability: Coefficient alpha was .88.

Validity: Correlations with other variables ranged from −.41 to .19.

Author: Spector, P. E., et al.

Article: A longitudinal study of relations between job stressors and job strains while controlling for prior negative affectivity and strains.

Journal: *Journal of Applied Psychology*, April 2000, *85*(2), 211–218.

Related Research: Levine, E. L., & Weitz, J. (1968). Job satisfaction among graduate students: Intrinsic versus extrinsic variables. *Journal of Applied Psychology*, *52*, 263–271.

7547

Test Name: SENSITIVITY TO CRITICISM SCALE

Purpose: To assess sensitivity to criticism among college students.

Number of Items: 15

Format: 7-point scales are anchored by (1) not at all critical or not hurt at all and (7) extremely critical or extremely hurt. Sample items are presented.

Reliability: Alphas ranged from .82 to .92. Test-retest reliability was .82.

Validity: Correlations with other variables ranged from −.30 to .65.

Author: White, J. D., et al.

Article: Validity of the perceived criticism measure in an undergraduate sample.

Journal: *Psychological Reports*, August 1998, *83*(1), 83–97.

Related Research: Atlas, G. D. (1994). Sensitivity to criticism: A new measurement of responses to everyday criticisms. *Journal of Psychoeducational Assessment*, *12*, 241–253.

7548

Test Name: SOCIAL INTEGRATION AND PERSISTENCE INTENTIONS SCALE

Purpose: To assess a student's connection to the institution and to the faculty.

Number of Items: 25

Format: Scales range from 1 (strongly disagree) to 5 (strongly agree). Sample items are presented.

Reliability: Alpha coefficients ranged from .73 to .84.

Author: Solberg, V. S., et al.

Article: The Adaptive Success Identity Plan (ASIP): A career intervention for college students.

Journal: *Career Development Quarterly*, September 1998, 47(1), 48–95.

Related Research: Pascarella, E. T., & Terenzini, P. T. (1977). Patterns of student-faculty informal interaction beyond the classroom and voluntary attrition. *Journal of Higher Education*, 48, 540–552.

7549

Test Name: STATISTICAL ANXIETY RATING SCALE

Purpose: To assess statistical anxiety.

Number of Items: 51

Format: Includes 6 subscales: Worth of Statistics, Interpretation Anxiety, Test and Class Anxiety, Computational Self-Concept, Fear of Asking for Help, and Fear of the Statistics Instructor.

Reliability: Alpha coefficients ranged from .68 to .94. Test-retest (5 weeks) reliability ranged from .67 to .83.

Validity: Correlations with other variables ranged from −.47 to −.04.

Author: Onwuegbuzie, A. J.

Article: Statistics anxiety and the role of self-perceptions.

Journal: *Journal of Educational Research*, May/June 2000, 93(5), 323–330.

Related Research: Cruise, R. J., & Wilkins, E. M. (1980). *STARS: Statistical Anxiety Rating Scale.* Unpublished manuscript,

Andrews University, Berrien Springs, MI.

7550

Test Name: STUDENT ADAPTATION TO COLLEGE QUESTIONNAIRE

Purpose: To assess adjustment to college.

Number of Items: 67

Format: Nine-point scales range from "applies very closely to me" to "doesn't apply to me at all."

Reliability: Coefficient alpha was .92.

Validity: Correlations with other variables ranged from .30 to .53.

Author: Mathis, M., and Lecci, L.

Article: Hardiness and college adjustment: Identifying students in need of services.

Journal: *Journal of College Student Development*, May/June 1999, 40(3), 305–309.

Related Research: Baker, R. W., & Siryk, B. (1986). Exploratory intervention with a scale measuring adjustment to college. *Journal of Counseling Psychology*, 33, 31–38.

7551

Test Name: STUDENT ADAPTATION TO COLLEGE QUESTIONNAIRE

Purpose: To measure student adaptation to college.

Number of Items: 68

Format: Includes 4 subscales: Academic Adjustment, Social Adjustment, Personal/Emotional Adjustment, and General Institutional Attachment. Responses are made on a 5-point Likert-type scale ranging from 1

(strongly disagree) to 5 (strongly agree).

Reliability: Internal consistency was .93.

Validity: Correlations with other variables ranged from .38 to .58.

Author: Zea, M. C., et al.

Article: Reliability, ethnic comparability, and validity evidence for a condensed measure of proactive coping: The BAPC-C.

Journal: *Educational and Psychological Measurement*, April 1996, 56(2), 330–343.

Related Research: Baker, R. W., & Siryk, B. (1984). Student adaptation to college questionnaire. *Journal of Counseling Psychology*, 2, 179–189.

7552

Test Name: STUDENT COPING SCALE

Purpose: To measure students' coping style.

Number of Items: 48

Format: Responses are made on a 10-point scale ranging from 1 (extremely uncharacteristic) to 10 (extremely characteristic). Items are presented.

Reliability: Alpha coefficients ranged from .70 to .80.

Author: Struthers, C. W., et al.

Article: An examination of the relationship among academic stress, coping, motivation, and performance in college.

Journal: *Research in Higher Education*, October 2000, 41(5), 581–592.

Related Research: Carver, C. S., et al. (1989). Assessing coping strategies: A theoretically based approach. *Journal of Personality* *and Social Psychology, 56,* 267–283.

7553

Test Name: STUDENT PROBLEM INVENTORY

Purpose: To assess adjustment problems of students.

Number of Items: 229

Format: 5-point response scales are anchored by (SA) Strongly agreed and (SD) strongly disagreed.

Reliability: Spearman Brown (prophecy formula) reliability was .76.

Author: Cherian, V. I., and Cherian, L.

Article: University students' adjustment problems.

Journal: *Psychological Reports,* June 1998, *82*(3) Part 2, 1135–1138.

Related Research: Wilson, B. (1984). Problems of university adjustment experiences by undergraduates in a developing country. *Higher Education, 13,* 1–22.

7554

Test Name: STUDENT STRESS SCALE

Purpose: To measure student stress.

Number of Items: 31

Format: Yes/no format. Sample items are presented.

Reliability: Test-retest, Cronbach alpha and split-half reliabilities were all equal to .81.

Author: Peltzer, K., et al.

Article: Minor psychiatric morbidity in South African secondary school pupils.

Journal: *Psychological Reports,* October 1999, *85*(2), 397–402.

Related Research: Zimbardo, P. G. (1992). *Psychology and life.* (13th ed.). New York: Harper Collins.

7555

Test Name: STUDENT-TEACHER RELATIONSHIP SCALE

Purpose: To assess teachers' perceptions of their relationship with a particular student.

Number of Items: 28

Format: Includes 3 subscales: Conflict, Closeness, and Dependency. Examples are presented.

Reliability: Alpha coefficients ranged from .61 to .92.

Author: Kesner, J. E.

Article: Teacher characteristics and the quality of child-teacher relationships.

Journal: *Journal of School Psychology,* March/April 2000, *38*(2), 133–149.

Related Research: Pianta, R. C. (1991). *The Student-Teacher Relationship Scale.* Unpublished manuscript.

7556

Test Name: STUDENT-TEACHER RELATIONSHIP SCALE

Purpose: To assess teacher perceptions of their relationship with the child.

Number of Items: 30

Format: Provides three relationship quality scores: Closeness, Conflictual, and Dependency. Responses are made on a 5-point scale.

Reliability: Alpha coefficients ranged from .66 to .92.

Author: Howes, C. E., et al.

Article: The consistency of perceived teacher-child relationships between preschool and kindergarten.

Journal: *Journal of School Psychology,* March/April 2000, *38*(2), 113–132.

Related Research: Pianta, R. C., & Steinberg, M. (1992). Teacher-child relationships and adjusting to school. In R. C. Pianta (Ed.), *Beyond the parent* (pp. 61–80). San Francisco: Jossey-Bass.

7557

Test Name: STUDENT-TEACHER RELATIONSHIP SCALE

Purpose: To identify teacher-child relationship.

Number of Items: 35

Format: Includes 3 factors: Closeness, Conflict, and Dependency. Responses are made on a 5-point scale ranging from 1 (definitely does not apply) to 5 (definitely applies). Sample items are presented.

Reliability: Alpha coefficients ranged from .69 to .93.

Author: Ladd, G. W., and Burgess, K. B.

Article: Charting the relationship trajectories of aggressive, withdrawn, and aggressive/withdrawn children during early grade school.

Journal: *Child Development,* July/August 1999, *70*(4), 910–929.

Related Research: Rianta, R. C., et al. (1995). The first two years of school: Teacher-child relationship and deflections in children's classroom adjustment.

Development and Psychopathology, 7, 295–312.

7558

Test Name: STUDY HABITS INVENTORY

Purpose: To assess the study habits of college students.

Number of Items: 63

Format: True/false format.

Reliability: Alpha was .85. Test-retest reliabilities (2 weeks) ranged from .71 to .82.

Validity: Correlations with other variables ranged from −.54 to .40.

Author: Onwuegbuzie, A. J., and Daley, C. E.

Article: Study skills of undergraduates as a function of academic locus of control, self-perception, and social interdependence.

Journal: *Psychological Reports*, October 1998, *83*(2), 595–598.

Related Research: Jones, C. H., & Slate, J. R. (1992). Technical manual for the Study Habits Inventory. (Unpublished manuscript, Arkansas State University, Jonesboro, AR).

7559

Test Name: SURVEY OF ACADEMIC ORIENTATIONS

Purpose: To measure how undergraduates interpret the academic environment.

Number of Items: 36

Format: Includes 6 factors: Structure Dependence, Creative Expression, Reading for Pleasure, Academic Efficacy, Academic Apathy, and Mistrust of Instructors. Responses are on a 5-point Likert-type scale ranging from 1 (strongly disagree) to 5 (strongly agree).

Reliability: Alpha coefficients ranged from .59 to .85.

Validity: Correlations with other variables ranged from −.55 to .67.

Author: Davidson, W. B., et al.

Article: Development and validation of scores on a measure of six academic orientations in college students.

Journal: *Educational and Psychological Measurement*, August 1999, *59*(4), 678–693.

7560

Test Name: TEACHER RATING SCALE OF ACTUAL COMPETENCE AND SOCIAL ACCEPTANCE

Purpose: To enable the teacher to note the child's cognitive and physical competence and social acceptance.

Number of Items: 18

Format: Includes 3 subscales: Cognitive Competence, Physical Competence, and Social Acceptance. Responses are made on a 4-point scale.

Reliability: Alpha coefficients ranged from .85 to .91.

Author: Verschueren, K., et al.

Article: The internal working model of the self, attachment, and competence in five-year-olds.

Journal: *Child Development*, October 1996, *67*(5), 2493–2511.

Related Research: Harter, S., & Pike, R. (1984). The Pictorial Scale of Perceived Competence and Social Acceptance for Young Children. *Child Development, 55*, 1969–1983.

7561

Test Name: TEACHER REPORT INDEX OF ANXIETY

Purpose: To assess anxiety by teacher report.

Number of Items: 12

Format: Four-point Likert scales are anchored by 1 (never) and 4 (often).

Reliability: Alpha coefficient was .90.

Validity: Correlations with other variables ranged from .07 to .81.

Author: Cole, D. A., et al.

Article: Relation between symptoms of anxiety and depression: A multitrait-multimethod-multigroup assessment.

Journal: *Journal of Consulting and Clinical Psychology*, February 1997, *65*(1), 110–119.

7562

Test Name: TEACHER SUPPORT SCALE

Purpose: To assess student perceptions of the degree to which they experience teacher support.

Number of Items: 27

Format: Responses are made on a 5-point Likert scale ranging from 5 (strongly agree) to 1 (strongly disagree). Sample items are presented.

Reliability: Alpha coefficients were .96 and .68.

Validity: Correlation with a 6-item measure of teacher support was .72.

Author: McWhirter, E. H., et al.

Article: The effects of high school career education on social-cognitive variables.

Journal: *Journal of Counseling*

Psychology, July 2000, *47*(3), 330–341.

7563

Test Name: TEACHER-CHILD RATING SCALE

Purpose: To measure elementary children's school problem behaviors and competencies.

Number of Items: 38

Format: Includes 2 parts: Class Problems and Children's Classroom Competencies. Five-point scales are used for each part.

Reliability: Alpha coefficients ranged from .85 to .95. Stability coefficients (10–20 weeks) ranged from .66 to .85.

Validity: Correlations with other variables ranged from −.69 to .67.

Author: Pigott, R. L., and Cowen, E. L.

Article: Teacher race, child race, racial congruence, and teacher ratings of children's school adjustments.

Journal: *Journal of School Psychology*, March/April 2000, *38*, 177–196.

Related Research: Hightower, A. D., et al. (1986). The Teacher-Child Rating Scale: A brief objective measure of elementary children's school problem behaviors and competencies. *School Psychology Review*, *15*, 393–409.

7564

Test Name: TEACHER-CHILD RATING SCALE-MODIFIED

Purpose: To measure child adjustment.

Number of Items: 17

Format: Includes 2 parts: Child Adjustment and Peer Social Skills. Responses are made on 5-point scales. Sample items are presented.

Reliability: Alpha coefficients ranged from .93 to .95.

Author: Sutton, S. E., et al.

Article: Pathways to aggression in young, highly stressed urban children.

Journal: *Child Study Journal*, 1999, *29*(1), 49–67.

Related Research: Hightower, A. D., et al. (1986). The Teacher-Child Rating Scale: A brief objective measure of elementary children's school problem behavior and competencies. *School Psychology Behavior*, *15*, 393–409.

7565

Test Name: TEACHER-CHILD RELATIONSHIP SCALE

Purpose: To enable teachers to rate the teacher-child relationship.

Number of Items: 9

Format: Includes 3 subscales: Mentorship/Communicative/Supportive, Autonomy/Directive/Instructive, and Control/Primitive/Disciplinary. Responses are made on a 5-point scale ranging from 1 (false) to 5 (true). Examples are presented.

Reliability: Alpha coefficients ranged from .74 to .90.

Author: McCall, R. B., et al.

Article: The nature and correlates of underachievements among elementary school children in Hong Kong.

Journal: *Child Development*, May/June 2000, *71*(3), 785–801.

Related Research: Lau, S. (1995). *Psychological adjustment in the development of primary school children: A longitudinal study.* Unpublished report, Hong Kong Baptist University.

7566

Test Name: THINGS I WORRY ABOUT SCALE

Purpose: To identify adolescent school pupils' self-expressed personal and social concerns.

Number of Items: 138

Format: Includes 13 categories: myself, at home, obtaining a job or course, social confidence/assertiveness, choosing a job or course, opposite sex, verbal communications, starting work or college, information seeking, powerlessness, finances/money, school/college work, and change. Responses are made on a 4-point scale ranging from 1 (never worry) to 4 (always worry).

Reliability: Alpha coefficients ranged from .81 to .98.

Author: Millar, R., and Gallagher, M.

Article: The "Things I Worry About" Scale: Further developments in surveying the worries of postprimary school pupils.

Journal: *Educational and Psychological Measurement*, December 1996, *56*(6), 972–994.

Related Research: Millar, R., et al (1993). Surveying adolescent worries: Development of the Things I Worry About Scale. *Pastoral Care in Education*, *11*, 43–51.

7567

Test Name: UNIVERSITY ALIENATION SCALE

Purpose: To assess alienation in the college context.

Number of Items: 24

Format: Scales range from 1 (strongly disagree) to 5 (strongly agree).

Reliability: Split-half reliabilities ranged from .72 to .89 across subscales.

Author: Thomlinson-Clarke, S., and Clarke, D.

Article: Institutional effects on alienation and student effort at three campus environments.

Journal: *Journal of College Student Development*, January/ February 1996, *37*(1), 60–67.

Related Research: Burbach, H. J. (1972). The development of a contextual measure of alienation. *Pacific Sociological Review, 15*, 225–234.

7568

Test Name: WORK-SCHOOL CONFLICT AND SCHOOL READINESS SCALES

Purpose: To measure work-school conflict among students and perceived school readiness.

Number of Items: 18

Format: Five-point scales ranged from 1 (never) to 5 (very often). All items are presented.

Reliability: Coefficient alpha was .86 (work-school conflict). Alpha coefficients ranged from .72 to .81 across readiness subscales.

Author: Markel, K. S., and Frone, M. R.

Article: Job characteristics, work-school conflict, and school outcomes among adolescents: Testing a structural model.

Journal: *Journal of Applied Psychology*, April 1998, *83*(2), 277–287.

Related Research: Frone, M. R., et al. (1997). Developing and testing an integrative model of the work-family interface. *Journal of Vocational Behavior, 50*, 145–167.

7569

Test Name: WORRY-EMOTIONALITY SCALE

Purpose: To assess test anxiety.

Number of Items: 10

Format: Responses are made on a 5-point agreement scale.

Reliability: Internal consistency coefficients ranged in the .80's.

Author: Williams, J. E.

Article: The relation between efficacy for self-regulated learning and domain-specific academic performance, controlling for test anxiety.

Journal: *Journal of Research and Development in Education*, Winter 1996, *29*(2), 77–80.

Related Research: Morris, L. W., et al. (1981). Cognitive and emotional components of anxiety: Literature review and a revised worry emotionality scale. *Journal of Educational Psychology, 73*, 541–555.

7570

Test Name: WRITING APPREHENSION TEST

Purpose: To measure the degree to which writing is associated with apprehension, anxiety and failure.

Number of Items: 26

Format: Five-point Likert format.

Reliability: Coefficient alpha was .96.

Author: Onwuegbuzie, A. J.

Article: The relationship between writing anxiety and learning styles among graduate students.

Journal: *Journal of College Student Development*, November/ December 1998, *39*(6), 589–598.

Related Research: Daley, J. A., & Miller, M. D. (1975). The empirical development of an instrument to measure writing apprehension. *Research in the Teaching of English, 9*, 242–249.

7571

Test Name: WRITING APPREHENSION TEST-REVISED

Purpose: To measure writing anxiety.

Number of Items: 9

Format: Responses are made on an 8-point scale.

Reliability: Coefficient alpha was .83.

Validity: Correlations with other variables ranged from −.13 to −.52.

Author: Pajares, F., and Valiante, G.

Article: Influence of self-efficacy on elementary students' writing.

Journal: *Journal of Educational Research*, July/August 1997, *90*(6), 353–360.

Related Research: Daly, J. A., & Miller, M. D. (1975). The empirical development of an instrument to measure writing apprehension. *Research in the Teaching of English, 9*, 272–289.

CHAPTER 3
Adjustment—Psychological

7572

Test Name: ABILITY TO COPE SCALE

Purpose: To measure ability to cope.

Number of Items: 5

Format: Responses are made on a 7-point Likert-type scale ranging from 1 (strongly disagree) to 7 (strongly agree). Examples are presented.

Reliability: Coefficient alpha was .87.

Validity: Correlations with other variables ranged from −.50 to .32.

Author: Saks, A. M., and Ashforth, B. E.

Article: Proactive socialization and behavioral self-management.

Journal: *Journal of Vocational Behavior*, June 1996, *48*(3), 301–323.

Related Research: House, R. I., et al. (1982). *An empirical examination of the construct validity of the Rizzo, House and Litzman role scales: Toward a clarification of the nature of role conflict.* Paper presented at the annual mid-west meeting of the Academy of Management, Columbus, Ohio.

7573

Test Name: ACCEPTANCE OF DISABILITY SCALE

Purpose: To measure an individual's acceptance of his or her own disability.

Number of Items: 10

Format: Scales range from 1 (strongly disagree) to 5 (strongly agree). All items are presented.

Reliability: Coefficient alpha was .79.

Validity: Correlations with other variables ranged from −.37 to .53.

Authors: Li, L., and Moore, D.

Article: Acceptance of disability and its correlates.

Journal: *Journal of Social Psychology*, February 1998, *138*(1), 13–25.

Related Research: Linkowski, D. C. (1971). A scale to measure acceptance of disability. *Rehabilitation Counseling Bulletin, 4,* 236–244.

7574

Test Name: ADHD RATING SCALE-IV

Purpose: To measure inattention and hyperactivity-impulsivity as symptoms of ADHD.

Number of Items: 18

Format: Four-point scales are anchored by 0 (never or rarely) and 3 (very often). All items are presented.

Validity: In a two-factor model, the correlation between factors was .92. The two-factor model had a significantly better fit with the observed data than the one-factor model ($p < .01$).

Author: DuPaul, G. J., et al.

Article: Parent ratings of attention-deficit/hyperactivity disorder symptoms: Factor structure and normative data.

Journal: *Journal of Psychopathology and Behavioral Assessment*, March 1998, *20*(1), 83–102.

Related Research: DuPaul, G. J., et al. (1994). *ADHD rating scale-IV.* Unpublished rating scale.

7575

Test Name: ADHD SYMPTOMS RATING SCALE

Purpose: To assess ADHD in K-12 populations.

Number of Items: 50

Format: Five-point scales are anchored by 1 (poor) and 5 (excellent). All items are presented.

Reliability: Alpha coefficients were .98 (parent data) and .99 (teacher data). Test-retest (2 weeks) reliabilities ranged from .72 to .97.

Validity: Correlations with criterion measures ranged from .30 to .97.

Author: Holland, M. L., et al.

Article: Innovations in assessing ADHD: Development, psychometric properties, and factor structure of the ADHD Symptoms Rating Scale (ADHD-SRS).

Journal: *Journal of Psychopathology and Behavioral Assessment*, December 1998, *20*(4), 307–322.

7576

Test Name: ADOLESCENT COPING ORIENTATION FOR PROBLEM EXPERIENCES

Purpose: To identify adolescent coping strategies used by them to manage problem or difficult situations.

Number of Items: 54

Format: Responses are made on a 5-point scale ranging from 1 (never) to 5 (most of the time).

Reliability: Alpha coefficients ranged from .50 to .76.

Validity: A validity coefficient was reported as .40.

Author: Chapman, P. L., and Mullis, R. L.

Article: Adolescent coping strategies and self-esteem.

Journal: *Child Study Journal*, 1999, *29*(1), 69–77.

Related Research: Patterson, J. M., & McCubbin, H. I. (1986). Adolescent Coping Orientation for Problem Experiences. In H. I. McCubbin and A. I. Thompson (Eds.), *Family assessment inventories research and practice* (pp. 227–246). Madison: Family Stress, Coping and Health Project, University of Wisconsin-Madison.

7577

Test Name: ADOLESCENT DECISION PROCESSES SCALE

Purpose: To measure how actively adolescents make decisions when facing a variety of problems.

Number of Items: 17

Format: Includes 3 factors: Vacillation, Undeliberated Conclusion, and Thoughtful Determination. Responses are made on a 6-point scale ranging from 1 (never) to 6 (always). All items are presented.

Reliability: Alpha coefficients ranged from .79 to .83.

Author: Friedman, I. A.

Article: Deliberation and resolution in decision-making processes: A self-report scale for adolescents.

Journal: *Educational and Psychological Measurement*, October 1996, *56*(5), 881–890.

Related Research: Friedman, I. A., & Mann, L. (1993). Coping patterns in adolescent decision-making: An Israeli-Austrian comparison. *Journal of Adolescence*, *16*, 187–199.

7578

Test Name: ADOLESCENT INJURY CHECKLIST

Purpose: To measure recent injuries.

Number of Items: 14

Format: True/false format.

Reliability: Coefficient alpha was .89.

Author: Monti, P. M., et al.

Article: Brief intervention for harm reduction with alcohol-positive older adolescents in a hospital emergency department.

Journal: *Journal of Consulting and Clinical Psychology*, December 1999, *67*(6), 989–994.

Related Research: Jelalian, E., et al. (1997). Risk-taking, reported injury, and perception of future injury among adolescents. *Journal of Pediatric Psychology*, *22*, 513–532.

7579

Test Name: ADOLESCENT PERCEIVED EVENTS SCALE—SHORT FORM

Purpose: To assess life events experienced by adolescents.

Number of Items: 100

Format: Includes positive and negative: Daily events and major events. Examples are presented.

Reliability: Test-retest (2 weeks) reliabilities ranged from .74 to .89.

Validity: Correlations with Academic Self-Efficacy ranged from −.20 to .33.

Author: Huebner, E. S., and McCullough, G.

Article: Correlates of school satisfaction among adolescents.

Journal: *Journal of Educational Research*, May/June 2000, *93*(5), 331–335.

Related Research: Campas, D., et al. (1987). Assessment of major and daily life events during adolescence: The Adolescent Perceived Events Scale. *Journal of Consulting and Clinical Psychology*, *55*, 534–541.

7580

Test Name: ADOLESCENT PHYSICAL HEALTH QUESTIONNAIRE

Purpose: To assess the physical health of adolescents by self-report.

Number of Items: 12

Format: Yes/no format. Sample items are presented.

Reliability: Internal consistencies ranged from .68 to .76.

Author: Wickrama, K. A. S., et al.

Article: Parental education and adolescent self-reported physical health.

Journal: *Journal of Marriage and the Family*, November 1998, *60*(4), 967–978.

Related Research: Mechanic, D., & Hansell, S. (1987). Adolescent competence, psychological well-being, and self-assessed physical health. *Journal of Health and Social Behavior, 28,* 364–374.

7581

Test Name: AFFECT AND AROUSAL SCALE

Purpose: To assess positive affect, negative affect, and physiological hyperarousal.

Number of Items: 49

Format: Four-point scales are anchored by 0 (never true) and 3 (always true). All items are presented. Items are from other scales.

Reliability: Alphas ranged from .77 to .81 across subscales.

Validity: Goodness of fit indexes ranged from .67 to .93.

Author: Chorpita, B. F., et al.

Article: Assessment of tripartite factors of emotion in children and adolescents I: Structural validity and normative data of an affect and arousal scale.

Journal: *Journal of Psychopathology and Behavioral Assessment,* June 2000, *22*(2), 141–160.

Related Research: Daleiden, E., et al. (2000). Assessment of tripartite factors of emotion in children and adolescents II: Concurrent validity of the affect and arousal scales for children. *Journal of Psychopathology and Behavioral Assessment, 22,* 161–182.

7582

Test Name: AFFECT BALANCE SCALE

Purpose: To assess social psychological well-being as a balance between positive and negative affect.

Number of Items: 10

Format: All items are presented.

Reliability: Alpha coefficients ranged from .36 to .64.

Author: MacIntosh, R.

Article: A confirmatory factor analysis of the Affect Balance Scale in 38 nations: A research note.

Journal: *Social Psychology Quarterly,* March 1998, *61*(1), 83–91.

Related Research: Bradburn, N. (1969). *The structure of psychological well-being.* Chicago: Aldine.

Sastry, J., & Ross, C. E. (1998). Asian ethnicity and the sense of personal control. *Social Psychology Quarterly, 61,* 101–120.

7583

Test Name: AFFECT INTENSITY MEASURE

Purpose: To measure the magnitude of both positive and negative emotions.

Number of Items: 40

Format: Responses are made on a 6-point scale ranging from 1 (never) to 6 (always). An example is presented.

Reliability: Alpha coefficients ranged from .90 to .94. Stability over 1, 2, and 3-month periods was .80 and .81.

Author: Searle, B., and Meara, N. M.

Article: Affective dimensions of attachment styles: Exploring self-reported attachment style, gender, and emotional experience among college students.

Journal: *Journal of Counseling Psychology,* April 1999, *46*(2), 147–158.

Related Research: Larsen, R. J., et al. (1986). Affect intensity and reactions to daily life events. *Journal of Personality and Social Psychology, 51,* 803–814.

7584

Test Name: AFFECT REGULATION AND EXPERIENCE AND Q-SORT

Purpose: To measure affect regulation and experience by observer-based rating.

Number of Items: 47

Format: All items are presented.

Reliability: Alphas ranged from .71 to .92.

Validity: Correlations with other variables ranged from −.47 to .75.

Author: Westen, D., et al.

Article: Affect regulation and affective experience: Individual differences, group differences, and measurement using a Q-sort.

Journal: *Journal of Consulting and Clinical Psychology,* June 1997, *65*(3), 429–439.

7585

Test Name: AFFECTIVE COMMITMENT SUBSCALE

Purpose: To assess affective commitment.

Number of Items: 8

Format: Responses are made on a 5-point Likert-type scale ranging from 1 (strongly disagree) to 5 (strongly agree). Sample items are presented.

Reliability: Alpha coefficients were .86 and .91.

Validity: Correlations with other variables ranged from −.17 to .36.

Author: Marsour-Cole, D. M., and Scott, S. G.

Article: Hearing it through the grapevine: The influence of source, leader-relations, and legitimacy on survivors' fairness perceptions.

Journal: *Personnel Psychology*, Spring 1998, *51*(1), 25–54.

Related Research: Allen, N., & Meyer, J. (1990). The measurement and antecedents of affective, continuance, and normative commitment to the organization. *Journal of Occupational Psychology*, *63*, 1–18.

7586

Test Name: AFFECTOMETER 2

Purpose: To measure positive affect.

Number of Items: 40

Format: Scales range from 1 (not at all) to 5 (all the time). Sample items are presented.

Reliability: Coefficient alpha was .92.

Validity: Correlations with other variables ranged from .06 to .22.

Author: Deluga, R. J., and Masson, S.

Article: Relationship of resident assistant conscientiousness, extraversion, and positive affect with rated performance.

Journal: *Journal of Research in Personality*, June 2000, *34*(2), 225–235.

Related Research: Kammann, R., & Flett, R. (1983). Affectometer 2: A scale to measure current level of general happiness. *Australian Journal of Psychology*, *35*, 259–265.

7587

Test Name: ANGER, DEPRESSION, AND ANXIETY RATING SCALES

Purpose: To measure anger, depression, and anxiety.

Number of Items: 22

Format: Includes 3 scales: Anger, Depression, and Anxiety. Responses are made on 4-point scales ranging from 1 (no) to 4 (a lot).

Reliability: Alpha coefficients ranged from .68 to .93.

Author: Deffenbacher, J. L., and Swaim, R. C.

Article: Anger expression in Mexican American and White non-Hispanic adolescents.

Journal: *Journal of Counseling Psychology*, January 1999, *46*(1), 61–69.

Related Research: Oetting, E. R., et al.(1989). Indian and Anglo adolescent alcohol use and emotional distress: Path models. *American Journal of Drug and Alcohol Abuse*, *15*, 153–172.

7588

Test Name: ANOMALOUS EXPERIENCES INVENTORY

Purpose: To measure anomalous/paranormal beliefs, experiences, abilities, and fears.

Number of Items: 70

Format: True-false format. Sample items are presented.

Reliability: Alphas ranged from .68 to .87 across subscales.

Author: Houran, J., and Williams, C.

Article: Relation of tolerance of ambiguity to global and specific paranormal experience.

Journal: *Psychological Reports*, December 1998, *83*(3) Part 1, 807–818.

Related Research: Kumar, V. K., et al. (1994). The Anomalous Experiences Inventory, West

Chester University (Unpublished test, West Chester, PA).

7589

Test Name: ANTIOCH SENSE OF HUMOR INVENTORY

Purpose: To measure enjoyment of a joke or cartoon.

Number of Items: 50

Format: Five-point scales are anchored by 5 (very much) and 1 (not at all).

Reliability: Test-retest reliability was .88 (2 weeks). Internal consistency was .82.

Author: Kelly, F. D., and Osborne, D.

Article: Ego states and preference for humor.

Journal: *Psychological Reports*, December 1999, *85*(3, Part I), 1031–1039.

Related Research: Mindness, H., et al. (1985). *The Antioch Humor Test: Making sense of humor*. New York: Avon.

7590

Test Name: ANXIETY, DEPRESSION, AND PSYCHOSOCIAL DYSFUNCTION QUESTIONNAIRE

Purpose: To measure anxiety, depression and psychosocial dysfunction in Persian and English speaking populations.

Number of Items: 39

Format: Five-point scale ranged from "never" to "always."

Reliability: Alpha coefficients ranged from .83 to .92 across subscales.

Authors: Ghaffarian, S.

Article: The acculturation of Iranian immigrants in the United

States and the implications for mental health.

Journal: *Journal of Social Psychology,* October 1998, *138*(5), 645–654.

Related Research: Warheit, G. J., & Buhl, J. M. (1979). *Symptoms and dysfunction scales used as part of the southeastern U.S. mental health needs and utilization studies.* Mineographed manuscript, Department of Psychology, University of Florida, Gainesville.

7591

Test Name: ANXIETY RATING SCALE

Purpose: To measure cognitive anxiety, somatic anxiety, and self-confidence.

Number of Items: 3

Format: Responses are made on a 7-point Likert scale.

Validity: Correlations with other variables ranged from .68 to .76.

Author: Cox, R. H., et al.

Article: Order of scale administration and concurrent validity of the Anxiety Rating Scale.

Journal: *Perceptual and Motor Skills,* February 1999, *88*(1), 271–272.

Related Research: Cox, R. H., & Rabb, M. (1998). Concurrent validity of the Revised Anxiety Rating Scale. *Journal of Applied Sport Psychology,* 10 (Suppl.), S160.

7592

Test Name: ANXIETY SCALE

Purpose: To measure anxiety.

Number of Items: 15

Format: Scales range from 1 (rarely) to 5 (very often).

Reliability: Coefficient alpha was .94.

Validity: Correlations with other variables ranged from −.19 to .43.

Author: Schaubroeck, J., et al.

Article: Collective efficacy versus self-efficacy in coping responses to stressors and control: A cross-cultural study.

Journal: *Journal of Applied Psychology,* August 2000, *85*(4), 512–525.

Related Research: Parker, D. F., & DeCotiis, T. A. (1983). Organizational determinants of job stress. *Organizational Behavior and Human Decision Processes, 32,* 160–177.

7593

Test Name: ANXIETY SENSITIVITY INDEX

Purpose: To measure concern with aversive consequences of anxiety symptoms.

Number of Items: 16

Format: Five-point scales are anchored by 0 (very little) and 4 (very much).

Reliability: Alpha coefficients ranged from .79 to .90.

Validity: Correlations with other variables ranged from −.08 to .31.

Author: Eifert, G. H., et al.

Article: Predictors of self-reported anxiety and panic symptoms: An evaluation of anxiety sensitivity, suffocation fear, heart-focused anxiety, and breath-holding duration.

Journal: *Journal of Psychopathology and Behavioral Assessment,* December 1999, *21*(4), 293–305.

Related Research: Reiss, S., et al. (1986). Anxiety, sensitivity,

anxiety frequency, and the prediction of fearfulness. *Behavior Research and Therapy, 24,* 1–8.

7594

Test Name: ARABIC CHILDREN'S DEPRESSION INVENTORY

Purpose: To measure depression in children.

Number of Items: 27

Format: Response rating scale ranges from "rarely" to "sometimes" to "often." All items are presented in English.

Reliability: Alpha coefficients ranged from .88 to .90.

Author: Abdel-Khalek, A. M., and Soliman, H. H.

Article: A cross-cultural evaluation of depression in children in Egypt, Kuwait, and the United States.

Journal: *Psychological Reports,* December 1999, *85*(3, Part I), 973–980.

Related Research: Abdel-Khalek, A. M. (1993). The construction and validation of the Arabic Children's Depression Inventory. *European Journal of Psychological Assessment, 9,* 41–50.

7595

Test Name: ATHLETE STRESS INVENTORY

Purpose: To measure athletes' life event stressors.

Number of Items: 49

Format: Includes 4 factors: Negative Mood, Team Compatibility, Physical Well-Being, and Academic Efficiency. Responses are made on an 11-point scale ranging from 0 (absence of stress) to 10 (extreme amount of stress). All items are presented.

Reliability: Test-retest (one hour) reliability ranged from .82 to .97.

Validity: Correlations with athletic performance scores ranged from −.94 to .38.

Author: Seggar, J. F., et al.

Article: A measure of stress for athletic performance.

Journal: *Perceptual and Motor Skills*, February 1997, *84*(1), 227–236.

7596

Test Name: ATTENTION TO FEELING SUBSCALE

Purpose: To measure valuing and paying attention to one's emotions.

Number of Items: 13

Format: Responses are made on a 5-point Likert scale ranging from 1 (strongly disagree) to 5 (strongly agree).

Reliability: Alpha coefficients were .86 and .88.

Validity: Correlations with other variables ranged from −.22 to .17.

Author: Searle, B., and Meara, N. M.

Article: Affective dimensions of attachment styles: Exploring self-reported attachment style, gender, and emotional experience among college students.

Journal: *Journal of Counseling Psychology*, April 1999, *46*(2), 147–158.

Related Research: Salovey, P., et al. (1995). Emotional attention, clarity, and repair: Exploring emotional intelligence using the Trait Meta-Mood Scale. In J. Pennebaker (Ed.), *Emotion, disclosure, and health* (pp. 125–

154). Washington, DC: American Psychological Association.

7597

Test Name: AUTOMATIC THOUGHTS QUESTIONNAIRE

Purpose: To measure depression.

Number of Items: 30

Format: Responses are made on a 7-point scale ranging from "strongly disagree" to "strongly agree."

Reliability: Reliability coefficient was .94.

Author: Boles, J. S., et al.

Article: The dimensionality of the Maslach Burnout Inventory across small business owners and educators.

Journal: *Journal of Vocational Behavior*, February 2000, *56*(1), 12–34.

Related Research: Hollon, S. D., & Kendall, P. C. (1980). Cognitive self-statements in depression: Development of an Automatic Thoughts Questionnaire. *Cognitive Therapy and Research*, 4, 383–395.

7598

Test Name: AUTOMATICITY IRRATIONALITY QUESTIONNAIRE

Purpose: To measure reaction to spiders.

Number of Items: 20

Format: Five-point Likert format. All items are presented.

Reliability: Alphas were .97 (automaticity) and .70 (irrationality).

Validity: Correlations with other variables ranged from −.47 to .41.

Author: Mayer, B., et al.

Article: Self-reported automaticity and irrationality in spider phobia.

Journal: *Psychological Reports*, October 2000, *87*(2), 395–405.

7599

Test Name: BEHAVIORAL ATTRIBUTES OF PSYCHOSOCIAL COMPETENCE SCALE-C

Purpose: To measure competent coping.

Number of Items: 13

Format: All items are presented.

Reliability: Coefficient alpha was .76. Test-retest (6 weeks) reliability was .86 (*n* = 62).

Validity: Correlation with other variables ranged from −.51 to .55.

Author: Zea, M. C., et al.

Article: Reliability, ethnic comparability, and validity evidence for a condense measure of proactive coping: The BAPC-C.

Journal: *Educational and Psychological Measurement*, April 1996, *56*(2), 330–343.

Related Research: Tyler, F. B. (1978). Individual psychological competence: A personality configuration. *Educational and Psychological Measurement*, 38, 309–323.

7600

Test Name: BEHAVIORAL ATTRIBUTES OF PSYCHOSOCIAL COMPETENCE SCALE— FORM AR

Purpose: To measure competent coping.

Number of Items: 39

Format: Includes 4 types of competent coping: Active, General, Self-Maintenance or Emotion-Focuses, and Autonomy. The following domains are reflected: Personal, Interpersonal, Task-Related, and General Coping.

Reliability: Reliabilities ranged from .84 to .86.

Validity: Correlations with other variables ranged from −.51 to .58.

Author: Zea, M. C., et al.

Article: Reliability, ethics, and validity evidence for personality measure of proactive coping: The BAPC-C.

Journal: *Educational and Psychological Measurement*, April 1996, *56*(2), 330–343.

Related Research: Tyler, F. B. (1978). Individual psychosocial competence: A personality configuration. *Educational and Psychological Measurement*, *38*, 309–323.

7601

Test Name: (BERKELEY) EXPRESSIVITY QUESTIONNAIRE

Purpose: To measure positive and negative expressivity and impulse strength.

Number of Items: 16

Format: Scales range from 1 (strongly disagree) to 5 (strongly agree).

Reliability: Coefficient alpha was .80.

Author: Totterdell, P.

Article: Catching moods and hitting runs: Mood linkage and subjective performance in professional sports teams.

Journal: *Journal of Applied*

Psychology, December 2000, *85*(6), 848–859.

Related Research: Gross, J. J., & John, O. P. (1997). Revealing feelings: Facts of emotional expressivity in self-reports, peer ratings, and behavior. *Journal of Personality and Social Psychology,* 72, 435–448.

7602

Test Name: BLUSHING, TREMBLING, AND SWEATING QUESTIONNAIRE

Purpose: To assess severity, the problems associated with, strategies to hide, and the positive and negative affect associated with blushing, trembling, and sweating.

Number of Items: 154

Format: Likert scales and visual analogue scales are employed.

Reliability: Alphas ranged from .67 to .98 across subscales.

Validity: Correlations with criterion measures ranged from −.19 to .70.

Author: Bogels, S. M., and Reith, W.

Article: Validity of two questionnaires to assess social fears: The Dutch Social Phobia and Anxiety Inventory and the Blushing, Trembling, and Sweating Questionnaire.

Journal: *Journal of Psychopathology and Behavioral Assessment,* March 1999, *21*(1), 51–66.

Related Research: Bogels, S. M. (1994). *Cognitive therapy vs. applied social skills training for social fear of blushing, trembling, and sweating.* Paper presented at the 2nd Congress of the European Association for Behavioral and Cognitive Therapies, Corfu, September 6–10.

7603

Test Name: BODY SENSATIONS INTERPRETATION QUESTIONNAIRE

Purpose: To assess body sensations related and unrelated to panic.

Number of Items: 14

Format: Open-ended, multiple-choice rating formats are used. A detailed description of one item is described.

Reliability: Alphas ranged from .74 to .94. Test-retest reliabilities ranged from .48 to .81.

Author: Clark, D. M., et al.

Article: Misinterpretation of body sensations in panic disorder.

Journal: *Journal of Consulting and Clinical Psychology*, April 1997, *65*(2), 203–213.

Related Research: McNally, R. J., & Foa, E. B. (1987). Cognition and agoraphobia. Bias in the interpretation of threat. *Cognitive Therapy and Research*, *11*, 567–581.

7604

Test Name: BOREDOM PRONENESS SCALE

Purpose: To measure college student boredom proneness.

Number of Items: 22

Format: Responses are "true" or "false." All items are presented.

Reliability: KR-20 formula reliability was .82.

Validity: Correlation with Farmer and Sundberg's Boredom Proneness Scale was .30 (*n* = 61).

Author: Nasir, S. J., et al.

Article: Internal consistency of Boredom Proneness Scale for a sample of Pakistani students.

Journal: *Perceptual and Motor*

Skills, April 1996, *82*(2), 367–370.

7605

Test Name: BOREDOM PRONENESS SCALE

Purpose: To assess the tendency to experience boredom.

Number of Items: 28

Format: Scales range from 1 (highly disagree) to 7 (highly agree).

Reliability: Reliability coefficients ranged from .77 to .84.

Author: Vodanovich, S. J., and Watt, J. D.

Article: The relationship between time structure and boredom proneness: An investigation within two cultures.

Journal: *Journal of Social Psychology*, April 1999, *139*(2), 143–152.

Related Research: Farmer, R., & Sundberg, N. D. (1986). Boredom proneness: The development and correlates of a new scale. *Journal of Personal Assessment, 50*, 4–17.

7606

Test Name: BRIEF COPE INVENTORY

Purpose: To assess aspects of coping.

Number of Items: 28

Format: Includes 14 scales. Responses are made on a 4-point scale ranging from 1 (I didn't do this at all) to 4 (I did this a lot).

Reliability: Alpha coefficients ranged from .57 to .94.

Author: Perczek, R., et al.

Article: Coping, mood, and aspects of personality in Spanish translation and evidence of

convergence with English versions.

Journal: *Journal of Personality Assessment*, February 2000, *74*(1), 63–87.

Related Research: Carver, C. S. (1997). You want to measure coping but your protocol's too long: Consider the Brief COPE. *International Journal of Behavioral Medicine, 4,* 92–100.

7607

Test Name: BRIEF PSYCHIATRIC RATING SCALE

Purpose: To assess psychological symptoms by interview.

Number of Items: 24

Format: Four-point scales.

Reliability: Interrater reliabilities ranged from .56 to .97.

Author: Toro, P. A., et al.

Article: Evaluating an intervention for homeless persons: Results of a field experiment.

Journal: *Journal of Consulting and Clinical Psychology*, June 1997, *65*(3), 476–484.

Related Research: Overall, J. E., & Gorham, D. R. (1962). The Brief Psychiatric Rating Scale. *Psychological Reports, 10*, 799–812.

7608

Test Name: CARDIAC ANXIETY QUESTIONNAIRE

Purpose: To measure heart-focused anxiety.

Number of Items: 18

Format: Five-point scales are anchored by 0 (never) and 4 (always).

Reliability: Alpha was .83.

Validity: Correlations with other

variables ranged from −.09 to .41.

Author: Eifert, G. H., et al.

Article: Predictors of self-reported anxiety and panic symptoms: An evaluation of anxiety sensitivity, suffocation fear, heart-focused anxiety and breath-holding duration.

Journal: *Journal of Psychopathology and Behavioral Assessment*, December 1999, *21*(4), 293–305.

7609

Test Name: CENTER FOR EPIDEMIOLOGICAL STUDIES —DEPRESSION SCALE—10-ITEM VERSION

Purpose: To measure depression.

Number of Items: 10

Format: Yes/No response scales. All items are presented.

Reliability: Alpha was .78.

Validity: Correlations with other variables ranged from −.31 to −.48. Imputing values for missing data altered the factor structure of these items.

Author: Kimberlin, C. L., et al.

Article: Issues related to using a short-form of the Center for Epidemiological Studies—Depression Scale.

Journal: *Psychological Reports*, October 1998, *83*(2), 411–421.

Related Research: Radloff, L. S. (1977). The CES-D Scale: A self-report depression scale for research in the general population. *Applied Psychological Measurement, 1*, 385–401.

7610

Test Name: CES-D

Purpose: To measure depressive symptoms.

Number of Items: 20

Format: Each symptom is rated by the number of days in the past week in which it was experienced. Responses are 0 days, 1–2 days, 2–4 days, or 5–7 days.

Reliability: Alpha coefficients were .77 (boys) to .83 (girls).

Validity: Correlations with other variables ranged from .02 to .86.

Author: Whitbeck, L. B., et al.

Article: Depressive symptoms and co-occurring depressive symptoms, substance abuse and conduct problems among runaway and homeless adolescents.

Journal: *Child Development*, May/June 2000, *71*(3), 721–732.

Related Research: Radloff, L. (1977). The CES-D scale: A self-report depression scale for research in the general population. *Applied Psychological Measurement*, *1*, 385–401.

7611

Test Name: CHILD BEHAVIOR INVENTORY

Purpose: To assess children's mental health symptoms and adaptational outcomes.

Number of Items: 42

Format: Includes 5 subscales: Anxiety, Depression, Aggression, Planful Behavior, and Prosocial Behavior.

Reliability: Alpha coefficients ranged from .51 to .74.

Author: MacKsoud, M. S., and Abner, J. L

Article: The war experiences and psychosocial development of children in Lebanon.

Journal: *Child Development*, February 1996, *67*(1), 70–88.

Related Research: MacKsoud, M., et al. (1990). *Child Behavior Inventory*. New York: Columbia University, Center for the Study of Human Rights, Project on Children and War.

7612

Test Name: CHILD DEPRESSION INVENTORY-CHILD AND PARENT FORMS

Purpose: To assess affective, cognitive, and behavioral symptoms of depression by self-report.

Number of Items: 27

Format: Three-point severity scales ranged from 0 to 2.

Reliability: Alpha was .91 (child form) and .88 (parent form).

Author: Cole, D. A., et al.

Article: Relation between symptoms of anxiety and depression in children: A multitrait-multimethod-multigroup assessment.

Journal: *Journal of Consulting and Clinical Psychology*, February 1997, *65*(1), 110–119.

Related Research: Kovacs, M. (1985). The Children's Depression Inventory. *Psychopharmacology Bulletin*, *21*, 995–998.

Kazdin, A. E., et al. (1983). Child, mother, and father evaluations of depression in psychiatric inpatient children. *Journal of Abnormal Child Psychology*, *11*, 167–180.

7613

Test Name: CHILD POST-TRAUMATIC STRESS REACTION INDEX

Purpose: To measure post-traumatic stress in children.

Number of Items: 20

Format: Five-point scales range from 1 (now) to 5 (most of the time).

Reliability: Interrater reliability was .88.

Author: Dubner, A. E., and Motta, R. W.

Article: Sexually and physically abused foster care children and posttraumatic stress disorder.

Journal: *Journal of Consulting and Clinical Psychology*, June 1999, *67*(3), 367–373.

Related Research: Frederick, C. J., et al. (1992). Child Post-Traumatic Stress Index. Unpublished manuscript.

7614

Test Name: CHILD RATING SCALE-MODIFIED

Purpose: To provide a child self-report measure of adjustment.

Number of Items: 12

Format: Includes two subscales: Rule Compliance and Peer Social Skills. Responses are made on a 3-point scale of: 1 (usually no), 2 (sometimes), and 3 (usually yes). Examples are presented.

Reliability: Alpha coefficients were .75 and .63.

Author: Sutton, S. E., et al.

Article: Pathways to aggression in young, highly stressed urban children.

Journal: *Child Study Journal*, 1999, *29*(1), 49–67.

Related Research: Hightower, A. D., et al. (1987). The Child Rating Scale: The development and psychometric refinement of a socioemotional self-rating scale for young school children. *School Psychology Review*, *16*, 239–255.

7615

Test Name: CHILDHOOD WAR TRAUMA QUESTIONNAIRE

Purpose: To assess children's exposure to war trauma.

Number of Items: 45

Format: Includes 10 categories: Exposure to shelling or combat, Separation from parents, Bereavement, Witnessing violent acts, Suffering physical injuries, Victim of violent acts, Emigration, Displacement, Involvement in the hostilities, and Extreme deprivation.

Reliability: Alpha coefficient was .66.

Author: MacKsoud, M. S., and Abner, J. L

Article: The war experiences and psychosocial development of children in Lebanon.

Journal: *Child Development*, February 1996, *67*(1), 70–88.

Related Research: Macksoud, M. (1992). Assessing war trauma in children: A case study of Lebanese children. *Journal of Refugee Studies*, *5*(1), 1–15.

7616

Test Name: CHILDREN'S COPING STRATEGIES CHECKLIST

Purpose: To assess children's coping styles.

Number of Items: 50

Format: Includes 12 types of coping behavior: Cognitive Avoidance, Active Avoidance, Distracting Actions, Positive Cognitive Restructuring, Expressing Feelings, Cognitive Decision Making, Direct Problem Solving, Problem-Focused Support, Emotion-Focused Support, Aggressive Actions, Physical Release of Emotion, and Seeking Understanding.

Responses are made on a 5-point scale ranging from 1 (never) to 5 (very often). Examples are presented.

Reliability: Alpha coefficients ranged from .36 to .86.

Author: Eisenberg, N., et al.

Article: Parents' reactions to children's negative emotions: Relations to children's social competence and comforting behavior.

Journal: *Child Development*, October 1996, *67*(5), 2227–2247.

Related Research: Sandler, I. N., et al. (1994). Coping, stress, and the psychological symptoms of children of divorce: A cross-sectional and longitudinal study. *Child Development*, *65*, 1744–1763.

7617

Test Name: CHILDREN'S COPING STRATEGIES CHECKLIST—ADAPTED

Purpose: To assess children's coping styles.

Number of Items: 28

Format: Responses are made on a 5-point scale ranging from 1 (never) to 5 (very often). Includes the following scales: Positive Cognitive Structuring, Cognitive Decision Making, Direct Problem Solving, Problem-Focused Support, Emotion-Focused Support, and Seeking Understanding.

Reliability: Alpha coefficients ranged from .72 to .86.

Author: Eisenberg, N., et al.

Article: The relations of children's dispositional prosocial behavior to emotionality, regulation, and social functioning.

Journal: *Child Development*, June 1996, *67*(3), 974–992.

Related Research: Program for Prevention Research. (1992, October). *Divorce Adjustments Project Documentation*. Available from the Program for Prevention Research, Arizona State University, Tempe, AZ.

7618

Test Name: CHILDREN'S DEPRESSION INVENTORY

Purpose: To measure depression among children and adolescents (a downward extension of the Beck Depression Inventory).

Number of Items: 27

Format: Frequency rating scales indicate how often a symptom occurred in the past 2 weeks.

Validity: Correlations with the Brief Symptoms Inventory Scales ranged from −.40 to .55.

Author: Greco-Vigorito, C., et al.

Article: Affective symptoms in young children of substance abusers correlate with parental distress.

Journal: *Psychological Reports*, October 1996, *79*(2), 547–552.

Related Research: Kovacs, M. (1979). *Children's Depression Inventory*. Pittsburgh, PA: University of Pittsburgh.

7619

Test Name: CHILDREN'S GLOBAL RATING SCALE

Purpose: To assess young children's experience of pain and anxiety.

Number of Items: 5

Format: Includes 5 progressively more wavy lines representing pain and anxiety. Employs a 5-point scale ranging from 1 (flat line: no pain or anxiety) to 5 (high frequency wave; the most pain or anxiety possible).

Validity: Correlations with other variables ranged from .53 to .67.

Author: Smith, J. T., et al.

Article: Comparison of hypnosis and distraction in severely ill children undergoing painful medical procedures.

Journal: *Journal of Counseling Psychology*, April 1996, *43*(2), 187–195.

Related Research: Carpenter, P. J. (1992). Perceived control as a predictor of distress in children undergoing invasive medical procedures. *Journal of Pediatric Psychology*, 17(6), 757–809.

7620

Test Name: CHINESE REVISED LIFE ORIENTATION TEST

Purpose: To measure optimism.

Number of Items: 5

Format: Five-point scales are anchored by 0 (strongly disagree) and 4 (strongly agree).

Reliability: Alpha was .61.

Validity: Correlations with age, sex, and education were .11, .06, and −.06, respectively.

Author: Lai, J. C. L., et al.

Article: Health beliefs and optimism as predictors of preventive health decisions in Hong Kong Chinese.

Journal: *Psychological Reports*, June 2000, *86*(3, Part 2), 1059–1070.

Related Research: Lai, J. C. L., et al. (1998). The utility of the revised Life Orientation Test to measure optimism among Hong Kong Chinese. *International Journal of Psychology*, 33, 45–56.

7621

Test Name: CHINESE SYMPTOM CHECKLIST

Purpose: To assess physical symptoms and psychological symptoms.

Number of Items: 20

Format: Five-point scales range from (1) never to (2) frequently.

Reliability: Alphas were .91 (physical) and .95 (psychological).

Validity: Correlation with stress was .25.

Author: Hamid, P. N., and Chan, W. T.

Article: Locus of control and occupational stress in Chinese professionals.

Journal: *Psychological Reports*, February 1998, *82*(1), 75–79.

7622

Test Name: CHINESE SYMPTOM CHECKLIST

Purpose: To identify physical and psychological symptoms.

Number of Items: 40

Format: Responses are made on a 5-point scale ranging from 1 (never) to 5 (frequently). Examples are presented.

Reliability: Alpha coefficient ranged from .87 to .92.

Author: Hamid, P. N., and Cheng, S-T.

Article: The development and validation of an index of emotional disposition and mood state: The Chinese Affect Scale.

Journal: *Educational and Psychological Measurement*, December 1996, *56*(6), 995–1014.

Related Research: Cheng, S-T., & Hamid, P. N. (1996). The Chinese Symptom Checklist: Preliminary data concerning reliability and validity. *Journal*

of Social Behavior and Personality, *11*, 241–252.

7623

Test Name: COGNITION CHECKLIST

Purpose: To assess frequency of automatic thoughts relevant to depression and anxiety.

Number of Items: 26

Format: Five-point scales are anchored by 0 (never) and 4 (always).

Reliability: Alphas were .91 (depression) and .90 (anxiety).

Author: Epkins, C. C.

Article: Cognitive specificity and affective confounding in social anxiety and dysphoria in children.

Journal: *Journal of Psychopathology and Behavioral Assessment*, March 1996, *18*(1), 83–101.

Related Research: Beck, A. T., et al. (1987). Differentiating anxiety and depression: A test of the cognitive content-specific hypothesis. *Journal of Abnormal Psychology*, 96, 179–183.

7624

Test Name: COGNITION CHECKLIST (FARSI VERSION)

Purpose: To measure depression and anxiety.

Number of Items: 43

Format: Five-point scales are anchored by 0 (never) and 5 (always).

Reliability: Alpha was .76. Test-retest (10-days) reliability was .79.

Author: Makaremi, A.

Article: Relation of depression and anxiety to personal and academic problems among Iranian college students.

Journal: *Psychological Reports*, October 2000, *87*(2), 693–698.

Related Research: Beck, A. T., et al. (1987). Differentiating anxiety and depression: A test of the cognitive content-specificity hypothesis. *Journal of Abnormal Psychology*, *96*, 179–183.

7625

Test Name: COGNITIVE-SOMATIC ANXIETY QUESTIONNAIRE

Purpose: To assess cognitive and somatic aspects of anxiety.

Number of Items: 14

Format: Includes two subscales: Somatic and Cognitive. Responses are made on a 5-point scale ranging from "not at all" to "very much so."

Reliability: Alpha coefficients were .85 and .74.

Validity: Correlation with other variables ranged from −.47 to .52.

Author: Joiner, Jr., T. E., et al.

Article: Development and factor analytic validation of the SPANAS among women in Spain: (More) cross-cultural convergence in the structure of mood.

Journal: *Journal of Personality Assessment*, June 1997, *68*(3), 600–615.

Related Research: Schwartz, G. E., et al. (1978). Patterning of cognitive and somatic processes in the self-regulation of anxiety: Effects of mediation versus exercise. *Psychosomatic Medicine*, *40*, 321–328.

7626

Test Name: COLLEGE STUDENT REASONS FOR LIVING INVENTORY

Purpose: To assess suicidal risk in college populations.

Number of Items: 46

Format: Scales range from 1 (not at all important/does not apply) to 6 (extremely important). All items are presented.

Reliability: Alpha coefficients ranged from .59 to .87 across subscales.

Author: Rogers, J. R., and Hanlon, P. J.

Article: Psychometric analysis of the College Student Reasons for Living Inventory.

Journal: *Measurement and Evaluation in Counseling and Development*, April 1996, *29*(1), 13–24.

Related Research: Westefeld, J. S., et al. (1992). Development of the College Student Reasons for Living Inventory. *Suicide and Life-Threatening Behavior*, *22*, 442–452.

Westefeld, J. S., et al. (1998). Psychometric analysis of the College Student Reasons for Living Inventory using a clinical population. *Measurement and Evaluation in Counseling and Development*, April 1996, *31*, 86–94.

7627

Test Name: COMMON EXPERIENCE QUESTIONNAIRE

Purpose: To assess likelihood of seeking counseling for personal problems.

Number of Items: 20

Format: Scales range from 1 (very unlikely) to 6 (very likely).

Reliability: Coefficient alpha was .89.

Author: Kahn, J. H., and Nauta, M. M.

Article: The influence of student problem-solving appraisal and nature of problem on likelihood of seeking counseling services.

Journal: *Journal of College Student Development*, January/February 1997, *38*(1), 32–39.

Related Research: Baumgardner, A. H., et al. (1986). Role of causal attribution in personal problem solving. *Journal of Personality and Social Psychology*, *50*, 636–643.

7628

Test Name: COMPETITIVE STATE ANXIETY INVENTORY-2

Purpose: To measure cognitive and somatic anxiety.

Number of Items: 27

Format: Includes 2 subscales: Cognitive Anxiety and Somatic Anxiety. Responses are made on a 4-point scale ranging from 1 (not at all) to 4 (very much so).

Reliability: Internal consistencies ranged from .79 to .90.

Validity: Correlations with other variables ranged from −.45 to .28.

Author: Williams, D. M., et al.

Article: Predicting anxiety in competitive sports.

Journal: *Perceptual and Motor Skills*, June 2000, *90*(3) Part 1, 847–850.

Related Research: Martens, R., et al. (1982). *Competitive State Anxiety Inventory-2*. Symposium conducted at the meeting of the North American Society for the Psychology of Sport and Physical Activity, College Park, MD, May.

7629

Test Name: COPE SCALE

Purpose: To measure and identify the use of reactive responses to life situations.

Number of Items: 60

Format: Four-point scales are anchored by 1 (I usually don't do this at all) and 4 (I usually do this a lot).

Reliability: Alphas ranged from .45 to .92 across subscales. Test-retest reliabilities ranged from .46 to .86 (8 weeks).

Validity: Scale intercorrelations ranged from −.29 to .67.

Author: Leitschuh, G. A.

Article: How college students' physical health relates to coping.

Journal: *Psychological Reports*, August 1999, *85*(1), 220–226.

Related Research: Carver, C. S., et al. (1989). Assessing coping strategies: A theoretically based approach. *Journal of Personality and Social Psychology, 66*, 184–195.

7630

Test Name: COPING BEHAVIORS SCALE

Purpose: To measure coping behaviors.

Number of Items: 8

Format: Includes 2 factors: Emotion-Focused Coping and Problem-Focused Coping. Responses are made on a 5-point scale ranging from 1 (never) to 5 (always). Sample items are presented.

Reliability: Alpha coefficients were .74 to .78.

Validity: Correlations with other variables ranged from −.26 to .42.

Author: Aryee, S., et al.

Article: Role stressors, inter-role conflict, and well-being: The moderating influence of spousal support and coping behaviors among employed parents in Hong Kong.

Journal: *Journal of Vocational Behavior*, April 1999, *54*(2), 259–278.

Related Research: Steffy, B. D., & Jones, J. W. (1988). The impact of family and career planning variables or the organizational, career and community commitment of professional women. *Journal of Vocational Behavior, 32*, 196–212.

7631

Test Name: COPING HUMOR SCALE

Purpose: To assess how much a person uses humor to cope with stress.

Number of Items: 7

Format: Four-point scales are anchored by (1) strongly disagree and (4) strongly agree.

Reliability: Cronbach alpha was .61.

Author: Perlini, A. H., et al.

Article: Effects of humor on test anxiety and performance.

Journal: *Psychological Reports*, June 1999, *84*(3) Part 2, 1203–1213.

Related Research: Martin, R. A., & Lefcourt, H. M. (1983). Sense of humor as a moderator of the relation between stressors and moods. *Journal of Personality and Social Psychology, 45*, 1313–1324.

7632

Test Name: COPING INVENTORY FOR STRESSFULL SITUATIONS

Purpose: To measure three basic coping strategies.

Number of Items: 48

Format: Includes three factors: Task-Oriented, Emotion-Oriented, and Avoidance-Oriented.

Reliability: Alpha reliability coefficient ranged from .76 to .92. Test-retest (6 weeks) reliability coefficients ranged from .51−.73.

Author: Cook, S. W., and Hefpner, P. P.

Article: A psychometric study of three coping measures.

Journal: *Educational and Psychological Measurement*, December 1997, *57*(6), 906–923.

Related Research: Endler, N. S., & Parker, J. D. A. (1994). Assessment of multidimensional coping: Task, emotion, and avoidance strategies. *Psychological Assessment, 6*, 50–60.

7633

Test Name: COPING STRATEGIES INVENTORY

Purpose: To assess situational coping.

Number of Items: 23

Format: Responses are made on a 5-point Likert-type format.

Reliability: Coefficient alpha ranged from .71 to .94. Test-retest (2 weeks) ranged from .67 to .83.

Author: Cook, S. W., and Heppner, P. P.

Article: A psychometric study of three coping measures.

Journal: *Educational and Psychological Measurement*, December 1997, 57(6), 906–923.

Related Research: Tobin, D. L., et al. (1989). The hierarchical factor structure of the Coping Strategies Inventory. *Cognitive Therapy and Research*, 13, 343–361.

7634

Test Name: COPING STRATEGIES INVENTORY

Purpose: To assess how respondents use strategies to cope with rape and to assess cognitive avoidance.

Number of Items: 32

Format: Five-point scales are anchored by 1 (not at all) and 5 (very much).

Reliability: Alpha coefficients ranged from .71 to .78. Test-retest reliabilities ranged from .68 to .72.

Author: Mechanic, M. B., et al.

Article: A comparison of normal forgetting, psychopathology, and information-processing models of reported amnesia for recent sexual trauma.

Journal: *Journal of Consulting and Clinical Psychology*, December 1998, 66(6), 948–957.

Related Research: Tobin, D. L., et al. (1989). The hierarchical factor structure of the Coping Strategies Inventory. *Cognitive Therapy and Research*, 13, 343–361.

7635

Test Name: COPING STRATEGIES INVENTORY

Purpose: To measure coping strategies.

Number of Items: 72

Format: Includes two factors: Engaged Coping and Disengaged Coping. Responses are made on a 5-point scale ranging from 1 (none) to 5 (very much). Examples are presented.

Reliability: Alpha coefficients were .89 and .91.

Validity: Correlations with other variables ranged from −.40 to .37.

Author: Chang, E. C., and Strunk, D. R.

Article: Dysphoria: Relations to appraisals, coping, and adjustments.

Journal: *Journal of Counseling Psychology*, January 1999, 46(1), 99–108.

Related Research: Tobin, L. D., et al. (1989). The hierarchical factor structure of the Coping Strategies Inventory. *Cognitive Therapy and Research*, 13, 343–361.

7636

Test Name: COPING STRATEGIES INVENTORY— SHORT FORM

Purpose: To measure coping strategies.

Format: Includes 8 factors: Problem-Solving, Cognitive Restructuring, Express Emotions, Social Support, Problem Avoidance, Wishful Thinking, Social Withdrawal, and Self-Criticism. Responses are made on a 5-point scale varying from 1 (none) to 5 (very much).

Reliability: Test-retest (2 weeks) reliabilities ranged from .67 to .83. Alpha coefficients ranged from .80 to .90.

Validity: Correlations with other

varieties ranged from −.36 to .46.

Author: Chang, E. C.

Article: Cultural differences in optimism, pessimism, and coping. Predictors of subsequent adjustment in Asian American and Caucasian American college students.

Journal: *Journal of Counseling Psychology*, January 1996, 43(1), 113–123.

Related Research: Tobin, L. D., et al. (1989). The hierarchical factor structure of the Coping Strategies Inventory. *Cognitive Therapy and Research*. 13, 343–361.

7637

Test Name: COPING STYLE IN SPORT SURVEY

Purpose: To assess coping style in competitive sport.

Number of Items: 65

Format: Scales ranged from 1 (very untrue) to 5 (very true). All items are presented.

Validity: Correlations among factors ranged from −.66 to .57.

Author: Anshel, M. H., et al.

Article: Coping style following acute stress in competitive sport.

Journal: *Journal of Social Psychology*, December 2000, 140(6), 751–773.

Related Research: Carver, C. S., et al. (1989). Assessing coping strategies: A theoretically-based approach. *Journal of Personality and Social Psychology*, 56, 267–283.

7638

Test Name: COPING WITH CHANGE SCALE

Purpose: To measure reactance to change and leading change.

Number of Items: 12

Format: Five-point Likert format. All items are presented.

Reliability: Coefficient alpha ranged from .77 to .79.

Validity: Correlations with other variables ranged from −.38 to .52.

Author: Judge, T. A., et al.

Article: Managerial coping with organizational change: A dispositional perspective.

Journal: *Journal of Applied Psychology*, February 1999, *84*(1), 107–122.

7639

Test Name: COPING WITH HARASSMENT SCALE

Purpose: To identify how one deals with harassment.

Number of Items: 20

Format: Includes two factors: Internal and External coping. Responses are made on a 5-point scale ranging from "not at all descriptive" to "extremely descriptive."

Reliability: Reliabilities ranged from .56 to .88.

Validity: Correlations of External coping with other variables ranged from −.21 to .36.

Author: Munson, L. J., et al.

Article: Longitudinal analysis of dispositional influences and sexual harassment: Effects on job and psychological outcomes.

Journal: *Personnel Psychology*, Spring 2000, *53*(1), 21–46.

7640

Test Name: COPING WITH STRESS SCALE

Purpose: To assess the degree to which individuals respond to stress by active coping, positive reinterpretation, acceptance, denial and behavioral disengagement.

Number of Items: 20

Format: Scales range from 1 (I usually don't do this at all) to 4 (I usually do this a lot).

Reliability: Alpha coefficients ranged from .62 to .75.

Validity: Correlations with other variables ranged from −.16 to .75.

Author: Bray, N. J., et al.

Article: The influence of stress-related coping strategies on college student departure decisions.

Journal: *Journal of College Student Development*, November/December 1999, *40*(6), 645–656.

Related Research: Carver, C. S., et al. (1989). Assessing coping strategies: A theoretically based approach. *Journal of Personality and Social Psychology, 56,* 267–283.

7641

Test Name: CRIME-RELATED PTS SCALE—REVISED

Purpose: To assess psychological well-being and psychological distress.

Number of Items: 28

Format: Five-point scales are anchored by 0 (not at all) and 4 (extremely). Sample items are presented.

Reliability: Coefficient alpha was .96.

Author: Campbell, R., et al.

Article: Community services for rape survivors: Enhancing psychological well-being or increasing trauma?

Journal: *Journal of Consulting and Clinical Psychology*, December 1999, *67*(6), 847–858.

Related Research: Saunders, B. E., et al. (1990). Development of a crime-related post-traumatic stress disorder scale for women within the Symptom Checklist-90-Revised. *Journal of Traumatic Stress, 3,* 439–448.

7642

Test Name: DAILY ENVIRONMENTAL HASSLES SCALE

Purpose: To assess one's dissatisfaction with living arrangements.

Number of Items: 10

Format: Response indicates whether the item identifies a problem with the place they stayed the night before. Examples are given.

Reliability: Internal consistencies were .78 and .87.

Author: Ingram, K. M., et al.

Article: The relationship of victimization experiences to psychological well-being among homeless women and low-income housed women.

Journal: *Journal of Counseling Psychology*, April 1996, *43*(2), 218–227.

Related Research: LaGory, M., et al. (1990). Depression among the homeless. *Journal of Health and Social Behavior, 19,* 2–21.

7643

Test Name: DAILY HASSLES AND UPLIFTS SCALE—SHORT FORM

Purpose: To measure common events that can be rated as hassles or uplifts.

Number of Items: 53

Format: Three-point scales.

Reliability: Mean interitem correlations were .79 (frequency of hassles) and .48 (intensity of hassles).

Validity: Correlations with other variables ranged from −.25 to .63.

Author: Jung, J.

Article: Balance and source of social support in relation to well-being.

Journal: *Journal of General Psychology*, January 1997, *124*(1), 77–90.

Related Research: DeLongis, A., et al. (1988). The impact of daily stress on health and mood: Psychological and social resources as mediators. *Journal of Personality and Social Psychology, 54*, 486–495.

7644

Test Name: DAILY HASSLES QUESTIONNAIRE

Purpose: To measure day-to-day concerns of school-age adolescents.

Number of Items: 81

Format: Four-point scales are anchored by 1 (not at all a hassle) and 4 (a very big hassle).

Reliability: Alpha was .95.

Author: Hastings, T. L., et al.

Article: Gender differences in coping and daily stress in conduct-disordered and non-conduct-disordered adolescents.

Journal: *Journal of Psychopathology and Behavioral Assessment*, September 1996, *18*(3), 213–226.

Related Research: Rowlinson, R. T., & Felner, R. D. (1988). Major life events, hassles, and adaptation in adolescence: Confounding in the

conceptualization and measurement of life stress and adjustment revisited. *Journal of Personality and Social Psychology, 55*, 432–444.

7645

Test Name: DEATH ANXIETY SCALE

Purpose: To measure anxiety about death.

Number of Items: 15

Format: True/false format.

Reliability: Internal consistency reliability was .76. Test-retest (3-week) was .83.

Validity: Correlations with other variables ranged from −.42 to .63.

Author: Slanger, E., and Rudestam, K. E.

Article: Motivation and disinhibition in high risk sports: Sensation-seeking and self-efficacy.

Journal: *Journal of Research in Personality*, September 1997, *31*(3), 355–374.

Related Research: Templer, D. I. (1969). *Death Anxiety Scale*. Proceedings, 77th Annual Convention, American Psychological Association.

7646

Test Name: DEATH ANXIETY SCALE

Purpose: To measure components of death anxiety: fear of pain of dying, uncertainty of life beyond death and of not existing, burial and decomposition fears, and helplessness and loss of control.

Number of Items: 25

Format: Five-point Likert format. All items are presented.

Validity: Morticians score higher than nonmorticians.

Author: Thorson, J. A., and Powell, F. C.

Article: Undertakers and death anxiety.

Journal: *Psychological Reports*, June 1996, *78*(3) Part 2, 1228–1230.

Related Research: Thorson, J. A., & Powell, F. C. (1992). A Revised Death Anxiety Scale. *Death Studies, 16*, 507–521.

7647

Test Name: DEATH TRANSCENDENCE SCALE

Purpose: To measure the cognitive and mystical modes of death transcendence.

Number of Items: 25

Format: Four-point scales are anchored by 1 (strongly disagree) and 4 (strongly agree).

Reliability: Interitem reliability coefficients ranged from .62 to .79.

Author: MacDonald, D. A., and Gagnier, J. J.

Article: The Self-Expansiveness Level Form: Examination of its validity and relation to the NEO Personality Inventory—Revised.

Journal: *Psychological Reports*, June 2000, *86*(3, Part 1), 707–726.

Related Research: Vandcreek, L., & Nye, C. (1993). Testing the Death Transcendence Scale. *Journal for the Scientific Study of Religion, 32*, 279–283.

7648

Test Name: DEFENSE STYLE QUESTIONNAIRE

Purpose: To assess 13 defense

strategies used to cope with stressful events.

Number of Items: 36

Format: Nine-point scales.

Reliability: Alpha coefficients ranged from .47 to .79.

Validity: Correlations with other variables ranged from −.27 to .30.

Author: Ungerer, J. A., et al.

Article: Defense style and adjustment in interpersonal relationships.

Journal: *Journal of Research in Personality*, September 1997, *31*(3), 375–384.

Related Research: Andrews, G. (1991). Anxiety, personality and anxiety disorders. *International Review of Psychiatry, 3,* 293–302.

7649

Test Name: DEFENSIVE COPING SCALE

Purpose: To measure defensive coping.

Number of Items: 12

Format: Scales range from 1 (I usually don't do this at all) to 4 (I usually do this a lot). All items are presented.

Reliability: Alpha coefficients ranged from .38 to .79 across subscales and time. Total alphas ranged from .72 to .81.

Author: Knee, C. R., and Zuckerman, M.

Article: A nondefensive personality: Autonomy and control as moderators of defensive coping and self-handicapping.

Journal: *Journal of Research in Personality,* March 1998, *32*(1), 115–130.

Related Research: Carver, C. S.,

et al. (1989). Assessing coping strategies: A theoretically-based approach. *Journal of Personality and Social Psychology, 56,* 267–283.

7650

Test Name: DEPRESSION-HAPPINESS SCALE

Purpose: To assess positive and negative thoughts, feelings, and bodily experiences.

Number of Items: 25

Format: Four-point scales range from 0 (rarely) to 3 (often).

Reliability: Alphas ranged from .89 to .92. Test-retest correlation (2 weeks) was .70.

Author: Lewis, C. A., and McCollum, M. A.

Article: The Depression-Happiness Scale: Test-retest data over two weeks.

Journal: *Psychological Reports*, December 1999, *85*(3, Part I), 889–892.

Related Research: McGreal, R., & Joseph, S. (1993). The Depression-Happiness Scale. *Psychological Reports, 73,* 1279–1282.

7651

Test Name: DEPRESSION SELF-RATING SCALE

Purpose: To assess moderate to severe depression in children and early adolescents aged 8 to 14 years.

Number of Items: 18

Format: Items are rated on a 0–2 scale which includes "most of the time," "sometimes," or "never." Includes 2 factors: Dysphoria and Social Isolation; and Positive Affect. All items are presented.

Reliability: Alpha coefficients ranged from .65 to .75. Spearman-Brown split-half coefficients ranged from −.55 to .54.

Validity: Correlations with variables ranged from −.55 to .54.

Author: Cheung, S-K.

Article: Reliability and factor structure of the Chinese version of the Depression Self-Rating Scale.

Journal: *Educational and Psychological Measurement*, February 1996, *56*(1), 142–154.

Related Research: Birleson, P. (1981). The validity of depressive disorders and the development of a self-rating scale: A research report. *Journal of Child Psychology and Psychiatry, 22,* 73–88.

7652

Test Name: DEPRESSIVE EXPERIENCES QUESTIONNAIRE

Purpose: To measure dependency, self-criticism, and efficacy.

Number of Items: 66

Format: Likert format.

Reliability: Alpha coefficients ranged from .80 to .81. Test-retest reliabilities ranged from .75 to .91.

Validity: Correlations with other variables ranged from −.35 to .65.

Author: Alden, L. E., and Bieling, P. J.

Article: Interpersonal convergence of personality constructs in dynamic and cognitive models of depression.

Journal: *Journal of Research in Personality,* March 1996, *30*(1), 60–75.

Related Research: Blatt, S. J., et al. (1976). Experiences of depression in young adults. *Journal of Abnormal Psychology*, 85, 383–389.

7653

Test Name: DEPRESSIVE MOOD SCALE

Purpose: To determine how of 10 high school students are bothered or troubled by certain situations in the last 2 weeks.

Number of Items: 6

Format: Responses are made on a 3-point scale ranging from 1 (not at all) to 3 (somewhat too much).

Reliability: Coefficient alpha was .79. Test-retest (5–6 months) reliability was .76.

Validity: Correlation with SCL-90 Scale was .72.

Author: Wolfson, A. R., and Carskadon, M. A.

Article: Sleep schedules and daytime functioning in adolescents.

Journal: *Child Development*, August 1998, 69(4), 875–887.

Related Research: Kandel, D. B., & Davies, M. (1982). Epidemiology of depressive mood in adolescents. *Archives of General Psychiatry*, 39, 1205–1212.

7654

Test Name: DIFFERENTIAL EMOTIONS SCALE

Purpose: To measure anxiety related symptoms and behavior.

Number of Items: 36

Format: Five-point scales are anchored by 1 (rarely or never) and 5 (very often).

Reliability: Coefficient alpha was .92.

Validity: Correlations with other variables ranged from −.23 to .68.

Author: Youngstrom, E., et al.

Article: Dysphoria-related bias in maternal ratings of children.

Journal: *Journal of Consulting and Clinical Psychology*, December 1999, 67(6), 905–916.

Related Research: Izard, C. E., et al. (1993). Stability of emotion experiences and their relations to traits of personality. *Journal of Personality and Social Psychology*, 64, 847–860.

7655

Test Name: DISPOSITIONAL RESILIENCE SCALE

Purpose: To provide three indicators of hardiness.

Number of Items: 45

Format: Includes 3 dimensions: Commitment, Control, and Challenge. Responses are made on a 4-point scale ranging from 0 (not at all true) to 3 (completely true).

Reliability: Internal consistency estimates ranged from .62 to .82.

Validity: Correlations with other variables ranged from −.53 to .60.

Author: Robitschek, C., and Keshubeck, S.

Article: A structural model of parental alcoholism, family functioning, and psychological health: The mediating effects of hardiness and personal growth orientation.

Journal: *Journal of Counseling Psychology*, April 1999, 46(2), 159–172.

Related Research: Bartone, P. T., et al. (1989). The impact of a military air disaster on the health of assistance workers: A prospective study. *Journal of Nervous and Mental Disease*, 177, 317–328.

7656

Test Name: DISSOCIATIVE DISORDERS INTERVIEW SCHEDULE

Purpose: To assess symptoms of schizophrenia, major depression, borderline personality disorder, somatization disorder, and dissociative disorders.

Number of Items: 131

Format: Interview format.

Reliability: Interrater reliability was .68.

Author: Ellason, J. W., and Ross, C. A.

Article: Childhood trauma and psychiatric symptoms.

Journal: *Psychological Reports*, April 1997, 80(2), 447–450.

Related Research: Ross, C. A., & Joshi, S. (1992). Shneiderian symptoms and childhood trauma in the general population. *Comprehensive Psychiatry*, 33, 269–273.

7657

Test Name: DISTRESS SCALE

Purpose: To measure depression, anxiety, unhappiness, anger, resentment, and other related concepts.

Number of Items: 10

Format: Five-point scales are anchored by 1 (not at all) and 5 (extremely).

Reliability: Coefficient alpha was .89.

Validity: Correlations with other variables ranged from −.23 to .34.

Author: Carrier, C. S., et al.

Article: Responsiveness to threats and incentives, expectancy of recurrence, and distress and disengagement: Moderator effects in women with early stage breast cancer.

Journal: *Journal of Consulting and Clinical Psychology*, December 2000, *68*(6), 965–975.

Related Research: Carrier, C. S., et al. (1993). How coping mediates the effect of optimism on distress: A study of women with early stage breast cancer. *Journal of Personality and Social Psychology*, 65, 375–390.

7658

Test Name: EMOTION RECOGNITION QUESTIONNAIRE

Purpose: To assess a child's skills in identifying the emotions likely to be elicited in everyday situations.

Number of Items: 16 vignettes/pictures

Format: Child is asked to identify the emotion in the vignette (happy, sad, mad, or scared).

Reliability: Coefficient alpha was .66.

Author: Conduct Problems Prevention Research Group

Article: Initial impact of the fast track prevention trial for conduct problems: I. The high risk sample.

Journal: *Journal of Consulting and Clinical Psychology*, October 1999, *67*(5), 631–647.

Related Research: Ribordy, S. C., et al. (1988). Vignettes for emotion recognition research and affective therapy with children. *Journal of Clinical Child Psychology*, 17, 322–325.

7659

Test Name: EMOTIONAL CONTAGION SCALE

Purpose: To measure susceptibility to love, anger, fear, sadness, happiness and the ability to decode emotional communication.

Number of Items: 18

Format: Scales range from 1 (never true for me) to 4 (always true for me).

Reliability: Coefficient alpha was .67.

Author: Totterdell, P.

Article: Catching moods and hitting runs: Mood linkage and subjective performance in professional sports teams.

Journal: *Journal of Applied Psychology*, December 2000, *85*(6), 848–859.

Related Research: Hatfield, E., et al. (1994). *Emotional contagion*. Cambridge, England: Cambridge University Press.

7660

Test Name: EMOTIONAL STABILITY AND CONSCIENTIOUSNESS INVENTORY

Purpose: To measure emotional stability and conscientiousness.

Number of Items: 28

Format: Five-point rating scales.

Reliability: Alpha coefficients ranged from .80 to .89.

Validity: Correlations with other variables ranged from .02 to .67.

Author: Vasilopoulos, N. J., et al.

Article: The difference of job familiarity and impression management on self-report measure scale scores and response latencies.

Journal: *Journal of Applied Psychology*, February 2000, *85*(1), 50–64.

7661

Test Name: EMOTIONALITY SCALE

Purpose: To measure the propensity to become affectively distressed.

Number of Items: 8

Format: Five-point scales are anchored by 1 (never true of me) and 5 (always true of me).

Reliability: Cronbach's alpha was .77.

Author: Stice, E., et al.

Article: Support for the continuity hypotheses of bulimic pathology.

Journal: *Journal of Consulting and Clinical Psychology*, October 1998, *66*(5), 784–790.

Related Research: Buss, A. H., & Plomin, R. (1984*). Temperament: Early developing personality traits*. Hillsdale, NJ: Erlbaum.

7662

Test Name: EXERCISE-INDUCED FEELING INVENTORY

Purpose: To measure feelings associated with a single bout of exercise.

Number of Items: 12

Format: Includes 4 subscales: Positive Engagement, Revitalization, Tranquility, and Physical Exhaustion. Responses are made on a 5-point scale ranging from 0 (do not feel) to 4 (feel very strongly).

Reliability: Alpha coefficients ranged from .72 to .91.

Author: Annesi, J. J.

Article: Effects of minimal exercise and cognitive behavior identification on adherence, emotional change, self-image, and physical change in obese women.

Journal: *Perceptual and Motor Skills*, August 2000, *91*(1), 322–336.

Related Research: Gauvin, L., & Rejeski, W. J. (1993). The Exercise-Induced Feeling Inventory: Development and initial validation. *Journal of Sport and Exercise Psychology, 15*, 403–423.

7663

Test Name: EXPATRIATE ADAPTATION INVENTORY

Purpose: To assess adaptation to life abroad in terms of satisfaction with life abroad, feelings toward the host country, and satisfaction with life in the home country.

Number of Items: 58

Format: Response categories ranged from 0 (not true) to 2 (very true or often true). All items are presented.

Reliability: Correlations with other variables ranged from −.36 to .38.

Author: Fukunishi, I., et al.

Article: Alexthymic traits as predictors of difficulties with adjustment in an outpatient cohort of expatriates in Tokyo.

Journal: *Psychological Reports*, August 1999, *85*(1), 67–77.

Related Research: Cui, G., & Njoku, A. E. (1992). Measuring intercultural effectiveness: An integrative approach. *International Journal of Intercultural Relations, 16*, 311–328.

7664

Test Name: EXPLORATORY AND DECISIONAL STRESS SCALES

Purpose: To measure contextual anxiety.

Number of Items: 9

Format: Responses are made on a 7-point scale. Examples are presented.

Reliability: Alpha coefficients ranged from .72 to .88.

Author: Bartley, D. F., and Robitschek, C.

Article: Career exploration: A multivariate analysis of predictors.

Journal: *Journal of Vocational Behavior*, February 2000, *56*(1), 63–81.

Related Research: Blustein, D. L., & Phillips, S. D. (1988). Individual and contextual factors in career exploration. *Journal of Vocational Behavior, 33*, 203–216.

7665

Test Name: EXTENDED LIFE ORIENTATION TEST

Purpose: To measure optimism and pessimism.

Number of Items: 20

Format: Includes a 6-item optimism scale, a 9-item pessimism scale, and 5 filler items. Responses are made on a 5-point Likert-type scale ranging from 1 (strongly disagree) to 5 (strongly agree).

Reliability: Test-retest (6 weeks) reliability was .73 (optimism) and .84 (pessimism). Alpha coefficients ranged from .86 to .93

Validity: Correlations with other variables ranged from −.37 to .31.

Author: Chang, E. C.

Article: Cultural differences in optimism, pessimism, and coping. Predictors of subsequent adjustments in Asian American and Caucasian American college students.

Journal: *Journal of Counseling Psychology*, January 1996, *43*(1), 113–123.

7666

Test Name: EXTERNAL COPING SCALE

Purpose: To measure external coping.

Number of Items: 15

Format: Assesses avoidance, seeking social support, appeasement, assertion, and reporting to organizational authorities. Responses are made on a 5-point scale ranging from "not at all descriptive" to "extremely descriptive."

Reliability: Reliability coefficients were .85 and .88.

Validity: Correlations with other variables ranged from −.21 to .18.

Author: Munson, L. J., et al.

Article: Longitudinal analysis of dispositional influences and sexual harassment: Effects on job and psychological outcomes.

Journal: *Personnel Psychology*, Spring 2000, *53*(1), 21–46.

7667

Test Name: FEAR AROUSAL SCALE

Purpose: To measure the extent of feeling distracted, worried and fearful.

Number of Items: 7

Format: Scales range from 1 (not at all) to 7 (very much so).

Reliability: Coefficient alpha was .82.

Author: Keller, P. A.

Article: Converting the unconverted: The effect of inclination and opportunity to discount health-related fear appeals.

Journal: *Journal of Applied Psychology*, June 1999, *84*(3), 403–415.

Related Research: Rogers, R. W. (1983). Cognitive and psychological processes in fear appeals and attitude change: A revised theory of protection motivation. In J. Cacioppo & R. E. Petty (Eds.), *Social psychology* (pp. 153–176). New York: Guilford Press.

7668

Test Name: FEAR OF AIDS SCALE

Purpose: To measure fear of AIDS

Number of Items: 14

Format: Items are rated on 5-point scales anchored by "strongly agree" and "strongly disagree."

Reliability: Alphas ranged from .75 to .80.

Validity: Three of four known-groups' comparisons yielded statistically significant mean differences.

Author: Miller, D. B., et al.

Article: Fear of AIDS and homophobia scales: Additional estimates of reliability and validity.

Journal: *Psychological Reports*, December 1997, *81*(3, Part I), 783–786.

Related Research: Bouton, R. A., et al. (1987). Scales for measuring fear of AIDS and homophobia. *Journal of Personality Assessment, 51*, 606–614.

7669

Test Name: FEAR OF BEING INCOMPETENT SCALE

Purpose: To measure fear of appearing incompetent.

Number of Items: 36

Format: True/false format.

Reliability: Alpha was .92.

Author: Tomkiewicz, J., and Bass, K.

Article: Changes in women's fear of success and fear of appearing incompetent in business.

Journal: *Psychological Reports*, December 1999, *85*(3, Part I), 1003–1010.

Related Research: Good, L. R., & Good, K. C. (1973). An objective measure of the motive to avoid success. *Psychological Reports, 32*, 1075–1078.

7670

Test Name: FEAR OF CRIME SCALE

Purpose: To measure fear of crime.

Number of Items: 6

Format: Four-point scales range from 0 (disagree strongly) to 3 (agree strongly).

Reliability: Coefficient alpha was .82.

Author: Herek, G. M., et al.

Article: Psychological sequelae of hate-crime victimization among lesbian, gay, and bisexual adults.

Journal: *Journal of Consulting and Clinical Psychology*, December 1999, *67*(6), 945–951.

Related Research: Norris, F. H., & Kaniasty, K. (1991). The psychological experience of crime: A test of the mediating role of beliefs in explaining the distress of victims. *Journal of Social and Clinical Psychology, 10*, 239–261.

7671

Test Name: FEAR OF FLYING INVENTORY

Purpose: To measure fear of flying.

Number of Items: 33

Format: Nine-point scales range from 0 (not at all) to 8 (very severely disturbing).

Reliability: Test-retest reliability was .92.

Validity: Correlation with anxiety symptoms was .45.

Author: Rothbaum, B. O., et al.

Article: A controlled study of virtual reality exposure therapy for the fear of flying.

Journal: *Journal of Consulting and Clinical Psychology*, December 2000, *68*(6), 1020–1026.

Related Research: Scott, W. (1987). A fear of flying inventory. In P. Keller & S. Hayman (Eds.), *Innovations of clinical practice* (Vol. 7). Professional Resource Exchange.

7672

Test Name: FEAR OF FLYING QUESTIONNAIRE

Purpose: To measure fear of flying.

Number of Items: 36

Format: Eleven-point scales range from 0 (no fear) to 10 (extreme fear).

Reliability: Test-retest reliability

was .92. Split-half reliability was .99.

Author: Rothbaum, B. O., et al.

Article: A controlled study of virtual reality exposure therapy for the fear of flying.

Journal: *Journal of Consulting and Clinical Psychology*, December 2000, *68*(6), 1020–1026.

Related Research: Howard, W. A., et al. (1983). The nature and treatment of fear of flying: A controlled investigation. *Behavior Therapy, 14*, 557–567.

7673

Test Name: FEAR OF SUCCESS SCALE

Purpose: To measure fear of success.

Number of Items: 29

Format: True/false format.

Reliability: Alpha was .86.

Author: Tomkiewicz, J., and Bass, K.

Article: Changes in women's fear of success and fear of appearing incompetent in business.

Journal: *Psychological Reports*, December 1999, *85*(3, Part I), 1003–1010.

Related Research: Good, L. R., & Good, K. C. (1973). An objective measure of the motive to avoid success. *Psychological Reports, 33*, 1009–1010.

7674

Test Name: FEAR PERCEPTION INDEX

Purpose: To assess phobic populations.

Number of Items: 108

Format: Five-point scales are anchored by ''none at all'' and

''very much.'' All items are presented.

Reliability: Alpha was .97.

Validity: Correlations with Right-Wing Authoritarianism Scale ranged from .29 to .59.

Author: Eigenberger, M. E.

Article: Fear as a correlate of authoritarianism.

Journal: *Psychological Reports*, December 1998, *83*(3) Part 2, 1395–1409.

7675

Test Name: FEAR QUESTIONNAIRE

Purpose: To assess the presence of agoraphobia, social and blood-injury fears.

Number of Items: 17

Format: Ten-point scales are anchored by 0 (would not avoid it) and 9 (would always avoid it).

Reliability: Test-retest reliability (1-week) was .96 for the blood-injury scale.

Author: Wenzel, A., and Holt, C. S.

Article: Situation-specific scripts for threat in two specific phobias.

Journal: *Journal of Psychopathology and Behavioral Assessment*, March 2000, *22*(1), 1–21.

Related Research: Marks, I. M., & Mathews, A. (1979). Brief standard self-rating for phobic patients. *Behavior Research and Therapy, 17*, 263–267.

7676

Test Name: FEAR SURVEY SCHEDULE FOR CHILDREN—REVISED

Purpose: To assess specific fears in children.

Number of Items: 80

Format: Three-point scales.

Reliability: Alphas were in the range of .92.

Validity: Correlations with trait anxiety ranged from .46 to .51.

Author: Kendall, P. C., et al.

Article: Therapy for youths with anxiety disorders: A second randomized clinical trial.

Journal: *Journal of Consulting and Clinical Psychology*, June 1997, *65*(3), 366–380.

Related Research: Ollendick, T. (1983). Reliability and validity of the Revised Fear Survey Schedule for Children. *Behavior Research and Therapy, 21*, 685–692.

7677

Test Name: FINANCIAL STRAIN QUESTIONNAIRE

Purpose: To measure financial strain.

Number of Items: 5

Format: All items are presented. Four-point scales range from 0 (never) to 3 (most of the time).

Reliability: Cronbach alpha was .78.

Author: Paschall, M. J., and Hubbard, M. L.

Article: Effects of neighborhood and family stressors on African American male adolescents' self-worth and propensity for violent behavior.

Journal: *Journal of Consulting and Clinical Psychology*, October 1998 *66*(5), 825–831.

Related Research: McLoyd, V. (1990). The impact of economic hardship on Black families and children: Psychological distress, parenting, and socioemotional development. *Child Development, 61*, 311–346.

7678

Test Name: FRUSTRATION SCALE

Purpose: To measure frustration.

Number of Items: 3

Format: Scales range from 1 (strongly disagree) to 2 (agree strongly).

Reliability: Coefficient alpha was .73.

Validity: Correlations with other variables ranged from −.30 to .44.

Author: Spector, P. E., et al.

Article: A longitudinal study of relations between job stressors and job strains while controlling for prior negative affectivity and strains.

Journal: *Journal of Applied Psychology*, April 2000, *85*(2), 211–218.

Related Research: Peters, L. H., et al. (1980). The behavioral and affective consequences of performance-relevant situational variables. *Organizational Behavior and Human Performance, 25*, 79–96.

7679

Test Name: FUNCTIONAL INDEPENDENCE MEASURE

Purpose: To provide an indication of disability severity.

Number of Items: 18

Format: Includes 2 subscales: Motor and Cognitive. Items are rated on a 7-point scale ranging from 1 (total assistance necessary) to 7 (complete independence).

Validity: Correlations with other

variables ranged from −.41 to .24.

Author: Elliott, T. R., et al.

Article: Goal instability and adjustment to physical disability.

Journal: *Journal of Counseling Psychology*, April 2000, *47*(2), 251–265.

Related Research: Linacre, J. M., et al. (1995). *The Functional Independence Measure as a measure of disability*. (Research Report No. 91–01). Chicago: Rehabilitation Institute of Chicago.

7680

Test Name: FUNCTIONAL STATUS SCALE

Purpose: To assess the ability to perform instrumental daily activities.

Number of Items: 8

Format: Responses were: could do activity without help, with some help, or were unable to do the activity.

Reliability: Alpha was .82.

Validity: Correlation with depression was −.34.

Author: Kimberlin, C. L., et al.

Article: Issues related to using a short-form of the Center for Epidemiological Studies—Depression Scale.

Journal: *Psychological Reports*, October 1998, *83*(2), 411–421.

Related Research: Duke University. (1978). Multidimensional functional assessment: The OARS methodology. (2nd ed.) Durham, NC: Duke University Medical Center, Center for the Study of Aging and Human Development.

7681

Test Name: GAY LIFESTYLES HASSLES SCALE

Purpose: To measure hassles in the everyday life of gay men.

Number of Items: 26

Format: Four-point response scales.

Reliability: Alphas ranged from .72 to .89 across subscales.

Author: Siegel, K., and Epstein, J.

Article: Ethnic-racial differences in psychological stress related to gay lifestyle among HIV-positive men.

Journal: *Psychological Reports*, August 1996, *79*(1), 303–312.

Related Research: Kanner, A. D., et al. (1981). Comparisons of two models of stress measurement: Daily hassles and uplifts versus major life events. *Journal of Behavioral Medicine, 4*, 1–39.

7682

Test Name: GENERAL BEHAVIOR INVENTORY

Purpose: To assess symptoms of depression, hypomania, or cyclothymia.

Number of Items: 73

Format: Four-point scales are anchored by "never or hardly ever" and "very often or almost constantly."

Reliability: Internal consistency ranged from .90 to .96. Test-retest reliabilities (12 to 16 weeks) ranged from .71 to .74.

Author: Meyer, B., et al.

Article: Exploring behavioral activation and inhibition sensitivities among college students at risk for bipolar spectrum symptomatology.

Journal: *Journal of*

Psychopathology and Behavioral Assessment, December 1999, *21*(4), 275–292.

Related Research: Depue, R. A., et al. (1989). General behavior inventory identification of unipolar and bipolar conditions in a non-clinical university population. *Journal of Abnormal Psychology, 98*, 117–126.

7683

Test Name: GENERAL HEALTH QUESTIONNAIRE

Purpose: To measure mental health.

Number of Items: 12

Format: Four-point scales range from 1 (not at all) to 4 (much more than usual).

Reliability: Coefficient alpha was .92.

Validity: Correlations with other variables ranged from −.13 to .66.

Author: Wanberg, C. R.

Article: Antecedents and outcomes of coping behaviors among unemployed and reemployed individuals.

Journal: *Journal of Applied Psychology*, October 1997, *82*(5), 731–744.

Related Research: Banks, M. H., et al. (1980). The use of the General Health Questionnaire as an indicator of mental health in occupational studies. *Journal of Occupational Psychology, 53*, 187–194.

7684

Test Name: GENERAL HEALTH RATING INDEX

Purpose: To measure perceived health status.

Number of Items: 22

Format: Responses are made on a 5-point scale.

Reliability: Coefficient alpha was .84.

Author: Mahon, N. E., et al.

Article: Loneliness and health-related variables in young adults.

Journal: *Perceptual and Motor Skills*, December 1997, *85*(3, Part 1), 800–802.

Related Research: Davies, A. R., & Ware, J. E. (1981). *Measuring health perception in the Health Insurance Experiment* (R-2711-HHS). Santa Monica, CA: RAND Corp.

7685

Test Name: GERIATRIC DEPRESSION SCALE—SHORT FORM

Purpose: To measure depression.

Number of Items: 15

Format: Yes/no format.

Validity: Correlations with other variables ranged from −.09 to .24.

Author: Ferraro, F. R., et al.

Article: Relationship of Maudsley obsessional-compulsive inventory subscales with negative priming.

Journal: *Journal of General Psychology*, July 1997, *124*(3), 341–349.

Related Research: Ferraro, F. R., & Chelminski, I. (1996). Preliminary normative data on the Geriatric Depression Scale—Short Form (GSD-SF) in a sample of young adults. *Journal of Clinical Psychology, 52*, 443–447.

7686

Test Name: GERIATRIC DEPRESSION SCALE—CHINESE VERSION

Purpose: To measure depression in the elderly.

Number of Items: 30 (15 on short version).

Reliability: Alphas ranged from .77 to .86.

Validity: Correlations between the long form and short form were .94 (old) and .91 (new).

Author: Liu, C-Y, et al.

Article: Correlations between scores on Chinese versions of long and short forms of the Geriatric Depression Scale among elderly Chinese.

Journal: *Psychological Reports*, February 1998, *82*(1), 211–214.

7687

Test Name: (GOLDFARB) FEAR OF FAT SCALE

Purpose: To measure the fear of becoming fat.

Number of Items: 10

Format: Scales range from 1 (very untrue) to 4 (very true). Sample items are presented.

Reliability: Coefficient alpha was .85. Test-retest reliability (1 week) was .88.

Authors: Sjostedt, J. P., et al.

Article: Eating disorders among Indian and Australian university students.

Journal: *Journal of Social Psychology*, June 1998, *138*(3), 351–357.

Related Research: Goldfarb, L. A., et al. (1988). The Goldfarb Fear of Fat Scale. *Journal of Personality Assessment, 49*, 329–332.

7688

Test Name: HAMILTON ANXIETY RATING SCALE—REVISED

Purpose: To measure anxiety symptoms.

Number of Items: 16

Reliability: Coefficient alpha was .83.

Validity: Correlations with other variables ranged from .32 to .66.

Author: Bowman, D., et al.

Article: Efficacy of self-examination therapy in the treatment of generalized anxiety disorders.

Journal: *Journal of Counseling Psychology*, July 1997, *44*(3), 267–273.

Related Research: Riskind, J., et al. (1987). Taking the measure of anxiety and depression: Validity of the reconstructed Hamilton scales. *Journal of Nervous and Mental Disease*, *175*, 474–479.

7689

Test Name: HAMILTON DEPRESSION RATING SCALE

Purpose: To provide a clinical interview measure of the severity of depressive symptoms.

Number of Items: 17

Reliability: Internal consistency coefficient was .91. Interrater reliability ranged from .90 to .97.

Validity: Correlation with the Reynolds Adolescent Depression Scale was .76.

Author: Reynolds, W. M., and Mazza, J. J.

Article: Reliability and validity of the Reynolds Adolescent Depression Scale with young adolescents.

Journal: *Journal of School Psychology*, Fall 1998, *36*(3), 295–312.

Related Research: Hamilton, M. (1967). Development of a rating scale for primary depressive

illness. *British Journal of Social and Clinical Psychology*, *6*, 278–296.

7690

Test Name: HASSLES SCALE

Purpose: To measure stress in everyday life from work, health, family, friends, the environment, and chance events.

Number of Items: 117

Format: Three-point severity scales.

Reliability: Test-retest reliabilities ranged from .60 to .79 across subscales.

Author: Schuldberg, D., et al.

Article: Stress, coping, and social support in hypothetically psychosis-prone subjects.

Journal: *Psychological Reports*, June 1996, *78*(3) Part 2, 1267–1283.

Related Research: Kanner, A. D., et al. (1981). Comparison of two modes of stress management: Daily hassles and uplifts versus major life events. *Journal of Behavioral Medicine*, *4*, 1–39.

7691

Test Name: HEALTH BEHAVIORS QUESTIONNAIRE

Purpose: To assess health behaviors and emotions.

Number of Items: 34

Format: Scales range from 1 (never) to 4 (almost always). A sample item is presented.

Reliability: Coefficient alpha was .80 for the total scale. Subscale alphas ranged from .56 to .83.

Author: McCarthy, C. J., et al.

Article: Predicting emotional and behavioral risk factors in adolescents.

Journal: *The School Counselor*, March 1996, *43*(4), 277–286.

Related Research: Ingersoll, G. M., & Orr, D. P. (1989). Behavioral and emotional risk in early adolescents. *Journal of Early Adolescence*, *9*, 396–408.

7692

Test Name: HELPLESSNESS SCALE

Purpose: To assess the extent of helplessness behaviors with respect to women.

Number of Items: 7

Format: Scales range from 0 (never participate/ engage in) to 10 (always participate/engage in). All items are presented.

Reliability: Coefficient alpha was .73.

Author: Foster, M. D.

Article: Positive and negative responses to personal discrimination: Does coping make a difference?

Journal: *Journal of Social Psychology*, February 2000, *140*(1)93–106.

Related Research: Peterson, C. (1993). Helplessness behavior. *Behavior Research and Therapy*, *31*, 289–295.

7693

Test Name: HELPLESSNESS SCALE

Purpose: To measure general and specific helplessness.

Number of Items: 14

Format: Response scales are anchored by (−3) "strongly disagree" and (+3) "strongly agree." Sample items are presented.

Reliability: Cronbach's alpha was .90.

Validity: Correlations with other variables ranged from −.53 to .65.

Author: Ozmet, J. M., and Lester, D.

Article: Helplessness and depression.

Journal: *Psychological Reports*, April 1998, *82*(2), 434.

7694

Test Name: HOPE SCALE

Purpose: To assess hope.

Format: Subjects write a detailed essay on the most significant event in their lives in the past 4 years.

Reliability: Interrater agreement ranged from .61 to .88.

Validity: Correlation with optimism was .40 and −.14 with depression.

Author: McLenon, J.

Article: A prospective study of hope, optimism, and health.

Journal: *Psychological Reports*, December 1997, *81*(3, Part I), 723–733.

Related Research: Gottschalk, L. A. (1974). A hope scale applicable to verbal samples. *Archives of General Psychiatry*, *30*, 779–785.

7695

Test Name: HOPE SCALE

Purpose: To measure the agency and pathways dimensions of hope.

Number of Items: 8

Format: 4-point scales are anchored by (1) disagree and (4) agree.

Reliability: Cronbach alphas ranged from .88 (agency) to .83 (pathways).

Validity: Correlations with other variables ranged from −.43 to −.17.

Author: Cramer, K. M., and Dyrkacz, L.

Article: Differential predictions of maladjustment scores with Snyder Hope Subscales.

Journal: *Psychological Reports* December 1998, *83*(3) Part 1, 1035–1041.

Related Research: Snyder, C. R., et al. (1996). Development and validation of the State Hope Scale. *Journal of Personality and Social Psychology*, *70*, 321–335.

7696

Test Name: HOPE SCALE

Purpose: To measure hope.

Number of Items: 12

Format: Includes 2 factors: Agency and Pathways

Reliability: Test-retest reliability .85 (3 weeks), .76 and .82 (10 weeks). Alpha coefficients ranged from .71 to .76 (Agency) and from .63 to .80 (Pathways).

Validity: Correlations with other variables ranged from .05 to .47.

Author: Onwuegbuzie, A. J., and Daley, C. E.

Article: Relation of hope to self-perception.

Journal: *Perceptual and Motor Skills*, April 1999, *88*(2), 535–540.

Related Research: Snyder, C. R., et al. (1991). The will and the ways: Development and validation of an individual differences measure of hope. *Journal of Personality and Social Psychology*, *60*, 570–585.

7697

Test Name: HOPE SCALE

Purpose: To assess the optimism toward the future in areas of parental relationships.

Number of Items: 30

Format: Five-point scales are anchored by 1 (it probably won't happen) and 5 (it will happen to a greater extent than I now realize). Sample items are presented.

Reliability: Alpha was .93.

Author: Freedman, S. R., and Enright, R. D.

Article: Forgiveness as an intervention goal with incest survivors.

Journal: *Journal of Consulting and Clinical Psychology*, October 1996, *64*(5), 983–992.

Related Research: Al-Mabuk, R. H., et al. Forgiveness therapy with parents of adolescent suicide victims. *Journal of Family Psychotherapy*, 7, 21–39.

7698

Test Name: HOPELESSNESS SCALE

Purpose: To measure hopelessness.

Number of Items: 5

Format: Five-point Likert format. A sample item is presented.

Reliability: Reliability was .49.

Author: Cheung, C.-K., and Kwok, S.-T.

Article: Conservative orientation as a determinant of hopelessness.

Journal: *Journal of Social Psychology*, June 1996, *136*(3), 333–347.

Related Research: Kovacs, M., et al. (1975). Hopelessness: An indication of suicidal risk. *Suicide, 5,* 98–103.

7699

Test Name: HOPELESSNESS SCALE

Purpose: To measure an individual's negative expectancies of the future.

Number of Items: 20

Format: True/false format.

Reliability: Internal consistencies ranged from .39 to .72. Test-retest reliability was .85.

Validity: Correlations with clinical ratings of depression ranged from .60 to .74.

Author: Kapci, E. G.

Article: Test of the hopelessness theory of depression: Drawing negative inference from negative life events.

Journal: *Psychological Reports,* April 1998, *82*(2), 355–363.

Related Research: Beck, A. T., et al. (1974). The measurement of pessimism: The Hopelessness Scale. *Journal of Consulting and Clinical Psychology, 42,* 861–865.

7700

Test Name: HOPELESSNESS SCALE FOR CHILDREN

Purpose: To measure hopelessness.

Number of Items: 17

Format: Includes two factors: Giving Up and Future Expectations. Responses are either "true" or "false."

Reliability: Alpha coefficients ranged from .69 to .97. Split-half reliability was .70.

Validity: Correlation with Nowicki-Strickland Internal-

External Scale was .42. Intellectual Achievement Responsibility Questionnaire was −.29.

Author: Wehmeyer, M. L., and Palmer, S. B.

Article: Factor structure and construct validity of scores on the Hopelessness Scale for Children with students with cognitive disabilities.

Journal: *Educational and Psychological Measurement,* August 1998, *58*(4), 661–667.

Related Research: Kazdin, A. E., et al. (1986). The Hopelessness Scale for Children: Psychometric characteristics and concurrent validity. *Journal of Consulting and Clinical Psychology, 54,* 241–245.

7701

Test Name: HOPKINS SYMPTOM CHECKLIST

Purpose: To provide a self-report of psychological symptoms.

Format: Responses are made on a 4-point scale ranging from 1 (not at all) to 4 (extremely).

Reliability: Alpha coefficients ranged from .84 to .86. Test-retest reliabilities ranged from .75 to .81.

Validity: Correlation with other variables ranged from −.07 to .34.

Author: Simonsen, G., et al.

Article: Gender role conflict and psychological well-being among gay men.

Journal: *Journal of Counseling Psychology,* January 2000, *47*(1), 85–89.

Related Research: Derogatis, L., et al. (1974). The Hopkins Symptom Checklist. *Psychological Measurements in Psychopharmacology, 7,* 79–110.

7702

Test Name: HOPKINS SYMPTOM CHECKLIST

Purpose: To assess a client's current symptoms.

Number of Items: 90

Format: Responses are made on a 0–4 Likert scale.

Reliability: Test-retest reliability was .74.

Validity: Convergent validity ranged from .40 to .75.

Author: Jobes, D. A., et al.

Article: Assessment and treatment of suicidal clients in a university counseling center.

Journal: *Journal of Counseling Psychology,* October 1997, *44*(4), 368–377.

Related Research: Derogatis, L. R., et al. (1974). The Hopkins Symptom Checklist: A self-report symptom inventory. *Behavioral Science, 19,* 1–15.

7703

Test Name: HOPKINS SYMPTOM CHECKLIST— REVISED

Purpose: To measure psychological distress.

Number of Items: 30

Format: Includes 3 of the 5 subscales: Anxiety, Depression, and Somatization. Responses are made on a 5-point scale ranging from 1 (not at all) to 5 (extremely).

Reliability: Internal consistency reliability coefficients ranged from .84 to .87. Test-retest (one week) reliability coefficients range from .75 to .82.

Author: Ingram, K. M., et al.

Article: The relationship of victimization experiences to psychological well-being among homeless women and low-income housed women.

Journal: *Journal of Counseling Psychology*, April 1996, *43*(2), 218–227.

Related Research: Derogatis, L. R., et al. (1974). The Hopkins Symptom Checklist (HSCL): A self-report symptom inventory. *Behavioral Science*, 19(1), 1–15.

7704

Test Name: HOPKINS SYMPTOM CHECKLIST— SHORT VERSION

Purpose: To measure mental health (depression and anxiety).

Number of Items: 25

Format: Four-point scale range from 1 (not at all) to 4 (often).

Reliability: Alpha coefficients ranged from .85 to .91.

Author: Ickovics, J. R., et al.

Article: "A grief observed": The experience of HIV-related illness and death among women in a clinic-based sample in New Haven, Connecticut.

Journal: *Journal of Consulting and Clinical Psychology*, December 1998, *66*(6), 958–966.

Related Research: Derogatis, L. R., et al. (1974*)*. The Hopkins Symptom Checklist (HSCL). *Modern Problems of Pharmacopsychiatry*, 7, 79–110.

7705

Test Name: HUMOR SCALES

Purpose: To assess the degree to which individuals use humor to cope with stress and the situations in which they would have used humor.

Number of Items: 28

Format: Coping scales range from 1 (strongly disagree) to 4

(strongly agree). Use scales range from 1 (I would not have been amused) to 5 (I would laugh heartily).

Reliability: Alpha coefficients ranged from .60 to .70 (Coping) and from .70 to .79 (Use).

Author: Lefcourt, H. M., et al.

Article: Humor as a stress moderator in the prediction of blood pressure obtained during five stressful events.

Journal: *Journal of Research in Personality*, December 1997, *31*(4), 523–542.

Related Research: Martin, R. A., & Lefcourt, H. M. (1983). Sense of humor as a moderator in the relation between stressors and moods. *Journal of Personality and Social Psychology*, 45, 1313–1324.

Martin, R. A., & Lefcourt, H. M. (1984). The Situational Humor Response Questionnaire: A quantitative measure of the sense of humor. *Journal of Personality and Social Psychology*, 47, 145–155.

7706

Test Name: IMPACT OF EVENTS SCALE

Purpose: To assess signs of both intrusion and avoidance in cognition and affect related to a designated stressor.

Number of Items: 15

Format: Includes 2 subscales: Intrusion and Avoidance. Responses are made on a 4-point scale ranging from "not at all" to "often." Sample items are presented.

Reliability: Split-half reliability was .86. Alpha coefficients were .78 (Intrusion) and .82 (Avoidance).

Validity: Correlations with other

variables ranged from −.09 to .46.

Author: Kemp, M. A., and Neimeyer, G. J.

Article: Interpersonal attachment: Experiencing, expressing, and coping with stress.

Journal: *Journal of Counseling Psychology*, July 1999, *46*(3), 388–394.

Related Research: Horowitz, M. J., et al. (1979). Impact of Events Scale: A study of subjective distress. *Psychosomatic Medicine, 41*, 209–218.

7707

Test Name: IMPACT OF EVENTS SCALE—REVISED

Purpose: To assess subjective, posttraumatic stress associated with a specific life event.

Number of Items: 22

Format: Responses are made on a 5-point scale ranging from 0 (not at all) to 4 (extremely). An example is presented.

Reliability: Split-half reliability was .86.

Author: Hill, C. E., et al.

Article: Structured brief therapy with a focus on dreams or loss for clients with troubling dreams and recent loss.

Journal: *Journal of Counseling Psychology*, January 2000, *47*(1), 90–101.

Related Research: Weiss, D. S., & Marmar, C. R. (1997). The Impact of Events Scale— Revised. In J. P. Wilson and T. M. Keane (Eds.), *Assessing psychological trauma and PTSD: A practitioner's handbook* (pp. 339–411). New York: Guilford Press.

7708

Test Name: INDEX OF WELL-BEING

Purpose: To rate present feeling about life.

Number of Items: 9

Format: Bipolar scales range from 1 to 7. Sample items are presented.

Reliability: Internal consistency was .87.

Author: Helgeson, V. S., and Fritz, H. L.

Article: Unmitigated agency and unmitigated communion: Distinctions from agency and communion.

Journal: *Journal of Research in Personality*, June 1999, *33*(2), 131–158.

Related Research: Campbell, A., et al. (1976). *The quality of American life: Perceptions, evaluations, and satisfactions.* New York: Russell Sage Foundation.

7709

Test Name: INTERNAL STATE SCALE

Purpose: To measure current mania and depression symptoms.

Number of Items: 17

Format: Five-point scales are anchored by 1 (not at all today) and 5 (extremely today). Visual analog scales can also be used.

Reliability: Alphas ranged from .81 to .92.

Validity: Correlations with criterion measures ranged from .60 to .84.

Author: Meyer, B., et al.

Article: Exploring behavioral activation and inhibition sensitivities among college

students at risk for bipolar spectrum symptomatology.

Journal: *Journal of Psychopathology and Behavioral Assessment*, December 1999, *21*(4), 275–292.

Related Research: Bauer, M. S., et al. (1991). Independent assessment of manic and depressive symptoms by self-rating: Scale characteristics and implications for the study of mania. *Archives of General Psychiatry, 48,* 807–812.

7710

Test Name: INVENTORY OF COPING SCHEMAS

Purpose: To measure self-reported coping strategies.

Number of Items: 81

Format: Scales range from 1 (not at all) to 5 (a great amount). Sample items are presented.

Reliability: Alpha coefficients ranged from .80 to .97.

Validity: Correlations with other variables ranged from −.18 to .58.

Author: Peacock, E. J., and Wong, P. T. P.

Article: Anticipatory stress: The relation of locus of control, optimism, and control appraisals to coping.

Journal: *Journal of Research in Personality*, June 1996, *30*(2), 204–222.

Related Research: Wong, P. T. P., et al. (1991). *An inventory of coping schemas.* Unpublished manuscript, Trent University, Peterborough, Canada.

7711

Test Name: THE INVENTORY OF HEALTH STATUS

Purpose: To assess health status.

Number of Items: 60

Format: Multiple-choice format. All items are presented.

Validity: Beta weights ranged from −.20 to .49.

Author: Sheridan, C. L., et al.

Article: The role of social desirability, negative affectivity, and female reproductive system symptoms in differences in reporting symptoms by men and women.

Journal: *Psychological Reports*, August 1999, *85*(1), 54–62.

Related Research: Sheridan, C. L., et al. (1998). Validation of a brief, self-report inventory of organic health status independent of social desirability and negative affectivity. *Psychological Reports, 82,* 679–687.

7712

Test Name: INVENTORY TO DIAGNOSE DEPRESSION

Purpose: To measure depressive behavior.

Number of Items: 22

Format: Responses are made on a 5-point Likert-type scale.

Reliability: Test-retest (over 2 days) reliability was .98. Coefficients alpha was .92.

Validity: Correlation with other variables ranged from −.18 to .52.

Author: Elliott, T. R., et al.

Article: Goal instability and adjustment to physical disability.

Journal: *Journal of Counseling Psychology*, April 2000, *47*(2), 251–265.

Related Research: Zimmerman, M., & Coryell, W. (1987). The Inventory to Diagnose Depression (IDD): A self-report scale to diagnose major depressive disorder. *Journal of Consulting and Clinical Psychology*, 55, 55–59.

7713

Test Name: IRRATIONAL BELIEFS SCALE

Purpose: To assess irrational beliefs.

Reliability: Alpha was .73.

Validity: Correlation with need for cognition was −.29.

Author: Mahoney, J. M., and Kaufman, D.

Article: Need for cognition and irrational beliefs.

Journal: *Psychological Reports*, October 1997, *81*(2), 685–690.

Related Research: Watson, C. G., et al. (1989). Contributions to self-defeating philosophies, helplessness, and repression to anxiety among psychiatric patients. *Journal of Clinical Psychology*, 67, 1049–1062.

7714

Test Name: JAPANESE MENTAL-PHYSICAL HEALTH SCALES

Purpose: To measure mental and physical health.

Number of Items: 48

Format: Scales range from 1 (doesn't at all) to 5 (very much). Sample items are presented.

Reliability: Alpha coefficients ranged from .82 to .91 across scales.

Authors: Jou, Y. H., and Fukada, H.

Article: The causes and influence of transitional stress among Chinese students in Japan.

Journal: *Journal of Social*

Psychology, August 1996, *136*(4), 501–509.

Related Research: Matsuoka, Y. (1990). Psychological measurement and medical psychodiagnosis (Clinical scale): KMI. In T. Kawano et al. (Eds.), *Psychological test for psychosomatic medicine*. Tokyo: Asa kura Syoten (In Japanese).

Ueda, S., et al. (1992). The psychological study of happiness (2): An attempt to develop a happiness scale. *Bulletin of the Faculty of Education, Hiroslunia University, Part 1* (Psychology), *41*, 35–40. (In Japanese)

7715

Test Name: JEWISH IDENTIFICATION AND PSYCHOLOGICAL WELL-BEING SCALES

Purpose: To measure Jewish identification and well-being.

Number of Items: 46

Format: Six-point rating scales.

Reliability: Alphas ranged from .74 to .90.

Validity: Correlations with other variables ranged from .00 to .26.

Author: Ressler, W. H.

Article: Jewishness and well-being: Specific identification and general psychological adjustment.

Journal: *Psychological Reports*, October 1997, *81*(2), 515–518.

7716

Test Name: KANDEL DEPRESSION SCALE.

Purpose: To provide an epidemiological assessment of depressed mood.

Number of Items: 6

Format: Includes either 3-point or 5-point scales.

Reliability: Alpha coefficient was .79. Test-retest (5 to 6 months) was .76.

Author: Rice, K. G., et al.

Article: Attachment to parents, social competence, and emotional well-being: A comparison of black and white late adolescents.

Journal: *Journal of Counseling Psychology*, January 1997, *44*(1), 89–101.

Related Research: Kandel, D. B., & Davies, M. (1982). Epidemiology of depressive mood in adolescents. *Archives of General Psychiatry*, 39, 1205–1212.

7717

Test Name: KIDCOPE

Purpose: To measure frequency of use of 10 coping strategies.

Number of Items: 13

Format: Four-point scales are anchored by 1 (not at all) and 4 (almost all of the time). Sample items are presented.

Reliability: Internal consistencies ranged from .43 to .77 across subscales.

Author: LaGreca, A. M., et al.

Article: Symptoms of posttraumatic stress in children after Hurricane Andrew: A prospective study.

Journal: *Journal of Consulting and Clinical Psychology*, August 1996, *64*(4), 712–723.

Related Research: Vernberg, E. M., et al. (1996). Prediction of posttraumatic stress symptoms in children after Hurricane Andrew. *Journal of Abnormal Psychology*, 105, 237–248.

7718

Test Name: KUWAIT UNIVERSITY ANXIETY SCALE

Purpose: To measure the predisposition to develop anxiety.

Number of Items: 20

Format: Four-point scales are anchored by 1 (rarely) and 4 (always). All items are presented.

Reliability: Alphas ranged from .88 to .92. Test-retest reliabilities (1 week) ranged from .70 to .93.

Validity: Correlations with other anxiety measures ranged from .71 to .88. Correlations with depression measures ranged from .70 to .88.

Author: Abdel-Khalek, A. M.

Article: The Kuwait University Anxiety Scale: Psychometric properties.

Journal: *Psychological Reports*, October 2000, *87*(2), 478–492.

7719

Test Name: LARSON DRIVER'S STRESS PROFILE

Purpose: To assess drivers' stress in terms of anger, impatience, competing, and punishing.

Number of Items: 40

Format: Four-point scales are anchored by 0 (never) and 3 (always).

Reliability: Reliability coefficients ranged from .84 to .96.

Validity: Correlations with other variables ranged from −.37 to .57.

Author: Blanchard, E. B., et al.

Article: Psychometric properties of a measure of aggressive driving: The Larson Driver's Stress Profile.

Journal: *Psychological Reports*, December 2000, *87*(3, Part 1), 881–892.

Related Research: Larson, J. A. (1996). Driver's Stress Profile. In J. A. Larson (Ed.), *Steering*

clear of highway madness (pp. 25–28). Wilsonville, OR: Bookpartners.

7720

Test Name: LAUFER COMBAT SCALE

Purpose: To assess Gulf War combat exposure.

Number of Items: 33

Format: Three-point scales range from 0 (never) to 2 (three or more times).

Reliability: Coefficient alpha was .73.

Author: Wolfe, J., et al.

Article: Course and predictors of posttraumatic stress disorder among Gulf War veterans: A prospective analysis.

Journal: *Journal of Consulting and Clinical Psychology*, August 1999, *67*(4), 520–528.

Related Research: Gallops, M., et al. (1981). The combat scale revised. In A. Egendorf, et al., (Eds.), *Legacies of Vietnam: Comparative adjustment of veterans and their peers* (pp. 125–129). New York: Center for Policy Research.

7721

Test Name: LEISURE SATISFACTION MEASURE

Purpose: To measure leisure satisfaction.

Number of Items: 51

Format: Five-point Likert format.

Reliability: Reliability coefficients ranged from .92 to .96.

Author: Pearson, Q. M.

Article: Job satisfaction, leisure satisfaction, and psychological health.

Journal: *Career Development*

Quarterly, June 1998, *46*(4), 416–426.

Related Research: Beard, J. G., & Ragheb, M. G. (1980). Measuring leisure satisfaction. *Journal of Leisure Research, 12,* 20–33.

7722

Test Name: LEVINSON'S SELF-REPORT PSYCHOPATHY SCALE

Purpose: To assess both primary and secondary psychopathy.

Number of Items: 26

Format: Responses are made on a 4-point scale ranging from 1 (strongly disagree) to 4 (strongly agree). All items are presented.

Reliability: Test-retest (8 weeks) reliability was .83.

Validity: Correlations with other variables ranged from −.59 to .37.

Author: Lynam, D. R., et al.

Article: Self-reported psychopathy: A validation study.

Journal: *Journal of Personality Assessment*, August 1999, *73*(1), 110–132.

Related Research: Levenson, M. R., et al. (1995). Assessing psychopathic attributes in a noninstitutional population. *Journal of Personality and Social Psychology, 68,* 151–158.

7723

Test Name: LIFE EVENTS CHECKLIST

Purpose: To measure life events among children, to assess events as "good" or "bad," and to assess the impact the event had.

Number of Items: 46

Format: Four-point impact scales

range from 0 (no impact) to 3 (great impact).

Validity: Correlations with other variables ranged from −.14 to .24 (negative life events only).

Author: Holmes, C. S., et al.

Article: Chronic and discrete stress as predictors of children's adjustment.

Journal: *Journal of Consulting and Clinical Psychology*, June 1999, *67*(3), 411–419.

Related Research: Johnson, J. H., & McCutcheon, S. (1980). Assessing life stress in older children and adolescents: Preliminary findings with the Life Events Checklist. In I. G. Sarason & C. D. Spielberger (Eds.), *Stress and anxiety* (pp. 111–125). Washington, DC: Hemisphere.

7724

Test Name: LIFE EVENTS CHECKLIST—MODIFIED

Purpose: To measure life events.

Number of Items: 42

Format: The respondents indicate whether each item has been either a positive or negative event for them. All items are presented.

Reliability: Test-retest (2 weeks) reliability was .72.

Author: Jackson, Y., and Warren, J. S.

Article: Appraisal, social support, and life events: Predicting outcome behavior in school-age children.

Journal: *Child Development*, September/October 2000, *71*(5), 1441–1457.

Related Research: Johnson, J., & McCutcheon, S. (1980). Assessing life stress in older children and adolescents: Preliminary findings

with the Life Events Checklist. In G. Sarason & C. Spielberger (Eds.), *Stress and anxiety*. Washington, DC: Hemisphere.

7725

Test Name: LIFE EXPERIENCES SURVEY

Purpose: To measure life stress.

Number of Items: 57

Format: Seven-point desirability scales are anchored by −3 and 3.

Reliability: Test-retest (6 weeks) reliability was .64.

Validity: Correlations with other variables ranged from −.32 to .00.

Author: Clum, G. A., et al.

Article: An expanded etiological model for suicide behavior in adolescents: Evidence for its specificity relative to depression.

Journal: *Journal of Psychopathology and Behavioral Assessment*, September 1997, *19*(3), 207–222.

Related Research: Sarason, I., et al. (1978). Assessing the impact of life changes: Development of the Life Experiences Survey. *Journal of Consulting and Clinical Psychology*, *46*, 932–946.

7726

Test Name: LIFE EXPERIENCES SURVEY

Purpose: To assess a wide range of life experiences and events.

Number of Items: 60

Format: Responses are made on a 7-point scale.

Reliability: Test-retest (8 weeks) reliability ranged from .60 to .82.

Author: Napoli, A. R., and Wortman, P. M.

Article: Psychosocial factors related to retention and early departure of two-year community college students.

Journal: *Research in Higher Education*, August 1998, *39*(4), 419–455.

Related Research: Sarason, I. G., et al. (1978). Assessing the impact of life changes: Development of the life experiences survey. *Journal of Consulting and Clinical Psychology*, *46*(5), 932–946.

7727

Test Name: LIFE MEANING AND PURPOSE SCALE

Purpose: To measure life meaning and purpose.

Number of Items: 4

Format: Responses are made on 7-point scales. All items are presented.

Validity: Correlations with other variables ranged from −.24 to .43.

Author: Sumerlin, J. R., and Bundrick, C. M.

Article: Happiness and self-actualization under conditions of strain: A sample of homeless men.

Journal: *Perceptual and Motor Skills*, February 2000, *90*(1), 191–203.

Related Research: Dinkmeyer, D. C., et al. (1987). *Adlerian counseling and psychotherapy*. Columbus, OH: Merrill.

7728

Test Name: LIFE ORIENTATION TEST

Purpose: To measure optimism.

Number of Items: 8

Format: Five-point scales.

Reliability: Coefficient alpha was .82.

Validity: Correlations with other variables ranged from −.18 to .55.

Author: Wanberg, C. R., and Banas, J. T.

Article: Predictors and outcomes of openness to changes in a reorganizing workplace.

Journal: *Journal of Applied Psychology*, February 2000, *85*(1), 132–142.

Related Research: Scheier, M. F., et al. (1994). Distinguishing optimism from neuroticism and trait anxiety, self-mastery, and self-esteem: A reevaluation of the Life Orientation Test. *Journal of Personality and Social Psychology, 67,* 1063–1078.

7729

Test Name: LIFE ORIENTATION TEST—REVISED

Purpose: To measure individuals' possession of favorable expectations concerning life outcomes.

Number of Items: 6

Format: Responses are made on a 5-point scale ranging from 1 (strongly agree) to 5 (strongly disagree). An example is given.

Reliability: Alpha coefficients were .78 and .80. Test-retest correlations ranged from .56 to .79. (4 months to 2 years).

Validity: Correlations with other variables ranged from −.38 to .51.

Author: Pallant, J. F.

Article: Development and validation of a scale to measure perceived control of internal states.

Journal: *Journal of Personality*

Assessment, October 2000, *75*(2), 308–337.

Related Research: Scheier, M. F., et al. (1994). Distinguishing optimism from neuroticism (and trait anxiety, self-mastery, and self-esteem): A reevaluation of the Life Orientation Test. *Journal of Personality and Social Psychology, 67,* 1063–1078.

7730

Test Name: LIFE SATISFACTION INDEX-A

Purpose: To assess adjustment.

Number of Items: 20

Format: Responses are either "agreement," "disagreement," or "cannot say." Sample items are presented.

Validity: Correlations with other variables ranged from −.45 to .54.

Author: Elliott, T. R., et al.

Article: Goal instability and adjustment to physical disability.

Journal: *Journal of Counseling Psychology*, April 2000, *47*(2), 251–265.

Related Research: Adams, D. (1969). Analysis of a life satisfaction index. *Journal of Gerontology, 24,* 470–474.

7731

Test Name: LIFE SATISFACTION SCALE

Purpose: To measure satisfaction with life.

Number of Items: 5

Format: Responses are made on a 7-point Likert scale. An example is presented.

Reliability: Coefficient alpha was .87.

Validity: Correlations with other variables ranged from −.45 to .67.

Author: Munson, L. J., et al.

Article: Longitudinal analysis of dispositional influences and sexual harassment: Effects on job and psychological outcomes.

Journal: *Personnel Psychology*, Spring 2000, *53*(1), 21–46.

Related Research: Diener, E., et al. (1985). The Satisfaction With Life Scale. *Journal of Personality Assessment, 49,* 71–75.

7732

Test Name: LIFE SATISFACTION SCALE

Purpose: To measure life satisfaction.

Number of Items: 8

Format: Five-point scales are anchored by 1 (strongly disagree) and 5 (strongly agree). A sample item is presented.

Reliability: Alpha was .77.

Validity: Correlations with other variables ranged from −.18 to .40.

Author: Beutell, N. J., and Wittig-Berman, U.

Article: Predictors of work-family conflict and satisfaction with family, job, career and life.

Journal: *Psychological Reports*, December 1999, *85*(3, Part I), 893–903.

Related Research: Beutell, N. J., & Greenhaus, J. H. (1992). Interrole conflict among married women: The influence of husband and wife characteristics on conflict and coping behavior. *Journal of Vocational Behavior, 21,* 99–110.

7733

Test Name: LIFE SATISFACTION SCALE

Purpose: To assess life satisfaction.

Number of Items: 10

Reliability: Alpha coefficient was .79.

Validity: Correlations with other variables ranged from −.96 to .12.

Author: Aquino, J. A., et al.

Article: Employment status, social support, and life satisfaction among the elderly.

Journal: *Journal of Counseling Psychology*, October 1996, *43*(4), 480–489.

Related Research: Lohman, N. (1980). A factor analysis of life satisfaction, adjustment and morale measures with elderly adults. *International Journal of Aging and Human Development*, *11*, 35–43.

7734

Test Name: LIFE SKILLS DEVELOPMENT INVENTORY —COLLEGE FORM

Purpose: To assess life-skills mastery for students aged 17 to 24 years.

Number of Items: 90

Reliability: Internal consistency coefficients ranged from .77 to .85 across subscales (total internal consistency was .94).

Validity: Correlations with other variables ranged from .26 to .64.

Author: Picklesimer, B. K., and Miller, T. K.

Article: Life-Skills Development Inventory-College Form: An assessment measure.

Journal: *Journal of College*

Student Development, January/ February 1998, *39*(1), 100–110.

Related Research: Brooks, D. K., Jr. (1984). *A life-skills taxonomy: Defining elements of effective functioning through the use of the Delphi technique.* Unpublished doctoral dissertation, The University of Georgia.

7735

Test Name: LIFE STRESS SCALE

Purpose: To assess life stress.

Number of Items: 10

Reliability: Coefficient alpha was .89.

Validity: Correlations with other variables ranged from −.20 to .53.

Author: Parasuraman, S., et al.

Article: Work and family variables, entrepreneurial career success, and psychological well-being.

Journal: *Journal of Vocational Behavior*, June 1996, *48*(3), 275–300.

Related Research: Parasuraman, S., et al. (1992). Role stressors, social support, and well-being among two-career couples. *Journal of Organizational Behavior*, *13*, 339–356.

7736

Test Name: LONELINESS SCALE

Purpose: To measure loneliness.

Number of Items: 11

Format: Agreement scales are implied. Sample items are presented.

Reliability: Reliability coefficient was .81.

Author: Peters, A., and Liefbroer, A. C.

Article: Beyond marital status: Partner history and well-being in old age.

Journal: *Journal of Marriage and the Family*, August 1997, *59*(3), 687–699.

Related Research: Jong Gierveld, J. de., & Kamphuis, F. (1985). The development of a Rash-type loneliness scale. *Applied Psychological Measurement*, *9*, 289–299.

7737

Test Name: MANIC DEPRESSIVENESS SCALE

Purpose: To measure manic-depressive-like experiences and behavior.

Number of Items: 18

Format: True-false format. All items are presented.

Validity: Correlations with other variables ranged from .45 to .52.

Author: Thalbourne, M. A., and Bassett, D. L.

Article: The Manic Depressiveness Scale: A preliminary effort at replication and extension.

Journal: *Psychological Reports*, August 1998, *83*(1), 75–80.

Related Research: Thalbourne, M. A., et al. (1994). An attempt to construct short scales measuring manic depressive-like experience and behavior. *British Journal of Clinical Psychology*, *33*, 205–207.

7738

Test Name: MASCULINE GENDER ROLE STRESS SCALE

Purpose: To assess a man's experience of stress that is often tied to cognitive, behavioral, and environmental events associated with the male gender role.

Number of Items: 40

Format: Includes 5 factors: Physical Inadequacy, Emotional Inexpressiveness, Subordination to Women, and Intellectual Inferiority.

Reliability: Internal consistency ranged from .77 to .90.

Validity: Correlation with other variables ranged from −.28 to .50.

Author: Fischer, A. R., and Good, G. E.

Article: Perceptions of parent-child relationships and masculine role conflicts of college men.

Journal: *Journal of Counseling Psychology*, July 1998, *45*(3), 346–352.

Related Research: Fisher, R. M., & Skidmore, J. R. (1987). Masculine gender role stress: Scale development and component factors in the appraisal of stressful situations. *Behavior Modifications*, *11*, 123–136.

7739

Test Name: MAUDSLEY OBSESSIVE-COMPULSIVE INVENTORY

Purpose: To measure various types of obsessions and compulsions, including cleaning, checking, slowness, and doubting.

Number of Items: 30

Format: True/false format.

Reliability: Alpha coefficients ranged from .70 to .80 across subscales.

Author: Harrell, J. P., and Wright, L. W., Jr.

Article: The development and

validation of the Multicomponent AIDS Phobia Scale.

Journal: *Journal of Psychopathology and Behavioral Assessment*, September 1998, *20*(3), 201–216.

Related Research: Hodgson, R. J., & Rachman, S. (1977). Obsessional-compulsive complaints. *Behavior Research and Therapy, 15*, 389–395.

7740

Test Name: MCGILL PAIN QUESTIONNAIRE—SHORT FORM

Purpose: To assess pain.

Number of Items: 15

Format: Four-point rating scales range from 0 (none) to 3 (severe).

Validity: Correlations with criterion measures ranged from .64 to .88.

Author: Kvaal, S. A., and Patodia, S.

Article: Relations among positive affect, negative affect, and somantic symptoms in a medically ill patient sample.

Journal: *Psychological Reports*, August 2000, *87*(1), 227–233.

Related Research: Melzack, R., & Katz, J. (1992). The McGill Pain Questionnaire: Appraisal and current status. In D. C. Turk & R. Melzack (Eds.), *Handbook of pain assessment* (pp. 152–168). New York: Guilford.

7741

Test Name: MEN'S ADULT LIFE EXPERIENCE INVENTORY

Purpose: To measure men's functioning at middle age with respect to relationships with parents, spouse, children and friends; death, health, job,

leisure, sex, self-reflection, and pressure of time.

Number of Items: 97

Format: Self-report format ranges from 1 ("not at all") to 4 ("very much").

Reliability: Alphas ranged from .72 to .84.

Author: Tikoo, M.

Article: An exploratory study of differences in developmental concerns of middle-aged men and women in India

Journal: *Psychological Reports*, June 1996, *78*(3) Part 1, 883–887.

Related Research: Deluccie et al. (1989). The Men's Adult Life Experiences Inventory: An instrument for assessing developmental concerns of middle age. *Psychological Reports*, *64*, 479–485.

7742

Test Name: MENTAL AND PHYSICAL HEALTH SCALE

Purpose: To measure depression, somatic complaints, and happiness.

Number of Items: 48

Format: Five-point scales range from (1) not at all to (5) very much.

Reliability: Alphas ranged from .82 to .89 across subscales.

Author: Jou, Y. U., and Fukada, H.

Article: Stress and social support in mental and physical health of Chinese students in Japan.

Journal: *Psychological Reports*, December 1997, *81*(3, Part II), 1303–1312.

Related Research: Ueda, S., et al. (1992). [The psychological study of happiness (2): An attempt to

develop a happiness scale].
[*Bulletin of the Faculty of Education*, Hiroshima University, Part I (*Psychology*)], *41*, 35–40. [In Japanese. English summary].

7743

Test Name: MENTAL HEALTH INDEX

Purpose: To measure adult psychological functioning.

Number of Items: 38

Format: Includes two factors: Psychological Distress and Positive Well-Being.

Reliability: Alpha coefficients were .94 and .95.

Author: Speltz, M. L., et al.

Article: Early predictors of attachment in infants with cleft lip and/or palate.

Journal: *Child Development*, February 1997, *68*(1), 12–25.

Related Research: Veit, C. T., & Ware, J. E. (1983). The structure of psychological distress and well-being in general populations. *Journal of Consulting and Clinical Psychology*, *51*, 730–742.

7744

Test Name: MENTAL HEALTH INDEX—ADAPTED

Purpose: To determine how one felt during the past month.

Number of Items: 9

Format: Responses are made on a 6-point scale ranging from "never" to "most of the time." Examples are presented.

Reliability: Internal consistencies were .88 and .87.

Validity: Correlations with other variables ranged from −.54 to .67.

Author: Munson, L. J., et al.

Article: Longitudinal analysis of dispositional influences and sexual harassment: Effects on job and psychological outcomes.

Journal: *Personnel Psychology*, Spring 2000, *53*(1), 21–46.

Related Research: Veit, C. T., & Ware, J. E. (1983). The structure of psychological distress and well-being in general populations. *Journal of Consulting and Clinical Psychology*, *51*, 730–742.

7745

Test Name: MENTAL HEALTH INVENTORY

Purpose: To assess parent mental health.

Number of Items: 5

Format: Responses are made on a 6-point scale ranging from 1 (none of the time) to 6 (all of the time).

Reliability: Coefficient alpha was .81.

Author: Sutton, S. E., et al.

Article: Pathways to aggression in young, highly stressed urban children.

Journal: *Child Study Journal*, 1999, *29*(1), 49–67.

Related Research: Sutton, S. E. (1995). Pathways to aggression in highly stressed 2nd and 3rd grade urban children. Unpublished Ph.D. dissertation, University of Rochester.

7746

Test Name: MENTAL HEALTH INVENTORY

Purpose: To measure psychological health.

Number of Items: 18

Format: Includes 5 subscales: Anxiety, Depression, Loss of Behavioral/Emotional Control, General Positive Affect, and Interpersonal Ties. Responses are made on a 6-point scale ranging from "all the time" to "none of the time."

Reliability: Alpha coefficients ranged from .51 to .90.

Validity: Correlations with other variables ranged from −.72 to .51.

Author: Hanson, K. M., and Mintz, L. B.

Article: Psychological health and problem solving self-appraisal in older adults.

Journal: *Journal of Counseling Psychology*, October 1997, *44*(4), 433–441.

Related Research: Veit, C. T., & Ware, J. E. (1983). The structure of psychological distress and well-being in general populations. *Journal of Consulting and Clinical Psychology*, *51*, 730–742.

7747

Test Name: MENTAL HEALTH INVENTORY

Purpose: To measure psychological health.

Number of Items: 38

Format: Likert format (two items are forced choice).

Reliability: Coefficient alpha was .96. Test-retest reliabilities (1 year) ranged from .60 to .76.

Author: Pearson, Q. M.

Article: Job satisfaction, leisure satisfaction, and psychological health.

Journal: *Career Development Quarterly*, June 1998, *46*(4), 416–426.

Related Research: Ware, J., et al.

(1979). *Conceptualization and measurement of health for adults in the health insurance study: Vol. 3. mental health* (R-1987/3-HEW). Washington, DC: U. S. Government Printing Office.

7748

Test Name: MENTAL HEALTH INVENTORY

Purpose: To measure mental health and well-being.

Number of Items: 42

Format: Six-point severity scales are used. Sample items are presented.

Reliability: Alphas were .96 (total), .95 (distress), and .93 (well-being).

Validity: Correlations with Ways of Coping subscales ranged from −.22 to .46.

Author: Siegel, K., et al.

Article: Coping and mood in HIV-positive women.

Journal: *Psychological Reports*, October 1997, *81*(2), 435–442.

Related Research: Viet, C., and Ware, J. (1983). The structure of psychological distress and well-being in general populations. *Journal of Consulting and Clinical Psychology, 51*, 730–742.

7749

Test Name: MENTAL HEALTH INVENTORY—MODIFIED

Purpose: To measure well-being and psychological distress.

Number of Items: 35

Format: Responses are made on 5- or 6-point scales. A sample item is presented.

Reliability: Test-retest (1 year) reliability was .64 (*N* = 3,525).

Internal consistency was .96 (*N* = 5,089).

Validity: Correlations with other variables ranged from −.14 to .26.

Author: Fischer, A. R., and Shaw, C. M.

Article: African Americans' mental health and perceptions of racist discrimination. The moderating effects of racial socialization experiences and self-esteem.

Journal: *Journal of Counseling Psychology*, July 1999, *46*(3), 395–407.

Related Research: Veit, C. T., & Ware, J. E. (1983). The structure of psychological distress and well-being in the general population. *Journal of Consulting and Clinical Psychology, 51*, 730–742.

7750

Test Name: MENTAL, PHYSICAL, AND SPIRITUAL WELL-BEING SCALE

Purpose: To measure holistic health.

Number of Items: 30

Reliability: Alphas ranged from .75 to .85. One-month test-retest reliabilities ranged from .87 to .97.

Author: Vella-Brodrick, D. A., and White, V.

Article: Response set of social desirability in relation to the mental, physical, and spiritual well-being scale.

Journal: *Psychological Reports*, August 1997, *81*(1), 127–130.

Related Research: Vella-Brodrick, D. A., & Allen, F. C. L. (1995). Development and psychometric validation of the Mental, Physical, and Spiritual Well-

Being Scale. *Psychological Reports*, 77, 659–674.

7751

Test Name: MENTAL READINESS FORM—LIKERT

Purpose: To measure competitive state anxiety.

Number of Items: 3

Format: Responses are made on an 11-point Likert scale.

Validity: Correlations with other variables ranged from .52 to .67.

Author: Cox, R. H., et al.

Article: Order of scale administration and concurrent validity of the Anxiety Rating Scale.

Journal: *Perceptual and Motor Skills*, February 1999, *88*(1), 271–272.

Related Research: Murphy, S. M., et al. (1989). Development of a brief rating instrument of competitive state anxiety comparisons with the Competitive State Anxiety Inventory-2. *Proceedings of the Association for the Advancement of Applied Sport Psychology*. Seattle, WA: The Association, p. 82.

7752

Test Name: MISSISSIPPI SCALE FOR COMBAT RELATED PTSD

Purpose: To measure PTSD.

Number of Items: 35

Format: Five-point Likert format.

Reliability: Various reliability coefficients ranged from .89 to .97.

Author: Wolfe, J., et al.

Article: Course and predictors of posttraumatic stress disorder among Gulf War veterans: A prospective analysis.

Journal: *Journal of Consulting and Clinical Psychology*, August 1999, *67*(4), 520–528.

Related Research: Keane, T. M., et al (1988). The Mississippi Scale for Combat Related Posttraumatic Stress Disorder: Three studies in reliability and validity. *Journal of Consulting and Clinical Psychology, 56*, 85–90.

7753

Test Name: MODIFIED CHILD DENTAL ANXIETY SCALE

Purpose: To assess anxiety associated with dental procedures.

Number of Items: 8

Format: Five-point scales are anchored by (1) relaxed/not worried and (5) very worried. All items are presented.

Reliability: Alpha was .84.

Validity: Correlations with related measures ranged from .66 to .98.

Author: Wong, H-M., et al.

Article: Preliminary validation and reliability of the Modified Child Dental Anxiety Scale.

Journal: *Psychological Reports*, December 1998, *83*(3) Part 2, 1179–1186.

Related Research: Coran, N. L., et al. (1978). Assessment of a dental anxiety scale. *Journal of the American Dental Association, 97*, 816–819.

7754

Test Name: MODIFIED LIFE EVENTS INTERVIEW

Purpose: To measure life events experienced in the last 6 months.

Number of Items: 88

Format: Checklist format.

Reliability: Test-retest reliability was .84.

Author: Toro, P. A., et al.

Article: Evaluating an intervention for homeless persons: Results of a field experiment.

Journal: *Journal of Consulting and Clinical Psychology*, June 1997, *65*(3), 476–484.

Related Research: Lovell, A. M. (1984). *Modified Life Events Interview*. Unpublished manuscript. Epidemiology of Mental Disorders. Research Department, New York State Psychiatric Institute, New York.

7755

Test Name: MODIFIED SCALE FOR SUICIDE IDEATION

Purpose: To assess symptoms of suicide ideation.

Number of Items: 18

Format: Three-point scales.

Reliability: Coefficient alpha was .94.

Validity: Correlations with other variables ranged from .04 to .81.

Author: Joiner, T. E., Jr., and Rudd, M. D.

Article: Intensity and duration of suicidal crises vary as a function of previous suicide attempts and negative life events.

Journal: *Journal of Consulting and Clinical Psychology*, October 2000, *68*(5), 909–916.

Related Research: Miller, I., et al. (1986). The Modified Scale for Suicide Ideation: Reliability and validity. *Journal of Consulting and Clinical Psychology, 54*, 724–725.

7756

Test Name: MOOD AND ANXIETY SYMPTOM QUESTIONNAIRE—REVISED

Purpose: To measure and discriminate between anxiety and depression.

Number of Items: 60

Format: Includes 3 scales: General Distress, Positive Affect, and Somatic Anxiety. Responses are made on a 5-point scale ranging from 1 (not at all) to 5 (extremely).

Reliability: Alpha coefficients ranged from .88 to .95.

Author: Keogh, E., and Reidy, J.

Article: Exploring the factor structure of the Mood and Anxiety Symptom Questionnaire (MASQ).

Journal: *Journal of Personality Assessment*, February 2000, *74*(1), 106–125.

Related Research: Watson, D., & Clark, A. L. (1991). *The Mood and Anxiety Symptom Questionnaire (MASQ)*. Unpublished manuscript, University of Iowa, Iowa City.

7757

Test Name: MOOD AND ANXIETY SYMPTOM QUESTIONNAIRE—SHORT FORM

Purpose: To measure distress.

Number of Items: 62

Format: Includes 4 scales: Depressive Symptoms, Anxious Symptoms, Anhedonic Depression, and Anxious Arousal.

Reliability: Internal consistency coefficients ranged from .78 to .93.

Author: Dunkley, D. M., et al.

Article: The relation between perfectionism and distress: Hassles, coping and perceived social support as mediators and moderators.

Journal: *Journal of Counseling Psychology*, October 2000, 47(4), 437–453.

Related Research: Watson, D., & Clark, L. A. (1991). *The Mood and Anxiety Symptom Questionnaire*. Unpublished manuscript. University of Iowa, Iowa City.

7758

Test Name: MOOD DIMENSIONS SCALES

Purpose: To measure nonspecific depression, semantic arousal, anhedonia, and nonspecific anxiety.

Number of Items: 12

Format: All items are presented.

Reliability: Alpha reliabilities ranged from .53 to .84.

Author: Burns, D. D., and Eidelson, R. J.

Article: Why are depression and anxiety correlated? A test of the tripartite model.

Journal: *Journal of Consulting and Clinical Psychology*, June 1998, 66(3), 461–473.

Related Research: Watson, D., & Clark, L. A. (1991). *The Mood and Anxiety Symptom Questionnaire*. Unpublished manuscript. University of Iowa.

7759

Test Name: MOOD REGULATION EXPECTANCIES SCALE

Purpose: To measure mood regulation expectancies.

Number of Items: 30

Format: Items are rated on the extent to which the person agrees or disagrees with each item.

Reliability: Alpha coefficients were .88 and .90.

Validity: Correlations with other variables ranged from −.52 to .40.

Author: Bensur, B. J., et al.

Article: An exploratory study of motivational predictors which influence graduation from two- and four-year colleges.

Journal: *Perceptual and Motor Skills*, June 1999, 88(3) Part 1, 997–1008.

Related Research: Kirsch, L., et al. (1990). Mood regulation expectancies as determinants of dysphoria in college students. *Journal of Counseling Psychology*, 37, 306–312.

7760

Test Name: MOTHER IMMIGRATION STRESS SCALE

Purpose: To measure stress resulting from immigration.

Number of Items: 10

Format: Four-point scales use construct-specific anchors.

Reliability: Internal consistency was .66.

Author: Short, K. H., and Johnston, C.

Article: Stress, maternal distress, and children's adjustment following immigration: The buffering role of social support.

Journal: *Journal of Consulting and Clinical Psychology*, June 1997, 65(3), 494–503.

Related Research: Vega, W. A., et al. (1987). Migration and mental health: An empirical test of depression risk factors among immigrant Mexican women.

International Migration Review, 21, 512–530.

7761

Test Name: MULTI-ATTITUDE SUICIDE TENDENCY SCALE

Purpose: To measure attraction and repulsion by life/death.

Number of Items: 30

Format: Five-point scales are anchored by 1 (strongly agree) and 5 (strongly disagree).

Reliability: Alpha ranged from .57 to .88 across subscales.

Validity: Correlations with criterion measures ranged from −.58 to .66.

Author: Hagstrom, A. H., and Gutierrez, P. M.

Article: Confirmatory factor analysis of the Multi-Attitude Suicide Tendency Scale.

Journal: *Journal of Psychopathology and Behavioral Assessment*, June 1998, 20(2), 173–186.

Related Research: Orbach, I., et al. (1993). The Multi-Attitude Suicidal Tendency Scale: Psychometric characteristics in an American sample. *Journal of Clinical Psychology*, 49, 847–855.

7762

Test Name: MULTICOMPONENT AIDS PHOBIA SCALE

Purpose: To measure unfounded fear of AIDS.

Number of Items: 20

Format: Six-point scales are anchored by 0 (strongly disagree) and 5 (strongly agree). All items are presented.

Reliability: Alpha were .70 (fear of others/avoidance) and .73 (fear of infection).

Validity: Correlations with other variables ranged from .21 to .57.

Author: Harrell, J. P., and Wright, L. W., Jr.

Article: The development and validation of the Multicomponent AIDS Phobia Scale.

Journal: *Journal of Psychopathology and Behavioral Assessment*, September 1998, *20*(3), 201–216.

7763

Test Name: MULTIDIMENSIONAL ANXIETY SCALE FOR CHILDREN

Purpose: To measure anxiety in children.

Number of Items: 39

Format: Includes 4 subscales: Physical Symptoms, Social Anxiety, Separation Anxiety, and Harm Avoidance. Responses are made on a 4-point rating scale.

Reliability: Alpha coefficients ranged from .85 to .70.

Author: Muris, P., et al.

Article: Correlations between two multidimensional anxiety scales for children.

Journal: *Perceptual and Motor Skills*, August 1998, *87*(1), 269–270.

Related Research: March, J. S., et al. (1997). The Multidimensional Anxiety Scale for Children (MASC): Factor structure, reliability, and validity. *Journal of the American Academy of Child and Adolescent Psychiatry, 36*, 554–565.

7764

Test Name: MULTIDIMENSIONAL ASSESSMENT OF STRESSFUL LIFE EVENTS

Purpose: To measure stress.

Number of Items: 39

Format: Scales range from 1 (very unhappy) to 5 (very happy). Frequency scales range from "never happened" to "happened in the last 12 months."

Validity: Correlations with health variables ranged from −.25 to .21.

Author: Damush, T. M., et al.

Article: Stressful life events and health-related quality of life in college students.

Journal: *Journal of College Student Development*, March/April 1997, *38*(2), 181–190.

Related Research: Newcomb, M. D., et al. (1981). A multidimensional assessment of stressful life events among adolescents: Derivation and correlates. *Journal of Health and Social Behavior, 22*, 400–415.

7765

Test Name: MULTIDIMENSIONAL FATIQUE INVENTORY—20

Purpose: To measure fatigue: general, mental, physical, reduction activity, and reduction motivation.

Number of Items: 20

Time Required: 10 minutes.

Format: 5-point scales.

Reliability: Alphas ranged from .37 to .82 across subscales.

Validity: Correlations with the Beck Depression Inventory ranged from .52 to .61.

Author: Schneider, R. A.

Article: Concurrent validity of the Beck Depression Inventory and the Multidimensional Fatigue Inventory—20 in assessing fatigue among cancer patients.

Journal: *Psychological Reports*, June 1998, *82*(3) Part 1, 883–886.

Related Research: Smets, E. M. A., et al. (1995). The Multidimensional Fatigue Inventory (MFI): Psychometric qualities of an instrument to assess fatigue. *Journal of Psychosomatic Research, 39*, 315–325.

7766

Test Name: MULTIDIMENSIONAL SENSE OF HUMOR SCALE

Purpose: To measure sense of humor.

Number of Items: 24

Format: Items are scored on a five-point scale ranging from (0) strongly disagree to (4) strongly agree.

Reliability: Alphas ranged from .88 to .91.

Validity: Correlations with other variables ranged from .55 to .91.

Author: Thorson, J. A., et al.

Article: Factor-analytic study of sense of humor in Croatia and the USA.

Journal: *Psychological Reports*, December 1997, *81*(3, Part I), 971–977.

Related Research: Thorson, J. A., & Powell, F. C. (1993). Development and validation of a multidimensional sense of humor scale. *Journal of Clinical Psychology, 49*, 13–23.

7767

Test Name: NEGATIVE AFFECTIVITY SCALE

Purpose: To measure negative moods and emotional reactivity.

Number of Items: 6

Format: Six-point scales ranged from "strongly disagree" to "strongly agree." A sample item is presented.

Reliability: Coefficient alpha was .86.

Validity: Correlations with other variables ranged from −.13 to .55.

Author: Frone, M. R.

Article: Predictors of work injuries among employed adolescents.

Journal: *Journal of Applied Psychology*, August 1998, *83*(4), 565–576.

Related Research: Tellegen, A., & Waller, N. G. (1992). *Exploring the personality through test construction: Development of the multidimensional personality questionnaire.* Unpublished manuscript, University of Minnesota.

7768

Test Name: NEGATIVE AFFECTIVITY SCALE

Purpose: To measure negative affectivity.

Number of Items: 21

Format: Responses are made on a 5-point Likert-type scale ranging from 1 (strongly disagree) to 5 (strongly agree). An example is given.

Reliability: Coefficient alpha was .86.

Validity: Correlation with other variables ranged from .06 to .55.

Author: Carlson, D. S.

Article: Personality and role variables as predictors of three forms of work-family conflict.

Journal: *Journal of Vocational Behavior*, October 1999, *55*(2), 236–253.

Related Research: Levin, I., & Stokes, J. P. (1989). Dispositional approach to job satisfaction: Role of negative affectivity. *Journal of Applied Psychology*, *74*, 752–758.

7769

Test Name: NEGATIVE MOOD REGULATION SCALE

Purpose: To measure beliefs about one's ability to alleviate negative moods.

Number of Items: 30

Format: Scales range from 1 (strongly disagree) to 5 (strongly agree). Sample items are presented.

Reliability: Internal consistency coefficients ranged from .86 to .92.

Validity: Correlations with other variables ranged from .28 to .51.

Author: McCarthy, C. J., et al.

Article: The relationship of beliefs about mood to coping resource effectiveness.

Journal: *Journal of College Student Development*, March/April 1997, *38*(2), 157–165.

Related Research: Kirsch, I., et al. (1990). Mood regulation expectancies as determinants of dysphoria in college students. *Journal of Counseling Psychology*, *37*, 306–312.

7770

Test Name: NEUTRAL OBJECTS SATISFACTION QUESTIONNAIRE

Purpose: To measure affective predisposition.

Number of Items: 13

Format: Responses are "satisfied," "neutral," and "dissatisfied."

Reliability: Coefficient alpha was .75.

Validity: Correlations with other variables ranged from −.19 to .25.

Author: Glomb, T. M., et al.

Article: Structural equation models of sexual harassment: Longitudinal explorations and cross-sectional generalizations.

Journal: *Journal of Applied Psychology*, February 1999, *84*(1), 14–28.

Related Research: Weitz, J. (1952). A neglected concept in the study of job satisfaction. *Personnel Psychology*, *5*, 201–205.

7771

Test Name: NIMH TRICHOTILLOMANIA SEVERITY AND IMPAIRMENT SCALES

Purpose: To assess duration, resistance, distress, and interference associated with hair pulling.

Number of Items: 6

Format: Five-, six-, and ten-point rating scales are used.

Reliability: Alphas ranged from .36 to .71.

Validity: Correlations with criterion measures ranged from −.22 to .87.

Author: Stanley, M. A., et al.

Article: Clinician-rated measures of hair pulling: A preliminary psychometric evaluation.

Journal: *Journal of Psychopathology and Behavioral Assessment*, June 1999, *21*(2), 157–170.

Related Research: Swedo, S. E., et al. (1997). A double-blind comparison of clomipramine and desipramine in the treatment of trichotillomania (hair pulling). *New England Journal of Medicine, 321,* 497–501.

7772

Test Name: ONTARIO CHILD HEALTH STUDY—REVISED

Purpose: To measure oppositional defiant disorders and attention deficit-hyperactivity disorders.

Number of Items: 23

Format: Three-point scales range from 0 (never or not true) to 2 (often or very true). All items are presented.

Reliability: Coefficient alpha ranged from .92 to .95 across scales at baseline and at follow-up.

Validity: Correlations with other variables ranged from −.19 to .19.

Author: Bennett, K. J., et al.

Article: Predicting conduct problems: Can high-risk children be identified in kindergarten and Grade 1?

Journal: *Journal of Consulting and Clinical Psychology,* August 1999, *67*(4), 470–480.

Related Research: Boyle, M. H., et al. (1992). Evaluation of the Revised Ontario Child Health Study Scales. *Journal of Child Psychology and Psychiatry, 34,* 189–213.

7773

Test Name: OUTCOME QUESTIONNAIRE

Purpose: To provide repeated measurement of patient changes occurring throughout the course of mental health.

Number of Items: 45

Format: Includes 3 subscales: Subjective Distress, Interpersonal

Relations, and Social Role. Responses are made on a 5-point scale ranging from 0 (never) to 4 (almost always). All items are presented.

Reliability: Test-retest (3 weeks) reliability was .84. Internal consistency reliability was .93.

Author: Vermeersch, D. A., et al.

Article: Outcome Questionnaire: Item sensitivity to change.

Journal: *Journal of Personality Assessment,* April 2000, *74*(2), 242–261.

Related Research: Lambert, M. J., et al. (1996). The reliability and validity of the Outcome Questionnaire. *Clinical Psychology and Psychotherapy, 3,* 249–258.

7774

Test Name: OXFORD HAPPINESS INVENTORY (HEBREW VERSION)

Purpose: To measure trait happiness.

Number of Items: 29

Reliability: Internal reliability was .85.

Validity: Correlations with other variables ranged from −.14 to .42.

Author: Francis, L. J., and Katz, Y. J.

Article: Internal consistency, reliability, and validity of the Hebrew translation of the Oxford Happiness Inventory.

Journal: *Psychological Reports,* August 2000, *87*(1), 193–196.

Related Research: Argyle, M., et al. (1989). Happiness as a function of personality and social encounters. In J. P. Forgas & J. M. Innes (Eds.), *Recent advances in social psychology: An international perspective* (pp.

189–203). Amsterdam: North Holland-Elsevier Science.

7775

Test Name: PAIN SEVERITY SCALE

Purpose: To measure the severity of pain.

Number of Items: 3

Format: Seven-point rating scales.

Reliability: Coefficient alpha was .72. Test-retest reliability was .82.

Author: Currie, S. R., et al.

Article: Cognitive-behavioral treatment of insomnia secondary to chronic pain.

Journal: *Journal of Consulting and Clinical Psychology,* June 2000, *68*(3), 407–416.

Related Research: Buysse, D. J., et al. (1989). The Pittsburgh Sleep Quality Index: A new instrument for psychiatric practice and research. *Psychiatry Research, 28,* 193–213.

7776

Test Name: PANAS-C

Purpose: To measure positive and negative affect in children.

Number of Items: 20

Format: Five-point scales are anchored by "very slightly or not at all" and "extremely." All items are presented.

Reliability: Test-retest reliability (2 weeks) ranged from .67 to .82. Alpha reliability was .86.

Validity: Correlations with anxiety and depression measures ranged from −.50 to .76.

Author: Crook, K., et al.

Article: Anxiety and depression in children: A preliminary examination of the utility of the PANAS-C.

Journal: *Journal of Psychopathology and Behavioral Assessment*, December 1998, *20*(4), 333–350.

Related Research: Laurent, J., et al. (1994). *Assessing positive and negative affect in children: The development of the PANAS-C*. Poster session at the annual meeting of the National Association of School Psychologists, Seattle, WA: March.

7777

Test Name: PARANOIA SCALES

Purpose: To measure lack of trust, perceived hostility, and abnormal beliefs.

Format: Five-point response scales ranged from 0 (somewhat agree) to 4 (strongly agree) or from 0 (never) to 3 (very often).

Reliability: Alphas ranged from .75 to .85.

Validity: Correlations with other demoralization scales ranged from .36 to .67.

Author: Whaley, A. L.

Article: Ethnicity, race, paranoia, and psychiatric diagnosis: Clinician bias versus sociocultural differences.

Journal: *Journal of Psychopathology and Behavioral Assessment*, March 1997, *19*(1), 1–20.

Related Research: Dohrenwend, B. P., et al. (1986). Screening scales from the Psychiatric Epidemiology Research Interview (PERI). In M. M. Wiseman et al. (Eds.), *Community surveys of psychiatric disorders* (pp. 349–375). New Brunswick, NJ: Rutgers University Press.

7778

Test Name: PARENT RATED ADJUSTMENT SCALE

Purpose: To enable parents to rate their children's adjustment.

Number of Items: 10

Format: Includes 3 subscales: Emotional Disturbance, Conduct Disturbance, and Good Adjustment. Examples are presented.

Reliability: Alpha coefficients ranged from .43 to .67.

Author: McCall, R. B., et al.

Article: The nature and correlates of underachievements among elementary school children in Hong Kong.

Journal: *Child Development*, May/June 2000, *71*(3), 785–801.

Related Research: Spivack, G., et al (1986). Early classroom behaviors and later misconduct. *Developmental Psychology*, 22, 124–131.

7779

Test Name: PARENT RATING FORM

Purpose: To assess depression and anxiety in children.

Number of Items: 66

Format: Seven-point Likert format.

Reliability: Alpha was .94.

Validity: Correlations with related variables was .47 and .54.

Author: Epkins, C. C.

Article: Cognitive specificity and affective confounding in social anxiety and dysphoria in children.

Journal: *Journal of Psychopathology and Behavioral Assessment*, March 1996, *18*(1), 83–101.

7780

Test Name: PARENTAL POSITIVE AND NEGATIVE AFFECT SCALE

Purpose: To measure positive and negative affect directed toward a targeted adolescent.

Number of Items: 7

Format: Five-point scales.

Reliability: Intraobserver reliability ranged from .57 to .96. Alpha coefficients ranged from .72 to .83.

Validity: Correlations with other variables ranged from −.21 to .27

Author: Paley, B., et al.

Article: Parents' affect, adolescent cognitive representations, and adolescent social development.

Journal: *Journal of Marriage and the Family*, August 2000, *62*(3), 761–776.

Related Research: Conger, R. D., et al. (1995). *A comprehensive approach to assessing family and observer reports of parent-child interactions: The Iowa family interaction rating scales*. Unpublished technical report, Iowa State University, Ames.

7781

Test Name: PEER NOMINATION INDEX OF DEPRESSION AND ANXIETY

Purpose: To assess symptoms of depression and anxiety.

Number of Items: 25

Format: Scales are anchored by 0 (no nominations) to 12 or 13 (all persons nominated).

Reliability: Alphas were .83 (depression) and .79 (anxiety).

Author: Cole, D. A., et al.

Article: Relation between

symptoms of anxiety and depression in children: A multitrait-multimethod-multigroup assessment.

Journal: *Journal of Consulting and Clinical Psychology*, February 1997, *65*(1), 110–119.

Related Research: Lefkowitz, M. M., & Tesiny, E. P. (1980). Assessment of childhood depression. *Journal of Consulting and Clinical Psychology, 48*, 43–50.

7782

Test Name: PENN STATE WORRY QUESTIONNAIRE

Purpose: To measure frequency and intensity of worry.

Number of Items: 16

Format: Responses are made on a 5-point Likert scale.

Reliability: Internal consistency was .94. Test-retest (2 weeks) reliability was .75. Test-retest (4 weeks) reliability was .74.

Author: Vivona, J. M.

Article: Parental attachment styles of late adolescents: Qualities of attachment relationships and consequences for adjustment.

Journal: *Journal of Counseling Psychology*, July 2000, *47*(3), 316–329.

Related Research: Meyer, T. J., et al. (1990). Development and validation of the Penn State Worry Questionnaire. *Behavioral Research and Therapy, 28*, 487–495.

7783

Test Name: PENNEBAKER INVENTORY OF LIMBIC LANGUIDNESS

Purpose: To assess somatic

symptoms of multiple organ systems.

Number of Items: 54

Format: Five-point scales are anchored by 1 (have never or almost never experienced) and 5 (more than once every week).

Reliability: Alpha was .91. Test-retest reliability (2 months) was .83.

Validity: Correlations with other variables ranged from .02 to .38.

Author: Kvaal, S. A., and Patodia, S.

Article: Relations among positive affect, negative affect, and semantic symptoms in a medically ill patient sample.

Journal: *Psychological Reports*, August 2000, *87*(1), 227–233.

Related Research: Pennebaker, J. W. (1982). *The psychology of physical symptoms*. New York: Springer-Verlag.

7784

Test Name: PERCEIVED STRESS SCALE

Purpose: To measure perceived stress.

Number of Items: 14

Format: Responses are made on a 5-point scale ranging from 1 (never) to 5 (very often). An example is presented.

Reliability: Coefficient alpha was .89.

Validity: Correlations with other variables ranged from −.53 to .68.

Author: O'Connell, C. E., and Korabik, K.

Article: Sexual harassment: The relationship of personal vulnerability, work context, perpetrator status, and types of harassment to outcomes.

Journal: *Journal of Vocational Behavior*, June 2000, *56*(3), 299–329.

Related Research: Cohen, S., et al. (1983). A global measure of perceived stress. *Journal of Health and Social Behavior, 24*, 385–396.

7785

Test Name: PERCEIVED STRESS SCALE—REVISED

Purpose: To measure levels of perceived or appraised stress.

Number of Items: 10

Format: Responses are made on a 5-point scale ranging from 1 (never) to 5 (very often).

Reliability: Coefficient alpha was .85.

Validity: Correlations with other variables ranged from −.58 to .58.

Author: Pallant, J. F.

Article: Development and validation of a scale to measure perceived control of internal states.

Journal: *Journal of Personality Assessment*, October 2000, *75*(2), 308–337.

Related Research: Cohen, S., et al (1983). A global measure of perceived stress. *Journal of Health and Social Behavior, 24*, 385–396.

7786

Test Name: PERCEIVED STRESS SCALE—SHORT FORM

Purpose: To measure perceived stress.

Number of Items: 4

Format: Five-point scales range from "never" to "very often." All items are presented.

Reliability: Alpha coefficients ranged from .73 to .88 across 3 days.

Validity: Correlations with other variables ranged from .10 to .62.

Author: Carney, M. A., et al.

Article: Positive and negative daily events, perceived stress, and alcohol use: A diary study.

Journal: *Journal of Consulting and Clinical Psychology*, October 2000, *68*(5), 788–798.

Related Research: Cohen, S., et al. (1983). A global measure of perceived stress. *Journal of Health and Social Behavior*, *24*, 385–396.

7787

Test Name: PERCEPTUAL ALTERATION SCALE

Purpose: To measure dissociative tendencies.

Number of Items: 27

Format: Four-point scales range from 1 (low dissociation) to 4 (high dissociation).

Reliability: Alpha was .95.

Validity: Correlations with other variables ranged from −.20 to .34.

Author: Orbach, I., et al.

Article: Thresholds and tolerance of physical pain in suicidal and nonsuicidal adolescents.

Journal: *Journal of Consulting and Clinical Psychology*, August 1997, *65*(4), 646–652.

Related Research: Sanders, B. (1986). The Perceptual Alteration Scale: A scale measuring dissociation. *American Journal of Clinical Hypnosis*, *29*, 95–102.

7788

Test Name: PERSONAL GROWTH SCALE

Purpose: To measure personal growth orientation.

Number of Items: 14

Format: Responses are made on a 6-point Likert type scale ranging from 1 (strongly disagree) to 6 (strongly agree).

Reliability: Internal consistency coefficients were .85 and .86.

Validity: Correlations with other variables ranged from −.29 to .51.

Author: Robitschek, C., and Keshubeck, S.

Article: A structural model of parental alcoholism, family functioning, and psychological health: The mediating effects of hardiness and personal growth orientation.

Journal: *Journal of Counseling Psychology*, April 1999, *46*(2), 159–172.

Related Research: Ryff, C. D. (1989). Happiness is everything, or is it? Explorations on the meaning of psychological well-being. *Journal of Personality and Social Psychology*, *57*, 1069–1081.

7789

Test Name: PERSONAL PROBLEMS INVENTORY— REVISED

Purpose: To assess participants' current levels of self-reported problems.

Number of Items: 20

Format: Includes two factors: Personal–Social Problems and Academic Adjustment Problems. Responses are made on a 6-point scale ranging from 1 (not at all) to 6 (very significant problem).

Reliability: Coefficient alpha was .83.

Validity: Correlations with other variables ranged from .01 to .10.

Author: Lopez, F. G., et al.

Article: Internal working models, self-reported problems, and help-seeking attitudes among college students.

Journal: *Journal of Counseling Psychology*, January 1998, *45*(1), 79–83.

Related Research: Cash, T. F., et al. (1975). When counselors are heard but not seen: Initial impact of physical attractiveness. *Journal of Counseling Psychology*, *22*, 273–279.

7790

Test Name: PHYSICAL STRAIN SCALE

Purpose: To measure stress-related physical strain.

Number of Items: 24

Format: Yes/no format.

Reliability: Group mean reliability was .14.

Validity: Correlations with other variables ranged from −.10 to .49.

Author: Jex, S. M., and Bliese, P. D.

Article: Efficacy beliefs as a moderator of the impact of work-related stressors: A multilevel study.

Journal: *Journal of Applied Psychology*, June 1999, *84*(3), 349–361.

7791

Test Name: PHYSICAL SYMPTOM CHECKLIST

Purpose: To provide a physical symptoms checklist.

Number of Items: 12

Format: Responses are made on a 5-point scale ranging from 1 (not at all) to 5 (extremely).

Reliability: Coefficient alpha was .73.

Validity: Correlations with other variables ranged from −.46 to −.14.

Author: Pallant, J. F.

Article: Development and validation of a scale to measure perceived control of internal states.

Journal: *Journal of Personality Assessment*, October 2000, 75(2), 308–337.

Related Research: Brophy, C. J., et al. (198). An examination of the factor structure and convergent and discriminant validity of the SCL-90R in an outpatient clinic population. *Journal of Personality Assessment*, 52, 334–340.

7792

Test Name: PHYSICAL SYMPTOM INVENTORY

Purpose: To measure health symptoms.

Number of Items: 18

Format: Yes/no format.

Validity: Correlations with other variables ranged from −.38 to .51.

Author: Spector, P. E., et al.

Article: A longitudinal study of relations between job stressors and job strains while controlling for prior negative affectivity and strains.

Journal: *Journal of Applied Psychology*, April 2000, 85(2), 211–218.

Related Research: Spector, P. E., & Jex, S. M. (1988). Development of four self-report

measures of job stressors and strain: Interpersonal Conflict at Work Scale, Organizational Constraints Scale, Quantitative Workload Inventory, and Physical Symptoms Inventory. *Journal of Occupational Health Psychology*, 3, 356–367.

7793

Test Name: PHYSICAL SYMPTOMS SCALE

Purpose: To measure stress symptoms.

Number of Items: 7

Format: Responses are made on a 6-point scale ranging from 1 (almost never) to 6 (several times a week). An example is presented.

Reliability: Alpha coefficients were .76 and .79.

Validity: Correlations with other variables ranged from −.37 to .68.

Author: Saks, A. M., and Ashforth, B. E.

Article: A longitudinal investigation of the relationships between job information sources, applicant perceptions of fit, and work outcomes.

Journal: *Personnel Psychology*, Summer 1997, 50(2), 395–426.

Related Research: Patchen, M. (1970). *Participation, achievement and involvement on the job*. Englewood Cliffs, NJ: Prentice-Hall.

7794

Test Name: POSITIVE AND NEGATIVE AFFECT

Purpose: To measure positive and negative affect.

Number of Items: 12

Format: Seven-point scales are anchored by "does not apply at all" and "applies very much." Sample items are presented.

Reliability: Coefficient alpha was .89 (positive) and .95 (negative).

Validity: Correlations with other variables ranged from −.67 to .32.

Author: Keeping, L. M., and Levy, P. E.

Article: Performance appraisal reactions: Measurement, modeling and method bias.

Journal: *Journal of Applied Psychology*, October 2000, 85(5), 708–723.

Related Research: Zuwerink, J. R., & Devine, P. G. (1996). Attitude importance and resistance to persuasion: It's not just the thought that counts. *Journal of Personality and Social Psychology*, 70, 931–944.

7795

Test Name: POSITIVE AND NEGATIVE AFFECT SCHEDULE

Purpose: To measure positive and negative affect.

Number of Items: 20

Format: Includes 2 subscales: Positive Affect and Negative Affect. Responses are made on a 5-point scale ranging from 1 (very slightly, not at all) to 5 (extremely).

Reliability: Alpha coefficients exceeded .80.

Validity: Correlations with other variables ranged from −.12 to .32.

Author: Hibbard, S., et al.

Article: Differential validity of the defense mechanism manual for the TAT between Asian Americans and whites.

Journal: *Journal of Personality Assessment*, December 2000, 75(3), 351–372.

Related Research: Watson, D., et al. (1988). Development and validation of brief measures of positive and negative affect: The PANAS scales. *Journal of Personality and Social Psychology, 54*, 1063–1070.

7796

Test Name: POSITIVE AND NEGATIVE AFFECT SCHEDULE—EXTENDED VERSION

Purpose: To measure positive and negative affect.

Number of Items: 60

Format: Five-point scales ranged from 1 (very slightly/not at all) to 5 (extremely).

Reliability: Alpha coefficients ranged from .68 to .82 across samples.

Validity: Correlations with other variables ranged from −.42 to .57.

Author: Lonigan, C. J., et al.

Article: Positive and negative affectivity in children: Confirmatory factor analysis of a two-factor model and its relation to symptoms of anxiety and depression.

Journal: *Journal of Consulting and Clinical Psychology*, June 1999, 67(3), 374–386.

Related Research: Watson, D., & Clark, L. A. (1991). *The PANAS-X: Preliminary manual for the Positive and Negative Affect Schedule—Expanded Form.* Dallas, TX: Author.

7797

Test Name: POSITIVE AND NEGATIVE AFFECT SCHEDULE—GERMAN SHORT VERSION

Purpose: To assess emotional balance.

Number of Items: 20

Format: Includes adjectives denoting positive and negative affect. Responses are made on a 5-point scale ranging from 1 (very often) to 5 (not at all).

Reliability: Coefficient alpha was .70.

Validity: Correlations with other variables ranged from −.40 to .65.

Author: Wiese, B. S., et al.

Article: Selection, optimization, and compensation: An action-related approach to work and partnership.

Journal: *Journal of Vocational Behavior*, December 2000, 57(3), 273–300.

Related Research: Smith, J., et al. (1999). Well-being in very old age: Predictions from objective life conditions and subjective experience. In P. B. Baltes & K. U. Mayer (Eds.), *The Berlin Aging Study: Aging from 70 to 100* (pp. 450–471). New York: Cambridge University Press.

7798

Test Name: POSITIVE AND NEGATIVE AFFECT SCHEDULES

Purpose: To measure social positive and negative affectivity.

Number of Items: 10

Format: 5-point scales are anchored by (1) very slightly or not at all and (5) extremely.

Reliability: Cronbach alphas ranged from .85 to .87.

Validity: Correlations with other variables ranged from −.23 to .43 (positive affectivity) and from −.33 to .62 (negative affectivity).

Author: Smith, D., and Tinzer, A.

Article: Moderating effects of affective disposition and social support on the relationship between person-environment fit and strain.

Journal: *Psychological Reports*, June 1998, 82(3) Part 1, 963–983.

Related Research: Watson, D., et al (1988). Development and validation of brief measures of positive and negative affect: The PANAS scales. *Journal of Personality and Social Psychology, 54*, 1063–1070.

7799

Test Name: POSITIVE PSYCHOLOGICAL WELLNESS SCALES

Purpose: To assess self-acceptance, environmental mastery, positive relations with others, purpose in life, autonomy and personal growth.

Number of Items: 42

Format: Scales range from "strongly disagree" to "strongly agree." Sample items are presented.

Reliability: Alpha coefficients ranged from .70 to .79.

Author: Marks, N. F.

Article: Flying solo at midlife: Marital status and psychological well-being.

Journal: *Journal of Marriage and the Family*, November 1996, 58(4), 917–932.

Related Research: Ryff, C. D., &

Keyes, C. L. M. (1995). The structure of psychological well-being revisited. *Journal of Personality and Social Psychology, 69,* 719–727.

Marks, N. F. (1998). Does it hurt to care? Caregiving, work-family conflict, and midlife well-being. *Journal of Marriage and the Family, 60,* 951–966.

7800

Test Name: POSTTRAUMATIC STRESS DISORDER— REACTION INDEX FOR CHILDREN

Purpose: To assess posttraumatic stress symptoms in children.

Number of Items: 20

Format: Five-point scales are anchored by 0 (none of the time) and 4 (most of the time).

Reliability: Alpha coefficients ranged from .83 to .89.

Author: La Greca, A. M., et al.

Article: Children's predisaster functioning as a predictor of posttraumatic stress following Hurricane Andrew.

Journal: *Journal of Consulting and Clinical Psychology,* December 1998, *66*(6), 883–892.

Related Research: Frederick, C., et al. (1992). *Reaction Index to Psychic Trauma Form C (Child).* Unpublished manuscript, University of California, Los Angeles.

7801

Test Name: POSTTRAUMATIC STRESS DISORDER SYMPTOM SCALE

Purpose: To measure symptoms of PTSD.

Number of Items: 10

Format: Scales range from 1

(none) to 5 (extreme discomfort). Sample symptoms are presented.

Reliability: Coefficient alpha was .76.

Validity: Correlations with other variables ranged from −.54 to .32.

Author: Glomb, T. M., et al.

Article: Structural equation models of sexual harassment: Longitudinal explorations and cross-sectional generalizations.

Journal: *Journal of Applied Psychology,* February 1999, *84*(1), 14–28.

Related Research: Saunders, B. F., et al. (1990). Development of a crime-related post-traumatic stress disorder for women within the Symptom Checklist-90— Revised. *Journal of Traumatic Stress, 3,* 439–448.

7802

Test Name: POST-TRAUMATIC STRESS REACTION CHECKLIST

Purpose: To measure post-traumatic stress disorder symptoms in relation to one trauma.

Number of Items: 14

Format: Items are rated 1 (present) or 0 (absent). Examples are presented.

Reliability: Alpha coefficient was .77.

Author: MacKsoud, M. S., and Abner, J. L

Article: The war experiences and psychosocial development of children in Lebanon.

Journal: *Child Development,* February 1996, *67*(1), 70–88.

Related Research: MacKsoud, M., et al. (1990). *Post-Traumatic Stress Disorder Reaction Checklist for Children.* New

York: Columbia University, Center for the Study of Human Rights, Project on Children and War.

7803

Test Name: PRELIMINARY STRATEGIC APPROACH TO COPING SCALE

Purpose: To assess personal strengths and coping abilities.

Number of Items: 34

Format: Five-point Likert format.

Reliability: Alpha was .81.

Author: Kaslow, N. J., et al.

Article: Factors that mediate and moderate the link between partner abuse and suicidal behavior in African American women.

Journal: *Journal of Consulting and Clinical Psychology,* June 1998, *66*(3), 533–540.

Related Research: Hobfoll, S. E., et al. (1994). Gender and coping: The dual-axis model of coping. *American Journal of Community Psychology, 22,* 49–82.

7804

Test Name: PRESSURE INVENTORY

Purpose: To identify specific pressures.

Number of Items: 48

Format: Responses are made on a 5-point mild–severe scale. Includes 6 sectors of interaction: family, work, intimate, school, and neighbor relationships; and self-imposed.

Reliability: Test-retest (2 weeks) reliability was .72.

Validity: Average correlation with Life Experiences Survey was .57.

Author: Jobes, D. A., et al.

Article: Assessment and treatment

of suicidal clients in a university counseling center.

Journal: *Journal of Counseling Psychology*, October 1997, *44*(4), 368–377.

Related Research: Weiten, W. (1988). Pressure as a form of stress and its relationship to psychological symptomtology. *Journal of Social and Clinical Psychology*, *6*, 127–139.

7805

Test Name: PRIMARY AND SECONDARY PSYCHOPATHY SCALE

Purpose: To measure primary and secondary psychopathology.

Number of Items: 26

Format: Four-point scales are anchored by "disagree strongly" and "agree strongly."

Reliability: Internal consistency reliabilities were .82 (primary) and .63 (secondary).

Author: Wilson, D. L., et al.

Article: Gender, somatization, and psychopathic traits in a college sample.

Journal: *Journal of Psychopathology and Behavioral Assessment*, September 1999, *21*(3), 221–235.

Related Research: Levenson, M. R., et al. (1995). Assessing psychopathic attributes in a noninstitutionalized population. *Journal of Personality and Social Psychology*, *68*, 151–158.

7806

Test Name: PROBLEM-FOCUSED STYLE OF COPING

Purpose: To assess coping style.

Number of Items: 18

Format: Includes 3 coping styles: Reactive, Reflective, and

Suppressive. A 5-point Likert response scale is used. Sample items are presented.

Reliability: Internal consistency ranged from .68 to .80. Test-retest (3 weeks) reliability ranged from .65 to .71.

Validity: Correlations with other variables ranged from −.47 to .42.

Author: Robitschek, C., and Cook, S. W.

Article: The influence of personal growth initiative and coping styles on career exploration and vocational identity.

Journal: *Journal of Vocational Behavior*, February 1999, *54*(1), 127–141.

Related Research: Heppner, P. P., et al. (1995). Progress in resolving problems: A problem-focused style of coping. *Journal of Counseling Psychology*, *42*, 279–293.

7807

Test Name: PROFESSIONAL LIFE STRESS SCALE (CHINESE)

Purpose: To measure professional stress including general work satisfaction, self-determination, interpersonal conflict, emotional pressure, and time pressure.

Number of Items: 20

Format: Seven-point scales are anchored by 1 (not at all characteristic) and 7 (extremely characteristic).

Reliability: Alpha was .83.

Author: Hamid, P. N.

Article: Self-disclosure and occupational stress in Chinese professionals

Journal: *Psychological Reports*, December 2000, *87*(3), Part 2, 1075–1082.

Related Research: Hamid, P. N., & Chan, W. T. (1998) Locus of control and occupational stress in Chinese professionals. *Psychological Reports*, *82*, 75–79.

7808

Test Name: PSYCHIATRIC INSTITUTE TRICHOTILLOMANIA SCALE

Purpose: To assess several dimensions of hair-pulling.

Number of Items: 6

Format: Seven-point Likert scales.

Reliability: Alphas ranged from .22 to .61.

Validity: Correlations with criterion measures ranged from −.50 to .75.

Author: Stanley, M. A., et al.

Article: Clinician-rated measures of hair pulling: A preliminary psychometric evaluation.

Journal: *Journal of Psychopathology and Behavioral Assessment*, June 1999, *21*(2), 157–170.

Related Research: Winchel, R. M., et al. (1992). The Psychiatric Institute Trichotillomania Scale. *Psychopharmacology Bulletin*, *22*, 463–476.

7809

Test Name: PSYCHOLOGICAL DISTRESS INVENTORY

Purpose: To measure life stress of college students.

Number of Items: 50

Format: 5-point scales range from "not at all aversive" to "extremely aversive."

Reliability: Test-retest reliabilities ranged from .72 to .83 across subscales.

Validity: Concurrent criterion-related validity coefficients ranges from .65 to .74 across subscales.

Author: Brazelton, E., et al.

Article: Femininity, bulimia, and distress in college women.

Journal: *Psychological Reports*, August 1998, *83*(1), 355–363.

Related Research: Lustman, P. J., et al. (1984). Factors influencing college students' health: Development of the Psychological Distress Inventory. *Journal of Counseling Psychology, 31,* 28–35.

7810

Test Name: PSYCHOLOGICAL EMPOWERMENT SCALE

Purpose: To provide a self-report measure of psychological empowerment.

Number of Items: 32

Format: Includes 4 factors: Attitudes, Formal Participation, Informal Participation, and Skills. Items are presented.

Reliability: Reliability coefficients ranged from .91 to .94.

Author: Akey, T. M., et al.

Article: Validation of scores on the Psychological Empowerment Scale: A measure of empowerment for parents of children with a disability.

Journal: *Educational and Psychological Measurement*, June 2000, *60*(3), 419–438.

Related Research: Akey, T. M. (1996). *Exploratory factor analysis and item analysis of the Psychological Empowerment Scale.* Unpublished manuscript, Auburn University, AL.

7811

Test Name: PSYCHOLOGICAL MINDEDNESS SCALE— REVISED

Purpose: To assess psychological mindedness.

Number of Items: 45

Format: Responses are made on a 4-point Likert scale ranging from "strongly agree" to "strongly disagree." A sample item is presented.

Reliability: Coefficient alpha was .82.

Author: Connolly, M. B., et al.

Article: The reliability and validity of a measure of self-understanding of interpersonal patterns.

Journal: *Journal of Counseling Psychology*, October 1999, *46*(4), 472–482.

Related Research: Lotterman, A. C. (1979). *A questionnaire measure of psychological mindedness and the capacity to benefit from psychotherapy.* Unpublished manuscript.

7812

Test Name: PSYCHOLOGICAL STRESS MEASURE

Purpose: To measure stress.

Number of Items: 25

Format: Frequency scales ranged from 1 (not at all) to 8 (extremely).

Reliability: Coefficient alpha was .92.

Authors: Damji, T., et al.

Article: Acculturation mode, identity variation, and psychosocial adjustment.

Journal: *Journal of Social Psychology*, August 1996, *136*(4), 493–500.

Related Research: Lemyre, L., et al. (1990). *Measure du stress psychologique (MSP): Manuel d'utilisation* [Psychological Stress Measure: User's manual]. Brossard, Quebec: Editions Behavoria.

7813

Test Name: PSYCHOLOGICAL WELL-BEING SCALE

Purpose: To measure psychological well-being.

Number of Items: 9

Format: Responses are made on a 6-point scale ranging from "never" to "most of the time." Examples are presented.

Reliability: Internal consistency was .88 and .87.

Validity: Correlations with other variables ranged from −.54 to .67.

Author: Munson, L. J., et al.

Article: Longitudinal analysis of disproportional influences and sexual harassment: Effects on job and psychological outcomes.

Journal: *Personnel Psychology*, Spring 2000, *53*(1), 21–46.

Related Research: Veit, C. T., & Ware, J. E. (1983). The structure of psychological distress and well-being in general populations. *Journal of Consulting and Clinical Psychology, 51,* 730–742.

7814

Test Name: PSYCHOPATHY CHECKLIST—REVISED

Purpose: To assess adult antisociality.

Number of Items: 20

Format: Checklist format. All items are presented.

Reliability: Alpha coefficients ranged from .76 to .87.

Author: McDermott, P. A., et al.

Article: Generality of Psychopathy Checklist—Revised factors over prisoners and substance-dependent patients.

Journal: *Journal of Consulting and Clinical Psychology*, February 2000, *68*(1), 181–186.

Related Research: Hare, R. D. (1991). *The Revised Psychopathy Checklist*. Toronto, Ontario, Canada: Multihealth Systems.

7815

Test Name: PSYCHOSOMATIC HEALTH SCALE

Purpose: To assess the presence of health problems.

Number of Items: 22

Format: Responses are made on a 5-point scale. An example is presented.

Reliability: Coefficient alpha was .89.

Validity: Correlations with other variables ranged from −.54 to .21.

Author: O'Connell, C. E., and Korabik, K.

Article: Sexual harassment: The relationship of personal vulnerability, work context, perpetrator status, and types of harassment to outcomes.

Journal: *Journal of Vocational Behavior*, June 2000, *56*(3), 299–329.

Related Research: Spence, J. T., et al. (1987). Impatience versus achievement strivings in the Type A pattern: Differential effects on students' health and academic performance. *Journal of Applied Psychology*, *72*, 522–528.

7816

Test Name: PSYCHOSOMATIC SUBSCALE

Purpose: To measure psychosomatic symptoms.

Number of Items: 36

Format: Responses are made on 5-point scales.

Reliability: Alpha coefficients were .92. Test-retest reliabilities were .81 and .83.

Author: Li, S., et al.

Article: Validation of a single-item measure of usual physical activity.

Journal: *Perceptual and Motor Skills*, October 2000, *91*(2), 593–602.

Related Research: Li, S., et al. (1999). The relationship between physical activity and perimenopause. *Health Care for Women International*, *20*, 163–178.

7817

Test Name: PSYCHOSOMATIC SYMPTOMS SUBSCALE

Purpose: To measure psychosomatic symptoms.

Number of Items: 47

Format: Includes 4 subscales: Vasomotor, Psychosomatic, Menstrual, and Sexual symptoms.

Reliability: Alpha coefficients were .91 and .94. Test-retest reliabilities were .80 and .85.

Author: Li, S., et al.

Article: Validation of a single-item measure of usual physical activity.

Journal: *Perceptual and Motor Skills*, October 2000, *91*(2), 593–602.

Related Research: Li, S., et al. (1999). The relationship between

physical activity and perimenopause. *Health Care for Women International*, *20*, 163–178.

7818

Test Name: PTSD CHECKLIST

Purpose: To measure posttraumatic stress disorder.

Number of Items: 17

Format: Five-point scales.

Reliability: Coefficient alpha was .97. Test-retest reliability was .96.

Validity: Validity coefficients were .83 (specificity) and .82 (sensitivity).

Author: Schnurr, P. P., et al.

Article: Predictors and outcomes of posttraumatic stress disorder in World War II veterans exposed to mustard gas.

Journal: *Journal of Consulting and Clinical Psychology*, April 2000, *68*(2), 258–268.

Related Research: Weathers, F. W., et al. (1996). *PTSD Checklist: Description, use, and psychometric properties*. Unpublished manuscript.

7819

Test Name: PTSD SYMPTOM SCALE—SELF-REPORT REVISED VERSION

Purpose: To measure symptoms of posttraumatic stress.

Number of Items: 17

Format: Four-point scales are anchored by 1 (not at all) and 4 (almost always).

Reliability: Alpha was .85.

Author: Boney-McCoy, S., and Finkelhor, D.

Article: Is youth victimization related to trauma symptoms and depression after controlling for prior symptoms and family relationships? A longitudinal prospective study.

Journal: *Journal of Consulting and Clinical Psychology,* December 1996, *64*(6), 1406–1416.

Related Research: Foa, E. B., et al. (1993). Reliability and validity of a brief measure for assessing post-traumatic stress disorder. *Journal of Traumatic Stress, 6,* 459–473.

7820

Test Name: QUALITY OF LIFE SCALE

Purpose: To measure quality of life of women.

Number of Items: 9

Format: Seven-point scales are anchored by 1 (terrible) and 7 (extremely pleased).

Reliability: Cronbach's alpha was .88. Corrected item-total correlations ranged from .56 to.79.

Author: Sullivan, C. M., and Bybee, D. I.

Article: Reducing violence using community-based advocacy for women with abusive partners.

Journal: *Journal of Consulting and Clinical Psychology,* February 1999, *67*(1), 43–53.

Related Research: Andrews, F., & Withey, S. (1976). *Social indicators of well-being: Americans' perceptions of life quality.* New York: Plenum.

7821

Test Name: RAPE AFTERMATH SYMPTOM TEST

Purpose: To measure fears and other symptoms present following rape.

Number of Items: 70

Format: Five-point Likert format.

Reliability: Alpha was .95. Test-retest reliability was .85 (2.5 weeks).

Author: Mechanic, M. B., et al.

Article: A comparison of normal forgetting, psychopathology, and information-processing models of reported amnesia for recent sexual trauma.

Journal: *Journal of Consulting and Clinical Psychology,* December 1998, *66*(6) 948–957.

Related Research: Kilpatrick, D. G. (1998). Rape aftermath symptom test. In *Dictionary of behavioral assessment techniques* (pp. 366–367). Oxford, England: Pergamon Press.

7822

Test Name: REALISTIC CONTROL MEASURE

Purpose: To enable children to assess the extent to which each of a series of problems is controllable.

Number of Items: 18

Format: Responses are made on a 4-point scale ranging from 1 (almost always) to 4 (almost never). An example is given.

Reliability: Alpha coefficients ranged from .74 to .83.

Author: Fagen, D. B., et al.

Article: Relationships between parent-child relational variables and child test variables in highly stressed urban families.

Journal: *Child Study Journal,* 1996, *26*(2), 87–108.

Related Research: Wannon, M. (1990). *Children's control attributions about controllable and uncontrollable events: Their relationship to stress-resiliency and psychological adjustment.*

Unpublished doctoral dissertation, University of Rochester.

7823

Test Name: REASONS FOR LIVING INVENTORY

Purpose: To measure reasons for living when suicide is considered.

Number of Items: 48

Format: Includes 6 subscales: Survival and Coping Beliefs, Responsibility to Family, Moral Objections, Fear of Suicide, Fear of Social Disapproval, and Child-Related Concerns. Responses are made on a 6-point scale ranging from 1 (not at all important) to 6 (extremely important).

Reliability: Alpha coefficients ranged from .76 to .91.

Validity: Correlations with other variables ranged from −.56 to .65.

Author: Gutierrez, P. M., et al.

Article: Suicide risk assessment in a college student population.

Journal: *Journal of Counseling Psychology,* October 2000, *47*(4), 403–413.

Related Research: Linehan, M. M., et al. (1983). Reasons for staying alive when you are thinking of killing yourself. The Reasons for Living Inventory. *Journal of Consulting and Clinical Psychology, 51,* 276–286.

7824

Test Name: RELIGIOUS COPING

Purpose: To assess the degree to which individuals use religious coping to deal with transplant-related stress.

Number of Items: 10

Format: Five-point scales are

anchored by 1 (not at all) and 5 (very much). Sample items are presented.

Reliability: Alpha coefficients ranged from .92 to .94.

Author: Tix, A. P., and Frazier, P. A.

Article: The use of religious coping during stressful life events: Main effects, moderation, and mediation.

Journal: *Journal of Consulting and Clinical Psychology*, April 1998, *66*(2), 411–422.

Related Research: Carrier, C. S., et al. (1989). Assessing coping strategies: A theoretically based approach. *Journal of Personality and Social Psychology, 56*, 267–283.

7825

Test Name: REPORTING QUESTIONNAIRE FOR CHILDREN

Purpose: To assess emotional, behavioral, intellectual, and neurological problems.

Number of Items: 10

Format: Yes/no format.

Reliability: Split-half reliabilities ranged from .86 to .87.

Author: Peltzer, K.

Article: Posttraumatic stress symptoms in a population of rural children in South Africa.

Journal: *Psychological Reports*, October 1999, *85*(2), 646–650.

Related Research: De Jong, J. T. V. M. (1986/'87). A study on mental disorders among children attending general healthcare facilities in Guinea-Bissau. *Psychopathologie Africaine, 21*, 67–90.

7826

Test Name: RESILIENCY SCALE

Purpose: To measure future orientation, active skill acquisition, and risk-taking.

Number of Items: 35

Format: Five-point scales are anchored by (1) strongly disagree and (5) strongly agree. Sample items are presented.

Reliability: Alphas ranged from .68 to .91.

Author: Jew, C. L., and Green, K. E.

Article: Effects of risk factors on adolescents' resiliency and coping.

Journal: *Psychological Reports*, April 1998, *82*(2), 675–678.

Related Research: Jew, C. L., & Green, K. E. (1995). *Resiliency and coping.* Paper presented at the annual meeting of the American Educational Research Association., San Francisco, CA.

7827

Test Name: RESILIENCY SCALE

Purpose: To measure future orientation, active skill acquisition, and independence/risk taking.

Number of Items: 49

Format: Likert format.

Reliability: Internal consistency reliabilities ranged from .36 to .95.

Validity: Correlations with other variables ranged from .26 to .60.

Author: Jew, C. L., et al.

Article: Development and validation of a measure of resiliency.

Journal: *Measurement and Evaluation in Counseling and*

Development, July 1999, *32*(2), 75–89.

7828

Test Name: RESPONSES TO SOCIAL STRESS QUESTIONNAIRE—ADOLESCENT VERSION

Purpose: To measure voluntary coping methods and involuntary responses to stress.

Number of Items: 57

Format: Various formats are used. The complete questionnaire is presented.

Reliability: Internal consistency coefficients ranged from .32 to .92. Test-retest reliabilities ranged from .49 to .81.

Validity: Correlations with coping ranged from −.05 to .58. Correlations with other variables ranged from −.44 to .64.

Author: Connor-Smith, J. K., et al.

Article: Responses to stress in adolescence: Measurement of coping and involuntary stress responses.

Journal: *Journal of Consulting and Clinical Psychology*, December 2000, *68*(6), 976–992.

7829

Test Name: REVISED DEATH ANXIETY SCALE

Purpose: To assess fear of pain, fear of the unknown, fear of not being, concern over the possibility of life after death, fear of helplessness and loss of control.

Number of Items: 25

Format: Five-point scales are anchored by (0) strongly disagree and (4) strongly agree. All items are presented.

Reliability: Alphas ranged from .84 to .91.

Author: Thorson, J. A., et al.

Article: African- and Euro-American samples differ little in scores on death anxiety.

Journal: *Psychological Reports*, October 1998, *83*(2), 623–626.

Related Research: Thorson, J. A., & Powell, F. C. (1992) A revised death anxiety scale. *Death Studies*, *16*, 507–521.

7830

Test Name: ROLE DEMANDS SCALE

Purpose: To assess stress.

Number of Items: 8

Format: Scales range from 1 (none or very little) to 7 (very much/to a great extent). Sample items are presented.

Reliability: Coefficient alpha was .75.

Author: Sinclair, R. R., and Tetrick, L. E.

Article: Implications of item wording for hardiness structure, relation with neuroticism, and stress buffering.

Journal: *Journal of Research in Personality*, March 2000, *34*(1), 1–25.

Related Research: House, R. J., & Rizzo, J. L. (1972). Role conflict and ambiguity as critical variables in a model of organizational behavior. *Organizational Behavior and Human Decision Processes*, *7*, 467–505.

7831

Test Name: ROLE STRESSORS SCALE

Purpose: To measure two role stressors.

Number of Items: 10

Format: Includes two sub-scales: Work Overload and Parental Overload. Responses are made on a 5-point scale.

Reliability: Alpha coefficients were .84 (Work Overload) and .85 (Parental Overload).

Validity: Correlations with other variables ranged from −.20 to .52.

Author: Aryee, S., et al.

Article: Role stressors, internal conflict, and well-being: The moderating influence of spousal support and coping behaviors among employed parents in Hong Kong.

Journal: *Journal of Vocational Behavior*, April 1999, *54*(2), 259–278.

Related Research: Cook, J. D., et al. (1981). *The experience of work: A compendium and review of 249 measures and their use.* London: Academic Press.

7832

Test Name: RUMINATION ON SADNESS SCALE

Purpose: To measure rumination on sadness.

Number of Items: 13

Format: Responses are made on a 5-point scale ranging from 1 (not at all) to 5 (very much). All items are presented.

Reliability: Coefficient alpha was .91. Test-retest (2–3 weeks) reliability was .70 ($N = 76$).

Validity: Correlations with other variables ranged from −.39 to .81.

Author: Conway, M., et al.

Article: On assessing individual differences in rumination on sadness.

Journal: *Journal of Personality Assessment*, December 2000, *75*(3), 404–425.

7833

Test Name: RYFF SCALES— SHORT VERSION

Purpose: To measure overall psychological well-being.

Number of Items: 18

Format: Includes 6 subdimensions: Self-Acceptance, Positive Relations With Others, Autonomy, Environmental Mastery, Purpose in Life, and Growth. Sample items are given.

Reliability: Coefficient alpha was .85.

Validity: Correlations with other variables ranged from −.54 to .57.

Author: Wiese, B. S., et al.

Article: Selection, optimization, and compensation: An action-related approach to work and partnership.

Journal: *Journal of Vocational Behavior*, December, 2000, *57*(3), 273–300.

Related Research: Ryff, C. D., & Keyes, C. L. (1995). The structure of psychological well-being revisited. *Journal of Personality and Social Psychology*, *69*, 719–727.

7834

Test Name: SATISFACTION WITH LIFE SCALE

Purpose: To measure life satisfaction.

Number of Items: 5

Format: Responses are made on a 7-point scale ranging from 1

(strongly disagree) to 7 (strongly agree). Sample items are presented.

Reliability: Coefficients alpha was .87. Test-retest (2 months) reliability was .82. Test-retest reliability (4 years) was .54.

Validity: Correlations with other variables ranged from −.24 to .53.

Author: Bonebright, C. A., et al.

Article: The relationship of workaholism with work-life conflict, life satisfaction, and purpose in life.

Journal: *Journal of Counseling Psychology*, October 2000, 47(4), 469–477.

Related Research: Diener, E., et al. (1985). The Satisfaction with Life Scales. *Journal of Personality Assessment, 49*, 71–75.

7835

Test Name: SCALE FOR SUICIDE IDEATION

Purpose: To assess and quantify the degree of intent for suicide ideators.

Number of Items: 19

Format: Interview-rated format.

Reliability: KR-20 was .89. Interrater reliability was .83.

Author: Clum, G. A., et al.

Article: An investigation of the validity of the SPSI and SPSI-R in differentiating high suicidal from depressed, low suicidal college students.

Journal: *Journal of Psychopathology and Behavioral Assessment*, June 1996, 18(2), 119–132.

Related Research: Beck, A., et al. (1979). Assessment of suicidal ideation: The Scale for Suicide Ideators. *Journal of Consulting*

and Clinical Psychology, 47, 343–352.

7836

Test Name: SCALES OF PSYCHOLOGICAL WELL-BEING

Purpose: To measure psychological well-being in older adults.

Number of Items: 84

Format: Includes 6 subscales: Self-Acceptance, Positive Relations with Others, Autonomy, Environmental Mastery, Purpose in Life, and Personal Growth. Responses are made on a 6-point scale ranging from 1 (strongly disagree) to 6 (strongly agree).

Reliability: Alpha coefficients ranged from .83 to .96.

Validity: Correlations with other variables ranged from −.72 to .73.

Author: Hanson, K. M., and Mintz, L. B.

Article: Psychological health and problem-solving self-appraisal in older adults.

Journal: *Journal of Counseling Psychology*, October 1997, 44(4), 433–441.

Related Research: Ryff, C. D. (1989). Happiness is everything, or is it? Explorations of the meaning of psychological well-being. *Journal of Personality and Social Psychology, 57,* 1069–1081.

7837

Test Name: SCREEN FOR CHILD ANXIETY RELATED EMOTIONAL DISORDERS

Purpose: To measure anxiety in children.

Number of Items: 38

Format: Includes 5 subscales: Somatic/Panic, General Anxiety, Separation Anxiety, Social Phobia, and School Phobia. Responses are made on a 3-point rating scale.

Reliability: Alpha coefficients ranged from .63 to .91.

Author: Muris, P., et al.

Article: Correlations between two multidimensional anxiety scales for children.

Journal: *Perceptual and Motor Skills*, August 1998, 87(1), 269–270.

Related Research: Birmaher, B., et al. (1997). The Screen for Child Anxiety Related Educational Disorders (SCARED): Scale construction and psychometric characteristics. *Journal of the American Academy of Child and Adolescent Psychiatry, 36*, 545–553.

7838

Test Name: SCREEN FOR CHILD ANXIETY RELATED EMOTIONAL DISORDERS

Purpose: To measure the entire spectrum of anxiety disorders.

Number of Items: 66

Format: Three-point scales are anchored by 0 (almost never) and 2 (often).

Reliability: Alpha coefficients ranged from .68 to .95.

Validity: Correlation with other variables ranged from .67 to .89.

Author: Muris, P., et al.

Article: Sensitivity for treatment effects of the screen for child anxiety related emotional disorders.

Journal: *Journal of Psychopathology and Behavioral Assessment*, December 1999, 21(4), 323–335.

Related Research: Muris, P., et al. (1999). The revised version of the Screen for Child Anxiety Related Emotional Disorders (SCARED-R): Factor structure in normal children. *Personality and Individual Differences, 26*, 99–112.

7839

Test Name: SCREEN TEST FOR CHILD ANXIETY RELATED EMOTIONAL DISORDERS

Purpose: To measure symptoms of a *DSM-IV* defined anxiety disorder in children.

Number of Items: 66

Format: Three-point scales are anchored by 0 (almost never) to 2 (often).

Reliability: Alphas ranged from .49 to .84 across disorders. Total alpha was .91.

Validity: Correlations with self-reported disorders ranged from −.18 to .77.

Author: Muris, P., et al.

Article: Associations of symptoms of anxiety disorders and self-reported behavior problems in normal children.

Journal: *Psychological Reports,* February 2000, *86*(1), 157–162.

Related Research: Birmaher, B., et al. (1997). The Screen for Child Anxiety Related Emotional Disorders (SCARED): Scale construction and psychometric characteristics. *Journal of the American Academy of Child and Adolescent Psychiatry, 36*, 545–553.

7840

Test Name: SEASONAL LIGHT INVENTORY

Purpose: To measure seasonal-depressive symptomatology when combined with a seasonal depressive measure and to assess exposure to outdoor and bright indoor light.

Number of Items: 20

Format: Includes two subscales: Seasonality and Light Exposure.

Reliability: Alpha coefficients were .58 (Light Exposure) and .85 (Seasonality).

Author: Groom, K. N., and O'Connor, M. E.

Article: Relation of light and exercise to seasonal depressive symptoms: Preliminary development of a scale.

Journal: *Perceptual and Motor Skills,* October 1996, *83*(2), 379–383.

Related Research: Radloff, L. S. (1987). The CES-D scale. In K. Corcoran and J. Fisher (Eds.), *Measures for clinical practice* (pp. 118–119). New York: Free Press.

7841

Test Name: SECONDARY TRAUMA QUESTIONNAIRE

Purpose: To measure symptoms of secondary post-traumatic syndrome.

Number of Items: 20

Format: Five-point scales are anchored by 1 (rarely/never) and 5 (very often). All items are presented.

Reliability: Alphas ranged from .75 to .88.

Validity: Correlations with other trauma measures ranged from .41 to .56.

Author: Motta, R. W., et al.

Article: Initial evaluation of the Secondary Trauma Questionnaire.

Journal: *Psychological Reports,*
December 1999, *85*(3, Part I), 997–1002.

Related Research: Motta, R. W., & Joseph, J. M. (1988). *The Secondary Trauma Questionnaire.* (Unpublished scale. Hofstra University, New York).

7842

Test Name: SELF-DEPRECATION/DEPRESSION SCALES

Purpose: To assess self-image in terms of anxiety, irascibility, and depression.

Number of Items: 26

Format: Checklist format. All items are presented.

Reliability: Alpha coefficients ranged from .76 to .92.

Author: Tallman, I., et al.

Article: The intergenerational transmission of marital conflict: Testing a process model.

Journal: *Social Psychology Quarterly,* September 1999, *62*(3), 219–239.

Related Research: Lipman, R. S., et al. (1969). Factors of symptom distress. *Archives of General Psychiatry, 21*, 328–338.

7843

Test Name: SELF-PERCEIVED STRESS IN RETIREMENT SCALE

Purpose: To measure stress in retirement.

Number of Items: 14

Format: Five-point scales range from 1 (low) to 5 (extreme). All items are presented.

Reliability: Alpha was .88. Item-total correlations ranged from .31 to .74.

Validity: Correlations with other variables ranged from .50 to .55.

Author: Sharpley, C. F.

Article: Psychometric properties of the Self-Perceived Stress in Retirement Scale.

Journal: *Psychological Reports*, August 1997, *81*(1), 319–322.

7844

Test Name: SELF-RATING ANXIETY SCALE

Purpose: To measure affective and somatic symptoms of anxiety.

Number of Items: 20

Reliability: Split-half reliability was .71.

Validity: Correlation with the Taylor Manifest Anxiety Scale was .30.

Author: Whatley, S. L., et al.

Article: The relationship of coping style to dysphoria, anxiety, and anger.

Journal: *Psychological Reports*, December 1998, *83*(3) Part 1, 738–791.

Related Research: Zung, W. (1971). A rating instrument for anxiety disorders, *Psychomatics*, *12*, 371–379.

7845

Test Name: SELF-RATING DEPRESSION SCALE

Purpose: To measure depression.

Number of Items: 20

Format: Scales range from 1 (rarely) to 5 (very often).

Reliability: Coefficient alpha was .96.

Validity: Correlations with other variables ranged from −.17 to .43.

Author: Schaubroeck, J., et al.

Article: Collective efficacy versus self-efficacy in coping responses to stressors and control: A cross-cultural study.

Journal: *Journal of Applied Psychology*, August 2000, *85*(4), 512–525.

Related Research: Zung, W. W. K. (1965). Self-rating depression scale. *Archives of General Psychiatry, 12*, 63–70.

7846

Test Name: SELF-RATING DEPRESSION SCALE (JAPANESE VERSION)

Purpose: To measure depression.

Number of Items: 20

Format: Frequency rating scales range from 1 (none or little of the time) to 4 (most all of the time).

Reliability: Alpha was .78.

Author: Matsui, T., et al.

Article: Long-term outcomes of early victimization by peers among Japanese male university students: Model of a vicious cycle.

Journal: *Psychological Reports*, December 1996, *79*(3) Part 1, 711–720.

Related Research: Zung, W. (1965). A self-rating depression scale. *Archives of General Psychiatry, 12*, 63–67.

7847

Test Name: SELF-REPORT COPING SCALE

Purpose: To measure children's coping strategies.

Number of Items: 34

Format: Five-point scales are anchored by "never" and "always."

Reliability: Alpha coefficients ranged from .68 to .90. Test-retest reliabilities (2 weeks) ranged from .58 to .78.

Author: Crook, K., et al.

Article: Anxiety and depression in children: A preliminary examination of the utility of the PANAS-C.

Journal: *Journal of Psychopathology and Behavioral Assessment*, December 1998, *20*(4), 333–350.

Related Research: Causey, D. L., & Dubow, E. F. (1992). Development of a self-report coping measure for elementary school children. *Journal of Clinical Child Psychology, 21*, 47–59.

7848

Test Name: SELF-REPORT OF PSYCHOPATHY SCALE—2ND EDITION

Purpose: To measure psychopathy.

Number of Items: 60

Format: Seven-point scales are anchored by 1 (strongly disagree) and 7 (strongly agree).

Validity: Correlations with criterion measures ranged from .55 to .62.

Author: Wilson, D. L., et al.

Article: Gender, somatization, and psychopathic traits in a college sample.

Journal: *Journal of Psychopathology and Behavioral Assessment*, September 1999, *21*(3), 221–235.

Related Research: Zagon, I. K., & Jackson, H. J. (1994). Construct validity of a psychopathy instrument. *Personality and Individual Differences, 17*, 125–135.

7849

Test Name: SEXUAL RESPONSE CYCLE SCALE

Purpose: To assess psychophysiologic phases of the sexual response cycle.

Number of Items: 27

Format: Five-point scales are anchored by 0 (never) and 4 (always). Sample items are presented.

Reliability: Internal consistency ranged from .72 to .86 across subscales.

Validity: Correlations with other variables ranged from .35 to .66.

Author: Yurek, D., et al.

Article: Breast cancer surgery: Comparing surgical groups and determining individual differences in postoperative sexuality and body change stress.

Journal: *Journal of Consulting and Clinical Psychology*, August 2000, *68*(4), 697–709.

Related Research: Cyranowski, J. C., & Andersen, B. L. (1988). Schemas, sexuality, and romantic attachment. *Journal of Personality and Social Psychology*, 74, 1364–1379.

7850

Test Name: SICKNESS IMPACT PROFILE—MOBILITY SCALE

Purpose: To assess psychosocial mobility.

Number of Items: 10

Format: Responses are either "True" or "False." Sample items are presented.

Validity: Correlations with other variables ranged from −.46 to .82.

Author: Elliott, T. R., et al.

Article: Goal instability and adjustment to physical disability.

Journal: *Journal of Counseling Psychology*, April 2000, 47(2), 251–265.

Related Research: Bergner, M., et al. (1981). The Sickness Impact Profile: Development and final revision of a health status measure. *Medical Care, 19*, 787–805.

7851

Test Name: SLEEP DIFFICULTIES SCALE

Purpose: To measure problems of falling asleep, coping with that problem, and fatigue on awakening.

Number of Items: 4

Reliability: Alpha was .60.

Validity: Correlation with a longer version of the scale was .61.

Author: Hener, T., et al.

Article: Supportive versus cognitive-behavioral intervention programs in achieving adjustment to home peritoneal kidney dialysis.

Journal: *Journal of Consulting and Clinical Psychology*, August 1996, *64*(4), 731–741.

Related Research: Lavie, P. (1981). Sleep habits and sleep disturbance in industrial workers in Israel: Main findings and some characteristics of workers complaining of excessive daytime sleepiness. *Sleep, 4*, 147–158.

7852

Test Name: SMITH QUICK STRESS TEST

Purpose: To measure somatic stress, negative affect, and worry.

Number of Items: 27

Format: Includes 3 dimensions:

Somatic Stress, Worry, and Negative Affect.

Reliability: Alpha coefficients ranged from .71 to .83.

Validity: Correlations with other variables ranged from −.36 to .45.

Author: Khasky, A. D., and Smith, J. C.

Article: Stress, relaxation states, and creativity.

Journal: *Perceptual and Motor Skills*, April 1999, *88*(2), 409–416.

Related Research: Smith, J. C. (1999). *ABC relaxation theory: An evidence-based approach.* New York: Springer.

7853

Test Name: SOCIAL COGNITION AND OBJECT RELATIONS SCALE

Purpose: To assess an array of psychological functioning.

Format: Includes 8 variables: Complexity, Affect, Relationships, Morals, Causality, Aggression, Self-Esteem, and Identity. Responses are made on a 7-point scale ranging from 1 (pathological) to 7 (healthy).

Reliability: Interrater reliability ranged from .36 to .95.

Validity: Correlations with other variables ranged from .30 to .47.

Author: Ackerman, S. J., et al.

Article: Use of the TAT in the assessment of DSM-IV Cluster B personality disorders.

Journal: *Journal of Personality Assessment*, December 1999, 73(3), 422–448.

Related Research: Westen, D., et al. (1985). *Object relations and social cognition TAT scoring manual.* Unpublished

manuscript, University of
Michigan, Ann Arbor.

7854

Test Name: SOCIAL PHOBIA
AND ANXIETY INVENTORY
(SPANISH)

Purpose: To assess social phobia
and agoraphobia.

Number of Items: 45

Time Required: 40 minutes.

Format: Seven-point scales are
anchored by 1 (never) and 7
(always).

Reliability: Alphas ranged from
.78 to .96.

Author: Olivares, J., et al.

Article: The Social Phobia and
Anxiety Inventory: Reliability
and validity in an adolescent
Spanish population.

Journal: *Journal of
Psychopathology and Behavioral
Assessment*, March 1999, *21*(1),
67–78.

Related Research: Osman, A., et
al. (1996). The Social Phobia and
Anxiety Inventory: Further
validation in two nonclinical
samples. *Journal of
Psychopathology and Behavioral
Assessment, 18*, 35–47.

7855

Test Name: SOCIAL PHOBIA
SCALE

Purpose: To measure fears or the
affective experience of anxiety.

Number of Items: 20

Format: Five-point Likert format.

Reliability: Internal consistency
ranged from .89 to .94.

Validity: Correlations with other
variables ranged from .05 to .69.

Author: Habke, A. M., et al.

Article: The Social Phobia and
Social Interaction Anxiety scales:
An exploration of the dimension
of social anxiety and sex
differences in structure and
relations with pathology.

Journal: *Journal of
Psychopathology and Behavioral
Assessment*, March 1997, *19*(1),
21–39.

Related Research: Mattick, R. P.,
& Clark, J. C. (1989).
*Development and validation of
measures of social phobia
scrutiny fears and social
interaction anxiety*. Unpublished
manuscript.

Osman, A., et al. (1998). The
Social Phobia and Social
Interaction Anxiety scales:
Evaluation of psychometric
properties. *Journal of
Psychopathology and Behavioral
Assessment, 20*, 249–264.

7856

Test Name: SOCIAL PHYSIQUE
ANXIETY SCALE

Purpose: To measure anxiety
about social physique.

Number of Items: 12

Format: Responses are made on a
5-point scale ranging from 1 (not
at all true for me) to 5
(extremely true for me).

Reliability: Internal reliability was
.9. Test-retest (2 weeks)
reliability was .82.

Author: Frederick, C. M., and
Morrison, C. S.

Article: Social physique anxiety:
Personality constructs,
motivations, exercise attitudes,
and behaviors.

Journal: *Perceptual and Motor
Skills*, June 1996, *82*(3) Part 1,
963–972.

Related Research: Hart, E. A., et
al. (1989). The measurement of

social physique anxiety. *Journal
of Sport and Exercise
Psychology, 11*, 94–104.

7857

Test Name: SOMATIC,
COGNITIVE, BEHAVIORAL
ANXIETY INVENTORY

Purpose: To measure the somatic,
behavioral, and cognitive
components of anxiety.

Number of Items: 36

Format: Eight-point Likert
format.

Reliability: Split-half reliability
coefficients ranged from .91 to
.93.

Author: Harrell, J. P., and
Wright, L. W., Jr.

Article: The development and
validation of the Multicomponent
AIDS Phobia Scale.

Journal: *Journal of
Psychopathology and Behavioral
Assessment*, September 1998,
20(3), 201–216.

Related Research: Lehrer, P. M.,
& Woolfolk, R. L. (1982). Self-
report assessment of anxiety:
Somatic, cognitive, and
behavioral modalities. *Behavioral
Assessment, 4*, 167–177.

7858

Test Name: SOMATIC
COMPLAINTS SCALE

Purpose: To assess the frequency
of somatic complaints.

Number of Items: 10

Format: 3-point scales are
anchored by (1) never and (3)
three or more times. A sample
item is presented.

Reliability: Cronbach's alpha was
.79.

Validity: Correlations with other

variables ranged from −.25 to .43.

Author: Smith, D., and Tinzer, A.

Article: Moderating effects of affective disposition and social support on the relationship between person-environment fit and strain.

Journal: *Psychological Reports*, June 1998, 82(3) Part 1, 963–983.

Related Research: Caplan, R. D., et al. (1975). *Job demands and worker health: Main effects and occupational differences* (pp. 75–160). (Report to National Institute for Occupational Safety and Health, NIOSH) Washington, DC: Health, Environment, and Welfare.

Langer, T. S. (1962). A 22-item screening score of psychological symptoms indicating impairment. *Journal of Health and Human Behavior, 3,* 269–276.

7859

Test Name: SPORT ANXIETY SCALE

Purpose: To measure sport-specific cognitive and somatic trait anxiety.

Number of Items: 21

Format: Includes 3 subscales: Worry scale, Concentration Disruption scale, and Somatic Anxiety scale. Responses are made on a 4-point scale ranging from 1 (not at all) to 4 (very much so). Sample items are presented.

Reliability: Test-retest (7 days) reliability exceeded .85 on all scales. Alpha coefficients ranged from .74 to .88.

Validity: Correlations with other variables ranged from −.44 to .32.

Author: Robazza, C., et al.

Article: Performance related emotions in skilled athletes: Hedonic tone and functional impact.

Journal: *Perceptual and Motor Skills*, October 1998, 87(2), 547–564.

Related Research: Smith, R. E., et al. (1990). Measurement and correlates of sport-specific cognitive and somatic trait anxiety: The Sport Anxiety Scale, *Anxiety Research, 2,* 263–280.

7860

Test Name: SPORT COPING STRATEGIES INVENTORY

Purpose: To measure coping styles in sports.

Number of Items: 26

Format: Scales range from 1 (not at all like me) to 5 (very much like me). All items are presented.

Reliability: Alpha coefficients ranged from .81 to .90 across subscales.

Validity: Interfactor correlations ranged from .42 to .78.

Author: Anshel, M.

Article: Coping styles among adolescent competitive athletes.

Journal: *Journal of Social Psychology*, June 1996, 136(3), 311–323.

7861

Test Name: STATE ANXIETY SCALE

Purpose: To assess anxiety.

Number of Items: 10

Format: Scales range from 1 (almost never) to 4 (almost always).

Reliability: Coefficient alpha was .90.

Validity: Correlations with other

variables ranged from −.40 to .70.

Author: Spector, P. E., et al.

Article: A longitudinal study of relations between job stressors and job strains while controlling for prior negative affectivity and strains.

Journal: *Journal of Applied Psychology*, April 2000, 85(2), 211–218.

Related Research: Spector, P. E., et al. (1988). Relation of job stressors to affective, health, and performance outcomes: A comparison of multiple data sources. *Journal of Applied Psychology, 73,* 11–19.

7862

Test Name: STATE COMPETITIVE WORRIES INVENTORY FOR CHILDREN

Purpose: To measure precompetitive worries.

Number of Items: 10

Format: Includes 2 factors: Performance Worries and Social Evaluation Worries. Employs a 4-point response scale.

Reliability: Alpha coefficients were .68 and .66.

Validity: Correlations with other variables ranged from −.10 to −.13.

Author: Psychountaki, M., and Zervas, Y.

Article: Competitive worries, sport confidence, and performance ratings for young swimmers.

Journal: *Perceptual and Motor Skills*, August 2000, 91(1), 87–94.

Related Research: Kakkos, V., et al. (1996). *State competitive worries inventory for children.*

Unpublished manuscript, University of Athens.

7863

Test Name: STRAIN CHECKLIST

Purpose: To measure strain symptoms.

Number of Items: 10

Format: Checklist format. Sample items are presented.

Reliability: Coefficient alpha was .80.

Author: Bram, A. D., et al.

Article: A longitudinal investigation of object relations: Child-rearing antecedents, stability in adulthood, and construct validation.

Journal: *Journal of Research in Personality*, June 1999, *33*(2), 159–188.

Related Research: Franz, C. E., et al. (1991). Childhood antecedents of conventional social accomplishment in mid life adults: A 36-year prospective study. *Journal of Personality and Social Psychology, 4*, 586–595.

7864

Test Name: STRAIN-FREE NEGATIVE AFFECTIVITY SCALE

Purpose: To measure strain-free negative affectivity.

Number of Items: 28

Format: Responses are made on a Likert-type scale. All items are presented.

Reliability: Coefficient alpha was .86.

Validity: Correlation with other variables ranged from −.15 to .64.

Author: Fortunato, V. J., and Stone-Romero, E. F.

Article: Taking the strain out of negative affectivity: Development and initial validation of scores on a strain-free measure of negative affectivity.

Journal: *Educational and Psychological Measurement*, February 1999, *59*(1), 77–97.

Related Research: Watson, D., & Clark, L. A. (1984). Negative affectivity: The disposition to experience aversive emotional states. *Psychological Bulletin*, *96*, 465–490.

7865

Test Name: STRESS FACTORS AND HIGH-RISK BEHAVIOR SCALES

Purpose: To measure incidence of emotional stress of interpersonal stress and of high risk behavior.

Number of Items: 51

Format: Scales range from 0 (never) to 9 (nine or more times).

Reliability: Alpha coefficients ranged from .36 to .95 across 12 subscales.

Validity: Correlations between stress and childhood rape and oral sex ranged from −.09 to .06.

Author: Duane, E. A., et al.

Article: Consequences of childhood sexual abuse for college students.

Journal: *Journal of College Student Development*, January/February 1997, *38*(1), 13–23.

7866

Test Name: STRESS INTENSITY AND APPRAISAL SCALE

Purpose: To assess perceived

stressfulness in a situation in competitive sports.

Number of Items: 8

Format: Scales range from 1 (not at all) to 5 (very much).

Reliability: Alpha coefficients range from .68 to .81.

Author: Anshel, M. H., and Wells, B.

Article: Personal and situational variables that describe coping with acute stress in competitive sports.

Journal: *The Journal of Social Psychology*, October 2000, *140*(4), 434–450.

Related Research: Kaissidis, A. N. (1993). *Sources of and responses to acute stress in sport as a function of selected personal dispositions, situational appraisals, and cultural differences.* Unpublished doctoral dissertation, University of Wollongong, New South Wales, Australia.

7867

Test Name: STRESS OUTCOMES SCALE

Purpose: To measure anxiety and depression by frequency of psychosomatic events.

Number of Items: 16

Format: Scales range from 1 (rarely or never) to 5 (always). Sample items are presented.

Reliability: Alpha coefficients ranged from .71 to .79.

Author: Sinclair, R. R., and Tetrick, L. E.

Article: Implications of item wording for hardiness structure, relation with neuroticism, and stress buffering.

Journal: *Journal of Research in Personality*, March 2000, *34*(1), 1–25.

Related Research: Watson, D., et al. (1995). Testing a tripartite model: II. Exploring the symptom structure of anxiety in student, adult, and patient samples. *Journal of Abnormal Psychology, 104,* 15–25.

7868

Test Name: STRESS REACTIONS CHECKLIST

Purpose: To measure reaction to stress.

Number of Items: 18

Format: Four-point rating scales. All items are presented.

Reliability: Alpha was .87.

Validity: Correlations with ego-strength ranged from −.31 to −.11.

Author: Torki, M. A.

Article: Ego strength and stress reaction in Kuwaiti students after the Iraqi invasion.

Journal: *Psychological Reports,* August 2000, *87*(1), 188–192.

Related Research: Vocational Instructional Material Laboratory. (1983). Managing stress before it manages you. Columbus, OH: The Ohio State University.

7869

Test Name: STRESS RESPONSE SCALE

Purpose: To assess children's behavioral adjustments.

Number of Items: 40

Format: Responses are made on a scale ranging from 0 (never) to 5 (always). Includes 3 subscales: School Adjustment, Disruptive/Impulsive Behavior, and Withdrawn Behavior.

Reliability: Alpha coefficients ranged from .83 to .94.

Author: Verschueren, K., et al.

Article: The internal working model of the self, attachment, and competence in five-year-olds.

Journal: *Child Development,* October 1996, *67*(5), 2493–2511.

Related Research: Chandler, L. A., & Shermis, M. D. (1985). Assessing behavioral responses to stress. *Educational and Psychological Measurement, 45,* 825–844.

7870

Test Name: STRESS SCALE

Purpose: To measure stress.

Number of Items: 2

Format: Responses are made on a 5-point scale ranging from two or three a week to less than once a month. The items are presented.

Reliability: Coefficients alpha was .04.

Validity: Correlations with other variables ranged from −.22 to .56.

Author: Greenhaus, J. H., et al.

Article: Work and family influences or departure from public accounting.

Journal: *Journal of Vocational Behavior,* April 1997, *50*(2), 249–270.

Related Research: Patchen, M. (1970). *Participation, achievement, and involvement on the job.* Englewood Cliffs, NJ: Prentice-Hall.

7871

Test Name: SUBJECTIVE STRESS SCALE

Purpose: To measure subjective stress.

Number of Items: 7

Format: Six-point scales are anchored by 1 (low perceived stress) and 6 (high perceived stress).

Reliability: Coefficient alpha was .77.

Validity: Correlations with other variables ranged from −.74 to .20.

Author: Johnston, J. H., et al.

Article: Vigilant and hypervigilant decision making.

Journal: *Journal of Applied Psychology* August, 1997, *82*(4), 614–622.

Related Research: Driskel, J. E., & Salas, E. (1991). Group decision making under stress. *Journal of Applied Psychology, 76,* 473–478.

7872

Test Name: SUFFOCATION FEAR SCALE

Purpose: To measure fear of suffocation as a claustrophobic-related phenomenon.

Number of Items: 16

Format: Five-point scales are anchored by 0 (no anxiety) and 4 (maximum anxiety).

Reliability: Alpha was .78.

Validity: Correlations with other variables ranged from .13 to .31.

Author: Eifert, G. H., et al.

Article: Predictors of self-reported anxiety and panic symptoms: An evaluation of anxiety sensitivity, suffocation fear, heart-focused anxiety and breath-holding duration.

Journal: *Journal of Psychopathology and Behavioral Assessment,* December 1999, *21*(4), 293–305.

Related Research: Rachman, S., & Taylor, S. (1993). Analyses of claustrophobia. *Journal of Anxiety Disorders, 7,* 281–291.

7873

Test Name: SUICIDE INTENT SCALE

Purpose: To assess degree of suicidal attempt.

Number of Items: 15

Format: Responses are made on an ordinal scale ranging from 0 to 2.

Reliability: Interrater reliability was .95. Internal consistency was .82.

Validity: Correlations with other variables ranged from −.9 to .35.

Author: Spirito, A., et al.

Article: Factor analysis of the suicide intent scale with adolescent suicide attempters.

Journal: *Journal of Personality Assessment,* August 1996, *67*(1), 90–101.

Related Research: Beck, A. T., et al. (1974). Development of suicidal intent scales. In A. T. Beck, et al. (Eds.), *The prediction of suicide* (pp. 45–56). Bowie, MD: Charles Press.

7874

Test Name: SURVEY OF HEALTH CONCERNS

Purpose: To measure health concerns.

Number of Items: 20

Format: Five-point scales are anchored by 1 (not at all like me) and 5 (very much like me). All items are presented.

Reliability: Alpha was .84. Test-retest reliability (2 weeks) was .85.

Validity: Correlation with the

Penn State Worry Questionnaire was .62.

Author: Katz, R. C., and Zenger, N.

Article: Assessing hypochondriasis: Findings on the Survey of Health Concerns.

Journal: *Journal of Psychopathology and Behavioral Assessment,* September 1999, *21*(3), 183–189.

7875

Test Name: SYMPTOM CHECKLIST

Purpose: To assess physical symptoms experienced over the past 3 months.

Number of Items: 17

Format: Checklist format.

Reliability: Coefficient alpha was .83.

Author: Larson, R., and Lee, M.

Article: The capacity to be alone as a stress buffer.

Journal: *Journal of Social Psychology,* February 1996, *136*(1), 5–16.

Related Research: Mechanic, D. (1980). The experience and reporting of common physical complaints. *Journal of Health and Social Behavior, 21,* 146–155.

7876

Test Name: SYMPTOM PATTERN SCALE

Purpose: To identify one's symptoms.

Number of Items: 17

Format: Responses are made on a 5-point scale.

Reliability: Coefficient alpha was .78.

Author: Mahon, N. E., et al.

Article: Loneliness and health-related variables in young adults.

Journal: *Perceptual and Motor Skills,* December 1997, *85*(3, Part 1), 800–802.

Related Research: Gurin, G., et al. (1960). *Americans view their mental health.* New York: Basic Books.

7877

Test Name: SYMPTOM PATTERN SCALE—KOREAN VERSION

Purpose: To measure psychological, physical, and psychosomatic manifestations of psychological distress.

Number of Items: 20

Format: Four-point scales ranged from "nearly all the time" to "never."

Reliability: Alpha was .83.

Author: Kim, O.

Article: Loneliness: A prediction of health perception among older Korean immigrants.

Journal: *Psychological Reports,* October 1997, *81*(2), 591–594.

Related Research: Gurin, G., et al. (1960). *Americans view their mental health.* New York: Basic.

7878

Test Name: TASK-SPECIFIC ANXIETY SCALE

Purpose: To measure task-specific anxiety.

Number of Items: 10

Format: Responses are made on a 7-point Likert-type scale ranging from 1 (strongly disagree) to 7 (strongly agree). All items are presented.

Reliability: Coefficient alpha was .80.

Validity: Correlations with other variables ranged from −.50 to .44.

Author: Saks, A. M., and Ashforth, B. E.

Article: Proactive socialization and behavioral self-management.

Journal: *Journal of Vocational Behavior*, June 1996, *48*(3), 301–323.

7879

Test Name: THANATOPHOBIA SCALE

Purpose: To assess caregivers' uncomfortable feelings and sense of helplessness when confronting patients who are terminally ill.

Number of Items: 7

Format: 7-point scales are anchored by (1) strongly disagree and (7) strongly agree. All items are presented.

Reliability: Alphas ranged from .82 to .87.

Author: Merrill, J., et al.

Article: Caring for terminally ill persons: Comparative analysis of attitudes (thanatophobia) of practicing physicians, student nurses and medical students.

Journal: *Psychological Reports*, August 1998, *83*(1), 123–128.

Related Research: Merrill, J. M., et al. (1989). AIDS and student attitudes. *Southern Medical Journal*, *82*, 426–432.

7880

Test Name: TRAIT COMPETITIVE WORRIES INVENTORY FOR CHILDREN

Purpose: To measure precompetitive worries.

Number of Items: 10

Format: Includes 2 factors: Performance Worries and Social Evaluation Worries.

Reliability: Alpha coefficients were .68 and .66.

Validity: Correlations with other variables ranged from −.55 to .72.

Author: Psychountaki, M., and Zervas, Y.

Article: Competitive worries, sport confidence, and performance ratings for young swimmers.

Journal: *Perceptual and Motor Skills*, August 2000, *91*(1), 87–94.

Related Research: Kakkos, V., et al. (1999). Psychological assessment procedures for young athletes: Part I. Development of instruments. *Proceedings of 10th European Congress of Sport Psychology: Psychology of Sport and Exercise: Enhancing the quality of life* (pp. 292–294). Prague.

7881

Test Name: TRAUMA SYMPTOM CHECKLIST

Purpose: To assess adult symptoms of emotional distress such as anxiety and sleep problems.

Number of Items: 40

Format: Three-point frequency scales ask respondents to report symptoms in past 2 months.

Reliability: Alpha coefficients ranged from .77 to .85 across subscales.

Author: Banyard, V. L., and Williams, L. M.

Article: Characteristics of child sexual abuse as correlates of women's adjustment: A prospective study.

Journal: *Journal of Marriage and the Family*, November 1996, *58*(4), 853–865.

Related Research: Briere, J., & Runtz, M. (1987). *A brief measure of victimization affects: The Trauma Symptom Checklist (TSC-33)*. Paper presented at the Third National Family Violence Research Conference, Durham, NH.

7882

Test Name: TRAUMATIC EXPERIENCES INVENTORY

Purpose: To measure the existence, intensity, and duration of biopsychological symptoms of traumatic experiences following a crime or natural disaster.

Number of Items: 38

Format: Yes/no format. Sample items are presented.

Reliability: KR-20 reliability was .91. Alphas ranged from .81 to .94 across samples.

Validity: Similar factor structures were obtained in two samples that experienced a traumatic event.

Author: Sprang, G.

Article: The Traumatic Experiences Inventory: A test of psychometric properties.

Journal: *Journal of Psychopathology and Behavioral Assessment*, September 1997, *19*(3), 257–271.

7883

Test Name: UNDERSTANDING MOOD DISORDERS QUESTIONNAIRE

Purpose: To assess knowledge of mood disorders by family members of individuals with mood disorders.

Number of Items: 49

Format: Yes/No/Don't Know and checklist formats are used. All items are presented.

Reliability: Alpha was .73.

Validity: No significant differences were measured between mother and father responses.

Author: Gavazzi, S. M., et al.

Article: The Understanding Mood Disorders Questionnaire.

Journal: *Psychological Reports*, August 1997, *81*(1), 172–174.

7884

Test Name: URSIN HEALTH INVENTORY

Purpose: To assess health complaints.

Number of Items: 36

Format: Intensity and duration of each health problem are rated on 3-point scales. Examples are given.

Reliability: Coefficient alpha was .79.

Author: Brand, N., et al.

Article: Chronic stress affects blood pressure and speed of short-term memory.

Journal: *Perceptual and Motor Skills*, August 2000, *91*(1), 291–298.

Related Research: Ursin, H., et al. (1988). Psychological factors and self-reports of muscle pain. *European Journal of Applied Physiology, 57*, 282–290.

7885

Test Name: VISUAL ANALOGUE MOOD SCALE

Purpose: To assess depressive mood states.

Number of Items: 1

Format: 5.5" long scale is anchored by "not at all depressed" and "most depressed I've ever felt."

Validity: Hit rates ranged from .75 to .80. Other classification indexes ranged from .45 to .91.

Author: Killgore, W. D. S.

Article: The Visual Analogue Mood Scale: Can a single item scale accurately classify depressive mood state?

Journal: *Psychological Reports*, December 1999, *85*(3, Part 2), 1238–1243.

Related Research: Luria, R. E. (1975). The validity and reliability of the Visual Analogue Mood Scale. *Journal of Psychiatric Research, 12*, 51–57.

7886

Test Name: VITALITY SCALE

Purpose: To assess energy and enthusiasm for living.

Number of Items: 7

Format: Responses are made on a 7-point Likert-type scale ranging from 1 (strongly disagree) to 7 (strongly agree). A sample item is presented.

Reliability: Alpha coefficients were .92 and .95.

Validity: Correlations with other variables ranged from .33 to .79.

Author: Patrick, B. C., et al.

Article: "What's everybody so excited about?": The effects of teacher enthusiasm on student intrinsic motivation and vitality.

Journal: *Journal of Experimental Education*, Spring 2000, *68*(3), 217–236.

Related Research: Ryan, R. M.,

& Frederick, C. (1997). On energy, personality, and health: Subjective vitality as a dynamic reflection of well-being. *Journal of Personality, 65*, 529–565.

7887

Test Name: WEINBERGER ADJUSTMENT INVENTORY

Purpose: To assess distress, self-restraint, and repressive defensiveness in children.

Number of Items: 36

Format: Five-point scales are anchored by 1 (almost never) and 5 (almost always).

Reliability: Alpha coefficients ranged from .80 to.82.

Author: Crick, N. R., and Bigbee, M. A.

Article: Relational and overt forms of peer victimization: A multi-informant approach.

Journal: *Journal of Consulting and Clinical Psychology*, April 1998, *66*(2), 337–347.

Related Research: Weinberger, D. A., et al. (1989). Preadolescents' socio-emotional adjustment and relative attrition in family research. *Child Development, 61*, 1374–1386.

7888

Test Name: WEINBERGER ADJUSTMENT INVENTORY

Purpose: To assess distress, self-restraint, denial of distress, repressive defensiveness, and validity.

Number of Items: 84

Format: Responses are made on 5-point Likert scales. Several items are presented.

Reliability: Test-retest (7 months) reliability coefficients ranged from .73 to .76.

Validity: Correlations with other variables ranged from −.71 to .71.

Author: Weinberger, D. A.

Article: Distorted self-perceptions: Divergent self-reports as statistical outliers in the multimethod assessment of children's social-emotional adjustment.

Journal: *Journal of Personality Assessment*, February 1996, *66*(1), 126–143.

Related Research: Weinberger, D. A. (1991). Social-emotional adjustment in older children and adults: *Psychometric properties of the Weinberger Adjustment Inventory*. Unpublished manuscript, Case Western Reserve University.

7889

Test Name: WELL-BEING INDICATORS

Purpose: To measure three areas of satisfaction

Number of Items: 16

Format: Includes 3 scales: Life Satisfaction, Job Satisfaction, and Family Satisfaction. Responses are made on a 5-point scale ranging from 1 (strongly disagree) to 5 (strongly agree). Sample items are presented.

Reliability: Alpha coefficients ranged from .83 to .88.

Validity: Correlations with other variables ranged from −.22. to .42.

Author: Aryee, S., et al.

Article: Role stressors, inter-role conflict, and well-being: The moderating influence of spousal support and coping behaviors among employed parents in Hong Kong.

Journal: *Journal of Vocational*

Behavior, April 1999, *54*(2), 259–278.

Related Research: Diener, E., et al. (1985). The Satisfaction with Life Scales. *Journal of Personality Assessment*, *49*, 71–75.

Agbo, A. O., et al. (1992). Discriminant validity measures of job satisfaction, positive affectivity, and negative affectivity. *Journal of Occupational Psychology*, *65*, 185–196.

Parasuraman, S., et al. (1996). Work and family variables, entrepreneurial career success, and psychological well-being. *Journal of Vocational Behavior*, *48*, 275–300.

7890

Test Name: WELLNESS EVALUATION OF LIFESTYLE

Purpose: To assess holistic wellness.

Number of Items: 98

Time Required: 15–20 minutes.

Format: Likert format.

Reliability: Alpha coefficients ranged from .58 to .89 across subscales.

Validity: Correlations with the Testwell ranged from .35 to .77.

Author: Garrett, M. T.

Article: Soaring on the wings of the eagle: Wellness of Native American high school students.

Journal: *Professional School Counseling*, October 1999, *3*(1), 57–64.

Related Research: Myers, J. E., et al. (1995). *The WEL manual*. Greensboro, NC: Authors.

7891

Test Name: WILLINGNESS SCALE

Purpose: To assess what people do to cope when they feel depressed.

Number of Items: 45

Format: Three-point scales are anchored by 0 (definitely not) and 2 (definitely).

Reliability: Coefficient alpha was .95.

Author: Burns, D. D., and Spangler, D. L.

Article: Does psychotherapy homework lead to improvements in depression in cognitive-behavioral therapy or does improvement lead to increased homework compliance?

Journal: *Journal of Consulting and Clinical Psychology*, February 2000, *68*(1), 46–56.

Related Research: Burns, D. D., et al. (1987). Thinking styles and coping strategies of depressed women: An empirical investigation. *Behavioral Research and Therapy*, *25*, 223–225.

7892

Test Name: WOMEN'S HEALTH QUESTIONNAIRE

Purpose: To assess symptoms of somatic as well as psychological distress.

Number of Items: 18

Format: Each item is rated for frequency of experience ranging from rarely or never to frequently.

Reliability: Alpha coefficient was .82.

Validity: Correlations with the Child Behavior Checklist ranged from .21 to .33

Author: Miller, K. E.

Article: The effects of state terrorism and exile on indigenous Guatemalan refugee children: A mental health assessment and an analysis of children's narratives.

Journal: *Child Development*, February 1996, *67*(1), 89–106.

7893

Test Name: WORK ORIENTATION AND SELF-RELIANCE SCALES

Purpose: To assess adolescent pride in successful completion of tasks and feelings of internal control.

Number of Items: 20

Format: Scales range from 1 (strongly agree) to 4 (strongly disagree). Sample items are presented.

Reliability: Alpha coefficients ranged from .76 to .81.

Validity: Correlations with other variables ranged from −.10 to .24.

Author: Fletcher, A. C., et al.

Article: Adolescents' well-being as a function of perceived interparental consistency.

Journal: *Journal of Marriage and the Family*, August 1999, *61*(3), 599–610.

Related Research: Greenberger, E., et al. (1974). The measurement and structure of psychosocial maturity. *Journal of Youth and Adolescence*, *4*, 127–143.

7894

Test Name: WORRY DOMAINS QUESTIONNAIRE

Purpose: To indicate how much an individual engages in normal worrying.

Number of Items: 25

Format: Includes 5 factors: Relationships, Lack of Confidence, Aimless Future,

Work Incompetence, and Financial Issues. Responses are made on a 5-point scale ranging from 0 (not at all) to 4 (extremely).

Reliability: Internal consistency was .92.

Validity: Correlations with other variables ranged from −.50 to .63.

Author: Wang, L., et al.

Article: Role of gender-related personality traits, problem-solving appraisal, and perceived social support in developing a mediational model of psychological adjustment.

Journal: *Journal of Counseling Psychology*, April 1997, *44*(2), 245–255.

Related Research: Tallis, F., et al. (1992). A questionnaire for the measurement of nonpathological worry. *Personality and Individual Differences*, *13*, 161–168.

7895

Test Name: WORRY DOMAINS QUESTIONNAIRE

Purpose: To assess worry.

Number of Items: 30

Format: Includes 6 domains: Relationships, Lack of Confidence, Aimless Future, Work Incompetence, Financial, and Socio-Political. Responses are made on a 5-point scale ranging from 0 (not at all) to 4 (extremely). Examples are presented.

Reliability: Test-retest (4 weeks) reliability was .85. Alpha coefficients were .92 and .94.

Validity: Correlations with other variables ranged from −.37 to .59.

Author: Chang, E. C.

Article: Perfectionism as a predictor of positive and negative psychological outcomes: Examining a mediation model in younger and older adults.

Journal: *Journal of Counseling Psychology*, January 2000, *47*(1), 18–26.

Related Research: Tallis, R., et al. (1992). A questionnaire for the measurement of nonpathological worry. *Personality and Individual Differences*, *12*, 21–27.

7896

Test Name: WORRY SURVEY

Purpose: To assess youngsters' concerns about a variety of development issues.

Number of Items: 28

Format: Scales range from 1 (not at all) to 5 (very much). All items are presented.

Reliability: Alpha coefficients ranged from .66 to .81 across subscales.

Validity: Correlations between subscales ranged from .38 to .69.

Author: O'Andrea, M., et al.

Article: Testing the validity and reliability of the Worry Survey among urban African American youth.

Journal: *Measurement and Evaluation in Counseling and Development*, January 1998, *30*(4), 170–181.

Related Research: Adolescent Health Program. (1987). *The Adolescent Health Survey*. St. Paul, MN: University of Minnesota.

7897

Test Name: ZEST SCALE

Purpose: To measure psychological health.

Number of Items: 5

Format: Scales range from 1 (never) to 5 (frequently). All items are presented.

Reliability: Coefficient alpha was .77.

Author: Bram, A. D., et al.

Article: A longitudinal investigation of object relations: Child-rearing antecedents, stability in adulthood, and construct validation.

Journal: *Journal of Research in Personality*, June 1999, *33*(2), 159–188.

Related Research: Veroff, J., et al. (1981). *The inner American: A self-portrait from 1957 to 1976.* New York: Basic Books.

7898

Test Name: ZUNG ANXIETY SCALE

Purpose: To measure anxiety level.

Number of Items: 20

Format: Contains 15 somatic and 5 affective symptoms of anxiety. Responses are made on a 4-point scale ranging from 1 (none or little of the time) to 4 (most or all of the time).

Reliability: Internal consistencies were .77 and .85.

Validity: Correlations with other

variables ranged from −.57 to −.30.

Author: Pallant, J. F.

Article: Development and validation of a scale to measure perceived control of internal states.

Journal: *Journal of Personality Assessment*, October 2000, *75*(2), 308–337.

Related Research: Zung, W. W. K. (1971). A rating instrument for anxiety disorder. *Psychosomatics, 12,* 371–379.

7899

Test Name: ZUNG DEPRESSION SCALE

Purpose: To measure depression level.

Number of Items: 20

Format: Includes Psychic-Affective, Physiological Disturbance, Psychomotor Disturbance, and Psychological Disturbance. Responses are made on a 4-point scale ranging from 1 (none or little of the time) to 4 (most or all of the time).

Reliability: Alpha coefficients ranged from .73 to .92.

Validity: Correlations with other variables ranged from −.69 to −.36.

Author: Pallant, J. F.

Article: Development and validation of a scale to measure perceived control of internal states.

Journal: *Journal of Personality Assessment*, October 2000, *75*(2), 308–337.

Related Research: Zung, W. W. K. (1965). A self-rating depression scale. *Archives of General Psychiatry, 12,* 63–70.

7900

Test Name: ZUNG SELF-RATING DEPRESSION SCALE (JAPANESE VERSION)

Purpose: To measure depression.

Number of Items: 20

Format: Four-point scales.

Validity: Correlations with Temperament and Character scales ranged from −.60 to .51.

Author: Tanaka, E., et al.

Article: Correlations between the Temperament and Character Inventory and the Self-Rating Depression Scale among Japanese students.

Journal: *Psychological Reports*, February 1997, *80*(1), 251–254.

Related Research: Fukuda, K., & Kobayashi, S. (1973). Jiko hyouka-shiki yokuutsu-sei shakudo no kenkyu [A study of a self-rating depression scale]. *Psychiatrica et Neurologia Japonica, 75,* 673–679.

CHAPTER 4

Adjustment—Social

7901

Test Name: ACCULTURATION QUESTIONNAIRE

Purpose: To assess several dimensions of acculturation.

Number of Items: 20

Format: Includes the following dimensions: Language Familiarity and Usage, Ethnic Interaction, Ethnic Pride and Identity, and Generational Status.

Reliability: Alpha coefficients ranged from .81 to .88.

Author: Patel, N., et al.

Article: Socialization values and practices of Indian immigrant parents: Correlates of modernity and acculturation.

Journal: *Child Development*, April 1996, *67*(2), 302–313.

Related Research: Cuellar, I., et al. (1980). An acculturation scale for Mexican-American normal and clinical populations. *Hispanic Journal of Behavioral Sciences*, *2*, 199–217.

7902

Test Name: ACCULTURATION RATING SCALE FOR MEXICAN AMERICANS

Purpose: To measure level of acculturation in the United States.

Number of Items: 21

Format: Assesses language preference, identity, generational and geographical history, friendship choice, behavior, and attitudes.

Reliability: Coefficient alpha was .91.

Validity: Correlations with demographic variables ranged from .41 to .61.

Author: Tsai, D. C., and Pike, P. L.

Article: Effects of acculturation on the MMPI-2 scores of Asian American students.

Journal: *Journal of Personality Assessment*, April 2000, *74*(2), 216–230.

Related Research: Cuellar, I., et al. (1980). An acculturation scale for Mexican American normal and clinical populations. *Hispanic Journal of Behavioral Sciences*, *2*, 199–217.

7903

Test Name: ACCULTURATION RATING SCALE FOR MEXICAN AMERICANS—II

Purpose: To provide a multidimensional, bilingual (English and Spanish) measure of Mexican American acculturation.

Number of Items: 30

Format: Includes 2 subscales: the Anglo Orientation Scale and the Mexican Orientation Scale. Responses are made on a 5-point scale ranging from 1 (not at all) to 5 (extremely often or almost always).

Reliability: Alpha coefficients ranged from .83 to .96. Test-retest reliability was .96.

Validity: Correlation with other

variables ranged from −. 33 to .29.

Author: Ruelas, S. R., et al.

Article: Counselor helping model, participant ethnicity and acculturation level, and perceived counselor credibility.

Journal: *Journal of Counseling Psychology*, January 1998, *45*(1), 98–103.

Related Research: Cuellar, I., et al. (1995). Acculturation Rating Scale for Mexican Americans— II: A revision of the original ARSMA scale. *Hispanic Journal of Behavioral Sciences*, *17*, 275–304.

7904

Test Name: ADOLESCENT RELATIONSHIP SCALES QUESTIONNAIRE

Purpose: To measure relationships and patterns of attachment.

Number of Items: 17

Format: Five-point scales range from (1) not characteristic of me to (5) very characteristic of me.

Reliability: Alpha was .60.

Author: Domingo, M., et al.

Article: Relations of early maternal employment and attachment in introvertive and extrovertive adults.

Journal: *Psychological Reports*, October 1997, *81*(2), 403–410.

Related Research: Scharfe, E., and Bartholomew, K. (1995). Accommodation strategies and attachments in young couples. *Journal of Personality and Social Psychology, 67,* 53–61.

7905

Test Name: ADULT ATTACHMENT MEASURE

Purpose: To measure adult attachment style.

Number of Items: 4

Format: Each of four paragraphs is rated on a 7-point Likert scale.

Validity: Correlations with other variables ranged from −.55 to .46.

Author: Buelow, G., et al.

Article: A new measure for an important construct: The Attachment and Object Relation Inventory.

Journal: *Journal of Personality Assessment,* June 1996, *66*(3), 604–623.

Related Research: Bartholomew, K., & Horowitz, L. M. (1991). Attachment styles among young adults: A text of a four-category model. *Journal of Personality and Social Psychology, 61,* 226–244.

7906

Test Name: ADULT ATTACHMENT QUESTIONNAIRE

Purpose: To measure two primary dimensions assumed to underlie adult attachment orientations.

Number of Items: 13

Format: Includes 2 factors: Avoidance and Anxiety. Responses are made on a 7-point scale ranging from 1 (strongly disagree) to 7 (strongly agree). Examples are presented.

Reliability: Alpha coefficients ranged from .58 to .81. Test-

retest (2 months) reliability coefficients were .79 (Avoidance) and .64 (Anxiety).

Author: Lopez, F. G., et al.

Article: Parental divorce, parent-child bonds, and adult attachment orientations among college students: A comparison of three racial/ethnic groups.

Journal: *Journal of Counseling Psychology,* April 2000, *47*(2), 177–186.

Related Research: Simpson, J. A., et al. (1992). Support-seeking and support-giving within couples in an anxiety-provoking situation: The role of attachment styles. *Journal of Personality and Social Psychology, 62,* 434–446.

7907

Test Name: ADULT ATTACHMENT SCALE

Purpose: To estimate the clients' self-reported ability to develop healthy intimate relationships.

Number of Items: 18

Format: Includes 3 subscales: Depend, Anxiety, and Close. Responses are made on a 5-point scale ranging from 1 (not at all characteristic of me) to 5 (very characteristic of me).

Reliability: Test-retest (2 months) reliabilities ranged from .52 to .71. Internal consistency coefficients ranged from .82 to 91.

Validity: Correlations with other variables ranged from −.19 to .38 (*N* = 40).

Author: Kivlighan, Jr., D. M., et al.

Article: Moderating effects of client attachment on the counselor experience—working alliance relationship.

Journal: *Journal of Counseling*

Psychology, July 1998, *45*(3), 274–278.

Related Research: Collins, N. L., & Read, S. J.(1990). Adult attachment, working models, and relationship quality in dating couples. *Journal of Personality and Social Psychology, 58,* 644–663.

7908

Test Name: HIV RISK REDUCTION INTENSIONS SCALE

Purpose: To assess intentions to engage in risk reduction behaviors.

Number of Items: 9

Format: Eleven-point scales.

Reliability: Cronbach alpha was .79.

Author: Belcher, L., et al.

Article: A randomized trial of a brief HIV risk reduction counseling intervention for women.

Journal: *Journal of Consulting and Clinical Psychology,* October 1998, *66*(5), 856–861.

Related Research: Kalichman, S. C., et al. (1996). Experimental component analysis of a behavioral HIV-AIDS prevention intervention for inner-city women. *Journal of Consulting and Clinical Psychology, 64,* 687–693.

7909

Test Name: AFRICAN AMERICAN ACCULTURATION SCALE—SHORT FORM REVISED

Purpose: To measure level of cultural identification.

Number of Items: 29

Format: Includes 10 areas:

Preference for African American Things, Religious Beliefs and Practices, Traditional Foods, Traditional Childhood, Superstitions, Interracial Attitudes and Cultural Mistrust, Falling Out, Traditional Games, Family Values, and Family Practices. Responses are made on a 7-point scale ranging from 1 (I totally disagree, this is not true of me) to 7 (I totally agree, this is absolutely true of me).

Reliability: Coefficient alpha was .83.

Validity: Correlations with other variables ranged from −.12 to .14.

Author: Lester, R., and Petrie, T. A.

Article: Physical, psychological, and societal correlates of bulimic symptomatology among African American college women.

Journal: *Journal of Counseling Psychology*, July 1998, *45*(3), 315–321.

Related Research: Landrine, H., & Klonoff, E. (1995). The African American Acculturation Scale II: Cross-validation and short form. *Journal of Black Psychology, 21*, 124–152.

7910

Test Name: AFRICAN AMERICAN MULTIDIMENSIONAL RACIAL IDENTITY SCALE

Purpose: To measure four aspects of racial identity: physical, sociopolitical, cultural, and psychological.

Number of Items: 24

Reliability: Alpha coefficients ranged from .80 to .92 across subscales.

Validity: Correlations with identity salience ranged from .26 to .82.

Authors: Thompson-Sanders, V. L.

Article: Variables affecting racial-identity salience among African Americans.

Journal: *The Journal of Social Psychology*, December 1997, *139*(6), 748–761.

Related Research: Myers, M., & Thompson-Sanders, V. L. (1994). An evaluation of two culture-specific instruments. *Western Journal of Black Studies, 18*, 179–184.

7911

Test Name: AFRICAN AMERICAN RACIAL-IDENTITY SALIENCE SCALE

Purpose: To measure the salience of racial identity among African Americans.

Number of Items: 5

Format: Scales range from 0 (not very important) to 3 (very important).

Reliability: Coefficient alpha was .91.

Validity: Correlations with other variables ranged from −.08 to .34.

Authors: Thompson-Sanders, V. L.

Article: Variables affecting racial identity salience among African Americans.

Journal: *The Journal of Social Psychology*, December 1999, *139*(6), 748–761.

Related Research: White, C. L., & Burke, P. J. (1987). Ethnic role identity and Black and White college students: An interactionist approach. *Sociological Perspectives, 30*, 310–331.

7912

Test Name: AFRICAN AMERICAN RACIAL SOCIALIZATION AND SOCIAL NETWORK SCALES

Purpose: To measure attitudes about race relations and participation in African American groups.

Number of Items: 26.

Format: Scales range from 0 (never) to 4 (very often) for socialization items and from 0 (never) to 10 (frequently) for network items.

Reliability: Coefficient alpha was .93 (socialization). Internal consistency was .82 for network items.

Validity: Correlations with other variables ranged from −.41 to .34.

Authors: Thompson-Sanders, V. L.

Article: Variables affecting racial identity salience among African Americans.

Journal: *The Journal of Social Psychology*, December 1999, *139*(6), 748–761.

Related Research: Thompson-Sanders, V. L. (1994). Socialization to race and its relationships to racial identification among African Americans. *Journal of Black Psychology, 20*, 175–188.

7913

Test Name: ALTERNATIVE PARTNER QUALITY SCALE

Purpose: To assess how easy it would be to find a new dating partner that more closely resembles an ideal partner than a current partner.

Number of Items: 2

Format: Nine-point scale. Both items are presented.

Reliability: Alpha coefficients ranged from .81 to .86.

Validity: Correlations with other variables ranged from −.70 to .38.

Author: Sacher, J. A., and Fine, M. A.

Article: Predicting relationship status and satisfaction after 6 months among dating couples.

Journal: *Journal of Marriage and the Family*, February 1996, 58(1), 21–32.

Related Research: Hatfield, E., et al. (1979). Equity theory and intimate relationships. In R. L. Burgess & T. L. Huston (Eds.), *Social exchange in developing relationships* (pp. 93–134). New York: Academic Press.

7914

Test Name: ANXIOUS ROMANTIC ATTACHMENT SCALE

Purpose: To measure adult attachment.

Number of Items: 33

Format:

Reliability: Coefficient alpha was .90.

Validity: Correlations with other variables ranged from −.16 to .57.

Author: Sperling, M. B., et al.

Article: Measuring adult attachment: Are self-report instruments congruent?

Journal: *Journal of Personality Assessment*, August 1996, 67(1), 37–51.

Related Research: Hindy, C. G., & Schwartz, J. C. (1984, July). *Individual differences in the tendency toward anxious*

romantic attachment. Paper presented at the Second International Conference on Personal Relationships, Madison, WI.

7915

Test Name: ASIAN SELF-IDENTITY ACCULTURATION SCALE

Purpose: To assess acculturation.

Number of Items: 21

Format: Multiple-choice format.

Reliability: Alpha was .88.

Author: Kim, E. J., and O'Neil, J. M.

Article: Asian-American men's acculturation and gender role conflict.

Journal: *Psychological Reports*, August 1996, 79(1), 95–104.

Related Research: Suinn, R. M., et al. (1987). The Suinn-Lew Asian Self-Identity Acculturation Scale: An initial report. *Educational and Psychological Measurement*, 47, 401–407.

7916

Test Name: ATTACHMENT STYLE INVENTORY

Purpose: To measure adult attachment.

Number of Items: 24

Format: Includes 5 subscales: Secure, Avoidant, Dependent, Hostile, and Resistant/Ambivalent.

Reliability: Alpha coefficients ranged from .39 to .53.

Validity: Correlations with other variables ranged from −.54 to .55.

Author: Sperling, M. B., et al.

Article: Measuring adult

attachment: Are self-report instruments congruent?

Journal: *Journal of Personality Assessment*, August 1996, 67(1), 37–51.

Related Research: Sperling, M. B., & Berman, W. H. (1991). An attachment classification of desperate love. *Journal of Personality Assessment*, 56, 45–55.

7917

Test Name: ATTACHMENT STYLE MEASURE

Purpose: To measure adult attachment.

Number of Items: 13

Format: Includes 3 subscales: Secure, Avoidant, and Anxious.

Reliability: Alpha coefficients ranged from .42 to .80.

Validity: Correlations with other variables ranged from −.84 to .79.

Author: Sperling, M. B., et al.

Article: Measuring adult attachment: Are self-report instruments congruent?

Journal: *Journal of Personality Assessment*, August 1996, 67(1), 37–51.

Related Research: Simpson, J. A. (1990). Influence of attachment styles on romantic relationships. *Journal of Personality and Social Psychology*, 59, 971–980.

7918

Test Name: ATTACHMENT STYLE QUESTIONNAIRE

Purpose: To measure secure, anxious, and avoidant attachment styles.

Number of Items: 15

Format: Five-point scales are

anchored by "strongly agree" and "strongly disagree."

Validity: Correlations with other variables ranged from −.14 to .15. Correlations between subscales ranged from −.59 to .22.

Author: Doverspike, D., et al.

Article: Correlations between leadership style as measured by the least preferred co-worker scale and adults' attachment styles.

Journal: *Psychological Reports*, December, 1997, *81*(3, Part II), 1148–1150.

Related Research: Hazan, C., and Shaver, P. (1987). Romantic love conceptualized as an attachment process. *Journal of Personality and Social Psychology, 52*, 511–524.

7919

Test Name: ATTACHMENT STYLE QUESTIONNAIRE

Purpose: To measure attachment style.

Number of Items: 25

Format: Includes 3 factors: Preoccupied Attachment Style, Fearful Attachment Style, and Secure Attachment Style. Responses are made on a 7-point scale ranging from 1 (strongly disagree) to 7 (strongly agree). All items are presented.

Reliability: Alpha coefficients ranged from .80 to .84.

Author: Becker, T. E., et al.

Article: Validity of scores on three attachment style scales: Explanatory and confirmatory evidence.

Journal: *Educational and Psychological Measurement*, June 1997, *57*(3), 477–493.

Related Research: Bartholomew,

K., & Horowitz, L. M. (1991). Attachment styles among young adults: A test of a four-category model, *Journal of Personality and Social Psychology, 61*, 226–244.

7920

Test Name: AUTONOMOUS-RELATIONAL ORIENTATION SCALE—REVISED

Purpose: To assess orientation to group behavior.

Number of Items: 5

Format: Scales range from 1 (strongly disagree) to 5 (strongly agree). All items are presented.

Reliability: Alpha coefficients ranged from .58 to .59 across two subscales.

Author: Brown, R., and Uriddendorf, J.

Article: The underestimated role of temporal comparison: A test of the life-span model.

Journal: *Journal of Social Psychology*, June 1996, *136*(3), 325–331.

Related Research: Brown, R., et al. (1992). Recognizing group diversity: Individualist-collectivist and autonomous-relational social orientations and their implications for intergroup processes. *British Journal of Social Psychology, 31*, 327–342.

7921

Test Name: AUTONOMY SCALE

Purpose: To assess autonomy on three dimensions.

Number of Items: 42

Format: Includes 3 dimensions: Self-Awareness, Capacity to Manage New Situations, and Sensitivity to Others.

Reliability: Internal consistency ranged from .80 to .85.

Author: Vivona, J. M.

Article: Parental attachment styles of late adolescents: Qualities of attachment relationships and consequences for adjustment.

Journal: *Journal of Counseling Psychology*, July 2000, *47*(3), 316–329.

Related Research: Bekker, M. H. J. (1993). The development of an autonomy scale based on recent insights into gender identity. *European Journal of Personality, 7*, 177–194.

7922

Test Name: AVAILABILITY OF INSTRUMENTAL SUPPORT SCALE

Purpose: To measure the level of instrumental support mothers could receive from others if it were needed.

Number of Items: 4

Format: Scales range from 0 (never true) to 5 (true all of the time). All items are presented.

Reliability: Coefficient alpha was .63.

Author: Jackson, A. P., et al.

Article: Employment status, psychological well-being, social support, and physical discipline practices of single Black mothers.

Journal: *Journal of Marriage and the Family*, November 1998, *60*(4), 894–902.

Related Research: McLoyd, V. C., et al. (1994). Unemployment and work interruption among African American single mothers: Effects of parenting and adolescent socioemotional functioning. *Child Development, 65*, 562–589.

7923

Test Name: BEHAVIORAL ACCULTURATION SCALE

Purpose: To assess to what extent an individual is acculturated into Anglo-Australian society.

Number of Items: 7

Format: Scales range from 1 (immigrant culture) to 5 (host culture). All items are presented.

Reliability: Coefficient alpha was .79.

Validity: Significant relationships between scores and proportion of life in host country, age of respondent, level of education, and income.

Author: Marino, R., et al.

Article: Acculturation of values and behavior: A study of Vietnamese immigrants.

Journal: *Measurement and Evaluation in Counseling and Development*, April 2000, *33*(1), 21–41.

7924

Test Name: BELL OBJECT RELATIONS INVENTORY

Purpose: To measure individuals' capacity for interpersonal interaction.

Number of Items: 45

Format: Includes 4 subscales: Alienation, Insecurity, Egocentricity, Social Incompetence.

Validity: Correlations with other variables ranged from −.04 to −.41.

Author: Buelow, G., et al.

Article: A new measure for an imported construct: The Attachment and Object Relations Inventory.

Journal: *Journal of Personality Assessment*, June 1996, *66*(3), 604–623.

Related Research: Bell, M. D. (1994, April). *Construct validity of the Bell object relations and reality testing inventory.* Paper presented at the Society for Personality Assessment, Chicago.

7925

Test Name: BYRNES-KIGER SOCIAL SCENERIOS SCALE

Purpose: To identify responses to descriptions of racial bias toward African Americans.

Number of Items: 12

Format: One of four responses is selected for each item.

Reliability: Test-retest reliability was .93. Internal consistency was .75.

Author: Carroll, J. J.

Article: Responses to descriptions of bias against African Americans among Euro-American students enrolled in colleges of education and journalism.

Journal: *Perceptual and Motor Skills*, June 1997, *84*(3, Part 1), 1058.

Related Research: Byrnes, D., & Kiger, G. (1998). Contemporary measures of attitudes towards Blacks. *Educational and Psychological Measurement, 48*, 107–118.

7926

Test Name: CAPACITY TO BE ALONE SCALE

Purpose: To measure solitary coping and solitary comfort.

Number of Items: 20

Format: Sample items are presented.

Reliability: Reliability coefficients were .82 (coping) and .83 (comfort). Test-retest reliabilities (3 weeks) were .60 (coping) and .70 (comfort).

Author: Larson, R., and Lee, M.

Article: The capacity to be alone as a stress buffer.

Journal: *Journal of Social Psychology*, February 1996, *136*(1), 5–16.

Related Research: Winnicott, D. W. (1958). The capacity to be alone. *International Journal of Psychoanalysis, 39*, 416–420.

7927

Test Name: CAREGIVER CONFLICT SCALE

Purpose: To assess the frequency of conflict between caregivers in the children's presence.

Number of Items: 10

Format: Five-point scales ranged from "never/very little" to "a lot." Sample items are presented.

Reliability: Alpha coefficients exceeded .77.

Author: Brody, G. H., et al.

Article: Sibling relationships in rural African American families.

Journal: *Journal of Marriage and the Family*, December 1999, *61*(4), 1046–1057.

Related Research: Porter, B., & O'Leary, K. D. (1980). Marital discord and childhood behavior problems. *Journal of Abnormal Child Psychology, 8*, 287–295.

7928

Test Name: CHILDREN'S LONELINESS SCALE

Purpose: To measure children's loneliness.

Number of Items: 16

Format: Responses are made on a 5-point scale ranging from "that's always true about me" to "that's not true at all about me."

Reliability: Coefficient alpha was .89.

Author: Cheung, S-K.

Article: Reliability and factor structure of the Chinese version of the Depression Self-Rating Scale.

Journal: *Educational and Psychology Measurement*, February 1996, *56*(1), 142–154.

Related Research: Asher, S. R., & Wheeler, V. A. (1985). Children's loneliness: A comparison of rejected and neglected peer status. *Journal of Consulting and Clinical Psychology*, *53*(4), 500–505.

7929

Test Name: CLIMATE FOR RACISM SCALE

Purpose: To assess acceptance of minorities and their participation in an organization.

Number of Items: 6

Format: Likert format.

Reliability: Coefficient alpha was .76.

Author: Jeanquart-Barone, S., and Sekaran, U.

Article: Institutional racism: An empirical study.

Journal: *Journal of Social Psychology*, August 1996, *136*(4), 477–482.

Related Research: Barbarian, O. A., & Gilbert, R. (1981). Institutional Racism Scale: Assessing self and organizational attributes. In O. A. Barbarian, et al. (Eds.), *Institutional racism and community competence* (pp. 147–171). Rockville, MD: U. S. Department of Health and Human Services.

7930

Test Name: COHESION SCALE

Purpose: To measure cohesion.

Number of Items: 15

Format: Items refer to other students, subject matter, and the professor.

Reliability: Coefficient alpha was .75.

Validity: Correlation with the FIRO-4 Scale was .81.

Author: Slavin, R. L.

Article: Perception of self-attitude toward one's college class, cohesion, and grade.

Journal: *Perceptual and Motor Skills*, August 1996, *83*(1), 211–217.

Related Research: Schutz, W. C. (1958). *FIRO: Three-dimensional theory of interpersonal behavior.* New York: Holt, Winston.

7931

Test Name: COLLECTIVE SELF-ESTEEM SCALE

Purpose: To assess the esteem of an entire group.

Number of Items: 16

Reliability: Alpha coefficients ranged from .34 to .88.

Validity: Correlations with personal self-esteem ranged from −.11 to .45.

Authors: Lay, C., and Verkuyten, M.

Article: Ethnic identity and its relation to personal self-esteem: A comparison of Canadian-born and foreign-born Chinese adolescents.

Journal: *Journal of Social Psychology*, June 1999, *139*(3), 288–299.

Related Research: Crocker, J., et al. (1994). Collective self-esteem

and psychological well-being among White, Black, and Asian college students. *Personality and Social Psychology Bulletin, 20,* 503–513.

Sato, T., & Cameron, J. E. (1999). The relationship between collective self-esteem and self-construal in Japan and Canada. *Journal of Social Psychology, 139,* 426–435.

DeCremer, D., et al. (1999). Effect of collective self-esteem on in-group evaluations. *Journal of Social Psychology, 139,* 530–532.

7932

Test Name: COLLECTIVISM SCALE

Purpose: To measure emotional involvement with family, peers, and society.

Number of Items: 24

Format: Five-point Likert format. All items are presented.

Reliability: Alpha coefficients ranged from .66 to .82 across subscales.

Validity: Correlations with other variables ranged from −.27 to .42.

Author: Realo, A., et al.

Article: The hierarchical structure of collectivism.

Journal: *Journal of Research in Personality*, March 1997, *31*(1), 93–116.

7933

Test Name: COLOR-BLIND RACIAL ATTITUDES SCALE

Purpose: To assess cognitive dimensions of color-blind racial attitudes.

Number of Items: 20

Format: Includes 3 factors: Unawareness of Racial Privilege,

Institutional Discrimination, and Blatant Racial Issues. All items are presented.

Reliability: Alpha coefficients ranged from .70 to .91. Test-retest (2 weeks) reliability ranged from .34 to .80.

Validity: Correlations with other variables ranged from .03 to .61.

Author: Neville, H. A., et al.

Article: Construction and initial validation of the Color-Blind Racial Attitudes Scale (CoBRAS).

Journal: *Journal of Counseling Psychology*, January 2000, *47*(1), 59–70.

7934

Test Name: COMMITMENT INVENTORY

Purpose: To measure personal dedication and commitment to a relationship.

Number of Items: 60

Format: Seven-point Likert format. Sample items are presented.

Reliability: Alpha coefficients ranged from .70 to .94 across subscales.

Author: Pistole, M. C., and Vocaturo, L. C.

Article: Attachment and commitment in college students' romantic relationships.

Journal: *Journal of College Student Development*, November/December 1999, *40*(6), 710–720.

Related Research: Stanley, S. M., & Markman, H. J. (1992). Assessing commitment in personal relationships. *Journal of Marriage and the Family, 54,* 595–608.

7935

Test Name: COMMITMENT SCALE

Purpose: To measure commitment to a dating partner.

Number of Items: 7

Format: Scales range from 1 (not at all true) to 9 (extremely true). A sample item is presented.

Reliability: Alpha coefficients ranged from .90 to .92.

Validity: Correlations with other variables ranged from −.68 to .70.

Author: Sacher, J. A., and Fine, M. A.

Article: Predicting relationship status and satisfaction after six months among dating couples.

Journal: *Journal of Marriage and the Family*, February 1996, *58*(1), 21–32.

Related Research: Sternberg, R. J. (1988). Triangulating love. In R. J. Sternberg & M. L. Barnes (Eds.), *The psychology of love* (pp. 119–138). New Haven, CT: Yale University Press.

7936

Test Name: COMMITMENT TO RELATIONSHIP SCALE

Purpose: To measure commitment to a relationship.

Number of Items: 5

Format: Scales range from 1 (not at all committed) to 7 (very committed). Sample items are presented.

Reliability: Alpha coefficients ranged from .66 to .93. Test-retest reliabilities ranged from .43 to .70.

Validity: Correlations with other variables ranged from −.21 to .28.

Author: Sprecher, S.

Article: The effect of exchange orientation on close relationships.

Journal: *Social Psychology*

Quarterly, September 1998, *61*(3), 220–231.

Related Research: Lund, M. (1985). The development of investment and commitment scales for predicting continuity of personal relationships. *Journal of Social and Personal Relationships, 2,* 3–23.

7937

Test Name: COMPANION ANIMAL BONDING SCALE

Purpose: To measure bonding between pets and owners.

Number of Items: 8

Format: Five-point scales are anchored by (1) never and (5) always.

Reliability: Alphas ranged from .77 to .82.

Validity: Correlation with bonding scale was .40.

Author: Kogan, L. R., and Viney, W.

Article: Reported strength of human-animal bonding and method of acquiring a dog.

Journal: *Psychological Reports*, April 1998, *82*(2), 647–650.

7938

Test Name: CONCERN FOR OTHERS SCALE

Purpose: To measure concern for others.

Number of Items: 12

Format: Forced-choice format. A sample item is presented.

Reliability: Test-retest reliability (4- weeks) was .70.

Validity: Correlations with other variables ranged from −.22 to −.04.

Author: Korsgaard, M. A., et al.

Article: Beyond helping: Do other-oriented values have broader implications in organizations?

Journal: *Journal of Applied Psychology*, February 1997, *82*(1), 160–177.

Related Research: Ralvin, E. C., & Meglino, B. M. (1987). Effect of values on perceptions and decision-making: A study of alternative work values measures. *Journal of Applied Pschology*, 72, 666–673.

7939

Test Name: CONFLICT APPROACHES SCALES

Purpose: To measure cooperative and competitive approaches to conflict.

Number of Items: 10

Format: Includes 2 scales: Cooperative Approach and Competitive Approach to conflict. Responses are made on a 7-point scale ranging from 1 (strongly agree) to 7 (strongly disagree). Examples are presented.

Reliability: Alpha coefficients were .88 and .92 ($N = 61$).

Validity: Correlations with other variables ranged from −.61 to .78.

Author: Alper, S., et al.

Article: Conflict-management, efficacy, and performance in organizational teams.

Journal: *Personnel Psychology*, Autumn 2000, *53*(3), 625–642.

Related Research: Tjosvold, D. (1985). Implications of controversy research for management. *Journal of Management*, 11, 21–37.

7940

Test Name: CONTACT WITH AMERICANS SCALE

Purpose: To measure the degree of contact Saudi Arabian students had with American students in a university setting.

Number of Items: 12

Format: Scales range from 1 (never) to 4 (often). Items are described.

Reliability: Coefficient alpha was .80.

Validity: Correlations with other variables ranged from .21 to .62.

Authors: Alreshoud, A., and Koeske, G. F.

Article: Arab students' attitudes towards the amount of contact with Americans: A causal process analysis of cross-sectional data.

Journal: *Journal of Social Psychology*, April 1997, *137*(2), 235–245.

7941

Test Name: CRAIG HANDICAP ASSESSMENT AND REPORTING TECHNIQUES

Purpose: To assess the degree of handicap in social roles imposed by a disability and the immediate environment of the respondents.

Number of Items: 27

Format: Includes 5 subscales: mobility, occupational activity, social integration, physical independence, and economic self-sufficiency.

Reliability: Test-retest (1 week) reliabilities ranged from .81 to .95 for four subscales which did not include Economic Self-Sufficiency.

Validity: Correlations with other variables ranged from −.01 to .77 for all subscales except economic self-sufficiency.

Author: Elliott, T. R., et al.

Article: Goal instability and adjustment to physical disability.

Journal: *Journal of Counseling Psychology*, April 2000, *47*(2), 251–265.

Related Research: Whiteneck, G. G., et al. (1992). Quantifying handicap: A new measure of long-term rehabilitation outcomes. *Archives of Physical Medicine and Rehabilitation*, 73, 519–526.

7942

Test Name: CROSS-CULTURAL ADJUSTMENT QUESTIONNAIRE—REVISED

Purpose: To measure cross-cultural adjustment.

Number of Items: 9

Format: Includes two factors: General Adjustment and Interaction Adjustment. Responses are made on a 7-point scale ranging from 1 (unadjusted) to 7 (adjusted). All items are presented.

Reliability: Alpha coefficients were .86 (General Adjustment) and .95 (Interaction Adjustment).

Author: Robie, C., and Ryan, A. M.

Article: Structural equivalence of a measure of cross-cultural adjustment.

Journal: *Educational and Psychological Measurement*, June 1996, *56*(3), 514–521.

Related Research: Black, J. S., & Stephens, G. K. (1989). The influence of the spouse on American expatriate adjustment and intent to stay in Pacific Rim overseas assignments. *Journal of Management*, 15, 529–544.

7943

Test Name: CUELLAR ACCULTURATION SCALE

Purpose: To measure the

acculturation in English and Spanish.

Number of Items: 20

Format: Includes 5 levels of acculturation: Mexican, Mexican-oriented bicultural, "true" bicultural, Anglo-oriented, and very very Anglicized.

Reliability: Test-retest reliability was .80. Coefficient alpha was .96.

Validity: Correlation with other variables ranged from .20 to .60.

Author: Newcomb, M. D., et al.

Article: Acculturation, sexual risk taking, and HIV health promotion among Latinas.

Journal: *Journal of Counseling Psychology*, October 1998, *45*(4), 454–467.

Related Research: Cuellar, I., et al. (1993). An acculturation scale of Mexican Americans. In. C. Ellias and L. Heise (Eds.). *The development of microbicides: A new mthod of HIV prevention for women.* New York: Population Council.

7944

Test Name: CULTURAL AFFILIATION SCALE

Purpose: To measure acculturation.

Number of Items: 20

Format: Five-point response categories.

Reliability: Alpha was .88. Test-retest reliability was .80.

Author: Shokovhi-Behnam, S., and Chambliss, C.

Article: Value priorities of Iranian and American college students.

Journal: *Psychological Reports*, August 1996, *79*(1), 251–256.

Related Research: Cuellar, I., et al. (1980). An acculturation scale

for Mexican and American normal and clinical populations. *Hispanic Journal of Behavioral Sciences, 2*, 197–213.

7945

Test Name: CULTURAL IDENTITY QUESTIONNAIRE

Purpose: To provide a measure of cultural identity.

Number of Items: 12

Format: Responses are made on a 7-point Likert scale.

Validity: Correlation with homesickness intensity was .20.

Author: Thurber, C. A., and Sigman, M. D.

Article: Preliminary models of risk and prospective factors for childhood homesickness: Review and empirical synthesis.

Journal: *Child Development*, August 1998, *69*(4), 903–934.

Related Research: Ward, C., & Kennedy, A. (1992). Locus of control, mood disturbance, and social difficulty during cross-cultural transitions. *International Journal of Intercultural Relations, 16*, 175–194.

7946

Test Name: CULTURAL LIFE STYLE INVENTORY

Purpose: To measure acculturation.

Number of Items: 29

Format: Includes 4 factors: Intra-Family Language, Extra Family Language, Social Affiliation and Activities, and Cultural Familiarity and Pride. Responses are made on a 5-point Likert-type scale.

Reliability: Alpha coefficients ranged from .64 to .87.

Author: De Leon, B., and Mendez, S.

Article: Factorial structure of a measure of acculturation in a Puerto Rican population.

Journal: *Educational and Psychological Measurement*, February 1996, *56*(1), 155–165.

Related Research: Mendoza, Ritt (1989). An empirical scale to measure type and degree of acculturation in Mexican American adolescents and adults. *Journal of Cross-Cultural Psychology, 20*(4), 372–385.

7947

Test Name: CULTURAL TOLERANCE SCALE

Purpose: To measure cultural tolerance.

Number of Items: 288

Format: Likert-type items.

Reliability: Alpha coefficients ranged from .50 to .95.

Author: Gasser, M. B., and Tan, R. N.

Article: Cultural tolerance: Measurement and latent structure of attitudes toward the cultural practice of others.

Journal: *Educational and Psychological Measurement*, February 1999, *59*(1), 111–126.

Related Research: Gasser, M. B. (1995). Measurement and validation. *Dissertation Abstracts International, 56*, 10B.

7948

Test Name: CULTURE NOVELTY SCALE

Purpose: To assess culture novelty.

Number of Items: 8

Reliability: Reliability was .75.

Validity: Correlations with other variables ranged from −.35 to .23.

Author: Gregersen, H. B., and Stroh, L. K.

Article: Coming home to the arctic cold: Antecedents to Finnish expatriate and spouse repatriation adjustment.

Journal: *Personnel Psychology*, Autumn 1997, *50*(3), 635–654.

Related Research: Black, J. S., & Gregersen, H. B. (1991). When Yankee comes home: Factors related to repatriate and spouse repatriation adjustment. *Journal of International Business Studies*, *22*, 671–694.

7949

Test Name: DATING COMPETENCE SCALE

Purpose: To assess dating competence.

Number of Items: 5

Format: Responses are made on a 5-point scale ranging from 1 (never) to 5 (always).

Reliability: Coefficient alpha was .83.

Validity: Correlations with other variables ranged from −.12 to .30.

Author: Goodyear, R. K., et al.

Article: Predictors of Latino men's paternity in teen pregnancy: Test of a mediational model of childhood experiences, gender role attitudes, and behaviors.

Journal: *Journal of Counseling Psychology*, January 2000, *47*(1), 116–128.

Related Research: Levenson, R. W., & Gottman, J. M. (1978). Toward the assessment of social competence. *Journal of*

Consulting and Clinical Psychology, *46*, 453–462.

7950

Test Name: DEPEND SUBSCALE

Purpose: To measure the extent to which individuals trust others and depend on their availability when needed.

Number of Items: 6

Format: Responses are made on a 5-point scale ranging from 1 (not at all characteristic) to 5 (very characteristic). An example is presented.

Reliability: Test-retest reliability was .71.

Validity: Correlation with other variables ranged from −.37 to .24 (*N* = 125).

Author: Rochlen, A. B., et al.

Article: Development of the Attitudes Toward Career Counseling Scale.

Journal: *Journal of Counseling Psychology*, April 1999, *46*(2), 196–206.

Related Research: Collins, N. L., and Read, S. J. (1990). Adult attachment, working models, and relationship quality in dating couples. *Journal of Personality and Social Psychology*, *58*, 644–663.

7951

Test Name: DYADIC TRUST SCALE

Purpose: To measure trust in close relationships.

Number of Items: 8

Format:

Reliability: Coefficient alpha was .93.

Validity: Correlations with other variables ranged from .38 to .84.

Author: Couch, L. L., et al.

Article: The assessment of trait orientation.

Journal: *Journal of Personality Assessment*, October 1996, *67*(2), 305–323.

Related Research: Lazelere, R. E., & Huston, T. L. (1980). The Dyadic Trust Scale: Toward understanding interpersonal trust in close relationships. *Journal of Marriage and the Family*, *42*, 595–604.

7952

Test Name: ETHNIC ATTACHMENT SCALE

Purpose: To measure ethnic attachment as pride, ethnic introjection, and ethnic importance.

Number of Items: 12

Format: Scales range from 1 (low degree of ethnic attachment) to 4 (high level of ethnic attachment).

Reliability: Alpha coefficients ranged from .67 to .83 across subscales.

Validity: Correlations with other variables ranged from −.14 to .70.

Authors: Share-Pour, M.

Article: Self-categorization in in-group formation among Iranian children in Australia: A replication and extension.

Journal: *Journal of Social Psychology*, April 1999, *139*(2), 180–190.

7953

Test Name: ETHNIC IDENTIFICATION SCALE

Purpose: To measure ethnic identification.

Number of Items: 19

Format: Scales range from "strongly agree" to "strongly disagree."

Reliability: KR-20 reliability coefficients ranged from .56 to .88 across subscales.

Authors: Bornman, E.

Article: Self-image and ethnic identification in South Africa.

Journal: *Journal of Social Psychology*, August 1999, *139*(4), 411–425.

Related Research: Phinney, J. S. (1992). The Multigroup Ethnic Identity Measure: A new scale for use with diverse groups. *Journal of Adolescent Research, 7*, 156–177.

Saylor, E. S., & Aries, E. (1999). Ethnic identity and change in social context. *Journal of Social Psychology, 139*, 549–566.

Sam, D. L. (1999). Psychological adaptation of adolescents with immigrant backgrounds. *Journal of Social Psychology, 140*, 5–25.

7954

Test Name: ETHNIC SELF-EVALUATION SCALE

Purpose: To assess ethnic self-evaluation.

Number of Items: 3

Format: Five-point scales ranged from "No, I disagree" to "Yes, I agree." Sample items are presented.

Reliability: Coefficient alpha was .70.

Author: Kinket, B., and Verkuyten, M.

Article: Levels of ethnic self-identification and social context.

Journal: *Social Psychology Quarterly*, December 1997, *60*(4), 338–354.

Related Research: Luhtanen, R.,

& Crocker, J. (1992). A collective self-esteem scale: Self-evaluation of one's social identity. *Personality and Social Psychology Bulletin, 18*, 302–318.

Crocker, J., & Luhtanen, R. (1990). Collective self-esteem and ingroup bias. *Journal of Personality and Social Psychology, 58*, 60–67.

7955

Test Name: ETHNICITY QUESTIONNAIRE

Purpose: To assess ethnic pride, ethnic worry, and ethnic discrimination.

Number of Items: 24

Format: Scales range from 1 (strongly disagree) to 5 (strongly agree).

Reliability: Alpha coefficients ranged from .63 to .89 across subscales.

Author: Phelps, R. E., et al.

Article: Roommate satisfaction and ethnic pride in same-race and mixed-race university roommate pairs.

Journal: *Journal of College Student Development*, July/August 1996, *37*(4), 377–388.

Related Research: Phelps, R. E., & Day, J. D. (1992). *Ethnicity-related self-esteem and worry: Development of a scale.* Unpublished manuscript, University of Georgia at Athens.

Phelps, R. E. (1998). Roommate satisfaction and ethnic identity in mixed-race and White university roommate dyads. *Journal of College Student Development, 39*, 194–203.

7956

Test Name: EVALUATION OF ETHNIC IDENTITY SCALE

Purpose: To measure a child's evaluation of his or her ethnic identity.

Number of Items: 4

Format: Scales range from 1 (negative evaluation of ethnic identity) to 5 (positive evaluation of ethnic identity).

Reliability: Coefficient alpha was .70.

Validity: Correlations with other variables ranged from −.49 to .70.

Authors: Share-Pour, M.

Article: Self-categorization and in-group formation among Iranian children in Australia: A replication and extension.

Journal: *Journal of Social Psychology*, April 1999, *139*(2), 180–190.

Related Research: Verkuyten, M. (1991). Self-definition and in-group formation among ethnic minorities in the Netherlands. *Social Psychology Quarterly, 54*, 280–286.

7957

Test Name: EXPANDED CULTURAL ESTRANGEMENT SCALE

Purpose: To measure alienation.

Number of Items: 7

Format: Two-point scales are anchored by (0) rarely and (1) frequently

Reliability: KR-20 reliability was .79. Test-retest reliability was .78.

Author: Juni, S.

Article: Cultural estrangement revisited: A contemporary adaptation with reference to gender and to ethnic and racial foci.

Journal: *Psychological Reports*,

December 1998, *83*(3) Part 2,
1251–1256.

Related Research: Seeman, M.
(1959). On the meaning of
alienation. *American Sociological
Review, 24,* 783–791.

7958

Test Name: FEAR OF INTIMACY
SCALE

Purpose: To assess a specific
variable that influences intimacy
in a close relationship or at the
prospect of a close relationship.

Number of Items: 35

Format: Responses are made on a
5-point scale ranging from 1 (not
at all characteristic of me) to 5
(extremely characteristic of me).

Reliability: Internal consistency
was .93. Test-retest (1 month)
reliability was .89.

Validity: Correlations with other
variables ranged from −.58 to
.41.

Author: Wang. L., et al.

Article: Role of gender-related
personality traits, problem-
solving appraisal, and perceived
social support in developing a
mediational model of
psychological adjustment.

Journal: *Journal of Counseling
Psychology,* April 1997, *44*(2),
245–255.

Related Research: Descutner,
C. J., & Thelen, M. H. (1991).
Development and validation of a
Fear-of-Intimacy Scale.
Psychological Assessment, 3,
218–225.

7959

Test Name: FRIENDSHIP
QUALITIES SCALE

Purpose: To assess children's
perception of the qualities of
their best friends' friendships.

Number of Items: 23

Format: Includes 5 categories:
companionship, security-intimacy
and trust, closeness, help, and
conflict. Responses are made on
a 5-point scale ranging from 1
(not at all true) to 5 (very true).
Examples are presented.

Reliability: Alpha coefficients
ranged from .71 to .86.

Validity: Correlations with other
variables ranged from −.62 to
.54.

Author: Bauminger, N., and
Kasari, C.

Article: Loneliness and friendship
in high-functioning children with
autism.

Journal: *Child Development,*
March/April 2000, *71*(2), 447–
456.

Related Research: Bukowski,
W. M., et al. (1994). Measuring
friendship quality during pre-
and early adolescence: The
development and psychometric
properties of the Friendship
Qualities Scale. *Journal of Social
and Personal Relationships, 11,*
471–484.

7960

Test Name: GENERAL
MATTERING SCALE

Purpose: To measure the extent
to which people consider
themselves significant to others.

Number of Items: 5

Format: Four-point scales range
from 4 (very much) to 1 (not at
all). All items are presented.

Reliability: Cronbach's alpha was
.85.

Validity: Interitem correlations
ranged from .42 to .65.

Author: DeForge, B. R., and
Barclay, D. M., III

Article: The internal reliability of

a general mattering scale in
homeless men.

Journal: *Psychological Reports,*
April 1997, *80*(2), 429–430.

Related Research: Marcus, F. M.
(1991). *Mattering, self-esteem,
gender and the Protestant ethic.*
Paper presented at the annual
meeting of the American
Sociological Association.

7961

Test Name: GIFT-RECEIVING
DISCOMFORT AND
INTENTION TO REPAY SCALE

Purpose: To assess the discomfort
in receiving a gift and the
intention to repay.

Number of Items: 10

Format: Six-point scales are
anchored by (1) strongly disagree
and (6) strongly agree. All items
are presented.

Reliability: Alphas were .83
(Discomfort) and .73 (Repay).

Validity: A two-factor model
yielded the best fit for the 10
items.

Author: Dorsch, M. J., et al.

Article: Responses to gift-giving in
a business context: An empirical
examination.

Journal: *Psychological Reports,*
December 1997, *81*(3, Part I),
947–955.

7962

Test Name: GLOBAL TRUST
SCALES

Purpose: To measure
interpersonal trust and belief in
the general trustworthiness of
people in general.

Number of Items: 39

Reliability: Coefficient alpha was
.79. Other reliabilities ranged
from .58 to .76.

Validity: Correlations with other variables ranged from .29 to .59.

Author: Couch, L. L., and Jones, W. H.

Article: Measuring levels of trust.

Journal: *Journal of Research in Personality*, September 1997, *31*(3), 319–336.

Related Research: Rotter, J. B. (1967). A new scale for the measurement of interpersonal trust. *Journal of Personality, 35*, 651–665.

Chun, K., & Campbell, J. B. (1975). Notes on the internal structure of Wrightman's measure of trustworthiness. *Psychological Reports, 37*, 323–330.

7963

Test Name: (GOULD) MANIFEST ALIENATON MEASURE

Purpose: To measure alienation.

Number of Items: 20

Format: Seven-point scales are anchored by 1 (disagree strongly) and 7 (agree strongly). A sample item is presented.

Reliability: Alphas ranged from .58 to .83.

Author: Mahoney, J. M., and Quick, B. G.

Article: Personality correlates of alienation in a university sample.

Journal: *Psychological Reports*, December 2000, *87*(3), Part 2, 1094–1100.

Related Research: Gould, L. J. (1964) *The alienation syndrome: Psycho-social correlates and behavioral consequences.* Unpublished doctoral dissertation, University of Connecticut (No. 66–848, University Microfilms, Ann Arbor, MI).

7964

Test Name: GREEK-AMERICAN ACCULTURATION SCALE

Purpose: To measure degree of acculturation of Greek Americans.

Number of Items: 44

Format: Seven-point scales. Sample items are presented.

Reliability: Alphas ranged from .76 to .94 across subscales.

Author: Harris, A. C., and Verven, R.

Article: Acculturation as a determinant of Greek-American family values.

Journal: *Psychological Reports*, December 1998, *83*(3) Part 2, 1163–1176.

Related Research: Harris, A. C., & Verven, R. (1996). The Greek-American Acculturation Scale: Development and validity. *Psychological Reports, 78*, 599–610.

7965

Test Name: GRONINGEN ENJOYMENT QUESTIONNAIRE

Purpose: To measure enjoyment in leisure-time physical activity.

Number of Items: 10

Format: All items are presented.

Reliability: Test-retest reliability was .84.

Validity: Correlations with other variables were .26 and .61.

Author: Stevens, M., et al.

Article: The Groningen Enjoyment Questionnaire: A measure of enjoyment in leisure-time physical activity.

Journal: *Perceptual and Motor Skills*, April 2000, *90*(2), 601–604.

Related Research: Snaith, R. P., et al. (1995). A scale for the assessment of hedonic tone: The Snaith-Hamilton Pleasure Scale. *British Journal of Psychiatry, 167*, 99–103.

7966

Test Name: GROUP CLIMATE QUESTIONNAIRE—SHORT FORM

Purpose: To measure participant's perception of the group atmosphere.

Number of Items: 12

Format: Includes 3 scales: Engagement, Avoidance, and Conflict. Responses are made on a 6-point scale from 1 (not at all) to 6 (extremely).

Author: Kivlighan, Jr., D. M., et al.

Article: Helpful impacts in group counseling: Development of a multidimensional rating system.

Journal: *Journal of Counseling Psychology*, July 1996, *43*(3), 347–355.

Related Research: MacKenzie, K. R. (1983). Therapeutic factors in group psychotherapy: A contemporary view. *Group, 11*, 26–34.

7967

Test Name: GROUP ENVIRONMENT QUESTIONNAIRE

Purpose: To measure group cohesion.

Number of Items: 18

Format: Includes 4 scales: Individual Attraction to Group-Task, Individual Attraction to Group-Social, Group Integration-Task, and Group Integration-Social. Responses are made on a 9-point scale.

Reliability: Internal consistencies ranged from .64 to .76.

Author: Meyer, B. B.

Article: The ropes and challenge course: A quasi-experimental examination.

Journal: *Perceptual and Motor Skills*, June 2000, *90*(3) Part 2, 1249–1257.

Related Research: Carron, A. V., et al. (1985). The development of an instrument to assess cohesion in sport teams: The Group Environment Questionnaire. *Journal of Sport Psychology, 7,* 244–246.

7968

Test Name: GROUP PROCESS SCALES

Purpose: To measure openness of communication, task focus, leader emergence, and group cohesion.

Number of Items: 20

Format: Five-point scales are anchored by "to a very little extent" and "to a very great extent." All items are presented.

Reliability: Alpha coefficients ranged from .69 to .96.

Validity: Correlations with other variables ranged from −.13 to .15.

Author: Barry, B., and Stewart, G. L.

Article: Composition, process, and performance in self-managed groups: The role of personality.

Journal: *Journal of Applied Psychology*, February 1997, *82*(1), 62–78.

Related Research: Rosenfeld, L. B., & Gilbert, J. R. (1989). The measurement of cohesion and its relationship to dimensions of self-disclosure in classroom settings. *Small Group Behavior, 20,* 291–301.

7969

Test Name: HARMONY CONTROL SCALE

Purpose: To measure to what extent people are flexible and adjusting and that agency resides in spiritual and social forces.

Number of Items: 21

Format: Seven-point scales range from 1 (strongly disagree) to 7 (strongly agree). All items are presented.

Reliability: Alpha coefficients ranged from .70 to .78 across samples. Test-retest reliability was .78.

Validity: Correlations with other variables ranged from −.36 to .37.

Author: Morling, B., and Fiske, S. T.

Article: Defining and measuring harmony control.

Journal: *Journal of Research in Personality*, December 1999, *33*(4), 379–414.

7970

Test Name: IDENTITY SCALES

Purpose: To measure American, Global, and Ethnic Identity.

Number of Items: 17

Format: Six-point scales range from 1 (strongly disagree) to 6 (strongly agree). All items are presented.

Reliability: Alphas ranged from .70 to .81.

Validity: Correlations with other variables ranged from −.40 to .43.

Author: Der-Karabetian, A., and Ruiz, Y.

Article: Affective bicultural and global-human identity scales for Mexican-American adolescents.

Journal: *Psychological Reports*, June 1997, *80*(3) Part 1, 1027–1039.

7971

Test Name: INDEX OF RACE-RELATED STRESS

Purpose: To assess race-related stress as cultural racism, institutional racism, individual racism and global racism.

Number of Items: 22

Format: Scales range from 0 (this never happened to me) to 4 (this event happened and I was extremely upset). All items are presented.

Reliability: Alpha coefficients ranged from .69 to .78 across subscales.

Validity: Black respondent means were significantly higher than White respondent means.

Author: Utsey, S. O.

Article: Development and validation of a short form of the index of race-related stress.

Journal: *Measurement and Evaluation in Counseling and Development*, October 1999, *32*(3), 149–167.

Related Research: Utsey, S. O., & Ponterotto, J. G. (1996). Development and validation of the index of race-related stress (IRRS). *Journal of Counseling Psychology, 43,* 490–502.

7972

Test Name: INDEX OF RACE RELATED STRESS

Purpose: To measure stress associated with the experiences of racism in the daily lives of African Americans.

Number of Items: 46

Format: Includes 4 components of racism: Cultural, Institutional, Individual, and Collective. All items are presented.

Reliability: Test-retest reliability coefficients ranged from .54 to .79. Internal consistency coefficients ranged from .74 to .89.

Validity: Correlations with the Index of Race Related Stress ranged from −.02 to .46.

Author: Utsey, S. O., and Ponterott, J. G.

Article: Developments and validation of the Index of Race-Related Stress (IRRS).

Journal: *Journal of Personality Assessment*, October 1996, *43*(4), 490–501.

Related Research: Lazarus, R. S., & Folkman, S. (1984). *Stress, appraisal, and coping*, New York: Springer.

7973

Test Name: INDIAN ACCULTURATION SCALES

Purpose: To assess attitudes, behavior and possessions that indicate traditional Indian values.

Number of Items: 34

Format: Various frequency and rating scales are used. Sample items are described.

Reliability: Alpha coefficients ranged from .60 to .93.

Author: Jain, A., and Belsky, J.

Article: Fathering and acculturation: Immigrant Indian families with young children.

Journal: *Journal of Marriage and the Family*, November 1997, *59*(4), 873–883.

Related Research: Patel, N., et al.

(1996). Socialization values and practices of Indian immigrant parents: Correlates of modernity and acculturation. *Child Development*, *67*, 302–313.

7974

Test Name: INTERDEPENDENCE SCALE

Purpose: To assess interdependence.

Number of Items: 10

Format: Includes task interdependence and outcome interdependence. Responses are made on a 7-point scale ranging from 1 (completely false) to 7 (completely true). Examples are presented.

Reliability: Alpha coefficients ranged from .61 to .89.

Validity: Correlations with other variables ranged from −.49 to .80.

Author: Janz, B. D., et al.

Article: Knowledge worker team effectiveness: The role of autonomy, interdependence, team development, and contextual support variables.

Journal: *Personnel Psychology*, Winter 1997, *50*(4), 877–904.

Related Research: Johnson, D. W., et al. (1988). The effect of prolonged implementation of support within the classroom. *Journal of Psychology*, *119*, 405–411.

7975

Test Name: INTERNAL-EXTERNAL ETHNIC IDENTITY MEASURE

Purpose: To measure the internal and external aspects of ethnic identity.

Number of Items: 24

Format: Includes 4 factors: Ethnic Friendship and Affiliation, Ethno-Communal Expression, Ethnic Food Orientation, and Family-Collectivism. All items are presented. Responses are made on a 6-point Likert-type scale ranging from 6 (agree strongly) to 1 (disagree strongly).

Reliability: Alpha coefficients ranged from .72 to .90.

Author: Kwan, K.-L. K.

Article: The Internal-External Ethnic Identity Measure: Factor analytic structures based on a sample of Chinese Americans.

Journal: *Educational and Psychological Measurement*, February 2000, *60*(1), 142–152.

Related Research: Kwan, K.-L. K., & Sodowsky, G. R. (1997). Internal and external ethnic identity and their correlates: A study of Chinese American immigrants. *Journal of Multicultural Counseling and Development*, *25*, 51–67.

7976

Test Name: INTERPERSONAL AND INTERGROUP-CONTACT SCALES

Purpose: To measure the importance of interpersonal and intergroup contact.

Number of Items: 17

Format: Scales range from 1 (totally unimportant) to 5 (very important). All items are presented.

Reliability: Alpha coefficients were .80 (intergroup) and .65 (interpersonal).

Validity: The correlations between intergroup and interpersonal scores was .28 (Arab respondents) and .36 (Jewish respondents).

Authors: Eshel, Y.

Article: Effects on in-group bias on planned encounters of Jewish and Arab youths.

Journal: *The Journal of Social Psychology*, December 1999, *139*(6), 768–783.

7977

Test Name: INTERPERSONAL COMPETENCE QUESTIONNAIRE

Purpose: To measure 5 domains of interpersonal competence.

Number of Items: 40

Format: Includes 5 domains: Relationship Initiation, Disclosure of Personal Information, Assertion of Displeasure with Others, Provision of Emotional Support, and Interpersonal Conflict Management.

Reliability: Alpha coefficients were .82 and .76.

Author: Jackson, T., et al.

Article: Culture and self-presentation as predictors of shyness among Japanese and American female college students.

Journal: *Perceptual and Motor Skills*, April 2000, *90*(2), 475–482.

Related Research: Buhrmester, D., et al. (1988). Five domains of interpersonal competence in peer relationships. *Journal of Personality and Social Psychology*, 55, 991–1008.

7978

Test Name: INTERPERSONAL COMPETENCE SCALE

Purpose: To rate boys' and girls' social behavior and academic competence.

Number of Items: 18

Format: Includes 3 factors: Aggression, Popularity, and Academic Competence. Each item is rated on a 7-point scale.

Reliability: Alpha coefficients ranged from a median of .71 to a median of .82. Three-week reliabilities ranged from .73 to .89. Median 1-year stabilities ranged from .39 to .51.

Author: Mahoney, J. L.

Article: School extracurricular activity participation as a moderator in the development of antisocial patterns.

Journal: *Child Development*, March/April 2000, *71*(2), 502–516.

Related Research: Cairns, R. B., et al. (1995). A brief method for assessing social development: Structure, reliability, stability, and developmental validity of the Interpersonal Competence Scale. *Behavior Research and Therapy Incorporating Behavioral Assessment*, *33*, 725–736.

7979

Test Name: INTERPERSONAL CONTROL SCALE

Purpose: To measure perceived control.

Number of Items: 10

Reliability: Test-retest (4 weeks) reliability was above .90. Test-retest (6 months) reliability was above .70.

Validity: Correlation with other variables ranged from −.34 to .39 (N = 152).

Author: Mothersead, P. K., et al.

Article: Attachment, family dysfunction, parental alcoholism, and interpersonal distress in late adolescence: A structural model.

Journal: *Journal of Counseling Psychology*, April 1998, *45*(2), 196–203.

Related Research: Paulhus, D. (1983). Sphere-specific measures of perceived control. *Journal of Personality and Social Psychology*, *44*, 1253–1265.

7980

Test Name: INTERPERSONAL DEPENDENCY INVENTORY

Purpose: To measure dependency.

Number of Items: 48

Format: Includes 3 subscales: Emotional Reliance on Others, Lack of Social Self-Confidence, and Assertion of Autonomy. Responses are made on a 4-point scale ranging from 1 (Disagree) to 4 (Agree). Sample items are presented.

Validity: Correlations with other variables ranged from −.64 to .55.

Author: Bornstein, R. F., et al.

Article: Relationships of objective and projective dependency scores to sex role orientation in college student participants.

Journal: *Journal of Personality Assessment*, June 1996, *66*(3), 555–568.

Related Research: Bornstein, R. F. (1994). Construct validity of the Interpersonal Dependency Inventory: 1977–1992. *Journal of Personality Disorders*, *8*, 64–76.

7981

Test Name: INTERPERSONAL JEALOUSY SCALE

Purpose: To measure negative emotion from loss of a loved one to a rival.

Number of Items: 28

Reliability: Coefficient alpha was .92.

Validity: Correlations with other

variables ranged from −.26 to −.29.

Author: Couch, L. L., and Jones, W. H.

Article: Measuring levels of trust.

Journal: *Journal of Research in Personality*, September 1997, *31*(3), 319–336.

Related Research: Mathes, E. W., & Severa, N. (1981). Jealousy, romantic love, and liking: Theoretical considerations and preliminary scale development. *Psychological Reports, 49,* 23–31.

7982

Test Name: INTERPERSONAL MISTRUST-TRUST MEASURE

Purpose: To assess trust and mistrust in interpersonal situations.

Number of Items: 18

Format: Scales range from 1 (not likely to respond in this way) to 7 (very likely to respond in this way). All items are presented.

Reliability: Coefficient alpha was .81.

Validity: Correlations with other variables ranged from −.53 to .41.

Author: Omodel, M. M., and McLennan, J.

Article: Conceptualizing and measuring global interpersonal mistrust-trust.

Journal: *Journal of Social Psychology*, June 2000, *140*(3), 279–294.

7983

Test Name: INTERPERSONAL REACTIVITY INDEX

Purpose: To measure an individual's responsiveness to others.

Number of Items: 28

Format: Five-point scales are anchored by 1 (not at all like me) and 5 (very much like me).

Reliability: Alphas ranged from .54 to .69 across subscales.

Author: Ehrenberg, M. F., et al.

Article: Shared parenting agreements after marital separation: The roles of empathy and narcissism.

Journal: *Journal of Consulting and Clinical Psychology*, August 1996, *64*(4), 808–818.

Related Research: Davis, M. H. (1983). Measuring individual differences in empathy: Evidence for a multidimensional approach. *Journal of Personality and Social Psychology, 44,* 113–126.

7984

Test Name: INTERPERSONAL RELATIONSHIP ASSESSMENT TECHNIQUE

Purpose: To measure peer relations that range from casual to intimate.

Number of Items: 7

Format: Guttman scale.

Reliability: Scalability was .67. Reproducibility was .93.

Authors: Kurman, J., and Eshel, Y.

Article: Self-enhancement, general level of self-evaluation, and emotional adjustment.

Journal: *Journal of Social Psychology*, October 1998, *138*(5), 549–563.

Related Research: Schwartzwald, J., & Cohen, S. (1982). Relationship between academic tracking and the degree of inter-ethnic acceptance. *Journal of Educational Psychology, 74,* 588–597.

Eshel, Y. (1999). Effects of in-group bias on planned encounters of Jewish and Arab youths. *Journal of Social Psychology, 139,* 768–783.

7985

Test Name: INTERPERSONAL SUPPORT EVALUATION LIST

Purpose: To assess perceived availability of four types of social support: tangible, appraisal, self-esteem, and belonging.

Number of Items: 40

Format: Sample items are presented.

Reliability: Coefficient alpha was .90. Test-retest reliability (6 months) was .74.

Validity: Correlations with other variables ranged from −.57 to .21.

Author: Igreja, I., et al.

Article: Social motives, social support, and distress in gay men differing in HIV status.

Journal: *Journal of Research in Personality*, September 2000, *34*(3), 287–304.

Related Research: Cohen, S., et al. (1985). Measuring the functional components of social support. In I. Sarason & B. Sarason (Eds.), *Social support: Theory, research and applications* (pp. 73–94). The Hague, Netherlands: Martinus Nijhoff.

7986

Test Name: INTERPERSONAL TRUST SCALE

Purpose: To measure global trust.

Number of Items: 25

Format:

Reliability: Coefficient alpha was .79. Split-half reliability was .76.

Test-retest reliabilities were .58 and .68.

Validity: Correlations with other variables ranged from .51 to .66.

Author: Couch, L. L., et al.

Article: The assessment of trait orientation.

Journal: *Journal of Personality Assessment*, October 1996, *67*(2), 305–323.

Related Research: Rotter, J. B. (1967). A new scale for the measurement of interpersonal trust. *Journal of Personality, 35,* 651–665.

7987

Test Name: INTIMACY, PASSION, AND COMMITMENT SCALE

Purpose: To measure levels of intimacy, passion, and commitment.

Number of Items: 19

Format: Seven-point scales are anchored by 1 (strongly disagree) and 7 (strongly agree). All items are presented.

Reliability: Alphas ranged from .89 to .94.

Author: Limieux, R., and Hale, J. I.

Article: Intimacy, passion, and commitment among married individuals: Further testing of the Triangular Theory of Love.

Journal: *Psychological Reports*, December 2000, *87*(3, Part 1), 941–948.

Related Research: Limieux, R., & Hale, J. I. (1999). Intimacy, passion, and commitment in young romantic relationships: Successfully measuring the Triangular Theory of Love. *Psychological Reports, 85,* 497–503.

7988

Test Name: INTIMACY SCALE

Purpose: To measure intimacy.

Number of Items: 8

Format: Responses are made on a 5-point scale ranging from "not at all" to "very much."

Reliability: Alpha coefficients were .78 and .81.

Author: Updegraff, K. A., et al.

Article: Adolescents' sex-typed friendship experiences: Does having a sister versus having a brother matter?

Journal: *Child Development*, November/December 2000, *71*(6), 1597–1610.

Related Research: Blyth, D. A., et al. (1982). Early adolescents' significant others: Grade and gender differences in perceived relationships with familial and nonfamilial adults and young people. *Journal of Youth and Adolescence, 11,* 425–450.

7989

Test Name: INTIMATE RELATIONS SCALE

Purpose: To assess maintenance/communication, conflict, love and ambivalence.

Number of Items: 25

Format: Includes two composites: A positive and a negative marriage composite.

Reliability: Alpha coefficients ranged from .83 to .87.

Validity: Correlations with other variables ranged from .46 to −.53.

Author: Belsky, J., et al.

Article: Troubles in the second year: Three questions about family interaction.

Journal: *Child Development*, April 1996, *67*(2), 556–578.

Related Research: Braiker, H., & Kelley, H. (1979). Conflicts in the development of close relationships. In R. Burgess and T. Huston (Eds.), *Social exchange and developing relationships*, New York: Academic Press.

7990

Test Name: INTRAGROUP TRUST SCALE

Purpose: To measure perceptions of trust, truthfulness, and integrity in groups.

Number of Items: 5

Format: Scales range from 1 (never) to 7 (always). All items are presented.

Reliability: Coefficient alpha was .89.

Validity: Correlations with other variables ranged from −.62 to .39.

Author: Simons, T. L., and Peterson, R. S.

Article: Task conflict and relationship conflict in top management teams: The pivotal role of intragroup trust.

Journal: *Journal of Applied Psychology*, February 2000, *85*(1), 102–111.

Related Research: McAllister, D. J. (1995). Affect- and cognition-based trust as foundations for interpersonal cooperation in organizations. *Academy of Management Journal, 38,* 24–59.

7991

Test Name: INVENTORY OF INTERPERSONAL PROBLEMS

Purpose: To determine the

amount of interpersonal distress that a person is experiencing.

Number of Items: 127

Format: Responses are made on a 5-point scale ranging from 0 (not at all) to 4 (extremely). Examples are presented.

Reliability: Alpha coefficients ranged from .94 to .97. Test-retest (10 weeks) reliability was .86.

Author: Kivlighan, Jr., D. M., and Shaughnessy, P.

Article: Patterns of working alliance development: A typology of client's working alliance ratings.

Journal: *Journal of Counseling Psychology*, July 2000, 47(3), 362–371.

Related Research: Horowitz, L. M., et al. (1988). Inventory of Interpersonal Problems: Psychometric properties and clinical applications. *Journal of Consulting and Clinical Psychology*, 56, 885–892.

7992

Test Name: INVENTORY OF INTERPERSONAL PROBLEMS —CIRCUMPLEX

Purpose: Eight scales measure two dimensions: domineering vs. nonassertive and overly nurturant vs. cold.

Format: Sample items are presented.

Reliability: Alpha coefficients ranged from .72 to .85.

Validity: Correlations with other variables ranged from −.35 to .39.

Author: Alden, L. E., and Bieling, P. J.

Article: Interpersonal convergence of personality constructs in

dynamic and cognitive models of depression.

Journal: *Journal of Research in Personality*, March 1996, 30(1), 60–75.

Related Research: Horowitz, L. M., et al. (1988). Inventory of interpersonal problems: Psychometric properties and clinical applications. *Journal of Consulting and Clinical Psychology*, 56, 885–892.

7993

Test Name: INVENTORY OF INTERPERSONAL PROBLEMS —REVISED

Purpose: To assess the severity and type of an individual's interpersonal difficulties.

Number of Items: 64

Format: Includes 8 subscales: Domineering, Vindictive, Cold, Socially Avoidant, Nonassertive, Overly Nurturant, Exploitable, and Intrusive. Responses are made on a 5-point scale ranging from 0 (not at all) to 4 (extremely).

Reliability: Test-retest (10 weeks) reliability ranged from .80 to .90.

Validity: Correlations with the Symptom Checklist–90—Revised was .64.

Author: Barber, J. P., et al.

Article: The Central Relationship Questionnaire: Initial report.

Journal: *Journal of Counseling Psychology*, April 1998, 45(2), 131–142.

Related Research: Horowitz, L. M., et al. (1988). Inventory of Interpersonal Problems: Psychometric properties and clinical applications. *Journal of Consulting and Clinical Psychology*, 56, 885–892.

7994

Test Name: INVENTORY OF INTERPERSONAL PROBLEMS —SHORT FORM

Purpose: To assess the level of distress about interpersonal problems.

Number of Items: 64

Format: Responses are made on a 5-point scale ranging from 0 (not at all) to 4 (extremely). Examples are presented.

Reliability: Alpha coefficients ranged from .72 to .85. Test-retest reliabilities ranged from .74 to .89.

Author: Hill, C. E., et al.

Article: Structured brief therapy with a focus on dreams or loss for clients with troubling dreams and recent loss.

Journal: *Journal of Counseling Psychology*, January 2000, 47(1), 90–101.

Related Research: Alden, L. E., et al. (1990). Construction of circumplex scales for the Inventory of Interpersonal Problems. *Journal of Personality Assessment*, 55, 521–536.

7995

Test Name: INVENTORY OF INTERPERSONAL PROBLEMS —SHORT VERSION

Purpose: To assess the extent of interpersonal problems.

Number of Items: 32

Format: Five-point scales are anchored by 0 (not at all) and 4 (extremely).

Validity: Correlations with the long version ranged from .94 to .96.

Author: Barkham, M., et al.

Article: Dose-effect relations in

time-limited psychotherapy for depression.

Journal: *Journal of Consulting and Clinical Psychology*, October 1996, *64*(5), 927–935.

Related Research: Barkham, M., et al. (1988). The IIP-32: A short version of the Inventory of Interpersonal Problems. *British Journal of Clinical Psychology*, *35*, 21–35.

7996

Test Name: ISRAELI ACCULTURATION SCALE

Purpose: To assess acculturation in Israel.

Number of Items: 17

Format: Scales range from 1 (totally disagree) to 5 (totally agree). All items are presented.

Reliability: Alpha coefficients ranged from .51 to .72 across subscales.

Validity: Correlations with other variables ranged from−.39 to .16.

Author: Eshel, Y., and Rosenthal-Sokolov, M.

Article: Acculturation attitudes and sociocultural adjustment of sojourner youth in Israel.

Journal: *Journal of Social Psychology*, December 2000, *140*(6), 677–691.

Related Research: Horenczyk, G. (1994). *Acculturation conflicts and the migrants' construction of their social worlds.* Paper presented at the Congress on Migration and Identity, Jerusalem, Israel.

7997

Test Name: ISRAELI PERCEIVED ADJUSTMENT SCALE

Purpose: To assess perceived adjustment to Israel.

Number of Items: 19

Format: Scales range from 1 (do not agree at all) to 5 (totally agree). All items are presented.

Reliability: Alpha coefficients ranged from .68 to .91 across subscales.

Validity: Correlations with other variables ranged from −.33 to .16.

Author: Eshel, Y., and Rosenthal-Sokolov, M.

Article: Acculturation attitudes and sociocultural adjustment of sojourner youth in Israel.

Journal: *Journal of Social Psychology*, December 2000, *140*(6), 677–691.

Related Research: Aronson, N. (1994). [Absorption of immigrants in light of reference group theory.] Unpublished master's thesis, University of Haifa, Israel (in Hebrew).

7998

Test Name: JEALOUSY SCALE

Purpose: To assess the appropriateness, experience, and expression of jealousy.

Number of Items: 8

Format: Scales ranged from 1 (not at all) to 7 (very much). All items are presented.

Reliability: Alpha coefficients ranged from .87 to .94.

Authors: Aune, K. S., and Comstock, J.

Article: Effect of relationship length on the experience, expression, and perceived appropriateness of jealousy.

Journal: *Journal of Social Psychology*, February 1997, *137*(1), 23–31.

Related Research: Aune, K. S., & Comstock, J. (1991). Experience and expression of jealousy: Comparison between friends and romantics. *Psychological Reports*, *69*, 315–319.

7999

Test Name: KINDNESS SCALE

Purpose: To measure the reasons for being kind.

Number of Items: 25

Format: Five-point scales range from (1) not at all true to (5) exactly true. All items are presented in English and Italian.

Reliability: Alphas ranged from .65 to.80.

Validity: Correlations with other variables ranged from −.36 to .35.

Author: Comunian, A. L.

Article: The Kindness Scale.

Journal: *Psychological Reports*, December 1998, *83*(3) Part 2, 1351–1361.

8000

Test Name: LACK OF AGREEMENT SCALE

Purpose: To measure disagreements between couples.

Number of Items: 12

Format: Five-point scales are anchored by 1 (not at all) to 5 (daily disagreement).

Reliability: Alpha was .78.

Validity: Correlations with other variables ranged from −.23 to .54.

Author: Hener, T., et al.

Article: Supportive versus cognitive-behavioral intervention programs in achieving adjustment to home peritoneal kidney dialysis.

Journal: *Journal of Consulting and Clinical Psychology*, August 1996, *64*(4), 731–741.

Related Research: Spanier, G. B. (1976). Measuring dyadic adjustment: New scales for assessing the quality of marriage and similar dyads. *Journal of Marriage and the Family, 38*, 15–28.

8001

Test Name: LEVEL OF SOCIALIZATION SCALE-REVISED

Purpose: To assess level of socialization.

Number of Items: 28

Format: Includes six dimensions: Politics, History, Organizational Goals/Values, People, Performance Proficiency, and Language. Responses are made on a 5-point Likert scale.

Reliability: Alpha coefficients ranged from .63 to .86.

Author: Klein, H. J., and Weaver, N. A.

Article: The effectiveness of an organizational-level orientation training program in the socialization of new hires.

Journal: *Personnel Psychology*, Spring 2000, *53*(1), 47–66.

Related Research: Chao, G. T., et al. (1994). Organizational socialization: Its content and consequences. *Journal of Applied Psychology, 79*, 730–743.

8002

Test Name: LIFE SPACE SCALE—SHORT FORM

Purpose: To depict a person's external life space: biological foundations, groups, and interactions with the environment.

Number of Items: 77

Format: Multiple formats are used and described. All items are presented, along with scoring rules.

Reliability: Split-half reliabilities ranged from .74 to .87.

Validity: Correlations with other variables ranged from −.20 to .26.

Author: Mayer, J. D., et al.

Article: Describing the person's external environment: Conceptualizing and measuring the life space.

Journal: *Journal of Research in Personality*, September 1998, *32*(3), 253–296.

8003

Test Name: LONELINESS AND SOCIAL DISSATISFACTION QUESTIONNAIRE

Purpose: To measure loneliness distinct from relationship satisfaction.

Number of Items: 19

Format: Includes two subscales: Loneliness and Social Satisfaction. Responses are made on a 3-point scale ranging from 1 (no) to 3 (yes). Examples are presented.

Reliability: Coefficient alpha was .75.

Author: Ladd, G. W., and Burgess, K. B.

Article: Charting the relationship trajectories of aggressive, withdrawn, and aggressive/withdrawn children during early grade school.

Journal: *Child Development*, July/August 1999, *70*(4), 910–929.

Related Research: Cassidy, J., & Asher, S. R. (1992). Loneliness and peer relations in young children. *Child Development, 63*, 350–365.

8004

Test Name: LONELINESS AND SOCIAL DISSATISFACTION QUESTIONNAIRE

Purpose: To measure loneliness.

Number of Items: 24

Format: Responses are made on a 5-point scale ranging from 1 (That's not true about me) to 5 (That's always true about me). Examples are presented.

Reliability: Coefficient alpha was .81.

Validity: Correlations with other variables ranged from −.22 to .27.

Author: Gresham, F. M., et al.

Article: Effects of positive and negative illusory biases: Comparisons across social and academic self-concept domains.

Journal: *Journal of School Psychology*, March/April 2000, *38*(2), 151–175.

Related Research: Asher, S., & Wheeler, V. (1985). Children's loneliness: A comparison of rejected and neglected peer status. *Journal of Consulting and Clinical Psychology, 53*, 500–505.

8005

Test Name: LONELINESS AND SOCIAL DISSATISFACTION QUESTIONNAIRE—GREEK VERSION

Purpose: To measure children's loneliness and social dissatisfaction.

Number of Items: 21

Format: Responses are made on a 3-point scale of 1 (yes), 2

(sometimes), and 3 (no). All items are presented.

Reliability: Alpha coefficients ranged from .57 to .87.

Validity: Correlation with other variables ranged from −.09 to −.42.

Author: Galanaki, E. P., and Kalantzi-Azizi, A.

Article: Loneliness and social dissatisfaction: Its relation with children's self-efficacy for peer interaction.

Journal: *Child Study*, 1999, *29*(1), 1–22.

Related Research: Asher, S. R., et al. (1984). Loneliness in children. *Child Development*, *55*, 1456–1464.

8006

Test Name: LONELINESS EXPERIENCE SCALE

Purpose: To measure loneliness as emotional distress, social alienation and inadequacy, growth and discovery, isolation, and self-alienation.

Number of Items: 82

Time Required: 10 minutes.

Format: Unspecified rating scales. Sample items are presented.

Reliability: Total reliability was .92. Reliabilities ranged from .75 to .86 across subscales.

Author: Rokach, A.

Article: Loneliness and the life cycle.

Journal: *Psychological Reports*, April 2000, *86*(2), 629–642.

Related Research: Rokach, A. (1988). The experience of loneliness: A tri-level model. *Journal of Psychology, 122*, 531–544.

8007

Test Name: LONELINESS QUESTIONNAIRE

Purpose: To measure loneliness.

Number of Items: 15

Reliability: Alpha was .52.

Validity: Factor structure of the 15-item scale was largely the same as for an 82-item version.

Author: Rokach, A., and Koledin, S.

Article: Perceived sources of loneliness of incarcerated men.

Journal: *Psychological Reports*, October 1997, *81*(2), 643–654.

Related Research: Rokach, A., and Brock, H. (1996). The causes of loneliness. *Psychology: A Journal of Human Behavior, 33*, 1–11.

8008

Test Name: LONELINESS QUESTIONNAIRE

Purpose: To assess childrens' feelings of loneliness and social dissatisfaction.

Number of Items: 20

Format: Responses are made on a 3-point scale: yes, sometimes, no.

Reliability: Alpha coefficients ranged from .78 to .82.

Author: Parker, J. G., and Seal, J.

Article: Forming, losing, renewing, and replacing friendships: Applying temporal parameters to the assessment of children's friendship experiences.

Journal: *Child Development*, October 1996, *67*(5), 2248–2268.

Related Research: Williams, G. A., & Asher, S. R. (1992). Assessment of loneliness at school among children with mild mental retardation. *American Journal of Mental Retardation*, *96*, 373–385.

8009

Test Name: LONELINESS RATING SCALE

Purpose: To assess children's global feelings of loneliness.

Number of Items: 24

Format: Responses are made on a 5-point scale ranging from 1 (not true at all) to 5 (always true). Examples are given.

Reliability: Coefficient alpha was .90.

Author: Bauminger, N., and Kosari, C.

Article: Loneliness and friendship in high-functioning children with autism.

Journal: *Child Development*, March/April 2000, *71*(2), 447–456.

Related Research: Asher, S. R., et al. (1984). Loneliness in children. *Child Development*, *55*, 1456–1464.

8010

Test Name: LONELINESS SCALE

Purpose: To measure loneliness.

Number of Items: 5

Format: Responses were 3 (yes), 2 (sometimes), or 1 (no). Two items are presented.

Reliability: Coefficient alpha was .78.

Validity: Correlations with other variables ranged from −.35 to .33.

Author: Kochenderfer, B. J., and Ladd, G. W.

Article: Peer victimization: Cause or consequence of school maladjustment?

Journal: *Child Development*, August 1996, *67*(4), 1305–1317.

Related Research: Cassidy, J., & Asher, S. R. (1992). Loneliness and peer relations in young children. *Child Development*, *63*, 350–365.

8011

Test Name: LONELINESS SCALE

Purpose: To measure loneliness in children.

Number of Items: 18

Format: Five-point response scales.

Reliability: Alpha was .92.

Author: Crick, N. R., and Bigbee, M. A.

Article: Relational and overt forms of peer victimization: A multi-informant approach.

Journal: *Journal of Consulting and Clinical Psychology*, April 1998, *66*(2), 337–347.

Related Research: Asher, S. R., & Wheeler, V. A. (1985). Children's loneliness: A comparison of rejected and neglected peer status. *Journal of Consulting and Clinical Psychology*, *53*, 500–505.

8012

Test Name: LONELINESS SCALE

Purpose: To measure aloneness, peer-related loneliness, and parent-related loneliness.

Number of Items: 28

Format: Scales range from 1 (very seldom) to 4 (very often).

Reliability: Alpha coefficients ranged from .53 to .90 across subscales. Total alpha was .92.

Validity: Correlations with other variables ranged from .33 to .71.

Authors: Lau, S., et al.

Article: Facets of loneliness and depression among Chinese children and adolescents.

Journal: *The Journal of Social Psychology*, December 1999, *139*(6), 713–729.

Related Research: Marcoen, A., & Brumagne, M. (1985). Loneliness among children and young adolescents. *Developmental Psychology*, *21*, 1025–1031.

8013

Test Name: LONELINESS SCALES

Purpose: To measure loneliness and its causes.

Number of Items: 164

Time Required: 20 minutes

Format: Checklist format.

Reliability: Kuder-Richardson internal consistencies ranged from .75 to .97.

Author: Rokach, A.

Article: Relations of perceived causes and the experience of loneliness.

Journal: *Psychological Reports*, June 1997, *80*(3) Part 2, 1067–1074.

Related Research: Rokach, A. (1988). The experience of loneliness: A tri-level model. *The Journal of Psychology*, *122*, 531–544.

8014

Test Name: LOVE SCALE

Purpose: To measure feelings of romantic love.

Number of Items: 9

Format: Five-point scales are anchored by "strongly disagree" and "strongly agree." A sample item is presented.

Reliability: Alpha was .88.

Validity: Correlations with other variables ranged from .09 to .33.

Author: Murstein, B. I., and Tuerkheimer, A.

Article: Gender differences in love, sex, and motivation for sex.

Journal: *Psychological Reports*, April 1998, *82*(2), 435–450.

Related Research: Rubin, Z. (1970). Measurement of romantic love. *Journal of Personality and Social Psychology*, *16*, 265–273.

8015

Test Name: LOW SELF-CONTROL SCALE

Purpose: To measure low self-control.

Number of Items: 12

Format: Responses are made on a 5-point scale ranging from 1 (never) to 5 (very often).

Reliability: Coefficient alpha was .86.

Author: Tibbetts, S. G.

Article: Differences between women and men regarding decisions to commit test cheating.

Journal: *Research in Higher Education*, June 1999, *40*(3), 323–342.

Related Research: Grasnick, H., et al. (1993). Testing the core implications of Gottfredson and Hirschi's general theory of crime. *Journal of Research in Crime and Delinquency*, *30*(1), 5–22.

8016

Test Name: MARLOWE-CROWNE SOCIAL DESIRABILITY SCALE

Purpose: To measure social desirability.

Number of Items: 33

Format: Responses are true-false.

Reliability: Internal consistency was .88.

Validity: Correlations with other variables ranged from .22 to .54.

Author: Buelow, G., et al.

Article: A new measure for an important construct: The Attachment and Object Relation Inventory.

Journal: *Journal of Personality Assessment*, June 1996, *66*(3), 604–623.

Related Research: Crowne, D. P., & Marlowe, D. (1960). A new scale of social desirability independent of psychopathology. *Journal of Counseling Psychology*, 24, 349–354.

8017

Test Name: MARLOWE-CROWNE SOCIAL DESIRABILITY SCALE— FORM C

Purpose: To measure social desirability.

Number of Items: 13

Format: True–false format. Examples are presented.

Reliability: Coefficient alpha was .68.

Validity: Correlation with other variables ranged from −.09 to .26.

Author: Kelly, A. E.

Article: Clients' secret keeping in outpatient therapy.

Journal: *Journal of Counseling Psychology*, January 1998, *45*(1), 50–57.

Related Research: Reynolds, W. M. (1982). Development of

reliable and valid short forms of the Marlowe-Crowne Social Desirability Scale. *Journal of Clinical Psychology*, 38, 119–125.

8018

Test Name: MARLOWE-CROWNE SOCIAL DESIRABILITY SCALE— SHORT FORM

Purpose: To measure an individual's tendencies to respond in a socially desirable manner.

Number of Items: 10

Format: Employs a true-false format.

Reliability: Internal consistencies ranged from .61 to .70.

Author: Johnson, C. E., and Petrie, T. A.

Article: Relationship of gender discrepancy to psychological correlates of disordered eating in female undergraduates.

Journal: *Journal of Counseling Psychology*, October 1996, *43*(4), 473–479.

Related Research: Strahan, R., & Gerbesi, K. C. (1972). Short, homogenous versions of the Marlowe-Crowne Social Desirability Scale. *Journal of Clinical Psychology*, 28, 191–193.

8019

Test Name: MIVILLE-GUZMAN UNIVERSALITY–DIVERSITY SCALE

Purpose: To measure universal diversity.

Number of Items: 45

Format: Includes 3 subscales: Relativistic Appreciation, Diversity of Contact, and Sense of Connectedness. Responses were made on a 6-point Likert

scale ranging from 1 (strongly disagree) to 6 (strongly agree). Examples are presented.

Reliability: Alpha coefficients range from .89 to .94. Coefficient of stability (1–2 weeks) was .94.

Validity: Correlations with other variables ranges from −.60 to .54.

Author: Miville, M. L., et al.

Article: Appreciating similarities and valuing differences: The Miville-Guzman Universality– Diversity Scale.

Journal: *Journal of Counseling Psychology*, July 1999, *46*(3), 291–307.

8020

Test Name: MULTICULTURAL COMPETENCE IN STUDENT AFFAIRS—PRELIMINARY 2 SCALE

Purpose: To measure multicultural competence in a higher education context (among nonstudents).

Number of Items: 34

Format: Scales range from 1 (not at all accurate) to 7 (very accurate). Sample items are presented.

Reliability: Coefficient alpha was .91.

Validity: Correlations with other variables ranged from −.01 to .66.

Author: Pope, R. L., and Mueller, J. A.

Article: Development and initial validation of the Multicultural Competence in Student Affairs— preliminary 2 scale.

Journal: *Journal of College Student Development*, November/ December 2000, *41*(6), 599–608.

8021

Test Name: MULTICULTURAL SOCIAL DESIRABILITY SCALE

Purpose: To measure a preference to make a good impression on others.

Number of Items: 26

Format: Responses are true or false. Examples are presented.

Reliability: Alpha coefficients were .75 and .80.

Validity: Correlations with other variables ranged from −.11 to .23.

Author: Sodowsky, G. R., et al.

Article: Correlates of self-reported multicultural competencies: Counselor multicultural social desirability, race, social inadequacy, locus of control racial ideology, and multicultural training.

Journal: *Journal of Counseling Psychology*, July 1998, *45*(3), 256–264.

Related Research: Sodowsky, G. R., et al. (1993, August). *Investigating multicultural counseling competencies: Training and service relevance.* Paper presented at the 101st annual convention of the American Psychological Association, Toronto, Ontario, Canada.

8022

Test Name: MULTIDIMENSIONAL ASSESSMENT OF INTERPARENTAL CONFLICT SCALE

Purpose: To assess interparental conflict.

Number of Items: 40

Format: Formats vary. All items are presented.

Reliability: Alpha coefficients

ranged from .52 to .89 across subscales and groups.

Validity: Correlations with other variables ranged from −.47 to .57.

Author: Tschann, J. M., et al.

Article: Assessing interparental conflict: Reports of parents and adolescents in European American and Mexican American families.

Journal: *Journal of Marriage and the Family*, May 1999, *61*(2), 269–283.

8023

Test Name: MULTIDIMENSIONAL INVENTORY OF BLACK IDENTITY

Purpose: To assess racial centrality, racial ideology, and racial regard.

Number of Items: 51

Format: Scales range from 1 (strongly disagree) to 7 (strongly agree).

Reliability: Alpha coefficients ranged from .60 to .79 across racial ideology subscales.

Author: Cokley, K.

Article: Reconceptualizing the impact of college racial composition on African American students' racial identity.

Journal: *Journal of College Student Development*, May/June 1999, *40*(3), 235–246.

Related Research: Sellers, R. M., et al. (1997). Multidimensional Inventory of Black Identity: A preliminary investigation of reliability and validity. *Journal of Personality and Social Psychology, 73*, 808–815.

8024

Test Name: MULTIDIMENSIONAL SCALE OF PERCEIVED SOCIAL SUPPORT

Purpose: To measure social support from family, friends, and a significant other.

Number of Items: 12

Format: Seven-point scales are anchored by 1 (very strongly disagree) and 7 (very strongly agree).

Reliability: Internal consistency was .94.

Author: Short, K. H., and Johnston, C.

Article: Stress, maternal distress, and children's adjustment following immigration: The buffering role of social support.

Journal: *Journal of Consulting and Clinical Psychology*, June 1997, *65*(3), 494–503.

Related Research: Zimet, G. D., et al. (1988). The Multidimensional Scale of Social Support. *Journal of Personality Assessment, 52*, 30–41.

8025

Test Name: MULTIGROUP ETHNIC IDENTITY MEASURE

Purpose: To assess ethnic identity.

Number of Items: 14

Format: Includes items measuring: Ethnic Identity Achievement, Ethnic Behaviors and Practices, and Ethnic Affirmation and Belonging.

Reliability: Alpha coefficients ranged from .77 to .80.

Author: Markstrom, C. A., and Hunter, C. L.

Article: The roles of ethnic and ideological identity in predicting fidelity in African American and European American adolescents.

Journal: *Child Study Journal*, 1999, *29*(1), 23–38.

Related Research: Phinney, J. S. (1992). The Multigroup Ethnic Identity Measure: A new scale for use with adolescents and young adults from diverse groups. *Journal of Adolescent Research*, 2, 156–176.

8026

Test Name: MULTIGROUP ETHNIC IDENTITY MEASURE

Purpose: To assess identification with and degree of interaction with a subculture.

Number of Items: 20

Format: Scales range from 1 (strongly disagree) to 4 (strongly agree). Sample items are presented for lesbian/gay/bisexual subcultures.

Reliability: Coefficient alpha was .80.

Validity: Correlations with other variables ranged from −.47 to .37.

Author: Mohr, J., and Fassinger, R.

Article: Measuring dimensions of lesbian and gay male experience.

Journal: *Measurement and Evaluation in Counseling and Development*, July 2000, *33*(2), 66–90.

Related Research: Phinney, J. S. (1992). The multigroup ethnic identity measure: A new scale for use with diverse groups. *Journal of Adolescent Research*, 7, 156–176.

8027

Test Name: MULTIGROUP ETHNIC IDENTITY MEASURE

Purpose: To measure ethnic identity and achievement, affirmation and belonging, behavior, and group orientation.

Number of Items: 23

Format: Scales range from 1 (strongly disagree) to 4 (strongly agree). All items are presented.

Reliability: Internal reliabilities ranged from .74 to .90 across two scales.

Validity: Correlations with other variables ranged from −.04 to .46.

Author: Lee, R. M., and Davis, C., III.

Article: Cultural orientation, past multicultural experience, and a sense of belonging on campus for Asian American college students.

Journal: *Journal of College Student Development*, January/February 2000, *41*(1), 110–115.

Related Research: Phinney, J. (1992). The Multigroup Identity Measure: A new scale for use with diverse groups. *Journal of Adolescent Research*, 7, 156–176.

8028

Test Name: MULTILEVEL ASSESSMENT INSTRUMENT

Purpose: To assess participation in social and recreational activities.

Number of Items: 16

Format: Frequency scales range from 0 (never) to 5 (12 or more times).

Reliability: Alphas were .57 and .60 in two subgroups.

Author: Haley, W. E., et al.

Article: Appraisal, coping and social support as mediators of well-being in Black and White caregivers of patients with Alzheimer's disease.

Journal: *Journal of Consulting and Clinical Psychology*, February 1996, *64*(1), 121–129.

Related Research: Lawton, M. P., et al. (1982). A research and service oriented multilevel assessment instrument. *Journal of Gerontology*, 37, 91–99.

8029

Test Name: NAME CALLING SURVEY

Purpose: To measure the extent to which children experience being called different types of names.

Number of Items: 35

Format: Yes/no format.

Reliability: Coefficient alpha was .89.

Author: Dennis, M. J. B., and Satcher, J.

Article: Name calling and the peer beliefs of elementary school children.

Journal: *Professional School Counseling*, December 1999, *3*(2), 76–80.

Related Research: Embry, S. L. (1995). Types of name calling experienced by second, third, fourth, fifth and sixth graders and their beliefs about their peers. *Dissertation Abstracts International*, 56, 3905. (Doctoral dissertation, University of Alabama, Tuscaloosa).

8030

Test Name: NEGATIVE DOMINANCE SCALE

Purpose: To assess to what extent a person feels driven to actions that are opposed to those of another person or agency.

Number of Items: 14

Format: Three-point response

scales are "negativistic,"
"conformist," and "not sure."

Reliability: Alpha was .80.

Author: Turner, S., and
Heskin, K.

Article: Metamotivational
dominance and use of tobacco
and alcohol among adolescents.

Journal: *Psychological Reports*,
August 1998, *83*(1), 307–315.

Related Research: McDermott,
M. R., & Apter, M. J. (1988).
The Negative Dominance Scale.
In M. J. Apter et al. (Eds.),
Progress in reversal theory (pp.
373–376). Amsterdam: Elsevier.

8031

Test Name: NETWORK
ACTIVITY SCALE

Purpose: To measure church/
community activities and leisure
activities.

Number of Items: 6

Format: Scale anchors are 1
(much less) and 5 (much more).
Sample items are presented.

Reliability: Coefficient alpha was
.73 (church) and .69 (leisure).

Validity: Correlations with other
variables ranged from −.24 to
.19.

Author: Gowan, M. A., et al.

Article: Test of a model of coping
with involuntary job loss
following a company closing.

Journal: *Journal of Applied
Psychology*, February 1999,
84(1), 75–86.

8032

Test Name: NETWORK OF
RELATIONSHIPS INVENTORY

Purpose: To assess adolescents'
perceptions of supportive and

negative interactions with mother
and best friend.

Number of Items: 30

Format: Includes two factors:
Support and Negative
Interactions. Responses are made
on a 5-point scale ranging from 1
(little or none) to 5 (the most).

Reliability: Alpha coefficients for
the factors were greater than .90.

Author: Gavin, L. A., and
Furman, W.

Article: Adolescent girls'
relationships with mothers and
best friends.

Journal: *Child Development*,
April 1996, *67*(2), 375–386.

Related Research: Furman, W., &
Buhrmester, D. (1985).
Children's perceptions of the
personal relationship in their
social networks. *Developmental
Psychology*, *21*, 1016–1024.

8033

Test Name: NETWORK OF
RELATIONSHIPS INVENTORY

Purpose: To measure children's
perceptions of specific, significant
personal relationships in their
social environment.

Number of Items: 33

Format: Includes 9 Relationship
Attributes: Reliable Alliance,
Admiration, Companionship,
Instrumental Aid, Affection,
Intimacy, Relative Power,
Satisfaction, and Relationship
Importance. Employs a 5-point
Likert scale.

Reliability: Internal consistency
coefficients were .80 and .92.

Author: Jackson, Y., and Warren,
J. S.

Article: Appraisal, social support,
and life events: Predicting
outcome behavior in school-age
children.

Journal: *Child Development*,
September/October 2000, *71*(5),
1441–1457.

Related Research: Furman, W., &
Buhrmester, D. (1985).
Children's perceptions of the
social relationships in their social
networks. *Developmental
Psychology*, *22*, 297–304.

8034

Test Name: NETWORKING
COMFORT AND NETWORKING
INTENSITY SCALES

Purpose: To assess comfort level
with the idea of networking and
the frequency and thoroughness
of using networking.

Number of Items: 17

Format: Scales range from 1
(strongly disagree) to 5 (strongly
agree) for the comfort scale.
Frequency scales are employed in
the Use scale. All items are
presented.

Reliability: Coefficient alpha was
.79 (comfort) and .89 (intensity).

Validity: Correlations with other
variables ranged from −.19 to
.49.

Author: Wanberg, C. R., et al.

Article: Predictors and outcomes
of networking intensity among
unemployed job seekers.

Journal: *Journal of Applied
Psychology*, August 2000, *85*(4),
491–503.

8035

Test Name: OTHER GROUP
ORIENTATION SUBSCALE

Purpose: To measure regularity
of social interaction with
heterosexual people.

Number of Items: 6

Format: Responses are made on a
4-point scale ranging from 1

(strongly agree) to 5 (strongly disagree). An example is presented

Reliability: Alpha coefficients were .75 and .85.

Validity: Correlations with other variables ranged from .00 to .45.

Author: Mohr, J. J., and Rochlen, A. B.

Article: Measuring attitudes regarding bisexuality in lesbian, gay male, and heterosexual populations.

Journal: *Journal of Counseling Psychology*, July 1999, *46*(3), 353–369.

Related Research: Phinney, J. S. (1992). The multigroup ethnic identity measure: A new scale for use with diverse groups. *Journal of Adolescent Research*, 7, 156–176.

8036

Test Name: PEER NOMINATION INVENTORY

Purpose: To measure social rejection and bullying by peers.

Number of Items: Up to 3 peers are nominated. Three bullying/ aggression items.

Format: Liking and disliking scores are used to calculate social preference scores.

Reliability: Alpha coefficients for bullying/aggression ranged from .91 to .94.

Author: Schwartz, D., and Proctor, L. J.

Article: Community violence exposure and children's social adjustment in the school peer group: The mediating roles of emotion regulation and social cognition.

Journal: *Journal of Consulting and Clinical Psychology*, August 2000, *68*(4), 670–683.

Related Research: Schwartz, D., et al (1987). The early socialization of aggressive victims of bullying. *Child Development*, *68*, 665–675.

8037

Test Name: PERCEIVED CONTROL OVER LONELINESS SCALE

Purpose: To measure perceived control over loneliness.

Number of Items: 4

Format: Sample items are presented.

Reliability: Alpha coefficients ranged from .58 to .83.

Validity: Correlations with other variables ranged from −.28 to .28.

Author: Neto, F.

Article: Loneliness and adaptation among second-generation Portuguese migrants to France: Roles of perceived responsibility and control.

Journal: *Perceptual and Motor Skills*, August 2000, *91*(1), 115–119.

Related Research: Moore, D., and Schultz, N. (1987). Loneliness among elderly: The role of perceived responsibility and control. In M. Hojat & R. Crandall (Eds.), *Loneliness: Theory, research, and applications* (pp. 215–224). Newbury Park, CA: Sage.

8038

Test Name: PERCEIVED SOCIAL SUPPORT (FRIENDS AND FAMILY)

Number of Items: 40

Format: Respondents do or do not endorse each item.

Reliability: Internal consistency ranged from .88 to .90.

Author: Schuldberg, D., et al.

Article: Stress, coping, and social support in hypothetically psychosis-prone subjects.

Journal: *Psychological Reports*, June 1996, *78*(3) Part 2, 1267–1283.

Related Research: Procidano, M. E., & Heller, K. (1983). Measures of perceived social support from friends and from family: Three validation studies. *American Journal of Community Psychology*, *11*, 1–24.

8039

Test Name: PERCEPTIONS OF INCLUSION / EXCLUSION SURVEY

Purpose: To measure isolation.

Number of Items: 18

Format: Five-point scales are anchored by (1) strongly disagree and (5) strongly agree. All items presented.

Reliability: Alpha was .84.

Validity: Correlations with Dean's Alienation Scale ranged from .19 to .36.

Author: Smith, J. W.

Article: Preliminary development of an alternative measure of isolation: The construct of institution isolation.

Journal: *Psychological Reports*, June 1998, *83*(2) Part 2, 1323–1330.

8040

Test Name: PERSONAL ASSESSMENT OF INTIMACY IN RELATIONSHIPS

Purpose: To measure ambivalence, conflict and love.

Number of Items: 20

Format: Five-point scales.

Reliability: Alpha coefficients ranged from .69 to .84.

Validity: Correlations with other variables ranged from −.40 to .22.

Author: Bradley, R. H., et al.

Article: Parents' socioemotional investment in children.

Journal: *Journal of Marriage and the Family*, February 1997, *59*(1), 77–90.

Related Research: Schaefer, M. T., & Olson, D. H. (1981). Assessing intimacy: The Pair Inventory. *Journal of Marital and Family Therapy*, 7, 47–59.

8041

Test Name: PERSONAL STYLE INVENTORY

Purpose: To measure social desirability and negative affectivity.

Number of Items: 75

Format: Yes/no format. Sample items are presented.

Reliability: Alpha was .88. Test-retest reliability was .89 (2 weeks).

Author: Sheridan, C. L., et al.

Article: The role of social desirability, negative affectivity, and female reproductive system symptoms in differences in reporting symptoms by men and women.

Journal: *Psychological Reports*, August 1999, *85*(1), 54–62.

Related Research: Sheridan, C. L., & Radmacher, S. A. (1998). The Personal Style Inventory: A measure of stress resiliency. In C. P. Zalaquett & R. J. Woods (Eds.), *Evaluating stress: A book of resources*. Vol.

2. Landham, MD: Scarecrow/ University Press.

8042

Test Name: PICTORIAL SCALE OF PERCEIVED COMPETENCE AND SOCIAL ACCEPTANCE FOR YOUNG CHILDREN

Purpose: To assess self-concept: cognitive competence, peer acceptance, physical competence and maternal acceptance.

Number of Items: 24

Format: Pictorial format. Children point to pictures designed to elicit their self-perceptions.

Reliability: Internal consistency coefficients ranged from .50 to .80 across scales and subgroups.

Validity: Correlations with teacher ratings ranged from −.09 to .51.

Author: Strein, W., and Simonson, T.

Article: Kindergartners' self-perceptions: Theoretical and measurement issues.

Journal: *Measurement and Evaluation in Counseling and Development*, April 1999, *32*(1), 31–42.

Related Research: Harter, S., & Pike, R. (1984). The pictorial scale of perceived competence and social acceptance for young children. *Child Development*, 55, 1969–1982.

8043

Test Name: POSITIVE RELATIONS SCALE

Purpose: To measure one's degree of positive relations with others.

Number of Items: 14

Format: Responses are made on a

6-point Likert-type scale ranging from 1 (strongly disagree) to 6 (strongly agree).

Reliability: Internal consistency estimate was .88.

Validity: Correlations with other variables ranged from −.43 to .73 (*N* = 294).

Author: Robitschek, C., and Kashubeck, S.

Article: A structural model of parental alcoholism, family functioning, and psychological health: The mediating effects of hardiness and personal growth orientation.

Journal: *Journal of Counseling Psychology*, April 1999, *46*(2), 159–172.

Related Research: Ryff, C. D. (1989). Happiness is everything, or is it? Explorations on the meaning of psychological well-being. *Journal of Personality and Social Psychology*, 57, 1069–1081.

8044

Test Name: POWER SCALES

Purpose: To assess perceived level and satisfaction with power in an intimate relationship.

Number of Items: 11

Format: Various formats are used. All items are described.

Reliability: Alpha coefficients ranged from .62 (perceived power) to .74 (power satisfaction).

Validity: Correlations with other variables ranged from −.23 to .20.

Author: Ronfeldt, H. M., et al.

Article: Satisfaction with relationship power and the perpetration of dating violence.

Journal: *Journal of Marriage and*

the Family, February 1998, *60*(1), 70–78.

8045

Test Name: PREMARITAL RELATIONSHIP QUESTIONNAIRE

Purpose: To measure feelings of belonging, amount of communication, feelings of confusion, and amount of conflict.

Number of Items: 25

Reliability: Alpha coefficients ranged from .65 to .84 across subscales and gender.

Validity: Correlations between three subscales and other variables ranged from −.58 to .59.

Author: Houts, R. M., et al.

Article: Compatibility and the development of premarital relationships.

Journal: *Journal of Marriage and the Family*, February 1996, *58*(1), 7–20.

Related Research: Braiker, H. B., & Kelley, H. H. (1979). Conflict in the development of close relationships. In R. L. Burgess & T. L. Huston (Eds.), *Social exchange in developing relationships* (pp. 135–168). New York: Academic Press.

Christopher, F. S., et al. (1998). Premarital sexual aggressors: A multivariate analysis of social, relational, and individual variables. *Journal of Marriage and the Family*, *60*, 56–69.

Rubin, Z. (1970). Measurement of romantic love. *Journal of Personality and Social Psychology*, *16*, 591–604.

Johnson, M. P. (1999). The tripartite nature of marital commitment: Personal, moral and structural reasons to stay

married. *Journal of Marriage and the Family*, *61*, 160–177.

Bumpas, M. F., et al. (1999). Work demands of dual-earner couples: Implications for parents' knowledge about children's daily lives in middle childhood. *Journal of Marriage and the Family*, *61*, 465–475.

8046

Test Name: PRESCHOOL COMPETENCE QUESTIONNAIRE

Purpose: To measure social competence.

Format: Includes 3 dimensions: Peer Behavior, Cooperativeness, and Empathy.

Reliability: Alpha coefficients were .89 and .85.

Validity: Correlations with other variables ranged from −.16 to .22.

Author: Denham, S. A., and Burton, R.

Article: A social-emotional intervention for at-risk 4-year-olds.

Journal: *Journal of Child Psychology*, Fall 1996, *33*(3), 225–245.

Related Research: Olson, S. L. (1989). Assessment of impulsivity in preschoolers: Cross-measure convergences, longitudinal stability, and relevance to social competence. *Journal of Clinical Child Psychology*, *18*, 176–183.

8047

Test Name: PRESCHOOL SOCIAL BEHAVIOR QUESTIONNAIRE

Purpose: To measure preschoolers' positive and negative aspects of social behavior.

Number of Items: 29

Format: Includes 3 subscales: Disruptive, Anxious, and Prosocial. Responses are made on a 3-point scale ranging from 0 (does not apply) to 2 (frequently/certainly applies).

Reliability: Alpha coefficients ranged from .66 to .81.

Author: Verschueren, K., and Marcoen, A.

Article: Representation of self and socioemotional competence in kindergartners: Differential and combined effects of attachment to mother and to father.

Journal: *Child Development*, January/February 1999, *70*(1), 183–201

Related Research: Tremblay, R. E., et al. (1992). A prosocial scale for the Preschool Behavior Questionnaire: Concurrent and predictive correlates. *International Journal of Behavioral Development*, *15*, 227–245.

8048

Test Name: RACIAL STRUGGLES SOCIALIZATION SUBSCALE

Purpose: To measure teenager experiences of racial socialization.

Number of Items: 8

Format: Responses are made on a 3-point scale ranging from 1 (never) to 3 (lots of times). An example is presented.

Reliability: Alpha coefficients were .71 and .74.

Validity: Correlations with other variables ranged from −.05 to .10.

Author: Fischer, A. R., and Shaw, C. M.

Article: African Americans' mental health and perceptions of racist discrimination. The moderating effects of racial socialization experiences and self-esteem.

Journal: *Journal of Counseling Psychology*, July 1999, *46*(3), 395–407.

Related Research: Stevenson, H. C., et al. (1998). *Merging the ideal and the real: Relationship of racial socialization beliefs and experiences.* Unpublished manuscript, University of Pennsylvania, Philadelphia.

8049

Test Name: RACISM AND LIFE EXPERIENCE SCALE—BRIEF VERSION

Purpose: To measure minority group members' perceptions of the impact of racism on their lives.

Number of Items: 32

Format: Includes two parts: Perceived Racism-Self and Perceived Racism-Group.

Reliability: Alpha coefficients ranged from .83 to .90.

Validity: Correlations with the Index of Race Related Stress ranged from −.02 to .46.

Author: Utsey, S. O., and Ponterott, J. G.

Article: Developments and validation of the index of race-related stress (IRRS).

Journal: *Journal of Personality Assessment*, October 1996, *43*(4), 490–501.

Related Research: Wells, T. (1995). *Learned effectiveness: The role of self-efficacy, racial identity, and perceptions of racism in the adaptive functioning of African American youth.* Unpublished doctoral dissertation, California School of Professional Psychology, Los Angeles.

8050

Test Name: RACISM AND POLITICAL ACTIVISM SCALES

Purpose: To assess experiences involving racial slurs or comments and extent of involvement in political activism stemming from social inequity.

Number of Items: 17

Format: Racism Experience scales range from 0 (did not occur) to 3 (frequently occurs), and racism Impact scales from 0 (none) to 4 (severe). Five-point Activism scales were used.

Reliability: Coefficient alpha was .80 (Racism). Inter-item consistency was .96 (Activism).

Validity: Correlations with other variables ranged from −.41 to .59.

Authors: Thompson-Sanders, V. L.

Article: Variables affecting racial identity salience among African Americans.

Journal: *The Journal of Social Psychology*, December 1999, *139*(6), 748–761.

Related Research: Thompson-Sanders, V. L. (1995). Socio-cultural influences on African American racial identification. *Journal of Applied Social Psychology, 25*, 1411–1429.

8051

Test Name: RELATEDNESS QUESTIONNAIRE

Purpose: To measure children's perceptions of the emotional quality of their relationships and how close they feel to their relationship partners.

Number of Items: 17

Format: Includes two subscales: emotional quality and psychological proximity seeking.

Four-point scales are used for responding to the items. Sample items are presented.

Reliability: Alpha coefficients ranged from .67 to .93.

Author: Lynch, M., and Cicchetti, D.

Article: Children's relationships with adults and peers: An examination of elementary and junior high school students.

Journal: *Journal of School Psychology*, Spring 1997, *35*(1), 81–99.

Related Research: Lynch, M. (1992). *Modes of linkage between relationship disturbances and maladaptation: Issues in the area of child maltreatment.* Unpublished doctoral dissertation, University of Rochester.

8052

Test Name: RELATIONAL REPAIR STRATEGY SCALES

Purpose: To assess attempts to repair relationships damaged by deception.

Number of Items: 24

Format: Seven-point scales range from "not relevant" to "very relevant." All items are presented.

Reliability: Alpha coefficients ranged from .27 to .83 across subscales.

Validity: Correlations with other variables ranged from −.12 to .45.

Authors: Aune, R. K., et al.

Article: Managing outcomes of discovered deception.

Journal: *Journal of Social Psychology*, December 1998, *138*(6), 677–689.

Related Research: Aune, R. K., et al. (1990). *Managing the*

discovery of deception. Paper presented at the speech communication convention, Chicago, IL.

8053

Test Name: RELATIONAL TRUST SCALES

Purpose: To measure confidence in romantic relationships, confidence in self-disclosure, and confidence in close relationships.

Number of Items: 27

Reliability: Alpha coefficients ranged from .71 to .93.

Validity: Correlations with other variables ranged from to .42 to .82.

Author: Couch, L. L., and Jones, W. H.

Article: Measuring levels of trust.

Journal: *Journal of Research in Personality,* September 1997, *31*(3), 319–336.

Related Research: Rempel, J. K., et al. (1985). Trust in close relationships. *Journal of Personality and Social Psychology, 49,* 95–112.
Johnson-George, C., & Swap, W. (1982). Measurement of specific interpersonal trust: Construction and validation of a scale to assess trust in a specific order. *Journal of Personality and Social Psychology, 43,* 1306–1317.
Lazelere, R. E., & Huston, T. L. (1980). The Dyadic Trust Scale: Toward understanding interpersonal trust in close relationships. *Journal of Marriage and the Family, 42,* 595–604.

8054

Test Name: RELATIONSHIP ASSESSMENT SCALE

Purpose: To measure general satisfaction in a relationship.

Number of Items: 7

Format: Five-point scales. Sample items are presented.

Reliability: Alpha coefficients ranged from .75 to .87. Test-retest reliabilities ranged from .54 to .64.

Validity: Correlations with other variables ranged from −.17 to .29.

Author: Sprecher, S.

Article: The effect of exchange orientation on close relationships.

Journal: *Social Psychology Quarterly,* September 1998, *61*(3), 220–231.

Related Research: Hendrick, S. (1988). A generic measure of relationship satisfaction. *Journal of Marriage and the Family, 50,* 93–98.

8055

Test Name: RELATIONSHIP CLOSENESS INVENTORY

Purpose: To measure the degree of closeness in relationships.

Number of Items: 3

Format: Ten-point scales rate frequency, diversity, and strength of relationships.

Reliability: Test-retest reliability (5 weeks) was .82.

Authors: Yaugn, E., and Nowicki, S., Jr.

Article: Close relationships and complementary interpersonal styles among men and women.

Journal: *The Journal of Social Psychology,* August 1999, *139*(4), 473–478.

Related Research: Berscheid, E., et al. (1989). The Relationship Closeness Inventory: Assessing the closeness of interpersonal

relationships. *Journal of Personality and Social Psychology, 57,* 792–807.

8056

Test Name: RELATIONSHIP COMMITMENT SCALE

Purpose: To measure commitment to a relationship.

Number of Items: 5

Format: Nine-point Likert format.

Reliability: Alphas ranged from .91 to .93.

Author: Christopher, F. S., et al.

Article: Premarital sexual aggressors: A multivariate analysis of social, relational, and individual variables.

Journal: *Journal of Marriage and the Family,* February 1998, *60*(1), 56–69.

Related Research: Rusbult, C. (1983). A longitudinal test of the investment model: The development (and deterioration) of satisfaction and commitment in heterosexual involvement. *Journal of Personality and Social Psychology, 45,* 101–117.

8057

Test Name: RELATIONSHIP ORIENTATION SCALE

Purpose: To measure exchange and communal orientation.

Number of Items: 11

Format: Scales range from 1 (strongly disagree) to 19 (strongly agree). A sample item is presented.

Reliability: Coefficient alpha was .76.

Authors: Zak, A. M, et al.

Article: Assessments of trust in intimate relationships and the self-perception process.

Journal: *Journal of Social Psychology*, April 1998, *138*(2), 217–228.

Related Research: Zak, A. M., & Gold, J. A. (1991). *Relation styles revisited*. Unpublished manuscript, University of Maine.

8058

Test Name: RESPONSIBILITY FOR LONELINESS SCALE

Purpose: To measure responsibility for loneliness.

Number of Items: 4

Format: Examples are presented.

Reliability: Alpha coefficients ranged from .66 to .85.

Validity: Correlations with other variables ranged from −.17 to .22.

Author: Neto, F.

Article: Loneliness and adaptation among second-generation Portuguese migrants to France: Roles of perceived responsibility and control.

Journal: *Perceptual and Motor Skills*, August 2000, *91*(1), 115–119.

Related Research: Moore, D., & Schultz, N. (1987). Loneliness among elderly: The role of perceived responsibility and control. In M. Hojat & R. Crandall (Eds.), *Loneliness: Theory, research, and applications* (pp. 215–224). Newbury Park, CA: Sage.

8059

Test Name: THE REVERSE SOCIAL DISTANCE SCALE

Purpose: To assess how respondents perceive how they are accepted by others in five roles.

Number of Items: 5

Format: Yes/no format. All items are presented.

Reliability: Guttman's coefficient of reproducibility was .99.

Author: Lee, M. Y., et al.

Article: The Reverse Social Distance scale.

Journal: *Journal of Social Psychology*, February 1996, *136*(1), 17–24.

Related Research: Bogardus, E. S. (1925). Measuring social distance. *Journal of Applied Sociology*, *9*, 299–308.

8060

Test Name: REVISED EXCHANGE ORIENTATION SCALE

Purpose: To measure under-benefiting and overbenefiting exchange orientations.

Number of Items: 40

Format: Scales range from 1 (strongly disagree/definitely not) to 5 (strongly agree/definitely yes). All items are presented.

Reliability: Alpha coefficients ranged from .66 to .84. Test-retest reliabilities ranged from .60 to .75.

Validity: Correlations with other variables ranged from −.22 to .29.

Author: Sprecher, S.

Article: The effect of exchange orientation on close relationships.

Journal: *Social Psychology Quarterly*, September 1998, *61*(3), 220–231.

Related Research: Murstein, B. I., et al. (1987). The Revised Exchange Orientation Scale. *Small Group Behavior*, *18*, 212–223.

8061

Test Name: RIGHT-WING EXTREMISM SCALE

Purpose: To assess ethnocentrism, negative attitude towards democratic values, and exaggerated nationalism.

Number of Items: 16

Format: Scales range from 1 (strongly disagree) to 5 (strongly agree). All items are presented.

Reliability: Alpha coefficients ranged from .51 to .81.

Validity: Correlations with a left-right criterion variable ranged from .42 to .55

Author: Rippl, S., and Seipel, C.

Article: Gender differences in right wing extremism: Intergroup validity of a second-order construct.

Journal: *Social Psychology Quarterly*, December 1999, *62*(4), 381–393.

8062

Test Name: RISK IN INTIMACY INVENTORY

Purpose: To assess one's perception of risk in close relationships.

Number of Items: 10

Format: Responses are made on a 6-point Likert scale.

Reliability: Coefficient alpha was .80.

Validity: Correlation with other variables ranged from −.43 to .38 ($N = 152$).

Author: Mothersead, P. K., et al.

Article: Attachment, family dysfunction, parental alcoholism, and interpersonal distress in late adolescence: A structural model.

Journal: *Journal of Counseling*

Psychology, April 1998, *45*(2), 196–203.

Related Research: Pilkington, C. J., & Richardson, D. R. (1988). Perceptions of risk in intimacy. *Journal of Social and Personal Relationships*, 5, 503–508.

8063

Test Name: ROMANTIC RELATIONSHIP SATISFACTION AND COMMITMENT SCALE

Purpose: To measure satisfaction with and commitment to a romantic relationship.

Number of Items: 25

Reliability: Coefficient alpha exceeded .75.

Validity: Correlations with other variables ranged from .35 to .81.

Author: Couch, L. L., and Jones, W. H.

Article: Measuring levels of trust.

Journal: *Journal of Research in Personality*, September 1997, *31*(3), 319–336.

Related Research: Jones, W. H., et al. (1995). A psychometric exploration of marital satisfaction and commitment. *Journal of Social Behavior and Personality*, 10, 923–932.

8064

Test Name: SCALE OF SOCIAL SKILL

Purpose: To measure basic and high-level skills, skills for dealing with feelings, stress, and planning.

Number of Items: 17

Format: Five-point scales are anchored by 1 (not at all) and 5 (very strongly). All items are presented in English.

Reliability: Alphas ranged from .36 to .79 across subscales.

Author: Matsushima, R., et al.

Article: Shyness in self-disclosure mediated by social skill.

Journal: *Psychological Reports*, February 2000, *86*(1), 333–338.

Related Research: Kikuchi, A. (1998). [Scientific study of thoughtfulness]. Tokyo: Kawashimasyoten [in Japanese].

8065

Test Name: SCHEDULE OF RACIAL EVENTS—REVISED

Purpose: To measure how often African Americans report experiencing particular racist events.

Number of Items: 18

Format: Includes 2 subscales: Year and Lifetime. Responses are made on a 6-point scale ranging from 1 (never) to 6 (almost all of the time). A sample item is presented.

Reliability: Internal consistency estimates ranged from .89 to .95. Split-half reliability coefficients were .93 (Year) and .91 (Lifetime).

Validity: Correlations with other variables ranged from −.14 to .19.

Author: Fischer, A. R., and Shaw, C. M.

Article: African Americans' mental health and perceptions of racist discrimination. The moderating effects of racial socialization experiences and self-esteem.

Journal: *Journal of Counseling Psychology*, July 1999, *46*(3), 395–407.

Related Research: Landrine, H., & Klonoff, E. A. (1996). The Schedule of Racist Events: A

measure of racial discrimination and a study of its negative physical and mental health consequences. *Journal of Black Psychology*, 22, 144–168.

8066

Test Name: SELF-EVALUATION OF BIASES AND PREJUDICES SCALE

Purpose: To assess biases and prejudices in regard to ethnic groups.

Number of Items: 10

Format: Scales are anchored by 1 (very much) and 3 (not at all). All items are presented.

Reliability: Alpha was .87.

Author: Paniagua, F. A., et al.

Article: Self-evaluation of unintended biases and prejudices.

Journal: *Psychological Reports*, December 2000, *87*(3, Part 1), 823–829.

Related Research: Paniagua, F. A. (1998). Assessing and treating culturally diverse clients: A practical guide (2nd ed.). Newbury Park, CA: Sage.

8067

Test Name: SENSE OF COMMUNITY SCALE

Purpose: To measure sense of community.

Number of Items: 5

Format: Four-point closeness scales ranged from "very close" to "not close at all." All items are presented.

Reliability: Alphas ranged from .64 to .70.

Author: Davidson, W. B., and Cotter, P. R.

Article: Psychological sense of

community and newspaper readership.

Journal: *Psychological Reports*, April 1997, *80*(2), 659–665.

Related Research: Davidson, W. B., & Cotter. P. R. (1986). Measurement of sense of community within the sphere of city. *Journal of Applied Social Psychology*, *16*, 608–619.

8068

Test Name: SENSITIVITY TO REJECTION SCALE

Purpose: To examine participant concerns with others' possible rejection of them.

Number of Items: 24

Format: Responses are made on a 7-point scale of agreement-disagreement.

Reliability: Alpha coefficients were .69 and .75.

Author: Jackson, T., et al.

Article: Culture and self-presentation as predictors of shyness among Japanese and American female college students.

Journal: *Perceptual and Motor Skills*, April 2000, *90*(2), 475–482.

Related Research: Mehrabian, A., & Ksionsky, M. (1974). *A theory of affiliation*. Lexington, MA: Lexington Books.

8069

Test Name: SHORT ACCULTURATION SCALE

Purpose: To assess acculturation.

Number of Items: 12

Format: Includes 3 domains: Language Use, Ethnic Social Relations, and Media. Responses are made on a 5-point scale.

Reliability: Alpha coefficients were .87 and .92.

Validity: Correlations with other variables ranged from −.19 to .29.

Author: Abreu, J. M., and Gabarain, G.

Article: Social desirability and Mexican American counselor preferences: Statistical control for a potential confound.

Journal: *Journal of Counseling Psychology*, April 2000, *47*(2), 165–176.

Related Research: Marin, G., et al. (1987). Development of a short acculturation scale for Hispanics. *Hispanic Journal of Behavioral Sciences*, *9*, 183–205.

8070

Test Name: SITUATED IDENTITY SCALE

Purpose: To assess acculturation in terms of Anglophone or Francophone.

Number of Items: 22

Format: Scales range from 0 (not at all Anglophone [or Francophone]) to (very Anglophone [or Francophone]).

Reliability: Coefficient alpha was .93.

Authors: Damji, T., et al.

Article: Acculturation mode, identity variation, and psychosocial adjustment.

Journal: *Journal of Social Psychology*, August 1996, *136*(4), 493–500.

Related Research: Clement, R., & Noels, K. (1992). Toward a situated approach to ethnolinguistic identity: The effects of status on individuals and groups. *Journal of Language and Social Psychology*, *11*, 203–232.

8071

Test Name: SITUATIONAL SOCIAL AVOIDANCE SCALE

Purpose: To assess social avoidance as a behavioral correlate of anxiety.

Number of Items: 15

Format: Seven-point scales are anchored by 1 (almost never) and 7 (almost always). All items are presented.

Reliability: Cronbach alphas ranged from .82 to .92. Test-retest reliability was .86 (65 weeks).

Validity: Correlations with other variables ranged from .21 to .78.

Author: Ishiyama, F. I.

Article: Development and validation of a situational social avoidance scale.

Journal: *Psychological Reports*, August 1999, *85*(1), 114–120.

8072

Test Name: SOCIAL ACCEPTANCE SCALE

Purpose: To measure the social acceptability of persons with habit disorders such as motor tics.

Number of Items: 15

Format: Seven-point Likert format.

Reliability: Alpha was .88. Test-retest reliability (1 week) was .87.

Author: Woods, D. W., et al.

Article: Evaluating the social acceptability of persons with habit disorders: The effects of topography, frequency, and manipulation.

Journal: *Journal of Psychopathology and Behavioral Assessment*, March 1999, *21*(1), 1–18.

Related Research: Woods, D. W., et al. (1997). *Evaluating the social acceptability of persons with tic disorders*. Paper presented at the meeting of the Association of Behavior Analysis, Chicago, IL.

8073

Test Name: SOCIAL ACTIVITY SCALE

Purpose: To assess participation, emotional security, and perceived social competence.

Number of Items: 47

Format: Includes 3 dimensions: Participation, Emotional Security, and Perceived Social Competence. Four-and five-point response scales are employed.

Reliability: Alpha coefficients ranged from .67 to .88.

Author: Stinson, M. S., et al.

Article: Self-perceptions of social relationships in hearing-impaired adolescents.

Journal: *Journal of Educational Psychology*, March 1996, *88*(1), 132–143.

Related Research: Connell, J., & Wellborn, J. (1987). *Manual for the Rochester Assessment Package for Schools (RAPS)*. Unpublished manuscript, University of Rochester.

8074

Test Name: SOCIAL ADJUSTMENT SCALE FOR CHILDREN AND ADOLESCENTS—SPANISH

Purpose: To measure social adjustment.

Number of Items: 22

Format: Three-point scales.

Reliability: Coefficient alpha was .99.

Author: Rossello, J., and Bernal, G.

Article: The efficacy of cognitive-behavioral and interpersonal treatments for depression in Puerto Rican adolescents.

Journal: *Journal of Consulting and Clinical Psychology*, October 1999, *67*(5), 734–745.

Related Research: Beiser, M. (1990). *Final report submitted in fulfillment of requirements for the grants at the United States National Institute of Mental Health (5-RO1-MH36678–04) and the Canada Health and Welfare National Research Directorate Program (NHRDP 6610–1322–04)*. Unpublished manuscript.

8075

Test Name: SOCIAL ADJUSTMENT SUBSCALE

Purpose: To measure social competence.

Number of Items: 20

Format: A subscale of the student Adaptation to College Questionnaire. Responses are made on a 9-point scale ranging from 1 (applies very closely to me) to 9 (doesn't apply to me at all).

Reliability: Alpha coefficient ranged from .76 to .92.

Author: Rice, K. G., et al.

Article: Attachment to parents, social competence, and emotional well-being: A comparison of Black and White adolescents.

Journal: *Journal of Counseling Psychology*, January 1997, *44*(1), 89–101.

Related Research: Baker, R. W., & Siryk, B. (1984). Measuring adjustment to college. *Journal of Counseling Psychology*, *31*, 179–189.

8076

Test Name: SOCIAL ANXIETY SCALE

Purpose: To measure social anxiety.

Number of Items: 5

Format: Responses are made on a 7-point Likert scale.

Reliability: Alpha coefficients ranged from .83 to .85.

Validity: Correlation with other variables ranged from −.77 to .63.

Author: Bruch, M. A., et al.

Article: Shyness, masculine ideology, physical attractiveness, and emotional inexpressiveness: Testing a mediational model of men's interpersonal competence.

Journal: *Journal of Counseling Psychology*, January 1998, *45*(1), 84–97.

Related Research: Fleming, J. S., & Whalen, D. J. (1990). The Personal and Academic Self-Concept Inventory: Factor structure and gender differences in high school and college samples. *Educational and Psychological Measurement*, *50*, 957—967.

8077

Test Name: SOCIAL ANXIETY SCALE

Purpose: To access children's anxiety in terms of social anxiety and social avoidance.

Number of Items: 12

Format: Five-point scales are anchored by 1 (not at all true about me) and 5 (always true about me). Sample items are presented.

Reliability: Alphas ranged from .77 to .81.

Author: Crick, N. R., and Bigbee, M. A.

Article: Relational and overt forms of peer victimization: A multi-informant approach.

Journal: *Journal of Consulting and Clinical Psychology*, April 1998, *66*(2), 337–347.

Related Research: Crick, N. R., & Grotpeter, J. K. (1995). Relational aggression, gender and social-psychological adjustment. *Child Development, 66*, 710–722.

8078

Test Name: SOCIAL ANXIETY SCALE FOR CHILDREN

Purpose: To measure children's feelings of social anxiety.

Number of Items: 10

Format: Includes 3 components: Fear of Negative Evaluation, Social Avoidance, and Social Distress.

Reliability: Coefficient alpha was .76. Test-retest (2 weeks) was .67.

Author: Granger, D. A., et al.

Article: Reciprocal influences among adrenocortical activation, psychological processes, and the behavioral adjustment of clinic-referred children.

Journal: *Child Development*, December 1996, *67*(6), 3250–3362.

Related Research: La Greca, A. M., et al. (1988). Development and validation of the Social Anxiety Scale for Children: Reliability and concurrent validity. *Journal of Clinical Child Psychology, 17*, 84–91.

8079

Test Name: SOCIAL, ATTITUDINAL, FAMILIAL AND ENVIRONMENTAL ACCULTURATION STRESS SCALE

Purpose: To measure Hispanics' acculturation stress.

Number of Items: 21

Format: Scales range from 1 (not stressful) to 5 (extremely stressful). All items are presented.

Reliability: Alpha coefficients ranged from .70 to .88 across subscales.

Validity: Correlations with other variables ranged from .77 to .83.

Author: Fuertes, J. N., and Westbrook, F. D.

Article: Using the Social, Attitudinal, Familial, and Environmental (SAFE) Acculturation Stress Scale to assess the adjustment needs of Hispanic college students.

Journal: *Measurement and Evaluation in Counseling and Development*, July 1996, *29*(2), 67–76.

Related Research: Mena, F. J., et al. (1987). Acculturative stress and specific coping strategies among immigrant and later generation college students. *Hispanic Journal of Behavioral Sciences, 9*, 207–225.

8080

Test Name: SOCIAL, ATTITUDINAL, FAMILIAL, AND ENVIRONMENTAL ACCULTURATION STRESS SCALE—REVISED

Purpose: To measure acculturative stress in social, attitudinal, familial, and environmental contexts.

Number of Items: 24

Format: Responses are made on a 5-point scale ranging from 1 (not stressful) to 5 (extremely stressful). Examples are presented.

Reliability: Alpha coefficients ranged from .65 to .89.

Author: Lee, R. M., et al.

Article: Construction of the Asian American Family Conflicts Scale.

Journal: *Journal of Counseling Psychology*, April 2000, *47*(2), 211–222.

Related Research: Mena, F. J., et al. (1987). Acculturative stress and specific coping strategies among immigrants and later generation college students. *Hispanic Journal of Behavioral Sciences, 9*, 207–225.

8081

Test Name: SOCIAL AVOIDANCE AND DISTRESS SCALE

Purpose: To measure to what extent individuals avoid social situations and experience distress when confronted by situations.

Number of Items: 28

Format: True/false format.

Reliability: KR-2 reliability was .94. Test-retest reliability ranged from .68 to .79.

Validity: Correlation with Social Desirability was −.25.

Author: Avants, S. K., et al.

Article: When is less treatment better? The role of social anxiety in matching methadone patients to psychosocial treatments.

Journal: *Journal of Consulting and Clinical Psychology*, December 1998, *66*(6), 924–931.

Related Research: Watson, D., & Friend, R. (1969). Measurement of social-evaluative anxiety. *Journal of Consulting and Clinical Psychology, 33*, 448–457.

8082

Test Name: SOCIAL BEHAVIOR INHIBITION SCALE

Purpose: To measure discomfort and behavioral inhibition in a variety of social settings.

Number of Items: 20

Format: Responses are made on a 5-point scale ranging from 1 (no discomfort at all with this behavior) to 5 (extreme discomfort engaging in this behavior). Examples are presented.

Reliability: Coefficient alpha was .89, split-half reliability was .81.

Validity: Correlations with other variables ranged from .13 to .46.

Author: Fredrick, C. M., and Morrison, C. S.

Article: A mediational model of social physique anxiety and eating disordered behaviors.

Journal: *Perceptual and Motor Skills*, February 1998, *86*(1), 139–145.

8083

Test Name: SOCIAL BEHAVIOR TOWARD OUTGROUP MEMBER SCALE

Purpose: To measure behavior toward an out-group.

Number of Items: 7

Format: Four-point scales range from ''almost never'' to ''very often.'' All items are presented.

Reliability: K-R 20 reliabilities were .80 (Black) and .90 (White).

Validity: Correlations with other variables ranged from −.20 to .49.

Authors: Bornman, E., and Applegryn, A. E. M.

Article: Ethnolinguistic vitality under a new political dispensation in South Africa.

Journal: *Journal of Social Psychology*, December 1997, *137*(6), 690–707.

8084

Test Name: SOCIAL COMPETENCE RATING SCALE FOR CHILDREN—MODIFIED

Purpose: To measure social competencies of children.

Format: Includes 3 factors: School Competence, Social Competence, and Good Peer Relations.

Reliability: Alpha coefficients ranged from .77 to .84.

Validity: Correlations with other variables ranged from −.31 to .50.

Author: Murray, C., and Greenberg, M. T.

Article: Children's relationship with teachers and bonds with school: An investigation of patterns and correlates in middle school.

Journal: *Journal of School Psychology*, September/October 2000, *38*(5), 425–445.

Related Research: Hightower, D. A., et al. (1986). The Teacher-Child Rating Scale: A brief objective measure of elementary children's school problem behaviors and competencies. *School Psychology Review*, 15, 393–409.

8085

Test Name: SOCIAL COMPETENCE SCALE

Purpose: To assess social competence.

Number of Items: 4

Format: Two-step response procedure. An example is presented.

Reliability: Alpha coefficients ranged from .53 to .92.

Author: Smith, T., and Brody, G. H.

Article: Intra- and extracultural perceptions of competence in rural African-American youth.

Journal: *Journal of School Psychology*, September/October 2000, *38*(5), 407–422.

Related Research: Harter, S. (1982). The Perceived Competence Scale for Children. *Child Development*, 53, 87–97.

8086

Test Name: SOCIAL COMPETENCE SCALE

Purpose: To measure a child's social competence with peers.

Number of Items: 14

Format: Includes 3 scores: Difficult, Hesitant, and Sociable.

Reliability: Alpha coefficients ranged from .90 to .94.

Author: Farver, J. A. M., and Frosch, D. L.

Article: L. A. stories: Aggression in preschoolers' spontaneous narratives after the riots of 1992.

Journal: *Child Development*, February 1996, *67*(1), 19–32.

Related Research: Howes, C. (1988). Peer interaction of young children. *Monographs of the Society for Research in Child Development*, 53, (Serial No. 217).

8087

Test Name: SOCIAL COMPETENCE SCALE— PARENT FORM

Purpose: To assess prosocial behavior and emotion regulation.

Number of Items: 12

Format: Five-point scales.

Reliability: Coefficient alpha was .87.

Author: Conduct Problems Prevention Research Group

Article: Initial impact of the fast track prevention trial for conduct problems: I. The high risk sample.

Journal: *Journal of Consulting and Clinical Psychology*, October 1999, *67*(5), 631–647.

Related Research: Conduct Problems Prevention Research Group. (1999). *Technical reports for the Fast Track Assessment Battery*. Unpublished manuscript.

8088

Test Name: SOCIAL DESIRABILITY QUESTIONNAIRE

Purpose: To measure social desirability.

Number of Items: 14

Format: Yes/no format.

Reliability: Coefficient alpha was .80.

Author: Eisenberg, N., et al.

Article: The relations of children's dispositional prosocial behavior to emotionality, regulation, and social functioning.

Journal: *Child Development*, June 1996, *67*(3), 974–992.

Related Research: Crandall, V. C., et al. (1965). A child's social desirability questionnaire. *Journal of Consulting Psychology*, *29*, 27–36.

8089

Test Name: SOCIAL DESIRABILITY QUESTIONNAIRE

Purpose: To measure social desirability.

Number of Items: 22

Format: True/false format.

Reliability: Coefficient alpha was .73.

Author: Eisenberg, N., et al.

Article: The relations of children's dispositional prosocial behavior to emotionality, regulation, and social functioning.

Journal: *Child Development*, June 1996, *67*(3), 974–992.

Related Research: Crowne, D. P., & Marlowe, D. (1964). *The approval motive*. New York: Wiley.

8090

Test Name: SOCIAL DESIRABILITY SCALE

Purpose: To measure one's tendency to present one's self in a socially desirable light by biasing self-reports.

Number of Items: 33

Format: Responses are made on a 7-point scale.

Reliability: Coefficient alpha was .58.

Author: Crowell, J. A., et al.

Article: Discriminant validity of the Adult Attachment Interview.

Journal: *Child Development*, October 1996, *67*(5), 2584–2599.

Related Research: Bakermans-Kranenburg, M., & van Ijzendoorn, M. (1993). A psychometric study of the Adult Attachment Interview: Reliability and discriminant validity. *Developmental Psychology*, *29*, 870–879.

8091

Test Name: SOCIAL EXPERIENCE QUESTIONNAIRE—PEER AND SELF-REPORT

Purpose: To assess peer perception of children's positive and negative treatment by peers.

Number of Items: 26

Format: All items are presented. Scales are anchored by 1 (never) and 5 (all the time).

Reliability: Alpha coefficients ranged from .68 to .93.

Validity: Correlations with reported victimization ranged from .31 to .39.

Author: Crick, N. R., and Bigbee, M. A.

Article: Relational and overt forms of peer victimization: A multi-informant approach.

Journal: *Journal of Consulting and Clinical Psychology*, April 1998, *66*(2), 337–347.

8092

Test Name: SOCIAL INFLUENCE SCALES

Purpose: To measure social influences on nutrition, alcohol and sex behavior.

Number of Items: 34

Format: Sample items are presented.

Reliability: Alpha coefficients ranged from .72 to .81.

Author: Sands, T., et al.

Article: Prevention of health-risk behaviors in college students: Evaluating seven variables.

Journal: *Journal of College Student Development*, July/August 1998, *39*(4), 331–342.

Related Research: Perkins, H., & Berkowitz, A. (1991). *Student Life, Health and Well-Being Survey*. Geneva, NY: Hobart and William Smith Colleges.

8093

Test Name: SOCIAL INFORMATION PROCESSING INTERVIEW—MODIFIED

Purpose: To measure children's responses to ambiguous peer provocations.

Number of Items: Four scenarios. Three evaluation items per scenario.

Format: Four-point rating scales.

Reliability: Alpha coefficients ranged from .68 to .83 across subscales.

Author: Schwartz, D., and Proctor, L. J.

Article: Community violence exposure and children's social adjustment in the school peer group: The mediating roles of emotion regulation and social cognition.

Journal: *Journal of Consulting and Clinical Psychology*, August 2000, *68*(4), 670–683.

Related Research: Quiggle, N. L., et al. (1992). Social-information-processing in aggressive and depressed children. *Child Development, 63*, 1305–1320.

8094

Test Name: SOCIAL INTERACTION ANXIETY SCALE

Purpose: To measure generalized social apprehension.

Number of Items: 20

Format: Five-point Likert format.

Reliability: Alphas ranged from .88 to .93.

Validity: Correlations with other variables ranged from −.05 to .90.

Author: Habke, A. M., et al.

Article: The Social Phobia and Social Interaction Anxiety Scales:

An exploration of the dimensions of social anxiety and sex differences in structure and relations with pathology.

Journal: *Journal of Psychopathology and Behavioral Assessment*, March 1997, *19*(1), 21–39.

Related Research: Mattick, R. P., and Clark, J. C. (1989). *Development and validation of measures of social phobia scrutiny fears and social interaction anxiety*. Unpublished manuscript.

Osman, A., et al. (1998). The Social Phobia and Social Interaction Anxiety Scales: Evaluation of psychometric properties. *Journal of Psychopathology and Behavioral Assessment, 20*, 249–264.

8095

Test Name: SOCIAL INTERACTION INVENTORY

Purpose: To measure interaction in its interpersonal, personal, and extrapersonal dimensions.

Number of Items: 18

Format: Scales range from 1 (extremely uncharacteristic) to 5 (extremely characteristic). All items are presented.

Reliability: Test-retest reliability (3 weeks) was .79.

Authors: Dadkhah, A., et al.

Article: Pattern of social interaction in societies of the Asia-Pacific region.

Journal: *The Journal of Social Psychology*, December 1999, *139*(6), 730–735.

Related Research: Triandis, H. C. (1996). The psychological measurement of cultural syndromes. *American Psychologist, 51*, 407–415.

8096

Test Name: SOCIAL INTERDEPENDENCE SCALE

Purpose: To measure one's cooperative, competitive, and individualistic perceptions.

Number of Items: 22

Format: Responses are made on a 5-point Likert-type scale.

Reliability: Alpha coefficients ranged from .73 to .94.

Validity: Correlations with other variables ranged from −.40 to .62.

Author: Onwuegbuzie, A. J., et al.

Article: Cognitive, affective, personality, and demographic predictions of foreign-language achievement

Journal: *Journal of Educational Research*, September/October 2000, *94*(1), 3–15

Related Research: Johnson, D. W. and Norem-Hebeisen, A. A. (1979). A measure of cooperative, competitive, and individualistic attitudes. *The Journal of Social Psychology, 109*, 253–261.

8097

Test Name: SOCIAL INTIMACY SCALE

Purpose: To assess closeness, affection, and personal disclosure in a relationship.

Number of Items: 17

Format: Ten-point Likert format. Sample items are presented.

Reliability: Alphas were .90 (wives) and .92 (husbands).

Author: Roberts, L. J., and Leonard, K. E.

Article: An empirical typology of drinking partnerships and their relationship to marital functioning and drinking consequences.

Journal: *Journal of Marriage and the Family*, May 1998, *60*(2), 515–526.

Related Research: Miller, R. S., & Lefcourt, H. M. (1982). The assessment of social intimacy. *Journal of Personality Assessment, 46*, 514–518.

8098

Test Name: SOCIAL PHOBIA AND ANXIETY INVENTORY (SPAI)

Purpose: To assess the range of social anxiety symptoms in clinical and nonclinical samples. There are two subscales: Social Phobia and Agoraphobia.

Number of Items: 45

Format: Seven-point scales are anchored by 1 (never) and 7 (always).

Reliability: Alphas ranged from .83 to .96 across samples and scales.

Validity: Correlations with other variables ranged from .12 to .76.

Author: Osman, A., et al.

Article: The Social Phobia and Anxiety Inventory: Further validation in two nonclinical samples.

Journal: *Journal of Psychopathology and Behavioral Assessment*, March 1996, *18*(1), 35–47.

Related Research: Beidel, D. C., et al. (1989). The Social Phobia and Anxiety Inventory: Concurrent and external validity. *Behavior Therapy, 20*, 417–427.

8099

Test Name: SOCIAL PROVISIONS SCALE

Purpose: To measure social support.

Number of Items: 24

Format: Scales range from -4 (very strongly disagree) to +4 (very strongly agree). A sample item is presented.

Reliability: Alpha coefficients ranged from .92 to .95.

Author: Pratt, M. W., et al.

Article: Facilitating the transition to university: Evaluation of a social support discussion intervention program.

Journal: *Journal of College Student Development*, July/August 2000, *41*(4), 427–441.

Related Research: Cutrona, C. E. (1984). Social support and stress in the transition to parenthood. *Journal of Abnormal Psychology, 93*, 378–390.

8100

Test Name: SOCIAL RECEPTIVITY SCALE

Purpose: To measure perceived social receptivity.

Number of Items: 3

Format: Five-point scales are anchored by 1 (strongly disagree) and 5 (strongly agree). All items are presented.

Reliability: Coefficient alpha was .75. Test-retest reliability (3-months) was .59.

Validity: Correlations with other variables ranged from .34 to .36.

Author: Stanton, A. L., et al.

Article: Emotionally expressive coping predicts psychological and physical adjustment to breast cancer.

Journal: *Journal of Consulting and Clinical Psychology*, October 2000, *68*(5), 875–882.

8101

Test Name: SOCIAL SKILLS RATING SCALE

Purpose: To rate how well one's partners performed social skills.

Number of Items: 11

Format: Responses are made on a 5-point scale ranging from 1 (poor) to 5 (extremely good).

Reliability: Alpha coefficients ranged from .83 to .88.

Author: Gavin, L. A., and Furman, W.

Article: Adolescent girls' relationships with mothers and best friends.

Journal: *Child Development*, April 1996, *67*(2), 375–386.

Related Research: Buhrmester, D., et al. (1988). Five domains of interpersonal competence in peer relations. *Journal of Personality and Social Psychology, 55*, 991–1008.

8102

Test Name: SOCIAL SUPPORT-APPRAISAL SCALE—MODIFIED

Purpose: To measure African American professionals' appraisals of social support.

Number of Items: 25

Format: An example is presented. Includes 2 parts: work support, and nonwork support.

Reliability: Coefficients alpha was .89.

Validity: Correlations with other variables ranged from −.66 to .62.

Author: Holder, J. C., and Vaux, A.

Article: African American professionals: Coping with occupational stress in predominantly White work environments.

Journal: *Journal of Vocational Behavior*, December 1998, *53*(3), 315–333.

8103

Test Name: SOCIAL SUPPORT FOR EXERCISE BEHAVIORS SCALE—DUTCH VERSION

Purpose: To measure social support for exercise behavior.

Number of Items: 18

Format: Includes 3 subscales: Participation and Involvement, Rewards and Punishment, and Exercising Together. All items are presented.

Reliability: Alpha coefficients ranged from .26 to .71.

Author: Stevens, M., et al.

Article: A Dutch version of the Social Support for Exercise Behaviors Scale.

Journal: *Perceptual and Motor Skills*, June 2000, *90*(3) Part 1, 771–774.

Related Research: Sallis, J. F., et al. (1995). The development of scales to measure social support for diet and exercise behaviors. *Preventative Medicine, 16*, 825–836.

8104

Test Name: SOCIAL SUPPORT FROM FRIENDS AND FAMILY

Purpose: To measure the extent to which one feels supported by one's friends and family.

Number of Items: 40

Format: Yes/no/don't know format.

Reliability: Alpha coefficients ranged from .87 to .91.

Validity: Correlations with other

variables ranged from −.41 to −.23.

Author: Langhinrichsen-Rohling, J., et al.

Article: Retrospective reports of the family of origin environment and the transition to college.

Journal: *Journal of College Student Development*, January/ February 1997, *38*(1), 49–61.

Related Research: Procidano, M., & Heller, K. (1983). Measures of perceived social support from friends and from family: Three validation studies. *American Journal of Community Psychology, 11*, 1–24.

Gloria, A. M., et al. (1999). African American students' persistence at a predominately White university: Influences of social support, university comfort and self-beliefs. *Journal of College Student Development, 40*, 257–268.

8105

Test Name: SOCIAL SUPPORT INVENTORY

Purpose: To assess satisfaction with social support.

Number of Items: 39

Format: Scales range from 1 (not at all satisfied) to 7 (very satisfied).

Reliability: Alpha coefficients ranged from .94 to .96.

Validity: Correlations with other variables ranged from −.53 to .77.

Author: Petrie, T. A., and Stoever, S.

Article: Academic and nonacademic predictors of female student athletes' academic performances.

Journal: *Journal of College*

Student Development, November/ December 1997, *38*(6), 599–608.

Related Research: Brown, S., et al. (1987). Perceived social support among college students: Three studies of the psychometric characteristics and counseling uses of the Social Support Inventory. *Journal of Counseling Psychology, 34*, 337–354.

8106

Test Name: SOCIAL SUPPORT QUESTIONNAIRE

Purpose: To measure the number of people persons can rely on and how satisfied they are with these social supports.

Number of Items: 27

Format: Six-point scales.

Reliability: Alphas ranged from .94 to .97. Test-retest reliabilities (4 weeks) ranged from .83 to .90.

Author: Pretorius, T. B.

Article: Measuring life events in a sample of South African students: Comparison of the Life Experiences Survey of the Schedule of Recent Experiences.

Journal: *Psychological Reports*, December 1998, *83*(3) Part 1, 771–780.

Related Research: Sarason, I. G., et al. (1983). Assessing social support: The Social Support Questionnaire, *Journal of Personality and Social Psychology, 44*, 127–137.

8107

Test Name: SOCIAL SUPPORT QUESTIONNAIRE—ADAPTED

Purpose: To assess interpersonal influence.

Number of Items: 6

Format: Includes 2 parts. First part: Respondent indicated number of supports she believes she has for each situation. Second part: Respondent indicates on a 6-point scale ranging from 1 (very dissatisfied) to 6 (very satisfied) the degree of satisfaction with the supports.

Reliability: Alpha coefficients ranged from .90 to .96.

Author: Ingram, K. M., et al.

Article: The relationship of victimization experiences to psychological well-being among homeless women and low-income housed women.

Journal: *Journal of Counseling Psychology*, April 1996, *43*(2), 218–227.

Related Research: Sarason, I. G., et al. (1987). A brief measure of social support: Practical and theoretical implications. *Journal of Social and Personal Relationships*, *4*, 497–510.

8108

Test Name: SOCIAL SUPPORT QUESTIONNAIRE—SHORT FORM

Purpose: To measure perceived availability of and satisfaction with support.

Number of Items: 3

Format: Each item includes 2 parts: the number of available others and the degree of satisfaction with the perceived support.

Reliability: Internal reliabilities were .75 and .79. Test-retest correlations were .84 and .85.

Author: Perrine, R. M.

Article: Please see me: Students' reactions to professor's request as a function of attachment and perceived support.

Journal: *Journal of Experimental Education*, Fall 1999, *68*(1), 60–72.

Related Research: Sarason, I. G., et al. (1987). A brief measure of social support: Practical and theoretical implications. *Journal of Social and Personal Relationships*, *4*, 497–510.

8109

Test Name: SOCIAL SUPPORT SCALE

Purpose: To measure social support from family and friends.

Number of Items: 4

Format: Five-point scales are anchored by 1 (strongly agree) and 5 (strongly disagree). All items are presented.

Reliability: Alpha was .82.

Validity: Correlation with job satisfaction was .14.

Author: Tan, P. P., et al.

Article: Job satisfaction and intent to continue working among individuals with serious mental illness.

Journal: *Psychological Reports*, December 1999, *85*(3, Part I), 801–807.

Related Research: Maynard, M. (1986). Measuring work and support network satisfaction. *Journal of Employment Counseling*, *23*, 9–19.

8110

Test Name: SOCIAL SUPPORT SCALE

Purpose: To measure support from friends and support from relatives.

Number of Items: 8

Format: Scale anchors are 0 (don't have any such person) and 4 (very much). Sample items are presented.

Reliability: Coefficients alpha were .88 (friends) and .93 (relatives).

Validity: Correlations with other variables ranged from −.29 to .23.

Author: Gowan, M. A., et al.

Article: Test of a model of coping with involuntary job loss following a company closing.

Journal: *Journal of Applied Psychology*, February 1999, *84*(1), 75–86.

Related Research: Caplan, R. D., et al. (1975). *Job demands and worker health*. Cincinnati, OH: National Institute of Occupational Safety and Health.

8111

Test Name: SOCIAL SUPPORT SCALE

Purpose: To measure social support from supervisors, co-workers, family and friends.

Number of Items: 12

Format: 6-point scales are anchored by (5) very much and (0) don't have such person.

Reliability: Cronbach's alpha was .79.

Validity: Correlations with other variables ranged from −.25 to .39.

Author: Smith, D., and Tinzer, A.

Article: Moderating effects of affective disposition and social support on the relationship between person-environment fit and strain.

Journal: *Psychological Reports*, June 1998, *82*(3) Part 1, 963–983.

Related Research: Caplan, R. D., et al. (1975). *Job demands and worker health: Main effects and occupational differences* (pp. 75–160). (Report to National Institute for Occupational Safety and Health, NIOSH) Washington,

DC: Department of Health, Environment, and Welfare.

8112

Test Name: SOCIAL SUPPORT SCALE FOR CHINESE STUDENTS IN JAPAN

Purpose: To measure needed and actual social support.

Number of Items: 15

Format: Four-point response scales. Sample items are presented.

Reliability: Alphas ranged from .90 to .95.

Author: Jou, Y. H., and Fukada, H.

Article: Comparison of differences in the association of social support and adjustment between Chinese and Japanese students in Japan: A research note.

Journal: *Psychological Reports*, August 1996, *79*(1), 107–112.

Related Research: Jou, Y. H. (1993). [An attempt to construct a social support scale for Chinese students in Japan.] [*Research in Social Psychology*], *8*, 235–245. [Japanese-English summary]

8113

Test Name: SOCIAL SUPPORT SCALE FOR CHINESE STUDENTS IN JAPAN

Purpose: To measure social support.

Number of Items: 29

Format: Five-point scales are anchored by (1) not at all and (5) very much. Sample items are presented.

Reliability: Alphas ranged from .95 to .96.

Author: Jou, Y. H., and Fukada, H.

Article: Stress and social support in mental and physical health of Chinese students in Japan.

Journal: *Psychological Reports*, December 1997, *81*(3, Part II), 1302–1312.

Related Research: Jou, Y. H. (1993). [An attempt to construct a social support scale for Chinese students in Japan]. [*Research in Social Psychology*], *10*, 196–207. [In Japanese. English summary]

8114

Test Name: SOCIAL WELL-BEING SCALE

Purpose: To assess social integration, social acceptance, social contribution, social actualization and social coherence.

Number of Items: 50

Format: Scales range from "strongly disagree" to "strongly agree." All items are presented.

Reliability: Alpha coefficients ranged from .41 to .81 across subscales.

Validity: Correlations with other variables ranged from −.55 to .49.

Author: Keyes, C. L. M.

Article: Social well-being.

Journal: *Social Psychology Quarterly*, June 1998, *61*(2), 121–140.

8115

Test Name: SPORT COHESIVENESS QUESTIONNAIRE

Purpose: To measure team cohesion

Number of Items: 9

Format: Unspecified rating scale. A sample item is presented.

Reliability: Alpha was .88.

Validity: Correlations with other variables ranged from −.79 to .74.

Author: Miles, J. A.

Article: Relationships of collective orientation and cohesion to team outcomes.

Journal: *Psychological Reports*, April 2000, *86*(2), 435–444.

Related Research: Martens, R., et al. (1972). *Sport cohesiveness questionnaire*. Unpublished report, University of Illinois, Department of Physical Education, Champaign, IL.

8116

Test Name: SUINN-LEW ASIAN SELF-IDENTITY ACCULTURATION SCALE

Purpose: To measure Asian students' acculturation level.

Number of Items: 21

Format: Five-point scales are anchored by 1 (very Asian) and 5 (very Anglicized).

Reliability: Alpha was .82.

Author: Hirai, M., and Clum, G. A.

Article: Development, reliability, and validity of the Beliefs Toward Mental Illness Scale.

Journal: *Journal of Psychopathology and Behavioral Assessment*, September 2000, *22*(3), 221–236.

Related Research: Suinn, R. W., et al. (1987). The Suinn-Lew Asian Self-Identity Acculturation Scale: Concurrent and factorial validation. *Educational and Psychological Measurement*, 47, 401–407.

8117

Test Name: SUINN-LEW ASIAN SELF-IDENTITY ACCULTURATION SCALE

Purpose: To measure levels of acculturation

Number of Items: 26

Format: Assesses comfort level with the American language, parents' racial identity, one's own identity, friendship, behaviors, generational/ geographic background, and attitudes.

Validity: Correlations with other variables ranged from $-.60$ to .62

Author: Tang, M., et al.

Article: Asian Americans' career choices: A path model to examine factors influencing their career choices.

Journal: *Journal of Vocational Behavior*, February 1999, *54*(1), 142–157.

Related Research: Suinn, R. M., et al. (1987). The Suinn-Lew Asian Self Identity acculturation scale: An initial report. *Educational and Psychological Measurement, 47,* 401–407.

8118

Test Name: SUINN-LEW ASIAN SELF-IDENTITY ACCULTURATION SCALE

Purpose: To quantify the degree of acculturation of Asian Americans.

Number of Items: 30

Format: Includes 5 factors: Language and Cultural Preferences, Ethnic Interaction, Ethnic Pride, General Identity, and Food Preferences.

Reliability: Internal consistency was .91.

Validity: Correlation with other

variables ranged from $-.22$ to .14.

Author: Hibbard, S., et al.

Article: Differential validity of the defense mechanism manual for the TAT between Asian Americans and whites.

Journal: *Journal of Personality Assessment*, December 2000, *75*(3), 351–372.

Related Research: Suinn, R. M., et al. (1992). The Suinn-Lew Asian Self-Identity Acculturation Scale: Concurrent and factorial validity. *Educational and Psychological Measurement, 52,* 1041–1046.

8119

Test Name: SUPERIORITY SCALE

Purpose: To assess how people view themselves in relation to others.

Number of Items: 10

Format: Responses are made on a 6-point Likert scale.

Reliability: Test-retest (2 weeks) reliability was .76. Internal consistency coefficients ranged from .78 to .82.

Validity: Correlations with other variables ranged from .61 to .75.

Author: Patton, M. J., et al.

Article: The Missouri Psychoanalytic Counseling Project: Relation of changes in counseling process to client outcomes.

Journal: *Journal of Counseling Psychology*, April 1997, *44*(2), 189–208.

Related Research: Robbins, S. B., & Patton, M. J. (1985). Self-psychology and career development: Construction of the Superiority and Goal Instability

Scales. *Journal of Counseling Psychology, 32,* 221–231.

8120

Test Name: TAXONOMY OF PROBLEMATIC SOCIAL SITUATIONS

Purpose: To enable teachers to rate children's situational social competence.

Number of Items: 44

Format: Responses are made on a 5-point scale ranging from 1 (never) to 5 (almost always). Includes 6 factors: Peer Group Entry, Response to Provocation, Response to Failure, Response to Success, Social Expectations, and Teacher Expectations.

Reliability: Alpha coefficients ranged from .81 to .96. Test-retest (6 months) reliability coefficients ranged from .57 to .79.

Author: Shah, F., and Morgan, S. B.

Article: Teachers' ratings of social competence of children with their high versus low levels of depressive symptoms.

Journal: *Journal of School Psychology*, Winter 1996, *34*(4), 337–349.

Related Research: Dodge, K. A., et al. (1985). Situational approach to the assessment of social competence in children. *Journal of Consulting and Clinical Psychology, 53,* 344–353.

8121

Test Name: TEACHER CHECKLIST OF PEER RELATIONS

Purpose: To identify social skills and aggressiveness.

Number of Items: 17

Format: Includes: Peer Acceptance, Social Skills, and Aggressiveness with Peers. Examples are presented.

Reliability: Alpha coefficients were .93 and .88.

Validity: Correlations with other variables ranged from −.39 to .29.

Author: Mize, J., and Pettit, G. S.

Article: Mothers' social coaching, mother-child relationship style, and children's peer competence: Is the medium the message?

Journal: *Child Development*, April 1997, *68*(2), 312–332.

Related Research: Coie, J. D., & Dodge, K. A. (1988). Multiple sources of data on social behavior and social status in the school: A cross-age comparison. *Child Development*, *59*, 815–829.

8122

Test Name: TEST OF NEGATIVE SOCIAL EXCHANGE

Purpose: To measure interpersonal influences.

Number of Items: 16

Format: Includes 4 subscales: Hostility/Impatience, Interference, Insensitivity, and Ridicule. Responses are made on a 5-point scale ranging from 0 (not at all) to 4 (about every day).

Reliability: Internal consistency estimates ranged from .70 to .88.

Author: Ingram, K. M., et al.

Article: The relationship of victimization experiences to psychological well-being among homeless women and low-income housed women.

Journal: *Journal of Counseling Psychology*, April 1996, *43*(2), 218–227.

Related Research: Ruehlman, L. S., & Karoly, P. (1991). With a little flak from my friends: Development and preliminary validation of the Test of Negative Social Exchange (TENSE). *Psychological Assessment*, *3*, 97–104.

8123

Test Name: TEST OF NEGATIVE SOCIAL EXCHANGE

Purpose: To measure social conflict.

Number of Items: 20

Format: Likert format.

Reliability: Coefficient alpha ranged from .70 to .83 across subscales.

Author: Gallo, L. C., and Smith, T. W.

Article: Patterns of hostility and social support: Conceptualizing psychosocial risk factors as characteristics of the person and the environment.

Journal: *Journal of Research in Personality*, September 1999, *33*(3), 281–310.

Related Research: Ruehlman, L. S., & Karoly, P. (1991). With a little flak from my friends: Development and preliminary validation of the test of negative social exchange (TENSE). *Psychological Assessment*, *3*, 97–104.

8124

Test Name: TOLERANCE SCALE

Purpose: To measure social acceptance.

Number of Items: 6

Format: Yes/no format.

Reliability: Test-retest reliability (1 week) was .96.

Author: Woods, D. W., et al.

Article: Evaluating the social acceptability of persons with habit disorders: The effects of topography, frequency, and manipulation.

Journal: *Journal of Psychopathology and Behavioral Assessment*, March 1999, *21*(1), 1–18.

Related Research: Yamamoto, K., and Dizney, H. F. (1967). Rejection of the mentally ill: A study of attitudes of student teachers. *Journal of Counseling Psychology*, *14*, 263–268.

8125

Test Name: TRIANGULAR LOVE SCALE—COMPOSITE VERSION

Purpose: To assess intimacy, passion, and commitment in romantic relationships.

Number of Items: 20

Format: Seven-point Likert format. All items are presented.

Reliability: Alpha coefficients ranged from .87 to .88 across subscales.

Validity: Correlations between subscales ranged from .39 to .83.

Author: Limieux, R., and Hale, J. L.

Article: Intimacy, passion, and commitment in young romantic relationships: Successfully measuring the triangular theory of love.

Journal: *Psychological Reports*, October 1999, *85*(2), 497–503.

8126

Test Name: TRUST IN LEADER SCALE

Purpose: To measure trust in a leader.

Number of Items: 9

Format: Scales range from 1 (strongly disagree) to 7 (strongly agree). All items are presented.

Reliability: Coefficient alpha was .96.

Validity: Correlations with other variables ranged from −.11 to .60.

Author: Dirks, K. T.

Article: Trust in leadership and team performance: Evidence for NCAA basketball.

Journal: *Journal of Applied Psychology*, December 2000, *85*(6), 1004–1012.

8127

Test Name: TRUST IN MEDIATOR SCALE

Purpose: To measure how much negotiators trust mediators.

Number of Items: 3

Format: All items are presented.

Reliability: Coefficient alpha was .58.

Validity: Correlations with other variables ranged from .04 to .25.

Author: Ross, W. H., and Wieland, C.

Article: Effects of interpersonal trust and time pressure on managerial mediation strategy in a simulated organizational dispute.

Journal: *Journal of Applied Psychology*, June 1996, *81*(3), 228–248.

8128

Test Name: TRUST INVENTORY

Purpose: To measure trust in generalized others and romantic partners.

Number of Items: 40

Format: All items are presented,

which include Partners Trust and Generalized Trust.

Reliability: Alpha coefficients were .92 (Partner Trust) and .91 (Generalized Trust). Test-retest reliabilities were .82 (Partner Trust) and .80 (Generalized Trust).

Validity: Correlations with other variables ranged from −.44 to .84.

Author: Couch, L. L., et al.

Article: The assessment of trait orientation.

Journal: *Journal of Personality Assessment*, October 1996, *67*(2), 305–323.

8129

Test Name: TRUST INVENTORY

Purpose: To measure partner trust, network trust, and generalized trust.

Number of Items: 50

Format: Sample items are presented.

Reliability: Alpha coefficients ranged from .87 to .92. Test-retest reliabilities (9 weeks) ranged from .74 to .82.

Validity: Correlations with other variables ranged from .29 to .82.

Author: Couch, L. L., and Jones, W. H.

Article: Measuring levels of trust.

Journal: *Journal of Research in Personality*, September 1997, *31*(3), 319–336.

Related Research: Couch, L. L., et al. (1996). The assessment of trust orientation. *Journal of Personality Assessment, 67*, 305–323.

8130

Test Name: TRUST SCALE

Purpose: To measure trust.

Number of Items: 36

Format: Responses are made on a 4-point scale ranging from 0 (strongly disagree) to 3 (strongly agree). All items are presented.

Reliability: Alpha coefficients were .90 and .96.

Author: Adams, K. S., and Christenson, S. L.

Article: Trust and the family-school relationship examination of parent-teacher differences in elementary and secondary grades.

Journal: *Journal of School Psychology*, September/October 2000, *38*(5), 477–497.

Related Research: Adams, K. S., & Christenson, S. L. (1998). Differences in parent and teacher trust levels: Implications for creating collaborative family-school relationships. *Special Services in the Schools, 14*(1/2), 1–22.

8131

Test Name: TRUST SCALES

Purpose: To measure ability, benevolence, integrity, propensity and trust of top management.

Number of Items: 30

Format: Five-point Likert format. All items are presented.

Reliability: Alpha coefficients ranged from .55 to .88.

Author: Mayer, R. C., and Davis, J. H.

Article: The effect of the performance appraisal system on trust for management: A field quasi-experiment.

Journal: *Journal of Applied Psychology*, February 1999, *84*(1), 123–136.

Related Research: Schoorman, F. D., et al. (1996). *Empowerment in veterinary* *clinics: The role of trust in delegation*. Paper presented at the 11th annual meeting of the Society for Industrial and Organizational Psychology, San Diego, CA.

8132

Test Name: TRUSTWORTHINESS OF HUMAN NATURE SUBSCALE

Purpose: To measure one's beliefs about humans being trustworthy, moral, and responsible.

Number of Items: 14

Format: A subscale of the Philosophies of Human Nature Scale.

Reliability: Coefficient alpha was .79.

Validity: Correlations with other variables ranged from .32 to .76.

Author: Couch, L. L., et al.

Article: The assessment of trait orientation.

Journal: *Journal of Personality Assessment*, October 1996, 67(2), 305–323.

Related Research: Wrightsman, L. S. (1974). *Assumptions about human nature: A social-psychological approach*. Monterey, CA: Brooks Cole.

8133

Test Name: UCLA LONELINESS SCALE—VERSION 3

Purpose: To assess loneliness.

Number of Items: 20

Format: Responses are made on a 4-point scale ranging from 1 (never) to 4 (always). All items are presented.

Reliability: Alpha coefficients ranged from .89 to .94.

Validity: Correlations with other

variables ranged from −.68 to .72.

Author: Russell, D. W.

Article: UCLA Loneliness Scale (Version 3): Reliability, validity, and factor structure.

Journal: *Journal of Personality Assessment*, February 1996, 66(1), 20–40.

Related Research: Russell, D., et al. (1980). The revised UCLA Loneliness Scale: Concurrent and discriminant validity evidence. *Journal of Personality and Social Psychology*, 39, 472–480.

8134

Test Name: UNIVERSAL ORIENTATION SCALE

Purpose: To assess nonprejudice.

Number of Items: 20

Format: Responses are made on a 5-point scale ranging from 1 (does not describe me well) to 5 (describes me very well). Sample items are presented.

Reliability: Internal reliability coefficient was .76. Test-retest reliability was .75.

Author: Heesacker, M., et al.

Article: Gender-based emotional stereotyping.

Journal: *Journal of Counseling Psychology*, October 1999, 46(4), 483–495.

Related Research: Phillips, S. T., & Ziller, R. C. (1997). Toward a theory and measure of the nature of nonprejudice. *Journal of Personality and Social Psychology*, 72, 420–434.

8135

Test Name: UNIVERSALITY—DIVERSITY SCALE

Purpose: To measure tolerance

and appreciation of differences and similarities of people.

Number of Items: 45

Format: Six-item scales are anchored by (1) strongly disagree and (6) strongly agree.

Reliability: Internal consistency was .93.

Author: Fuertes, J. N., and Gelso, C. J.

Article: Asian-American, Euro-American, and African-American Students' universal-diverse orientation and preferences for characteristics of psychologists.

Journal: *Psychological Reports*, August 1998, 83(1), 280–282.

Related Research: Miville, M. L., et al (1995). *Universality-Diversity Scale: Appreciating the Similarities and Differences Among People*. Poster session presented at the 103rd annual convention of the American Psychological Association, New York, August, 1995.

8136

Test Name: UNMITIGATED COMMUNION SCALE

Purpose: To measure concern for others to the exclusion of concern for self.

Number of Items: 9

Format: Five-point scales. Sample items are presented.

Reliability: Internal consistency coefficients ranged from .69 to .76.

Author: Helgeson, V. S., and Fritz, H. L.

Article: Unmitigated agency and unmitigated communion: Distinctions from agency and communion.

Journal: *Journal of Research in Personality*, June 1999, 33(2), 131–158.

Related Research: Fritz, H. L., & Helgeson, V. S. (1998). Distinctions of unmitigated communion from communion: Self-neglect and overinvolvement with others. *Journal of Personality and Social Psychology*, 75, 121–140.

8137

Test Name: VISIBLE RACIAL AND ETHNIC IDENTITY SCALE

Purpose: To assess racial or ethnic identity development of Asian, Latino and Native American individuals in terms of conformity, dissonance, resistance, and awareness.

Number of Items: 43

Format: Scales range from 1 (strongly disagree) to 5 (strongly agree).

Reliability: Alpha coefficients ranged from .87 to .95 across four subscales.

Author: Pope, R. L.

Article: The relationship between psychosocial development and racial identity of college students of color.

Journal: *Journal of College Student Development*, May/June 2000, 41(3), 301–312.

Related Research: Helms, J. E., & Carter, R. T. (1986). *Manual for the Visible Racial/Ethnic Identity Attitude Scale.* Paper presented at the annual convention of the American Psychological Association, Washington, DC.

8138

Test Name: WHITE RACIAL IDENTITY ATTITUDE SCALE

Purpose: To measure white racial identity attitudes.

Number of Items: 50

Format: Includes 5 subscales: Contact, Disintegration, Reintegration, Pseuso-Independence, and Autonomy. Responses are made on a 5-point Likert scale ranging from 1 (strongly disagree) to 5 (strongly agree).

Reliability: Alpha coefficients ranged from .38 to .80.

Validity: Correlations with other variables ranged from −.28 to .35.

Author: Gushue, G. V., and Carter, R. T.

Article: Remembering race: White racial identity attitudes and two aspects of social memory.

Journal: *Journal of Counseling Psychology*, April 2000, 47(2), 199–210.

Related Research: Helms, J. E., & Carter, R. T. (1990). The development of the White Racial Identity Inventory. In J. E. Helms (Ed.), *Black and White racial identity attitude: Theory, research and practice* (pp. 67–80). Westport, CT: Greenwood Press.

8139

Test Name: WHITE RACIAL IDENTITY ATTITUDE SCALE

Purpose: To measure white racial identity.

Number of Items: 60

Format: includes 6 subscales: Contact, Disintegration, Reintegration, Pseudo-Independence, Immersion-Emersion, and Autonomy. Responses are made on a 5-point Likert scale ranging from 1 (strongly disagree) to 5 (strongly agree).

Reliability: Alpha coefficients ranged from .32 to .77.

Validity: Correlations with other variables ranged from −.31 to .52.

Author: Ladany, N., et al.

Article: Supervisee multicultural case conceptualization ability and self-reported multicultural competence as functions of supervisee racial identity and supervisor focus.

Journal: *Journal of Counseling Psychology*, July 1997, 44(3), 284–293.

Related Research: Helms, J. E., & Carter, R. T. (1990). Development of the White Racial Identity Scale. In J. Helms (Eds.), *Black and White racial identity: Theories, research, and practice* (pp. 67–80). Westport, CT: Greenwood Press.

8140

Test Name: WILCOX SOCIAL SUPPORT NETWORK SURVEY

Purpose: To indicate extent of a social support network.

Number of Items: 18

Format: Responses are "yes-no."

Reliability: Reliability coefficients were .81 and .86.

Validity: Correlation with other variables ranged from −.28 to .12.

Author: Cepeda-Benito, A., and Short, P.

Article: Self-concealment, avoidance of psychological services, and perceived likelihood of seeking professional help.

Journal: *Journal of Counseling Psychology*, January 1998, 45(1), 58–64.

Related Research: Reis, J. (1988). A factorial analysis of a compound measure of social support. *Journal of Clinical Psychology*, 44, 876–890.

CHAPTER 5
Adjustment—Vocational

8141

Test Name: ADMINISTRATIVE STRESS INDEX

Purpose: To identify sources of occupational stress among school administrators.

Number of Items: 35

Format: Five-point scales ranged from (1) rarely or never bothers me to (5) frequently bothers me. Sample items are presented.

Reliability: Alphas ranged from .73 to .80.

Author: Allison, D. G.

Article: Assessing stress among public school principals in British Columbia.

Journal: *Psychological Reports*, June 1997, *80*(3) Part 2, 1103–1114.

Related Research: Swent, B., & Gmelch, W. H. (1977). *Stress at the desk and how to creatively cope.* Eugene, OR: Oregon School Study Council Bulletin, 21 (ERIC Document Reproduction Service No. ED 146 658).

8142

Test Name: ADULT'S AUTHOR CHECKLIST

Purpose: To enable parents to identify authors of adults' books from a list of authors and foils.

Number of Items: 60

Format: Parents check those book authors believed to be those of adults' books. All items are presented.

Reliability: Spearman-Brown coefficient was .95.

Validity: Correlations with other variables ranged from −.14 to .64.

Author: Senechal, M., et al.

Article: Knowledge of storybooks as a predictor of young children's vocabulary.

Journal: *Journal of Educational Psychology*, September 1996, *88*(3), 520–536.

8143

Test Name: ANXIETY-STRESS QUESTIONAIRE—ABBRIEVIATED

Purpose: To measure job-induced stress.

Number of Items: 3

Format: Responses are made on a 5-point scale. An example is presented.

Reliability: Internal consistency estimate of reliability was .81.

Validity: Correlations with other variables ranged from −.18 to .08.

Author: Allen, T. D., et al.

Article: A field study of factors related to supervisors' willingness to mentor others.

Journal: *Journal of Vocational Behavior*, February 1997, *50*(1), 1–22.

Related Research: House , R. J., & Rizzo, J. R. (1972). Role conflict and ambiguity as initial variables in a model of organizational behavior.

Organizational Behavior and Human Performance, 7, 467–505.

8144

Test Name: BURNOUT INDEX

Purpose: To measure burnout.

Number of Items: 21

Format: Seven-point scales are anchored by 1 (low frequency of occurrence) to 7 (high frequency of occurrence).

Reliability: Alpha coefficients ranged from .93 to .95.

Validity: Correlations with other variables ranged from .23 to .69.

Author: Westman, M., and Eden, D.

Article: Effects of a respite from work on burnout: Vacation relief and fade-out.

Journal: *Journal of Applied Psychology* August, 1997, *82*(4), 516–527.

Related Research: Pines, A., et al. (1981). *Burnout: From tedium to personal growth.* New York: Free Press.

8145

Test Name: BURNOUT SCALE

Purpose: To measure burnout.

Number of Items: 16

Format: Responses are made on a 6-point scale. Examples are presented.

Reliability: Coefficient alpha was .92.

Validity: Correlations with other variables ranged from −.55 to .17.

Author: Krausz, M., et al.

Article: Actual and preferred work schedules and scheduling control as determinants of job-related attitudes.

Journal: *Journal of Vocational Behavior,* February 2000, *56*(1), 1–11.

Related Research: Melamed, S., et al. (1992). Burnout and risk factors for cardiovascular diseases. *Behavioral Medicine, 18,* 53–60.

8146

Test Name: CAREER AUTONOMY SCALE

Purpose: To measure career autonomy.

Number of Items: 4

Format: Responses are made on a 5-point scale ranging from 1 (not at all true) to 5 (very true). Sample items are presented.

Reliability: Coefficient alpha was .94.

Validity: Correlations with other variables ranged from −.17 to .22.

Author: Aryee, S., and Luk, V.

Article: Work and nonwork influences on the career satisfaction of dual-earner couples.

Journal: *Journal of Vocational Behavior*, August 1996, *49*(1), 38–52.

Related Research: Rosin, H. (1990). The effects of dual career participation on men: Some determinants of variation in career and personal satisfaction. *Human Relations, 43,* 169–182.

8147

Test Name: CAREER LOYALTY SCALE

Purpose: To measure career loyalty.

Number of Items: 2

Format: Responses are made on a 5-point scale ranging from "strongly agree" to "strongly disagree." Examples are given.

Validity: Correlations with other variables ranged from −.47 to .42.

Author: Stroh, L. K., et al.

Article: Family structure, glass ceiling, and traditional explanations for the differential rate of turnover of female and male managers.

Journal: *Journal of Vocational Behavior*, August 1996, *49*(1), 99–118.

Related Research: Reilly, A. H., et al. (1993). The impact of corporate turbulence on managers' attitudes. *Strategic Management Journal*, *14*, 167–179.

8148

Test Name: CAREER RESILIENCE SCALE

Purpose: To measure career flexibility, creativeness, self-reliance, ambition, desire to learn new things, confidence, and career ownership.

Number of Items: 8

Format: Five-point scales are anchored by 1 (strongly disagree) and 5 (strongly agree).

Reliability: Alpha was .77.

Validity: Correlations with other variables ranged from −.31 to .53.

Author: Gowan, M. A., et al.

Article: Response to work

transitions by United States Army personnel: Effects on self-esteem, self-efficacy, and career resilience.

Journal: *Psychological Reports*, June 2000, *86*(3, Part 1), 911–921.

8149

Test Name: CAREER SATISFACTION SCALE

Purpose: To assess one's satisfaction with one's career progress.

Number of Items: 8

Reliability: Alpha coefficients were .88 and .89.

Validity: Correlation with the Work Locus of Control Scale ranged from .-02 to −.47.

Author: Macan, T. H., et al.

Article: Spector's Work Locus of Control Scale: Dimensionality and validity evidence.

Journal: *Educational and Psychological Measurement*, April 1996, *56*(2), 349–357.

Related Research: Trimble, S. K. (1992). *Testing a model of organizational career development*. Unpublished doctoral dissertation, University of Missouri-St. Louis, Department of Psychology.

8150

Test Name: CAREER SATISFACTION SCALE

Purpose: To assess career satisfaction.

Number of Items: 9

Format: Responses are made on a 7-point scale ranging from 1 (very dissatisfied) to 7 (very satisfied). All items are presented.

Reliability: Coefficient alpha was .87.

Author: Tharenou, P., and Terry, D. J.

Article: Reliability and validity of scores on scales to measure managerial aspirations.

Journal: *Educational and Psychological Measurement*, June 1998, *58*(3), 475–492.

Related Research: Schneer, J. A., & Reitman, F. (1990). Effects of unemployment gaps on the careers of M.B.As. *Academy of Management Journal*, *33*, 391–406.

8151

Test Name: CAREER SATISFACTION SCALE

Purpose: To measure career satisfaction.

Number of Items: 23

Format: Five-point response scales ranged from 1 (disagree completely) to 5 (agree completely).

Reliability: Alpha was .83.

Author: Bozionelos, N.

Article: Organizational promotion and career satisfaction.

Journal: *Psychological Reports*, October 1996, *79*(2), 371–375.

Related Research: Gattiker, U., & Larwood, L. (1986). Subjective career success: A study of managers and support personnel. *Journal of Business and Psychology*, *1*, 78–94.

8152

Test Name: CAREER SEARCH SELF-EFFICACY SCALE

Purpose: To assess the degree of perceived confidence in performing various career search tasks.

Number of Items: 35

Format: Includes 4 factors: Job Exploration Efficacy, Interviewing Efficacy, Networking Efficacy, and Personal Exploration Efficacy.

Reliability: Coefficient alpha was .97.

Validity: Correlations with other variables ranged from −.36 to .35.

Author: Ryan, N. E., et al.

Article: Family dysfunction, parental attachment, and career search self-efficacy among community college students.

Journal: *Journal of Counseling Psychology*, January 1996, *43*(1), 84–89.

Related Research: Solberg, V. S., et al. (1993). *The Career Search Efficacy Scale*. Available from V. Scott Solberg, Department of Educational Psychology, University of Wisconsin, Enderis Hall, Room 745, Milwaukee, WI 53201.

8153

Test Name: CAREER SUCCESS EXPECTATIONS SCALE

Purpose: To measure expectations of career success.

Number of Items: 13

Format: Includes 3 factors: career development, career achievement, and career balance. Responses are made on a 5-point Likert-type scale ranging from "strongly disagree" to "strongly agree." All items are presented.

Reliability: Internal consistency ranged from .74 to .83.

Author: Stephens, G. K., et al.

Article: The Career Success Expectations Scale: An exploratory and confirmatory factor analysis.

Journal: *Educational Psychological Measurement*, February 1988, *58*(1), 129–141.

Related Research: Derr, C. B. (1988). *Managing the new careerists*. San Francisco: Jossey-Bass.

8154

Test Name: CHALLENGE- AND HINDRANCE-RELATED STRESS MEASURES

Purpose: To measure stress from job challenges and stress from organizational hindrances.

Number of Items: 11

Format: Scales range from 1 (produces no stress) to 5 (produces a great deal of stress). All items are presented.

Reliability: Coefficient alpha was .87 (challenge) and .75 (hindrances).

Validity: Correlations with other variables ranged from −.52 to .35.

Author: Cavanaugh, M. A., et al.

Article: An empirical examination of self-reported work stress among U.S. managers.

Journal: *Journal of Applied Psychology*, February 2000, *85*(1), 65–74.

8155

Test Name: COGNITIVE APPRAISAL SCALES

Purpose: To assess the transition from military to civilian jobs.

Number of Items: 15

Format: Five-point scales are anchored by 1 (not at all) and 5 (a lot).

Reliability: Alphas ranged from .84 to .91 across subscales.

Validity: Correlations with other

variables ranged from $-.35$ to $.16$.

Author: Gowan, M. A., et al.

Article: Response to work transitions by United States Army personnel: Effects on self-esteem, self-efficacy, and career resilience.

Journal: *Psychological Reports*, June 2000, *86*(3, Part 1), 911–921.

8156

Test Name: COLLECTIVE ORIENTATION SCALE

Purpose: To measure how valuable and useful teamwork is perceived.

Number of Items: 2

Format: Unspecified rating scale. All items are presented.

Reliability: Alpha was .86.

Validity: Correlation with other variables ranged from $-.64$ to $.86$.

Author: Miles, J. A.

Article: Relationships of collective orientation and cohesion to team outcomes.

Journal: *Psychological Reports*, April 2000, *86*(2), 435–444.

Related Research: Driskell, J. E., & Salas, E. (1992). Collective behavior and team performance. *Human Factors, 34*, 277–288.

8157

Test Name: COMPLIANCE/ COMPLAINT QUESTIONNAIRE

Purpose: To assess the extent to which an employee will comply and complain about a supervisor's request.

Number of Items: 12

Format: Scales range from 1

(certain not to) to 5 (certain to). All items presented.

Reliability: Coefficient alpha was .83. Spearman-Brown split half reliability was .82.

Validity: Correlations with other variables ranged from $-.20$ to $.73$.

Authors: Sachau, D. A., et al.

Article: Predictors of employee resistance to supervisors' requests.

Journal: *The Journal of Social Psychology*, October 1999, *139*(5), 611–621.

8158

Test Name: CONCERN FOR DISPUTANT OUTCOMES SCALE

Purpose: To assess how important approval from a manager is to a proposal.

Number of Items: 6

Format: Six-point scales ranged from 1 (very unimportant) to 6 (very important). All items are presented.

Reliability: Coefficient alpha was .79.

Validity: Correlations with other variables ranged from $-.09$ to $.19$.

Author: Ross, W. H., and Wieland, C.

Article: Effects of interpersonal trust and time pressure on managerial mediation strategy in a simulated organizational dispute.

Journal: *Journal of Applied Psychology*, June 1996, *81*(3), 228–248.

8159

Test Name: CONSEQUENCES OF PLATEAUING SCALE

Purpose: To measure respondents' perceived consequences of plateauing.

Time Required: 6

Format: Responses are made on a 5-point scale ranging from 1 (definitely false) to 5 (definitely true). A sample item is presented.

Reliability: Coefficient alpha was .67.

Validity: Correlations with other variables ranged from .12 to .36.

Author: Ettington, D. R.

Article: Successful career plateauing.

Journal: *Journal of Vocational Behavior*, February 1998, *52*(1), 72–88.

8160

Test Name: COPING WITH JOB LOSS SCALE

Purpose: To measure coping with job loss.

Number of Items: 17

Format: Five-point scales range from 1 (hardly ever do this) to 5 (almost always do this). Sample items are presented.

Reliability: Alpha coefficients ranged from .67 to .91.

Validity: Correlations with other variables ranged from $-.14$ to $.36$.

Author: Wanberg, C. R.

Article: Antecedents and outcomes of coping behaviors among unemployed and reemployed individuals.

Journal: *Journal of Applied Psychology*, October 1997, *82*(5), 731–744.

Related Research: Kinicki, A. J., & Latack, J. C. (1990). Explication of the construct of coping with involuntary job loss.

Journal of Vocational Behavior,
36, 339–360.

8161

Test Name: COPING WITH JOB
LOSS SCALES

Purpose: To measure efforts to
look for work and the extent of
use of contacts.

Number of Items: 5

Format: Scales range from 1
(hardly ever do this) to 5 (almost
always do this).

Reliability: Coefficient alphas
were .91 (looking for work) and
.89 (use of contacts).

Validity: Correlations with other
variables ranged from −.13 to
.38.

Author: Gowan, M. A., et al.

Article: Test of a model of coping
with involuntary job loss
following a company closing.

Journal: *Journal of Applied*
Psychology, February 1999,
84(1), 75–86.

Related Research: Kinicki, A. J.,
& Latack, J. C. (1990).
Explication of the construct of
coping with involuntary job loss.
Journal of Vocational Behavior,
36, 339–360.

8162

Test Name:
DEPERSONALIZATION SCALE

Purpose: To measure
depersonalization in the
workplace.

Number of Items: 5

Format: Eleven-point scales are
anchored by (1) applies very
little to me and (11) applies very
much to me. A sample item is
presented.

Reliability: Alpha was .68.

Author: Cheuk, W. H., and
Wong, K. S.

Article: Depersonalization in
kindergarten teachers in relation
to rejection of help by fellow
teachers and emotional support
from family.

Journal: *Psychological Reports,*
December 1998, *83*(3) Part 1,
939–942.

Related Research: Cheuk, W. H.,
and Rosen, S. (1994). Validating
a "spurning scale" for teachers.
Current Psychology, 13, 241–
247.

8163

Test Name: DESIRE TO
TERMINATE SCALE

Purpose: To measure one's desire
to terminate the assignment.

Number of Items: 3

Format: Responses are made on a
4-point scale ranging from 1
(definitely not) to 4 (yes
definitely). All items are
presented.

Reliability: Coefficient alpha was
.82.

Validity: Correlations with other
variables ranged from −.31 to
.09.

Author: Caligiuri, P. M.

Article: The Big Five personality
characteristics as predictors of
expatriate's desire to terminate
the assignment and supervisor-
rated performance.

Journal: *Personnel Psychology,*
Spring 2000, *53*(1), 67–88.

8164

Test Name: DISTANCING JOB
LOSS SCALE

Purpose: To assess the extent to
which an individual removes

himself or herself from the
stressor of job loss.

Number of Items: 4

Format: Scale anchors are 1
(hardly ever do this) and 5
(almost always do this). Sample
items are presented.

Reliability: Coefficient alpha was
.71.

Validity: Correlations with other
variables ranged from −.05 to
.38.

Author: Gowan, M. A., et al.

Article: Test of a model of coping
with involuntary job loss
following a company closing.

Journal: *Journal of Applied*
Psychology, February 1999,
84(1), 75–86.

8165

Test Name: ECONOMIC
HARDSHIP SCALE

Purpose: To assess economic
hardship.

Number of Items: 3

Format: Five-point scales are
anchored by 1 (not at all
difficult) and 2 (extremely
difficult or impossible). A sample
item is presented.

Reliability: Coefficient alpha was
.86.

Validity: Correlations with other
variables ranged from −.19 to
.29.

Author: Wanberg, C. R., et al.

Article: Individuals without jobs:
An empirical study of job-seeking
behavior and reemployment.

Journal: *Journal of Applied*
Psychology, February 1996,
81(1), 76–87.

Related Research: Vinokur, A., &
Caplon, R. D. (1987) Attitudes
and social support: Determinants
of job-seeking behavior and well-

being among the unemployed. *Journal of Applied Social Psychology, 17,* 1007–1024.

8166

Test Name: EFFECTIVENESS SCALE

Purpose: To measure perceived effectiveness in work groups.

Number of Items: 9

Format: All items are presented.

Reliability: Coefficient alpha was .88.

Authors: Van Der Vegt, G., and Van De Vliert, E.

Article: Effects on interdependencies in project teams.

Journal: *Journal of Social Psychology,* April 1999, *139*(2), 202–214.

Related Research: Tjosvold, D., et al. (1991). Power and interdependence in work groups. *Group and Organization Studies, 16,* 285–299.

8167

Test Name: EMPLOYEE ABSENTEEISM SCALE

Purpose: To assess the frequency of and type of absenteeism at work in terms of its voluntary or involuntary character.

Number of Items: 13

Format: Five-point scales. All items are presented.

Reliability: Cronbach alphas were .67 (involuntary) and .87 (voluntary).

Validity: Correlations with other variables ranged from −.47 to −.04.

Author: Paget, K. J., et al.

Article: Development and

validation of an Employee Absenteeism Scale.

Journal: *Psychological Reports,* June 1998, *82*(3) Part 2, 1144–1146.

Related Research: Nicholson, N., & Payne, R. (1987). Absence from work: Explanations and attributions. *Applied Psychology: An International Journal, 36,* 121–132.

8168

Test Name: EMPLOYEE SATISFACTION INVENTORY

Purpose: To measure job satisfaction: work, pay, promotion, working conditions, and organization as a whole.

Number of Items: 24

Format: Five-point scales are anchored by (1) strongly agree and (5) strongly disagree.

Reliability: Alphas ranged from .62 to .81 across subscales.

Validity: Correlations with other variables ranged from −.45 to .45.

Author: Koustelios, A., and Kousteliou, I.

Article: Relations among measures of job satisfaction, role conflict and role ambiguity for a sample of Greek teachers.

Journal: *Psychological Reports,* February 1998, *82*(1), 131–136.

Related Research: Koustelios, A. D. , & Bagiatis, K. (1997). The Employee Satisfaction Inventory (ESI): Development of a scale to measure satisfaction of Greek employees. *Educational and Psychological Measurement, 57,* 469–476.

8169

Test Name: EMPLOYMENT ALTERNATIVES SCALE

Purpose: To measure job security and possibility of alternative employment.

Number of Items: 3

Format: Five-point Likert format. All items are presented.

Reliability: Internal consistency was .72.

Validity: Correlations with other variables ranged from −.12 to .35.

Author: Pisnar-Sweeney, M.

Article: Role of normative commitment in predicting member's participation in the union.

Journal: *Psychological Reports,* June 1997, *80*(3) Part 2, 1183–1207.

Related Research: Faber, H. S., & Saks, D. H. (1980). Why workers want unions: The role of relative wages and job characteristics. *Journal of Political Economy, 88,* 349–369.

8170

Test Name: EMPLOYMENT OUTCOME MEASURES

Purpose: To provide employment outcome measures

Number of Items: 12

Format: Includes the following: Perceived Fairness of the Layoff, Organizational Endorsement, Desire to Sue Past Employers, and Future Organizational Commitment.

Reliability: Alpha coefficients ranged from .86 to .96.

Validity: Correlations with other variables ranged from −.48 to .75

Author: Wanberg, C. R., et al.

Article: Perceived fairness of layoffs among individuals who have been laid off: A longitudinal study.

Journal: *Personnel Psychology*, Spring 1999, *52*(1), 59–84.

8171

Test Name: EMPLOYMENT PREDICTOR MEASURES

Purpose: To provide employment predictors.

Number of Items: 35

Format: Includes the following: Explanation, Correctability, Severance Benefits, Negative Affectivity, and Prior Commitment to the Organization.

Reliability: Alpha coefficients ranged from .71 to .93

Validity: Correlations with other variables ranged from −.42 to .66

Author: Wanberg, C. R., et al.

Article: Perceived fairness of layoffs among individuals who have been laid off: A longitudinal study.

Journal: *Personnel Psychology*, Spring 1999, *52*(1), 59–84.

8172

Test Name: EMPOWERMENT SCALE

Purpose: To assess the degree to which a person has a degree of control in his or her place of work in terms of meaning, impact, competence, and self-determination.

Number of Items: 12

Format: Scales range from 1 (strongly disagree) to 7 (strongly agree). A sample item is presented.

Reliability: Alpha coefficients ranged from .77 to .92.

Validity: Correlations with other variables ranged from .04 to .63.

Author: Liden, R. C., et al.

Article: An examination of the mediating role of psychological empowerment on the relations between the job, interpersonal relationships, and work outcomes.

Journal: *Journal of Applied Psychology*, June 2000, *85*(3), 407–416.

Related Research: Spreitzer, G. M. (1995). Psychological empowerment in the workplace: Construct definition, measurement, and validation. *Academy of Management Journal, 38*, 1442–1465.

8173

Test Name: ENJOYMENT OF WORK SCALE

Purpose: To measure enjoyment of work.

Number of Items: 10

Format: Sample items are presented.

Reliability: Alpha coefficients ranged from .85 to .86.

Validity: Correlations with other variables ranged from −.14 to .42.

Author: Bonebright, C. A., et al.

Article: The relationship of workaholism with work-life conflict, life satisfaction, and purpose in life.

Journal: *Journal of Counseling Psychology*, October 2000, *47*(4), 469–477.

Related Research: Spence, J. T., & Robbins, A. S. (1992). Workaholism: Definition, measurement, and preliminary results. *Journal of Personality Assessment, 58*(1), 60–178.

8174

Test Name: EXPATRIATE ASSIGNMENT WITHDRAWAL SCALE

Purpose: To assess the likelihood of leaving an overseas job assignment.

Number of Items: 6

Format: Scales range from 1 (strongly disagree) to 6 (strongly agree). Sample items are presented.

Reliability: Coefficient alpha was .76.

Validity: Correlations with other variables ranged from .11 to .51.

Author: Garonzik, R., et al.

Article: Identifying international assignees at risk for premature departure: The interactive effect of outcome favorability and procedural fairness.

Journal: *Journal of Applied Psychology*, February 2000, *85*(1), 13–20.

8175

Test Name: FRAME MANAGEMENT QUESTIONAIRE

Purpose: To measure goals, freedom of action and coupling in management actions.

Number of Items: 11

Format: Seven-point scales anchored by (1) very little and (7) very much. All items are presented.

Reliability: Alpha was .83.

Validity: Correlations with other variables ranged from −.11 to .60.

Author: Kirkhaug, R., and Haluari, H.

Article: Relations among freedom of action, goal orientation, coupling and satisfaction with frame management among school managers.

Journal: *Psychological Reports*, August 1998, *83*(1), 339–352.

8176

Test Name: INDEX OF JOB SATISFACTION

Purpose: To measure job satisfaction.

Number of Items: 5

Format: Eleven-point scales are anchored by 0 (strongly disagree) and 10 (strongly agree). All items are presented.

Reliability: Reliability was .88.

Validity: The average correlation with the Job Description Index was .89.

Author: Judge, T. A., et al.

Article: Dispositional effects on job and life satisfaction: The role of core evaluations.

Journal: *Journal of Applied Psychology,* February 1998, *83*(1), 17–34.

Related Research: Brayfield, A. H., & Rothe, H. F. (1951). An index of job satisfaction. *Journal of Applied Psychology, 35*, 307–311.

8177

Test Name: INDOCTRINATION SCALE

Purpose: To assess the extent to which employee values mesh with organizational values.

Number of Items: 8

Format: Scales range from "low levels of absorption" to "high levels." A sample item is presented.

Reliability: Coefficient alpha was .70.

Authors: Jeonquart-Barone, S., and Sekaran, U.

Article: Institutional racism: An empirial study.

Journal: *Journal of Social Psychology,* August 1996, *136*(4), 477–482.

Related Research: Hood, J. (1989). Acculturation and assimilation as applied to business organizations. Unpublished doctoral dissertation, University of Colorado, Boulder.

8178

Test Name: INDSALES— REVISED

Purpose: To measure overall job satisfaction.

Number of Items: 6

Reliability: Alpha coefficient was .91.

Validity: Correlations with other variables ranged from −.09 to .71.

Author: Murrell, A. J., et al.

Article: Mobility strategies and career outcomes: A longitudinal study of MBAs.

Journal: *Journal of Vocational Behavior,* December 1996, *49*(3), 324–335.

Related Research: Comer, J. M., et al. (1989). Psychometric assessment of a reduced version of INDSALES. *Journal of Business Research, 18*, 291–302.

8179

Test Name: INTENT TO TURNOVER SCALE

Purpose: To measure turnover intentions.

Number of Items: 3

Format: Responses are made on a

5-point scale ranging from "strongly agree" to "strongly disagree." Sample items are presented.

Reliability: Reliability estimate was .83.

Validity: Correlations with other variables ranged from −.67 to .45.

Author: Hochwarter, W. A., et al.

Article: Commitment as an antidote to the tension and turnover consequences of organizational politics.

Journal: *Journal of Vocational Behavior*, December 1999, *55*(3), 277–297.

Related Research: Cammann, C., et al. (1979). *Michigan Organizational Assessment Questionnaire*. Unpublished manuscript, University of Michigan, Ann Arbor.

8180

Test Name: INTENT TO TURNOVER SCALE

Purpose: To measure intent to turnover.

Number of Items: 5

Reliability: Coefficient alpha was .91 ($N = 419$).

Validity: Correlations with other variables ranged from −.62 to −.27 ($N = 419$).

Author: Sturman, M. C., and Short, J. C.

Article: Lump-sum bonus satisfaction: Testing the construct validity of a new pay satisfaction dimension.

Journal: *Personnel Psychology*, Autumn 2000, *53*(3), 673–700.

Related Research: Netemeyer, R. G., et al. (1996). Development and validation of work-family conflict and family-work conflict scales. *Journal of Applied Psychology, 81*, 400–410.

8181

Test Name: INTENT TO TURNOVER SCALE

Purpose: To measure intent to turnover.

Number of Items: 7

Format: Responses are made on a 5-point Likert scale ranging from 1 (strongly disagree) to 5 (strongly agree). Sample items are presented.

Reliability: The reliability estimate was .91.

Validity: Correlations with other variables ranged from −.65 to .47.

Author: Hochwarter, W. A., et al.

Article: Commitment as an antidote to the tension and turnover consequences of organizational politics.

Journal: *Journal of Vocational Behavior*, December 1999, *55*(3), 277–297.

Related Research: Mowday, R. T., et al. (1984). The psychology of the withdrawal process: A cross validation test of Mobley's intermediate linkages model of turnover in two samples. *Academy of Management Journal, 27*, 79–94.

8182

Test Name: INTENTION TO LEAVE MEASURE

Purpose: To measure intention to stay in the employ of the hospital.

Number of Items: 3

Format: Responses are made on a 5-point scale. A sample item is presented.

Reliability: Coefficient alpha was .69.

Validity: Correlations with other variables ranged from −.36 to .17.

Author: Krausz, M., et al.

Article: Actual and preferred work schedules and scheduling control as determinants of job-related attitudes.

Journal: *Journal of Vocational Behavior*, February 2000, *56*(1), 1–11.

Related Research: Seashore, S. E., et al. (Eds.). (1982). *Observing and measuring organizational change: A guide to field practice.* New York: Wiley.

8183

Test Name: INTENTION TO LEAVE THE ORGANIZATION SCALE

Purpose: To measure intention to leave the organization.

Number of Items: 3

Format: Responses are made on a 5-point scale. All items are presented.

Reliability: Reliability was .82.

Validity: Correlations with other variables ranged from −.53 to .01.

Author: Cohen, A.

Article: On the discriminant validity of the Meyers and Allen measure of organized commitment: How does it fit with the work commitment construct?

Journal: *Educational and Psychological Measurement*, June 1996, *56*(6), 494–503.

Related Research: Mobley, W. H., et al (1979). Review and conceptual analysis of the employee turnover process.

Psychological Bulletin, 86, 493–522.

8184

Test Name: INTENTIONS OF EXIT AND NEGLECT SCALE

Purpose: To measure intentions of exit and neglect.

Number of Items: 11

Format: Includes 2 scales: Intentions of Exit and Neglect. Responses are made on a 5-point scale ranging from 1 (strongly disagree) to 5 (strongly agree). Sample items are presented.

Reliability: Reliability coefficients ranged from .58 to .84.

Validity: Correlation with other variables ranged from −.41 to .29.

Author: Vigoda, E.

Article: Organizational politics, job attitudes, work outcomes: Exploration and implications for the public sector.

Journal: *Journal of Vocational Behavior*, December 2000, *57*(3), 326–347.

Related Research: Farrell, D., and Rusbult, C. E. (1992). Exploring the exit, voice, loyalty, and neglect typology: The influence of job satisfaction, quality of alternatives, and investment size. Special Issue: Research on Hirshman's Exit, Voice, and Loyalty model. *Employee Responsibilities and Rights Journal, 5*, 201–218.

8185

Test Name: INTENTIONS TO LEAVE SCALE

Purpose: To assess intentions to leave.

Number of Items: 3

Format: Responses are made on a

5-point scale ranging from 1 (never) to 5 (all the time). All items are presented.

Reliability: Coefficient alpha was .90.

Author: Tharenou, P., and Terry, D. J.

Article: Reliability and validity of scores on scales to measure managerial aspirations.

Journal: *Educational and Psychological Measurement*, June 1998, *58*(3), 475–492.

Related Research: Blau, G. J. (1988). The measurement and prediction of career commitment. *Journal of Occupational Psychology*, *58*, 277–288

8186

Test Name: INTENTIONS TO QUIT SCALE

Purpose: To measure intentions to quit.

Number of Items: 3

Format: Sample items are presented.

Reliability: Alpha coefficients were .86 and .82.

Validity: Correlations with other variables ranged from −.82 to .60.

Author: Saks, A. M., and Ashforth, B. E.

Article: A longitudinal investigation of the relationships between job information sources, applicant perception of fit, and work outcomes.

Journal: *Personnel Psychology*, Summer 1997, *50*(2), 395–426.

Related Research: Colarelli, S. M. (1984). Methods of communication and mediating processes in realistic job previews. *Journal of Applied Psychology*, *69*, 633–642.

8187

Test Name: INTERPERSONAL FACILITATION SCALE

Purpose: To measure helpful, considerate and cooperative aspects of performance on the job.

Number of Items: 7

Format: Five-point scales. All items are presented.

Reliability: Coefficient alpha was .89.

Validity: Correlations with other variables ranged from .06 to .36.

Author: Van Scotter, J. R., et al.

Article: Effects of task performance and contextual performance on systemic rewards.

Journal: *Journal of Applied Psychology*, August 2000, *85*(4), 526–535.

8188

Test Name: INTERPERSONAL SATISFACTION SUB-SCALE

Purpose: To identify satisfaction with co-workers and supervision.

Number of Items: 6

Format: Responses are made on a 7-point agree-disagree scale.

Reliability: Coefficient alpha was .80.

Author: Fried, Y., et al.

Article: Changes in job decision latitude: The influence of personality and interpersonal satisfaction.

Journal: *Journal of Vocational Behavior*, April 1999, *54*(2), 233–243.

Related Research: Hackman, J. R., & Oldham, G. R. (1975). Development of the Job Diagnostic Survey. *Journal of*

Applied Psychology, *60*, 159–170.

8189

Test Name: INTERROLE WORK TRANSITION SCALES

Purpose: To measure interrole work transition variables.

Number of Items: 7

Format: Includes 3 variables: Organizational Withdrawal Intent, Profession Withdrawal Intent, and Retirement Age Intent. Sample items are presented.

Validity: Correlations with other variables ranged from −.41 to .17.

Author: Blau, G.

Article: Job, organizational, and professional context antecedents as predictors of intent for interrole work transitions.

Journal: *Journal of Vocational Behavior*, June 2000, *56*(3), 330–345.

Related Research: Michaels, C., & Spector, P. (1982). Causes of employee turnover: A test of the Mobley, Griffeth, Hand and Meglino model. *Journal of Applied Psychology*, *67*, 53–59.

Blau, G. (1989). Testing the generalizability of a career commitment measure and its impact on employee turnover. *Journal of Vocational Behavior*, *35*, 88–103.

8190

Test Name: INTRINSIC CAREER SUCCESS MEASURE

Purpose: To assess overall job satisfaction.

Number of Items: 8

Format: Interviewers coded responses on a 5-point scale

ranging from 1 (dislike it very much) to 5 (like it very much).

Reliability: Coefficient alpha was .92.

Validity: Correlations with other variables ranged from −.26 to .40.

Author: Judge, T. A., et al.

Article: The Big Five personality traits, general mental ability, and career success across the life span.

Journal: *Personnel Psychology,* Autumn 1999, *52*(3), 621–652.

8191

Test Name: JOB BOREDOM SCALE

Purpose: To assess the extent to which individuals find their job boring and uninteresting.

Number of Items: 5

Format: Scales range from ''never'' to ''often.'' A sample item is presented.

Reliability: Coefficient alpha was .80.

Validity: Correlations with other variables ranged from −.29 to .49.

Author: Frone, M. R.

Article: Predictors of work injuries among employed adolescents.

Journal: *Journal of Applied Psychology,* August 1998, *83*(4), 565–576.

8192

Test Name: JOB DIAGNOSTIC SURVEY—ABBREVIATED

Purpose: To measure job satisfaction.

Number of Items: 3

Format: Responses are made on a

7-point rating scale ranging from 1 (disagree strongly) to 7 (agree strongly). Sample items are presented.

Reliability: Coefficient alpha was .76.

Validity: Correlation with other variables ranged from −.33 to .42.

Author: Adams, G. A.

Article: Career-related variables and planned retirement age: An extension of Beehr's model.

Journal: *Journal of Vocational Behavior,* October 1999, *55*(2), 221–235.

Related Research: Hackman, J. R., & Oldham, G. R. (1975). Development of the Job Diagnostic Survey. *Journal of Applied Psychology, 60,* 159–170.

8193

Test Name: JOB DISSATISFACTION SCALE

Purpose: To measure dissatisfaction with job.

Number of Items: 2

Format: Five- and six-point scales are used.

Reliability: Coefficient alpha was .84.

Author: Markel, K. S., and Frone, M. R.

Article: Job characteristics, work-school conflict, and school outcomes among adolescents: Testing a structural model.

Journal: *Journal of Applied Psychology,* April 1998, *83*(2), 277–287.

Related Research: Johnston, L. D., et al. (1995). *Monitoring the future: Questionnaire responses from the nation's high school seniors, 1993.* Ann Arbor:

University of Michigan, Institute for Social Research.

8194

Test Name: JOB DISSATISFACTION SCALE

Purpose: To measure dissatisfaction with job.

Number of Items: 6

Format: Five-point scales are anchored by 1 (not at all) and 5 (extremely).

Reliability: Coefficient alpha ranged from .81 to .84 across subscales.

Author: Markel, K. S., and Frone, M. R.

Article: Job characteristics, work-school conflict, and school outcomes among adolescents: Testing a structural model.

Journal: *Journal of Applied Psychology,* April 1998, *83*(2), 277–287.

Related Research: Kandel, D. B., et al. (1985). The stressfulness of daily social roles for women: Marital, occupational and household roles. *Journal of Health and Social Behavior, 26,* 64–78.

8195

Test Name: JOB HASSLES SCALE

Purpose: To measure hassles encountered in an electrical contracting organization.

Number of Items: 17

Format: Four-point scales are anchored by 1 (not at all) and 4 (great extent).

Reliability: Cronbach alpha was .85.

Author: Mayes, B. T., et al.

Article: Personality, job level, job

stressors, and their interaction as predictors of coping behavior.

Journal: *Psychological Reports*, August 2000, *87*(1), 61–81.

Related Research: Newton, T. J., & Keenan, P. T., Jr. (1985). Coping with work-related stress. *Human Relations, 38*, 107–126.

8196

Test Name: JOB INSECURITY MEASURE

Purpose: To measure job insecurity by self-report.

Number of Items: 18

Format: Five-point scales are anchored by 1 (strongly disagree) and 5 (strongly agree). A sample item is presented.

Reliability: Coefficient alpha ranged from .70 to .87.

Validity: Correlations with other variables ranged from −.21 to .48.

Author: Barling, J., et al.

Article: Effects of parents' job insecurity on children's work beliefs and attitudes.

Journal: *Journal of Applied Psychology*, February 1998, *83*(1), 112–118.

Related Research: Kuhnert, K. W., & Vance, R. T. (1992). Job insecurity and moderators of the relation between job insecurity and employee adjustment. In J. C. Quick et al. (Eds.), *Stress and well-being at work: Assessments and interventions for occupational mental health* (pp. 48–63). Washington, DC: American Psychological Association.

8197

Test Name: JOB INSECURITY SCALE

Purpose: To measure threats to job security.

Number of Items: 5

Format: Likert format.

Reliability: Coefficient alpha was .87.

Validity: Correlations with other variables ranged from −.24 to .23.

Author: Kivimaki, M., et al.

Article: Psychosocial factors predicting employee sickness absence during economic decline.

Journal: *Journal of Applied Psychology*, December 1997, *82*(6), 858–872.

Related Research: Lehto, A.-M. (1991). *Työe lämän laatuja tasa-arvo tuotannossa* [Quality of working life and equity]. Helsinki: Statistics Finland.

8198

Test Name: JOB LOSS DISTRESS SCALES

Purpose: To measure anxiety, irritation, and depression.

Number of Items: 13

Format: Scale anchors are 1 (never or a little of the time) and 4 (most of the time). Sample items are presented.

Reliability: Alpha coefficients ranged from .75 to .90 across subscales.

Validity: Correlations with other variables ranged from −.29 to .15.

Author: Gowan, M. A., et al.

Article: Test of a model of coping with involuntary job loss following a company closing.

Journal: *Journal of Applied Psychology*, February 1999, *84*(1), 75–86.

Related Research: Harris, M. M.,

et al. (1988). Sex differences in psychological well-being during a facility closure. *Journal of Management, 14*, 391–402.

8199

Test Name: JOB SATISFACTION BLANK

Purpose: To assess overall job satisfaction.

Number of Items: 4

Format: Responses are made to one of seven alternatives that most accurately reflects how one feels about his/her present job.

Reliability: Alpha coefficients ranged from .76 to .89.

Validity: Correlations with other variables ranged from −.18 to .16.

Author: Tokar, D. M., and Subich, L. M.

Article: Relative contributions of congruences and personality dimensions to job satisfaction.

Journal: *Journal of Vocational Behavior*, June 1997, *50*(3), 482–491.

Related Research: Hoppock, R. (1935). *Job satisfaction*. New York: Harper and Row.

8200

Test Name: JOB SATISFACTION INDEX

Purpose: To measure job satisfaction.

Format: Responses are either "yes", "no", or "?."

Reliability: Alpha coefficients ranged from .82 to .92.

Validity: Correlations with other variables ranged from −.23 to .27.

Author: Morrow, P. C., and Crum, M. R.

Article: The effects of perceived and objective safety risk on employee outcomes.

Journal: *Journal of Vocational Behavior*, October 1998, *53*(2), 300–313.

Related Research: Smith, P. C., et al. (1969*). The measurements of job satisfaction in work and retirement*, Chicago: Rand McNally.

8201

Test Name: JOB SATISFACTION INDEX

Number of Items: 10

Format: Four-point scales range from 1 (not true at all) to 4 (very true). Sample items are presented.

Validity: Correlations with other variables ranged from −. 02 to .15.

Author: Dickter, D. N., et al.

Article: Temporal tempering: An event history analysis of the process of voluntary turnover.

Journal: *Journal of Applied Psychology*, December 1996, *81*(6), 705–716.

Related Research: Smith, P. C., et al. (1969). *The measurement of satisfaction in work and retirement*. Chicago: Rand-McNally.

8202

Test Name: JOB SATISFACTION INDEX

Purpose: To measure employees' degree of satisfaction they feel towards their jobs.

Number of Items: 18

Reliability: Split-half reliability was .87.

Validity: Correlation with the

Hoppock Job Satisfaction Blanks was .92.

Author: Leong, F. T. L., et al.

Article: An evaluation of the cross-cultural validity of Holland's theory: Career choices by workers in India.

Journal: *Journal of Vocational Behavior*, June 1998, *52*(3), 441–455.

Related Research: Brayfield, A. H., & Rothe, H. F. (1951). An index of job satisfaction. *Journal of Applied Psychology*, *35*, 307–311.

8203

Test Name: JOB SATISFACTION INVENTORY FOR FAMILY PHYSICIANS

Purpose: To measure job satisfaction among family physicians.

Number of Items: 80

Format: Semantic differential format.

Reliability: Alphas ranged from .77 to .94.

Author: Garcia-Pena, M. D. C., et al.

Article: Development and validation of an inventory for measuring job satisfaction among family physicians.

Journal: *Psychological Reports*, August 1996, *79*(1), 291–299.

Related Research: Lichtenstein, R. (1994). Measuring the job satisfaction of physicians in organized settings. *Medical Care*, *22*, 56–68.

8204

Test Name: JOB SATISFACTION QUESTIONNAIRE

Purpose: To measure job satisfaction.

Number of Items: 5

Format: Seven-point scales range from 1 (terrible) to 7 (delighted).

Reliability: Alpha coefficients ranged from .79 to .81.

Validity: Correlation with the Minnesota Satisfaction Questionnaire was .70.

Author: Steel, R. P., and Rentsch, J. R.

Article: The dispositional model of job attitudes revisited: Findings of a 10-year study.

Journal: *Journal of Applied Psychology*, December 1997, *82*(6), 873–879.

Related Research: Andrews, F. M., & Withey, S. B. (1976). *Social indicators of well-being: Americans' perceptions of life quality*. New York: Plenum Press.

8205

Test Name: JOB SATISFACTION QUESTIONNAIRE/ ORGANIZATIONAL COMMITMENT SCALE

Purpose: To measure job satisfaction in the United Arab Emirates.

Number of Items: 60

Format: Five-point response scales.

Reliability: Alphas ranged from .68 to .80. Total alphas were .94 (job satisfaction) and .70 (organizational commitment).

Validity: Correlations between job satisfaction and organizational commitment ranged from .09 to .34.

Author: Alnajjar, A. A.

Article: Relationship between job satisfaction and organizational commitment among employees in the United Arab Emirates.

Journal: *Psychological Reports*, August 1996, *79*(1), 315–321.

8206

Test Name: JOB SATISFACTION SCALE

Purpose: To measure job satisfaction.

Format: Includes 6 job aspects: current job, co-workers, supervisors, current salary, opportunities for promotion, and work in general. Responses are made on a 5-point scale ranging from 1 (very dissatisfied) to 5 (very satisfied).

Reliability: Reliability coefficient was .77.

Validity: Correlations with other variables ranged from −.40 to .56.

Author: Vigoda, E.

Article: Organizational politics, job attitudes, work outcomes: Exploration and implications for the public sector.

Journal: *Journal of Vocational Behavior*, December 2000, *57*(3), 326–347.

Related Research: Schriesheim, C., & Tsui, A. S. (1980). *Development and validation of a short satisfaction instrument for use in survey feedback interventions*. Paper presented at the Western Academy of Management meeting.

8207

Test Name: JOB SATISFACTION SCALE

Purpose: To measure job satisfaction.

Number of Items: 3

Format: Responses are made on a 5-point Likert-type scale ranging from 1 (strongly disagree) to 5

(strongly agree). An example is given.

Reliability: Coefficient alpha was .84.

Validity: Correlations with other variables ranged from −.71 to .71 (*N* = 116).

Author: Nielsen, I. K., et al.

Article: Development and validation of scores on a two-dimensional workplace friendship scale.

Journal: *Educational and Psychological Measurement*, August 2000, *60*(4), 628–643.

Related Research: Cammann, C., et al. (1979). *The Michigan Organizational Assessment Questionnaire*, Unpublished manuscript, University of Michigan, Ann Arbor.

8208

Test Name: JOB SATISFACTION SCALE

Purpose: To measure job satisfaction.

Number of Items: 3

Format: Responses are made on a 5-point scale ranging from 1 (strongly disagree) to 5 (strongly agree). A sample item is presented.

Reliability: Coefficient alpha was .89.

Validity: Correlations with other variables ranged from −.52 to .39.

Author: Shaffer, M. A., et al.

Article: Gender discrimination and job-related outcomes: A cross-cultural comparison of working women in the United States and China.

Journal: *Journal of Vocational Behavior*, December 2000, *57*(3), 395–427.

Related Research: Hackman, J. R., & Oldham, G. R. (1975). Development of the job diagnostic survey. *Journal of Applied Psychology, 60*, 159–170.

8209

Test Name: JOB SATISFACTION SCALE

Purpose: To measure job satisfaction.

Number of Items: 4

Format: Responses are made on a 5-point Likert-type scale.

Reliability: Coefficient alpha was .85.

Validity: Correlations with other variables ranged from −.55 to .54.

Author: Krausz, M., et al.

Article: Actual and preferred work schedules and scheduling control as determinants of job-related attitudes.

Journal: *Journal of Vocational Behavior*, February 2000, *56*(1), 1–11.

Related Research: Beehr, A. T. (1976). Perceived situational moderators of the relationships between subjective role ambiguity and role strain. *Journal of Applied Psychology, 61*, 35–40.

8210

Test Name: JOB SATISFACTION SCALE

Purpose: To measure global satisfaction with the job.

Number of Items: 5

Format: Responses are made on a 7-point scale ranging from "strongly disagree" to "strongly agree."

Reliability: Reliability coefficients were .94 and .93.

Author: Boles, J. S., et al.

Article: The dimensionality of the Maslach Burnout Inventory across small business owners and educators.

Journal: *Journal of Vocational Behavior*, February 2000, *56*(1), 12–34.

Related Research: Netemeyer, R. G., et al. (1996). Development and validation of work-family conflict and family-work conflict scales. *Journal of Applied Psychology, 81*, 1–11.

8211

Test Name: JOB SATISFACTION SCALE

Purpose: To measure job satisfaction.

Number of Items: 5

Format: Scales range from 1 (strongly disagree) to 5 (strongly agree). All items are presented.

Reliability: Coefficient alpha was .89.

Validity: Correlations with other variables ranged from −.27 to .84.

Author: Judge, T. A., et al.

Article: Personality and job satisfaction: The mediating role of job characteristics.

Journal: *Journal of Applied Psychology*, April 2000, *85*(2), 237–249.

Related Research: Brayfield, A. H., & Rothe, H. F. (1951). An index of job satisfaction. *Journal of Applied Psychology, 35*, 307–311.

8212

Test Name: JOB SATISFACTION SCALE

Purpose: To identify one's feelings about one's job.

Number of Items: 6

Format: Responses are made on a 5-point scale ranging from 1 (never) to 5 (most of the time). All items are presented.

Reliability: Coefficient alpha was .82.

Validity: Correlations with other variables ranged from −.15 to .43.

Author: Ettington, D. R.

Article: Successful career plateauing.

Journal: *Journal of Vocational Behavior*, February 1998, *52*(1), 72–88.

Related Research: Quinn, R. P., & Shepard, L. J. (1974). *The 1972 Quality of Employment Survey*. Ann Arbor, MI: Survey Research Center, Institute for Social Research.

8213

Test Name: JOB SATISFACTION SCALE

Purpose: To measure job satisfaction for workers with modest educational attainment.

Number of Items: 7

Format: Scales range from 1 (extremely satisfied) to 7 (extremely dissatisfied).

Reliability: Internal reliability was .84.

Validity: Correlations with other variables ranged from −.10 to .39.

Author: Wright, B. M., and Cordery, J. L.

Article: Production uncertainty as a contextual moderator of employee reactions to job design.

Journal: *Journal of Applied Psychology*, June 1999, *84*(3), 456–463.

Related Research: Warr, P. B., et al. (1979). Scales for the measurement of some work attitudes and aspects of psychological well-being. *Journal of Occupational Psychology, 52*, 129–148.

8214

Test Name: JOB SATISFACTION SCALE

Purpose: To assess job satisfaction among industrial salespersons.

Number of Items: 11

Format: Scales ranged from "completely untrue" to "completely true."

Reliability: Coefficient alpha was .90.

Author: Klein, D. J., and Verbeke, W.

Article: Autonomic feedback in stressful environments: How do individual differences in autonomic feedback relate to burnout, job performance, and job attitudes in salespeople?

Journal: *Journal of Applied Psychology*, December 1999, *84*(6), 911–924.

Related Research: Churchill, G., et al. (1974). Measuring the job satisfaction of industrial salesmen. *Journal of Marketing Research, 11*, 254–260.

8215

Test Name: JOB SATISFACTION SCALE

Purpose: To measure satisfaction within the work environment.

Number of Items: 14

Format: Includes 5 satisfactions: pay, job security, social, supervisory, and growth satisfaction.

Reliability: Alpha coefficients were .88 and .89.

Validity: Correlations with the Work of Locus Control Scale ranged from −.53 to .02.

Author: Macan, T. H., et al.

Article: Spector's Work of Locus Control Scale: Dimensionality and validity evidence.

Journal: *Educational and Psychological Measurement*, April 1996, *56*(2), 349–357.

Related Research: Hackman, J. R., & Oldham, G. R. (1975). Development of the job survey. *Journal of Applied Psychology*, *60*, 159–170.

8216

Test Name: JOB SATISFACTION SCALE

Purpose: To measure job satisfaction.

Number of Items: 15

Format: Responses are made on a 4-point scale ranging from 1 (strongly disagree) to 4 (strongly agree).

Reliability: Coefficient alpha was .86.

Validity: Correlation with other variables ranged from −.05 to .12.

Author: Blau, G., and Lunz, M.

Article: Testing the incremental effect of professional commitment on intent to leave one's profession beyond effects of external, personal, and work-related variables.

Journal: *Journal of Vocational Behavior*, April 1998, *52*(2), 260–269.

Related Research: Hackman, J., & Oldham, G. (1975). Development of the Job Diagnostic Survey. *Journal of*

Applied Psychology, *60*, 159–170.

8217

Test Name: JOB SATISFACTION SCALE

Purpose: To measure job satisfaction.

Number of Items: 15

Format: Five-point Likert format. Items are described.

Reliability: Alpha coefficients ranged from .73 to .86 across subscales.

Validity: Correlations with other variables ranged from −.31 to .42.

Author: Riipinen, M.

Article: The relation of work involvement to occupational needs, need satisfaction, locus of control and affect.

Journal: *Journal of Social Psychology*, June 1996, *136*(3), 291–303.

Related Research: Gorn, G. J., & Kanungo, R. N. (1980). Job involvement and motivation: Are intrinsically motivated managers more job involved? *Organizational Behavior and Human Performance*, *26*, 265–277.

8218

Test Name: JOB SATISFACTION SCALE

Purpose: To measure job satisfaction.

Number of Items: 16

Format: Seven-point scales are anchored by 1 (extremely dissatisfied) and 7 (extremely satisfied). All items are presented.

Reliability: Alpha was .89.

Author: Rout, U.

Article: Job stress among general practitioners and nurses in primary care in England.

Journal: *Psychological Reports*, December 1999, *85*(3, Part I), 981–986.

Related Research: Warr, P., et al. (1979). Scales for the measurement of some work attitudes and aspects of psychological well-being. *Journal of Occupational Psychology*, *52*, 129–148.

8219

Test Name: JOB SATISFACTION SURVEY

Purpose: To measure job satisfaction.

Number of Items: 36

Format: Includes 9 subscales: Pay, Promotion, Supervision, Benefits, Contingent Rewards, Operating Procedures, Co-workers, Nature of Work, and Communication. Responses are made on a 4-point scale ranging from 1 (strongly disagree) to 4 (strongly agree).

Reliability: Alpha coefficients were .89 and .91.

Validity: Correlations with other variables ranged from −.19 to .29.

Author: Blau, G.

Article: Job, organizational, and professional context antecedents as predictors of intent for interrole work transitions.

Journal: *Journal of Vocational Behavior*, June 2000, *56*(3), 330–345.

Related Research: Spector, P. (1985). Measurement of human service staff satisfaction: Development of the Job Satisfaction Survey. *American*

Journal of Community Psychology, 39, 693–713.

8220

Test Name: JOB STRESS QUESTIONNAIRE

Purpose: To measure job stress.

Number of Items: 42

Format: Five-point scales are anchored by 1 (no stress at all) and 5 (source of extreme stress).

Reliability: Alpha was .90.

Author: Rout, U.

Article: Job stress among general practitioners and nurses in primary care in England.

Journal: *Psychological Reports,* December 1999, *85*(3, Part I), 981–986.

Related Research: Rout, U., et al. (1996). Job stress among British general practitioners: Predictors of job dissatisfaction and mental ill-health. *Stress Medicine, 12,* 155–166.

8221

Test Name: JOB STRESS SCALE

Purpose: To assess job stress.

Number of Items: 15

Format: Includes 3 aspects of job stress: supervisor, coworkers, and subordinates. Responses are made on a 5-point scale ranging from "no stress at all" to "extreme stress." An example is presented.

Reliability: Alpha coefficients ranged from .89 to .91.

Validity: Correlations with other variables ranged from −.39 to .56.

Author: O'Connell, C. E., and Korabik, K.

Article: Sexual harassment: The relationship of personal

vulnerability, work context, perpetrator status, and types of harassment to outcomes.

Journal: *Journal of Vocational Behavior,* June 2000, *56*(3), 299–329.

Related Research: Chemers, M. M., et al. (1985). A person-environment analysis of job stress: A contingency model explanation. *Journal of Personality and Social Psychology, 49,* 628–635.

8222

Test Name: JOB STRESSOR QUESTIONNAIRE

Purpose: To measure perceived job stressors.

Number of Items: 8

Format: Seven-point scales are anchored by 1 (low prevalence) and 7 (high prevalence).

Reliability: Alpha coefficients ranged from .76 to .79 across five occasions.

Validity: Correlations with other variables ranged from .22 to .69.

Author: Westman, M., and Eden, D.

Article: Effects of a respite from work on burnout: Vacation relief and fade-out.

Journal: *Journal of Applied Psychology* August, 1997, *82*(4), 516–527.

Related Research: Etzion, D. (1984). Moderating effect of social support on the stress-burnout relationship. *Journal of Applied Psychology, 69,* 615–622.

8223

Test Name: JOB TENSION SCALE

Purpose: To assess job-induced tension.

Number of Items: 7

Format: Responses are made on a 6-point scale ranging from "strongly agree" to "strongly disagree." Sample items are presented.

Reliability: Reliability estimate was .84.

Validity: Correlations with other variables ranged from −.39 to .48.

Author: Hochwarter, W. A., et al.

Article: Commitment as an antidote to the tension and turnover consequences of organizational politics.

Journal: *Journal of Vocational Behavior,* December 1999, *55*(3), 277–297.

Related Research: House, R., & Rizzo, J. (1972). Toward the measurement of organizational practices: Scale development and validation. *Journal of Applied Psychology, 56,* 338–396.

8224

Test Name: LIKING SCALE

Purpose: To measure liking in an organizational setting.

Number of Items: 4

Format: Five-point scales are anchored by 5 (strongly agree) and 1 (strongly disagree). A sample item is presented.

Reliability: Coefficient alpha was .87.

Validity: Correlations with other variables ranged from −.49 to .74.

Author: Allen, T. D., and Rush, M. C.

Article: The effects of organizational citizenship behavior on performance judgments: A field study and a laboratory experiment.

Journal: *Journal of Applied Psychology*, April 1998, *83*(2), 247–260.

Related Research: Wayne, S. J., & Ferris, G. R. (1990). Influence tactics, affect, and exchange quality in supervisor-subordinate interactions: A laboratory experiment and a field study. *Journal of Applied Psychology*, 73, 487–499.

8225

Test Name: LOCALISM SCALE

Purpose: To assess the importance of on-the-job training and success in an organization.

Number of Items: 4

Format: Five-item scales are anchored with "very important" and "not very important." Sample items are presented.

Reliability: Alpha was .72.

Author: Wright, T. A., and Larwood, L.

Article: Further examination of the cosmopolitan-local latent role construct.

Journal: *Psychological Reports*, December 1997, *81*(3, Part I), 897–898.

Related Research: Grimes, A. J., & Berger, P. K. (1970). Cosmopolitan-local: Evaluation of the construct. *Administrative Science Quarterly*, 2, 281–306.

8226

Test Name: LUMP-SUM BONUS SATISFACTION MEASURE

Purpose: To measure lump-sum bonus satisfaction.

Number of Items: 4

Format: Responses are made on a 5-point scale ranging from 1 (very dissatisfied) to 5 (very satisfied). All items are presented.

Reliability: Coefficient alpha was .93 (*N* = 419).

Validity: Correlations with other variables ranged from −.27 to .66 (*N* = 419).

Author: Sturman, M. C., and Short, J. C.

Article: Lump-sum bonus satisfaction: Testing the construct validity of a new pay satisfaction dimension.

Journal: *Personnel Psychology*, Autumn 2000, *53*(3), 673–700.

8227

Test Name: MANIFEST NEEDS SCALE

Purpose: To measure manifest needs in work settings.

Number of Items: 5

Format: Seven-point Likert format. A sample item is presented.

Reliability: Coefficient alpha was .75.

Validity: Correlations with other variables ranged from −.75 to .38.

Authors: Rotono, D.

Article: Individual-difference variables and career-related coping.

Journal: *The Journal of Social Psychology*, August 1999, *139*(4), 458–471.

Related Research: Steers, R. M., & Braunstein, D. N. (1976). A behaviorally-based measure of manifest needs in work settings. *Journal of Vocational Behavior*, 9, 251–266.

8228

Test Name: MENTAL WORKLOAD SCALE

Purpose: To measure mental workload.

Number of Items: 6

Format: Responses are made on a 5-point Likert scale. A sample item is presented.

Reliability: Internal consistency reliability was .87.

Validity: Correlations with other variables ranged from −.48 to .39.

Author: Fisher, S. L., and Ford, J. K.

Article: Differential effects of learner effort and goal orientation on two learning outcomes.

Journal: *Personnel Psychology*, Summer 1998, *51*(2), 397–420.

Related Research: Hart, S. G., & Staveland, L. E. (1988). Development of NASA-TLX (Task Load Index): Results of empirical and theoretical research. In P. A. Hancock & N. Meshkati (Eds.), *Human mental workload* (pp. 77–106). New York: Elsevier Science Publishers B. V. (North-Holland).

8229

Test Name: MILITARY JOB SATISFACTION SCALE

Purpose: To measure satisfaction with military jobs.

Number of Items: 3

Format: Scales range from 1 (strongly disagree) to 5 (strongly agree). A sample item is presented.

Reliability: Reliability was .84.

Validity: Correlations with other variables ranged from −.27 to .53.

Author: Jex, S. M., and Bliese, P. D.

Article: Efficacy beliefs as a

moderator of the impact of work-related stressors: A multilevel study.

Journal: *Journal of Applied Psychology*, June 1999, *84*(3), 349–361.

Related Research: Hackman, J. R., & Oldham, G. R. (1980). *Work redesign*. Reading, MA: Addison-Wesley.

8230

Test Name: MINNESOTA SATISFACTION QUESTIONNAIRE

Purpose: To measure job satisfaction.

Number of Items: 20

Format: Five-point scales range from "very dissatisfied" to "very satisfied."

Reliability: Internal consistency was .91.

Author: George, J. M., and Jones, G. R.

Article: The experience of work and turnover intention: Interactive effects of value attainment, job satisfaction, and positive mood.

Journal: *Journal of Applied Psychology*, June 1996, *81*(3), 318–325.

Related Research: Weiss, D. J., et al. (1967). *Manual for the Minnesota Satisfaction Questionnaire*. Minneapolis: University of Minnesota Press.

8231

Test Name: NONWORK SATISFACTION SCALE

Purpose: To measure nonwork satisfaction.

Number of Items: 8

Format: Responses are made on a 5-point scale ranging from 1

(strongly disagree) to 5 (strongly agree). An example is presented.

Reliability: Internal consistency reliability estimate was .70.

Validity: Correlations with other variables ranged from −.11 to .63.

Author: Kacmar, K. M., et al.

Article: Antecedents and consequences of organizational commitment: A comparison of two scales.

Journal: *Educational and Psychological Measurement*, December 1999, *59*(6), 976–994.

Related Research: Romzek, B. S. (1989). Personal consequences of employee commitment. *Academy of Management Journal, 32*, 649–661.

8232

Test Name: NONWORK SATISFACTION SCALE

Purpose: To assess police officers' levels of satisfaction in nonwork domains.

Number of Items: 10

Format: Scales range from 1 (very dissatisfied) to 5 (very satisfied). All items are presented.

Reliability: Alpha coefficients ranged from .81 to .84.

Validity: Correlations with other variables ranged from −.50 to .56.

Author: Hart, P. M.

Article: Predicting employee life satisfaction: A coherent model of personality, work and nonwork experiences, and domain satisfactions.

Journal: *Journal of Applied Psychology*, August 1999, *84*(4), 564–584.

8233

Test Name: OCCUPATIONAL STRESS QUESTIONNAIRE

Purpose: To assess psychic strain symptoms.

Number of Items: 3

Format: Scales range from 1 (very seldom) to 5 (very often).

Reliability: Coefficient alpha was .75.

Authors: Kivimäki, M., et al.

Article: Effects of components of personal need for structure on occupational strain.

Journal: *Journal of Social Psychology*, December 1996, *136*(6), 769–777.

Related Research: Elo, A- L., et al. (1992). *Occupational stress questionnaire: Users' instructions*. Finnish Institute of Occupational Health, Review number 19. Helsinki: Työterveyslaitos.

8234

Test Name: OCCUPATIONAL STRESS QUESTIONNAIRE

Purpose: To measure perceived stressors at the workplace.

Number of Items: 11

Format: Five-point scales are anchored by (1) very seldom and (5) very often.

Reliability: Alphas ranged from .68 to .78 across subscales. Test-retest reliabilities ranged from .59 to .69.

Author: Kivimaki, M., et al.

Article: Sense of coherence as a modifier of occupational stress exposure, stress perception, and experienced strain: A study of industrial managers.

Journal: *Psychological Reports*, December 1998, *83*(3) Part 1, 971–981.

Related Research: Elo, A. L., et al. (1992). *Occupational Stress Questionnaire: User's instructions*. (Reviews No. 19), Helsinki: Finish Institute of Occupational Health.

8235

Test Name: OCCUPATIONAL STRESS SCALE

Purpose: To measure occupational stress.

Number of Items: 6

Format: Includes 2 subscales: Responsibility Pressures and Job vs. Non-Job Conflict. Examples are presented.

Reliability: Alpha coefficients ranged from .59 to .76.

Validity: Correlations with other variables ranged from −.39 to .59.

Author: Holder, J. C., and Vaux, A.

Article: African American professionals: Coping with occupational stress in predominantly White work environments.

Journal: *Journal of Vocational Behavior*, December 1998, *53*(3), 315–333.

Related Research: House, J. S., et al. (1979). Occupational stress and health among factory workers. *Journal of Health and Social Behavior*, *20*, 139–160.

8236

Test Name: ORGANIZATIONAL IDENTIFICATION SCALE

Purpose: To assess organizational identification.

Number of Items: 6

Format: Sample items are presented.

Reliability: Alpha coefficients were .80 and .85.

Validity: Correlations with other variables ranged from −.51 to .75.

Author: Saks, A. M., and Ashforth, B. E.

Article: A longitudinal investigation of the relationships between job information sources, applicant perceptions of fit, and work outcomes.

Journal: *Personnel Psychology*, Summer 1997, *50*(2), 395–426.

Related Research: Mael, F., & Ashforth, B. E. (1992). Alumni and their alma mater: A partial test of the reformulated model of organizational identification. *Journal of Organizational Behavior*, *13*, 103–123.

8237

Test Name: OVERALL JOB SATISFACTION

Purpose: To measure job satisfaction.

Number of Items: 4

Format: Seven-point scales range from 1 (strongly agree) to 7 (strongly disagree). All items are presented.

Reliability: Coefficient alpha was .72.

Validity: Correlations with other variables ranged from .45 to .60.

Author: Eisenberger, R., et al.

Article: Perceived organizational support, discretionary treatment, and job satisfaction.

Journal: *Journal of Applied Psychology*, October 1997, *82*(5), 812–820.

Related Research: Quinn, R. P., & Sheppard, L. G. (1974). *The 1972–1973 Quality of Employment Survey*. Ann Arbor:

Institute for Social Research, University of Michigan.

8238

Test Name: OVERALL JOB SATISFACTION SCALE

Purpose: To measure overall job satisfaction.

Number of Items: 3

Format: All items are presented.

Reliability: Coefficient alpha was .80 ($N = 419$).

Validity: Correlations with other variables ranged from −.62 to .65 ($N = 419$).

Author: Sturman, M. C., and Short, J. C.

Article: Lump-sum bonus satisfaction: Testing the construct validity of a new pay satisfaction dimension.

Journal: *Personnel Psychology*, Autumn 2000, *53*(3), 673–700.

Related Research: Judge, T. A., et al. (1995). An empirical investigation of the predictors of executive career success. *Personnel Psychology*, *48*, 485–519.

8239

Test Name: PAY SATISFACTION QUESTIONNAIRE

Purpose: To measure pay satisfaction.

Number of Items: 14

Format: Includes 4 dimensions: Benefits, Pay Level, Raises, and Structure/Administration. All items are presented.

Reliability: Alpha coefficients ranged from .84 to .95.

Author: DeConinck, J. B., et al.

Article: A construct validity analysis of scores on measures of distributive justice and pay satisfaction.

Journal: *Educational and Psychological Measurement*, December 1996, *56*(6), 1026–1036.

Related Research: Heneman, H. G., III, & Schwab, D. P. (1985). Pay satisfaction: Its multidimensional nature and measurement. *International Journal of Psychology*, *20*, 129–141.

8240

Test Name: PAY SATISFACTION QUESTIONNAIRE

Purpose: To measure dimensions of pay satisfaction.

Number of Items: 18

Format: Includes 4 dimensions: Pay Level, Benefits, Raise, and Structure/Administration. Responses are made on a 5-point scale ranging from 1 (very dissatisfied) to 5 (very satisfied).

Reliability: Alpha coefficients ranged from .90 to .96 ($N = 419$).

Validity: Correlations with other variables ranged from −.38 to .66 ($N = 419$).

Author: Sturman, M. C., and Short, J. C.

Article: Lump-sum bonus satisfaction: Testing the construct validity of a new pay satisfaction dimension.

Journal: *Personnel Psychology*, Autumn 2000, *53*(3), 673–700.

Related Research: Heneman, H. G., III, & Schwab, D. (1985). Pay satisfaction: Its multidimensional nature and measurement. *International Journal of Psychology*, *20*, 129–141.

8241

Test Name: PERCEIVED COMMON GROUND SCALE

Purpose: To measure the degree of agreement over managerial proposals.

Number of Items: 3

Format: All items are presented.

Reliability: Coefficient alpha was .59.

Validity: Correlations with other variables ranged from −.27 to .08.

Author: Ross, W. H., and Wieland, C.

Article: Effects of interpersonal trust and time pressure on managerial mediation strategy in a simulated organizational dispute.

Journal: *Journal of Applied Psychology*, June 1996, *81*(3), 228–248.

8242

Test Name: PERCEIVED FINANCIAL HARDSHIP SCALE

Purpose: To assess the difficulty of living on current household income.

Number of Items: 3

Format: Scales range from 1 (not at all difficult) to 5 (extremely difficult or impossible). All items are presented.

Reliability: Coefficient alpha was .85.

Validity: Correlations with other variables ranged from −.17 to .39.

Author: Wanberg, C. R., et al.

Article: Unemployed individuals: Motives, job-search competencies, and job-search constraints as predictors of job seeking and reemployment.

Journal: *Journal of Applied Psychology*, December 1999, *84*(6), 897–910.

Related Research: Vinokur, A., & Caplan, R. D. (1987). Attitudes and social support: Determinants of job-seeking behavior and well-being among the unemployed. *Journal of Applied Social Psychology*, *17*, 1007–1024.

8243

Test Name: PERCEIVED SOCIAL SUPPORT SCALE

Purpose: To measure social support by supervisor and colleague report.

Number of Items: 8

Format: Scales range from 1 (never) to 5 (always).

Reliability: Alpha coefficients ranged from .85 to .89 across subscales.

Author: van Dierendonck, D., et al.

Article: The evaluation of an individual burnout intervention program: The role of inequity and social support.

Journal: *Journal of Applied Psychology*, June 1998, *83*(3), 392–407.

Related Research: House, J. S. (1981). *Work stress and social support*. Reading, MA: Addison-Wesley.

8244

Test Name: PERCEIVED TASK INDEPENDENCE SCALE

Purpose: To assess the degree to which team tasks are dependent on cooperation and communication.

Number of Items: 4

Format: Scales range from 1

(strongly disagree) to 6 (strongly agree). All items are presented.

Reliability: Coefficient alpha was .78.

Validity: Correlations with other variables ranged from −.04 to .14.

Author: Bishop, J. W., and Scott, K. D.

Article: An examination of organizational and team commitment in a self-directed team environment.

Journal: *Journal of Applied Psychology*, June 2000, *85*(3), 439–450.

8245

Test Name: PERCEPTIONS OF FAIR INTERPERSONAL TREATMENT SCALE

Purpose: To assess employees' perceptions of interpersonal treatment where they work.

Number of Items: 18

Format: Yes/no format. All items are presented.

Reliability: Coefficient alpha was .90 (Total), .91 (Supervisor subscale), and .76 (Coworker subscale).

Validity: Correlations with other variables ranged from −.35 to .56.

Author: Donovan, M. A., et al.

Article: The Perceptions of Fair Interpersonal Treatment Scale: Development and validation of a measure of interpersonal treatment in the workplace.

Journal: *Journal of Applied Psychology*, October 1998, *83*(5), 683–692.

8246

Test Name: PERFORMANCE VALANCE SCALE

Purpose: To measure performance valance as the average of satisfaction with five performance areas.

Number of Items: 5

Format: Seven-point scales ranged from 1 (extremely dissatisfied) to 7 (extremely satisfied).

Reliability: Coefficient alpha was .90.

Validity: Correlations with other variables ranged from −.43 to .09.

Author: Gellatly, I. R.

Article: Conscientiousness and task performance: Test of a cognitive process model.

Journal: *Journal of Applied Psychology*, October 1996, *81*(5), 474–482.

8247

Test Name: PHYSICAL WORKING CONDITIONS CHECKLIST

Purpose: To measure job stress.

Number of Items: 16

Format: yes/no format.

Validity: Correlations with other variables ranged from −.45 to .57.

Author: Gorgievski—Duijvesteijn, M., et al.

Article: Protestant work ethic as a moderator of mental and physical well-being.

Journal: *Psychological Reports*, December 1998, *83*(3) Part 1, 1043–1050.

Related Research: Kompier, M. A. J., & Marcelissen, F. H. G. (1990). *Handboek werkstress [Handbook of work stress]*. Amsterdam: NIA.

8248

Test Name: PLATEAUING SCALE

Purpose: To measure content and hierarchical career plateauing.

Number of Items: 10

Format: Scales range from 1 (strongly disagree) to 5 (strongly agree). Sample items are presented.

Reliability: Alpha coefficients were .81 (hierarchical) and .84 (content).

Validity: Correlations with other variables ranged from −.19 to .48.

Author: Allen, T. D., et al.

Article: Attitudes of managers who are more or less career plateaued.

Journal: *Career Development Quarterly*, December 1998, *47*(2), 159–172.

Related Research: Milliman, J. F. (1992). *Causes and moderators of career plateauing: An empirical investigation*. Unpublished doctoral dissertation, University of Southern California.

8249

Test Name: POLICE DAILY HASSLES SCALE

Purpose: To assess positive and negative experiences of police work encountered on a day-to-day basis.

Number of Items: 86

Format: Five-point frequency and intensity scales ranged from 0 (definitely does not apply to me) to 4 (strongly applies to me).

Reliability: Alpha coefficients ranged from .93 to .98.

Validity: Correlations with other

variables ranged from −.54 to .62.

Author: Hart, P. M.

Article: Predicting employee life satisfaction: A coherent model of personality, work and nonwork experiences, and domain satisfactions.

Journal: *Journal of Applied Psychology*, August 1999, *84*(4), 564–584.

Related Research: Hart, P. M., et al. (1994). Perceived quality of life, personality and work experiences: Construct validation of the police daily hassles and uplifts scales. *Journal of Criminal Justice and Behavior, 21*, 283–311.

8250

Test Name: POLICE DAILY UPLIFTS SCALE

Purpose: To assess a wide range of organizational experiences common to police work.

Number of Items: 50

Format: Five-point frequency and positive intensity scales.

Reliability: Alpha coefficients ranged from .93 to .95.

Validity: Correlations with other variables ranged from −.36 to .54.

Author: Hart, P. M.

Article: Predicting employee life satisfaction: A coherent model of personality, work and nonwork experiences, and domain satisfactions.

Journal: *Journal of Applied Psychology*, August 1999, *84*(4), 564–584.

Related Research: Hart, P. M., et al. (1993). Assessing police work experiences: Development of the police daily hassles and uplifts scales. *Journal of Criminal*

Justice and Behavior, 21, 283–311.

Kanner, A. D., et al. (1981). Comparison of two modes of stress measurement: Daily hassles and uplifts versus major life events. *Journal of Behavioral Medicine, 4*, 1–39.

8251

Test Name: PROACTIVE SOCIALIZATION TACTICS SCALES

Purpose: To measure proactive tactics that individuals might use to increase feelings of control in a new job situation.

Number of Items: 24

Format: All items are presented.

Reliability: Alpha coefficients ranged from .61 to .95.

Author: Ashford, S. J., and Black, J. S.

Article: Proactivity during organizational entry: The role of desire for control.

Journal: *Journal of Applied Psychology*, April 1996, *81*(2), 199–214.

Related Research: Ostroff, C., & Kozlowski, S. W. (1992). Organizational socialization on a learning process: The role of information acquisition. *Personnel Psychology, 45*, 849–874.

8252

Test Name: PROPENSITY TO LEAVE SCALE

Purpose: To assess propensity to leave the current job or occupation.

Number of Items: 5

Format: Responses are made on a 7-point scale.

Reliability: Alpha coefficients were .98 and .94.

Author: Boles, J. S., et al.

Article: The dimensionality of the Maslach Burnout Inventory across small business owners and educators.

Journal: *Journal of Vocational Behavior,* February 2000, *56*(1), 12–34.

Related Research: Bluedorn, A. C. (1982). A unified model of turnover from organizations. *Human Relations, 35*, 135–153.

8253

Test Name: PROPENSITY TO LEAVE THE ORGANIZATION SCALE

Purpose: To measure one's intention to quit the organization.

Number of Items: 3

Format: Responses are made on a 7-point scale ranging from 1 (not at all likely) to 7 (extremely likely). All items are presented.

Reliability: Coefficient alpha was .87.

Validity: Correlation with other variables ranged from −.46 to .01.

Author: Koberg, C. S., et al.

Article: Factors and outcomes associated with mentoring among health-care professionals.

Journal: *Journal of Vocational Behavior*, August 1998, *53*(1), 58–72.

Related Research: Lyons, T. F. (1971). Role clarity, need for clarity, satisfaction, tension, and withdrawal. *Organizational Behavior and Human Performance, 6*, 99–110.

8254

Test Name: PSYCHOLOGICAL EMPOWERMENT QUESTIONNAIRE (HEBREW)

Purpose: To assess the job as an enabling situation.

Number of Items: 12

Format: All items are presented in English.

Reliability: Alphas ranged from .78 to .90 across subscales.

Validity: Correlations with other variables ranged from $-.46$ to .43.

Author: Vardi, Y.

Article: Psychological empowerment as a criterion for adjustment to a new job.

Journal: *Psychological Reports*, December 2000, *87*(3), Part 2, 1083–1093.

8255

Test Name: PSYCHOLOGICAL EMPOWERMENT SCALE

Purpose: To measure empowerment.

Number of Items: 12

Format: Includes four dimensions: Meaning, Competence, Self-Determination, and Impact. Responses are made on a 7-point scale ranging from 1 (strongly disagree) to 7 (strongly agree).

Reliability: Alpha coefficients ranged from .76 to .85.

Validity: Correlations with other variables ranged from .08 to .74.

Author: Kraimer, M. L., et al.

Article: Psychological empowerment as a multidimensional construct: A test of construct validity.

Journal: *Educational and*

Psychological Measurement, February 1999, *59*(1), 127–142.

Related Research: Spreitzer, G. M. (1995). Individual empowerment in the workplace: Dimensions, measurement, and validation. *Academy of Management Journal, 38,* 1442–1465.

8256

Test Name: PSYCHOLOGICAL REACTIONS SCALE

Purpose: To measure subjective experiences and psychological reactions to unemployment.

Number of Items: 10

Format: Five-point Likert format. All items are presented.

Reliability: Alphas ranged from .34 to .73 across subscales.

Author: Sightler, K. W., et al.

Article: Dimensionality of a scale of adjustment to unemployment.

Journal: *Psychological Reports,* August 1996, *79*(1), 19–23.

Related Research: Kaufman, H. G. (1982). *Professionals in search of work: Coping with the stress of job loss and underemployment.* New York: Wiley.

8257

Test Name: QUALITY OF RELATIONSHIP WITH SUPERVISOR SCALE

Purpose: To assess the quality of an individual's relationship with his or her supervisor.

Number of Items: 4

Format: Responses are made on a 1 to 5 point scale.

Reliability: Internal consistency estimate of reliability was .90.

Validity: Correlations with other

variables ranged from .-17 to .15.

Author: Allen, T. D., et al.

Article: A field study of factors related to supervisors' willingness to mentor others.

Journal: *Journal of Vocational Behavior,* February 1997, *50*(1), 1–22.

Related Research: Scandura, T. A., & Graen, G. B. (1984). Moderating effects of initial leader-member exchange status on the effects of a leadership intervention. *Journal of Applied Psychology, 69,* 428–436.

8258

Test Name: RACIAL DISTINCTIVENESS SCALE

Purpose: To assess the degree to which minority individuals are singled out in the workplace.

Number of Items: 13

Format: Seven-point scales are anchored by 1 (strongly agree) and 7 (strongly disagree). All items are presented.

Reliability: Coefficient alpha was .91.

Validity: Correlations with other variables ranged from $-.56$ to .28.

Author: Niemann, Y. F., and Dovidio, J. F.

Article: Relationship of solo status, academic rank, and perceived distinctiveness to job satisfaction of racial/ethnic minorities.

Journal: *Journal of Applied Psychology,* February 1998, *83*(1), 55–71.

8259

Test Name: REASONS FOR ABSENTEEISM AND ATTENDANCE

Purpose: To assess acceptability of the reason to be absent from work or to go to work.

Number of Items: 14

Format: Five- and seven-point scales are described.

Reliability: Alpha coefficients ranged from .60 to .77 across subscales.

Validity: Correlations with other variables ranged from −.06 to .42.

Author: Johns, G., and Xie, J. L.

Article: Perceptions of absence from work: People's Republic of China versus Canada.

Journal: *Journal of Applied Psychology*, August 1998, *83*(4), 515–530.

Related Research: Johns, G. (1994). Absenteeism estimates by employees and managers: Divergent perspectives and self-serving perceptions. *Journal of Applied Psychology, 79,* 229–239.

8260

Test Name: RECIPROCATION WARINESS SCALE

Purpose: To measure employee wariness regarding relations with others.

Number of Items: 10

Format: Scales range from 1 (strongly disagree) to 7 (strongly agree). All items are presented.

Reliability: Coefficient alphas ranged from .77 to .82.

Validity: Correlations with other variables ranged from −.16 to .07.

Author: Lynch, P. D., et al.

Article: Perceived organizational support: Inferior versus superior performance by wary employees.

Journal: *Journal of Applied*

Psychology, August 1999, *84*(4), 467–483.

8261

Test Name: RELATIONSHIP WITH LAYOFF VICTIMS SCALE

Purpose: To measure relationship with layoff victims.

Number of Items: 3

Format: Responses are made on a 5-point Likert-type scale ranging from 1 (strongly disagree) to 5 (strongly agree). All items are presented.

Reliability: Coefficient alpha was .75.

Validity: Correlations with other variables ranged from −.28 to .16.

Author: Mansour-Cole, D. M., and Scott, S. G.

Article: Hearing it through the grapevine: The influence of source, leader-relations, and legitimacy on survivors' fairness perceptions.

Journal: *Personnel Psychology,* Spring 1998, *51*(1), 25–54.

Related Research: Brockner, J., & Greenberg, J. (1990). The impact of layoffs on survivors: An organizational justice perspective. In Carroll, J. (Ed.), *Applied social psychology and organizational settings* (pp. 45–75). Hillsdale, NJ: Erlbaum.

8262

Test Name: RESOURCE AND COWORKER CONFLICT SCALES

Purpose: To measure work-related resources and material problems and communication conflicts.

Number of Items: 10

Format: Scales range from 1 (strongly disagree) to 6 (strongly agree). All items are presented.

Reliability: Coefficient alpha was .83 (coworker communication) and .82 (resource-related).

Validity: Correlations with other variables ranged from −.59 to .14.

Author: Bishop, J. W., and Scott, K. D.

Article: An examination of organizational and team commitment in a self-directed team environment.

Journal: *Journal of Applied Psychology,* June 2000, *85*(3), 439–450.

8263

Test Name: RETIREMENT ACTIVITIES SCALE

Purpose: To identify expected retirement activities.

Number of Items: 16

Format: Includes 5 variables: Social Activities, Growth Activities, Passive Activities, Tinkering Activities, and Employment Activities. Responses are made on a 5-point scale ranging from 1 (never) to 5 (very often). Examples are presented.

Reliability: Alpha coefficients ranged from .41 to .72. Test-retest reliabilities ranged from .49 to .68.

Validity: Correlations with other variables ranged from −.27 to .29.

Author: Beehr, T. A., et al.

Article: Work and nonwork predictors of employees' retirement ages.

Journal: *Journal of Vocational Behavior,* October 2000, *57*(2), 206–225.

Related Research: Beehr, T. A.,

& Nielson, N. L. (1995). Description of job characteristics and retirement activities during the transition to retirement. *Journal of Organizational Behavior, 16*, 681–690.

8264

Test Name: RETRIBUTIVE INTENTIONS SCALE

Purpose: To assess reactions to an organization's treatment of employees.

Number of Items: 7

Format: Likert format.

Reliability: Coefficient alpha was .81 (customer intentions) and .68 (employee intentions).

Validity: Correlations with other variables ranged from −.52 to .77.

Author: Skarlicki, D. P., et al.

Article: Third-party perceptions of a layoff: Procedural, derogation, and retributive aspects of justice.

Journal: *Journal of Applied Psychology*, February 1998, *83*(1), 119–127.

8265

Test Name: REWARDS AND COSTS OF WORK SCALES

Purpose: To assess perception of the rewards and costs involved in the work role.

Number of Items: 9

Format: Includes two subscales: Work-Reward and Work-Cost. Responses are made on 5-point scales. All items are presented.

Reliability: Alpha coefficients were .75 (Work-Reward) and .80 (Work-Cost).

Validity: Correlations with other

variables ranged from −.20 to .43

Author: Matsui, T., et al.

Article: Some motivational bases for work and home orientation among Japanese college women: A rewards/costs analysis.

Journal: *Journal of Vocational Behavior*, February 1999, *54*(1), 114–126

Related Research: Matsui, T., et al. (1991). Personality and career commitment among Japanese female clerical employees. *Journal of Vocational Behavior, 38*, 351–360.

8266

Test Name: RISK AVERSION SCALE

Purpose: To assess risk aversion.

Number of Items: 8

Format: Five-point Likert format. Sample items are presented.

Reliability: Coefficient alpha was .76.

Author: Judge, T. A., et al.

Article: Managerial coping with organizational change: A dispositional perspective.

Journal: *Journal of Applied Psychology*, February 1999, *84*(1), 107–122.

Related Research: Cable, D. M., & Judge, T. A. (1994). Pay preferences and job search decisions: A person-organization fit perspective. *Personnel Psychology, 47*, 317–348.

8267

Test Name: ROLE OVERLOAD SCALE

Purpose: To measure pressures experienced by individuals while on the job.

Number of Items: 5

Format: Nine-point scales. Sample items are presented.

Reliability: Coefficient alpha was .91.

Validity: Correlations with other variables ranged from −.18 to .24.

Author: Zohar, D.

Article: A group-level model of safety climate: Testing the effect of group climate on microaccidents in manufacturing jobs.

Journal: *Journal of Applied Psychology*, August 2000, *85*(4), 587–596.

Related Research: Hart, S. G., & Staveland, L. E. (1988). Development of NASA-TLX: Task load index. In P. A. Hancock & M. Meshkati (Eds.), *Human mental workload* (pp. 139–183). Amsterdam, the Netherlands: Elsevier North-Holland.

8268

Test Name: SATISFACTION WITH CAREER PROGRESS SCALE

Purpose: To measure satisfaction with attainment of income, skill and income goals.

Number of Items: 5

Format: Five-point scales are anchored by 1 (very dissatisfied) and 5 (very satisfied). A sample item is presented.

Reliability: Alpha was .80.

Validity: Correlations with other variables ranged from −.23 to .42.

Author: Beutell, N. J., and Wittig-Berman, U.

Article: Predictors of work-family conflict and satisfaction with family, job, career and life.

Journal: *Psychological Reports,* December 1999, *85*(3, Part I), 893–903.

Related Research: Parasuraman, S., et al. (1992). Role stressors, social support, and well-being among two-career couples. *Journal of Organizational Behavior, 13,* 339–356.

8269

Test Name: SATISFACTION WITH GRIEVANCE SYSTEM SCALE

Purpose: To measure satisfaction with a union grievance system.

Number of Items: 5

Format: Five-point Likert format. All items are presented.

Reliability: Alpha was .78.

Validity: Correlations with other variables ranged from −.21 to .64.

Author: Pisnar-Sweeney, M.

Article: Role of normative commitment in predicting member's participation in the union.

Journal: *Psychological Reports,* June 1997, *80*(3) Part 2, 1183–1207.

Related Research: Clark, P. F., & Gallagher, D. G. (1988). *Membership perceptions on value and effect of grievance procedures* (pp. 406–414). Proceedings of the 40th annual meeting of the Industrial Relations Research Association.

8270

Test Name: SATISFACTION WITH MEETING SCALE

Purpose: To measure participant satisfaction with group discussion.

Number of Items: 4

Format: All items are presented.

Reliability: Coefficient alpha was .69.

Validity: Correlations with other variables ranged from −.14 to .46.

Author: Bluedorn, A. C., et al.

Article: The effects of stand-up and sit-down meeting formats on meeting outcomes.

Journal: *Journal of Applied Psychology,* April 1999, *84*(2), 277–285.

8271

Test Name: SATISFACTION WITH SUPERVISION AND COWORKERS SCALES

Purpose: To measure job satisfaction.

Number of Items: 8

Format: Scales range from 1 (extremely dissatisfied) to 6 (extremely satisfied). All items are presented.

Reliability: Coefficient alpha was .88 (coworkers) and .94 (supervision).

Validity: Correlations with other variables ranged from −.59 to .63.

Author: Bishop, J. W., and Scott, K. D.

Article: An examination of organizational and team commitment in a self-directed team environment.

Journal: *Journal of Applied Psychology,* June 2000, *85*(3), 439–450.

8272

Test Name: SATISFACTION WITH SUPERVISORS AND COWORKERS SCALE

Purpose: To measure satisfaction with supervisors and coworkers.

Number of Items: 36

Format: Includes two scales: Satisfaction with Supervisors and Satisfaction with Coworkers.

Reliability: Alpha coefficients ranged from .86 to .91.

Validity: Correlations with other variables ranged from −.36 to .31.

Author: Munson, L. J., et al.

Article: Longitudinal analysis of dispositional influences and sexual harassment: Effects on job and psychological outcomes.

Journal: *Personnel Psychology,* Spring 2000, *53*(1), 21–46.

Related Research: Roznowski, M. (1989). Examination of the measurement properties of the JDI with experimental items. *Journal of Applied Psychology, 74,* 805–814.

8273

Test Name: SATISFACTION WITH THE WORK ITSELF SCALE

Purpose: To measure work satisfaction.

Number of Items: 18

Format: Response categories are "yes," "no," and "cannot decide." Sample items are presented.

Reliability: Coefficient alpha was .81.

Validity: Correlations with other variables ranged from .11 to .63.

Author: Liden, R. C., et al.

Article: An examination of the mediating role of psychological empowerment on the relations between the job, interpersonal relationships, and work outcomes.

Journal: *Journal of Applied Psychology*, June 2000, *85*(3), 407–416.

Related Research: Smith, P. C., et al. (1987). *Manual for the revised JDI and job in general scales*. Bowling Green, OH: Bowling Green State University.

8274

Test Name: SATISFACTION WITH WORK SCALE

Purpose: To assess growth satisfaction, pay satisfaction, coworker satisfaction, and supervision satisfaction.

Number of Items: 13

Format: Seven-point scales range from "extremely dissatisfied" to "extremely satisfied."

Reliability: Alpha coefficients ranged from .76 to .90 across subscales.

Validity: Correlations with other variables ranged from −.19 to .81.

Author: Ellingson, J. E., et al.

Article: Factors related to the satisfaction and performance of temporary employees.

Journal: *Journal of Applied Psychology*, December 1998, *83*(6), 913–921.

Related Research: Hackman, J. R., & Oldham, G. R. (1980). *Work redesign*. Reading, MA: Addison-Wesley.

8275

Test Name: SOCIAL COHESIVENESS SCALE

Purpose: To measure social cohesiveness in work teams.

Number of Items: 7

Format: Five-point Likert format. Sample items are presented.

Reliability: Coefficient alpha was .87.

Author: Barrick, M. R., et al.

Article: Relating member ability and personality to work-team processes and team effectiveness.

Journal: *Journal of Applied Psychology*, June 1998, *83*(3), 377–391.

Related Research: Stokes, J. P. (1983). Components of group cohesion: Intermember attraction, instrumental value, and risk-taking. *Small Group Behavior, 14,* 163–173.

8276

Test Name: SOCIAL INTEGRATION SCALE

Purpose: To measure how well an individual gets along with coworkers.

Number of Items: 4

Format: Seven-point Likert scales. Sample items are presented.

Reliability: Coefficient alpha was .84.

Validity: Correlations with other variables ranged from −.35 to .45.

Author: Wanberg, C. R., and Kammeyer-Mueller, J. D.

Article: Predictors and outcomes of proactivity in the socialization process.

Journal: *Journal of Applied Psychology*, June 2000, *85*(3), 373–385.

Related Research: Morrison, E. W. (1977). Career adaptivity: The effective adaptation of managers to changing role demands. *Journal of Applied Psychology, 62,* 549–558.

8277

Test Name: SOURCES OF STRESS QUESTIONNAIRE

Purpose: To assess sources of teacher stress.

Number of Items: 35

Format: Includes 4 sources-of-stress factors: Pupil Misbehavior, Poor Working Conditions, Poor Staff Relations, and Time Pressures. Responses are made on a 5-point scale ranging from 1 (no stress) to 5 (extreme stress).

Reliability: Alpha coefficients ranged from .73 to .92.

Validity: Correlations with other variables ranged from −.56 to .69.

Author: Abel, M. H., and Sewell, J.

Article: Stress and burnout in rural and urban secondary school teachers.

Journal: *Journal of Educational Research*, May/June 1999, *92*(5), 287–293.

Related Research: Borg, M. G., & Riding, R. J. (1991). Towards a model for the determinants of occupational stress among schoolteachers. *European Journal of Psychology of Education, 6,* 355–373.

8278

Test Name: SPURNING SCALE

Purpose: To measure the extent of rejection classroom teachers experience when helping students.

Number of Items: 12

Format: Eleven-point scales are anchored by (1) "applies very little to me" and (11) "applies very much to me." A sample item is presented.

Reliability: Alpha was .53.

Author: Cheuk, W. H., and Wong, K. S.

Article: Depersonalization in kindergarten teachers in relation to rejection of help by fellow teachers and emotional support from family.

Journal: *Psychological Reports*, December 1998, *83*(3) Part 1, 939–942.

Related Research: Cheuk, W. H., et al. (1996). The effects of spurning and social support on teacher burnout. *Journal of Social Behavior and Personality*, 9, 657–664.

8279

Test Name: STRESS IN GENERAL SCALE

Purpose: To measure job stress.

Number of Items: 18

Reliability: Alpha coefficients were .91 and .89.

Validity: Correlations with other variables ranged from −.32 to .25.

Author: Munson, L. J., et al.

Article: Longitudinal analysis of dispositional influences and sexual harassment: Effects on job and psychological outcomes.

Journal: *Personnel Psychology*, Spring 2000, *53*(1), 21–46.

Related Research: Smith, P. C., et al. (1992, May). *Development and validation of the Stress in General (SIG) Scale.* Paper presented at the Annual Conference for the Society for Industrial and Organizational Psychology, Montreal, Canada.

8280

Test Name: STRESS QUESTIONNAIRE

Purpose: To measure job stress.

Number of Items: 21

Format: Yes/moderate/no format. All items are presented.

Reliability: Alphas ranged from .62 to .75 across subscales.

Author: Kawada, T.

Article: Psychometric properties of a stress questionnaire and its use in the workplace.

Journal: *Psychological Reports*, August 1999, *85*(1), 131–137.

Related Research: Kawada, T., et al. (1997). Psychometric properties of a stress check list for self and its relationship to health satisfaction and psychological traits (introversion and extraversion). *Journal of Occupational Health*, *39*, 223–227.

8281

Test Name: TASK AND RELATIONSHIP CONFLICT SCALE

Purpose: To measure friction and conflict in a task executive group.

Number of Items: 4

Format: Scales range from 1 (none) to 5 (a very great deal). All items are presented.

Reliability: Alpha coefficients were .78 (task) and .87 (relationship).

Validity: Correlations with other variables ranged from −.62 to .29.

Author: Simons, T. L., and Peterson, R. S.

Article: Task conflict and relationship conflict in top management teams: The pivotal role of intragroup trust.

Journal: *Journal of Applied Psychology*, February 2000, *85*(1), 102–111.

Related Research: Jehn, K. A. (1995). A multimethod examination of the benefits and detriments of intragroup conflict. *Administrative Science Quarterly*, *40*, 256–282.

8282

Test Name: TASK SATISFACTION SCALE

Purpose: To assess global satisfaction with a task.

Number of Items: 3

Format: Seven-point scales are anchored by 1 (strongly disagree) and 7 (strongly agree). A sample item is presented.

Reliability: Alpha was .85.

Author: Houston, J. M., et al.

Article: Competitiveness and conflict behavior in a simulation of a social dilemma.

Journal: *Psychological Reports*, June 2000, *86*(3, Part 2), 1219–1225.

Related Research: Houston, J. M. (1989). *Perceived goal relationships within small work groups.* Unpublished doctoral dissertation, New York University.

8283

Test Name: TASK SATISFACTION SCALE

Purpose: To measure task satisfaction.

Number of Items: 4

Format: Scales ranged from ''strongly disagree'' to ''strongly agree.'' All items are presented.

Reliability: Coefficient alpha was .80.

Author: Roberson, Q. M., et al.

Article: Identifying a missing link between participation and satisfaction: The mediating role of procedural justice perceptions.

Journal: *Journal of Applied Psychology*, August 1999, *84*(4), 585–593.

Related Research: Dunnette, M. D., et al. (1967). Factors contributing to job satisfaction and job dissatisfaction in six occupational groups. *Organizational Behavior and Human Decision Processes, 2,* 143–174.

8284

Test Name: TEAM EFFECTIVENESS SCALE

Purpose: To assess team effectiveness.

Number of Items: 9

Format: Includes Team Performance, Team Commitment, and Team Satisfaction. Sample items are presented.

Reliability: Alpha coefficients ranged from .73 to .89.

Validity: Correlations with other variables ranged from −.48 to .89.

Author: Janz, B. D., et al.

Article: Knowledge worker team effectiveness: The role of autonomy, interdependence, team development, and contextual support variables.

Journal: *Personnel Psychology,* Winter 1997, *50*(4), 877–904.

Related Research: Henderson, J. C., & Lee, S. (1992). Managing I/S design teams: A control theories perspective. *Management Science, 6,* 757–777.

8285

Test Name: TEAM SATISFACTION SCALE

Purpose: To assess satisfaction with working with a teammate.

Number of Items: 8

Format: Unspecified rating scales. All items are presented.

Reliability: Alpha was .82.

Validity: Correlation with other variables ranged from −.71 to .74.

Author: Miles, J. A.

Article: Relationships of collective orientation and cohesion to team outcomes.

Journal: *Psychological Reports,* April 2000, *86*(2), 435–444.

8286

Test Name: TEAMWORK FUNCTIONING SCALES

Purpose: To measure cohesion, coordination, and task-coordination.

Number of Items: 24

Reliability: Alpha coefficients ranged from .86 to .95.

Validity: Correlations with other variables ranged from .01 to .83.

Author: Lindell, M. K., and Brandt, C. J.

Article: Climate quality and climate consensus as mediators of the relationship between organizational antecedents and outcomes.

Journal: *Journal of Applied Psychology,* June 2000, *85*(3), 331–348.

Related Research: Seers, A. (1989). Team-member exchange quality: A new construct for role-making research. *Organizational Behavior and Human Decision Processes, 43,* 118–135.

8287

Test Name: TOLERANCE FOR DISAGREEMENT SCALE

Purpose: To measure employees' orientation to disagreement with superiors.

Number of Items: 14

Format: Five-point scales are used to indicate how true each statement is about respondent.

Reliability: Alpha was .92.

Author: Lamude, K. G., and Torres, P.

Article: Supervisors' tactics of influence and subordinates' tolerance for disagreement.

Journal: *Psychological Reports,* December 2000, *87*(3), Part 2, 1050–1052.

Related Research: Teven, J. J., et al. (1998). Measurement of tolerance for disagreement. *Communication Research Reports, 15,* 209–217.

8288

Test Name: TRUST SCALE

Purpose: To measure trust supervisors have for an employee.

Number of Items: 2

Format: Responses are made on a 7-point scale ranging from "strongly disagree" to "strongly agree." Both items are presented.

Reliability: Coefficient alpha was .87.

Validity: Correlations with other variables ranged from −.26 to .72.

Author: Thacker, R. A.

Article: Perceptions of trust, upward influence tactics, and performance ratings.

Journal: *Perceptual and Motor Skills,* June 1999, *88*(3) Part 2, 1059–1070.

8289

Test Name: TURNOVER INTENTION SCALE

Purpose: To measure turnover intention.

Number of Items: 3

Format: Scales range from 1 (extremely disagree) to 5 (extremely agree). All items are presented.

Reliability: Coefficient alpha was .78.

Validity: Correlations with other variables ranged from −.26 to .30.

Author: Chen, X-P., et al.

Article: The role of organizational citizenship behavior in turnover: Conceptualization and preliminary tests of key hypotheses.

Journal: *Journal of Applied Psychology*, December 1998, *83*(6), 922–931.

Related Research: Camman, C., et al. (1979). *The Michigan Organizational Assessment Questionnaire*. Unpublished manuscript, University of Michigan, Ann Arbor.

8290

Test Name: TURNOVER INTENTION SCALE

Purpose: To assess intention to quit the current job.

Number of Items: 3

Format: Responses are made on 5-point and 6-point scales. A sample item is presented.

Reliability: Coefficient alpha was .91.

Validity: Correlations with other variables ranged from −.04 to .71 ($N = 116$).

Author: Nielsen, I. K., et al.

Article: Development and validation of scores on a two-dimensional workplace friendship scale.

Journal: *Educational and*

Psychological Measurement, August 2000, *60*(4), 628–643.

Related Research: Beehr, R. A., & O'Driscoll, M. P. (1990, May). *Employee uncertainty as a factor in occupational stress.* Paper presented at the 62nd annual meeting of the Midwestern Psychological Association, Chicago.

8291

Test Name: TURNOVER INTENTIONS SCALE

Purpose: To measure the likelihood of changing jobs.

Number of Items: 3

Format: Scales range from "very unlikely" to "very likely." All items are presented.

Reliability: Coefficient alpha was .87.

Validity: Correlations with other variables ranged from −.56 to .40.

Author: Maslyn, J. M., and Fedor, D. B.

Article: Perceptions of politics: Does measuring different foci matter?

Journal: *Journal of Applied Psychology*, August 1998, *83*(4), 645–653.

Related Research: Konovsky, M. A., & Cropanzano, R. (1991). Perceived fairness of employee drug testing as a predictor of employee attitudes and job performance. *Journal of Applied Psychology, 76,* 698–707.

8292

Test Name: TURNOVER INTENTIONS SCALE

Purpose: To measure turnover intentions.

Number of Items: 4

Format: Responses are made on a 5-point scale ranging from 1 (strongly disagree) to 5 (strongly agree). A sample item is presented.

Reliability: Coefficient alpha was .83.

Validity: Correlations with other variables ranged from −.52 to .24.

Author: Shaffer, M. A., et al.

Article: Gender discrimination and job-related outcomes: A cross-cultural comparison of working women in the United States and China.

Journal: *Journal of Vocational Behavior*, December 2000, *57*(3), 395–427.

Related Research: Hom, P. W., & Griffeth, R. W. (1991). Structural equations modeling test of turnover theory: Cross-cultural and longitudinal analyses. *Journal of Applied Psychology, 76,* 350–366.

8293

Test Name: TURNOVER INTENTIONS SCALE

Purpose: To assess turnover intentions.

Number of Items: 7

Format: Responses are made on a 5-point scale ranging from 1 (strongly disagree) to 5 (strongly agree). An example is presented.

Reliability: Coefficient alpha was .82.

Validity: Correlations with other variables ranged from −.49 to .54.

Author: O'Connell, C. E., and Korabik, K.

Article: Sexual harassment: The relationship of personal vulnerability, work context, perpetrator status, and types of harassment to outcomes.

Journal: *Journal of Vocational Behavior*, June 2000, 56(3), 299–329.

Related Research: Rosin, H. M., & Korabik, K. (1991). Workplace variables, affective responses, and intention to leave among women managers. *Journal of Occupational Psychology, 64,* 1–14.

8294

Test Name: UNEMPLOYMENT NEGATIVITY SCALE

Purpose: To measure how upset and depressed unemployed people are.

Number of Items: 3

Format: Seven-point scales.

Reliability: Internal consistency was .92.

Validity: Correlations with other variables ranged from −.31 to .54.

Author: Wanberg, C. R., et al.

Article: Individuals without jobs: An empirical study of job-seeking behavior and reemployment.

Journal: *Journal of Applied Psychology*, February 1996, 81(1), 76–87.

Related Research: Wanberg, C. R., & Marchese, M. C. (1994). Heterogeneity in the unemployment experience: A cluster analytic investigation. *Journal of Applied Social Psychology, 24,* 473–488.

8295

Test Name: WILLINGNESS TO RELOCATE MEASURES

Purpose: To provide measures that indicate willingness to relocate.

Format: Includes Employee Willingness to Relocate, Relocation Beliefs, Normative Beliefs, Self-Efficacy for Developing Career Related Skills, Difficulty Associated With Moving, Employee Satisfaction With the Relocation Policy, General Job Satisfaction, Organizational Commitment, Desire for Career Progress, Spouse Willingness to Relocate, Spouse Satisfaction With the Relocation Policy, Spouse General Job-Satisfaction, and Spouse Organizational Commitments.

Reliability: Alpha coefficients ranged from .60 to .92.

Validity: Correlations with other variables ranged from −.39 to .69.

Author: Eby, L. T., and Russell, J. E. A.

Article: Predictors of employee willingness to relocate for the firm.

Journal: *Journal of Vocational Behavior*, August 2000, 57(1), 42–61.

Related Research: Brett, J. M., et al. (1993). Pulling up roots in the 1990s: Who's willing to relocate: *Journal of Organizational Behavior, 14,* 49–60.

8296

Test Name: WITHDRAWAL INTENTIONS SCALE

Purpose: To measure withdrawal intentions.

Number of Items: 6

Format: Seven-point rating scales. All items are presented.

Reliability: Coefficient alpha was .89.

Validity: Correlations with other variables ranged from .15 to .45.

Author: Somers, J. M.

Article: Application of two neural network paradigms to the study of voluntary employee turnover.

Journal: *Journal of Applied Psychology*, April 1999, 84(2), 177–185.

Related Research: Bluedorn, A. C. (1982). The theories of turnover: Causes, effects and meaning. In S. Bacharach (Ed.), *Research in the sociology of organizations* (pp. 75–128). Greenwich, CT: JAI Press.

8297

Test Name: WORK AND CAREER OUTCOMES SCALES

Purpose: To measure work and career outcomes.

Number of Items: 19

Format: Includes 5 scales: Job Satisfaction, Intention to Quit, Career Satisfaction, Job Involvement, and Future Career Prospects. Examples are presented.

Reliability: Alpha coefficients ranged from .68 to .86.

Validity: Correlations with other variables ranged from −.22 to .24.

Author: Burke, R. J., and McKeen, C. A.

Article: Benefits of mentoring relationships among managerial and professional women: A cautionary tale.

Journal: *Journal of Vocational Behavior*, August 1997, 51(1), 43–57.

Related Research: Burke, R. J. (1991). Early work and career experiences of female and male managers: Reasons for optimism? *Canadian Journal of Administrative Sciences, 8,* 224–230.

Greenhaus, J. H., et al. (1990). Organizational experiences and career success of Black and White managers. *Academy Journal, 33,* 64–86.

8298

Test Name: WORK AND JOB WITHDRAWAL SCALES

Purpose: To assess behavioral attempts of an employee to escape from work or engage in job withdrawal behaviors.

Format: Scales range from 1 (never) to 7 (all of the time). Items are described.

Reliability: Coefficient alpha was .63 (work withdrawal) and .88 (job withdrawal).

Validity: Correlations with other variables ranged from −.28 to .32.

Author: Glomb, T. M., et al.

Article: Structural equation models of sexual harassment: Longitudinal explorations and cross-sectional generalizations.

Journal: *Journal of Applied Psychology,* February 1999, *84*(1), 14–28.

Related Research: Hanish, K. A., & Hulin, C. L. (1991). General attitudes and organizational withdrawal: An evaluation of a causal model. *Journal of Vocational Behavior, 39,* 110–128.

8299

Test Name: WORK AND JOB WITHDRAWAL SCALES

Purpose: To assess task-avoidance at work and intention to leave a job.

Number of Items: 20

Format: Five-point multiple choice format.

Reliability: Coefficient alpha was

.71 (work withdrawal) and .76 (intention to leave).

Validity: Correlations with other variables ranged from −.21 to .24.

Author: Donovan, M. A., et al.

Article: The Perceptions of Fair Interpersonal Treatment Scale: Development and validation of a measure of interpersonal treatment in the workplace.

Journal: *Journal of Applied Psychology,* October 1998, *83*(5), 683–692.

Related Research: Hanish, K. A., & Hulin, C. L. (1991). General attitudes and organizational withdrawal: An evaluation of a causal model. *Journal of Vocational Behavior, 37,* 60–78.

8300

Test Name: WORK CHALLENGE SCALE

Purpose: To measure work challenge.

Number of Items: 5

Format: Responses are made on a 5-point scale ranging from 1 (always) to 5 (never).

Reliability: Coefficient alpha was .79.

Validity: Correlations with other variables ranged from −.13 to .43.

Author: Ettington, D. R.

Article: Successful career plateauing.

Journal: *Journal of Vocational Behavior,* February 1998, *52*(1), 72–88.

Related Research: Smith, P. C., et al. (1969). *The measurement of satisfaction in work and retirement: A strategy for the study of attitudes.* Chicago, IL: Rand McNally.

8301

Test Name: WORK CONFLICT SCALES

Purpose: To measure conflict with supervisor and coworkers and between work and school.

Number of Items: 13

Format: Scales range from "never" to "very often." Sample items are presented.

Reliability: Alpha coefficients ranged from .85 to .86 across subscales.

Validity: Correlations with other variables ranged from −.07 to .36.

Author: Frone, M. R.

Article: Predictors of work injuries among employed adolescents.

Journal: *Journal of Applied Psychology,* August 1998, *83*(4), 565–576.

Related Research: Spector, P. (1987). Interactive effects of perceived control and job stressors on affective reactions and health outcomes for clinical workers. *Work and Stress, 1,* 155–162.

8302

Test Name: WORK DISTRESS SCALE

Purpose: To assess work distress.

Number of Items: 6

Format: Respondents indicate on a 5-point scale their frequency of feeling six emotional reactions while at work.

Reliability: Coefficient alpha was .85.

Validity: Correlations with other variables ranged from −.43 to .41.

Author: Frone, M. R., et al.

Article: Developing and testing an integrative model of the work-family interface.

Journal: *Journal of Vocational Behavior*, April 1997, *50*(2), 145–167.

Related Research: Kandel, D. B., et al. (1985). The stressfulness of daily social roles for women: Marital, occupational, and household roles. *Journal of Health and Social Behavior*, *26*, 64–78.

8303

Test Name: WORK GROUP RATING SCALES

Purpose: To measure work group members' ratings of open communication, task motivation, group viability, group cohesion, and satisfaction with group.

Number of Items: 23

Reliability: Alpha coefficients ranged from .56 to .87.

Validity: Correlations between subscales ranged from −.74 to .76.

Author: Druskat, V. U., and Wolff, S. B.

Article: Effects of timing of developmental peer appraisals in self-managing work groups.

Journal: *Journal of Applied Psychology*, February 1999, *84*(1), 58–74.

Related Research: Stokes, J. P. (1983). Components of group cohesion: Intermember attraction, instrumental value, and risk taking. *Small Group Behavior*, *14*, 163–173.

Zaccaro, S. J., & McCoy, M. C. (1988). The effects of task and interpersonal cohesiveness on performance of a disjunctive group task. *Journal of Applied Social Psychology*, *18*, 837–851.

Hackman, J. R. (1988). *Flight*

Crew Questionnaire. Cambridge, MA: Author.

Harkins, S. G., & Jackson, J. J. (1985). The role of evaluation in eliminating social loafing. *Personality and Social Psychology Bulletin*, *11*, 457–465.

8304

Test Name: WORK OVERLOAD SCALE

Purpose: To measure to what extent persons feel overworked.

Number of Items: 3

Format: Scales range from 1 (strongly disagree) to 5 (strongly agree). A sample item is presented.

Reliability: Coefficient alpha was .55.

Validity: Correlations with other variables ranged from −.24 to .17.

Author: Jex, S. M., and Bliese, P. D.

Article: Efficacy beliefs as a moderator of the impact of work-related stressors: A multilevel study.

Journal: *Journal of Applied Psychology*, June 1999, *84*(3), 349–361.

Related Research: Camman, C., et al. (1983). Michigan Organizational Assessment Questionnaire. In S. E. Seashore et al. (Eds.), *Assessing organizational change: A guide to methods, measures, and practices* (pp. 71–138). New York: Wiley-Interscience.

8305

Test Name: WORK OVERLOAD SCALE

Purpose: To measure work overload.

Number of Items: 4

Format: Responses are made on a 5-point Likert scale ranging from 1 (strongly disagree) to 5 (strongly agree).

Reliability: Coefficient alpha was .80.

Validity: Correlations with other variables ranged from −.20 to .65.

Author: Wallace, J. E.

Article: It's about time: A study of hours worked and work spillover among law firm lawyers.

Journal: *Journal of Vocational Behavior*, April 1997, *50*(2), 227–248.

Related Research: Caplan, R. D., et al .(1975). Relationship of cessation of smoking with job stress, personality and social support. *Journal of Applied Psychology*, *60*, 211–219.

8306

Test Name: WORK-RELATED NEGATIVE MOOD SCALE

Purpose: To assess work-related negative mood.

Number of Items: 15

Format: Includes 3 types of items: anger, anxiety, and sadness. Responses are made on a 5-point scale ranging from "not at all" to "all of the time."

Reliability: Coefficient alpha was .92.

Validity: Correlations with other variables ranged from −.17 to .46.

Author: O'Connell, C. E., and Korabik, K.

Article: Sexual harassment: The relationship of personal vulnerability, work context, perpetrator status, and types of harassment to outcomes.

Journal: *Journal of Vocational Behavior*, June 2000, *56*(3), 299–329.

Related Research: Barling, J., et al. (1996). Prediction and replication of the organizational and personal consequences of workplace sexual harassment. *Journal of Managerial Psychology, 11*, 3–22.

8307

Test Name: WORK SPILLOVER AND HOURS WORKED SCALE

Purpose: To measure work spillover and hours worked.

Number of Items: 4

Format: Responses are made on a 5-point Likert scale ranging from 1 (strongly disagree) to 5 (strongly agree).

Reliability: Coefficient alpha for work spillover was .85.

Validity: Correlation with other variables ranged from −.29 to .65.

Author: Wallace, J. E.

Article: It's about time: A study of hours worked and work spillover among law firm lawyers.

Journal: *Journal of Vocational Behavior*, April 1997, *50*(2), 227–248.

Related Research: Kopelman, R. E., et al. (1983). A model of work, family, and interrole conflict: A construct validation study. *Organizational Behavior and Human Performance, 32*, 198–215.

8308

Test Name: WORK STRESS SCALE—CHINESE

Purpose: To measure work stress.

Number of Items: 20

Format: Seven-point scales are anchored by (1) not at all characteristic and (7) extremely characteristic. Sample items are presented.

Reliability: Alpha was .83.

Validity: Correlation with locus of control was .35 and with psychological symptoms was .25.

Author: Hamid, P. N., and Chan, W. T.

Article: Locus of control and occupational stress in Chinese professionals.

Journal: *Psychological Reports*, February 1998, *82*(1), 75–79.

8309

Test Name: WORK WITHDRAWAL SCALE

Purpose: To assess how often the participant engages in work withdrawal behaviors.

Number of Items: 12

Format: Responses are made on a 7-point scale.

Reliability: Alpha coefficients were .63 and .69.

Validity: Correlations with other variables ranged from −.28 to .34.

Author: Munson, L. J., et al.

Article: Longitudinal analysis of dispositional influences and sexual harassment: Effects on job and psychological outcomes.

Journal: *Personnel Psychology*, Spring 2000, *53*(1), 21–46.

Related Research: Hanisch, K. A., & Hulin, C. L. (1990). Job attitudes and organizational withdrawal: An examination of retirement and other voluntary withdrawal behavior. *Journal of Vocational Behavior, 37*, 60–78.

CHAPTER 6
Aptitude

8310

Test Name: FIGURAL INTERSECTION TEST

Purpose: To measure mental capacity.

Format: A detailed description of the format is presented.

Reliability: Spearman-Brown internal reliability coefficient was .80.

Validity: Correlations with other variables ranged from .16 to .38.

Author: Niaz, M., et al.

Article: Academic performance of high school students as a function of mental capacity, cognitive style, mobility-fixity dimension, and creativity.

Journal: *Journal of Creative Behavior*, First Quarter 2000, *34*(1), 18–29.

Related Research: DeRibaupierre, A., & Pascual-Leone, J. (1979). Formal operations and M power: A neo-Piagetan investigation. In D. Kuhn (Ed.), *New directions in child development: Intellectual development beyond childhood* (pp. 1–44). San Francisco: Jossey-Bass.

8311

Test Name: MATH OUTCOME EXPECTATIONS SCALE

Purpose: To assess math outcome expectations.

Number of Items: 10

Format: Responses are made on a 10-point scale ranging from 0 (strongly disagree) to 9 (strongly agree).

Reliability: Alpha coefficients were .90 and .89. Test-retest (2 weeks) coefficient was .91.

Validity: Correlations with other variables ranged from .07 to 55

Author: Gainor, K. A., and Lent, R. W.

Article: Social cognitive expectations and racial identity attitudes in predicting the math choice intentions of Black college students.

Journal: *Journal of Counseling Psychology*, October 1998, *45*(4), 403–413.

Related Research: Lent, R. W., et al. (1991). Mathematics self-efficacy: Sources and relation to science-based career choice. *Journal of Counseling Psychology, 38*, 424–430.

8312

Test Name: QUICK WORD TEST

Purpose: To assess general aptitude.

Number of Items: 80

Format: Respondents are presented a five-letter word and asked to choose between four meanings.

Reliability: Alternate forms reliability was .88.

Author: Hickman, G. P., et al.

Article: Influence of parenting styles on the adjustment and academic achievement of traditional college freshmen.

Journal: *Journal of College Student Development*, January/February 2000, *41*(1), 41–54.

Related Research: Merwin, J. C. (1965). The Quick Word Test. *Journal of Counseling Psychology, 12*, 436–437.

8313

Test Name: TALENT IDENTIFICATION INSTRUMENTS

Purpose: To assess music and dance talent.

Number of Items: 18

Format: Rater must be trained to make observations in classes of 25–35 students. Talent profiles are presented.

Reliability: Interrater reliabilities ranged from .65 to .82.

Validity: Average correlations with other talent variables ranged from .40 to .49. Correlations with academic achievement ranged from .08 to .25. Other validity data are presented.

Author: Baum, S. M., et al.

Article: Talent beyond words: Identification of potential talent in dance and music in elementary schools.

Journal: *Gifted Child Quarterly*, Spring 1996, *40*(2), 93–101.

CHAPTER 7
Attitudes

8314

Test Name: ADOLESCENT ATTITUDES SCALES

Purpose: To measure two adolescent attitudes representing adherence to mainstream values toward social behavior and future success.

Number of Items: 24

Format: Includes 2 scales: One scale measures the extent of adolescents' moral disengagement and the other scale measures the adolescent's perception that such activities as getting good grades and furthering one's education will help in getting ahead in life. Examples are presented.

Reliability: Alpha coefficients were .84 and .62.

Author: Kalil, A., and Eccles, J. S.

Article: Does welfare affect family processes and adolescent adjustment?

Journal: *Child Development*, December 1998, *69*(6), 1597–1613

Related Research: Wilson, W. J. (1987). *The truly disadvantaged: The inner city, the underclass, and public policy*. Chicago: University of Chicago Press.

8315

Test Name: ADVERSARIAL SEXUAL BELIEFS SCALE

Purpose: To assess the perception that sexual relationships between men and women are inherently exploitive.

Number of Items: 9

Reliability: Coefficient alpha was .85.

Validity: Correlations with other variables ranged from −.24 to .69.

Author: Hamburger, M. E., et al.

Article: Assessing hypergender ideologies: Development and initial validation of a gender-neutral measure of adherence to extreme gender-role beliefs.

Journal: *Journal of Research in Personality*, June 1996, *30*(2), 157–178.

Related Research: Burt, M. R. (1980). Cultural myths and support for rape. *Journal of Personality and Social Psychology, 38*, 217–230.

8316

Test Name: AIDS ATTITUDE SCALE

Purpose: To assess attitudes toward AIDS.

Number of Items: 54

Format: Scales range from 1 (strongly agree) to 5 (strongly disagree).

Reliability: Alpha coefficients ranged from .90 to .97.

Author: Guth, L. J., et al.

Article: Student attitudes toward AIDS and homosexuality: The effects of a speaker with HIV.

Journal: *Journal of College Student Development*, September/October 2000, *41*(5), 503–512.

Related Research: Shrum, J. C., et al. (1989). Development of an instrument to measure attitudes toward acquired immune deficiency syndrome. *AIDS Education and Prevention, 1*, 222–230.

8317

Test Name: AIDS VICTIM BLAMING SCALES

Purpose: To measure the blaming of AIDS victims.

Number of Items: 18

Format: Five-point response scales. All items are presented.

Reliability: Alphas ranged from .77 to .87 across subscales.

Validity: Correlations with other variables ranged from −.27 to .36.

Author: Mulford, C. L., and Lee, M. Y.

Article: Reliability and validity of AIDS Victim Blaming Scales.

Journal: *Psychological Reports*, August 1996, *79*(1), 191–201.

8318

Test Name: ALCOHOL EFFECTS QUESTIONNAIRE

Purpose: To assess participants' beliefs about alcohol's effects on their own behavior.

Number of Items: 40

Format: True/false format. A sample item is presented.

Reliability: Alphas ranged from .49 to .74 across subscales.

Author: McNair, L. D.

Article: Alcohol use and stress in women: The role of prior vs. anticipated stressors.

Journal: *Journal of Psychopathology and Behavioral Assessment*, December 1996, *18*(4), 331–346.

Related Research: Rohsenow, D. J. (1983). Drinking habits and expectancies about alcohol's effects for self vs. others. *Journal of Consulting and Clinical Psychology, 51*, 752–756.

8319

Test Name: ANIMAL RIGHTS ATTITUDE SURVEY

Purpose: To measure attitudes toward using animals in biomedical research and general attitudes toward animals.

Number of Items: 10

Time Required: 20 minutes

Format: Five-point Likert format. All items are presented.

Validity: Correlations between subscales (factors) ranged from .76 to .46.

Author: Vigorito, M.

Article: An animal rights attitude survey of undergraduate psychology students.

Journal: *Psychological Reports*, August 1996, *79*(1), 131–142.

Related Research: Bowd, A. (1984). Development and validation of a scale of attitudes toward the treatment of animals. *Educational and Psychological Measurement, 44*, 513–515.

8320

Test Name: ANTI-FAT ATTITUDES SCALE

Purpose: To measure negative

attitudes toward overweight individuals.

Number of Items: 5

Format: Scales range from 1 (strongly disagree) to 5 (strongly agree). All items are presented.

Reliability: Alpha coefficients ranged from .70 to .80.

Validity: Correlations with other variables ranged from −.29 to .37.

Authors: Morrison, T. G., & O'Connor, W. E.

Article: Psychometric properties of a scale measuring negative attitudes toward overweight individuals.

Journal: *The Journal of Social Psychology*, August 1999, *139*(4), 436–445.

8321

Test Name: ANTI-JEWISH AND ANTI-ARAB SCALES

Purpose: To measure negative sentiments towards Jews and Arabs.

Number of Items: 10

Format: Five-point Likert format.

Reliability: Alpha coefficients were .84 (anti-Arab sentiment) and .87 (anti-Jewish sentiment).

Validity: Correlations with other variables ranged from −.45 to .46.

Author: Ruttenberg, J., et al.

Article: Collective identity and intergroup prejudice among Jewish and Arab students in the United States.

Journal: *Journal of Social Psychology*, April 1996, *136*(2), 209–220.

Related Research: Lewinson, D. J., & Sanford, R. (1944). A scale for the measurement of

anti-Semitism. *The Journal of Psychology, 17*, 339–370.

8322

Test Name: ATTITUDE REGARDING BISEXUALITY SCALE

Purpose: To assess attitudes regarding bisexuality.

Number of Items: 18

Format: Includes 2 factors: Tolerance and Stability. Responses are made on a 5-point scale ranging from 1 (strongly agree) to 5 (strongly disagree). All items are presented.

Reliability: Test-retest (3 weeks) reliability ranged from .69 to .92.

Validity: Correlations with other variables ranged from −.22 to .87.

Author: Mohr, J. J., and Rochlen, A. B.

Article: Measuring attitudes regarding bisexuality in lesbian, gay male, and heterosexual populations.

Journal: *Journal of Counseling Psychology*, July 1999, *46*(3), 353–369.

8323

Test Name: ATTITUDES TO GUNS SCALE

Purpose: To measure attitudes to guns in terms of rights, protection, and crime.

Number of Items: 17

Format: Scales range from 1 (strongly disagree) to 8 (strongly agree). All items are presented.

Reliability: Alpha coefficients ranged from .78 to .90 across subscales.

Author: Cooke, C. A., and Puddifoot, J. E.

Article: Gun culture and symbolism among U.K. and U.S. women.

Journal: *Journal of Social Psychology*, August 2000, *140*(4), 423–433.

Related Research: Branscombe, N. R., et al. (1992). A three-factor scale of attitudes towards guns. *Aggressive Behavior, 17,* 261–273.

8324

Test Name: ATTITUDE TOWARD EDUCATIONAL MEASUREMENT INVENTORY

Purpose: To measure attitude toward educational measurement.

Number of Items: 31

Format: Includes 3 factors: Relevance, Affective, and Course. Responses are made on a 5-point Likert-type scale ranging from "strongly agree" to "strongly disagree." Abbreviated versions of all items are presented.

Reliability: Internal consistency reliabilities ranged from .88 to .93. Test-retest (3 weeks) reliabilities ranged from .60 to .74.

Author: Bryant, N. C., and Barnes, L. L. B.

Article: Development and validation of the Attitude Toward Educational Measurement Inventory.

Journal: *Educational and Psychological Measurement,* October 1997, *57*(5), 870–875.

Related Research: Wise, S. L. (1985). The development and validation of a scale measuring attitudes toward statistics. *Educational and Psychological Measurement, 45,* 401–405.

8325

Test Name: ATTITUDE TO MATHEMATICS SURVEY

Purpose: To measure dimensions of attitude toward mathematics.

Number of Items: 24

Format: Includes 2 factors: Enjoyment and Value. Responses are made on a 5-point Likert-type format ranging from "strongly disagree" to "strongly agree." All items are presented.

Reliability: Alpha coefficients ranged from .50 to .91.

Author: Taylor, J. A.

Article: Factorial validity of scores on the Aiken Attitude to Mathematics scales for adult pretertiary students.

Journal: *Educational and Physiological Measurement,* February 1997, *57*(1), 125–130.

Related Research: Aiken, L. (1979). Attitudes toward mathematics and science in Iranian middle schools. *School Science and Mathematics, 79,* 229–234.

8326

Test Name: ATTITUDE TOWARD ROLE MODELING SCALE

Purpose: To measure attitudes regarding the importance of role modeling in physical activity and fitness behaviors among Health, Physical Education, Recreation, and Dance Professionals.

Number of Items: 16

Format: Responses are made on a 5-point scale ranging from 1 (strongly diasagree) to 5 (strongly agree). All items are presented.

Reliability: Coefficient alpha was .95. Split-half reliability was .97.

Author: Cardinal, B. J., et al.

Article: Preliminary development of a scale to measure attitudes regarding the importance of role modeling in physical activity and fitness behaviors among health, physical education, recreation, and dance professionals.

Journal: *Perceptual and Motor Skills,* April 1998, *86*(2), 627–630.

Related Research: National Association for Sport and Physical Education (1994). *Physical fitness and physical activity patterns of physical education teachers: Position statement sponsored by CUPEC.* Reston, VA: Author.

8327

Test Name: ATTITUDE TOWARD STUDENTS' EDUCATIONAL RIGHTS QUESTIONNAIRE.

Purpose: To determine attitude toward students' educational rights.

Number of Items: 28

Format: Responses are made on a 5-point Likert scale ranging from "strongly agree" to "strongly disagree." All items are presented.

Reliability: Coefficient alpha was .79.

Author: Jones, C. H., and Slate, J. R.

Article: Educators' attitudes toward educational practices based in behavior analysis.

Journal: *Journal of Research and Development in Education,* Fall 1996, *30*(1), 31–41.

Related Research: Barrett, B., et al. (1991). The right to effective education. *The Behavior Analyst, 14,* 79–82.

8328

Test Name: ATTITUDE TOWARD WOMEN SCALE

Purpose: To assess adolescents' attitudes toward women's rights and roles.

Number of Items: 12

Format: Four-point Likert format.

Reliability: Alphas ranged from .62 to .86.

Author: Daley, C. E., and Onwuegbuzie, A. J.

Article: Relationship between sex-role attitudes and attitudes toward violence among incarcerated male juvenile offenders.

Journal: *Psychological Reports*, October 2000, *87*(2), 552–554.

Related Research: Galambos, N. L., et al. (1985). The Attitudes Toward Women Scale for Adolescents (AWSA): A study of reliability and validity. *Sex Roles, 13*, 343–356.

8329

Test Name: ATTITUDE TOWARD WOMEN SCALE

Purpose: To assess the rights and roles of women.

Number of Items: 25

Format: Likert format. Sample items are presented.

Reliability: Alpha was .80.

Author: Tomkiewicz, J., and Bass, K.

Article: Changes in women's fear of success and fear of appearing incompetent in business.

Journal: *Psychological Reports*, December 1999, *85*(3, Part I), 1003–1010.

Related Research: Spence, J. T., et al. (1973). A short version of

the Attitudes Toward Women Scale (AWS). *Bulletin of the Psychonomic Society, 2*, 219–220.

8330

Test Name: ATTITUDE TOWARD WOMEN'S WORK SCALE

Purpose: To assess attitudes towards women's work.

Number of Items: 4

Format: Scales ranged from 1 (strongly disagree) to 5 (strongly agree). All items are presented.

Reliability: Coefficient alpha was .59.

Author: Sidani, Y. M., and Gardner, W. L.

Article: Work values among Lebanese workers.

Journal: *Journal of Social Psychology*, October 2000, *140*(5), 597–607.

Related Research: Peters, L. H., et al. (1974). Women as Managers Scale (WAMS): A measure of attitudes toward women in management positions. *JSHS Catalog of Selected Documents in Psychology, 4*, 27.

8331

Test Name: ATTITUDE TOWARD WORK SCALE

Purpose: To measure attitude toward work as a positive influence in life.

Number of Items: 5

Format: Five-point scales are anchored by 1 (strongly agree) and 5 (strongly disagree). All items are presented.

Reliability: Alpha was .83.

Validity: Correlation with job satisfaction was .35.

Author: Tan, P. P., et al.

Article: Job satisfaction and intent to continue working among individuals with serious mental illness.

Journal: *Psychological Reports*, December 1999, *85*(3, Part I), 801–807.

8332

Test Name: ATTITUDES ABOUT AIDS SCALE

Purpose: To assess attitudes about AIDS.

Number of Items: 15

Format: All items are presented.

Reliability: Alpha coefficients ranged from .64 to .85 across subscales.

Validity: Correlations with AIDS knowledge ranged from −.16 to .21.

Author: Zagumny, M. J., and Fuller, A. J.

Article: Current and preservice teachers' knowledge and attitudes about HIV positive students: Examination in a southern rural community.

Journal: *Educational Research Quarterly*, September 2000, *24*(1), 30–41.

8333

Test Name: ATTITUDES ABOUT REALITY SCALE

Purpose: To assess belief in a social constructionist or a logical positivist position.

Number of Items: 40

Format: Seven-point summated rating format.

Reliability: Alpha was .72.

Validity: Correlations with other variables ranged from −.44 to .66.

Author: Evans, W. J.

Article: Construct validity of the Attitudes about Reality Scale.

Journal: *Psychological Reports*, June 2000, *86*(3, Part 1), 738–744.

Related Research: Jackson, L. A., & Jeffers, D. L. (1989). The Attitudes about Reality Scale: A new measure of personal epistemology. *Journal of Personality Assessment, 53,* 353–365.

8334

Test Name: ATTITUDES OF HRS MANAGERS TOWARDS ACADEMIC RESEARCH

Purpose: To measure the relevance, credibility, and validity of research among human resource managers.

Number of Items: 9

Format: Five-point Likert format. All items are presented.

Reliability: Reliability coefficients ranged from .68 to .86.

Validity: Correlations between items ranged from .02 to .74. Correlations with other variables ranged from −.29 to −.16.

Author: Terpstra, D. E., and Rozell, E. J.

Article: Psychology of the scientist: LXXI. Attitudes of practitioners in human resource management toward information from academic research.

Journal: *Psychological Reports*, April 1997, *80*(2), 403–411.

8335

Test Name: ATTITUDES TOWARD BANDING SCALE

Purpose: To assess the understanding and perceived

fairness of test score banding in the hiring process.

Number of Items: 8 and 24 item versions

Format: Scales range from 1 (strongly disagree) to 5 (strongly agree). All items are presented.

Reliability: Alpha coefficients ranged from .77 to .94 across subscales and test versions.

Author: Truxillo, D. M., and Bauer, T. N.

Article: Applicant reactions to test score banding in entry-level and promotional contexts.

Journal: *Journal of Applied Psychology*, June 1999, *84*(3), 322–339.

Related Research: Smither, J. W., et al. (1993). Applicant reaction to selection procedures. *Personnel Psychology, 46,* 49–76.

8336

Test Name: ATTITUDES TOWARD CAREER COUNSELING SCALE

Purpose: To measure attitudes toward career counseling.

Number of Items: 16

Format: Includes 2 subscales: Value of Career Counseling and Stigma Related to Career Counseling. All items are included.

Reliability: Internal consistency reliability coefficients were .86 and .83. Test-retest correlation coefficients were .80 for both subscales. Adjusted test-retest correlations were .79 for both subscales.

Validity: Correlations with other variables ranged from −.45 to .46 (*N* = 125). Correlations with other variables ranged from −.41 to .46 (*N* = 69).

Author: Rochlen, A. B., et al.

Article: Development of the Attitudes Toward Career Counseling Scale.

Journal: *Journal of Counseling Psychology*, April 1999, *46*(2), 196–206.

8337

Test Name: ATTITUDES TOWARD COLLEGIATE CLASSROOM TESTING

Purpose: To assess attitudes toward classroom testing in college.

Number of Items: 20

Format: Likert format. All items are presented.

Reliability: Alpha coefficients ranged from .64 to .93 across subscales.

Validity: Concurrent validity was .84.

Author: Shifflet, B., et al.

Article: Attitudes toward collegiate level classroom testing.

Journal: *Educational Research Quarterly*, September 1997, *21*(1), 15–26.

Related Research: Green, K. E. (1992). Differing opinions on testing between preservice and inservice teachers. *Journal of Educational Research, 86,* 37–42.

8338

Test Name: ATTITUDES TOWARD COMPUTER SCALES

Purpose: To measure attitude toward computers.

Number of Items: 10

Format: 7-point scales are anchored by (1) completely disagree and (7) completely agree.

Reliability: Alpha was .75.

Author: Jawahar, I. M., &
Elango, B.

Article: Predictors of performance
in software training: Attitudes
towards computers versus
attitudes toward working with
computers.

Journal: *Psychological Reports*,
August 1998, *83*(1), 227–233.

Related Research: Lee, R. S.
(1970). Social attitudes and the
computer revolution. *Public
Opinion Quarterly*, *34*, 53–59.

8339

Test Name: ATTITUDES
TOWARD COMPUTER USAGE
SCALE—MODIFIED

Purpose: To measure attitudes
toward computers.

Number of Items: 19

Format: Responses are made on a
5-point Likert scale ranging from
"strongly agree" to "strongly
disagree". All items are
presented.

Reliability: Coefficient alpha was
.84. Test-retest reliability was
.91.

Author: Bures, E. M., et al.

Article: Student motivation to
learn via computer conferencing.

Journal: *Research in Higher
Education*, October 2000, *41*(5),
593–621.

Related Research: Popovich, P.,
et al. (1987). Redevelopment of
the attitudes toward computer
usage scale. *Educational and
Psychological Measurement*, *47*,
261–269.

8340

Test Name: ATTITUDES
TOWARD COMPUTER USE

Purpose: To assess attitudes
about computer use.

Number of Items: 11

Format: Five-point Likert format.

Reliability: Chronbach's alpha
was .70.

Validity: Correlations with other
variables ranged from −.61 to
.27.

Author: Bozionelos, N.

Article: Psychology and computer
use: XLV. Cognitive spontaneity
as a correlate of computer
anxiety and attitudes toward
computer use.

Journal: *Psychological Reports*,
April 1997, *80*(2), 395–402.

Related Research: Ingbaria, M.,
& Chakrabarti, A. (1990).
Computer anxiety and attitudes
toward microcomputer use.
*Behavior and Information
Technology*, *9*, 229–241.

8341

Test Name: ATTITUDES
TOWARD CREDIT CARD USE

Purpose: To assess attitudes
toward credit card use.

Number of Items: 14

Format: Five-point Likert format.

Reliability: Alphas ranged from
.64 to .83 across subscales.

Author: Pinto, M. D., et al.

Article: Materialism and credit
card use by college students.

Journal: *Psychological Reports*,
April 2000, *86*(2), 643–652.

Related Research: Brobeck, S.
(1992, July-August). Consumers'
attitude toward credit cards.
Credit World, *80*(July/August),
8–13.

8342

Test Name: ATTITUDES
TOWARD DIVORCE SCALE

Purpose: To assess attitudes
toward divorce.

Number of Items: 6

Format: Scales range from 1
(strongly agree) to 4 (strongly
disagree). Sample items are
presented.

Reliability: Coefficient alpha was
.58.

Author: Amato, P. R.

Article: Explaining the
intergenerational transmission of
divorce.

Journal: *Journal of Marriage and
the Family*, August 1996, *58*(3),
628–640.

Related Research: Booth, A., et
al. (1993). *Marital instability
over the life course: Methodology
report for fourth wave*. Lincoln:
University of Nebraska Bureau
of Sociological Research.

White, L. K., & Rogers, S. J.
(1997). Strong support but
uneasy relationships: Coresidence
and adult children's relationships
with their parents. *Journal of
Marriage and the Family*, *59*,
62–76.

8343

Test Name: ATTITUDES
TOWARD DREAMS MEASURE

Purpose: To assess how
participants perceived the value
of dreams.

Number of Items: 11

Format: True-false, yes-no, and
4- and 5-point scales are used for
responding.

Reliability: Internal consistency
was .79.

Validity: Correlations with other
variables ranged from .32 to .44.

Author: Rochlen, A. B., et al.

Article: Effects of training in
dream recall and dream

interpretation skills on dream recall, attitudes, and dream interpretation outcome.

Journal: *Journal of Counseling Psychology*, January 1999, *46*(1), 27–34.

Related Research: Hill, C. E., et al. (1997). Dream interpretation sessions: Who volunteers, who benefits, and what participants view as most and least helpful. *Journal of Counseling Psychology*, 44, 53–62.

8344

Test Name: ATTITUDES TOWARD EARTH SCIENCE INVENTORY

Purpose: To survey students' attitudes toward earth science.

Number of Items: 13

Format: Includes 3 subscales: Class Involvement, Confidence in the Subject Matter, and Learning Interest in Earth Science.

Reliability: Alpha coefficients were .84 and .85.

Author: Chang, C. Y., and Mao, S. L.

Article: Comparison of Taiwan science students' outcomes with inquiry-group versus traditional instruction.

Journal: *Journal of Educational Research*, July/August 1999, *92*(6), 340–346.

Related Research: Mao, S. L., & Chang, C. Y. (1997). *The effects of instructional strategies on ninth-grade students' skills of data interpretation and concept formation.* Unpublished report. National Science Council No. NSC 86–2511-S-003–024.

8345

Test Name: ATTITUDES TOWARD FAMILY LIFE SCALES

Purpose: To measure attitudes toward family life.

Number of Items: 14

Format: Includes 3 scales: Marital Burnout, Parental Stress, and Parental Rewards.

Reliability: Alpha coefficients were .64 and .89.

Validity: Correlations with days absent ranged from .04 to .14.

Author: Erickson, R. J., et al.

Article: Family influences on absenteeism: Testing an expanded process model.

Journal: *Journal of Vocational Behavior*, October 2000, *57*(2), 246–272.

8346

Test Name: ATTITUDES TOWARD FEMINISM AND THE WOMEN'S MOVEMENT SCALE

Purpose: To measure attitudes toward feminism.

Number of Items: 10

Format: Five-point agreement scales. A sample item is presented.

Reliability: Alpha coefficients ranged from .86 to .89 across samples.

Validity: Correlations with other variables ranged from .02 to .15.

Author: Hartung, P. J., and Rogers, J. R.

Article: Work-family commitment and attitudes toward feminism in medical students.

Journal: *The Career Development Quarterly*, March 2000, *48*(3), 264–275.

Related Research: Fassinger, L. F. (1994). Development and testing of the Attitudes Toward Feminism and the Women's Movement (FWM) Scale.

Psychology of Women Quarterly, 18, 389–402.

8347

Test Name: ATTITUDES TOWARD FOREIGN LANGUAGE STUDY

Purpose: To measure attitudes toward foreign language study.

Number of Items: 32

Format: Likert scales range from "strongly disagree" to "strongly agree." All items are presented.

Reliability: Internal consistency coefficients ranged from .53 to .94 across subscales.

Author: Corbin, S. S., and Chiachiere, F. J.

Article: Attitudes toward and achievement in foreign language study.

Journal: *Educational Research Quarterly*, September 1997, *21*(1), 3–13.

Related Research: Briem, H. (1974). *Development of an instrument to measure attitudes toward the study of foreign languages.* Unpublished dissertation for Ph.D., Ann Arbor: University of Michigan. University Microfilms No. 75–652.

8348

Test Name: ATTITUDES TOWARD GAY MEN SCALE

Purpose: To measure attitudes toward gay men.

Number of Items: 10

Format: Responses are made on a 9-point scale ranging from 1 (strongly disagree) to 9 (strongly agree).

Reliability: Coefficient alpha was .93.

Author: Slusher, M. P., and Anderson, C. A.

Article: Using causal persuasive arguments to change beliefs and teach new information: The mediating note of explanation availability and evaluation bias in the acceptance of knowledge.

Journal: *Journal of Educational Psychology*, March 1996, *88*(1), 110–122.

Related Research: Herek, G. M. (1987). Religious orientation and prejudice: A comparison of racial and sexual attitudes. *Personality and Social Psychology Bulletin*, *13*, 34–44.

8349

Test Name: ATTITUDES TOWARD GENDER ROLES SCALE

Purpose: To measure gender role attitudes for in-home and out-of-home roles.

Number of Items: 12

Format: Scales range from 1 (disagree) to 5 (agree). Sample items are presented.

Reliability: Coefficient alpha was .68 (in-home roles) and .69 (out-of-home roles).

Authors: Kulik, L.

Article: Gendered personality disposition and gender role attitudes among Israeli students.

Journal: *The Journal of Social Psychology*, December 1999, *139*(6), 736–747.

Related Research: Singleton, R., Jr., & Christiansen, J. B. (1977). The construct validity of a short-form Attitudes Towards Feminism Scale. *Sociology and Social Research*, *61*, 294–303.

8350

Test Name: ATTITUDES TOWARD ILLEGAL ALIENS SCALE

Purpose: To measure attitudes toward illegal aliens.

Number of Items: 30

Format: Likert format. All items are presented.

Reliability: Item-total correlations ranged from .59 to .72.

Validity: Correlations with other variables ranged from .27 to .44.

Authors: Ommundsen, R., and Larsen, K. S.

Article: Attitudes toward illegal aliens: The reliability and validity of a Likert-type scale.

Journal: *Journal of Social Psychology*, October 1997, *137*(5), 665–667.

8351

Test Name: ATTITUDES TOWARD LESBIANS AND GAY MEN

Purpose: To measure heterosexist attitudes.

Number of Items: 20

Format: Scales range from 1 (strongly disagree) to 5 (strongly agree). All items are presented.

Reliability: Alpha coefficients ranged from .90 to .94.

Validity: Correlations with other variables ranged from −.66 to −.12.

Author: Simoni, J. M.

Article: Pathways to prejudice: Predicting students' heterosexist attitudes with demographics, self-esteem, and contact with lesbians and gay men.

Journal: *Journal of College Student Development*, January/February 1996, *37*(1), 68–78.

Related Research: Herek, G. M. (1988). Heterosexuals' attitudes toward lesbians and gay men: Correlates and gender differences. *The Journal of Sex Research*, *25*, 451–477.

8352

Test Name: ATTITUDES TOWARD LESBIANS AND GAY MEN SCALE

Purpose: To measure attitudes toward lesbians and gay men.

Number of Items: 10

Format: Scales range from 1 (strongly disagree) to 9 (strongly agree).

Reliability: Alpha coefficient ranged from .93 (attitudes toward lesbians) to .90 (attitudes toward gay men).

Validity: Correlations with other variables ranged from −.19 to .16.

Authors: Smith, M. R., and Gordon, R. A.

Article: Personal need for structure and attitudes toward homosexuality.

Journal: *Journal of Social Psychology*, February 1998, *138*(1), 83–87.

Related Research: Herek, G. M. (1988). Heterosexuals' attitudes toward lesbians and gay men: Correlates and gender differences. *The Journal of Sex Research*, *25*, 451–477.

8353

Test Name: ATTITUDES TOWARD MALE SOCIAL WORKERS SCALE

Purpose: To assess attitudes towards male social workers.

Number of Items: 15

Format: Five-point scales are

anchored by "strongly agree" and "strongly disagree." All items are presented.

Reliability: Cronbach alpha was .85.

Validity: Correlations with other variables ranged from −.10 to .40.

Author: Green, R. G., et al.

Article: Psychometric evaluation of a questionnaire modified to assess attitudes toward male social workers.

Journal: *Psychological Reports*, June 2000, *86*(3, Part 1), 756–762.

Related Research: Laroche, E., & Livneh, H. (1983). Regressional analysis of attitudes toward male nurses. *Journal of Psychology*, *113*, 67–71.

8354

Test Name: ATTITUDES TOWARD MATHEMATICS AND ITS TEACHING SCALE

Purpose: To measure attitudes and experiences associated with mathematics and its teaching.

Number of Items: 29

Format: Responses are made on a 6-point Likert scale ranging from "very strongly agree" to "very strongly disagree." All items are presented.

Reliability: Alpha coefficients ranged from .95 to .97.

Author: Ludlow, L. H., and Bell, K. N.

Article: Psychometric characteristics of the Attitudes Toward Mathematics and Its Teaching (ATMAT) scale.

Journal: *Educational and Psychological Measurements*, October 1996, *56*(5), 864–880.

Related Research: Bell, K. N. (1995). *How assessment impacts attitudes towards mathematics held by prospective elementary teachers*. Unpublished doctoral dissertation, Boston College, MA.

8355

Test Name: ATTITUDES TOWARD MATHEMATICS— MODIFIED

Purpose: To measure attitudes toward mathematics.

Number of Items: 30

Format: Includes 15 positively and 15 negatively worded statements about mathematics. Responses are made on 5-point scales. Examples are presented.

Reliability: Split-half coefficient was .87.

Author: Alkhateeb, M. H., and Jumaa, M.

Article: Middle-school students in United Arab Emirates: Effects of heterogeneous small group work on attitudes toward mathematics.

Journal: *Perceptual and Motor Skills*, October 2000, *91*(2), 483–490.

Related Research: Jumaa, M. (1989). [The effects of mastery learning strategy on students' achievement in mathematics and attitudes towards it]. Unpublished master's thesis. Yarmouk University, Jordan [in Arabic].

8356

Test Name: ATTITUDES TOWARD MULTIPLE ROLE PLANNING SCALE

Purpose: To assess the degree of realism-unrealism embodied in individuals' attitudes toward multiple roles.

Number of Items: 40

Format: Includes 4 scales: Knowledge/Certainty, Commitment to Multiple Roles, Independence, and Involvement.

Reliability: Alpha coefficients ranged from high .70's to mid .80's. Test-retest (2 weeks) ranged from .62 to .90.

Validity: Correlations with other variables ranged from −.38 to .27 (*N* = 131).

Author: McCracken, R. S., and Weitzman, L. M.

Article: Relationships of personal agency, problem-solving appraisal, and traditionality of career choice to women's attitudes toward multiple role planning.

Journal: *Journal of Counseling Psychology*, April 1997, *44*(2), 149–159.

Related Research: Weitzman, L. M. (1996). The development and initial validation of scales to assess attitudes toward multiple role planning. *Journal of Career Assessment*, *4*, 269–284.

8357

Test Name: ATTITUDES TOWARD RAPE SCALE— REVISED

Purpose: To assess attitudes toward rape.

Number of Items: 25

Format: Scales range from 1 (strongly agree) to 5 (strongly disagree).

Reliability: Alpha coefficients ranged from .68 to .79.

Author: Anderson, L. A., et al.

Article: The effectiveness of two types of rape prevention programs in changing rape-supportive attitudes of college students.

Journal: *Journal of College Student Development*, March/April 1998, *39*(2), 131–142.

Related Research: Harrison, P. F., et al. (1991). Date and acquaintance rape: Perceptions and attitude change strategies. *Journal of College Student Development, 32,* 131–139.

8358

Test Name: ATTITUDES TOWARD RESEARCH SCALES

Purpose: To assess intrinsic motivation to do research, research-related burnout, perceived rewards of research, and satisfaction with being a professor.

Number of Items: 19

Format: Five-point Likert scales. All items are presented.

Reliability: Cronbach alphas ranged from .76 to .90 across subscales.

Validity: Standardized path coefficients between variables ranged from −.55 to −.08.

Author: Singh, S. N., et al.

Article: Research-related burnout among faculty in higher education.

Journal: *Psychological Reports,* October 1998, *83*(2), 463–473.

8359

Test Name: ATTITUDES TOWARD SEEKING PROFESSIONAL PSYCHOLOGICAL HELP SCALE

Purpose: To identify general orientation toward seeking professional help for psychological problems.

Number of Items: 29

Format: Responses are indicated on a 1 to 4 scale measuring agreement or disagreement with each statement.

Reliability: Internal consistencies ranged from .83 to .86. Test-retest (8 and 2 weeks) reliabilities ranged from .84 to .89.

Validity: Correlations with other variables ranged from −.39 to .01.

Author: Simonsen, G., et al.

Article: Gender role conflict and psychological well-being among gay men.

Journal: *Journal of Counseling Psychology,* January 2000, *47*(1), 85–89.

Related Research: Fischer, E. H., & Turner, J. L. (1970). Orientation to seeking professional psychological help: Development and research utility of an attitude scale. *Journal of Consulting and Clinical Psychology, 35,* 79–90.

8360

Test Name: ATTITUDES TOWARD SEEKING PROFESSIONAL PSYCHOLOGICAL HELP— SHORT FORM

Purpose: To assess attitudes toward seeking professional help for psychological problems.

Number of Items: 10

Format: Responses are made on a 4-point Likert-type scale ranging from 0 (disagree) to 3 (agree).

Reliability: Coefficient alpha was .84. Test-retest (4 weeks) reliability was .80.

Validity: Correlations with other variables ranged from −.40 to .26.

Author: Komiya, N., et al.

Article: Emotional openness as a predictor of college students' attitudes toward seeking psychological help.

Journal: *Journal of Counseling*

Psychology, January 2000, *47*(1), 138–143.

Related Research: Fischer, E. H., & Farina, A. (1995). Attitudes toward seeking professional psychological help: A shortened form and considerations for research. *Journal of College Student Development, 36,* 368–373.

8361

Test Name: ATTITUDES TOWARD WOMEN SCALE

Purpose: To identify mothers' and fathers' attitudes concerning women's roles in society.

Number of Items: 15

Format: Responses are made on a 4-point scale ranging from 1 (strongly agree) to 4 (strongly disagree).

Reliability: Alpha coefficients were .81 (mothers) and .73 (fathers).

Author: Crouter, A. C., et al.

Article: Conditions underlying parents' knowledge about children's daily lives in middle childhood: Between and within family comparisons.

Journal: *Child Development,* January/February 1999, *70*(1), 246–259.

Related Research: Spence, J. T., & Helmreich, R. L. (1972). The Attitudes Toward Women Scale: An objective instrument to measure attitudes toward the rights and roles of women in contemporary society. *JSAS Catalog of Selected Documents in Psychology, 2,* 153.

8362

Test Name: ATTITUDES TOWARD WOMEN SCALE FOR ADOLESCENTS

Purpose: To provide a global

measure of adolescents' attitudes about the rights and roles of women in educational, vocational, and intellectual domains.

Number of Items: 12

Format: Responses are made on a 4-point scale ranging from 1 (strongly agree) to 4 (strongly disagree).

Reliability: Alpha coefficients ranged from .62 to .78.

Author: Rainey, L. M., and Borders, L. D.

Article: Influential factors in career orientation and career aspiration of early adolescent girls.

Journal: *Journal of Counseling Psychology*, April 1997, *44*(2), 160–172.

Related Research: Galambos, N. L., et al. (1985). The Attitude Toward Women Scale for Adolescents (AWSA): A study of reliability and validity. *Sex Roles, 13*, 343–356.

8363

Test Name: ATTITUDES TOWARD WOMEN SCALE— SHORT FORM

Purpose: To assess attitudes toward women.

Number of Items: 25

Format: Responses are made on a 4-point Likert scale ranging from 1 (agree strongly) to 4 (disagree strongly). Examples are presented.

Reliability: Test-retest reliability ranged from .74 and .85. Alpha coefficients were .86 and .90.

Author: Heesacker, M., et al.

Article: Gender-based emotional stereotyping.

Journal: *Journal of Counseling*

Psychology, October 1999, *46*(4), 483–495.

Related Research: Spence, J. T., et al. (1973). A short version of the Attitudes Toward Women Scale (AWS). *Bulletin of the Psychometric Society, 2*, 219–220.

8364

Test Name: ATTITUDES TOWARD WORKING WITH COMPUTERS SCALE

Purpose: To measure attitude toward working with computers.

Number of Items: 10

Format: Seven-point scales are anchored by (1) completely disagree and (7) completely agree.

Reliability: Alpha was .88.

Author: Jawahar, I. M., & Elango, B.

Article: Predictors of performance in software training: Attitudes towards computers versus attitudes toward working with computers.

Journal: *Psychological Reports*, August 1998, *83*(1), 227–233.

Related Research: Rafaeli, A. (1986). Employee attitudes toward working with computers. *Journal of Organizational Behavior, 1*, 89–106.

8365

Test Name: ATTITUDES TOWARDS LEARNING ARABIC

Purpose: To measure student attitudes towards learning Arabic.

Number of Items: 37

Format: Scales range from 1 (strongly disagree) to 5 (strongly agree). Sample items are presented.

Validity: Correlations with other variables ranged from −.09 to .48.

Authors: Abu-Rabia, S.

Article: The learning of Arabic by Israeli Jewish children.

Journal: *Journal of Social Psychology*, April 1998, *138*(2), 165–171.

8366

Test Name: ATTITUDES TOWARDS STATISTICS

Purpose: To assess attitudes toward the field of statistics and statistics courses.

Number of Items: 29

Format: Five-point scales are anchored by (1) strong disagreement and (5) strong agreement.

Reliability: Internal consistencies ranged from .90 to .92. Test-retest (2 weeks) ranged from .82 to .91.

Author: Onwuegbuzie, A. J.

Article: Teachers' attitudes towards statistics.

Journal: *Psychological Reports*, December 1998, *83*(3) Part 1, 1008–1010.

Related Research: Wise, S. L. (1985). The development and validation of a scale measuring attitudes toward statistics. *Educational and Psychological Measurement, 45*, 401–405.

8367

Test Name: ATTITUDES TOWARDS WOMEN SCALE

Purpose: To measure traditional role orientations.

Number of Items: 25

Reliability: Coefficient alpha was .92.

Validity: Correlations with other variables ranged from −.06 to .77.

Author: Hamburger, M. E., et al.

Article: Assessing hypergender ideologies: Development and initial validation of a gender-neutral measure of adherence to extreme gender-role beliefs.

Journal: *Journal of Research in Personality*, June 1996, *30*(2), 157–178.

Related Research: Spence, J. T., et al. (1973). A short version of the Attitudes Toward Women Scale (AWS). *Bulletin of the Psychonomic Society, 2*, 219–220.

Ross, R. R., & Allgeier, E. R. (1991). *Correlates of males' femininity with sexually coercive attitudes and behavior.* Paper presented at the meeting of the American Psychological Association, San Francisco, CA.

8368

Test Name: BELIEF IDENTIFICATION SCALE

Purpose: To identify one's beleifs.

Number of Items: 9

Format: Responses are made on a 6-point scale ranging from 1 (disagree strongly) to 6 (agree strongly). All items are presented.

Validity: Correlations with other variables ranged from −.53 to .55.

Author: Sa, W. C., et al.

Article: The domain specificity and generality of belief bias: Searching for a generalizable critical thinking skill.

Journal: *Journal of Educational Psychology*, September 1999, *91*(3), 497–510.

Related Research: Cederblom, J.

(1989). Willingness to reason and the identification of the self. In E. P. Maimon et al. (Eds.), Thinking, reasoning and writing (pp. 147–159). New York: Longman.

8369

Test Name: BELIEF IN CONVENTIONAL ROLES SCALE

Purpose: To measure belief in conventional roles.

Number of Items: 17

Format: Four-point scales are anchored by "not at all wrong" and "very wrong."

Reliability: Alpha was .78.

Author: Gottfredson, D. C., and Koper, C. S.

Article: Race and sex differences in the prediction of drug use

Journal: *Journal of Consulting and Clinical Psychology*, April 1996, *64*(2), 305–313.

Related Research: Patterson, G. R., & Stouthamer-Loeber, M. (1984). The correlation of family management practices and delinquency. *Child Development, 55*, 1299–1307.

8370

Test Name: BELIEF IN GOOD LUCK SCALE

Purpose: To measure belief in good luck.

Number of Items: 14

Format: Scales range from 1 (strongly disagree) to 6 (strongly agree). All items are presented.

Reliability: Coefficient alpha was .85.

Validity: Correlations with other variables ranged from −.34 to .43.

Author: Darke, P. R., and Freedman, J. L.

Article: The Belief in Good Luck Scale.

Journal: *Journal of Research in Personality*, December 1997, *31*(4), 486–511.

8371

Test Name: BELIEFS ABOUT ATTRACTIVENSS SCALE— REVISED

Purpose: To measure women's beliefs about attractiveness.

Number of Items: 19

Format: Includes 2 factors: Importance of Physical Fitness and Importance of Being Attractive and Thin. Responses are made on a 7-point Likert scale ranging from 1 (strongly disagree) to 7 (strongly agree). An example is given.

Reliability: Coefficient alphas were .88 and .89.

Validity: Correlations with other variables ranged from −.23 to .35.

Author: Johnson, C. E., and Petrie, T. A.

Article: Relationship of gender discrepancy to psychological correlates of disordered eating in female undergraduates.

Journal: *Journal of Counseling Psychology*, October 1996, *43*(4), 473–479.

Related Research: Petrie, T., et al. (1996, August). Development and validation of the Revised Beliefs About Attractiveness Scale. Paper presented at the 104th Annual Convention of the American Psychological Association, Toronto, Ontario, Canada.

8372

Test Name: BELIEFS TOWARD MENTAL ILLNESS SCALE

Purpose: To measure cross-cultural differences in beliefs about mental health and treatment beliefs.

Number of Items: 24

Format: Six-point scales are anchored by 0 (completely disagree) and 5 (completely agree). All items are presented.

Reliability: Cronbach alpha reliabilities ranged from .74 to .91.

Validity: Correlations with other variables ranged from −.21 to .31.

Author: Hirai, M., and Clum, G. A.

Article: Development, reliability, and validity of the Beliefs Toward Mental Illness Scale.

Journal: *Journal of Psychopathology and Behavioral Assessment*, September 2000, 22(3), 221–236.

8373

Test Name: BROAD VIEW OF CULTURAL MINORITIES SCALE

Purpose: To assess the extent to which counselors view a broad range of populations as a cultural minority.

Number of Items: 13

Format: Responses are made on a 5-point scale.

Reliability: Coefficient alpha was .92.

Validity: Correlations with other variables ranged from −.27 to .26.

Author: Bieschke, K. J., and Matthews, C.

Article: Career counselor attitudes and behaviors toward gay, lesbian, and bisexual clients.

Journal: *Journal of Vocational Behavior*, April 1996, 48(2), 243–255.

8374

Test Name: CALLOUSED SEXUAL BELIEFS

Purpose: To measure rape-supportive beliefs related to hypermasculinity.

Number of Items: 10

Format: Forced-choice format. Sample items are presented.

Reliability: Alpha was .79.

Author: Bernat, J. A., et al.

Article: Construct validity and test-retest reliability of a date-rape decision-latency measure.

Journal: *Journal of Psychopathology and Behavioral Assessment*, December 1997, 19(4), 315–330.

Related Research: Mosher, D. L., & Sirkin, M. (1984). Measuring a macho personality constellation. *Journal of Research in Personality*, 18, 150–163.

8375

Test Name: CEO ATTITUDE AND PERCEPTION SCALES

Purpose: To assess task-satisfaction, congruence of beliefs and values, trust in the leader, inspiration, and tack clarity.

Number of Items: 27

Format: Seven-point scales are anchored by 1 (strongly disagree) and 7 (strongly agree). All items are presented.

Reliability: Alpha coefficients ranged from .60 to .92 across subscales.

Validity: Correlations with other variables ranged from −.43 to .68.

Author: Kirkpatrick, S. A., and Locke, E. A.

Article: Direct and indirect effects of three core charismatic leadership components on performance and attitudes.

Journal: *Journal of Applied Psychology*, June 1996, 81(1) 36–51.

8376

Test Name: CHILDREN'S ATTITUDES TOWARD WOMEN SCALE

Purpose: To assess gender role attitudes.

Number of Items: 19

Format: Responses are made on a 4-point scale. A sample item is presented.

Reliability: Alpha coefficients were .83 and .80.

Validity:

Author: McHale, S. M., et al.

Article: Family context and gender role socialization in middle childhood: Comparing girls to boys and sisters to brothers.

Journal: *Child Development*, July/August 1999, 70(4), 990–1004.

Related Research: Antill, J., et al. (1994). *Measures of children's sex-typing in middle childhood II*. Unpublished manuscript, Macquarie University, Sydney, Australia.

8377

Test Name: COERCIVE SEX SCALE

Purpose: To measure endorsement of and willingness to engage in coercive sex.

Number of Items: 5

Format: Responses are made on a 5-point rating scale ranging from 1 (strongly agree) to 5 (strongly disagree). An example is presented.

Reliability: Coefficient alpha was .64.

Validity: Correlations with other variables ranged from −.15 to .25.

Author: Goodyear, R. K., et al.

Article: Predictions of Latino men's paternity in teen pregnancy: Test of a mediational model of childhood experiences, gender role attitudes, and behaviors.

Journal: *Journal of Counseling Psychology*, January 2000, 47(1), 116–128.

Related Research: Kirby, D. (1984). *Sexuality education: A handbook for evaluating programs*. Santa Cruz, CA: Network Publications.

8378

Test Name: COMMUNITY SERVICE ATTITUDES SCALE

Purpose: To measure college students' attitudes about community service.

Number of Items: 46

Format: Includes 8 factors: Normative Helping Attitudes, Connectedness, Costs, Awareness, Intentions, Benefits, Seriousness, and Career Benefits. Responses are made on 7-point scales. All items are presented.

Reliability: Alpha coefficients ranged from .72 to .93.

Author: Shiarella, A. H., et al.

Article: Development and construct validity of scores on the Community Service Attitudes Scale.

Journal: *Educational and Psychological Measurement*, April 2000, 60(2), 286–300.

Related Research: Schwartz, S. H. (1977). Normative influences on altruism. In L. Berkowitz (Ed.), *Advances in experimental social psychology* (Vol. 10, pp. 221–279). New York: Academic Press.

8379

Test Name: CONDOM ATTITUDES SCALE

Purpose: To measure attitudes toward condom use.

Number of Items: 7

Format: Four-point scales are anchored by 1 (strongly disagree) and 4 (strongly agree). Sample items are presented.

Reliability: Coefficient alpha was .66.

Author: Kalichman, S. C., et al.

Article: Effectiveness of a video-based motivational skills-building HIV risk-reduction intervention for inner-city African American men.

Journal: *Journal of Consulting and Clinical Psychology*, December 1999, 67(6), 959–966.

Related Research: Hewlig-Larsen, M., & Collins, B. (1991). *Framing messages to promote condom use*. Paper presented at the 99th Annual Convention of the American Psychological Association, San Francisco, CA.

8380

Test Name: CROSS-CULTURAL COUNSELING INVENTORY— REVISED

Purpose: To assess counselors' behaviors and attitudes.

Number of Items: 20

Format: Includes 3 subscales: Cross-Cultural Counseling Skill, Sociopolitical Awareness, and Cultural Sensitivity. Responses are made on a 6-point Likert scale ranging from 1 (strongly disagree) to 6 (strongly agree).

Reliability: Alpha coefficients were .95 and .97.

Author: Worthington, R. L., et al.

Article: Multicultural counseling competencies: Verbal content, counselor attributions, and social desirability.

Journal: *Journal of Counseling Psychology*, October 2000, 47(4), 460–468.

Related Research: LaFromboise, T. D., et al. (1991). Development and factor structure of the Cross-Cultural Counseling Inventory— Revised. *Professional Psychology: Research and Practice, 22*, 380–388.

8381

Test Name: CULTURAL IDENTITY ATTITUDE SCALE

Purpose: To assess racial identity for people of color.

Number of Items: 50

Format: Responses are made on a 5-point Likert-type scale ranging from 1 (strongly disagree) to 5 (strongly agree).

Reliability: Internal consistency coefficients ranged from .66 to .72.

Author: Ladany, N., et al.

Article: Supervisee multicultural case conceptualization ability and self-reported multicultural competence as functions of supervisee racial identity and supervisor focus.

Journal: *Journal of Counseling Psychology*, July 1997, 44(3), 284–293.

Related Research: Helms, J. E., & Carter, R. T. (1990). *Preliminary overview of the Cultural Identity Attitude Scale.* Unpublished manuscript.

8382

Test Name: DISGUST SCALE

Purpose: To measure whether a situation is disgusting.

Number of Items: 32

Format: Two scales are used (not, slightly, very) and true/false. All items are presented.

Validity: Correlations with other variables ranged from −.46 to .39.

Author: Rozin, P., et al.

Article: Individual differences in disgust sensitivity: Comparisons and evaluations of pencil-and-paper versus behavioral measures.

Journal: *Journal of Research in Personality,* September 1999, 33(3), 330–351.

Related Research: Haidt, J., et al. (1994). Individual differences in sensitivity to disgust: A scale sampling seven domains of disgust elicitors. *Personality and Individual Differences, 16,* 701–713.

8383

Test Name: DIVERGENT THINKING ATTITUDES SCALE

Purpose: To measure divergent thinking attitudes.

Number of Items: 44

Format: Includes 3 subscales: Valuing New Ideas, Belief That Creativity Is Not Only for a Select Few, and Not Feeling Too Busy for New Ideas. All items are presented.

Reliability: Alpha coefficients ranged from .70 to .83.

Author: Basadur, M., et al.

Article: Improving the measurement of divergent thinking attitudes in organizations.

Journal: *Journal of Creative Behavior,* Second Quarter 1999, 33(2), 75–111.

Related Research: Basadur, M. S., & Hausdorf, P. (1996). Measuring divergent thinking attitudes related to creative problem solving. *Creativity Research Journal, 9,* 21–32.

8384

Test Name: DYSFUNCTIONAL ATTITUDE SCALE

Purpose: To measure cognitive vulnerability to depression as perfectionism and need for approval.

Number of Items: 26

Format: Sample items are presented.

Reliability: Coefficient alphas were .91 (Need for Approval) and .82 (Perfectionism). Test-retest correlations ranged from .56 to .68.

Author: Zuroff, D. C., et al.

Article: Relations of therapeutic alliance and perfectionism to outcome in brief outpatient treatment of depression.

Journal: *Journal of Consulting and Clinical Psychology,* February 2000, 68(1), 114–124.

Related Research: Cane, D. B., et al. (1986). Factor structure of the Dysfunctional Attitude Scale in a student population. *Journal of Clinical Psychology, 42,* 307–309.

8385

Test Name: DYSFUNCTIONAL BELIEFS AND ATTITUDES ABOUT SLEEP

Purpose: To measure attributions about the effects of insomnia, perceptions of loss of control of sleep, perceived sleep needs, misattributions about the causes of insomnia, and expectations about sleep-promoting habits.

Number of Items: 28

Format: 100 mm visual analog scales. Sample items are presented.

Reliability: Alpha coefficients ranged from .80 to .82.

Author: Edinger, J. D., et al.

Article: Insomnia and the eye of the beholder: Are there clinical markers of objective sleep disturbances among adults with and without insomnia complaints?

Journal: *Journal of Consulting and Clinical Psychology,* August 2000, 68(4), 586–593.

Related Research: Morin, C. M., et al. (1993). Dysfunctional beliefs and attitudes about sleep among older adults with and without insomnia complaints. *Psychology and Aging, 8,* 463–467.

8386

Test Name: EATING ATTITUDE INVENTORY FOR DIABETES MELLITUS

Purpose: To measure eating attitudes.

Number of Items: 24

Format: Four-point rating scales range from (1) strongly disagree to (4) strongly agree. All items are presented.

Reliability: Total alpha was .72.

Alphas for subscales ranged from .69 to .92.

Validity: Correlations with other variables ranged from −.62 to .46.

Author: Fukunishi, I., and Akimoto, M.

Article: Development of the Eating Attitude Inventory for Diabetes Mellitus.

Journal: *Psychological Reports*, June 1997, *80*(3) Part 2, 1363–1371.

8387

Test Name: EATING ATTITUDES TEST–26

Purpose: To discover bulimic and anorexic patients in a population at risk.

Number of Items: 26

Format: Responses are made on a 6-point scale ranging from "always" to "never."

Reliability: Coefficient alpha was .94.

Validity: Concurrent validity of .87 was found with criterion group membership in an anorexia group or a control group.

Author: Berry, E. M., et al.

Article: Word association test and psychosexual cues in assessing persons with eating disorders.

Journal: *Perceptual and Motor Skills*, February 1998, *86*(1), 43–50.

Related Research: Garner, D. M., & Garfinkel, P. E. (1979). The Eating Attitudes Test: An index of the symptoms of anorexia nervosa. *Psychological Medicine*, *9*, 273–279.

8388

Test Name: ECOSCALE

Purpose: To measure beliefs and attitudes about the environment.

Number of Items: 22

Format: Five-point scales are anchored by 1 (strongly disagree) and 5 (strongly agree) or 1 (never) and 5 (always).

Reliability: Alphas ranged from .78 to .93.

Author: Ramanaiah, N. V., et al.

Article: Personality profiles of environmentally responsible groups.

Journal: *Psychological Reports*, August 2000, *87*(1), 176–178.

Related Research: Stone, G., et al. (1995). ECOSCALE: A scale for environmentally responsible consumers. *Psychology and Marketing*, *12*, 595–612.

8389

Test Name: ELEMENTARY EDUCATION STUDENTS' BELIEFS ABOUT TEACHING READING SCALE

Purpose: To assess beliefs about teaching reading, including meaningful comprehension, word recognition, and comprehension skills.

Number of Items: 21

Format: Five-point scales are anchored by 1 (almost always) and 5 (almost never). All items are presented.

Reliability: Alphas ranged from .60 to .73 across subscales.

Author: Knudson, R. E., and Anderson, K.

Article: Survey of elementary education students' reading instructional beliefs.

Journal: *Psychological Reports*, June 2000, *86*(3, Part 1), 883–892.

Related Research: Knudson, R. E. (1999). Student teachers' beliefs related to literacy instruction for normative English

speakers. *Psychological Reports*, *84*, 317–318.

8390

Test Name: ELEMENTARY READING ATTITUDE SURVEY

Purpose: To rate attitudes toward reading.

Number of Items: 20

Format: Includes 2 subscales: Recreational Reading Attitude and Academic Reading Attitude.

Reliability: Internal consistency ranged from .74 to .89.

Author: Kush, J. C., and Watkins, M. W.

Article: Long-term stability of children's attitudes toward reading.

Journal: *Journal of Educational Research*, May/June 1996, *89*, 315–319.

Related Research: McKenna, M. C., & Kear, D. J. (1990). Measuring attitude toward reading: A new tool for teachers. *The Reading Teacher*, *43*, 626–639.

8391

Test Name: EMPLOYEE ATTITUDE SCALE

Purpose: To measure employee attitude.

Number of Items: 74

Format: Includes 8 factors: Supervision, Job/Company Satisfaction, Teamwork, Quality Emphasis, External Customer Focus, Workload and Stress, Empowerment, and Training and Development. Responses are made on a 5-point scale ranging from "strongly agree" to "strongly disagree." Sample items are presented.

Reliability: Alpha coefficients ranged from .76 to .96.

Validity: Correlations with other variables ranged from −.27 to .41.

Author: Ryan, A. M., et al.

Article: Attitudes and effectiveness: Examining relations at an organizational level.

Journal: *Personnel Psychology*, Winter 1996, *49*(4), 853–882.

8392

Test Name: ENGLISH AS A SECOND LANGUAGE ATTITUDE SCALE

Purpose: To assess attitudes and motivation to learn English as a second language.

Number of Items: 8

Format: Scales range from 1 (strongly disagree) to 5 (strongly agree). All items are presented.

Reliability: Alpha coefficients ranged from .78 to .85 across subscales.

Authors: Abu-Rabia, S.

Article: Factors affecting the learning of English as a second language in Israel.

Journal: *Journal of Social Psychology*, October 1996, *136*(5), 589–595.

Related Research: Gardner, R. C., & Lambert, W. E. (1972). *Attitudes and motivation in second language learning.* Rowley, MA: Newbury House.

8393

Test Name: ESTES ATTITUDE SCALES—SECONDARY FORM

Purpose: To measure students' attitudes toward five school subjects.

Number of Items: 75

Format: Includes five subjects: English, math, reading, science, and social studies. Responses are made on 5-point Likert continua.

Reliability: Alpha coefficients ranged from .76 to .93.

Author: Ramsay, S. G., and Richards, H. C.

Article: Cooperative learning environments: Effects on academic attitudes of gifted students.

Journal: *Gifted Child Quarterly*, Fall 1997, *41*(4), 160–168.

Related Research: Estes, T. H., et al. (1981). *Estes Attitude Scales: Measures of attitudes toward school subjects.* Contact H. C. Richards, University of Virginia, Charlottesville, VA 22903.

8394

Test Name: ETHNOCENTRISM SCALE

Purpose: To measure attitudes towards ethnic minorities.

Number of Items: 7

Format: Five-point scales range from (1) completely agree to (5) completely disagree. Respondents could also check "never thought about it."

Reliability: Alpha was .90.

Validity: Correlations with other variables ranged from −.40 to .44.

Author: Vollebergh, W. A. M.

Article: Ethnocentrism in secondary school students in the Netherlands: Agreement, absence of opinion and education.

Journal: *Psychological Reports*, August 1997, *81*(1), 339–348.

8395

Test Name: EXTRASENSORY PERCEPTION SURVEY

Purpose: To measure beliefs in extrasensory phenomena.

Number of Items: 12

Format: Five-point scales are anchored by 1 (strongly disagree) and 5 (strongly agree). All items are presented.

Reliability: KR-20 reliabilities ranged from .51 to .58.

Author: Vitulli, W. F., et al.

Article: Beliefs in the paranormal: Age and sex differences among elderly persons and undergraduate students.

Journal: *Psychological Reports*, December 1999, *85*(3, Part I), 847–855.

Related Research: Crawford, H. J., & Christensen, L. B. (1995). *Developing research skills: A laboratory manual* (3rd ed.). Boston, MA: Allyn & Bacon.

8396

Test Name: FACES SCALES

Purpose: To assess attitudes (satisfaction) with work group.

Number of Items: 4

Format: Respondents note the number of the face (1=big frown; 7=big smile) that best expresses their feelings.

Reliability: Coefficient alpha was .86.

Validity: Correlations with other variables ranged from −.27 to .23.

Author: LePine, J. A., and Van Dyne, L.

Article: Predicting voice behavior in work groups.

Journal: *Journal of Applied Psychology*, December 1998, *83*(6), 853–868.

Related Research: Kunin, T. (1955). The construction of a new

type of attitude measure.
Personnel Psychology, 8, 65–78.

8397

Test Name: FACULTY BELIEFS
ABOUT GRADES INVENTORY

Purpose: To measure instructors'
attitudes toward norm- and
criterion-referenced grading
systems and their attitudes
toward the gate-keeping function
of grades.

Number of Items: 30

Format: Includes 3 scales: Frame
of Reference, Gate-Keeping, and
Tough Love. Responses are made
on a 7-point scale ranging from
"strongly agree" to "strongly
disagree."

Reliability: Alpha coefficients
ranged from .66 to .86.

Author: Barnes, L. L. B.

Article: Development of the
faculty belief about grades
inventory.

Journal: *Educational and
Psychological Measurement,* June
1997, *57*(3), 459–468.

Related Research: Geisinger,
K. F., & Rabinovitz, W. (1979,
November). Grading attitudes
and practices among college
faculty members at an American
University. In H. Dahl et al.
(Eds.), *A spotlight on
educational problems* (pp. 145–
171). Oslo, Norway:
Universitetsforlaget.

8398

Test Name: FENNEMA-
SHERMAN MATHEMATICS
ATTITUDES SCALES

Purpose: To measure attitudes
towards mathematics.

Number of Items: 108

Format: Includes 9 scales:
Attitude Toward Success in

Mathematics; Mathematics as a
Male Domain; Mother, Father,
and Teacher; Confidence in
Learning Mathematics;
Mathematics Anxiety; Effectance
Motivation in Mathematics; and
Usefulness of Mathematics.
Responses are made on a 5-point
Likert-type scale. All items are
presented.

Reliability: Split-half reliability
was .87, Alpha coefficients
ranged from .79 to .96.

Author: Mulhern, F., and Rae, G.

Article: Development of a
shortened form of the Fennema-
Sherman Mathematics Attitudes
Scales.

Journal: *Educational and
Psychological Measurement,*
April 1998, *58*(2), 295–306.

Related Research: Fennema, E.,
& Sherman, J. A. (1976).
Fennema-Sherman Mathematics
Attitude Scales: Instruments
designed to measure attitudes
towards the learning of
mathematics by males and
females. *JSAS Catalog of
Selected Documents in
Psychology,* 6(1), 3b.

8399

Test Name: FITNESS ATTITUDE
SCALE

Purpose: To measure attitude
toward fitness.

Number of Items: 19

Format: Responses are made on a
scale ranging from -3 (strongly
disagree) to 3 (strongly agree).
An example is presented.

Reliability: Coefficient alpha was
.87.

Validity: Correlations with other
variables ranged from −.10 to
.38.

Author: Kerner, M. S., and
Grossman, A. H.

Article: Attitudinal, social, and
practical correlates to fitness
behavior: A test of the theory of
planned behavior.

Journal: *Perceptual and Motor
Skills,* December 1998, *87*(3)
Part 2, 1139–1154.

Related Research: Kerner, M. S.
(1993). Fitness attitude scale.
Unpublished scale, New York
University.

8400

Test Name: FRANCIS SCALE OF
ATTITUDE TOWARD
CHRISTIANITY

Purpose: To assess affective
responses to God, Jesus, Bible,
prayer, and church.

Number of Items: 24

Format: Five-point Likert format.
All items are presented in
English.

Reliability: Alpha was .96.

Author: Francis, L. J., and
Hermans, C. A. M.

Article: Internal consistency
reliability and construct validity
of the Dutch translation of the
Francis Scale of Attitude Toward
Christianity among adolescents.

Journal: *Psychological Reports,*
February 2000, *86*(1), 301–307.

Related Research: Francis, L. J.
(1993). Reliability and validity of
a short scale of attitude to
Christianity among adults.
Psychological Reports, 72, 615–
618.

8401

Test Name: GAY LESBIAN
SCALE

Purpose: To measure
homophobia.

Number of Items: 32

Format: Scales range from 1

(strongly agree) to 5 (strongly disagree).

Reliability: Alpha coefficients ranged from .94 to .95.

Author: Brandyberry, L. J., and MacNair, R. R.

Article: The content and function of attitudes toward AIDS.

Journal: *Journal of College Student Development*, May/June 1996, *37*(3), 335–346.

Related Research: Daly, J. (1990). Measuring attitudes toward lesbians and gay men: Development and initial psychometric evaluation of an instrument. *Dissertation Abstracts International*, *52*(05), 2816B. (University Microfilms No. AAG9129812).

8402

Test Name: "GREEN BUYING" SCALES

Purpose: To measure environmental concerns of consumers.

Number of Items: 40

Format: Seven-point Likert scales. Sample items are presented.

Reliability: Alpha coefficients ranged from .59 to .86 across subscales.

Authors: Mainieri, T., et al.

Article: Green buying: The influence of environmental concern on consumer behavior.

Journal: *Journal of Social Psychology*, April 1997, *137*(2), 189–204.

Related Research: Weigel, R. H., & Weigel, J. (1970). Environmental concern: The development of a measure. *Environment and Behavior*, *10*, 3–15.

8403

Test Name: HOLYOAKE CODEPENDENCY INDEX

Purpose: To measure the extent to which a person endorses codependent beliefs and attribution.

Number of Items: 13

Format: All items are presented.

Reliability: Internal consistency ranged from .73 to .84.

Validity: Correlations with other variables ranged from −.67 to .64.

Author: Dear, G. E., and Roberts, C. M.

Article: The Holyoake Codependency Index: Investigation of the factor structure and psychometric properties.

Journal: *Psychological Reports*, December 2000, *87*(3), Part 1, 991–1002.

8404

Test Name: HOMOPHOBIA SCALE

Purpose: To assess homophobia.

Number of Items: 5

Format: Scales ranged from 1 (strongly disagree) to 7 (strongly agree). All items are presented.

Reliability: Coefficient alpha was .88.

Validity: Correlations with other variables ranged from −.22 to .55.

Author: Floyd, K.

Article: Affectionate same-sex touch: The influence of homophobia on observers' perceptions.

Journal: *Journal of Social Psychology*, December 2000, *140*(6), 774–788.

8405

Test Name: HOMOPHOBIA SCALE

Purpose: To measure homophobia.

Number of Items: 7

Format: Scales range from 1 (strongly disagree) to 5 (strongly agree). Sample items are presented.

Reliability: Reliability coefficient was .89.

Authors: Aberson, C. L., et al.

Article: Covert discrimination against gay men by U.S. college students.

Journal: *Journal of Social Psychology*, June 1999, *139*(3), 323–334.

Related Research: Bouton, R. A., et al. (1987). Scales for measuring fear of AIDS and homophobia. *Journal of Personality Assessment*, *51*, 606–614.

8406

Test Name: HOMOPHOBIA SCALE

Purpose: To assess the cognitive, affective and behavioral components of homophobia.

Number of Items: 25

Time Required: 5 minutes

Format: Five-point Likert format. All items are presented.

Reliability: Alpha was .93. Test-retest (1 week) was .96.

Validity: Correlation with the Index of Homophobia was .66.

Author: Wright, L. W., et al.

Article: Development and validation of the Homophobia Scale.

Journal: *Journal of Psychopathology and Behavioral*

Assessment, December 1999, *21*(4), 337–347.

8407

Test Name: HOMOPHOBIA SCALE

Purpose: To measure attitudes toward gay men and lesbians.

Number of Items: 32

Format: Responses are made on a 5-point Likert scale ranging from 1 (strongly disagree) to 5 (strongly agree).

Reliability: Internal consistency coefficients were .93 and .86. Test-retest (4 weeks) reliability was .93.

Validity: Correlations with other variables ranged from −.32 to .19.

Author: Bieschke, K. J., and Matthews, C.

Article: Career counselor attitudes and behaviors toward gay, lesbian, and bisexual clients.

Journal: *Journal of Vocational Behavior*, April 1996, *48*(2), 243–255.

Related Research: Daly, J. (1990). *Measuring attitudes toward lesbians and gay men: Development and initial psychometric evaluation of an instrument.* Unpublished doctoral dissertation. Carbondale, IL: Southern Illinois University at Carbondale.

8408

Test Name: HOMOPHOBIA SCALE—SHORT FORM

Purpose: To measure negative or prejudicial attitudes toward gays and lesbians.

Number of Items: 15

Format: Likert-type items.

Reliability: Alpha coefficient was .95

Validity: Correlations with other variables ranged from −.33 to .29.

Author: Miville, M. L., et al.

Article: Appreciating similarities and valuing differences: The Miville-Guzman Universality–Diversity Scale.

Journal: *Journal of Counseling Psychology*, July 1999, *46*(3), 291–307.

Related Research: Hansan, G. L. (1982). Measuring prejudice against homosexuality (homosexism) among college students. A new scale. *Journal of Social Psychology, 117*, 233–236.

8409

Test Name: HOMOSEXUAL ATTITUDES INVENTORY—MODIFIED SCALE

Purpose: To assess the degree to which respondents internalize antigay values.

Number of Items: 7

Format: Responses are made on a 7-point scale ranging from 1 (strongly disagree) to 7 (strongly agree). An example is presented.

Reliability: Coefficient alpha was .75.

Author: Mohr, J. J., and Rochlen, A. B.

Article: Measuring attitudes regarding bisexuality in lesbian, gay male, and heterosexual populations.

Journal: *Journal of Counseling Psychology*, July 1999, *46*(3), 353–369.

Related Research: Nungesser, L. (1983). *Homosexual acts, actors and identities.* New York: Praeger.

8410

Test Name: HYPERCOMPETITIVE ATTITUDE SCALE

Purpose: To assess individual differences in hypercompetitive attitudes.

Number of Items: 26

Format: Responses are made on a 5-point scale ranging from 1 (never true of me) to 5 (always true of me). Examples are presented.

Reliability: Alpha coefficient was .90.

Validity: Correlations with other variables ranged from −.48 to .44.

Author: Ryckman, R. M., et al.

Article: Construction of a personal development competitive attitude scale.

Journal: *Journal of Personality Assessment*, April 1996, *66*(2), 374–385.

Related Research: Rychman, R. M., et al. (1990). Construction of a hypercompetitive attitude scale. *Journal of Personal Assessment, 55*, 630–639.

8411

Test Name: HYPERMASCULINITY INDEX

Purpose: To assess to what extent individuals endorse hypermasculine behavior.

Number of Items: 20

Format: Seven-point scales range from 1 (extremely uncharacteristic of me) to 7 (extremely characteristic of me). Sample items are presented.

Reliability: Alpha was .78.

Author: Lasane, T. P., et al.

Article: Hypermasculinity and

academic goal-setting: An explanatory study.

Journal: *Psychological Reports*, October 1999, *85*(2), 487–496.

Related Research: Mosher, D. L., & Sirkin, M. (1994). Measuring a macho personality constellation. *Journal of Research in Personality, 18*, 150–163.

8412

Test Name: ILLINOIS RAPE MYTH ACCEPTANCE SCALE

Purpose: To measure the acceptance of the rape myth.

Number of Items: 40

Format: Scales range from 1 (not at all agree) to 7 (very much agree). Sample items are presented.

Reliability: Coefficient alpha was .93.

Author: Muir, G., et al.

Article: Rape myth acceptance among Scottish and American students.

Journal: *Journal of Social Psychology*, April 1996, *136*(2), 261–262.

Related Research: Payne, D. L. (1993). *The structure and assessment of rape myths.* Unpublished doctoral dissertation, University of Illinois, Champagne-Urbana.

8413

Test Name: ILLINOIS RAPE MYTH ACCEPTANCE SCALE

Purpose: To assess the degree of acceptance of cultural myths and supports of rape.

Number of Items: 45 (20 Short Form)

Format: Seven-point scales range from 1 (not at all agree) to 5

(very much agree). All items are presented.

Reliability: Coefficient alpha was .93 (.87, Short Form). Subscale alphas ranged from .74 to .84.

Validity: Correlations with other variables ranged from .47 to .74.

Author: Payne, D. L., et al.

Article: Rape myth acceptance: Exploration of its structure and its measurement using the Illinois Rape Myth Acceptance Scale.

Journal: *Journal of Research in Personality*, March 1999, *33*(1), 27–68.

8414

Test Name: ILLINOIS RAPE MYTH ACCEPTANCE SCALE

Purpose: To assess the degree of acceptance of cultural myths and supports of rape.

Number of Items: 45 (20 Short Form)

Format: Seven-point scales range from 1 (not at all agree) to 5 (very much agree). All items are presented.

Reliability: Coefficient alpha was .93 (.87, Short Form). Subscale alphas ranged from .74 to .84.

Validity: Correlations with other variables ranged from .47 to .74.

Author: Payne, D. L., et al.

Article: Rape myth acceptance: Exploration of its structure and its measurement using the Illinois Rape Myth Acceptance Scale.

Journal: *Journal of Research in Personality*, March 1999, *33*(1), 27–68.

8415

Test Name: ILLNESS ATTITUDE SCALE

Purpose: To measure attitudes,

fears and beliefs associated with hypochondriasis.

Number of Items: 28

Format: Five-point Likert format.

Reliability: Test-retest (4 weeks) correlations ranged from .62 to .92. Alphas ranged from .23 to .93.

Author: Harrell, J. P., and Wright, L. W., Jr.

Article: The development and validation of the Multicomponent AIDS Phobia Scale.

Journal: *Journal of Psychopathology and Behavioral Assessment*, September 1998, *20*(3), 201–216.

Related Research: Kellner, R., et al. (1985). Hostility, somatic symptoms, and hypochondriacal fears and beliefs. *Journal of Nervous and Mental Disease, 173*, 554–560.

8416

Test Name: ILLNESS ATTITUDES SCALE

Purpose: To assess attitudes, beliefs, and fears associated with hypochondriasis.

Number of Items: 27

Format: Includes 9 subscales: Worry About Illness, Concern About Pain, Health Habits, Hypochondriacal Beliefs, Themtophobia, Disease Phobia, Body Preoccupation, Treatment Experience, and Effect of Symptoms. Responses are made on a 5-point scale ranging from 0 (no) to 4 (most of the time). Sample items are presented.

Reliability: Alpha coefficients ranged from .50 to .94.

Validity: Correlations with other variables ranged from −.29 to .29.

Author: Joiner, Jr., T. E., et al.

Article: Development and factor analytic validation of the SPANAS among women in Spain: (More) cross-cultural convergence in the structure of mood.

Journal: *Journal of Personality Assessment*, June 1997, *68*(3), 600–615.

Related Research: Kellner, R. (1986). *Somatization and hypochondriasis*. New York: Praeger.

8417

Test Name: INDEX OF ATTITUDES TOWARDS HOMOSEXUALS

Purpose: To measure homophobia.

Number of Items: 25

Format: Scales range from 1 (strongly agree) to 5 (strongly disagree). Sample items are presented.

Reliability: Coefficient alpha was .90.

Author: Hogan, T. L., and Rentz, A. L.

Article: Homophobia in the academy.

Journal: *Journal of College Student Development*, May/June 1996, *37*(3), 301–314.

Related Research: Hudson, W. W., & Rickets, W. A. (1980). A strategy for the measurement of homophobia. *Journal of Homosexuality*, 5, 357–372.

Guth, L. J., et al. (2000). Student attitudes toward AIDS and homosexuality: The effects of a speaker with HIV. *Journal of College Student Development*, 41, 503–512.

8418

Test Name: INDEX OF HOMOPHOBIA

Purpose: To measure the affective response to homosexuals.

Number of Items: 25

Format: Scales range from 1 (strongly disagree) to 7 (strongly agree).

Reliability: Coefficient alpha was .93.

Validity: Correlations with other variables ranged from −.45 to .35.

Author: Sinn, J. S.

Article: The predictive and discriminant validity of masculinity ideology.

Journal: *Journal of Research in Personality*, March 1997, *31*(1), 117–135.

Related Research: Hudson, W. W., & Rickets, W. A. (1980). A strategy for the measurement of homophobia. *Journal of Homosexuality, 5*, 357–372.

8419

Test Name: INDEX OF HOMOPHOBIA—MODIFIED

Purpose: To identify homophobic attitudes.

Number of Items: 25

Format: Responses are made on a 5-point Likert-type scale ranging from (strongly agree) to 5 (strongly disagree).

Reliability: Alpha coefficients were .95 and .94.

Validity: Correlations with other variables ranged from .20 to 69.

Author: Tokar, D. M., and Jome, L. M.

Article: Masculinity, vocational interests, and career choice traditionality: Evidence for a fully mediated model.

Journal: *Journal of Counseling Psychology*, October 1998, *45*(4), 424–435.

Related Research: Hudson, W. W., & Rickets, W. A. (1980). A strategy for the measurement of homophobia. *Journal of Homosexuality*, 5, 357–372.

8420

Test Name: INTERNATIONAL ASSIGNEE TRAINING AND REPATRIATION SURVEY

Purpose: To assess preparation for international job assignments and beliefs about successful repatriation.

Number of Items: 15

Format: Scales range from 1 (thoroughly disagree) to 6 (thoroughly agree). Sample items are presented.

Reliability: Alpha coefficients ranged from .77 to .85 across subscales.

Validity: Subscale intercorrelations and correlations with other variables ranged from .11 to .52.

Author: Garonzik, R., et al.

Article: Identifying international assignees at risk for premature departure: The interactive effect of outcome favorability and procedural fairness.

Journal: *Journal of Applied Psychology*, February 2000, *85*(1), 13–20.

8421

Test Name: INTRINSIC JOB ATTRIBUTES SCALE

Purpose: To measure perceived intrinsic work characteristics.

Number of Items: 5

Format: Eleven-point scales are anchored by 0 (none at all) and 10 (a tremendous amount). All items are presented.

Reliability: Alpha coefficients ranged from .64 to .78.

Validity: Correlations with other variables ranged from −.24 to .44.

Author: Judge, T. A., et al.

Article: Dispositional effects on job and life satisfaction: The role of core evaluations.

Journal: *Journal of Applied Psychology*, February 1998, *83*(1), 17–34.

Related Research: Hackman, J. R., & Oldham, G. P. (1980). *Work redesign*. Reading, MA: Addison-Wesley.

8422

Test Name: INTRUSIVE MARKETING QUESTIONNAIRE

Purpose: To assess feelings about intrusive marketing practices such as junk mail and unsolicited phone calls.

Number of Items: 10

Format: Five-point scales range from (1) strongly disagree to (2) strongly agree.

Reliability: Alpha was .78.

Validity: Correlations with other variables ranged from −.07 to .49.

Author: Brown, D. J., and Browne, B. A.

Article: Vulnerability and attitudes toward intrusive marketing.

Journal: *Psychological Reports*, December 1998, *83*(3) Part 2, 1348–1350.

8423

Test Name: IRRATIONAL BELIEFS SCALE

Purpose: To measure irrational beliefs.

Number of Items: 11

Format: Five-point Likert format.

Reliability: Item-total correlations ranged from .38 to .55.

Validity: Only one dominant factor emerged.

Author: Mahoney, J. M.

Article: Factor structure of Ellis' Irrational Beliefs in a nonclinical college population.

Journal: *Psychological Reports*, April 1997, *80*(2), 511–514.

Related Research: Watson, C. G., et al. (1990). A factor analysis of Ellis' irrational beliefs. *Journal of Clinical Psychology, 46*, 412–415.

8424

Test Name: JACKSON RISK ATTITUDE SCALE

Purpose: To measure risk taking in four domains.

Number of Items: 6

Format: Includes 4 domains: Monetary, Ethical, Social, and Physical Well-Being.

Validity: Correlations with other variables ranged from −.20 to .36.

Author: Tinsley, B. J., et al.

Article: A multimethod analysis of risk perceptions and health behaviors in children.

Journal: *Educational and Psychological Measurement*, April 1997, *57*(2), 197–209.

Related Research: Jackson, D. N., et al. (1978). A four-dimensional interpretation of risk-taking. *Journal of Personality, 40*, 483–501.

8425

Test Name: LEARNING ORIENTATION-GRADE ORIENTATION SCALE–II

Purpose: To assess educational attitudes and behavior in terms of the importance of learning or grades.

Number of Items: 32

Format: Scales range from 1 (strongly disagree or never) to 5 (strongly agree or always). Sample items are presented.

Reliability: Alpha coefficients ranged from .52 to .82.

Validity: Correlations with other variables ranged from −.15 to .34.

Author: Alexitch, L. R.

Article: Students' educational orientation and preferences for advising from university professors.

Journal: *Journal of College Student Development*, July/August 1997, *38*(4), 333–343.

Related Research: Eison, J. A., et al. (1986). Educational and personal characteristics of four types of learning- and grade-oriented students. *Contemporary Educational Psychology, 11*, 54–67.

8426

Test Name: LEARNING PROCESS QUESTIONNAIRE

Purpose: To assess students' attitudes toward their studies and their usual ways of learning.

Number of Items: 20

Format: Five-point scales are anchored by 1 (never or rarely true of me) and 5 (always or almost always true of me). All items are presented.

Reliability: Alphas ranged from .73 to .86 across subscales.

Author: Marjoribanks, K., and Mboya, M.

Article: Family and individual correlates of academic goal orientations: Social context differences in South Africa.

Journal: *Psychological Reports*, October 2000, *87*(2), 373–380.

Related Research: Biggs, J. B. (1987). *Student approaches to learning*. Melbourne: Australian Council for Educational Research.

8427

Test Name: LOVE ATTITUDES SCALE

Purpose: To measure the love attitudes of eros, ludus, storge, progma, mania, and agape.

Number of Items: 42

Reliability: Alpha coefficients ranged from .62 to .84. Test-retest reliabilities ranged from .60 to .78.

Validity: Correlations with other variables ranged from to −.64 to .55.

Author: Couch, L. L., and Jones, W. H.

Article: Measuring levels of trust.

Journal: *Journal of Research in Personality*, September 1997, *31*(3), 319–336.

Related Research: Hendrick, C., & Hendrick, S. (1986). A theory and method of love. *Journal of Personality and Social Psychology, 50*, 392–402.

8428

Test Name: MALE ROLE NORMS SCALE

Purpose: To measure traditional attitudes about men.

Number of Items: 26

Format: Includes three subscales: Status, Toughness, and Antifemininity. Responses are made on a 5-point scale ranging from 1 (strongly disagree) to 5

(strongly agree). Examples are presented.

Reliability: Alpha coefficients ranged from .74 to .85.

Author: McCreary, D. R., et al.

Article: The male role, alcohol use, and alcohol problems: A structural modeling examination in adult women and men.

Journal: *Journal of Counseling Psychology*, January 1999, *46*(1), 109–124.

Related Research: Thompson, E. H., & Pleck, J. H. (1986). The structure of male role norms. *American Behavioral Scientist, 29*, 531–543.

8429

Test Name: MATHEMATICS ATTITUDE SCALE

Purpose: To measure self-confidence in approaching mathematics classes and problems.

Number of Items: 18

Format: Responses are made on a 7-point Likert-type scale. An example is presented.

Validity: Correlation with testosterone levels was −.43.

Author: Johnson, W., et al.

Article: Overall self-confidence, self-confidence in mathematics, and sex-role stereotyping in relation to salivary free testosterone in university women.

Journal: *Perceptual and Motor Skills*, October 2000, *91*(2), 391–401.

Related Research: Eccles, J. (Parsons) (1983). Expectancies, values, and academic behaviors. In J. Spence (Ed.), *Achievement and achievement motives* (pp. 75–146). San Francisco, CA: Freeman.

8430

Test Name: MATHEMATICS ATTITUDE SCALES— ADAPTED

Purpose: To measure perceptions of attitudes of social agents.

Number of Items: 18

Format: Includes 3 scales: Father's Attitude Scale, Mother's Attitude Scale, and Teacher's Attitude Scale. Responses are made on a 5-point Likert scale ranging from 1 (strongly disagree) to 5 (strongly agree). Examples are presented.

Reliability: Alpha coefficients ranged from .74 to .79.

Author: Vezeau, C., et al.

Article: The impact of single-sex versus coeducational school environment on girls' general attitudes, self-perceptions and performance in mathematics.

Journal: *Journal of Research and Development in Education*, Fall 2000, *34*(1), 49–59.

Related Research: Fennema, E., & Sherman, J. A. (1976). Fennema-Sherman Mathematics Attitudes Scales: Instruments designed to measure attitudes toward the learning of mathematics by females and males. *JASA: Catalog of Selected Documents in Psychology, 6*(1), 31 (Ms. No. 1225).

8431

Test Name: MATHEMATICS SEMANTIC DIFFERENTIAL

Purpose: To measure attitude toward mathematics.

Number of Items: 14

Format: Responses are made on 8-point bipolar scales.

Reliability: Alpha coefficients were .92 and .93.

Author: Wong, N. Y., and Watkins, D.

Article: A longitudinal study of the psychosocial environmental and learning approaches in the Hong Kong classroom.

Journal: *Journal of Educational Research*, March/April 1998, *91*(4), 247–254.

Related Research: Minato, S. (1983). Some mathematical attitudinal data on eighth grade students in Japan measured by a semantic differential. *Educational Studies in Mathematics*, *14*, 19–38.

8432

Test Name: METAMEMORY IN ADULTHOOD SCALES

Purpose: To assess an individual's knowledge, beliefs and feelings about memory.

Number of Items: 76

Format: Scales range from 1 (strongly disagree [or never]) to 5 (strongly agree [or always]).

Reliability: Alpha coefficients ranged from .54 to .87 across subscales.

Validity: Correlations with other variables ranged from −.34 to .55.

Author: McDonald-Miszczak, L., et al.

Article: Metamemory predictors of prospective and retrospective memory performance.

Journal: *Journal of General Psychology*, January 1999, *126*(1), 37–57.

Related Research: Dixon, A. R., et al. (1987). The metamemory in adulthood (MIA) questionnaire. *Psychopharmacology Bulletin*, *24*, 671–688.

8433

Test Name: MULTI-ATTITUDE SUICIDE TENDENCY SCALE

Purpose: To assess four conflicting attitudes related to life and death.

Number of Items: 30

Format: Includes 4 scales: Attraction to Life, Repulsion by Life, Attraction to Death, Repulsion by Death. Responses are made on a 5-point scale ranging from 1 (strongly agree) to 5 (strongly disagree).

Reliability: Alpha coefficients ranged from .59 to .81.

Validity: Correlations with other variables ranged from −.56 to .67.

Author: Gutierrez, P. M., et al.

Article: Suicide risk assessment in a college student population.

Journal: *Journal of Counseling Psychology*, October 2000, *47*(4), 403–413.

8434

Test Name: MULTICULTURAL COUNSELING INVENTORY

Purpose: To assess behaviors and attitudes related to multicultural counseling.

Number of Items: 40

Format: Includes 4 subscales: Multicultural Counseling Skills, Multicultural Awareness, Multicultural Counseling Relationship, and Multicultural Counseling Knowledge. Responses are made on a 4-point scale ranging from 1 (very inaccurate) to 4 (very accurate).

Reliability: Alpha coefficients ranged from .60 to .85.

Validity: Correlations with other variables ranged from −.17 to .36.

Author: Worthington, R. L., et al.

Article: Multicultural counseling competencies: Verbal content, counselor attributions, and social desirability.

Journal: *Journal of Counseling Psychology*, October 2000, *47*(4), 460–468.

Related Research: Sodowsky, G. R., et al. (1994). Development of the Multicultural Counseling Inventory. A self-report measure of multicultural competencies. *Journal of Counseling Psychology*, *41*, 137–148.

8435

Test Name: NEW ENVIRONMENTAL PARADIGM SCALE

Purpose: To assess the extent to which individuals view humans as an integral part of nature.

Number of Items: 12

Format: Seven-point scales range from 1 (strongly disagree) to 7 (strongly agree). Sample items are presented.

Reliability: Coefficient alpha was .82.

Author: Schultz, P. W., and Oskamp, S.

Article: Effort as a moderator of the attitude-behavior relationship: General environmental concern and recycling.

Journal: *Social Psychology Quarterly*, December 1996, *59*(4), 375–383.

Related Research: Dunlap, R., & Van Liere, K. (1978). The new environmental paradigm. *Journal of Environmental Education*, *9*, 10–19.

8436

Test Name: OKLAHOMA RACIAL ATTITUDES' SCALE

Purpose: To measure type of racial attitudes Whites hold regarding their own and other racial groups.

Number of Items: 50

Format: Responses are made on a 5-point Likert scale ranging from 1 (strongly disagree) to 5 (strongly agree).

Reliability: Alpha coefficients ranged from .68 to .82.

Author: Pope-Davis, D. B., et al.

Article: White racial identity attitude development: A psychometric examination of two instruments.

Journal: *Journal of Counseling Psychology*, January 1999, *46*(1), 70–79.

Related Research: Choney, S., & Behrens, J. (1996). Development of the Oklahoma Racial Attitudes' Scale—Preliminary Form (ORAS–P). In G. R. Sodowsky & J. Impara (Eds.), *Multicultural assessment in counseling and clinical psychology* (pp. 225–240). Lincoln, NE: Burows Institute of Mental Measurements.

8437

Test Name: OLDER WORKER BIAS INDEX

Purpose: To assess bias against older workers.

Number of Items: 7

Format: Semantic differential format. All bipolar adjectives are presented.

Reliability: Alpha coefficient was .70.

Validity: Correlations with other variables ranged from −.19 to −.12.

Author: Perry, E. L., et al.

Article: Moderating effects of personal and contextual factors in age discrimination.

Journal: *Journal of Applied Psychology*, December 1996, *81*(6), 628–647.

Related Research: Cleveland, J. N., et al. (1988). Applicant pool composition and job perceptions: Impact on decisions regarding an older applicant. *Journal of Vocational Behavior*, *32*, 112–125.

8438

Test Name: PAINTING SEMANTIC DIFFERENTIAL

Purpose: To provide reactions to paintings.

Number of Items: 12

Format: Items are 7-point semantic differential scales. All items are presented.

Reliability: Alpha coefficients ranged from .85 to .96.

Author: Polzella, D. J.

Article: Differences in reactions to paintings by male and female college students.

Journal: *Perceptual and Motor Skills*, August 2000, *91*(1), 251–258.

Related Research: Berlyne, D. E. (1973). Interrelations of verbal and nonverbal measures used in experimental aesthetics. *Scandinavian Journal of Psychology*, *14*, 177–184.

8439

Test Name: PARENT ATTITUDE SCALE

Purpose: To measure parent attitude.

Number of Items: 15

Format: Includes objective and open-ended items. Examples are given.

Reliability: Coefficient alpha was .76.

Author: Sutton, S. E., et al.

Article: Pathways to aggression in young, highly stressed urban children.

Journal: *Child Study Journal*, 1999, *29*(1), 49–67.

Related Research: Sutton, S. E. (1995). *Pathways to aggression in highly stressed 2nd and 3rd grade urban children.* Unpublished Ph.D. dissertation, University of Rochester.

8440

Test Name: PARENT ATTITUDES SCALE

Purpose: To measure parent attitudes.

Number of Items: 12

Format: Responses are made on 5-point scales. An example is given.

Reliability: Coefficient alpha was .77.

Author: Fagen, D. B., et al.

Article: Relationships between parent-child relational variables in highly stressed urban families.

Journal: *Child Study Journal*, 1996, *26*(2), 87–108.

Related Research: Gribble, P. A., et al. (1993). Parent and child views of parent-child relationship qualities and resilient outcomes among urban children. *Journal of Child Psychology and Psychiatry*, *34*, 507–519.

8441

Test Name: PAY SYSTEMS ATTITUDE SCALE

Purpose: To measure attitudes toward pay systems.

Number of Items: 9

Format: Scales range from 1 (highly unimportant) to 5 (highly important). Items are described.

Reliability: Coefficient alpha was .80.

Authors: Mamman, A.

Article: Employees' attitudes toward criteria for pay systems.

Journal: *Journal of Social Psychology*, February 1997, *137*(1), 33–41.

Related Research: Mamman, A. (1990). Employees' preferences for pay systems: Theoretical approaches and an empirical test. *International Journal of Human Resource Management*, *1*, 329–340.

8442

Test Name: PERCEIVED CONTINGENCY SCALE FOR CHILDREN

Purpose: To assess children's contingency beliefs.

Number of Items: 30

Format: Includes 3 contingency scores: Academic, Behavioral, and Social.

Reliability: Alpha coefficients ranged from .69 to .75. Test-retest (10 days) reliabilities ranged from .48 to .78.

Author: Granger, D. E., et al.

Article: Reciprocal influences among adrenocortical activation, psychosocial processes, and the behavioral adjustment of clinic-referred children.

Journal: *Child Development*, December 1996, *67*(6), 3250–3362.

Related Research: Weitz, J. R., et al. (1991). *The Perceived*

Contingency Scale for Children: Development and validation. Unpublished manuscript, University of California at Los Angeles.

8443

Test Name: PERSONAL BELIEFS SCALE

Purpose: To measure the strength of six mind-body beliefs.

Number of Items: 60

Format: 7-point scales are anchored by (0) very strongly disagree and (6) very strongly agree.

Reliability: Split-half reliability was .83.

Author: Embree, R. A.

Article: Attitudes toward elective abortion: Preliminary evidence of validity for the Personal Beliefs Scale.

Journal: *Psychological Reports*, June 1998, *82*(3) Part 2, 1267–1281.

Related Research: Embree, R. A., and Embree, M. C. (1993). The Personal Beliefs Scale on a measure of individual differences in commitment to the mind-body beliefs proposed by F. F. Centore. *Psychological Reports*, *73*, 411–428.

8444

Test Name: PERSONAL DEVELOPMENT COMPETITIVE ATTITUDE SCALE

Purpose: To assess individual differences in competitive attitude based on personal development goals.

Number of Items: 15

Format: Responses are made on a 5-point scale ranging from 1

(strongly disagree) to 5 (strongly agree). All items are presented.

Reliability: Coefficient alphas were .90 and .89.

Validity: Correlations with other variables ranged from −.07 to .20.

Author: Ryckman, R. M., et al.

Article: Construction of a personal development competitive attitude scale.

Journal: *Journal of Personality Assessment*, April 1996, *66*(2), 374–385.

8445

Test Name: PHYSICAL EDUCATORS' ATTITUDE TOWARD TEACHING THE INDIVIDUALS WITH DISABILITIES SURVEY

Purpose: To assess attitudes toward teaching students with disabilities in regular physical education classes.

Number of Items: 19

Format: Includes two parts: The first part has 4 areas: Emotional Behavior Disorder, Specific Learning Disability, Moderate Mental Retardation, and Orthopedic Impairment. The second part contains seven attributes.

Reliability: Internal consistency coefficients ranged from .83 to .90.

Author: Zanandrea, M., and Rizzo, T.

Article: Attitudes of undergraduate physical education majors in Brazil toward teaching students with disabilities.

Journal: *Perceptual and Motor Skills*, April 1998, *86*(2), 699–706.

Related Research: Rizzo, T. L. (1984). Attitudes of physical educators toward teaching handicapped pupils. *Adapted Physical Activity Quarterly, 1,* 263–274.

8446

Test Name: PLURALISM AND DIVERSITY ATTITUDE ASSESSMENT SCALE

Purpose: To measure the degree of positive attitudes toward cultural pluralism and one's comfort with diversity.

Number of Items: 19

Format: Includes four scales: Appreciate Cultural Pluralism, Value Cultural Pluralism, Implement Cultural Pluralism, and Uncomfortable With Cultural Diversity. Responses are made on a 6-point scale ranging from "strongly agree" to "strongly disagree."

Reliability: Coefficient alpha was .91 ($n = 35$). Test-retest reliability was .84.

Author: Stanley, L. S.

Article: The development and validation of an instrument to assess attitudes toward cultural diversity and pluralism among preservice physical educators.

Journal: *Educational and Psychological Measurement,* October 1996, *56*(5), 891–897.

Related Research: Gable, R. K. (1986). *Instrument development in the affective domain.* Boston: Kuwer-Nijoff.

8447

Test Name: PREDICTION OF FUTURE EVENTS SCALE

Purpose: To assess seven beliefs about predicting the future.

Number of Items: 21

Format: Scales range from 1

(strongly disagree) to 5 (strongly agree).

Reliability: Alpha coefficients ranged from −.52 to .83 across subscales.

Author: Van der Sijde, P. C., et al.

Article: Demographic differences in coping with uncertainty about the future.

Journal: *Journal of Social Psychology,* April 1996, *136*(2), 159–164.

Related Research: Tobycyk, J., et al. (1989). Prediction of Future Events Scale: Assessment of beliefs about predicting the future. *Journal of Social Psychology, 129,* 819–823.

8448

Test Name: PREJUDICE SCALE

Purpose: To measure prejudice.

Number of Items: 8

Format: Sample items are presented.

Reliability: Alpha coefficients ranged from .68 to .82 across groups.

Validity: Correlations with other variables ranged from .06 to .60.

Author: Verkuyten, M.

Article: Personal self-esteem and prejudice among ethnic majority and minority youth.

Journal: *Journal of Research in Personality,* June 1996, *30*(2), 248–263.

Related Research: Masson, C. H., & Verkuyten, M. (1993). Prejudice, ethnic identity, contact and ethnic group preferences among Dutch young adolescents. *Journal of Applied Social Psychology, 23,* 156–168.

8449

Test Name: PRIMARY TEACHER QUESTIONNAIRE

Purpose: To assess teacher endorsement of statements about developmentally appropriate and traditional practices in early childhood classrooms.

Number of Items: 42

Format: Includes 2 subscales: Developmentally Appropriate Practices and Traditional Practices. Responses are made on a 4-point Likert-type scale.

Reliability: Alpha coefficients were .80 and .87.

Validity: Correlations with other variables ranged from −.46 to .89.

Author: Ketner, C. S., et al.

Article: Relationship between teacher orientation to reading and endorsement of developmentally appropriate practice.

Journal: *Journal of Educational Research,* March/April 1997, *90*(4), 212–220.

Related Research: Smith, K. E. (1993). The development of the Primary Teacher Questionnaire. *The Journal of Educational Research, 87*(1), 23–29.

8450

Test Name: PROS AND CONS OF QUITTING SCALE

Purpose: To assess the anticipated physical, social, self-evaluative, and monetary outcomes of quitting smoking.

Number of Items: 21

Format: Four-point scales are anchored by 0 (not sure or not expecting) and 3 (strong expectation of the outcome).

Reliability: Alpha was .87 (pros) and .57 (cons).

Author: Dijkstra, A., et al.

Article: Tailored interventions to communicate staged-matched information to smoking in different motivational stages.

Journal: *Journal of Consulting and Clinical Psychology,* June 1998, *66*(3), 549–557.

Related Research: Dijkstra, A., et al. (1996). The pros and cons of quitting, self-efficacy, and the stages of change in smoking cessation. *Journal of Consulting and Clinical Psychology, 64,* 758–763.

8451

Test Name: PSI-EXPERIENCE QUESTIONNAIRE—REVISED

Purpose: To gauge PSI experiences.

Number of Items: 9

Format: Responses are made on a 5-point scale ranging from 0 (never) to 4 (weekly or more). Examples are presented.

Reliability: Coefficient alpha was .81.

Validity: Correlations with other variables ranged from −.09 to .50.

Author: Donavan, J. M.

Article: Reinterpreting telepathy as unusual experiences of empathy and charisma.

Journal: *Perceptual and Motor Skills,* August 1998, *87*(1), 131–146.

Related Research: Anthony, J. S. (1982). *Interrelationships among belief in psychic abilities, psychic experiences, and sensation-seeking.* Unpublished Ph.D. dissertation, United States International University.

8452

Test Name: PSYCHOTHERAPY AND STIGMA SCALE

Purpose: To measure stigma as it is attached to seeking therapy.

Number of Items: 23

Format: Includes 3 subscales: Secrecy of Therapy, Societal Stigmatization, and Who Belongs in Therapy. Responses are made on a 6-point Likert scale ranging from 1 (strongly disagree) to 6 (strongly agree). Examples are presented.

Reliability: Internal consistency estimates ranged from .81 to .90. Test-retest (2–3 weeks) correlation estimates ranged from .76 to .88.

Validity: Correlations with other variables ranged from −.57 to .58.

Author: Rochlen, A. B., et al.

Article: Development of the Attitudes Toward Career Counseling Scale.

Journal: *Journal of Counseling Psychology,* April 1999, *46*(2), 196–206.

Related Research: Judge, A. B., and Gelso, C. J. (1998). *Psychotherapy and Stigma Scale: Development and validation of an instrument to measure stigma as it is attached to seeking therapy.* Unpublished doctoral dissertation, University of Maryland, College Park.

8453

Test Name: QUANTITATIVE ATTITUDES QUESTIONNAIRE

Purpose: To measure graduate students' attitudes toward quantitative research methodology.

Number of Items: 20

Format: Includes 4 factors:

Utility, Value, Efficacy, and Knowledge. Responses are made on either a 4-point or a 6-point scale. All items are presented.

Reliability: Alpha coefficients ranged from .74 to .89.

Validity: Correlations with other variables ranged from .20 to .59.

Author: Chang, L.

Article: Quantitative Attitudes Questionnaire: Instrument development and validation.

Journal: *Educational and Psychological Measurement,* December 1996, *56*(6), 1037–1042.

8454

Test Name: QUICK DISCRIMINATION INDEX

Purpose: To assess general attitudes regarding racial diversity, specific attitudes regarding contract and personal comfort with racial diversity, and general attitudes regarding women's equality.

Number of Items: 30

Format: Includes 3 factors. A five-point Likert-type measure was used, ranging from 1 (strongly disagree) to 5 (strongly agree).

Reliability: Test-retest (15 weeks) reliability coefficients ranged from .78 to .96. Alpha coefficients ranged from .65 to .85.

Author: Utsey, S. O., and Ponterotto, J. G.

Article: Further factorial validity assessment of scores on the Quick Discrimination Index.

Journal: *Educational and Psychological Measurement,* April 1999, *59*(2), 325–335

Related Research: Ponterotto, J. G., et al. (1995). Development and initial validation of the Quick Discrimination Index (QDI). *Educational and Psychological Measurement*, 55, 1026–1031

8455

Test Name: RACE IDENTITY ATTITUDE SCALE

Purpose: To assess knowledge, appreciation, cognizance, and satisfaction with one's race.

Number of Items: 60

Format: Five-point Likert format.

Reliability: Test-retest reliabilities were less than .70. Alpha coefficients ranged from .33 to .70.

Validity: Correlations with other variables ranged from −.56 to .86 across subscales and across scale versions (Black and White).

Author: Lemon, R. L., and Waehler, C. A.

Article: A test of stability and construct validity of the Black Racial Identity Attitude Scale, Form B (RIAS-B), and the White Racial Identity Scale (WRIAS).

Journal: *Measurement and Evaluation in Counseling and Development*, July 1996, 29(2), 77–85.

Related Research: Helms, J. E., & Carter, R. T. (1990). Development of the White Racial Identity Inventory. In J. E. Helms (Ed.), *Black and White racial identity: Theory, research, and practice*. Westport, CT: Greenwood Press.

Tokar, D. M., & Fischer, A. R. (1998). Psychometric analysis of the Racial Identity Attitude Scale —Long Form. *Measurement and Evaluation in Counseling and Development*, 31, 138–149.

8456

Test Name: RACIAL IDENTITY ATTITUDE SCALE

Purpose: To assess attitudes associated with four racial identity ego statuses.

Number of Items: 50

Format: Includes subscales: Pre-encounter, Encounter, Immersion/Emersion, and Internalization. Responses are made on a 5-point scale ranging from 1 (strongly disagree) to 5 (strongly agree).

Reliability: Alpha coefficients ranged from 41 to .80.

Validity: Correlations with other variables ranged from −.29 to .14.

Author: Gainor, K. A., and Lent, R. W.

Article: Social cognitive expectations and racial identity attitudes in predicting the math choice intentions of Black college students.

Journal: *Journal of Counseling Psychology*, October 1998, 45(4), 403–413.

Related Research: Helms, J. E., & Parham, T. A. (1990). Black Racial Identity Attitudes Scale (Form RIAS-B). In J. E. Helms (Ed.), *Black and white racial identity* (pp. 245–247). New York: Greenwood.

8457

Test Name: RACISM AWARENESS TEACHING— SUBSCALE

Purpose: To measure racial socialization beliefs.

Number of Items: 11

Format: Responses are made on a 5-point scale ranging from 1 (disagree a lot) to 5 (agree a lot).

Reliability: Internal consistency estimates were .60 and .70.

Validity: Correlations with other variables ranged from .08 to .25.

Author: Fischer, A. R., and Shaw, C. M.

Article: African Americans' mental health and perceptions of racist discrimination. The moderating effects of racial socialization experiences and self-esteem.

Journal: *Journal of Counseling Psychology*, July 1999, 46(3), 395–407.

Related Research: Stevenson, H. C. (1995). Relationship of adolescent perceptions of racial socialization to racial identity. *Journal of Black Psychology*, 21, 49–70.

8458

Test Name: RAPE EMPATHY SCALE—REVISED

Purpose: To measure respondents' feelings associated with acquaintance rape victimization.

Number of Items: 19

Format: Scales range from 1 (strongly agree) to 7 (strongly disagree). Sample items are presented.

Reliability: Coefficient alpha was .76. Test-retest reliability (2 weeks) was .71.

Author: Berg, D. R., et al.

Article: Rape prevention education for men: The effectiveness of empathy-induction techniques.

Journal: *Journal of College Student Development*, May/June 1999, 40(3), 219–234.

Related Research: Dietz, S. R., et al. (1982). Measurement of empathy toward rape victims and rapists. *Journal of Personality and Social Psychology, 43*, 372–384.

8459

Test Name: RAPE MYTH ACCEPTANCE SCALE

Purpose: To measure adherence to false beliefs about rape, rape victims, and rapists.

Number of Items: 19

Reliability: Coefficient alpha was .86.

Validity: Correlations with other variables ranged from −.02 to .70.

Author: Hamburger, M. E., et al.

Article: Assessing hypergender ideologies: Development and initial validation of a gender-neutral measure of adherence to extreme gender-role beliefs.

Journal: *Journal of Research in Personality*, June 1996, *30*(2), 157–178.

Related Research: Burt, M. R. (1980). Cultural myths and supports for rape. *Journal of Personality and Social Psychology, 38*, 217–230.
Jones, M. E., et al. (1998). The structure of rape attitudes for men and women: A three-factor model. *Journal of Research in Personality, 32*, 331–350.

8460

Test Name: RAPE MYTH ACCEPTANCE SCALE

Purpose: To assess adherence to the cultural myths that support rape.

Number of Items: 20

Format: Scales range from 0 (never true) to 5 (always true). Sample items are presented.

Reliability: Alpha coefficients

ranged from .85 to .87. Test-retest reliability (2 weeks) was .82.

Author: Berg, D. R., et al.

Article: Rape prevention education for men: The effectiveness of empathy-induction techniques.

Journal: *Journal of College Student Development*, May/June 1999, *40*(3), 219–234.

Related Research: Payne, D. L., et al. (1999). Rape myth acceptance: Exploration of its structure and its measurement using the Illinois Rape Myth Acceptance (IRMA) Scale. *Journal of Research in Personality, 33*, 27–68.

8461

Test Name: REACTIONS TO INFERTILITY AND INFERTILITY TREATMENT

Purpose: To assess stress behavior and attitudes toward children, family, medicine, and religion.

Number of Items: 100

Format: Four-point scales are anchored by 1 (strongly agree) and 4 (strongly disagree). Sample items are presented.

Reliability: Alphas ranged from .78 to .90 across subscales.

Author: Nasseri, M.

Article: Cultural similarities in psychological reactions to infertility.

Journal: *Psychological Reports*, April 2000, *86*(2), 375–378.

Related Research: Nasseri, M., et al. (1998). *Psychological reactions to infertility in infertility treatment: The Persian experience.* Poster presented to the 18th annual conference of Society for Reproductive and Infant Psychology. Proceedings

published in *Journal of Reproductive and Infant Psychology, 16*, 239–240.

8462

Test Name: READER BELIEF INVENTORY

Purpose: To measure transmission and transaction beliefs.

Number of Items: 16

Format: Includes 2 subscales: Transmission Beliefs and Transaction Beliefs. Responses are made on a 5-point scale. All items are presented.

Reliability: Alpha coefficients were .81 and .78.

Author: Schraw, G.

Article: Reader beliefs and measuring construction in narrative text.

Journal: *Journal of Educational Psychology*, March 2000, *92*(1), 96–106.

Related Research: Schraw, G., & Bruning, R. (1996). Readers' implicit models of reading. *Reading Research Quarterly, 31*, 290–305.

8463

Test Name: RESEARCH ATTITUDES MEASURE

Purpose: To assess a student's global self-efficacy related to research productivity and competence.

Number of Items: 23

Format: Scales range from 0 (no confidence) to 4 (absolute confidence). Sample items are presented.

Reliability: Internal consistency was .94.

Validity: Correlations with other variables ranged from .41 to .49.

Author: Kahn, J. H., and Miller, S. A.

Article: Measuring global perceptions of the research training environment using a short form of the RTES-R.

Journal: *Measurement and Evaluation in Counseling and Development*, July 2000, *33*(2), 103–119.

Related Research: O'Brien, K. M., et al. (1998). *Research self-efficacy: Improvements in instrumentation*. Poster session presented at the annual conference of the American Psychological Association, San Francisco, CA.

8464

Test Name: RESEARCH ATTITUDES MEASURE

Purpose: To assess research self-efficacy.

Number of Items: 57

Format: Responses are made on a 5-point scale ranging from 0 (no confidence) to 4 (absolute confidence).

Reliability: Internal consistency estimate was .98.

Author: O'Brien, K. M., et al.

Article: The Career Counseling Self-Efficacy Scale: Instrument development and training applications.

Journal: *Journal of Counseling Psychology*, January 1997, *44*(1), 20–31.

Related Research: O'Brien, K. M., & Lucas, M. S. (1993). The Research Attitude Measure. (Available from K. M. O'Brien, Psychology Department, University of Maryland, College Park, MD 20732)

8465

Test Name: RISK ASSESSMENT SURVEY

Purpose: To measure attitudes and beliefs related to technological hazards.

Time Required: 30 minutes.

Format: Seven-point rating scales. Items, response categories, and scoring methods are described.

Reliability: Alpha coefficients ranged from .39 to .79 across subscales.

Author: Myers, J. R., et al.

Article: Facing technological risks: The importance of individual differences.

Journal: *Journal of Research in Personality*, March 1997, *31*(1), 1–20.

Related Research: Gould, L. C., et al. (1988). *Perceptions of technological risks and benefits*. New York: Russell Sage.

8466

Test Name: SCALE FOR THE IDENTIFICATION OF ACQUAINTANCE RAPE ATTITUDES

Purpose: To provide a measure of the identification of acquaintance rape attitudes.

Number of Items: 33

Format: Responses are made on a 6-point scale ranging from 0 (strongly disagree) to 5 (strongly agree).

Reliability: Internal consistency was .94.

Validity: Correlation with the Rape Myth Acceptance Scale was .28 and with the Adversarial Beliefs Scale was .17.

Author: Heppner, M. J., et al.

Article: Examining immediate and long-term efficacy of rape

prevention programming with racially diverse college men.

Journal: *Journal of Counseling Psychology*, January 1999, *46*(1), 16–26.

Related Research: Humphrey, C. F. (1996). *Scales for the Identification of Acquaintance Rape Attitudes (SIARA)*. Unpublished manuscript, University of Missouri—Columbia.

8467

Test Name: SEMANTIC DIFFERENTIAL SCALE

Purpose: To measure attitude toward reading.

Number of Items: 12

Format: Consists of 5-point bipolar adjectives.

Reliability: Coefficients alpha was .92.

Author: Braio, A., et al.

Article: Incremental implementation of learning style strategies among urban low achievers.

Journal: *Journal of Educational Research*, September/October 1997, *91*(1), 15–25.

Related Research: Pizzo, J. (1981). An investigation of the relationships between selected acoustic environments and sound, an element of learning style, as they affect sixth grade students' reading achievement and attitudes. (Doctoral dissertation, St. John's University). *Dissertation Abstracts International*, *42*, 2475A.

8468

Test Name: SEX-ROLE EGALITARIANISM SCALE

Purpose: To measure attitudes toward the equality of the sexes.

Number of Items: 25

Format: Scales range from 1 (strongly disagree) to 5 (strongly agree).

Reliability: Coefficient alpha was .91.

Validity: Correlations with other variables ranged from −.54 to .35.

Author: Sinn, J. S.

Article: The predictive and discriminant validity of masculinity ideology.

Journal: *Journal of Research in Personality*, March 1997, *31*(1), 117–135.

Related Research: King, L. A., & King, D. W. (1990). Abbreviated measures of sex role egalitarian attitudes. *Sex Roles, 23*, 659–673.

8469

Test Name: SEXUAL OPINION SURVEY

Purpose: To measure erotophobia and erotophilia.

Number of Items: 21

Format: Likert format.

Reliability: Coefficient alpha was .86.

Author: Smith, G. E., et al.

Article: Sexual attitudes, cognitive associative networks, and perceived vulnerability to unplanned pregnancy.

Journal: *Journal of Research in Personality*, March 1996, *30*(1), 88–102.

Related Research: Hedges, T. J. (1994). *The heat of the moment: The influence of sexual arousal on cognitive-emotional processes.* Unpublished masters' thesis, Iowa State University, Ames, IA.

Wright, T. M., & Reise, S. P. (1997). Personality and unrestricted sexual behavior: Correlations of sociosexuality in Caucasian and Asian college students. *Journal of Research in Personality, 31*, 166–192.

Jones, M. (1998). Sociosexuality and motivations for romantic involvement. *Journal of Research in Personality, 32*, 173–182.

8470

Test Name: SEXUAL PERMISSIVENESS SCALE

Purpose: To measure sexually permissive attitudes.

Number of Items: 5

Format: Scales range from 1 (strongly agree) to 5 (strongly disagree).

Reliability: Alpha coefficients ranged from .74 to .91.

Author: Whitbeck, L. B., et al.

Article: Early adolescent sexual activity: A developmental study.

Journal: *Journal of Marriage and the Family*, December 1999, *61*(4), 934–946.

Related Research: Reiss, I. (1967). *The social context of premarital sexual permissiveness.* New York: Holt.

8471

Test Name: SITUATIONAL ATTITUDE SURVEY

Purpose: To assess attitudes people hold about sexual orientation.

Number of Items: 10 situations/10 bipolar scales.

Format: All situations are presented, along with sample 5-point adjective scales.

Reliability: Alpha coefficients ranged from .36 to .96.

Author: Eagstrom, C. M., and Sedlacek, W.

Article: Attitudes of heterosexual students toward their gay male and lesbian peers.

Journal: *Journal of College Student Development*, November/December 1997, *38*(6), 565–576.

Related Research: Sedlacek, W. E., & Brooks, G. C. (1976). *Racism in American education: A model for change.* Chicago: Nelson-Hall.

8472

Test Name: SMOKING ATTITUDES SCALE

Purpose: To measure attitudes toward smoking and smokers.

Number of Items: 17

Format: Scales range from 1 (strongly disagree) to 7 (strongly agree). All items are presented.

Reliability: Total internal consistency was .90. Subscale reliabilities ranged from .69 to .88.

Author: Shore, T. H., et al.

Article: Development and validation of a scale measuring attitudes towards smoking.

Journal: *Journal of Applied Psychology*, October 2000, *140*(5), 615–623.

Related Research: Crowe, J. W., et al. (1994). Cross-cultured study of samples of adolescents' attitude, knowledge, and behaviors related to smoking. *Psychological Reports, 74*, 1155–1161.

8473

Test Name: STUDENT ATTITUDE TOWARD OTHERS SURVEY

Purpose: To assess positive and negative attitudes towards others.

Number of Items: 24

Format: Five-point Likert format.

Reliability: Test-retest reliability (1 week) was .75.

Author: Tobias, A. K., and Myrick, R. D.

Article: A peer facilitator-led intervention with middle school problem-behavior students.

Journal: *Professional School Counseling*, October 1999, *3*(1), 27–33.

Related Research: Campbell, C., & Myrick, R. D. (1990). Motivational group counseling with low performing students. *Journal for Specialists in Group Work, 15*, 43–50.

8474

Test Name: STUDENT SURVEY ABOUT CLASS ACTIVITIES

Purpose: To measure student attitudes toward their classes.

Number of Items: 40

Format: Includes 4 factors: Enjoyment, Interest, Choice, and Challenge. Responses are made on a 5-point Likert-type scale. All items are presented.

Reliability: Internal consistency estimates ranged from .70 to .93.

Author: Gentry, M., et al.

Article: Construct validity evidence for enrichment clusters and regular classrooms: Are they different as students see them?

Journal: *Educational and Psychological Measurement*, April 1998, *58*(2), 258–274.

Related Research: Renzulli, J. S. (1994). *Schools for talent development: A comprehensive plan for total school*

improvement. Mansfield Center, CT: Creative Learning Press.

8475

Test Name: STUDENT SURVEY ABOUT ENRICHMENT CLUSTERS

Purpose: To measure student attitudes toward their enrichment cluster.

Number of Items: 40

Format: Includes 4 factors: Interest/Enjoyment, Challenge, Meaning, and Choice. Responses are made on a 5-point Likert-type scale. All items are presented.

Reliability: Internal consistency estimates ranged from .74 to .91.

Author: Gentry, M., et al.

Article: Construct validity evidence for enrichment clusters and regular classrooms: Are they different as students see them?

Journal: *Educational and Psychological Measurements*, April 1998, *58*(2), 258–274.

Related Research: Renzulli, J. S. (1994). *Schools for talent development: A comprehensive plan for total school improvement*. Mansfield Center, CT: Creative Learning Press.

8476

Test Name: SUBJECTIVE CAREGIVER BURDEN SCALE

Purpose: To measure the perceptions, attitudes, and emotional reactions to caregiving.

Number of Items: 5

Format: Three-point scales range from "none of the time" to "most of the time."

Reliability: Coefficient alpha was .80.

Author: Call, K. T., et al.

Article: Caregiver burden from a social exchange perspective: Caring for older people after hospital discharge.

Journal: *Journal of Marriage and the Family*, August 1999, *61*(3), 688–699.

Related Research: Montgomery, R. J. V., et al. (1985). Caregiving and the experience of subjective and objective burden. *Family Relations, 34*, 19–26.

8477

Test Name: SUICIDE ATTITUDE QUESTIONNAIRE

Purpose: To measure attitudes toward suicide in the South African context.

Number of Items: 35

Format: Five-point scales ranged from (1) definitely yes to (5) definitely no. Sample items are presented.

Reliability: Alpha was .85. Split-half reliability was .94.

Author: Peltzer, K., et al.

Article: Attitudes toward suicide among South African secondary school pupils.

Journal: *Psychological Reports*, December 1998, *83*(3) Part 2, 1259–1265.

Related Research: Range, L. M., & Knott, E. C. (1997). Twenty suicide assessment instruments: Evaluations and recommendations. *Death Studies, 21*, 25–58.

8478

Test Name: TEACHER MULTICULTURAL ATTITUDE SURVEY

Purpose: To measure teachers' multicultural awareness and sensitivity.

Number of Items: 20

Format: Responses are made on a 5-point Likert-type scale ranging from 1 (strongly disagree) to 5 (strongly agree). All items are presented.

Reliability: Alpha coefficients ranged from .79 to .91.

Validity: Correlations with other variables ranged from .00 to .45.

Author: Ponterotto, J. G., et al.

Article: Development and initial score validation of the Teacher Multicultural Attitude Survey.

Journal: *Educational and Psychological Measurement*, December 1998, *58*(6), 1002–1016.

8479

Test Name: TEACHERS' ATTITUDES TOWARD TEACHING PHYSICAL ACTIVITY AND FITNESS SCALE

Purpose: To assess physical educators' belief system toward physical activity and fitness

Number of Items: 36

Format: Includes 4 domains: Physical Activity and Fitness, Individual Development/Self-Actualization, Motor Skill Development, and Social Development. Responses are made on a 5-point Likert-type scale. All items are presented.

Reliability: Alpha coefficients ranged from .81 to .89.

Author: Kulinna, P. H., and Silverman, S.

Article: The development and validation of scores on a measure of teachers' attitudes toward teaching physical activity and fitness.

Journal: *Educational and*

Psychological Measurement, June 1999, *59*(3), 507–517.

Related Research: Ennis, C. D. (1992). The influence of value orientations in curriculum decision making. *Quest*, *44*, 317–329.

8480

Test Name: TEACHERS' JOB ATTITUDES SCALE

Purpose: To describe teachers' job attitudes.

Number of Items: 17

Format: Includes Extrinsic Satisfaction, Intrinsic Satisfaction, Social Satisfaction, Influence Satisfaction, Role Clarity, Fair Role Loading, Job Meaning, and Job Responsibility. Responses are made on a 7-point scale.

Reliability: Alpha coefficients ranged from .50 to .82.

Validity: Correlations with Teachers' Professionalism ranged from .18 to .44.

Author: Cheng, Y. C.

Article: Relation between teachers' professionalism and job attitudes, educational outcomes, and organizational factors.

Journal: *Journal of Educational Research*, January/February, 1996, *89*(3), 163–171.

Related Research: Cammann, C., et al. (1983). Assessing the attitudes and perceptions of organizational members. In S. E. Seashore et al. (Eds.), *Assessing organization change* (pp. 71–138). New York: Wiley.

8481

Test Name: TESTIMONIAL VALIDITY SCALE

Purpose: To assess a data

source's judgments of qualitative analysis.

Number of Items: 10

Format: Responses are made on a 5-point scale ranging from 0 (not at all) to 4 (very much).

Reliability: Alpha coefficient was .81.

Author: Chwalisz, K., et al.

Article: A quasi-qualitative investigation of strategies used in qualitative categorization.

Journal: *Journal of Personality Assessment*, October 1996, *43*(4), 502–509.

Related Research: Stiles, W. B. (1993). Quality control in qualitative research. *Clinical Psychology Review*, *13*, 593–618.

8482

Test Name: THEORETICAL ORIENTATION TO READING PROFILE

Purpose: To ascertain a teacher's theoretical orientation toward reading.

Number of Items: 28

Format: Includes phonic, skill-oriented, and whole language statements. Responses are made on a 5-point Likert scale ranging from 5 (strongly disagree) to 1 (strongly agree).

Validity: Correlations with the Literacy Acquisition Perception Profile were −.75 and .32.

Author: McMahon, R., et al.

Article: Relationships between kindergarten teachers' perceptions of literacy acquisition and children's literacy involvement and classroom materials.

Journal: *Journal of Educational Research*, January/February 1998, *91*(3), 173–182.

Related Research: Deford, D. E. (1985). Validating the construct of theoretical orientation to reading. *Reading Research Quarterly, 20*(3), 351–367.

8483

Test Name: TIME-USE QUESTIONNAIRE—SHORT FORM

Purpose: To provide a self-report measure of attitudes and behaviors associated with procrastination.

Number of Items: 19

Format: Responses are made on a 5-point scale ranging from "true" to "false."

Reliability: Internal consistency was .85.

Validity: Correlations with other variables ranged from .37 to .48.

Author: Cook, P. F.

Article: Effects of counselors' etiology attributions on college students' procrastination.

Journal: *Journal of Counseling Psychology,* July 2000, *47*(3), 352–361.

Related Research: Aiken, M. E. (1982). *A personality profile of the college student procrastinator.* Unpublished doctoral dissertation, University of Pittsburgh.

8484

Test Name: TRADITIONALISM–MODERNISM INVENTORY

Purpose: To assess modernity of parents' attitudes.

Number of Items: 40

Format: Assess values and beliefs relating to sex roles, preferences for urban versus rural life-style, authority relations, political beliefs, and religion.

Reliability: Alpha coefficients were .93 and .94.

Author: Patel, N., et al.

Article: Socialization values and practices of Indian immigrant parents: Correlation of modernity and acculturation.

Journal: *Child Development,* April 1996, *67*(2), 302–313.

Related Research: Ramirez, M. (1991). Psychology and counseling with minorities: A cognitive approach to individual and cultural differences. New York: Pergamon.

8485

Test Name: WOMANIST IDENTITY ATTITUDE SCALE

Purpose: To assess attitudes associated with the four stages of womanist identity development.

Number of Items: 43

Format: Scales range from 1 (strongly disagree) to 5 (strongly agree).

Reliability: Alpha coefficients ranged from .43 to .82.

Author: Poindexter-Cameron, J. M., and Robinson, T. L.

Article: Relationships among racial identity attitudes, womanist identity attitudes, and self-esteem in African American college women.

Journal: *Journal of College Student Development,* May/June 1997, *38*(3), 288–296.

Related Research: Ossanna, S. M., et al. (1992). Do "womanist" identity attitudes influence college women's self-esteem and perceptions of environmental bias? *Journal of Counseling and Development, 70,* 402–408.

8486

Test Name: WORK ATTITUDE AND ALIENATION SCALES

Purpose: To measure motivation to do good work and alienation.

Number of Items: 14

Format: Four- and six-point Likert formats are used.

Reliability: Coefficient alpha was .70 (motivation) and .71 (alienation).

Validity: Correlations with other variables ranged from .−.21 to .57 (motivation) and from −.42 to .10 (alienation).

Author: Barling, J., et al.

Article: Effects of parents' job insecurity on children's work beliefs and attitudes.

Journal: *Journal of Applied Psychology,* February 1998, *83*(1), 112–118.

Related Research: Stern, D., et al. (1990). Quality of students' work experience and orientation toward work. *Youth and Society, 22,* 263–282.

8487

Test Name: WORK GROUPS ATTITUDES SCALE

Purpose: To measure work group cohesiveness, commitment, and productivity.

Number of Items: 14

Format: Four-point scales are anchored by 1 (strongly disagree) and 4 (strongly agree). All items are presented.

Reliability: Alpha coefficients ranged from .69 to .92 across subscales.

Validity: Correlations between subscales ranged from .28 to .65.

Author: Riordan, C. M., and Shore, L. M.

Article: Demographic diversity and employee attitudes: An empirical examination of relational demography within work units.

Journal: *Journal of Applied Psychology*, June 1997, 82(3), 342–358.

8488

Test Name: WRITING OUTCOME EXPECTATIONS SCALE—ADAPTED

Purpose: To assess students' perceived usefulness of writing.

Number of Items: 9

Format: Responses are made on a 6-point scale ranging from 1 (extremely unimportant) to 6 (extremely important).

Reliability: Alpha coefficients were .78 and .93.

Author: Pajares, F., et al.

Article: Gender differences in writing self-beliefs of elementary school students.

Journal: *Journal of Educational Psychology*, March 1999, 91(1), 50–61.

Related Research: Shell, D. F., et al. (1989). Self-efficacy and outcome expectancy mechanisms in reading and writing achievement. *Journal of Educational Psychology, 81*, 91–100.

CHAPTER 8
Behavior

8489

Test Name: ABUSE DISABILITY QUESTIONNAIRE

Purpose: To assess the extent to which a disabling psychological perspective has become associated with partner abuse.

Number of Items: 30

Format: Five-point rating scales. A sample item is presented.

Reliability: Internal consistencies ranged from .88 to .93. Test-retest reliability was .76.

Validity: Correlations with Holden subscales ranged from .21 to .70.

Author: McNamara, J. R., and Fields, S. A.

Article: Use of the Abuse Disability Questionnaire in screening a clinical outpatient sample of women.

Journal: *Psychological Reports*, April 2000, *86*(2), 466–470.

Related Research: McNamara, J. R., & Brooker, D. (2000). The Abuse Disability Questionnaire: A new scale for assessing the consequences of partner abuse. *Journal of Interpersonal Violence, 15*, 170–183.

8490

Test Name: ACADEMIC SELF-REGULATION TEST

Purpose: To measure academic self-regulation.

Number of Items: 16

Format: Includes 4 dimensions: Motives, Methods, Performance Outcomes, and Social-Environment Resources. All items are presented.

Reliability: Test-retest coefficient ranged from .49 to .93. Alpha coefficients were .75 and .80.

Author: Schunk, D. H., and Ertmer, P. A.

Article: Self-regulatory processes during computer skill acquisition: Goal and self-evaluative influences.

Journal: *Journal of Educational Psychology*, June 1999, *91*(2), 251–260.

Related Research: Zimmerman, B. J. (1994). Dimensions of academic self-regulation: A conceptual framework for education. In D. H. Schunk & B. J. Zimmerman (Eds.), *Self-regulation of learning and performance: Issues and educational applications* (pp. 3–21). Hillsdale, NJ: Erlbaum.

8491

Test Name: ACTION CONTROL SCALE

Purpose: To assess differences in action-state orientation: preoccupation, hesitation, and volatility.

Number of Items: 36

Format: Dichotomous (forced-choice) format. All items are presented.

Reliability: Alpha coefficients ranged from .56 to .75.

Author: Diefendorff, J. M., et al.

Article: Action-state orientation: Construct validity of a revised measure and its relationship to work-related variables.

Journal: *Journal of Applied Psychology*, April 2000, *85*(2), 250–263.

Related Research: Kuhl, J., & Beckmänn, J. (1994). *Volition and personality: Action versus state orientation*. Seattle, WA: Hogrefe & Huber.

8492

Test Name: ACTIVE AND PASSIVE LEISURE ACTIVITIES SCALE

Purpose: To measure the frequency of passive and active leisure time activities.

Number of Items: 11

Format: Five-point scales are anchored by 1 (not at all) and 5 (a great deal).

Reliability: Test-retest reliability (5 weeks) was .91.

Validity: The correlation with depression was −.26. Correlations with other variables ranged from −.37 to .31.

Author: Hener, T., et al.

Article: Supportive vs. cognitive-behavioral intervention programs in achieving adjustment to home peritoneal kidney dialysis.

Journal: *Journal of Consulting and Clinical Psychology*, August 1996, *64*(4), 731–741.

8493

Test Name: ACTIVITIES OF DAILY LIVING SCALE

Purpose: To measure the frequency of daily activities.

Number of Items: 11

Format: Scales range from "never" to "always." Sample items are presented.

Reliability: Alpha coefficients ranged from .78 to .86.

Author: Stein, C. H., et al.

Article: "Because they're my parents": An intergenerational study of felt obligation and parental caregiving.

Journal: *Journal of Marriage and the Family*, August 1998, *60*(3), 611–622.

Related Research: Brody, E. M., & Schoonover, C. B. (1986). Patterns of patient-care when adult daughters work and when they do not. *The Gerontologist*, *26*, 372–381.

8494

Test Name: ADD COMPREHENSIVE TEACHER RATING SCALE

Purpose: To assess oppositional behavior, attention, hyperactivity, and social skills.

Number of Items: 24

Format: Scales range from "almost never" to "almost always."

Reliability: Internal consistencies ranged from .73 to .97. Test-retest reliabilities (2 weeks) ranged from .78 to .82.

Author: Erford, B. T., et al.

Article: Analysis of teacher responses to the Conners Abbreviated Symptoms Questionnaire.

Journal: *Measurement and Evaluation in Counseling and Development*, April 1998, *31*(1), 2–14.

Related Research: Ullman, R. K., et al. (1984). A new rating scale for diagnosis and monitoring of ADD children. *Psychopharmacology Bulletin*, *20*, 160–164.

8495

Test Name: ADDICTION SCALE (SPANISH AND ENGLISH VERSIONS)

Purpose: To assess addicts using items from the Eysenck Personality Inventory.

Number of Items: 27

Format: Yes/no format. All items presented in Spanish and English.

Reliability: Alphas ranged from .28 to .84 across subscales.

Author: Porrata, J. L., and Rosa, A.

Article: Personality and psychopathology of drug addicts in Puerto Rico.

Journal: *Psychological Reports*, February 2000, *86*(1), 275–280.

Related Research: Eysenck, S. B. G., & Porrata, J. L. (1984). Un estudio transcultural de personalidad: Puerto Rico e Inglaterra. *Rivista Latino Americana de Psicologia*, *16*, 355–372.

8496

Test Name: ADOLESCENT ALCOHOL USE SCALE

Purpose: To measure alcohol use among adolescents by self-report.

Number of Items: 2

Format: Eight-point scales are anchored by 0 (not at all) and 7 (everyday). All items are presented.

Reliability: Alphas ranged from .86 to .91.

Validity: Correlations with other variables ranged from −.05 to .66.

Author: Curran, P. J., et al.

Article: The relation between adolescent alcohol use and peer alcohol use: A longitudinal random coefficients model.

Journal: *Journal of Consulting and Clinical Psychology*, February 1997, *65*(1), 130–140.

8497

Test Name: ADOLESCENT BEHAVIOR CHECKLIST

Purpose: To measure ADHD characteristics and associated difficulties in adolescents aged 11 to 17.

Number of Items: 44

Format: Four-point scales are anchored by 0 (not at all) and 3 (very much).

Validity: Correlations with criterion measures ranged from −.10 to .84.

Author: Adams, C. D., et al.

Article: The Adolescent Behavior Checklist: Validation using structured diagnostic interviews.

Journal: *Journal of Psychopathology and Behavioral Assessment*, March 1998, *20*(1), 103–125.

Related Research: Adams, C. D., et al. (1997). *The Adolescent Behavior Checklist*: Development and initial psychometric properties of a self-report measure for adolescents with ADHD. *Journal of Clinical Psychology*, *26*, 77–86.

8498

Test Name: ADOLESCENT ETHICAL BEHAVIOR IN LEISURE SCALE

Purpose: To measure the extent to which one engages in ethical leisure behaviors.

Number of Items: 62

Format: Includes 4 activity domains: Intellectual, Creative, Meaningful Relationships, and Moral.

Reliability: Alpha coefficients ranged from .89 to .98.

Validity: Correlations with other variables ranged from −.20 to .28.

Author: Munson, W. W., and Widmer, M. A.

Article: Leisure behavior and occupational identity in university students.

Journal: *Career Development Quarterly*, December 1997, 46(2), 190–198.

Related Research: Widmer, M. A., et al. (1996). Measurement of ethical behavior in leisure among high and low risk adolescents. *Adolescence*, 31(122), 397–408.

8499

Test Name: ADOLESCENT PLANFULNESS SCALE

Purpose: To measure whether adolescents plan their actions carefully or act spontaneously.

Number of Items: 4

Format: Scales range from 1 (not true) to 4 (true). A sample item is presented.

Reliability: Alpha coefficients ranged from .69 to .71.

Validity: Correlations with other variables ranged from −.28 to .18.

Author: Schmitt-Rodermund, E., and Silbereisen, R. K.

Article: Career maturity determinants: Individual

development, social context, and historical time.

Journal: *Career Development Quarterly*, September 1998, 47(1), 16–31.

Related Research: Cavelli, A. (1988). Zeiterfahrungen von jugendlichen [Time experiences of adolescents]. In R. Zoll (Ed.), *Zerstörung und Wiederaneignung von Zeit* (pp. 387–404). Frankfurt: Suhrkamp.

8500

Test Name: ADOLESCENT PROBLEM BEHAVIORS SCALE

Purpose: To assess delinquent behavior.

Number of Items: 26

Format: A scoring method is described. Sample items are described.

Reliability: Coefficient alpha was .76.

Author: Swinford, S. P., et al.

Article: Harsh physical discipline in childhood and violence in later romantic involvements: The mediating role of problem behaviors.

Journal: *Journal of Marriage and the Family*, May 2000, 62(2), 508–519.

Related Research: Elliott, D. S., & Ageton, S. S. (1980). Reconciling race and class differences in self-reported and official estimates of delinquency. *American Sociological Review*, 45, 95–110.

8501

Test Name: ADOLESCENT REBELLIOUSNESS SCALE

Purpose: To measure adolescent rebelliousness.

Number of Items: 8

Format: Five-point Likert scales are anchored by 1 (strongly disagree) and 5 (strongly agree). Sample items are presented.

Reliability: Alphas ranged from .79 to .81.

Validity: Correlations with other variables ranged from .26 to .32.

Author: Curran, P. J., et al.

Article: The relation between adolescent alcohol use and peer alcohol use: A longitudinal random coefficients model.

Journal: *Journal of Counseling and Clinical Psychology*, February 1997, 65(1), 130–140.

Related Research: Smith, G. M., & Fogg, C. P. (1979). Psychological correlates of teenage drug use. *Research in Community and Mental Health*, 1, 87–102.

8502

Test Name: ADULT BEHAVIOR CHECKLIST

Purpose: To screen for ADHD symptomatology.

Number of Items: 18

Format: Scales range from 1 (never/not at all) to 4 (very often/very much). All items are presented.

Reliability: Alpha coefficients ranged from .74 to .78.

Author: Smith, E. V., Jr., and Johnson, B. D.

Article: Factor structure of the *DSM-IV* criteria for college students using the Adult Behavior Checklist.

Journal: *Measurement and Evaluation in Counseling and Development*, October 1998, 31(3), 164–182.

Related Research: Johnson, B. D., & Lyonfields, S. (1995). *ADHD and college students: How* *useful are the DSM-IV criteria?* Paper presented at the 103rd annual convention of the American Psychological Association, New York.

8503

Test Name: ADULT BEHAVIORAL CLASSIFICATION PROJECT INVENTORY—ABBREVIATED FORM

Purpose: To classify behavior and emotional disorders.

Number of Items: 43

Format: All are presented. Observers use a true/false format.

Validity: A norm table is included to aid in deciding if further information is needed to confirm a pathological condition.

Author: Marullo, S., and Dreger, R. M.

Article: Background for development of a brief adult behavioral classification project inventory.

Journal: *Psychological Reports*, October 1998, *83*(2), 531–544.

Related Research: Marullo, S. (1981). An extension of the behavioral classification project to adults. (Doctoral dissertation, Louisiana State University, 1981). *Dissertation Abstracts International, 42*, 2539-B.

8504

Test Name: AGGRESSIVE BEHAVIOR SCALE

Purpose: To measure aggressive behavior.

Number of Items: 6

Format: Scales range from 0 (zero times) to 2 (three or more times). All items are described.

Reliability: Coefficient alpha was .88. Test-retest reliability (1 month) was .90.

Author: Magdol, L., et al.

Article: Hitting without a license: Testing explanations for differences in partner abuse between young adult daters and cohabitors.

Journal: *Journal of Marriage and the Family*, February 1998, *60*(1), 41–55.

Related Research: Moffit, T. E., & Silva, P. A. (1988). Self-reported delinquency: Results from an instrument for New Zealand. *Australian and New Zealand Journal of Criminology, 21*, 227–240.

8505

Test Name: AGGRESSIVE CONFLICT TACTICS SCALE

Purpose: To measure intragroup control tactics.

Number of Items: 4

Format: Unspecified agreement scales. All items are presented.

Reliability: Coefficient alpha was .65.

Validity: Correlations with other variables ranged from −.05 to .39.

Author: Simons, T. L., and Peterson, R. S.

Article: Task conflict and relationship conflict in top management teams: The pivotal role of intragroup trust.

Journal: *Journal of Applied Psychology*, February 2000, *85*(1), 102–111.

Related Research: Putnam, L. L., & Wilson, C. (1982). Communicative strategies in organizational conflict: Reliability and validity of a measurement scale. In M. Burgoon (Ed.),

Communication yearbook (Vol. 6, pp. 629–652). Newbury Park, CA: Sage.

8506

Test Name: AGGRESSIVE SEXUAL BEHAVIOR INVENTORY

Purpose: To measure sexual aggression.

Number of Items: 20

Format: Seven-point Likert format.

Reliability: Alpha was .88.

Author: Bernat, J. A., et al.

Article: Construct validity and test-retest reliability of a date-rape decision-latency measure.

Journal: *Journal of Psychopathology and Behavioral Assessment*, December 1997, *19*(4), 315–330.

Related Research: Mosher, D. L., & Anderson, R. D. (1986). Macho personality, sexual aggression, and reactions to guided imagery of realistic rape. *Journal of Research in Personality, 20*, 77–94.

8507

Test Name: ALCOHOL ADVERSE CONSEQUENCES SCALE

Purpose: To determine the extent of adverse consequences as a result of alcohol use.

Number of Items: 47

Format: Responses are made on a 4-point scale ranging from 1 (none) to 4 (more than 5 times). Examples are presented.

Reliability: Coefficient alpha was .92.

Author: McCreary, D. R., et al.

Article: The male role, alcohol

use, and alcohol problems: A structural modeling examination in adult women and men.

Journal: *Journal of Counseling Psychology*, January 1999, *46*(1), 109–124.

Related Research: White, H. R. (1987). Longitudinal stability and dimensional structure of problem drinking in adolescence. *Journal of Studies on Alcohol*, *48*, 541–550.

8508

Test Name: ALCOHOL DEPENDENCE SCALE

Purpose: To assess the negative psychological and physical aspects of drinking.

Number of Items: 25

Format: Two-, three-, and four-point scales are used.

Reliability: Coefficient alpha was .85.

Authors: Ricciardelli, L. A., et al.

Article: Relation of drinking and eating to masculinity and femininity.

Journal: *Journal of Social Psychology*, December 1998, *138*(6), 744–752.

Related Research: Skinner, H. A., & Allen, B. A. (1982). Alcohol dependence syndrome: Measurement and validation. *Journal of Abnormal Psychology*, *91*, 199–209.

8509

Test Name: ALCOHOL USE INTENSITY SCALE

Purpose: To assess the frequency, quantity, occasions for drinking, and frequency of drunkenness.

Number of Items: 4

Format: All items and frequency scales are presented.

Reliability: Coefficient alpha was .86.

Author: Thombs, D. L., and Briddick, W. C.

Article: Readiness to change among at-risk Greek student drinkers.

Journal: *Journal of College Student Development*, May/June 2000, *41*(3), 313–322.

Related Research: Thombs, D. L., et al. (1998). Social context, perceived norms, and drinking behavior in young people. *Journal of Substance Abuse*, *9*, 257–267.

8510

Test Name: ALTRUISTIC BEHAVIOR SCALE

Purpose: To assess altruistic behavior.

Number of Items: 11

Format: Scales range from 1 (highly uncharacteristic) to 5 (highly characteristic). Sample items are described.

Reliability: Coefficient alpha was .92.

Validity: Correlations with other variables ranged from −.23 to .89.

Author: Wagner, S. L., and Rush, M. L.

Article: Altruistic organizational citizenship behavior: context, disposition, and age.

Journal: *Journal of Social Psychology*, August 2000, *140*(3), 379–391.

Related Research: Smith, C. A., et al. (1983). Organizational citizenship behavior: It's nature and antecedents. *Journal of Applied Psychology*, *68*, 653–663.

8511

Test Name: ANOREXIA AND BULIMIA PROBLEM INVENTORY

Purpose: To assess coping effectiveness in women with eating disorders and college-age women at risk for developing disorders.

Number of Items: 36 (vignettes). All vignettes are described.

Time Required: 15–20 minutes.

Format: Responses to vignettes are tape recorded and rated by judges.

Reliability: Alphas for vignettes ranged from .93 to .98. Six scales constructed of vignettes had alphas that ranged from .49 to .83.

Validity: Correlations with other variables ranged from −.74 to .77.

Author: Espelage, D. L., et al.

Article: Assessment of problematic situations and coping strategies in women with eating disorders: Initial validation of a situation-specific inventory.

Journal: *Journal of Psychopathology and Behavioral Assessment*, September 2000, *22*(3), 271–296.

Related Research: Eason, B. J. (1983). Social competence and problem-solving abilities in anorexic, bulimic, and non-eating disordered females: Empirical development of a role-playing instrument (Doctoral dissertation, Indiana University). *Dissertation Abstracts International*, *44*, 3190.

8512

Test Name: ANOREXIA AND BULIMIA PROBLEM INVENTORY

Purpose: To assess competence in

dealing with anorexia and bulimia.

Number of Items: 44

Format: Four-point rating scales range from 1 (incompetent) to 4 (competent).

Reliability: Mean coefficient alpha was .93. Alphas ranged from .49 to .87 across subscales.

Validity: Non-eating-disordered participants had higher mean scores than eating-disordered participants (biserial correlation was .54).

Author: McFall, R. M., et al.

Article: Social competence and eating disorders: Development and validation of the Anorexia and Bulimia Problem Inventory.

Journal: *Journal of Psychopathology and Behavioral Assessment*, December 1999, *21*(4), 365–394.

8513

Test Name: ANTISOCIAL ACTS SCALE

Purpose: To measure the use of antisocial acts.

Number of Items: 11

Format: Scales range from 1 (used not at all) to 9 (used a great deal).

Reliability: Coefficient alpha was .90.

Author: Christopher, F. S., et al.

Article: Premarital sexual aggressors: A multivariate analysis of social, relational, and individual variables.

Journal: *Journal of Marriage and the Family*, February 1998, *60*(1), 56–69.

Related Research: Christopher, F. S., & Frandsen, M. M. (1990). Strategies of influence in sex and dating. *Journal of Social and*

Personal Relationships, 7, 89–105.

8514

Test Name: ANXIOUS SELF-STATEMENT QUESTIONNAIRE

Purpose: To assess frequency of anxious self-talk.

Number of Items: 32

Format: Five-point scales range from 1 (not at all) to 5 (all of the time).

Reliability: Alpha was .94. Split-half reliability was .94.

Author: Kendall, P. C., and Sugarman, A.

Article: Attrition in the treatment of childhood anxiety disorders.

Journal: *Journal of Consulting and Clinical Psychology*, October 1997, *65*(5), 883–888.

Related Research: Kendall, P. C., & Hollon, S. D. (1989). Development of the anxious self-statement questionnaire. *Cognitive Therapy and Research, 13*, 81–93.

8515

Test Name: APPETITE SUPPRESSANT AND LAXATIVE USE SCALE

Purpose: To measure use of suppressants, laxatives, and diuretics in adolescents.

Number of Items: 6

Format: Six and seven-point scales are used. Sample items are presented.

Reliability: Coefficient alpha was .82.

Author: Stice, E., et al.

Article: Naturalistic weight-reduction efforts prospectively predict growth in relative weight

and onset of obesity among female adolescents.

Journal: *Journal of Consulting and Clinical Psychology*, December 1999, *67*(6), 967–974.

Related Research: Cooper, Z., et al. (1989). The validity of the Eating Disorder Examination and its subscales. *British Journal of Psychiatry, 154*, 807–812.

8516

Test Name: APPROACH SUCCESS-AVOID FAILURE ACHIEVEMENT QUESTIONNAIRE

Purpose: To measure the tendency to approach success and to avoid failure.

Number of Items: 36

Format: Scales range from 1 (not very true of me) to 5 (very true of me).

Reliability: Coefficient alpha was .73.

Author: Simons, H. D., et al.

Article: Academic motivation and the student athlete.

Journal: *Journal of College Student Development*, March/April 1999, *40*(2), 151–162.

Related Research: Covington, M. V., & Omelich, C. L. (1991). Need achievement revisited: Verification of Atkinson's original 2 x 2 model. In C. D. Spielbeiger et al. (Eds.), *Stress and emotion: Anxiety, anger and curiosity* (Vol. 14, pp. 85–105). Washington, DC: Hemisphere.

8517

Test Name: AROUSAL PREDISPOSITION SCALE

Purpose: To measure physiological arousal.

Number of Items: 12

Format: Five-point (low/high) Likert format.

Reliability: Coefficient alpha was .83.

Validity: Correlations with other variables ranged from −.02 to .50.

Author: Saliba, A. J., et al.

Article: The Arousability Predisposition Scale: Validity and determinant of between-subject variability.

Journal: *Journal of General Psychology*, July 1998, *125*(3), 263–269.

Related Research: Coren, S. (1990). The Arousal Predisposition Scale: Normative data. *Bulletin of the Psychonomic Society*, 28, 551–552.

8518

Test Name: ASSERTIVENESS SCHEDULE

Purpose: To assess a range of assertive and nonassertive behaviors.

Number of Items: 30

Format: Scales range from -3 (strongly disagree) to 3 (strongly agree). Sample items are presented.

Reliability: Alpha coefficient was .77. Test-retest reliability (6 weeks) was .91.

Validity: Correlations with other variables ranged from −.33 to .74.

Author: Weitlauf, J. C., et al.

Article: Generalization effects of coping-skills training: Influence of self-defense training on women's efficacy beliefs, assertiveness and aggression.

Journal: *Journal of Applied Psychology*, August 2000, *85*(4), 625–633.

Related Research: Rathus, S. A. (1973). A 30-item schedule for assessing assertive behavior. *Behavior Therapy, 4,* 398–406.

8519

Test Name: ASSESSMENT SCHEDULE FOR ALTERED STATES OF CONSCIOUSNESS

Purpose: To assess the "altered states" experiences a person has had and is able to recall.

Number of Items: 325

Format: Four- and five-point scales.

Reliability: Alphas ranged from .80 to .98. Guttman split-half coefficients ranged from .81 to .96.

Author: MacDonald, D. A., and Gagnier, J. J.

Article: The Self-Expansiveness Level Form: Examination of its validity and relation to the NEO Personality Inventory—Revised.

Journal: *Psychological Reports*, June 2000, *86*(3, Part 1), 707–726.

Related Research: Van Quekelberghe, R., et al. (1991). Assessment Schedule for Altered States of Consciousness: A brief report. *Journal of Parapsychology, 55,* 377–390.

8520

Test Name: BEHAVIOR ALTERATION TECHNIQUES SCALES

Purpose: To measure how likely an immediate supervisor would use a message-based method of influence.

Number of Items: 22

Format: Five-point scales are anchored by 5 (strongly agree) and 1 (strongly disagree).

Reliability: Alpha was .87.

Author: Lamude, K. G., and Torres, P.

Article: Supervisors' tactics of influence and subordinates' tolerance for disagreement.

Journal: *Psychological Reports*, December 2000, *87*(3), Part 2, 1050–1052.

Related Research: Richmond, V. P., et al. (1986). The relationship of supervisor use of power and affinity-seeking strategies with subordinate satisfaction. *Communication Quarterly, 34,* 178–193.

8521

Test Name: BEHAVIOR IDENTIFICATION FORM

Purpose: To measure individual differences in level of personal agency.

Number of Items: 25

Format: Forced-choice format. A sample item is presented.

Reliability: Test-retest reliability (2 weeks) was .91. Alpha was .84.

Author: Bishop, D. I., et al.

Article: Levels of personal agency among academic majors.

Journal: *Psychological Reports*, February 2000, *86*(1), 221–224.

Related Research: Vallacher, R., and Wegner, D. (1989). Levels of personal agency: Individual variation in action identification. *Journal of Personality and Social Psychology, 57,* 660–671.

8522

Test Name: BEHAVIOR PROBLEMS INDEX

Purpose: To measure disruptive behavior problems in children at 6-months intervals between 3.5 and 6 years.

Number of Items: 10

Format: Responses are either "never true," "sometimes true," or "often true."

Reliability: Alpha coefficients ranged form .79 to .87.

Author: Spieker, S. J., et al.

Article: Developmental trajectories of disruptive behavior problems in preschool children of adolescent mothers.

Journal: *Child Development*, March/April 1999, *70*(2), 443–458.

Related Research: Baker, P. C., & Mott, F. L. (1989). *NLSY child handbook 1989*. Columbus, OH: The Ohio State University, Ohio Center for Human Resources Research.

8523

Test Name: BEHAVIOR RATING CHECKLIST

Purpose: To assess student classroom behavior as rated by teachers.

Number of Items: 10

Format: Scales range from "there is no evidence of this behavior" to "this behavior is frequent and typical."

Reliability: Internal consistency reliabilities ranged from .87 to .88 across subscales. Test-retest reliabilities (6 months) ranged from .71 to .73.

Author: Otwell, P. S., and Mullis, F.

Article: Counselor-led staff development: An efficient approach to teacher consultation.

Journal: *Professional School Counseling*, October 1997, *1*(1), 25–30.

Related Research: Doss, D., & Lignon, G. (1979). *A practical, economical, reliable and valid*

measure of student classroom behavior. Austin Independent School District, TX. (ERIC Document Reproduction Service No. ED 177212).

8524

Test Name: BEHAVIORAL ACTIVATION SYSTEM AND BEHAVIORAL INHIBITION SYSTEM SCALES

Purpose: To assess trait sensitivity levels of activation and inhibition.

Number of Items: 20

Format: Four-point scales are anchored by 1 (very false for me) and 4 (very true for me).

Reliability: Alpha reliabilities ranged from .66 to .76. Test-retest reliabilities (8 weeks) ranged from .59 to .69.

Validity: Correlations with other variables ranged from −.53 to .49.

Author: Meyer, B., et al.

Article: Exploring behavioral activation and inhibition sensitivities among college students at risk for bipolar spectrum symptomatology.

Journal: *Journal of Psychopathology and Behavioral Assessment*, December 1999, *21*(4), 275–292.

Related Research: Carver, C. S., & White, T. L. (1994). Behavioral inhibition, behavioral activation and affective responses to impending reward and punishment: The BIS/BAS scales. *Journal of Personality and Social Psychology, 67*, 319–333.

8525

Test Name: BEHAVIORAL ADJUSTMENT PROBLEMS QUESTIONNAIRE

Purpose: To measure behavioral adjustment problems in school.

Number of Items: 23

Format: Teachers respond on a 4-point scale ranging from "Most of the time" to "never." Sample items are presented.

Reliability: Coefficient alpha was .90.

Validity: Correlations with other variables ranged from −.41 to .30

Author: Evans, G. W. , et al.

Article: Chronic residential crowding and children's well-being: An ecological perspective.

Journal: *Child Development*, December 1998, *69*(6), 1514–1523.

Related Research: Peterson, J., & Zill, N. (1986). Marital disruption, parent-child relationships, and behavioral problems in children. *Journal of Marriage and the Family, 48*, 95–107.

8526

Test Name: BEHAVIORAL COMPETENCE INVENTORY

Purpose: To measure adaptive functioning.

Number of Items: 110

Format: Includes 7 scales: Self Care, Instrumental Activities, Activities of Daily Living, Memory, Social Interaction, Compensates for Incapacities, Behavioral Excesses, and Behavioral Deficits. Responses are either "yes," "no," "don't know," or "not applicable."

Reliability: Alpha coefficients ranged from .70 to .91.

Validity: Correlations with other variables ranged from −.69 to .68.

Author: Jarjoura, D., et al.

Article: Reliability and construct validity of scores on the Behavioral Competence Inventory: A measure of adaptive functioning.

Journal: *Educational and Psychological Measurement,* October 1999, *59*(5), 855–865.

8527

Test Name: BEHAVIORAL INHIBITION AND BEHAVIORAL APPROACH SCALES

Purpose: To measure drive, fun-seeking, and reward responsiveness.

Number of Items: 5

Format: Four-point response scales are anchored by 1 (very false for me) and 4 (very true for me). Sample items are presented.

Reliability: Alpha coefficients approximated or exceeded .50.

Validity: Correlations with other variables ranged from −.09 to .56.

Author: Carrier, C. S., et al.

Article: Responsiveness to threats and incentives, expectancy of recurrence, and distress and disengagement: Moderator effects in women with early stage breast cancer.

Journal: *Journal of Consulting and Clinical Psychology,* December 2000, *68*(6), 965–975.

Related Research: Carrier, C. S., & White, T. L. (1994). Behavioral inhibition, behavioral activation, and affective responses to impending reward and punishment: The BIS/BAS scales. *Journal of Personality and Social Psychology, 67*, 319–333.

8528

Test Name: BEHAVIORAL RATING SCALE OF PRESENTED SELF-ESTEEM

Purpose: To assess the behavioral manifestation of self-esteem.

Number of Items: 15

Format: The child's teacher responds to each item on a 4-point scale after first deciding which description best fits the child. A sample item is presented.

Reliability: Coefficient alpha was .94.

Author: Verschueren, K., and Marcoen, A.

Article: Representation of self and socioemotional competence in kindergartners: Differential and combined effects of attachment to mother and to father.

Journal: *Child Development,* January/February 1999, *70*(1), 183–201.

Related Research: Haltiwanger, J. (1989). *Behavioral referents of presented self-esteem in young children.* Poster presented at the biennial meetings of the Society of Research in Child Development, Kansas City, Missouri, April 1989.

8529

Test Name: BEHAVIORAL SELF-MANAGEMENT SCALE

Purpose: To measure behavioral self-management.

Number of Items: 15

Format: Includes 5 factors: Self-Observation, Self-Goal Setting, Self-Reward, Self-Punishment, and Rehearsal.

Reliability: Coefficient alphas ranged from .62 to .84.

Validity: Correlations with other

variables ranged from −.28 to .33.

Author: Saks, A. M., and Ashforth, B. E.

Article: Proactive socialization and behavioral self-management.

Journal: *Journal of Vocational Behavior,* June 1996, *48*(3), 301–323.

8530

Test Name: BEHAVIORAL STYLE QUESTIONNAIRE

Purpose: To measure child adaptability.

Number of Items: 112

Format: Reflects 9 dimensions of child temperament. Responses are made on a 6-point scale ranging from "almost never" to "almost always."

Reliability: Test-retest reliability was .89.

Author: Ackerman, B. P., et al.

Article: Contextual risk, caregiver emotionality, and the problem behaviors of six and seven-year-old children from economically disadvantaged families.

Journal: *Child Development,* November/December 1999, *70*(6), 1415–1427.

Related Research: McDevitt, S. C., & Carey, W. B. (1978). The measurement of temperament in 3–7 year old children. *Journal of Child Psychology and Psychiatry, 19,* 245–253.

8531

Test Name: BIPHASIC ALCOHOL EFFECTS SCALE

Purpose: To assess the stimulating and sedating effects of alcohol.

Number of Items: 14

Format: Scales range from 0 (not at all) to 10 (extremely).

Validity: Correlations with aggression ranged from −.12 to .69 (stimulation) and from −.38 to .27 (sedation).

Author: Giancala, P. R., et al.

Article: Alcohol-induced stimulation and sedation: Relation to physical aggression.

Journal: *Journal of General Psychology*, October 1998, *125*(4), 297–304.

Related Research: Martin, C., et al. (1993). Development and validation of the biphasic alcohol effects scale. *Alcoholism: Clinical and Experimental Research, 17,* 140–146.

8532

Test Name: BRIEF MICHIGAN ALCOHOLISM SCREENING TEST

Purpose: To screen for alcohol problems.

Number of Items: 10

Format: Yes-no format.

Reliability: Alpha was .84.

Author: Kaslow, N. J., et al.

Article: Factors that mediate and moderate the link between partner abuse and suicidal behavior in African American women.

Journal: *Journal of Consulting and Clinical Psychology*, June 1998, *66*(3), 533–540.

Related Research: Pokorny, A., et al. (1972). The Brief MAST: A shortened version of the Michigan Alcoholism Screening Test. *American Journal of Psychiatry, 129,* 342–345.

8533

Test Name: BULIMIA COGNITIVE DISTRESS SCALE

Purpose: To measure irrational beliefs.

Number of Items: 25

Format: Five-point scales are anchored by (1) strongly disagree and (5) strongly agree. Sample items are presented.

Reliability: Alpha was .97.

Author: Brazelton, E., et al.

Article: Femininity, bulimia, and distress in college women.

Journal: *Psychological Reports*, August 1998, *83*(1), 355–363.

Related Research: Schulman, R. G., et al. (1986). The development of a scale to measure cognitive distortions in bulimia. *Journal of Personality Assessment, 50,* 630–639.

8534

Test Name: BULIMIA TEST— REVISED

Purpose: To assess bulimia behaviors.

Number of Items: 28

Format: Responses are made on a 1 to 5 scale.

Reliability: Coefficient alpha was .94. Test-retest coefficients were .95 (2 months) and .85 (3 weeks).

Validity: Correlations with other variables ranged from −.60 to .80.

Author: Mazzeo, S. E.

Article: Modification of an existing measure of body image preoccupation and its relationship to disordered eating in female college students.

Journal: *Journal of Counseling Psychology*, January 1999, *46*(1), 42–50.

Related Research: Thelen, M. H., et al. (1991). A revision of the Bulimia Test: The BULIT–R. *Psychological Assessment, 3,* 119–124.

8535

Test Name: BULIMIA TEST— REVISED

Purpose: To measure individuals' levels of bulimic symptomatology.

Number of Items: 36

Format: Responses are made on a 5-point scale ranging from 1 (extreme normal) to 5 (extreme bulimic).

Reliability: Alpha coefficients were .98 and .90.

Validity: Correlation with other variables ranged from −.44 to .43.

Author: Lester, R., and Petrie, T. A.

Article: Physical, psychological, and societal correlates of bulimic symptomatology among African American college women.

Journal: *Journal of Counseling Psychology*, July 1998, *45*(3), 315–321.

Related Research: Thelen, M. H., et al. (1991). A revision of the Bulimia Test: The BULIT–R. *Psychological Assessment, 3,* 119–124.

8536

Test Name: BULLY SCALE

Purpose: To assess the tendency to bully.

Number of Items: 6

Format: Formats vary by question. Sample items are presented.

Reliability: Coefficient alpha was .85.

Validity: Partial correlations (controlling for age) with cooperativeness ranged from −.19 to −.01.

Authors: Rigby, K., et al.

Article: Cooperativeness and bully/victim problems among Australian school children.

Journal: *Journal of Social Psychology*, June 1997, *137*(3), 357–368.

Related Research: Rigby, K., & Slee, P. T. (1995). *Manual for the Peer Relations Questionnaire (PRQ)*. Adelaide: University of South Australia.

8537

Test Name: BULLY SCALE

Purpose: To describe bully behavior.

Number of Items: 7

Format: Items are scored either 0 or 1. Examples are presented.

Reliability: Alpha coefficients ranged from .78 to .93.

Validity: Correlations with other variables ranged from −.37 to .34.

Author: Curtner-Smith, M. E.

Article: Mechanisms by which family processes contribute to school-age boys' bullying.

Journal: *Child Study Journal*, 2000, *30*(3), 169–186.

Related Research: Wiggins, J. S., & Winder, C. L. (1961). The Peer Nomination Inventory: An empirically derived sociometric measure of adjustment in preadolescent boys. *Psychological Reports, 9*, 643–677.

8538

Test Name: CAREGIVER INTERACTION SCALE

Purpose: To identify caregiver interaction with children.

Number of Items: 26

Format: Provides 3 scores: Sensitivity, Harshness, and Detachment. Responses are made by an observer on a 4-point scale.

Reliability: Reliability coefficients ranged from .89 to .98.

Author: Howes, C. E., et al.

Article: The consistency of perceived teacher-child relationships between preschool and kindergarten.

Journal: *Journal of School Psychology*, March/April 2000, *38*(2), 113–132.

Related Research: Arnett, J. (1989). Caregivers in day-care centers: Does training matter? *Journal of Applied Developmental Psychology, 10*, 541–552.

8539

Test Name: CHILD ADAPTIVE BEHAVIOR INVENTORY— MODIFIED

Purpose: To assess children's behavior adjustment.

Number of Items: 91

Format: Includes 21 adaptive and maladaptive behaviors: Negative Engagement, Hostility, Hyperactivity, Antisocial Behavior, Tension, Fairness/ Responsibility, Kindness, Empathy, Calm Response, Intelligence, Creative Curiosity, Task Orientation, Distractibility, Immaturity, Introversion, Depression, Victimization by Others, Fantasizing, Somatic Complaints, Low Physical Skill, and Apathy. Responses are made on a 4-point scale ranging from 1 (not at all like the child) to 4 (very much like the child).

Reliability: Alpha coefficients ranged from .67 to .93.

Author: Parker, J. G., and Seal, J.

Article: Forming, losing, renewing, and replacing friendships: Applying temporal parameters to the assessment of children's friendship experiences.

Journal: *Child Development*, October 1996, *67*(5), 2248–2268.

Related Research: Cowan, P. A., & Cowan, C. P. (1990). Becoming a family: Research and intervention. In I. Sigel & E. Brody (Eds.), *Methods of family research* (Vol. 1, pp. 1–51). Hillsdale, NJ: Erlbaum.

8540

Test Name: CHILD BEHAVIOR QUESTIONNAIRE

Purpose: To enable parents and teachers to measure children's shyness.

Number of Items: 12 (for teachers) and 13 (for parents).

Format: Responses are made on a 7-point scale ranging from 1 (extremely untrue) to 7 (extremely true).

Reliability: Alpha coefficients ranged from .91 to .96.

Author: Eisenberg, N., et al.

Article: Shyness and children's emotionality, regulation and coping: Contemporaneous, longitudinal, and cross-context relations.

Journal: *Child Development*, June 1998, *69*(3), 767–790.

Related Research: Rothbart, M. K., et al. (1994). Temperament and social behavior in childhood. *Merrill-Palmer Quarterly, 40*, 21–39.

8541

Test Name: CHILD BEHAVIOR SCALE–2 SUBSCALES

Purpose: To measure physical and verbal aspects of aggression and passive-withdrawn behavior.

Number of Items: 13

Format: Includes two subscales: Aggression and Asocial.

Reliability: Alpha coefficients were .89 (Aggression) and .86 (Asocial).

Author: Ladd, G. W., and Burgess, K. B.

Article: Charting the relationship trajectories of aggressive, withdrawn, and aggressive/withdrawn children during early grade school.

Journal: *Child Development*, July/August 1999, *71*(4), 910–929.

Related Research: Ladd, G. W., & Profilet, S. M. (1996). The Child Behavior Scale: A teacher-report measure of young children's aggressive, withdrawn, and prosocial behaviors. *Developmental Psychology, 32,* 1008–1024.

8542

Test Name: CHILD PROBLEM BEHAVIOR CHECKLIST

Purpose: To identify child behavior problems.

Number of Items: 24

Format: Items are rated on a 4-point scale ranging from 1 (never) to 4 (often). Examples are presented.

Reliability: Alpha coefficients were .91 to .90.

Author: Eisenberg, N., et al.

Article: Contemporaneous and longitudinal prediction of

children's social functioning from regulation and emotionality.

Journal: *Child Development*, August 1997, *68*(4), 642–664.

Related Research: Lochman, J. E., & Conduct Problems Prevention Research Group. (1995). Screening of child behavior problems for prevention programs at school entry. *Journal of Consulting and Clinical Psychology, 63,* 549–559.

8543

Test Name: CHILD PROBLEM BEHAVIORS SCALE

Purpose: To measure mothers' perceptions of their children's behavior problems.

Number of Items: 26

Format: Scales range from 1 (very much like my child) to 3 (not at all like my child). Sample items are presented.

Reliability: Coefficient alpha was .86.

Author: Jackson, A. P., et al.

Article: Employment status, psychological well-being, social support, and physical discipline practices of single Black mothers.

Journal: *Journal of Marriage and the Family,* November 1998, *60*(4), 894–902.

Related Research: Peterson, J. L., & Zill, N. (1986). Marital disruption, parent-child relationships, and behavioral problems in children. *Journal of Marriage and the Family, 48,* 295–307.

8544

Test Name: CHILDHOOD ROUTINES INVENTORY

Purpose: To assess the construct

of compulsivity in the context of normative development.

Number of Items: 23

Format: Responses are made on a 5-point scale.

Reliability: Coefficient alpha was .89.

Author: Evans, D. W., and Gray, F. L.

Article: Compulsive-like behavior in individuals with Down's syndrome: Its relation to mental age level, adaptive and maladaptive behavior.

Journal: *Child Development*, March/April 2000, *71*(2), 288–300.

Related Research: Evans, D. W., et al. (1997). Ritual, habit and perfectionism: The prevalence and development of compulsive-like behavior in young children. *Child Development, 86,* 58–68.

8545

Test Name: CHILDREN'S AGGRESSION SCALE

Purpose: To enable mothers to rate their children's aggression.

Number of Items: 6

Format: Responses are made on a 7-point scale ranging from 1 (extremely untrue) to 7 (extremely true).

Reliability: Alpha coefficients were .82 and .69.

Author: Kochanska, G., et al.

Article: Children's narratives about hypothetical moral dilemmas and objective measures of their conscience: Mutual relations and socialization antecedents.

Journal: *Child Development*, August 1996, *67*(4), 1420–1436.

Related Research: Rothbart, M. K., et al. (1994).

Temperament and social behavior in childhood. *Merrill-Palmer Quarterly, 40,* 21–39.

8546

Test Name: CHILDREN'S AGGRESSION SCALE

Purpose: To enable teachers to rate children's aggression.

Number of Items: 13

Format: Includes Reactive Aggressive items, Proactive-Aggressive items, and filler items. Responses are made on a 5-point scale ranging from 1 (never true of this child) to 5 (always true of this child). Examples are presented.

Reliability: Alpha coefficients were .90.

Author: Crick, N. R., and Dodge, K. A.

Article: Social information-processing mechanisms in reactive and proactive aggression.

Journal: *Child Development,* June 1996, *67*(3), 993–1002.

Related Research: Dodge, K. A., & Coie, J. D. (1987). Social information-processing factors in reactive and proactive aggression in children's playgroups. *Journal of Personality and Social Psychology, 53,* 1146–1158.

8547

Test Name: CHILDREN'S BEHAVIORAL CLASSIFICATION PROJECT INVENTORY

Purpose: To measure children's behavior.

Number of Items: 274

Format: True-false format.

Reliability: Test-retest reliability was .79. Alphas averaged .65.

Alphas ranged from .75 to .95 across subscales.

Validity: Mother-father agreement correlations averaged .76.

Author: Dreger, R. M.

Article: A further validation of the Children's Behavioral Classification Project Inventory.

Journal: *Psychological Reports,* August 1997, *81*(1), 259–271.

Related Research: Dreger, R. M. (1994). *A manual for the Children's Behavioral Classification Project Inventory.* Unpublished manuscript, Louisiana State University.

8548

Test Name: CHILDREN'S PREKINDERGARTEN EXTERNALIZING BEHAVIOR PROBLEMS AT HOME SCALE

Purpose: To assess children's displays of proactive and reactive aggression.

Number of Items: 6

Format: Responses are made on a 5-point scale ranging from 1 (never or almost never true) to 5 (very often or always true).

Reliability: Coefficient alpha was .70.

Validity: Correlations with other variables ranged from .07 to .49.

Author: Nix, R. L., et al.

Article: The relation between mothers' hostile attribution tendencies and children's externalizing behavior problems: The mediating role of mothers' harsh discipline practices.

Journal: *Child Development,* July/August 1999, *70*(4), 896–909.

8549

Test Name: COGNITIVE BEHAVIORAL DIETING SCALE

Purpose: To measure thoughts and behaviors related to dieting within the past 2 weeks.

Number of Items: 14

Format: Five-point Likert format.

Reliability: Coefficient alpha was .95. Test-retest reliability (2-days) was .95.

Author: Martz, D. M., and Bazzini, D. G.

Article: Eating disorders prevention programming may be failing: Evaluation of 2 one-shot programs.

Journal: *Journal of College Student Development,* January/February 1999, *40*(1), 32–42.

Related Research: Martz, D. M., et al. (1996). Development and preliminary validation of the Cognitive Behavioral Dieting Scale. *International Journal of Eating Disorders, 19,* 297–309.

8550

Test Name: COGNITIVE DIFFICULTIES SCALE

Purpose: To assess behaviors associated with cognitive difficulties.

Number of Items: 12

Format: Scales range from 1 (never) to 7 (always). Sample items are presented.

Reliability: Coefficient alpha was .80.

Validity: Correlations with other variables ranged from −.19 to .31.

Author: Barling, J., et al.

Article: Parents' job insecurity affects children's academic performance through cognitive difficulties.

Journal: *Journal of Applied Psychology,* June 1999, *84*(3), 437–444.

Related Research: Fryer, D., & Warr, P. (1984). Unemployment and cognitive difficulties. *British Journal of Clinical Psychology, 23,* 67–68.

8551

Test Name: COLLEGE DATE RAPE ATTITUDE AND BEHAVIOR MEASURE—MODIFIED

Purpose: To measure attitudes and behaviors related to date rape.

Number of Items: 27

Format: Five-point Likert format. Scales range from "strongly agree" to "strongly disagree." A sample item is presented.

Reliability: Alpha coefficients ranged from .67 to .86. Test-retest reliabilities ranged from .89 to .94.

Author: Shultz, S. K., et al.

Article: Evaluation of a university-based date rape prevention program: Effect on attitudes and behavior related to rape.

Journal: *Journal of College Student Development,* March/April 2000, *41*(2), 193–201.

Related Research: Lanier, C. A., & Elliott, M. N. (1997). A new instrument for the evaluation of a date rape prevention program. *Journal of College Student Development, 38,* 673–676.

8552

Test Name: COMPULSIVE BUYING SCALE

Purpose: To measure the compulsion to buy.

Number of Items: 5

Format: Five-point scales are anchored by 1 (strongly agree)

and 5 (strongly disagree). All items are presented.

Validity: Correlations with other variables ranged from −.01 to .32.

Author: Roberts, J. A., and Tanner, J. F., Jr.

Article: Compulsive buying and risky behavior among adolescents.

Journal: *Psychological Reports,* June 2000, *86*(3, Part 1), 763–770.

Related Research: Edwards, E. A. (1993). Development of a new scale for measuring compulsive buying behavior. *Financial Counseling and Planning, 4,* 67–84.

8553

Test Name: CONCERN WITH DIETING SCALE

Purpose: To assess food intake inhibition.

Number of Items: 6

Format: Responses to items ranged from "never" to "always."

Reliability: Alpha was .52.

Author: Robinson, L. A., et al.

Article: Predictors of risk for different stages of adolescent smoking in a biracial sample.

Journal: *Journal of Consulting and Clinical Psychology,* August 1997, *65*(4), 653–662.

Related Research: Polivy, J., et al. (1978). Internal and external components of emotionality in restrained and unrestrained eaters. *Journal of Abnormal Psychology, 87,* 497–504.

8554

Test Name: CONDUCT PROBLEMS AND SELF-CONTROL (SUB) SCALES

Purpose: To assess self-regulation and problem behavior patterns.

Number of Items: 15

Format: Five-point rating scales.

Reliability: Alpha coefficients exceeded .80.

Author: Brody, G. H., et al.

Article: Sibling relationships in rural African American families.

Journal: *Journal of Marriage and the Family,* December 1999, *61*(4), 1046–1057.

Related Research: Humphrey, L. L. (1982). Children's and teachers' perspectives on children's self-control: The development of two rating scales. *Journal of Consulting and Clinical Psychology, 50,* 624–633.

8555

Test Name: CONFLICT TACTICS SCALE

Purpose: To measure negative control strategies.

Number of Items: 11

Format: Responses are made on a 7-point scale ranging from "never" to "nearly every day."

Reliability: Alpha coefficients were .79 and .74

Author: Spieker, S. J., et al.

Article: Developmental trajectories of disruptive behavior problems in preschool children of adolescent mothers.

Journal: *Child Development,* March/April 1999, *70*(2), 443–458

Related Research: Strauss, M. A. (1974). Leveling, civility, and violence in the family. *Journal of Marriage & the Family, 36,* 13–29, plus addendum, 442–445.

8556

Test Name: CONFLICT TACTICS SCALE—SCHOOL VIOLENT BEHAVIOR FORM

Purpose: To assess eight types of violent behavior a respondent has engaged in during the school year.

Number of Items: 8

Format: Scales range from 0 (never) to 5 (more than once a month).

Reliability: Coefficient alpha was .88.

Validity: Correlations with other variables ranged from −.31 to .34.

Author: Dykeman, C., et al.

Article: Psychological predictors of school based violence: Implications for school counselors.

Journal: *The School Counselor*, September 1996, *44*(1), 35–47.

Related Research: Kashani, J. H., et al. (1991). Aggression and anxiety: A new look at an old notion. *Journal for the American Academy of Child and Adolescent Psychiatry, 30*, 218–223.

8557

Test Name: CONSUMER ASSERTIVENESS, AGGRESSIVNESS AND VERBAL INTENTIONS QUESTIONNAIRE

Purpose: To assess the degree to which individuals resist sales persons, the extent to which individuals react to sales persons, and how much individuals influence their friends about a product or service.

Number of Items: 23

Format: Five-point scales are anchored by (1) strongly agree and (5) strongly disagree. Seven-

point scales are anchored by (1) definitely and (7) definitely not. All items are presented.

Reliability: Alphas ranged between .81 and .91.

Author: Swanson, S. R., and McIntyre, R. P.

Article: Assertiveness and aggressiveness as potential moderators of consumers' verbal behavior following a failure of service.

Journal: *Psychological Reports*, August 1998, *82*(3) Part 2, 1239–1247.

Related Research: Richins, M. L. (1993). An analysis of consumer interaction in the marketplace. *Journal of Consumer Research, 10*, 73–82.

Halstead, D., & Page, T. J., Jr. (1992). The effects of satisfaction and complaining behavior on consumer repurchase intentions. *Journal of Consumer Satisfaction, Dissatisfaction and Complaining Behavior, 5*, 1–11.

8558

Test Name: COOPERATIVENESS SCALE

Purpose: To measure cooperativeness.

Number of Items: 18

Format: Five-point scales. All items are presented.

Reliability: Coefficient alpha was .79.

Validity: Correlations with other variables ranged from .20 to .56.

Authors: Rigby, K., et al.

Article: Cooperativeness and bully/victim problems among Australian school children.

Journal: *Journal of Social Psychology*, June 1997, *137*(3), 357–368.

8559

Test Name: CREATIVITY FOSTERING TEACHER INDEX

Purpose: To measure teachers' creativity fostering behavior.

Number of Items: 45

Format: Includes 9 scales: Independence, Integration, Motivation, Judgment, Flexibility, Evaluation, Question, Opportunities, and Frustration. Responses are made on a 6-point scale ranging from 1–6. All items are presented.

Reliability: Alpha coefficients ranged from .69 to .86.

Author: Soh, K.-C.

Article: Indexing creativity fostering teacher behavior: A preliminary validation study.

Journal: *Journal of Creative Behavior*, Second Quarter 2000, *34*(2), 118–134.

Related Research: Cropley, A. J. (1997). Fostering creativity in the classroom: General principles. In M. A. Runco (Ed.), *Creativity research handbook* (Vol. 1, pp. 83–114). Creskill, NJ: Hampton Press.

8560

Test Name: CRIMINAL VICTIMIZATION INSTRUMENT

Purpose: To assess criminal victimization.

Number of Items: 5

Format: Responses are made on a 4-point scale ranging from 1 (never) to 4 (three or more times).

Reliability: Internal consistency ranged from .78 to .85.

Author: Ingram, K. M., et al.

Article: The relationship of victimization experiences to psychological well-being among homeless women and low-income housed women.

Journal: *Journal of Counseling Psychology*, April 1996, *43*(2), 218–227.

Related Research: Simons, R. L., et al. (1989). Life on the streets: Victimization and psychological distress among the adult homeless. *Journal of Interpersonal Violence*, *4*, 482–501.

8561

Test Name: DAILY FUNCTIONING SELF-REPORT QUESTIONNAIRE

Purpose: To permit respondents to report the extent to which they are able to perform eight selected daily activities.

Number of Items: 8

Format: Responses are made on a 5-point rating scale.

Reliability: Coefficient alpha was .91.

Validity: Correlations with other variables ranged from −.49 to .38.

Author: Netz, Y., and Argov, E.

Article: Assessment of functional fitness among independent older adults: A preliminary report.

Journal: *Perceptual and Motor Skills*, June 1997, *84*(3, Part 1), 1059–1074.

8562

Test Name: DATING SELF-PROTECTION AGAINST RAPE SCALE

Purpose: To measure what actions individuals take when on dates to protect against rape.

Number of Items: 15

Format: Scales range from 1

(never) to 6 (always). All items are presented.

Reliability: Coefficient alpha was .86. Spearman-Brown split-half reliability was .81.

Validity: Heterosexual women score higher than heterosexual men, $t(78) = -.6.54$, $p < .01$.

Author: Moore, C. D., and Waterman, C. K.

Article: Predicting self-protection against sexual assault in dating relationships among heterosexual men and women, gay men, lesbians and homosexuals.

Journal: *Journal of College Student Development*, March/April 1999, *40*(2), 132–140.

8563

Test Name: DECISIONAL PROCRASTINATION SCALE

Purpose: To assess the tendency to procrastinate.

Number of Items: 5

Format: Five-point scales.

Reliability: Coefficient alpha was .70. Test-retest reliability was .69.

Author: Ferrari, R. R., and Dovidio, J. F.

Article: Examining behavioral processes in indecision: Decisional procrastination and decision-making style.

Journal: *Journal of Research in Personality*, March 2000, *34*(1), 127–137.

Related Research: Mann, L. (1982). *Decision-Making Questionnaire*. Unpublished scale, Flinders University of South Australia.

8564

Test Name: DELAY OF GRATIFICATION QUESTIONNAIRE

Purpose: To measure preparedness to delay gratification.

Number of Items: 12

Format: Responses are either "yes" or "no."

Reliability: Coefficient alpha was .7.

Author: Hesketh, B., et al.

Article: Time-related discounting of value and decision-making about job options.

Journal: *Journal of Vocational Behavior*, February 1998, *52*(1), 89–105.

Related Research: Ray, J., & Najman, J. (1985). The generalizability of deferment of gratification. *The Journal of Social Psychology*, *126*(1), 117–119.

8565

Test Name: DELINQUENCY AND SUBSTANCE ABUSE SCALES

Purpose: To assess the frequency of delinquent behavior and substance use and abuse.

Number of Items: 48

Format: Scales range from 0 (never) to 5 (five [or six] or more times).

Reliability: Coefficient alpha was .80.

Validity: Correlations with other variables ranged from −.31 to .25.

Author: Simons, R. L., et al.

Article: Socialization in the family of origin and male dating violence: A prospective study.

Journal: *Journal of Marriage and the Family*, May 1998, *60*(2), 467–478.

Related Research: Elliott, D. S., et al. (1989). *Multiple-problem youth: Delinquency, substance*

use, and mental health problems.
New York: Springer.

8566

Test Name: DELINQUENT
FRIENDS QUESTIONNAIRE

Purpose: To measure association
with deviant peers.

Number of Items: 35 (delinquent
behaviors)

Format: Responses range from
"none" to "all" (number of
peers) and "rarely" to "almost
always" (frequency of behavior).

Reliability: Alpha coefficients
ranged from .93 to .94 across age
groups.

Author: Holtzworth-Munroe, A.,
et al.

Article: Testing to Holtzworth-
Munroe and Stuart (1994)
batterer typology.

Journal: *Journal of Consulting
and Clinical Psychology*,
December 2000, *68*(6), 1000–
1019.

Related Research: Johnston, L.,
et al. (1988). *Illicit drug use,
smoking and drinking by
America's high school students,
college students, and young
adults, 1975–1987.* Washington,
DC: U.S. Government Printing
Office.

8567

Test Name: DEVELOPMENTAL
FEEDBACK-SEEKING
BEHAVIORS SCALE

Purpose: To assess developmental
feedback-seeking behaviors.

Number of Items: 6

Format: Responses are made on a
5-point scale ranging from 1 (not
at all) to 5 (a great deal). All
items are presented.

Reliability: Coefficient alpha was
.76.

Validity: Correlation with other
variables ranged from −.15 to
.46.

Author: Kossek, E. E., et al.

Article: Career self-management:
A quasi-experimental assessment
of the effects of a training
intervention.

Journal: *Personnel Psychology*,
Winter 1998, *51*(4), 935–962.

8568

Test Name: DEVIANT
BEHAVIOR RATING SCALE

Purpose: To measure general
deviant behavior.

Number of Items: 5

Format: Responses are made on a
4-point scale ranging from 1 (no)
to 4 (a lot).

Reliability: Coefficient alpha was
.87.

Author: Deffenbacher, J. L., et
al.

Article: Anger reduction in early
adolescents.

Journal: *Journal of Counseling
Psychology*, April 1996, *43*(2),
149–157.

Related Research: Swaim, R. C.,
et al. (1989). Links from
emotional distress to adolescent
drug use: A path model. *Journal
of Counseling and Clinical
Psychology*, 57, 227–231.

8569

Test Name: DEVIANT PEERS
SCALE

Purpose: To measure the number
of deviant peers.

Number of Items: 6

Format: Scales range from 1

(none) to 5 (all). Items are
described.

Reliability: Coefficient alpha was
.79.

Author: Magdol, L., et al.

Article: Hitting without a license:
Testing explanations for
differences in partner abuse
between young adult daters and
cohabitors.

Journal: *Journal of Marriage and
the Family*, February 1998,
60(1), 41–55.

Related Research: Elliott, D. S.,
et al. (1985). *The dynamics of
delinquent behavior: A national
survey progress report.* Boulder:
University of Colorado, Institute
of Behavioral Sciences.

8570

Test Name: DIETER'S
INVENTORY OF EATING
TEMPTATIONS

Purpose: To provide a structured
behavioral assessment of
competence in weight control.

Number of Items: 30

Format: Includes 6 subscales:
Resisting Temptation, Positive
Social, Food Choice, Exercise,
Overeating, and Negative
Emotions.

Reliability: Alpha coefficients
ranged from .59 to .86.

Validity: Correlations with other
variables ranged from −.46 to
.28.

Author: Riva, G.

Article: An examination of the
reliability and validity of scores
on the Italian version of the
Dieter's Inventory of Eating
Temptations.

Journal: *Perceptual and Motor
Skills*, April 1998, *86*(2), 435–
439.

Related Research: Schlundt,

D. G., & Zimering, R. T. (1988). The Dieter's Inventory of Eating Temptations: A measure of weight control competence. *Addictive Behavior, 13,* 151–164.

8571

Test Name: DIETING READINESS TEST—REVISED

Purpose: To measure aspects of readiness to lose weight.

Number of Items: 20

Format: Includes 5 factors: Binging and Eating Cues, Exercise Patterns and Attitudes, Commitment and Expectation, Control Over Eating, and Purging.

Validity: Correlations with other variables ranged from −.11 to .08.

Author: Fontaine, K. R., et al.

Article: Predicting treatment attendance and weight loss: Assessing the psychometric properties and predictive validity of the Dieting Readiness Test.

Journal: *Journal of Personality Assessment,* February 1997, *68*(1), 173–183.

Related Research: Brownell, K. D. (1990). Dieting readiness. *Weight Control Digest, 1,* 5–10.

8572

Test Name: DRIVING ANGER SCALE

Purpose: To measure driving anger.

Number of Items: Two forms: 14-item form and a 33-item form.

Format: The short form contains at least one item from each of the long form's 6 subscales: Hostile Gestures, Illegal Driving, Police Presence, Slow Driving, and Discourtesy. Responses are made on a 5-point scale ranging from 1 (not at all) to 5 (very much).

Reliability: Alpha coefficients ranged from .79 to .90.

Author: Deffenbacher, J. L., et al.

Article: Characteristics and treatment of high-anger drivers.

Journal: *Journal of Counseling Psychology,* January 2000, *47*(1), 5–17.

Related Research: Deffenbacher, J. L., et al. (1994). Development of a driving anger scale. *Psychological Reports, 74,* 83–91.

8573

Test Name: DRIVING APPRAISAL INVENTORY

Purpose: To assess four driving-related factors.

Format: Included 4 factors: Carelessness, Drunken Driving, Vehicle Safety, and Self-Evaluation.

Reliability: Test-retest reliability coefficients ranged from .61 to .68. Alpha coefficients ranged from .59 to .75.

Validity: Correlations with Type A scores ranged from −.01 to .24.

Author: Perry, A. R., and Baldwin, D. A.

Article: Further evidence of association of Type A personality scores and driving-related attitudes and behaviors.

Journal: *Perceptual and Motor Skills,* August 2000, *91*(1), 147–154.

Related Research: Cutler, B. L., et al. (1993). The Driving Appraisal Inventory: Characteristics and construct validity. *Journal of Applied Social Psychology, 23,* 1196–1213.

8574

Test Name: DRIVING BEHAVIOR QUESTIONNAIRE

Purpose: To measure driving-related factors.

Format: Includes 5 factors: Aggression, Law-Breaking, Confidence, Excitement, and Risk Taking.

Reliability: Coefficient alpha was .79.

Validity: Correlations with Type A scores ranged from .00 to .41.

Author: Perry, A. R., and Baldwin, D. A.

Article: Further evidence of associations of Type A personality scores and driving-related attitudes and behaviors.

Journal: *Perceptual and Motor Skills,* August 2000, *91*(1), 147–154.

Related Research: Furnham, A., & Saipe, J. (1993). Personality correlates of convicted drivers. *Personality and Individual Differences, 14,* 329–336.

8575

Test Name: DRUG ABUSE SCREENING TEST

Purpose: To detect drug abuse (parents provide the responses).

Number of Items: 28

Format: yes/no format.

Reliability: Alpha was .95.

Author: Dorkin, P. L., et al.

Article: Predictors of outcome in drug treatment of adolescent inpatients.

Journal: *Psychological Reports,* August 1998, *83*(1), 175–186.

Related Research: Skinner, H. A. (1982). The Drug Abuse Screening Test. *Addictive Behavior*, 7, 363–371.

8576

Test Name: DRUG AND ALCOHOL USE SCALE

Purpose: To measure the frequency of use of drugs, alcohol and tobacco during the last month.

Number of Items: 5

Format: Scales range from "never" to "often."

Reliability: Coefficient alpha was .86.

Author: Gray, M. R., and Steinberg, L.

Article: Unpacking authoritative parenting: Reassessing a multidimensional construct.

Journal: *Journal of Marriage and the Family*, August 1999, *61*(3), 574–587.

Related Research: Greenberger, E., et al. (1981). Adolescents who work: Health and behavioral consequences of job stress. *Developmental Psychology*, 17, 691–703.

8577

Test Name: DRUG-USE PROBLEM SCALE

Purpose: To measure problems related to drug use.

Number of Items: 19

Format: Three-point rating scales are anchored by 0 (no problem) and 2 (serious problem).

Reliability: Mean alphas ranged from .77 to .92 across types of drug use.

Author: Stephens, R. S., et al.

Article: Comparison of extended

versus brief treatments for marijuana use.

Journal: *Journal of Consulting and Clinical Psychology*, October 2000, *68*(5), 898–908.

Related Research: Stephens, R. S., et al. (1994). Treating adult marijuana dependence: A test of the relapse prevention model. *Journal of Consulting and Clinical Psychology*, 62, 92–99.

8578

Test Name: EATING ATTITUDES TEST

Purpose: To assess behavior and attitudes concerning anorexia, bulimia, and obsessive dieting.

Number of Items: 40

Format: Responses are made on a 6-point scale ranging from "always" to "never."

Reliability: Test-retest reliabilities ranged from .74 to .92 (16 days) and from .81 to .88 (23 days).

Validity: Correlations with other variables ranged from −.27 to .73.

Author: Johnson, C. E., and Petrie, T. A.

Article: Relationship of gender discrepancy to psychological correlates of disordered eating in female undergraduates.

Journal: *Journal of Counseling Psychology*, October 1996, *43*(4), 473–479.

Related Research: Garner, D. M., & Garfinkel, P. E. (1979). The Eating Attitudes Test: An index of the symptoms of anorexia nervosa. *Psychological Medicine*, 9, 273–279.

8579

Test Name: EATING ATTITUDES TEST–26

Purpose: To assess eating disorder symptomatology.

Number of Items: 26

Format: Responses are made on a 6-point scale ranging from 1 (always) to 6 (never).

Reliability: Internal consistency ranged from .79 to .94. Test-retest (3 weeks) reliability coefficient was .86.

Validity: Correlations with other variables ranged from −.56 to .79.

Author: Mazzeo, S. E.

Article: Modification of an existing measure of body image preoccupation and its relationship to disordered eating in female college students.

Journal: *Journal of Counseling Psychology*, January 1999, *46*(1), 42–50.

Related Research: Garner, D. M., & Garfinkel, P. (1979). The Eating Attitudes Test: An index of the symptoms of anorexia nervosa. *Psychological Medicine*, 9, 273–279.

8580

Test Name: EATING DISORDER INVENTORY

Purpose: To measure symptoms associated with anorexia nervosa and bulimia nervosa.

Number of Items: 64

Format: Six-point scales are anchored by "always" and "never."

Reliability: Alpha coefficients ranged from .81 to .93.

Author: Espelage, D. L., et al.

Article: Assessment of problematic situations and coping strategies in women with eating disorders: Initial validation of a situation-specific inventory.

Journal: *Journal of Psychopathology and Behavioral Assessment*, September 2000, 22(3), 271–296.

Related Research: Garner, D. M., et al. (1983). Development and validation of a multidimensional eating disorder inventory for anorexia nervosa and bulimia. *International Journal of Eating Disorders*, 2, 1–15.

8581

Test Name: EATING RESTRAINT SCALE

Purpose: To assess to what extent individuals attempt to diet.

Number of Items: 10

Format: Five-point scales are used. A sample item is presented.

Reliability: Coefficient alpha was .80.

Authors: Ricciardelli, L. A., et al.

Article: Relation of drinking and eating to masculinity and femininity.

Journal: *Journal of Social Psychology*, December 1998, 138(6), 744–752.

Related Research: Heatherton, T. F. (1988). The mis(measurement) of restraint: An analysis of conceptual and psychometric issues. *Journal of Abnormal Psychology*, 97, 19–28.

8582

Test Name: EATING TO COPE SCALE

Purpose: To measure an increasing interest in eating before an upcoming exam.

Number of Items: 7

Format: Scales range from 0 (not at all true about me) to 4 (always true about me). A sample item is presented.

Reliability: Alpha coefficients ranged from .77 to .88.

Author: Toray, T., and Cooley, E.

Article: Coping in women college students: The influence of experience.

Journal: *Journal of College Student Development*, May/June, 1998, 39(3), 291–295.

Related Research: Cooley, E., & Toray, T. (1996). *Coping styles and class standing in a college population*. Poster session presented at the 76th Western Psychological Association annual convention, San Jose, CA.

8583

Test Name: EFFECTIVE BIRTH CONTROL MEASURE

Purpose: To provide indicators of a latent construct of birth control effectiveness.

Number of Items: 4

Format: Includes 4 contexts and 4 levels of response.

Reliability: Coefficient alpha was .86.

Validity: Correlations with other variables ranged from −.15 to .20.

Author: Goodyear, R. K., et al.

Article: Predictors of Latino men's paternity in teen pregnancy: Test of a mediational model of childhood experiences, gender role attitudes, and behaviors.

Journal: *Journal of Counseling Psychology*, January 2000, 47(1), 116–128.

8584

Test Name: ELEMENTARY SCHOOL CHILDREN'S SELF-REGUALTION QUESTIONNAIRE

Purpose: To assess self-regulation in elementary school children.

Number of Items: 32

Format: Includes 4 factors: Permissiveness, Self-Disclosure, Decision-Making, and Uniqueness. Responses are made on a 4-point scale ranging from 1 (not at all) to 4 (very strongly). All items are presented.

Reliability: Alpha coefficients ranged from .77 to .82.

Author: Nakata, S., and Shiomi, K.

Article: Construction of self-regulation questionnaire for Japanese elementary school children.

Journal: *Perceptual and Motor Skills*, June 1998, 86(3) Part 1, 827–833.

Related Research: Nakata, S., & Shiomi, K. (1997). Structures of self-regulation in Japanese preschool children. *Psychological Reports*, 81, 63–66.

8585

Test Name: EMOTION REGULATION CHECKLIST

Purpose: To assess children's capacities for emotional self-regulation as liability/negativity and emotion regulation.

Number of Items: 24

Format: Four-point scales are anchored by 1 (never true for child) and 4 (almost always true for child). Sample items are presented.

Reliability: Coefficient alpha was .94 for the total scale.

Author: Schwartz, D., and Proctor, L. J.

Article: Community violence exposure and children's social adjustment in the school peer group: The mediating roles of emotion regulation and social cognition.

Journal: *Journal of Consulting and Clinical Psychology*, August 2000, *68*(4), 670–683.

Related Research: Shields, A., & Cicchetti, D. (1997). Emotion regulation among school-age children: The development and validation of a new criterion Q-sort scale. *Developmental Psychology*, *33*, 906–916.

8586

Test Name: EMOTIONAL ABUSE QUESTIONNAIRE

Purpose: To assess threatening, controlling, degrading, and sexually abusive spousal behavior.

Number of Items: 66

Format: Four-point scales are anchored by 1 (never) and 4 (very often). Sample items are presented.

Reliability: Alpha coefficients ranged from .82 to .90.

Author: Waltz, J., et al.

Article: Testing a typology of batterers.

Journal: *Journal of Consulting and Clinical Psychology*, August 2000, *68*(4), 658–699.

Related Research: Rushe, R., et al. (1992). *The Emotional Abuse Questionnaire*. Unpublished manuscript.

8587

Test Name: EMOTIONAL AND PHYSICAL ABUSE QUESTIONNAIRE

Purpose: To measure levels of abuse in children and adolescents.

Number of Items: 32

Format: Six-point scales range

from 0 (never) to 5 (very frequently). Sample items are presented.

Reliability: Alpha coefficients ranged from .44 to .87 across samples.

Author: Meston, C. M., et al.

Article: Ethnicity, desirable responding, and self-reports of abuse: A comparison of European and Asian ancestry undergraduates.

Journal: *Journal of Consulting and Clinical Psychology*, February 1999, 67(1), 139–144.

Related Research: Carlin, A. S., et al. (1994). The effects of differences in objective and subjective definitions of childhood physical abuse on estimates of its incidents and relationship to psychopathology. *Child Abuse and Neglect*, *18*, 393–399.

8588

Test Name: (FAGERSTROM) TEST FOR NICOTINE DEPENDENCE (SPANISH VERSION)

Purpose: To assess dependence on nicotine.

Number of Items: 6.

Format: Yes/no and multiple-choice formats. All items are presented in English and Spanish.

Reliability: Estimated reliability was .66.

Author: Becona, E., and Vazquez, F. L.

Article: The Fagerstrom Test for Nicotine Dependence in a Spanish sample.

Journal: *Psychological Reports*, December 1998, *83*(3) Part 2, 1455–1458.

Related Research: Fagerstrom,

K. O., and Schnieder, N. G. (1989). Measuring nicotine dependence: a review of the Fagerstrom Taterome Questionnaire. *Journal of Behavioral Medicine*, *12*, 159–182.

8589

Test Name: FATHER—SHORT MICHIGAN ALCOHOLISM SCREENING TEST

Purpose: To assess the biological father's drinking behavior.

Number of Items: 13

Format: Responses are "yes," "no." An example is presented.

Reliability: Test-retest reliability was $K = .79$, Yule's $Y = .86$. Coefficient alpha was .74.

Author: Stout, M. L., and Mintz, L. B.

Article: Differences among non-clinical college women with alcoholic mothers, alcoholic fathers, and nonalcoholic parents.

Journal: *Journal of Counseling Psychology*, October 1996, *43*(4), 466–472.

Related Research: Sher, K. J., & Descutner, C. (1986). Reports of parental alcoholism: Reliability across siblings. *Addictive Behaviors*, *11*, 25–30.

8590

Test Name: HARASSMENT INCIDENTS RECOLLECTIONS SCALE

Purpose: To assess past harassment experiences.

Number of Items: 9

Format: Responses are made on a 4-point scale ranging from 0 (has not happened this year) to 3 (a couple of times this week).

Reliability: Coefficient alpha was .79.

Validity: Correlations with other variables ranged from −.36 to .60.

Author: Juvonen, J., et al.

Article: Peer harassment, psychological adjustment, and school functioning in early adolescence.

Journal: *Journal of Educational Psychology*, June 2000, *92*(2), 349–359.

Related Research: Nishina, A., & Juvonen, J. (1998, February). *Daily reports of peer harassment in middle school.* Paper presented at the biennial meeting of the Society for Research on Adolescence, Coronado, CA.

8591

Test Name: HEALTH BEHAVIORS CHECKLIST

Purpose: To assess health behaviors, including wellness behaviors, accident-control behaviors, and traffic-risk-taking behaviors.

Number of Items: 26

Format: Scales range from 1 (strongly disagree) to 5 (strongly agree).

Validity: Correlations with other variables ranged from −.26 to .55.

Author: Elliott, T. R., et al.

Article: Social problem solving and health behaviors of undergraduate students.

Journal: *Journal of College Student Development,* January/February 1997, *38*(1), 24–31.

Related Research: Vickers, R. R., et al. (1990). Demonstration of replicable dimensions of health behaviors. *Preventive Medicine, 19,* 337–401.

8592

Test Name: HELPING PROCESSES SCALES

Purpose: To measure costs of seeking help, help-seeking behavior, and helping behavior.

Number of Items: 30

Format: Five-point scales are anchored by 1 (strongly disagree) and 5 (strongly agree). All items are presented.

Reliability: Alpha coefficients ranged from .87 to .91 across subscales.

Validity: Correlations with other variable ranged from −.20 to .37.

Author: Anderson, S. E., and Williams, L. J.

Article: Interpersonal, job, and individual factors related to helping processes at work.

Journal: *Journal of Applied Psychology*, June 1996, *81*(3), 282–296.

Related Research: Pearce, P. L., & Amato, P. R. (1980). A taxonomy of helping: A multidimensional scaling analysis. *Social Psychology Quarterly, 43,* 363–371.

8593

Test Name: HISTORICAL, CLINICAL, AND RISK MANAGEMENT ASSESSMENT SCALE

Purpose: To screen for violent behavior.

Number of Items: 20

Format: Three-point scales are anchored by 0 (available information contraindicates the presence of the item) and 2 (available information indicates the presence of the item). All items are presented.

Validity: Predictive validity

coefficients ranged from .59 to .80 across subscales and across types of violence.

Author: Douglas, K. S., et al.

Article: Assessing risk for violence among psychiatric patients: The HCR-20 Violence Risk Assessment Schema and the Psychopathy Checklist: Screening Version.

Journal: *Journal of Consulting and Clinical Psychology,* December 1999, *67*(6), 917–930.

Related Research: Webster, C. D., et al. (1997). *HCR-20: Assessing risk for violence (Version 2).* Vancouver, British Columbia, Canada: Simon Fraser University and Forensic Psychiatric Services Commission of British Columbia.

8594

Test Name: HISTORY OF VICTIMIZATION QUESTIONNAIRE

Purpose: To assess mild, moderate, and severe child physical abuse.

Number of Items: 56

Format: Items are described.

Reliability: Coefficient alpha ranged from .77 to .86 across subscales.

Author: Mechanic, M. B., et al.

Article: A comparison of normal forgetting, psychopathology, and information-processing models of reported amnesia for recent sexual trauma.

Journal: *Journal of Consulting and Clinical Psychology,* December 1998, *66*(6), 948–957.

Related Research: Resnick, P. A. (1988*). History of Victimization Questionnaire.* Unpublished manuscript.

8595

Test Name: HIV RISK AVOIDANCE INTENTIONS SCALE

Purpose: To measure the intention to engage in HIV avoidance activities.

Number of Items: 9

Format: Six-point scales are anchored by 1 (definitely will not do) and 6 (definitely will do).

Reliability: Coefficient alpha was .89.

Author: Kalichman, S. C., et al.

Article: Effectiveness of a video-based motivational skills-building HIV risk-reduction intervention for inner-city African American men.

Journal: *Journal of Consulting and Clinical Psychology*, December 1999, *67*(6), 959–966.

Related Research: Kalichman, S. C., et al. (1996). Prevention of sexually transmitted HIV infection: Meta-analytic review and critique of the theory-based intervention outcome literature. *Annals of Behavioral Medicine*, *18*, 6–15.

8596

Test Name: HOME SITUATIONS QUESTIONNAIRE

Purpose: To identify where children presented behavior problems and how severe they were.

Number of Items: 16

Format: Ten-point severity scale.

Reliability: Alpha coefficient was .91.

Validity: Correlations with other variables ranged from .52 to .70.

Author: Erford, B. T.

Article: Technical analysis of father responses to the

Disruptive Behavior Rating Scale—Parent version (DBRS–P).

Journal: *Measurement and Evaluation in Counseling and Development*, January 1998, *30*(4), 199–210.

8597

Test Name: HONG PSYCHOLOGICAL REACTANCE SCALE

Purpose: To assess rebelliousness.

Number of Items: 11

Format: Responses are made on a 5-point agree–disagree scale.

Reliability: Coefficient alpha was .86.

Author: Voelkl, K. E., and Frone, M. R.

Article: Predictors of substance use at school among high school students.

Journal: *Journal of Educational Psychology*, September 2000, *92*(3), 583–592.

Related Research: Hong, S. M., & Faedda, S. (1996). Refinement of the Hong Psychological Reactance Scale. *Educational and Psychological Measurement*, *56*, 173–182.

8598

Test Name: HOSTILITY TOWARD WOMEN SCALE— SHORT FORM

Purpose: To measure hostility toward women.

Number of Items: 8

Format: Responses are "true" or "false."

Reliability: Coefficient alpha for the 30-item version was .80.

Author: Caron, S. L., et al.

Article: Athletes and rape: Is there a connection?

Journal: *Perceptual and Motor Skills*, December 1997, *85*(3, Part 2), 1379–1393.

Related Research: Koss, M. P., & Gaines, J. A. (1993). The prediction of sexual aggression by alcohol use, athletic participation, and fraternity affiliation. *Journal of Interpersonal Violence*, *8*, 94–108.

8599

Test Name: IMPULSE BUYING TENDENCY SCALE

Purpose: To measure the tendency to buy on impulse.

Number of Items: 5

Format: Seven-point scales are anchored by (1) very rarely and (7) very often. All items are presented.

Reliability: Composite reliabilities ranged from .81 to .86. Alphas ranged from .80 to .85.

Validity: Correlations with other variables ranged from .37 to .57.

Author: Weun, S., et al.

Article: Development and validation of the Impulse Buying Tendency Scale.

Journal: *Psychological Reports*, June 1998, *82*(3) Part 2, 1123–1133.

8600

Test Name: IMPULSIVITY SCALE

Purpose: To measure spur-of-the-moment behavior.

Number of Items: 6

Format: Six-point scales are anchored by 1 (strongly disagree) and 6 (strongly agree). A sample item is presented.

Reliability: Coefficient alpha was .75.

Validity: Correlations with other variables ranged from −.12 to .35.

Author: Frone, M. R.

Article: Predictors of work injuries among employed adolescents.

Journal: *Journal of Applied Psychology*, August 1998, *83*(4), 565–576.

8601

Test Name: INDEX OF PSYCHOLOGICAL ABUSE

Purpose: To assess the degree that assailants use ridicule, harassment, criticism, and emotional withdrawal against women.

Number of Items: 33

Format: Four-point scales are anchored by 1 (never) and 4 (often).

Reliability: Internal consistency was .97. Item–total correlations ranged from .51 to .90.

Author: Sullivan, C. M., and Bybee, D. I.

Article: Reducing violence using community-based advocacy for women with abusive partners.

Journal: *Journal of Consulting and Clinical Psychology*, February 1999, *67*(1), 43–53.

Related Research: Sullivan, C. M., et al. (1991). *The Index of Psychological Abuse: Development of a measure.* Poster session presented at the 99th annual convention of the American Psychological Association, San Francisco, CA.

8602

Test Name: INFLUENCE BEHAVIOR QUESTIONNAIRE

Purpose: To measure the use of influence tactics.

Number of Items: Eleven tactics are measured by 4 responses.

Format: Multiple-choice scales are used. All responses are presented.

Reliability: Alphas ranged from .66 to .82.

Validity: Convergent validity ranged from .45 to .62.

Author: Blickle, G.

Article: Assessing convergent and discriminant validity of the Influence Behavior Questionnaire.

Journal: *Psychological Reports*, June 1998, *82*(3) Part 1, 923–929.

Related Research: Yukl, G. (1997). *Scoring guide for the 1997 IBQ (short version).* New York: University of Albany.

8603

Test Name: INFLUENCE TACTICS SCALE

Purpose: To enable supervisors to measure subordinates' use of influence tactics.

Format: Responses are made on a 5-point scale ranging from ''never'' to ''almost always.'' Examples are presented.

Reliability: Alpha coefficients ranged from .72 to .82.

Validity: Correlations with other variables ranged from −.37 to .68.

Author: Thacker, R. A.

Article: Perceptions of trust, upward influence tactics, and performance ratings.

Journal: *Perceptual and Motor Skills*, June 1999, *88*(3) Part 2, 1059–1070.

Related Research: Kipnis, D., et al. (1980). Intraorganizational influence tactics: Exploration in getting one's way. *Journal of Applied Psychology, 65,* 440–452.

8604

Test Name: INFORMATION SEEKING SCALE

Purpose: To assess the frequency of information seeking behavior on the job.

Number of Items: 8

Format: Scales range from 1 (very infrequently) to 5 (very frequently).

Reliability: Coefficient alpha was .92.

Validity: Correlations with other variables ranged from −.13 to .44.

Author: Wanberg, C. R., and Kammeyer-Mueller, J. D.

Article: Predictors and outcomes of proactivity in the socialization process.

Journal: *Journal of Applied Psychology*, June 2000, *85*(3), 373–385.

Related Research: Major, D. A., & Kozlowski, S. W. J. (1997). Newcomer information seeking: Individual and contextual differences. *International Journal of Selection and Assessment, 5,* 16–28.

8605

Test Name: INITIATION OF STRUCTURE AND CONSIDERATION SCALES

Purpose: To measure supervisor leadership style.

Number of Items: 11

Format: Scales range from 1 (very false) to 7 (very true).

Reliability: Coefficient alpha was

.90 (consideration) and .71 (initiation).

Validity: Correlations with other variables ranged from −.44 to .23.

Author: VandeWalle, D., et al.

Article: An integrated model of feedback-seeking behavior: Disposition, context, and cognition.

Journal: *Journal of Applied Psychology*, December 2000, *85*(6), 996–1003.

Related Research: Teas, R. K. (1983). Supervisory behavior, role stress, and the job satisfaction of industrial salespeople. *Journal of Marketing Research, 20*, 84–91.

8606

Test Name: INSOMNIA SYMPTOM QUESTIONNAIRE

Purpose: To assess symptoms and behaviors associated with insomnia.

Number of Items: 13

Format: 100-mm visual analog scales are anchored by "never" and "always."

Reliability: Coefficient alpha was .90.

Author: Edinger, J. D., et al.

Article: Insomnia and the eye of the beholder: Are there clinical markers of objective sleep disturbances among adults with and without insomnia complaints?

Journal: *Journal of Consulting and Clinical Psychology*, August 2000, *68*(4), 586–593.

Related Research: Speilman, A. J., et al. (1987). Treatment of chronic insomnia by restriction of time in bed. *Sleep, 10*, 45–55.

8607

Test Name: INTROSPECTIVENESS SCALE

Purpose: To measure the extent to which a person thinks about himself or herself.

Number of Items: 10

Format: Scales range from 1 (very little) to 5 (very much). Sample items are presented.

Reliability: Reliability was .87.

Author: Schieman, S., and Van Gundy, K.

Article: The personal and social links between age and self-reported empathy.

Journal: *Social Psychology Quarterly*, June 2000, *63*(2), 152–174.

Related Research: Hansell, S., et al. (1986). Introspectiveness and adolescent development. *Journal of Youth and Adolescence, 15*, 115–132.

8608

Test Name: INVENTORY OF SOCIALLY SUPPORTIVE BEHAVIORS

Purpose: To measure the frequency with which supportive behaviors are received (or performed).

Number of Items: 40

Format: Scales are 1 (received and given in equal frequency), 2 (given more than received), and 3 (received more than given).

Reliability: Coefficient alphas ranged from .93 to .94.

Validity: Correlations with other variables ranged from −.22 to .47.

Author: Jung, J.

Article: Balance and source of social support in relation to well-being.

Journal: *Journal of General Psychology*, January 1997, *124*(1), 77–90.

Related Research: Barrera, M., Jr., et al. (1981). Preliminary development of a scale of social support: Studies on college students. *American Journal of Community Psychology, 9*, 435–447.

8609

Test Name: JOB SATISFACTION PREPAREDNESS BEHAVIORS SCALE

Purpose: To assess job mobility preparedness behaviors.

Number of Items: 9

Format: Responses are made on a 5-point scale ranging from 1 (not at all) to 5 (a great deal). All items are presented.

Reliability: Coefficient alpha was .84.

Validity: Correlation with other variables ranged from −.28 to .25.

Author: Kossek, E. E., et al.

Article: Career self-management: A quasi-experimental assessment of the effects of a training intervention.

Journal: *Personnel Psychology*, Winter 1998, *57*(4), 935–962.

8610

Test Name: JOB-SEARCH BEHAVIOR SCALE

Purpose: To assess the frequency and scope of job-search activity.

Number of Items: 7

Format: Scales range from 1 (never or zero times) to 5 (very often, at least 10 times). All items are presented.

Reliability: Coefficient alpha was .71.

Validity: Correlations with other variables ranged from −.21 to .49.

Author: Wanberg, C. R., et al.

Article: Predictors and outcomes of networking intensity among unemployed job seekers.

Journal: *Journal of Applied Psychology*, August 2000, *85*(4), 491–503.

Related Research: Blau, G. (1994). Testing a two-dimensional measure of job-search behavior. *Organizational Behavior and Human Decision Processes, 59,* 288–312.

8611

Test Name: JOB SEARCH BEHAVIORS SCALES

Purpose: To measure preparatory and active job-search behaviors.

Number of Items: 14

Format: Includes two scales: Preparatory Job-Search Behavior and Active Job-Search Behavior. Responses are made on a 5-point scale ranging from 1 (never) to 5 (very frequently, at least 10 times).

Reliability: Alpha coefficients ranged from .69 to .74.

Validity: Correlations with other variables ranged from −.29 to .44.

Author: Saks, A. M., and Ashforth, B. E.

Article: Change in job search behaviors and employment outcomes.

Journal: *Journal of Vocational Behavior*, April 2000, *56*(2), 277–287.

Related Research: Blau, G. (1994). Testing a two-dimensional measure of job search behavior.

Organizational Behavior and Human Decision Processes, 59, 288–312.

8612

Test Name: LEADER EMPOWERING BEHAVIOR QUESTIONNAIRE

Purpose: To measure empowering leader behavior.

Number of Items: 17

Format: Includes 6 dimensions: Delegation of Authority, Accountability, Self-Directed Decision-Making, Information Sharing, Skill Development, and Coaching for Innovative Performance. Responses are made on a 7-point Likert-type scale ranging from 1 (strongly disagree) to 7 (strongly agree). All items are presented.

Reliability: Alpha coefficients ranged from .82 to .93.

Validity: Correlations with other variables ranged from .31 to .63.

Author: Konczak, L. J., et al.

Article: Defining and measuring empowering leader behaviors: Development of an upward feedback instrument.

Journal: *Educational and Psychological Measurement*, April 2000, *60*(2), 301–313.

8613

Test Name: LEADERSHIP ORIENTATIONS (OTHER) SCALE

Purpose: To assess leadership style.

Number of Items: 38

Format: Scales range from 1 (never) to 5 (always).

Reliability: Alpha coefficients ranged from .92 to .95 across subscales.

Author: Short, P. M., et al.

Article: The relationship of teacher empowerment and principal leadership orientation.

Journal: *Educational Research Quarterly*, June 1999, *22*(4), 45–52.

Related Research: Bolman, L., & Deal, T. (1991). *Reframing organizations: Artistry, choice and leadership.* San Francisco, CA: Jossey-Bass.

8614

Test Name: LEADERSHIP STYLE QUESTIONNAIRE

Purpose: To identify respondents' methods they believed were important for managing people in their job.

Number of Items: 26

Format: Includes 3 factors: Machiavellian, Bureaucratic, and Transformational. Responses are made on a 7-point scale ranging from 1 (strongly disagree) to 7 (strongly agree). All items are presented.

Reliability: Alpha coefficients ranged from .62 to .86. Test-retest (3 weeks) reliability was .88.

Author: Girodo, M.

Article: Machiavellian, bureaucratic, and transformational leadership styles in police managers: Preliminary findings of interpersonal ethics.

Journal: *Perceptual and Motor Skills*, April 1998, *86*(2), 419–427.

Related Research: Hitt, W. D. (1990). *Ethics and leadership: Putting theory into practice.* Columbus, OH: Battelle Press.

8615

Test Name: LEISURE ACTIVITIES SCALE

Purpose: To enable adolescents to rate the frequency of leisure activities.

Number of Items: 26

Format: Includes the following activities: Peer, Family, Cultural, and Self-Improvement. Examples are presented.

Reliability: Alpha coefficients ranged from .40 to .77.

Author: Silbereisen, R. K., et al.

Article: Differential timing of initial vocational choice: The influence of early childhood family relocation and parental support behaviors in two cultures.

Journal: *Journal of Vocational Behavior*, February 1997, *50*(1), 41–59.

Related Research: Coleman, J. C., & Hendry, L. B. (1990). *The nature of adolescence* (2nd ed.). London: Routledge.

8616

Test Name: LIE/BET QUESTIONNAIRE

Purpose: To screen participants for pathological gambling.

Number of Items: 2

Format: Yes/no format. Both items are presented.

Validity: Specificities and predictive values all exceeded .78.

Author: Johnson, E. E., and Hamer, R. M.

Article: The Lie/Bet Questionnaire for screening pathological gamblers: A follow-up study.

Journal: *Psychological Reports*, December 1998, *83*(3) Part 2, 1219–1224.

Related Research: Johnson, E. E., et al. (1997). The Lie/Bet Questionnaire for screening

pathological gamblers. *Psychological Reports, 80*, 83–88.

8617

Test Name: LIFE EVENTS SCALE

Purpose: To predict concurrent and subsequent child functioning.

Number of Items: 40

Format: Includes the following topics: Family, Conflict, Difficulties with Neighbors, Instability of Living Situation, Work-Related Problems, Health Problems, and Trouble with the Law.

Reliability: Pearson correlations ranged from .86 to .96.

Author: Weinfield, N. S., et al.

Article: Attachment from infancy to early adulthood in a high-risk sample: Continuity, discontinuity, and their correlates.

Journal: *Child Development*, May/June 2000, *71*(3), 695–702.

Related Research: Egeland, B., & Deinard, A. (1975). *Life stress scale and manual*. Unpublished manuscript, University of Minnesota.

8618

Test Name: LOW SELF-CONTROL SCALE

Purpose: To measure low self-control.

Number of Items: 12

Format: Responses are made on a 5-point scale ranging from 1 (never) to 5 (very often).

Reliability: Coefficient alpha was .86.

Author: Tibbetts, S. G.

Article: Differences between

women and men regarding decisions to commit test cheating.

Journal: *Research in Higher Education*, June 1999, *40*(3), 323–342.

Related Research: Grasnick, H., et al. (1993). Testing the core implications of Gottfredson and Hirschi's general theory of crime. *Journal of Research in Crime and Delinquency*, 30(1), 5–22.

8619

Test Name: MATTHEWS YOUTH TEST FOR HEALTH

Purpose: To enable teachers to rate the competitiveness, impatience, and aggression of children.

Number of Items: 17

Format: Includes 2 subscales: Competitiveness and Impatience/Aggression. Responses are made on a 5-point scale ranging from 1 (extremely uncharacteristic) to 5 (extremely characteristic). Examples are presented.

Reliability: Alpha coefficients were .85 and .88.

Author: McCall, R. B., et al.

Article: The nature and correlates of underachievement among elementary school children in Hong Kong.

Journal: *Child Development*, May/June 2000, *71*(3), 785–801.

Related Research: Matthews, K. A., & Angulo, J. (1980). Measurement of the Type A behavior pattern in children: Assessment of children's competitiveness, impatience-anger, and aggression. *Child Development, 51*, 466–475.

8620

Test Name: MEASURE OF UPWARD INFLUENCE

Purpose: To measure upward influence behaviors in organizational settings.

Number of Items: 18

Format: Includes 6 factors: Assertiveness, Exchange, Rationality, Ingratiation, Upward Appeal, and Coalition Building.

Reliability: Alpha coefficients ranged from .50 to .80.

Author: Hochwarter, W. A., et al.

Article: A reexamination of Schriesheim and Hinkin's (1990) measure of upward influence.

Journal: *Educational and Psychological Measurement*, October 2000, *60*(5), 755–771.

Related Research: Schriesheim, C., & Hinkin, T. (1990). Influence tactics used by subordinates: A theoretical and empirical analysis and refinements of the Kipnis, Schmidt, and Wilkinson subscales. *Journal of Applied Psychology, 75*, 246–257.

8621

Test Name: MODELS FOR DRUG-USE SCALE

Purpose: To assess exposure to peer models for drug use.

Number of Items: 4

Format: Five-point scales are anchored by 1 (none) and 5 (all).

Reliability: Coefficient alpha was .86. Test-retest reliabilities ranged from .37 to .44.

Author: Farrell, A. D., and White, K. S.

Article: Peer influences and drug use among urban adolescents: Family structure and parent-adolescent relationship as protective factors.

Journal: *Journal of Consulting and Clinical Psychology*, April 1998, *66*(2), 248–258.

Related Research: Jessor, R., & Jessor, S. L. (1977). *Problem behavior and psychosocial development*. New York: Academic Press.

8622

Test Name: MOTHER—SHORT MICHIGAN ALCOHOLISM SCREENING TEST

Purpose: To assess the biological mother's drinking behavior.

Number of Items: 13

Format: Responses are "yes", "no." An example is presented.

Reliability: Test-retest reliability was $K = .85$, Yule's $Y = .86$. Coefficient alpha was .87.

Author: Stout, M. L., and Mintz, L. B.

Article: Differences among non-clinical college women with alcoholic mothers, alcoholic fathers, and nonalcoholic parents.

Journal: *Journal of Counseling Psychology*, October 1996, *43*(4), 466–472.

Related Research: Sher, K. J., & Descutner, C. (1986). Reports of parental alcoholism: Reliability across siblings. *Addictive Behaviors, 11*, 25–30.

8623

Test Name: NORMALCY AND EVALUATION OF TOUCHING BEHAVIOR SCALE

Purpose: To assess how expected and how positive touching behavior is evaluated.

Number of Items: 8

Format: Scales ranged from 1 (not at all) to 7 (very much). All items are presented.

Reliability: Coefficient alpha was .76.

Author: Floyd, K.

Article: Affectionate same-sex touch: The influence of homophobia on observers' perceptions.

Journal: *Journal of Social Psychology*, December 2000, *140*(6), 774–788.

Related Research: Burgoon, J. K., & Walther, J. B. (1990). Nonverbal expectancies and evaluative consequences of violations. *Human Communication Research, 17*, 232–265.

8624

Test Name: NURSES' OBSERVATION SYSTEM FOR GERIATRIC REFERRALS—ENGLISH VERSION

Purpose: To assess functioning relevant to geriatric treatment in terms of positive social interest, neatness, negative social behavior, memory, and negative affect.

Number of Items: 30

Format: Checklist format.

Reliability: Internal consistencies ranged from .78 to .89.

Validity: A six-factor model was not confirmed.

Author: Grimmell, D., et al.

Article: Confirmatory factor analysis of the nurses' observation system for geriatric referrals.

Journal: *Psychological Reports*, June 1998, *82*(3) Part 1, 719–722.

Related Research: Speigel, R., et al. (1991). A new behavioral assessment scale for geriatric out- and in-patients: The NOSGER (Nurses' Observation Scale for Geriatric Referrals). *Journal of the American Geriatrics Society, 39*, 339–347.

8625

Test Name: OBSERVATIONAL SCALE OF BEHAVIORAL DISTRESS—REVISED

Purpose: To measure children's observable behaviors during acute pain episodes.

Number of Items: 11

Format: Examples of each item are presented. Indicators are marked either "present" or "absent."

Validity: Correlations with other variables ranged from .13 to .80.

Author: Smith, J. T., et al.

Article: Comparison of hypnosis and distraction in severely ill children undergoing painful medical procedures.

Journal: *Journal of Counseling Psychology*, April 1996, *43*(2), 187–195.

Related Research: Jay, S., et al. (1983). Assessment of children's distress during painful medical procedures. *Health Psychology*, 2, 133–147.

8626

Test Name: ORGANIZATIONAL CITIZENSHIP BEHAVIOR

Purpose: To measure organizational citizenship.

Number of Items: 24

Format: Five-point scales are anchored by 1 (strongly disagree) and 5 (strongly agree). A sample item is presented.

Reliability: Coefficient alpha was .93.

Validity: Correlations with other variables ranged from −.59 to .74.

Author: Allen, T. D., and Rush, M. C.

Article: The effects of organizational citizenship behavior on performance judgments: A field study and a laboratory experiment.

Journal: *Journal of Applied Psychology*, April 1998, *83*(2), 247–260.

Related Research: Podsakoff, P. M., et al. (1990). Transformational leader behaviors and their effects on followers' trust in leader, satisfaction, and organizational citizenship behaviors. *Leadership Quarterly*, 1, 107–142.

8627

Test Name: ORGANIZATIONAL CITIZENSHIP BEHAVIOR MEASURE

Purpose: To measure contextual performance.

Number of Items: 16

Format: Includes 2 factors: Altuism and Conscientiousness.

Reliability: Alpha coefficients were .86 for each factor.

Author: Goodman, S. A., and Svyantek, D. J.

Article: Person-organization fit and contextual performance: Do shared values matter?

Journal: *Journal of Vocational Behavior*, October 1999, *55*(2), 254–275.

Related Research: Smith, C. A., et al. (1983). Organizational citizenship behavior: Its nature and antecedents. *Journal of Applied Psychology*, 68, 653–663.

8628

Test Name: ORGANIZATIONAL CITIZENSHIP BEHAVIOR SCALE

Purpose: To measure organizational citizenship behavior.

Format: Includes 2 types of citizenship: Altruism and Compliance. Responses are made on a 5-point scale ranging from 1 (disagree completely) to 5 (agree completely).

Reliability: Alpha coefficients were .80 and .84.

Validity: Correlations with other variables ranged from −.14 to .70.

Author: Shore, L. M., et al.

Article: Construct validity of measures of Becker's side bet theory.

Journal: *Journal of Vocational Behavior*, December 2000, *57*(3), 428–444.

Related Research: Smith, C. A., et al. (1983). Organizational citizenship behavior: Its nature and antecedents. *Journal of Applied Psychology*, 68, 653–663.

8629

Test Name: ORGANIZATIONAL CITIZENSHIP BEHAVIOR SCALE

Purpose: To measure altruism and compliance.

Number of Items: 10

Format: Five-point scales ranged from "strongly agree" to "strongly disagree." Sample items are presented.

Reliability: Alpha coefficients ranged from .91 to .93.

Validity: Correlations with other variables ranged from −.18 to .67.

Author: Hui, C., et al.

Article: Instrumental values of organizational citizenship behavior for promotion: A field quasi-experiment.

Journal: *Journal of Applied Psychology*, October 2000, *85*(5), 822–828.

Related Research: Smith, C. A., et al. (1983). Organizational citizenship behavior: Its nature and antecedents. *Journal of Applied Psychology, 68,* 653–663.

8630

Test Name: ORGANIZATIONAL CITIZENSHIP BEHAVIOR SCALE

Purpose: To measure altruism, conscientiousness, and sportsmanship.

Number of Items: 11

Format: Scales range from 1 (extremely disagree) to 5 (extremely agree). All items are presented.

Reliability: Alpha coefficients ranged from .69 to .87 across subscales.

Validity: Correlations with other variables ranged from −.28 to .14.

Author: Chen, X-P., et al.

Article: The role of organizational citizenship behavior in turnover: Conceptualization and preliminary tests of key hypotheses.

Journal: *Journal of Applied Psychology,* December 1998, *83*(6), 922–931.

Related Research: Podsakoff, P. M., et al. (1990). Transformational leader behaviors and their effects on followers' trust in leader, satisfaction, and organizational citizenship behaviors. *Leadership Quarterly, 1,* 107–142.

8631

Test Name: ORGANIZATIONAL CITIZENSHIP BEHAVIOR SCALE

Purpose: To measure organizational citizenship

behavior among members of a machine crew.

Number of Items: 13

Format: Seven-point scales ranged from 1 (strongly disagree) to 7 (strongly agree). All items are presented.

Reliability: Alpha coefficients exceed .70.

Author: Podaskoff, P. M., et al.

Article: Organizational citizenship behavior and its quantity and quality of work group performance.

Journal: *Journal of Applied Psychology,* April, 1997, *82*(2), 262–270.

Related Research: Podaskoff, P. M., & Mackenzie, S. B. (1994). Organizational citizenship behavior and sales unit effectiveness. *Journal of Marketing Research, 31,* 351–363.

8632

Test Name: ORGANIZATIONAL CITIZENSHIP BEHAVIOR SCALE

Purpose: To measure courtesy, altruism, and conscientiousness.

Number of Items: 15

Format: Scales range from 1 (strongly disagree) to 7 (strongly agree). Sample items are presented.

Reliability: Coefficient alpha was .94.

Validity: Correlations with other variables ranged from −.12 to .30.

Author: Findley, H. M., et al.

Article: Performance appraisal process and system facets: Relationships with contextual performance.

Journal: *Journal of Applied*

Psychology, August 2000, *85*(4), 634–640.

Related Research: Podsakoff, P. M., et al. (1990). Transformational leader behaviors and their effects on followers' trust in leader, satisfaction, and organizational citizenship behaviors. *Leadership Quarterly, 1,* 107–142.

8633

Test Name: PARENT-CHILD RATING SCALE

Purpose: Provides parent ratings of children's problem behaviors and competencies.

Number of Items: 18

Format: Responses are made on a 5-point scale ranging from 1 (not at all true) to 5 (very true).

Reliability: Alpha coefficients for two factors were .75 and .80.

Author: Sutton, S. E., et al.

Article: Pathways to aggression in young, highly stressed urban children.

Journal: *Child Study Journal,* 1999, *29*(1), 49–67.

Related Research: Cowen, E. L., et al. (1996). *School based prevention for children at risk: The Primary Mental Health Project.* Washington, DC: American Psychological Association.

8634

Test Name: PARENTAL CULTURAL CAPITAL SCALE

Purpose: To measure the frequency of beaux arts participation and reading habits.

Number of Items: 10

Format: Scales range from 1 (never) to 3 (more than once a year). All items are described.

Reliability: Coefficient alpha was .84.

Validity: The correlation between parental and respondent reports was .37.

Author: DeGraaf, N. D., et al.

Article: Parental cultural capital and educational attainment in the Netherlands: A refinement of the cultural capital perspective.

Journal: *Sociology of Education,* April 2000, *73*(2), 92–111.

8635

Test Name: PEER ALCOHOL USE SCALE

Purpose: To measure alcohol use among adolescents.

Number of Items: 2

Format: Five-point frequency scales are anchored by 0 (none) to 4 (all). All items are presented.

Reliability: Alphas ranged from .85 to .87.

Validity: Correlations with other variables ranged from −.13 to .66.

Author: Curran, P. J., et al.

Article: The relation between adolescent alcohol use and peer alcohol use: A longitudinal random coefficients model.

Journal: *Journal of Consulting and Clinical Psychology,* February 1997, *65*(1), 130–140.

8636

Test Name: PEER ASSESSMENT OF BEHAVIOR SCALE

Purpose: To enable children to evaluate peer behavior.

Number of Items: 12

Format: Includes 3 subscales: Aggression, Withdrawal, and

Prosocial Behavior. All items are presented.

Reliability: Alpha coefficients ranged from .83 to .97.

Author: Erdley, C. A., and Asher, S. R.

Article: Children's social goals and self-efficacy perceptions as influences on their responses to ambiguous provocation.

Journal: *Child Development,* August 1996, *67*(4), 1329–1344.

Related Research: Asher, S. R., et al. (1991, April). Self-referral for peer relationship problems among aggressive and withdrawn low-accepted children. In J. T. Parkhurst & D. L. Rabiner (Chairs), *The behavioral characteristics and the subjective experience of aggressive and withdrawn/submissive rejected children.* Symposium conducted at the biennial meeting of the Society for Research in Child Development, Seattle.

8637

Test Name: PEER DELINQUENCY SCALE

Purpose: To measure peer delinquency.

Number of Items: 10

Format: Items include delinquency and substance abuse. Responses are made on a 4-point scale ranging from "very much like" to "very much unlike." An example is given.

Reliability: Alpha coefficients were .84 (mother), .88 (father).

Author: Kim, J. E., et al.

Article: Association among family relationships, antisocial peers, and adolescents' externalizing behaviors: Gender and family type differences.

Journal: *Child Development,*

September/October 1999, *70*(5), 1209–1230.

Related Research: Reiss, D., et al. (1994). The separate worlds of teenage siblings: An introduction to the study of the nonshared environment and adolescent development. In E. M. Hetherington et al. (Eds.), *Separate social worlds of siblings: Importance of nonshared environment on development* (pp. 63–109). Hillsdale, NJ: Erlbaum.

8638

Test Name: PEER NOMINATION INVENTORY

Purpose: To enable children to identify behaviors of peers.

Number of Items: 53

Format: Includes 12 scales: Aggression, Argumentativeness, Dishonesty, Pushy Peer Entry Style, Disruptiveness, Victimization, Immaturity, Withdrawal, Anxiety/Depression, Hovering Peer Entry Style, Prosocial Behavior, and Physical Strength. Examples are presented.

Reliability: Test-retest (1 year) reliability ranged from .69 to .84 (*N* = 173).

Author: Finnegan, R. A., et al.

Article: Preoccupied and avoidant coping during middle childhood.

Journal: *Child Development,* August 1996, *67*(4), 1318–1328.

Related Research: Wiggins, J. S., & Winder, C. L. (1961). The Peer Nominations Inventory: An empirically derived sociometric measure of adjustment in preadolescent boys. *Psychological Reports, 9,* 643–677.

8639

Test Name: PEER VICTIMIZATION SCALE

Purpose: To assess peer victimization.

Number of Items: 4

Format: Includes 4 types of peer aggression: Direct Verbal, Indirect Verbal, Physical, and General. Responses are made on a 3-point scale ranging from 1 (no, never) to 3 (a lot). Examples are presented.

Reliability: Coefficient alpha was .74.

Author: Ladd, G. W., and Burgess, K. B.

Article: Charting the relationship trajectories of aggressive, withdrawn, and aggressive/withdrawn children during early grade school.

Journal: *Child Development*, July/August 1999, 70(4), 910–929.

Related Research: Kochenderfer, B. J., & Ladd, G. W. (1997). Victimized children's response to peers' aggression: Behaviors associated with reduced versus continued victimization. *Developmental and Psychotherapy*, 9, 59–73.

8640

Test Name: PENN INTERACTIVE PEER PLAY SCALE

Purpose: To enable teachers to rate preschool children's interactive peer play.

Number of Items: 32

Format: Includes 3 dimensions: Play Interaction, Play Disruption, and Play Disconnection.

Reliability: Alpha coefficients ranged from .87 to .91.

Author: Coolahan, K., et al.

Article: Preschool peer interactions and readiness to learn: Relationships between classroom peer play and learning behaviors and conduct.

Journal: *Journal of Educational Psychology*, September 2000, 92(3), 458–465.

Related Research: Fontuzzo, J. W., et al. (1995). Assessment of play interaction behaviors in young, low-income children: Penn Interactive Peer Play Scale. *Early Childhood Research Quarterly, 10*, 105–120.

8641

Test Name: PERCEIVED BEHAVIORAL CONTROL SCALE

Purpose: To measure perceived behavioral control.

Number of Items: 3

Format: Scales from 0 to 6 are used for response to each item. An example is presented.

Reliability: Coefficient alpha was .82.

Validity: Correlation with other variables ranged from −.10 to .49.

Author: Kerner, M. S., and Grossman, A. H.

Article: Attitudinal, social, and practical correlates to fitness behavior: A test of the theory of planned behavior.

Journal: *Perceptual and Motor Skills*, December 1998, 87(3) Part 2, 1139–1154.

Related Research: Kerner, M. S. (1993). Perceived Behavioral Control Scale. Unpublished manuscript, New York University, New York.

8642

Test Name: PERSONAL ASSERTION ANALYSIS

Purpose: To measure passive aggressive and assertive behavior.

Number of Items: 30

Format: Four-point Likert format.

Reliability: Test-retest reliability (1 week) was .70.

Author: Nash, H. C., and Chrisler, J. C.

Article: Personality characteristics and coping styles of women working in and in training for nontraditional blue collar jobs.

Journal: *Psychological Reports*, December 2000, 87(3), Part 2, 1115–1122.

Related Research: Hedlund, B. L., & Lindquist, C. U. (1984). The development of an inventory for distinguishing among passive, aggressive, and assertive behavior. *Behavioral Assessment*. 6, 379–390.

8643

Test Name: PERSONAL LIFESTYLE QUESTIONNAIRE

Purpose: To measure six self-reported health-related practices.

Number of Items: 24

Format: Includes 6 health-related practices: nutrition, exercise, relaxation, safety, less substance use, and health promotion.

Reliability: Test-retest reliabilities were .88 (3 weeks) and .87 (4 weeks). Coefficient alpha was .79.

Validity: Correlations with future time perspective ranged from .20 to .52.

Author: Mahon, N. E., et al.

Article: Future time perspective and positive health practices among young adolescents: A further extension.

Journal: *Perceptual and Motor Skills*, February 2000, *90*(1), 166–168.

Related Research: Brown, N., et al. (1983). The relationship among health beliefs, health values, and health promotion activity. *Western Journal of Nursing Research*, 5, 155–163.

8644

Test Name: PHYSICAL ACTIVITY QUESTIONNAIRE— MODIFIED

Purpose: To estimate moderate and vigorous activity.

Number of Items: 10

Format: Includes 2 subscales: Current and Long-Term Physical Activity. Sample items are presented.

Reliability: Coefficient alpha was .79. Test-retest reliability was .92.

Author: Li, S., et al.

Article: Validation of a single-item measure of usual physical activity.

Journal: *Perceptual and Motor Skills*, October 2000, *91*(2), 593–602.

Related Research: Sturgeon, S. R., et al. (1993). Past and present physical activity and endometrial cancer risk. *British Journal of Cancer*, 68, 584–589.

8645

Test Name: PRINCIPAL'S LEADERSHIP SCALE

Purpose: To describe the principal's leadership.

Number of Items: 30

Format: Includes Human Leadership, Structural

Leadership, Political Leadership, Symbolic Leadership, and Education Leadership.

Reliability: Alpha coefficients ranged from .87 to .94.

Validity: Correlations with teachers' professionalism ranged from .47 to .56.

Author: Cheng, Y. C.

Article: Relation between teachers' professionalism and job attitudes, educational outcomes, and organizational factors.

Journal: *Journal of Educational Research*, January/February, 1996, *89*(3), 163–171.

Related Research: Sergiovanni, T. J. (1984). Leadership and excellence in schooling. *Educational Leadership*, *41*(5), 4–13.

8646

Test Name: PRIOR DELINQUENCY SCALE

Purpose: To assess the frequency of prior delinquency.

Number of Items: 28

Format: Scales range from 1 (never) to 9 (2–3 times per day).

Reliability: Alpha coefficients ranged from .73 to .82.

Author: Heimer, K.

Article: Gender, interaction, and delinquency: Testing a theory of differential social control.

Journal: *Social Psychology Quarterly*, March 1996, *59*(1), 39–61.

Related Research: Elliott, D. S., et al. (1985). *Explaining delinquency and drug use*. Beverly Hills, CA: Sage.

8647

Test Name: PROACTIVE CAREER BEHAVIORS SCALE

Purpose: To measure proactive career behaviors.

Number of Items: 11

Format: Includes 4 factors: Skill Development, Career Planning, Consultation, and Networking.

Reliability: Alpha coefficients ranged from .65 to .76.

Validity: Correlations with other variables ranged from −.22 to .11.

Author: Claes, R., and Ruiz-Quintanilla, S. A.

Article: Influences of early career experience, occupational group, and national culture on proactive career behavior.

Journal: *Journal of Vocational Behavior*, June 1998, *52*(3), 357–378.

Related Research: Penley, L., & Gould, S. (1981). *Measuring career strategies: The psychometric characteristics of the Career Strategies Inventory*. San Antonio, TX: Center for Studies in Business, Economics and Human Resources, University of Texas.

8648

Test Name: PROCRASTINATION LOG

Purpose: To measure procrastination-related behavior during the past week.

Number of Items: 9

Format: Responses are made on a 7-point scale ranging from "true" to "false."

Reliability: Test-retest (1 week) reliability was .62. Coefficient alpha was .63.

Author: Cook, P. F.

Article: Effects of counselors' etiology attributions on college students' procrastination.

Journal: *Journal of Counseling Psychology*, July 2000, 47(3), 352–361.

Related Research: Strong, S. R., et al. (1979). Motivational and equipping functions of interpretation in counseling. *Journal of Counseling Psychology, 26*, 98–107.

8649

Test Name: PROCRASTINATION SCALE

Purpose: To measure procrastination.

Number of Items: 20

Format: True/false format.

Reliability: Coefficient alpha was .82.

Author: Martin, T. R., et al.

Article: Personality correlates of depression and health symptoms: A test of a self-regulation model.

Journal: *Journal of Research in Personality*, June 1996, 30(2), 264–277.

Related Research: Lay, C. H. (1995). Trait procrastination, agitation, dejection and self-discrepancy. In J. Ferrari et al. (Eds.), *Procrastination and task avoidance: Theory, research, and treatment* (pp. 97–112). New York: Plenum.

Ferrari, J. R., & Tice, D. M. (2000). Procrastination as a self-handicap for men and women: A task-avoidance strategy in a laboratory setting. *Journal of Research in Personality, 34*, 73–83.

8650

Test Name: PROCRASTINATION SCALE

Purpose: To measure level of procrastination.

Number of Items: 32

Format: Examples are presented.

Reliability: Coefficient alpha was .86.

Validity: Correlations with other variables ranged from −.19 to .54.

Author: Tuckman, B. W.

Article: Using tests as an incentive to motivate procrastinators to study.

Journal: *Journal of Experimental Education*, Winter 1997, 66(2), 141–147.

Related Research: Tuckman, B. W. (1991). The development and concurrent validity of the Procrastination Scale. *Educational and Psychological Measurement, 57*, 473–480.

8651

Test Name: PROCRASTINATION SCALE

Number of Items: 35 (16)

Format: Four-point scales are anchored by (1) that's not me for sure and (4) that's me for sure.

Reliability: Alpha was .90 (long version) and .86 (short version).

Validity: Correlations with time structure ranged from −.64 to −.29.

Author: Vodanovich, S. J., and Seib, H. M.

Article: Relationship between time structure and procrastination.

Journal: *Psychological Reports*, February 1997, 80(1), 211–215.

Related Research: Tuckman, B. W. (1991). The development and concurrent validity of the Procrastination Scale. *Educational and Psychological Measurement, 51*, 473–480.

8652

Test Name: PROFILE OF ORGANIZATIONAL INFLUENCE STRATEGIES (GERMAN VERSION)

Purpose: To measure the strategies people use to influence their managers at work.

Number of Items: 16

Format: Five-point scales are anchored by 1 (never) and 5 (often). Sample items are presented.

Reliability: Cronbach alphas ranged from .60 to .77.

Validity: Convergent validity coefficients ranged from .43 to .89.

Author: Blickle, G.

Article: Influence tactics used by subordinates: An empirical analysis of the Kipnis and Schmidt subscales.

Journal: *Psychological Reports*, February 2000, 86(1), 143–154.

Related Research: Kipnis, D., & Schmidt, S. M. (1982). Profiles of Organizational Influence Strategies (POIS). University Associates, Inc., Production Avenue, San Diego, CA, 92121.

8653

Test Name: PROS AND CONS OF QUITTING SMOKING SCALE

Purpose: To assess physical, social, self-evaluative, and monetary outcomes of quitting smoking.

Number of Items: 35

Format: Four-point scales are anchored by 1 (not expecting a certain outcome) and 5 (strong expectation of the outcome).

Reliability: Alphas were .85 (total), .89 (Pros), and .73 (Cons).

Author: Dijkstra, A., et al.

Article: Pros and cons of quitting, self-efficacy, and the stages of change in smoking cessation.

Journal: *Journal of Consulting and Clinical Psychology*, August 1996, *64*(4), 758–763.

Related Research: DeVries, H., & Backbier, E. (1994). Self-efficacy as an important determinant of quitting among pregnant women who smoke: The Q-pattern. *Preventive Medicine, 23*, 167–174.

8654

Test Name: PROSOCIAL BEHAVIOR SCALE

Purpose: To enable children, mothers, teachers, and peers to rate the children's level of prosocial behavior.

Number of Items: 10

Reliability: Alpha coefficients ranged from .75 to .88.

Validity: Correlations with other variables ranged from −.47 to .55.

Author: Bandura, A., et al.

Article: Multifaceted impact of self-efficacy beliefs on academic functioning.

Journal: *Child Development*, June 1996, *67*(3), 1206–1222.

Related Research: Caprara, G. V., & Pastorelli, C. (1993). Early emotional instability, prosocial behavior, and aggression: Some methodological aspects. *European Journal of Personality, 7*, 19–36.

8655

Test Name: PSYCHOLOGICAL MALTREATMENT OF WOMEN INVENTORY

Purpose: To assess attempts to

isolate, dominate, humiliate, or threaten a partner.

Number of Items: 58

Format: Scales range from 1 (never) to 5 (very frequently).

Reliability: Coefficient alpha was .96.

Validity: Correlations with other variables ranged from −.16 to .50.

Author: Ronfeldt, H. M., et al.

Article: Satisfaction with relationship power and the perpetration of dating violence.

Journal: *Journal of Marriage and the Family*, February 1998, *60*(1), 70–78.

Related Research: Tolman, R. M. (1989). The development of a measure of maltreatment of women by their male partners. *Violence and Victims, 4*, 159–177.

8656

Test Name: PSYCHOLOGICAL PROFILE OF FORGIVENESS SCALE

Purpose: To assess the degree to which an incest victim forgives the perpetrator.

Number of Items: 30

Format: Four-point scales are anchored by 1 (strongly disagree) and 4 (strongly agree). Sample items are presented.

Reliability: Alphas ranged from .90 to .95.

Author: Freedman, S. R., and Enright, R. D.

Article: Forgiveness as an intervention goal with incest survivors.

Journal: *Journal of Consulting and Clinical Psychology*, October 1996, *64*(5), 983–992.

Related Research: Hebl, J. H., &

Enright, R. D. (1993). Forgiveness as a psychotherapeutic goal with elderly females. *Psychotherapy, 30*, 658–667.

8657

Test Name: PSYCHOLOGICAL REACTANCE SCALE

Purpose: To measure rebelliousness resulting from frustration with regulations.

Number of Items: 11

Format: Five-point scales range from 1 (strongly disagree) to 5 (strongly agree).

Reliability: Coefficient alpha was .85.

Validity: Correlations with other variables ranged from −.06 to .35.

Author: Frone, M. R.

Article: Predictors of work injuries among employed adolescents.

Journal: *Journal of Applied Psychology*, August 1998, *83*(4), 565–576.

Related Research: Hong, S. M., & Faedda, S. (1996). Refinement of the Hong Kong Psychological Reactance Scale. *Educational and Psychological Measurement, 56*, 173–182.

8658

Test Name: PSYCHOLOGICAL REACTANCE SCALE

Purpose: To assess the degree to which individuals desire control over their environments.

Number of Items: 14

Format: Sample items are represented.

Reliability: Coefficient alpha was .80.

Validity: Correlations with other variables ranged from −.20 to .26.

Authors: Sachau, D. A., et al.

Article: Predictors of employee resistance to supervisors' requests.

Journal: *The Journal of Social Psychology*, October 1999, *139*(5), 611–621.

Related Research: Hong, S-M., & Page, S. (1989). A psychological resistance scale: Effects of age and gender. *The Journal of Social Psychology, 134*, 223–229.

8659

Test Name: PUPIL EVALUATION INVENTORY

Purpose: To assess children's social behavior.

Number of Items: 34

Format: Includes 3 scales: Aggressiveness-Disturbance, Social-Withdrawal, and Likability.

Reliability: Alpha coefficients were .97 and .96.

Author: Vitaro, F., et al.

Article: Disruptiveness, friends' characteristics, and delinquency in early adolescence: A test of two competing models of development.

Journal: *Child Development*, August 1997, *68*(4), 676–689.

Related Research: Pekarik, E. G., et al. (1976). The Pupil Evaluation Inventory: A sociometric technique for assessing children's social behavior. *Journal of Abnormal Child Psychology, 4*, 83–97.

8660

Test Name: QUANTITATIVE INVENTORY OF ALCOHOL DISORDERS

Purpose: To measure the severity of alcoholism in individuals.

Number of Items: 22

Format: Five-point scales.

Reliability: Test-retest reliability (14–18 days) was .96.

Validity: Correlation with reported drinking behavior was .52.

Author: Kashubeck, S., and Mintz, L. B.

Article: Eating disorder symptomatology and substance use in college females.

Journal: *Journal of College Student Development*, July/ August 1996, *37*(4), 396–404.

Related Research: Stinnett, J. J., & Schechter, J. O. (1982–1983). A Quantitative Inventory Of Alcohol Disorders (QIAD): A severity scale for alcohol abuse. *American Journal of Drug and Alcohol Abuse, 9*, 413–430.

8661

Test Name: QUESTIONNAIRE OF ALCOHOL URGES— MODIFIED

Purpose: To measure desire to drink.

Number of Items: 3

Format: Eight-point scales are anchored by 1 (definitely false) and 8 (definitely true). All items are presented.

Reliability: Alpha coefficients ranged from .71 to .78 across 52 days.

Validity: Correlations with other variables ranged from −.24 to .44.

Author: Carney, M. A., et al.

Article: Positive and negative daily events, perceived stress, and alcohol use: A diary study.

Journal: *Journal of Consulting and Clinical Psychology*, October 2000, *68*(5), 788–798.

Related Research: Bohn, M. J., et al. (1995). Development and validation of an initial measure of drinking urges in abstinent alcoholics. *Alcoholism: Clinical and Experimental Research, 19*, 600–606.

8662

Test Name: QUESTIONNAIRE ON TEACHER INTERACTION

Purpose: To measure teacher interaction in eight dimensions: Leadership, Friendliness, Understanding, Student Freedom, Certainty, Satisfaction, Anger, and Strictness.

Number of Items: 48

Format: Three-point response categories. Sample items are presented.

Reliability: Alphas ranged from .58 to .96.

Validity: Predictive validity coefficients ranged from −.75 to .68.

Author: Goh, S. C., and Fraser, B. J.

Article: Validation of an elementary version of the Questionnaire on Teacher Interaction.

Journal: *Psychological Reports*, October 1996, *79*(2), 515–522.

Related Research: Wubbels, T., & Levy, T. (1991). A comparison of interpersonal behavior of Dutch and American teachers. *International Journal of Intercultural Relations, 15*, 1– 18.

8663

Test Name: RAHIM LEADER POWER INVENTORY

Purpose: To measure five bases of

social power through subscales depicting each type of power.

Number of Items: 29

Format: Includes 5 factors: Expert Power, Referent Power, Coercive Power, Legitimate Power, and Reward Power. Responses are made on a 5-point Likert-type scale ranging from "strongly disagree" to "strongly agree."

Reliability: Alpha coefficients ranged from .76 to .90.

Author: Hess, C. W., and Wagner, B. T.

Article: Factor structure of the Rahim Leader Power Inventory (RLPI) with clinical female student supervisees.

Journal: *Educational and Psychological Measurement*, December 1999, *59*(6), 1004–1015.

Related Research: Rahim, M. A. (1988). The development of a leader power inventory. *Multivariate Behavioral Research*, *23*, 491–503.

8664

Test Name: REBELLIOUS BEHAVIOR SCALE

Purpose: To measure misconduct, both major and minor.

Number of Items: 14

Format: Responses are "often," "sometimes," and "never."

Reliability: Alpha was .80.

Author: Gottfredson, D. C., and Koper, D. S.

Article: Race and sex differences in the prediction of drug use.

Journal: *Journal of Consulting and Clinical Psychology*, April 1996, *64*(2), 305–313.

Related Research: Bachman, J. G. (1975). *Youth in Transition*

documentation manual. Ann Arbor: University of Michigan, Institute for Social Research.

8665

Test Name: RECENT SEXUAL HARASSMENT SCALE

Purpose: To measure sexual harassment.

Number of Items: 5

Format: Responses are made on a 5-point scale ranging from 0 (never) to 4 (very often).

Reliability: Alpha coefficients were .84 and .87.

Author: Ingram, K. M., et al.

Article: The relationship of victimization experiences to psychological well-being among homeless women and low-income housed women.

Journal: *Journal of Counseling Psychology*, April 1996, *43*(2), 218–227.

Related Research: D'Ercole, A., & Struening, E. (1990). Victimization among homeless women: Implications for service delivery. *Journal of Community Psychology*, *18*, 141–152.

8666

Test Name: REPRESSION–SENSITIZATION SCALE

Purpose: To measure the tendency to approach or to avoid elevated emotional material.

Number of Items: 127

Reliability: Split-half reliability was .94. Test-retest (3 month) reliability was .82.

Validity: Correlations with other variables ranged from −.65 to .63.

Author: Slanger, E., and Rudestam, K. E.

Article: Motivation and disinhibition in high risk sports: Sensation-seeking and self-efficacy.

Journal: *Journal of Research in Personality*, September 1997, *31*(3), 355–374.

Related Research: Byrne, D., et al. (1963). Relation of Revised Repression–Sensitization Scale to measures of self-description. *Psychological Reports*, *13*, 323–334.

8667

Test Name: RESISTANCE SCALE

Purpose: To evaluate the frequency and intensity of client behaviors indicative of resistance.

Number of Items: 19

Format: Includes 4 factors: Abrupt/Shifting, Oppositional, Flat/Halting, and Vague/Doubting.

Reliability: Alpha coefficients ranged from .50 to .71.

Author: Patton, M. J., et al.

Article: The Missouri Psychoanalytic Counseling Project: Relation of changes in counseling process to client outcomes.

Journal: *Journal of Counseling Psychology*, April 1997, *44*(2), 189–208.

Related Research: Schuller, R., et al. (1991). The Resistance Scale: Background and psychometric properties. *Psychoanalytic Psychology*, *8*, 195–211.

8668

Test Name: RETROSPECTIVE OVERT AGGRESSION SCALE

Purpose: To assess aggression histories in psychiatric patients. Verbal and physical aggression are assessed.

Number of Items: 16

Format: Items are scored 0 (never) or 1 (sometimes).

Reliability: Alpha was .75.

Author: Huang, D. B., et al.

Article: Laboratory measurement of aggression in high school age athletes: Provocation in a nonsporting context.

Journal: *Psychological Reports*, December 1999, *85*(3, Part 2), 1251–1262.

Related Research: Sorgi, R., et al. (1991). Rating aggression in the clinical setting: A retrospective adaptation of the Overt Aggression Scale: Preliminary results. *Journal of Neuropsychiatry and Clinical Neuroscience, 3*, S52–S56.

8669

Test Name: REVISED BEHAVIOR PROBLEM CHECKLIST

Purpose: To assess behavior problems children and adolescents might display.

Number of Items: 89

Format: Two-point scales.

Reliability: Test-retest reliability was .67.

Author: Hastings, T. L., et al.

Article: Gender differences in coping and daily stress in conduct-disordered and non-conduct-disordered adolescents.

Journal: *Journal of Psychopathology and Behavioral Assessment*, September 1996, *18*(3), 213–226.

Related Research: Quay, H. C., & Peterson, D. R. (1987). Manual for the Revised Problem Behavior Checklist. Coral Gables, FL: University of Miami.

8670

Test Name: REVISED PROBLEM BEHAVIOR CHECKLIST

Purpose: To assess disruptive behavior in children as reported by teachers and parents.

Number of Items: 22

Format: Scales range from "no," to "sometimes," to "yes."

Reliability: Coefficient alpha was .90.

Author: Brown, A. C., et al.

Article: Rural Black women and depression: A contextual analysis.

Journal: *Journal of Marriage and the Family*, February 2000, *62*(1), 187–198.

Related Research: Quay, H. C. (1983). A dimensional approach to behavior disorder: The Revised Behavior Problem Checklist. *School Psychology Review, 12*, 244–249.

8671

Test Name: RUTGERS ALCOHOL/MARIJUANA PROBLEM INDEX

Purpose: To assess presence or absence of specified alcoholic/marijuana problems over one's lifetime.

Number of Items: 23

Format: Sample items are presented.

Reliability: Alpha coefficients were .86 (marijuana) and .89 (alcohol).

Validity: Correlation with other variables ranged from .07 to .59.

Author: Simons, J., et al.

Article: Validating a five-factor marijuana motives measure: Relations with use, problems, and alcohol motives.

Journal: *Journal of Counseling Psychology*, July 1998, *45*(3), 265–273.

Related Research: White, H. R., & Labouvie, E. W. (1989). Towards the assessment of adolescent problem drinking. *Journal of Studies on Alcohol, 50*, 30–37.

8672

Test Name: SCALE OF STRATEGIES FOR RECALLING PACE

Purpose: To measure three aspects of cue utilization for recalling pace.

Number of Items: 34

Format: Includes 3 aspects of cue utilization for recalling pace: Attention Strategies (has 5 subcategories: 1) attending to exertion of the whole body, 2) attending to running tempo, 3) attending to exertion of the legs, 4) imaging past running, and 5) attending to self-motivation), Strategy of Following Other Runners, and Strategy of Checking the Time. Responses are made on a 7-point scale ranging from 1 (never) to 7 (very often).

Reliability: Internal consistency coefficients were .87 and .64.

Author: Takai, K.

Article: Cognitive strategies and recall of pace by long-distance runners.

Journal: *Perceptual and Motor Skills*, June 1998, *86*(3) Part 1, 763–770.

Related Research: Takai, K. (1996). Cognitive strategies of long-distance runners for recalling pace. *Japan Journal of Physical Education, 41*, 104–114.

8673

Test Name: SCHOOL DEVIANCE SCALE

Purpose: To measure the frequency of deviant school behavior such as cheating and being tardy.

Number of Items: 5

Format: Scales range from "never" to "often."

Reliability: Coefficient alpha was .68.

Author: Gray, M. R., and Steinberg, L.

Article: Unpacking authoritative parenting: Reassessing a multidimensional construct.

Journal: *Journal of Marriage and the Family*, August 1999, *61*(3), 574–587.

Related Research: Ruggerio, M. (1984). *Work as an impetus to delinquency: An examination of theoretical and empirical connections.* Unpublished doctoral dissertation, University of California, Irvine.

8674

Test Name: SCREEN FOR ADOLESCENT VIOLENCE EXPOSURE—ADAPTED VERSION

Purpose: To measure exposure to violence among children. The scale assesses frequency and impact.

Number of Items: 45

Format: Frequency scales are anchored by 0 (never) and 2 (a lot). Impact scales are anchored by 0 (not at all upsetting) and 2 (very upsetting). All items are presented.

Reliability: Alphas ranged from .60 to .91 across subscales. Test-retest reliabilities (3 weeks) ranged from .58 to .86.

Validity: Correlations with other variables ranged from .17 to .54.

Author: Flowers, A. L., et al.

Article: Development of a screening instrument for exposure to violence in children: The KID-SAVE.

Journal: *Journal of Psychopathology and Behavioral Assessment*, March 2000, *22*(1), 91–104.

Related Research: Hastings, T., & Kelley, M. L. (1997). Development and validation of the Screen for Adolescent Violence Exposure (SAVE). *Journal of Abnormal Child Psychology, 25*, 511–520.

8675

Test Name: SELF-CONTROL RATING SCALE—REVISED

Purpose: To rate children's self-control.

Number of Items: 22

Format: Items are rated on a 7-point scale. Examples are presented.

Reliability: Alpha coefficients ranged from .64 to .79.

Author: Eisenberg, N., et al.

Article: Shyness and children's emotionality, regulation and coping: Contemporaneous, longitudinal, and cross-context relations.

Journal: *Child Development*, June 1998, *69*(3), 767–790.

Related Research: Kendall, P. C., & Wilcox, L. E. (1979). Self-control in children: The development of a rating scale. *Journal of Consulting and Clinical Psychology, 47*, 1020–1030.

8676

Test Name: SELF-CONTROL SUBSCALE

Purpose: To assess self-regulation.

Number of Items: 5

Format: Responses are made on a 5-point scale. All items are presented.

Reliability: Alpha coefficients were .72 (mothers) and .91 (teachers).

Author: Brody, G. H., et al.

Article: Linking maternal efficiency, beliefs, developmental goals, parenting practices, and child competence in rural single-parent African American families.

Journal: *Child Development*, September/October 1999, *70*(5), 1197–1208.

Related Research: Humphrey, L. L. (1982). Children's and teachers' perspectives on children's self-control: The development of two rating scales. *Journal of Consulting and Clinical Psychology, 50*, 624–633.

8677

Test Name: SELF-HANDICAPPING SCALE

Purpose: To assess self-handicapping behaviors.

Number of Items: 25

Format: A sample item is presented.

Reliability: Coefficient alpha was .71. Test-retest reliability (7 months) was .94.

Author: Knee, C. R., and Zuckerman, M.

Article: A nondefensive personality: Autonomy and control as moderators of defensive coping and self-handicapping.

Journal: *Journal of Research in Personality*, March 1998, *32*(1), 115–130.

Related Research: Jones, E. E., & Rhodewalt, F. (1982). *The self-handicapping scale* [Available from F. Rhodewalt, Department of Psychology, University of Utah, Salt Lake City, Utah].

8678

Test Name: SELF-MANAGEMENT LEADERSHIP QUESTIONNAIRE

Purpose: To measure leader behaviors encouraging self-management.

Number of Items: 22

Format: Includes 6 factors: Encourage, Rehearsal, Self-Goal Setting, Self-Criticism, Self-Reinforcement, Self-Expectation, and Self-Observation.

Reliability: Reliability ranged from .72 to .94.

Author: Cohen, S. G., et al.

Article: A hierarchical construct of self-management leadership and its relationship to quality of work life and perceived work group effectiveness.

Journal: *Personnel Psychology*, Summer 1997, *50*(2), 275–308.

Related Research: Manz, C. C., & Sims, H. P. (1987). Leading workers to lead themselves: The external leadership of self-managed working teams. *Administrative Science Quarterly*, *32*, 106–128.

8679

Test Name: SELF-REGULATED LEARNING SCALE

Purpose: To measure high school students' perceived capability to use self-regulated learning strategies.

Number of Items: 11

Format: Responses are made on a 7-point scale ranging from 1 (not very well at all) to 7 (very well).

Reliability: Coefficient alpha was .86.

Author: Williams, J. E.

Article: The relation between efficacy for self-regulated learning and domain-specific academic performance, controlling for test anxiety.

Journal: *Journal of Research and Development in Education*, Winter 1996, *29*(2), 77–80.

Related Research: Bandura, A. (1989). *Multidimensional scales of perceived self efficacy.* Unpublished manuscript, Stanford University, CA.

8680

Test Name: SELF-REGULATED LEARNING SCALE— JAPANESE VERSION

Purpose: To assess perceived learning orientation, goal orientation, performance orientation, and learning strategies.

Number of Items: 36

Format: Sample items presented.

Reliability: Alphas ranged from .51 to .81.

Validity: Correlations with other variables ranged from −.42 to .62.

Author: Yammauchi, H., and Tanaka, K.

Article: Relations of autonomy, self-referenced beliefs, and self-regulated learning among Japanese children.

Journal: *Psychological Reports*, June 1998, *82*(3) Part 1, 803–816.

Related Research: Niemivirta, M.

(1996). *Motivational-cognitive components in self-regulated learning.* Paper presented at the 5th International Conference on Motivation, March 1996, Landau, Germany.

8681

Test Name: SELF-REGULATED LEARNING STRATEGIES SCALE (JAPANESE)

Purpose: To measure cognitive strategy use and self-regulation when studying.

Number of Items: 17

Format: Five-point scales are anchored by 1 (not at all) and 5 (always). All items are presented in English.

Reliability: Alphas ranged from .73 to .78 across two factor subscales.

Author: Yamauchi, H., et al.

Article: Perceived control, autonomy, and self-regulated learning strategies among Japanese high school students.

Journal: *Psychological Reports*, December 1999, *85*(3, Part I), 779–798.

Related Research: Pintrich, P. R., & DeGroot, E. V. (1990). Motivational and self-regulated learning components of classroom academic performance. *Journal of Educational Psychology*, *82*, 33–40.

8682

Test Name: SELF-REGULATION INVENTORY

Purpose: To measure participants' self-regulatory attitudes and behaviors.

Number of Items: 50

Format: Responses are made on a 5-point, Likert-type scale ranging from 5 (strongly agree) to 1 (strongly disagree).

Reliability: Coefficient alpha was .91.

Author: Orange, C.

Article: Using peer modeling to teach self-regulation.

Journal: *Journal of Experimental Education*, Fall 1999, *68*(1), 21–39.

Related Research: Schunk, D. H. (1996). *Learning theories: An educational perspective.* Englewood Cliffs, NJ: Prentice Hall.

8683

Test Name: SELF-REPORT DELINQUENCY MEASURE

Purpose: To measure deviant peer involvement.

Number of Items: 41

Format: Scales range from 0 (none) to 4 (all).

Reliability: Coefficient alpha was .97.

Validity: Correlations with other variables ranged from −.23 to .77.

Author: Cashwell, C. S., and Vacc, N. A.

Article: Family functioning and risk behaviors: Influences on adolescent delinquency.

Journal: *The School Counselor*, November 1996, *44*(2), 105–114.

Related Research: Hindelang, M. J., et al. (1981). *Measuring delinquency.* Newbury Park, CA: Sage.

8684

Test Name: SELF-REPORTED ACADEMIC DISHONESTY SCALE

Purpose: To measure students'

self-reported academic dishonesty.

Number of Items: 12

Format: Responses are made on a 5-point scale ranging from 1 (never) to 5 (many times). All items are presented.

Reliability: Coefficient alpha was .83.

Author: McCabe, D. L., and Trevino, L. K.

Article: Individual and contextual influences on academic dishonesty: A multicampus investigation.

Journal: *Research in Higher Education*, June 1997, *38*(3), 379–396.

Related Research: McCabe, D. L., & Trevino, L. K. (1993). Academic dishonesty: Honor codes and other contextual influences. *Journal of Higher Education*, *64*(5), 520–538.

8685

Test Name: SELF-REPORTED DELINQUENCY QUESTIONNAIRE

Purpose: To assess involvement in delinquent behaviors over the last 12 months.

Number of Items: 27

Format: Includes 4 areas: Physical Violence, Theft, Vandalism, and Substance Use. Responses are made on a 4-point scale ranging from "never" to "very often."

Reliability: Alpha coefficients ranged from .74 to .77.

Author: Vitaro, F., et al.

Article: Disruptiveness, friends' characteristics, and delinquency in early adolescence: A test of two competing models of development.

Journal: *Child Development*, August 1997, *68*(4), 676–689.

Related Research: Tremblay, R. E., et al. (1994). Predicting early onset of male antisocial behavior from preschool behavior. *Archives of General Psychiatry*, *51*, 732–739.

8686

Test Name: SELF-TALK INVENTORY

Purpose: To identify self-talk of elementary school children.

Number of Items: 33

Format: Includes two scales: Positive Self-Talk and Negative Self-Talk.

Reliability: Reliability coefficients were .89 (positive) and .86 (negative).

Author: Burnett, P. C., and McCrindle, A. R.

Article: The relationship between significant others' positive and negative statements, self-talk, and self-esteem.

Journal: *Child Study Journal*, 1999, *29*(1), 39–48.

Related Research: Burnett, P. C. (1996). Children's self-talk and significant others' positive and negative statements. *Educational Psychology*, *16*, 57–67.

8687

Test Name: SENIOR BULLY/ VICTIM QUESTIONNAIRE

Purpose: To measure bullying.

Number of Items: 14

Format: Includes 2 factors: Bullying and Victimization. Employs a Likert scoring format.

Reliability: Alpha coefficients ranged from .76 to .95.

Author: Pelligrini, A. D., and Bartini, M.

Article: An empirical comparison of methods of sampling aggression and victimization in school settings.

Journal: *Journal of Educational Psychology*, June 2000, *92*(2), 360–366.

Related Research: Alweus, D. (1993). *Bullying at school.* Cambridge, MA: Blackwell.

8688

Test Name: SEVERITY OF ALCOHOL DEPENDENCE QUESTIONNAIRE

Purpose: To measure alcohol dependence.

Number of Items: 20

Format: Scales range from 0 (never or almost never) to 3 (nearly always). A sample item is presented.

Reliability: Alpha was .97.

Author: Sitharthan, T., et al.

Article: Cue exposure in moderation drinking: A comparison with cognitive-behavior therapy.

Journal: *Journal of Consulting and Clinical Psychology*, October 1997, *65*(5), 878–882.

Related Research: Stockwell, T., et al. (1994). The measurement of alcohol dependence and impaired control in community samples. *Addiction, 89,* 167–174.

8689

Test Name: SEVERITY OF VICTIMIZATION SCALE (JAPANESE VERSION)

Purpose: To measure the severity of victimization in school.

Number of Items: 7

Format: Frequency and type of bullying are rated on scales.

Reliability: Test-retest reliability (3 weeks) was .70.

Validity: Correlations with depression and self-esteem ranged from −.24 to .25.

Author: Matsui, T., et al.

Article: Long-term outcomes of early victimization by peers among Japanese male university students: Model of a vicious cycle.

Journal: *Psychological Reports*, December 1996, *79*(3) Part 1, 711–720.

8690

Test Name: SEXUAL ABUSE EXPOSURE QUESTIONNAIRE

Purpose: To measure exposure and duration of sexual abuse.

Number of Items: 10

Format: Each of 10 categories of abuse are rated for exposure and duration.

Reliability: Alphas ranged from .73 to .94.

Author: Rodriguez, N., et al.

Article: Posttraumatic stress disorder in adult female survivors of childhood sexual abuse: A comparison study.

Journal: *Journal of Consulting and Clinical Psychology*, February 1997, *65*(1), 53–59.

Related Research: Rowan, A. B., et al. (1994). Posttraumatic stress disorder in a clinical sample of adults sexually abused as children. *Child Abuse and Neglect, 18,* 51–61.

8691

Test Name: SEXUAL BEHAVIOR SCALE

Purpose: To assess intention for future sexual behavior.

Number of Items: 4

Format: Scales range from 1 (very unlikely or very unsure) to 5 (very likely or very sure). All items are presented.

Reliability: Coefficient alpha was .77.

Author: East, P. L.

Article: Racial and ethnic differences in girls' sexual, marital, and birth expectations.

Journal: *Journal of Marriage and the Family*, February 1998, *60*(1), 150–162.

Related Research: Olsen, J., et al. (1992). The effects of abstinence sex education programs on virgin versus nonvirgin students. *Journal of Research and Development in Education, 25,* 69–75.

8692

Test Name: SEXUAL EXPERIENCES QUESTIONNAIRE

Purpose: To identify gender harassment, unwanted sexual attention, and sexual coercion.

Number of Items: 18

Format: Responses are made on a 5-point scale ranging from "never" to "most of the time."

Reliability: Reliability coefficients were .77 and .81.

Validity: Correlations with other variables ranged from −.36 to .27.

Author: Munson, L. J., et al.

Article: Longitudinal analysis of dispositional influences and sexual harassment: Effects on job and psychological outcomes.

Journal: *Personnel Psychology*, Spring 2000, *53*(1), 21–46.

Related Research: Fitzgerald, L. F., et al. (1988). Academic harassment: Sex and denial in scholarly garb. *Psychology of Women Quarterly, 12,* 329–340.

8693

Test Name: SEXUAL EXPERIENCES QUESTIONNAIRE

Purpose: To determine the prevalence of sexual harassment.

Number of Items: 19

Format: Includes 3 subscales: Gender Harassment, Unwanted Sexual Attention, and Sexual Coercion. Also, one item assessing attempted sexual assault. Responses are made on a 5-point scale ranging from 1 (never) to 5 (most of the time). Examples are presented.

Reliability: Alpha coefficients ranged from .77 to .83.

Validity: Correlations with other variables ranged from −.42 to .46.

Author: O'Connell, C. E., and Korabik, K.

Article: Sexual harassment: The relationship of personal vulnerability, work context, perpetrator status, and types of harassment to outcomes.

Journal: *Journal of Vocational Behavior,* June 2000, *56*(3), 299–329.

Related Research: Fitzgerald, L. F., et al. (1993). *Sexual Experiences Questionnaire, Form W.* Unpublished research scale, Department of Psychology, University of Illinois at Urbana-Champaigne.

8694

Test Name: SEXUAL EXPERIENCES QUESTIONNAIRE

Purpose: To measure sexual harassment, gender harassment, unwanted sexual attention, and sexual coercion.

Number of Items: 23

Format: Scales range from 1 (never) to 5 (most of the time).

Reliability: Coefficient alpha was .93.

Validity: Correlations with other variables ranged from −.28 to .41.

Author: Donovan, M. A., et al.

Article: The Perceptions of Fair Interpersonal Treatment Scale: Development and validation of a measure of interpersonal treatment in the workplace.

Journal: *Journal of Applied Psychology,* October 1998, *83*(5), 683–692.

Related Research: Fitzgerald, L. F., et al. (1995). Measuring sexual harassment: Theoretical and psychometric advances. *Basic and Applied Social Psychology, 17,* 425–427.

8695

Test Name: SEXUAL EXPERIENCES QUESTIONNAIRE—REVISED

Purpose: To measure sexual harassment experiences.

Number of Items: 18

Format: Five-point scales.

Reliability: Alpha coefficients ranged from .79 to .86 across samples.

Validity: Correlations with other variables ranged from −.36 to .21.

Author: Schnieder, K. T., et al.

Article: Job-related and psychological effects of sexual harassment in the workplace:

Empirical evidence from two organizations.

Journal: *Journal of Applied Psychology,* June 1997, *82*(3), 401–415.

Related Research: Fitzgerald, L. F., et al. (1995). Measuring sexual harassment: Theoretical and psychometric advances. *Basic and Applied Social Psychology, 17,* 425–445.

8696

Test Name: SEXUAL EXPERIENCE SURVEY

Purpose: To measure participation in a range of sexually aggressive situations.

Number of Items: 10

Reliability: Internal consistency was .89. Test-retest (1 week) reliability was .89.

Validity: Correlations with responses to an interviewer several months later was .93.

Author: Heppner, M. J., et al.

Article: Examining immediate and long-term efficacy of rape prevention programming with racially diverse college men.

Journal: *Journal of Counseling Psychology,* January 1999, *46*(1), 16–26.

Related Research: Koss, M. P., & Gidycz, C. A. (1987). Sexual Experiences Survey: Reliability and validity. *Journal of Consulting and Clinical Psychology, 53,* 422–423.

8697

Test Name: SEXUAL EXPERIENCES SURVEY

Purpose: To identify extent of sexual experiences with women.

Number of Items: 11

Format: Responses are never,

once, twice, several times, and often.

Reliability: Coefficient alpha was .89.

Author: Caron, S. L., et al.

Article: Athletes and rape: Is there a connection?

Journal: *Perceptual and Motor Skills*, December 1997, *85*(3, Part 2), 1379–1393.

Related Research: Koss, M. P., & Gaines, J. A. (1993). The prediction of sexual aggression by alcohol use, athletic participation, and fraternity affiliation. *Journal of Interpersonal Violence*, *8*, 94–108.

8698

Test Name: SEXUAL EXPERIENCES SURVEY

Purpose: To assess women's sexual victimization by men.

Number of Items: 13

Format: Responses to each item are either "yes" or "no."

Reliability: Internal consistency estimate was .74. Test-retest (1 week) reliability was .93.

Author: Ingram, K. M., et al.

Article: The relationship of victimization experiences to psychological well-being among homeless women and low-income housed women.

Journal: *Journal of Counseling Psychology*, April 1996, *43*(2), 218–227.

Related Research: Koss, M. P., & Oros, C. J. (1982). Sexual Experiences Survey: A research instrument investigating sexual aggression and victimization. *Journal of Consulting and Clinical Psychology*, *50*, 455–457.

8699

Test Name: SEXUAL EXPERIENCES SURVEY— MODIFIED

Purpose: To measure childhood sexual abuse by retrospective self-report by adults with limited reading ability.

Number of Items: 9

Format: Sample items are presented.

Reliability: Coefficient alpha was .84.

Author: Roosa, M. W., et al.

Article: The relationship of childhood sexual abuse to teenage pregnancy.

Journal: *Journal of Marriage and the Family*, February 1997, *59*(1), 119–130.

Related Research: Koss, M. P., & Oros, C. J. (1982). Sexual Experiences Survey: A research instrument in investigating sexual aggression and victimization. *Journal of Consulting and Clinical Psychology*, *50*, 455–457.

Christopher, F. S., et al. (1998). Premarital sexual aggressors: A multivariate analysis of social, relational, and individual variables. *Journal of Marriage and the Family*, *60*, 56–69.

8700

Test Name: SEXUAL OPINION SURVEY

Purpose: To assess personal sexual behaviors.

Number of Items: 21

Format: Scales range from 1 (strongly disagree) to 5 (strongly agree). A sample item is presented.

Reliability: Test-retest reliabilities (2 months) were .80 (women) and .85 (men).

Authors: Caron, S. L., and Carter, D. B.

Article: The relationships among sex role orientation, egalitarianism, attitudes toward sexuality, and attitudes toward violence against women.

Journal: *Journal of Social Psychology*, October 1997, *137*(5), 568–587.

Related Research: Fisher, W. A., et al. (1983). Emotional barriers to contraception. In J. Byrne & W. A. Fisher (Eds.), *Adolescents, sex, and contraception* (pp. 207–239). Hillsdale, NJ: Erlbaum.

8701

Test Name: SEXUALITY SCALES

Purpose: To assess the dimensions of sexuality by rating descriptive adjectives.

Number of Items: 67

Format: Scales range from 1 (extremely inaccurate) to 9 (extremely accurate). All items are presented.

Reliability: Alpha coefficients ranged from .74 to .96. Test-retest reliabilities (4 scales) ranged from .70 to .92.

Validity: Validity indexes ranged from −.51 to .61. Correlations with Big Five factors ranged from −.39 to .45.

Author: Schmitt, D. P., and Buss, D. M.

Article: Sexual dimensions of person description: Beyond or subsumed by the Big Five?

Journal: *Journal of Research in Personality*, June 2000, *34*(2), 141–177.

8702

Test Name: SHORT MICHIGAN ALCOHOLISM SCREENING TEST

Purpose: To detect alcoholism.

Number of Items: 13

Format: Includes two versions: one for mother, one for father.

Reliability: Alpha coefficients ranged from .76 to 93.

Validity: Correlation with other variables ranged from -06 to 34 ($N = 152$).

Author: Mothersead, P. K., et al.

Article: Attachment, family dysfunction, parental alcoholism, and interpersonal distress in late adolescence: A structural model.

Journal: *Journal of Counseling Psychology*, April 1998, *45*(2), 196–203.

Related Research: Selzer, M. L., & Vinokur, A. (1975). A self-administered Short Michigan Alcoholism Screening Test (SMAST). *Journal of Studies on Alcohol*, *36*, 117–126.

8703

Test Name: SITUATIONAL HUMOR RESPONSE SCALE

Purpose: To assess the frequency of responding with humor in a variety of situations.

Number of Items: 21

Format: Five-point Guttman-type Scale.

Reliability: Cronbach alphas ranged from .70 to .83. Test-retest reliability was .70.

Author: Perlini, A. H., et al.

Article: Effects of humor on test anxiety and performance.

Journal: *Psychological Reports*, June 1999, *84*(3) Part 2, 1203–1213.

Related Research: Martin, R. A., & Leftcourt, H. M. (1984). Situational humor response questionnaire: Quantitative measure of sense of humor.

Journal of Personality and Social Psychology, *47*, 145–155.

8704

Test Name: SLEEP HYGIENE SELF-TEST

Purpose: To measure adaptive and non-adaptive sleep-related activities engaged in during the past month.

Number of Items: 30

Format: Yes/no Format. All items are presented.

Reliability: Alpha was .54.

Validity: Correlations with other variables ranged from .10 to .20.

Author: Blake, D. D., and Gomez, M. H.

Article: A scale for assessing sleep hygiene: Preliminary data.

Journal: *Psychological Reports*, December 1998, *83*(3) Part 2, 1175–1178.

8705

Test Name: SLEEP QUESTIONNAIRE

Purpose: To assess sleep patterns.

Number of Items: 55

Format: Includes 7 factors: Depth of Sleep, Difficulties in Waking Up, Quality and Latency of Sleep, Negative Affect in Dreams, Length of Sleep, Dream Recall and Vividness, and Sleep Irregularity. Employs Likert-type items.

Reliability: Alpha coefficients ranged from .58 to .88.

Author: Verlander, L. A., et al.

Article: Stress and sleep patterns of college students.

Journal: *Perceptual and Motor Skills*, June 1999, *88*(3) Part 1, 893–898.

Related Research: Domino, G., et al. (1984). Subjective assessment of sleep by sleep questionnaire. *Perceptual and Motor Skills*, *59*, 163–170.

8706

Test Name: SLEEP/WAKE BEHAVIOR PROBLEMS SCALE

Purpose: To determine frequency of indicators of erratic sleep/wake behaviors over the course of the last 2 weeks.

Number of Items: 10

Format: Responses are made on a 5-point scale ranging from 5 (everyday) to 1 (never).

Reliability: Coefficient alpha was .75.

Author: Wolfson, A. R., and Carskadon, M. A.

Article: Sleep schedules and daytime functioning in adolescents.

Journal: *Child Development*, August 1998, *69*(4), 875–887.

Related Research: Carskadon, M. A., et al. (1991). Reliability of six scales in a sleep questionnaire for adolescents. *Sleep Research*, *20*, 421.

8707

Test Name: SOCIAL AND PERSONAL COMPETENCE MEASURES FOR ADOLESCENTS

Purpose: To measure skills use in drug prevention programs.

Number of Items: 24

Format: Five-point scales range from (1) definitely would to (5) definitely would not, or from (1) never to (5) always. Sample items are presented.

Reliability: Alphas ranged from .73 to .89 across subscales.

Author: Epstein, J. A., et al.

Article: Reliability of social and personal competence measures for adolescents.

Journal: *Psychological Reports*, October 1997, *81*(2), 449–450.

Related Research: Botvin, G. J., et al. (1997). School-based drug abuse prevention with inner-city minority youth. *Journal of Child and Adolescent Substance Abuse*, *6*, 5–19.

8708

Test Name: SOCIAL BEHAVIOR QUESTIONNAIRE

Purpose: To provide teachers' behavioral ratings of externalizing behavior problems.

Number of Items: 10

Format: Includes 3 problem areas: Physical Aggression, Opposition, and Hyperactivity. All items are included.

Reliability: Alpha coefficients ranged from .78 to .89.

Author: Nagin, D., and Tremblay, R. E.

Article: Trajectories of boys' physical aggression, opposition, and hyperactivity on the path to physically violent and nonviolent juvenile delinquency.

Journal: *Child Development*, September/October 1999, *70*(5), 1181–1196.

Related Research: Tremblay, R. E., et al. (1991). Disruptive boys with stable and unstable high fighting behavior patterns during junior elementary school. *Journal of Abnormal Child Psychology*, *19*, 285–300.

8709

Test Name: SOCIAL BEHAVIOR QUESTIONNAIRE

Purpose: To measure social behavior.

Number of Items: 32

Format: Includes Disruptiveness, Inattention, Anxiety Withdrawal, and Prosocial Behavior. Responses are made on a scale ranging from 0 (did not apply) to 2 (applied often).

Reliability: Alpha coefficients ranged from .85 to .75.

Author: Vitaro, F., et al.

Article: Disruptiveness, friends' characteristics, and delinquency in early adolescence: A test of two competing models of development.

Journal: *Child Development*, August 1997, *68*(4), 676–689.

Related Research: Tremblay, R. E., et al. (1991). Disruptive boys with stable and unstable high fighting behavior patterns during elementary school. *Journal of Abnormal Child Psychology*, *19*, 285–300.

8710

Test Name: SOCIAL BEHAVIOR SCALE

Purpose: To assess a child's social behavior.

Number of Items: 20

Format: Includes Disruptive Behavior, Aggression, and Prosocial Behavior. Sample items are presented. Items are rated from 1 (never) to 7 (almost always).

Reliability: Alpha coefficients ranged from .75 to .94.

Author: Eisenberg, N., et al.

Article: Contemporaneous and longitudinal prediction of children's social functioning from regulation and emotionality.

Journal: *Child Development*, August 1997, *68*(4), 642–664.

Related Research: Coie, J. D., et al. (1993). *A teacher checklist of children's social behavior*. Unpublished manuscript, Duke University.

8711

Test Name: SOUTH OAKS GAMBLING SCREEN

Purpose: To measure gambling behavior.

Number of Items: 16

Format: Yes/no format.

Reliability: Test-retest (30 days or more) was .71. Alpha was .97.

Validity: Correlation with OSM-III-R was .94.

Author: Kweitel, R., and Allen, F. C. L.

Article: Cognitive processes associated with gambling behavior.

Journal: *Psychological Reports*, February 1998, *82*(1), 147–153.

Related Research: Lesieur, H. R., & Blume, S. B. (1987). The South Oaks Gambling Screen (SOGS): A new instrument for the identification of pathological gamblers. *American Journal of Psychiatry*, *144*, 1184–1188.

8712

Test Name: STANFORD HYPNOTIC CLINICAL SCALE FOR CHILDREN

Purpose: To measure children's hypnotizability.

Number of Items: 6

Format: Includes 6 tasks: suggested hand lowering, arm rigidity, visual and auditory hallucinations, a dream, and age regression.

Validity: Correlations with the adult scale was .67.

Author: Smith, J. T., et al.

Article: Comparison of hypnosis and distraction in severely ill children undergoing painful medical procedures.

Journal: *Journal of Counseling Psychology*, April 1996, *43*(2), 187–195.

Related Research: Morgan, A. H., & Hilgard, J. R. (1979). The Stanford Hypnotic Clinical Scale for Children. *American Journal of Clinical Hypnosis*, *21*, 148–169.

8713

Test Name: STUDENT SCALE OF SELF-REGULATION

Purpose: To measure students' self-regulatory behavior.

Number of Items: 16

Format: Responses are made on a 7-point scale ranging from 1 (I never do this) to 7 (I always do this). All items are presented.

Reliability: Coefficient alpha was .82 ($N = 105$).

Author: Martinez-Pons, M.

Article: Test of a model of parental inducement of academic self-regulation.

Journal: *Journal of Experimental Education*, Spring 1996, *64*(3), 213–227.

Related Research: Martinez-Pons, M. (1996, April). *Perceived self-efficacy to self-regulate academic learning: Emerging evidence of construct validity*. Paper presented at the annual meeting of the American Educational Research Association, New York.

8714

Test Name: STUDY HABITS INVENTORY

Purpose: To assess typical study behaviors of college students.

Number of Items: 63

Format: True-false format. Includes both effective and ineffective study behaviors.

Reliability: The mean alpha coefficient was .85. Two-week test-retest coefficient was .82.

Validity: Correlation with foreign-language achievement was −.06.

Author: Onwueghuzie, A. J., et al.

Article: Cognitive, affective, personality, and demographic predictors of foreign-language achievement.

Journal: *Journal of Educational Research*, September/October 2000, *94*(1), 3–15.

Related Research: Jones, C. H., & Slate, J. R. (1992). *Technical manual for the Study Habits Inventory*. Unpublished manuscript. Arkansas State University, AR: State University.

8715

Test Name: SUBSTANCE USE SCALES

Purpose: To measure general and on-the-job substance use.

Number of Items: 16

Format: Scales range from "never" to "every day" or "very often."

Reliability: Coefficient alpha was .93 (general use) and .85 (on-the-job use).

Validity: Correlations with other variables ranged from −.12 to .56.

Author: Frone, M. R.

Article: Predictors of work injuries among employed adolescents.

Journal: *Journal of Applied*

Psychology, August 1998, *83*(4), 565–576.

8716

Test Name: TEACHER BEHAVIOR SCALES

Purpose: To assess teacher organization and preparation, and skill and clarity.

Number of Items: 10

Format: Scales range from 1 (never) to 4 (very often). All items are presented.

Reliability: Alpha coefficients ranged from .86 to .87 across two subscales.

Author: Pascarella, E., et al.

Article: Effects of teacher organization/preparation and teacher skill/clarity on general cognitive skills in college.

Journal: *Journal of College Student Development*, January/February 1996, *37*(1), 7–19.

Related Research: Pace, C. (1984). *Measuring the quality of college student experiences*. Los Angeles: Higher Education Research Institute, Graduate School of Education, University of California at Los Angeles.

8717

Test Name: TEACHER BEHAVIORAL INDICANTS OF IMMEDIACY SCALE

Purpose: To measure a teacher's immediacy (the behavior that diminishes physical and psychological distance between people).

Number of Items: 16

Format: Seven-point scales. A sample item is presented.

Reliability: Internal consistency was .83.

Validity: Correlations with other

variables ranged from −.60 to −.37.

Author: Rowden, G. V., and Carlson, R. E.

Article: Gender issues and student perceptions of instructors' immediacy and evaluation of teaching and course.

Journal: *Psychological Reports*, June 1996, 78(3) Part 1, 835–839.

Related Research: Andersen, J. F. (1979). Teacher immediacy as a predictor of teaching effectiveness. In D. Nimmo (Ed.), *Communication Yearbook 3* (pp. 543–559), New Brunswick, NJ: Transaction Books.

8718

Test Name: TEACHER–CHILD RATING SCALE—PROBLEM BEHAVIORS SECTION

Purpose: To identify problem behaviors of elementary school children.

Number of Items: 18

Format: Responses are made on a 5-point scale ranging from 1 (not a problem) to 5 (very serious problem). Includes 3 subscales: Acting Out, Shy/Anxious, and Learning Problems.

Reliability: Interitem subscale reliabilities ranged from .85 to .95. Test-retest (20 weeks) reliabilities ranged from .66 to .86.

Author: Zellman, G. L., and Waterman, J. M.

Article: Understanding the impact of parent school involvement on children's educational outcomes.

Journal: *Journal of Educational Research*, July/August 1998, 91(6), 370–380.

Related Research: Hightower, A., et al. (1986). The Teacher-Child Rating Scale: A brief objective

measure of elementary children's school problem behaviors and competencies. *School Psychology Review*, 15, 393–409.

8719

Test Name: TEACHER RATED ADJUSTMENT SCALE

Purpose: To enable teachers to rate students' behavior.

Number of Items: 10

Format: Includes 3 subscales: Emotional Disturbance, Conduct Disturbance, and Good Adjustment. Examples are presented.

Reliability: Alpha coefficients ranged from .43 to .67.

Author: McCall, R. B., et al.

Article: The nature and correlates of underachievement among elementary school children in Hong Kong.

Journal: *Child Development*, May/June 2000, 71(3), 785–801.

Related Research: Spivack, G., et al. (1986). Early classroom behaviors and later misconduct. *Developmental Psychology*, 22, 124–131.

8720

Test Name: TEACHER'S RATING SCALE OF CHILD'S ACTUAL BEHAVIOR

Purpose: To provide for teacher's appraisals for children's competencies.

Number of Items: 15

Format: Includes 5 subscales.

Reliability: Alpha coefficients ranged from .93 to .97. Test-retest (4 months) reliability ranged from .67 to .73.

Author: Cole, D. A., et al.

Article: Children's over- and

underestimation of academic competence: A longitudinal study of gender differences, depression, and anxiety.

Journal: *Child Development*, March/April 1999, 70(2), 459–473.

Related Research: Harter, S. (1985). *Self-Perception Profile for Children*. Denver, CO: University of Denver.

8721

Test Name: TEACHING BEHAVIOR RATING SCALE

Purpose: To measure teacher behavior.

Number of Items: 15

Format: Eleven-point rating scales range from (1) very poor to (11) excellent. All items are presented.

Reliability: Alpha was .98.

Validity: Correlations with other variables ranged from −.55 to .73.

Author: Randhawa, B. S., and Pavelich, B.

Article: Evidence of validity for the Teacher Behavior Rating Scale.

Journal: *Psychological Reports*, October 1997, 81(2), 451–461.

8722

Test Name: TEAM-TASK ASSERTIVENESS SCALE

Purpose: To assess team-task assertiveness.

Number of Items: 9

Format: Responses are made on a 6-point Likert scale.

Reliability: Reliability coefficients were .67 and .73.

Validity: Correlations with other variables ranged from .21 to .63.

Author: Smith-Jentsch, K. A., et al.

Article: Training team performance-related assertiveness.

Journal: *Personnel Psychology*, Winter 1996, *49*(4), 909–936.

Related Research: Smith, K., et al. (1993, April). *Development of a scale to measure assertiveness in team situations*. Poster presented at the eighth annual conference of the Society for Industrial and Organizational Psychology, San Francisco.

8723

Test Name: TIME MANAGEMENT BEHAVIOR SCALE

Purpose: To assess time management practices and behaviors.

Number of Items: 46

Format: Includes 4 subscales: Setting Goals and Priorities, Mechanics, Perceived Control of Time, and Preference for Organization. Responses are made on a 5-point scale ranging from 1 (seldom true) to 5 (very often true). All items are presented.

Reliability: Alpha coefficients ranged from .62 to .80.

Author: Mudrak, P. E.

Article: The structure of perceptions of time.

Journal: *Educational and Psychological Measurement*, April 1997, *57*(2), 222–240.

Related Research: Macan, T. H., et al. (1990). College students' time management: Co-relations with academic performance and stress. *Journal of Educational Psychology*, *82*, 760–768.

8724

Test Name: TIME MANAGEMENT QUESTIONNAIRE

Purpose: To assess short-term and long-term time management.

Number of Items: 7

Format: Five-point scales are anchored by 1 (never) and 5 (always).

Reliability: Alpha coefficients ranged were .85 (short-term) and .73 (long-term).

Author: Barling, J., et al.

Article: Time management and achievement striving interact to predict car sales performance.

Journal: *Journal of Applied Psychology*, December 1996, *81(6)*, 821–826.

Related Research: Britton, B. K., & Tesser, A. (1991). Effects of time management practices on college grades. *Journal of Educational Psychology*, *83*, 405–410.

8725

Test Name: TIME STRUCTURE QUESTIONNAIRE

Purpose: To assess time structuring.

Number of Items: 20

Format: Includes 5 subscales: Sense of Purpose, Structure Routine, Present Orientation, Effective Organization, and Persistence. Responses are made on a 7-point scale ranging from 1 (never) to 7 (always). All items are presented.

Reliability: Alpha coefficients ranged from .68 to .77.

Author: Mudrak, P. E.

Article: The structure of perceptions of time.

Journal: *Educational and*

Psychological Measurement, April 1997, *57*(2), 222–240.

Related Research: Feather, N. T., & Bond, M. J. (1983). Time structure and purposeful activity among employed and unemployed university graduates. *Journal of Occupational Psychology*, 56, 241–354.

8726

Test Name: TIMED SELF-INJURIOUS BEHAVIOR SCALE

Purpose: To score the frequency of self-injurious behaviors in a short period of time.

Number of Items: 16

Time Required: 10 minutes

Format: Raters rate behavior in 10-second subdivisions. All items are presented.

Reliability: Rater agreement ranged from .38 to .82 across behaviors.

Author: Brasic, J. R., et al.

Article: Clinical assessment of self-injurious behavior.

Journal: *Psychological Reports*, February 1997, *80*(1), 155–160.

Related Research: Campbell, M. (1985). Protocol for rating drug-related AIMS, stereotyping and CPRS assessments. *Psychopharmacology Bulletin*, *21*, 1081–1082.

8727

Test Name: TODDLER BEHAVIOR CHECKLIST

Purpose: To enable parents to assess the social-emotional characteristics of young preschoolers.

Number of Items: 36

Format: Includes 2 factors: Opposition and Physical Aggression.

Reliability: Alpha coefficients were .91 to .83.

Author: Shaw, D. S., et al.

Article: A prospective study of the effects of marital status and family relations on young children's adjustment among African American and European American families.

Journal: *Child Development*, May/June 1999, *70*(3), 742–755.

Related Research: Larzelere, R. E., et al. (1989). The Toddler Behavior Checklist: A parent completed assessment of social-emotional characteristics of young preschoolers. *Family Relations*, *38*, 418–425.

8728

Test Name: TODDLER BEHAVIOR CHECKLIST

Purpose: To measure frequency of behavior in the past 2 months.

Number of Items: 103

Format: Checklist format.

Reliability: Alpha coefficients on two subscales were .80 and .91.

Author: Larzelere, R. E., et al.

Article: Punishment enhances reasoning's effectiveness as a disciplinary response to toddlers.

Journal: *Journal of Marriage and the Family*, May 1998, *60*(2), 388–403.

Related Research: Larzelere, R. E., et al. (1989). The Toddler Behavior Checklist: A parent-completed assessment of socio-emotional characteristics of young preschoolers. *Family Relations*, *38*, 418–425.

8729

Test Name: TRAINER BEHAVIOR SCALE

Purpose: To measure group leader behavior.

Number of Items: 28

Format: Includes 7 dimensions: Congruence-Empathy, Conceptual Input, Conditionality, Perceptiveness, Openness, Affection, and Dominance. Responses are made on a 5-point Likert scale ranging from 1 (strongly agree) to 5 (strongly disagree). Examples are presented.

Reliability: Alpha coefficients ranged from .87 to .94.

Author: Kivlighan, Jr., D. M., et al.

Article: Helpful impacts in group counseling: Development of a multidimensional rating system.

Journal: *Journal of Counseling Psychology*, July 1996, *43*(3), 347–355.

Related Research: Bolman, L. (1971). Some effects of trainers on their T groups. *The Journal of Applied Behavioral Science*, 7, 309–325.

8730

Test Name: TREATMENT-SEEKING BEHAVIOR SCALE

Purpose: To assess treatment seeking behavior.

Number of Items: 14

Format: Six-point scales are anchored by 0 (completely disagree) and 5 (completely agree).

Reliability: Alphas ranged from .65 to .70.

Validity: Correlations with other variables ranged from −.21 to .31.

Author: Hirai, M., and Clum, G. A.

Article: Development, reliability,

and validity of the Beliefs Toward Mental Illness Scale.

Journal: *Journal of Psychopathology and Behavioral Assessment*, September 2000, *22*(3), 221–236.

8731

Test Name: UNION PARTICIPATION SCALE

Purpose: To measure amount and strength of participation in union activities.

Number of Items: 15

Format: Each item is scored yes or no on participation. Frequency of participation is rated from 1 (never) to 5 (very often).

Reliability: Coefficient alpha was .91.

Validity: Correlations with other variables ranged from −.31 to .51.

Author: Bulger, C. A., and Mellor, S.

Article: Self-efficacy as a mediator of the relationship between perceived union barriers and women's participation in union activities.

Journal: *Journal of Applied Psychology*, December 1997, *82*(6), 935–944.

8732

Test Name: UPWARD CONTROLLINGNESS SCALE

Purpose: To assess subordinates use of influence.

Number of Items: 20

Format: Scales range from 1 (never) to 5 (usually).

Reliability: Coefficient alpha was .77.

Validity: Correlations with other

variables ranged from −.09 to .44.

Author: Schriesheim, C. A., et al.

Article: Investigating contingencies: An examination of the impact of span of supervision and upward controllingness on leader-member exchange using traditional and multivariate within- and between-entities analysis.

Journal: *Journal of Applied Psychology*, October 2000, *85*(5), 659–677.

Related Research: Tepper, B. J. (1990). *Influence tactics endorsed in charismatic and non-charismatic leader-follower interactions.* Unpublished doctoral dissertation, Department of Psychology, University of Miami.

8733

Test Name: VERBAL AND ACTUAL COMMITMENT SUBSCALES

Purpose: To measure future commitments to action and self-reported actual behavior.

Number of Items: 20

Format: Includes two subscales of the Ecology Scale: Verbal Commitment and Actual Commitment. Responses are true-false.

Reliability: Alpha coefficients ranged from .57 to .75.

Validity: Correlations with other variables ranged from .15 to .63.

Author: Der-Karabetian, A., et al.

Article: Environmental risk perception, activism and world-mindedness among samples of British and U.S. college students.

Journal: *Perceptual and Motor Skills*, October 1996, *83*(2), 451–462.

Related Research: Maloney, M. P., et al. (1975). A revised measurement of ecological attitudes and knowledge. *American Psychologist*, *30*, 787–790.

8734

Test Name: WEIGHT MANAGEMENT QUESTIONNAIRE

Purpose: To measure current and previous eating behaviors, type of exercise, and binge eating.

Number of Items: 31

Format: Frequency scales.

Reliability: Test-retest reliabilities (2 weeks) ranged from .73 to .90 across subscales.

Author: Baldo, T. D., et al.

Article: Effects of intrafamilial sexual assault on eating behaviors.

Journal: *Psychological Reports*, October 1996, *79*(2), 531–536.

Related Research: Mintz, L. B., & Betz, N. E. (1988). Prevalence and correlates of disordered behaviors among undergraduate women. *Journal of Counseling Psychology*, *35*, 463–471.

8735

Test Name: WELL-BEING SCALE FOR ALCOHOLICS

Purpose: To assess well-being as perceived by abstinent and non-abstinent alcoholics.

Number of Items: 10

Format: Scales range from 0 (disagree completely) to 8 (agree completely). Sample items are presented.

Reliability: Coefficient alpha was .90.

Author: Kairouz, S., and Dube, L.

Article: Abstinence and well being among alcoholics anonymous: Personal experience and social perceptions.

Journal: *Journal of Social Psychology*, October 2000, *140*(5), 565–579.

Related Research: Ryff, C. D. (1989). Happiness is everything, or is it? Explorations on the meaning of psychological well-being. *Journal of Personality and Social Psychology*, *57*, 1069–1081.

8736

Test Name: WORK ADDICTION RISK TEST

Purpose: To measure work addiction.

Number of Items: 25

Format: Responses are made on a 4-point scale ranging from "never true" to "always true." All items are presented.

Reliability: Test-retest (2 weeks) reliability was .83. Coefficient alpha was .85. Spearman-Brown split-half coefficient was .85.

Validity: Correlations with other variables ranged from .20 to .40.

Author: Robinson, B. E.

Article: The Work Addiction Risk Test: Development of a tentative measure of workaholism.

Journal: *Perceptual and Motor Skills*, February 1999, *88*(1), 199–210.

Related Research: Robinson, B. E., and Post, P. (1995). Split-half reliability of the Work Addiction Risk Test: Development of a measure of workaholism. *Psychological Reports*, *76*, 1226.

8737

Test Name: WORK-PERFORMANCE SCALE

Purpose: To assess work performance.

Number of Items: 5

Format: Responses are made on a 5-point frequency-based scale. A sample item is presented.

Reliability: Coefficient alpha was .77.

Validity: Correlations with other variables ranged from −.32 to .37.

Author: Frone, M. R., et al.

Article: Developing and testing an integrative model of the work-family interface.

Journal: *Journal of Vocational Behavior*, April 1997, *50*(2), 145–167.

Related Research: Williams, L. J., & Anderson, S. E. (1991). Job satisfaction and organizational commitment as predictors of organizational citizenship and in-role behaviors. *Journal of Management*, *17*(3), 601–617.

8738

Test Name: YALE-BROWN OBSESSIVE-COMPULSIVE SCALE

Purpose: To measure symptom severity and change in obsessive-compulsive behavior.

Number of Items: 10

Format: Five-point scales are anchored by 0 (none) and 5 (extreme).

Reliability: Alpha coefficients ranged from .85 to .91.

Author: McKay, D., et al.

Article: The Yale-Brown Obsessive-Compulsive Scale: Confirmatory factor analysis.

Journal: *Journal of Psychopathology and Behavioral Assessment*, September 1998, *20*(3), 265–274.

Related Research: Goodman, W. K., et al. (1989). The Yale-Brown Obsessive-Compulsive Scale I: Developmental use and reliability. *Archives of General Psychiatry*, *46*, 1006–1011.

8739

Test Name: YOUTH SELF-REPORT

Purpose: To evaluate behavior and emotional psychopathology in youth and adolescents.

Number of Items: 112

Format: Three-point scales are anchored by 0 (not) and 2 (often).

Reliability: Alphas ranged from .59 to .89 across problem types.

Validity: Correlations with symptoms of anxiety ranged from −.18 to .77.

Author: Muris, P., et al.

Article: Associations of symptoms of anxiety disorders and self-reported behavior problems in normal children.

Journal: *Psychological Reports*, February 2000, *86*(1), 157–162.

Related Research: Achenbach, T. M. (1991). *Manual for the Youth Self-Report and 1991 Profile*. Burlington, VT: University of Vermont, Department of Psychiatry.

CHAPTER 9
Communication

8740

Test Name: AFFECTIVE COMMUNICATION TEST

Purpose: To provide a self-report measure for emotional expressiveness.

Number of Items: 13

Format: Responses are made on a 11-point scale ranging from 0 (not at all true of me) to 10 (very true of me).

Reliability: Alpha coefficients were .77 and .76. Test-retest (2 months) reliability was .90.

Validity: Correlations with other variables ranged from −.15 to .31.

Author: Donavan, J. M.

Article: Reinterpreting telepathy as unusual experiences of empathy and charisma.

Journal: *Perceptual and Motor Skills*, August 1998, *87*(1), 131–146.

Related Research: Friedman, H. S., et al. (1980). Understanding and assessing nonverbal expressiveness: The Affective Communication Test. *Journal of Personality and Social Psychology*, *39*, 333–351.

8741

Test Name: AUTONOMIC NERVOUS SYSTEM REACTIVITY SCALE

Purpose: To measure intensity of autonomic feedback in response to positive and negative evocative stimuli.

Number of Items: 20

Format: Likert format. All items are presented.

Reliability: Coefficient alpha was .90.

Validity: Correlations with other variables ranged from −.30 to .38.

Author: Klein, D. J., and Verbeke, W.

Article: Autonomic feedback in stressful environments: How do individual differences in autonomic feedback relate to burnout, job performance, and job attitudes in salespeople?

Journal: *Journal of Applied Psychology*, December 1999, *84*(6), 911–924.

8742

Test Name: BALANCED INVENTORY OF DESIRABLE RESPONDING

Purpose: To measure the tendency to give self-reports that are positively balanced.

Number of Items: 20

Format: Seven-point scales range from 1 (not true) to 7 (very true). A sample item is presented.

Reliability: Coefficient alpha was .77.

Validity: Correlations with other variables ranged from −.29 to .20.

Author: Martocchio, J. J., and Judge, T. A.

Article: Relationship between conscientiousness and learning in employee training: Mediating influences of self-deception and self-efficacy.

Journal: *Journal of Applied Psychology*, October 1997, *82*(5), 764–773.

Related Research: Paulhus, D. L. (1991). Measurement and control of response bias. In J. P. Robinson et al. (Eds.), *Measures of personality and social psychological attitudes* (pp. 17–59). San Diego, CA: Academic Press.

8743

Test Name: BALANCED INVENTORY OF DESIRABLE RESPONDING

Purpose: To measure self-deception and impression management.

Number of Items: 40

Format: Five-point Likert format.

Reliability: Alpha coefficients ranged from .74 to .86.

Validity: Correlations with other variables ranged from −.10 to .54.

Author: Barrick, M. R., and Mount, M. K.

Article: Effects of impression management and self-deception on the predictive validity of personality constructs.

Journal: *Journal of Applied Psychology*, June 1996, *81*(3), 261–272.

Related Research: Paulhus, D. L. (1988). Measurement and control of response bias. In J. P. Robinson et al. (Eds.), *Measures of personality and social psychological attitudes* (Vol. 1, pp. 17–60) New York: Academic Press.

8744

Test Name: COMMUNICATION PATTERNS QUESTIONNAIRE

Purpose: To measure spouse perceptions of communication about relationship problems.

Number of Items: 5

Format: All items are described. Response scales range from 1 (very unlikely) to 9 (very likely).

Reliability: Alpha coefficients ranged from .63 to .75.

Author: Holtzworth-Munroe, A., et al.

Article: Demand and withdraw communication among couples experiencing husband violence.

Journal: *Journal of Consulting and Clinical Psychology*, October 1998, *66*(5), 731–743.

Related Research: Christensen, A., & Sulloway, M. (1984). *Communications Patterns Questionnaire*. Unpublished manuscript, University of California, Los Angeles.

8745

Test Name: COMMUNICATION SCALE

Purpose: To measure parent-adolescent communication.

Number of Items: 10

Format: Four-point Likert format. All items are presented.

Reliability: Alpha was .85.

Author: Forehand, R., et al.

Article: Role of parenting in adolescent deviant behavior:

Replication across and within two ethnic groups.

Journal: *Journal of Consulting and Clinical Psychology*, December 1997, *65*(6), 1036–1041.

Related Research: Barnes, H., & Olson, D. H. (1985). Parent-adolescent communication and the circumplex model. *Child Development, 56*, 438–447.

8746

Test Name: COMMUNICATION WITH INSTRUCTOR SCALE

Purpose: To measure relational, functional, and sycophantic communication with instructors.

Number of Items: 30

Format: Five-point scales are anchored by 1 (not at all like me) and 5 (exactly like me).

Reliability: Alphas ranged from .86 to .90 across subscales.

Validity: Correlations with other variables ranged from .16 to .24.

Author: Martin, M. W., et al.

Article: Students' motives for communicating with their instructors and affective and cognitive learning.

Journal: *Psychological Reports*, December 2000, *87*(3, Part 1), 830–834.

Related Research: Martin, M. W., et al. (1999). Students' motives for communicating with their instructors. *Communication Education, 48*, 155–164.

8747

Test Name: CONSTRUCTIVE COMMUNICATIONS (SUB) SCALE

Purpose: To assess family communication patterns related to problem-solving.

Number of Items: 7 (35 items in the total questionnaire).

Format: Scales range from 1 (very unlikely) to 9 (very likely). All items are described.

Reliability: Alpha coefficients ranged from .81 to .84. Total scale alphas ranged from .55 to .72.

Validity: Correlations with other variables ranged from .54 to .78.

Author: Heavy, C. L., et al.

Article: The Communication Patterns Questionnaire: The reliability and validity of a constructive communication subscale.

Journal: *Journal of Marriage and the Family*, August 1996, *58*(3), 796–800.

Related Research: Christensen, A., & Sulloway, M. (1984). *Communication Patterns Questionnaire*. Unpublished manuscript, University of California, Los Angeles.

Klinetob, N. A., & Smith, D. A. (1996). Demand-withdraw communication in marital interaction: Tests of interspousal contingency and gender role hypotheses. *Journal of Marriage and the Family, 58*, 945–957.

Kluwer, E. S., et al. (1997). The marital dynamics of conflict over the division of labor. *Journal of Marriage and the Family, 59*, 635–653.

Hahlweg, K., et al. (2000). Self-report and observational assessment of couples' conflict: The concordance between the Communication Patterns Questionnaire and the KPT Observation System. *Journal of Marriage and the Family, 62*, 61–67.

8748

Test Name: FEEDBACK PROPENSITIES QUESTIONNAIRE

Purpose: To measure individual differences in feedback propensities.

Number of Items: 28

Format: Includes 3 factors: Internal Propensity, Internal Ability, and External Propensity. All items are presented.

Reliability: Alpha coefficients ranged from .59 to .69.

Validity: Correlations with other variables ranged from −.39 to .54.

Author: Harold, D. M., et al.

Article: Individual differences in the generation and processing of performance feedback.

Journal: *Educational and Psychological Measurement*, February 1996, 56(1), 5–25.

8749

Test Name: FEEDBACK SCALES

Purpose: To assess feedback consequences following an episode in which negative feelings were experienced.

Number of Items: 56

Format: Bipolar scales range from "not at all" to "very much" on some items. Other items use 5-point agreement scales. Sample items are presented.

Reliability: Alpha coefficients ranged from .72 to .92 across subscales.

Author: Lundgren, D. C., and Rudawsky, D. J.

Article: Speaking one's mind or biting one's tongue: When do angered persons express or withhold feedback in transactions with male and female peers?

Journal: *Social Psychology Quarterly*, September 2000, 63(3), 253–263.

Related Research: Lundgren,

D. C., & Rudawsky, D. J. (1998). Female and male college students' responses to negative feedback from parents and peers. *Sex Roles, 39,* 409–429.

8750

Test Name: FEEDBACK-SEEKING BEHAVIOR SCALE

Purpose: To measure individual-sought feedback from supervisors.

Number of Items: 5

Format: Scales range from 1 (almost never) to 7 (very frequently). All items are presented.

Reliability: Coefficient alpha was .88.

Validity: Correlations with other variables ranged from −.25 to .32.

Author: VandeWalle, D., et al.

Article: An integrated model of feedback-seeking behavior: Disposition, context, and cognition.

Journal: *Journal of Applied Psychology*, December 2000, 85(6), 996–1003.

Related Research: Morrison, E. W. (1993). Newcomer information seeking: Exploring types, modes, sources, and outcomes. *Academy of Management Journal, 36,* 173–183.

8751

Test Name: INFORMATION-SEEKING SCALE

Purpose: To measure proactive information seeking.

Number of Items: 10

Format: Seven-point scales are anchored by 1 (never) and 7 (a few times per day). All items are described.

Reliability: Alpha coefficients were .80 (task information) and .83 (social information).

Validity: Correlations with other variables ranged from −.09 to .25.

Author: Bauer, T. N., and Green, S. G.

Article: Testing the combined effects of newcomer information seeking and manager behavior on socialization.

Journal: *Journal of Applied Psychology*, February 1998, 83(1), 72–83.

Related Research: Morrison, E. W. (1993). Newcomer information seeking: Exploring types, modes, sources and outcomes. *Academy of Management Journal, 36,* 557–589.

8752

Test Name: LEADER-MEMBER EXCHANGE SCALE

Purpose: To assess negotiating latitude that groups can use to develop their jobs to suit their own interests.

Number of Items: 4

Format: Scales range from 4 (low latitude) to 16 (high latitude).

Reliability: Coefficient alpha was .84.

Authors: Ashkanasy, N. M., and O'Connor, C.

Article: Value congruence in leader-member exchange.

Journal: *Journal of Social Psychology*, October 1997, 137(5), 647–662.

Related Research: Liden, R. C., & Graen, G. B. (1980). Generalizability of the vertical dyad linkage model of leadership. *Academy of Management Journal, 23,* 451–465.

8753

Test Name: LEADER-MEMBER EXCHANGE SCALE

Purpose: To measure leader-member exchange.

Number of Items: 7

Format: Scales range from 1 (not at all) to 5 (to a very large extent). Sample items are described.

Reliability: Coefficient alpha was .87.

Validity: Correlations with other variables ranged from −.32 to .54.

Author: Hofmann, D. A., and Morgeson, F. P.

Article: Safety-related behavior as a social exchange: The role of perceived organizational support and leader-member exchange.

Journal: *Journal of Applied Psychology*, April 1999, *84*(2), 286–296.

Related Research: Graen, G. B., & Uhl-Bien, M. (1995). Relationship-based approach to leadership: Development of leader-member exchange (LMX) theory of leadership over 25 years: Applying a multi-level multi-domain perspective. *Leadership Quarterly, 6*, 219–247.

8754

Test Name: LEADER-MEMBER EXCHANGE SCALE

Purpose: To measure leader-member relationships.

Number of Items: 13

Format: Scales range from 1 (strongly disagree) to 7 (strongly agree). A sample item is presented.

Reliability: Coefficient alpha was .96.

Validity: Correlations with other variables ranged from .04 to .36.

Author: Liden, R. C., et al.

Article: An examination of the mediating role of psychological empowerment on the relations between the job, interpersonal relationships, and work outcomes.

Journal: *Journal of Applied Psychology*, June 2000, *85*(3), 407–416.

Related Research: Settoon, R. P., et al. (1996). Social exchange in organizations: Perceived organizational support, leader-member exchange, and employment reciprocity. *Journal of Applied Psychology, 81*, 219–227.

8755

Test Name: MOTHER-ADOLESCENT GENERAL COMMUNICATION SCALE

Purpose: To measure general communication between parent and adolescent.

Number of Items: 10

Format: Scales range from 1 (strongly disagree) to 4 (strongly agree). All items are presented.

Reliability: Coefficient alpha was .76.

Author: Miller, K. S.

Article: Adolescent sexual behavior and two ethnic minority samples: The role of family variables.

Journal: *Journal of Marriage and the Family*, February 1999, *61*(1), 85–98.

Related Research: Barnes, H. L., & Olsen, D. H. (1985). Parent-adolescent communication and the circumplex model. *Child Development, 56*, 438–447.

8756

Test Name: OPENER SCALE

Purpose: To measure the tendency to elicit intimate disclosure from other people.

Number of Items: 10

Format: An example is presented.

Reliability: Alpha coefficients were .79 and .85. Test-retest (6 weeks) reliability was .69.

Validity: Correlation with other variables ranged from −. 41 to .52.

Author: Bruch, M. A., et al.

Article: Shyness, masculine ideology, physical attractiveness, and emotional inexpressiveness: Testing a mediational model of men's interpersonal competence.

Journal: *Journal of Counseling Psychology*, January 1998, *45*(1), 84–97.

Related Research: Miller, L. C., et al. (1983). Openers: Individuals who elicit intimate self-disclosure. *Journal of Personality and Social Psychology, 44*, 1234–1244.

8757

Test Name: PARENT ADOLESCENT COMMUNICATION SCALE

Purpose: To assess open communication and problem communication.

Number of Items: 20

Format: Scales range from 1 (strongly disagree) to 5 (strongly agree). Sample items are presented.

Reliability: Coefficient alpha was .87 (open communication) and .78 (problem communication).

Author: White, F. A.

Article: Relationship of family

socialization processes to adolescent moral thought.

Journal: *Journal of Social Psychology*, Aug, 2000, *140*(1), 75–91.

Related Research: Barnes, H. L., & Olsen, D. H. (1985). Parent-adolescent communication and the circumplex model. *Child Development, 56*, 438–447.

8758

Test Name: PARENT-PERCEIVED AMOUNT OF TEACHER COMUNICATIONS SCALE

Purpose: To assess parents' perceptions of the amount of communications they received from their children's teachers.

Number of Items : 8

Format: Responses are made on a 5-point scale ranging from 1 (not enough) to 5 (more than enough). All items are presented.

Reliability: Coefficient alpha was .92.

Validity: Correlations with other variables ranged from −.19 to .32.

Author: Watkins, T. J.

Article: Teacher communications, child achievement, and parent traits in parent involvement models.

Journal: *Journal of Educational Research*, September/October 1997, *91*(1), 3–14.

Related Research: Ames, C., et al. (1993, April). *Effects of parent involvement strategies on parents' perceptions and the development of children's motivation.* Paper presented at the annual meeting of the American Educational Association, Atlanta.

8759

Test Name: PATIENT IMPAIRMENT LEXICON

Purpose: To provide a common language to describe and communicate specific treatment needs for clinical disorders.

Number of Items: 63

Format: Each item (impairment) is followed by a 4-point severity scale ranging from (1) distressing to (4) imminently dangerous.

Reliability: Alphas were .67 (presence or absence) and .86 (severity).

Validity: Only one false-negative and no false-positive impairments were noted.

Author: Klewicki, L. L., et al.

Article: Patient impairment lexicon: A psychometric analysis.

Journal: *Psychological Reports*, October 1998, *83*(2), 547–570.

8760

Test Name: PERCEIVED ACCURACY OF FEEDBACK SCALE

Purpose: To measure perceived accuracy of feedback.

Number of Items: 9

Format: Responses are made on a 7-point scale ranging from "strongly disagree" to "strongly agree." An example is presented.

Reliability: Alpha coefficients ranged from .94 to .96.

Author: Hammer, L. B., and Stone-Romero, E. F.

Article: Effects of mood state and favorability of feedback on reactions to performance feedback.

Journal: *Perceptual and Motor Skills*, December 1996, *83*(1) Part 3, 923–934.

Related Research: Stone, E. F., & Stone, D. L. (1984) The effects of multiple sources of performance feedback and feedback favorability on self-perceived task competence and perceived feedback accuracy. *Journal of Management, 10*, 371–378.

8761

Test Name: PERCEIVED COMMUNICATION SELF-EFFICACY SCALE

Purpose: To measure ability to communicate in a group context.

Number of Items: 8

Format: Scales range from 1 (strongly agree) to 7 (strongly disagree).

Reliability: Coefficient alpha was .88.

Validity: Correlations with other variables ranged from −.24 to .47.

Author: Karakowsky, L., and Siegel, J. P.

Article: The effects of proportional representation and gender orientation of the task on emergent leadership behavior in mixed-gender workgroups.

Journal: *Journal of Applied Psychology*, August 1999, *84*(4), 620–631.

Related Research: Klauss, R., & Bass, B. M. (1982). *Interpersonal communication in organizations.* New York: Academic Press.

8762

Test Name: PERSONAL REPORT OF COMMUNICATION APPREHENSION SCALE

Purpose: To measure individual differences on several domains of communication apprehension:

dyadic, group meetings, and public.

Number of Items: 24

Format: Items are anchored by "strongly disagree" and "strongly agree."

Validity: Correlations with other variables ranged from −.59 to .61.

Author: Schroeder, J. E., and Ketrow, S. M.

Article: Social anxiety and performance in an interpersonal perception task.

Journal: *Psychological Reports*, December 1997, *81*(3, Part I), 991–996.

Related Research: McCroskey, J. C. (1978). Validity of the PRCA as an index of oral communication apprehension. *Communication Monographs, 45*, 192–203.

8763

Test Name: PROACTIVE SOCIALIZATION SCALES

Purpose: To assess feedback-making, relationship building, and positive framing.

Number of Items: 7

Format: Scales range from 1 (to no extent) to 5 (to a great extent). Sample items are presented.

Reliability: Alpha coefficients ranged from .73 to .87.

Validity: Correlations with other variables ranged from −.22 to .36.

Author: Wanberg, C. R., and Kammeyer-Mueller, J. D.

Article: Predictors and outcomes of proactivity in the socialization process.

Journal: *Journal of Applied*

Psychology, June 2000, *85*(3), 373–385.

Related Research: Ashford, S. J., & Black, J. S. (1996). Proactivity during organizational entry: The role of desire for control. *Journal of Applied Psychology, 81,* 199–214.

8764

Test Name: SELF-CONCEALMENT SCALE

Purpose: To measure the predisposition to conceal personal information perceived to be negative or distressing.

Number of Items: 10

Format: Responses are made on a 5-point scale ranging from 1 (strongly disagree) to 5 (strongly agree). Examples are provided.

Reliability: Test-retest (4 weeks) reliability was .81. Alpha coefficients were .83 and .87 (*N* = 42).

Validity: Correlations with other variables ranged from −.27 to 42.

Author: Kelly, A. E.

Article: Clients' secret keeping in outpatient therapy.

Journal: *Journal of Counseling Psychology*, January 1998, *45*(1), 50–57.

Related Research: Larson, D. G., & Chastain, R. L. (1990). Self-concealment: Conceptualization, measurement, and health implications. *Journal of Social and Clinical Psychology, 9*, 439–455.

8765

Test Name: SELF-DISCLOSURE INDEX

Purpose: To measure the extent of disclosure on various topics to closest male friend.

Number of Items: 10

Format: Scales range from 1 (not at all) to 5 (fully and completely).

Reliability: Coefficient alpha was .90.

Validity: Correlations with other variables ranged from −.12 to .31.

Author: Sinn, J. S.

Article: The predictive and discriminant validity of masculinity ideology.

Journal: *Journal of Research in Personality*, March 1997, *31*(1), 117–135.

Related Research: Miller, L. C., et al. (1983). Openers: Individuals who elicit intimate self-disclosure. *Journal of Personality and Social Psychology, 44*, 1234–1244.

8766

Test Name: SELF-DISCLOSURE QUESTIONAIRE

Purpose: To measure how much information people disclose to others.

Number of Items: 25

Format: 5-point scales anchored by (1) never and (5) always. All items are presented.

Reliability: Alphas ranged from .90 (depth of disclosure) to .93 (breadth of disclosure).

Author: Myers, S. A.

Article: Students' self disclosure in the college classroom.

Journal: *Psychological Reports*, December 1998, *83*(3) Part 1, 1067–1070.

Related Research: Jourard, S. M. (1971). *Self-disclosures: An experimental analysis of the transparent self.* New York; Wiley-Interscience.

8767

Test Name: SELF-DISCLOSURE QUESTIONNAIRE

Purpose: To measure self-disclosure of intimate topics.

Number of Items: 30

Format: Includes 3 subscales: Sexuality, One's Body, and One's Personality.

Reliability: Alpha coefficients ranged from .75 to .92.

Validity: Correlations with other variables ranged from −. 33 to .25.

Author: Bruch, M. A., et al.

Article: Shyness, masculine ideology, physical attractiveness, and emotional inexpressiveness: Testing a mediational model of men's interpersonal competence.

Journal: *Journal of Counseling Psychology*, January 1998, *45*(1), 84–97.

Related Research: Lavine, L. O., & Lombardo, J. P. (1984). Self-disclosure: Intimate and non-intimate disclosures to parents and best friends as a function of Bem sex-role category. *Sex Roles*, *11*, 735—744.

8768

Test Name: SELF-DISCLOSURE SCALE (CHINESE)

Purpose: To measure shared intimacy with others. Subscales include Personal Feelings, Tastes and Attitudes, Social Relationships, Body Image, and Opinions.

Number of Items: 35

Format: Four-point scales are anchored by "not at all" and "a great deal" Sample items are presented.

Validity: Significant correlations with other variables ranged from −.40 to .26.

Author: Hamid, P. N.

Article: Self-disclosure and occupational stress in Chinese professionals.

Journal: *Psychological Reports*, December 2000, *87*(3), Part 1, 1075–1082.

Related Research: Cozby, P. C. (1973). Self-disclosure: A literature review. *Psychological Bulletin*, *79*, 73–91.

8769

Test Name: STATE MEASURE OF CENTRAL ROUTE PROCESSING

Purpose: To assess how motivated people are to hear a message, how much of it they understand, and how favorable they regard it.

Number of Items: 7

Format: Seven-point scales.

Reliability: Coefficient alpha was .69.

Author: Foubert, J. D., and McEwen, M. K.

Article: An all-male rape prevention peer education program: Decreasing men's behavioral intent to rape.

Journal: *Journal of College Student Development*, November/December 1998, *39*(6), 548–556.

Related Research: Gilbert, B. J., et al. (1991). Changing the sexual aggression-supportive attitudes of men: A psychoeducational intervention. *Journal of Counseling Psychology*, *38*, 197–203.

8770

Test Name: TASK-RELATED IDEAS CONTRIBUTION SCALE

Purpose: To measure the extent to which group members contribute ideas to a task.

Number of Items: 4

Format: All items are presented.

Reliability: Coefficient alpha was .75.

Validity: Correlations with other variables ranged from −.20 to .30.

Author: Bluedorn, A. C., et al.

Article: The effects of stand-up and sit-down meeting formats on meeting outcomes.

Journal: *Journal of Applied Psychology*, April 1999, *84*(2), 277–285.

8771

Test Name: TEAM FUNCTIONS SCALE

Purpose: To measure communication and resource utilization in groups, both internally and externally.

Number of Items: 6

Format: Scales range from "strongly disagree" to "strongly agree."

Reliability: Coefficient alpha was .70 (internal) and .86 (external).

Validity: Correlations with other variables ranged from −.37 to .65.

Author: Choi, J. N., and Kim, M. U.

Article: The organizational application of groupthink and its limitations in organizations.

Journal: *Journal of Applied Psychology*, April 1999, *84*(2), 297–306.

8772

Test Name: TEAM-MEMBER EXCHANGE SCALE

Purpose: To measure team-member exchange as a role making construct to supplement the leader-member exchange construct.

Number of Items: 9

Format: Scales range from 1 (strongly disagree) to 7 (strongly agree). A sample item is presented.

Reliability: Coefficient alpha was .88.

Validity: Correlations with other variables ranged from .13 to .30.

Author: Liden, R. C., et al.

Article: An examination of the mediating role of psychological empowerment on the relations between the job, interpersonal relationships, and work outcomes.

Journal: *Journal of Applied*

Psychology, June 2000, *85*(3), 407–416.

Related Research: Seers, A. (1989). Team-member exchange quality: A new construct for role-making research. *Organizational Behavior and Human Decision Processes, 43,* 118–135.

8773

Test Name: VOICE SCALE

Purpose: To measure the expression of constructive challenge with the intent to improve, not merely criticize.

Number of Items: 6

Format: Scales range from 1 (strongly disagree) to 7 (strongly agree). All items are presented.

Reliability: Coefficient alpha was .95.

Validity: Correlations with other variables ranged from −.15 to .22.

Author: LePine, J. A., and Van Dyne, L.

Article: Predicting voice behavior in work groups.

Journal: *Journal of Applied Psychology,* December 1998, *83*(6), 853–868.

Related Research: Van Dyne, L., & LePine, J. A. (1998). Helping and voice extra-role behavior: Evidence of construct and predictive validity. *Academy of Management Journal, 41,* 108–119.

CHAPTER 10
Concept Meaning

8774

Test Name: BELIEF SYSTEMS TEST

Purpose: To measure one's conceptual thinking level.

Number of Items: 21

Format: Includes 4 categories: Mutability of Truth, Polarity, Knowledge via Faith, and Effectance via God. Responses are made on a 5-point scale ranging from 1 (strongly disagree) to 5 (strongly agree). Examples are presented.

Reliability: Coefficient alpha was .90.

Author: Johnson, P. E., and Johnson, R. E.

Article: The role of concrete-abstract-thinking levels in teachers' multiethnic beliefs.

Journal: *Journal of Research and Development in Education,* Spring 1996, *29*(3), 134–140.

Related Research: Gore, E. J. (1986). Development of an objective measure of belief systems (Doctoral dissertation, University of Colorado, 1985). *Dissertation Abstracts International,* 47(02), 850B.

8775

Test Name: PHONEMIC ANALYSIS TEST

Purpose: To provide phonemic analysis of single words.

Number of Items: 10

Format: Participants find a spoken sound in one of four words at the same position as in a stimulus word. An example is given.

Validity: Correlations with other variables ranged from .66 to .78.

Author: Dalby, M. A., et al.

Article: Temporal lobe asymmetry and dyslexia: An *in vivo* study using MRI.

Journal: *Brain and Language,* March 1998, *62*(1), 51–69.

Related Research: Nielson, I., & Petersen, D. K. (1992). *Diavok. Et materiale der afdoekker eventuelle loese-og stavevanskeligheder.* [Diavok. A screening test for reading and spelling disabilities in adults]. Copenhagen: Workers Educational Association (ADF).

8776

Test Name: PHONOLOGICAL DISCRIMINATION TASK

Purpose: To measure phonological discrimination.

Number of Items: 34

Format: Pairs of pictures are presented with participants pointing to the picture matching a spoken word.

Validity: Correlations with other variables ranged from .33 to .71.

Author: Dalby, M. A., et al.

Article: Temporal lobe asymmetry and dyslexia: An *in vivo* study using MRI.

Journal: *Brain and Language,* March 1998, *62*(1), 51–69.

Related Research: Elbro, C. (1990). *Differences in dyslexia: A study of reading strategies and deficits in a linguistic perspective.* Copenhagen: Munksgaard International Publishers.

8777

Test Name: VERBALIZER–VISUALIZER QUESTIONNAIRE

Purpose: To assess the part that linguistic and imagery representations play in cognition.

Number of Items: 30

Format: Includes half target and half filler items. Responses are either "true" or "false." Sample items are presented.

Reliability: Test-retest reliabilities ranged from .48 to .91 with intervals ranging from 7 days to 8 weeks.

Validity: Split-half coefficients ranged from .39 to .45.

Author: Antonietti, A., and Giorgetti, M.

Article: The Verbalizer–Visualizer Questionnaire: A review.

Journal: *Perceptual and Motor Skills,* February 1998, *86*(1), 227–239.

Related Research: Richardson, A. (1977). Verbalizer-visualizer: A cognitive style dimension. *Journal of Mental Imagery, 1,* 109–126.

CHAPTER 11
Creativity

8778

Test Name: COGNITIVE SPONTANEITY SCALE

Purpose: To measure curiosity and inventiveness in hypothesis-testing behavior.

Number of Items: 22

Format: Seven-point scales ranged from 1 (strongly disagree) to 7 (strongly agree).

Reliability: Chronbach's alpha was .80.

Validity: Correlations with other variables ranged from −.20 to .13.

Author: Bozionelos, N.

Article: Psychology and computer use: XLV. Cognitive spontaneity as a correlate of computer anxiety and attitudes toward computer use.

Journal: *Psychological Reports*, April 1997, *80*(2), 395–402.

Related Research: Webster, J., & Martochhio, J. J. (1992). Microcomputer playfulness: Development of a measure with workplace implications. *MIS Quarterly*, June 16, 201–226.

8779

Test Name: CREATIVE PERSONALITY SCALE

Purpose: To measure creative personality.

Number of Items: 9

Format: Responses are either "true" or "false." All items are presented.

Validity: Correlations with other variables were −.15 and .41.

Author: Thalbourne, M. A.

Article: Transliminality and creativity.

Journal: *Journal of Creative Behavior*, Third Quarter 2000, *34*(3), 193–202.

Related Research: Thalbourne, M. A., & Delin, P. S. (1994). A common thread underlying belief in the paranormal, creative personality, mystical experience and psychopathology. *Journal of Parapsychology, 58*, 3–38.

8780

Test Name: CREATIVITY STYLES QUESTIONNAIRE— REVISED

Purpose: To measure one's beliefs concerning how to be creative and strategies one uses to facilitate one's creative work.

Number of Items: 76

Format: Includes 7 subscales: Belief in Unconscious Processes, Use of Techniques, Use of Other People, Final Product Orientation, Superstition, Environmental Control, and Use of Senses.

Reliability: Alpha coefficients ranged from .23 to .83.

Author: Pollick, M. F., and Kumar, V. K.

Article: Creativity styles of supervising managers.

Journal: *Journal of Creative Behavior*, 1997, *31*(4), 260–270.

Related Research: Kumar, V. K., & Holman, E. R. (1989). *Creativity Styles Questionnaire*. Unpublished manuscript, Department of Psychology, West Chester University, West Chester, PA.

8781

Test Name: INDIVIDUAL INNOVATION SCALE

Purpose: To measure individual innovations in work situations.

Number of Items: 5

Format: Five-point scales are anchored by 1 (strongly disagree) to 5 (strongly agree). A sample item is presented.

Reliability: Cronbach alphas ranged from .77 to .85.

Author: West, M. A., and Anderson, N. R.

Article: Innovation in top management teams.

Journal: *Journal of Applied Psychology*, December 1996, *81*(6), 680–693.

Related Research: Bunce, D., & West, M. A. (1995). Personality and perceptions of group climate factors as predictors of individual innovation at work. *Applied Psychology: An International Review, 44*, 199–215.

8782

Test Name: INVENTION EVALUATION SCALE

Purpose: To assess the originality,

technical goodness, and aesthetic appeal of inventions.

Number of Items: 11

Format: Responses are made on a 5-point rating scale. Includes 3 factors: Originality, Technical Goodness, and Aesthetic Appeal.

Reliability: Alpha coefficients ranged from .90 to .94. Interrater reliabilities ranged from .69 to .92.

Validity: Correlation with achievement was .24.

Author: Westberg, K. L.

Article: The effects of teaching students how to invent.

Journal: *Journal of Creative Behavior*, 1996, *30*(4), 249–267.

8783

Test Name: SURVEY OF CREATIVE AND INNOVATIVE PERFORMANCE

Purpose: To measure creative performance.

Number of Items: 14

Format: Includes 3 scales: Novelty, Resolution, and Elaboration and Synthesis.

Reliability: Alpha coefficients ranged from .55 to .80.

Author: Puccio, G. J., et al.

Article: Examining creative performance in the workplace through a person-environment fit model.

Journal: *Journal of Creative Behavior*, Fourth Quarter 2000, *34*(4), 227–247.

Related Research: Bessemer, S. P., & O'Quin, K. (1987). Creative product analysis: Testing a model by developing a judging instrument. In S. G. Isaksen (Ed.), *Frontiers of creativity research: Beyond the basics* (pp. 341–357). Buffalo, NY: Bearly Limited.

CHAPTER 12
Development

8784

Test Name: COGNITION QUESTIONNAIRE FOR CHILDREN—DUTCH

Purpose: To assess children's cognition.

Number of Items: 50

Format: Four-point scales range from "never" to "all the time."

Reliability: Coefficient alpha ranged from .73 to .89 across subscales.

Validity: Correlations between subscales ranged from −.14 to .69.

Author: Prins, P. J. M., and Hanewald, G. J. F. P.

Article: Coping self-talk and cognitive interference in anxious children.

Journal: *Journal of Consulting and Clinical Psychology*, June 1999, *67*(3), 435–439.

Related Research: Zatz, S., & Chassin, L. (1985). Cognitions of test-anxious children under naturalistic test-taking conditions. *Journal of Consulting and Clinical Psychology, 53,* 393–401.

8785

Test Name: COGNITIVE COMPETENCE SCALE

Purpose: To assess cognitive competence.

Number of Items: 6

Format: Two-step response procedure. Examples are presented.

Reliability: Alpha coefficients ranged from .82 to .92.

Author: Smith, T., and Brody, G. H.

Article: Intra- and extracultural perceptions of competence in rural African-American youth.

Journal: *Journal of School Psychology*, September/October 2000, *38*(5), 407–422.

Related Research: Harter, S. (1982). The Perceived Competence Scale for Children. *Child Development, 53,* 87–97.

8786

Test Name: COGNITIVE UNDERSTANDING OF TRAITS

Purpose: To assess children's understanding of the consistency of personality.

Number of Items: 24

Format: Includes 3 scores: Trait Label, Future Stability, and Situational Stability.

Reliability: Alpha coefficients ranged from .79 to .87.

Author: Shell, R. M., and Eisenberg, N.

Article: Children's reactions to the receipt of direct and indirect help.

Journal: *Child Development*, August 1996, *67*(4), 1391–1405.

Related Research: Eisenberg, N., et al. (1987). Consistency based compliance: When and why do children become vulnerable? *Journal of Personality and Social Psychology, 58,* 1174–1181.

8787

Test Name: CONCEPTS OF DEVELOPMENT QUESTIONNAIRE

Purpose: To measure parents' interpretations of their child's developmental behavior.

Number of Items: 20

Format: Responses are made on a 4-point scale ranging from 3 (strongly agree) to 0 (strongly disagree).

Reliability: Alpha coefficients ranged from .60 to .78.

Validity: Correlations with other variables ranged from −.55 to .33.

Author: Benasich, A. A., and Brooks-Gunn, J.

Article: Maternal attitudes and knowledge of child-rearing: Associations with family and child outcomes.

Journal: *Child Development*, June 1996, *67*(3), 1186–1205.

Related Research: Sameroff, A. J., & Feil, L. A. (1985). Parental concepts of development. In I. E. Sigel (Ed.), *Parental belief systems* (pp. 83–105). Hillsdale, NJ: Erlbaum.

8788

Test Name: ERICKSON PSYCHOSOCIAL STAGE INVENTORY—MODIFIED

Purpose: To measure Erickson's

stages of psychosocial development.

Number of Items: 24

Format: Includes 6 subscales: Trust, Autonomy, Initiative, Industry, Identity, and Intimacy. Responses are made on a 4-point scale.

Validity: Correlations with other variables ranged from −.10 to .60.

Author: Brookins, C. L.

Article: Exploring psychological task resolution and self-concept among African-American adolescents.

Journal: *Perceptual and Motor Skills*, June 1996, *82*(3) Part 1, 803–810.

Related Research: Rosenthal, D., et al. (1981). From trust to intimacy: A new inventory for examining Erickson's stages of psychosocial development. *Journal of Youth and Adolescence*, *10*, 525–537.

8789

Test Name: GROWTH NEED STRENGTH MEASURES

Purpose: To measure growth need strength.

Number of Items: 18

Format: Includes two measures: Would Like measure and Job Choice measure. Sample items are presented.

Reliability: Coefficient alpha was .81.

Author: Fried, Y., et al.

Article: Changes in job decision latitude: The influence of personality and interpersonal satisfaction.

Journal: *Journal of Vocational Behavior*, April 1999, *54*(2), 233–243.

Related Research: Hackman, J. R., & Oldham, G. R. (1980). *Work redesign*. Reading, MA: Addison-Wesley.

8790

Test Name: HEALTH RESOURCES QUESTIONNAIRE

Purpose: To assess teachers' perceptions of a child's school-related competencies.

Number of Items: 44

Format: Five-point scales range from 1 (describes child not at all) to 5 (describes child very well).

Reliability: Test-retest reliabilities of three scales ranged from .72 to .91.

Author: Ketsetzis, M., et al.

Article: Family processes, parent-child interactions, and child characteristics influencing school-based social adjustment.

Journal: *Journal of Marriage and the Family*, May 1998, *60*(2), 374–387.

Related Research: Gesten, E. L. (1976). A Health Resources Inventory: The development of a measure of personal and social competence of primary grade children. *Journal of Consulting and Clinical Psychology*, *44*, 775–786.

8791

Test Name: INVENTORY OF PSYCHOLOGICAL BALANCE

Purpose: To provide an Eriksonian lifestyle measure.

Number of Items: 120

Format: Includes 8 scores corresponding to Erikson's eight life stages. Responses are made on a 5-point Likert-type scale ranging from "strongly disagree" to "strongly agree." Some items are presented.

Reliability: Alpha coefficients ranged from .40 to .79. Test-retest coefficients ranged from .78 to .90.

Validity: Correlations with other variables ranged from .04 to .26.

Author: Hannah, M. T., et al.

Article: The prediction of ego integrity in older persons.

Journal: *Educational and Psychological Measurement*, December 1996, *56*(6), 930–950.

Related Research: Domino, G., & Alfonso, D. (1990). The IPB: A personality measure of Erikson's life stages. *Journal of Personality Assessment*, *54*, 576–588.

8792

Test Name: INVENTORY OF PSYCHOSOCIAL DEVELOPMENT—INTIMACY AND ISOLATION SCALES

Purpose: To assess resolution of two of Erikson's stages.

Number of Items: 20

Format: Includes two stages: Intimacy and Isolation. Responses are made on a 7-point Likert scale.

Reliability: Test-retest (1 week) reliability ranged from .71 to .89.

Author: Vivona, J. M.

Article: Parental attachment styles of late adolescents: Qualities of attachment relationships and consequences for adjustment.

Journal: *Journal of Counseling Psychology*, July 2000, *47*(3), 316–329.

Related Research: Constantinople, A. (1969). An Eriksonian measure of personality development in college students. *Developmental Psychology*, *1*, 357–372.

8793

Test Name: KNOWLEDGE OF INFANT DEVELOPMENT INVENTORY

Purpose: To measure parental knowledge of infant development.

Number of Items: 75

Format: Includes parental knowledge of child-rearing practice, developmental processes, and infant developmental norms and milestones. Items are answered as 1 (right), 0 (wrong), or 0 (not sure). An example is presented.

Reliability: Coefficient alpha for a 20-item Accuracy score was .63.

Validity: Correlations with other variables ranged from −.55 to .49.

Author: Benasick, A. A., and Brooks-Gunn, J.

Article: Maternal attitudes and knowledge of child-rearing: Associations with family and child outcomes.

Journal: *Child Development*, June 1996, *67*(3), 1186–1205.

Related Research: MacPhee, D. (1981). *Manual: Knowledge of Infant Development Inventory.* Unpublished manuscript, University of North Carolina.

8794

Test Name: MY CHILD

Purpose: To enable mothers to rate their child's conscience development.

Number of Items: 100

Format: Includes two dimensions: Affect Discomfort and Active Moral Regulation/Vigilance.

Reliability: Alpha coefficients ranged from .73 to .90.

Author: Kochanska, G., et al.

Article: Children's narratives

about hypothetical moral dilemmas and objective measures of their conscience: Mutual relations and socialization antecedents.

Journal: *Child Development*, August 1996, *67*(4), 1420–1436.

Related Research: Kochanska, G., et al. (1994). Maternal reports of conscience development and temperament in young children. *Child Development, 65,* 852–868.

8795

Test Name: PERSONAL GROWTH INITIATIVE SCALE

Purpose: To assess personal growth initiative.

Number of Items: 9

Format: Responses are made on a 6-point scale. Examples are presented.

Reliability: Internal consistency ranged from .78 to .90. Test-retest correlations ranged from .73 to .84.

Validity: Correlations with other variables ranged from −.47 to .43

Author: Robitschek, C., and Cook, S. W.

Article: The influence of personal growth initiative and coping styles on career exploration and vocational identity.

Journal: *Journal of Vocational Behavior*, February 1999, *54*(1), 127–141

8796

Test Name: PUBERTAL DEVELOPMENT SCALE

Purpose: To assess pubertal development among adolescent girls and boys.

Number of Items: 6

Format: Scales range from 1 (this

change has not begun) to 2 (these changes seem to be completed). Sample items are presented.

Reliability: Alpha coefficients ranged from .54 to .85 across groups.

Author: Whitbeck, L. B., et al.

Article: Early adolescent sexual activity: A developmental study.

Journal: *Journal of Marriage and the Family*, December 1999, *61*(4), 934–946.

Related Research: Robertson, E., et al. (1992). The Pubertal Development Scale: A rural and suburban comparison. *Journal of Early Adolescence, 12,* 174–186.

8797

Test Name: SCALE OF INTELLECTUAL DEVELOPMENT

Purpose: To assess Perry's developmental theory.

Number of Items: 119

Format: Scales range from "strongly agree" to "strongly disagree."

Reliability: Alpha coefficients ranged from .70 to .84.

Author: Zhang, Z., and RiCharde, R. S.

Article: Intellectual and megacognitive development of male college students: A repeated measures approach.

Journal: *Journal of College Student Development*, November/December 1999, *40*(6), 721–738.

Related Research: Erwin, T. D. (1983). The Scale of Intellectual Development: Measuring Perry's Scheme. *Journal of College Student Personnel, 24,* 6–12.

8798

Test Name: STAGES OF CHANGE SCALE

Purpose: To assess readiness for change.

Number of Items: 32

Format: Scales range from 1 (strongly disagree) to 5 (strongly agree). A sample item is presented.

Reliability: Alpha coefficients ranged from .71 to .84 across subscales.

Author: Badura, A. S., et al.

Article: Effects of peer training on peer educators: Leadership, self-esteem, health knowledge, and health behaviors.

Journal: *Journal of College Student Development*, September/October 2000, *41*(5), 471–478.

Related Research: McConnaughy, E. A., et al. (1983). Stages of change in psychotherapy: Measurement and sample profiles. *Psychotherapy: Theory, Research, and Practice, 20,* 368–375.

8799

Test Name: ZHANG COGNITIVE DEVELOPMENT INVENTORY

Purpose: To measure cognitive development of Chinese college students in terms of dualism, relativism and commitment.

Number of Items: 137

Time Required: 30–60 minutes

Format: Four-point scales.

Relibility: Alphas ranged from .68 to .85.

Author: Zhang, L-F, and Hood, A. B.

Article: Cognitive development of students in China and the USA: Opposite directions?

Journal: *Psychological Reports*, June 1998, *82*(3) Part 2, 1251–1263.

CHAPTER 13
Family

8800

Test Name: ADOLESCENT LIFE EVENTS CHECKLIST

Purpose: To assess normative and nonnormative family stress.

Number of Items: 42

Format: Scales range from 0 (no, life event did not occur) to 3 (yes, life event occurred and was highly stressful).

Reliability: Alpha coefficients ranged from .60 to .85 across subscales.

Author: Plunkett, S. W., et al.

Article: Adolescent life events, stress and coping: A comparison of communities and genders.

Journal: *Professional School Counseling*, June 2000, *3*(5), 356–366.

Related Research: Fournier, D. G. (1981). *Adolescent Life Events Checklist (ALEC)*. Unpublished manuscript, Oklahoma State University at Stillwater.

8801

Test Name: AFFECTION TOWARDS PARENTS MEASURE

Purpose: To measure intimacy with parents.

Number of Items: 17

Format: Scales range from "not true" to "always true."

Reliability: Alpha coefficients ranged from .96 to .97.

Author: Stein, C. H., et al.

Article: "Because they're my parents": An intergenerational study of felt obligation and parental caregiving.

Journal: *Journal of Marriage and the Family*, August 1998, *60*(3), 611–622.

Related Research: Walker, A. J., & Thompson, L. (1983). Intimacy and intergenerational aid and contact among mothers and daughters. *Journal of Marriage and the Family, 45,* 841–849.

8802

Test Name: AFFECTUAL SOLIDARITY SCALE

Purpose: To measure affective closeness between spouses.

Number of Items: 5

Format: Scales range from 1 (not at all) to 6 (very much/a great deal).

Reliability: Coefficient alpha was .92.

Author: Feng, D., et al.

Article: Intergenerational transmission of marital quality and marital instability.

Journal: *Journal of Marriage and the Family*, May 1999, *61*(2), 451–463.

Related Research: Mangen, D. J., et al. (Eds.). (1988). *Measurement of intergenerational relations*. Newbury Park, CA: Sage.

8803

Test Name: AREAS OF CHANGE QUESTIONNAIRE

Purpose: To evaluate parent-child relationships in specified problem areas.

Number of Items: 34

Format: Seven-point scales are anchored by −3 (less change) and +3 (much more change).

Reliability: Internal consistency reliabilities ranged from .91 to .94.

Author: Kolko, D. J., et al.

Article: Cognitive and family therapies for adult depression: Treatment specificity, mediation, and moderation

Journal: *Journal of Consulting and Clinical Psychology*, August 2000, *68*(4), 603–614.

Related Research: Jacob, T., & Seilhamer, R. A. (1985). Adaption of the areas of change questionnaire for parent-child relationship assessment. *American Journal of Family Therapy, 13,* 28–38.

8804

Test Name: ASIAN AMERICAN FAMILY CONFLICTS SCALE

Purpose: To measure typical generational family conflicts.

Number of Items: 20

Format: Includes 2 subscales: Likelihood and Seriousness. Responses are made on a 5-point scale ranging from 1 (not at all)

to 5 (extremely). All items are presented.

Reliability: Alpha coefficients ranged from .81 to .89.

Validity: Correlations with other variables ranged from −.36 to .53.

Author: Lee, R. M., et al.

Article: Construction of the Asian American Family Conflicts Scale.

Journal: *Journal of Counseling Psychology*, April 2000, 47(2), 211–222.

8805

Test Name: ATTACHMENT HISTORY QUESTIONNAIRE

Purpose: To examine recollections of an individual's childhood attachment history.

Number of Items: 51

Format: Includes 4 factors: Secure Attachment Base, Parental Discipline, Separation, and Peer Affectional Support. Responses are made on a 7-point scale ranging from 1 (never) to 7 (always).

Reliability: Alpha coefficients ranged from .68 to .91.

Author: Kesner, J. E.

Article: Teacher characteristics and the quality of child-teacher relationships.

Journal: *Journal of School Psychology*, March/April 2000, 38(2), 133–149.

Related Research: Pottharst, K., & Kessler, R. (1990). The search for methods and measures. In K. Pottharst (Ed.), *Research explanations in adult attachment* (pp. 9–37). New York: Lang.

8806

Test Name: BEHAVIORAL CONTROL SCALE

Purpose: To measure behavioral control.

Number of Items: 5

Format: Responses are made on a 3-point scale ranging from 1 (doesn't know) to 3 (knows a lot). All items are presented.

Reliability: Alpha coefficients ranged from .75 to .82.

Validity: Correlations with psychological control ranged from −.17 to −.26.

Author: Barber, B. K.

Article: Parental psychological control: Revisiting a neglected construct.

Journal: *Child Development*, December 1996, 67(6), 3296–3319.

Related Research: Brown, B. B., et al. (1993). Parenting practices and peer group affiliation in adolescence. *Child Development*, 63, 391–400.

8807

Test Name: BEHAVIORAL NURTURANCE SCALE

Purpose: To assess mothers' behaviors relevant to nurturance.

Number of Items: 11

Format: Six-point scales ranged from "0 times" to "11 or more times" during the previous 2 days.

Reliability: Alpha coefficients ranged from .64 to .78 across two subscales.

Author: Larzelere, R. E., et al.

Article: Punishment enhances reasoning's effectiveness as a disciplinary response to toddlers.

Journal: *Journal of Marriage and the Family*, May 1998, 60(2), 388–403.

Related Research: Chamberlain, P., & Reid, J. B. (1987). Parent

observation and report of child symptoms. *Behavioral Assessment*, 9, 97–109.

8808

Test Name: BOUNDARY AMBIGUITY SCALE FOR DIVORCED ADULTS

Purpose: To assess the degree of clarity of family roles after divorce.

Number of Items: 22

Format: Five-point scales range from "never" to "almost always." Sample items are presented.

Reliability: Coefficient alpha was .80.

Author: Madden-Derdich, D. A., et al.

Article: Boundary ambiguity and coparental conflict after divorce: An empirical test of a family systems model of the divorce process.

Journal: *Journal of Marriage and the Family*, August 1999, 61(3), 588–598.

Related Research: Boss, P., & Pearce-McCall, D. (1990). *Boundary Ambiguity Scale for Divorced Adults: Manual for the measurement of boundary ambiguity in families*. Unpublished manuscript, University of Minnesota, St. Paul.

8809

Test Name: BURDEN INTERVIEW

Purpose: To measure the burden associated with functional and behavioral impairments in the home care situation.

Number of Items: 22

Format: Five-point scales are anchored by 1 (never) and 5 (nearly always present). A sample item is presented.

Reliability: Alpha was .91. Test-retest reliability (4–12 weeks) was .71.

Author: Beckham, J. C., et al.

Article: Caregiver burden in partners of Vietnam war veterans with posttraumatic stress disorder.

Journal: *Journal of Consulting and Clinical Psychology*, October 1996, *64*(5), 1068–1072.

Related Research: Zarit, S. H. (1989). Do we need another stress and caregiving study? *Gerontologist, 29,* 147–148.

8810

Test Name: CHILDBEARING PERCEPTIONS SCALES

Purpose: To measure rewards and regrets associated with childbearing.

Number of Items: 11

Format: Five-point scales ranged from "strongly agree" to "strongly disagree." All items are presented.

Reliability: Alpha coefficients ranged from .68 (rewards) to .69 (regrets).

Validity: The correlation between rewards and regrets scores was −.22.

Author: Groat, H. T., et al.

Article: Attitudes toward childbearing among young parents.

Journal: *Journal of Marriage and the Family*, August 1997, *59*(3), 568–581.

8811

Test Name: CHILDREARING PRACTICES REPORT

Purpose: To measure autonomy given to children and conformity expected of them.

Number of Items: 26

Format: Scales range from 1 (not at all descriptive of me) to 6 (highly descriptive of me). Sample items are presented.

Reliability: Alpha coefficient was .75.

Validity: Correlations with other variables ranged from −.47 to .29.

Author: Gerris, J. R. M., et al.

Article: The relationship between social class and childrearing behaviors: Parents' perspective taking and value orientations.

Journal: *Journal of Marriage and the Family*, November 1997, *59*(4), 834–847.

Related Research: Block, J. H. (1981). *The Child Rearing Practice Report (CRPR): A set of items for the description of parental socialization attitudes and values.* Unpublished manuscript, Institute of Human Development, University of California, Berkeley.

Van Ijzendoorn, M. H., et al. (1998). Attunement between parents and professional caregivers: A comparison of childrearing attitudes in different child-care settings. *Journal of Marriage and the Family, 60,* 771–781.

8812

Test Name: CHILD REARING PRACTICES REPORT

Purpose: To measure maternal child-rearing attitudes.

Number of Items: 65

Format: Six-point response scales range from 1 ("not at all descriptive of me") to 6 ("highly descriptive of me").

Reliability: Alphas ranged from .14 to .81 across subscales.

Author: Andersson, H. W., et al.

Article: Maternal child-rearing attitudes, IQ, and socioeconomic status as related to cognitive abilities of five-year-old children.

Journal: *Psychological Reports*, August 1996, *79*(1), 3–14.

Related Research: Greenberger, E., & Goldberg, W. A. (1989). Work, parenting, and the socialization of children. *Developmental Psychology, 25,* 22–35.

8813

Test Name: CHILDREN'S EXPECTATIONS OF SOCIAL BEHAVIOR QUESTIONNAIRE

Purpose: To assess children's perceptions of their relationships with their mother and teacher.

Number of Items: 20

Format: For each vignette, the child selects one of three possible responses.

Reliability: Alpha coefficients ranged from .74 to .83. Test-retest (1 month) reliability was .86. Test-retest (5 months) reliability was .82

Author: Howes, C., et al.

Article: Stability and continuity of child-caregiver and child-peer relationships.

Journal: *Child Development*, April 1998, *69*(2), 418—426.

Related Research: Rudolph, K., et al. (1995). Cognitive representations of self, family, and peers in school age children: Links with social competence and sociometric status. *Child Development, 66,* 1385–1402.

8814

Test Name: CHILDREN'S PERCEPTIONS OF INTERPARENTAL CONFLICT SCALE

Purpose: To assess interparental conflict.

Number of Items: 13

Format: Includes 2 groups of items: Items reflecting frequency of interparental arguments and items reflecting intensity of arguments. Examples are presented.

Reliability: Alpha coefficients were .82 and .89.

Author: Sandler, I. N., et al.

Article: Coping efficacy and psychological problems of children of divorce.

Journal: *Child Development*, July/August 2000, *71*(4), 1099–1118

Related Research: Grych, J. H., et al. (1992). Assessing marital conflict from the child's perspective: The Children's Perception of Interpersonal Conflict Scale. *Child Development*, *63*, 558–572.

8815

Test Name: CHILDREN'S PERCEPTION OF INTER-PARENTAL CONFLICT SCALE

Purpose: To assess children's perception of interparental conflict.

Number of Items: 40

Format: Responses are either "true", "sort of true", or "false." Includes 3 subscales: Conflict Properties, Perceived Threat, and Self-Blame.

Reliability: Alpha coefficients ranged from .79 to .92.

Author: Grych, J. H., et al.

Article: Interpersonal conflict and child adjustments: Testing the mediational role of appraisals in the cognitive-contextual framework.

Journal: *Child Development*, November/December 2000, *71*(6), 1648–1661.

Related Research: Grych, J. H., et al. (1992). Assessing marital conflict from the child's perspective. *Child Development*, *63*, 558–572.

8816

Test Name: CHILDREN'S PERCEPTION OF INTERPARENTAL CONFLICT SCALE

Purpose: To measure aspects of interparental conflict from the child's viewpoint.

Number of Items: 51

Format: Response categories are "true," "sort of true," and "false."

Reliability: Alpha coefficients ranged from .71 to .86 across subscales.

Author: Grych, J. H., et al.

Article: Patterns of adjustment among children of battered women

Journal: *Journal of Consulting and Clinical Psychology*, February 2000, *68*(1), 84–94.

Related Research: Grych, J. H., et al. (1992). Assessing marital conflict from the child's perspective. *Child Development*, *63*, 558–572.

8817

Test Name: CHILDREN'S ROLE INVENTORY

Purpose: To measure affiliation with the four family roles.

Number of Items: 60

Format: Includes 4 factors: Hero, Lost Child, Mascot, and Scapegoat.

Reliability: Alpha coefficients ranged from .87 to .91.

Author: Kier, F. J., and Buras, A. R.

Article: Perceived affiliation with family member roles: Validity and reliability of scores on the Children's Role Inventory.

Journal: *Educational and Psychological Measurement*, August 1999, *59*(4), 640–650.

Related Research: Potter, A. E., & Williams, D. E. (1991). Development of a measure examining children's roles in alcohol families. *Journal of Studies on Alcohol*, *52*, 70–77.

8818

Test Name: COGNITIVE STIMULATION SCALE

Purpose: To assess a parent's active cognitive stimulation.

Number of Items: 19

Format: Includes parent's Active Encouragement of Language Development, Imagination and Curiosity, and Problem-Solving Skills.

Reliability: Coefficient alpha was .84.

Validity: Correlation with mothers' level of education was .36 and with occupational prestige was .22. With other variables correlations ranged from −.24 to .19.

Author: Goldberg, W. A., et al.

Article: Employment and achievement: Mothers' work involvement in relation to children's achievement behaviors and mothers' parenting behaviors.

Journal: *Child Development,* August 1996, *67*(4), 1512–1527.

Related Research: O'Neil, R. (1992). *Maternal occupational experiences and psychological well-being: Influences on parental achievement-facilitation and children's academic achievement.* Unpublished doctoral dissertation, School of Social Ecology, University of California, Irvine.

8819

Test Name: COMMUNICATION PATTERNS QUESTIONNAIRE

Purpose: To assess how couples navigate the different stages of problem solving.

Number of Items: 35

Format: Nine-point scales are anchored by 1 (very unlikely) and 9 (very unlikely).

Reliability: Coefficient alpha was .74 (husbands) and .75 (wives).

Validity: Correlations with other variables ranged from −.57 to .51.

Author: Rogge, R. D., and Bradbury, T. N.

Article: Till violence do us part? The differing rules of communication and aggression in predicting adverse marital outcomes.

Journal: *Journal of Consulting and Clinical Psychology,* June 1999, *67*(3), 340–351.

Related Research: Christensen, A., & Sullaway, M. (1984). *Communication Patterns Questionnaire.* Unpublished manuscript, University of California, Los Angeles.

8820

Test Name: COMPLEX FAMILY SCALE

Purpose: To assess family integration and family challenge.

Number of Items: 32

Format: Includes two subscales: Family Integration and Family Challenge. Responses are made on a 4-point scale ranging from 1 (least agree) to 4 (most agree).

Reliability: Alpha coefficients ranged from .74 to .91.

Validity: Correlations with other variables ranged from −.29 to .79.

Author: Bensur, B. J., et al.

Article: An exploratory study of motivational predictors which influence graduation from two- and four-year colleges.

Journal: *Perceptual and Motor Skills,* June 1999, *88*(3) Part 1, 997–1008.

Related Research: Csikszentmihalya, M., et al. (1993). *Talented teenagers: The roots of success and failure.* Cambridge, MA: Cambridge University Press.

8821

Test Name: CONFLICT BEHAVIOR QUESTIONNAIRE

Purpose: To assess the quality and interaction patterns of parent-child relationships.

Number of Items: 20

Format: Yes/no format.

Reliability: Alpha coefficients were greater than .88.

Validity: Correlation with a 75-item version of the scale was .96.

Author: Summers, P., et al.

Article: Parental divorce during early adolescence in Caucasian families: The role of family process variables in predicting the long-term consequences for

early adult psychosocial adjustment.

Journal: *Journal of Consulting and Clinical Psychology,* April 1998, *66*(2), 327–336.

Related Research: Robin, A. L., & Weiss, J. G. (1980). Criterion-related validity of behavioral and self-report measures of problem solving. Communication skills in distressed and non-distressed parent-adolescent dyads. *Behavioral Assessment, 2,* 339–352.

8822

Test Name: CONFLICT TACTICS SCALES—REVISED

Purpose: To measure mothers' harsh discipline practices.

Number of Items: 16

Format: Responses are made on a 7-point scale ranging from "never" to "almost every day." Examples are presented.

Reliability: Coefficient alpha was .90.

Validity: Correlations with other variables ranged from .00 to .40.

Author: Nix, R. L., et al.

Article: The relation between mothers' hostile attribution tendencies and children's externalizing behavior problems: The mediating role of mothers' harsh discipline practices.

Journal: *Child Development,* July/August 1999, *70*(4), 896–909.

Related Research: Straus, M. A. (1979). Measuring intrafamily conflict and violence: The Conflict Tactics (CT) Scales. *Journal of Marriage and the Family, 21,* 75–88.

8823

Test Name: CONFLICT WITH PARENTS SCALE

Purpose: To measure conflict with parents over chores, friends, habits, and family relationships.

Number of Items: 11

Format: Four-point scales are anchored by 1 (never) and 4 (almost every day).

Reliability: Alphas were .88 (U.S. sample) and .76 (Chinese sample).

Author: Greenberger, E., et al.

Article: Family, peer, and individual correlates of depressive symptomatology among U.S. and Chinese adolescents.

Journal: *Journal of Consulting and Clinical Psychology*, April 2000, *68*(2), 209–219.

Related Research: Chen, C., et al. (1998). A cross-cultural study of family and peer correlates of adolescent misconduct. *Developmental Psychology, 34*, 770–781.

8824

Test Name: CONFLICTUAL INDEPENDENCE SUBSCALE

Purpose: To assess parent–child relationships.

Number of Items: 25

Format: Responses are made on a 5-point scale ranging from 1 (not at all true of me) to 5 (very true of me).

Reliability: Internal consistencies were .92 and .88.

Validity: Correlation with other variables ranged from −.66 to .78.

Author: Fisher, A. R., and Good, G. E.

Article: Perceptions of parent-child relationships and masculine role conflicts of college men.

Journal: *Journal of Counseling*

Psychology, July 1998, *45*(3), 346–352.

Related Research: Hoffman, J. A. (1984). Psychological separation of late adolescents from their parents. *Journal of Counseling Psychology, 31*, 170–178.

8825

Test Name: CONTINUED ATTACHMENT SCALE

Purpose: To assess cognitive elements of parental relationships and behavioral features of attachments.

Number of Items: 6

Format: Includes two subscales: Parental Preoccupation and Parental Concern.

Reliability: Internal consistency reliability was .76 for the mother and .74 for the father.

Author: Heiss, G. E., et al.

Article: Five scales in search of a construct: Exploring continued attachments to parents in college students.

Journal: *Journal of Personality Assessment*, August 1996, *67*(1), 102–115.

Related Research: Berman, W. H., et al. (1994). Measuring continued attachment to parents: The Continued Attachment Scale —Parent Version. *Psychological Reports, 75*, 171–182.

8826

Test Name: CONTROL SCALE

Purpose: To measure control.

Number of Items: 10

Format: Responses are made on a 5-point scale.

Reliability: Alpha coefficients were .75 and .76.

Author: Updegraff, K. A., et al.

Article: Adolescents' sex-typed friendship experiences: Does having a sister versus having a brother matter?

Journal: *Child Development*, November/December 2000, *71*(6), 1597–1610.

Related Research: Stets, J. E. (1995). Modeling control in relationships. *Journal of Marriage and the Family, 57*, 489–501.

8827

Test Name: COPARENTING SUPPORT SCALE

Purpose: To assess frequency of agreement on issues of parenting support.

Number of Items: 3

Format: Five-point scales range from "always" to "never." All items are presented.

Reliability: Alpha coefficients ranged from .55 to .60.

Author: Brody, G. H., et al.

Article: Sibling relationships in rural African American families.

Journal: *Journal of Marriage and the Family*, December 1999, *61*(4), 1046–1057.

Related Research: Ahrons, C. R. (1981). The continuing coparental relationship between divorced spouses. *American Journal of Orthopsychiatry, 51*, 415–428.

Brown, A. C., et al. (2000). Rural Black women and depression: A contextual analysis. *Journal of Marriage and the Family, 62*, 187–198.

8828

Test Name: COPING WITH CHILDREN'S NEGATIVE EMOTIONS SCALE

Purpose: To assess parental reactions.

Number of Items: 12

Format: For each of 12 situations, parents indicate on a 7-point scale how likely they are to react in each of six types of alternative fashions.

Reliability: Alpha coefficients ranged from .71 to .89.

Author: Eisenberg, N., et al.

Article: Parents' reactions to children's negative emotions: Relations to children's social competence and comforting behavior.

Journal: *Child Development*, October 1996, 67(5), 2227–2247.

Related Research: Fabes, R. A., et al. (1990). *The Coping with Children's Negative Emotions Scale: Description and scoring.* Unpublished manuscript, Department of Family Resources and Human Development, Arizona State University.

8829

Test Name: DIFFERENTIATION IN THE FAMILY SYSTEM SCALE

Purpose: To assess the level of differentiation in reciprocal relationships in the family system.

Number of Items: 11

Format: Scales range from "never" to "always." Scoring rules are described.

Reliability: Alpha coefficients ranged from .77 to .88.

Author: Chun, Y. -J., and MacDermid, S. M.

Article: Perceptions of family differentiation, individuation, and self-esteem among Korean adolescents.

Journal: *Journal of Marriage and*

the Family, May 1997, 59(2), 451–462.

Related Research: Anderson, S. A., & Sabatelli, R. M. (1992). The Differentiation in the Family System Scales: DIFS. *American Journal of Family Therapy, 20,* 89–101.

Bartle-Haring, S., & Sabatelli, R. M. (1998). An intergenerational examination of patterns of individual and family adjustment. *Journal of Marriage and the Family, 60,* 903–911.

Bartle-Haring, S., et al. (1999). Multiple perspectives on family differentiation: Analyses by multitrait multimethods matrix and triadic social relations models. *Journal of Marriage and the Family, 61,* 491–503.

8830

Test Name: DIFFERENTIATION OF SELF INVENTORY

Purpose: To identify adults' significant relationships and their current relations with family of origin.

Number of Items: 43

Format: Includes 4 subscales: Emotional Reactivity, I-Position, Emotional Cutoff, and Fusion with Others. Responses are made on a 6-point scale ranging from 1 (not at all true of me) to 6 (very true of me).

Reliability: Alpha coefficients ranged from .59 to .90.

Author: Skowron, E. A.

Article: The role of differentiation of self in marital adjustment.

Journal: *Journal of Counseling Psychology*, April 2000, 47(2), 229–237.

Related Research: Skowron, E. A., & Friedlander, M. L. (1998). The Differentiation of Self Inventory: Development and

initial validation. *Journal of Counseling Psychology, 45,* 1–11.

8831

Test Name: DISCIPLINE QUESTIONNAIRE

Purpose: To measure discipline style and discipline techniques used by parents.

Number of Items: 62

Format: Various formats are used. Each is briefly described.

Reliability: Internal consistency ranged from .63 to .97.

Author: Webster-Stratton, C.

Article: Preventing conduct problems in Head Start children: Strengthening parenting competencies.

Journal: *Journal of Consulting and Clinical Psychology*, October 1998, 66(5), 715–730.

Related Research: Webster-Stratton, C., & Spitzer, A. (1991). Development, reliability and validity of a daily telephone discipline interview: DDI. *Behavioral Assessment, 13,* 221–239.

8832

Test Name: DIVORCE ADJUSTMENT AND LIFE SATISFACTION SCALES

Purpose: To assess adjustment to divorce, attachment to ex-spouse, and general life satisfaction.

Number of Items: 21

Format: Four-point formats vary. All items are presented for divorce adjustment and attachment to ex-spouse. Sample items are presented for general life satisfaction.

Reliability: Alpha coefficients ranged from .76 to .82 across subscales.

Validity: Correlations between scales ranged from −.42 to .23.

Author: Wang, H., and Amato, P. R.

Article: Predictors of divorce adjustment: Stressors, resources, and definitions.

Journal: *Journal of Marriage and the Family*, August 2000, *62*(3), 655–668.

Related Research: Booth, A., et al. (1988). *Marital instability over the life course: Methodology report and code book for the fifth wave.* Lincoln, NE: Bureau of Sociological Research, University of Nebraska— Lincoln.

8833

Test Name: EMPLOYEES' CAREGIVING STRESS SCALE

Purpose: To measure stress experienced by employees as a result of caregiving responsibilities.

Number of Items: 3

Format: Five-point scales are used. All items and scales are presented.

Reliability: Coefficient alpha was .73.

Validity: Correlations with other variables ranged from −.04 to .37.

Author: Starrels, M. E., et al.

Article: The stress of caring for a parent: Effects of the elder's impairment on an employed adult child.

Journal: *Journal of Marriage and the Family*, November 1997, *59*(4), 860–872.

Related Research: Ingersall-Dayton, B., et al. (1996). Caregiving for parents and parents-in-law: Is gender

important? *The Gerontologist, 36*, 483–491.

8834

Test Name: ESSENTIAL CHARACTERISTICS OF SPOUSE SCALE

Purpose: To assess young adults' perceptions of desired spouse characteristics.

Number of Items: 27

Format: Includes 3 scales: Career Success Traits, Emotional/ Relational Traits, and Views of Family Life. Responses are made on a 5-point scale ranging from ''not at all essential'' to ''very essential.'' Sample items are presented.

Reliability: Alpha coefficients ranged from .67 to .87.

Author: Hallet, M. B., and Gilbert, L. A.

Article: Variables differentiating university women considering role-sharing and conventional dual-career marriages.

Journal: *Journal of Vocational Behavior*, April 1997, *50*(2), 308–322.

Related Research: Gilbert, L. A., et al. (1991). Assessing perceptions of occupational-family integration. *Sex-Roles, 24*, 107–119.

8835

Test Name: FAMILY ADAPTABILITY AND COHESION EVALUATION SCALE (FACES-III)

Purpose: To measure family cohesion.

Number of Items: 10

Format: Five-point scales are anchored by 1 (almost never) and 5 (almost always).

Reliability: Alpha coefficients ranged from .77 to .85.

Author: Huey, S. J., et al.

Article: Mechanisms of change in multisystemic therapy: Reducing delinquent behavior through therapist adherence and improved family and peer functioning.

Journal: *Journal of Consulting and Clinical Psychology*, June 2000, *68*(3), 451–467.

Related Research: Olson, D. H., et al. (1985). *FACES-III*. St. Paul, MN: University of Minnesota, Department of Family Social Science.

8836

Test Name: FAMILY ADAPTABILITY AND COHESION EVALUATION SCALES II

Purpose: To measure the dimensions of family cohesion and adaptability.

Number of Items: 30

Format: Likert format.

Reliability: Alpha coefficients ranged from .78 to .87 across subscales. Total alpha was .90.

Validity: Correlations with other variables ranged from −.26 to .65.

Author: Cashwell, C. S., and Vacc, N. A.

Article: Family functioning and risk behaviors: Influences on adolescent delinquency.

Journal: *The School Counselor*, November 1996, *44*(2), 105–114.

Related Research: Olson, D. H., et al. (1992). *Family inventories: Inventories used in a national survey of families across the lifecycle*. St. Paul, MN: University of Minnesota.

8837

Test Name: FAMILY ASSESSMENT DEVICE

Purpose: To assess family functioning.

Number of Items: 60

Format: Includes Problem-Solving, Communication, Roles, Affective Involvement, and General Functioning.

Reliability: Alpha coefficients ranged from .13 to .77

Author: Gavidia-Payne, S., and Stoneman, Z.

Article: Family predictors of maternal and paternal involvement in programs for young children with disabilities.

Journal: *Child Development*, August 1997, *68*(4), 701–717.

Related Research: Miller, I. W., et al. (1985). The McMaster Family Assessment Device: Reliability and validity. *Journal of Marital and Family Therapy*, *11*, 345–356.

8838

Test Name: FAMILY BACKGROUND QUESTIONNAIRE

Purpose: To measure memories of family of origin characteristics.

Number of Items: 169

Format: Includes 22 subscales.

Reliability: Alpha coefficients ranged from .76 to .98, Test-retest correlations ranged from .59 to .96.

Validity: Correlation with the Marlowe-Crowne Social Desirability Scale ranged from .06 to .29.

Author: Melchert, T. P., and Sayger, T. V.

Article: The development of an instrument for measuring memories of family of origin characteristics.

Journal: *Educational and Psychological Measurement*, February 1998, *58*(1), 99–118.

8839

Test Name: FAMILY COHESION AND ENMESHMENT SCALES

Purpose: To assess social support from family members and family members' reaction to giving and receiving support.

Number of Items: 8

Format: Scales range from 1 (very untrue for my family) to 4 (very true for my family).

Reliability: Alpha coefficients ranged from .53 to .83 across subscales.

Author: Barber, B. K., and Buehler, C.

Article: Family cohesion and enmeshment: Different constructs, different effects.

Journal: *Journal of Marriage and the Family*, May 1996, *58*(2), 433–441.

Related Research: Bloom, B. L. (1985). A factor analysis of self-report measures of family functioning. *Family Process, 24*, 225–239.

8840

Test Name: FAMILY COHESION SCALE

Purpose: To measure the closeness of family relationships.

Number of Items: 10

Format: Scales range from 1 (almost never) to 5 (almost always). Sample items are presented.

Reliability: Alpha coefficients ranged from .82 to .85.

Author: Tseng, V., and Fuligni, A. J.

Article: Parent-adolescent language use and relationships among immigrant families with East Asian, Filipino, and Latin American backgrounds.

Journal: *Journal of Marriage and the Family*, May 2000, *62*(2), 465–476.

Related Research: Olsen, D. H., et al. (1979). Circumplex model of marital and family systems: I. Cohesion and adaptability dimensions, family types, and clinical applications. *Family Process, 18*, 3–28.

8841

Test Name: FAMILY CONFLICT SCALE

Purpose: To assess family conflict.

Number of Items: 5

Format: Responses are made on a 5-point scale ranging from 1 (never) to 5 (always).

Reliability: Coefficient alpha was .79.

Validity: Correlations with other variables ranged from −.60 to .35.

Author: Duxbury, L. E., et al.

Article: Work and family environments and the adoption of computer-supported supplemental work-at-home.

Journal: *Journal of Vocational Behavior*, August 1996, *49*(1), 1–23.

Related Research: Nye, F., & MacDougall, E. (1959). The dependent variable in marital research. *Pacific Sociological Review, 2*, 67–70.

8842

Test Name: FAMILY DECISION-MAKING SCALE

Purpose: To identify type of family decision-making.

Number of Items: 24

Format: Responses are made on a 5-point scale ranging from 5 (parents decided each issue without discussing it) to 1 (left it entirely to the child).

Reliability: Alpha coefficients ranged from .86 to .91.

Author: Smetana, J., and Gaines, C.

Article: Adolescent-parent conflict in middle-class African American families.

Journal: *Child Development,* November/December 1999, 70(6), 1447–1463.

Related Research: Steinberg, L. (1987). Single-parents, stepparents, and the susceptibility of adolescents to antisocial peer pressure. *Child Development, 58,* 269–275.

8843

Test Name: FAMILY DISTRESS SCALE

Purpose: To assess family distress.

Number of Items: 6

Format: Responses are made on a 5-point scale.

Reliability: Coefficient alpha was .84.

Validity: Correlations with other variables ranged from −.41 to .40.

Author: Frone, M. R., et al.

Article: Developing and testing an integrative model of the work-family interface.

Journal: *Journal of Vocational*

Behavior, April 1997, 50(2), 145–167.

Related Research: Kandel, D. B., et al. (1985). The stressfulness of daily social roles for women: Marital, occupational, and household roles. *Journal of Health and Social Behavior, 26,* 64–78.

8844

Test Name: FAMILY EMOTIONAL INVOLVEMENT AND CRITICISM SCALE

Purpose: To measure how one family member perceives the emotional expressions of the entire family.

Number of Items: 14

Format: Five-point scales.

Reliability: Reliability indexes ranged from .54 to .82.

Author: Rossello, J., and Bernal, G.

Article: The efficacy of cognitive-behavioral and interpersonal treatments for depression in Puerto Rican adolescents.

Journal: *Journal of Consulting and Clinical Psychology,* October 1999, 67(5), 734–745.

Related Research: Shields, C., et al. (1992). Development of the Family Emotional Involvement and Criticism Scale (FEICS): A self-report scale to measure expressed emotion. *Journal of Marriage and Family Therapy, 18,* 395–407.

8845

Test Name: FAMILY EXPECTATIONS SCALE

Purpose: To measure family expectations.

Number of Items: 5

Format: All items are presented.

Reliability: Coefficient alpha was .81.

Validity: Correlations with other variables ranged from −.15 to .17.

Author: Duxbury, L. E., et al.

Article: Work and family environments and the adoption of computer-supported supplemental work-at-home.

Journal: *Journal of Vocational Behavior,* August 1996, 49(1), 1–23.

Related Research: Cooke, R., & Rousseau, D. 1984. Stress and strain from family roles and work role expectations. *Journal of Applied Psychology, 69,* 252–260.

8846

Test Name: FAMILY EXPRESSIVENESS QUESTIONNAIRE

Purpose: To determine the family expressiveness climate.

Number of Items: 40

Format: Provides 3 scores: FEQ Positive, FEQ Negative Dominant, and the FEQ Negative Submissive. Responses are made on a 9-point scale ranging from 1 (not at all frequently in my family) to 9 (very frequently in my family).

Reliability: Alpha coefficients ranged from .81 to .90.

Author: Jones, D. C., et al.

Article: The development of display rule knowledge: Linkages with family expressiveness and social competence.

Journal: *Child Development,* August 1998, 69(4), 1209–1222.

Related Research: Halberstadt, A. G. (1986). Family socialization of emotional expression and nonverbal communication styles and skills. *Journal of Personality and Social Psychology*, *51*, 827–836.

8847

Test Name: FAMILY-FRIEND SUPPORT SCALE

Purpose: To measure family and friend support in a job search, family and friend emotional sustenance, and influence of family and friends.

Number of Items: 13

Format: Five-point Likert format.

Reliability: Alpha coefficients ranged from .77 to .89.

Validity: Correlations with other variables ranged from −.21 to .60.

Author: Ryan, A. M., et al.

Article: Applicant self-selection: Correlates of withdrawal from a multiple hurdle process.

Journal: *Journal of Applied Psychology*, April 2000, *85*(2), 163–179.

Related Research: Ryan, A. M., & McFarland, L. A. (1997). *Organizational influences on applicant withdrawal from selection processes.* Paper presented at the twelfth annual conference of the Society for Industrial and Organizational Psychology, St. Louis, MO.

8848

Test Name: FAMILY IDENTITY SCALE

Purpose: To measure family identity.

Number of Items: 4

Format: Responses are made on a 5-point scale ranging from 1 (strongly disagree) to 5 (strongly

agree). Sample items are presented.

Reliability: Coefficient alpha was .82.

Validity: Correlations with other variables ranged from −.24 to −.16.

Author: Aryee, S., and Luk, V.

Article: Work and nonwork influences on the career satisfaction of dual-earner couples.

Journal: *Journal of Vocational Behavior*, August 1996, *49*(1), 38–52.

Related Research: Lodahl, T., & Kejner, M. (1965). The definition and measurement of job involvement. *Journal of Applied Psychology*, *49*, 24–33.

8849

Test Name: FAMILY INVOLVEMENT SCALE

Purpose: To assess family involvement.

Number of Items: 3

Format: Responses are made on a 5-point scale ranging from "strongly agree" to "strongly disagree." An example is presented.

Reliability: Coefficient alpha was .85.

Validity: Correlations with other variables ranged from −.18 to .27.

Author: Greenhaus, J. H., et al.

Article: Work and family influences on departure from public accounting.

Journal: *Journal of Vocational Behavior*, April 1997, *50*(2), 249–270.

Related Research: Parasuraman, S., et al. (1992). Role stressors, social support and well being

among two-career couples. *Journal of Organizational Behavior*, *13*, 339–356.

8850

Test Name: FAMILY INVOLVEMENT SCALE

Purpose: To measure family involvement.

Number of Items: 4

Reliability: Coefficient alpha was .76.

Validity: Correlations with other variables ranged from −.33 to .40.

Author: Parasuraman, S., et al.

Article: Work and family variables, entrepreneurial career success, and psychological well-being.

Journal: *Journal of Vocational Behavior*, June 1996, *48*(3), 275–300.

Related Research: Kopelman, R. E., et al. (1983). A model of work, family and interrole conflict: A construct validation study. *Organizational Behavior and Human Performance*, *32*, 198–215.

8851

Test Name: FAMILY INVOLVEMENT SCALE

Purpose: To measure family involvement.

Number of Items: 6

Format: An example is presented.

Reliability: Coefficient alpha was .83.

Validity: Correlations with other variables ranged from −.11 to .23.

Author: Duxbury, L. E., et al.

Article: Work and family environments and the adoption of computer-supported supplemental work-at-home.

Journal: *Journal of Vocational Behavior*, August 1996, *49*(1), 1–23.

Related Research: Yogev, S., & Brett, J. (1985). Patterns of work and family involvement among single and dual-earner couples. *Journal of Applied Psychology*, *70*, 754–786.

8852

Test Name: FAMILY INVOLVEMENT SCALES

Purpose: To assess spouse, parental, and family involvement.

Number of Items: 11

Format: All items are presented.

Reliability: Alpha coefficients ranged from .66 to .97.

Validity: Correlations with other variables ranged from −.14 to .25.

Authors: Eagle, B. W., et al.

Article: The importance of employee demographic profiles for understanding experiences of work-family internal conflicts.

Journal: *Journal of Social Psychology*, December 1998, *138*(6), 690–709.

8853

Test Name: FAMILY OBLIGATIONS SCALE

Purpose: To assess family relationships.

Number of Items: 8

Format: Responses are made on a scale ranging from "strongly disagree" to "strongly agree."

Reliability: Alpha coefficients ranged from .70 to .77.

Author: Phinney, J. S., et al.

Article: Cultural values and intergenerational value discrepancies in immigrant and non-immigrant families.

Journal: *Child Development*, March/April 2000, *71*(2), 528–539.

Related Research: Berry, J., et al. (1995). *The ICSEY Questionnaire.* Working document of the International Comparative Study of Ethnocultural Youth.

8854

Test Name: FAMILY-OVERLOAD SCALE

Purpose: To measure parenting overload.

Number of Items: 4

Format: Responses are made on a 5-point frequency-based response scale. A sample item is presented.

Reliability: Coefficient alpha was .72.

Validity: Correlations with other variables ranged from −.22 to .42.

Author: Frone, M. R., et al.

Article: Developing and testing an integrative model of the work-family interface.

Journal: *Journal of Vocational Behavior*, April 1997, *50*(2), 145–167.

Related Research: Kessler, R. C. (1985). *1985 Detroit area survey.* Unpublished manuscript. University of Michigan, Ann Arbor, MI: Institute for Social Research.

Frone, M. R., et al. (1992). Antecedents and outcomes of work-family conflict: Testing a model of the work-family interface. *Journal of Applied Psychology*, *77*, 65–78.

8855

Test Name: FAMILY-PERFORMANCE SCALE

Purpose: To assess family performance.

Number of Items: 5

Format: Responses are made on a 5-point frequency-based scale. A sample item is presented.

Reliability: Coefficient alpha was .84.

Validity: Correlations with other variables ranged from −.44 to .37.

Author: Frone, M. R., et al.

Article: Developing and testing an integrative model of the work-family interface.

Journal: *Journal of Vocational Behavior*, April 1997, *50*(2), 145–167.

Related Research: Williams, L. J., & Anderson, S. E. (1991). Job satisfaction and organizational commitment as predictors of organizational citizenship and in-role behaviors. *Journal of Management*, *17*(3), 601–617.

8856

Test Name: FAMILY PROBLEM SOLVING SCALE

Purpose: To assess to what degree family members rely on each other to solve problems.

Number of Items: 7 (for each family member).

Format: Scales range from 1 (never or almost never) to 5 (always or almost always). All items are described.

Reliability: Alpha coefficients ranged from .49 to .75.

Author: Vuchinich, S., and DeBaryshe, B.

Article: Factor structure and predictive validity of

questionnaire reports on family problem solving.

Journal: *Journal of Marriage and the Family,* November 1997, *59*(4), 915–927.

Related Research: Conger, R. D., & Elder, G. H., Jr. (1994). *Families in troubled times: Adapting to change in rural America.* New York: Aldine de Gruyter.

8857

Test Name: FAMILY PROCESS SCALES

Purpose: To assess a child's perceptions of parental expectations of general academic performance, grades, interest in academic performance, involvement in school activities and parent–child communication.

Number of Items: 16

Format: All items are presented.

Reliability: Alpha coefficients ranged from .25 to .92 across grade levels.

Author: Hoge, D. R., et al.

Article: Four family process factors predicting academic achievement in sixth and seventh grade.

Journal: *Educational Research Quarterly,* December 1997, *21*(2), 27–42.

Related Research: Brookover, W. B., et al. (1962). *Self-concept of ability and school achievement* (Report of Cooperative Research Project No. 845, U.S. Office of Education). East Lansing, Michigan State University.

8858

Test Name: FAMILY PROFILE II

Purpose: To measure family functioning.

Number of Items: 58

Format: Seven-point scales range from (1) never to (7) always. All items are presented. Scoring methods are also presented.

Reliability: Cronbach alphas ranged from .72 to .95 across subscales.

Validity: Multiple correlations with other variables ranged from .20 to .78.

Author: Lee, T. R., et al.

Article: The Family Profile II: A self-scored brief family assessment tool.

Journal: *Psychological Reports,* October 1997, *81*(2), 467–477.

8859

Test Name: FAMILY RESOURCE SCALE—MODIFIED

Purpose: To evaluate the adequacy of mothers' families' financial resources.

Number of Resources: 17

Format: Includes 3 subscales: Necessities, General Money, and Money for Extras. Responses are made on a 5-point scale ranging from 1 (not at all) to 5 (almost always).

Reliability: Alpha coefficients ranged from .69 to .84.

Validity: Correlations with other variables ranged from −.14 to .17.

Author: Brody, G. H., et al.

Article: Linking maternal efficacy beliefs, developmental goals, parenting practices, and child competence in rural single-parent African American families.

Journal: *Child Development,* September/October 1999, *70*(5), 1197–1208.

Related Research: Dunst, C. J., & Leet, H. E. (1987). Measuring the adequacy of resources in households with young children. *Child: Care, Health, and Development, 13*(2), 111–125.

8860

Test Name: FAMILY ROUTINES INVENTORY

Purpose: To assess family routines.

Number of Items: 28

Format: Responses are made on a frequency scale ranging from "almost never" to "almost every day." Examples are presented.

Reliability: Coefficient alpha was .67.

Author: Brody, G. H., et al.

Article: Linking maternal efficacy beliefs, developmental goals, parenting practices, and child competence in rural single-parent African American families.

Journal: *Child Development,* September/October 1999, *70*(5), 1197–1208.

Related Research: Jensen, E. W., et al. (1983). The Family Routines Inventory: Development and validation. *Social Science and Medicine, 17*(4), 201–211.

8861

Test Name: FAMILY SATISFACTION SCALE

Purpose: To measure family satisfaction.

Number of Items: 3

Format: Responses are made on a 5-point scale ranging from 1 (strongly agree) to 5 (strongly disagree). An example is given.

Reliability: Coefficient alpha was .76.

Validity: Correlations with other variables ranged from −.28 to .21.

Author: Parasuraman, S., et al.

Article: Work and family variables, entrepreneurial career success, and psychological well-being.

Journal: *Journal of Vocational Behavior*, June 1996, *48*(3), 275–300.

Related Research: Kopelman, R. E., et al. (1983). A model of work, family and interrole conflict: A construct validation study. *Organizational Behavior and Human Performance*, *32*, 198–215.

8862

Test Name: FAMILY SATISFACTION SCALE

Purpose: To assess satisfaction with family adaptability and cohesion.

Number of Items: 14

Reliability: Coefficient alpha was .92. Test-retest reliability (5 weeks) was .75.

Validity: Correlations with other variables ranged from −.49 to .65.

Author: Cashwell, C. S., and Vacc, N. A.

Article: Family functioning and risk behaviors: Influences on adolescent delinquency.

Journal: *The School Counselor*, November 1996, *44*(2), 105–114.

Related Research: Olson, D. H., et al. (1992). *Family inventories: Inventories used in a national survey of families across the lifecycle.* St. Paul, MN: University of Minnesota.

8863

Test Name: FAMILY STRENGTHS SCALE

Purpose: To assess an individual's family strengths and weaknesses.

Number of Items: 12

Format: Five-point Likert format.

Reliability: Alpha was .88.

Author: Kaslow, N. A., et al.

Article: Factors that mediate and moderate the link between partner abuse and suicidal behavior in African American women.

Journal: *Journal of Consulting and Clinical Psychology*, June 1998, *66*(3), 533–540.

Related Research: Olson, D. H., et al. (1982). Family strengths. In D. H. Olson et al. (Eds.), *Family inventories* (pp. 56–70). St. Paul: University of Minnesota Family Social Science.

8864

Test Name: FAMILY STRUCTURE SURVEY

Purpose: To measure adults' recalled perceptions of their family interactions on four dimensions of dysfunctional family structure.

Number of Items: 50

Format: Includes 4 dimensions: Overinvolvement, Fear of Separation, Role Reversal, and Marital Conflict. Responses are made on a 5-point scale ranging from 1 (completely false) to 5 (completely true).

Reliability: Alpha coefficients ranged from .51 to .90.

Validity: Correlations with other variables ranged from −.36 to .53.

Author: Mallinckrodt, B., et al.

Article: Family dysfunction, alexithymia, and client attachment to therapist.

Journal: *Journal of Counseling*

Psychology, October 1998, *45*(4), 497–504.

Related Research: Lopez, F. G., et al. (1988). Family structure, psychological separation, and college adjustment: A canonical analysis and cross-validation. *Journal of Counseling Psychology*, *35*, 402–409.

8865

Test Name: FAMILY SUPPPORT SCALE

Purpose: To measure the social supports construct.

Number of Items: 18

Format: Responses are made on a 5-point scale ranging from 1 (not at all helpful) to 5 (extremely helpful).

Reliability: Alpha coefficients were .76 and .78.

Author: Gavidia-Payne, S., and Stoneman, Z.

Article: Family predictors of maternal and paternal involvement in programs for young children with disabilities.

Journal: *Child Development*, August 1997, *68*(4), 701–717.

Related Research: Dunst, C. J., et al. (1988). *Enabling and empowering families: Principles and guidelines for practice.* Cambridge, MA: Brookline.

8866

Test Name: FAMILY UNPREDICTABILITY SCALE

Purpose: To assess the lack of consistency in family behavior and regulatory systems.

Number of Items: 22

Format: Scales range from 1 (not at all) to 5 (extremely). All items are presented.

Reliability: Alpha coefficients ranged from .75 to .88.

Validity: Correlations with other variables ranged from −.52 to .54.

Author: Ross, L. T., and Hill, E. M.

Article: The Family Unpredictability Scale: Reliability and validity.

Journal: *Journal of Marriage and the Family*, May 2000, *62*(2), 549–562.

8867

Test Name: FATHER INVOLVEMENT AND SATISFACTION SCALES

Purpose: To measure the perceived involvement and satisfaction of fathers in their family role.

Number of Items: 15

Format: Involvement scales range from 1 (not at all) to 5 (very much). Satisfaction scales are bipolar adjectives. Sample items are presented.

Reliability: Alpha coefficients were .78 (involvement) and .90 (satisfaction).

Validity: Correlations with other variables ranged from −.33 to .46.

Author: Lev-Wiesel, R.

Article: The effect of children's sleeping arrangements (communal vs. familial) on fatherhood among men in an Israeli kibbutz.

Journal: *The Journal of Social Psychology*, October 2000, *140*(5), 580–588.

8868

Test Name: FELT OBLIGATION MEASURE

Purpose: To measure expectations

of appropriate interactions in relationships with kin.

Number of Items: 34

Format: Five-point scales.

Reliability: Internal consistency coefficients ranged from .61 to .88 across subscales.

Author: Stein, C. H., et al.

Article: "Because they're my parents": An intergenerational study of felt obligation and parental caregiving.

Journal: *Journal of Marriage and the Family*, August 1998, *60*(3), 611–622.

Related Research: Stein, C. H. (1992). Ties that bind: Three studies of obligation on adult relationships with family. *Journal of Social and Personal Relationships*, *9*, 525–547.

8869

Test Name: FILIAL RESPONSIBILITY COMPONENT INDEX

Purpose: To assess attitudes of adult children about responsibilities to aging parents.

Number of Items: 10

Format: Five-point scales. Sample items are presented.

Reliability: Internal consistency coefficients ranged from .84 to .86.

Author: Stein, C. H., et al.

Article: "Because they're my parents": An intergenerational study of felt obligation and parental caregiving.

Journal: *Journal of Marriage and the Family*, August 1998, *60*(3), 611–622.

Related Research: Finley, N. J., et al. (1988). Motivators and inhibitors of attitudes of filial

obligation toward aging parents. *The Gerontologist*, *28*, 73–78.

8870

Test Name: FILIAL RESPONSIBILITY EXPECTATIONS SCALE

Purpose: To measure perceptions of filial responsibilities.

Number of Items: 4

Format: Scales range from 1 (strongly disagree) to 4 (strongly agree). All items are presented.

Reliability: Coefficient alpha was .79.

Author: Lee, G. R., et al.

Article: Race differences in filial responsibility expectations among older parents.

Journal: *Journal of Marriage and the Family*, May 1998, *60*(2), 404–412.

Related Research: Seelbach, W. C. (1978). Correlates of aged parents' filial responsibility expectations and realizations. *Family Coordinator*, *27*, 341–350.

8871

Test Name: FINANCIAL STRAIN SCALE

Purpose: To measure financial strain in the family

Number of Items: 3

Format: Four-point scales range from 1 (not at all) to 4 (a lot) on two items and from 1 (not at all difficult) to 4 (very difficult) on one item. All items are presented.

Reliability: Coefficient alpha was .56.

Author: Jackson, A. P., et al.

Article: Employment status, psychological well-being, social support, and physical discipline practices of single Black mothers.

Journal: *Journal of Marriage and the Family,* November 1998, *60*(4), 894–902.

Related Research: McLoyd, V. C., et al. (1994). Unemployment and work interruption among African American single mothers: Effects on parenting and adolescent socioemotional functioning. *Child Development, 65,* 562–589.

8872

Test Name: FIRM-RESPONSIVE PARENTING SCALE

Purpose: To measure firm-responsive parenting.

Number of Items: 9

Format: Responses are made on a 4-point scale ranging from 1 (definitely false) to 4 (definitely true). Examples are presented.

Reliability: Coefficient alpha was .76.

Validity: Correlations with other variables ranged from −.24 to .22.

Author: Shumow, L., et al.

Article: School choice, family characteristics, and home–school relations: Contributors to school achievement.

Journal: *Journal of Educational Psychology,* September 1996, *88*(3), 457–460.

8873

Test Name: GRANDPARENT–GRANDCHILDREN INTEGRATION SCALE

Purpose: To assess affectual solidarity and social-structural integration of grandparents and grandchildren.

Number of Items: 7

Format: Solidarity scales range

from "extremely close/well" to "not at all close/well." Solidarity scales range from 1 (none) to 4 (at least once a week) or 1 (greater than 500 miles) to 4 (less than 5 miles). All items are presented.

Reliability: Alpha coefficients exceed .80.

Author: Silverstein, M., and Long, J. D.

Article: Trajectories of grandparents' perceived solidarity with adult grandchildren: A growth curve analysis over 23 years.

Journal: *Journal of Marriage and the Family,* November 1998, *60*(4), 912–923.

Related Research: Silverstein, M., & Bergston, V. L. (1997). Intergenerational solidarity and the structure of adult child-parent relationships in American families. *American Journal of Sociology, 103,* 429–460.

Silverstein, M., & Chen, X. (1999). The impact of acculturation in Mexican American families on the quality of adult-grandchild-grandparent relationships. *Journal of Marriage and the Family, 61,* 188–198.

8874

Test Name: HENDERSON ENVIRONMENTAL LEARNING PROCESS SCALE

Purpose: To assess environmental process variables in the home that are relevant to intellectual development and academic achievement of young children.

Number of Items: 44

Format: Includes 6 factors: Reinforcement of Education, Outside Activities, Attitude About Education, Direct Teaching, Parent Education, and Play.

Responses are made on a 5-point scale. All items are presented.

Reliability: Alpha coefficients ranged from .35 to .80.

Author: Curtis, W. J., and Singh, N. N.

Article: The psychometric characteristic of the Henderson Environmental Learning Process Scale.

Journal: *Educational and Psychological Measurement,* April 1997, *57*(2), 280–291.

Related Research: Henderson, R., et al. (1972). Development and validation of the Henderson Environmental Learning Process Scale. *Journal of Social Psychology, 88,* 185–196.

8875

Test Name: HOME LITERACY QUESTIONNAIRE

Purpose: To identify parental initiatives to enhance their children's at-home literacy experience.

Number of Items: 5

Format: For each item, one of five frequency of occurrence or date of onset of literacy activities is checked. All items are presented.

Reliability: Spearman-Brown split-half reliability was .77.

Validity: Correlations with other variables ranged from −.16 to .76.

Author: Frijters, J. C., et al.

Article: Direct and mediated influences of home literacy and literacy interest on prereaders' oral vocabulary and early written language skill.

Journal: *Journal of Educational Psychology,* September 2000, *92*(3), 466–477.

Related Research: Bus, A. G., &

van Ijzendoorn, M. H. (1995). Mothers reading to their 3-year-olds: The role of mother-child attachment security in becoming literate. *Reading Research Quarterly, 30*, 998–1015.

8876

Test Name: HOME OBSERVATION FOR MEASUREMENT OF THE ENVIRONMENT

Purpose: To assess the quality and quantity of support for children in the home.

Number of Items: 45

Format: Observation/interview format yields binary responses.

Reliability: Alpha coefficients ranged from .50 to .76.

Validity: Correlations with other variables ranged from .16 to .41.

Author: Bradley, R. H., et al.

Article: Parents' socioemotional investment in children.

Journal: *Journal of Marriage and the Family,* February 1997, *59*(1), 77–90.

Related Research: Caldwell, B. M., & Bradley, R. H. (1984). *Home Observation for Measurement of the Environment.* University of Arkansas at Little Rock.

8877

Test Name: HOUSEHOLD DISCONTENT SCALE

Purpose: To assess the frequency of discontent concerning the division of household labor and paid work.

Number of Items: 9

Format: Scales range from 1 (never) to 7 (very often). A sample item is presented.

Reliability: Alpha coefficients

ranged from .81 (housework) to .85 (paid work).

Validity: Correlations with other variables ranged from −.25 to .45.

Author: Kluwer, E. S., et al.

Article: The marital dynamics of conflict over the division of labor.

Journal: *Journal of Marriage and the Family,* August 1997, *59*(3), 635–653.

Related Research: Kluwer, E. S., et al. (1996). Marital conflict about the division of household labor and paid work. *Journal of Marriage and the Family, 58*, 958–969.

8878

Test Name: HUSBAND'S EMOTIONAL AND PRACTICAL SUPPORT INVENTORY

Purpose: To measure women's perception of their husband's instrumental and emotional support of their out-of-home world.

Number of Items: 9

Format: Includes 2 subscales: Emotional Support and Practical Support. Responses are made on a 5-point scale ranging from 1 (not at all) to 5 (to a very large extent). Examples are given.

Reliability: Alpha coefficients ranged from .78 to .83

Validity: Correlations with other variables ranged from −.38 to .12

Author: Rosenbaum, M., and Cohen, E.

Article: Equalitarian marriages, spousal support, resourcefulness, and psychological distress among Israeli working women.

Journal: *Journal of Vocational*

Behavior, February 1999, *54*(1), 102–113

Related Research: Tovel, C. (1984). *Personality, family, and environmental variables as determinants of career development among Air-Force pilots' wives.* Unpublished master's thesis, Tel Aviv University, Israel.

8879

Test Name: HUSBAND EVALUATION SCALE

Purpose: To rate the qualities of a former husband.

Number of Items: 7

Format: Semantic differential format.

Reliability: Alpha coefficients ranged from .85 to .92.

Author: DeGarmo, D. S., and Kitson, G. C.

Article: Identity relevance and disruption as predictors of psychological distress for widowed and divorced women.

Journal: *Journal of Marriage and the Family,* November 1996, *58*(4), 983–997.

Related Research: Lopata, H. Z. (1979). *Women as widows: Support systems.* New York: Elsevier North Holland.

8880

Test Name: IDENTIFICATION WITH PARENTS SCALE

Purpose: To assess to what degree children identify with parents.

Number of Items: 4

Format: Scales range from 1 (not true at all) to 7 (very true). Sample items are presented.

Reliability: Alpha coefficients ranged from .83 to .85.

Validity: Correlations with other variables ranged from −.19 to .09.

Author: Barling, J., et al.

Article: Parents' job insecurity affects children's academic performance through cognitive difficulties.

Journal: *Journal of Applied Psychology*, June 1999, *84*(3), 437–444.

Related Research: MacEwen, K. E., & Barling, J. (1991). Effects of maternal employment experiences on children's behavior via mood, cognitive difficulties and parenting behavior. *Journal of Marriage and the Family, 53*, 635–644.

8881

Test Name: IMPACT OF CAREGIVING SCALE

Purpose: To measure the restriction on personal time resulting from involvement with spouse with cancer.

Number of Items: 8

Format: Three-point scales are anchored by 0 (not at all) to 3 (a great deal). Sample items are presented.

Reliability: Coefficient alpha was .90.

Author: Manne, S. L., et al.

Article: Spousal negative responses to cancer patients: The role of social restriction, spouse mood, and relationship satisfaction.

Journal: *Journal of Consulting and Clinical Psychology*, June 1999, *67*(3), 352–361.

Related Research: Poulshock, S. W., & Deimling, G. T. (1984). Families caring for elders in residence: Issues in the measurement of burden. *Journal of Gerontology, 39*, 230–239.

8882

Test Name: INDEX OF SEXUAL SATISFACTION

Purpose: To measure sexual satisfaction in heterosexual couples.

Number of Items: 25

Format: Five-point Likert format.

Reliability: Alpha coefficients ranged from .89 to .91. Test-retest reliability was .93 (1 week).

Author: Purnine, D. M., and Carey, M. P.

Article: Interpersonal communication and sexual adjustment: The roles of understanding and agreement.

Journal: *Journal of Consulting and Clinical Psychology*, December 1997, *65*(6), 1017–1025.

Related Research: Hudson, W. W., et al. (1981). A short-form scale to measure sexual discord in dyadic relationships. *Journal of Sex Research, 17*, 157–174.

8883

Test Name: INDIVIDUALISM–COLLECTIVISM SCALE

Purpose: To measure individualism–collectivism in the context of relations with family members and others.

Number of Items: 64

Format: Responses are made on a 6-point scale ranging from "strong agreement" to "strong disagreement."

Reliability: Alpha coefficients were .65 and .75.

Author: Jackson, T., et al.

Article: Culture and self-presentation as predictors of

shyness among Japanese and American female college students.

Journal: *Perceptual and Motor Skills*, April 2000, *90*(2), 475–482.

Related Research: Hui, C. H. (1988). Measurement of individualism-collectivism. *Journal of Research in Personality, 22*, 17–36.

8884

Test Name: INTERACTION RESPONSE PATTERNS QUESTIONNAIRE

Purpose: To assess partners' perceptions of the behavioral response patterns in interactions with spouses in terms of avoidance, conflict avoidance, angry withdrawal, and hostile reciprocity.

Number of Items: 24

Format: Likelihood ratings ranged from "unlikely" to "likely."

Reliability: Alpha coefficients ranged from .83 to .85 across subscales.

Validity: Correlations with other variables ranged from −.01 to .37.

Author: Roberts, L. J.

Article: Fire and ice in marital communication: Hostile and distancing behaviors as predictors of marital distress.

Journal: *Journal of Marriage and the Family*, August 2000, *62*(3), 693–707.

8885

Test Name: INTERGENERATIONAL FUSION SCALE

Purpose: To assess adolescent individuation in the family system.

Number of Items: 6

Format: Five-point scales range from "strongly disagree" to "strongly agree." A sample item is presented.

Reliability: Coefficient alpha was .69.

Author: Chun, Y.-J., and MacDermid, S. M.

Article: Perceptions of family differentiation, individuation, and self-esteem among Korean adolescents.

Journal: *Journal of Marriage and the Family,* May 1997, *59*(2), 451–462.

Related Research: Bray, J. H., et al. (1984). Personal authority in the family system: Development of a questionnaire to measure personal authority in intergenerational family processes. *Journal of Marital and Family Therapy, 10,* 167–178.

8886

Test Name: INVENTORY OF PARENT AND PEER ATTACHMENT

Purpose: To ascertain children's relationships with their primary caregiver.

Number of Items: 23

Format: Responses are made on a 4-point scale ranging from 1 (hardly ever true) to 4 (very often true). Includes 3 subscales: Communication, Trust, and Alienation. Examples are presented.

Reliability: Alpha coefficients ranged from .76 to .83.

Author: Rhodes, J. E., et al.

Article: Agents of change: Pathways through which mentoring relationships influence adolescents' academic adjustment.

Journal: *Child Development,* November/December 2000, *71*(6), 1662–1671.

Related Research: Armsden, G. C., & Greenberg, M. T. (1987). The Inventory of Parent and Peer Attachment (IPPA): Relationship to well being in adolescence. *Journal of Youth and Adolescence, 16,* 427–454.

8887

Test Name: INVENTORY OF PARENT AND PEER ATTACHMENT

Purpose: To assess adolescents' perceptions of the current degree of trust, communication, and alienation in their relationships with their mothers.

Number of Items: 25

Format: Responses are made on a 5-point Likert scale.

Reliability: Coefficient alpha was .95.

Author: Allen, J. P., et al.

Article: Attachment and adolescent psychological functioning.

Journal: *Child Development,* October 1998, *69*(5), 1406–1419.

Related Research: Armsden, G. C., & Greenberg, M. T. (1987). The Inventory of Parent and Peer Attachment: Individual differences and their relationship to psychological well-being in adolescence. *Journal of Youth and Adolescence, 16,* 427–454.

8888

Test Name: INVENTORY OF PARENT AND PEER ATTACHMENT

Purpose: To measure the overall quality or security in the attachment bond with mother and with father.

Number of Items: 50

Format: Includes 2 subscales: Attachment to Mother and Attachment to Father. Responses are made on a 5-point scale ranging from 1 (almost always true or always true) to 5 (almost never or never true).

Reliability: Alpha coefficients ranged from .72 to .91. Test-retest (3 weeks) reliability coefficients ranged from .86 to .93.

Author: Rice, K. G., and Mirzadeh, S. A.

Article: Perfectionism, attachment, and adjustment.

Journal: *Journal of Counseling Psychology,* April 2000, *47*(2), 238–250.

Related Research: Armsden, G. C., & Greenberg, M. T. (1987). The Inventory of Parent and Peer Attachment: Individual differences and their relationship to psychological well-being in adolescence. *Journal of Youth and Adolescence, 16,* 427–453.

8889

Test Name: INVENTORY OF PARENT AND PEER ATTACHMENT

Purpose: To measure the quality of attachment of adolescents to parents and peers.

Number of Items: 53

Format: Includes 3 factors: Trust, Communication, and Alienation. Responses are made on a 5-point scale ranging from 1 (almost never or never) to 5 (almost always or always).

Reliability: Alpha coefficients ranged from .72 to .91.

Validity: Correlations with other variables ranged from −.36 to .70 ($N = 152$).

Author: Mothersead, P. K., et al.

Article: Attachment, family dysfunction, parental alcoholism, and interpersonal distress in late adolescence: A structural model.

Journal: *Journal of Counseling Psychology*, April 1998, *45*(2), 196–203.

Related Research: Armsden, G. C., & Greenberg, M. T. (1987). The Inventory of Parent and Peer Attachment: Individual differences and their relationship to psychological well-being in adolescence. *Journal of Youth and Adolescence, 16,* 427–453.

8890

Test Name: INVENTORY OF PARENT AND PEER ATTACHMENT

Purpose: To assess the degree of attachment that adolescents experience with respect to their parents and friends.

Number of Items: 75

Format: Includes peer, mother, and father attachment subscales. Responses are made on a 5-point Likert-type scale.

Reliability: Internal reliabilities ranged from .87 to .92.

Validity: Correlations with other variables ranged from −.22 to .48.

Author: Felsman, D. E., and Blustein, D. L.

Article: The role of peer relatedness in late adolescent career development.

Journal: *Journal of Vocational Behavior*, April 1999, *54*(2), 279–295.

Related Research: Armsden, G. C., & Greenberg, M. T. (1987). The Inventory of Parent and Peer Attachment: Individual differences and their relationship to psychological well-being in

adolescence. *Journal of Youth and Adolescence, 16,* 427–454.

8891

Test Name: INVENTORY OF PARENT AND PEER ATTACHMENTS—MOTHER & FATHER SUBSCALES

Purpose: To indicate level of attachment to parents.

Number of Items: 50

Format: Includes 2 subscales: Mother Attachment and Father Attachment. Responses are made on a 5-point scale ranging from 0 (almost never or never true) to 4 (almost always or always true).

Reliability: Alpha coefficients ranged from .88 to .96.

Validity: Correlations with other variables ranged from −.69 to .46.

Author: O'Brien, K. M., et al.

Article: Attachment, separation, and women's vocational development: A longitudinal analysis.

Journal: *Journal of Counseling Psychology*, July 2000, *47*(3), 301–315.

Related Research: Armsden, G. C., & Greenberg, M. T. (1987). The Inventory of Parent and Peer Attachment: Individual differences and their relationship to psychological well-being in adolescence. *Journal of Youth and Adolescence, 16,* 427–454.

8892

Test Name: INVENTORY OF PARENT AND PEER ATTACHMENT—PARENT SCALE

Purpose: To assess affective and cognitive dimensions of relationships with parents.

Number of Items: 28

Format: Includes 3 subscales: Trust, Communication, and Alienation. Responses are made on a 5-point Likert scale.

Reliability: Internal consistencies ranged from .86 to .91. Average test-retest (3 weeks) reliability was .93.

Author: Vivona, J. M.

Article: Parental attachment styles of late adolescents: Qualities of attachment relationships and consequences for adjustment.

Journal: *Journal of Counseling Psychology*, July 2000, *47*(3), 316–329.

Related Research: Armsden, G. C., & Greenberg, M. T. (1987). The Inventory of Parent and Peer Attachment: Individual differences and their relationship to psychological well-being in adolescence. *Journal of Youth and Adolescence, 16,* 427–454.

8893

Test Name: INVENTORY OF PARENT AND PEER ATTACHMENT—REVISED

Purpose: To assess parental attachments.

Number of Items: 50

Format: Includes Mother and Father scales.

Reliability: Alpha coefficients were .96.

Validity: Correlations with other variables ranged from −.48 to .35.

Author: Ryan, N. E., et al.

Article: Family dysfunction, parental attachment, and career search self-efficacy among community college students.

Journal: *Journal of Counseling Psychology*, January 1996, *43*(1), 84–89.

Related Research: Armsden, G. C., & Greenburg, M. T. (1987). The Inventory of Parent and Peer Attachment: Individual differences and their relationships to psychological well-being in adolescence. *Journal of Youth and Adolescence, 16*, 427–453.

8894

Test Name: ISSUES CHECKLIST

Purpose: To measure adolescents' perceptions of conflict with their parents.

Number of Items: 12

Format: Responses are made on a 5-point scale ranging from 1 (very calm) to 5 (very angry).

Reliability: Alpha coefficients ranged from .70 to .83.

Author: Fuligni, A. J., et al.

Article: Attitudes toward family obligations among American adolescents with Asian, Latin American, and European backgrounds.

Journal: *Child Development,* July/August 1999, *70*(4), 1030–1044.

Related Research: Prinz, R. J., et al. (1979). Multivariate assessment of conflict in distressed and non-distressed mother-adolescent dyads. *Journal of Applied Behavioral Analysis, 12*, 691–700.

8895

Test Name: ISSUES CHECKLIST

Purpose: To measure sources of conflict between parents and children.

Number of Items: 44

Format: Multiple formats are used. All are described.

Reliability: Test-retest reliability (1–2 weeks) was .80.

Author: Reed, J. S., and Dubow, E. F.

Article: Cognitive and behavioral predictors of communication in clinic-referred and nonclinical mother-adolescent dyads.

Journal: *Journal of Marriage and the Family,* February 1997, *59*(1), 91–102.

Related Research: Prinz, R. J., et al. (1979). Multivariate assessment of conflict in distressed and nondistressed mother-adolescent dyads. *Journal of Applied Behavior Analysis, 12*, 691–700.

Tseng, V., & Fuligni, A. J. (2000). Parent-adolescent language use and relationships among immigrant families with East Asian, Filipino, and Latin American backgrounds. *Journal of Marriage and the Family, 62*, 465–476.

8896

Test Name: JOB INSECURITY QUESTIONNAIRE—MODIFIED & STANDARD VERSIONS

Purpose: To measure job insecurity of parents as perceived by children and as perceived by parents themselves.

Number of Items: 18

Format: Scales range from 1 (strongly disagree) to 5 (strongly agree). Sample items are presented.

Reliability: Alpha coefficients ranged from .82 to .89.

Validity: Correlations with other variables ranged from −.19 to .31.

Author: Barling, J., et al.

Article: Parents' job insecurity affects children's academic performance through cognitive difficulties.

Journal: *Journal of Applied Psychology,* June 1999, *84*(3), 437–444.

Related Research: Barling, J., et al. (1988). Effects of parents' job insecurity on children's work beliefs and attitudes. *Journal of Applied Psychology, 83*, 112–118.

8897

Test Name: KANSAS MARITAL SATISFACTION SCALE

Purpose: To measure marital satisfaction.

Number of Items: 3

Format: Five-point scales range from (1) very dissatisfied to (5) very satisfied. All items are presented.

Reliability: Alphas ranged from .95 to .96.

Validity: Correlations with other variables ranged from −.41 to .52.

Author: Green, R. G., et al.

Article: Reliability and validity of the Kansas Marital Satisfaction Scale in a sample of African-American husbands and wives.

Journal: *Psychological Reports,* February 1998, *82*(1), 255–258.

Related Research: Schumm, W., et al. (1986). Concurrent and discriminant validity of the Kansas Marital Satisfaction Scale. *Journal of Marriage and the Family, 48*, 381–387.

8898

Test Name: KERNS SECURITY SCALE

Purpose: To assess child attachment security.

Number of Items: 15

Format: A forced-choice, self-report measure.

Reliability: Coefficient alpha was .93. Test-retest reliability was .75

Author: Lieberman, M. L., et al.

Article: Developmental patterns in security of attachment to mother and father in late childhood and early adolescence: Associations with peer relations

Journal: *Child Development*, January/February 1999, *70*(1), 202–213

Related Research: Kerns, K. A., et al. (1996). Peer relations and preadolescents' perceptions of security in the mother-child relationship. *Development Psychology*, *32*, 457–466.

8899

Test Name: KNOWLEDGE SUBSCALE

Purpose: To assess parental monitoring.

Number of Items: 13

Format: Responses are made on a 5-point scale ranging from "always" to "never."

Reliability: Alpha coefficients were .89 (mother) and .90 (father).

Author: Kim, J. E., et al.

Article: Associations among family relationships, antisocial peers, and adolescents' externalizing behaviors: Gender and family type differences.

Journal: *Child Development*, September/October 1999, *70*(5), 1209–1230.

Related Research: Hetherington, E. M., & Clingempeel, W. G. (1992). Coping with marital transitions: A family system perspective. *Monographs of the Society for Research in Child Development*, *57* (2–3, Serial No. 227).

8900

Test Name: LOCKE-WALLACE MARITAL ADJUSTMENT TEST

Purpose: To measure marital adjustment.

Number of Items: 15

Reliability: Cronbach's alphas ranged from .63 to .89 across subgroups. Test-retest reliabilities ranged from .75 to .84.

Validity: Correlations with other variables ranged from .90 to .93.

Author: Freestom, M. H., and Plechaty, M.

Article: Reconsideration of the Locke-Wallace Marital Adjustment Test: Is it still relevant for the 1990's?

Journal: *Psychological Reports*, October 1997, *81*(2), 419–434.

Related Research: Locke, H., and Wallace, K. (1959) Short marital adjustment and prediction tests: Their reliability and validity. *Marriage and Family Living*, *2*, 251–255.

8901

Test Name: LOVE SCALE

Purpose: To assess the emotional attachment between spouses.

Number of Items: 13

Format: Scales range from 0 (not at all true) to 8 (definitely true).

Reliability: Omega reliability was .88.

Author: Burke, P. J., and Stets, J. E.

Article: Trust and commitment through self-verification.

Journal: *Social Psychology Quarterly*, December 1999, *62*(4), 347–360.

Related Research: Rubin, Z. (1973). *Liking and loving: An invitation to social psychology.*

New York: Holt, Rinehart, and Winston.

8902

Test Name: MARITAL ATTRIBUTION STYLE QUESTIONNAIRE

Purpose: To assess attributions for responsibility of husbands and wives.

Number of Items: 6

Format: For each of 3 positive and 3 negative behaviors respondents indicate whether the partner's behavior was intentional, praiseworthy, or selfish.

Reliability: Alpha were .84 (husbands) and .83 (wives).

Author: Bradbury, T. N., et al.

Article: Attributions and behavior in functional and dysfunctional marriages.

Journal: *Journal of Consulting and Clinical Psychology*, June 1996, *64*(3), 569–576.

Related Research: Fincham, F. D., & Bradbury, T. N. (1987). The impact of attributions in marriage: A longitudinal analysis. *Journal of Personality and Social Psychology*, *53*, 510–517.

8903

Test Name: MARITAL CONFLICT BEHAVIOR SCALE

Purpose: To measure constructive and destructive conflict behavior.

Number of Items: 11

Format: Scales range from "very true" to "not at all true." Sample items are described.

Reliability: Alpha coefficients ranged from .70 to .79.

Author: Crohan, S. E.

Article: Marital quality and

conflict across the transition to parenthood in African American and White couples.

Journal: *Journal of Marriage and the Family*, November 1996, 58(4), 933–944.

Related Research: Crohan, S. E. (1988). *The relationship between conflict behavior and marital happiness: Conflict beliefs as moderators.* Unpublished doctoral dissertation, University of Michigan, Ann Arbor.

8904

Test Name: MARITAL DISAFFECTION SCALE

Purpose: To measure emotional estrangement in marriage.

Number of Items: 21

Format: Four-point scales are anchored by 1 (not at all true) and 4 (very true).

Reliability: Alpha was .97.

Validity: Correlations with other variables ranged from −.14 to .48.

Author: Flowers, C., et al.

Article: Criterion-related validity of the Marital Disaffection Scale as a measure of marital estrangement.

Journal: *Psychological Reports*, June 2000, 86(3, Part 2), 1101–1103.

Related Research: Kayser, K. (1996). The Marital Disaffection Scale: An inventory for assessing emotional estrangement in marriage. *The American Journal of Family Therapy, 24*, 83–88.

8905

Test Name: MARITAL HAPPINESS SCALE

Purpose: To assess marital happiness.

Number of Items: 6

Format: Four-point rating scales. All items are described.

Reliability: Alpha coefficients ranged from .85 to .90.

Author: Crohan, S. E.

Article: Marital quality and conflict across the transition to parenthood in African American and White couples.

Journal: *Journal of Marriage and the Family*, November 1996, 58(4), 933–944.

Related Research: Crohan, S. E., & Veroff, J. (1989). Dimensions of marital well-being among White and Black newlyweds. *Journal of Marriage and the Family, 51*, 373–383.

8906

Test Name: MARITAL LOCUS OF CONTROL SCALE

Purpose: To measure the extent to which respondents view their marriage as due to factors inside or outside the marriage.

Number of Items: 20

Format: Four-point scales range from "strongly agree" to "strongly disagree." All items are presented.

Reliability: Coefficient alpha was .98.

Author: Meyers, S. M., and Booth, A.

Article: Marital strains and marital quality: The role of high and low locus of control.

Journal: *Journal of Marriage and the Family*, May 1999, 61(2), 423–430.

Related Research: Miller, P. C., et al. (1983). The construction and development of the Miller Marital Locus of Control Scale. *Canadian Journal of Behavioral Science, 15*, 266–279.

8907

Test Name: MARITAL PARTNER'S MATERNAL EMPLOYMENT PREFERENCE AND INTENT

Purpose: To measure perceived marital partner's maternal employment preference and maternal employment intent.

Number of Items: 8

Format: Includes two scales: Perceived Marital Partner's Maternal Employment Preference and Maternal Employment Intent. Responses are made on a 5-point Likert scale ranging from 1 (strongly disagree) to 5 (strongly agree). All items are presented.

Reliability: Alpha coefficients were .78 (preference) and .84 (intent).

Validity: Correlations with other variables ranged from −.59 to .76.

Author: Werbel, J.

Article: Intent and choice regarding maternal employment following childbirth.

Journal: *Journal of Vocational Behavior*, December 1998, 53(3), 372–385.

8908

Test Name: MARITAL QUALITY AND PARENT-CHILD RELATIONS SCALES

Purpose: To measure parent–child affection and parents' marriage quality.

Number of Items: 15

Format: Multiple-choice rating scales vary in format. Sample items are presented.

Reliability: Alpha coefficients ranged from .70 to .87.

Author: Amato, P. R., and Booth, A.

Article: A prospective study of divorce and parent-child relationships.

Journal: *Journal of Marriage and the Family*, May 1996, *58*(2), 356–365.

Related Research: Booth, A., et al. (1991). *Marital instability over the life course: Methodology report and code book for three wave panel study.* Lincoln, NE: Bureau of Sociological Research.

8909

Test Name: MARITAL SATISFACTION SCALE

Purpose: To measure the positive and negative sentiments that define marital satisfaction.

Number of Items: 10

Format: Scales range from 1 (hardly ever) to 5 (almost always).

Reliability: Alpha coefficients ranged from .84 to .87.

Author: Feng, D., et al.

Article: Intergenerational transmission of marital quality and marital instability.

Journal: *Journal of Marriage and the Family*, May 1999, *61*(2), 451–463.

Related Research: Gilford, R., & Bengston, V. (1979). Measuring marital satisfaction in three generations: Positive and negative dimensions. *Journal of Marriage and the Family, 41*, 387–398.

8910

Test Name: MARITAL WELL-BEING SCALE

Purpose: To measure harmony in marriage.

Number of Items: 4

Format: Scales range from 1

(strongly disagree) to 4 (strongly agree). All items are presented.

Reliability: Coefficient alpha was .72.

Author: Broman, C. L., et al.

Article: Traumatic events and marital well-being.

Journal: *Journal of Marriage and the Family*, November 1996, *58*(4), 908–916.

Related Research: House, J. S. (1986). *Americans' changing lives: Wave I* (Electronic data file). Ann Arbor, MI: Survey Research Center (Producer), Inter-university Consortium for Political and Social Research.

8911

Test Name: MATERNAL DISCIPLINARY PRACTICES SCALE

Purpose: To measure mother's reliance upon inappropriate methods of discipline.

Number of Items: 4

Format: Responses are made on a 3-point scale ranging from 1 (almost never) to 3 (almost always). Examples are presented.

Reliability: Coefficient alpha was .40.

Validity: Correlations with other variables ranged from −.46 to .34.

Author: Curtner-Smith, M. E.

Article: Mechanisms by which family processes contribute to school-age boys' bullying.

Journal: *Child Study Journal*, 2000, *30*(3), 169–186.

Related Research: Loeber, R. (1990). *Caretaker Self-Administered Questionnaire: The Pittsburgh Youth Study.* Western Psychiatric Institute and Clinic, The University of Pittsburgh School of Medicine.

8912

Test Name: MATERNAL GATEKEEPING SCALE

Purpose: To assess the degree of maternal gatekeeping in families.

Number of Items: 11

Format: Four-point scales range from "not at all like me" to "very much like me." Five-point Likert scales are also used on some items. All items are presented.

Reliability: Alpha coefficients ranged from .66 to .79 across subscales.

Validity: Gatekeepers did more family work than others, $F(2, 613) = 2.87$, $p = .05$.

Author: Allen, S. M., and Hawkins, A. J.

Article: Maternal gatekeeping: Mothers' beliefs and behaviors that inhibit greater father involvement in family work.

Journal: *Journal of Marriage and the Family*, February 1999, *61*(1), 199–212.

8913

Test Name: MATERNAL SEPARATION ANXIETY QUESTIONNAIRE

Purpose: To assess worry, sadness, and guilt.

Number of Items: 21

Format: Five-point scales range from "strongly disagree" to "strongly agree."

Reliability: Coefficient alpha was .93.

Validity: Correlations with other variables ranged from −.35 to .69.

Author: Bradley, R. H., et al.

Article: Parents' socioemotional investment in children.

Journal: *Journal of Marriage and the Family*, February 1997, *59*(1), 77–90.

Related Research: DeMeis, D., et al. (1986). Effects of early maternal employment on toddlers, mothers and fathers. *Developmental Psychology, 22*, 627–632.

8914

Test Name: MATERNAL SEPARATION ANXIETY SCALE

Purpose: To measure feelings and attributions about separation.

Number of Items: 35

Format: Includes 3 domains: Maternal Separation Anxiety, Maternal Perception of Separation Effects on the Child, and Employment-Related Separation Concerns. Responses are made on a 5-point scale ranging from "strongly disagree" to "strongly agree."

Reliability: Coefficient alpha was .90.

Author: Scher, A., and Mayseless, O.

Article: Mothers of anxious/ambivalent infants: Maternal characteristics and child-care context.

Journal: *Child Development*, November/December 2000, *71*(6), 1629–1639.

Related Research: Hock, E., et al. (1989). Maternal separation anxiety: Mother-infant separation from the maternal perspective. *Child Development, 60*, 793–802.

8915

Test Name: MCMASTER FAMILY ASSESSMENT DEVICE

Purpose: To measure family functioning, including problem solving, communication, roles,

affective responses, and affective involvement.

Number of Items: 60

Format: Five-point Likert format.

Reliability: Test-retest reliabilities ranged from .67 to .75.

Author: Robinson, B. E., and Post, P.

Article: Risk of addiction to work and family functioning.

Journal: *Psychological Reports*, August 1997, *81*(1), 91–95.

Related Research: Epstein, N. B., et al. (1983). The McMaster Family Assessment Device. *Journal of Marital and Family Therapy, 9* 171–180.

8916

Test Name: MOTHER, FATHER, AND TEACHER SUPPORT SCALES

Purpose: To assess students' perceptions of the degree of support for their academic achievement by parents and teachers.

Number of Items: 32

Format: Includes scales for mother, father, and teachers. Responses are made on a 5-point scale ranging from *strongly agree* to *strongly disagree*.

Reliability: Alpha coefficients ranged from .68 to .95.

Author: McWhirter, E. H., et al.

Article: A causal model of the educational plan and career expectations of Mexican American high school girls.

Journal: *Journal of Counseling Psychology*, April 1998, *45*(2), 166–181.

Related Research: Farmer, H., et al. (1981). Career Motivation and Achievement Planning (C-MAP). (Measure available with scoring

manual and interpretive materials from Helen S. Farmer, Department of Educational Psychology, University of Illinois, 310 South Sixth Street, Champaign, IL 61820).

8917

Test Name: MOTHER-FATHER-PEER SCALE

Purpose: To measure attitudes of parents and peers as respondents remember them from childhood.

Number of Items: 60

Format: Scales range from 1 (strongly disagree) to 5 (strongly agree). Sample items are presented.

Reliability: Internal consistencies ranged from .71 to .91.

Author: Guerra, A. L., and Braungart-Rieker, J. M.

Article: Predicting career indecision in college students: The roles of identity formation and parental relationship factors.

Journal: *Career Development Quarterly*, March 1999, *47*(3), 255–266.

Related Research: Epstein, S. (1983). *The Mother-Father-Peer Scale*. Unpublished manuscript, University of Massachusetts, Amherst.

8918

Test Name: MOTHER'S MARITAL SATISFACTION

Purpose: To measure mother's marital satisfaction.

Number of Items: 10

Format: Responses are made on a 6-point scale ranging from 0 (all the time) to 5 (never).

Reliability: Coefficient alpha was .89.

Validity: Correlations with other

variables ranged from −.46 to .77.

Author: Curtner-Smith, M. E.

Article: Mechanisms by which family processes contribute to school-age boys' bullying.

Journal: *Child Study Journal*, 2000, *30*(3), 169–186.

Related Research: Spanier, G. B. (1976). Measuring dyadic adjustments: New scales for assessing the quality of marriage and similar dyads. *Journal of Marriage and the Family, 38*, 15–28.

8919

Test Name: MOTHERS' MONITORING SCALE

Purpose: To measure mothers' monitoring of children.

Number of Items: 5

Format: Scales range from 1 (don't know at all) to 5 (know a lot).

Reliability: Coefficient alpha was .80.

Author: East, P. L.

Article: The first teenage pregnancy in the family: Does it affect mothers' parenting, attitudes, or mother-adolescent communication?

Journal: *Journal of Marriage and the Family,* May 1999, *61*(2), 306–319.

Related Research: Brown, B., et al. (1993). Parenting practices and peer group affiliation in adolescence. *Child Development, 64*, 467–482.

8920

Test Name: MULTIGENERATIONAL INTERCONNECTEDNESS SCALE

Purpose: To assess financial, functional, and psychological connections between adolescents and their families.

Number of Items: 31

Format: Seven-point frequency rating scales. All items are presented.

Reliability: Cronbach alphas ranged from .82 to .86 across subscales. Total alpha was .87.

Validity: Correlations with age ranged from. −.36 to −.24.

Author: Gavazzi, S. M., et al.

Article: Measurement of financial, functional, and psychological connections in families: Conceptual development and empirical use of the Multigenerational Interconnectedness Scale.

Journal: *Psychological Reports*, June 1999, *84*(3) Part 1, 1361–1371.

8921

Test Name: NETWORK SUPPORT SCALE

Purpose: To measure the extent to which low levels of support from family and friends is a barrier to participation in development activities.

Number of Items: 2

Format: Five-point scales range from 1 (strongly disagree) to 5 (strongly agree). A sample item is presented.

Reliability: Coefficient alpha was .61.

Validity: Correlations with other variables ranged from −.39 to .36.

Author: Birdi, K., et al.

Article: Correlates and perceived outcomes of four types of employee development activity.

Journal: *Journal of Applied Psychology*, December 1997, *82*(6), 845–857.

8922

Test Name: O'LEARY-PORTER SCALE

Purpose: To assess conflict between family caregivers.

Number of Items: 10

Reliability: Test-retest (2 weeks) reliability was .96. Coefficient alpha was .86.

Validity: Correlation with the Marital Adjustment Test was .63.

Author: Stoneman, Z., et al.

Article: Effects of residential instability on Head Start children and their relationships with older siblings: Influences of child emotionality and conflict between family caregivers.

Journal: *Child Development*, September/October 1999, *70*(5), 1246–1262.

Related Research: Porter, B., & O'Leary, K. D. (1980). Marital discord and childhood behavior problems. *Journal of Abnormal Child Psychology, 8*, 287–295.

8923

Test Name: PARENT-ADOLESCENT RELATIONSHIP QUESTIONNAIRE

Purpose: To rate the parent-adolescent relationship from the perspective of both the parent and adolescent.

Number of Items: 51

Format: Six-point rating scales.

Reliability: Alpha coefficients ranged from .94 (adolescent) and .95 (parent).

Author: Reed, J. S., and Dubow, E. F.

Article: Cognitive and behavioral predictors of communication in clinic-referred and nonclinical mother-adolescent dyads.

Journal: *Journal of Marriage and the Family*, February 1997, *59*(1), 91–102.

Related Research: Robin, A. L., et al. (1990). Multidimensional assessment of parent–adolescent relations. *Psychological Assessment: A Journal of Consulting and Clinical Psychology, 2,* 451–459.

8924

Test Name: PARENT–ADOLESCENT RELATIONSHIP SCALE

Purpose: To assess parent–adolescent relationships

Number of Items: 9

Format: Includes 2 scales: Conflict and Communication. Responses are made on 5-point and 6-point scales.

Reliability: Internal consistency was .75 and .68.

Author: Kahil, A., and Eccles, J. S.

Article: Does welfare affect family processes and adolescent adjustment?

Journal: *Child Development*, December 1998, *69*(6), 1597–1613.

Related Research: Montemayor, R. (1983). Parents and adolescents in conflict: All families some of the time and some families most of the time. *Journal of Early Adolescence, 3,* 83–103.

8925

Test Name: PARENT ADOLESCENT SUPPORT SCALE

Purpose: To measure the degree to which parents and adolescents can count on each other.

Number of Items: 13

Format: Five-point scale.

Reliability: Alpha was .95.

Author: Valtolina , G. G., and Marta, E.

Article: Family relations and psychosocial risks in families with an obese adolescent.

Journal: *Psychological Reports*, August 1998, *83*(1), 251–260.

Related Research: Scabini, E., & Cigoli, V. (1992). Per una episteme del rischio. In E. Scabini & P. Domati, (Eds.), *Famiglie in diffoculta tra rischio e risorse: Studi interdisciplinari sulla famiglie* (pp. 101–121). (Monograph).

8926

Test Name: PARENT–CHILD BEHAVIORAL INTERACTIION SCALES

Purpose: To assess parent–child affective quality.

Number of Items: 13

Format: Responses are made on a 7-point scale ranging from ''always'' to ''never.'' Examples are presented.

Reliability: Coefficient alpha was .83.

Validity: Correlations with other variables ranged from −.70 to .41.

Author: Spoth, R., et al.

Article: A protective process model of parent-child affective quality and child mastery effects on oppositional behaviors: A test and replication.

Journal: *Journal of School Psychology*, Spring 1999, *37*(1), 49–71.

Related Research: Conger, R. D. (1989). *Iowa Youth and Families Projects*, *Wave A* (Technical report). Ames, IA: Iowa State University Center for Family Research in Rural Mental Health.

8927

Test Name: PARENT DISCIPLINE PRACTICES

Purpose: To assess parent discipline practices.

Number of Items: 9

Format: Includes two practices: Approach and Consistency. The 3 Approach items are open-ended. The 6 Consistency items are each rated on a 5-point scale.

Reliability: Coefficient alpha was .71.

Author: Sutton, S. E., et al.

Article: Pathways to aggression in young, highly stressed urban children.

Journal: *Child Study Journal*, 1999, *29*(1), 49–67.

Related Research: Sutton, S. E. (1995). *Pathways to aggression in highly stressed 2nd and 3rd grade urban children.* Unpublished Ph.D. dissertation, University of Rochester.

8928

Test Name: PARENT EXPERIENCE SCALE

Purpose: To assess parenting concerns.

Number of Items: 24

Format: Includes six areas: Sibling Relationships, Family Issues, Community Issues, Development of the Child, Educational Issues, and Parental Self-Concept. Responses are made on a 5-point scale ranging

from 1 (strongly disagree) to 5 (strongly agree).

Reliability: Reliability was .82.

Validity: Correlations with other variables ranged from −.15 to −.42.

Author: Windecker-Nelson, E., et al.

Article: Intellectually gifted preschoolers' perceived competence: Relations to maternal attitudes, concerns, and support.

Journal: *Gifted Child Quarterly*, Fall 1997, *41*(4), 133–144.

Related Research: Keirouz, K. S. (1990). Concerns of parents of gifted children: A research review. *Gifted Child Quarterly*, *34*, 56–63.

8929

Test Name: PARENT INVOLVEMENT SCALE

Purpose: To assess parent involvement.

Number of Items: 15

Format: Ten activities are each rated on a 4-point scale ranging from 1 (rarely or not at all) to 4 (very often), and 5 items are rated on a 5-point scale ranging from 1 (very true) to 5 (not true). Examples are presented.

Reliability: Coefficient alpha was .60.

Author: Sutton, S. E., et al.

Article: Pathways to aggression in young, highly stressed urban children.

Journal: *Child Study Journal*, 1999, *29*(1), 49–67.

Related Research: Sutton, S. E. (1995). *Pathways to aggression in highly stressed 2nd and 3rd grade urban children.* Unpublished Ph.D. dissertation, University of Rochester.

8930

Test Name: PARENT INVOLVEMENT SCALE

Purpose: To assess joint activities and parent participation in the child's life.

Number of Items: 24

Format: Includes two rating scales: a 4-point scale ranging from 1 (rarely or not at all) to 4 (very often); and a 5-point scale ranging from 1 (not true) to 5 (very true). Examples are presented.

Reliability: Coefficient alpha was .83.

Author: Fergen, D. B., et al.

Article: Relationships between parent-child relational variables and child test variables in highly stressed urban families.

Journal: *Child Study Journal*, 1996, *26*(2), 87–108.

Related Research: Gribble, P. A. (1993). Parent and child views of parent-child relationship qualities and resilient outcomes among urban children. *Journal of Child Psychology and Psychiatry*, *34*, 507–519.

8931

Test Name: PARENT SENSE OF COMPETENCE SCALE

Purpose: To measure parenting satisfaction.

Number of Items: 16

Format: Includes 2 subscales: Parenting Satisfaction and Parenting Self-Efficacy. Responses arc made on a 6-point scale ranging from 1 (strongly agree) to 6 (strongly disagree).

Reliability: Internal consistency was .89.

Author: Black, M. M., et al.

Article: African American fathers

in low income, urban families: Development, behavior, and home environment of their three-year-old children.

Journal: *Child Development*, July/August 1999, *70*(4), 967–978.

Related Research: Johnson, C., & Mash, E. J. (1989). A measure of parenting satisfaction and efficacy. *Journal of Clinical Child Psychology*, *18*, 167–175.

8932

Test Name: PARENT SENSE OF EFFICACY IN INVOLVEMENT SCALE

Purpose: To measure parents' sense of efficacy in helping their children at home.

Number of Items: 2

Format: Responses are made on a 5-point scale ranging from 1 (not effective) to 5 (very effective). Both items are presented.

Validity: Correlations with other variables ranged from .06 to .34.

Author: Watkins, T. J.

Article: Teacher communications, child achievement, and parent traits in parent involvement models.

Journal: *Journal of Educational Research*, September/October 1997, *91*(1), 3–14.

Related Research: Ames, C., et al. (1993, April). *Effects of parent involvement strategies on parents' perceptions and the development of children's motivation.* Paper presented at the meeting of the American Educational Research Association, Atlanta.

8933

Test Name: PARENTAL ACCEPTANCE–REJECTION QUESTIONNAIRE

Purpose: To assess children's perceptions of parental acceptance–rejection.

Number of Items: 60

Format: Four-point scales range from "almost always true" to "almost never true." Sample items are presented.

Reliability: Alpha coefficients ranged from .83 to .95 across subscales. Total alpha was .77.

Author: Veneziano, R. A., and Rohner, R. P.

Article: Perceived paternal acceptance, paternal involvement, and youths' psychological adjustment in a rural, biracial southern community.

Journal: *Journal of Marriage and the Family*, May 1998, *60*(2), 335–343.

Related Research: Rohner, R. (1998). *Parental acceptance and rejection bibliography.* Storrs: University of Connecticut, Center for the Study of Parental Acceptance and Rejection.

Bluestone, C., & Tamis-LeMonda, C. S. (1999). Correlates of parenting styles in predominantly working and middle-class African American women. *Journal of Marriage and the Family, 61*, 881–893.

8934

Test Name: PARENTAL ATTACHMENT QUESTIONNAIRE

Purpose: To assess late adolescents' perceptions of parental availability, understanding, and support in addition to the extent of help seeking from parents and satisfaction with help received.

Number of Items: 55

Format: Includes 3 scales:

Affective Quality of Attachment, Fostering of Autonomy, and Emotional Support. Responses are made on a 5-point Likert scale.

Reliability: Alpha coefficients ranged from .88 to .96. Test-retest reliabilities (2 weeks) ranged from .82 to .92.

Author: Vivona, J. M.

Article: Parental attachment styles of late adolescents: Qualities of attachment relationships and consequences for adjustment.

Journal: *Journal of Counseling Psychology*, July 2000, *47*(3), 316–329.

Related Research: Kenny, M. E. (1990). College seniors' perceptions of parental attachments: The value and stability of family ties. *Journal of College Student Development, 31*, 39–46.

8935

Test Name: PARENTAL ATTACHMENT QUESTIONNAIRE

Purpose: To assess college students' continued attachment to parents.

Number of Items: 70

Format: Includes 3 dimensions: Parents as a Source of Support, Parents as Facilitators of Independence, and Affective Quality of the Parent–Child Relationship.

Reliability: Alpha coefficients were .93 (men) and .95 (women).

Author: Heiss, G. E., et al.

Article: Five scales in search of a construct: Exploring continued attachments to parents in college students.

Journal: *Journal of Personality*

Assessment, August 1996, *67*(1), 102–115.

Related Research: Kenny, M. (1987). The extent and function of parental attachment among first year college students. *Journal of Youth and Adolescence, 16*, 17–29.

8936

Test Name: PARENTAL ATTACHMENT QUESTIONNAIRE—MODIFIED

Purpose: To measure attachment to parents.

Number of Items: 55

Format: Scales range from 1 (not at all) to 5 (very much). Item modifications are described.

Reliability: Alpha coefficients ranged from .75 to .88 across subscales.

Validity: Correlations with other variables ranged from $-.26$ to .03.

Author: Kenny, M. E., and Perez, V.

Article: Attachment and psychological well-being among racially and ethnically diverse first-year college students.

Journal: *Journal of College Student Development*, September/October 1996, *37*(5), 527–535.

Related Research: Kenny, M. E. (1990). College seniors' perceptions of personal attachments: The value and stability of family ties. *Journal of College Student Development, 31*, 39–46.

Taub, D. J. (1997). Autonomy and parental attachment in traditional-age undergraduate women. *Journal of College Student Development, 38*, 645–653.

8937

Test Name: PARENTAL ATTITUDES TOWARD CHILD-REARING

Purpose: To assess parents' perceptions of their parenting behavior.

Number of Items: 51

Format: Includes four dimensions of parenting attitudes: Independence, Warmth, Strictness, and Aggravation. Responses are made on a 6-point Likert-type scale ranging from 1 (strongly disagree) to 6 (strongly agree).

Reliability: Alpha coefficients ranged from .58 to .78.

Author: Windecker-Nelson, E., et al.

Article: Intellectually gifted preschoolers' perceived competence: Relations to maternal attitudes, concerns, and support.

Journal: *Gifted Child Quarterly,* Fall 1997, *41*(4), 133–144.

Related Research: Easterbrooks, A., & Goldberg, J. A. (1984). Toddler development in the family: Impact of father involvement and parenting characteristics. *Child Development, 55,* 740–752.

8938

Test Name: PARENTAL AUTHORITY QUESTIONNAIRE

Purpose: To assess parental authority as authoritarian, permissive, or authoritative.

Number of Items: 30

Format: Scales range from 1 (strongly disagree) to 5 (strongly agree). Sample items are presented.

Reliability: Alpha reliabilities

ranged from .82 to .89 across subscales.

Author: Hickman, G. P., et al.

Article: Influence of parenting styles on the adjustment and academic achievement of traditional college freshmen.

Journal: *Journal of College Student Development,* January/February 2000, *41*(1), 41–54.

Related Research: Buri, J. R. (1991). Parental Authority Questionnaire. *Journal of Personality Assessment, 57,* 110–119.

8939

Test Name: PARENTAL BEHAVIOR INVENTORY SCALE—REVISED

Purpose: To assess perception of parenting styles.

Number of Items: 76

Format: Includes 4 dimensions: Punishment and Rejection, Intimacy and Love, Strictness and Control, and Concern. Examples are presented.

Reliability: Alpha coefficients ranged from .57 to .89.

Author: Punamaeki, R.-L., et al.

Article: Models of traumatic experiences and children's psychological adjustment: The roles of perceived parenting and the children's own resources and activity.

Journal: *Child Development,* August 1997, *64*(4), 718–728.

Related Research: Schaefer, E. S. (1965). Children's reports of parental behavior: An inventory. *Child Development, 36,* 413–424.

8940

Test Name: PARENTAL BEHAVIORS SCALE

Purpose: To measure parenting style, parental openness to adolescent issues, parent–adolescent relationship, and parental support of occupational preparation.

Number of Items: 18

Format: Scales range from 1 (does not apply) to 4 (fully applies). Most items are presented.

Reliability: Alpha coefficients ranged from .75 to .83 across subscales.

Author: Kracke, B.

Article: Parental behaviors and adolescents' career exploration.

Journal: *Career Development Quarterly,* June 1997, *45*(4), 341–350.

Related Research: Steinberg, L. D., et al. (1989). Authoritative parenting, psychosocial maturity, and academic success among adolescents. *Child Development, 60,* 1424–1436.

8941

Test Name: PARENTAL BELIEFS SURVEY

Purpose: To measure beliefs about infant care.

Number of Items: 20

Format: Includes two subscales: Spoiling and Discipline. Examples are presented.

Author: Coe, G., et al.

Article: Infant childrearing: Beliefs of parents and child care providers.

Journal: *Child Study Journal,* 1996, *26*(2), 109–124.

Related Research: Luster, T. (1986). *Influences or maternal behavior: Childrearing beliefs, social support and infant temperament.* Paper presented at the International Conference on Infant Studies, Los Angeles

(ERIC Document Reproduction Services No. 275 416).

8942

Test Name: PARENTAL BONDING INSTRUMENT

Purpose: To measure childhood attachment to mother and father by adult retrospective self-report.

Number of Items: 12 (25)

Format: Sample items are presented.

Reliability: Alpha coefficients ranged from .90 to .91.

Author: Davies, L., et al.

Article: Significant life experiences and depression among single and married mothers.

Journal: *Journal of Marriage and the Family*, May 1997, 59(2), 294–308.

Related Research: Parker, G., et al. (1979). A parental bonding instrument. *British Journal of Medical Psychology*, 52, 1–10.

Woodward, L., et al. (2000). Timing of parental separation and attachment to parents in adolescence: Results of a prospective study from birth to age 16. *Journal of Marriage and the Family*, 62, 162–174.

8943

Test Name: PARENTAL BONDING INSTRUMENT

Purpose: To assess parents' retrospective self-reports of the quality of their childhood emotional bonds with each parent during their first 16 years of life.

Number of Items: 25

Format: Includes 2 subscales: Care and Overprotection. Responses are made on a 4-point scale ranging from 1 (very like) to 4 (very unlike). Examples are presented.

Reliability: Test-retest (3 weeks) reliabilities were .76 and .63. Split-half reliabilities were .88 and .74

Author: Lopez, F. G., et al.

Article: Parental divorce, parent-child bonds, and adult attachment orientations among college students: A comparison of three racial/ethnic groups.

Journal: *Journal of Counseling Psychology*, April 2000, 47(2), 177–186.

Related Research: Parker, G. B., et al. (1979). A parental bonding instrument. *British Journal of Medical Psychology*, 52, 1–10.

8944

Test Name: PARENTAL BONDING INVENTORY (JAPANESE VERSION)

Purpose: To measure parental care and parental overprotection.

Number of Items: 25

Format: Four-point rating scales. Sample items are presented.

Validity: Correlations with the Toronto Alexithymia Scale ranged from −.44 to .24.

Author: Fukunishi, I., et al.

Article: Mothers' low care in the development of alexithymia: A preliminary study in Japanese college students.

Journal: *Psychological Reports*, February 1997, 80(1), 143–146.

Related Research: Ogawa, M. (1991). [Reliability and validation of the Japanese version of the PBI]. *Seishinka chiryogaku*, 6, 1193–1201. [In Japanese]

8945

Test Name: PARENTAL COMPARISON LEVEL INDEX

Purpose: To assess the experience of parenthood in terms of costs and rewards.

Number of Items: 40

Format: All items are presented.

Reliability: Alpha coefficients ranged from .92 (cost) to .95 (rewards).

Validity: Correlations with other variables ranged from .14 to .40.

Author: Waldron-Hennessey, R., and Sabatelli, R. M.

Article: The Parental Comparison Level Index: A measure for assessing parental rewards and costs relative to expectations.

Journal: *Journal of Marriage and the Family*, November 1997, 59(4), 824–833.

8946

Test Name: PARENTAL CONTROL SCALE

Purpose: To assess psychological control versus autonomy.

Number of Items: 12

Format: Responses are made on a 3-point scale ranging from 1 (not like the parent) to 3 (a lot like the parent).

Reliability: Alpha coefficients ranged from .70 to .80.

Validity: Correlations with other variables ranged from −.19 to .02.

Author: Smetana, J., and Gaines, C.

Article: Adolescent-parent conflict in middle-class African American families.

Journal: *Child Development*, November/December 1999, 70(6), 1447–1463.

Related Research: Dornbusch, S. M., et al. (1985). Single parents, extended households, and control of adolescents. *Child Development, 56,* 326–341.

Stienberg, L., et al. (1991). Authoritative parenting and adolescents' adjustments across varied ecological niches. *Journal of Research on Adolescence, 1,* 19–36.

8947

Test Name: PARENTAL EVALUATION SCALE

Purpose: To enable parents to rate their children on academics, appearance, and behavior.

Number of Items: 8

Format: Includes 4 subscales: Academic, Appearance, Social, and General. Responses are made on a 5-point scale ranging from 1 (disagree) to 5 (agree). All items are presented.

Reliability: Alpha coefficients ranged from .58 to .74.

Author: McCall, R. B., et al.

Article: The nature and correlates of underachievement among elementary school children in Hong Kong.

Journal: *Child Development,* May/June 2000, 71(3), 785–801.

Related Research: Lau, S., & Pun, K. L. (1991, November). *Parental evaluation and children's self-concept.* Paper presented at the Eighth Annual Conference of the Hong Kong Educational Research Association, Hong Kong.

8948

Test Name: PARENTAL INDUCEMENT OF ACADEMIC SELF-REGULATION SCALE.

Purpose: To assess four areas of

parental self-regulation inducement.

Number of Items: 20

Format: Includes 4 areas of parental inducement: modeling, encouragement, facilitation, and rewarding. Five-point response scales are employed. All items are presented.

Reliability: Alpha coefficients were .80 and .90.

Validity: Correlations with other variables ranged from .13 to .31.

Author: Martinez-Pons, M.

Article: Test of a model of parental inducement of academic self-regulation.

Journal: *Journal of Experimental Education,* Spring 1996, 64(3), 213–227.

8949

Test Name: PARENTAL INVESTMENT IN THE CHILD QUESTIONNAIRE

Purpose: To measure acceptance of parenting role, delight in being a parent, knowledge/sensitivity, and separation anxiety.

Number of Items: 24

Format: Scales range from "strongly disagree" to "strongly agree." All items are presented.

Reliability: Alpha coefficients ranged from .70 to .84 across subscales. Test-retest reliabilities ranged from .63 to .86.

Validity: Correlations with other variables ranged from −.52 to .70.

Author: Bradley, R. H., et al.

Article: Parents' socioemotional investment in children.

Journal: *Journal of Marriage and the Family,* February 1997, 59(1), 77–90.

8950

Test Name: PARENTAL INVOLVEMENT IN SCHOOLING SCALE

Purpose: To measure student perceptions of parents' involvement in schooling.

Number of Items: 5

Format: Scales range from 1 (never) to 3 (usually). Sample items are described.

Reliability: Alpha coefficients ranged from .71 to .77.

Author: Bogenschneider, K.

Article: Parental involvement in adolescent schooling: A proximal process with transcontextual validity.

Journal: *Journal of Marriage and the Family,* August 1997, 59(3), 718–733.

Related Research: Steinberg, L., & Brown, B. B. (1989). *Beyond the classroom: Parental and peer influences on high school achievement.* Paper presented at the annual meeting of the American Educational Research Association, San Francisco.

8951

Test Name: PARENTAL MONITORING QUESTIONNAIRE

Purpose: To assess parent's monitoring of their children.

Number of Items: 10

Format: Responses are made on a 5-point scale.

Reliability: Internal consistency ranged from .56 to .73.

Validity: Correlations with other variables ranged from −.37 to .35.

Author: Smetana, J., and Gaines, C.

Article: Adolescent-parent conflict

in middle-class African American families.

Journal: *Child Development*, November/December 1999, *70*(6), 1447–1463.

Related Research: Steinberg, L., et al. (1991). Authoritative parenting and adolescent adjustment across varied ecological niches. *Journal of Research on Adolescence*, *1*, 19–36.

8952

Test Name: PARENTAL MONITORING SCALE

Purpose: To assess how closely parents monitor the behavior and activities of a child.

Number of Items: 4

Format: Five-point scales range from "never" to "always." Items are described.

Reliability: Coefficient alpha was .82.

Author: Luster, T., and Small, S. A.

Article: Sexual abuse history and problems in adolescence: Exploring the effects of moderating variables.

Journal: *Journal of Marriage and the Family*, February 1997, *59*(1), 131–142.

Related Research: Small, S., & Kerns, D. (1993). Unwanted sexual activity among peers during early and middle adolescence: Incidence and risk factors. *Journal of Marriage and the Family*, *55*, 941–952.

Rodgers, K. S. (1999). Parenting processes related to sexual risk-taking behaviors of adolescent males and females. *Journal of Marriage and the Family*, *61*, 99–109.

8953

Test Name: PARENTAL NEGLECT, HOSTILITY AND REJECTION (SUB)SCALES

Purpose: To assess parental (and caretaker) relationships to children.

Number of Items: 40

Format: Scales range from "almost always true" to "almost never true." Sample items are presented.

Reliability: Alpha coefficients ranged from .78 to .94.

Author: Rohner, R. P., et al.

Article: Children's perceptions of corporal punishment, caretaker acceptance, and psychological adjustment in a poor, biracial, southern community.

Journal: *Journal of Marriage and the Family*, November 1996, *58*(4), 842–852.

Related Research: Rohner, R. P. (1990). *Handbook for the study of parental acceptance and rejection*. Center for the Study of Parental Acceptance and Rejection, University of Connecticut at Storrs.

Veneziano, R. A. (2000). Perceived paternal and maternal acceptance and rural African American and European American youth's psychological adjustment. *Journal of Marriage and the Family*, *62*, 123–132.

8954

Test Name: PARENTAL OVERT CONFLICT STYLE QUESTIONNAIRE

Purpose: To measure youth perceptions of parental conflict.

Number of Items: 6

Format: Scales range from 1 (never) to 4 (very often). Sample items are presented.

Reliability: Coefficient alpha was .87.

Validity: Correlations with other variables ranged from .51 to .67.

Author: Gerard, J. M., and Buehler, C.

Article: Multiple risk factors in the family environment and youth problem behaviors.

Journal: *Journal of Marriage and the Family*, May 1999, *61*(2), 343–361.

Related Research: Ahrons, C. R. (1983). Predictors of paternal involvement postdivorce: Mothers' and fathers' perceptions. *Journal of Divorce*, *6*, 55–69.

Ahrons, C. R. (1981). The continuing coparental relationship between divorced spouses. *American Journal of Orthopsychiatry*, *5*, 415–428.

8955

Test Name: PARENTAL RELATIONSHIP INVENTORY

Purpose: To assess a respondent's relationships with parents.

Number of Items: 50

Format: Scales range from 4 (strongly agree) to 1 (strongly disagree).

Reliability: Alpha coefficients ranged from .72 to .95 across subscales.

Validity: Correlations with other variables ranged from −.45 to .69.

Author: Perosa, S. L., and Perosa, L. M.

Article: Intergenerational family theory and Kohut's self-psychology constructs applied to college females.

Journal: *Journal of College Student Development*, March/April 1997, *38*(2), 143–156.

Related Research: Stutman, S., & Lich, S. (1984). *The development and validation of the Parental Relationship Inventory.* Los Angeles.

8956

Test Name: PARENTAL RESPONSIVENESS SCALE

Purpose: To measure the extent to which adolescents perceive parents to be responsive and involved.

Number of Items: 7

Format: Response categories are "usually true" and "usually false." A sample item is presented.

Reliability: Alpha coefficients ranged from .74 to .77.

Validity: Correlations with other variables ranged from −.16 to .26.

Author: Fletcher, A. C., et al.

Article: Adolescents' well-being as a function of perceived interparental consistency.

Journal: *Journal of Marriage and the Family,* August 1999, *61*(3), 599–610.

Related Research: Rodgers, R. R. (1966). *Cornell Parent Behavior Description: An interim report.* Unpublished manuscript, Department of Human Development and Family Studies, Cornell University, Ithaca, New York.

8957

Test Name: PARENTAL ROLE QUESTIONNAIRE

Purpose: To measure the strength of task clarity, personal control, and personal obligation and parental psychological engagement in and expectations for the future of children.

Number of Items: 22

Format: Scales range from 1 (strong agreement) to 7 (strong disagreement). Most items are presented or described.

Reliability: Alpha coefficient ranged from .45 to .78 across subscales.

Validity: Correlations between subscales ranged from .11 to .60.

Author: Khazanovich, G., and Schlenker, B. R.

Article: Psychological involvement in parenthood among Ukranians.

Journal: *Journal of Social Psychology,* April 2000, *140*(2), 180–195.

8958

Test Name: PARENTAL SUPPORT BEHAVIORS DURING CHILDHOOD SCALE

Purpose: To assess parental support behaviors during childhood.

Number of Items: 13

Format: Includes the following variables: Cultural Encouragement, Expectations to Succeed, and School Involvement. Responses are made on a 4-point scale.

Reliability: Alpha coefficients ranged from .66 to .77.

Author: Silbereisen, R. K., et al.

Article: Differential timing of initial vocational choice: The influence of early childhood family relocation and parental support behaviors in two cultures.

Journal: *Journal of Vocational Behavior,* February 1997, *50*(1), 41–59.

Related Research: Steinberg, L., et al. (1992). Impact of parenting practices on adolescent achievement: Authoritative

parenting, school involvement, and encouragement to succeed. *Child Development,* 63, 1266–1281.

8959

Test Name: PARENTAL SUPPORT SCALE

Purpose: To measure an adolescent's perception of his or her relationship with each parent.

Number of Items: 6

Format: Scales range from 0 (never) to 4 (always). Sample items are presented.

Reliability: Alpha coefficients ranged from .89 to .93.

Author: Rodgers, K. B.

Article: Parenting processes related to sexual risk-taking behaviors of adolescent males and females.

Journal: *Journal of Marriage and the Family,* February 1999, *61*(1), 99–109.

Related Research: Armsden, G. C., & Greenberg, M. T. (1987). Inventory of Parents and Peer Attachment: Individual differences in their relationship to psychological well-being in adolescence. *Journal of Youth and Adolescence,* 16, 427–454.

Woodward, L., et al. (2000). Timing of parental separation and attachments to parents in adolescence: Results of a prospective study from birth to age 16. *Journal of Marriage and the Family,* 62, 162–174.

8960

Test Name: PARENTING CONVERGENCE SCALE

Purpose: To measure parenting support received by the mother from a secondary caregiver.

Number of Items: 12

Format: Scales range from 1 (often) to 5 (never).

Reliability: Internal consistency estimates ranged from .75 to .88.

Validity: Correlations with other variables ranged from −.08 to .01.

Author: Dorsey, S. D., et al.

Article: Parenting self-efficacy of HIV-infected mothers: The role of social support.

Journal: *Journal of Marriage and the Family,* May 1999, *61*(2), 295–305.

Related Research: Ahrons, C. (1979). The binuclear family: Two households, one family. *Alternative Lifestyles, 2,* 499–515.

8961

Test Name: PARENTING DIMENSIONS INVENTORY–2 SCALES

Purpose: To measure mother responsiveness to child distress, shared good times, and enjoyment of mother–child interaction.

Number of Items: 10

Format: Includes 2 scales: Nurturance and Responsiveness to Child Input. Employs a 6-point scale ranging from 1 (not at all descriptive of me) to 6 (highly descriptive of me).

Reliability: Coefficient alpha was .77.

Author: Kochanska, G., and Murray, K. T.

Article: Mother-child mutually responsive orientation and conscience development: From toddler to early school age.

Journal: *Child Development,* March/April 2000, *71*(2), 417–431.

Related Research: Power, T. G. (1991). *Parenting Dimensions Inventory (PDI): A research manual.* Unpublished manuscript, University of Houston, Houston, TX.

8962

Test Name: PARENTING PERFORMANCE SCALE

Purpose: To assess parents' satisfaction with their childrearing skills.

Number of Items: 9

Format: Four-point scales ranged from "strongly agree" to "strongly disagree." Sample items are presented.

Reliability: Coefficient alpha was .84.

Author: Madden-Derdich, D. A., et al.

Article: Boundary ambiguity and coparental conflict after divorce: An empirical test of a family systems model of the divorce process.

Journal: *Journal of Marriage and the Family,* August 1999, *61*(3), 588–598.

Related Research: Guidabaldi, J., & Cleminshaw, H. K. (1985). The development of the Cleminshaw-Guidabaldi Parent Satisfaction Scale. *Journal of Clinical Child Psychology, 14,* 293–298.

8963

Test Name: PARENTING POSSIBILITIES QUESTIONNAIRE

Purpose: To identify mothers' hostile attribution tendencies.

Number of Items: Nine vignettes

Format: Includes three kinds of situations: No Affect/No Control, No Affect/Control, and Negative Affect/Control. Responses are made on a 4-point scale. Sample items are presented.

Reliability: Alpha coefficients ranged from .14 to .64.

Validity: Correlations with other variables ranged from −.04 to .21.

Author: Nix, R. L., et al.

Article: The relation between mothers' hostile attribution tendencies and children's externalizing behavior problems: The mediating role of mothers' harsh discipline practices.

Journal: *Child Development,* July/August 1999, *70*(4), 896–909.

Related Research: Pettit, G. S., et al. (1988). Early family experience, social problem solving patterns, and children's social competence. *Child Development, 59,* 107–120.

8964

Test Name: PARENTING SCALES

Purpose: To measure parental warmth, monitoring, disciplining, and reasoning as child-care strategies.

Number of Items: 23

Format: Various 5-point scales are used and all are presented. Sample items are presented.

Reliability: Alpha coefficients ranged from .60 to .81.

Validity: Correlations with other variables ranged from −.67 to −.06.

Author: Simons, R. L., et al.

Article: Socialization in the family of origin and male dating violence: A prospective study.

Journal: *Journal of Marriage and the Family,* May 1998, *60*(2), 467–478.

8965

Test Name: PARENTING SCALES/PARENT–CHILD RELATIONS SCALES

Purpose: To measure 11 dimensions of parenting and parent–child relations.

Number of Items: 46

Format: All items are presented.

Reliability: Alpha coefficients range from .30 to .86.

Author: Aquilino, W. S.

Article: From adolescent to young adult: A prospective study of parent-child relations during the transition to adulthood.

Journal: *Journal of Marriage and the Family,* August 1997, *59*(3), 670–686.

Related Research: Sweet, J., et al. (1988). *The design and content of the national survey of families and households.* (Working Paper NSFH-1). Madison: University of Wisconsin, Center for Demography and Ecology.

8966

Test Name: PARENTING SELF-EFFICACY SCALE

Purpose: To assess mothers' sense of self-efficacy in the mother role.

Number of Items: 25

Format: Four-point Likert format. Sample items are presented.

Reliability: Coefficient alpha was .94.

Validity: Correlations with other variables ranged from −.16 to −.06.

Author: Dorsey, S. D., et al.

Article: Parenting self-efficacy of HIV-infected mothers: The role of social support.

Journal: *Journal of Marriage and the Family,* May 1999, *61*(2), 295–305.

Related Research: Allen, C. (1993). *An investigation of parenting efficacy.* Unpublished manuscript, University of Georgia, Athens.

8967

Test Name: PARENTING STRESS SCALE

Purpose: To measure stress due to parenting.

Number of Items: 20

Format: Four-point scales range from "not at all concerned" to "extremely concerned."

Reliability: Coefficient alpha was .82.

Validity: Correlations with other variables ranged from −.51 to .01.

Author: Bradley, R. H., et al.

Article: Parents' socioemotional investment in children.

Journal: *Journal of Marriage and the Family,* February 1997, *59*(1), 77–90.

Related Research: Marshall, N. L., & Barnett, R. (1993). Work-family strains and gains among two-earner couples. *Journal of Community Psychology, 21,* 64–78.

8968

Test Name: PARENTING STYLE INDEX

Purpose: To assess parenting style.

Number of Items: 19

Format: Includes two scales: Acceptance/Involvement and Strictness/Supervision. A 3-point format was used with some items, and a true-false format was used with other items.

Reliability: Alpha coefficients were .72 and .76.

Author: Glasgow, K. L, et al.

Article: Parenting styles, adolescents' attributions, and educational outcomes in nine heterogeneous high schools.

Journal: *Child Development,* June 1997, *68*(3), 507–529.

Related Research: Lamborn, S., et al. (1991). Patterns of competence and adjustment from authoritative, authoritarian, indulgent, and neglectful families. *Child Development, 62,* 1049–1065.

8969

Test Name: PARENTING STYLE SCALE

Purpose: To assess the underlying socialization process of autonomy and involvement.

Number of Items: 9

Format: Responses are made on a 4-point scale ranging from 1 (strongly disagree) to 4 (strongly agree). An example is given.

Reliability: Alpha coefficients were .73 and .80.

Author: Bensur, B. J., et al.

Article: An exploratory study of motivational predictors which influence graduation from two- and four-year colleges.

Journal: *Perceptual and Motor Skills,* June 1999, *88*(3) Part 1, 997–1008.

Related Research: Steinberg, L., et al. (1989). Authoritative parenting, psychosocial maturity, and academic success among adolescents. *Child Development, 60,* 1424–1436.

8970

Test Name: PARENTS' BELIEFS AND AWARENESS OF ADOLESCENT ALCOHOL USE QUESTIONNAIRE

Purpose: To assess parents' beliefs, awareness (monitoring), and response to adolescent alcohol use.

Number of Items: 37

Format: Formats vary. Sample items and all formats are presented.

Reliability: Alpha coefficients ranged from .67 to .93 across scales for mothers and fathers.

Author: Bogenschneider, K., et al.

Article: "Other teens drink, but not my kid": Does parental awareness of adolescent alcohol use protect adolescents from risky consequences?

Journal: *Journal of Marriage and the Family*, May 1998, *60*(2), 356–373.

Related Research: Small, S. A., & Kerns, D. (1993). Unwanted sexual activity among peers during early and middle adolescence: Incidence and risk factors. *Journal of Marriage and the Family*, 55, 941–952.

Armsden, G., & Greenberg, M. T. (1987). Inventory of Parents and Peer Attachment: Individual differences in their relationship to psychological well-being in adolescence. *Journal of Youth and Adolescence*, 16, 427–454.

Bogenschneider, K., & Stone, M. (1997). Delivering parent education to low- and high-risk parents of adolescents via age-posed newsletters. *Family Relations*, 46, 123–134.

Bennon, P., et al. (1987). *The quicksilver years: The hopes and fears of early adolescence*. San Francisco: Harper Row.

Rodgers, K. B. (1999). Parenting processes related to sexual risk-taking behaviors of adolescent males and females. *Journal of Marriage and the Family, 61*, 99–109.

8971

Test Name: PARTNERSHIP QUESTIONNAIRE

Purpose: To measure marital quality in terms of quarreling, tenderness, and togetherness.

Number of Items: 30

Format: Scales range from "never/very seldom" to "very often." Sample items are presented.

Reliability: Coefficient alpha was .95.

Author: Hahlweg, K., et al.

Article: Self-report and observational assessment of couples' conflict: The concordance between the Communication Patterns Questionnaire and the KPI Observation System.

Journal: *Journal of Marriage and the Family*, February 2000, *62*(1), 61–67.

Related Research: Hahlweg, K., et al. (1984). The Munich Marital Therapy Study. In K. Hahlweg & N. S. Jacobson (Eds.), *Marital interaction: Analysis and modification* (pp. 3–26). New York: Guilford Press.

8972

Test Name: PATERNAL INVOLVEMENT IN CHILD CARE INDEX

Purpose: To measure frequency of fathers' behavior related to preteens and adolescents.

Number of Items: 16

Format: Scales range from

"frequently" to "infrequently," "husband always" to "wife only," or "very involved" to "very uninvolved." Sample items are presented.

Reliability: Alpha coefficients ranged from .67 to .78.

Author: Veneziano, R. A., and Rohner, R. P.

Article: Perceived paternal acceptance, paternal involvement, and youths' psychological adjustment in a rural, biracial southern community.

Journal: *Journal of Marriage and the Family*, May 1998, *60*(2), 335–343.

Related Research: Radin, N. (1981). Childrearing fathers in intact families I: Some antecedents and consequences. *Merrill-Palmer Quarterly*, 27, 489–514.

8973

Test Name: PERCEIVED INSTRUMENTAL SPOUSE'S AND OTHER FAMILY MEMBERS' SOCIAL SUPPORT SCALE

Purpose: To measure perceived instrumental social support from one's spouse and other family members.

Number of Items: Eight items for spouse and 8 items from other family members.

Format: Includes two parallel forms: spouse and other family members. Responses are made on a 6-point agree/disagree scale.

Reliability: Alpha coefficients were .88 (spouse) and .87 (family).

Validity: Correlations with other variables ranged from −.41 to .23.

Author: Frone, M. R., et al.

Article: Developing and testing an

integrative model of the work-family interface.

Journal: *Journal of Vocational Behavior*, April 1997, *50*(2), 145–167.

Related Research: Cutrona, C. E., & Russell, D. W.(1987). The provisions of social relationships and adaptation to stress. In W. H. Jones & D. Perlman (Eds.), *Advances in personal relationships*. Greenwich, CT: JAI Press.

8974

Test Name: PERCEIVED NEGATIVE SPOUSE BEHAVIORS SCALE

Purpose: To assess criticism and avoidance of cancer patient spouses.

Number of Items: 13

Format: Four-point scales are anchored by 1 (never responds this way) and 4 (often responds this way). Sample items are presented.

Reliability: Coefficient alpha was .83.

Validity: Correlations with other variables ranged from .14 to .29.

Author: Manne, S. L., et al.

Article: Spousal negative responses to cancer patients: The role of social restriction, spouse mood, and relationship satisfaction.

Journal: *Journal of Consulting and Clinical Psychology*, June 1999, *67*(3), 352–361.

Related Research: Manne, S. L., et al. (1997). Supportive and negative responses in the partner relationship: Their association with psychological adjustment among individuals with cancer. *Journal of Behavioral Medicine*, *20*, 101–126.

8975

Test Name: PERCEIVED PARENTAL BEHAVIOR INVENTORY

Purpose: To measure students' perceptions of their proximal family environment.

Number of Items: 23

Format: 5-point scales are anchored by (1) strongly disagree and (5) strongly agree. All items are presented.

Reliability: Alpha was .87.

Author: Marjoribanks, K., and Mboya, M.

Article: Family correlates of South African students' self-concept: A regression surface analysis.

Journal: *Psychological Reports*, August 1998, *83*(1), 163–172.

Related Research: Mboya, M. M. (1993). Development and initial validation of a perceived behavior inventory for African students. *Perceptual and Motor Skills*, *76*, 1003–1008.

8976

Test Name: PERCEIVED PARENTING STYLE SCALE

Purpose: To measure perceived parenting style.

Number of Items: 14

Format: Includes 3 subscales: Mentorship/Communicative/Support, Autonomy/Directives/Instructive, and Control/Punitive/Disciplinary. Responses are made on a 4-point scale ranging from 1 (false) to 4 (true). Sample items are presented.

Reliability: Alpha coefficients ranged from .73 to .84

Author: McCall, R. B., et al.

Article: The nature and correlates of underachievements among

elementary school children in Hong Kong.

Journal: *Child Development*, May/June 2000, *71*(3), 785–801.

Related Research: Lau, S., et al (1993, November). *Perceived parenting style and primary school children's self-concept*. Paper presented at the Tenth Annual Conference of the Hong Kong Educational Research Association, Hong Kong.

8977

Test Name: PERCEPTIONS OF PARENTS SCALE

Purpose: To measure perceptions of parents held by younger and older adolescents who may not have contact with them.

Number of Items: 15

Format: Scales range from 1 (not at all or never) to 6 (extremely or always). All items are presented.

Reliability: Alpha coefficients ranged from .76 to .96.

Validity: Correlations with other variables ranged from −.41 to .71.

Author: Phares, V., and Renk, K.

Article: Perceptions of Parents: A measure of adolescents' feelings about their parents.

Journal: *Journal of Marriage and the Family*, August 1998, *60*(3), 646–659.

8978

Test Name: PERSONAL AUTHORITY IN THE FAMILY SYSTEM QUESTIONNAIRE— COLLEGE

Purpose: To assess authority, individuation, triangulation, and intimacy in the two-generational family system.

Number of Items: 84

Format: Scales range from 1 (strongly disagree) to 5 (strongly agree).

Reliability: Alpha coefficients ranged from .75 to .92. Test-retest reliabilities ranged from .58 to .80.

Validity: Correlations with other variables ranged from −.45 to .69.

Author: Perosa, S. L., and Perosa, L. M.

Article: Intergenerational family theory and Kohut's self-psychology constructs applied to college females.

Journal: *Journal of College Student Development*, March/April 1997, *38*(2), 143–156.

Related Research: Bray, J., & Harvey, D. (1992). Intimacy and individuation in young adults: Development of the college version of the Personal Authority in the Family Questionnaire. *Journal of Family Psychology, 6*, 152–163.

Fraser, K. P., & Tucker, C. M. (1997). Individuation, stress, and problem-solving abilities of college students. *Journal of College Student Development, 38*, 461–467.

8979

Test Name: POSITIVE FEELINGS QUESTIONNAIRE

Purpose: To measure feelings about one's spouse.

Number of Items: 17

Format: Seven-point Likert scales.

Reliability: Coefficient alpha was .95.

Author: Burleson, B. R., and Denton, W. H.

Article: The relationship between communication skill and marital

satisfaction: Some moderating effects.

Journal: *Journal of Marriage and the Family*, November 1997, *59*(4), 884–902.

Related Research: O'Leary, K. D., et al. (1983). Assessment of positive feelings toward spouse. *Journal of Consulting and Clinical Psychology, 51*, 947–951.

8980

Test Name: PROBLEM LIST

Purpose: To assess the number of problem areas in a marital relationship.

Number of Items: 23

Format: Scales are anchored by 0 (no problems) and 3 (problems we cannot find solutions to and don't discuss anymore).

Reliability: Internal consistency was .84.

Author: Kaiser, A., et al.

Article: The efficacy of a compact psychoeducational group training program for married couples.

Journal: *Journal of Consulting and Clinical Psychology*, October 1998, *66*(5), 753–760.

Related Research: Hahlweg, K., et al. (1984). The Munich Marital Therapy Study. In K. Hahlweg & N. S. Jacobson (Eds.), *Marital interaction: Analysis and modification* (pp. 3–26). New York: Guilford Press.

8981

Test Name: PSYCHOLOGICAL CONTROL SCALE—YOUTH SELF-REPORT REVISED

Purpose: To measure psychological control

Number of Items: 8

Format: Responses are made on a

3-point scale ranging from 1 (not like him/her) to 3 (a lot like her/him). All items are presented.

Reliability: Alpha coefficients ranged from .80 to .83.

Author: Barber, B. K.

Article: Parental psychological control: Revisiting a neglected construct.

Journal: *Child Development*, December 1996, *67*(6), 3296–3319.

Related Research: Darling, N., & Steinberg, L. (1993). Parenting style as context: An integrative model. *Psychological Bulletin, 113*, 487–496.

8982

Test Name: PSYCHOLOGICAL CONTROL SUBSCALE (REVISED) OF CHILDREN'S REPORT OF PARENTAL BEHAVIOR INVENTORY

Purpose: To measure psychological control.

Number of Items: 6

Format: Responses are made on a 3-point scale ranging from 1 (not like her or him) to 3 (a lot like her or him). All items are presented.

Reliability: Alpha coefficients ranged from .77 to .80.

Author: Barber, B. K.

Article: Parental psychological control: Revisiting a neglected construct.

Journal: *Child Development*, December 1996, *67*(6), 3296–3319.

Related Research: Schaefer, E. S. (1965). A configurational analysis of children's reports of parent behavior. *Journal of Consulting Psychology, 29*, 552–557.

8983

Test Name: PSYCHOLOGICAL SEPARATION INVENTORY

Purpose: To assess separation from both mother and father.

Number of Items: 35

Format: Includes 4 types of separation: Emotional Independence, Attitudinal Independence, Functional Independence, and Conflictual Independence. Responses are made on a 5-point scale ranging from 0 (not at all true of me) to 4 (very true of me). Examples are presented.

Reliability: Internal consistencies ranged from .77 to .94.

Validity: Correlations with other variables ranged from −.70 to .54.

Author: O'Brien, K. M., et al.

Article: Attachment, separation, and women's vocational development: A longitudinal analysis.

Journal: *Journal of Counseling Psychology*, July 2000, 47(3), 301–315.

Related Research: Hoffman, J. (1984). Psychological separation of late adolescents from their parents. *Journal of Counseling Psychology*, 31, 170–178.

8984

Test Name: PSYCHOLOGICAL SEPARATION INVENTORY

Purpose: To assess feelings of separation and independence from parents.

Number of Items: 138

Format: Scales range from 1 (not at all true of me) to 5 (very much true of me).

Reliability: Alpha coefficients ranged from .70 to .90 across subscales.

Author: Leonardi, A., and Kiosseoglou, G.

Article: The relationship of parental attachment and psychological separation to the psychological functioning of young adults.

Journal: *Journal of Social Psychology*, October 2000, 140(4), 451–464.

Related Research: Hoffman, J. A. (1984). Psychological separation of late adolescents from their parents. *Journal of Counseling Psychology*, 31, 170–178.

8985

Test Name: PSYCHOLOGICAL SEPARATION INVENTORY— REVISED

Purpose: To assess the degree of psychological separation from parents.

Number of Items: 70

Format: Responses are made on a 5-point Likert-type scale.

Reliability: Test-retest (2 to 3 weeks) reliabilities ranged from .49 to .96. Alpha coefficients ranged from .77 to .88.

Author: O'Brien, K. M.

Article: The influence of psychological separation and parental attachment on the career development of adolescent women.

Journal: *Journal of Vocational Behavior*, June 1996, 48(3), 257–274.

Related Research: Hoffman, J. (1984). Psychological separation of late adolescents from their parents. *Journal of Counseling Psychology*, 31, 170–178.

8986

Test Name: QUALITY OF MARRIAGE INDEX

Purpose: To provide a global assessment of an individual's marriage.

Number of Items: 6

Format: Sample items are presented. Agreement scales are implied.

Reliability: Coefficient alpha was .97.

Validity: Correlations with other variables ranged from .14 to .22.

Author: Waldron-Hennessey, R., and Sabatelli, R. M.

Article: The Parental Comparison Level Index: A measure for assessing parental rewards and costs relative to expectations.

Journal: *Journal of Marriage and the Family*, November 1997, 59(4), 824–833.

Related Research: Norton, R. (1983). Measuring marital quality: A critical look at the dependent variable. *Journal of Marriage and the Family*, 45, 141–151.

Katz, J., & Beach, S. R. (1997). Self-verification and depressive symptoms in marriage and courtship: A multiple pathway model. *Journal of Marriage and the Family*, 59, 903–914.

8987

Test Name: QUALITY OF PARENTING SCALE

Purpose: To measure quality of parenting in terms of talking to child, supporting the decisions of the mother, and use of consistent discipline.

Number of Items: 14

Format: Scales range from 1 (strongly disagree) to 5 (strongly agree).

Reliability: Coefficient alpha was .90.

Author: Simons, R. L., et al.

Article: Explaining the higher incidence of adjustment problems among children of divorce compared with those in two-parent families.

Journal: *Journal of Marriage and the Family*, December 1999, *61*(4), 1020–1033.

Related Research: Simons, R. L., et al. (1994). The impact of mothers' parenting, involvement by nonresidential fathers, and parental conflict on adjustment of adolescent children. *Journal of Marriage and the Family, 56*, 356–374.

8988

Test Name: QUALITY OF SIGNIFICANT RELATIONSHIP SCALE

Purpose: To measure marital satisfaction.

Format: Responses are made on a 5-point scale ranging from 1 (never) to 5 (always). Examples are presented.

Reliability: Coefficient alpha was .85.

Validity: Correlations with other variables ranged from −.60 to .33.

Author: Duxbury, L. E., et al.

Article: Work and family environments and the adoption of computer-supported supplemental work-at-home.

Journal: *Journal of Vocational Behavior*, August 1996, *49*(1), 1–23.

Related Research: Moos, R. H., et al. (1988). *Health and Daily Living Form manual.* Unpublished manuscript, Social Ecology Laboratory, Department of Psychiatry, Stanford University.

8989

Test Name: RAISING CHILDREN CHECKLIST

Purpose: To measure parenting practices.

Number of Items: 30

Format: Includes 3 factors: Firm/Responsive Parenting, Permissive (Lax) Parenting, and Harsh Parenting. Responses are made on a 4-point scale ranging from 1 (definitely no) to 4 (definitely yes). Examples are presented.

Reliability: Alpha coefficients ranged from .66 to .76.

Author: Pierce, K. M., et al.

Article: Experiences in after-school programs and children's adjustment in first-grade classrooms.

Journal: *Child Psychology*, May/June 1999, *70*(3), 756–767.

Related Research: Shumow, L., et al. (1998). Harsh, firm, and permissive parenting in low-income families: Relations to children's academic achievement and behavioral adjustment. *Journal of Family Issues, 19*, 483–507.

8990

Test Name: RATINGS OF PARENT CHANGE SCALE

Purpose: To assess change in parenting practices and cognitions.

Number of Items: 11

Format: Seven-point scales ranged from −3 (much worse) to +3 (much better).

Reliability: Coefficient alpha ranged from .63 to .86.

Author: Conduct Problems Prevention Research Group

Article: Initial impact of the fast track prevention trial for conduct problems: I. The high risk sample.

Journal: *Journal of Consulting and Clinical Psychology*, October 1999, *67*(5), 631–647.

Related Research: Conduct Problems Prevention Research Group. (1999). *Technical reports for the Fast Track Assessment Battery.* Unpublished manuscript.

8991

Test Name: REJECTION SCALE

Purpose: To assess adolescents' perceptions of parental trust, caring, and blame.

Number of Items: 5

Format: Scales range from 1 (strongly agree) to 5 (strongly disagree). All items are described.

Reliability: Alpha coefficients ranged from .82 to .86.

Validity: Correlations with other variables ranged from .02 to .18.

Author: Bao, W. -N., et al.

Article: Perceived parental acceptance as a moderator of religious transmission among adolescent boys and girls.

Journal: *Journal of Marriage and the Family*, May 1999, *61*(2), 362–374.

Related Research: Brennen, T. (1974). *Evaluation and validation regarding the national strategy for youth development.* Boulder, CO: Behavior Research Evaluation Program.

8992

Test Name: RELATIONSHIP QUALITY SCALES

Purpose: To measure intimacy, autonomy, equality, constructive problem solving, and barriers in partner relationships.

Number of Items: 36

Format: Scales range from 1 (not at all true) to 9 (very true) on three subscales. Scales range from 1 (never) to 5 (always) on one subscale and from 1 (strongly disagree) to 5 (strongly agree) on one subscale. All items are presented.

Reliability: Alpha coefficients ranged from .67 to .90.

Validity: Correlations with other variables ranged from −.14 to .48.

Author: Kurdek, L. A.

Article: Relationship outcomes and their predictors: Longitudinal evidence from heterosexual married, gay cohabiting, and lesbian cohabiting couples.

Journal: *Journal of Marriage and the Family*, August 1998, *60*(3), 553–568.

Related Research: Kurdek, L. A. (1994). Conflict resolution styles in gay, lesbian and heterosexual couples. *Journal of Marriage and the Family, 56*, 705–722.

8993

Test Name: RELATIONSHIP WITH FATHER AND CHILDHOOD RELATIONSHIP SCALE

Purpose: To measure paternal independence–encouragement versus overprotection and acceptance.

Number of Items: 30

Format: Five-point Likert scales. Sample items are described.

Reliability: Alphas ranged from .86 to .91.

Author: McCormick, C. B., and Kennedy, J. H.

Article: Father-child separation: Retrospective and current views of attachment relationship with father and self-esteem in late adolescence.

Journal: *Psychological Reports*, June 2000, *86*(3, Part 1), 827–834.

Related Research: Epstein, S. (1983). *The Mother-Father-Peer Scale*. Unpublished manuscript, University of Massachusetts.

8994

Test Name: RELATIONSHIP WITH FATHER INVENTORY

Purpose: To measure current emotional attachment to father and father–child coalition.

Number of Items: 22

Format: Sixteen item are anchored by (1) very untrue and (4) very true. Six items are anchored by (1) not at all and (5) a great deal. Sample items are presented.

Reliability: Internal consistencies ranged from low .80s to low .90s.

Validity: Correlations with Parental Bonding Scale ranged from −.33 to .78.

Author: Zazzaro, J. A., et al.

Article: Concurrent validity of the Relationship with Father Inventory.

Journal: *Psychological Reports*, October 1998, *83*(2), 403–409.

Related Research: Southworth, S., & Schwartz, J. C. (1987). Post-divorce contact, relationship with father and heterosexual trust in female college students. *American Journal of Orthopsychiatry, 57*, 371–382.

8995

Test Name: REWARDS AND COSTS OF HOMEMAKING SCALES

Purpose: To assess perception of the rewards and costs involved in the homemaking role.

Number of Items: 10

Format: Includes two subscales: Homemaking Reward and homemaking Cost. Responses are made on 5-point scales. All items are presented.

Reliability: Alpha coefficients were .83 (homemaking reward) and .75 (homemaking cost).

Validity: Correlations with other variables ranged from −.36 to .55.

Author: Matsui, T., et al.

Article: Some motivational bases for work and home orientation among Japanese college women: A rewards/costs analysis.

Journal: *Journal of Vocational Behavior*, February 1999, *54*(1), 114–126

Related Research: Matsui, T., et al. (1995). Work-family conflict and the stress-buffering effects of husband support and coping behavior among Japanese married working women. *Journal of Vocational Behavior, 47*, 178–192.

8996

Test Name: ROLE OVERLOAD SCALE

Purpose: To measure demands placed on parents.

Number of Items: 13

Format: Five-point scales.

Reliability: Alpha coefficients ranged from .72 to .79.

Author: Bumpas, M. F., et al.

Article: Work demands of dual-earner couples: Implications for parents' knowledge about children's daily lives in middle childhood.

Journal: *Journal of Marriage and the Family,* May 1999, *61*(2), 465–475.

Related Research: Reilly, M. D. (1982). Working wives and convenience consumption. *Journal of Consumer Research, 8,* 407–418.

8997

Test Name: ROLE-TAKING SCALE

Purpose: To assess the degree to which a person is able to take his or her spouse's perspective.

Number of Items: 5

Format: Scales range from 0 (never) to 4 (often). Sample items are presented.

Reliability: Omega reliability was .78.

Author: Burke, P. J., and Cast, A. D.

Article: Stability and change in gender identities of newly married couples.

Journal: *Social Psychology Quarterly,* December 1997, *60*(4), 277–290.

Related Research: Davis, M. H. (1983). Measuring individual differences in empathy: Evidence for a multidimensional approach. *Journal of Personality and Social Psychology, 53,* 397–410.

8998

Test Name: SELF-EXPRESSIVENESS IN THE FAMILY QUESTIONNAIRE

Purpose: To assess verbal and nonverbal, and positive and negative expressiveness in the family.

Number of Items: 12

Reliability: Alphas ranged from .82 to .88.

Validity: Correlations with other variables ranged from −.52 to .34.

Author: Yelsma, P., et al.

Article: Clients' positive and negative expressiveness within their families and alexithymia

Journal: *Psychological Reports,* April 1998, *82*(2), 563–569.

Related Research: Halberstadt, A. G., et al. (1995). Self-expressiveness within the family context: Psychometric support for a new measure. *Psychological Assessment, 7,* 93–103.

8999

Test Name: SEXUAL SATISFACTION SCALE

Purpose: To measure sexual satisfaction.

Number of Items: 27

Format: Unspecified response scales. All items are presented.

Reliability: Alphas ranged from .63 to .91 across subscales.

Validity: Correlation with other variables ranged from .05 to .57.

Author: Young, M., et al.

Article: Sexual satisfaction among married women age 50 and older.

Journal: *Psychological Reports,* June 2000, *86*(3, Part 2), 1107–1122.

9000

Test Name: SIBLING RELATIONSHIP SCALE

Purpose: To measure negativity in the sibling relationship.

Number of Items: 5

Format: Five-point frequency scales.

Reliability: Alpha coefficients ranged from .75 to .80.

Author: McHale, S. M., et al.

Article: Step in or stay out? Parents' roles in adolescent siblings' relationships.

Journal: *Journal of Marriage and the Family,* August 2000, *62*(3), 746–760.

Related Research: Stocker, C., & McHale, S. (1992). Linkages between sibling and parent-child relationships in early adolescence. *Journal of Social and Personal Relationships, 9,* 179–195.

9001

Test Name: SONS' GENERAL INVOLVEMENT SCALE

Purpose: To assess sons' general involvement with parents and family.

Number of Items: 4

Format: Responses are made on a 3-point scale ranging from 1 (hardly ever) to 3 (often). Sample items are presented.

Reliability: Coefficient alpha was .57.

Author: Curtner-Smith, M. E.

Article: Mechanisms by which family processes contribute to school-age boys' bullying.

Journal: *Child Study Journal,* 2000, *30*(3), 169–186.

Related Research: Loeber, R. (1990). *Caretaker Self-Administered Questionnaire: The Pittsburgh Youth Study.* Western Psychiatric Institute and Clinic, The University of Pittsburgh School of Medicine.

9002

Test Name: SONS' PERCEPTION OF MOTHERS' MONITORING INSTRUMENTS

Purpose: To measure the son's

perception of mother's monitoring and strictness of supervision.

Number of Items: 10

Format: A variety of response formats is used. Examples of items are presented.

Validity: Correlations with other variables ranged from −.14 to .12.

Author: Curtner-Smith, M. E.

Article: Mechanisms by which family processes contribute to school-age boys' bullying.

Journal: *Child Study Journal,* 2000, *30*(3), 169–186.

Related Research: Lamborn, S. D., et al. (1991). Patterns of competence and adjustment among adolescents from authoritative, authoritarian, indulgent, and neglectful families. *Child Development, 62*, 1049–1065.

9003

Test Name: SPOUSAL STYLE OF CONFLICT RESOLUTION QUESTIONNAIRE

Purpose: To assess constructive methods of resolving marital disagreements.

Number of Items: 10

Format: Includes Compromise and Intimacy scales. Examples are presented.

Reliability: Alpha coefficients were > .70.

Author: Davies, P. T., and Cummings, E. M.

Article: Exploring children's emotional security as a mediator of the link between marital relations and child development.

Journal: *Child Development,* February 1998, *69*(1), 124–139.

Related Research: Rands, M., et

al. (1981). Patterns of conflict resolution and marital satisfaction. *Journal of Family Issues, 2*, 297–321.

9004

Test Name: SPOUSAL SUPPORT SCALE

Purpose: To measure spousal support.

Number of Items: 5

Format: Responses are made on a 5-point scale ranging from 1 (strongly disagree) to 5 (strongly agree). Sample items are presented.

Reliability: Coefficient alpha was .85.

Validity: Correlations with other variables ranged from −.11 to .33.

Author: Aryee, S., et al.

Article: Role stressors, inter-role conflict, and well-being: The moderating influence of spousal support and coping behaviors among employed parents in Hong Kong.

Journal: *Journal of Vocational Behavior,* April 1999, *54*(2), 259–278.

Related Research: Matsui, T., et al. (1995). Work-family conflict and the stress buffering effects of husband support and coping behavior among Japanese married working women. *Journal of Vocational Behavior, 47*, 178–192.

9005

Test Name: SPOUSE SUPPORT SCALE

Purpose: To measure spouse support.

Number of Items: 4

Format: Responses are made on a

5-point scale ranging from 1 (very inaccurate) to 5 (very accurate). Examples are presented.

Reliability: Coefficient alpha was .77.

Validity: Correlations with other variables ranged from −.22 to .34.

Author: Aryee, S., and Luk, V.

Article: Work and nonwork influences on the career satisfaction of dual-earner couples.

Journal: *Journal of Vocational Behavior,* August 1996, *49*(1), 38–52.

9006

Test Name: STRICTNESS/ SUPERVISION SCALE

Purpose: To measure parental monitoring.

Number of Items: 4

Format: Scales range from 1 (doesn't/don't know at all) to 4 (always knows/know).

Reliability: Alpha coefficients range from .68 to .73.

Author: Miller, K. S.

Article: Adolescent sexual behavior and two ethnic minority samples: The role of family variables.

Journal: *Journal of Marriage and the Family,* February 1999, *61*(1), 85–98.

Related Research: Steinberg, L., et al. (1992). Impact of parenting practices in adolescent achievement: Authoritative parenting, school involvement and encouragement to succeed. *Child Development, 63*, 1266–1281.

9007

Test Name: STUDENT ATTITUDES AND PERCEPTIONS SURVEY—ADAPTED

Purpose: To identify the characteristics of respondents' relationships with their parents.

Number of Items: 32

Format: Includes 6 scales: Autonomy Granting, Demandingness, Supportiveness, Childhood Autonomy, Childhood Demandingness, and Child Supportiveness.

Reliability: Alpha coefficients ranged from .67 to .87.

Validity: Correlations with other variables ranged from −.19 to .44.

Author: Strage, A., and Brandt, T. S.

Article: Authoritative parenting and college students' academic adjustment and success.

Journal: *Journal of Educational Psychology*, March 1999, *91*(1), 146–156.

Related Research: Baumrind, D. (1991). The influence of parenting style on adolescent competence and substance use. *Journal of Early Adolescence*, *11*, 56–95.

9008

Test Name: TRADITIONAL FAMILY IDEOLOGY SCALE

Purpose: To measure family ideology on the authoritarian–democratic continuum.

Number of Items: 40

Reliability: Split-half reliability was .84.

Validity: Correlations with other variables ranged from .05 to .73.

Author: Hamburger, M. E., et al.

Article: Assessing hypergender ideologies: Development and initial validation of a gender-neutral measure of adherence to extreme gender-role beliefs.

Journal: *Journal of Research in Personality*, June 1996, *30*(2), 157–178.

Related Research: Levinson, D. J., & Huffman, P. E. (1955). Traditional family ideology and its relation to personality. *Journal of Personality*, *23*, 251–275.

CHAPTER 14
Institutional Information

9009

Test Name: AFTER-SCHOOL ENVIRONMENT SCALE

Purpose: To measure children's perceptions of the psychosocial climate of their after-school programs.

Number of Items: 36

Format: Responses are made on a 4-point scale ranging from 1 (never) to 4 (always). Includes 3 factors: Emotional Support, Autonomy/Privacy, and Peer Affiliation.

Reliability: Alpha coefficients ranged from .79 to .95. Test-retest correlations ranged from .70 to .91 ($N = 65$).

Author: Rosenthal, R., and Vandell, D. L.

Article: Quality of care at school-aged child-care programs: Regulatable features, observed experiences, child perspectives, and parent perspectives.

Journal: *Child Development*, October 1996, 67(5), 2434–2445.

Related Research: Albrecht, K. (1991). *Quality criteria for school-age child-care programs.* Alexandria, VA: Project Home Safe, American Home Economics Association; and Benton Harbor, MI: Whirlpool Foundation.

9010

Test Name: APPRAISAL SCALES

Purpose: To measure supervisor observation, supervisor feedback, supervisor guidance, system openness, system commitment, and system complexity.

Number of Items: 25

Format: Scales range from 1 (strongly disagree) to 7 (strongly agree). Sample items are presented.

Reliability: Alpha coefficients ranged from .64 to .92.

Author: Findley, H. M., et al.

Article: Performance appraisal process and system facets: Relationships with contextual performance.

Journal: *Journal of Applied Psychology*, August 2000, 85(4), 634–640.

Related Research: Giles, W. F., et al. (1997). Procedural fairness in performance appraisal: Beyond the review session. *Journal of Business and Psychology, 11,* 493–506.

Folger, R., et al. (1992). Due process metaphor for performance appraisal. *Research in Organizational Behavior, 14,* 129–177.

9011

Test Name: ASSESSMENT PERCEPTIONS AND ATTITUDES SCALES

Purpose: To measure perceived validity and fairness of assessments, and the extent to which assessments are enjoyable, brief, satisfying, and modern.

Number of Items: 36

Format: Scales range from 1 (strongly disagree) to 10 (strongly agree). Sample items are presented.

Reliability: Alpha coefficients ranged from .54 to .86 across subscales.

Author: Richman-Hirsch, W. L., et al.

Article: Examining the impact of administration medium on examinee perceptions and attitudes.

Journal: *Journal of Applied Psychology,* December 2000, 85(6), 880–887.

Related Research: Macan, T. H., et al. (1994). The effects of applicants' reactions to cognitive ability tests and an assessment center. *Personnel Psychology, 47,* 715–738.

9012

Test Name: ATTRIBUTES OF STRATEGIC MANAGEMENT INVENTORY

Purpose: To measure perceptions of strategic management in terms of process and outcome.

Number of Items: 22

Format: 7-point scales range from (1) low to (7) high.

Reliability: Alpha was .94.

Author: Budd, J. L., and Carraher, S. M.

Article: Validation of an inventory to measure attributes of strategic management.

Journal: *Psychological Reports,* June 1998, 82(3) Part 2, 1220–1222.

Related Research: Budd, J., & Shinde, J. (1995). Toward a theory of strategy. *Proceedings of the Association of Management, 13*, 106–111.

9013

Test Name: BARRIERS TO ADVANCEMENT SCALE

Purpose: To assess perceived barriers to career advancement.

Number of Items: 26

Format: Scales range from 1 (no problem at all) to 5 (a very serious problem). All items are presented.

Reliability: Alpha coefficients ranged from .69 to .84 across subscales.

Validity: Correlations with other variables ranged from −.37 to .20.

Author: Lyness, K. S., and Thompson, D. E.

Article: Climbing the corporate ladder: Do female and male executives follow the same route?

Journal: *Journal of Applied Psychology,* February 2000, *85*(1), 86–101.

9014

Test Name: BARRIERS TO MENTORING SCALE

Purpose: To measure perceived barriers to mentoring.

Number of Items: 6

Format: Responses are made on a 5-point Likert-type scale ranging from 1 (strongly disagree) to 5 (strongly agree). An example is presented.

Reliability: Internal consistency reliability estimate was .83.

Validity: Correlations with other variables ranged from −.18 to .56.

Author: Allen, T. D., et al.

Article: A field study of factors related to supervisors' willingness to mentor others.

Journal: *Journal of Vocational Behavior,* February 1997, *50*(1), 1–22.

Related Research: Ragins, B. R., & Cotton, J. L. (1993). Gender and willingness to mentor in organizations. *Journal of Management, 19*, 97–111.

9015

Test Name: BARRIERS-TO-TREATMENT PARTICIPATION SCALE

Purpose: To assess barriers to treatment that could occur over the course of treatment or perceived by patient and therapist.

Number of Items: 44

Format: Five-point scales are anchored by 1 (never a problem) and 5 (very often a problem).

Reliability: Alphas ranged from .69 to .90 across subscales and patient and therapist versions.

Validity: Correlations with other variables ranged from −.24 to .27.

Author: Kazdin, A. E., et al.

Article: Family experience of barriers to treatment and premature termination from child therapy.

Journal: *Journal of Consulting and Clinical Psychology,* June 1997, *65*(3), 453–463.

Related Research: Kazdin, A. E., et al. (1991). *Barriers to Participation in Treatment Scale —parent and therapist versions.* New Haven, CT: Yale University.

9016

Test Name: BUREAUCRATIC PROCEDURES SCALE

Purpose: To determine the amount of the organization's internal structures.

Number of Items: 5

Format: Responses are made on a scale ranging from 1 (agree) to 5 (disagree). Sample items are presented.

Reliability: Coefficient alpha was .69.

Validity: Correlations with other variables ranged from −.17 to .29.

Author: Timmermin, G., and Bajema, C.

Article: The impact of organizational culture on perceptions and experiences of sexual harassment.

Journal: *Journal of Vocational Behavior,* October 2000, *57*(2), 188–205.

9017

Test Name: CAMPUS ENVIRONMENT QUESTIONNAIRE

Purpose: To assess campus peer pressure and respondents' campus behavior.

Number of Items: 19

Format: Pressure scales range from 1 (none/not at all satisfied) to 5 (a lot/very satisfied). Behavior scales range from 1 (never) to 5 (all the time/ frequently).

Reliability: Alpha coefficients ranged from .72 to .85 across pressure subscales.

Validity: Correlations with other variables ranged from −.16 to .62.

Author: Kashubeck, S., et al.

Article: Sorority membership, campus pressures, and bulimic symptomatology in college women: A preliminary investigation.

Journal: *Journal of College Student Development*, January/February 1997, *38*(1), 40–48.

9018

Test Name: CAMPUS ENVIRONMENT SURVEY—MODIFIED

Purpose: To determine students' perception of the campus environment.

Number of Items: 40

Format: Responses are made on a 5-point Likert scale ranging from 1 (strongly disagree) to 5 (strongly agree). Examples are presented.

Reliability: Internal consistency was .87.

Author: Serex, C. P., and Townsend, B. K.

Article: Student perceptions of chilling practices in sex-atypical majors.

Journal: *Research in Higher Education*, October 1999, *40*(5), 527–538.

Related Research: Leonard, M. M., & Ossana, S. (1987). *Technical manual for the Campus Environment Survey.* Unpublished manual, University of Maryland Counseling Center.

9019

Test Name: CAREER DEVELOPMENT OPPORTUNITIES SCALE

Purpose: To assess career development opportunities.

Number of Items: 7

Format: Responses are made on a

5-point scale ranging from "very frequently" to "never."

Reliability: Coefficient alpha was .76.

Validity: Correlations with other variables ranged from −.09 to .28.

Author: Greenhaus, J. H., et al.

Article: Work and family influences on departure from public accounting.

Journal: *Journal of Vocational Behavior*, April 1997, *50*(2), 249–270.

9020

Test Name: CAREER GROWTH OPPORTUNITY SCALE

Purpose: To measure career growth opportunity.

Number of Items: 4

Format: All items are presented.

Reliability: Coefficient alpha was .89.

Validity: Correlations with other variables ranged from −.26 to .44.

Author: Adams, G. A.

Article: Career-related variables and planned retirement age: An extension of Beehr's model.

Journal: *Journal of Vocational Behavior*, October 1999, *55*(2), 221–235.

Related Research: Bedeian, A. G., et al. (1991). Career commitment and expected utility of present job as predictors of turnover intentions and turnover behavior. *Journal of Vocational Behavior, 39*, 331–343.

9021

Test Name: CAREER TRANSITION INVENTORY

Purpose: To assess the

psychological resources of and barriers to adults in career transition.

Number of Items: 40

Format: Includes 5 factors: Readiness, Confidence, Control, Perceived Support, and Decision Independence. Responses are made on a 6-point Likert scale ranging from 1 (strongly disagree) to 6 (strongly agree).

Reliability: Internal consistency coefficients ranged from .66 to .87.

Validity: Correlations with other variables ranged from −.29 to .56.

Author: Heppner, M. J., et al.

Article: The relationship of trainee self-efficacy to the process and outcome of career counseling.

Journal: *Journal of Counseling Psychology*, October 1998, *45*(4), 392–402.

Related Research: Heppner, M. J. (1991). *The Career Transitions Inventory* (Available from M. J. Heppner, Department of Educational and Counseling Psychology, 16 Hill Hall, University of Missouri, Columbia, MO 65211).

9022

Test Name: CHARLES F. KETTERING CLIMATE SCALE FOR JUNIOR HIGH SCHOOL

Purpose: To measure school climate.

Number of Items: 105

Format: Includes 4 sections: Part A—General Climate Factors, Part B—Program Determinants, Part C—Process Determinants, and Part D—Material Determinants. Responses for Part A range from 1 (almost never) to

4 (almost always). All 40 items are presented.

Reliability: Alpha coefficients for Part A ranged from .40 to .85.

Author: Johnson, W. L., et al.

Article: Assessing the validity of scores on the Charles F. Kettering Scale for the junior high school.

Journal: *Educational and Psychological Measurement*, October 1997, 57(5), 858–869.

Related Research: Howard, E., et al. (1987). Handbook for conducting school climate improvement projects. Bloomington, IN: Phi Delta Kappa Educational Foundation (ERIC Document Reproduction Service No. ED 290 211).

9023

Test Name: CLASSROOM-CLIMATE QUESTIONNAIRE

Purpose: To assess the perceived traditional and experimental writing class climates.

Number of Items: 21

Format: Includes 6 dimensions: Teacher-Student Relations, Peer Relations, Writing Processes, Role of the Computer, Classroom Management, and Student Responsibility. Responses are made on a 4-point Likert scale ranging from *strongly agree* to *strongly disagree*.

Reliability: Reliability estimates ranged from .51 to .88.

Author: Levine, T., et al.

Article: Student perception of classroom climate in a communicative and computer-supported approach to writing instruction.

Journal: *Journal of Research and Development in Education*, Winter 1996, 29(2), 94–103.

Related Research: Donitsa-Schmidt, S. (1994). *Development of a classroom environment questionnaire for writing classes in high school*. Unpublished master's thesis, Tel-Aviv University.

9024

Test Name: CLASSROOM ENVIRONMENT SCALE

Purpose: To measure peer affiliation and teacher support in the classroom experience.

Number of Items: 20

Format: True/false format.

Reliability: Alpha coefficients ranged from .74 to .84 across subscales. Test-retest reliability (2 weeks) was .95.

Author: Schwitzer, A. M., and Lovell, C.

Article: Effects of goal instability, peer affiliation and teacher support on distance learners.

Journal: *Journal of College Student Development*, January/February 1999, 40(1), 43–53.

Related Research: Tricket, E. J., & Moos, R. H. (1973). Social environment of junior high and high school classrooms. *Journal of Educational Psychology*, 65, 92–102.

9025

Test Name: CLASSROOM LIFE MEASURE

Purpose: To measure 12 dimensions of classroom life.

Number of Items: 65

Format: Scales range from 1 (very untrue) to 5 (very true).

Reliability: Alpha coefficients ranged from .51 to .83 across subscales.

Authors: Dudley, B. S., et al.

Article: Using cooperative learning to enhance the academic and social experiences of freshman student athletes.

Journal: *Journal of Social Psychology*, June 1997, 137(4), 449–459.

Related Research: Johnson, D. W., et al. (1983). Social interdependence and classroom climate. *Journal of Psychology*, 114, 135–142.

9026

Test Name: CLIMATE FOR SERVICE SCALES

Purpose: To measure organizational climate within which services are provided.

Number of Items: 22

Format: Sample items are presented.

Reliability: Average alpha coefficients ranged from .82 to .91 across subscales and across time.

Validity: Correlations with other variables ranged from .11 to .69.

Author: Schneider, B., et al.

Article: Linking service climate and customer perceptions of service quality: Test of a causal model.

Journal: *Journal of Applied Psychology*, April 1998, 83(2), 150–163.

9027

Test Name: CLIMATE SCALE—MODIFIED

Purpose: To measure race-related workplace climate.

Number of Items: 20

Reliability: Alpha coefficients were .83 and .91.

Validity: Correlations with other

variables ranged from −.66 to .75.

Author: Holder, J. C., and Vaux, A.

Article: African American professionals: Coping with occupational stress in predominantly White work environments.

Journal: *Journal of Vocational Behavior*, December 1998, *53*(3), 315–333.

Related Research: Watts, R. J., & Carter, R. J. (1991). Psychological aspects of racism in organizations. *Group and Organization Studies*, *16*, 328–344.

9028

Test Name: CLINICAL MENTAL HEALTH ASSESSMENT SURVEY

Purpose: To rate mental health instruments on usefulness, need, and frequency of use.

Number of Items: 43

Format: Scales range from 1 (not useful) to 5 (essential).

Reliability: Reliability coefficient was .97. Split-half reliability was .90 (adjusted Spearman Brown formula).

Author: Giordano, F. G., et al.

Article: School counselors' perceptions of the usefulness of standardized tests, frequency of their use and assessment training needs.

Journal: *The School Counselor*, January 1997, *44*(3), 198–205.

Related Research: Juhnke, G., et al. (1994). *The Clinical Mental Health Assessment Survey*. Unpublished manuscript, University of North Carolina, Greensboro, NC.

9029

Test Name: COLLEGE AND UNIVERSITY CLASSROOM ENVIRONMENT INSTRUMENT

Purpose: To evaluate perceptions of classroom environments in small seminar and tutorial-style college classes.

Format: Includes 7 scales: Personalization, Involvement, Student Cohesiveness, Satisfaction, Task Orientation, Innovation, and Individualization.

Reliability: Alpha coefficients ranged from .64 to .89.

Validity: Correlations with cheating neutralization ranged from −.01 to .29.

Author: Pulvers, K., and Diekhoff, G. M.

Article: The relationship between academic dishonesty and college classroom environment.

Journal: *Research in Higher Education*, August 1999, *40*(4), 487–498.

Related Research: Fraser, B. J., et al. (1986). Development of an instrument for assessing classroom psychosocial environments at universities and colleges. *Studies in Higher Education*, 11, 43–54.

9030

Test Name: COMMUNITY EXPERIENCES QUESTIONNAIRE

Purpose: To measure exposure to violence in the community by self-report.

Number of Items: 25

Format: Four-point scales are anchored by 1 (never) and 4 (lots of times). All items are presented.

Reliability: Alpha coefficients were

.81 (direct victimization) and .89 (witnessing).

Validity: The correlation between subscales was .54.

Author: Schwartz, D., and Proctor, L. J.

Article: Community violence exposure and children's social adjustment in the school peer group: The mediating roles of emotion regulation and social cognition.

Journal: *Journal of Consulting and Clinical Psychology*, August 2000, *68*(4), 670–683.

Related Research: Richters, J. E., & Saltzman, W. (1990). *Survey of Exposure to Community Violence—Self-Report Version*. Rockville, MD: National Institute of Mental Health.

9031

Test Name: CONTEXT-SPECIFIC ORGANIZATION CHANGE VARIABLES

Purpose: To measure context-specific organizational variables that are responsive to intervention: information, participation, change self-efficacy and social support.

Number of Items: 15

Format: Scales range from 1 (strongly disagree) to 7 (strongly agree). All items are presented.

Reliability: Alpha coefficients ranged from .44 to .87.

Validity: Correlations with other variables ranged from −.29 to .26.

Author: Wanberg, C. R., and Banas, J. T.

Article: Predictors and outcomes of openness to changes in a reorganizing workplace.

Journal: *Journal of Applied*

Psychology, February 2000, *85*(1), 132–142.

9032

Test Name: CUSTOMER PERCEPTIONS OF SERVICE SCALES

Purpose: To measure the elements of the quality of service.

Number of Items: 30

Format: Sample items are presented.

Reliability: Average alpha coefficients ranged from .74 to .94 across subscales and across time.

Validity: Correlations with other variables ranged from .00 to .31.

Author: Schneider, B., et al.

Article: Linking service climate and customer perceptions of service quality: Test of a causal model.

Journal: *Journal of Applied Psychology*, April 1998, *83*(2), 150–163.

9033

Test Name: DEVELOPMENT CHALLENGE PROFILE— SHORT VERSION

Purpose: To measure the developmental characteristics of positions and difficulties participants face in those positions.

Number of Items: Subscales contain 3–5 items.

Format: Five-point scales range from 1 (not at all descriptive) to 5 (extremely descriptive).

Reliability: Coefficient alphas ranged from .56 to .81 across subscales.

Author: Lyness, K. S., and Thompson, D. E.

Article: Above the glass ceiling? A comparison of matched samples of female and male executives.

Journal: *Journal of Applied Psychology*, June 1997, *82*(3), 359–375.

Related Research: Ohlott, P. J., et al. (1994). Gender differences in managers' developmental job experiences. *Academy of Management Journal*, 37, 46–67.

9034

Test Name: DISTRIBUTUVE AND PROCEDURAL JUSTICE SCALE

Purpose: To measure distributive and procedural justice.

Number of Items: 11

Format: Includes distributive and procedural justice. Responses are made on a 5-point scale ranging from 1 (strongly disagree) to 5 (strongly agree). Examples are presented.

Reliability: Alpha coefficients were .85 and .71.

Validity: Correlations with other variables ranged from .18 to .54.

Author: Scandura, T. A.

Article: Mentoring and organizational justice: An empirical investigation.

Journal: *Journal of Vocational Behavior*, August 1997, *51*(1), 58–69.

Related Research: Moorman, R. H. (1991). Relationship between organizational justice and organizational citizenship behavior: Do fairness perceptions influence employee citizenship? *Journal of Applied Psychology*, 76, 845–855.

9035

Test Name: DISTRIBUTIVE FAIRNESS SCALE

Purpose: To measure the extent to which a respondent judges current facets of his or her work context to be fair.

Number of Items: 5

Format: Responses are made on a 5-point Likert type scale ranging from 1 (strongly disagree) to 5 (strongly agree). All items are presented.

Reliability: Coefficient alpha was .75.

Validity: Correlations with other variables ranged from .13 to .36.

Author: Mansour-Cole, D. M., and Scott, S. G.

Article: Hearing it through the grapevine: The influence of source, leader-relation, and legitimacy on survivors' fairness perceptions.

Journal: *Personnel Psychology*, Spring 1998, *51*(1), 25–54.

Related Research: Price, J., & Mueller, C. (1986). *Handbook of organizational measurement.* Marshfield, MA: Pitman Publishing.

9036

Test Name: DISTRIBUTIVE JUSTICE SCALE

Purpose: To measure appraisal distributive justice.

Number of Items: 4

Format: Scales range from "strongly disagree" to "strongly agree." A sample item is presented.

Reliability: Coefficient alpha was .95.

Validity: Correlations with other variables ranged from −.27 to .88.

Author: Keeping, L. M., and Levy, P. E.

Article: Performance appraisal

reactions: Measurement, modeling and method bias.

Journal: *Journal of Applied Psychology*, October 2000, *85*(5), 708–723.

Related Research: Korsgaard, M. A., & Roberson, L. (1995). Procedural justice in performance evaluation: The role of instrumental and non-instrumental voice in performance appraisal discussions. *Journal of Management, 21,* 657–669.

9037

Test Name: DIVERSITY PRACTICES SURVEYS

Purpose: To measure the extent to which an organization engages in management of diversity practices.

Number of Items: 22

Format: Six-point scales are anchored by 0 (not at all) and 5 (a great deal). All items are presented.

Reliability: Total alpha was .75. Subscale alphas ranged from .85 to .88.

Author: Gilbert, J. A., and Ones, D. S.

Article: Development of the diversity practices survey.

Journal: *Psychological Reports*, August 1999, *85*(1), 101–104.

Related Research: Thomas, R. R., Jr. (1992). Managing diversity: A conceptual framework. In S. E. Jackson & Associates (Eds.), *Diversity in the workplace* (pp. 306–317). New York: Guilford.

9038

Test Name: EDUCATIONAL OUTCOMES AND EXPERIENCES SCALES

Purpose: To assess alumni

perceptions of multicultural gains, creative thinking gains, communication and problem solving gains, instructional satisfaction, and satisfaction with student services.

Number of Items: 41

Format: All items are presented. Response scales are described.

Reliability: Alpha coefficients ranged from .74 to .83 across subscales.

Author: Graham, S. W., and Gisi, S. L.

Article: The effects of instructional climate and student affairs services on college outcomes and satisfaction.

Journal: *Journal of College Student Development*, May/June 2000, *41*(3), 279–291.

Related Research: American College Testing. (1996). *College outcomes survey user norms.* Iowa City, IA: Author.

9039

Test Name: ELABORATION LIKELIHOOD MODEL QUESTIONNAIRE

Purpose: To assess components necessary for central route attitude change to occur.

Number of Items: 12

Format: Includes 2 factors: Cognitive Involvement and Presentation Quality. Responses are made on a 5-point scale. All items are presented.

Reliability: Alpha coefficients ranged from .37 to .83.

Author: Heppner, M. J., et al.

Article: Examining immediate and long-term efficacy of rape prevention programming with racially diverse college men.

Journal: *Journal of Counseling*

Psychology, January 1999, *46*(1), 16–26.

Related Research: Heppner, M. J. (1995). The differential effects of rape prevention programming on attitudes, behavior, and knowledge. *Journal of Counseling Psychology, 42,* 508–518.

9040

Test Name: EMPLOYEE SUPPORT, AFFECTIVITY, AUTONOMY AND WORKLOAD SCALES

Purpose: To assess perceived support at work, positive affectivity, autonomy at work, and workload.

Number of Items: 18

Format: Scales range from 1 (strongly disagree) to 5 (strongly agree). All items are presented.

Reliability: Alpha coefficients ranged from .65 to .70 across subscales.

Validity: Correlations with other variables ranged from −.43 to .70.

Author: Yoon, J., and Thye, S.

Article: Supervision support in the workplace: Legitimacy and positive affectivity.

Journal: *Journal of Social Psychology*, June 2000, 140(3), 295–316.

9041

Test Name: ENVIRONMENTAL DEPRIVATION SCALE

Purpose: To measure how well an individual functions in his or her surroundings.

Number of Items: 17

Format: Responses are coded "1" or "0." A sample item is presented.

Reliability: Alpha was .58.

Author: Long, C. K., and Witherspoon, A. D.

Article: The environmental deprivation scale as a predictor of academic performance.

Journal: *Psychological Reports*, June, 1998, *82*(3) Part 2, 1295–1298.

Related Research: Jenkins, W. O., & Sanford, W. L. (1972). *A manual for the use of the Environmental Deprivation Scale in corrections: The prediction of criminal behavior.* Rehabilitation Research Foundation, Contract No. 82–01–69–06, Manpower Administration, U. S. Department of Labor.

9042

Test Name: EQUITY SENSITIVITY INSTRUMENT

Purpose: To measure sensitivity to equity at the workplace.

Number of Items: 5

Format: Ten-point, forced distribution scales. A sample item is presented.

Reliability: Coefficient alpha was .86.

Validity: Correlations with other variables ranged from −.30 to .30.

Author: O'Neill, B. S., and Mone, M. A.

Article: Investigating equity sensitivity as a moderator of relations between self-efficacy and workplace attitudes.

Journal: *Journal of Applied Psychology*, October 1998, *83*(5), 805–816.

Related Research: Huseman, R. C., et al. (1985). Test for individual perceptions of job equity: Some preliminary

findings. *Perceptual and Motor Skills, 61*, 1055–1064.

9043

Test Name: ETHICAL CLIMATE QUESTIONNAIRE

Purpose: To assess the ethical climate within organizations.

Number of Items: 36

Format: Six-point scales ranged from 0 ("completely false") to 5 ("completely true").

Reliability: Alphas ranged from .60 to .89 across subscales.

Author: Vaicys, C., et al.

Article: An analysis of the factor structure of the Ethical Climate Questionnaire.

Journal: *Psychological Reports*, August 1996, *79*(1), 115–120.

Related Research: Cullen, J. B., et al. (1993). The Ethical Climate Questionnaire: An assessment of its development and validity. *Psychological Reports, 73*, 667–674.

9044

Test Name: FACE VALIDITY PERCEPTIONS SCALE

Purpose: To assess the face validity of a test to measure what is required by a job.

Number of Items: 5

Format: Five-point scales range from 1 (strongly disagree) to 5 (strongly agree). All items are presented.

Reliability: Alpha coefficients were .90 (paper-and-pencil judgment) and .78 (video-based judgment).

Validity: Correlations with other variables ranged from −.40 to .38.

Author: Chan, D., and Schmitt, N.

Article: Video-based versus paper-and-pencil method of assessment in situational judgement tests: Subgroup differences in test performance and face validity perceptions.

Journal: *Journal of Applied Psychology*, February 1997, *82*(1), 143–159.

Related Research: Smither, J. W., et al. (1993). Applicant reactions to selection procedures. *Personnel Pschology, 46*, 49–76.

9045

Test Name: FACILITATORS OF ADVANCEMENT SCALE

Purpose: To assess perceived facilitators of career advancement.

Number of Items: 21

Format: Scales range from 1 (not a facilitator) to 5 (a very important facilitator). All items are presented.

Reliability: Alpha coefficients ranged from .70 to .90 across subscales.

Validity: Correlations with other variables ranged from −.37 to .32.

Author: Lyness, K. S., and Thompson, D. E.

Article: Climbing the corporate ladder: Do female and male executives follow the same route?

Journal: *Journal of Applied Psychology*, February 2000, *85*(1), 86–101.

9046

Test Name: FACULTY EXPERIENCES IN WORKING TOWARD TENURE QUESTIONNAIRE

Purpose: To identify specific worklife issues faculty perceive to be barriers to their retention and tenure at research universities.

Number of Items: 96

Format: Includes 13 scales. Responses are made on a 5-point scale ranging from 1 (not a problem) to 5 (a significant problem).

Reliability: Alpha coefficients ranged from .72 to .94.

Author: Johnsrud, L. K., and Heck, R. H.

Article: Faculty worklife: Establishing benchmarks across groups.

Journal: *Research in Higher Education*, October 1998, *39*(5), 539–555.

Related Research: Johnsrud, L. K., and Desjarlais, C. D. (1994). Barriers to tenure for women and minorities. *Review of Higher Education*, 17(4), 335–353, summer.

9047

Test Name: FAIRNESS PERCEPTIONS MEASURE

Purpose: To assess participants' reactions to the information policies.

Number of Items: 6

Format: Responses are made on a 7-point Likert scale ranging from 1 (strongly disagree) to 7 (strongly agree). Examples are presented.

Reliability: Coefficient alpha was .94.

Author: Eddy, E. E., et al.

Article: The effects of information management policies on reactions to human resource information systems: An integration of privacy and procedural justice perspectives.

Journal: *Personnel Psychology*, Summer 1999, *52*(2), 335–358.

Related Research: Greenberg, J. (1990). Organizational justice: Yesterday, today, and tomorrow, *Journal of Management*, *16*, 399–432.

9048

Test Name: FLEXIBILITY OF WORK HOURS SCALE

Purpose: To measure flexibility of work hours.

Number of Items: 4

Format: A coding system of 0 or 1 was used. All items are presented.

Reliability: Coefficient alpha was .78.

Validity: Correlation with days absent was −.12.

Author: Erickson, R. J., et al.

Article: Family influences on absenteeism: Testing an expanded process model.

Journal: *Journal of Vocational Behavior*, October 2000, *57*(2), 246–272.

9049

Test Name: FORMALIZATION SCALE

Purpose: To measure how rule-bound an organization is in structure.

Number of Items: 5

Format: Scales range from 5 (very accurate) to 1 (very inaccurate). All items are presented.

Reliability: Coefficient alpha was .70.

Validity: Correlations with other variables ranged from −.06 to .08.

Author: Schminke, M., et al.

Article: The effect of organizational structure on

perceptions of procedural fairness.

Journal: *Journal of Applied Psychology*, April 2000, *85*(2), 294–304.

Related Research: Pugh, D. S., et al. (1968). Dimensions of organizational structure. *Administrative Science Quarterly*, *13*, 65–105.

9050

Test Name: FOUNDATION ISSUES SCALES

Purpose: To measure contextual factors that sustain work in organizations.

Number of Items: 25

Format: Sample items are presented.

Reliability: Average alpha ranged from .79 to .97 across subscales and across time.

Validity: Correlations with other variables ranged from .04 to .86.

Author: Schneider, B., et al.

Article: Linking service climate and customer perceptions of service quality: Test of a causal model.

Journal: *Journal of Applied Psychology*, April 1998, *83*(2), 150–163.

9051

Test Name: GROUP BEHAVIOR INVENTORY

Purpose: To measure work-group characteristics and processes.

Number of Items: 34

Format: Includes five subgroups: Group Effectiveness, Intergroup Trust, Mutual Influence, Worth of Group, and Leader Approachability. Both 5 and 7-point Likert formats are used.

Reliability: Kuder-Richardson Formula 20 reliabilities ranged from .72 to .91. Alpha coefficients ranged from .70 to .89.

Validity: Correlations with other variables ranged from −.33 to .42.

Author: Koberg, C. S., et al.

Article: Factors and outcomes associated with mentoring among health-care professionals.

Journal: *Journal of Vocational Behavior*, August 1998, *53*(1), 58–72.

Related Research: Friedlander, F. A. (1966). Performance and interactional dimensions of organizational work groups. *Journal of Applied Psychology*, *50*(3), 257–265.

9052

Test Name: GROUP SAFETY CLIMATE SCALE

Purpose: To measure safety climate perceptions.

Number of Items: 10

Format: Scales range from 1 (completely disagree) to 5 (completely agree). All items are presented.

Reliability: Alpha coefficients ranged from .91 to .93 across two factors.

Validity: Correlations with other variables ranged from −.23 to .37.

Author: Zohar, D.

Article: A group-level model of safety climate: Testing the effect of group climate on microaccidents in manufacturing jobs.

Journal: *Journal of Applied Psychology*, August 2000, *85*(4), 587–596.

9053

Test Name: HIERARCHY OF AUTHORITY SCALE

Purpose: To measure the extent to which decisions must be evaluated by higher authorities.

Number of Items: 5

Format: Scales range from 4 (definitely true) to 1 (definitely false). All items are presented.

Reliability: Coefficient alpha was .89.

Validity: Correlations with other variables ranged from −.37 to .14.

Author: Schminke, M., et al.

Article: The effect of organizational structure on perceptions of procedural fairness.

Journal: *Journal of Applied Psychology*, April 2000, *85*(2), 294–304.

Related Research: Hage, J., & Aiken, M. (1967). Relationship of centralization to other structural properties. *Administrative Science Quarterly*, *12*, 72–92.

9054

Test Name: INDIVIDUALIZED CLASSROOM ENVIRONMENT QUESTIONNAIRE

Purpose: To identify students' perceptions of their learning environments.

Number of Items: 25

Format: Includes 5 dimensions: Personalization, Participation, Independence, Investigation, and Differentiation. Responses are made on a 5-point scale ranging from 5 (very often) to 1 (almost never).

Reliability: Alpha coefficients were .76 and .72.

Author: Dart, B. C., et al.

Article: Students' conceptions of learning, the classroom environment, and approaches to learning.

Journal: *Journal of Educational Research*, March/April 2000, *93*(4), 262–270.

Related Research: Fraser, B. (1991). Two decades of classroom environment research. In B. Fraser & H. Walburg (Eds.), *Educational environments: Evaluation, antecedents and consequences* (pp. 3–27). Oxford: Pergamon.

9055

Test Name: INTERACTIONAL JUSTICE SCALE

Purpose: To measure interactional justice.

Number of Items: 14

Format: Responses are made on a 5-point Likert-type scale ranging from 1 (strongly disagree) to 5 (strongly agree). Examples are presented.

Validity: Correlation with procedural justice was .78.

Author: Skarlicki, D. P., and Latham, G. P.

Article: Leadership training in organizational justice to increase citizenship behavior within a labor union: A replication.

Journal: *Personnel Psychology*, Autumn 1997, *50*(3), 617–633.

Related Research: Moorman, R. H. (1991). Relationship between organizational justice and organizational citizenship behaviors: Do fairness perceptions influence employee citizenship? *Journal of Applied Psychology*, *76*, 845–855.

9056

Test Name: INVASION OF PRIVACY PERCEPTIONS MEASURE

Purpose: To assess invasion of privacy perceptions.

Number of Items: 20

Format: Responses are made on a 7-point Likert-type scale ranging from 1 (strongly disagree) to 7 (strongly agree).

Reliability: Coefficient alpha was .95.

Author: Eddy, E. R., et al.

Article: The effects of information management policies on reactions to human resource information systems: An integration of privacy and procedural justice perspectives.

Journal: *Personnel Psychology*, Summer 1999, *52*(2), 335–358.

Related Research: Stone, E. F., et al. (1983). A field experiment comparing information-privacy values, beliefs, and attitudes across several types of organizations. *Journal of Applied Psychology*, *68*, 459–468.

9057

Test Name: INVITING SCHOOL SAFETY SURVEY

Purpose: To assess how students and teachers perceive the relative safety of their school.

Number of Items: 50

Format: Scales range from 1 (strongly agree) to 5 (strongly disagree). All items are presented.

Reliability: Internal consistency reliabilities ranged from .61 to .73 across subscales.

Author: Shoffner, M. F., and Vacc, N. A.

Article: Psychometric analysis of the Inviting School Safety Survey.

Journal: *Measurement and Evaluation in Counseling and Development*, July 1999, *32*(2), 66–74.

Related Research: Lehr, J. B., & Purkey, W. W. (1997). *Inviting School Safety Survey*. Unpublished manuscript, University of North Carolina at Greensboro, International Alliance for Invitational Education.

9058

Test Name: JOB ATTRIBUTE SCALE

Purpose: To measure attributes of a job such as pay and coworkers.

Number of Items: 12

Format: Scales range from "very unfavorable" to "very favorable."

Reliability: Coefficient alpha was .84.

Validity: Correlations with other variables ranged from −.04 to .13.

Author: Ryan, A. M., et al.

Article: Applicant self-selection: Correlates of withdrawal from a multiple hurdle process.

Journal: *Journal of Applied Psychology*, April 2000, *85*(2), 163–179.

Related Research: Turban, D. B., et al. (1993). Job attributes: Preferences compared with reasons given for accepting and rejecting job offers. *Journal of Occupational and Organizational Psychology*, *66*, 71–81.

9059

Test Name: JOB CHARACTERISTICS SCALES

Purpose: To assess opportunity for involvement, job enlargement, and job enrichment.

Format: Scales range from 1 (not at all) to 5 (a great deal). Sample items are presented.

Reliability: Alpha coefficients ranged from .73 to .94 across subscales.

Validity: Correlations between enlargement and other variables ranged from −.06 to .41.

Author: Parker, S. K.

Article: Enhancing role breadth self-efficacy: The roles of job enrichment and other organizational interventions.

Journal: *Journal of Applied Psychology*, December 1998, *83*(6), 835–852.

Related Research: Wall, T. D., et al. (1995). Further evidence on some new measures of job control, cognitive demand and production responsibility. *Journal of Organizational Behavior*, *16*, 431–455.

9060

Test Name: JOB CONDITIONS SCALES

Purpose: To measure 4 job conditions.

Number of Items: 16

Format: Includes 4 scales: Work Overload, Job Complexity, Job Autonomy, and Opportunities for Advancement. Responses are made on a 4-point Likert-type scale ranging from 1 (strongly disagree) to 4 (strongly agree). Sample items are presented.

Reliability: Alpha coefficients ranged from .76 to .85.

Validity: Correlations with days absent ranged from −.14 to .03.

Author: Erickson, R. J., et al.

Article: Family influences on

absenteeism: Testing an expanded process model.

Journal: *Journal of Vocational Behavior*, October 2000, 57(2), 246–272.

9061

Test Name: JOB DEMANDS AND CONTROL SCALES

Purpose: To measure job demands, such as complexity, and how much an employ can control job demands.

Number of Items: 39

Format: Scales range from 1 (almost never) to 5 (very often).

Reliability: Coefficients alpha were .94 (demands) and .96 (control).

Validity: Correlations with other variables ranged from −.08 to .22.

Author: Schaubroeck, J., et al.

Article: Collective efficacy versus self-efficacy in coping responses to stressors and control: A cross-cultural study.

Journal: *Journal of Applied Psychology*, August 2000, 85(4), 512–525.

Related Research: Caplan, R. D., et al. (1975). *Job demands and worker health*. (NIOSH Publication No. 75–160). Washington, DC: Department of Health, Education, and Welfare.

Ganster, D. C. (1989). Worker control and well-being: A review of research in the workplace. In S. Sauter et al. (Eds.), *Job control and worker health* (pp. 3–24). Chichester, England: Wiley.

9062

Test Name: JOB DIAGNOSTIC SURVEY—MODIFIED

Purpose: To measure work-related variables.

Format: Includes 4 variables: Autonomy, Skill Variety, Task Significance, and Required Interaction. Responses are made on 7-point Likert-type scales.

Reliability: Alpha coefficients ranged from .53 to .67. Test-retest (6 months) reliabilities ranged from .45 to .74.

Validity: Correlations with other variables ranged from −.24 to .29.

Author: Beehr, T. A., et al.

Article: Work and nonwork predictors of employees' retirement ages.

Journal: *Journal of Vocational Behavior*, October 2000, 57(2), 206–225.

Related Research: Hackman, J. R., & Oldham, G. R. (1976). Motivation through the design of work: Test of a theory. *Organizational Behavior and Human Performance*, 16, 250–279.

9063

Test Name: JOB DIAGNOSTIC SURVEY—REVISED

Purpose: To assess job characteristics.

Format: Includes 3 job characteristics: Job Meaningfulness, Task Feedback, and Job Autonomy. Responses are made on a 7-point scale ranging from 1 (strongly disagree) to 7 (strongly agree).

Reliability: Alpha coefficients ranged from .69 to .85.

Validity: Correlations with other variables ranged from .10 to .74.

Author: Kraimer, M. L., et al.

Article: Psychological empowerment as a

multidimensional construct: A test of construct validity.

Journal: *Educational and Psychological Measurement*, February 1999, 59(1), 127–142.

Related Research: Idaszak, J. R., & Drasgow, F. (1987). A revision of the Job Diagnostic Survey: Elimination of a measurement artifact. *Journal of Applied Psychology*, 72, 69–74.

9064

Test Name: JOB DIAGNOSTIC SURVEY—SHORT VERSION

Purpose: To measure job characteristics.

Number of Items: 14

Format: Scales range from 1 (very inaccurate) to 7 (very accurate). Sample items are presented.

Reliability: Coefficient alpha was .73.

Validity: Correlations with other variables ranged from −.27 to .62.

Author: Judge, T. A., et al.

Article: Personality and job satisfaction: The mediating role of job characteristics.

Journal: *Journal of Applied Psychology*, April 2000, 85(2), 237–249.

Related Research: Dunham, R. B., et al. (1977). Dimensionality of task design as measured by the Job Diagnostic Inventory. *Academy of Management Journal*, 20, 209–233.

9065

Test Name: JOB DIAGNOSTIC SURVEY—SKILL VARIETY

Purpose: To measure skill variety.

Number of Items: 3

Format: Responses are made on 7-point scales. All items are presented.

Reliability: Coefficient alpha was .79.

Validity: Correlations with other variables ranged from −.25 to .27 (N = 116).

Author: Nielsen, I. K., et al.

Article: Development and validation of scores on a two-dimensional workplace friendship scale.

Journal: *Educational and Psychological Measurement,* August 2000, *60*(4), 628–643.

Related Research: Hackman, J. R., & Oldham, G. R. (1975). Development of the Job Diagnostic Survey. *Journal of Applied Psychology, 60,* 159–170.

9066

Test Name: JOB DIAGNOSTIC SURVEY—TASK IDENTITY

Purpose: To measure task identity.

Number of Items: 3

Format: Responses are made on 7-point scales. All items are presented.

Reliability: Coefficient alpha was .86.

Validity: Correlations with other variables ranged from −.04 to .20 (N = 116).

Author: Nielsen, I. K., et al.

Article: Development and validation of scores on a two-dimensional workplace friendship scale.

Journal: *Educational and Psychological Measurement,* August 2000, *60*(4), 628–643.

Related Research: Hackman, J. R., & Oldham, G. R. (1980).

Work redesign. Reading, MA: Addison-Wesley.

9067

Test Name: JOB DIMENSIONS INSTRUMENT—ADAPTED

Purpose: To measure workplace friendship.

Number of Items: 6

Format: Responses are made on a 5-point scale ranging from 1 (strongly disagree) to 5 (strongly agree).

Reliability: Coefficient alpha was .88.

Validity: Correlations with other variables ranged from −.27 to .76 (N = 116).

Author: Nielsen, I. K., et al.

Article: Development and validation of scores on a two-dimensional workplace friendship scale.

Journal: *Educational and Psychological Measurement,* August 2000, *60*(4), 628–643.

Related Research: Riordan, C. M., & Griffeth, R. W. (1995). The opportunity for friendship in the workplace: An underexplored construct. *Journal of Business and Psychology, 10,* 141–154.

9068

Test Name: JOB IMPROVEMENT SCALE

Purpose: To measure the extent to which a company emphasizes continuous job training.

Number of Items: 8

Format: Scales range from 1 (strongly disagree) to 7 (strongly agree). Sample items are presented.

Reliability: Alpha coefficients ranged from .74 to .82.

Validity: Correlations with other variables ranged from −.47 to .59.

Author: Robert, C., et al.

Article: Empowerment and continuous improvement in the United States, Mexico, Poland, and India: Predicting fit on the basis of the dimensions of power distance and individualism.

Journal: *Journal of Applied Psychology,* October 2000, *85*(5), 643–658.

9069

Test Name: JOB RELATEDNESS SCALE

Purpose: To assess the perceptions of biodata information requested from potential employees.

Number of Items: 5

Format: All items are presented.

Reliability: Coefficient alpha was .74.

Validity: Correlations with other variables ranged from −.51 to −.21.

Author: Elkins, T. J., and Phillips, J. S.

Article: Job context, selection decision outcome, and the perceived fairness of selection tests: Biodata as an illustrative case.

Journal: *Journal of Applied Psychology,* June 2000, *85*(3), 479–484.

Related Research: Smither, J. W., et al. (1993). Applicant reactions to selection procedures. *Personnel Psychology, 46,* 49–76.

9070

Test Name: JOB RICHNESS SCALE

Purpose: To measure job richness.

Number of Items: 3

Format: Employs 5-point scales. A sample is presented.

Reliability: Alpha was .62.

Validity: Correlations with other variables ranged from −.27 to .63.

Author: Gorgievski-Duijvesteijn, M., et al.

Article: Protestant work ethic as a moderator of mental and physical well-being.

Journal: *Psychological Reports*, December 1998, *83*(3) Part 1, 1043–1050.

Related Research: Steensma, H. O. (1988). Opgeruimd staat netjes-Organisatie-ontwikkeling bij een reinigingsdienst [That thing is nice and tidy again—Organizational development in a sanitary service organization]. Leiden: DSWO-Press.

9071

Test Name: JOB-SEARCH CONSTRAINT SCALE

Purpose: To measure the extent to which external factors interfere with a job search.

Number of Items: 7

Format: Scales range from 1 (not at all or no negative influence at all) to 5 (a great deal or extreme negative influence). All items are presented.

Reliability: Coefficient alpha was .73.

Validity: Correlations with other variables ranged from −.29 to .39.

Author: Wanberg, C. R., et al.

Article: Unemployed individuals: Motives, job-search competencies, and job-search constraints as predictors of job seeking and reemployment.

Journal: *Journal of Applied Psychology*, December 1999, *84*(6), 897–910.

9072

Test Name: JUSTICE INDEX

Purpose: To assess distributive, procedural, and interactional justice.

Number of Items: 27

Format: Seven-point scales are anchored by 1 (extremely unlikely) and 7 (extremely likely). Sample items are presented.

Reliability: Alphas ranged from .77 to .91 across subscales and several cultural groups.

Author: Tata, J.

Article: Differences between Caucasian and Hispanic undergraduates in emphasis on distributive, procedural, and interactional justice.

Journal: *Psychological Reports*, August 2000, *87*(1), 151–155.

Related Research: Tata, J., & Bowes-Sperry, L. (1996). Emphasis on distributed, procedural, and interactional justice: Differential perceptions of men and women. *Psychological Reports*, 79, 1327–1330.

9073

Test Name: JUSTICE PERCEPTIONS OF THE EDITORIAL REVIEW PROCESS SCALES

Purpose: To assess justice perceptions of the editorial review process.

Number of Items: 26

Format: Includes 6 factors: Distributive Justice, Feedback Timeliness, Editorial Review Process Consistency, Reviewer Consistency, Interpersonal Sensitivity, and Explanation. Responses are made on a 5-point scale.

Reliability: Internal consistency estimates ranged from .75 to .91.

Validity: Correlations with other variables ranged from −.52 to .60.

Author: Gilliland, S. W., and Beckstein, B. A.

Article: Procedural and distributive justice in the editorial review process.

Journal: *Personnel Psychology*, Autumn 1996, *49*(3), 669–691.

Related Research: Gilliland, S. W., & Honig, H. (1994, April). *Development of selection fairness survey.* Poster session presented at the ninth annual conference of the Society for Industrial and Organizational Psychology, Nashville.

9074

Test Name: JUSTICE PERCEPTIONS SCALE

Purpose: To measure procedural and distributive justice.

Number of Items: 9

Format: All items are presented.

Reliability: Coefficient alpha was .85 (procedural) and .81 (distributive).

Validity: Correlations with other variables ranged from −.29 to .51.

Author: Elkins, T. J., and Phillips, J. S.

Article: Job context, selection decision outcome, and the perceived fairness of selection tests: Biodata as an illustrative case.

Journal: *Journal of Applied Psychology*, June 2000, *85*(3), 479–484.

Related Research: Gilliland, S. W. (1994). Effects of procedural and distributive justice on reactions to a selection system. *Journal of Applied Psychology, 79,* 691–701.

9075

Test Name: LEARNING AND PERFORMANCE ORIENTED PHYSICAL EDUCATION CLASSES QUESTIONNAIRE

Purpose: To measure the perceptions of Greek students of the motivational climate of their physical education classes.

Number of Items: 27

Format: Responses are made on a 5-point scale.

Reliability: Alpha coefficients were .90 and .80.

Author: Papaioannou, A.

Article: Perceptions of motivational climate, perceived competence, and motivation of students of varying age and sport experience.

Journal: *Perceptual and Motor Skills,* October 1997, *85*(2), 419–430.

Related Research: Papaioannou, A. (1994). The development of a questionnaire to measure achievement orientations in physical education. *Research Quarterly for Exercise and Sport, 65,* 11–20.

9076

Test Name: LEGITIMACY OF ORGANIZATIONAL ACCOUNT SCALE

Purpose: To assess belief in the letter explaining the organization's layoffs and reorganization.

Number of Items: 3

Format: Responses are made on a 5-point Likert-type scale ranging from 1 (strongly disagree) to 5 (strongly agree). All items are presented.

Reliability: Coefficient alpha was .76.

Validity: Correlations with other variables ranged from −.16 to .55.

Author: Mansour-Cole, D. M., and Scott, S. G.

Article: Hearing it through the grapevine: The influence of source, leader-relations, and legitimacy on survivors' fairness perceptions.

Journal: *Personnel Psychology,* Spring 1998, *51*(1), 25–54.

Related Research: Mellor, S. (1992). The influence of layoff severity on post-layoff union commitment among survivors: The moderating effect of the perceived legitimacy of a layoff account. *Personnel Psychology, 45,* 579–600.

9077

Test Name: LEIDEN QUALITY OF WORK QUESTIONNAIRE

Purpose: To assess work characteristics.

Number of Items: 64

Format: Five-point scales are anchored by "disagree completely" and "agree completely." All items are presented.

Reliability: Alphas ranged from .73 to .93 across 12 subscales.

Validity: Goodness of fit indexes were .88 (number of factors, factor structure, loadings, and between-factor correlations).

Author: Van Der Doef, M., and Maes, S.

Article: The Leiden Quality of Work Questionnaire: Its construction, factor structure, and psychometric properties.

Journal: *Psychological Reports,* December 1999, *85*(3, Part I), 954–962.

9078

Test Name: LEVEL OF INFORMATIONAL/EMOTIONAL SUPPORT SCALE

Purpose: To measure level of informational or emotional support received by the entrepreneur.

Number of Items: 6

Format: Responses are made on a 5-point scale ranging from 1 (almost none) to 5 (a great deal). Examples are given.

Reliability: Coefficient alpha was .86.

Validity: Correlations with other variables ranged from −.38 to .40.

Author: Parasuraman, S., et al.

Article: Work and family variables, entrepreneurial career success, and psychological well-being.

Journal: *Journal of Vocational Behavior,* June 1996, *48*(3), 275–300.

Related Research: Parasurman, S., et al. (1992). Role stressors, social support and well-being among two-career couples. *Journal of Organizational Behavior, 13,* 339–356.

9079

Test Name: MEASUREMENT SUPPORT SCALE

Purpose: To measure the extent to which low levels of management support are a barrier to participation and development activities.

Number of Items: 3

Format: Five-point scales range from 1 (strongly disagree) to 5 (strongly agree). A sample item is presented.

Reliability: Coefficient alpha was .75.

Validity: Correlations with other variables ranged from −.25 to .41.

Author: Birdi, K., et al.

Article: Correlates and perceived outcomes of four types of employee development activity.

Journal: *Journal of Applied Psychology,* December 1997, *82*(6), 845–857.

Related Research: Maurer, T. J., & Taraulli, B. A. (1994). Investigation of perceived environment, perceived outcome, and person variables in relationship to voluntary development activities by employees. *Journal of Applied Psychology, 79,* 3–14.

9080

Test Name: MATHEMATICS CLASSROOM ENVIRONMENT SCALE

Purpose: To assess preferred and actual learning environments of the mathematics classroom.

Number of Items: 54

Format: Responses are made on a 5-point scale ranging from "almost never" to "very often." Sample items are presented.

Reliability: Coefficient of determination coefficients ranged from .61 to .85.

Author: Wong, N. Y., and Watkins, D.

Article: A longitudinal study of the psychosocial environmental

and learning approaches in the Hong Kong classroom.

Journal: *Journal of Educational Research,* March/April 1998, *91*(4), 247–254.

Related Research: Wong, N. Y. (1995). Discrepancies between preferred and actual mathematics classroom environment as perceived by students and teachers in Hong Kong. *Psychologia, 38,* 124–131.

9081

Test Name: MEASURE OF INGRATIATORY BEHAVIORS IN ORGANIZATIONAL SETTINGS SCALE

Purpose: To measure the frequency with which ingratiatory tactics are used by subordinates in superior-subordinate relationships.

Number of Items: 24

Format: Includes 4 factors: Other Enhancement, Opinion Conformity, Self-Presentation, and Favor Rendering. Responses are made on a 5-point rating scale ranging from 1 (never do) to 5 (almost always do). All items are presented.

Reliability: Alpha coefficients ranged from .74 to 89.

Author: Kacmar, K. M., and Valle, M.

Article: Dimensionality of the Measure of Ingratiatory Behaviors in Organizational Settings (MIBOS) Scale.

Journal: *Educational and Psychological Measurement,* April 1997, *57*(2), 314–328.

Related Research: Kumar, K., & Beyerlein, M. (1991). Construction and validation of an instrument for measuring ingratiatory behaviors in organizational settings. *Journal*

of Applied Psychology, 76, 619–627.

9082

Test Name: MULTICULTURAL ASSESSMENT OF CAMPUS PROGRAMMING QUESTIONNAIRE

Purpose: To assess several dimensions of campus multiculturalism.

Number of Items: 42

Format: Five-point Likert format. All items are presented.

Reliability: Coefficient alpha was .87. Test-retest reliability (4 weeks) was .79. Alpha coefficients ranged from .62 to .82 across subscales.

Author: McClellan, S. A., et al.

Article: Development of the Multicultural Assessment of Campus Programming (MAC-P) Questionnaire.

Journal: *Measurement and Evaluation in Counseling and Development,* July 1996, *29*(2), 86–99.

Related Research: Cooper, D. L. (1991). *UNCG Black student survey.* Greensboro, NC: Author.

9083

Test Name: MULTIMETHOD JOB DESIGN QUESTIONNAIRE

Purpose: To provide a general measure of work.

Format: Includes 10 factors: Feedback, Skill, Rewards, Specialization, Task Simplicity, Physical Ease, Work Conditions, Work Scheduling, Ergonomics, and Cognitive Simplicity. All items are presented.

Number of Items: 35

Reliability: Reliabilities ranged from .67 to greater than .70.

Author: Edwards, J. R., et al.

Article: The measurement of work: Hierarchical representation of the multi-method job design questionnaire.

Journal: *Personnel Psychology*, Summer 1999, *52*(2), 305–334.

Related Research: Campion, M. A. (1988). Interdisciplinary approaches to job design: A constructive replication with extensions. *Journal of Applied Psychology*, *73*, 467–481.

9084

Test Name: MULTIMETHOD JOB DESIGN QUESTIONNAIRE

Purpose: To measure four work-design approaches: motivational, mechanistic, biological, and perceptual–motor.

Number of Items: 48

Format: Scales range from 1 (strongly disagree) to 5 (strongly agree).

Reliability: Alpha coefficients ranged from .53 to .87 across subscales.

Validity: Correlations with other variables ranged from −.50 to .78.

Author: Edwards, J. R., et al.

Article: The nature and outcomes of work: A replication and extension of interdisciplinary work-design research.

Journal: *Journal of Applied Psychology*, December 2000, *85*(6), 860–868.

Related Research: Campion, M. A. (1998). Interdisciplinary approaches to job design: A constructive replication with extensions. *Journal of Applied Psychology*, *73*, 467–481.

9085

Test Name: MY CLASS INVENTORY

Purpose: To assess student perceptions of the classroom environment in terms of satisfaction, friction, competitiveness, difficulty, and cohesion.

Number of Items: 25

Format: Yes/no format.

Reliability: Alpha reliabilities ranged from .73 to .88 across subscales.

Author: Otwell, P. S., and Mullis, F.

Article: Counselor-led staff development: An efficient approach to teacher consultation.

Journal: *Professional School Counseling*, October 1997, *1*(1), 25–30.

Related Research: Fraser, B. J. (1989). Assessing and improving classroom environment. *The Key Centre for School Science and Mathematics*, *2*, 1–8.

9086

Test Name: NATIONAL SURVEY OF TEACHER EDUCATION GRADUATES

Purpose: To provide information for program evaluation.

Number of Items: 130

Format: Includes 9 sections. All items are included.

Reliability: Alpha coefficients ranged from .75 to .89.

Author: Loadman, W. E., et al.

Article: Development of a national survey of teacher education program graduates.

Journal: *Journal of Educational Research*, November/December 1999, *93*(2), 76–89.

Related Research: Loadman, W. E. (1989). *Developing a national database for pre-service teacher education follow-up studies*. Paper presented at the meeting of the American Association of Colleges of Teacher Education, Anaheim, CA.

9087

Test Name: NEIGHBORHOOD DISORDER SCALE

Purpose: To measure perceptions of disorder in a person's neighborhood.

Number of Items: 14

Format: Scales range from 1 (strongly disagree) to 5 (strongly agree). All items are presented.

Reliability: Coefficient alpha was .91.

Validity: Correlations with other variables ranged from −.32 to .26.

Author: Geis, K. J., and Ross, C. E.

Article: A new look at urban alienation: The effect of neighborhood disorder on perceived powerlessness.

Journal: *Social Psychology Quarterly*, September 1998, *61*(3), 232–246.

9088

Test Name: NONCOGNITIVE QUESTIONNAIRE

Purpose: To collect psychological, cultural, and social information for college admission purposes.

Number of Items: 23

Format: Eighteen items are in a Likert format, two are multiple-choice and three are open-ended.

Reliability: Test-retest reliabilities (2 weeks) ranged from .70 to .94 across items.

Author: Ting, S.-M. R.

Article: Estimating academic success in the 1st year of college for specially admitted White students: A model combining cognitive and psychosocial factors.

Journal: *Journal of College Student Development*, July/ August 1997, *38*(4), 401–409.

Related Research: Tracey, T. J., & Sedlacek, W. E. (1984). Noncognitive variables in predicting academic success by race. *Management and Evaluation in Guidance, 16,* 171–178.

9089

Test Name: NONHETEROSEXIST ORGANIZATIONAL CLIMATE SCALE

Purpose: To assess respondents' perceptions of their organizational climate as it pertains to gay, lesbian, and bisexual issues.

Number of Items: 15

Format: Statements are rated on a 5-point scale according to the degree to which they are true about the organization.

Reliability: Coefficient alpha was .85.

Validity: Correlations with other variables ranged from −.22 to .42.

Author: Bieschke, K. J., and Matthews, C.

Article: Career counselor attitudes and behaviors toward gay, lesbian, and bisexual clients.

Journal: *Journal of Vocational Behavior*, April 1996, *48*(2), 243–255.

Related Research: Eldridge, N. S., & Barnett, D. C. (1991). Counseling gay and lesbian

students. In N. J. Evans & V. A. Wall (Eds.), *Beyond tolerance: Gays, lesbians, and bisexuals on campus* (pp. 147– 178). Alexandria, VA: American College Personnel Association.

9090

Test Name: NURSING HOME SERVICE QUALITY INVENTORY

Purpose: To assess service quality in nursing homes from the perspective of residents in terms of staff and environmental responsiveness, dependability and trust, personal control, and food-related services.

Number of Items: 32

Format: Seven-point Likert scales and four-point rating scales are used. All items are presented.

Reliability: Alphas ranged from .68 to .93 across subscales.

Validity: Correlations with other variables ranged from −.30 to .13.

Author: Davis, M. A., et al.

Article: Measuring quality of nursing home service: Residents' perspective.

Journal: *Psychological Reports*, October 1997, *81*(2), 531–542.

Related Research: Parasuraman, A., et al. (1988) SERVQUAL: A multi-item scale for measuring consumer perceptions of service quality. *Journal of Retailing*, 64, 12–40.

9091

Test Name: NURTURANT LEARNING ENVIRONMENT SCALES

Purpose: To measure to what extent students perceive professors to contribute to a nurturant learning environment.

Number of Items: 7

Format: Scales range from 0 (this does not apply to any of my professors) to 5 (this applies to all of my professors). All items are presented.

Reliability: Coefficient alpha was .81.

Validity: Correlations with other variables ranged from −.22 to .27.

Author: Côté, J. E., and Levine, C.

Article: Student motivation, learning environments, and human capital acquisition: Toward an integrated paradigm of student development.

Journal: *Journal of College Student Development*, May/June 1997, *38*(3), 229–243.

9092

Test Name: OPPORTUNITIES FOR ADVANCEMENT SCALE

Purpose: To measure perceived opportunities for advancement.

Number of Items: 4

Format: Four-point scales are anchored by 1 (strongly disagree) and 4 (strongly agree). All items are presented.

Reliability: Coefficient alpha was .82.

Validity: Correlations with other variables ranged from .28 to .42.

Author: Riordan, C. M., and Shore, L. M.

Article: Demographic diversity and employee attitudes: An empirical examination of relational demography within work units.

Journal: *Journal of Applied Psychology*, June 1997, *82*(3), 342–358.

Related Research: Smith, P. C., et

al. (1969) *The measurement of satisfaction in work and retirement: A strategy for the study of attitudes.* Chicago: Rand McNally.

9093

Test Name: ORGANIZATION CLIMATE SURVEY

Purpose: To measure affirmative action/equal opportunity, procedural justice, distributive justice, career development, satisfaction, and loyalty.

Number of Items: 21

Format: Five-point scales are anchored by 1 (strongly disagree) and 5 (strongly agree). All items are presented.

Reliability: Alpha coefficients ranged from .66 to .88 across subscales.

Author: Parker, C. P., et al.

Article: Support for affirmative action, justice perceptions, and work attitudes: A study of gender and racial-ethnic group differences.

Journal: *Journal of Applied Psychology*, June 1997, *82*(3), 376–389.

Related Research: Parker, C. P., et al. (1995) Perceptions of organizational politics: An investigation of antecedents and consequences. *Journal of Management*, *21*, 891–912.

9094

Test Name: ORGANIZATION PERCEPTIONS QUESTIONNAIRE

Purpose: To rate perceptions of characteristics of fraternity and sorority houses.

Number of Items: 7

Format: Scales range from −3 (far below average) to 3 (far above average). All items are described.

Reliability: Coefficient alpha was .65.

Author: Larimer, M. E., et al.

Article: College drinking and the Greek system: Examining the role of perceived norms for high-risk behavior.

Journal: *Journal of College Student Development*, November/December 1997, *38*(6), 587–598.

Related Research: Larimer, M. E. (1992). *Alcohol abuse and the Greek system: An exploration of fraternity and sorority drinking.* Unpublished doctoral dissertation, University of Washington, Seattle.

9095

Test Name: ORGANIZATIONAL CLIMATE QUESTIONNAIRE

Purpose: To assess organizational culture.

Number of Items: 50

Format: Includes 9 dimensions: Structure, Responsibility, Reward, Risk, Warmth, Support, Standards, Conflict, and Identity.

Reliability: Alpha coefficients ranged from .10 to .80.

Author: Goodman, S. A., and Svyantek, D. J.

Article: Person-organization fit and contextual performance: Do shared values matter?

Journal: *Journal of Vocational Behavior*, October 1999, *55*(2), 254–275.

Related Research: Litwin, G. H., & Stringer, R. A. (1968). *Motivation and organizational climate.* Cambridge, MA: Harvard University Press.

9096

Test Name: ORGANIZATIONAL CONSTRAINTS SCALE

Purpose: To measure the extent to which doing one's job is made difficult by organizational constraints.

Number of Items: 11

Format: Scales range from 1 (less than once per month or never) to 5 (several times per day).

Reliability: Coefficient alpha was .85.

Validity: Correlations with other variables ranged from −.26 to .65.

Author: Spector, P. E., et al.

Article: A longitudinal study of relations between job stressors and job strains while controlling for prior negative affectivity and strains.

Journal: *Journal of Applied Psychology*, April 2000, *85*(2), 211–218.

9097

Test Name: ORGANIZATIONAL CULTURE SCALES

Purpose: To measure different facets of organizational culture.

Number of Items: 74

Format: Includes 12 scales: Positive Feedback, Peer Cohesion, Human Development, Participation, Conflict Tolerance, Innovation, Regulation, Communication, Reward, Work pressure, Effort, and Competition.

Reliability: Alpha coefficients ranged from .71 to .93.

Author: Van Vianen, A. E. M.

Article: Person-organization fit: The match between newcomers' and recruiters' preferences for organizational cultures.

Journal: *Personnel Psychology,* Spring 2000, *53*(1), 113–149.

Related Research: Van Vianen, A. E. M., & Kmieciek, Y. E. (1998). The match between recruiters' perceptions of organizational climate and personality of the ideal applicant for a management position. *International Journal of Selection and Assessment, 6,* 153–163.

9098

Test Name: ORGANIZATIONAL DEPENDABILITY QUESTIONNAIRE

Purpose: To measure an employee's belief that an organization can be trusted to look out for the well being of the employees.

Number of Items: 12

Format: Responses are made on a 7-point Likert-type scale ranging from 1 (strongly disagree) to 7 (strongly agree). Examples are presented.

Reliability: Coefficient alpha was .91.

Validity: Correlation with other variables ranged from .62 to .84.

Author: Hutchison, S.

Article: Perceived organizational support: Further evidence of construct validity.

Journal: *Educational and Psychological Measurement,* December 1997, *57*(6), 1025–1034.

Related Research: Lance, C. E. (1991). Evaluation of a structural model relating job satisfaction, organizational commitment, and precursors to voluntary turnover. *Multivariate Behavioral Research, 25,* 137–162.

9099

Test Name: ORGANIZATIONAL IMAGE SCALE

Purpose: To assess an applicant's view of an organization as a place to work.

Number of Items: 4

Format: Five-point Likert format. A sample item is presented.

Reliability: Coefficient alpha was .74.

Validity: Correlations with other variables ranged from −.10 to .70.

Author: Ryan, A. M., et al.

Article: Applicant self-selection: Correlates of withdrawal from a multiple hurdle process.

Journal: *Journal of Applied Psychology,* April 2000, *85*(2), 163–179.

Related Research: Goltz, S. M., & Giannantonio, C. M. (1995). Recruiter friendliness and attraction to the job: The mediating role of inferences about the organization. *Journal of Vocational Behavior, 46,* 109–118.

9100

Test Name: ORGANIZATIONAL JUSTICE QUESTIONNAIRE

Purpose: To measure hiring expectations, fairness, performance intentions and expectations, and other issues related to distributive justice.

Number of Items: 22

Format: Various Likert-type formats.

Reliability: Alpha coefficients ranged from .75 to .95.

Author: Ployhart, R. E., and Ryan, A. M.

Article: Applicants' reactions to the fairness of selection procedures: The effects of positive rule violations and time of measurement.

Journal: *Journal of Applied Psychology,* February 1998, *83*(1), 3–16.

Related Research: Gilliland, S. W., & Honig, H. (1994). *Development of the Selection Fairness Survey.* Paper presented at the ninth annual conference for the Society for Industrial and Organizational Psychology, Nashville, TN.

9101

Test Name: ORGANIZATIONAL JUSTICE SCALE

Purpose: To measure organizational justice.

Number of Items: 6

Format: Responses are made on a 5-point scale ranging from 1 (very fairly) to 5 (not at all fairly). A sample item is presented.

Reliability: Coefficient alpha was .94.

Validity: Correlations with other variables ranged from −.42 to .61.

Author: Kacmar, K. M., et al.

Article: Antecedents and consequences of organizational commitment: A comparison of two scales.

Journal: *Educational and Psychological Measurement,* December 1999, *59*(6), 976–994.

Related Research: Price, J. L., & Mueller, C. W. (1986). *Handbook of organizational measurement.* Marshfield, MA: Pitman.

9102

Test Name: ORGANIZATIONAL SANCTIONS AGAINST SEXUAL HARASSMENT SCALE

Purpose: To assess the perceived seriousness of the organization's response to sexual harassment and the harassment grievance policy.

Number of Items: 8

Format: Responses are made on a 5-point scale ranging from "strongly disagree" to "strongly agree."

Reliability: Coefficient alpha was .79.

Author: O'Connell, C. E., and Korabik, K.

Article: Sexual harassment: The relationship of personal vulnerability, work context, perpetrator status, and types of harassment to outcomes.

Journal: *Journal of Vocational Behavior*, June 2000, *56*(3), 299–329.

Related Research: Dekker, I., & Barling, J. (1998). Personal and organizational predictors of workplace sexual harassment of women by males. *Journal of Occupational Health Psychology*, *3*, 7–18.

9103

Test Name: ORGANIZATIONAL SOCIALIZATION SCALE

Purpose: To measure organizational socialization.

Number of Items: 34

Format: Includes 6 dimensions: Politics, History, Organizational Goals/Values, People, Performance Proficiency, and Language.

Reliability: Alpha coefficients ranged from .63 to .86.

Author: Klein, H. J., and Weaver, N. A.

Article: The effectiveness of an organizational-level orientation

training program in the socialization of new hires.

Journal: *Personnel Psychology*, Spring 2000, *53*(1), 47–66.

Related Research: Chao, G. T., et al. (1994). Organizational socialization: Its content and consequences. *Journal of Applied Psychology*, *79*, 730–743.

9104

Test Name: ORIENTATION HELPFULNESS SCALE

Purpose: To measure the helpfulness of an orientation program.

Number of Items: 4

Format: Scales range from 1 (to a very little extent) to 5 (to a very great extent). All items are presented.

Reliability: Coefficient alpha was .83.

Validity: Correlations with other variables ranged from −.63 to .58.

Author: Buckley, M. R., et al.

Article: Investigating newcomer expectations and job related outcomes.

Journal: *Journal of Applied Psychology*, June 1998, *83*(3), 452–461.

9105

Test Name: OUTCOMES OF INTERDEPENDENCE SCALE

Purpose: To measure how goals are linked and rewards are distributed in work groups.

Number of Items: 13

Format: Scales range from 1 (strongly disagree) to 5 (strongly agree). All items are presented.

Reliability: Alpha coefficients

ranged from .70 to .75 across subscales.

Validity: Correlations with other variables ranged from −.42 to .28.

Authors: Van Der Vegt, G., and Van de Vliert, E.

Article: Effects of interdependencies in project teams.

Journal: *Journal of Social Psychology*, April 1999, *139*(2), 202–294.

9106

Test Name: PARTICIPATION IN DECISION MAKING

Purpose: To assess employee participation in decision making.

Number of Items: 4

Format: Scales range from 5 (always) to 1 (never). All items are presented.

Reliability: Coefficient alpha was .84.

Validity: Correlations with other variables ranged from −.37 to −.02.

Author: Schminke, M., et al.

Article: The effect of organizational structure on perceptions of procedural fairness.

Journal: *Journal of Applied Psychology*, April 2000, *85*(2), 294–304.

Related Research: Hage, J., & Aiken, M. (1967). Relationship of centralization to other structural properties. *Administrative Science Quarterly*, *12*, 72–92.

9107

Test Name: PATIENT SATISFACTION QUESTIONNAIRE III

Purpose: To assess satisfaction with health care.

Number of Items: 50

Format: Five-point scales range from "strongly agree" to "strongly disagree."

Reliability: Alphas ranged from .81 to .89 across subscales.

Author: Marshall, G. N., et al.

Article: Health status and satisfaction with health care: Results from the medical outcomes study.

Journal: *Journal of Consulting and Clinical Psychology*, April 1996, *64*(2), 380–390.

Related Research: Marshall, G. N., et al. (1993). The structure of patient satisfaction with outpatient care. *Psychological Assessment, 5,* 477–483.

9108

Test Name: PERCEIVED BARRIERS SCALE

Purpose: To measure high school students' perceptions of potential educational and career barriers.

Number of Items: 24

Format: Responses are made on a 5-point Likert-type scale ranging from 1 (strongly agree) to 5 (strongly disagree). All items are presented.

Reliability: Alpha coefficients ranged from .74 to .89.

Author: McWhirter, E. H.

Article: Perceived barriers to education and career: Ethic and gender differences.

Journal: *Journal of Vocational Behavior*, February 1997, *50*(1), 124–140.

Related Research: McWhirter, E. H. (1992). *A test of a model of the career commitment and*

aspirations of Mexican American high school girls. Unpublished doctoral dissertation. Tempe, AZ: Arizona State University.

9109

Test Name: PERCEIVED BARRIERS TO UNION PARTICIPATION SCALE

Purpose: To assess barriers to labor union participation.

Number of Items: 12

Format: Yes/no format is used along with a 0–100 point scale anchored by "does not influence me at all" and "greatly influences me." Sample items are described.

Reliability: Alpha coefficients ranged from .72 to .81 across subscales.

Validity: Correlations with other variables ranged from −.26 to .38.

Author: Bulger, C. A., and Mellor, S.

Article: Self-efficacy as a mediator of the relationship between perceived union barriers and women's participation in union activities.

Journal: *Journal of Applied Psychology*, December 1997, *82*(6), 935–944.

9110

Test Name: PERCEIVED CHILLY CLIMATE FOR WOMEN SCALE

Purpose: To assess experience and observation of gender discrimination.

Number of Items: 8

Format: Scales range from 1 (strongly agree) to 5 (strongly disagree). All items are presented.

Reliability: Coefficient alpha was .81.

Author: Whitt, E. J., et al.

Article: Women's perceptions of a "chilly climate" and cognitive outcomes in college: Additional evidence.

Journal: *Journal of College Student Development*, March/ April 1999, *40*(2), 163–177.

Related Research: Hall, R. M., & Sandler, B. R. (1984). *Out of the classroom: A chilly campus climate for women?* Washington, DC: Association of American Colleges.

9111

Test Name: PERCEIVED CONTROL SCALE

Purpose: To assess the perceived control an individual has at work.

Number of Items: 6

Format: Scales range from 1 (never) to 6 (very often).

Reliability: Coefficient alpha was .83.

Validity: Correlations with other variables ranged from −.38 to .46.

Author: O'Driscoll, M. P., and Beehr, T. A.

Article: Moderating effects of perceived control and need for clarity on the relationship between role stressors and employee affective reactions.

Journal: *Journal of Social Psychology*, August 2000, *140*(2), 151–159.

Related Research: Tetrick, L., & LaRocco, J. (1987). Understanding, prediction, and control as moderators of the relationship between perceived stress, satisfaction, and psychological well being. *Journal*

of Applied Psychology, 72, 538–543.

9112

Test Name: PERCEIVED INSTRUMENTAL SOCIAL SUPPORT OF SUPERVISOR AND CO-WORKERS MEASURE

Purpose: To measure perceived instrumental social support from supervisors and from co-workers.

Number of Items: Eight items for supervisor and 8 items for co-workers.

Format: Includes two parallel versions: supervisors and co-workers. Responses are made on a 6-point agree/disagree scale. Sample items are presented.

Reliability: Alpha coefficients were .93 (supervisor) and .84 (co-workers).

Validity: Correlation with other variables ranged from −.43 to .23.

Author: Frone, M. R., et al.

Article: Developing and testing an integrative model of the work-family interface.

Journal: *Journal of Vocational Behavior,* April 1997, *50*(2), 145–167.

Related Research: Cutrone, C. E., & Russell, D. W. (1987). The provisions of social relationships and adaptation to stress. In W. H. Jones & D. Perlman (Eds.), *Advances in personal relationships.* Greenwich, CT: JAI Press.

9113

Test Name: PERCEIVED MOTIVATIONAL CLIMATE IN SPORT QUESTIONNAIRE

Purpose: To assess how basketball players perceive the

mastery and performance climates of their teams.

Number of Items: 21

Format: Includes 2 subscales: Mastery and Performance Climates.

Reliability: Alpha coefficients were .82 and .80.

Author: Yoo, J.

Article: Motivational-behavioral correlates of goal orientation and perceived motivational climate in physical education contexts.

Journal: *Perceptual and Motor Skills,* August 1999, *89*(1), 262–274.

Related Research: Seifrez, J., et al. (1992). The relationship of perceived motivational climate to intrinsic motivation and beliefs about success in basketball. *Journal of Sport & Exercise Psychology, 14,* 375–391.

9114

Test Name: PERCEIVED MOTIVATIONAL CLIMATE IN SPORT QUESTIONNAIRE (GREEK VERSION)

Purpose: To assess athletes' perceptions of motivational climate.

Number of Items: 12

Format: Includes 2 subscales: Mastery and Performance.

Reliability: Alpha coefficients were .72 and .67.

Validity: Correlations with other variables ranged from −.18 to .62.

Author: Goudas, M.

Article: Motivational climate and intrinsic motivation of young basketball players.

Journal: *Perceptual and Motor Skills,* February 1998, *86*(1), 323–327.

Related Research: Walling, M. D., et al. (1993). The Perceived Motivational Climate in Sport Questionnaire: Construct and predictive validity. *Journal of Sport and Exercise Psychology, 15,* 172–183.

9115

Test Name: PERCEIVED ORGANIZATIONAL SUPPORT SCALE

Purpose: To measure the degree of support an employee can expect from an employing organization.

Number of Items: 8

Format: Seven-point scales range from 1 (strongly agree) to 7 (strongly disagree). All items are presented.

Reliability: Coefficient alpha was .90.

Validity: Correlations with other variables ranged from .24 to .61.

Author: Eisenberger, R., et al.

Article: Perceived organizational support, discretionary treatment, and job satisfaction.

Journal: *Journal of Applied Psychology,* October 1997, *82*(5), 812–820.

Related Research: Eisenberger, R., et al. (1986). Perceived organizational support. *Journal of Applied Psychology, 71,* 500–507.

9116

Test Name: PERCEIVED ORGANIZATIONAL SUPPORT SCALE

Purpose: To assess employee beliefs about the orientation of the organization.

Number of Items: 11

Format: Seven-point scales range

from 1 (strongly disagree) to 7 (strongly agree).

Reliability: Coefficient alpha was .82.

Validity: Correlations with other variables ranged from −.06 to .20.

Author: Armeli, S., et al.

Article: Perceived organizational support and police performance: The moderating influence of socioemotional needs.

Journal: *Journal of Applied Psychology*, April 1998, *83*(2), 288–297.

Related Research: Eisenberger, R., et al. (1986). Perceived organizational support. *Journal of Applied Psychology, 71,* 500–507.

9117

Test Name: PERCEIVED SCHOOL CULTURE INVENTORY

Purpose: To identify teachers' perceived school culture.

Number of Items: 30

Format: Includes 6 factors: Academic Emphasis, Norm of Continuous School Improvement, Norm of Orderliness, Norm of Teamwork, Adaptation to Customer Demands, and Student Participation. All items are presented.

Reliability: Alpha coefficients ranged from .70 to .88.

Author: Gaziel, H. H.

Article: Impact of school culture on effectiveness of secondary schools with disadvantaged students.

Journal: *Journal of Educational Research*, May/June 1997, *90*(5), 310–318.

Related Research: Steinhoff, C., & Owens, R. (1989). The

Organizational Culture Assessing Inventory: A metaphorical analysis in an educational setting. *Journal of Educational Administration, 27,* 17–23.

9118

Test Name: PERCEPTION OF HOSPITAL SCALES

Purpose: To measure employee perceptions of the internal and external environment of a hospital.

Number of Items: 10

Format: All items are presented.

Reliability: Alphas were .87 (internal environment) and .99 (external environment).

Authors: Roy, D. D., and Ghose, M.

Article: Awareness of hospital environment and organizational commitment.

Journal: *Journal of Social Psychology*, June 1997, *137*(3), 380–386.

Related Research: Dutta Roy, D. (1989). *The study of organizational health and its effect on quality of working life.* Unpublished dissertation, Indian Institute of Technology, Kharagpur.

9119

Test Name: PERCEPTIONS OF EDUCATIONAL BARRIERS

Purpose: To assess possible barriers to the pursuit of postsecondary education.

Number of Items: 84

Format: Includes 3 subscales: Likelihood, Magnitude, and Difficulty. Sample items are presented.

Reliability: Alpha coefficients ranged from .88 to .96. Test-

retest (9 weeks) reliability was .57 (*N* = 95).

Validity: Correlations with other variables ranged from −.12 to −.43.

Author: McWhirter, E. H., et al.

Article: The effects of high school career education on social-cognitive variables.

Journal: *Journal of Counseling Psychology,* July 2000, *47*(3), 330–341.

Related Research: McWhirter, E. H. (1997). Perceived barriers to education and career: Ethnic and gender differences. *Journal of Vocational Behavior, 50,* 124–140.

9120

Test Name: PERCEPTION OF ORGANIZATIONAL POLITICS —REVISED

Purpose: To measure perceived politics.

Number of Items: 15

Format: Responses are made on a 5-point scale ranging from "strongly agree" to "strongly disagree." Sample items are presented.

Reliability: Reliability estimate was .86.

Validity: Correlations with other variables ranged from −.51 to .48.

Author: Hochwarter, W. A., et al.

Article: Commitment as an antidote to the tension and turnover consequences of organizational politics.

Journal: *Journal of Vocational Behavior*, December 1999, *55*(3), 277–297.

Related Research: Kacmar, K. M., & Carlson, D. (1997). Further validation of the Perception of Politics Scale

(POPS): A multiple sample investigation. *Journal of Management*, 23, 627–658.

9121

Test Name: PERCEPTIONS OF ORGANIZATIONAL POLITICS SCALE

Purpose: To measure the extent of organizational politics at the organizational and work-group level.

Number of Items: 7

Format: All items are presented.

Reliability: Coefficient alpha was .76 (organizational level) and .75 (work group).

Validity: Correlations with other variables ranged from −.61 to .62.

Author: Maslyn, J. M., and Fedor, D. B.

Article: Perceptions of politics: Does measuring different foci matter?

Journal: *Journal of Applied Psychology*, August 1998, *83*(4), 645–653.

Related Research: Kacmar, K. M., & Ferris, G. R. (1991). Perceptions of Organizational Politics Scale (POPS): Development and construct validity. *Educational and Psychological Measurement*, 51, 193–205.

9122

Test Name: PERCEPTIONS OF ORGANIZATIONAL POLITICS SCALE

Purpose: To measure perceptual politics.

Number of Items: 12

Format: Responses are made on a 5-point Likert scale ranging from 1 (strongly disagree) to 5

(strongly agree). Sample items are presented.

Reliability: Internal reliability estimate was .76.

Validity: Correlations with other variables ranged from −.56 to .30.

Author: Hochwarter, W. A., et al.

Article: Commitment as an antidote to the tension and turnover consequences of organizational politics.

Journal: *Journal of Vocational Behavior*, December 1999, *55*(3), 277–297.

Related Research: Kacmar, K. M & Ferris, G. R. (1991). Perceptions of Organizational Politics Scale (POPS): Development and construct validation. *Educational and Psychological Measurement*, 51, 193–205.

9123

Test Name: PERCEPTION OF ORGANIZATIONAL POLITICS SCALE—REVISED

Purpose: To measure one's view of the work environment as political, unfair, or unjust.

Number of Items: 12

Format: Responses are made on a 5-point scale ranging from 1 (strongly disagree) to 5 (strongly agree). Sample items are presented.

Reliability: Reliability coefficients ranged from .74 to .77.

Validity: Correlations with other variables ranged from −.30 to .29.

Author: Vigoda, E.

Article: Organizational politics, job attitudes, work outcomes: Exploration and implications for the public sector.

Journal: *Journal of Vocational*

Behavior, December 2000, *57*(3), 326–347.

Related Research: Kacmar, K. M., & Carlson, D. S. (1994). *Further validation of the Perceptions of Politics Scale (POPS): A multiple sample investigation.* Paper presented at the Academy of Management Meeting, Dallas, TX.

9124

Test Name: PERCEPTIONS OF PROCEDURAL JUSTICE SCALE

Purpose: To assess perceptions of procedural justice.

Number of Items: 3

Format: Scales range from 1 (not at all) to 9 (extremely). All items are presented.

Reliability: Coefficient alpha was .94.

Author: Roberson, Q. M., et al.

Article: Identifying a missing link between participation and satisfaction: The mediating role of procedural justice perceptions.

Journal: *Journal of Applied Psychology*, August 1999, *84*(4), 585–593.

Related Research: Tyler, T. R., & Lind, E. A. (1992). A relational model of authority in groups. In M. Zanna (Ed.), *Advances in experimental social psychology* (Vol. 25, pp. 115–191). New York: Academic Press.

9125

Test Name: PERCEPTIONS OF SAFETY CLIMATE

Purpose: To measure safety climate.

Number of Items: 9

Format: Includes 2 subscales: Management's Commitment to

Safety and Worker Involvement in Safety Activities. Responses are made on a 5-point scale of "strongly disagree" to "strongly agree."

Reliability: Alpha coefficients were .80 and .52.

Validity: Correlations with other variables ranged from −.66 to .57.

Author: Hofmann, D. A., and Stetzer, A.

Article: A cross-level investigation of factors influencing unsafe behaviors and accidents.

Journal: *Personnel Psychology*, Summer 1996, *49*(2), 307–339.

Related Research: Dedobbeleer, N., & BeLand, F. (1991). A safety climate measure for construction sites. *Journal of Safety Research*, *22*, 97–103.

9126

Test Name: PERFORMANCE BARRIER SCALE

Purpose: To measure the frequency and severity of problems encountered in a job task.

Number of Items: 7

Format: Frequency scales range from 1 (never is a problem) to 5 (always is a problem). Severity scales range from 1 (has no impact on performance) to 5 (greatly impacts performance). All items are presented.

Validity: Correlations between frequency and performance barriers ranged from .58 to .74.

Author: Tesluk, P. E., and Mathieu, J. E.

Article: Overcoming roadblocks to effectiveness: Incorporating management of performance barriers into models of work group effectiveness.

9127

Test Name: PERFORMANCE-NORMS QUESTIONNAIRE

Purpose: To assess each team's performance-norms.

Number of Items: 6

Format: Responses are made on a 5-point response scale ranging from 1 (strongly disagree) to 5 (strongly agree).

Reliability: Coefficient alpha was .84.

Author: Kim, M.-S.

Article: Self-monitoring and individual expectation of performance-norms in sport teams.

Journal: *Perceptual and Motor Skills*, December 1999, *89*(3, Part 2), 1129–1132.

Related Research: Kim, M.-S. (1992). Types of leadership and performance norms in school athletic teams. *Perceptual and Motor Skills*, *74*, 803–806.

9128

Test Name: PERSONAL DISCRIMINATION SCALE— MODIFIED

Purpose: To measure the overall amount of workplace discrimination.

Number of Items: 6

Format: An example is presented.

Reliability: Alpha coefficients were .84 and .94.

Validity: Correlations with other variables ranged from −.59 to .67.

Author: Holder, J. C., and Vaux, A.

Article: African American professionals: Coping with occupational stress in predominantly White work environments.

Journal: *Journal of Vocational Behavior*, December 1998, *53*(3), 315–333.

Related Research: Watts, R. J., & Carter, R. J. (1991). Psychological aspects of racism in organizations. *Group and Organization Studies*, *16*, 328–344.

9129

Test Name: PHYSICAL EDUCATION CLASS CLIMATE SCALE

Purpose: To assess perceptions of the prevailing motivational climate in school physical education.

Number of Items: 26

Format: Includes 6 subscales: Class Mastery Orientation, Teacher's Promotion of Mastery Orientation, Student Perception of Choice, Class Performance Orientation, and Worries About Mistakes. Responses are made on 5-point scales ranging from 1 (strongly disagree) to 5 (strongly agree).

Reliability: Alpha coefficients were .79 and .67.

Validity: Correlations with other variables ranged from −.01 to .47.

Author: Spray, C. M.

Article: Predicting participation in noncompulsory physical education: Do goal perspectives matter?

Journal: *Perceptual and Motor Skills*, June 2000, *90*(3) Part 2, 1207–1215.

Related Research: Biddle, S. J. H., et al. (1995).

Development of scales to measure perceived physical education class climate: A cross-national project. *British Journal of Educational Psychology, 65,* 341–358.

9130

Test Name: POWER SCALE

Purpose: To measure a customer's perception of a manufacturer's influence over the customer's business.

Number of Items: 10

Format: Five-point scales.

Reliability: Alpha was .87.

Author: Zemanek, Jr., J. E., and McIntyre, R. P.

Article: Is customers' dependence on manufacturers equivalent to manufacturers' power?

Journal: *Psychological Reports,* December 1998, *83*(3) Part 1, 1003–1007.

Related Research: Gaski, J. F., & Nevin, J. (1985). The differential effects of exercised and unexercised power sources in a marketing channel. *Journal of Marketing Research, 22,* 130–142.

9131

Test Name: PRISON PROBLEM SCALE

Purpose: To assess the perceptions of events in prison as problematic, for example, unsafe.

Number of Items: 40

Format: Five-point scales are anchored by "not at all" and "all the time."

Validity: Correlation with the Prison Control Scale was −.48.

Author: Pugh, D. N.

Article: Studies of validity for the prison control scale.

Journal: *Psychological Reports,* June 1998, *82*(3) Part 1, 739–744.

Related Research: Zamble, E., & Porporino, F. J. (1988). *Coping, behavior, and adaptation in prison inmates.* New York: Springer-Verlag.

9132

Test Name: PROCEDURAL FAIRNESS MEASURE

Purpose: To measure fairness of organizational procedures and the respect shown during the enactment of these procedures.

Number of Items: 14

Format: Responses are made on a 5-point Likert-type scale ranging from 1 (strongly disagree) to 5 (strongly agree). All items are presented.

Reliability: Coefficient alpha was .88.

Validity: Correlations with other variables ranged from −.25 to .52.

Author: Mansour-Cole, D. M., and Scott, S. G.

Article: Hearing it through the grapevine: The influence of source, leader-relation, and legitimacy on survivors' fairness perceptions.

Journal: *Personnel Psychology,* Spring 1998, *51*(1), 25–54.

Related Research: Moorman, R. (1991). Relationship between organizational justice and organizational citizenship behaviors: Do fairness perceptions influence employee citizenship? *Journal of Applied Psychology, 76,* 845–855.

9133

Test Name: PROCEDURAL FAIRNESS SCALE

Purpose: To assess how much input an organizational member has on decisions that affect him or her.

Number of Items: 3

Format: Scales range from 1 (very) to 7 (not at all). All items are presented.

Reliability: Coefficient alpha was .71.

Validity: Correlations with other variables ranged from −.20 to .53.

Author: Schminke, M., et al.

Article: The effect of organizational structure on perceptions of procedural fairness.

Journal: *Journal of Applied Psychology,* April 2000, *85*(2), 294–304.

Related Research: Tyler, T. R., & Schuller, R. (1990). *A relational model of authority in work organizations: The psychology of procedural justice.* Unpublished manuscript, American Bar Foundation.

9134

Test Name: PROCEDURAL FAIRNESS SCALE

Purpose: To measure the fairness of layoff decisions.

Number of Items: 4

Format: Seven-point Likert scales are anchored by 0 (strongly disagree) and 7 (strongly agree). A sample item is presented.

Reliability: Coefficient alpha was .92.

Validity: Correlations with other variables ranged from −.52 to .42.

Author: Skarlicki, D. P., et al.

Article: Third-party perceptions of a layoff: Procedural, derogation, and retributive aspects of justice.

Journal: *Journal of Applied Psychology*, February 1998, *83*(1), 119–127.

Related Research: Tyler, T. R., & Lind, E. A. (1992). A relational model of authority in groups. *Advances in experimental social psychology* (Vol. 25, pp. 115–191). San Francisco: Academic Press.

9135

Test Name: PROCEDURAL FAIRNESS SCALE

Purpose: To measure employee judgments of organizational climate.

Number of Items: 5

Format: Six-point rating scales with endpoints representing diametrically opposed statements. A sample item is provided.

Reliability: Reliability coefficient was .61.

Validity: Correlations with other variables ranged from .25 to .49.

Author: Garonzik, R., et al.

Article: Identifying international assignees at risk for premature departure: The interactive effect of outcome favorability and procedural fairness.

Journal: *Journal of Applied Psychology*, February 2000, *85*(1), 13–20.

9136

Test Name: PROCEDURAL JUSTICE AND DECISION CONTROL SCALES

Purpose: To measure procedural justice and decision control.

Number of Items: 3

Format: Nine-point bipolar adjectives. Items are described.

Reliability: Coefficient alpha was .87 (procedural justice) and .69 (decision control).

Author: Hunton, J. E., et al.

Article: The value of voice in participative decision making.

Journal: *Journal of Applied Psychology*, October 1998, *83*(5), 788–797.

Related Research: Early, P. C., & Lind, E. A. (1987). Procedural justice and participation in task selection: The role of control in mediating justice judgments. *Journal of Personality and Social Psychology, 52*, 1148–1160.

9137

Test Name: PROCEDURAL JUSTICE AND INTERACTIONAL JUSTICE SCALE

Purpose: To measure the consistency, bias suppression, accuracy, correctability, representativeness, and ethicality of union procedures.

Number of Items: 25

Format: Five-point scales are anchored by 1 (strongly disagree) and 5 (strongly agree).

Reliability: Internal consistency was .95.

Validity: Correlations with other variables ranged from −.10 to .19.

Author: Skarlicki, D. P., and Latham, G. P.

Article: Increasing citizen behavior within a labor union: A test of organizational justice theory.

Journal: *Journal of Applied*

Psychology, April 1996, *81*(2), 161–169.

Related Research: Folger, R., & Konousky, M. A. (1989). Effects of procedural and distributive justice on reactions to pay raise decisions. *Academy of Management Journal, 32*, 115–130.

Moorman, R. H. (1991). Relationship between organizational justice and organizational citizenship behavior: Do fairness perceptions influence employee citizenship? *Journal of Applied Psychology, 76*, 845–855.

9138

Test Name: PROCEDURAL JUSTICE PERCEPTIONS SCALE

Purpose: To measure information, chance, treatment, consistency, and job-relatedness as procedural justice rules.

Format: Scales range from 1 (strongly disagree) to 5 (strongly agree). Sample items are presented.

Reliability: Alpha coefficients exceeded .70 on all subscales.

Validity: Correlations with other variables ranged from .01 to .56.

Author: Bauer, T. N., et al.

Article: Longitudinal assessment of applicant reactions to employment testing and test outcome feedback.

Journal: *Journal of Applied Psychology*, December 1998, *83*(6), 892–903.

Related Research: Gilliland, S. W. (1993). The perceived fairness of selection systems: An organizational justice perspective. *Academy of Management Review, 18*, 694–734.

9139

Test Name: PROCEDURAL JUSTICE SCALE

Purpose: To measure procedural justice specific to the performance appraisal context.

Number of Items: 4

Format: Scales range from "strongly disagree" to "strongly agree." A sample item is presented.

Reliability: Coefficient alpha was .96.

Validity: Correlations with other variables ranged from −.20 to .76.

Author: Keeping, L. M., and Levy, P. E.

Article: Performance appraisal reactions: Measurement, modeling and method bias.

Journal: *Journal of Applied Psychology*, October 2000, *85*(5), 708–723.

9140

Test Name: PROCEDURAL JUSTICE SCALE

Purpose: To measure procedural justice.

Number of Items: 11

Format: Responses are made on a 5-point Likert-type scale ranging from 1 (strongly disagree) to 5 (strongly agree). Examples are presented.

Validity: Correlations with other interactional justice was .78.

Author: Skarlicki, D. P., and Latham, G. P.

Article: Leadership training in organizational justice to increase citizenship behavior within a labor union: A replication.

Journal: *Personnel Psychology*, Autumn 1997, *50*(3), 617–633.

Related Research: Folger, R., & Konovsky, M. A. (1989). Effects of procedural and distributive justice of reactions to pay raise decisions. *Academy of Management Journal*, 32, 115–130.

9141

Test Name: PROCEDURAL JUSTICE SCALE

Purpose: To assess perceived fairness of the means to establish employee compensation.

Number of Items: 23

Format: Likert format.

Reliability: Coefficient alpha was .93.

Authors: Jeanquart-Barone, S., and Sekaran, U.

Article: Institutional racism: An empirial study.

Journal: *Journal of Social Psychology*, August 1996, *136*(4), 477–482.

Related Research: Folger, R., & Konovsky, M. A. (1989). Effects of procedural and distributive justice on reactions to pay increases. *Academy of Management Journal*, 32, 115–130.

9142

Test Name: PRODUCTION JOB CONTROL SCALE

Purpose: To measure the degree of job control in production environments.

Number of Items: 9

Format: Scales range from 1 (not at all) to 5 (a great deal).

Reliability: Coefficient alpha was .85.

Validity: Correlations with other variables ranged from −.12 to .23.

Author: Parker, S. K., and Sprigg, C. A.

Article: Minimizing strain and maximizing learning: The role of job demands, job control and proactive personality.

Journal: *Journal of Applied Psychology*, December 1999, *84*(6), 925–939.

Related Research: Jackson, P. R., et al. (1993). New measures of job control, cognitive demand, and production responsibility. *Journal of Applied Psychology*, 78, 753–762.

9143

Test Name: PROFESSIONAL EXPERIENCE SCALES

Purpose: To enable graduates to evaluate the challenges in the teachers' relationships with students and others.

Number of Items: 11

Format: Includes 2 scales: Professional Challenges in Teachers' Relationships with Students, and with Others. All items are presented.

Reliability: Reliability coefficients were .72 and .88.

Author: Delaney, A. M.

Article: Quality assessment of professional degree programs.

Journal: *Research in Higher Education*, April 1997, *38*(2), 241–264.

Related Research: Pike, G. R. (1990, April). *Dimensions of alumni perceptions of cognitive and affective growth during college.* Paper presented at the annual meeting of the American Educational Research Association, Boston.

9144

Test Name: PROGRAM EVALUATION SCALES

Purpose: To evaluate four aspects of the teacher education program.

Number of Items: 30

Format: Includes four elements: Satisfaction with Courses, Perceived Professional Growth, Preparation for Diversity, and Assessment of the Program's Intellectual Challenge. All items are presented.

Reliability: Reliability coefficients ranged from .83 to .93.

Validity: Correlations with graduates' overall evaluation ranged from .47 to .72.

Author: Delaney, A. M.

Article: Quality assessment of professional degree programs.

Journal: *Research in Higher Education*, April 1997, *38*(2), 241–264.

9145

Test Name: PROGRESSIVISM SCALE

Purpose: To assess the extent to which teachers subscribe to a pedagogical approach that stresses development of higher order mental processes, general understandings, and cognitive power.

Number of Items: 10

Format: All items are presented.

Reliability: Coefficient alpha was .83.

Author: Bidwell, C. E., and Yasumoto, J. Y.

Article: The collegial focus: Teaching fields, collegial relationships, and instructional practice in American high schools.

Journal: *Sociology of Education*, December 1999, *72*(4), 234–256.

Related Research: Stodolsky,

S. S., & Grossman, P. L. (1995). The impact of subject matter on curricular activity: An analysis of five academic subjects. *American Educational Research Journal*, *32*, 227–250.

9146

Test Name: PROMOTIONAL OPPORTUNITY SCALE

Purpose: To measure promotional opportunity.

Number of Items: 3

Format: Responses are made on a 5-point Likert scale ranging from 1 (strongly disagree) to 5 (strongly agree).

Reliability: Coefficient alpha was .89.

Validity: Correlations with other variables ranged from −.25 to .45.

Author: Wallace, J. E.

Article: It's about time: A study of hours worked and work spillover among law firm lawyers.

Journal: *Journal of Vocational Behavior*, April 1997, *50*(2), 227–248.

Related Research: Price, J. L., & Mueller, C. W. (1986). *Handbook of organizational measurement*. New York: Harper-Collins.

9147

Test Name: PSYCHOLOGICAL CLIMATE SCALE

Purpose: To measure the psychological climate of a work situation.

Number of Items: 21

Format: Seven-point scales are anchored by "strongly disagree" and "strongly agree." All items are presented.

Reliability: Alpha coefficients

ranged from .79 to .85 across subscales.

Author: Brown, S. P., and Leigh, T. W.

Article: A new look at psychological climate and its relationship to job involvement, effort and performance.

Journal: *Journal of Applied Psychology*, August 1996, *81*(4), 358–368.

Related Research: Kahn, W. A. (1990). Psychological conditions of personal engagement and disengagement at work. *Academy of Management Journal*, *33*, 692–724.

9148

Test Name: QUALITY CULTURE AND ORGANIZATIONAL CLIMATE SURVEY

Purpose: To assess the degree to which employees believe that quality improvement practices are employed where they work and organizational climate related to quality improvement.

Number of Items: 86

Format: Seven-point scales are anchored by (1) strongly disagree and (7) strongly agree. Sample items are presented.

Reliability: Alphas coefficients ranged from .86 to .96.

Validity: Correlations between culture and climate ranged from .69 to 1.00.

Author: Johnson, J. J., and McIntye, C. L.

Article: Organizational culture and climate correlates of job satisfaction.

Journal: *Psychological Reports*, June, 1998, *82*(3) Part 1, 843–850.

9149

Test Name: QUANTITATIVE WORKLOAD INVENTORY

Purpose: To measure the extent to which people work hard and have a lot to do.

Number of Items: 5

Format: Scales range from 1 (never) to 2 (extremely often).

Reliability: Coefficient alpha was .84.

Validity: Correlations with other variables ranged from −.08 to .61.

Author: Spector, P. E., et al.

Article: A longitudinal study of relations between job stressors and job strains while controlling for prior negative affectivity and strains.

Journal: *Journal of Applied Psychology,* April 2000, *85*(2), 211–218.

9150

Test Name: REACTIONS TO RATINGS PROCESS SCALE

Purpose: To assess raters' reactions to job performance ratings.

Number of Items: 13

Format: Seven-point scales. All items are presented.

Reliability: Alpha coefficients ranged from .58 to .83 across subscales.

Author: DeNisi, A. S., and Peters, L. H.

Article: Organization of information in memory and the performance appraisal process: Evidence from the field.

Journal: *Journal of Applied Psychology,* December 1996, *81*(6), 717–737.

9151

Test Name: REACTIONS TO TRAINING SCALE

Purpose: To measure reactions to a computer training program.

Number of Items: 6

Format: Five-point Likert format ranged from "strongly disagree" to "strongly agree."

Reliability: Coefficient alpha was .92.

Validity: Correlations with other variables ranged from −.20 to .27.

Author: Simon, S. J., and Werner, J. M.

Article: Computer training through behavior modeling, self-paced, and instructional approaches: A field experiment.

Journal: *Journal of Applied Psychology,* December 1996, *81*(6), 648–659.

Related Research: Werner, J. M., et al. (1994). Augmenting behavior-modeling training: Testing the effects of pre- and post-training interventions. *Human Resource Development Quarterly, 5,* 169–183.

9152

Test Name: RECRUITER TRAINING SCALE

Purpose: To measure the amount and type of training offered to recruiters.

Number of Items: 8

Format: Responses were checked 1 (for yes) or 0 (for not checked).

Reliability: Coefficient alpha was .83.

Validity: Correlations with other variables ranged from −.11 to .64.

Author: Barber, A. E., et al.

Article: A tale of two job markets: Organizational size and its effects on hiring practices and job search behavior.

Journal: *Personnel Psychology,* Winter 1999, *52*(4), 841–867.

Related Research: Rynes, S. L., & Boudreau, J. W. (1986). College recruiting in large organizations: Practice, evaluation, and research implications. *Personnel Psychology, 39,* 729–757.

9153

Test Name: RECRUITMENT SOURCES SCALE

Purpose: To determine sources used by employers to recruit college graduates.

Number of Items: 9

Format: Sources include campus, internal networking, external agencies, advertising, and walk-ins/direct application. Responses are made on a 5-point scale ranging from "we do not use this source at all" to "we use this source on a regular basis."

Reliability: Alpha coefficients ranged from .48 to .72.

Validity: Correlations with other variables ranged from −.26 to .48.

Author: Barber, A. E., et al.

Article: A tale of two job markets: Organizational size and its effects on hiring practices and job search behavior.

Journal: *Personnel Psychology,* Winter 1999, *52*(4), 841–867.

9154

Test Name: REWARDS SCALES

Purpose: To measure the likelihood that supervisors would recognize and reward a subordinate, and to measure the rewards received by subordinates as determined by subordinate self-reports.

Number of Items: 8, 16

Format: Supervisor's scales range from 1 (strongly disagree) to 5 (strongly agree). Self-report scales range from 1 (never) to 7 (constantly). All items are presented.

Reliability: Coefficients alpha were .95 (supervisor) and .84 (self-report).

Validity: Correlations with other variables ranged from .12 to .92 (supervisor) and from .04 to .26 (self-report).

Author: Van Scotter, J. R., et al.

Article: Effects of task performance and contextual performance on systemic rewards.

Journal: *Journal of Applied Psychology*, August 2000, *85*(4), 526–535.

9155

Test Name: SAFTEY CULTURE MEASURE

Purpose: To measure safety climate appropriate for the railroad industry.

Number of Items: 9

Format: Responses are made on a 4-point scale ranging from 1 (definitely disagree) to 4 (definitely agree). Examples are presented.

Reliability: Coefficient alpha was .86.

Validity: Correlations with other variables ranged from −.38 to .48.

Author: Morrow, P. C., and Crum, M. R.

Article: The efforts of perceived and objective safety risk on employee outcomes.

Journal: *Journal of Vocational Behavior*, October 1998, *53*(2), 300–313.

Related Research: Coyle, I. R., et al. (1995). Safety climate. *Journal of Safety Research, 26,* 247–254.

9156

Test Name: SAFETY SCALES

Purpose: To measure the extent to which a group leader is committed to safety and how comfortable group members are in discussing safety with a group leader.

Number of Items: 10

Format: Five-point scales. All items are described.

Reliability: Coefficient alphas were .85 (communication) and .89 (commitment).

Validity: Correlations with other variables ranged from −.26 to .28.

Author: Hofmann, D. A., and Morgeson, F. P.

Article: Safety-related behavior as a social exchange: The role of perceived organizational support and leader-member exchange.

Journal: *Journal of Applied Psychology*, April 1999, *84*(2), 286–296.

Related Research: Hofmann, D. A., & Stetzer, A. (1996). The role of safety climate and communication in accident interpretation: Implications from negative events. *Academy of Management Journal, 41,* 644–657.

9157

Test Name: SATISFACTION QUESTIONNAIRE

Purpose: To assess an individual's

satisfaction with a career interest inventory.

Number of Items: 8

Format: Scales range from 1 (strongly disagree) to 5 (strongly agree). All items are presented.

Reliability: Alpha coefficients ranged from .79 to .80.

Author: Jones, L. K., et al.

Article: Comparing the effects of the Career Key with Self-Directed Search and Job-OE among eighth grade students.

Journal: *Professional School Counseling*, April 2000, *3*(4), 238–247.

Related Research: Jones, L. K. (1990). The Career Key: An investigation of the reliability and validity of its scales and its helpfulness to college students. *Measurement and Evaluation in Counseling and Development, 23,* 67–76.

9158

Test Name: SATISFACTION WITH APPRAISAL SESSION AND THE APPRAISAL SYSTEM SCALES

Purpose: To assess employee satisfaction with a performance appraisal.

Number of Items: 6

Format: Scales range from 1 (strongly disagree) to 6 (strongly agree). Sample items are presented.

Reliability: Coefficient alpha was .95 (session) and .90 (system).

Validity: Correlations with other variables ranged from −.29 to .82.

Author: Keeping, L. M., and Levy, P. E.

Article: Performance appraisal reactions: Measurement, modeling and method bias.

Journal: *Journal of Applied Psychology*, October 2000, *85*(5), 708–723.

Related Research: Giles, W. F., & Mossholder, K. W. (1990). Employee reactions to contextual and session components of performance appraisal. *Journal of Applied Psychology, 75*, 371–377.

9159

Test Name: SCHEDULE INFLEXIBILITY SCALE

Purpose: To assess schedule inflexibility.

Number of Items: 3

Format: Responses are made on a 4-point scale ranging from 1 (not at all flexible) to 4 (very flexible). Responses to one item were on a scale ranging from 1 (almost none) to 5 (a great deal). An example is given.

Reliability: Coefficient alpha was .68.

Validity: Correlations with other variables ranged from −.33 to .26.

Author: Parasuraman, S., et al.

Article: Work and family variables, entrepreneurial career success, and psychological well-being.

Journal: *Journal of Vocational Behavior*, June 1996, *48*(3), 275–300.

Related Research: Greenhaus, J. H., et al. (1989). Sources of work-family conflict among two-career couples. *Journal of Vocational Behavior, 34*, 133–153.

9160

Test Name: SCHOOL EFFECTIVENESS QUESTIONNAIRE

Purpose: To assess school effectiveness.

Number of Items: 39

Format: Scales range from 1 (not important) to 4 (extremely important).

Reliability: Guttman split-half reliability was .92. Alpha coefficients ranged from .35 to .85.

Author: Holdaway, E. A., et al.

Article: A factor-analytic approach to school effectiveness.

Journal: *Educational Research Quarterly*, June 1997, *20*(4), 15–35.

Related Research: Gunn, J. A., & Holdaway, E. A. (1986). Perceptions of effectiveness, influence, and satisfaction of senior high school principals. *Educational Administration Quarterly, 22*, 43–62.

9161

Test Name: SCHOOL ENVIRONMENT QUESTIONNAIRE

Purpose: To measure students' perceptions of the middle school environment.

Number of Items: 52

Format: Includes 9 subscales: Involvement, Affiliation, Teacher Support, Task Orientation, Competition, Order, and Organization, Rule Clarity, Teacher Control, and Innovation. Responses are "true" or "false."

Reliability: Internal consistency coefficients ranged from .67 to .85.

Author: Chung, H., et al.

Article: Patterns of individual adjustment changes during middle school transition.

Journal: *Journal of School Psychology*, Spring 1998, *36*(1), 83–101.

Related Research: Moos, R. H. (1979). *Evaluating educational environments*. San Francisco: Jossey-Bass.

9162

Test Name: SCHOOL PARTICIPANT EMPOWERMENT SCALE

Purpose: To assess teachers' level of empowerment.

Number of Items: 38

Format: Scales range from 1 (strongly disagree) to 5 (strongly agree).

Reliability: Alpha coefficients ranged from .81 to .86 across subscales.

Author: Short, P. M., et al.

Article: The relationship of teacher empowerment and principal leadership orientation.

Journal: *Educational Research Quarterly*, June 1999, *22*(4), 45–52.

Related Research: Short, P. M., & Rinehart, J. S. (1992). School Participant Empowerment Scale: Assessment of empowerment with the school environment. *Educational and Psychological Measurement, 52*, 951–960.

9163

Test Name: SCHOOL'S ORGANIZATIONAL STRUCTURE SCALE

Purpose: To assess the school's organizational structure.

Number of Items: 10

Format: Includes Formalization, Hierarchy of Authority, and Participation in Decision-Making.

Reliability: Alpha coefficients ranged from .67 to .71.

Author: Cheng, Y. C.

Article: Relation between teachers' professionalism and job attitudes, educational outcomes, and organizational factors.

Journal: *Journal of Educational Research*, January/February, 1996, *89*(3), 163–171.

Related Research: Oldham, G. R., & Hackman, J. R. (1981). Relationships between organizational structure and employees' reactions: Comparing alternative frameworks. *Administrative Science Quarterly*, 26, 66–83.

9164

Test Name: SELECTION, OPTIMIZATION, AND COMPENSATION QUESTIONNAIRE

Purpose: To assess selection, optimization, and compensation.

Number of Items: 9

Format: Includes 3 versions: domain-general, work-specific, and partnership-specific. Responses are made on a 5-point scale from 0–4. Sample items are presented.

Reliability: Test-retest (4 weeks) reliabilities ranged from .56 to .75. Alpha coefficients ranged from .47 to .70.

Validity: Correlations with other variables ranged from −.34 to .49.

Author: Wiese, B. S., et al.

Article: Selection, optimization, and compensation: An action-related approach to work and partnership.

Journal: *Journal of Vocational Behavior*, December 2000, *57*(3), 273–300.

Related Research: Baltes, P. B., et al. (1999). *The measurement of selection, optimization, and*

compensation (SOC) by self-report: Technical report 1999. Berlin, Germany: Max Planck Institute for Human Development.

9165

Test Name: SENSE OF COMMUNITY MEASURES

Purpose: To assess sense of community experienced by teachers.

Number of Items: 62

Format: Includes 3 factors: School-Related, Co-Worker Related, and Student-Related. Responses are made on 5-point formats ranging from "never" to "always" or from "strongly agree" to "strongly disagree."

Reliability: Alpha coefficients ranged from .80 to .94.

Author: Royal, M. A., and Rossi, R. J.

Article: Predictors of within-school differences in teachers' sense of community.

Journal: *Journal of Educational Research*, May/June 1999, *92*(5), 259–266.

Related Research: Royal, M. A., & Rossi, R. I. (1996). Individual-level correlates of sense of community: Findings from workplace and school. *Journal of Community Psychology*, 24, 395–416.

9166

Test Name: SITUATIONAL CONSTRAINTS QUESTIONNAIRE

Purpose: To assess the importance of the physical work environment, its availability and its quality.

Number of Items: 28

Format: Semantic differential

format. Sample items are presented.

Reliability: Alpha coefficients ranged from .93 to .94.

Validity: Correlations with other variables ranged from −.30 to .06.

Author: Villanova, P.

Article: Predictive validity of situational constraints in general versus specific performance domains.

Journal: *Journal of Applied Psychology*, October 1996, *81*(5), 532–547.

9167

Test Name: SITUATIONAL OUTLOOK QUESTIONNAIRE

Purpose: To assess creative climate.

Number of Items: 50

Format: Four-point scales are anchored by 0 (not at all applicable) and 3 (applicable to a high degree).

Reliability: Alphas ranged from .62 to .90 across dimensions.

Author: Isaksen, S. G., et al.

Article: Situational Outlook Questionnaire: A measure of the climate for creativity and change.

Journal: *Psychological Reports*, October 1999, *85*(2), 665–674.

Related Research: Lauer, K. J. (1994). *The assessment of creative climate: An investigation of Ekvall's Creative Climate Questionnaire.* Unpublished Master's thesis, State University College at Buffalo, New York.

9168

Test Name: SOCIAL CLIMATE IN THE ORGANIZATION SCALE

Purpose: To measure social climate in the organization.

Number of Items: 9

Format: Includes positively and negatively worded items. Responses are made on a 5-point Likert-type scale ranging from 1 (agree) to 5 (disagree). Examples are presented.

Reliability: Coefficient alpha was .82.

Validity: Correlation with other variables ranged from −.46 to .29.

Author: Timmermin, G., and Bajema, C.

Article: The impact of organizational culture on perceptions and experiences of sexual harassment.

Journal: *Journal of Vocational Behavior*, October 2000, *57*(2), 188–205.

Related Research: Hofstede, G., et al. (1990). Measuring organizational cultures: A qualitative and quantitative study across twenty cases. *Administrative Science Quarterly*, *35*, 286–316.

9169

Test Name: STUDENT ORGANIZATION ENVIRONMENT SCALES

Purpose: To measure student perceptions of the climate of college student organizations.

Number of Items: 51

Format: Scales range from 1 (never or almost never true) to 4 (always or almost always true). Sample items are presented.

Reliability: Alpha coefficients ranged from .70 to .90 across subscales and samples. Test-retest reliabilities (4 weeks) ranged from .37 to .98.

Validity: Correlations with other variables ranged from −.05 to .37.

Author: Winston, R. B., et al.

Article: Describing the climate of student organizations: The Student Organization Environment Scales.

Journal: *Journal of College Student Development*, July/August 1997, *38*(4), 417–428.

9170

Test Name: STUDENT'S EVALUATION OF COURSE

Purpose: To assess the qualities of a college course.

Number of Items: 6

Time Required: 3 minutes

Format: Six-point rating scales vary by item. All items are presented.

Reliability: Alpha was .86.

Author: Dreger, R. M.

Article: Longitudinal study of a "Student's Evaluation of a Course," including the effects of a professor's life experiences on students' evaluations.

Journal: *Psychological Reports*, October 1997, *81*(2), 563–588.

Related Research: Dreger, R. M. (1954). Further validational data on "A simple course evaluation scale." *Journal of Genetic Psychology*, *85*, 165–169.

9171

Test Name: SUPERVISOR MONITORING SCALE

Purpose: To measure closeness of supervision.

Number of Items: 5

Format: Scales range from "never" to "often." A sample item is presented.

Reliability: Coefficient alpha was .79.

Validity: Correlations with other variables ranged from −.29 to .26.

Author: Frone, M. R.

Article: Predictors of work injuries among employed adolescents.

Journal: *Journal of Applied Psychology*, August 1998, *83*(4), 565–576.

Related Research: Neihoff, B. P., & Moorman, R. H. (1993). Justice as a mediator of the relationship between methods of monitoring and organizational citizenship behavior. *Academy of Management Journal*, *36*, 527–556.

9172

Test Name: SURVEY OF PERCEIVED ORGANIZATIONAL SUPPORT —SHORT VERSION

Purpose: To assess employee perceptions of the extent to which the organization values employees' contributions and is concerned about their well being.

Number of Items: 8

Format: Responses are made on a 7-point Likert type scale ranging from 1 (strongly disagree) to 7 (strongly agree).

Reliability: Coefficient alpha was .92.

Validity: Correlation with other variables ranged from .66 to .88.

Author: Hutchison, S.

Article: Perceived organizational support: Further evidence of construct validity.

Journal: *Educational and Psychological Measurement*, December 1997, *57*(6), 1025–1034.

Related Research: Eisenberger, R., et al. (1986). Perceived organizational support. *Journal of Applied Psychology, 71,* 500–507.

9173

Test Name: TASK RESPONSIBILITIES SCALE

Purpose: To measure task responsibilities.

Number of Items: 30

Format: Responses are made on a 4-point scale ranging from 1 (never) to 4 (frequently). Examples are presented.

Reliability: Coefficient alpha was .88.

Validity: Correlations with other variables ranged from −.07 to .14.

Author: Blau, G., and Lunz, M.

Article: Testing the incremental effect of professional commitment on intent to leave one's profession beyond effects of external, personal, and work-related variables.

Journal: *Journal of Vocational Behavior,* April 1998, *52*(2), 260–269.

Related Research: Rudman, S., et al. (1995). Entry-level technologists report job preparedness. *Laboratory Medicine, 26,* 717–719.

9174

Test Name: TEACHER WORK-AUTONOMY

Purpose: To measure teacher sense of work autonomy.

Number of Items: 32

Format: Includes 4 factors: Student Teaching and Assessment, School Mode of Operating, Staff Development, and Curriculum Development. All items are presented.

Reliability: Alpha coefficients ranged from .80 to .91.

Author: Friedman, I. A.

Article: Teacher-perceived work autonomy: The concept and its measurement.

Journal: *Educational and Psychological Measurement,* February 1999, *59*(1), 58–76.

Related Research: Charters, W. W. (1974). *Sense of teacher work autonomy: Measurement and findings.* Eugene: Center for Educational Policy and Management, University of Oregon.

9175

Test Name: TEACHERS' SOCIAL NORMS SCALE

Purpose: To assess teachers' social norms.

Number of Items: 21

Format: Includes Esprit, Intimacy, Disengagement, and Hindrance.

Reliability: Alpha coefficients ranged from .66 to .80.

Validity: Correlations with teachers' professionalism ranged from −.41 to .46.

Author: Cheng, Y. C.

Article: Relation between teachers' professionalism and job attitudes, educational outcomes, and organizational factors.

Journal: *Journal of Educational Research,* January/February, 1996, *89*(3), 163–171.

Related Research: Halpin, A. W., & Croft, D. B. (1963) *The organization climate of schools.* Chicago: Midwest Administration Center, University of Chicago.

9176

Test Name: TEAM EFFECTIVENESS SCALE

Purpose: To rate team effectiveness.

Number of Items: 18

Format: Items include Productivity, Quality, and Cost Savings. All items are presented.

Reliability: Coefficient alpha was .94.

Validity: Correlations with other variables ranged from −.27 to .25.

Author: Alper, S., et al.

Article: Conflict management, efficacy, and performance in organizational teams.

Journal: *Personnel Psychology,* Autumn 2000, *53*(3), 625–642.

9177

Test Name: TEAM VIABILIT'. SCALE

Purpose: To measure a work team's capability to maintain itself over time.

Number of Items: 12

Format: Five-point scales are anchored by 1 (strongly disagree) and 5 (strongly agree). Sample items are presented.

Reliability: Coefficient alpha was .82.

Author: Barrick, M. R., et al.

Article: Relating member ability and personality to work-team processes and team effectiveness.

Journal: *Journal of Applied Psychology,* June 1998, *83*(3), 377–391.

Related Research: DeStephen, R. S., & Hirokawa, R. Y. (1988). Small group consensus: Stability and group support of the decision, task process, and group relationships. *Small Group Behavior, 19,* 227–239.

9178

Test Name: TELECOURSE EVALUATION QUESTIONNAIRE

Purpose: To assess student satisfaction with interactive telecourses.

Number of Items: 32

Format: Includes 7 dimensions: Instructor/Instruction Characteristics, Technological Characteristics, Course Management and Coordination, At-Site Personnel, Promptness of Material Delivery, Support Services, and Communication. Responses are made on a 5-point scale ranging from 1 (very poor) to 5 (very good). All items are presented.

Reliability: Alpha coefficients ranged from .35 to .96.

Author: Summers, M., et al.

Article: The camera adds more than pounds: Gender differences in course satisfaction for campus and distance learning students.

Journal: *Journal of Research & Development in Education,* Summer 1996, *29*(4).

Related Research: Biner, P. M. (1993). Redevelopment of an instrument to measure student attitudes toward televised courses. *The American Journal of Distance Education,* 7(1), 62–73.

9179

Test Name: UNION BENEFITS SCALE

Purpose: To measure the tangible benefits of union membership.

Number of Items: 6

Format: Five-point Likert format. All items are presented.

Reliability: Internal consistency was .79.

Validity: Correlations with other variables ranged from −.01 to .64.

Author: Pisnar-Sweeney, M.

Article: Role of normative commitment in predicting members' participation in the union.

Journal: *Psychological Reports,* June 1997, *80*(3) Part 2, 1183–1207.

Related Research: DeCotiis, T. A., & LeLouarn, J. (1981). A predictive study of voting behavior in a representative election using union instrumentality and work perceptions. *Organizational Behavior and Human Performance,* 27, 103–118.

9180

Test Name: UNIVERSITY ENVIRONMENT SCALE

Purpose: To assess concerns of racial and ethnic minority students.

Number of Items: 14

Format: Subscales range from 1 (not at all true) to 7 (very true). Sample items are presented.

Reliability: Alpha coefficients ranged from .81 to .84.

Validity: Correlations with other variables ranged from −.50 to .46.

Author: Gloria, A. M., et al.

Article: African American students' persistence at a predominately White university: Influences of social support, university comfort and self-beliefs.

Journal: *Journal of College Student Development,* May/June 1999, *40*(3), 257–268.

Related Research: Gloria, A. M., et al. (1996). The validation of the University Environment Scale and the College Congruity Scale. *Hispanic Journal of Behavioral Science,* 18, 533–549.

9181

Test Name: WHAT IS HAPPENING IN THIS CLASS QUESTIONNAIRE

Purpose: To measure students' perceptions of their classroom environments.

Number of Items: 56

Format: Includes 7 dimensions: Student Cohesiveness, Teacher Support, Involvement, Investigation, Task Orientation, Cooperation, and Equity. Responses are made on a 5-point scale ranging from 1 (almost never) to 5 (almost always). All items are presented.

Reliability: Alpha coefficients ranged from .81 to .93.

Author: Aldridge, J. M., et al.

Article: Investigating classroom environments in Taiwan and Australia with multiple research methods.

Journal: *Journal of Educational Research,* September/October 1999, *93*(1), 48–62.

Related Research: Fraser, B. J., et al. (1996, April). *Development, validation and use of personal and class forms of a new classroom environments instrument.* Paper presented at the annual meeting of the American Educational Research Association, New York.

9182

Test Name: WORK ENVIRONMENT SCALE

Purpose: To measure workplace climate.

Number of Items: 45

Format: Responses are made on a 5-point Likert scale ranging from 1 (strongly disagree) to 5 (strongly agree).

Reliability: Coefficient alpha was .90.

Validity: Correlations with other variables ranged from −.42 to .58.

Author: Driscoll, J. M., et al.

Article: Lesbian identity and disclosure in the workplace: Relation to occupational stress and satisfaction.

Journal: *Journal of Vocational Behavior*, April 1996, *48*(2), 229–242.

Related Research: Cranston, P., & Leonard, M. M. (1990). The relationship between undergraduate experiences of campus micro-inequities and their self-esteem and aspirations. *Journal of College Student Development*, *31*, 395–401.

9183

Test Name: WORK ENVIRONMENT SURVEY

Purpose: To survey the quality of the work environment.

Number of Items: 190

Format: Includes 13 categories.

Reliability: Reliabilities ranged from .53 to .96.

Author: Putten, J. V., et al.

Article: Comparing union and nonunion staff perceptions of the higher education work environment.

Journal: *Research in Higher Education*, February 1997, *38*(1), 131–149.

Related Research: Jones, A., &

James, L. (1979). Psychological climate: Dimensions and relationships of individual and aggregate work environment perceptions. *Organizational Behavior and Human Performance*, *23*, 201–250.

9184

Test Name: WORK HAZARD SCALE

Purpose: To measure physical hazards at work.

Number of Items: 7

Format: Five-point scales ranged from "never" to "often." A sample item is presented.

Reliability: Coefficient alpha was .79.

Validity: Correlations with other variables ranged from .00 to .35.

Author: Frone, M. R.

Article: Predictors of work injuries among employed adolescents.

Journal: *Journal of Applied Psychology*, August 1998, *83*(4), 565–576.

Related Research: Frone, M. R., & McFarlin, D. B. (1989). Chronic occupational stressors, self-focused attention, and well-being: Testing a cybernetic model of stress. *Journal of Applied Psychology*, *74*, 876–883.

9185

Test Name: WORK TEAM CHARACTERISTICS QUESTIONNAIRE

Purpose: To measure work team characteristics.

Number of Items: 53

Format: Includes 7 factors: Process, Context, Job Design, Flexibility, Task Significance, Interdependence, and Cross-

Functionalism. Responses are made on a 7-point response scale ranging from 7 (strongly agree) to 1 (strongly disagree).

Reliability: Internal consistency reliability ranged from .70 to .92.

Author: Campion, M. A., et al.

Article: Relations between work team characteristics and effectiveness: A replication and extension.

Journal: *Personnel Psychology*, Summer 1996, *49*(2), 429–452.

Related Research: Campion, M. A., et al. (1993). Relations between work group characteristics and effectiveness: Implications for designing effective work groups. *Personal Psychology*, *46*, 823–850.

9186

Test Name: WORKLOAD SCALE

Purpose: To measure workload demands.

Number of Items: 3

Format: Five-point scales range from 1 (never) to 5 (very often). A sample item is presented.

Reliability: Coefficient alpha was .70.

Author: Markel, K. S., and Frone, M. R.

Article: Job characteristics, work-school conflict, and school outcomes among adolescents: Testing a structural model.

Journal: *Journal of Applied Psychology*, April 1998, *83*(2), 277–287.

Related Research: Quinn, R. P., & Staines, G. L. (1970). *The 1977 Quality of Employment Survey*. Ann Arbor: University of Michigan, Institute for Social Research.

9187

Test Name: WORKPLACE DEVIANCE SCALE

Purpose: To measure interpersonal and organizational deviance.

Number of Items: 19

Format: Scales range from 1 (never) to 7 (daily). All items are presented.

Reliability: Coefficient alpha was .81 (organizational) and .78 (interpersonal).

Validity: Correlations with other variables ranged from −.35 to .79.

Author: Bennett, R. J., and Robinson, S. L.

Article: Development of a measure of workplace deviance.

Journal: *Journal of Applied Psychology,* June 2000, *85*(3), 349–360.

9188

Test Name: WORKPLACE FRIENDSHIP SCALE

Purpose: To assess workplace friendship.

Number of Items: 12

Format: Includes two dimensions: Opportunity and Prevalence. Responses are made on a 5-point Likert-type scale ranging from 1 (strongly disagree) to 5 (strongly agree). All items are presented.

Reliability: Internal consistency reliabilities ranged from .84 to .89.

Validity: Correlations with other variables ranged from −.28 to .76 (*N* = 116).

Author: Nielsen, I. K., et al.

Article: Development and validation of scores on a two-dimensional workplace friendship scale.

Journal: *Educational and Psychological Measurement,* August 2000, *60*(4), 628–643.

Related Research: Winstead, B. A., et al. (1995). The quality of friendships at work and job satisfaction. *Journal of Social and Personal Relationships, 12,* 199–215.

9189

Test Name: WORKPLACE RACIAL TREATMENT SCALE

Purpose: To measure the extent to which African American professionals perceive interaction and treatment at work as racially biased.

Number of Items: 15

Format: Examples are presented.

Reliability: Coefficient alpha was .91.

Validity: Correlations with other variables ranged from −.58 to .75.

Author: Holder, J. C., and Vaux, A.

Article: African American professionals: Coping with occupational stress in predominantly White work environments.

Journal: *Journal of Vocational Behavior,* December 1998, *53*(3), 315–333.

Related Research: Holder, J. C. (1994). *Workplace racial treatment scale.* Unpublished measure. Southern Illinois University.

9190

Test Name: WORKPLACE SITUATION INSTRUMENT

Purpose: To assess responses to concerns about the workplace.

Number of Items: 120

Format: Self-assessed likelihood-of-responding scales range from "I would never respond this way" to "I would most likely respond this way" Sample items are presented.

Reliability: Alphas ranged from .47 to .96 across subscales.

Validity: Correlations between subscales ranged from −.28 to .80.

Author: Juhasz, J. B., and Griffin, G. H.

Article: Predictiveness of orientation toward God at the workplace.

Journal: *Psychological Reports,* June 1996, *78*(3) Part 1, 739–752.

CHAPTER 15
Motivation

9191

Test Name: ACADEMIC MOTIVATION SCALE

Purpose: To assess intrinsic, extrinsic, and amotivation.

Number of Items: 28

Reliability: Internal consistency ranged from .83 to .86 across subscales.

Validity: Correlations between subscales ranged from −.31 to .68.

Author: Cokely, K. O.

Article: Examining the validity of the Academic Motivation Scale by comparing scale construction to self-determination theory.

Journal: *Psychological Reports*, April 2000, *86*(2), 560−564.

Related Research: Vallerand, R. J., et al. (1992). The Academic Motivation Scale: A measure of intrinsic, extrinsic and amotivation in education. *Educational and Psychological Measurement, 52,* 1003−1007.

9192

Test Name: ACHIEVABILITY OF FUTURE GOALS SCALE

Purpose: To measure an individual's effective evaluation of the future.

Number of Items: 8

Format: Responses are made on a 7-point scale ranging from 0 (not at all) to 6 (perfectly). An example is presented.

Reliability: Alpha coefficients ranged from .69 to .76.

Author: Marko, K. W., and Savickas, M. L.

Article: Effectiveness of a career time perspective intervention.

Journal: *Journal of Vocational Behavior*, February 1998, *52*(1), 106−119.

Related Research: Heinberg, L. (1961). *Development and construct validation of an inventory for the measurement of future time perspective.* Unpublished master's thesis, Vanderbilt University.

9193

Test Name: ACHIEVEMENT GOAL TENDENCIES SCALE

Purpose: To measure counselor trainees' achievement goal tendencies.

Number of Items: 20

Format: Includes 3 factors: Learning Goals, Performance Goals—Approval Seeking, and Performance Goals—Advancement. Responses are made on a 5-point scale ranging from 1 (never) to 5 (always).

Reliability: Alpha coefficients ranged from .71 to .89. Test-retest (2 weeks) reliability coefficients ranged from .70 to .87.

Author: Kivlighan, D. N., Jr., et al.

Article: Counselor trainee achievement goal orientation and the acquisition of time-limited dynamic psychotherapy skills.

Journal: *Journal of Counseling*

Psychology, April 1998, *45*(2), 189−195.

Related Research: Hayamizu, T., et al. (1989). Cognitive motivational processes mediated by achievement goal tendencies. *Japanese Psychological Research, 31,* 179−189.

9194

Test Name: ACHIEVEMENT MOTIVE GRID

Purpose: To measure achievement motivation by combining the validity of TAT type methods and the reliability of questionnaire methods.

Number of Items: 18 pictures, 18 statements.

Format: Subjects select statements that they believe apply to each picture. Four pictures and all statements are presented.

Reliability: Various reliability coefficients ranged from .67 to .93 across three subscales.

Author: Schmalt, H.-D.

Article: Assessing the achievement motive using the grid technique.

Journal: *Journal of Research in Personality*, June, 1999, *33*(2), 109−130.

Related Research: Schmalt, H.-D. (1976). Die messung des leistungsmotivs. Göttingen: Hogrefe.

9195

Test Name: ACHIEVEMENT MOTIVES SCALE

Purpose: To measure motive to succeed and motive to avoid failure.

Number of Items: 15

Format: Responses ranged from 1 ("is very true of me") to 4 ("is not at all true of me"). Sample items are presented.

Reliability: Alphas ranged from .81 to .86.

Author: Halvari, H.

Article: Personality and educational choice of general versus vocational students among 16-to-19 year-olds.

Journal: *Psychological Reports*, June 1996, *78*(3) Part 2, 1379–1388.

Related Research: Gjesme, T., & Nygard, R. (1970). *Achievement-related motives: Theoretical considerations and construction of a measuring instrument.* Unpublished manuscript, University of Oslo.

9196

Test Name: ACHIEVEMENT MOTIVES SCALE

Purpose: To assess achievement motives.

Number of Items: 16

Format: Includes 2 subscales: Motive to Achieve Success and Motive to Avoid Failure. Responses are made on a 4-point scale ranging from 4 (very true) to 1 (not at all true). Examples are presented.

Reliability: Alpha coefficients were .78 and .83.

Validity: Correlations with other variables ranged from −.47 to .48.

Author: Halvari, H., and Kjørmo, O.

Article: A structural model of achievement motives,

performance approach and avoidance goals, and performance among Norwegian Olympic athletes.

Journal: *Perceptual and Motor Skills*, December 1999, *89*(3) Part 1, 997–1022.

Related Research: Nygärd, R., & Gjesme, T. (1973). Assessment of achievement motives: Comments and suggestions. *Scandinavian Journal of Educational Research, 17*, 39–46.

9197

Test Name: ACHIEVEMENT MOTIVES SCALE

Purpose: To assess one's motive to achieve success and avoid failure.

Number of Items: 30

Format: Includes two subscales: Motive to Achieve Success and Motive to Avoid Failure. Responses are made on a 4-point scale ranging from 1 (is not at all true of me) to 4 (is very true of me). Examples are presented.

Reliability: Alpha coefficients were .76 (success) and .88 (failure).

Validity: Correlations with other variables ranged from −.29 to .33.

Author: Thomassen, T. O., and Halvari, H.

Article: Achievement motivation and involvement in sport competitions.

Journal: *Perceptual and Motor Skills*, December 1996, *83*(3) Part 2, 1363–1372.

Related Research: Gjesme, T., & Nygard, R. (1970). *Achievement-related motives: Theoretical considerations and construction of a measuring instrument.* Unpublished manuscript, University of Oslo.

9198

Test Name: ATTENTIONAL FOCUSING SCALE

Purpose: To assess the tendency to maintain attentional focus upon task-related channels.

Number of Items: 11

Format: An example is presented.

Reliability: Alpha coefficients ranged from .59 to .85.

Validity: Correlations with other variables ranged from −.60 to .33.

Author: Lengua, L. J., et al.

Article: Temperament as a predictor of symptomatology in children: Addressing contamination of measures.

Journal: *Child Development*, February 1998, *69*(1), 164–181.

Related Research: Goldsmith, H. H., & Rothbart, M. K. (1991). Contemporary inducements for assessing early temperament by questionnaire and in the laboratory. In J. Strelau & A. Angleitner (Eds.), *Explorations in temperament: International perspective on theory and measurement* (pp. 249–272). New York: Plenum.

9199

Test Name: AUTONOMY SCALE (JAPANESE)

Purpose: To assess intrinsic and extrinsic motivation and amotivation.

Number of Items: 26

Format: Five-point scales are anchored by 1 (not at all) and 5 (always). All items are presented in English.

Reliability: Alphas ranged from .77 to .90 across seven factor subscales.

Author: Yamauchi, H., et al.

Article: Perceived control, autonomy, and self-regulated learning strategies among Japanese high school students.

Journal: *Psychological Reports*, December 1999, *85*(3, Part I), 779–798.

Related Research: Vallerand, R. J., et al. (1992). The Academic Motivation Scale: A measure of intrinsic, extrinsic, and amotivation in education. *Educational and Psychological Measurement, 52*, 1003–1017.

9200

Test Name: BEHAVIORAL PREFERENCES CHECKLIST

Purpose: To measure academic goal-setting.

Number of Items: 17

Format: Five-point scales are anchored by 1 (never) and 5 (always).

Reliability: Alpha was .84.

Author: Lasane, T. P., et al.

Article: Hypermasculinity and academic goal-setting: An explanatory study.

Journal: *Psychological Reports*, October 1999, *85*(2), 487–496.

Related Research: Lasane, T. P., & Jones, J. M. (1999). Temporal orientation and academic goal-setting: The mediating properties of a motivational self. *Journal of Social Behavior and Personality, 14*, 31–44.

9201

Test Name: CAREER ASPIRATION SCALE

Purpose: To assess the degree to which participants valued their careers and aspired to advancement and leadership positions within their careers.

Number of Items: 10

Format: Responses are made on a 10-point scale ranging from 1 (not at all true of me) to 5 (very true of me). Sample items are presented.

Reliability: Internal consistency reliability estimates ranged from .73 to .77.

Validity: Correlations with other variables ranged from −.04 to .53.

Author: O'Brien, K. M., et al.

Article: Attachment, separation, and women's vocational development: A longitudinal analysis.

Journal: *Journal of Counseling Psychology*, July 2000, *47*(3), 301–315.

Related Research: O'Brien, K. M., et al. (1996, August). The operationalization of women's career choices: The Career Aspiration Scale. In V. S. Solberg & K. M. O'Brien (Chairs), *Promoting women's career development into the next millennium and beyond.* Symposium conducted at the 104th annual convention of the American Psychological Association, Toronto, Ontario, Canada.

9202

Test Name: DATING MOTIVATIONS SCALE

Purpose: To measure intrinsic, extrinsic, and instrumental motivations for dating.

Number of Items: 24

Format: Nine-point bipolar scales. Sample items are presented.

Reliability: Alpha coefficients ranged from .70 to .88 across subscales.

Validity: Correlations with the

other variables ranged from −.28 to .51.

Author: Jones, M.

Article: Sociosexuality and motivations for romantic involvement.

Journal: *Journal of Research in Personality*, March 1998, *32*(1), 173–182.

Related Research: Rempel, J. K., et al. (1985). Trust in close relationships. *Journal of Personality and Social Psychology, 49*, 95–112.

9203

Test Name: DEVELOPMENTAL GOALS SCALE

Purpose: To determine the importance of 4 developmental goals.

Number of Items: 4

Format: Includes being respectful, getting along with others, being well educated, and being well behaved. Responses are made on a 5-point scale ranging from 1 (slightly important) to 5 (extremely important).

Reliability: Coefficient alpha was .70.

Validity: Correlations with other variables ranged from −.08 to .29.

Author: Brody, G. H., et al.

Article: Linking maternal efficacy beliefs, developmental goals, parenting practices, and child competence in rural single-parent African American families.

Journal: *Child Development*, September/October 1999, *70*(4), 1197–1208.

Related Research: Brody, G. H., & Stoneman, Z. (1992). Child competence and developmental goals among rural Black families: Investigating the links. In I. E.

Sigel et al (Eds.), *Parental belief systems: The psychological consequences for children* (2nd ed., pp. 415–431). Hillsdale, NJ: Erlbaum.

9204

Test Name: DRINKING/ MARIJUANA MOTIVES MEASURE

Purpose: To assess motives for drinking/marijuana.

Number of Items: 20

Format: The motives are enhancement, coping, social, and conformity. Responses are made on a 5-point scale ranging from 1 (almost never/never) to 5 (almost always/always). Examples are presented.

Reliability: Alpha coefficients ranged from .84 to .94.

Validity: Correlations with other variables ranged from .07 to .59.

Author: Simons, J., et al.

Article: Validating a five-factor marijuana motives measure: Relations with use, problems, and alcohol motives.

Journal: *Journal of Counseling Psychology*, July 1998, *45*(3), 265–273.

Related Research: Cooper, M. L. (1994). Motivations for alcohol use among adolescents: Development and validation of a four-factor model. *Psychological Assessment, 6*, 117–128.

9205

Test Name: DRIVEN SCALE

Purpose: To measure a person's internal pressures or intrinsic drive to work.

Number of Items: 7

Format: Sample items are

presented. Scores range from 0 to 28.

Reliability: Alpha coefficients ranged from .67 to .81.

Validity: Correlations with other variables ranged from −.20 to .42.

Author: Bonebright, C. A., et al.

Article: The relationship of workaholism with work-life conflict, life satisfaction, and purpose in life.

Journal: *Journal of Counseling Psychology*, October 2000, *47*(4), 469–477.

Related Research: Spence, J. T., & Robbins, A. S. (1992). Workaholism: Definition, measurement, and preliminary results. *Journal of Personality Assessment, 58*, 160–178.

9206

Test Name: EMOTION AND MOTIVATION CONTROL SCALES

Purpose: To assess job-search-related emotions and motivations.

Number of Items: 11

Format: Scales range from 1 (not at all true of me) to 5 (extremely true of me). All items are presented.

Reliability: Coefficients alpha were .81 (emotion) and .74 (motivation).

Validity: Correlations with other variables ranged from −.29 to .39.

Author: Wanberg, C. R., et al.

Article: Unemployed individuals: Motives, job-search competencies, and job-search constraints as predictors of job seeking and reemployment.

Journal: *Journal of Applied Psychology*, December 1999, *84*(6), 897–910.

9207

Test Name: EMPLOYEE INTRINSIC MOTIVATION SCALE

Purpose: To measure employee intrinsic motivation.

Number of Items: 5

Format: Responses are made on a 6-point scale. All items are presented.

Reliability: Coefficient alpha was .74.

Validity: Correlations with other variables ranged from −.09 to .28.

Author: Tierney, P., et al.

Article: An examination of leadership and employee creativity: The relevance of traits and relationships.

Journal: *Personnel Psychology*, Autumn 1999, *52*(3), 591–620.

Related Research: Amabile, T. M. (1985). Motivation and creativity: Effects of motivational orientation on creative writers. *Journal of Personality and Social Psychology, 48*, 393–399.

9208

Test Name: EMPLOYEE PERFORMANCE QUESTIONNAIRE

Purpose: To measure the extent to which employees seek to increase organizational effectiveness.

Number of Items: 16

Format: Scales range from 1 (disagree) to 5 (very strongly agree). All items are presented.

Reliability: Coefficient alphas ranged from .87 to .91 across subscales.

Validity: Correlations with other variables ranged from −.16 to .13.

Author: Lynch, P. D., et al.

Article: Perceived organizational support: Inferior versus superior performance by wary employees.

Journal: *Journal of Applied Psychology*, August 1999, *84*(4), 467–483.

9209

Test Name: EXERCISE ENJOYMENT QUESTIONNAIRE

Purpose: To measure dimensions of exercise-related affect.

Number of Items: 20

Format: Includes 5 subscales: Exercise Fulfillment, Psychological Dependence on Exercise, Psychological Drive for Exercise, Physical Drive for Exercise, and Perceived Weight Satisfaction. Responses are made on a 5-point scale ranging from 1 (low endorsement) to 5 (high endorsement).

Reliability: Test-retest reliability was .68.

Author: Frederick, C. M., and Morrison, C. S.

Article: Social physique anxiety: Personality constructs, motivations, exercise attitudes, and behaviors.

Journal: *Perceptual and Motor Skills*, June 1996, *82*(3) Part 1, 963–972.

Related Research: Manning, T., & Morrison, C. S. (1994). Excessive exercise, family environment and perception of family environment. In F. Bell & G. Van Gyn (Eds.), *Proceedings of the 10th Commonwealth and International Scientific Congress* (pp. 108–112), Victoria, B.C.

9210

Test Name: FLOW SCALE

Purpose: To measure the

motivating psychological state of flow.

Number of Items: 15

Format: Includes measures of Intrinsic Motivation, Task Focus, Task Feedback, Match Between Challenge and Skills, and Altered Sense of Time. Examples are presented.

Reliability: Alpha coefficients ranged from .64 to .80.

Validity: Correlations with other variables ranged from −.01 to .51.

Author: Sosik, J. J., et al.

Article: Leadership style, anonymity, and creativity in group decision support systems: The mediating role of optimal flow.

Journal: *Journal of Creative Behavior*, Fourth Quarter 1999, *33*(4), 227–256.

Related Research: Csikszentmihalyi, M. (1990). *Flow: The psychology of optimal experience.* New York: Harper & Row.

9211

Test Name: FLOW STATE SCALE

Purpose: To assess swimmers' experiences of flow.

Number of Items: 36

Format: Sample items are presented.

Reliability: Alpha coefficients ranged from .76 to .89 across subscales. Total alpha was .94.

Validity: Correlations with other variables ranged from −.31 to .75.

Authors: Kowal, J., and Fortier, M. S.

Article: Motivational determinants

of flow: Contributions from self-determination theory.

Journal: *Journal of Social Psychology*, June 1999, *139*(3), 355–368.

Related Research: Jackson, S. A., & Marsh, H. (1996). Development and validation of a scale to measure optimal experience: The Flow State Scale. *The Journal of Sport and Exercise Psychology, 18*, 17–35.

9212

Test Name: GENERAL EFFORT JOB SEARCH SCALE

Purpose: To measure job search intensity.

Number of Items: 4

Format: Responses are made on a 5-point Likert-type scale ranging from 1 (strongly disagree) to 5 (strongly agree).

Reliability: Alpha coefficients were .94 and .90.

Validity: Correlations with other variables ranged from .01 to .68.

Author: Saks, A. M., and Ashforth, B. E.

Article: Change in job search behaviors and employment outcomes.

Journal: *Journal of Vocational Behavior*, April 2000, *56*(2), 277–287.

Related Research: Blau, G. (1993). Further exploring the relationship between job search and voluntary individual turnover. *Personnel Psychology, 46*, 213–330.

9213

Test Name: GOAL CONTENT SCALE

Purpose: To measure the importance of avoidance, skill

refinement, positive comparison, and skill development.

Number of Items: 13

Format: Scales range from 1 (very unimportant) to 7 (very important). All items are presented.

Reliability: Alpha coefficients ranged from .75 to .83.

Validity: Correlations with other variables ranged from −.10 to .28.

Author: Brett, J. F., and VandeWalle, D.

Article: Goal orientation and goal content as predictors of performance in a training program.

Journal: *Journal of Applied Psychology,* December 1999, *84*(6), 863–873.

9214

Test Name: GOAL INSTABILITY SCALE

Purpose: To assess goal directedness.

Number of Items: 10

Format: Responses are made on a 6-point Likert-type scale ranging from 1 (strongly disagree) to 6 (strongly agree). Examples are presented.

Reliability: Test-retest (2 weeks) reliability was .75. Coefficient alpha was .80.

Validity: Correlations with other variables ranged from −.64 to .64.

Author: Elliott, T. R., et al.

Article: Goal instability and adjustment to physical disability.

Journal: *Journal of Counseling Psychology,* April 2000, *47*(2), 251–265.

Related Research: Robbins, S. B., & Patton, M. J. (1985). Self-

psychology in career development: Construction of the Superiority and Goal Instability Scales. *Journal of Counseling Psychology, 32,* 221–231.

9215

Test Name: GOAL ORIENTATION AND GOAL COMMITMENT SCALES

Purpose: To assess learning orientation, performance orientation, and goal commitment.

Number of Items: 12

Format: Scales range from "strongly disagree" to "strongly agree." Sample items are presented.

Reliability: Coefficient alpha ranged from .69 to .83 across subscales.

Author: Colquitt, J. A., and Simmering, M. J.

Article: Conscientiousness, goal orientation, and motivation to learn during the learning process: A longitudinal study.

Journal: *Journal of Applied Psychology,* August 1998, *83*(4), 654–665.

Related Research: Hollenbeck, J. R., et al. (1989). An empirical examination of the antecedents of commitment to difficult goals. *Journal of Applied Psychology, 74,* 18–23.

Button, S. B., et al. (1996). Goal orientation in organizational research: A conceptual and empirical foundation. *Organizational Behavior and Human Decision Processes, 67,* 26–48.

9216

Test Name: GOAL ORIENTATION INSTRUMENT

Purpose: To assess goal orientation.

Number of Items: 13

Format: Includes 3 factors: Learning, Prove, and Avoid.

Reliability: Alpha coefficients ranged from .85 to .89. Test-retest reliability ranged from .57 to 66.

Validity: Correlations with other variables ranged from .44 to .60.

Author: Vandewalle, D.

Article: Development and validation of a work domain goal orientation instrument.

Journal: *Educational and Psychological Measurement,* December 1997, *57*(6), 995–1015.

9217

Test Name: GOAL ORIENTATION INVENTORY

Purpose: To assess task orientation and ego orientation with regard to mathematics.

Number of Items: 13

Format: Includes 2 goal orientations: task and ego. Responses are made on a scale ranging from 10 (not at all) to 100 (very much). Sample items are presented.

Reliability: Alpha coefficients were .75 and .83.

Author: Shih, S.-S., and Alexander, J. M.

Article: Interacting effects of goal setting and self- or other-referenced feedback on children's development of self-efficacy and cognitive skill within the Taiwanese classroom.

Journal: *Journal of Educational Psychology,* September 2000, *92*(3), 536–543.

Related Research: Nicholls, J. G., et al. (1990). Assessing students' theories of success in mathematics: Individual and classroom differences. *Journal of Research in Mathematics Education, 21,* 109–122.

9218

Test Name: GOAL ORIENTATION SCALE

Purpose: To measure orientation to learning as a goal, the desire to perform competently, and the extent to which expression of competence is avoided.

Number of Items: 13

Format: Scales range from 1 (strongly disagree) to 7 (strongly agree). All items are presented.

Reliability: Alpha coefficients ranged from .78 to .88 across subscales.

Validity: Correlations with other variables ranged from −.10 to .37.

Author: Brett, J. F., and VandeWalle, D.

Article: Goal orientation and goal content as predictors of performance in a training program.

Journal: *Journal of Applied Psychology,* December 1999, *84*(6), 863–873.

9219

Test Name: GOAL ORIENTATIONS SCALE

Purpose: To measure learning and performance goals.

Number of Items: 16

Format: Scales range from 1 (strongly disagree) to 5 (strongly agree). Sample items are presented.

Reliability: Alpha coefficients were .79 (learning) and .74 (performance).

Validity: Correlations with other variables ranged from −.11 to .34.

Author: Chen, G., et al.

Article: Examination of relationships among trait-like individual differences, state-like individual differences, and learning performance.

Journal: *Journal of Applied Psychology,* December 2000, *85*(6), 835–847.

Related Research: Button, S. B., et al. (1996). Goal orientation in organizational research: A conceptual and empirical foundation. *Organizational Behavior and Human Decision Processes, 67,* 26–48.

9220

Test Name: GOALS AND RELATIVE WEIGHTS QUESTIONNAIRE

Purpose: To assess weight loss goals and the expectations and evaluations of weight loss outcomes.

Number of Items: 44

Format: Ten-point scales are anchored by one of two sets of anchors: 1 (not at all important or extremely negative) and 10 (very important or extremely positive). Five items ask for weight responses in pounds.

Reliability: Test-retest reliability correlations ranged from .60 to .96.

Validity: Selected correlations with other variables ranged from −.75 to .33.

Author: Foster, G. D., et al.

Article: What is a reasonable weight loss? Patients' expectations and evaluations of obesity treatment outcomes.

Journal: *Journal of Consulting and Clinical Psychology,* February 1997, *65*(1), 79–85.

9221

Test Name: GOALS INVENTORY MEASURE

Purpose: To measure learning and performance goals.

Number of Items: 25

Format: Includes 2 subscales: Performance and Learning. All items are presented.

Reliability: Alpha coefficients were .80 and .75. Test-retest reliabilities were .73 and .76.

Author: Bures, E. M., et al.

Article: Student motivation to learn via computer conferencing.

Journal: *Research in Higher Education,* October 2000, *41*(5), 593–621.

Related Research: Roedel, T. B., et al. (1994). Validation of a measure of learning and performance goal orientations. *Educational and Psychological Measurement, 54,* 1013–1021.

9222

Test Name: GOALS QUESTIONNAIRE

Purpose: To assess students' self-reported adaption of mastery, performance, and work avoidance goals in their introductory psychology class.

Number of Items: 18

Format: Includes 4 parts: Mastery, Performance, Work Avoidance, and Initial Performance Expectations.

Reliability: Alpha coefficients ranged from .51 to .80.

Validity: Correlations with other variables ranged from −.30 to .48.

Author: Harackiewicz, J. M., et al.

Article: Short-term and long-term consequences of achievement goals: Predicting intent and performance over time.

Journal: *Journal of Educational Psychology*, June 2000, *92*(2), 316–330.

Related Research: Harackiewicz, J. M., et al. (1997). Predictors and consequences of achievement goals in the college classroom: Maintaining interest and making the grade. *Journal of Personality and Social Psychology, 73*, 1284–1295.

9223

Test Name: GOALS SCALE

Purpose: To assess goals.

Number of Items: 6

Format: Responses are made on a 5-point scale ranging from 0 (not at all true) to 4 (really true). All items are presented.

Reliability: Alpha coefficients were .85 and .90.

Author: Strough, J., and Cheng, S.

Article: Dyad gender and friendship differences in shared goals for mutual participation on a collaborative task.

Journal: *Child Study Journal*, 2000, *30*(2), 103–126.

Related Research: Strough, J., & Berg, C. A. (2000). Goals as a mediator of gender differences in high affiliation dyadic conversations. *Developmental Psychology, 36*, 117–125.

9224

Test Name: HIV RISK REDUCTION INTENSIONS SCALE

Purpose: To assess intentions to engage in risk reduction behaviors.

Number of Items: 9

Format: Eleven-point scales.

Reliability: Cronbach alpha was .79.

Author: Belcher, L., et al.

Article: A randomized trial of a brief HIV risk reduction counseling intervention for women.

Journal: *Journal of Consulting and Clinical Psychology*, October 1998, *66*(5), 856–861.

Related Research: Kalichman, S. C., et al. (1996). Experimental component analysis of a behavioral HIV-AIDS prevention intervention for inner-city women. *Journal of Consulting and Clinical Psychology, 64*, 687–693.

9225

Test Name: INNER- AND OTHER-MOTIVATION SCALES

Purpose: To measure the motivation to maintain an inner image of competence and the motivation to maintain an external image of competence.

Number of Items: 9

Format: All items are presented.

Reliability: Alpha were .73 (inner) and .88 (other).

Authors: Rao, V. S., and Monk, A.

Article: The effects of individual differences and anonymity on commitment decisions: Preliminary evidence.

Journal: *The Journal of Social Psychology*, August 1999, *139*(4), 496–515.

Related Research: Collins, B. E., et al. (1973). Some dimensions of the internal-external metaphor in theories of personality. *Journal of Personality, 41*, 471–492.

9226

Test Name: INTENT TO PERSIST SCALE

Purpose: To measure students' intent to persist.

Number of Items: 4

Format: Responses are made on a 5-point Likert scale.

Reliability: Coefficient alpha was .69.

Validity: Correlations with other variables ranged from −.20 to .24.

Author: Sandler, M. E.

Article: Career decision-making self-efficacy, perceived stress, and an integrated model of student persistence: A structural model of finances, attitudes, behavior, and career development.

Journal: *Research in Higher Education*, October 2000, *41*(5), 537–580.

Related Research: Bean, J. P., & Metzner, B. S. (1985). A conceptual model of nontraditional undergraduate student attrition. *Review of Educational Research, 55*(4), 485–540.

9227

Test Name: INTENTIONS OF SEEKING COUNSELING INVENTORY

Purpose: To rate one's likelihood of seeking counseling.

Number of Items: 17

Format: Responses are made on a 6-point scale ranging from 1 (very unlikely) to 6 (very likely). Examples are presented.

Reliability: Internal consistency was .88.

Validity: Correlations with other variables ranged from −.33 to .42.

Author: Rochlen, A. B., et al.

Article: Development of the Attitudes Toward Career Counseling Scale.

Journal: *Journal of Counseling Psychology*, April 1999, *46*(2), 196–206.

Related Research: Cash, T. F., et al. (1975). When counselors are heard but not seen: Initial impact of physical attractiveness. *Journal of Counseling Psychology*, 30, 215–220.

9228

Test Name: INTERNAL MOTIVATION SCALE

Purpose: To measure internal motivation.

Number of Items: 4

Format: Responses are made on a 7-point Likert-type scale ranging from 1 (strongly disagree) to 7 (strongly agree). Examples are presented.

Reliability: Coefficient alpha was .56.

Validity: Correlations with other variables ranged from −.10 to .33.

Author: Saks, A. M., and Ashforth, B. E.

Article: Proactive socialization and behavioral self-management.

Journal: *Journal of Vocational Behavior*, June 1996, *48*(3), 301–323.

Related Research: Hackman, J. R., & Oldham, G. R. (1980). *Work redesign*. Reading, MA: Addison-Wesley.

9229

Test Name: INTRINSIC MOTIVATION INVENTORY

Purpose: To measure intrinsic motivation in a sport setting.

Number of Items: 18

Format: Includes 4 subscales: Interest or Enjoyment, Perceived Competence, Effort or Importance, and Pressure or Tension.

Reliability: Alpha coefficients ranged from .65 to .83.

Author: Yoo, J.

Article: Motivational-behavioral correlates of goal orientation and perceived motivational climate in physical education's contexts.

Journal: *Perceptual and Motor Skills*, August 1999, *89*(1), 262–274.

Related Research: McAuley, E., et al. (1989). Psychometric properties of the Intrinsic Motivation Inventory in a sport setting: A confirmatory factor analysis. *Research Quarterly for Exercise and Sports*, 60, 48–58.

9230

Test Name: INTRINSIC MOTIVATION INVENTORY— REVISED

Purpose: To measure intrinsic motivation.

Format: Includes 3 subscales: Enjoyment/Interest, Effort/ Importance, and Pressure/ Tension. Examples are presented.

Reliability: Alpha coefficients ranged from .64 to .71.

Validity: Correlations with other variables ranged from −.03 to .62.

Author: Goudas, M.

Article: Motivational climate and

intrinsic motivation of young basketball players.

Journal: *Perceptual and Motor Skills*, February 1998, *86*(1), 323–327.

Related Research: McAuley, E., et al. (1989). Psychometric properties of the Intrinsic Motivation Inventory in a competitive sport setting: A confirmatory factor analysis. *Research Quarterly for Exercise and Sport*, 60, 48–58.

9231

Test Name: INTRINSIC MOTIVATION SCALE

Purpose: To measure an employee's intrinsic motivation to perform well.

Number of Items: 4

Reliability: Alpha coefficients were .90 and .91.

Validity: Correlations with the Work Locus of Control Scale ranged from −.13 to −.33.

Author: Macan, T. H., et al.

Article: Spector's Work Locus of Control Scale: Dimensionality and validity evidence.

Journal: *Educational and Psychological Measurement*, April 1996, *56*(2), 349–357.

Related Research: Lawler, E. E., & Hall, D. T. (1990). Relationship of job characteristics to job involvement, satisfaction, and intrinsic motivation. *Journal of Applied Psychology*, 54, 305–312.

9232

Test Name: INTRINSIC MOTIVATION SCALE

Purpose: To assess employee intrinsic motivation.

Number of Items: 6

Format: Scales range from 1 (strongly agree) to 5 (strongly disagree).

Reliability: Internal reliability was .77.

Validity: Correlations with other variables ranged from −.10 to .59.

Author: Wright, B. M., and Cordery, J. L.

Article: Production uncertainty as a contextual moderator of employee reactions to job design.

Journal: *Journal of Applied Psychology*, June 1999, *84*(3), 456–463.

Related Research: Warr, P. B. (1990). The measurement of well-being and other aspects of mental health. *Journal of Occupational Psychology*, *63*, 193–210.

9233

Test Name: INTRINSIC MOTIVATION SCALE

Purpose: To measure students' intrinsic motivation to learn.

Number of Items: 9

Format: Responses are made on a 7-point Likert scale ranging from 1 (strongly disagree) to 7 (strongly agree). A sample item is presented.

Reliability: Coefficient alpha was .96.

Validity: Correlations with other variables ranged from .24 to .69.

Author: Patrick, B. C., et al.

Article: "What's everybody so excited about?": The effects of teacher enthusiasm on student intrinsic motivation and vitality.

Journal: *Journal of Experimental Education*, Spring 2000, *68*(3), 217–236.

9234

Test Name: INTRINSIC MOTIVATION SCALE

Purpose: To measure intrinsic motivation.

Number of Items: 21

Format: Scales range from 1 (strongly disagree) to 7 (strongly agree). Sample items are presented.

Reliability: Internal consistency reliabilities ranged from .76 to .84.

Author: Steele-Johnson, D., et al.

Article: Goal orientation and task demand effects on motivation, affect, and performance.

Journal: *Journal of Applied Psychology*, October 2000, *85*(5), 724–738.

Related Research: McAuley, E., et al. (1991). Self-efficacy, perceptions of success, and intrinsic motivation for exercise. *Journal of Applied Social Psychology*, *21*, 139–155.

9235

Test Name: INTRINSIC READING MOTIVATION SCALE

Purpose: To measure intrinsic reading motivation.

Format: Includes Curiosity, Involvement, Strategy Use, Recognition, and Competition. Four-item response scales are used. All items are presented.

Reliability: Alpha coefficients ranged from .52 to .70.

Validity: Correlations with past achievement ranged from −.17 to .14.

Author: Guthrie, J. T., et al.

Article: Effects of integrated instruction on motivation and strategy use in reading.

Journal: *Journal of Educational*

Psychology, June 2000, *92*(2), 331–341.

Related Research: Wigfield, A., & Guthrie, J. T. (1997). Relations of children's motivation for reading to the amount and breadth of their reading. *Journal of Educational Psychology*, *89*, 420–433.

9236

Test Name: JOB DESIRE SCALE

Purpose: To assess the motivation to pursue police work.

Number of Items: 24

Format: Five-point Likert format. A sample item is presented.

Reliability: Coefficient alpha was .94.

Validity: Correlations with other variables ranged from −.13 to .60.

Author: Ryan, A. M., et al.

Article: Applicant self-selection: Correlates of withdrawal from a multiple a hurdle process.

Journal: *Journal of Applied Psychology*, April 2000, *85*(2), 163–179.

Related Research: Arvey, R. D., et al. (1990). Motivational components of test taking. *Personnel Psychology*, *43*, 695–716.

9237

Test Name: JOB MOTIVATION SCALE

Purpose: To measure job motivation.

Number of Items: 12

Format: Includes internal motivation and growth satisfaction. Responses are made on a 7-point scale ranging from 1 (disagree strongly) to 7 (agree strongly). Sample items are presented.

Reliability: Alpha coefficients ranged from .71 to .84.

Validity: Correlations with other variables ranged from −.12 to .75.

Author: Janz, B. D., et al.

Article: Knowledge worker team effectiveness: The role of autonomy, interdependence, team development, and contextual support variables.

Journal: *Personnel Psychology*, Winter 1997, *50*(4), 877–904.

Related Research: Hackman, J. R., & Oldham, G. R. (1975). Development of the job diagnostic survey. *Journal of Applied Psychology*, *60*, 159–170.

9238

Test Name: LEARNING AND PERFORMANCE GOAL ORIENTATION SCALES

Purpose: To measure learning and performance goal orientations.

Number of Items: 16

Format: Sample items are presented.

Reliability: Alpha coefficients ranged from .70 to .80.

Author: Phillips, J. M., and Gully, S. M.

Article: Role of goal orientation, ability, need for achievement, and locus of control in the self-efficacy and goal-setting process.

Journal: *Journal of Applied Psychology*, October 1997, *82*(5), 792–802.

Related Research: Button, S. B., et al. (1996). Goal orientation in organizational research: A conceptual and empirical foundation. *Organizational*

Behavior and Human Decision Processes, *67*, 26–48.

9239

Test Name: LEARNING GOAL ORIENTATION SCALE

Purpose: To measure learning goal orientation.

Number of Items: 9

Format: Scales range from 1 (strongly disagree) to 7 (strongly agree).

Reliability: Coefficient alpha was .84.

Validity: Correlations with other variables ranged from −.24 to .31.

Author: VandeWalle, D., et al.

Article: An integrated model of feedback-seeking behavior: Disposition, context, and cognition.

Journal: *Journal of Applied Psychology*, December 2000, *85*(6), 996–1003.

Related Research: Sujan, H., et al. (1994). Learning orientation, working smart, and effective selling. *Journal of Marketing*, *58*, 39–52.

9240

Test Name: LEARNING GOALS RELATED TO MATHEMATICS SCALES

Purpose: To measure learning goals related to mathematics.

Number of Items: 23

Format: Includes 3 subscales: Avoidance Goals, Mastery Goals, and Performance Goals.

Reliability: Alpha coefficients ranged from .73 to .90.

Author: Vezeau, C., et al.

Article: The impact of single-sex versus coeducational school

environment on girls' general attitudes, self-perceptions and performance in mathematics.

Journal: *Journal of Research and Development in Education*, Fall 2000, *34*(1), 49–59.

Related Research: Bouffard, T., et al. (1998). Elaboration et validation d'un instrument pour evaluer les buts des eleves, en contexte scolaire. *Revue Canadienne des Sciences due Comportement*, *30*, 203–206.

9241

Test Name: LEARNING MOTIVATION SCALE

Purpose: To measure learning motivation.

Number of Items: 5

Format: Five-point scales range from 1 (strongly disagree) to 5 (strongly agree). Sample items are presented.

Reliability: Coefficient alpha was .81.

Validity: Correlations with other variables ranged from −.40 to .62.

Author: Birdi, K., et al.

Article: Correlates and perceived outcomes of four types of employee development activity.

Journal: *Journal of Applied Psychology*, December 1997, *82*(6), 845–857.

Related Research: Warr, P. B., & Bunce, D. J. (1995). Trainee characteristics and the outcomes of open learning. *Personnel Psychology*, *48*, 347–375.

9242

Test Name: LEARNING PROCESS QUESTIONNAIRE

Purpose: To measure students'

motives and strategies for learning.

Number of Items: 36

Format: Includes 6 components. Responses are made on a 5-point scale ranging from 5 (always or almost always true of me) to 1 (never or rarely true of me).

Reliability: Alpha coefficients were .76 and .67.

Author: Dart, B. C., et al.

Article: Students' conceptions of learning, the classroom environment, and approaches to learning.

Journal: *Journal of Educational Research*, March/April 2000, 93(4), 262–270.

Related Research: Biggs, J. (1996). Enhancing teaching through constructive alignment. *Higher Education, 32*, 347–364.

9243

Test Name: LONG-TERM PERSONAL DIRECTION SCALE

Purpose: To identify one's long-term personal direction.

Number of Items: 20

Format: Responses are made on a 7-point scale ranging from 0 (not at all) to 6 (perfectly). Examples are presented.

Reliability: Alpha coefficients ranged from .80 to .87.

Author: Marko, K. W., and Savickas, M. L.

Article: Effectiveness of a career time perspective intervention.

Journal: *Journal of Vocational Behavior*, February 1998, 52(1), 106–119.

Related Research: Wessman, A. (1973). Personality and the subjective experience of time.

Journal of Personality Assessment, 37, 103–114.

9244

Test Name: MASTERY ORIENTATION SCALE

Purpose: To measure the importance of mastering a task.

Number of Items: 8

Format: Five-point scales are anchored by 1 (strongly disagree) and 5 (strongly agree). A sample item is presented.

Reliability: Coefficient alpha was .79.

Validity: Correlations with other variables ranged from −.06 to .31.

Author: Ford, J. K., et al.

Article: Relationships of goal orientation, metacognitive activity, and practice strategies with learning outcomes and transfer.

Journal: *Journal of Applied Psychology*, April 1998, 83(2), 218–233.

Related Research: Button, S. B., et al. (1996). The development and psychometric evaluation of learning goal and performance goal orientation. *Organizational Behavior and Human Decision Processes, 67*, 26–48.

9245

Test Name: MATH/SCIENCE GOALS SUBSCALE

Purpose: To identify middle school math/science goals.

Number of Items: 7

Format: Responses are made on a 6-point Likert scale. Sample items are presented.

Reliability: Internal consistency was .84.

Validity: Correlation with other variables ranged from −.47 to .02.

Author: Ferry, T. R., et al.

Article: The role of family context in a social cognitive model for career-related choice behavior: A math and science perspective.

Journal: *Journal of Vocational Behavior*, December 2000, 57(3), 348–364.

Related Research: Fouad, N., et al. (1995). Reliability and validity evidence for the Middle School Self-Efficacy Scale. *Measurement and Evaluation in Counseling and Development, 30*, 17–31.

9246

Test Name: ME AND MY READING SCALE

Purpose: To assess students' reading motivation and literacy behavior.

Number of Items: 15

Format: Includes Likert scale and forced-choice responses.

Reliability: Test-retest reliability was .68.

Author: Koskinen, P. S., et al.

Article: Book access, shared reading, and audio models: The effects of supporting the literacy learning of linguistically diverse students in school and at home.

Journal: *Journal of Educational Psychology*, March 2000, 92(1), 23–36.

Related Research: Gambrell, L. B. (1993). *The impact of Running Start on the reading motivation and behavior of first-grade children*. Unpublished manuscript, University of Maryland, National Reading Research Center.

9247

Test Name: MOTIVATED STRATEGIES FOR LEARNING QUESTIONNAIRE

Purpose: To assess positive motivational orientation, self-regulated strategy use, and test anxiety.

Number of Items: 81

Time Required: 30 minutes.

Format: Seven-point scales.

Reliability: Alpha coefficients ranged from .83 to .92.

Author: VanZile-Tamsen, C., and Livingston, J. A.

Article: The differential impact of motivation on the self-regulated strategy use of high- and low-achieving college students.

Journal: *Journal of College Student Development*, January/February 1999, *40*(1), 54–59.

Related Research: Pintrich, P. R., et al. (1991). *A manual for the use of the Motivated Strategies for Learning Questionnaire (MSLQ).* Ann Arbor, MI: National Center for Research to Improve Postsecondary Teaching and Learning.

9248

Test Name: MOTIVATION FOR PHYSICAL ACTIVITY MEASURE—REVISED

Purpose: To assess motives for participation in sport, exercise, or physical activity.

Number of Items: 32

Format: Reflects 5 motives for participation: Interest/Enjoyment motives, Skill Development motives, Fitness motives, Enhancement of Body Appearance, and Social motives.

Reliability: Interitem reliability ranged from .69 to .90.

Author: Frederick, C. M., et al.

Article: Motivation to participate, exercise affect, and outcome behaviors toward physical activity.

Journal: *Perceptual and Motor Skills*, April 1996, *82*(2), 691–701.

Related Research: Frederick, C. M., & Ryan, R. M. (1994). *Motivation for Physical Activity Measure—Revised.* Unpublished manuscript, University of Rochester, Rochester, New York.

9249

Test Name: MOTIVATION SOURCES INVENTORY

Purpose: To measure motivation in terms of intrinsic process, instrumental concerns, external self-concept, internal self-concept, and goal internalization.

Number of Items: 30

Format: Seven-point scales are anchored by (1) strongly disagree and (7) strongly agree. All items are presented.

Reliability: Alphas ranged from .83 to .92 across subscales.

Validity: Goodness of fit of the five subscales (nonorthogonal) was .92.

Author: Barbuto, J. E., Jr., and Scholl, R. W.

Article: Motivation Sources Inventory: Development and validation of new scales to measure an integrated taxonomy of motivation.

Journal: *Psychological Reports*, June 1998, *83*(2, Part I), 1011–1022.

9250

Test Name: MOTIVATION TO LEAD MEASURE

Purpose: To measure the motivation to lead.

Number of Items: 27

Format: Includes 3 factors: Affective-Identity, Social-Normative, and Noncalculative. Responses are made on a 5-point Likert-type scale ranging from "strongly disagree" to "strongly agree." Examples are presented.

Reliability: Alpha coefficients ranged from .74 to .92.

Validity: Correlations with other variables ranged from −.17 to .36.

Author: Chan, K.-Y., et al.

Article: The relation between vocational interests and the motivation to lead.

Journal: *Journal of Vocational Behavior*, October 2000, *57*(2), 226–245.

Related Research: Chan, K. (1999). *Toward a theory of individual differences and leadership: Understanding the motivation to lead.* Unpublished doctoral dissertation, University of Illinois at Urbana-Champaigne.

9251

Test Name: MOTIVATION TO LEARN SCALE

Purpose: To measure motivation to learn.

Number of Items: 3

Format: Seven-point scales range from 1 (strongly disagree) to 7 (strongly agree). A sample item is presented.

Reliability: Coefficient alphas ranged from .75 to .83.

Validity: Correlations with other variables ranged from −.21 to .65.

Author: Colquitt, J. A., and Simmering, M. J.

Article: Conscientiousness, goal orientation, and motivation to learn during the learning process: A longitudinal study.

Journal: *Journal of Applied Psychology,* August 1998, *83*(4), 654–665.

Related Research: Noe, R. A., & Schmitt, N. (1986). The influence of learner attitudes on training effectiveness: Test of a model. *Personnel Psychology, 39,* 497–523.

9252

Test Name: MOTIVATIONAL BELIEF SCALES

Purpose: To measure motivational beliefs.

Number of Items: 14

Format: Includes 3 scales: Self-Efficacy, Task Value, and Test Anxiety. Responses are made on a 7-point Likert scale ranging from 1 (strongly disagree) to 7 (strongly agree). Sample items are presented.

Reliability: Alpha coefficients ranged from .75 to .90.

Author: Pintrich, P. R.

Article: Multiple goals, multiple pathways: The role of goal orientation in learning and achievement.

Journal: *Journal of Educational Psychology,* September 2000, *92*(3), 544–555.

Related Research: Pintrich, P. R., & DeGroot, E. V. (1990). Motivational and self-regulated learning components of classroom academic performance. *Journal of Educational Psychology, 82,* 33–40.

9253

Test Name: MOTIVATIONAL STRATEGIES SCALES

Purpose: To measure two motivational strategies.

Number of Items: 9

Format: Includes 2 scales: Self-Handicapping and Risk Taking. Responses are made on a 7-point scale ranging from 1 (strongly disagree) to 7 (strongly agree). Sample items are presented.

Reliability: Alpha coefficients ranged from .50 to .62.

Author: Pintrich, P. R.

Article: Multiple goals, multiple pathways: The role of goal orientation in learning and achievement.

Journal: *Journal of Educational Psychology,* September 2000, *92*(3), 544–555.

Related Research: Clifford, M. (1988). Failure tolerance and academic risk-taking in ten-to-twelve-year-old students. *British Journal of Educational Psychology, 58,* 15–27.

9254

Test Name: MOTIVATIONAL STRUCTURAL QUESTIONNAIRE—CZECH VERSION

Purpose: To assess a person's joys, hopes, anxieties, goals and disappointments.

Number of Items: 33

Reliability: Most items have 9-point response scales.

Validity: Correlations between subscales ranged from −.78 to .57.

Author: Man, F., et al.

Article: Motivational structures of alcoholic and non-alcoholic Czech men.

Journal: *Psychological Reports,* June 1998, *82*(3, Part II), 1091–1106.

Related Research: Klinger, E., et al. (1965). The Motivational Structure Questionnaire. In J. P. Allen (Ed.), *Assessing alcohol problems: A guide for clinicians and researchers* (pp. 399–411). Bethesda, MD: National Institute on Alcohol Abuse and Alcoholism.

9255

Test Name: MOTIVES FOR USING COCAINE SCALE

Purpose: To assess sociability, emotionality, and the fun and excitement of using cocaine.

Number of Items: 15

Format: Five-point scales are anchored by "never" and "always."

Reliability: Alphas ranged from .77 to .85 across subscales.

Author: Ward, L. C., et al.

Article: Psychometric assessment of motives for using cocaine in men with substance abuse disorders.

Journal: *Psychological Reports,* February 1997, *80*(1), 189–190.

Related Research: Cooper, M. L., et al. (1992). Development and validation of a three-dimensional measure of drinking motives. *Psychological Assessment, 4,* 123–132.

9256

Test Name: NEED FOR ACHIEVEMENT SCALE

Purpose: To measure the motive to achieve.

Number of Items: 31

Format: Nine-point scales anchored by (−4) very strong disagreement and (+4) very strong agreement.

Reliability: Alphas ranged from

.90 to .92. Test-retest reliability (15 days) was .64.

Validity: Correlations with other variables ranged from −.52 to .74.

Author: Spratt, C. L., et al.

Article: Silencing the self and sex as predictors of achievement motivation.

Journal: *Psychological Reports*, February 1998, *82*(1), 259–263.

Related Research: Mehrabian, A., & Bank, L. (1978). A questionnaire measure of individual differences in achieving tendency. *Educational and Psychology Measurement*, *29*, 445–451.

9257

Test Name: NEED FOR COGNITION SCALE—SHORT FORM

Purpose: To measure tendencies to seek challenging intellectual experiences and to enjoy the pursuit of knowledge.

Number of Items: 18

Format: Responses are made on a 9-point scale ranging from 1 (strongly disagree) to 9 (strongly agree). An example is presented.

Reliability: Coefficient alpha was .90.

Author: Klaczynski, P. A.

Article: Motivated scientific reasoning biases, epistemological beliefs, and theory polarization: A two-process approach to adolescent cognition.

Journal: *Child Development*, September/October 2000, *71*(5), 1347–1366.

Related Research: Cacioppo, J. T., & Petty, R. E. (1982). The need for cognition. *Journal of Personality and Social Psychology*, *42*, 116–131.

9258

Test Name: OFF-TASK MENTAL EFFORT SCALE

Purpose: To measure the amount of off-task mental effort.

Number of Items: 13

Format: Responses are made on a 5-point Likert-type scale ranging from ''strongly agree'' to ''strongly disagree.'' A sample item is presented.

Reliability: Internal consistency reliability was .87.

Validity: Correlations with other variables ranged from −.48 to .34.

Author: Fisher, S. L., and Ford, J. K.

Article: Differential effects of learner effort and goal orientation on two learning outcomes.

Journal: *Personnel Psychology*, Summer 1998, *51*(2), 397–420.

Related Research: Kanfer, R., et al. (1994). Goal setting, conditions of practice, and task performance: A resource allocation perspective. *Journal of Applied Psychology*, *79*, 826–835.

9259

Test Name: ON-LINE MOTIVATION QUESTIONNAIRE— SHORTENED VERSION

Purpose: To obtain students' perceptions about relevant aspects of the learning situation during actual learning tasks.

Number of Items: 22

Format: Includes the topics Subjective Competence, Task Attraction, Personal Relevance, Learning Intention, and Attributions. Responses are made on 4-point scales. All items are presented.

Reliability: Alpha coefficients ranged from .72 to .86.

Author: Vermeer, H. J., et al.

Article: Motivational and gender differences: Sixth-grade students' mathematical problem-solving behavior.

Journal: *Journal of Educational Psychology*, June 2000, *92*(2), 308–315.

Related Research: Boekaerts, M. (1987). Situation specific judgments of a learning task versus overall measures of motivational orientation. In E. De Corte et al. (Eds.), *Learning and instruction* (pp. 169–179). Oxford, England: Pergamon Press; and Leuven, Belgium: Leuven University Press.

9260

Test Name: PARATELIC DOMINANCE SCALE

Purpose: To measure the degree to which individuals are oriented to the ongoing experience of behavior (not to goals).

Number of Items: 30

Format: True/false format.

Reliability: Alpha was .76.

Author: Turner, S., and Heskin, K.

Article: Metamotivational dominance and use of tobacco and alcohol among adolescents.

Journal: *Psychological Reports*, August 1998, *83*(1), 307–315.

Related Research: Apter, M. J. (1982). *The experience of motivation: The theory of psychological reversals*. London: Academic Press.

9261

Test Name: PARTICIPATION MOTIVATION QUESTIONNAIRE

Purpose: To assess children's motives for involvement in sport.

Number of Items: 30

Format: Responses are made on a 3-point scale ranging from 1 (not at all important) to 3 (very important). Examples are presented.

Reliability: Alpha coefficients ranged from .78 to .90.

Author: Kirkby, R. J., et al.

Article: Participation motives of young Australian and Chinese gymnasts.

Journal: *Perceptual and Motor Skills*, April 1999, *88*(2), 363–373.

Related Research: Gill, D. L., et al. (1983). Participation motivation in youth sport. *International Journal of Sport Psychology*, *14*, 1–14.

9262

Test Name: PERCEIVED MOTIVATIONAL CONTEXT SCALE

Purpose: To assess perceived teacher, peer, and economic contexts.

Number of Items: 75

Format: Includes 3 factors: Teacher Context, Peer Context, and Economic Context. Responses are made on a 5-point scale ranging from 1 (agree) to 5 (disagree). Items are presented.

Validity: Correlations with other variables ranged from −.36 to .44.

Author: Murdock, T. B.

Article: The social context of risk: Status and motivational

predictors of alienation in middle school.

Journal: *Journal of Educational Psychology*, March 1999, *91*(1), 62–75.

Related Research: Murdock, T. B. (1994). *Understanding alienation: Towards ecological perspectives on student motivation*. Unpublished doctoral dissertation, University of Delaware, Newark.

9263

Test Name: PERCEPTION OF SUCCESS QUESTIONNAIRE

Purpose: To measure goal orientations.

Format: Includes two subscales: Task Orientation and Ego Orientation.

Reliability: Alpha coefficients ranged from .48 to .82.

Validity: Correlations with other variables ranged from −.04 to .49.

Author: Pensgaard, A. M.

Article: The dynamics of motivation and perceptions of control when competing in the Olympic games.

Journal: *Perceptual and Motor Skills*, August 1999, *89*(1), 116–125.

Related Research: Roberts, G. C., et al. (1998). Achievement goals in sport: Development and validation of the Perception of Success Questionnaire. *Journal of Sports Sciences*, *16*, 337–347.

9264

Test Name: PERCEPTION OF SUCCESS QUESTIONNAIRE

Purpose: To assess habitual achievement and goal dispositions.

Number of Items: 12

Format: Scales range from 1 (strongly disagree) to 5 (strongly agree). A sample item is presented.

Reliability: Alpha coefficients ranged from .77 to .86 over two subscales.

Authors: Ryska, T. A., and Yin, Z.

Article: Dispositional and situational goal orientations as discriminators among recreational and competitive league athletes.

Journal: *Journal of Social Psychology*, June 1999, *139*(3), 335–342.

Related Research: Treasure, D. C., & Roberts, G. C. (1994). Cognitive and affective concomitants of task and ego orientation during the middle school years. *Journal of Sport and Exercise Psychology*, *16*, 15–28.

9265

Test Name: PERSISTENCE MEASURE

Purpose: To assess persistence.

Number of Items: 4

Format: Responses are made on a 6-point scale ranging from "strongly disagree" to "strongly agree." All items are presented.

Reliability: Coefficient alpha was .63.

Validity: Correlations with other variables ranged from −.36 to .62.

Author: Dai, D. Y.

Article: To be or not to be (challenged), that is the question: Task and ego orientation among high-ability, high-achieving adolescents.

Journal: *Journal of Experimental*

Education, Summer 2000, *68*(4), 311–330.

Related Research: Dai, D. Y., & Feldhusen, J. F. (1996). Goal orientations of gifted students. *Gifted and Talented International, 11*, 84–88.

9266

Test Name: PERSISTENT EFFORT TEST

Purpose: To measure persistence.

Number of Items: Twelve- and 6-item versions.

Format: Each item consists of 6-letter randomly arranged nonsense words. The 6 letters originally formed words selected from a Swedish dictionary. The subject is to rearrange the letters of each nonsense word to form as many words as possible.

Reliability: Alpha coefficients were .86 (12-item version) and .87 (6-item version).

Validity: Correlations with other variables were .69 (12-item version) and .71 (6-item version).

Author: Gustafson, R., and Norlander, T.

Article: Psychometric properties of a paper-and-pencil test measuring the personality trait of persistence.

Journal: *Perceptual and Motor Skills*, December 1996, *83*(3) Part 1, 979–986.

9267

Test Name: PERSONAL GOAL ORIENTATION SCALE

Purpose: To measure personal goal orientation.

Number of Items: 11

Format: Includes 2 scales: Mastery and Performance. Responses are made on a 7-point Likert scale ranging from 1 (strongly disagree) to 7 (strongly agree). Sample items are presented.

Reliability: Alpha coefficients were .70 and .76.

Author: Pintrich, P. R.

Article: Multiple goals, multiple pathways: The role of goal orientation in learning and achievement.

Journal: *Journal of Educational Psychology*, September 2000, *92*(3), 544–555.

Related Research: Midgley, C., et al. (1998). The development and validation of scales assessing students' achievement goal orientations. *Contemporary Educational Psychology, 23*, 113–131.

9268

Test Name: PERSONAL GOALS SCALE

Purpose: To assess how well defined personal job goals are regarded.

Number of Items: 4

Format: Scales range from 1 (almost never) to 5 (almost always). Sample items are presented.

Reliability: Coefficient alpha was .79.

Validity: Correlations with other variables ranged from −.11 to .40.

Author: O'Neill, B. S., and Mone, M. A.

Article: Investigating equity sensitivity as a moderator of relations between self-efficacy and workplace attitudes.

Journal: *Journal of Applied Psychology*, October 1998, *83*(5), 805–816.

Related Research: Locke, E. A., & Latham, G. P. (1990). *A theory of goal setting and task performance*. Englewood Cliffs, NJ: Prentice-Hall.

9269

Test Name: PERSONAL GROWTH INITIATIVE SCALE

Purpose: To measure an individual's active engagement in the process of self-change.

Number of Items: 9

Format: Responses are made on a Likert-type scale ranging from 1 (definitely disagree) to 6 (definitely agree).

Reliability: Internal consistency estimates ranged from .78 to .90. Test-retest (over 8 weeks) reliability was .74.

Validity: Correlations with other variables ranged from −.30 to .51.

Author: Robitschek, C., and Keshubeck, S.

Article: A structural model of parental alcoholism, family functioning, and psychological health: The mediating effects of hardiness and personal growth orientation.

Journal: *Journal of Counseling Psychology*, April 1999, *46*(2), 159–172.

Related Research: Robitschek, C. (1998). Personal growth initiative: The construct and its measure. *Measurement and Evaluation in Counseling and Development, 30*, 183–198.

9270

Test Name: PRECOLLEGE ACADEMIC MOTIVATION SCALE

Purpose: To measure motivation to work hard on academic tasks.

Number of Items: 8

Format: Scales range from 5 (strongly agree) to 1 (strongly disagree). Sample items are presented.

Reliability: Internal consistency reliability was .65.

Author: Pascarella, E., et al.

Article: Effects of teacher organization/preparation and teacher skill/clarity on general cognitive skills in college.

Journal: *Journal of College Student Development*, January/February 1996, *37*(1), 7–19.

Related Research: Ball, S. (Ed.). (1977). *Motivation in education.* New York: Academic Press.

9271

Test Name: PROFIT-DRIVEN SCALE

Purpose: To measure profit-driven behavior.

Number of Items: 3

Format: Responses are made on a 5-point Likert scale ranging from 1 (strongly disagree) to 5 (strongly agree).

Reliability: Coefficient alpha was .63.

Validity: Correlations with other variables ranged from −.30 to .38.

Author: Wallace, J. E.

Article: It's about time: A study of hours worked and work spillover among law firm lawyers.

Journal: *Journal of Vocational Behavior*, April 1997, *50*(2), 227–248.

9272

Test Name: READING MOTIVES SCALE

Purpose: To measure the motivation to read.

Number of Items: 43

Format: Five-point scales are anchored by (5) very interested and (1) not interested at all. All items are described.

Reliability: Alphas ranged from .49 to .84 across subscales.

Author: Halvari, H., and White, C.

Article: Effects of reading motivation on the belief in and consumption of newspapers among youth.

Journal: *Psychological Reports*, December 1997, *81*(3, Part I), 899–914.

Related Research: Halvari, H. (1991). The Reading Motives Scale (RMS). Oslo: Unpublished report.

9273

Test Name: REASONS FOR EXERCISE INVENTORY

Purpose: To measure the importance of each motive for exercise.

Number of Items: 25

Format: Includes 4 factors: Fitness/Health Management, Appearance/Weight Management, Stress/Mood Management, and Socializing.

Reliability: Alpha coefficients ranged from .73 to .91.

Author: Smith, B. L., et al.

Article: Sex differences in exercise motivation and body-image satisfaction among college students.

Journal: *Perceptual and Motor Skills*, April 1998, *86*(2), 723–732.

Related Research: Silberstein, L. R., et al. (1988). Behavioral and psychological implications of body dissatisfaction: Do men and women differ? *Sex Roles, 19,* 219–232.

9274

Test Name: SALESPERSON GOAL ORIENTATION SCALE

Purpose: To measure learning goal and performance goal orientation.

Number of Items: 11

Format: Scales ranged from 1 (strongly disagree) to 7 (strongly agree). All items are presented.

Reliability: Coefficients alpha were .74 (learning) and .81 (performance).

Validity: Correlations with other variables ranged from .01 to .44.

Author: VandeWalle, D., et al.

Article: The influences of goal orientation and self-regulation tactics on sales performance: A longitudinal field test.

Journal: *Journal of Applied Psychology*, April 1999, *84*(2), 249–259.

Related Research: Sujan, H., et al. (1994). Learning orientation, working smart, and effective selling. *Journal of Marketing, 58,* 39–52.

9275

Test Name: SCHOOL ACHIEVEMENT MOTIVATION RATING SCALE

Purpose: To measure achievement motivation for Grades K–12.

Number of Items: 15

Format: Responses are made on a 5-point scale ranging from "always" to "never."

Reliability: Alpha coefficients ranged from .61 to .90 (*n* ranged from 19 to 201). Test-retest (6–8 weeks) reliability ranged from .79 to .98 (*n* ranged from 17 to 27).

Validity: Correlations with variables ranged from .30 to .90 (*n* ranged from 15 to 85). Correlations with measures of motivation ranged from −.30 to .56 (*n* ranged from 9 to 50).

Author: Chiu, L.-H.

Article: Development and validation of the School Achievement Motivating Rating Scale.

Journal: *Educational and Psychological Measurement,* April 1997, *57*(2), 292–305.

9276

Test Name: SELF-EXPRESSION INVENTORY

Purpose: To measure goal instability and superiority.

Number of Items: 20

Format: Scales range from 1 (strongly agree) to 6 (strongly disagree).

Reliability: Internal consistencies ranged from .76 to .77. Test-retest reliabilities ranged from .76 to .80.

Validity: Correlations with other variables ranged from −.08 to .51.

Author: Perosa, S. L., and Perosa, L. M.

Article: Intergenerational family theory and Kohut's self-psychology constructs applied to college females.

Journal: *Journal of College Student Development,* March/April 1997, *38*(2), 143–156.

Related Research: Robbins, S., & Patton, M. (1985). Self-psychology and career development: Construction of the Superiority and Goal Instability Scales. *Journal of Counseling Psychology, 32,* 221–231.

9277

Test Name: SELF-MOTIVATION INVENTORY

Purpose: To measure level of self-motivation.

Number of Items: 40

Format: A self-report with a range from 40 to 200.

Reliability: Internal consistency was .86. Test-retest reliabilities were .92 (1 month) and .86 (over 20 weeks).

Author: Annesi, J. J.

Article: Effects of minimal exercise and cognitive behavior identification on adherence, emotional change, self-image, and physical change in obese women.

Journal: *Perceptual and Motor Skills,* August 2000, *91*(1), 322–336.

Related Research: Dishman, R. K., & Gettman, L. R. (1980). Psychobiologic influence on exercise adherence. *Journal of Sport Psychology, 2,* 295–310.

9278

Test Name: SERVICE ETHIC SCALE

Purpose: To assess to what degree individuals are committed to volunteer work and community service.

Number of Items: 10

Format: Scales ranged from 1 (strongly disagree) to 5 (strongly agree). All items are presented.

Reliability: Coefficient alpha was .92.

Validity: Correlations with other variables ranged from .29 to .41.

Authors: Tang, T. L.-P., and Weatherford, E. J.

Article: Perception of enhancing self-worth through service: The

development of a service ethic scale.

Journal: *Journal of Social Psychology,* December 1998, *138*(6), 734–743.

9279

Test Name: SEX INTEREST SCALE

Purpose: To measure preoccupation and interest in sex.

Number of Items: 7

Format: Response scales are anchored by ''strongly disagree'' and ''strongly agree.'' All items are presented.

Reliability: Alpha was .75.

Validity: Correlations with other variables ranged from −.27 to .57.

Author: Murstein, B. I., and Tuerkheimer, A.

Article: Gender differences in love, sex, and motivations for sex.

Journal: *Psychological Reports,* April 1998, *82*(2), 435–450.

9280

Test Name: SITUATIONAL MOTIVATION SCALE

Purpose: To measure intrinsic and extrinsic motivation.

Number of Items: 16

Format: Sample items are presented.

Reliability: Alpha coefficients ranged from .73 to .89 across subscales.

Validity: Correlations with other variables ranged from −.30 to .75.

Authors: Kowal, J., and Fortier, M. S.

Article: Motivational determinants of flow: Contributions from self-determination theory.

Journal: *Journal of Social Psychology*, June 1999, *139*(3), 355–368.

Related Research: Guay, F., & Vallerand, R. J. (1995). *The Situational Motivation Scale*. Paper presented at the annual convention of the American Psychological Society, New York.

9281

Test Name: SPORT FAN MOTIVATION SCALE

Purpose: To assess sport fan motivation.

Number of Items: 23

Format: Includes 8 subscales: Eustress, Self-Esteem, Escape, Entertainment, Economics, Aesthetic Value, Group Affiliation, and Family Needs.

Reliability: Alpha coefficients ranged from .65 to .87.

Author: Wann, D. L., et al.

Article: An exploratory investigation of the relationship between sport fans' motivation and race.

Journal: *Perceptual and Motor Skills*, June 1999, *88*(3) Part 2, 1081–1084.

Related Research: Wann, D. L. (1995). Preliminary validation of the Sport Fan Motivation Scale. *Journal of Sport and Social Issues*, *19*, 377–396.

9282

Test Name: SPORT ORIENTATION QUESTIONNAIRE

Purpose: To measure individual differences in approaches to competitive sport.

Number of Items: 25

Format: Includes 3 scales: Competitiveness, Desire to Win in Sport, and Desire to Achieve Personal Goals in Sport. Responses are made on a 5-point Likert scale.

Reliability: Internal consistencies were .73 and .94.

Author: Meyer, B. B.

Article: The ropes and challenge course: A quasi-experimental examination.

Journal: *Perceptual and Motor Skills*, June 2000, *90*(3) Part 2, 1249–1257.

Related Research: Gill, D. L., & Deeter, T. E. (1988). Development of the Sport Orientation Questionnaire. *Research Quarterly for Exercise and Sport*, *59*, 191–202.

9283

Test Name: STUDENT ASPIRATIONS SURVEY

Purpose: To measure the level of student aspirations.

Number of Items: 98

Format: Includes 13 scales. Responses are made on a 4-point scale ranging from 1 (strongly agree) to 4 (strongly disagree).

Reliability: Alpha coefficients ranged from .65 to .86.

Author: Plucker, J. A., and Quaglia, R. J.

Article: The Student Aspirations Survey: Assessing student effort and goals.

Journal: *Educational and Psychological Measurements*, April 1998, *58*(2), 252–257.

Related Research: University of Maine. (1994). *Student aspirations: A decade of inquiry, 1984–1994*. Orono: Center for Research and Evaluation, College of Education, University of Maine.

9284

Test Name: STUDENT MOTIVATION SCALE

Purpose: To assess state motivation.

Number of Items: 12

Format: Seven-point scales are anchored by 1 (strongly disagree) and 7 (strongly agree).

Reliability: Alpha was .93.

Author: Myers, S. A., and Rocca, K. A.

Article: Students' state motivation and instructors' use of verbally aggressive messages.

Journal: *Psychological Reports*, August 2000, *87*(1), 291–294.

Related Research: Christophel, D. M. (1990). The relationship among teacher immediacy behaviors, student motivation, and learning. *Communication Education*, *37*, 233–240.

9285

Test Name: STUDENT MOTIVATIONS FOR ATTENDING SCHOOL

Purpose: To assess motivations to attend school.

Number of Items: 23

Format: Scales range from 0 (strongly disagree) to 6 (strongly agree). All items are presented.

Reliability: Alpha coefficients ranged from .66 to .80.

Validity: Correlations with other variables ranged from −.37 to .40.

Author: Côté, J. E., and Levine, C.

Article: Student motivation, learning environments, and

human capital acquisition: Toward an integrated paradigm of student development.

Journal: *Journal of College Student Development*, May/June 1997, *38*(3), 229–243.

9286

Test Name: STUDENTS' COMMITMENT TO LEARN MATHEMATICS SCALES

Purpose: To assess students' commitment to learn mathematics.

Number of Items: 25

Format: Includes 3 scales: Effectance Motivation, Cognitive Strategies, and Metacognitive Strategies.

Reliability: Alpha coefficients ranged from .71 to .80.

Author: Vezeau, C., et al.

Article: The impact of single-sex versus coeducational school environment on girls' general attitudes, self-perceptions and performance in mathematics.

Journal: *Journal of Research and Development in Education*, Fall 2000, *34*(1), 49–59.

Related Research: Pintrick, P. R., & DeGroot, E. V. (1990). Motivational and self-regulated learning components of classroom academic performance. *Journal of Educational Psychology*, *82*, 33–40.

9287

Test Name: TASK AND EGO IN SPORT QUESTIONNAIRE

Purpose: To measure achievement by ascertaining sport participants' goal orientation in competitive sport contexts.

Number of Items: 13

Format: Includes 2 subscales: Inclination Toward Task and Ego Involvement in Sport. Responses are made on a 5-point Likert scale ranging from 1 (strongly disagree) to 5 (strongly agree). Examples are presented.

Reliability: Alpha coefficients were .78 and .81. Test-retest (3 weeks) reliabilities were .68 and .75.

Author: Stephens, D. E., et al.

Article: Goal orientation and ratings of perceived exertion in graded exercises testing of adolescents.

Journal: *Perceptual and Motor Skills*, June 2000, *90*(3) Part 1, 813–822.

Related Research: Duda, J. L., & Whitehead, J. (1998). Measurement of goal perspectives in the physical domain. In J. L. Duda (Ed.), *Advances in sport and exercise psychology measurement* (pp. 21–48). Morgantown, WV: Fitness Information Technology.

9288

Test Name: TASK-ORIENTATION MEASURE

Purpose: To measure task orientation.

Number of Items: 4

Format: Responses are made on a 6-point Likert-type scale ranging from "strongly agree" to "strongly disagree." All items are presented.

Reliability: Coefficient alpha was .80.

Validity: Correlations with other variables ranged from −.19 to .49.

Author: Dai, D. Y.

Article: To be or not to be (challenged), that is the question: Task and ego orientation among

high-ability, high-achieving adolescents.

Journal: *Journal of Experimental Education*, Summer 2000, *68*(4), 311–330.

Related Research: Nichols, J. G. (1989). *The competitive ethos and democrative education*. Cambridge, MA: Harvard University Press.

9289

Test Name: TELIC-PARATELIC ORIENTATION SCALE

Purpose: To measure telic-paratelic orientation.

Number of Items: 4

Format: Items are bipolar. Responses are made on a 6-point scale.

Reliability: Alpha coefficients were .86 and .92.

Author: Hudson, J., and Bates, M. D.

Article: Factors affecting metamotivational reversals during motor task performance.

Journal: *Perceptual and Motor Skills*, October 2000, *91*(2), 373–384.

Related Research: Cook, M. R., et al. (1993). Instruments for the assessment of reversal theory states. *Patient Education and Counseling*, *22*, 99–106.

9290

Test Name: TRAINING MOTIVATION SCALE

Purpose: To measure training motivation.

Number of Items: 8

Format: Responses are made on a 5-point scale ranging from 1 (strongly agree) to 5 (strongly disagree). All items are presented.

Reliability: Coefficient alpha was .94.

Validity: Correlations with other variables ranged from −.40 to .24.

Author: Kossek, E. E., et al.

Article: Career self-management: A quasi-experimental assessment of the effects of a training intervention.

Journal: *Personnel Psychology*, Winter 1998, *51*(4), 935–962.

Related Research: Noe, R. A., & Schmitt, N. (1986). The influence of trainee attitude on training effectiveness: Test of a model. *Personnel Psychology, 39,* 497–523.

9291

Test Name: VALANCE, INSTRUMENTALITY AND EXPECTANCY MOTIVATION SCALE

Purpose: To measure test-taking motivation.

Number of Items: 10

Format: Scales range from 1 (strongly disagree) to 5 (strongly agree). All items are presented.

Reliability: Alpha coefficients ranged from .86 to .94 across subscales.

Validity: Correlations with other variables ranged from .07 to .37.

Author: Sanchez, R. J., et al.

Article: Development and examination of an expectancy-based measure of test-taking motivation.

Journal: *Journal of Applied Psychology*, October 2000, *85*(5), 739–750.

9292

Test Name: VALENCE SCALE

Purpose: To assess valence.

Number of Items: 3

Format: Scales range from 1 (very undesirable) to 7 (very desirable). All items are presented.

Reliability: Coefficient alphas ranged from .63 to .64.

Validity: Correlations with other variables ranged from −.11 to .69.

Author: Colquitt, J. A., and Simmering, M. J.

Article: Conscientiousness, goal orientation, and motivation to learn during the learning process: A longitudinal study.

Journal: *Journal of Applied Psychology*, August 1998, *83*(4), 654–665.

Related Research: Lawler, E. E., & Suttle, J. L. (1973). Expectancy theory and job behavior. *Organizational Behavior and Human Decision Processes, 9,* 482–503.

9293

Test Name: WORK DIMENSIONS SCALE

Purpose: To measure parental self-direction in the workplace.

Number of Items: 20

Format: Four-point scales. Sample items are presented.

Reliability: Alpha coefficients ranged from .84 to .89.

Validity: Correlations with other variables ranged from −.20 to .18.

Author: McHale, S. M., et al.

Article: Step in or stay out? Parents' roles in adolescent siblings' relationships.

Journal: *Journal of Marriage and the Family*, August 2000, *62*(3), 746–760.

Related Research: Lennon, M. C.

(1994). Women, work, and well-being. *Journal of Health and Social Behavior, 35,* 235–247.

9294

Test Name: WORK EFFORT SCALE

Purpose: To assess the tendency to work long and hard as a means of achieving success.

Number of Items: 10

Format: Seven-point scales ranged from "strongly agree" to "strongly disagree." All items are presented.

Reliability: Alpha coefficients ranged from .82 to .86 across subscales.

Author: Brown, S. P., and Leigh, T. W.

Article: A new look at psychological climate and its relationship to job involvement, effort, and performance.

Journal: *Journal of Applied Psychology*, August, 1996, *81*(4), 358–368.

Related Research: Naylor, J. C., et al. (1980). *A theory of behavior in oganizations*. New York: Academic Press.

9295

Test Name: WORK MOTIVATION QUESTIONNAIRE

Purpose: To measure work motivation.

Number of Items: 20

Format: Seven-point rating scales range from 3 (I strongly agree) to −3 (I strongly disagree).

Reliability: Split-half reliability was .82.

Author: Kamalanabhan, T. J., et al.

Article: A Delphi study of

motivational profile of scientists in research and development organizations.

Journal: *Psychological Reports*, December 1999, *85*(3, Part I), 743–749.

Related Research: Luthans, F. (1989). *Organizational behavior*. New York: McGraw-Hill.

9296

Test Name: WORK PREFERENCE INVENTORY

Purpose: To assess intrinsic and extrinsic motivation.

Number of Items: 30

Format: Includes 2 scales: Intrinsic Motivation and Extrinsic Motivation. Examples are presented.

Validity: Correlations with other variables ranged from −.33 to .62.

Author: Davidson, W. B., et al.

Article: Development and validation of scores on a measure of six academic orientations in college students.

Journal: *Educational and Psychological Measurement*, August 1999, *59*(4), 678–693.

Related Research: Amabile, T. A., et al. (1994). The Work Preference Inventory: Assessing intrinsic and extrinsic motivational orientations. *Journal of Personality and Social Psychology, 66*, 950–967.

CHAPTER 16
Perception

9297

Test Name: ACADEMIC ABILITY SCALE

Purpose: To measure general feelings of self-esteem regarding school performance.

Number of Items: 5

Format: Responses are made on a 7-point Likert scale.

Reliability: Alpha coefficients were .76 and .77.

Validity: Correlations with other variables ranged from −.34 to .43.

Author: Hamer, R. J., and Bruch, M. A.

Article: Personality factors and inhibited career development: Testing the unique contribution of shyness.

Journal: *Journal of Vocational Behavior*, June 1997, *50*(3), 382–400.

Related Research: Fleming, J. S., & Whalen, D. J. (1990). The Personal and Academic Self-Concept Inventory: Factor structure and gender differences in high school and college samples. *Educational and Psychological Measurement, 50,* 957–967.

9298

Test Name: ACADEMIC LOCUS OF CONTROL SCALE

Purpose: To determine college students' academic locus of control.

Number of Items: 28

Format: True-false format.

Reliability: Alpha coefficients ranged from .68 to .70.

Validity: Correlation with foreign language achievement was −.08.

Author: Onwuegbuzie, A. J., et al.

Article: Cognitive, affective, personality, and demographic predictors of foreign-language achievement.

Journal: *Journal of Educational Research*, September/October 2000, *94*(1), 3–15.

Related Research: Trice, A. (1985). An academic locus of control scale for college students. *Perceptual and Motor Skills, 61,* 1043–1046.

9299

Test Name: ACADEMIC SELF-CONCEPT SCALE

Purpose: To index the general academic facets of college students' self-concept.

Number of Items: 40

Format: Responses are made on a 4-point scale ranging from 1 (strongly disagree) to 4 (strongly agree). Sample items are presented.

Reliability: Coefficient alpha was .92. Test-retest (2 weeks) reliability was .88.

Validity: Correlations with other variables ranged from .20 to .77.

Author: Lent, R. W., et al.

Article: Discriminant and predictive validity of academic self-concept, academic self-efficacy, and mathematics-specific self-efficacy.

Journal: *Journal of Counseling Psychology*, July 1997, *44*(3), 307–315.

Related Research: Reynolds, W. M. (1988). Measurement of academic self-concept in college students. *Journal of Personality Assessment, 52,* 223–240.

9300

Test Name: ACADEMIC SELF-DESCRIPTION QUESTIONNAIRE—ADAPTED

Purpose: To assess writing self-concept.

Number of Items: 6

Format: Responses are made on a 6-point scale ranging from 1 (definitely false) to 6 (definitely true). A sample item is presented.

Reliability: Coefficient alpha was .86.

Author: Pajares, F., et al.

Article: Gender differences in writing self-beliefs of elementary school students.

Journal: *Journal of Educational Psychology*, March 1999, *91*(1), 50–61.

Related Research: Marsh, H. W. (1990). The structure of academic self-concept: The Marsh-Shavelson model. *Journal of Educational Psychology, 82,* 623–636.

9301

Test Name: ACADEMIC SELF-EFFICACY SCALE

Purpose: To measure how confident an individual is in his or her ability to perform an academic task.

Number of Items: 36

Format: Nine-point Likert-type scales.

Reliability: Alpha coefficients ranged from .91 to .92 across two subscales.

Author: Elias, S. M., and Loomis, R. J.

Article: Using an academic self-efficacy scale to address university major persistence.

Journal: *Journal of College Student Development*, July/August 2000, *41*(4), 450–454.

Related Research: Lent, R. W., et al. (1986). Self-efficacy in the prediction of academic performance in perceived career options. *Journal of Counseling Psychology, 33*, 265–269.

9302

Test Name: ADULT NOWICKI–STRICKLAND INTERNAL–EXTERNAL CONTROL SCALE

Purpose: To measure locus of control.

Number of Items: 40

Format: Yes/no format.

Reliability: Internal consistency reliabilities ranged from .71 to .84. Test-restest reliabilities ranged from .88 (6 weeks) to .70 (1 year).

Authors: Nowicki, S., Jr., et al.

Article: Physical fitness as a function of psychological and situational factors.

Journal: *Journal of Social Psychology*, October 1997, *137*(5), 549–588.

Related Research: Nowicki, S., Jr. (1991). *A manual for the Nowicki–Strickland Internal–External Control Scale.* Atlanta: Department of Psychology, Emory University.

9303

Test Name: AFFECT SUBSCALE

Purpose: To measure the emotional aspect of the perception of environmental risks.

Number of Items: 10

Format: A subscale of the Ecology Scale. Contains 10 items. Each item is answered "true" or "false." Examples are presented.

Reliability: Alpha coefficients were .80 and .72.

Validity: Correlations with other variables ranged from .24 to .63.

Author: Der-Karabetian, A., et al.

Article: Environmental risk perception, activism and world-mindedness among samples of British and U.S. college students.

Journal: *Perceptual and Motor Skills*, October 1996, *83*(2), 451–462.

Related Research: Maloney, M. P., et al. (1975). A revised measurement of ecological attitudes and knowledge. *American Psychologist, 30*, 787–790.

9304

Test Name: AFFIRMATIVE COUNSELING BEHAVIORS SURVEY

Purpose: To assess counselors' perceptions of their affirmative behaviors with all clients and with clients who identify as gay, lesbians, or bisexual.

Number of Items: 30

Format: Includes 2 subscales: Affirmative Behaviors with GLB clients and Affirmative Behaviors with All clients. Responses are made on a 5-point scale ranging from 1 (almost never true) to 5 (almost always true).

Reliability: Alpha coefficients were .95 and .84.

Validity: Correlations with other variables ranged from −.24 to .42.

Author: Bieschke, K. J., and Matthews, C.

Article: Career counselor attitudes and behaviors toward gay, lesbian, and bisexual clients.

Journal: *Journal of Vocational Behavior*, April 1996, *48*(2), 243–255.

9305

Test Name: AGE IDENTITY MEASURE

Purpose: To measure age-related social identities.

Number of Items: 12

Format: Five-point Likert format.

Reliability: Internal consistency reliability was .72.

Author: Finkelstein, L. M., and Burke, M. J.

Article: Age stereotyping at work: The roles of rater and contextual factors on evaluations of job applicants.

Journal: *Journal of General Psychology*, October 1998, *125*(4), 317–345.

Related Research: Jackson, S. E. (1981). Measurement of commitment to role identities. *Journal of Personality and Social Psychology, 40*, 138–146.

9306

Test Name: AGENTIC AND COMMUNAL RATING SCALES

Purpose: To assess the agentic and communal attribute of a target subject.

Number of Items: 17

Format: Five-point rating scales. All attributes are presented.

Reliability: Alpha was .69 for the agentic scale and .88 for the communal scale.

Author: Martasian, P. J., and Goldstein, S. B.

Article: Students' beliefs about animal researchers as a function of researcher's sex.

Journal: *Psychological Reports*, December 1997, *81*(3, Part I), 803–811.

Related Research: Deaux, K., & Lewis, L. L. (1984). Structure of gender stereotypes: Interrelationships among components and general label. *Journal of Personality and Social Psychology, 46*, 991–1004.

9307

Test Name: AIDS-PREVENTIVE SELF-EFFICACY SCALE

Purpose: To assess confidence in engaging in safe-sex behavior.

Number of Items: 22

Format: Scales range from 1 (very sure) to 5 (not at all sure).

Reliability: Alpha coefficients ranged from .76 to .81.

Author: Sands, T., et al.

Article: Prevention of health-risk behaviors in college students: Evaluating seven variables.

Journal: *Journal of College Student Development*, July/August 1998, *39*(4), 331–342.

Related Research: Kasen, S., et al. (1992). Self-efficacy for AIDS preventive behaviors among 10th grade students. *Health Education Quarterly, 19*, 187–202.

9308

Test Name: ALCOHOL ABSTINENCE SELF-EFFICACY SCALE

Purpose: To assess alcohol abstinence self-efficacy.

Number of Items: 20

Format: Five-point Likert format.

Reliability: Alpha coefficients ranged from .81 to .92.

Author: Sands, T., et al.

Article: Prevention of health-risk behaviors in college students: Evaluating seven variables.

Journal: *Journal of College Student Development*, July/August 1998, *39*(4), 331–342.

Related Research: DiClemente, C., et al. (1994). The Alcohol Abstinence Self-Efficacy Scale. *Journal of Studies on Alcohol, 55*, 141–148.

9309

Test Name: ARTS SELF-PERCEPTION INVENTORY

Purpose: To provide a measure of arts self-perception.

Number of Items: 40

Format: Includes 4 subscales: Music, Visual Art, Dance, and Drama. Responses are made on a 6-point scale ranging from 1 (false) to 6 (true).

Reliability: Reliability coefficients were all .92.

Validity: Correlations with other variables ranged from −.007 to .500.

Author: Marsh, H. W., and Roche, L. A.

Article: Structure of artistic self-concepts for performing arts and non-performing arts students in a performing arts high school: "Setting the stage" with multigroup confirmatory factor analysis.

Journal: *Journal of Educational Psychology*, September 1996, *88*(3), 461–477.

Related Research: Vispoel, W. P. (1993). The development and validation of the Arts Self-Perception Inventory for Adolescents. *Educational and Psychological Measurement, 53*, 1023–1033.

9310

Test Name: ARTS SELF-PERCEPTION INVENTORY

Purpose: To measure perceptions of skill in music, visual art, dance, and dramatic art.

Number of Items: 48

Format: Includes subscales of music, art, dance, and drama.

Reliability: Alpha coefficients ranged from .95 to .96.

Validity: Correlations with other variables ranged from −.16 to .37.

Author: Vispoel, W. P.

Article: The development and validation of the Arts Self-Perception Inventory for Adults.

Journal: *Educational and Psychological Measurement*, August 1996, *56*(4), 719–735.

9311

Test Name: ASPECTS OF IDENTITY QUESTIONNAIRE–III

Purpose: To measure college student identity.

Number of Items: 31

Format: Responses are made on a 5-point scale ranging from 1 (not important to my sense of who I am) to 5 (extremely important to my sense of who I am).

Reliability: Coefficient alpha was .70.

Author: Dollinger, S. J.

Article: Autophotographic identities of young adults: With special references to alcohol, athletics, achievement, religion, and work.

Journal: *Journal of Personality Assessment*, October 1996, *67*(2), 384–398.

Related Research: Cheek, J. M. (1989). Identity orientations and self-interpretation. In D. M. Buss & N. Cantor (Eds.), *Personality psychology: Recent trends and emerging directions* (pp. 275–285). New York: Springer-Verlag.

9312

Test Name: ASSESSMENT OF ACADEMIC SELF-CONCEPT AND MOTIVATION SCALE

Purpose: To measure academic self-concept and motivation.

Number of Items: 80

Format: Scales range from 1 (very capable) to 7 (not very capable). All items are described.

Reliability: Alpha coefficients ranged from .80 to .94 across subscales.

Author: Rouse, K. A. G., and Cashin, S. E.

Article: Assessment of academic self-concept: Results from three ethnic groups.

Journal: *Measurement and Evaluation in Counseling and Development*, July 2000, *33*(2), 91–102.

Related Research: Gordon, K. A. (1995). *The assessment of*

academic self-concept and motivation. Unpublished manuscript, Ohio State University.

9313

Test Name: ASSESSMENT OF ATTRIBUTIONS FOR CAREER DECISION-MAKING SCALE

Purpose: To assess an individual's attributional style associated with the process of making career decisions.

Number of Items: 9

Format: Includes three factors: controllability, stability, and causality. Responses are made on a 5-point Likert scale ranging from 1 (strongly disagree) to 5 (strongly agree). Examples are presented.

Reliability: Alpha coefficients ranged from .64 to .89.

Validity: Correlations with other variables ranged from −.46 to .56.

Author: Luzzo, D. A., and Jenkins-Smith, A.

Article: Development and initial validation of the assessment of attributions for career decision-making.

Journal: *Journal of Vocational Behavior*, April 1998, *52*(2), 224–245.

9314

Test Name: ATHLETIC COPING SKILLS INVENTORY–28

Purpose: To measure athletes' perceptions regarding their reactions in typical situations in practice and competition.

Number of Items: 28

Format: Includes 7 factors: Coping with Adversity, Peaking Under Pressure, Goal Setting/

Mental Preparation, Concentration, Freedom From Worry, Confidence and Achievement Motivation, and Coachability. Responses are made on a 6-point scale ranging from 1 (never) to 6 (always).

Reliability: Alpha coefficients ranged from .54 to .81.

Author: Goudas, M., et al.

Article: Psychological skills in basketball: Preliminary study for development of a Greek form of the Athletic Coping Skills Inventory–28.

Journal: *Perceptual and Motor Skills*, February 1998, *86*(1), 59–65.

Related Research: Smith, R. E., et al. (1995). Development and validation of a multidimensional measure of sport specific psychological skills: The Athletic Coping Skills Inventory–28. *Journal of Sport and Exercise Psychology*, 17, 379–398.

9315

Test Name: ATHLETIC IDENTITY MEASUREMENT SCALE

Purpose: To measure the strength and exclusivity of identification with the athlete role.

Number of Items: 10

Format: Responses are made on a 7-point Likert-type scale ranging from "strongly disagree" to "strongly agree."

Reliability: Coefficient alpha was .93. Test-retest (2 weeks) reliability was .89.

Validity: Correlations with other variables ranged from −.06 to .79.

Author: Brown, C., and Glastetter-Fender, C.

Article: Psychosocial identity and

career control in college student-athletes.

Journal: *Journal of Vocational Behavior*, February 2000, *56*(1), 53–62.

Related Research: Brewer, B. W., et al. (1993). Athletic identity: Hercules' muscles or Achilles' heel? *International Journal of Sport Psychology, 24*, 237–254.

9316

Test Name: ATTACHMENT AND OBJECT RELATIONS INVENTORY

Purpose: To measure internal representations of significant others and views of the self as worthy of acceptance.

Number of Items: 60

Format: Includes 6 factors: Peers, Parents, Independent, Partners, Close, and Secure. Responses are made on a 5-point scale ranging from 1 (not at all like me) to 5 (very much like me).

Reliability: Alpha coefficients ranged from .70 to .91.

Validity: Correlations with other variables ranged from −.55 to .46.

Author: Buelow, G., et al.

Article: A new measure for an important construct: The Attachment and Object Relation Inventory.

Journal: *Journal of Personality Assessment*, June 1996, *66*(3), 604–623.

9317

Test Name: ATTITUDE SCALE

Purpose: To measure self-confidence.

Number of Items: 18

Format: Includes 4 factors: Overall Self-Confidence,

Reluctance to Give Up, Confidence in One's Ability to Act Independently, and Confidence in One's Life Course.

Reliability: Coefficient alpha was .81.

Author: Johnson, W., and McCoy, N.

Article: Self-confidence, self-esteem, and assumption of sex role in young men and women.

Journal: *Perceptual and Motor Skills*, June 2000, *90*(3) Part 1, 751–756.

Related Research: Garant, V., et al. (1995). Development and validation of a self-confidence scale. *Perceptual and Motor Skills, 81*, 401–402.

9318

Test Name: ATTRIBUTION OF MOTIVE SCALE

Purpose: To measure attribution of motive to altruistic and instrumental causes.

Number of Items: 12

Format: Five-point scales are anchored by 1 (strongly disagree) and 5 (strongly agree).

Reliability: Coefficient alpha was .83 (altruistic) and .89 (instrumental).

Validity: Correlations with other variables ranged from −.59 to .76.

Author: Allen, T. D., and Rush, M. C.

Article: The effects of organizational citizenship behavior on performance judgments: A field study and a laboratory experiment.

Journal: *Journal of Applied Psychology*, April 1998, *83*(2), 247–260.

9319

Test Name: ATTRIBUTIONAL SCALES

Purpose: To assess the dimensions of expectancy, causality, stability, and emotionality.

Number of Items: 46

Format: Includes 4 parts: Expectancy, Causality, Stability, and Emotionality. Responses are made on 8- and 9-point scales. Examples are presented.

Reliability: Alpha coefficients ranged from .39 to .91.

Validity: Correlations with other variables ranged from −.37 to .16

Author: Dunn, A., and Eliot, J.

Article: An exploratory study of undergraduates' attributions of success or failure on spatial tests.

Journal: *Perceptual and Motor Skills*, October 1999, *89*(2), 695–702.

Related Research: Badros, K. (1988). *Weiner's attribution theory and perceived success and failure in clinical second-year nursing students*. Unpublished dissertation, University of Maryland at College Park.

Roach, D. (1991). *Spatial ability and attribution of success and failure among art students*. Unpublished dissertation, University of Maryland at College Park.

9320

Test Name: ATTRIBUTIONAL STYLE QUESTIONNARIE

Purpose: To measure individual tendencies to select explanation for positive and negative events in terms of three dimensions: internal or external, stable or unstable, and global or specific.

Format: Self-report format.

Reliability: Reliabilities ranged from .44 to .75.

Validity: Correlations with other variables ranged from −.24 to .65.

Author: Ladd, E. R., et al.

Article: Narcissism and causal attribution.

Journal: *Psychological Reports*, February 1997, *80*(1), 171–178.

Related Research: Peterson, C., et al. (1982). The Attributional Style Questionnaire. *Cognitive Therapy and Research, 6*, 287–300.

9321

Test Name: ATTRIBUTIONAL STYLE QUESTIONNAIRE

Purpose: To measure explanatory style.

Number of Items: 12

Format: Responses are made on a 7-point summated scale. An example is presented.

Reliability: Interitem consistency was reported to be in the range of .75.

Author: Davis, H., IV, and Zaichkowsky, L.

Article: Explanatory style among elite ice hockey athletes.

Journal: *Perceptual and Motor Skills*, December 1998, *87*(3) Part 1, 1075–1080.

Related Research: Peterson, C., & Seligman, M. E. P. (1984). Causal explanations as a risk factor for depression: Theory and evidence. *Psychological Review, 91*, 347–374.

9322

Test Name: ATTRIBUTIONAL STYLE QUESTIONNAIRE

Purpose: To assess explanatory style.

Number of Items: 14

Format: Three 7-point response scales provide self-ratings on internality, collectivity, and globality.

Reliability: Alpha coefficients ranged from .80 to .87.

Authors: Kao, E. M., et al.

Article: Explanatory style, family expressiveness, and self-esteem among Asian American and European American college students.

Journal: *Journal of Social Psychology*, June 1997, *137*(4), 435–444.

Related Research: Peterson, C., & Villanova, P. (1988). An expanded Attributional Style Questionnaire. *Cognitive Therapy and Research, 6*, 287–299.

9323

Test Name: ATTRIBUTIONAL STYLE QUESTIONNAIRE

Purpose: To measure attributional style.

Number of Items: 36

Format: Includes 3 factors: Locus, Stability, and Globality, with a composite.

Reliability: Alpha coefficients ranged from .34 to .73.

Author: Higgins, H. C., et al.

Article: Construct validity of attributional style: Modeling context-dependent item sets in the Attributional Style Questionnaire.

Journal: *Educational and Psychological Measurement*, October 1999, *59*(5), 804–820.

Related Research: Peterson, C., et al. (1982). The Attributional Style Questionnaire. *Cognitive Therapy and Research, 6*, 287–300.

9324

Test Name: ATTRIBUTIONAL STYLE QUESTIONNAIRE

Purpose: To measure causal explanations attributed to six negative and six positive hypothetical events.

Number of Items: 48

Format: Seven-point rating scales ranged from 1 (external, unstable, or specific) to 7 (internal, stable, or global).

Reliability: Alpha was .74.

Validity: Correlations with other variables ranged from −.18 to .17.

Author: Johnson, J. G., et al.

Article: Attributional style, self-esteem and human immunodeficiency virus: A test of the hopelessness and self-esteem theories of depression.

Journal: *Journal of Psychopathology and Behavioral Assessment*, March 2000, *22*(1), 23–46.

Related Research: Seligman, M. E. P., et al. (1979). Depressive attributional style. *Journal of Abnormal Psychology, 88*, 242–247.

9325

Test Name: ATTRIBUTIONS RESPONSIBILITY SCALE

Purpose: To measure client's responsibility for the cause of and solution to the client's problems.

Number of Items: 6

Format: Includes 2 scales: Cause and Solution. Responses are made on a 7-point scale ranging from 1 (not at all) to 7 (very much).

Reliability: Internal consistencies ranged from .80 to .88 (Cause scale) and from .61 to .79 (Solution scale). Test-retest (2 weeks) reliabilities were .86 (Cause scale) and .70 (Solution scale).

Validity: Correlations with other variables ranged from −.49 to .36.

Author: Hayes, J. A., and Erkis, A. J.

Article: Therapist homophobia, client sexual orientation, and source of client HIV infection as predictors of therapist reactions to clients with HIV.

Journal: *Journal of Counseling Psychology*, January 2000, *47*(1), 71–78.

Related Research: Karuza, J., et al. (1990). Models of helping and coping, responsibility attributions, and well-being in community elderly and their helpers. *Psychology and Aging*, *5*, 194–208.

9326

Test Name: AUGMENTED SELF-EFFICACY FOR SELF-REGULATED LEARNING SCALE

Purpose: To assess self-regulated and other-directed regulation of learning.

Number of Items: 33

Format: Five-point Likert format. All items are presented.

Reliability: Alpha coefficients ranged from .68 to .87 across subscales.

Validity: Correlations between factors ranged from −.48 to .46.

Author: Gredler, M. E., and Garavalia, L. S.

Article: Students' perceptions of their self-regulatory and other-directed study strategies: A factor analysis.

Journal: *Psychological Reports*, February 2000, *86*(1), 102–108.

Related Research: Gredler, M. E., & Schwartz, L. (1997). Factorial structure of the Self-Efficacy for Self-Regulated Learning Scale. *Psychological Reports*, *81*, 51–57.

9327

Test Name: BODY AREAS SATISFACTION SCALE

Purpose: To identify satisfaction with specific physical attributes.

Number of Items: 8

Format: Responses are made on a 1 to 5 scale.

Reliability: Coefficient alpha was .80.

Author: Smith, B. L., et al.

Article: Sex differences in exercise motivation and body-image satisfaction among college students.

Journal: *Perceptual and Motor Skills*, April 1998, *86*(2), 723–732.

Related Research: Cash, T. F. (1989). Body-image affect: Gestalt versus summing the parts. *Perceptual and Motor Skills*, *69*, 17–18.

9328

Test Name: BODY-CATHEXIS SCALE

Purpose: To measure body satisfaction in terms of overall appearance and skin color.

Number of Items: 48

Format: Five-point Likert format.

Reliability: Coefficient alpha was .91.

Authors: Sahay, S., and Piran, N.

Article: Skin-color preference and body satisfaction among South Asian-Canadian and European-Canadian female university students.

Journal: *Journal of Social Psychology*, April 1997, *137*(2), 161–171.

Related Research: Secord, P. F., & Jourard, S. M. (1953). The appraisal of body cathexis: Body-cathexis and the self. *Journal of Consulting Psychology*, *17*, 343–347.

9329

Test Name: BODY CONSCIOUSNESS QUESTIONNAIRE—FARSI VERSION

Purpose: To measure cerebral palsied children's body consciousness.

Number of Items: 11

Format: Includes 2 factors: Private Body Consciousness and Public Body Consciousness. Responses are made on a 5-point scale ranging from 1 (extremely uncharacteristic) to 5 (extremely characteristic). All items are presented.

Reliability: Reliability was .64.

Author: Dadkhah, A.

Article: Body consciousness in DOHSA-HOU, a Japanese psychorehabilitative program.

Journal: *Perceptual and Motor Skills*, April 1998, *86*(2), 411–417.

Related Research: Miller, L. C., et al. (1981). Consciousness of body: Private and public. *Journal of Personality and Social Psychology*, *41*, 397–406.

9330

Test Name: BODY DISSATISFACTION SCALE

Purpose: To measure satisfaction with one's body.

Number of Items: 9

Format: Six-point scales are anchored by 1 (never) and 6 (always).

Reliability: Alpha was .90.

Author: Stice, E., et al.

Article: Support for the continuity hypothesis of bulimic pathology.

Journal: *Journal of Consulting and Clinical Psychology*, October 1998, *66*(5), 784–790.

Related Research: Garner, D. M., et al. (1983). Development and validation of a multidimensional eating disorder inventory for anorexia nervosa and bulimia. *International Journal of Eating Disorders*, *2*, 15–34.

9331

Test Name: BODY ESTEEM SCALE

Purpose: To assess body esteem among adolescents.

Number of Items: 32

Format: Includes 3 subscales that address specific components of body esteem separately for males and females. Responses are made on a 5-point Likert scale.

Reliability: Alpha coefficients ranged from .82 to .94.

Validity: Correlations with other variables ranged from −.24 to .53.

Author: Cecil, H., and Stanley, M. A.

Article: Reliability and validity of adolescents' scores on the Body Esteem Scale.

Journal: *Educational and*

Psychological Measurement, April 1997, *57*(2), 340–356.

Related Research: Frawzoi, S. L., & Shields, S. A. (1984). The Body-Esteem Scale: Multidimensional structure and sex differences in a college population. *Journal of Personality Assessment*, *48*, 173–178.

9332

Test Name: BODY ESTEEM SCALE

Purpose: To assess body image attitudes.

Number of Items: 35

Format: Responses are made on a 5-point scale ranging from 1 (have strong negative feelings) to 5 (have strong positive feelings).

Reliability: Alpha coefficients ranged from .78 to .90. Test-retest reliabilities were .85 (3 weeks) to .93 (3 months).

Validity: Correlations with other variables ranged from −.60 to .80.

Author: Mazzeo, S. E.

Article: Modification of an existing measure of body image preoccupation and its relationship to disordered eating in female college students.

Journal: *Journal of Counseling Psychology*, January 1999, *46*(1), 42–30.

Related Research: Franzoi, S. L., & Shields, S. A. (1984). The Body Esteem Scale: Multidimensional structure and sex differences in a college population. *Journal of Personality Assessment*, *48*, 173–178.

9333

Test Name: BODY ESTEEM SCALE—FEMALES

Purpose: To measure body esteem.

Number of Items: 35

Format: Includes 3 subscales: Sexual Attractiveness, Weight Concern, and Physical Condition. Responses are made on a 5-point scale ranging from 1 (I have strong negative feelings) to 5 (I have strong positive feelings).

Reliability: Alpha coefficients ranged from .78 to .87.

Author: Wiggins, M. S., and Moode, F. M.

Article: Analysis of body esteem in female college athletes and nonathletes.

Journal: *Perceptual and Motor Skills*, June 2000, *90*(3) Part 1, 851–854.

Related Research: Franzoi, S. L., & Shields, S. A. (1984). The Body Esteem Scale: Multidimensional structure and sex differences in a college population. *Journal of Personality Assessment*, *48*, 173–178.

9334

Test Name: BODY IMAGE AFFECT SCALE

Purpose: To measure affect associated with negative body image.

Number of Items: 6

Format: Five-point Likert format. Items are described.

Reliability: Cronbach alpha was .84.

Validity: Correlation with Coping Humor Scale was −.21.

Author: Campbell, M. E., and Chow, P.

Article: Preliminary development of the Body Image Affect Scale.

Journal: *Psychological Reports*, April 2000, *86*(2), 539–540.

9335

Test Name: BODY PARTS SATISFACTION SCALE

Purpose: Measures degree of satisfaction persons have with various parts of their bodies.

Number of Items: 24

Format: Responses are made on a 6-point scale ranging from 1 (extremely dissatisfied) to 6 (extremely satisfied).

Reliability: Alpha coefficients ranged from .89 to .93.

Validity: Correlations with other variables ranged from −.44 to .49.

Author: Lester, R., and Petrie, T. A.

Article: Physical, psychological, and societal correlates of bulimic symptomatology among African American college women.

Journal: *Journal of Counseling Psychology*, July 1998, *45*(3), 315–321.

Related Research: Mintz, L. B., & Betz, N. E. (1988). Prevalence and correlates of eating disordered behaviors among undergraduate women. *Journal of Counseling Psychology, 35,* 463–471.

9336

Test Name: BODY SELF-CONSCIOUSNESS QUESTIONNAIRE

Purpose: To assess self-consciousness about one's own body.

Number of Items: 25

Format: Five-point scales are anchored by 1 (extremely

uncharacteristic) and 5 (extremely characteristic).

Reliability: Internal consistencies ranged from .45 to .83.

Author: Wegner, B. S., et al.

Article: Effect of exposure to photographs of thin models on self-consciousness in female college students.

Journal: *Psychological Reports*, June 2000, *86*(3, Part 2), 1149–1154.

Related Research: Miller, L. C., et al. (1981). Consciousness of body: Private and public. *Journal of Personality and Social Psychology, 41,* 397–406.

9337

Test Name: BODY SHAPE QUESTIONNAIRE

Purpose: To assess body image preoccupations.

Number of Items: 34

Format: Responses are made on a 6-point scale ranging from 1 (never) to 6 (always). Examples are presented.

Reliability: Internal consistency was .93 and .97. Test-retest (3 weeks) reliabilities were .88 and .91.

Validity: Correlations with other variables ranged from −.76 to .80.

Author: Mazzeo, S. E.

Article: Modification of an existing measure of body image preoccupation and its relationship to disordered eating in female college students.

Journal: *Journal of Counseling Psychology*, January 1999, *46*(1), 42–50.

Related Research: Cooper, P. J., et al. (1987). The development and validation of the Body Shape Questionnaire. *International*

Journal of Eating Disorders, 6, 485–494.

9338

Test Name: BODY VIGILANCE SCALE

Purpose: To assess attentional focus to internal bodily sensations.

Number of Items: 19

Format: Ten- and 100-point rating scales are used. All items are presented.

Reliability: Alphas ranged from .58 to .69 across samples.

Validity: Correlations with other variables ranged from −.17 to .53.

Author: Schmidt, N. B., et al.

Article: Body vigilance in panic disorder: Evaluating attention to bodily pertubations.

Journal: *Journal of Consulting and Clinical Psychology*, April 1997, *65*(2), 214–220.

9339

Test Name: BRIEF INDEX OF SELF-ACTUALIZATION

Purpose: To measure self-actualization.

Number of Items: 40

Reliability: Internal consistency was .87. Test-retest (2 weeks) reliability was .89.

Validity: Correlations with other variables ranged from .32 to .79.

Author: Sumerlin, J. R., and Bundrick, C. M.

Article: Happiness and self-actualization under conditions of strain: A sample of homeless men.

Journal: *Perceptual and Motor Skills*, February 2000, *90*(1), 191–203.

Related Research: Sumerlin, J. R., & Bundrick, C. M. (1996). Brief Index of Self-Actualization: A measure of Maslow's model. *Journal of Social Behavior and Personality, 11,* 253–271.

9340

Test Name: BRIEF INDEX OF SELF-ACTUALIZATION— REVISED

Purpose: To measure the construct of self-actualization as proposed by Moslow.

Number of Items: 32

Format: Includes 4 factors: Core Self-Actualization, Autonomy, Openness to Experience, and Comfort with Solitude. All items are presented.

Reliability: Coefficient alpha was .86.

Author: Sumerlin, J. R., and Bundrick, C. M.

Article: Revision of the Brief Index of Self-Actualization.

Journal: *Perceptual and Motor Skills,* August 1998, *87*(1), 115–123.

Related Research: Sumerlin, J. R. (1995). Adaptation to homelessness: Self-actualization, loneliness, and depression in street homeless men. *Psychological Reports, 77,* 295–314.

9341

Test Name: BRONSTEIN–CRUZ CHILD/ADOLESCENT SELF-CONCEPT AND ADJUSTMENT SCALE—REVISED

Purpose: To assess self-esteem, self-evaluation, and interpersonal competence.

Number of Items: 40

Format: Includes 5 subscales: Self-Evaluation, Sense of Mastery, Social and Peer Relations, Family Relations, and Emotional Well-being and Distress. Responses are made on a 4-point scale ranging from 1 (that's very true about me) to 4 (that's not at all true about me). An example is presented.

Reliability: Alpha coefficients ranged from .50 to .85.

Validity: Correlations with other variables ranged from −.16 to .60.

Author: Brookins, C. C.

Article: Exploring psychological task resolution and self-concept among African-American adolescents.

Journal: *Perceptual and Motor Skills,* June 1996, *82*(3) Part 1, 803–810.

Related Research: Bronstein, P., et al. (1987) *A measure of child and adolescent self-concept and psychological adjustment.* Paper presented at the annual meeting of the American Psychological Association, New York.

9342

Test Name: BROWN LOCUS OF CONTROL SCALE

Purpose: To measure locus of control.

Number of Items: 25

Format: Includes 3 dimensions: Internal, External Social, and External Other. Responses are made on a 6-point Likert-type scale ranging from "strongly agree" to "strongly disagree." All items are presented.

Reliability: Test-retest (2 weeks) reliability was .90. Alpha coefficients ranged from .77 to .87.

Author: Brown, R.

Article: A cross-cultural comparison of the Brown Locus of Control scale.

Journal: *Educational and Psychological Measurement,* October 1996, *56*(6), 858–863.

Related Research: Brown, R. (1990). The construct and concurrent validity of the social dimension of the Brown Locus of Control scale. *Educational and Psychological Measurement, 50,* 377–382.

9343

Test Name: CAPACITY ABILITY SCALE

Purpose: To assess children's perceptions of their competence.

Number of Items: 6

Format: Responses are made on a 4-point scale ranging from 1 (not at all) to 4 (very true). Sample items are presented.

Author: Miserandino, M.

Article: Children who do well in school: Individual differences in perceived competence and autonomy in school-average children.

Journal: *Journal of Educational Psychology,* June 1996, *88*(2), 203–214.

Related Research: Skinner, E. S., et al. (1990). What it takes to do well in school and whether I've got it: The role of perceived contrast in children's engagement and school achievement. *Journal of Educational Psychology, 82,* 22–32.

9344

Test Name: CAREER CONFIDENCE SCALE

Purpose: To measure career self-efficacy beliefs.

Number of Items: 5

Format: Responses are made on a 5-point Likert scale.

Reliability: Coefficient alpha was .93. Internal consistency coefficient was .93.

Author: O'Brien, K. M.

Article: The influence of psychological separation and parental attachment on the career development of adolescent women.

Journal: *Journal of Vocational Behavior*, June 1996, *48*(3), 257–274.

Related Research: Fassinger, R. E. (1990). Causal models of career choice in two samples of college women. *Journal of Vocational Behavior*, *36*, 225–248.

9345

Test Name: CAREER CONFIDENCE SCALE (CHINESE VERSION)

Purpose: To assess self-efficacy for decision-making about careers. Subscales are Readiness Confidence, Self-Assessment Confidence, Implementation Confidence, Information-Seeking Confidence, and Deciding Confidence.

Number of Items: 40

Reliability: Alpha was .77. Test-retest reliability (1 month) was .74.

Validity: Correlations with other variables ranged from .20 to .50.

Author: Peng, H.

Article: Comparison of two counseling approaches to enhancing confidence in planning careers by undecided Taiwanese college women.

Journal: *Psychological Reports*, October 2000, *87*(2), 667–674.

Related Research: Pickering,

J. W., et al. (1992). *Career Confidence Scale*. Old Dominion University, Norfolk, VA 23529.

9346

Test Name: CAREER COUNSELING SELF-EFFICACY SCALE

Purpose: To indicate one's current level of confidence in performing activities related to career counseling.

Number of Items: 25

Format: Responses are made on a 5-point scale ranging from 0 (not confident) to 4 (highly confident). Includes 4 factors: Therapeutic Process and Alliance Skills, Vocational Assessment and Interpretation Skills, Multicultural Competency Skills, and Current Trends in the World of Work, Ethics, and Career Research. All items are presented.

Reliability: Alpha coefficients ranged from .55 to .97.

Validity: Correlations with other variables ranged from .21 to .72.

Author: O'Brien, K. M., et al.

Article: The Career Counseling Self-Efficacy Scale: Instrument development and training applications.

Journal: *Journal of Counseling Psychology*, January 1997, *44*(1), 20–31.

9347

Test Name: CAREER DECISION-MAKING OUTCOME EXPECTANCIES AND EXPLORATORY INTENTIONS

Purpose: To measure perceived relevance of education and its usefulness in career decision making.

Number of Items: 14

Format: Scales range from 1 (strongly disagree) to 5 (strongly agree). All items are presented.

Reliability: Alpha coefficients ranged from .73 to .79 across subscales.

Validity: Correlations with indecision ranged from −.25 to .25.

Author: Betz, N. E., and Voyten, K. K.

Article: Efficacy and outcome expectations influence career exploration and decidedness.

Journal: *Career Development Quarterly*, December 1997, *46*(2), 179–189.

Related Research: Fouad, N. A., & Smith, P. (1996). Test of a social cognitive model for middle school students: Math and science. *Journal of Counseling Psychology*, *43*, 338–346.

9348

Test Name: CAREER DECISION-MAKING SELF-EFFICACY SCALE

Purpose: To assess self-efficacy percepts with regard to career decision making.

Number of Items: 50

Format: Includes 5 subscales: Goal Selection, Gathering Occupational Information, Problem Solving, Planning, and Self-Appraisal. Responses are made on a 10-point scale ranging from 0 (no confidence) to 9 (complete confidence).

Reliability: Alpha coefficients ranged from .86 to .97.

Validity: Correlations with other variables ranged from −.51 to .46.

Author: Giauakos, I.

Article: Patterns of career choice

and career decision-making self-efficacy.

Journal: *Journal of Vocational Behavior*, April 1999, *54*(2), 244–258.

Related Research: Taylor, K. M., & Betz, N. E. (1983). Applications of self-efficacy theory to the understanding and treatment of career indecision. *Journal of Vocational Behavior*, *22*, 63–81.

9349

Test Name: CAREER DECISION-MAKING SELF-EFFICACY SCALE—SHORT FORM

Purpose: To measure one's degree of belief that one can successfully complete tasks necessary for making career decisions.

Number of Items: 25

Format: Includes 5 subscales: Self-Appraisal, Gathering Occupational Information, Selecting Goals, Making Plans, and Solving Problems. Responses are made on a 10-point confidence continuum ranging from 1 (no confidence at all) to 10 (complete confidence).

Reliability: Alpha coefficients ranged from .69 to .93.

Validity: Correlations with other variables ranged from −.53 to .53.

Author: Betz, N. E., and Voyten, K. K.

Article: Efficacy and outcome expectations influence career exploration and decidedness.

Journal: *Career Development Quarterly*, December 1997, *46*(2), 179–189.

Related Research: Taylor, K. M., & Popma, J. (1990). Construct validity of the Career Decision-Making Self-Efficacy Scale and the relationship of CDMSE to

vocational indecision. *Journal of Vocational Behavior*, *37*, 17–31.

9350

Test Name: CAREER EXPECTATIONS SCALE

Purpose: To measure one's perception of one's ability to progress in the organization.

Number of Items: 6

Format: Responses are made on a 5-point scale ranging from 1 (strongly disagree) to 5 (strongly agree). An example is presented.

Reliability: Coefficient alpha was .77.

Validity: Correlations with other variables ranged from .19 to .34.

Author: Scandura, T. A.

Article: Mentoring and organizational justice: An empirical investigation.

Journal: *Journal of Vocational Behavior*, August 1997, *51*(1), 58–69.

Related Research: Baugh, S. G., et al. (1996). An investigation of the effects of protégé gender on responses to mentoring. *Journal of Vocational Behavior*, *49*, 309–323.

9351

Test Name: CAREER LOCUS OF CONTROL SCALE

Purpose: To measure locus of control for career planning.

Number of Items: 18

Format: Responses are true/false.

Reliability: Test-retest (3 weeks) reliability was .93. Kuder-Richardson (20) reliability estimates ranged from .81 to .89.

Validity: Correlations with other variables ranged from −.21 to .10.

Author: Brown, C., and Glastetter-Fender, C.

Article: Psychosocial identity and career control in college student-athletes.

Journal: *Journal of Vocational Behavior*, February 2000, *56*(1), 53–62.

Related Research: Trice, A. D., et al. (1989). A career locus of control scale for undergraduate students. *Perceptual and Motor Skills*, *69*, 555–561.

9352

Test Name: CAREER SELF-EFFICACY SCALE

Purpose: To measure career self-efficacy.

Number of Items: 4 or 5

Format: Responses are made on a 4-point scale ranging from "strongly agree" to "strongly disagree."

Reliability: Internal consistency (4 items) was .77 ($n = 106$). Test-retest reliability (4 items) was .85. Standardized alphas were .75 (4 item, $n = 39$) and .77 (5 items).

Validity: Correlations with other variables ranged from −.67 to .77.

Author: Wulff, M. B., and Steitz, J. A.

Article: A measure of career self-efficacy.

Journal: *Perceptual and Motor Skills*, February 1996, *82*(1), 240–242.

9353

Test Name: CAREER SELF-EFFICACY SCALE

Purpose: To measure the belief that one is able to perform well at managing one's career.

Number of Items: 10

Format: Responses are made on a 5-point scale ranging from 1 (strongly agree) to 5 (strongly disagree). All items are presented.

Reliability: Coefficient alpha was .76.

Validity: Correlations with other variables ranged from −.10 to .43.

Author: Kossek, E. E., et al.

Article: Career self-management: A quasi-experimental assessment of the effects of a training intervention.

Journal: *Personnel Psychology*, Winter 1998, *51*(4), 935–962.

Related Research: Sherer, M., & Adams, C. (1983). Construct validation of the Self-Efficacy scale. *Psychological Reports*, *53*, 899–902.

9354

Test Name: CAUSAL ATTRIBUTION SCALE

Purpose: To measure causal attributions of 12–13-year-old students. Success and failure attributions are assessed.

Number of Items: 10

Format: Students rate effort, ability, strategy use, and luck on scales that range from "rarely" to "almost always." A sample item is presented.

Reliability: Reliability estimates ranged from .61 to .79.

Author: Chan, L. K. S.

Article: Motivational orientations and metacognitive abilities of intellectually gifted children.

Journal: *Gifted Child Quarterly*, Fall 1996, *40*(4), 184–193.

Related Research: Chan, L. K. S. (1994). Relationship of

motivation, strategic learning and reading achievement in Grades 5, 7, and 9. *Journal of Experimental Education*, *62*, 319–339.

9355

Test Name: CAUSAL DIMENSION SCALE

Purpose: To measure clients' attributions about their own psychological problems.

Number of Items: 9

Format: Includes 3 causal dimensions: Locus, Controllability, and Stability.

Reliability: Alpha coefficients ranged from .52 to .90.

Author: Worthington, R. L., et al.

Article: Multicultural counseling competencies: Verbal content, counselor attributions, and social desirability.

Journal: *Journal of Counseling Psychology*, October 2000, *47*(4), 460–468.

Related Research: Russell, D. (1982). The Causal Dimension Scale: A measure of how individuals perceive causes. *Journal of Personality and Social Psychology*, *42*, 1137–1145.

9356

Test Name: CAUSAL DIMENSION SCALE— REVISED

Purpose: To assess attributions of causality.

Number of Items: 12

Format: A semantic differential measure that includes 4 dimensions: Locus of Causality, Stability, Personal Control, and External Control.

Reliability: Alpha coefficients ranged from .60 to .92.

Validity: Correlations with other variables ranged from −.08 to .34.

Author: Naidoo, A. V., et al.

Article: Demographics, causality, work salience, and the career maturity of African-American students: A causal model.

Journal: *Journal of Vocational Behavior*, August 1998, *53*(1), 15–27.

Related Research: McAuley, E., et al. (1992). Measuring causal attributions: The revised Causal Dimension Scale (CDSII). *Personality and Social Psychology Bulletin*, *18*, 566–573.

9357

Test Name: CAUSES OF THIRD WORLD POVERTY QUESTIONNAIRE

Purpose: To measure attributions regarding Third World poverty.

Number of Items: 20

Format: Scales range from 1 (strongly disagree) to 5 (strongly agree).

Validity: Correlations with other variables ranged from −.25 to .30.

Authors: Carr, S. C., and MacLachlin, M.

Article: Actors, observers, and attributions for Third World poverty: Contrasting perspectives from Malawi and Australia.

Journal: *Journal of Social Psychology*, April 1998, *138*(2), 189–202.

Related Research: Harper, D. J., et al. (1990). Lay causal perceptions of Third World poverty and the just world theory. *Social Behavior and Personality, 18,* 235–238.

9358

Test Name: CENTRAL RELATIONSHIP QUESTIONNAIRE

Purpose: To measure central relationship patterns.

Number of Items: 139

Format: Includes 3 subscales: Wish, Response From Other, and Response From Self. Responses are made on a 7-point scale ranging from 1 (never true or typical of me) to 7 (always typical or true of me).

Reliability: Alpha coefficients ranged from .71 to .95. Test-retest coefficients ranged from .44 to .79 ($N = 54$)

Validity: Correlations with other variables ranged from −.35 to .42.

Author: Barber, J. P., et al.

Article: The Central Relationship Questionnaire: Initial report.

Journal: *Journal of Counseling Psychology,* April 1998, *45*(2), 131–142.

Related Research: Barber, J. P., et al., (1990). A guide to the standard categories and their classification. In L. Luborsky & P. Crits—Christoph (Eds.), *The core conflictual relationship theme* (pp. 37–50). New York: Basic Books.

9359

Test Name: CHANCE LOCUS OF CONTROL QUESTIONNAIRE

Purpose: To indicate factors influencing an individual's decision and behavior in life.

Number of Items: 24

Format: Includes 3 subscales:

Internality, Powerful Others, and Chance.

Validity: Correlations with other variables ranged from −.32 to .42.

Author: Gadzella, B. M., et al.

Article: Predicting students as deep and shallow processors of information.

Journal: *Perceptual and Motor Skills,* June 1997, *84*(3, Part 1), 875–881.

Related Research: Levenson, H. (1981). Differentiating among internality, powerful others, and chance. In H. M. Lefcourt (Ed.), *Research with locus of control: Vol. 1. Assessment method* (pp. 15–63). New York: Academic Press.

9360

Test Name: CHILD NOWICKI-STRICKLAND LOCUS OF CONTROL SCALE—SHORT FORM

Purpose: To measure locus of control.

Number of Items: 20

Reliability: KR-20 reliability coefficient was .54.

Validity: Correlations with other variables ranged from −.15 to .33.

Author: Dykeman, C., et al.

Article: Psychological predictors of school based violence: Implications for school counselors.

Journal: *The School Counselor,* September 1996, *44*(1), 35–47.

Related Research: Lindal, R. E., & Venables, P. H. (1983). Factor dimensions of the Child Nowicki-Strickland Internal-External Scale. *Personality and Individual Differences, 4,* 645–649.

Nowicki, S., Jr., & Strickland,

B. R. (1975). A locus of control scale for children. *Journal of Counseling and Clinical Psychology, 40,* 148–154.

9361

Test Name: CHILDREN'S INTERNAL–EXTERNAL CONTROL SCALE

Purpose: To measure locus of control.

Number of Items: 20

Format: Responses are either "yes" or "no." An example is presented.

Reliability: Split-half and test-retest reliabilities ranged from .63 to .81.

Author: Fagen, D. B., et al.

Article: Relationships between parent-child relational variables and child test variables in highly stressed urban families.

Journal: *Child Study Journal,* 1996, *26*(2), 87–108.

Related Research: Nowicki, S., & Strickland, B. R. (1973). A locus of control scale for children. *Journal of Consulting and Clinical Psychology, 40,* 148–154.

9362

Test Name: CHILDREN'S MULTIDIMENSIONAL SELF-EFFICACY SCALES—ADAPTED

Purpose: To assess students' judgments of their capability to use various self-regulated learning strategies.

Number of Items: 7

Format: Responses are made on a scale ranging from 1 (not well at all) to 6 (very well). A sample item is presented.

Reliability: Alpha coefficients were .80 and .87.

Author: Pajares, F., et al.

Article: Gender differences in writing self-beliefs of elementary school students.

Journal: *Journal of Educational Psychology*, March 1999, *91*(1), 50–61.

Related Research: Zimmerman, B. J., & Bandura, A. (1994). Impact of self-regulatory influences on writing course attainment. *American Educational Research Journal*, *31*, 845–862.

9363

Test Name: CHILDREN'S PERCEPTIONS OF THE GROUP EXPERIENCE QUESTIONNAIRE

Purpose: To identify children's perceptions of their group experiences.

Number of Items: 10

Format: Responses are made on a 5-point scale ranging from 1 (almost never happened) to 5 (almost always happened).

Reliability: Test-retest reliability ranged from .89 to .99.

Author: Ashman, A. F., and Gillies, R. M.

Article: Children's cooperative behavior and interactions in trained and untrained work groups in regular classrooms.

Journal: *Journal of School Psychology*, Fall 1997, *35*(3), 261–279.

Related Research: Johnson, D. W., & Johnson, R. T. (1990). Cooperative learning and achievement. In S. Sharan (Ed.), *Cooperative learning: Theory and research* (pp. 23–37). New York: Praeger.

9364

Test Name: CHILDREN'S SELF-EFFICACY FOR PEER INTERACTION SCALE

Purpose: To assess the two main children's tactics of requests and imperatives.

Number of Items: 20

Format: Responses are made on a 4-point scale ranging from 1 (Hard!) to 4 (Easy!). Examples are presented.

Reliability: Alpha coefficients ranged from .62 to .85.

Validity: Correlations with other variables ranged from −.09 to −.30.

Author: Galanaki, E. P., and Kalantzi-Azizi, A.

Article: Loneliness and social dissatisfaction: Its relation with children's self-efficacy for peer interaction.

Journal: *Child Study Journal*, 1999, *29*(1), 1–22.

Related Research: Wheeler, V., & Ladd, G. (1982). Assessment of children's self-efficacy for social interaction with peers. *Developmental Psychology*, *18*, 795–805.

9365

Test Name: CHINESE IMPLICIT LEADERSHIP QUESTIONNAIRE

Purpose: To assess perceptions of leadership.

Number of Items: 163

Format: Scales range from 1 (totally uncharacteristic of a leader) to 10 (very characteristic of a leader). Sample items are presented.

Reliability: Alpha coefficients ranged from .89 to .96 across subscales.

Author: Ling, W., et al.

Article: Chinese implicit leadership theory.

Journal: *Journal of Social Psychology*, December 2000, *140*(6), 729–739.

Related Research: Ling, W. Q. (1989). Pattern of leadership behavior assessment in China. *Psychologia*, *32*, 129–134.

9366

Test Name: CHINESE SELF-MONITORING SCALE

Purpose: To measure the ability and propensity to self-monitor.

Number of Items: 23

Format: Scales ranged from 0 (extremely uncharacteristic) to 6 (extremely characteristic).

Reliability: Alpha coefficients were .82 (ability) and .69 (propensity).

Validity: Correlations with other variables ranged from .16 to .47.

Authors: Li, F., and Zhang, Y.

Article: Measuring self-monitoring ability and propensity: A two-dimensional Chinese scale.

Journal: *Journal of Social Psychology*, December 1998, *138*(6), 758–765.

9367

Test Name: COGNITIVE TRIAD INVENTORY FOR CHILDREN

Purpose: To assess view of the self, view of the world, and view of the future.

Number of Items: 36

Format: Yes/no/maybe format.

Reliability: Alpha was .89 (.81 for Self subscale).

Validity: Correlations with other variables ranged from −.63 to .23.

Author: Epkins, C. C.

Article: Cognitive specificity and affective confounding in social anxiety and dysphoria in children.

Journal: *Journal of Psychopathology and Behavioral Assessment*, March 1996, *18*(1), 83–101.

Related Research: Kaslow, N. J., et al. (1992). Cognitive Triad Inventory for Children: Development and relation to depression and anxiety. *Journal of Clinical Child Psychology, 21*, 339–347.

9368

Test Name: COLLECTIVE SELF-ESTEEM SCALE

Purpose: To assess self-evaluation regarding one's social group memberships.

Number of Items: 16

Format: Includes 4 subscales: Membership, Public, Private, and Identity. Items are Likert-type.

Reliability: Alpha coefficient ranged from .58 to .80.

Validity: Correlations with other variables ranged from −.35 to .78.

Author: Miville, M. L., et al.

Article: Appreciating similarities and valuing differences: The Miville-Guzman Universality–Diversity Scale.

Journal: *Journal of Counseling Psychology*, July 1999, *46*(3), 291–307.

Related Research: Luhtamen, R., & Crocker, J. (1992). A collective self-esteem scale: Self-evaluation of one's social identity. *Personality and Social Psychology Bulletin, 18*, 302–318.

9369

Test Name: COLLEGE SELF-EFFICACY INVENTORY

Purpose: To assess student confidence in completing college-specific tasks.

Number of Items: 20

Format: Scales range from 1 (no confidence) to 7 (complete confidence).

Reliability: Coefficient alpha was .92 (excluding six items of one subscale).

Validity: Correlations with other variables ranged from −.21 to .36.

Author: Gloria, A. M., et al.

Article: African American students' persistence at a predominately White university: Influences of social support, university comfort and self-beliefs.

Journal: *Journal of College Student Development*, May/June 1999, *40*(3), 257–268.

Related Research: Solberg, V. S., et al. (1993). Self-efficacy and Hispanic college students: Validation of the College Self-Efficacy Instrument. *Hispanic Journal of Behavioral Science, 15*, 80–95.

9370

Test Name: COLLEGE STUDENT ROLE SCALE

Purpose: To measure students' conception of the role of college student.

Number of Items: 16

Format: All items are presented.

Reliability: Alpha coefficients ranged from .71 to .80 across subscales.

Author: Collier, P. J.

Article: The effects of completing a capstone course on student identity.

Journal: *Sociology of Education*, October 2000, *73*(4), 285–299.

Related Research: Collier, P. J., et al. (1998). *A role-identity approach to the assessment of general education*. Paper presented at the 93rd annual meeting of the American Sociological Association, San Francisco.

9371

Test Name: COMPUTER SELF-EFFICACY SCALE

Purpose: To assess perceptions of computer-related knowledge and skills.

Number of Items: 32

Format: Scales range from 1 (strongly agree) to 5 (strongly disagree). Sample items are presented.

Reliability: Coefficient alpha was .95.

Authors: Harrison, A. W., et al.

Article: Testing the self-efficacy–performance linkage of social–cognitive theory.

Journal: *Journal of Social Psychology*, February 1997, *137*(1), 79–87.

Related Research: Murphy, C. A., et al. (1989). Development and validation of the Computer Self-Efficacy Scale. *Educational and Psychological Measurement, 49*, 893–899.

9372

Test Name: CONCEPTIONS OF MATHEMATICS QUESTIONNAIRE

Purpose: To measure cohesive and fragmented conceptions of mathematics.

Number of Items: 19

Format: Five-point Likert format. All items are presented.

Reliability: Alphas ranged from .79 to .88 across samples.

Author: Mji, A.

Article: Reliability and validity of the Conceptions of Mathematics Questionnaire.

Journal: *Psychological Reports*, October 1999, *85*(2), 579–582.

Related Research: Crawford, K., et al. (1998). University mathematics students' conceptions of mathematics. *Studies in Higher Education, 23*, 87–94.

9373

Test Name: CONDOM USE SELF-EFFICACY SCALE

Purpose: To assess a person's level of confidence that he/she could engage in condom use.

Number of Items: 16 (4 in each of 4 scenarios).

Format: Eleven-point scales are anchored by 0 (not at all confident) and 10 (completely confident).

Reliability: Alpha was .93.

Author: Belcher, L., et al.

Article: A randomized trial of a brief HIV risk reduction counseling intervention for women.

Journal: *Journal of Consulting and Clinical Psychology*, October 1998, *66*(5), 856–861.

Related Research: DiIorio, C., et al. (1997). Measurement of condom use self-efficacy and outcome expectancies in a geographically diverse group of STD patients. *AIDS Education and Prevention, 9*, 1–13.

9374

Test Name: CONFLICT EFFICACY SCALE

Purpose: To measure team members' beliefs that their team could successfully manage different conflict situations.

Number of Items: 6

Format: Responses are made on a 7-point scale ranging from 1 (strongly agree) to 7 (strongly disagree). All items are presented.

Reliability: Coefficient alpha was .92.

Validity: Correlations with other variables ranged from −.61 to .78.

Author: Alper, S., et al.

Article: Conflicts management, efficacy, and performance in organizational teams.

Journal: *Personnel Psychology*, Autumn 2000, *53*(3), 625–642.

9375

Test Name: CONTROL ORIENTATION SCALE

Purpose: To measure the degree individuals see themselves in control of important forces affecting their lives.

Number of Items: 5

Format: Responses are made on a 5-point scale ranging from 1 (strongly disagree) to 5 (strongly agree). Sample items are presented.

Reliability: Coefficient alpha was .64.

Validity: Correlations with other variables ranged from .01 to .26.

Author: Mansour-Cole, D. M., and Scott, S. G.

Article: Hearing it through the grapevine: The influence of source, leader-relation, and

legitimacy on survivors' fairness perceptions.

Journal: *Personnel Psychology*, Spring 1990, *51*(1), 25–54.

Related Research: Pearlin, L., et al. (1981). The stress process. *Journal of Health and Social Behavior, 22*, 337–356.

9376

Test Name: CONTROL SCALES

Purpose: To measure dimensions of control appraisals: Controllable-by-Self, Controllable-by-Others, and Controllable-by-Anyone.

Number of Items: 12

Format: Scales range from 1 (not at all) to 5 (extremely).

Reliability: Alpha coefficients ranged from .69 to .89.

Author: Peacock, E. J., and Wong, P. T. P.

Article: Anticipatory stress: The relation of locus of control, optimism, and control appraisals to coping.

Journal: *Journal of Research in Personality*, June 1996, *30*(2), 204–222.

Related Research: Peacock, E. J., & Wong, P. T. P. (1990). The stress appraisal measure: A multidimensional approach to cognitive appraisal. *Stress Medicine, 6*, 227–236.

9377

Test Name: COUNSELING SELF-ESTIMATE INVENTORY

Purpose: To assess therapists' self-efficacy in counseling situations.

Number of Items: 37

Format: Includes 4 factors: Microskills, Counseling Process, Dealing with Difficult Client

Behaviors, and Cultural Competence. Responses are made on a 6-point scale ranging from 1 (strongly disagree) to 6 (strongly agree).

Reliability: Internal consistency was .93. Test-retest (3 weeks) was .87.

Author: Williams, E. N., et al.

Article: Experiences of novice therapists in practicum: Trainees', clients' and supervisors' perceptions of therapists' personal reactions and management strategies.

Journal: *Journal of Counseling Psychology*, October 1997, *44*(4), 390–399.

Related Research: Larson, L. M., et al. (1992). Development and validation of the Counseling Self-Estimate Inventory. *Journal of Counseling Psychology*, *39*, 105–120.

9378

Test Name: DESCRIPTIVE QUESTIONNAIRE

Purpose: To measure the extent to which characteristics describe groups.

Number of Items: 92

Format: Five-point scales. Sample items are presented.

Reliability: Alpha was .89.

Author: Tomkiewicz, J., and Ayeyemi-Bello, T.

Article: Perceptional differences in racial descriptions of Euro-American and Hispanic persons.

Journal: *Psychological Reports*, June 1997, *80*(3) Part 2, 1339–1343.

Related Research: Schein, V. (1973). The relation between sex role stereotypes and requisite management characteristics.

Journal of Applied Psychology, *57*, 95–100.

9379

Test Name: DIETING BELIEFS SCALE

Purpose: To assess women's dieting locus of control

Number of Items: 16

Format: Responses are made on a 6-point scale ranging from 1 (not at all descriptive of the belief) to 6 (very descriptive of their belief). Examples are presented.

Reliability: Test-retest (6 weeks) reliability was .81. Internal consistency reliabilities were .65 and .68.

Validity:

Author: Tylka, T. L, and Subich, L. M.

Article: Exploring the consistent validity of the eating disorder continuum.

Journal: *Journal of Counseling Psychology*, July 1999, *46*(2), 268–276.

Related Research: Stotland, S., & Zuroff, D. C. (1990). A new measure of weight locus of control. The Dieting Beliefs Scale. *Journal of Personality Assessment*, *54*, 191–203.

9380

Test Name: DIFFERENTIATION OF SELF INVENTORY

Purpose: To measure a person's level of differentiation.

Number of Items: 43

Format: Includes 4 subscales: Emotional Reactivity, Emotional Cutoff, Fusion with Others, and I-position. Responses are made on a 6-point scale ranging from 1 (not at all true of me) to 6 (very

true of me). Examples are presented.

Reliability: Alpha coefficients ranged from −.72 to .88.

Author: Tuason, M. T., and Friedlander, M. L.

Article: Do parents' differentiation levels predict those of their adult children? and other tests of Bowen Theory in a Philippine sample.

Journal: *Journal of Counseling Psychology*, January 2000, *47*(1), 27–35.

Related Research: Skowron, E., & Friedlander, M. (1998). The Differentiation of Self Inventory: Development and initial validation. *Journal of Counseling Psychology*, *28*, 235–246.

9381

Test Name: DRUG ABSTINENCE SELF-EFFICACY SCALE

Purpose: To measure self-rated confidence and temptation for high-risk relapse situations.

Number of Items: 20

Format: Five-point scales range from 1 (not at all) to 5 (extremely).

Reliability: Cronbach alpha coefficients ranged from .87 to .92 (Self-Efficacy) and from .72 to .90 (Temptation).

Author: Hiller, M. L., et al.

Article: Measuring self-efficacy among drug-involved probationers.

Journal: *Psychological Reports*, April 2000, *86*(2), 529–538.

Related Research: Di Clemente, C. C., et al. (1994). The Alcohol Abstinence Self-Efficacy Scale. *Journal of Studies on Alcohol*, *55*, 141–148.

9382

Test Name: EDUCATIONAL DEGREES SELF-EFFICACY SCALE

Purpose: To assess confidence in the ability to complete academic tasks for specific degrees.

Number of Items: 14

Format: Scales range from 1 (no confidence at all) to 7 (complete confidence). Sample items are presented.

Reliability: Coefficient alpha was .93.

Validity: Correlations with other variables ranged from −.27 to .71.

Author: Gloria, A. M., et al.

Article: African American students' persistence at a predominately White university: Influences of social support, university comfort and self-beliefs.

Journal: *Journal of College Student Development*, May/June 1999, *40*(3), 257–268.

9383

Test Name: EFFICACY BELIEFS SCALE

Purpose: To measure individual-level and group-level confidence to perform a task.

Number of Items: 5

Format: Scales range from 1 (strongly disagree) to 5 (strongly agree). Sample items are presented.

Reliability: Reliabilities ranged from .70 to .86 across subscales.

Validity: Correlations with other variables ranged from −.26 to .60.

Author: Jex, S. M., and Bliese, P. D.

Article: Efficacy beliefs as a

moderator of the impact of work-related stressors: A multilevel study.

Journal: *Journal of Applied Psychology*, June 1999, *84*(3), 349–361.

Related Research: Jones, G. R. (1986). Socialization tactics, self-efficacy and newcomers' adjustments to organizations. *Academy of Management Journal, 29*, 262–279.

9384

Test Name: EFFICACY SCALE

Purpose: To measure children's perceptions of self-efficacy for solving problems.

Number of Items: 10

Format: Responses are made on a scale ranging from 10 (high uncertainty) to 100 (complete certitude).

Reliability: Test-retest validity was .89.

Author: Shih, S.-S., and Alexander, J. M.

Article: Interacting effects of goal setting and self- or other-referenced feedback on children's development of self-efficacy and cognitive skill within the Taiwanese classroom.

Journal: *Journal of Educational Psychology*, September 2000, *92*(3), 536–543.

Related Research: Bandura, A., & Schunk, D. H. (1981). Cultivating competence, self-efficacy, and intrinsic interest through proximal self-motivation. *Journal of Personality and Social Psychology, 41*, 586–598.

9385

Test Name: EMPLOYEE PERCEPTIONS OF THEIR WORK PERFORMANCE SCALE

Purpose: To assess an employee's own conception of his/her work performance.

Number of Items: 5

Format: Scales range from 1 (strongly disagree) to 5 (strongly agree). A sample item is presented.

Reliability: Coefficient alpha was .93.

Validity: Correlations with other variables ranged from −.02 to .28.

Author: O'Neill, B. S., and Mone, M. A.

Article: Investigating equity sensitivity as a moderator of relations between self-efficacy and workplace attitudes.

Journal: *Journal of Applied Psychology*, October 1998, *83*(5), 805–816.

9386

Test Name: EMPLOYEES' PERCEPTIONS SCALE

Purpose: To measure employees' perceptions.

Number of Items: 39

Format: Includes Positive Affectivity, Negative Affectivity, Co-Worker Support, Supervisory Support, Peer Support, Autonomy, Role Stress, Emotional Exhaustion, Depersonalization, Personal Accomplishment, and Job Satisfaction. Responses are made on a 5-point Likert-type scale ranging from 1 (strongly disagree) to 5 (strongly agree). All items are presented.

Reliability: Reliabilities ranged from .65 to .91.

Author: Iverson, R. D., et al.

Article: Affectivity, organizational stressors, and absenteeism: A causal model of burnout and its consequences.

Journal: *Journal of Vocational Behavior*, February 1998, *52*(1), 1–23.

Related Research: Agho, O. A., et al. (1992). Discriminant validity of measures of job satisfaction, positive affectivity and negative affectivity. *Journal of Occupational and Organizational Psychology*, *65*, 185–196.

9387

Test Name: EMPOWERMENT SCALE

Purpose: To assess parents' perception of empowerment by the school.

Number of Items: 3

Format: Responses are made on a 4-point scale ranging from 1 (strongly disagree) to 4 (strongly agree).

Reliability: Alpha coefficient was .76.

Author: Griffith, J.

Article: Relation of parental involvement, empowerment, and school traits to student academic performance.

Journal: *Journal of Educational Research*, September/October 1996, *90*(1), 33–41.

Related Research: Goldring, E. B., & Shapira, R. (1993). Choice, empowerment, and involvement: What satisfies parents? *Educational Evaluation and Policy Analysis*, *15*(4), 396–409.

9388

Test Name: ENDORSEMENT OF INDIVIDUALIST CAUSES

Purpose: To measure the degree to which poverty and other

problems are attributed to individual character.

Number of Items: 6

Format: Five-point Likert format. All items are presented.

Reliability: Reliability was .66.

Author: Cheung, C.-K., and Kwok, S.-T.

Article: Conservative orientation as a determinant of hopelessness.

Journal: *Journal of Social Psychology*, June 1996, *136*(3), 333–347.

Related Research: Guimond, S., et al. (1989). Education and causal attributions: The development of person-blame and system-blame ideology. *Social Psychology Quarterly*, *52*, 126–140.

9389

Test Name: ENVIRONMENTAL RISK PERCEPTION SCALE

Purpose: To measure the cognitive aspect of risk perception.

Number of Items: 15

Format: Responses are made to each item on a 6-point scale ranging from 1 (very unlikely) to 6 (very likely). All items are presented.

Reliability: Alpha coefficients were .89 and .90.

Validity: Correlations with other variables ranged from .04 to .49.

Author: Der-Karabetian, A., et al.

Article: Environmental risk perception, activism and world-mindedness among samples of British and U.S. college students.

Journal: *Perceptual and Motor Skills*, October 1996, *83*(2), 451–462.

Related Research: Weinstein, N.

(1980). Unrealistic optimism about future life events. *Journal of Personality and Social Psychology*, *39*, 806–820.

9390

Test Name: ETIOLOGY ATTRIBUTION SCALE

Purpose: To identify etiological factors attributed to psychological problems.

Number of Items: 7

Format: Types of items include Interpersonal, Cognitive, Emotional, Somatic, Biophysical, Sociocultural, and Developmental. Items are rank-ordered according to importance and range from 1 (most important) to 7 (least important).

Reliability: Spearman rank-order correlation coefficients for 2-week test-retest ranged from .56 to .74 ($N = 32$).

Validity: Correlations with other variables ranged from −.36 to .43.

Author: Worthington, R. L., et al.

Article: Multicultural counseling competencies: Verbal content, counselor attributions, and social desirability.

Journal: *Journal of Counseling Psychology*, October 2000, *47*(4), 460–468.

Related Research: Worthington, R. L. (1995). *Etiology attributions, causal dimensions, responsibility attributions, treatment strategy recommendations, and theoretical commitment*. Unpublished doctoral dissertation, University of California, Santa Barbara.

9391

Test Name: EXAM STATE SELF-EFFICACY

Purpose: To measure confidence in performance on exams.

Number of Items: 9

Format: Scales range from 1 (strongly disagree) to 5 (strongly agree). Sample items are presented.

Reliability: Alpha coefficients ranged from .82 to .87.

Validity: Correlations with other variables ranged from −.35 to .54.

Author: Chen, G., et al.

Article: Examination of relationships among trait-like individual differences, state-like individual differences, and learning performance.

Journal: *Journal of Applied Psychology*, December 2000, 85(6), 835–847.

Related Research: Phillips, J. M., & Gully, S. M. (1997). Role of goal orientation, need for achievement, and locus of control in the self-efficacy and goal-setting process. *Journal of Applied Psychology, 82*, 792–802.

9392

Test Name: EXPECTATIONS ABOUT COUNSELING QUESTIONNAIRE

Purpose: To measure attitudes and behavior related to expectancies about counseling.

Number of Items: 68

Format: Scales range from 1 (definitely do not expect this to be true) to 7 (definitely do expect this to be true). Sample items are presented.

Reliability: Alpha coefficients ranged from .45 to .76 across 17

subscales and from .81 to .89 across factor scales.

Author: Ægisdóttir, S., et al.

Article: The factorial structure of the Expectations about Counseling Questionnaire—Brief Form: Some serious questions.

Journal: *Measurement and Evaluation in Counseling and Development*, April 2000, 33(1), 3–20.

Related Research: Tinsley, D. J., et al. (1991). A construct validation study of the Expectations about Counseling Questionnaire—Brief form: Factorial validity. *Measurement and Evaluation in Counseling and Development, 24*, 101–110.

9393

Test Name: EXPECTATIONS OF OTHERS SCALE

Purpose: To measure the perceptions of the participants that significant others in their lives thought that they should exercise.

Number of Items: 7

Format: Responses are made on a scale ranging from −3 (I should not) to 3 (I should). An example is presented.

Reliability: Coefficient alpha was .82.

Validity: Correlations with other variables ranged from −.16 to .35.

Author: Kerner, M. S., and Grossman, A. H.

Article: Attitudinal, social, and practical correlates to fitness behavior: A test of the theory of planned behavior.

Journal: *Perceptual and Motor Skills*, December 1998, 87(3) Part 2, 1139–1154.

Related Research: Kerner, M. S.

(1993). Expectations of Others Scale. Unpublished scale, New York University.

9394

Test Name: FAMILY-TO-WORK CONFLICT SCALE

Purpose: To measure family-to-work conflict.

Number of Items: 4

Format: An example is presented.

Reliability: Coefficient alpha was .64.

Validity: Correlations with other variables ranged from −.38 to .33.

Author: Parasuraman, S., et al.

Article: Work and family variables, entrepreneurial career success, and psychological well-being.

Journal: *Journal of Vocational Behavior*, June 1996, 48(3), 275–300.

Related Research: Kopelman, R. E., et al. (1983). A model of work, family and interrole conflict: A construct validation study. *Organizational Behavior and Human Performance, 32*, 198–215.

9395

Test Name: FAMILY-WORK CONFLICT SCALE

Purpose: To measure the extent to which family life interferes with work-related obligations.

Number of Items: 5

Format: Seven-point scales range from "strongly disagree" to "strongly agree." All items are presented.

Reliability: Alpha coefficients ranged from .83 to .89 across samples.

Validity: Correlations with other variables ranged from −.44 to .40.

Author: Netemeyer, R. G., et al.

Article: Development and validation of Work-Family Conflict and Family-Work Conflict Scales.

Journal: *Journal of Applied Psychology*, August 1996, *81*(4), 400–410.

9396

Test Name: FATALISM MEASURE

Purpose: To measure fatalistic thinking.

Number of Items: 7

Format: Seven-point scales range from 1 (completely disagree) to 7 (completely agree). Sample items are presented.

Reliability: Alpha was .70.

Author: Kalichman, S. C., et al.

Article: Fatalism, current life satisfaction, and risk for HIV infection among gay and bisexual men.

Journal: *Journal of Consulting and Clinical Psychology*, August 1997, *65*(4), 542–546.

Related Research: Heimberg, L. K. (1963). *The measurement of future time perspective.* Unpublished doctoral dissertation, Vanderbilt University.

9397

Test Name: FIVE ATTRIBUTIONAL DIMENSION SCALE

Purpose: To assess attributions across a wide variety of circumstances or events. Subscales are Internality,

Stability, Controllability, Globality, and Universality.

Number of Items: 20

Format: Five-point scales.

Reliability: Test-retest reliabilities ranged from .59 to .79.

Author: Kelly, K. T., and Campbell, J. L.

Article: Attribution of responsibility for alcohol related offenses.

Journal: *Psychological Reports*, June 1997, *80*(3) Part 2, 1159–1165.

Related Research: Benson, M. (1989). Attributional measurement techniques: Classification and comparison of attributions for measuring causal dimensions. *Journal of Social Psychology*, *129*, 307–323.

9398

Test Name: FOUR-ATTRIBUTIONAL DIMENSION SCALE

Purpose: To measure attributions across a wide variety of events.

Number of Items: 16

Format: Includes 4 dimensions: Internality, Stability, Globality, and Controllability. Responses are made on a 5-point Likert scale ranging from "strongly agree" to "strongly disagree."

Reliability: Test-retest reliability was .72.

Author: Crawford, P. M., and Brigham, F. J.

Article: Perceptions of causality in middle school.

Journal: *Journal of Research and Development in Education*, Fall 2000, *34*(1), 60–69.

Related Research: Benson, M. J. (1988). Attributional measurement techniques:

Classification and comparison of approaches for measuring causal dimensions. *Journal of Social Psychology*, *129*, 307–323.

9399

Test Name: FUTURE DIFFICULTIES SCALE

Purpose: To assess young adults' perceptions of dual-career lifestyle obstacles and realities.

Number of Items: 16

Format: Includes 3 scales: Childcare, Sharing Family Work, and Career Advancement. Responses are made on a 5-point scale ranging from "not at all an anticipated difficulty" to "very much an anticipated difficulty." Samples are presented.

Reliability: Alpha coefficients ranged from .61 to .78.

Author: Hallet, M. B., and Gilbert, L. A.

Article: Variables differentiating university women considering role-sharing and conventional dual-career marriages.

Journal: *Journal of Vocational Behavior*, April 1997, *50*(2), 308–322.

Related Research: Gilbert, L. A., et al. (1991). Assessing perceptions of occupational-family integration. *Sex Roles*, *24*, 107–119.

9400

Test Name: GENDER ROLE CONFLICT SCALE

Purpose: To measure gender role conflict.

Number of Items: 37

Format: Includes 4 subscales: Success, Power, and Competition; Restrictive Emotionality; Restrictive Affectionate Behavior between Men; and Conflict

Between Work and Family Relations. Responses are made on a 6-point Likert-type scale ranging from 1 (strongly disagree) to 6 (strongly agree).

Reliability: Internal consistencies ranged from .78 to .88. Test-retest (4 weeks) reliabilities ranged from .72 to .86.

Validity: Correlations with other variables ranged from −.39 to .38.

Author: Simonsen, G., et al.

Article: Gender role conflict and psychological well-being among gay men.

Journal: *Journal of Counseling Psychology*, January 2000, 47(1), 85–89.

Related Research: O'Neil, J. M., et al. (1986). Gender Role Conflict Scale: College men's fear of feminity. *Sex Roles, 14*, 335–350.

9401

Test Name: GENERAL CAUSALITY ORIENTATIONS SCALE

Purpose: To assess the strength of autonomous and controlled responses.

Number of Items: 15 vignettes

Format: Seven-point scales ranged from 1 (very unlikely) to 7 (very likely). A sample vignette and sample items are presented.

Reliability: Alpha coefficients ranged from .81 to .84. Test-retest reliabilities (3 months) ranged from .52 to .60.

Author: Knee, C. R., and Zuckerman, M.

Article: A nondefensive personality: Autonomy and control as moderators of defensive coping and self-handicapping.

Journal: *Journal of Research in Personality*, March 1998, 32(1), 115–130.

Related Research: Deci, E. L., & Ryan, R. M. (1985). The General Causality Orientations Scale: Self-determination in personality. *Journal of Research in Personality, 19*, 109–134.

9402

Test Name: GENERAL SELF-EFFICACY SCALE

Purpose: To measure general self-efficacy.

Number of Items: 2

Format: Five-point scales are anchored by 1 (never) and 5 (very often). All items are presented.

Reliability: Coefficient alpha was .82.

Validity: Correlations with other variables ranged from −.58 to .41.

Author: Bulger, C. A., and Mellor, S.

Article: Self-efficacy as a mediator of the relationship between perceived union barriers and women's participation in union activities.

Journal: *Journal of Applied Psychology*, December 1997, 82(6), 935–944.

9403

Test Name: GENERAL SELF-EFFICACY SCALE (CHINESE VERSION)

Purpose: To measure self-efficacy.

Number of Items: 10

Reliability: Cronbach alpha was .92. Test-retest reliability (6-months) was .70.

Validity: Correlations with other

variables ranged from −.64 to −.69.

Author: Cheung, S.-K., and Sun, S. Y. K.

Article: Assessment of optimistic self-beliefs: Further validation of the Chinese version of the General Self-Efficacy Scale.

Journal: *Psychological Reports*, December 1999, 85(3, Part II), 1221–1224.

Related Research: Jerusalem, M., & Schwarzer, R. (1992). Self-efficacy as a resource factor in stress appraisal process. In R. Schwarzer (Ed.), *Self-efficacy: Thought control of action* (pp. 195–213). Washington, DC: Hemisphere.

9404

Test Name: GENERAL SELF-EFFICACY SCALE (ENGLISH VERSION)

Purpose: To measure the strength of an individual's ability to deal with difficult situations, obstacles, and setbacks.

Number of Items: 10

Format: Four-point scales are anchored by 1 (not at all true) and 4 (exactly true). Sample items are presented.

Reliability: Test-retest reliability was .72. Cronbach's alpha and split-half reliabilities were .72.

Author: Peltzer, K., et al.

Article: Minor psychiatric morbidity in South African secondary pupils.

Journal: *Psychological Reports*, October 1999, 85(2), 397–402.

Related Research: Schwarzer, R. (1993). Measurement of perceived self-efficacy: Psychometric scales for cross-cultural research. Berlin: Freie Universitat Berlin.

9405

Test Name: GENERALIZED EXPECTANCY FOR SUCCESS SCALE

Purpose: To measure the expectancy for success in numerous situations without specifying the criteria for success.

Number of Items: 30

Format: Five-point scales range from 1 (highly improbable) to 5 (highly probable).

Reliability: Alpha was .89.

Author: Abel, M. H.

Article: Self-esteem: Moderator or mediator between perceived stress and expectancy of success.

Journal: *Psychological Reports*, October 1996, *79*(2), 635–641.

Related Research: Fibel, B., & Hale, W. D. (1978). The Generalized Expectancy of Success Scale—a new measure. *Journal of Consulting and Clinical Psychology, 46,* 924–931.

9406

Test Name: GENERALIZED SELF-EFFICACY SCALE

Purpose: To determine respondents' beliefs in their ability to respond to novel or difficult situations and to deal with any associated obstacles or setbacks.

Number of Items: 7

Format: Responses are made on a 4-point scale ranging from 1 (strongly agree) to 4 (strongly disagree). An example is presented.

Reliability: Coefficient alpha was .76.

Validity: Correlations with other variables ranged from −.34 to .54.

Author: Pallant, J. F.

Article: Development and validation of a scale to measure perceived control of internal states.

Journal: *Journal of Personality Assessment*, October 2000, *75*(2), 308–337.

Related Research: Schwarzer, R. (1992). *Self-efficacy: Thought control of action.* Washington, DC: Hemisphere.

9407

Test Name: GENERALIZED SELF-EFFICACY SCALE

Purpose: To assess generalized self-efficacy.

Number of Items: 8

Format: Eleven-point scales are anchored by 0 (strongly disagree) and 10 (strongly agree). Sample items are presented.

Reliability: Alpha coefficients ranged from .75 to .82.

Validity: Correlations with other variables ranged from −.55 to .82.

Author: Judge, T. A., et al.

Article: Dispositional effects on job and life satisfaction: The role of core evaluations.

Journal: *Journal of Applied Psychology*, February 1998, *83*(1), 17–34.

9408

Test Name: GENERALIZED SELF-EFFICACY SCALE

Purpose: To measure confidence to perform a task.

Number of Items: 10

Format: Five-point Likert format.

Reliability: Coefficient alpha was .75.

Author: Judge, T. A., et al.

Article: Managerial coping with organizational change: A dispositional perspective.

Journal: *Journal of Applied Psychology*, February 1999, *84*(1), 107–122.

Related Research: Scherer, M., et al. (1982). The Self-Efficacy Scale: Construction and validation. *Psychological Reports, 51,* 663–671.

9409

Test Name: GENERALIZED SELF-EFFICACY SCALE

Purpose: To measure the expectation that one can perform competently in a wide range of situations.

Number of Items: 23

Reliability: Alpha coefficients ranged from .71 to .86 across subscales.

Validity: Correlations with other variables ranged from −.65 to .57.

Author: Slanger, E., and Rudestam, K. E.

Article: Motivation and disinhibition in high risk sports: Sensation-seeking and self-efficacy.

Journal: *Journal of Research in Personality*, September 1997, *31*(3), 355–374.

Related Research: Scherer, M., & Adams, C. H. (1983). Construct validation of the self-efficacy scale. *Psychological Reports, 53,* 899–902.

9410

Test Name: (GLICKMAN) URGENT TASK INVOLVEMENT SCALE

Purpose: To assess the perceived urgency of tasks.

Number of Items: 10

Format: Seven-point scales are anchored by (1) entirely inaccurate to (7) entirely accurate. All items are presented.

Reliability: Alpha was .75.

Validity: An ADHD group scored higher than a control group.

Author: Glickman, M. M., and Dodd, D. K.

Article: GUTI: A measure of urgent task involvement among adults with attention-deficit hyperactivity disorder.

Journal: *Psychological Reports*, April 1998, *82*(2), 592–594.

9411

Test Name: GLOBAL SELF-ESTEEM SCALE

Purpose: To measure global self-esteem.

Number of Items: 10

Format: Responses are made on a 4-point scale ranging from "strongly agree" to "strongly disagree." A sample item is presented.

Reliability: Coefficient alpha was .87.

Author: Lamborn, S. D., et al.

Article: Ethnicity and community context as moderators of the relations between family decision making and adolescent adjustment.

Journal: *Child Development*, April 1996, *67*(2), 283–301.

Related Research: Rosenberg, M. (1965). *Society and the adolescent self-image*. Princeton, NJ: Princeton University Press.

9412

Test Name: POWERFUL OTHERS LOCUS OF CONTROL SCALE

Purpose: To measure locus of control.

Number of Items: 7

Format: Seven-point Likert scales. A sample item is presented.

Reliability: Coefficient alpha was .75.

Validity: Correlations with other variables ranged from −.09 to .14.

Author: Schaubroeck, J., et al.

Article: Organization and occupation influences in the attraction-selection-attrition process.

Journal: *Journal of Applied Psychology*, December 1998, *83*(6), 869–891.

Related Research: Levenson, H. (1973). Multidimensional locus of control in psychiatric patients. *Journal of Consulting and Clinical Psychology, 41*, 397–404.

9413

Test Name: GLOBAL SELF-WORTH SUBSCALE

Purpose: To provide an index of self-esteem.

Number of Items: 5

Format: Responses are made on a 4-point Likert scale.

Reliability: Alpha coefficients ranged from .72 to .79.

Validity: Correlations with emotionality were −.20 and −.33.

Author: Feinberg, M. E., et al.

Article: Sibling comparison of differential parental treatment in adolescence: Gender, self-esteem,

and emotionality as mediators of the parenting adjustment association.

Journal: *Child Development*, November/December 2000, *71*(6), 1611–1628.

Related Research: Harter, S. (1982). The Perceived Competence Scale for Children. *Child Development, 53*, 87–97.

9414

Test Name: HARE AREA-SPECIFIC SELF-ESTEEM SCALE

Purpose: To measure self-esteem among African American adolescents.

Number of Items: 10

Format: Four-point scales are anchored by 4 (strongly agree) and 1 (strongly disagree).

Reliability: Cronbach's alpha was .79.

Author: Paschall, M. J., and Hubbard, M. L.

Article: Effects of neighborhood and family stressors on African American male adolescents' self-worth and propensity for violent behavior.

Journal: *Journal of Counseling and Clinical Psychology*, October 1998, *66*(5), 825–831.

Related Research: Shoemaker, A. L. (1980). Construct validity of area-specific self-esteem: The Hare Self-Esteem Scale. *Educational and Psychological Measurement, 40*, 495–501.

9415

Test Name: HARE SELF-ESTEEM SCALE—REVISAL

Purpose: To measure self-esteem and to elicit information on use of and attitudes toward drugs, decision making, and relationship/communication skills.

Number of Items: 109

Format: Includes 10 subscales: Peer Self-Esteem, Home Self-Esteem, School Self-Esteem, Relationships/ Communication, Decision Making, Attitude-Cigarettes, Attitude-Alcohol, Attitude-Marijuana, Behavior Alcohol, and Behavior-Marijuana. All items are presented.

Reliability: Alpha coefficients ranged from .72 to .95.

Author: Young, M., et al.

Article: Evaluation of selected life-skill modules from the contemporary health series with students in Grade 6.

Journal: *Perceptual and Motor Skills*, June 1997, Part 1, *84*(3), 811–818.

Related Research: Shoemaker, A. L. (1980). Construct validity of area specific self-esteem: the Hare Self-Esteem Scale. *Educational and Psychological Measurement*, *40*, 495–501.

9416

Test Name: HEALTH STUDENT ACADEMIC LOCUS OF CONTROL SCALE

Purpose: To measure internal and external control beliefs of students in courses allied to medicine.

Number of Items: 20

Format: Includes internal and external control beliefs.

Reliability: Alpha coefficients were .75 (internal) and .84 (external).

Validity: Correlations with a 15-item Academic Locus of Control Scale were .64 (*n* = 154) and .42 (*n* = 164).

Author: Eachus, P., and Cassidy, S.

Article: The Health Student Academic Locus of Control Scale.

Journal: *Perceptual and Motor Skills*, December 1997, *85*(3, Part 1), 85.

9417

Test Name: IDENTITY STYLE INVENTORY

Purpose: To assess identity styles as diffuse–avoidant, informational, or normative.

Number of Items: 29

Format: Five-point scale. Sample items are presented.

Reliability: Alpha coefficients ranged from .61 to 77 across subscales.

Authors: Berzonsky, M. D.

Article: Identity styles and hypothesis testing strategies.

Journal: *The Journal of Social Psychology*, December 1999, *139*(6), 784–789.

Related Research: Berzonsky, M. D. (1992). Identity styles and coping strategies. *Journal of Personality*, *60*, 771–788.

9418

Test Name: IDENTITY STYLES INVENTORY—REVISED

Purpose: To measure identity styles in terms of information-seeking, normative conformance, and diffuse/avoidant orientation.

Number of Items: 40

Format: Five-point Likert format.

Reliability: Alpha coefficients ranged from .60 to .78.

Validity: Correlations with other variables ranged from −.43 to .38.

Author: Dollinger, S. J., and Dollinger, S. M. C.

Article: Individuality and identity exploration: An autophotographic study.

Journal: *Journal of Research in Personality*, September 1997, *31*(3), 337–354.

Related Research: Berzonsky, M. D. (1992). Identity style and coping strategies. *Journal of Personality*, *60*, 771–778.

9419

Test Name: INDEX OF SELF-ESTEEM

Purpose: To assess healthy self-esteem and severity of self-esteem problems.

Number of Items: 25

Time Required: 10 minutes.

Reliability: Coefficient alpha was .90.

Author: Scott, C. G.

Article: Modeling self-esteem: The potential impact of school personnel on students.

Journal: *Professional School Counseling*, June 1999, *2*(5), 367–372.

Related Research: Hudson, W. W. (1990). *Index of Self-Esteem*. Tempe, AZ: Walmyr.

9420

Test Name: INSTRUMENTALITY SCALE

Purpose: To assess perceived instrumentality of theoretical subject matter at school.

Number of Items: 7

Format: Response categories range from 1 ("is very true of me") to 4 ("is not at all true of me"). All items are presented.

Reliability: Alpha was .85.

Author: Halvari, H.

Article: Personality and educational choice of general versus vocational students among 16-to-19-year-olds.

Journal: *Psychological Reports*, June 1996, 78(3) Part 2, 1379–1385.

Related Research: Gjesme, T. (1981). Is there any future in achievement motivation? *Motivation and Emotion*, 5, 115–138.

9421

Test Name: INTENT ATTRIBUTION SCALE

Purpose: To assess children's intent attributions.

Number of Items: 12

Format: Includes 6 stories, each with two questions to determine the child's attributions of each story's provocateur's intent. Examples are presented.

Reliability: Coefficient alpha was .90.

Author: Crick, N. R., and Dodge, K. A.

Article: Social information-processing mechanisms in reactive and proactive aggression.

Journal: *Child Development*, June 1996, 67(3), 993–1002.

Related Research: Dell Fitzgerald, P., & Asher, S. R. (1987, August). *Aggressive-rejected children's attributional biases about liked and disliked peers.* Paper presented at the annual meeting of the American Psychological Association, New York.

9422

Test Name: INTERFERENCE SCALE

Purpose: To assess one's perception of the extent of work and family interference with each other.

Number of Items: 8

Format: A sample item is presented.

Reliability: Coefficient alpha was .71.

Validity: Correlations with other variables ranged from −.16 to .50.

Author: Duxbury, L. E., et al.

Article: Work and family environments and the adoption of computer-supported supplemental work-at-home.

Journal: *Journal of Vocational Behavior*, August 1996, 49(1), 1–23.

Related Research: Bohen, H., & Viveros-Long, A. (1981). *Balancing jobs and family life.* Philadelphia: Temple University Press.

9423

Test Name: INTERNAL CONTROL AND CHANCE CONTROL SCALES

Purpose: To measure perceptions of control.

Number of Items: 12

Format: Six-point scales are anchored by 1 (disagree strongly) and 6 (agree strongly).

Reliability: Alpha coefficients ranged from .65 to .77.

Author: Tix, A. P., and Frazier, P. A.

Article: The use of religious coping during stressful life events: Main effects, moderation, and mediation.

Journal: *Journal of Consulting and Clinical Psychology*, April 1998, 66(2), 411–422.

Related Research: Wallston, K., et al. (1978). Development of the Multidimensional Health Locus of Control (MHLC) scales. *Health Education Monographs*, 6, 160.

9424

Test Name: INTERNAL–EXTERNAL LOCUS OF CONTROL SCALE

Purpose: To determine one's belief concerning internal–external control of one's behavior.

Number of Items: 23

Reliability: Alpha coefficients ranged from .65 to .79.

Validity: Correlations with other variables ranged from −.36 to .30.

Author: Pallant, J. F.

Article: Development and validation of a scale to measure perceived control of internal states.

Journal: *Journal of Personality Assessment*, October 2000, 75(2), 308–337.

Related Research: Rotter, J. B. (1966). Generalized expectancies for internal versus external control of reinforcement. *Psychological Monographs*, 80 (Whole No. 609).

9425

Test Name: INTERNAL–EXTERNAL LOCUS OF CONTROL SCALE

Purpose: To measure locus of control.

Number of Items: 29

Reliability: Internal consistency was .66 and .75.

Validity: Correlations with other variables ranged from −.51 to .06.

Author: Zea, M. C., et al.

Article: Reliability, ethnic comparability, and validity evidence for a condensed measure of proactive coping: The BAPC-C.

Journal: *Educational and Psychological Measurement*, April 1996, *56*(2), 330–343.

Related Research: Rotter, J. B. (1966). Generalized expectancies for internal versus external locus of control. *Psychological Monographs*, *80*, 1–28.

9426

Test Name: INTERNAL–EXTERNAL LOCUS OF CONTROL SCALE—CHINESE VERSION

Purpose: To measure locus of control.

Number of Items: 19

Format: Forced-choice format.

Reliability: Alpha was .94.

Validity: Correlations with self-monitoring ranged from −.03 to .14.

Author: Li, F.

Article: Age differences in locus of control and self-monitoring in China.

Journal: *Psychological Reports*, December 1997, *81*(3, Part II), 1089–1090.

Related Research: Wang, D. (1991). [A norming study of a Chinese revision of Rotter's Internal–External Locus of Control Scale with Chinese college students]. *Acta Psychologica Sinica*, *23*, 292–298.

9427

Test Name: INTERNAL LOCUS OF ATTRIBUTON FOR ACADEMIC SUCCESS SCALE

Purpose: To measure internal attribution.

Number of Items: 4

Format: Responses are made on a Likert-type scale ranging from 5 (strongly agree) to 1 (strongly disagree). All items are presented.

Reliability: Alpha coefficients were .62 and .64.

Author: Pascarella, E. T., et al.

Article: Influences on students' internal locus of attribution for academic success in the first year of college.

Journal: *Research in Higher Education*, December 1996, *37*(6), 731–757.

Related Research: Pascarella, E., et al. (1994). Impacts of 2-year and 4-year colleges on learning orientations: A preliminary study. *Community College Journal of Research and Practice*, *18*, 577–589.

9428

Test Name: INTERNALITY, POWERFUL OTHERS, AND CHANCE SCALE

Purpose: To measure locus of control.

Number of Items: 12

Format: Eleven-point scales are anchored by 0 (strongly disagree) and 10 (strongly agree). Sample items are presented.

Reliability: Alpha coefficients ranged from .81 to .87.

Validity: Correlations with other variables ranged from −.48 to .57.

Author: Judge, T. A., et al.

Article: Dispositional effects on job and life satisfaction: The role of core evaluations.

Journal: *Journal of Applied Psychology*, February 1998, *83*(1), 17–34.

Related Research: Levenson, H. (1981). Differentiating among internality, powerful others and chance. In H. M. Lefcourt (Ed.), *Research with the locus of control construct* (Vol. 1, pp. 15–63). New York: Academic Press.

9429

Test Name: INTERNALITY SCALE

Purpose: To measure locus of control.

Number of Items: 10

Format: Five-point Likert format.

Reliability: Coefficient alpha was .66.

Author: Judge, T. A., et al.

Article: Managerial coping with organizational change: A dispositional perspective.

Journal: *Journal of Applied Psychology*, February 1999, *84*(1), 107–122.

Related Research: Levenson, H. (1981). Differentiating between internality, powerful others, and chance. In H. M. Lefcourt (Ed.), *Research with the locus of control construct* (Vol. 1, pp. 15–63). New York: Academic Press.

9430

Test Name: INTERROLE CONFLICT SCALE

Purpose: To measure family–work conflict and work–family conflict.

Number of Items: 10

Format: Includes 2 subscales: Work–Family Conflict and Family–Work Conflict. Responses are made on a 5-point scale ranging from 1 (strongly disagree) to 5 (strongly agree). Sample items are presented.

Reliability: Alpha coefficients ranged from .82 to .89.

Validity: Correlations with other variables ranged from −.26 to .52.

Author: Aryee, S., et al.

Article: Role stressors, inter-role conflict, and well being: The moderating influence of spousal support and coping behaviors among employed parents in Hong Kong.

Journal: *Journal of Vocational Behavior*, April 1999, 54(2), 259–278.

Related Research: Netemeyer, R. G., et al. (1996). Development and validation of work–family conflict and family–work conflict scales. *Journal of Applied Psychology*, 81, 400–410.

9431

Test Name: JANIS–FIELD FEELINGS OF INADEQUACY SCALE

Purpose: To measure self-esteem.

Number of Items: 20

Format: Responses are made on 5-point Likert scales. An example is given.

Reliability: Coefficient alpha was .70.

Author: Horan, J. J.

Article: Effects of computer-based cognitive restructuring on rationally mediated self-esteem.

Journal: *Journal of Counseling Psychology*, October 1996, 43(4), 371–375.

Related Research: Eagly, A. H. (1967). Involvement as a determinant of response to favorable information. *Journal of*

Personality and Social Psychology, 7, 1–15.

9432

Test Name: JAPANESE ATTRIBUTIONAL STYLES QUESTIONNAIRE

Purpose: To measure attributional style among Japanese undergraduates.

Number of Items: 60

Format: Seven-point scales.

Reliability: Alpha coefficients ranged from .69 to .80.

Authors: Sakamoto, S., and Kambara, M.

Article: A longitudinal study of the relationship between attributional style, life events, and depression in Japanese undergraduates.

Journal: *Journal of Social Psychology*, April 1998, *138*(2), 229–240.

Related Research: Peterson, C., et al. (1982). The Attributional Style Questionnaire. *Cognitive Theory and Research*, 6, 287–299.

9433

Test Name: JOB APPLICANT PERCEPTIONS SCALE

Purpose: To measure job applicant perceptions.

Number of Items: 61

Format: Includes Organizational Reputation, Pre-Job Attributes, Pre-Applicant Attraction, Recruiter Behaviors, Post-Job Attributes, Post-Applicant Attraction.

Reliability: Alpha coefficients ranged from .40 to .91.

Author: Turban, D. B., et al.

Article: Applicant attraction to

firms: Influences of organization reputation, job and organizational attributes, and recruiter behaviors.

Journal: *Journal of Vocational Behavior*, February 1998, 52(1), 24–44.

Related Research: Harris, M. M., & Fink, L. S. (1987). A field study of applicant reactions to employment opportunities: Does the recruiter make a difference? *Personnel Psychology*, 40, 765–784.

Turban, D. B., & Dougherty, T. W. (1992). Influences of campus recruiting on applicant attraction to firms. *Academy of Management Journal*, 35, 739–765.

9434

Test Name: JOB EXPECTATIONS SCALE

Purpose: To assess expectations about a job.

Number of Items: 5

Format: Scales range from 1 (to a very little extent) to 5 (to a very great extent). All items are presented.

Reliability: Alpha coefficients ranged from .86 to .93 across time.

Validity: Correlations with other variables ranged from −.63 to .76.

Author: Buckley, M. R., et al.

Article: Investigating newcomer expectations and job-related outcomes.

Journal: *Journal of Applied Psychology*, June 1998, 83(3), 452–461.

9435

Test Name: JOB SEARCH EFFICACY SCALE

Purpose: To assess competency in searching for a job.

Number of Items: 10

Format: Scales range from 1 (not at all confident) to 5 (highly confident). All items are presented.

Reliability: Coefficient alpha was .91.

Validity: Correlations with other variables ranged from −.24 to .51.

Author: Wanberg, C. R., et al.

Article: Unemployed individuals: Motives, job-search competencies, and job-search constraints as predictors of job seeking and reemployment.

Journal: *Journal of Applied Psychology*, December 1999, *84*(6), 897–910.

Related Research: Solberg, B. D., et al. (1994). Assessing career search expectations: Development and validation of the Career Search Efficacy Scale. *Journal of Career Assessment*, 2, 111–123.

9436

Test Name: JOB SEARCH SELF-EFFICACY SCALE

Purpose: To measure job search self-efficacy.

Number of Items: 10

Format: Responses are made on a 10-point scale ranging from 1 (not at all confident) to 10 (totally confident). Examples are presented.

Reliability: Coefficient alpha was .87.

Validity: Correlations with other variables ranged from .15 to .53.

Author: Saks, A. M., and Ashforth, B. E.

Article: Effects of individual differences and job search

behavior on the employment status of recent university graduates.

Journal: *Journal of Vocational Behavior*, April 1999, *54*(2), 335–349.

Related Research: Kaufer, R., & Hulin, C. L. (1985). Individual differences in successful job searches following lay-off. *Personnel Psychology*, 38, 835–847.

9437

Test Name: JOB-SEEKING SELF-EFFICACY SCALE

Purpose: To assess individuals' judgment about their competence at job-seeking.

Number of Items: 6

Format: Five-point scales are anchored by 1 (not at all) and 5 (a great deal).

Reliability: Internal consistency was .85.

Validity: Correlations with other variables ranged from −.31 to .55.

Author: Wanberg, C. R., et al.

Article: Individuals without jobs: An empirical study of job-seeking behavior and reemployment.

Journal: *Journal of Applied Psychology*, February 1996, *81*(1), 76–87.

Related Research: van Ryn, M., & Vinokur, A. D. (1991). *Mediators of intervention effects: The role of experimentally manipulated self-efficacy in determining job-search behavior among the unemployed.* Unpublished manuscript.

9438

Test Name: JOB SELF-EFFICACY AND COLLECTIVE EFFICACY SCALES

Purpose: To measure self-confidence in the ability to do a job and confidence in the members of a work group to do a job.

Number of Items: 17

Format: Scales range from 1 (very inaccurate) to 6 (very accurate). Sample items are presented.

Reliability: Coefficient alpha was .95 (self-efficacy) and .88 (collective efficacy).

Validity: Correlations with other variables ranged from −.10 to .08.

Author: Schaubroeck, J., et al.

Article: Collective efficacy versus self-efficacy in coping responses to stressors and control: A cross-cultural study.

Journal: *Journal of Applied Psychology*, August 2000, *85*(4), 512–525.

Related Research: Riggs, M. L., et al. (1994). Development and validation of self-efficacy and outcome expectancy scales for job-related applications. *Educational and Psychological Measurement*, 54, 793–802.

9439

Test Name: KUDER TASK SELF-EFFICACY SCALE

Purpose: To measure career-task self-efficacy.

Number of Items: 30

Format: Responses are made on a 5-point scale ranging from 0 (no confidence) to 4 (absolute confidence). Includes 10 subscales: Artistic, Musical, Mechanical, Scientific, Outdoor, Clerical, Computational, Literary, Social Service, and Persuasive.

Reliability: Test-retest reliabilities ranged from .66 to .84.

Validity: Correlations with other variables ranged from .00 to .76.

Author: Lucas, J. L., et al.

Article: Development of a career task self-efficacy scale: The Kuder Task Self-Efficacy Scale.

Journal: *Journal of Vocational Behavior*, June 1997, *50*(3), 432–459.

9440

Test Name: LEARNING AWARENESS QUESTIONNAIRE

Purpose: To measure the level of awareness of learning processes.

Number of Items: 17

Format: Three-point response scales are anchored by "minimum learning awareness" and "maximum learning awareness." All items are presented.

Reliability: Split-half reliability was .79.

Validity: Index of face validity was .70 ($n = 5$).

Author: Kumar, S., and Harizuka, S.

Article: Cooperative learning-based approach and development of learning awareness and achievement in mathematics in elementary school.

Journal: *Psychological Reports*, April 1998, *82*(2), 587–591.

9441

Test Name: LEARNING CONFIDENCE SCALE

Purpose: To measure learning confidence.

Number of Items: 4

Format: Five-point scales range from 1 (strongly disagree) to 5 (strongly agree). A sample item is presented.

Reliability: Coefficient alpha was .82.

Validity: Correlations with other variables ranged from −.29 to .40.

Author: Birdi, K., et al.

Article: Correlates and perceived outcomes of four types of employee development activity.

Journal: *Journal of Applied Psychology*, December 1997, *82*(6), 845–857.

Related Research: Noe, R. A., & Wilk, S. L. (1993). Investigation of the factors that influence employees' participation in development activities. *Journal of Applied Psychology, 78*, 291–302.

9442

Test Name: LEVEL OF ATTRIBUTION AND CHANGE SCALE

Purpose: To identify cause of procrastination.

Number of Items: 33

Format: Includes 11 factors: Environment, Interpersonal Conflicts, Intra-Personal Conflicts, Family of Origin, Biology, Bad Luck, Insufficient Effort, Fate, Maladaptive Thoughts, Deliberate Lifestyle, and Lack of Needed Skills. Responses are made on a 7-point Likert-type scale ranging from 1 (strongly disagree) to 7 (strongly agree). Examples are given.

Reliability: Average test-retest (4 weeks) reliability was .70.

Author: Cook, P. F.

Article: Effects of counselors' etiology attributions on college students' procrastination.

Journal: *Journal of Counseling Psychology*, July 2000, *47*(3), 352–361.

Related Research: Bellis, J. M. (1993). *The transtheoretical model of change applied to psychotherapy: A psychometric assessment of related instruments*. Unpublished doctoral dissertation, University of Rhode Island.

9443

Test Name: LITERACY ACQUISTION PERCEPTION PROFILE

Purpose: To determine teachers' perceptions of literacy acquisition.

Number of Items: 20

Format: Includes two subscales: Reading Readiness Skills and Emergent Literacy. Responses are made on a 5-point scale ranging from 1 (strongly disagree) to 5 (strongly agree). All items are presented.

Reliability: Alpha coefficients were .80 and .77. Test-retest (10 days) reliability were .85 and .73.

Validity: Correlations with other variables ranged from −.75 to .32.

Author: McMahon, R., et al.

Article: Relationships between kindergarten teachers' perceptions of literacy acquisition and children's literacy involvement and classroom materials.

Journal: *Journal of Educational Research*, January/February 1998, *91*(3), 173–182.

9444

Test Name: LOCUS OF CONTROL RACE IDEOLOGY FACTOR

Purpose: To measure beliefs about the operation of personal and external forces in the context of the race situation in the United States.

Number of Items: 12

Format: Uses an ipsative scoring format.

Validity: Correlation with other variables ranged from −.19 to .14.

Author: Sodowsky, G. R., et al.

Article: Correlates of self-reported multicultural competencies: Counselor multicultural social desirability, race, social inadequacy, locus of control racial ideology, and multicultural training.

Journal: *Journal of Counseling Psychology*, July 1998, 45(3), 256–264.

Related Research: Gurin, P., et al. (1969). Internal-external control in the motivational dynamics of Black youth. *Journal of Social Issues*, 25, 29–53.

9445

Test Name: LOCUS OF CONTROL SCALE

Purpose: To measure locus of control.

Number of Items: 6

Format: Responses are made on a 4-point scale ranging from "strongly disagree" to "strongly agree." Examples are presented.

Reliability: Coefficient alpha was .71.

Validity: Correlations with other variables ranged from −.03 to .57.

Author: Rojewski, J. W., and Yang, B.

Article: Longitudinal analysis of select influences on adolescents' occupational aspirations.

Journal: *Journal of Vocational Behavior*, December 1997, 51(3), 325–410.

Related Research: Ingels, S. J., et al. (1992). *National education longitudinal study of 1988: First follow-up-student component data file user's manual.* Washington, DC: U. S. Department of Education, National Center for Educational Statistics.

9446

Test Name: LOCUS OF CONTROL SCALE

Purpose: To measure locus of control.

Number of Items: 24

Format: Includes 3 factors: Internal, Chance, and Powerful Others. Responses are made on a 5-point Likert-type scale ranging from 1 (strongly disagree) to 5 (strongly agree).

Reliability: Alpha coefficients ranged from .66 to .74.

Validity: Correlations with the Work Locus of Control Scale ranged from −.38 to .46.

Author: Macan, T. H., et al.

Article: Spector's Work Locus of Control Scale: Dimensionality and validity evidence.

Journal: *Educational and Psychological Measurement*, April 1996, 56(2), 349–357.

Related Research: Levinson, H. (1974). Activism and powerful others: Distinction within the concept of internal-external control. *Journal of Personality Assessment*, 38, 377–383.

9447

Test Name: LOCUS OF CONTROL SCALES

Purpose: To assess locus of control.

Format: Five-point Likert format.

Reliability: Coefficient alpha exceeded .74.

Validity: Correlations with the variables ranged from −.23 to .87.

Authors: Leone, C., and Burns, J. T.

Article: Assessing contingency, power, and efficacy: A psychometric investigation of motivation.

Journal: *Journal of Social Psychology*, April 1997, 137(2), 255–265.

Related Research: Paulhus, P. (1983). Sphere-specific measures of perceived control. *Journal of Personality and Social Psychology*, 44, 1253–1265.

Leflourt, H. M., et al. (1979). The Multidimensional-Multi-Distributional Causality Scale: The development of a goal specific locus of control scale. *Canadian Journal of Behavioral Science*, 11, 286–304.

9448

Test Name: LOCUS OF CONTROL TEST

Purpose: To measure the degree of external/internal locus of control.

Number of Items: 23

Format: Forced-choice format.

Reliability: Cronbach alphas ranged from .75 to .78.

Author: Bernardi, R. A., and Nydegger, R. V.

Article: Changes in distribution of mean scores on locus of control by staff level in public accounting firms.

Journal: *Psychological Reports*, December 1999, 85(3, Part II), 1081–1087.

Related Research: Rotter, J. B. (1966). Generalized expectancies for internal versus external control of reinforcement. *Psychological Monographs, 80,* No. 1 (Whole No. 601).

9449

Test Name: MANAGERIAL SELF-AWARENESS SCALES

Purpose: To measure the ability to assess one's own behaviors and skills in the workplace.

Number of Items: 21 to 49, depending on workplace.

Format: Five and seven-point Likert formats. Scoring procedures are described.

Reliability: Alpha coefficients ranged from .89 to .97 (self-ratings) and from .90 to .98 (direct report ratings).

Author: Church, A. H.

Article: Managerial self-awareness in high-performing individuals in organizations.

Journal: *Journal of Applied Psychology,* April, 1997, *82*(2), 281–292.

Related Research: Harris, M. M., & Schaubroeck, J. (1988). A meta-analysis of self-supervisor, self-peer, and peer-supervisory ratings. *Personal Psychology, 41,* 43–62.

9450

Test Name: MASTERY SCALE

Purpose: To determine respondents' feelings on whether their life is under their control or whether it is fatalistically ruled.

Number of Items: 7

Format: Responses are made on a 4-point scale ranging from 1

(strongly agree) to 4 (strongly disagree).

Reliability: Coefficient alpha was .76.

Validity: Correlations with other variables ranged from −.39 to .52.

Author: Pallant, J. F.

Article: Development and validation of a scale to measure perceived control of internal states.

Journal: *Journal of Personality Assessment,* October 2000, *75*(2), 308–337.

Related Research: Pearlin, L. I., & Schooler, C. (1978). The structure of coping. *Journal of Health and Social Behavior, 19,* 2–21.

9451

Test Name: MASTERY SCALE— MODIFIED

Purpose: To measure internal locus of control regarding the professional's work environment.

Number of Items: 6

Format: An example is presented.

Reliability: Coefficient alpha was .79.

Validity: Correlations with other variables ranged from −.54 to .35.

Author: Holder, J. C., and Vaux, A.

Article: African American professionals: Coping with occupational stress in predominantly White work environments.

Journal: *Journal of Vocational Behavior,* December 1998, *53*(3), 315–333.

Related Research: Pearlin, L. I., & Schooler, C. (1978). The structure of coping. *Journal of*

Health and Social Behavior, 19, 2–21.

9452

Test Name: MATH COURSES SUBSCALE—REVISED

Purpose: To measure self-efficacy.

Number of Items: 27

Format: Respondents rate on a scale ranging from 0 (no confidence) to 9 (complete confidence) their confidence in their ability to complete each of the 27 mathematics-related courses.

Reliability: Coefficient alpha was .93.

Author: Schaefers, K. G., et al.

Article: Women's career development: Can theoretically derived variables predict persistence in engineering majors?

Journal: *Journal of Counseling Psychology,* April 1997, *44*(2), 173–183.

Related Research: Hackett, G. (1985). The role of mathematics self-efficacy in the choice of multi-related majors of college women and men: A path analysis. *Journal of Counseling Psychology, 32,* 47–56.

9453

Test Name: MATH–SCIENCE OUTCOME EXPECTANCIES SCALE

Purpose: To measure math–science outcome expectancies.

Number of Items: 7

Format: Responses are made on a 5-point scale. Examples are presented.

Reliability: Internal consistency was .80.

Validity: Correlation with the

Career Decision-Making Outcome Expectancies Scale was .71, corrected for attenuation.

Author: Fouad, N. A., and Smith, P. L.

Article: A test of a social cognitive model for middle school students: Math and science.

Journal: *Journal of Counseling Psychology*, July 1996, *43*(3), 338–346.

9454

Test Name: MATH/SCIENCE OUTCOME EXPECTANCIES SUBSCALE—MODIFIED

Purpose: To indicate outcome expectations.

Number of Items: 9

Format: Responses are made on a 6-point Likert scale. Sample items are presented.

Reliability: Internal consistency reliability was .81.

Validity: Correlation with other variables ranged from −.33 to .59.

Author: Ferry, T. R., et al.

Article: The role of family context in a social cognitive model for career-related choice behavior: A math and science perspective.

Journal: *Journal of Vocational Behavior*, December 2000, *57*(3), 348–364.

Related Research: Fouad, N., et al. (1995). Reliability and validity evidence for the Middle School Self-Efficacy Scale. *Measurement and Evaluation in Counseling and Development, 30,* 17–31.

9455

Test Name: MATH–SCIENCE SELF-EFFICACY SCALE

Purpose: To assess math-science self-efficacy.

Number of Items: 12

Format: Responses are made on a 5-point scale to indicate ability, ranging from 1 (very high) to 5 (very low).

Reliability: Internal consistency was .84.

Validity: Correlations with the Career Decision-Making Self-Efficacy Scale, corrected for attenuation, was .54.

Author: Fouad, N. A., and Smith, P. L.

Article: A test of a social cognitive model for middle school students: Math and science.

Journal: *Journal of Counseling Psychology*, July 1996, *43*(3), 338–346.

9456

Test Name: MATH/SCIENCE SELF-EFFICACY SCALES

Purpose: To measure math/science self-efficacy.

Number of Items: 35

Format: Includes 3 scales: Course, Technical Scientific Fields, and Occupational Self-Efficacy scales. Ten-point scales are used.

Reliability: Alpha coefficients ranged from .90 to .95.

Validity: Correlations with other variables ranged from .14 to .52.

Author: Luzzo, D. A., et al.

Article: Effects of self-efficacy-enhancing interventions on the math/science self-efficacy and career interests, goals, and actions of career undecided college students.

Journal: *Journal of Counseling Psychology*, April, 1999, *46*(2), 233–243.

Related Research: Cooper, S. E., & Robinson, D. A. G. (1991). The relationship of mathematics self-efficacy beliefs to mathematics anxiety and performance. *Measurement and Evaluation in Counseling and Development, 24,* 4–11.

9457

Test Name: MATH SELF-EFFICACY SUBSCALE

Purpose: To assess confidence in completing various tasks.

Number of Items: 7

Format: Responses are made on a 6-point Likert scale.

Reliability: Alpha coefficients were .90 and .93.

Author: Ferry, T. R., et al.

Article: The role of family context in a social cognitive model for career-related choice behavior: A math and science perspective.

Journal: *Journal of Vocational Behavior*, December 2000, *57*(3), 348–364.

Related Research: Bieschke, K. (1993). *A causal model of math/science career aspirations.* Unpublished doctoral dissertation, Michigan State University.

9458

Test Name: MATHEMATICS COURSE SELF-EFFICACY SCALE—REVISED

Purpose: To measure confidence in students' ability to complete each of 15 math-related college courses.

Number of Items: 15

Format: Responses are made on a 10-point scale ranging from 0 (no confidence) to 9 (complete confidence).

Reliability: Coefficient alpha was .93. Test-retest (2 weeks) correlation was .94

Author: Gainor, K. A., and Lent, R. N.

Article: : Social cognitive expectations and racial identity attitudes in predicting the math choice intentions of Black college students.

Journal: *Journal of Counseling Psychology*, October 1998, 45(4), 403–413.

Related Research: Betz, N. E., & Hackett, G. (1983). The relationship of math self-efficacy to the selection of science-based college majors. *Journal of Vocational Behaviors*, 23, 329–345.

9459

Test Name: MATHEMATICS SELF-CONCEPT SCALE

Purpose: To assess math self-concept.

Number of Items: 10

Format: Scales range from 1 (definitely false) to 8 (definitely true). A sample item is presented.

Reliability: Internal consistency estimates ranged from .84 to .95.

Author: Pajares, F., and Urdan, T.

Article: Exploratory factor analysis of the Mathematics Anxiety Scale.

Journal: *Measurement and Evaluation in Counseling and Development*, April 1996, 29(1), 35–47.

Related Research: Marsh, H. W. (1992). *SDQIII*. Campbelltown, Australia: University of Western Sydney, Publication Unit.

9460

Test Name: MATHEMATICS SELF-EFFICACY SCALE

Purpose: To assess confidence in the ability to solve math problems.

Number of Items: 18

Format: Scales range from 1 (no confidence) to 5 (complete confidence).

Reliability: Internal reliabilities ranged from .90 to .92.

Author: Pajares, F., and Urdan, T.

Article: Exploratory factor analysis of the Mathematics Anxiety Scale.

Journal: *Measurement and Evaluation in Counseling and Development*, April 1996, 29(1), 35–47.

Related Research: Pajares, F., & Kranzler, J. (1995). Self-efficacy beliefs and general mental ability in mathematical problem-solving: A path analysis. *Journal of Educational Psychology*, 86, 193–203.

9461

Test Name: MATHEMATICS SELF-EFFICACY SCALE

Purpose: To measure mathematics self-efficacy.

Number of Items: 52

Format: Responses are made on a 10-point scale ranging from 0 (no confidence) to 9 (complete confidence).

Reliability: Alpha coefficients ranged from .90 to .96.

Validity: Correlations with other variables ranged from −.39 to .68.

Author: Lapan, R. T., et al.

Article: Efficacy expectations and vocational interests as mediators between sex and choice of math/science college majors: A longitudinal study.

Journal: *Journal of Vocational Behavior*, December 1996, 49(3), 277–291.

Related Research: Betz, N. E., & Hackett, G. (1983). The relationship of mathematics self-efficacy expectations to the selection of science-based college majors. *Journal of Vocational Behavior*, 23, 329–345.

9462

Test Name: MATHEMATICS SELF-EFFICACY SCALE— REVISED (MODIFIED)

Purpose: To assess the math self-efficacy of college students in terms of solution of math problems, completion of everyday math tasks, and satisfactory performance in math-related college courses.

Number of Items: 52

Format: Five-point Likert format.

Reliability: Alpha coefficients ranged from .91 to .95.

Validity: Correlations between subscales ranged from .21 to .48.

Author: Kranzler, J. H., and Patares, F.

Article: An exploratory factor analysis of the Mathematics Self-Efficacy Scale—Revised (MSES–R).

Journal: *Measurement and Evaluation in Counseling and Development*, January 1997, 29(4), 215–228.

Related Research: Betz, N. E., & Hackett, G. (1983). The relationship of mathematics self-efficacy expectations to the selection of science-based college majors. *Journal of Vocational Behavior*, 23, 329–345.

9463

Test Name: MEASURE OF ACTUALIZATION OF POTENTIAL

Purpose: To measure actualization of potential.

Number of Items: 27

Format: Five-point scales. All items are presented.

Reliability: Test-retest reliability (1 week) was .87.

Validity: Correlations with clinical assessments ranged from .34 to .75 across subscales and across judges.

Author: Leclerc, G., et al.

Article: Criterion validity of a new measure of self-actualization.

Journal: *Psychological Reports*, December 1999, *85*(3, Part 2), 1167–1176.

9464

Test Name: MEASURE OF BODY APPERCEPTION

Purpose: To assess two aspects of psychological investment in body image.

Number of Items: 8

Format: Includes 2 factors: Concern about Appearance and Concern about Body Integrity. Responses are made on a 4-point scale ranging from 1 (strongly disagree) to 4 (strongly agree).

Reliability: Alpha coefficients ranged from .60 to .70.

Author: Perczek, R., et al.

Article: Coping, mood, and aspects of personality in Spanish translation and evidence of convergence with English versions.

Journal: *Journal of Personality Assessment*, February 2000, *74*(1), 63–87.

Related Research: Carver, C. S., et al. (1998). Concerns about aspects of body image and adjustment to early stage breast cancer. *Psychosomatic Medicine, 60,* 168–174.

9465

Test Name: MEASURE OF SELF-ACTUALIZATION OF POTENTIAL

Purpose: To evaluate the autonomy, adaptation, and psychological functioning of adults.

Number of Items: 54

Format: Five-point scales. Sample items presented.

Reliability: Alphas ranged from .14 to .77.

Validity: Various measures of reliabilities ranged from .6 to .90.

Author: Lafrancois, R., et al.

Article: Reliability of a new measure of self-actualization.

Journal: *Psychological Reports*, June 1998, *82*(3) Part 1, 875–878.

Related Research: Lefrancois, R., et al. (1997). The development and validation of self-report measure of self-actualization. *Social Behavior and Personality, an International Journal, 25,* 353–367.

9466

Test Name: MIDDLE SCHOOL SELF-EFFICACY SCALE

Purpose: To measure self-efficacy, outcome-expectancy, and intentions and goals in career decision-making or mathematics/science.

Number of Items: 49

Format: Five-point Likert format. All items are presented.

Reliability: Alpha coefficients ranged from .56 to .81 across subscales.

Validity: Confirmatory factor analytic and criterion-related validity evidence is provided.

Author: Fouad, N. A., et al.

Article: Reliability and validity evidence for the Middle School Self-Efficacy Scale.

Journal: *Measurement and Evaluation in Counseling and Development*, April 1997, *30*(1), 17–31.

9467

Test Name: MISSOURI COMPREHENSIVE GUIDANCE EVALUATION SURVEY

Purpose: To measure career self-efficacy.

Number of Items: 62

Format: Scales range from 1 (very low) to 7 (very high). Sample items are presented.

Reliability: Internal consistency reliabilities ranged from .71 to .96.

Author: O'Brien, K. M., et al.

Article: Broadening career horizons for students in at-risk environments.

Journal: *Career Development Quarterly*, March 1999, *47*(3), 215–228.

Related Research: Lapan, R. T., et al. (1997). Developing guidance competency self-efficacy scales for high school and middle school students. *Measurement and Evaluation in Counseling and Development, 30,* 4–16.

9468

Test Name: MISSOURI GUIDANCE COMPETENCY EDUCATION SURVEY

Purpose: To measure competency self-efficacy for high school and middle school students.

Number of Items: 98 (high school), 62 (middle school).

Format: Scales range from 1 (very low level of confidence) to 7 (very high level of confidence). Sample items are presented.

Reliability: Internal consistency reliabilities ranged from .71 to .87 (high school) and from .71 to .88 (middle school).

Validity: Correlations with other variables ranged from −.23 to .18.

Author: Lapan, R. T., et al.

Article: Developing guidance competency self-efficacy scales for high school and middle school students.

Journal: *Measurement and Evaluation in Counseling and Development,* April 1997, *30*(1), 4–16.

9469

Test Name: MODIFIED WORK LOCUS OF CONTROL SCALE

Purpose: To measure work locus of control that reflects control the respondent perceives he/she might have on the job.

Number of Items: 20

Format: Five-point Likert scales. All items are presented.

Reliability: Alphas ranged from .77 to .87. Total alpha was .88.

Author: Gupchup, G. V., and Wolfgang, A. P.

Article: A modified work locus of control scale: Preliminary investigation of reliability and validity in a sample of pharmacists.

Journal: *Psychological Reports,* October 1997, *81*(2), 640–642.

Related Research: Spector, P. E. (1988). Development of the Work Locus of Control Scale. *Journal of Occupational Psychology, 61,* 335–340.

9470

Test Name: MULTIDIMENSIONAL BODY–SELF RELATIONS QUESTIONNAIRE— APPEARANCE EVALUATION SUBSCALE

Purpose: To measure level of satisfaction and/or dissatisfaction with one's body.

Number of Items: 7

Format: Responses are made on a 5-point scale ranging from 1 (definitely disagree) to 5 (definitely agree). Examples are presented.

Reliability: Alpha coefficients were .88 and .89. Test-retest reliabilities were .91 (3 months) and .85 (3 weeks).

Validity: Correlations with other variables ranged from −.72 to .80.

Author: Mazzeo, S. E.

Article: Modification of an existing measure of body image preoccupation and its relationship to disordered eating in female college students.

Journal: *Journal of Counseling Psychology,* January 1999, *46*(1), 42–50.

Related Research: Cash, T. F. (1994). *The Multidimensional Body-Self Relations users' manual.* Unpublished manuscript, Old Dominion University, Norfolk, Virginia.

9471

Test Name: MULTIDIMENSIONAL SCALES OF PERCEIVED SELF-EFFICACY

Purpose: To measure confidence to organize and execute tasks.

Number of Items: 57

Format: Scales range from 1 (not well at all) to 7 (very well). Sample items are presented.

Reliability: Alpha coefficients ranged from .60 to .87 across subscales.

Author: Miller, J. C., et al.

Article: An examination of psychometric properties of Bandura's Multidimensional Scales of Perceived Self-Efficacy.

Journal: *Measurement and Evaluation in Counseling and Development,* January 1999, *31*(4), 186–196.

Related Research: Bandura, A. (1989). *The Multidimensional Self-Efficacy Scales.* Unpublished manuscript, Stanford University, Stanford, CA.

9472

Test Name: MULTI-PERSPECTIVE MULTI-DOMAIN SELF-CONCEPT INVENTORIES

Purpose: To measure domains of self-concept and perspectives on self-concept.

Number of Items: 80

Format: Two inventories include 8 subscales: Academic Ability, Appearance, Social, General, Reflected Parental Appraisal, Reflected School Appraisal, Downward Comparison, Upward Comparison, and Global Evaluation. Responses are made on a 4-point scale ranging from 1 (false) to 4 (true). Sample items are presented.

Reliability: Alpha coefficients ranged from .52 to .84.

Author: McCall, R. B., et al.

Article: The nature and correlates of underachievement among elementary school children in Hong Kong.

Journal: *Child Development*, May/June 2000, *71*(3), 785–801.

Related Research: Cheung, P. C., & Lau, S. (1995). *A multi-perspective multi-domain model of self-concept: Structure and sources of self-concept knowledge.* Unpublished manuscript, Chinese University of Hong Kong.

9473

Test Name: NEW IMAGINARY AUDIENCE SCALE

Purpose: To assess how often individuals think about an imaginary audience in given situations.

Number of Items: 42

Format: Four-point rating scales range from "never" to "often."

Reliability: Alpha was .92.

Validity: Correlations with alcohol use ranged from .22 to .36 across subscales.

Author: Montgomery, R. L., et al.

Article: The "imaginary audience," self-handicapping and drinking patterns among college students.

Journal: *Psychological Reports*, December 1996, *79*(3) Part 1, 783–786.

Related Research: Laisley, D. K., et al. (1989). Separation-individuation and the new look at the imaginary audience and personal fable: A test of an integrative theory. *Journal of Adolescent Research, 4,* 483–505.

9474

Test Name: NOWICKI-STRICKLAND LOCUS OF CONTROL SCALE

Purpose: To measure locus of control.

Number of Items: 40

Format: Responses are "yes" or "no."

Reliability: Split-half reliabilities ranged from .74 to .86.

Validity: Correlations with other variables ranged from −.38 to .24.

Author: Hall, C. W., et al.

Article: College students' perception of facial expressions.

Journal: *Perceptual and Motor Skills,* December 1999, *89*(3, Part 1), 763–770.

Related Research: Nowicki, S., & Strickland, B. (1973). *Adult Nowicki–Strickland Internal–External Locus of Control Scale.* (Available from Stephen Nowicki, Psychology Department, Emory University, Atlanta, GA 30322.)

9475

Test Name: NUTRITION SELF-EFFICACY SCALE

Purpose: To measure confidence in choosing healthy foods in 21 situations.

Number of Items: 21

Format: Scales range from 1 (highly confident) to 5 (not at all confident).

Reliability: Alpha coefficients ranged from .63 to .69.

Author: Sands, T., et al.

Article: Prevention of health-risk behaviors in college students: Evaluating seven variables.

Journal: *Journal of College*

Student Development, July/August 1998, *39*(4), 331–342.

Related Research: Ward, S. (1990). Characterizing adolescent eating behaviors with Bandura's social learning theory. (Doctoral dissertation, University of Virginia). *Dissertation Abstracts International, 51,* A4030.

9476

Test Name: OCCUPATIONAL SELF-EFFICACY SCALE

Purpose: To measure students' perceptions of self-efficacy.

Number of Items: 20

Format: Includes 10 female-dominated and 10 male-dominated occupations.

Reliability: Alpha coefficients were .91 and .92.

Author: Betz, N. E., and Schifano, R. S.

Article: Evaluation of an intervention to increase realistic self-efficacy and interests in college women.

Journal: *Journal of Vocational Behavior,* February 2000, *56*(1), 35–52.

Related Research: Betz, N. E., & Hackett, G. (1981). The relationship of career-related self-efficacy expectations to perceived career options in college women and men. *Journal of Counseling Psychology, 28,* 399–410.

9477

Test Name: ORGANIZATION-BASED SELF-ESTEEM SCALE

Purpose: To measure organization-based self-esteem.

Number of Items: 9

Format: Responses are made on a 5-point scale ranging from 1

(strongly disagree) to 5 (strongly agree). Sample items are presented.

Reliability: Alpha coefficients were .91 and .87. Test-retest reliability was .95.

Validity: Correlations with other variables ranged from −.14 to .46.

Author: Aryee, S., and Luk, V.

Article: Work and nonwork influences on the career satisfaction of dual-earner couples.

Journal: *Journal of Vocational Behavior*, August 1996, *49*(1), 38–52.

Related Research: Pierce, J, et al. (1989). Organization-based self-esteem: Construct definition, measurement and validation. *Academy of Management Journal, 32*, 622–648.

9478

Test Name: ORIENTATION TO OCCUPATIONAL AND FAMILY INTEGRATION SCALE

Purpose: To assess young adults' interest in combining occupational work and family roles.

Number of Items: 31

Format: Includes 3 scales: Male-Traditional/Conventional, Female-Traditional/Conventional, and Male and Female Role-Sharing. Responses are made on a 5-point scale ranging from "not at all" to "very much." Sample items are presented.

Reliability: Internal consistency and test-retest (1 month) reliability were greater than .76.

Author: Hallet, M. B., and Gilbert, L. A.

Article: Variables differentiating university women considering

role-sharing and conventional dual-career marriages.

Journal: *Journal of Vocational Behavior*, April 1997, *50*(2), 308–322.

Related Research: Gilbert, L. A., et al. (1991). Assessing perceptions of occupational-family integration. *Sex Roles, 24*, 107–119.

9479

Test Name: OSGOOD SEMANTIC DIFFERENTIAL: SELF-ESTEEM ADAPTATION

Purpose: To evaluate participants' feelings about themselves.

Number of Items: 25

Format: Responses are made on 7-point scales. Examples are given.

Reliability: Test-retest (2 weeks) reliability was .85.

Author: Jobes, D. A., et al.

Article: Assessment and treatment of suicidal clients in a university counseling center.

Journal: *Journal of Counseling Psychology*, October 1997, *44*(4), 368–377.

Related Research: Neuringer, C. (1974). Attitudes toward self in suicidal individuals. *Suicide and Life-Threatening Behavior, 4*, 96–106.

9480

Test Name: OUTCOME EXPECTATONS SCALE— REVISED

Purpose: To assess one's outcome expectations in taking mathematics courses.

Number of Items: 19

Format: Responses are made on a scale ranging from 0 (strongly

disagree) to 9 (strongly agree). Examples are presented.

Reliability: Coefficient alpha was .86.

Author: Schaefers, K. G., et al.

Article: Women's career development: Can theoretically derived variables predict persistence in engineering majors?

Journal: *Journal of Counseling Psychology*, April 1997, *44*(2), 173–183.

Related Research: Lent, R. W., et al. (1991). Mathematics self-efficacy: Sources and relation to science-based career choice. *Journal of Counseling Psychology, 38*, 424–430.

9481

Test Name: OUTCOME FAVORABILITY SCALE

Purpose: To measure the perceived favorability of outcomes associated with expatriate job assignments.

Number of Items: 7

Format: Scales range from 1 (very unadjusted) to 7 (very adjusted). Sample items are presented.

Reliability: Coefficient alpha was .85.

Validity: Correlations with other variables ranged from .15 to .49.

Author: Garonzik, R., et al.

Article: Identifying international assignees at risk for premature departure: The interactive effect of outcome favorability and procedural fairness.

Journal: *Journal of Applied Psychology*, February 2000, *85*(1), 13–20.

9482

Test Name: OVERALL SELF-CONFIDENCE SCALE

Purpose: To measure overall self-confidence.

Number of Items: 18

Format: Responses are made on a 7-point Likert scale. A sample item is presented.

Reliability: Coefficient alpha was .82.

Validity: Correlations with testosterone levels was −.49.

Author: Johnson, W., et al.

Article: Overall self-confidence, self-confidence in mathematics, and sex-role stereotyping in relation to salivary free testosterone in university women.

Journal: *Perceptual and Motor Skills*, October 2000, *91*(2), 391–401.

Related Research: Garant, V., et al. (1995). Development and validation of a self-confidence scale. *Perceptual and Motor Skills*, *81*, 401–402.

9483

Test Name: PARENTING EFFICACY SCALE

Purpose: To assess parenting efficacy beliefs.

Number of Items: 34

Format: Includes 3 subscales: Education, Communication and General Efficacy. Responses are made on a 5-point scale ranging from 1 (never) to 5 (always).

Reliability: Alpha coefficients ranged from .66 to .74.

Validity: Correlation with other variables ranged from −.12 to .67.

Author: Brody, G. H., et al.

Article: Linking maternal efficacy beliefs, developmental goals, parenting practices, and child competence in rural single-parent African American families.

Journal: *Child Development*, September/October 1999, *70*(5), 1197–1208.

Related Research: Duke, H. P., et al. (1996). *A new scale for measuring parents' feelings of confidence and competence: The Parenting Self-Efficacy Scale.* Unpublished manuscript, University of Georgia, Athens.

9484

Test Name: PARTICIPATIVE DECISION-MAKING SCALE FOR STUDENT NURSES

Purpose: To measure expectations for participative decision-making by student nurses in four dimensions: Clinical, Unit, Hospital-Wide, and Strategic.

Number of Items: 50

Format: Four- and five-point rating scales.

Reliability: Alpha ranged from .70 to .90 across subscales. Test-retest (6 weeks) ranged from .42 to .62.

Author: Wilson, A., et al.

Article: Test-retest reliability of the Participative Decision-Making Scale for Student Nurses.

Journal: *Psychological Reports*, December 1996, *79*(3) Part 1, 825–826.

Related Research: Pike, E., et al. (1996). Measuring expectations for participative decision-making among graduating nurses. *Journal of Nursing Measurement*, *4*, 17–30.

9485

Test Name: PEER BELIEFS INVENTORY

Purpose: To measure perceptions that children have of other children.

Number of Items: 12

Format: Scales range from 1 (not at all) to 5 (very much). A sample item is presented.

Reliability: Internal consistency coefficients ranged from .82 to .93.

Author: Dennis, M. J. B., and Satcher, J.

Article: Name calling and the peer beliefs of elementary school children.

Journal: *Professional School Counseling*, December 1999, *3*(2), 76–80.

Related Research: Rabiner, D., et al. (1993). Children's beliefs about familiar and unfamiliar peers in relation to sociometric status. *Developmental Psychology*, *29*, 236–243.

9486

Test Name: PEER VICTIMIZATION SCALE— ABBREVIATED

Purpose: To assess subjective feelings of victimization.

Number of Items: 4

Format: Responses are made on a 4-point scale ranging from "somewhat true for me" to "really true for me." All items are presented.

Reliability: Coefficient alpha was .82.

Validity: Correlations with other variables ranged from −.35 to .60.

Author: Juvonen, J., et al.

Article: Peer harassment, psychological adjustment, and school functioning in early adolescence.

Journal: *Journal of Educational Psychology*, June 2000, *92*(2), 349–359.

Related Research: Neary, A., & Joseph, S. (1994). Peer

victimization and its relationship to self-concept and depression among school girls. *Personality and Individual Differences, 16,* 183–186.

9487

Test Name: PERCEIVED COMPETENCE SCALE

Purpose: To measure the perceived competence of potential or new employees.

Number of Items: 2

Format: Nine-point competency scales. All items are presented.

Reliability: Correlation between the items was .85.

Author: Lee, J. A., et al.

Article: Sexual stereotypes and perceptions of competence and qualifications.

Journal: *Psychological Reports,* April 1997, *80*(2), 419–428.

Related Research: Heilman, M. E., et al. (1992). Presumed incompetent: Stigmatization and affirmative action efforts. *Journal of Applied Psychology,* 77, 536–544.

9488

Test Name: PERCEIVED COMPETENCE SCALE

Purpose: To measure perceived basketball competence.

Number of Items: 3

Format: Responses are made on a 5-point scale ranging from 1 (strongly disagree) to 5 (strongly agree). All items are presented.

Reliability: Coefficient alpha was .75.

Validity: Correlations with other variables ranged from −.18 to .43.

Author: Goudas, M.

Article: Motivational climate and intrinsic motivation of young basketball players.

Journal: *Perceptual and Motor Skills,* February 1998, *86*(1), 323–327.

9489

Test Name: PERCEIVED COMPETENCE SCALE FOR CHILDREN

Purpose: To enable children to assess their perceived competence.

Number of Items: 28

Format: Each item consists of two contrasting statements from which the children select the one that applies more to them. Includes 4 subscales: Social Competence, School Performance, Physical Abilities, and General Self-Worth.

Reliability: Alpha coefficients for Social Competence and General Self-Worth were .82 and .80 respectively.

Author: Gauze, C., et al.

Article: Interactions between family environment and friendship and associations with self-perceived well-being during early adolescence.

Journal: *Child Development,* October 1996, *67*(5), 2201–2216.

Related Research: Harter, S. (1982). The Perceived Competence Scale for Children. *Child Development,* 53, 87–97.

9490

Test Name: PERCEIVED COMPETENCE SCALE FOR CHILDREN

Purpose: To assess children's self-esteem and self-perception.

Number of Items: 36

Format: Includes 6 domains: Scholastic Competence, Social Competence, Athletic Competence, Physical Appearance, Behavioral Conduct, and Global Self-Worth or Self-Esteem.

Reliability: Alpha coefficients ranged from .72 to .75.

Author: Kovacs, D. M., et al.

Article: Behavioral, affective, and social correlates of involvement in cross-sex friendship in elementary school.

Journal: *Child Development,* October 1996, *67*(5), 2269–2286.

Related Research: Harter, S. (1983). *Revision of the Perceived Competence Scale for Children.* Unpublished manuscript, University of Denver.

9491

Test Name: PERCEIVED CONTROL OF INTERNAL STATES SCALE

Purpose: To measure the degree to which people feel they have control of their internal states.

Number of Items: 18

Format: Responses are made on a 5-point scale ranging from "strongly agree" to "strongly disagree." All items are presented.

Reliability: Coefficient alpha was .90. Mean interitem correlation was .34.

Validity: Correlations with other variables ranged from −.69 to .55.

Author: Pallant, J. F.

Article: Development and validation of a scale to measure perceived control of internal states.

Journal: *Journal of Personality*

Assessment, October 2000, 75(2), 308–337.

9492

Test Name: PERCEIVED CONTROL OVER JOB SEARCH OUTCOMES SCALE

Purpose: To measure perceived control over job search outcomes.

Number of Items: 5

Format: Responses are made on a 5-point Likert-type scale ranging from 1 (strongly disagree) to 5 (strongly agree). All items are presented.

Reliability: Coefficient alpha was .74.

Validity: Correlations with other variables ranged from −.06 to .53.

Author: Saks, A. M., and Ashforth, B. E.

Article: Effects of individual differences and job search behavior on the employment status of recent university graduates.

Journal: *Journal of Vocational Behavior*, April 1999, 54(2), 335–349.

9493

Test Name: PERCEIVED CONTROL OVER TIME SCALE

Purpose: To assess the extent to which individuals believe they can directly affect how their time is spent.

Number of Items: 5

Format: Responses are made on a 5-point scale ranging from 1 (seldom true) to 5 (very often true). Examples are presented.

Reliability: Alpha coefficients were .64 and .68.

Validity: Correlations with other variables ranged from .11 to .51.

Author: Nonis, S. A., et al.

Article: Influence of perceived control over time on college students' stress and stress-related outcomes.

Journal: *Research in Higher Education*, October 1998, 39(5), 587–605.

Related Research: Macan, T. H. (1994). Time management: Test of a process model. *Journal of Applied Psychology*, 79(3), 381–391.

9494

Test Name: PERCEIVED CONTROL SCALE (JAPANESE)

Purpose: To assess control beliefs, strategy beliefs, and capacity beliefs.

Number of Items: 60

Format: Five-point scales are anchored by 1 (not at all) and 5 (always). All items are presented in English.

Reliability: Alphas ranged from .68 to .83 across 10 factor subscales.

Author: Yamauchi, H., et al.

Article: Perceived control, autonomy, and self-regulated learning strategies among Japanese high school students.

Journal: *Psychological Reports*, December 1999, 85(3, Part I), 779–798.

Related Research: Skinner, E. A., et al. (1988). Control, means-ends, and agency beliefs: A new conceptualization and its measurement during childhood. *Journal of Personality and Social Psychology*, 54, 117–133.

9495

Test Name: PERCEIVED CRITICISM MEASURE

Purpose: To measure perceptions of being criticized and the perception of how upsetting it was.

Number of Items: 5

Format: Ten-point scales are anchored by (1) not at all critical or not at all upset and (10) very critical indeed or very upset.

Reliability: Alphas ranged from .72 to .80. Test-retest reliabilities ranged from .67 to .75.

Validity: Correlations with other variables ranged from .13 to .49.

Author: White, J. D., et al.

Article: Validity of the perceived criticism measure in an undergraduate sample.

Journal: *Psychological Reports*, August 1998, 83(1), 83–97.

Related Research: Hooley, J. M., & Tendale, J. D. (1989). Predictors of relapse in unipolar depressives: Expressed emotion, marital distress, and perceived criticism. *Journal of Abnormal Psychology*, 98, 229–235.

9496

Test Name: PERCEIVED DISCRIMINATION AGAINST DISABLED PERSONS SCALE

Purpose: To measure discrimination against disabled persons.

Number of Items: 4

Format: All items presented.

Reliability: Coefficient alpha was .72.

Validity: Correlations with other variables ranged from −.37 to .19.

Authors: Li, L., and Moore, D.

Article: Acceptance of disability and its correlates.

Journal: *Journal of Social Psychology*, February 1998, *138*(1), 13–25.

Related Research: Link, B. G., et al. (1989). A modified labeling theory approach to mental disorders: An empirical assessment. *American Sociological Review, 54*, 400–423.

9497

Test Name: PERCEIVED EFFORT SCALE

Purpose: To measure perceived effort.

Number of Items: 3

Format: Responses are made on a 6-point scale ranging from 1 (never) to 6 (almost all the time).

Reliability: Reliability was .67.

Validity: Correlations with other variables ranged from −.02 to .55.

Author: Cohen, A.

Article: On the discriminant validity of the Meyers and Allen measure of organized comment: How does it fit with the work commitment?

Journal: *Educational and Psychological Measurement*, June 1996, *56*(3), 494–503.

Related Research: Hall, D. T., & Hall, F. S. (1976). The relationship between goals, performance, self-image, and involvement under different organization climates. *Journal of Vocational Behavior, 9*, 267–278.

9498

Test Name: PERCEIVED EMPLOYMENT ALTERNATIVES SCALE

Purpose: To assess one's perception of available employment outside the current employer.

Number of Items: 4

Format: Responses are made on a 5-point scale ranging from 1 (strongly disagree) to 5 (strongly agree). Sample items are presented.

Reliability: Alpha coefficient was .79.

Validity: Correlations with other variables ranged from −.18 to .29.

Author: Baugh, S. G., et al.

Article: An investigation of the effects of protégé gender on responses to mentoring.

Journal: *Journal of Vocational Behavior*, December 1996, *49*(3), 309–323.

Related Research: Katerberg, R., & Green, S. G. (1982). Unpublished survey. University of Cincinnati, Ohio.

Kirschenbaum, A., & Weisberg, J. (1994). Job search, intentions, and turnover. The mismatched trilogy. *Journal of Vocational Behavior, 44*, 17–31.

9499

Test Name: PERCEIVED IMPORTANCE PROFILE

Purpose: To assess perceived importance.

Number of Items: 8

Format: Includes 4 subscales.

Reliability: Test-retest reliability ranged from .68 to .83.

Author: Daley, A. J., and Parfitt, G.

Article: Physical self-perceptions, aerobic capacity and physical activity in male and female

members of a corporate health and fitness club.

Journal: *Perceptual and Motor Skills*, December 1996, *83*(3) Part 1, 1075–1082.

Related Research: Fox, K. R., & Corbin, C. B. (1989). The Physical Self-Perception Profile: Development and preliminary validation. *Journal of Sport and Exercise Psychology, 11*, 408–430.

9500

Test Name: PERCEIVED JOB ALTERNATIVES SCALE

Purpose: To measure perceived job alternatives.

Number of Items: 3

Format: Responses are made on a 5-point Likert scale ranging from 1 (strongly disagree) to 5 (strongly agree). All items are presented.

Reliability: The reliability estimate was .64.

Validity: Correlations with other variables ranged from −.22 to .18.

Author: Hochwarter, W. A.

Article: Commitment as an antidote to the tension and turnover consequences of organizational politics.

Journal: *Journal of Vocational Behavior*, December 1999, *55*(3), 277–297.

Related Research: Ganster, D. (1984). Antecedents and consequences of employee stress. Final report: NIMH 1 ROI-MH 34408.

9501

Test Name: PERCEIVED JOB COMPETENCE SCALE

Purpose: To measure perceived job competence.

Number of Items: 6

Format: Scales range from 1 (strongly agree) to 5 (strongly disagree).

Reliability: Internal reliability was .75.

Validity: Correlations with other variables ranged from .00 to .59.

Author: Wright, B. M., and Cordery, J. L.

Article: Production uncertainty as a contextual moderator of employee reactions to job design.

Journal: *Journal of Applied Psychology*, June 1999, *84*(3), 456–463.

Related Research: Warr, P. B. (1990). The measure of well-being and other aspects of mental health. *Journal of Occupational Psychology*, *63*, 193–210.

9502

Test Name: PERCEIVED JOB IMAGE SCALE

Purpose: To assess perceptions of the police or another occupation in terms of prestige, integrity, competence, and routine.

Number of Items: 34

Format: Scales ranged from 1 (strongly disagree) to 5 (strongly agree). All items are presented.

Reliability: Alpha coefficients ranged from .60 to .87 across subscales.

Author: Lim, V. K. G., et al.

Article: Perceived job image among police officers in Singapore: Factorial dimensions and differential effects.

Journal: *Journal of Social Psychology*, December 2000, *140*(6), 740–750.

Related Research: Krau, E., &

Ziv, L. (1990). The hidden selection of the occupational appeal. The paradigm of nurses. *International Journal of Sociology and Social Policy*, *10*, 1–28.

9503

Test Name: PERCEIVED PERFORMANCE SCALE

Purpose: To measure perceived performance.

Number of Items: 3

Format: Responses are made on a 6-point scale ranging from 1 (never) to 6 (almost all the time).

Reliability: Reliability was .91.

Validity: Correlations with other variables ranged from −.10 to .55.

Author: Cohen, A.

Article: On the discriminant validity of the Meyers and Allen measure of organized comment: How does it fit with the work commitment?

Journal: *Educational and Psychological Measurement*, June 1996, *56*(3), 494–503.

Related Research: Hall, D. T., & Hall, F. S. (1976). The relationship between goals, performance, self-image, and involvement under different organization climates. *Journal of Vocational Behavior*, *9*, 267–278.

9504

Test Name: PERCEIVED SELF-CONTROL AND PERCEIVED SELF-EFFICACY

Purpose: To measure Bandura's concept of self-efficacy.

Number of Items: 19

Reliability: Alphas were .90 (self-control) and .70 (self-efficacy).

Validity: Correlations with

criterion measures ranged from .31 to .55. Correlations with other variables ranged from −.43 to .62.

Author: Hener, T., et al.

Article: Supportive versus cognitive-behavioral intervention programs in achieving adjustment to home peritoneal kidney dialysis.

Journal: *Journal of Consulting and Clinical Psychology*, August 1996, *64*(4), 731–741.

9505

Test Name: PERCEIVED SOCIAL STIGMA SCALE

Purpose: To measure negative stereotypes about individuals with disabilities.

Number of Items: 22

Format: Responses are made on a 4-point scale ranging from 1 (not at all true) to 4 (very much true).

Reliability: Coefficient alpha was .91.

Validity: Correlations with other variables ranged from −.54 to .42.

Author: Elliott, T. R., et al.

Article: Goal instability and adjustment to physical disability.

Journal: *Journal of Counseling Psychology*, April 2000, *47*(2), 251–265.

Related Research: Rybarczyk, B. D., et al. (1992). Social discomfort and depression in a sample of adults with leg amputations. *Archives of Physical Medicine and Rehabilitation*, *73*, 1169–1173.

9506

Test Name: PERCEIVED SOURCES OF MATHEMATICS SELF-EFFICACY SCALE

Purpose: To assess the perceived sources of mathematics self-efficacy.

Number of Items: 40

Format: Includes 4 subscales: Personal Performance Accomplishments, Vicarious Learning, Social Persuasion, and Physiological State/Emotional Arousal. Responses are made on a 5-point scale ranging from 1 (strongly disagree) to 5 (strongly agree). Examples are given.

Reliability: Alpha coefficients ranged from .55 to .91. Test-retest (2 weeks) reliability ranged from .85 to .96.

Author: Gainor, K. A., and Lent, R. W.

Article: Social cognitive expectations and racial identity attitudes in predicting the math choice intentions of Black college students.

Journal: *Journal of Counseling Psychology*, October 1998, *45*(4), 403–413.

Related Research: Lent, R. W., et al. (1991). Mathematics self-efficacy: Source and relation to science-based career choice. *Journal of Counseling Psychology*, *38*, 424–430.

9507

Test Name: PERCEIVED SPORTS COMPETENCE SUBSCALE

Purpose: To assess pupils' perceived ability in physical education.

Number of Items: 6

Format: Responses are made on a 5-point scale.

Reliability: Coefficient alpha was .78.

Validity: Correlations with other variables ranged from .07 to .45.

Author: Spray, C. M.

Article: Predicting participation in noncompulsory physical education: Do goal perspectives matter?

Journal: *Perceptual and Motor Skills*, June 2000, *90*(3) Part 2, 1207–1215.

Related Research: Fox, K. R., & Corbin, C. B. (1989). The Physical Self-Perception Profile, development and preliminary validation. *Journal of Sport and Exercise Psychology*, *11*, 408–430.

9508

Test Name: PERCEIVED USEFULNESS OF WRITING SCALE

Purpose: To assess students' perceptions of the usefulness of their writing.

Number of Items: 10

Reliability: Alpha coefficients were .93 and .84.

Validity: Correlations with other variables ranged from −.27 to .26.

Author: Pajares, F., and Valiante, G.

Article: Influences of self-efficacy on elementary students' writing.

Journal: *Journal of Educational Research*. July/August 1997, *90*(6), 353–360.

Related Research: Shell, D. F., et al. (1989). Self-efficacy and outcome expectancy mechanisms in reading and writing achievement. *Journal of Educational Psychology*, *81*, 91–100.

9509

Test Name: PERCEPTION OF SUCCESS QUESTIONNAIRE

Purpose: To assess the task and ego orientation in the team sport domain.

Number of Items: 11

Format: Includes two parts: Task and Ego. Responses are made on a 5-point scale ranging from 1 (strongly agree) to 5 (strongly disagree).

Reliability: Alpha coefficients were .81 (Ego-Orientation) and .60 (Task-Orientation).

Author: Ommundsen, Y., and Roberts, G. C.

Article: Goal orientations and perceived purposes of training among elite athletes.

Journal: *Perceptual and Motor Skills*, October 1996, *83*(2), 463–471.

Related Research: Roberts, G. C., & Ommundsen, Y. (1996). Effect of goal orientations on achievement beliefs, cognition and strategies in team sport. *Scandinavian Journal of Medicine and Science in Sport*, *6*, 46–56.

9510

Test Name: PERCEPTION OF SUCCESS QUESTIONNAIRE

Purpose: To assess the extent to which an individual defines success in terms of mastery and competition in physical activity settings.

Number of Items: 12

Format: Includes 2 subscales: Task and Ego goal orientation. Responses are made on a 5-point Likert-type scale ranging from 1 (strongly disagree) to 5 (strongly agree). Examples are presented.

Reliability: Alpha coefficients were .90 and .88.

Author: Yoo, J.

Article: Motivational-behavioral

correlates of goal orientation and perceived motivational climate in physical education contexts.

Journal: *Perceptual and Motor Skills*, August 1999, *89*(1), 262–274.

Related Research: Roberts, G. C., & Balague, G. (1989). *The development of a social-cognitive scale of motivation*. Paper presented at the Seventh World Congress, Cologne, Germany.

9511

Test Name: PERFORMANCE EFFICACY SCALE

Purpose: To measure an individual's confidence in engaging in work-related tasks.

Number of Items: 5

Format: Eleven-point scales are anchored by 0 (not at all confident) and 10 (very confident). A sample item is presented.

Reliability: Coefficient alpha was .97.

Validity: Correlations with other variables ranged from .00 to .59.

Author: Bauer, T. N., and Green, S. G.

Article: Testing the combined effects of newcomer information seeking and manager behavior on socialization.

Journal: *Journal of Applied Psychology*, February 1998, *83*(1), 72–83.

9512

Test Name: PERSONAL ATTRIBUTES QUESTIONNAIRE— EXTENDED VERSION

Purpose: To measure positive-other orientation (communion), positive-self orientation (agency)

and negative view of others (unmitigated agency).

Number of Items: 24

Format: Scales range from 1 (not at all) to 5 (very much). Sample items are described.

Reliability: Alpha coefficients ranged from .70 to .81 across subscales and samples.

Author: Helgeson, V. S., and Fritz, H. L.

Article: Unmitigated agency and unmitigated communion: Distinctions from agency and communion.

Journal: *Journal of Research in Personality*, June 1999, *33*(2), 131–158.

Related Research: Spence, J. T., et al. (1979). Negative and positive components of psychological masculinity and femininity and their relationship to self-reports of neurotic and acting out behaviors. *Journal of Personality and Social Psychology*, 37, 1673–1682.

9513

Test Name: PERSONAL CONCERN SCALE

Purpose: To measure to what extent a person believes God is guiding his or her life.

Number of Items: 10

Format: Three-point scales range from 0 (none) to 2 (high). A sample item is presented.

Reliability: Alpha was.66.

Author: Bourdeau, M. L., and George, D. M.

Article: Changes across age groups on measures of knowledge, faith and belief of God's personal concern.

Journal: *Psychological Reports*, June 1997, *80*(3) Part 2, 1359–1362.

Related Research: Donahue, M. J. (1985). Intrinsic and extrinsic religiousness: Review and meta-analysis. *Journal of Personality and Social Psychology*, 48, 400–419.

9514

Test Name: PERSONAL CONTROL SCALE

Purpose: To assess locus of control.

Number of Items: 4

Format: Responses are made on a 5-point scale ranging from 1 (strongly disagree) to 5 (strongly agree). An example is presented.

Reliability: Internal consistency reliability was .75.

Validity: Correlations with other variables ranged from −.16 to .27.

Author: Allen, T. D., et al.

Article: A field study of factors related to supervisors' willingness to mentor others.

Journal: *Journal of Vocational Behavior*, February 1997, *50*(1), 1–22.

Related Research: Paulhus, D. (1983). Sphere-specific measures of perceived control. *Journal of Personality and Social Psychology*, 44, 1253–1265.

9515

Test Name: PERSONAL PROBLEM-SOLVING INVENTORY

Purpose: To measure self-efficacy in overall problem-solving skills.

Number of Items: 11

Format: Responses are made on a 6-point scale ranging from 1 (strongly disagree) to 6 (strongly agree).

Reliability: Test-retest reliability

was .85. Coefficient alpha was .85.

Author: Kruger, L. J.

Article: Social support and self-efficacy in problem solving among teacher assistance teams and school staff.

Journal: *Journal of Educational Research*, January/February 1997, *90*(3), 164–168.

Related Research: Heppner, P. P., & Petersen. C. H. (1982). The development and implications of a personal problem-solving inventory. *Journal of Counseling Psychology*, *29*, 66–75.

9516

Test Name: PERSONAL REACTIONS INVENTORY

Purpose: To measure self-monitoring.

Number of Items: 18

Format: True-false format.

Reliability: Reliability was .73.

Author: Morrison, K. A.

Article: Personality correlates of the five-factor model for a sample of business owners/managers: Associations with scores on self-monitoring, Type A behavior, locus of control, and subjective well-being.

Journal: *Psychological Reports*, February 1997, *80*(1), 255–272.

Related Research: Snyder, M. (1987). *Public appearances/ private realities: The psychology of self monitoring*. New York: Freeman.

9517

Test Name: PICTORIAL SCALE OF PERCEIVED COMPETENCE AND SOCIAL ACCEPTANCE FOR YOUNG CHILDREN

Purpose: To measure self-competence.

Number of Items: 24

Format: Includes 4 subscales: Cognitive Competence, Physical Competence, Peer Acceptance, and Maternal Acceptance. An example is presented.

Validity: Correlations with other variables ranged from .05 to .38.

Author: Jambunathan, S., and Norris, J. A.

Article: Perception of self-competence in relation to language competence among preschoolers.

Journal: *Child Study Journal*, 2000, *30*(2), 91–102.

Related Research: Harter, S., & Pike, R. (1984). The Pictorial Scale of Perceived Competence and Social Acceptance for Young Children. *Child Development*, *55*, 1969–1982.

9518

Test Name: PICTORIAL SELF-EVALUATION SCALE

Purpose: To provide a young child's self-report of self-esteem.

Number of Items: 6

Format: Responses are made on a 4-point scale. A sample item is presented.

Reliability: Alpha coefficients were .71 and .82.

Author: Verschueren, K., et al.

Article: The internal working model of the self, attachment, and competence in five-year-olds.

Journal: *Child Development*, October 1996, *67*(5), 2493–2511.

Related Research: Verschueren, K., & Marcoen, A. (1993). *De Zefbelevingschaal voor Jange Kinderen [The Pictorial Self-Evaluation Scale]*. Unpublished

manual, Center for Developmental Psychology, University of Laurain.

9519

Test Name: PHYSICAL SELF-EFFICACY SCALE

Purpose: To measure physical self-efficacy.

Number of Items: 22

Format: Includes 2 subscales: Perceived Physical Ability and Physical Self-Presentation Confidence. Responses are made on a 6-point scale ranging from 1 (agree strongly) to 6 (disagree strongly). Examples are presented.

Reliability: Internal consistencies ranged from .74 to .85. Test-retest reliabilities ranged from .69 to .85.

Validity: Convergent validity using the Tennessee Self-Concept Scale ranged from .43 to .58.

Author: Gibbons, E. S., et al.

Article: Effects of sex composition by class and instructor's sex on physical self-efficacy of college men.

Journal: *Perceptual and Motor Skills*, February 2000, *90*(1), 105–110.

Related Research: Ryckman, R. M., et al. (1982). Development and validation of a physical self-efficacy scale. *Journal of Personality and Social Psychology*, *42*, 891–900.

9520

Test Name: PHYSICAL SELF-PERCEPTION PROFILE

Purpose: To measure individuals' physical self-perception.

Number of Items: 30

Format: Includes 5 factors:

Physical Self-Worth, Bodily Attractiveness, Sports Competence, Physical Strength and Musculature, and Fitness and Exercise.

Reliability: Test-retest reliabilities ranged from .74 to .92 (16 days) and from .81 to .88 (23 days). Alpha coefficients ranged from .81 to .92.

Validity: Correlations with other variables ranged from −.63 to .81.

Author: Johnson, C. E., and Petrie, T. A.

Article: Relationship of gender discrepancy to psychological correlates of disordered eating in female undergraduates.

Journal: *Journal of Counseling Psychology*, October 1996, *43*(4), 473–479.

Related Research: Fox, K. R., & Corbin, C. B. (1989). The Physical Self-Perception Profile: Development and preliminary validation. *Journal of Sport and Exercise Psychology, 11*, 408–430.

9521

Test Name: PHYSICAL SELF-PERCEPTION PROFILE

Purpose: To provide a physical self-perception profile.

Number of Items: 32

Format: Items are paired contrasting statements. A 4-category response scale is used. An example is given.

Reliability: Alpha coefficients were .71 and .82.

Author: Goni, A., and Zulaika, L.

Article: Relationships between physical education classes and the enhancement of fifth grade pupils' self-concept.

Journal: *Perceptual and Motor Skills*, August 2000, *91*(1), 246–250.

Related Research: Fox, K. R., & Corbin, C. B. (1989). The Physical Self-Perception Profile: Development and preliminary validation. *Journal of Sport and Exercise Psychology, 11*, 408–430.

9522

Test Name: PHYSICIAN PERCEPTION OF PATIENTS SCALE

Purpose: To assess how physicians perceive their patients in terms of their behaviors, attributes, and expectations that create frustration for physicians.

Number of Items: 32

Format: Nine-point rating scales ranged from 1 (not at all frustrating) to 9 (very frustrating). All items are presented.

Reliability: Alpha was .92.

Validity: Total scores were not related to the number of years the physician had been practicing.

Author: Katz, R. C.

Article: "Difficult patients" as family physicians perceive them.

Journal: *Psychological Reports*, October 1996, *79*(2), 539–544.

9523

Test Name: PHYSICIANS' REACTION TO UNCERTAINTY SCALE

Purpose: To measure physician uncertainty in patient care.

Number of Items: 16

Format: Six-point agreement scales range from 1 ("strongly disagree") to 6 ("strongly agree").

Reliability: Alpha was .75.

Author: Moore, S., and Katz, B.

Article: Psychiatric residents' scores on Machiavellianism.

Journal: *Psychological Reports*, June 1996, *78*(3) Part 1, 888–890.

Related Research: Gerrity, M. S., et al. (1990). Physicians' reactions to uncertainty in patient care. *Medical Care, 28*, 724–736.

9524

Test Name: POLITICAL SALIENCE SCALE

Purpose: To assess to what extent individuals have been attuned to late 20th-century political events.

Number of Items: 18

Format: Scales range from 1 (not at all important or personally meaningful) to 4 (extremely important or personally meaningful).

Reliability: Alpha coefficients ranged from .87 to .89.

Author: Peterson, B. E., and Duncan, L. E.

Article: Authoritarianism of parents and offspring: Intergenerational politics and adjustment to college.

Journal: *Journal of Research in Personality*, December 1999, *33*(4), 494–513.

Related Research: Duncan, L. E., & Stewart, A. J. (1999). *Finding meaning in social and historical events: A measure of political salience.* Unpublished manuscript.

9525

Test Name: POWERFUL OTHERS LOCUS OF CONTROL SCALE

Purpose: To measure locus of control.

Number of Items: 7

Format: Seven-point Likert scales. A sample item is presented.

Reliability: Coefficient alpha was .75.

Validity: Correlations with other variables ranged from −.09 to .14.

Author: Schaubroeck, J., et al.

Article: Organization and occupation influences in the attraction-selection-attrition process.

Journal: *Journal of Applied Psychology,* December 1998, 83(6), 869–891.

Related Research: Levenson, H. (1973). Multidimensional locus of control in psychiatric patients. *Journal of Consulting and Clinical Psychology, 41,* 397–404.

9526

Test Name: PREOCCUPATION AND HESITATION SUBSCALES

Purpose: To assess what we believe about our success or failure of a task after we have performed it and while we perform it.

Number of Items: 24

Format: Responses indicate that each item is either an action or a state condition. Examples are presented.

Reliability: Alpha coefficients were .80 and .81.

Validity: Correlations with other variables ranged from −.14 to −.52.

Author: Bensur, B. J., et al.

Article: An exploratory study of motivational predictors which influence graduation from two- and four-year colleges.

Journal: *Perceptual and Motor Skills,* June 1999, 88(3) Part 1, 997–1008.

Related Research: Kuhl, J. (1994). Action versus state orientation: Psychometric properties of the Action Control Scale (ACS-90). In J. Kuhl & J. Beckman (Eds.), *Volition and personality action versus state orientation.* (pp. 47–59). Seattle, WA: Hogrefe and Huber.

9527

Test Name: PREPARATION FOR SCIENTIFIC AND ENGINEERING OCCUPATIONS SELF-EFFICACY SCALE

Purpose: To measure self-efficacy.

Number of Items: 15

Format: Respondents rate on a scale ranging from 1 (no confidence) to 10 (complete confidence) their confidence in their ability to complete education and training for each of 15 scientific and engineering occupations.

Reliability: Alpha coefficients were .89 and .95. Test-retest (8 weeks) reliability was .89.

Author: Schaefers, K. G., et al.

Article: Women's career development: Can theoretically derived variables predict persistence in engineering majors?

Journal: *Journal of Counseling Psychology,* April 1997, 44(2), 173–183.

Related Research: Lent, R. W., et al. (1984). Relation of self-efficacy expectations to academic achievement and persistence.

Journal of Counseling Psychology, 31, 356–362.

9528

Test Name: PRISON CONTROL SCALE

Purpose: To assess locus of control in prison.

Number of Items: 30

Format: Five-point scales are anchored by "no control at all" and "complete or total control."

Validity: Correlations with other variables ranged from −.64 to −.48.

Author: Pugh, D. N.

Article: Studies of validity for the Prison Control Scale.

Journal: *Psychological Reports,* June 1998, 82(3) Part 1, 739–744.

Related Research: Pugh, D. N. (1992). Prisoners and locus of control: Initial studies of a specific scale. *Psychological Reports, 70,* 523–530.

Zamble, E., & Porporino, F. J. (1980). *Coping, behavior, and adaptation in prison inmates.* New York: Springer-Verlag.

9529

Test Name: PRISON LOCUS OF CONTROL SCALE

Purpose: To assess locus of control in a prison setting.

Number of Items: 20

Format: Ten-point scales are anchored by "agree" and "disagree." A sample item is presented.

Validity: Correlation with the Prison Control Scale was −.64.

Author: Pugh, D. N.

Article: Studies of validity for the Prison Control Scale.

Journal: *Psychological Reports*, June 1998, *82*(3) Part 1, 739–744.

Related Research: Pugh, D. N. (1992). Prisoners and locus of control: Initial studies of a specific scale. *Psychological Reports, 70*, 523–530.

9530

Test Name: PRIVATE BODY CONSCIOUSNESS SCALE

Purpose: To measure the tendency to focus on internal, physical sensations and body processes.

Number of Items: 5

Format: Likert format. Sample items are presented.

Reliability: Alpha was .64.

Validity: Correlations with other variables ranged from .10 to .45.

Author: Christensen, A. J., et al.

Article: Body consciousness, illness-related impairment, and patient adherence in hemodialysis.

Journal: *Journal of Consulting and Clinical Psychology*, February 1996, *64*(1), 147–152.

Related Research: Miller, L. C. (1981). Consciousness of body: Private and public. *Journal of Personality and Social Psychology, 41*, 397–406.

9531

Test Name: PROBLEM-SOLVING INVENTORY

Purpose: To measure the subjective appraisal of one's problem-solving ability.

Number of Items: 35

Format: Six-point Likert format.

Reliability: Alpha was .90. Test-

retest (2 weeks) reliability was .89.

Validity: Correlations with other variables ranged from −.27 to .84.

Author: Clum, G. A., et al.

Article: An expanded etiological model for suicide behavior in adolescents: Evidence for its specificity relative to depression.

Journal: *Journal of Psychopathology and Behavioral Assessment*, September 1997, *19*(3), 207–222.

Related Research: Heppner, P. P., & Peterson, E. H. (1982). The development and implications of a personal problem-solving inventory. *Journal of Counseling Psychology, 29*, 66–75.

9532

Test Name: PROFESSIONAL SELF-ESTEEM OF PHYSICIANS SCALE

Purpose: To measure the self-esteem of physicians.

Number of Items: 8

Format: Seven-point scales range from 1 (not at all true of me) to 7 (very true of me).

Reliability: Cronbach's alpha ranged from .81 to .82.

Validity: Correlations with other variables ranged from −.74 to .55.

Author: Carmel, S.

Article: The Professional Self-Esteem of Physicians Scale: Structure, properties, and the relationship to work outcomes and life satisfaction.

Journal: *Psychological Reports*, April 1997, *80*(2), 591–602.

9533

Test Name: PSYCHIATRIC EPIDEMIOLOGY RESEARCH

INTERVIEW SELF-ESTEEM SCALE

Purpose: To measure self-esteem.

Number of Items: 5

Reliability: Alpha was .75.

Validity: Correlations with other variables ranged from −.30 to .54.

Author: Johnson, J. G., et al.

Article: Attributional style, self-esteem and human immunodeficiency virus: A test of the hopelessness and self-esteem theories of depression.

Journal: *Journal of Psychopathology and Behavioral Assessment*, March 2000, *22*(1), 23–46.

Related Research: Dohrenwend, B. P., et al. (1980). Nonspecific psychological distress and other dimensions of psychopathology: Measures for use in the general population. *Archives of General Psychiatry, 37*, 1229–1236.

9534

Test Name: REASONS TO CHANGE QUESTIONNAIRE

Purpose: To measure reasons attributed by nurses to changes introduced in hospital procedures.

Number of Items: 27

Format: Scales ranged from 1 (not at all) to 5 (very great). All items are presented.

Reliability: Alpha reliabilities ranged from .67 to .87 across subscales.

Validity: Correlations between scales ranged from −.40 to .64.

Author: Rousseau, D. M., and Tijoriwala, S. A.

Article: What is a good reason to change? Motivated reasoning and social accounts in promoting organizational change.

Journal: *Journal of Applied Psychology*, August 1999, *84*(4), 514–528.

9535

Test Name: REFLECTIONS OF SELF BY YOUTH

Purpose: To measure progress toward self-actualization.

Number of Items: 67

Format: Four-point scales.

Reliability: Internal consistency ranged from .83 to .86.

Validity: Correlations with other variables ranged from −.49 to .42.

Author: Lewis, J. D.

Article: Scores on Self-Actualization for Gifted Junior High School students.

Journal: *Psychological Reports*, August 1996, *79*(1), 59–64.

Related Research: Schatz, E. M., & Buckmaster, L. R. (1984). Development of an instrument to measure self-actualizing growth in preadolescents. *Journal of Creative Behavior*, *18*, 263–272.

9536

Test Name: REP TEST

Purpose: To assess role types from a social environment.

Number of Items: 10

Time Required: 20 to 60 minutes

Format: Six-point bipolar adjective response scales.

Reliability: Test-retest reliabilities ranged from .71 to .86 (1 week).

Author: Carraher, S. W., and Buckley, M. R.

Article: Cognitive complexity and

the perceived dimensionality of pay satisfaction.

Journal: *Journal of Applied Psychology*, February 1996, *81*(1), 102–109.

Related Research: Bieri, J., et al. (1966). *Clinical and social judgement: The discrimination of behavioral information.* New York: Wiley.

9537

Test Name: RESEARCH OUTCOME EXPECTATIONS QUESTIONNAIRE

Purpose: To identify one's research outcome expectations.

Number of Items: 20

Format: Responses are made on a 5-point Likert scale ranging from 1 (strongly disagree) to 5 (strongly agree). Examples are presented.

Reliability: Alpha coefficients ranged from .89 to .90.

Validity: Correlations with other variables ranged from −.09 to .74.

Author: Bishop, R. M., and Bieschke, K. J.

Article: Applying social cognitive theory to interest in research among counseling psychology doctoral students: A path analysis.

Journal: *Journal of Counseling Psychology*, April 1998, *45*(2), 182–188.

Related Research: Bieschke, K. J., et al. (1995). Research interest among rehabilitation doctoral students. *Rehabilitation Education*, *9*, 51–66.

9538

Test Name: RESEARCH SELF-EFFICACY SCALE

Purpose: To measure one's perceived ability to perform research-related tasks.

Number of Items: 51

Format: Responses are made on a scale ranging from 0 (not confident) to 100 (totally confident). Examples are presented.

Reliability: Internal consistency was .96.

Validity: Correlation with other variables ranged from −.05 to .45.

Author: Bishop, R. M., and Bieschke, K. J.

Article: Applying social cognitive theory to interest in research among counseling psychology doctoral students: A path analysis.

Journal: *Journal of Counseling Psychology*, April 1998, *45*(2), 182–188.

Related Research: Greeley, A. T., et al. (1989). *Research Self-Efficacy Scale.* Unpublished scale, Pennsylvania State University, University Park.

9539

Test Name: RESIDENT ASSISTANT SELF-EFFICACY SCALE

Purpose: To assess the perceived confidence of resident assistants to perform their tasks.

Number of Items: 20

Format: Scales range from 1 (strongly disagree) to 6 (strongly agree). All items are presented.

Reliability: Coefficient alpha was .86 for the total score. Subscale alpha coefficients ranged from .72 to .85.

Validity: Correlations with other variables ranged from .17 to .48.

Author: Denzine, G. M., and Anderson, C. M.

Article: I can do it: Resident assistants' sense of self-efficacy.

Journal: *Journal of College Student Development*, May/June 1999, *40*(3), 247–256.

9540

Test Name: REVISED CAUSAL DIMENSION SCALE

Purpose: To assess causal perceptions as locus of control, stability, personal control, and external control.

Number of Items: 12

Format: Nine-point scales.

Reliability: Alphas ranged from .60 to .92.

Validity: Correlations between oblique factors ranged from .16 to .71.

Author: Kelly, K. T., and Campbell, J. L.

Article: Attribution of responsibility for alcohol-related offenses.

Journal: *Psychological Reports*, June 1997, *80*(3) Part 2, 1159–1165.

Related Research: McAuley, E., et al. (1992). Measuring causal attributions: The Revised Causal Dimension Scale (CD SII). *Personality and Social Psychology Bulletin*, *18*, 560–573.

9541

Test Name: REVISED JANIS–FIELD FEELINGS OF SOCIAL INADEQUACY SCALE

Purpose: To measure social self-esteem.

Number of Items: 20

Format: Responses are made on a 5-point scale ranging from 1 (very often) to 5 (never).

Reliability: Split-half reliabilities were .72 and .88.

Validity: Correlations with other variables ranged from −.30 to .10.

Author: Sodowsky, G. R., et al.

Article: Correlates of self-reported multicultural competencies: Counselor multicultural social desirability, race, social inadequacy, locus of control racial ideology, and multicultural training.

Journal: *Journal of Counseling Psychology*, July 1998, *45*(3), 256–264.

Related Research: Davis, C., et al. (1995). Psychological adjustment to age-related macular degeneration. *Journal of Visual Impairment and Blindness*, *89*, 16–27.

9542

Test Name: REVISED SELF-MONITORING QUESTIONNAIRE

Purpose: To measure managers' level of self-focus.

Number of Items: 18

Format: True-false format.

Reliability: Coefficient alpha was .79.

Validity: Correlations with other variables ranged from .31 to .36.

Author: Church, A. H.

Article: Managerial self-awareness in high-performing individuals in organizations.

Journal: *Journal of Applied Psychology*, April, 1997, *82*(2), 281–292.

Related Research: Snyder, M. (1987). *Public appearances/private realities: The psychology of self-monitoring.* San Francisco: Freeman.

9543

Test Name: ROLE AMBIGUITY–CLARITY SCALE

Purpose: To assess role clarity.

Number of Items: 6

Format: Seven-point scales are anchored by 1 (very false) and 7 (very true). A sample item is presented.

Reliability: Coefficient alpha was .90.

Validity: Correlations with other variables ranged from −.15 to .50.

Author: Bauer, T. N., and Green, S. G.

Article: Testing the combined effects of newcomer information seeking and manager behavior in socialization.

Journal: *Journal of Applied Psychology*, February 1998, *83*(1), 72–83.

Related Research: Rizzo, J., et al. (1970). Role conflict and ambiguity in complex organizations. *Administrative Science Quarterly*, *15*, 150–163.

9544

Test Name: ROLE AMBIGUITY SCALE

Purpose: To measure role ambiguity.

Number of Items: 6

Format: Responses are made on a 5-point Likert-type scale ranging from 1 (strongly disagree) to 5 (strongly agree). An example is given.

Reliability: Coefficient alpha was .82.

Validity: Correlations with other variables ranged from .05 to .49.

Author: Carlson, D. S.

Article: Personality and role variables as predictors of three forms of work-family conflict.

Journal: *Journal of Vocational Behavior*, October 1999, *55*(2), 236–253.

Related Research: Rizzo, J. R., et al. (1970). Role conflict and ambiguity in complex organizations. *Administrative Science Quarterly*, *15*, 150–163.

9545

Test Name: ROLE BREADTH SELF-EFFICACY SCALE

Purpose: To measure confidence in carrying out a wide variety of tasks.

Number of Items: 7

Format: Scales range from 1 (not at all confident) to 5 (very confident).

Reliability: Coefficient alpha was .93.

Validity: Correlations with other variables ranged from −.10 to .49.

Author: Parker, S. K., and Sprigg, C. A.

Article: Minimizing strain and maximizing learning: The role of job demands, job control and proactive personality.

Journal: *Journal of Applied Psychology*, December 1999, *84*(6), 925–939.

Related Research: Parker, S. K. (1988). Enhancing role breadth self-efficacy: The role of job enrichment and other organizational interventions. *Journal of Applied Psychology*, *83*, 835–852.

9546

Test Name: ROLE BREADTH SELF-EFFICACY SCALE

Purpose: To assess confidence across a wide array of tasks.

Number of Items: 10

Format: Scales range from 1 (not at all confident) to 5 (very confident). All items are presented.

Reliability: Coefficient alpha was .96.

Validity: Correlations with other variables ranged from −.19 to .49.

Author: Parker, S. K.

Article: Enhancing role breadth self-efficacy: The roles of job enrichment and other organizational interventions.

Journal: *Journal of Applied Psychology*, December 1998, *83*(6), 835–852.

9547

Test Name: ROLE CLARITY SCALE

Purpose: To measure role clarity.

Number of Items: 5

Reliability: Reliability was .88.

Validity: Correlations with other variables ranged from −.32 to .34.

Author: Gregersen, H. B., and Stroh, L. K.

Article: Coming home to the arctic cold: Antecedents to Finnish expatriate and spouse repatriation adjustment.

Journal: *Personnel Psychology*, Autumn 1997, *50*(3), 635–654.

Related Research: Rizzo, J. R., et al. (1970). Role conflict and ambiguity in complex organizations. *Administrative Science Quarterly*, *2*, 150–165.

9548

Test Name: ROLE CONFLICT AND AMBIGUITY SCALES

Purpose: To measure role conflict and ambiguity.

Number of Items: 7

Format: Scales range from 1 (never) to 6 (very often).

Reliability: Coefficient alpha was .86 (role ambiguity) and .79 (role conflict).

Validity: Correlations with other variables ranged from .60 to .50.

Author: O'Driscoll, M. P., and Beehr, T. A.

Article: Moderating effects of perceived control and need for clarity on the relationship between role stressors and employee affective reactions.

Journal: *Journal of Social Psychology*, April 2000 *140*(2), 151–159.

Related Research: House, R., et al. (1983). Role conflict and ambiguity scales. *Journal of Applied Psychology*, *68*, 334–337.

9549

Test Name: ROLE CONFLICT AND AMBIGUITY SCALES

Purpose: To measure role conflict and role ambiguity.

Number of Items: 13

Format: Responses are made on a 5-point Likert scale ranging from 1 (strongly disagree) to 5 (strongly agree). Includes 2 scales: Role Conflict and Role Ambiguity. Sample items are presented.

Reliability: Alpha coefficients were .80 (conflict) and .86 (ambiguity).

Validity: Correlations with other variables ranged from −.65 to .29.

Author: Baugh, S. G., et al.

Article: An investigation of the effects of protégé gender on responses to mentoring.

Journal: *Journal of Vocational Behavior*, December 1996, *49*(3), 309–323.

Related Research: Rizzo, J. R., et al. (1970). Role conflict and ambiguity in complex organizations. *Administrative Sciences Quarterly*, *15*, 150–163.

9550

Test Name: ROLE CONFLICT-ROLE AMBIGUITY SCALE

Purpose: To measure role conflict and role ambiguity.

Number of Items: 14

Format: Includes two subscales: Role Conflict and Role Ambiguity. Examples are presented.

Reliability: Alpha coefficients were .63 and .75.

Validity: Correlations with other variables ranged from −.51 to .59.

Author: Holder, J. C., and Vaux, A.

Article: African American professionals: Coping with occupational stress in predominantly White work environments.

Journal: *Journal of Vocational Behavior*, December 1998, *53*(3), 315–333.

Related Research: Rizzo, J. R., et al. (1970). Role conflict and ambiguity in complex organizations. *Administrative Science Quarterly*, *15*, 150–163.

9551

Test Name: ROLE CONFLICT SCALE

Purpose: To measure role conflict.

Number of Items: 4

Format: Responses are made on a Likert scale.

Reliability: Reliability was .82.

Validity: Correlations with other variables ranged from −.32 to .15.

Author: Gregersen, H. B., and Stroh, L. K.

Article: Coming home to the arctic cold: Antecedents to Finnish expatriate and spouse repatriation adjustment.

Journal: *Personnel Psychology*, Autumn 1997, *50*(3), 635–654.

Related Research: Rizzo, J. R., et al. (1970). Role conflict and ambiguity in complex organizations. *Administrative Science Quarterly*, *2*, 150–165.

9552

Test Name: ROLE CONFLICT SCALE

Purpose: To assess students' beliefs in the compatibility of science careers with marriage and family responsibilities for women.

Number of Items: 7

Format: Responses are made on a 5-point Likert-type scale ranging from 1 (strongly disagree) to 5 (strongly agree). Sample items are presented.

Reliability: Alpha coefficients were .75 and .81.

Author: Nauta, M. M., et al.

Article: A multiple-groups analysis of prediction of higher level career aspirations among women in mathematics, science, and engineering majors.

Journal: *Journal of Counseling Psychology*, October 1998, *45*(4), 483–496.

Related Research: Lips, H. M. (1992). Gender- and science-related attitudes as predictors of college students' academic choice. *Journal of Vocational Behavior*, *40*, 62–81.

9553

Test Name: ROLE CONFLICT SCALE

Purpose: To measure role conflict.

Number of Items: 8

Format: Responses are made on a 7-point scale.

Reliability: Coefficient alpha was .85.

Author: Boles, J. S., et al.

Article: The dimensionality of the Maslach Burnout Inventory across small business owners and educators.

Journal: *Journal of Vocational Behavior*, February 2000, *56*(1), 12–34.

Related Research: Rizzo, J., et al. (1970). Role conflict and ambiguity in complex organizations. *Administrative Science Quarterly*, *15*, 150–163.

9554

Test Name: ROLE DISCRETION SCALE

Purpose: To measure role discretion.

Number of Items: 8

Reliability: Reliability was .80.

Validity: Correlations with other variables ranged from −.08 to .30.

Author: Gregersen, H. B., and Stroh, L. K.

Article: Coming home to the arctic cold: Antecedents to Finnish expatriate and spouse repatriation adjustments.

Journal: *Personnel Psychology*, Autumn 1997, 50(3), 635–654.

Related Research: Black, J. S., & Gregersen, H. B.(1991). When Yankee comes home: Factors related to repatriate and spouse repatriation adjustment. *Journal of International Business Studies*, 22, 671–694.

9555

Test Name: ROLE OVERLOAD SCALE

Purpose: To measure role overload.

Number of Items: 5

Format: Responses are made concerning the extent of agreement or disagreement with each item. An example is given.

Reliability: Coefficient alpha was .88.

Validity: Correlations with other variables ranged from −.18 to .50.

Author: Duxbury, L. E., et al.

Article: Work and family environments and the adoption of computer-supported supplemental work-at-home.

Journal: *Journal of Vocational Behavior*, August 1996, 49(1), 1–23.

Related Research: Bohen, H., & Viveros-Long, A. (1981). *Balancing jobs and family life*. Philadelphia: Temple University Press.

9556

Test Name: ROLE QUESTIONNAIRE

Purpose: To measure role conflict and role ambiguity.

Number of Items: 14

Format: Scales range from 1 (strongly disagree) to 7 (strongly agree). All items are summarized.

Reliability: Alpha coefficients averaged .75.

Validity: A two-factor and three-factor solution are described.

Author: Freeman, B., and Coll, K. M.

Article: Factor structure of the Role Questionnaire: A study of high school counselors.

Journal: *Measurement and Evaluation in Counseling and Development*, April 1997, 30(1), 32–39.

Related Research: Rizzo, J. R., et al. (1970). Role conflict and ambiguity in complex organizations. *Administrative Science Quarterly*, 15, 150–163.

9557

Test Name: ROLE STRESS SCALES

Purpose: To measure parental and occupational stress.

Number of Items: 14

Format: Four-point Likert scales.

Reliability: Alpha coefficients exceeded or were equal to .90.

Author: Windle, M., and Dumenci, L.

Article: Parental and occupational stress as predictors of depressive symptoms among dual-income couples: A multilevel modeling approach.

Journal: *Journal of Marriage and the Family*, August 1997, 59(3), 625–634.

Related Research: Pearlin, L. I., & Schooler, C. (1978). The structure of coping. *Journal of Health and Social Behavior*, 19, 2–21.

Turner, R. J., et al. (2000).

Social contingencies in mental health: A seven-year follow-up study of teenage mothers. *Journal of Marriage and the Family*, 62, 777–791.

9558

Test Name: ROSENBERG SELF-ESTEEM SCALE—GERMAN VERSION

Purpose: To measure self-esteem.

Number of Items: 10

Format: An example is presented.

Reliability: Coefficient alpha was .79.

Validity: Correlation with other variables ranged from −.56 to .65.

Author: Wiese, B. S., et al.

Article: Selection, optimization, and compensation: An action-related approach to work and partnership.

Journal: *Journal of Vocational Behavior*, December 2000, 57(3), 273–300.

Related Research: Rosenberg, M. (1965). *Society and the adolescent self-image*. Princeton, NJ: Princeton University Press.

9559

Test Name: ROSENBERG SELF-ESTEEM SCALE (SPANISH VERSION)

Purpose: To measure self-esteem.

Number of Items: 10

Format: Four-point scales are anchored by 1 (I strongly agree) and 2 (I strongly disagree).

Reliability: Alphas ranged from .86 to .88.

Author: Banos, R. M., and Guillen, V.

Article: Psychometric characteristics in normal and

social phobic samples for a Spanish version of the Rosenberg Self-Esteem Scale.

Journal: *Psychological Reports*, August 2000, *87*(1), 269–274.

Related Research: Echeburua, E. (1995). Manual practico de evaluacion y tratamiento de la fokia social. Barcelona, Spain: Martinez Roca.

9560

Test Name: SCALE FOR INTERDEPENDENT AND INDEPENDENT CONSTRUAL OF THE SELF.

Purpose: To assess the Western and Japanese construal of the self.

Number of Items: 16

Format: Two-point scales. All items are described.

Reliability: Alphas ranged from .48 to .73 across subscales.

Author: Hasui, C., et al.

Article: Patients' desire to participate in decision-making in psychiatry: A questionnaire survey in Japan.

Journal: *Psychological Reports*, April 2000, *86*(2), 389–399.

Related Research: Kiuchi, A. (1995). [Construction of a scale for independent and interdependent construal of the self and its reliability and validity]. [*Japanese Journal of Psychiatry*], *66*, 100–106 [in Japanese].

9561

Test Name: SELF-ACCEPTANCE SCALE

Purpose: To assess self-acceptance.

Number of Items: 14

Format: Responses are made on a

6-point Likert-type scale ranging from 1 (strongly disagree) to 6 (strongly agree).

Reliability: Internal consistency was .91.

Validity: Correlations with other variables ranged from −.73 to .73.

Author: Robitschek, C., and Keshubeck, S.

Article: A structural model of parental alcoholism, family functioning, and psychological health: The mediating effects of hardiness and personal growth orientation.

Journal: *Journal of Counseling Psychology*, April 1999, *46*(2), 159–172.

Related Research: Ryff, C. D. (1989). Happiness is everything, or is it? Explorations on the meaning of psychological well-being. *Journal of Personality and Social Psychology*, 57, 1069–1081.

9562

Test Name: SELF-CONCEPT DISCONFIRMATION SCALE

Purpose: To measure self-concept.

Number of Items: 7

Format: Seven-point scales. All items are described. Scoring for disconfirmation is described.

Reliability: Alpha coefficients ranged from .78 to .82 before calculating disconfirmation scores.

Validity: Correlations with other variables ranged from −.27 to .31.

Author: Schafer, R. B., et al.

Article: Self-concept disconfirmation, psychological distress, and marital happiness.

Journal: *Journal of Marriage and*

the Family, February 1996, *58*(1), 167–177.

Related Research: Sherwood, J. J. (1970). Self-actualization and self-identity theory. *Personality*, *1*, 41–63.

9563

Test Name: SELF-CONCEPT OF ACADEMIC ABILITY SCALE

Purpose: To provide self-evaluation of general academic ability.

Number of Items: 8

Format: Responses are made on a scale ranging from 1 to 5.

Reliability: Reliability coefficients were .82 (boys) and .77 (girls).

Validity: Correlations with achievement ranged from .19 to .75.

Author: Mboya, M. M.

Article: Self-concept of academic ability as a function of sex, age, and academic achievement among African adolescents.

Journal: *Perceptual and Motor Skills*, August 1998, *87*(1), 155–161.

Related Research: Brookover, W. B., et al. (1967). Self-concept of ability and school achievement: 3. (Final report on cooperative research project No. 2831). Educational Publication Services, Michigan State University, East Lansing, MI.

9564

Test Name: SELF-CONFIDENCE IN INTELLECTUAL ABILITY MEASURE

Purpose: To measure self-confidence in intellectual ability.

Number of Items: 4

Format: Responses are made on a 6-point scale ranging from "strongly disagree" to "strongly agree." All items are presented.

Reliability: Coefficient alpha was .76.

Validity: Correlations with other variables ranged from −.35 to .35.

Author: Dai, D. Y.

Article: To be or not to be (challenged), that is the question: Task and ego orientation among high-ability, high-achieving adolescents.

Journal: *Journal of Experimental Education*, Summer 2000, *68*(4), 311–330.

Related Research: Dweck, C. S., & Henderson, V. L. (1988). *Theories of intelligence: Background and measures.* Unpublished manuscript.

9565

Test Name: SELF-CONSCIOUSNESS SCALE

Purpose: To measure self-consciousness.

Number of Items: 23

Format: Four-point Likert format.

Reliability: Alpha coefficients ranged from .77 to .86 across subscales.

Validity: Correlations with other variables ranged from −.47 to .67.

Author: Church, A. H.

Article: Managerial self-awareness in high-performing individuals in organizations.

Journal: *Journal of Applied Psychology*, April 1997, *82*(2), 281–292.

Related Research: Fenigstein, A., et al. (1975). Public and private self-consciousness: Assessment and theory. *Journal of*

Consulting and Clinical Psychology, *43*, 522–527.

9566

Test Name: SELF-CONSTRUAL SCALE

Purpose: To assess independent and interdependent dimensions of self-construal.

Number of Items: 24

Format: Scales range from 1 (strongly agree) to 7 (strongly disagree).

Reliability: Alpha coefficients ranged from .62 to .87 across subscales and groups.

Validity: Correlations with other variables ranged from −.14 to .57.

Authors: Sato, T., and Cameron, J. E.

Article: The relationship between collective self-esteem and self-construal in Japan and Canada.

Journal: *Journal of Social Psychology*, August 1999, *139*(4), 426–435.

Related Research: Singelis, T. M. (1994). The measurement of independent and interdependent self-construals. *Personality and Social Psychology Bulletin*, *20*, 580–591.

9567

Test Name: SELF-DESCRIPTION INVENTORY

Purpose: To measure need for achievement, need for self-actualization, need for job security, and need for high financial reward.

Number of Items: 39

Format: Adjective-pair format.

Reliability: Alpha coefficients ranged from .89 to .90.

Validity: Correlations with other variables ranged from −.57 to .27.

Author: Riipinen, M.

Article: The relation of work involvement to occupational needs, need satisfaction, locus of control and affect.

Journal: *Journal of Social Psychology*, June 1996, *136*(3), 291–303.

Related Research: Ghiselli, E. (1971). *Exploration in managerial talent.* Pacific Palisades, CA: Goodyear.

9568

Test Name: SELF-DESCRIPTION INVENTORY FOR AFRICAN STUDENTS

Purpose: To assess self-concept.

Number of Items: 15

Format: Five-point scales are anchored by 1 (I disagree very much) and 5 (I agree very much). All items are presented.

Reliability: Alpha was .78.

Author: Marjoribanks, K., and Mboya, M.

Article: Family and individual correlates of academic goal orientations: Social context differences in South Africa.

Journal: *Psychological Reports*, October 2000, *87*(2), 373–380.

Related Research: Marjoribanks, K., & Mboya, M. (1998). Family correlates of South African students' self-concepts: A regression surface analysis. *Psychological Reports*, *83*, 163–172.

9569

Test Name: SELF-DESCRIPTION INVENTORY FOR AFRICAN STUDENTS

Purpose: To measure self-concept.

Number of Items: 50

Format: Five-point Likert format.

Reliability: Alpha coefficients ranged from .65 to .85 across subscales.

Authors: Majoribanks, K., and Mboya, M. M.

Article: Factors affecting the self-concepts of South African students.

Journal: *Journal of Social Psychology,* October 1998, *138*(5), 572–580.

Related Research: Mboya, M. M. (1993). Development and construct validity of a self-description inventory for African students. *Psychological Reports, 72,* 183–191.

9570

Test Name: SELF-DESCRIPTION QUESTIONNAIRE

Purpose: To measure self-esteem.

Number of Items: 14

Format: Scales range from 1 (not like you) to 4 (very much like you). Sample items are presented.

Reliability: Internal reliability was .93. Test-retest (6 weeks) reliability was .81.

Validity: Correlations with other variables ranged from −.59 to .83.

Author: Weitlauf, J. C., et al.

Article: Generalization effects of coping-skills training: Influence of self-defense training on women's efficacy beliefs, assertiveness and aggression.

Journal: *Journal of Applied Psychology,* August, 2000 *85*(4), 625–633.

Related Research: Smoll, F. L., et al. (1993). Enhancement of children's self-esteem through social support training of youth sport coaches. *Journal of Applied Psychology, 78,* 602–610.

9571

Test Name: SELF-EFFICACY EXPECTATIONS SCALE

Purpose: To assess the ability to refrain from smoking in various situations.

Number of Items: 7

Format: Seven-point scales are anchored by −3 (not sure at all that I am able to refrain from smoking) and +3 (very sure I am able to refrain from smoking).

Reliability: Alpha coefficients ranged from .81 to .86 across subscales.

Author: Dijkstra, A., et al.

Article: Tailored interviews to communicate stage-matched information to smoking in different motivational stages.

Journal: *Journal of Consulting and Clinical Psychology,* June 1998, *66*(3), 549–557.

Related Research: Mudde, A. N., et al. (1995). Self-efficacy as a predictor for the cessation of smoking: Methodological issues and implications for smoking cessation programs. *Psychology and Health, 10,* 353–367.

9572

Test Name: SELF-EFFICACY FOR SELF-REGULATED LEARNING SCALE

Purpose: To measure cognitions, behaviors, and affects associated with attaining one's goals.

Number of Items: 24

Format: Seven-point scales range from (1) not well at all to (7) very well. All items are presented.

Reliability: Alphas ranged from .70 to .79.

Validity: Interfactor correlations ranged from .51 to .58.

Author: Gredler, M. E., and Schwartz, L. S.

Article: Factorial structure of the Self-Efficacy for Self-Regulated Learning Scale.

Journal: *Psychological Reports,* August 1997, *81*(1), 51–57.

Related Research: Zimmerman, B. J., & Bandura, A. (1994). Impact of self-regulatory influences on writing course attainment. *American Educational Research Journal, 1,* 845–862.

9573

Test Name: SELF-EFFICACY QUESTIONNAIRE

Purpose: To measure self-efficacy.

Number of Items: 32

Format: Includes 2 components: Efficacy Expectations and Outcome Expectations. Seven-point scales are used.

Reliability: Alpha coefficients ranged from .85 to .95.

Author: Romano, J. L.

Article: School personnel prevention training: A measure of self-efficacy.

Journal: *Journal of Educational Research,* September/October 1996, *90*(1), 58–63.

Related Research: Bandura, A. (1977). Self-efficacy: Toward a unifying theory of behavioral change. *Psychological Review, 84,* 191–215.

9574

Test Name: SELF-EFFICACY RATING FORM

Purpose: To measure self-efficacy directed toward labor union activities.

Number of Items: 15 (union activities).

Format: Each item is rated as 1 (yes, could participate) and 0 (no, could not participate). Each item was also rated as 0 (not confident in ability to participate) and 100 (entirely confident to participate). All items are presented. Scoring procedures are described.

Reliability: Alpha coefficient was .92.

Validity: Correlations with other variables ranged from −.58 to .82.

Author: Bulger, C. A., and Mellor, S.

Article: Self-efficacy as a mediator of the relationship between perceived union barriers and women's participation in union activities.

Journal: *Journal of Applied Psychology*, December 1997, *82*(6), 935–944.

9575

Test Name: SELF-EFFICACY SCALE

Purpose: To assess confidence in one's ability to do a job.

Number of Items: 3

Format: Scales range from 1 (never) to 7 (always). A sample item is presented.

Reliability: Coefficient alphas ranged from .66 to .70.

Author: Colquitt, J. A., and Simmering, M. J.

Article: Conscientiousness, goal orientation, and motivation to learn during the learning process: A longitudinal study.

Journal: *Journal of Applied Psychology*, August 1998, *83*(4), 654–665.

Related Research: McIntire, S. M., & Levine, E. L. (1984). Task-specific self-esteem: An empirical investigation. *Journal of Vocational Behavior, 25*, 290–303.

9576

Test Name: SELF-EFFICACY SCALE

Purpose: To assess self-efficacy.

Number of Items: 3

Format: Responses are made on a 5-point Likert-type scale ranging from "strongly disagree" to "strongly agree." A sample item is given.

Reliability: Coefficient alpha was .78.

Validity: Correlations with other variables ranged from −.27 to .77.

Author: Dulebohn, J. H., et al.

Article: Selection among employer-sponsored pension plans: The role of individual differences.

Journal: *Personnel Psychology*, Summer 2000, *53*(2), 405–432.

Related Research: Judge, T. A., & Martocchio, J. J. (1996). Dispositional influences on attributions concerning absenteeism. *Journal of Management, 22*, 837–861.

9577

Test Name: SELF-EFFICACY SCALE

Purpose: To measure self-efficacy.

Number of Items: 4

Format: Seven-point scales are anchored by (1) strongly agree and (7) strongly disagree.

Validity: Correlations with other variables ranged from −.47 to .19.

Author: Thompson, R. F., and Perlini, A. H.

Article: Feedback and self-efficacy, arousal, and performance of introverts and extroverts.

Journal: *Psychological Reports*, June 1998, *82*(3) Part 1, 707–716.

Related Research: Lust, J. A., et al.(1993). A note on issues concerning the measurement of self-efficacy. *Journal of Personality and Social Psychology, 46*, 1303–1312.

9578

Test Name: SELF-EFFICACY SCALE

Purpose: To measure self-efficacy.

Number of Items: 6

Format: Seven-point scales range from 1 (strongly disagree) to 7 (strongly agree). A sample item is presented.

Reliability: Alpha coefficients ranged from .88 to .94.

Validity: Correlations with other variables ranged from .05 to .63.

Author: Martocchio, J. J., and Judge, T. A.

Article: Relationship between conscientiousness and learning in employee training: Mediating influences of self-deception and self-efficacy.

Journal: *Journal of Applied Psychology*, October 1997, *82*(5), 764–773.

Related Research: Martocchio, J. J., & Dulebohn, J. (1994). Performance feedback effects in training: The role of perceived controllability. *Personnel Psychology, 47*, 357–373.

9579

Test Name: SELF-EFFICACY SCALE

Purpose: To measure students' self-efficacy for writing essays.

Number of Items: 6

Format: Responses are made on a 5-point Likert-type scale ranging from 1 (strongly disagree) to 5 (strongly agree). All items are presented.

Reliability: Coefficient alpha was .83.

Author: Page-Voth, V., and Graham, S.

Article: Effects of goal setting and strategy use on the writing performance and self-efficacy of students with writing and learning problems.

Journal: *Journal of Educational Psychology*, June 1999, *91*(2), 230–240.

Related Research: Graham, S., & Harris, K. R. (1989). A components analysis of cognitive strategy instruction: Effects on learning disabled students' composition and self-efficacy. *Journal of Educational Psychology, 81*, 353–361.

9580

Test Name: SELF-EFFICACY SCALE

Purpose: To measure confidence in the ability to perform a task successfully.

Number of Items: 8

Format: Five-point scales are anchored by 1 (strongly disagree) and 5 (strongly agree). A sample item is presented.

Reliability: Coefficient alpha was .90.

Validity: Correlations with other variables ranged from −.27 to .39.

Author: Ford, J. K., et al.

Article: Relationships of goal orientation, metacognitive activity, and practice strategies with learning outcomes and transfer.

Journal: *Journal of Applied Psychology*, April 1998, *83*(2), 218–233.

9581

Test Name: SELF-EFFICACY SCALE

Purpose: To measure self-efficacy.

Number of Items: 10

Format: Five-point scales range from 1 (strongly disagree) to 5 (strongly agree). Sample items are presented.

Reliability: Coefficient alpha was .86.

Author: Phillips, J. M., and Gully, S. M.

Article: Role of goal orientation, ability, need for achievement, and locus of control in the self-efficacy and goal-setting process.

Journal: *Journal of Applied Psychology*, October 1997, *82*(5), 792–802.

Related Research: Mone, M. A. (1994). Comparative validity of two measures of self-efficacy in predicting academic goals and performance. *Educational and Psychological Measurement, 54*, 516–529.

9582

Test Name: SELF-EFFICACY SCALE

Purpose: To measure self-efficacy.

Number of Items: 19

Format: Includes 2 factors: Self-Recognized and Consciousness of Potentiality. Responses are made on a 4-point scale ranging from 1 (not at all) to 4 (very strongly). All items are presented.

Reliability: Alpha coefficients were .81 and .72.

Author: Nakata, S., et al.

Article: Relationships between self-regulation and self-efficacy of Japanese school children.

Journal: *Perceptual and Motor Skills*, December 1999, *89*(3, Part 1), 885–889.

Related Research: Nakata, S. (1996). [*The roles and functions of self-control in Japanese preschool children.*] Unpublished master's thesis, Naruto University of Education in Japanese.

9583

Test Name: SELF-EFFICACY SCALE

Purpose: To assess general self-efficacy.

Number of Items: 22

Format: Scales range from 1 (not at all like me) to 5 (very much like me). Sample items are presented.

Reliability: Coefficient alpha was .91. Test-retest reliability (6 weeks) was .70.

Validity: Correlations with other variables ranged from −.51 to .83.

Author: Weitlauf, J. C., et al.

Article: Generalization effects of coping-skills training: Influence of self-defense training on women's efficacy beliefs, assertiveness and aggression.

Journal: *Journal of Applied*

Psychology, August 2000, *85*(4), 625–633.

Related Research: Coppel, D. B. (1980). *The relationship of perceived social support and self-efficacy to major and minor stressors.* Unpublished doctoral dissertation, University of Washington, Seattle.

9584

Test Name: SELF-EFFICACY SCALE

Purpose: To assess expectations of willingness to imitate behavior, willingness to expend effort in completing behavior, and persistence despite difficulties.

Number of Items: 23

Format: Responses are made on a 14-point Likert scale.

Reliability: Alpha coefficient was .82.

Author: Rice, K. G., et al.

Article: Attachment to parents' social competence, and emotional well-being: A comparison of Black and White adolescents.

Journal: *Journal of Counseling Psychology,* January 1997, *44*(1), 89–101.

Related Research: Sherer, M., et al. (1982). The Self-Efficacy Scale: Construction and validation. *Psychological Reports, 51,* 663–671.

9585

Test Name: SELF-EFFICACY SCALE

Purpose: To measure general and social self-efficacy.

Number of Items: 25

Reliability: Coefficient alpha was .86 (self) and .71 (social).

Validity: Correlations with other

variables ranged from −.54 to .11.

Author: Martin, T. R., et al.

Article: Personality correlates of depression and health symptoms: A test of a self-regulation model.

Journal: *Journal of Research in Personality,* June 1996, *30*(2), 264–277.

Related Research: Sherer, M., & Adams, C. H. (1983). Construct validity of the Self-Efficacy Scale. *Psychological Reports, 53,* 899–902.

9586

Test Name: SELF-EFFICACY SCALE

Purpose: To assess task-related confidence.

Number of Items: 32

Format: Scales range from 1 (totally unconfident) to 9 (totally confident).

Reliability: Coefficient alpha was .81.

Validity: Correlations with other variables ranged from −.03 to .22.

Author: O'Neill, B. S., and Mone, M. A.

Article: Investigating equity sensitivity as a moderator of relations between self-efficacy and workplace attitudes.

Journal: *Journal of Applied Psychology,* October 1998, *83*(5), 805–816.

9587

Test Name: SELF-EFFICACY SCALE—ADAPTED

Purpose: To measure leisure efficacy.

Number of Items: 12

Format: Includes 12 pairs of

adjectives. All items are presented.

Reliability: Coefficient alpha was .86.

Validity: Correlations with other variables ranged from .06 to .36.

Author: Munson, W. W., and Savickes, M. L.

Article: Relation between leisure and career development of college students.

Journal: *Journal of Vocational Behavior,* October 1998, *53*(2), 243–253.

Related Research: Gecas, V. (1971). Parental behavior and dimensions of adolescent self evaluation. *Sociometry, 34,* 466–482.

9588

Test Name: SELF-EFFICACY SCALE FOR QUITTING SMOKING

Purpose: To assess how difficult it would be to refrain from smoking among friends in social situations, in emotional situations, and in habitual-addictive situations.

Number of Items: 25

Format: Seven-point scales are anchored by −3 (I find it very difficult) and +3 (I find it very easy).

Reliability: Alpha was .97.

Author: Dijkstra, A., et al.

Article: Pros and cons of quitting, self-efficacy, and the stages of change in smoking cessation.

Journal: *Journal of Consulting and Clinical Psychology,* August 1996, *64*(4), 758–763.

Related Research: Mudde, A. N., et al. (1995). Self-efficacy as a predictor for the cessation of smoking: Methodological issues and implications for smoking cessation programs. *Psychology and Health, 10,* 353–367.

9589

Test Name: SELF-EFFICACY SCALES

Purpose: To measure self-efficacy for self-instruction and self-efficacy for learning from others.

Number of Items: 13

Format: Responses are made on a scale ranging from 0 to 10. Sample items are presented.

Reliability: Alpha coefficients were .86 and .87.

Validity: Correlations with other variables ranged from .02 to .35.

Author: Bergin, D. A.

Article: Adolescents' out-of-school learning strategies.

Journal: *Journal of Experimental Education,* Summer 1996, *64*(4), 309–323.

Related Research: Bergin, D. A. (1989). Student goals for out-of-school learning activities. *Journal of Adolescent Research, 4,* 92–109.

9590

Test Name: SELF-EFFICACY SCALE

Purpose: To measure self-efficacy.

Number of Items: Three forms of the scale: 70 items, 35 items, 21 items.

Format: One form is called Traditional, a second form is called Likert, and a third form is called Simplified.

Reliability: Alpha coefficients for Likert and Simplified versions ranged from .85 to .94.

Author: Maurer, T. J., and Andrews, K. D.

Article: Traditional, Likert, and

simplified measures of self-efficacy.

Journal: *Educational and Psychological Measurement,* December 2000, *60*(6), 965–973.

Related Research: Wood, R. E., & Locke, E. A. (1987). The relation of self-efficacy and grade goals to academic performance. *Educational and Psychological Measurement, 47,* 1013–1024.

9591

Test Name: SELF-EFFICACY TEST

Purpose: To assess students' perceived capabilities for performing.

Number of Items: 12

Format: Responses are made on a 7-point scale ranging from 1 (not confident) to 7 (very confident). All items are presented.

Reliability: Test-retest reliability was .94. Coefficient alpha was .96.

Validity: Correlations with other variables ranged from .54 to .80.

Author: Schunk, D. H., and Ertmer, P. A.

Article: Self-regulatory processes during computer skill acquisition: Goal and self-evaluation influences.

Journal: *Journal of Educational Psychology,* June 1999, *91*(2), 251–260.

9592

Test Name: SELF-ESTEEM INDEX

Purpose: To measure self-esteem.

Number of Items: 50

Format: Scales range from 0 (not true) to 3 (true).

Reliability: Coefficient alpha was .90.

Author: Badura, A. S., et al.

Article: Effects of peer training on peer educators: Leadership, self-esteem, health knowledge, and health behaviors.

Journal: *Journal of College Student Development,* September/October 2000, *41*(5), 471–478.

Related Research: Barksdale, L. S. (1972). *Building self-esteem.* Idyllwild, CA: Barksdale Foundation.

9593

Test Name: SELF-ESTEEM INVENTORY

Purpose: To measure global self-esteem.

Number of Items: 10

Format: Responses are made on a 5-point Likert-type scale ranging from 1 (strongly disagree) to 5 (strongly agree).

Reliability: Coefficient alpha was .83.

Validity: Correlations with other variables ranged from .12 to .47.

Author: Saks, A. M., and Ashforth, B. E.

Article: Effects of individual differences and job search behavior on the employment status of recent university graduates.

Journal: *Journal of Vocational Behavior,* April 1999, *54*(2), 335–349.

Related Research: Rosenberg, M. (1965). *Society and the adolescent self image.* Princeton, NJ: Princeton University Press.

9594

Test Name: SELF-ESTEEM SCALE

Purpose: To measure self-esteem.

Number of Items: 7

Format: Responses are made on a 4-point scale ranging from "strongly disagree" to "strongly agree." Examples are presented.

Reliability: Coefficient alpha was .81.

Validity: Correlations with other variables ranged from −.18 to .54.

Author: Rojewski, J. W., and Yang, B.

Article: Longitudinal analysis of select influences on adolescents' occupational aspirations.

Journal: *Journal of Vocational Behavior*, December 1997, *51*(3), 375–410.

Related Research: Kanouse, D. E., et al (1980). *Effects of postsecondary education on aspirations, attitudes, and self-conceptions.* Santa Monica, CA: RAND Corporation (ERIC Document Reproduction Service No. ED 214 430).

9595

Test Name: SELF-ESTEEM SCALE

Purpose: To measure self-esteem.

Number of Items: 9

Format: Scales range from 1 (very unpopular) to 7 (very popular).

Reliability: Coefficient alpha was .82.

Authors: Zea, M. C., et al.

Article: Predicting intention to remain in college among ethnic minority and non-minority students.

Journal: *Journal of Social Psychology*, April 1997, *137*(2), 149–160.

Related Research: Sherwood J. J. (1970). Self-actualization and

self-identity theory. *Personality, 1*, 41–63.

9596

Test Name: SELF-ESTEEM SCALE

Purpose: To measure self-esteem.

Number of Items: 11

Format: Eleven bipolar adjectives involving a 7-point semantic differential. All items are presented.

Reliability: Coefficient alpha was .82.

Validity: Correlations with other variables ranged from −.06 to .49.

Author: Sumerlin, J. R., and Bundrick, C. M.

Article: Happiness and self-actualization under conditions of strain: A sample of homeless men.

Journal: *Perceptual and Motor Skills*, February 2000, *90*(1), 191–203.

Related Research: Sumerlin, J. R. (1999). Cognitive-affective preparation for homelessness: Quantitative and qualitative analyses of childhood out-of-home placement and child abuse in a sample of homeless men. *Psychological Reports, 85*, 553–573.

9597

Test Name: SELF-EXPANSIVENESS LEVEL FORM

Purpose: To measure the extent to which an individual identifies with a constricted or an expansive view of self. Three levels are assessed: personal, middle, and transpersonal.

Number of Items: 18

Format: Five-point scales are anchored by A (very willing) and B (not at all willing).

Reliability: Alphas ranged from .72 to .79 across subscales.

Validity: Correlations with related constructs ranged from −.09 to .27.

Author: MacDonald, D. A., and Gagnier, J. J.

Article: The Self-Expansiveness Level Form: Examination of its validity and relation to the NEO Personality Inventory—Revised.

Journal: *Psychological Reports*, June 2000, *86*(3, Part 1), 707–726.

Related Research: Friedman, H. L. (1983). The Self-Expansiveness Level Form: A conceptualization and measurement of a transpersonal construct. *Journal of Transpersonal Psychology, 15*, 37–50.

9598

Test Name: SELF-EXPLORATION SCALE

Purpose: To assess self-exploration.

Number of Items: 5

Reliability: Alpha coefficients were .88 and .82. Test-retest (2 weeks) reliability was .83.

Validity: Correlation with other variables ranged from −.09 to .41.

Author: Hamer, R. J., and Bruch, M. A.

Article: Personality factors and inhibited career development: Testing the unique contribution of shyness.

Journal: *Journal of Vocational Behavior*, June 1997, *50*(3), 382–400.

Related Research: Stumpf, S. A.,

et al. (1983). Development of the career exploration survey. *Journal of Vocational Behavior*, 22, 191–226.

9599

Test Name: SELF-MONITORING SCALE

Purpose: To assess the tendency to adapt one's self-presentation in social interactions.

Number of Items: 18

Format: A true-false response format is used. An example is presented.

Reliability: Reliability estimates were .61 and .70.

Validity: Correlations with other variables ranged from .03 to .10.

Author: Mohr, J. J., and Rochlen, A. B.

Article: Measuring attitudes regarding bisexuality in lesbian, gay male, and heterosexual populations.

Journal: *Journal of Counseling Psychology*, July 1999, 46(3), 353–369.

Related Research: Snyder, M., & Gengstad, S. (1986). On the nature of self-monitoring: Matters of assessment, matters of validity. *Journal of Personality and Social Psychology, 51*, 125–139.

9600

Test Name: SELF-MOTHER SIMILARITY TEST

Purpose: To assess identification with one's mother.

Number of Items: 40

Format: Adjective rating scales range from 1 (a little) to 5 (very well). Each adjective is rated two times, once for self and once for mother.

Reliability: Split-half reliabilities ranged from .77 to .79.

Author: Sohlberg, S., et al.

Article: Symbiotic oneness and defensive autonomy: Yet another experiment demystifying Silverman's findings using "Mommy and I are One."

Journal: *Journal of Research in Personality*, March 2000, 34(1), 108–126.

Related Research: Sohlberg, S., et al. (1997). Depression, gender and identification. *British Journal of Clinical Psychology, 36*, 453–455.

9601

Test Name: SELF-PERCEIVED INVESTMENT KNOWLEDGE SCALE

Purpose: To assess what people think they know about financial investments.

Number of Items: 6

Format: Likert-like format. Sample items are presented.

Reliability: Alpha was .91.

Validity: Correlations with other variables ranged from −.15 to .32.

Author: Goldsmith, E., and Goldsmith, R. E.

Article: Gender differences in perceived and real knowledge of financial investments.

Journal: *Psychological Reports*, February 1997, 80(1), 236–238.

9602

Test Name: SELF-PERCEPTION PROFILE FOR ADOLESCENTS

Purpose: To assess perceived competence and self-worth.

Number of Items: 45

Format: Includes 9 subscales:

Scholastic, Social, and Athletic Competence; Physical Appearance, Morality, Friendship, Romantic Appeal, Job Competence, and Global Self-Worth.

Reliability: Internal consistency reliabilities ranged from .55 to .90.

Author: McGuire, S., et al.

Article: Perceived competence and self-worth during adolescence: A longitudinal behavioral genetic study.

Journal: *Child Development*, November/December 1999, 70(6), 1283–1296.

Related Research: Harter, S. (1988). *The Self-Perception Profile for Adolescents*. Unpublished manuscript, University of Denver, Denver, CO.

9603

Test Name: SELF-PERCEPTION PROFILE FOR CHILDREN

Purpose: To assess self-concept.

Number of Items: 36

Format: Statements are rated "really true" or "sort of true."

Reliability: Alphas ranged from .71 to .86.

Validity: Correlations with other variables ranged from −.30 to .63.

Author: Hagborg, W. J.

Article: The Child Rating Scale and its use with middle school students.

Journal: *Psychological Reports*, October 2000, 87(2), 381–388.

Related Research: Harter, S. (1985). *Manual for the Self-Perception Profile for Children*. Denver, CO: University of Denver.

9604

Test Name: SELF-PERCEPTION PROFILE FOR COLLEGE STUDENTS

Purpose: To enable college students to formulate a self-perception.

Number of Items: 54

Format: Includes 13 subscales. Each item is scored from 1 (low self-perception) to 4 (high self-perception).

Reliability: Alpha coefficients ranged from .76 to .92.

Validity: Correlations with other variables ranged from −.47 to −.04.

Author: Onwuegbuzie, A. J.

Article: Statistics anxiety and the role of self-perceptions.

Journal: *Journal of Educational Research*, May/June 2000, *93*(5), 323–330.

Related Research: Neemann, J., & Harter, S. (1986). *Manual for the Self-Perception Profile for College Students*. Unpublished manuscript, University of Denver, Colorado.

9605

Test Name: SELF-PERCEPTIONS OF INNOVATIVENESS SCALE

Purpose: To assess perceptions of the innovativeness of management teams.

Number of Items: 5

Format: Five-point scales are anchored by 1 (highly stable: few changes introduced) and 5 (highly innovative: many changes introduced).

Reliability: Cronbach's alpha was .81.

Validity: Correlations with other variables ranged from −.13 to .89.

Author: West, M. A., and Anderson, N. R.

Article: Innovation in top management teams.

Journal: *Journal of Applied Psychology*, December 1996, *81*(6), 680–693.

Related Research: West, M. A. (1987). Role innovation in the world of work. *British Journal of Social Psychology, 26,* 305–315.

9606

Test Name: SELF-RATING SCALE

Purpose: To assess multiple facets of self-esteem.

Number of Items: 36

Format: Responses are made on a 7-point scale.

Reliability: Alpha coefficients ranged from .90 to .95. Test-retest (1 week) reliability was .84.

Validity: Correlations with the Rosenberg Self-Esteem Scale was .66 (N = 259) and with depression was −.48 (N = 259).

Author: Kelly, A. E., et al.

Article: Client self-presentations at intake.

Journal: *Journal of Counseling Psychology*, July 1996, *43*(3), 300–309.

Related Research: Fleming, J. S., & Courtney, B. E. (1984). The dimensionality of self-esteem: II. Hierarchical facet model for revised measurement scales. *Journal of Personality and Social Psychology, 46,* 404–421.

9607

Test Name: SELF-REFERENCES BELIEFS SCALE—JAPANESE VERSION

Purpose: To assess perceived control beliefs, strategy beliefs, and capacity beliefs as well as self-esteem.

Number of Items: 32

Format: Sample items presented.

Reliability: Alphas ranged from .14 to .77.

Validity: Correlations with other variables ranged from −.14 to .41.

Author: Yammauchi, H., and Tanaka, K.

Article: Relations of autonomy, self-referenced beliefs, and self-regulated learning among Japanese children.

Journal: *Psychological Reports*, June 1998, *82*(3) Part 1, 803–816.

Related Research: Niemivirta, M. (1996). *Motivational-cognitive components in self-regulated learning*. Paper presented at the 5th International Conference on Motivation, March 1996, Landau, Germany.

9608

Test Name: SELF-REFERENCING CLOSED-ENDED VIGNETTES

Purpose: To assess the extent to which individuals make causal explanations in terms of internal or external, stable or unstable, and global or specific dimensions.

Number of Items: 12 vignettes.

Format: Seven-point scales.

Validity: Correlations with other variables ranged from −.27 to .65.

Author: Ladd, E. R., et al.

Article: Narcissism and causal attribution.

Journal: *Psychological Reports*, February 1997, *80*(1), 171–178.

Related Research: Ladd, E. R. (1995). *Narcissism and causal attribution*. Unpublished master's thesis, University of South Alabama.

9609

Test Name: SELF-WORTH SUBSCALE

Purpose: To describe the global self-worth of two groups.

Number of Items: 6

Format: Responses are made on a scale ranging from 1 to 4.

Reliability: Coefficient alpha was .75.

Author: Rhodes, J. E., et al.

Article: Agents of change: Pathways through which mentoring relationships influence adolescents' academic adjustment.

Journal: *Child Development*, November/December 2000, *71*(6), 1662–1671.

Related Research: Harter, S. (1986). Cognitive-developmental processes in the integration of concepts about emotions and the self. *Social Cognition, 4*, 119–151.

9610

Test Name: SELFISM SCALE

Purpose: To assess to what extent individuals view situations from a self-serving or an other-oriented perspective.

Number of Items: 40

Format: Five-point scales are anchored by 1 (strongly disagree) and 5 (strongly agree).

Reliability: Alpha was .84.

Author: Ehrenberg, M. F., et al.

Article: Shared parenting agreements after marital

separation: The roles of empathy and narcissism.

Journal: *Journal of Consulting and Clinical Psychology*, August 1996, *64*(4), 808–818.

Related Research: Phares, E. J., & Erskine, N. (1984). The measurement of selfism. *Educational and Psychological Measurement, 44*, 597–608.

9611

Test Name: SENSE OF COHERENCE SCALE

Purpose: To measure sense of coherence as comprehensibility, manageability, and meaningfulness.

Number of Items: 29

Format: Seven-point scales.

Reliability: Alphas ranged from .86 to .95.

Validity: Correlations with other variables ranged from −.71 to .64.

Author: Carstens, J. A., and Spangenberg, J. J.

Article: Major depression: A breakdown in sense of coherence?

Journal: *Psychological Reports*, June 1997, *80*(3) Part 2, 1211–1220.

Related Research: Antonovsky, A. (1993). The structure and properties of the Sense of Coherence Scale. *Social Science and Medicine, 36*, 725–733.

9612

Test Name: SENSE OF COHERENCE SCALE—SHORT FORM

Purpose: To assess sense of coherence.

Number of Items: 13

Format: Responses are made on a 7-point scale ranging from 1 (very often) to 7 (very seldom or never).

Reliability: Alpha coefficients ranged from .74 to .91.

Author: Ingram, K. M., et al.

Article: The relationship of victimization experiences to psychological well-being among homeless women and low-income housed women.

Journal: *Journal of Counseling Psychology*, April 1996, *43*(2), 218–227.

Related Research: Antonovsky, A. (1987). *Unraveling the mystery of health*. San Francisco: Jossey-Bass.

9613

Test Name: SENSE OF COMPETENCE QUESTIONNAIRE—REVISED

Purpose: To assess job competence.

Number of Items: 5

Format: Responses are made on a 7-point scale ranging from 1 (strongly disagree) to 7 (strongly agree). A sample item is presented.

Reliability: Coefficient alpha was .81.

Validity: Correlations with other variables ranged from −.05 to .60.

Author: Rentsch, J. R., and Steel, R. P.

Article: Testing the durability of job characteristics as predictors of absenteeism over a six-year period.

Journal: *Personnel Psychology*, Spring 1998, *51*(1), 165–190.

Related Research: Steel, R. P., et al. (1989). Psychometric properties of a measure of sense of competence. *Educational and Psychological Measurement, 49,* 433–446.

9614

Test Name: SEX ROLE IDENTITY SCALE

Purpose: To measure a person's self-perceived level of masculinity and femininity.

Number of Items: 6

Format: Responses are made on a 31-point scale ranging from 0 (most feminine) to 30 (most masculine).

Reliability: Internal consistency coefficients ranged from .66 to .80.

Author: Johnson, M. E., et al.

Article: Concurrent validity of the MMPI-2, feminine gender role (GF), and masculine gender role (GM) scales.

Journal: *Journal of Personality Assessment*, February 1996, 66(1), 153–168.

Related Research: Storms, M. D. (1979). Sex role identity and relationship to sex role attributes and sex role stereotypes. *Journal of Personality and Social Psychology, 37,* 1779–1789.

9615

Test Name: SEXUAL PREJUDICE ATTRIBUTION SCALE

Purpose: To assess the tendency to attribute negative life events to societal prejudice against gay and bisexual people.

Number of Items: 4

Format: Four-point scales are anchored by 0 (disagree strongly) and 3 (agree strongly).

Reliability: Coefficient alpha was .85.

Author: Herek, G. M., et al.

Article: Psychological sequelae of hate-crime victimization among lesbian, gay, and bisexual adults.

Journal: *Journal of Consulting and Clinical Psychology,* December 1999, 67(6), 945–951.

Related Research: Herek, G. M., & Glunt, E. K. (1995). Identity and community among gay and bisexual men in the AIDS era: Preliminary findings from the Sacramento Men's Health Study. In G. M. Herek & B. Green (Eds.), *AIDS, identity, and community* (pp. 55–84). Thousand Oaks, CA: Sage.

9616

Test Name: SEXUAL SELF-SCHEMA SCALE FOR WOMEN

Purpose: To measure passionate/romantic, open/direct, and embarrassed/conservative dimensions of sexuality.

Number of Items: 26 trait adjectives

Format: Seven-point scales are anchored by 0 (not at all descriptive of me) and 6 (very descriptive of me).

Reliability: Test-retest reliabilities were .89 (2 weeks) and .88 (2 months).

Author: Yurek, D., et al.

Article: Breast cancer surgery: Comparing surgical groups and determining individual differences in postoperative sexuality and body change stress.

Journal: *Journal of Consulting and Clinical Psychology,* August 2000, 68(4), 697–709.

Related Research: Andersen, B. L., & Cyranowski, J. M. (1994). Women's sexual self-schema. *Journal of Personality and Social Psychology, 67,* 1079–1100.

9617

Test Name: SEXUAL SELF-SCHEMA SCALE FOR WOMEN

Purpose: To assess the cognitive view about the sexual aspects of oneself.

Number of Items: 50

Format: Trait adjectives are followed by scales that range from 1 (not at all descriptive of me) to 6 (very descriptive of me).

Reliability: Internal consistency was .75. Test-retest reliabilities were (2 weeks) .89 and .88 (2 months).

Validity: Correlations with other variables ranged from −.13 to −.11 (negative affect and social desirability, respectively), thus indicating sexual self-schema was uncontaminated by these constructs.

Author: Andersen, B. L., et al.

Article: Sexual self-schema and sexual morbidity among gynecologic cancer survivors.

Journal: *Journal of Consulting and Clinical Psychology,* April 1997, 65(2), 221–229.

Related Research: Andersen, B. L., & Cryanowski, J. M. (1994). Women's sexual self-schema. *Journal of Personality and Social Psychology, 67,* 1079–1100.

9618

Test Name: SILENCING THE SELF SCALE

Purpose: To measure patterns of belief that guide behavior and gender-specific cognitions about how one should act to maintain a relationship.

Number of Items: 31

Format: Five-point scales are anchored by (1) strongly disagree and (5) strongly agree.

Reliability: Internal consistencies ranged from .86 to .94.

Validity: Correlations with achievement motivation ranged from −.57 to −.52.

Author: Spratt, C. L., et al.

Article: Silencing the self and sex as predictors of achievement motivation.

Journal: *Psychological Reports*, February 1998, *82*(1), 259–263.

Related Research: Jack, D. C., & Dill, D. (1992). The Silencing the Self Scale: Schemas of intimacy associated with depression in women. *Psychology of Women Quarterly, 16,* 97–106.

9619

Test Name: SITUATIONAL CONFIDENCE QUESTIONNAIRE

Purpose: To assess self-efficacy to resist heavy drinking.

Number of Items: 39

Format: Six-point scales range from 0% to 100%. All items are presented.

Reliability: Alpha coefficients ranged from .89 to .97 across subscales.

Author: Kirisci, L., and Moss, H. B.

Article: Reliability and validity of the Situational Confidence Questionnaire in an adolescent sample: Confirmatory factor analysis.

Journal: *Measurement and Evaluation in Counseling and Development*, October 1997, *30*(3), 146–155.

Related Research: Annis, H. M. (1987). *Situational Confidence Questionnaire, Short Form.* Toronto: Addiction Research Foundation.

9620

Test Name: SITUATIONAL INVENTORY OF BODY-IMAGE DYSPHORIA

Purpose: To identify frequency of experiencing negative feelings.

Number of Items: 48

Format: Responses are made on a scale ranging from 0 to 4.

Reliability: Coefficient alpha was .96.

Author: Smith, B. L., et al.

Article: Sex differences in exercise motivation and body-image satisfaction among college students.

Journal: *Perceptual and Motor Skills*, April 1998, *86*(2), 723–732.

Related Research: Cash, T. F. (1994). The Situational Inventory of Body-Image Dysphoria: Contextual assessment of a negative body image. *The Behavior Therapist, 17,* 133–134.

9621

Test Name: SIX-FACTOR SELF-CONCEPT SCALE

Purpose: To measure self-concept for adults.

Number of Items: 36

Format: Includes 6 subscales: Power, Task Accomplishment, Giftedness, Vulnerability, Likeability, and Morality. Responses are made on a 7-point scale ranging from 1 (never or almost never true of you) to 7 (always or almost always true of you).

Reliability: Alpha coefficients ranged from .79 to .86. Test-retest (4 weeks) reliabilities ranged from .74 to .88 (*N* = 57). Test-retest (6 weeks) reliabilities ranged from .68 to .85 (*N* = 61).

Author: Yanico, B. J., and Lu, T. G. C.

Article: A psychometric evaluation of the Six-Factor Self-Concept Scale in a sample of racial/ethnic minority women.

Journal: *Educational and Psychological Measurement*, February 2000, *60*(1), 86–99.

Related Research: Stake, J. E. (1994). Development and validation of the Six-Factor Self-Concept Scale for adults. *Educational and Psychological Measurement, 54,* 56–72.

9622

Test Name: SOCIAL PHYSIQUE ANXIETY SCALE

Purpose: To measure the extent of anxiety felt when one perceives his or her body to be observed and evaluated by others.

Number of Items: 12

Format: Responses are made on a 5-point scale ranging from 1 (not at all true for me) to 5 (extremely true for me).

Reliability: Interitem reliability was .9. Test-retest (2 weeks) reliability was .82.

Validity: Correlations with other variables ranged from .34 to .57.

Author: Fredrick, C. M., and Morrison, C. S.

Article: A mediational model of social physique anxiety and eating disordered behaviors.

Journal: *Perceptual and Motor Skills*, February 1998, *86*(1), 139–145.

Related Research: Hart, E. A., et al. (1989). The measurement of social physique anxiety. *Journal of Sports and Exercise Psychology, 11,* 94–104.

9623

Test Name: SOCIAL SELF-ESTEEM SCALE

Purpose: To assess differences in social self-esteem based on interpersonal competence.

Number of Items: 16

Format: Responses are made on a 5-point scale ranging from 1 (not at all characteristic of me) to 5 (very much characteristic of me).

Reliability: Alpha coefficient was .93.

Validity: Correlations with other variables were −.17 and .35.

Author: Ryckman, R. M., et al.

Article: Construction of a personal development competitive attitude scale.

Journal: *Journal of Personality Assessment*, April 1996, *66*(2), 374–385.

Related Research: Helmreich, R. L., & Stapp, J. (1974). Short forms of the Texas Social Behavior Inventory (TSBI): An objective measure of self-esteem. *Bulletin of the Psychonomic Society, 4*, 473–475.

9624

Test Name: SOURCES OF MATHEMATICS SELF-EFFICACY

Purpose: To assess perceived sources of mathematics self-efficacy.

Number of Items: 38

Format: Include 4 scales: Performance, Vicarious Learning, Social Persuasion, and Emotional Arousal. Responses are made on a 5-point scale ranging from 1 (strongly disagree) to 5 (strongly agree). Examples are presented.

Reliability: Alpha coefficients ranged from .62 to .91.

Validity: Correlations with other variables ranged from .15 to .64.

Author: Lopez, F. G., et al.

Article: Role of social-cognitive expectations in high school students' mathematics-related interest and performance.

Journal: *Journal of Counseling Psychology*, January 1997, *44*(1), 44–52.

Related Research: Lent, R. W. (1991). Mathematics self-efficacy: Sources and relation to science-based career choice. *Journal of Counseling Psychology, 38*, 424–430.

9625

Test Name: SPORT QUESTIONNAIRE

Purpose: To measure participants' perceptions of various purposes of sport.

Number of Items: 46

Format: Measures 7 purposes of sport participation: Competition, Affiliation, Being a Team Member, Release of Energy, Development of Skills, Improvement of Fitness, and Gaining Recognition or Status. Responses are made on a 5-point scale ranging from 1 (strongly disagree) to 5 (strongly agree).

Reliability: Alpha coefficients ranged from .75 to .83.

Author: Finkenberg, M. E., and Moode, F. M.

Article: College students' perceptions of the purpose of sports.

Journal: *Perceptual and Motor Skills*, February 1996, *82*(1), 19–22.

Related Research: Duda, J. L. (1989). Relationship between task and ego orientation and the perceived purpose of sport among high school athletes.

Journal of Sport and Exercise Psychology, 11, 318–335.

9626

Test Name: STATE SELF-ESTEEM SCALE

Purpose: To measure self-esteem.

Number of Items: 20

Format: Scales range from 1 (strongly disagree) to 7 (strongly agree).

Reliability: Alpha coefficents ranged from .76 to .86.

Author: Stewart, M. M., and Shapiro, D. L.

Article: Selection based on merit versus demography: Implications across race and gender lines.

Journal: *Journal of Applied Psychology*, April 2000, *85*(2), 219–231.

Related Research: Heatherton, T. F., & Polivy, P. J. (1991). Development and validation of a scale for measuring state self-esteem. *Journal of Personality and Social Psychology, 60*, 895–910.

9627

Test Name: STATE SPORT CONFIDENCE QUESTIONNAIRE

Purpose: To assess athletes' sports confidence prior to competition and their precompetitive feelings of confidence for that specific event.

Number of Items: 18

Format: Includes 3 factors: State General Self-Confidence, State Self-Confidence in Unfavorable Situations, and State Positive Thinking. Employs a 5-point response scale.

Reliability: Internal consistencies ranged from .77 to .80.

Validity: Correlations with other variables ranged from .16 to .27.

Author: Psychountaki, M., and Zervas, Y.

Article: Competitive worries, sport confidence, and performance ratings for young swimmers.

Journal: *Perceptual and Motor Skills*, August 2000, *91*(1), 87–94.

Related Research: Psychountaki, M., & Zervas, Y. (1998). Trait/State Sport-Confidence Questionnaire for Children. *Proceedings of 2nd International Congress of Sport Psychology* (pp. 234–236). Trikala, Greece: Congress.

9628

Test Name: STEREOTYPIC BELIEFS INVENTORY

Purpose: To measure ethnic stereotyping.

Number of Items: 24

Format: Seven-point scales are anchored by (1) not true and (7) very true. All items are presented.

Reliability: Alpha was .93. Test-retest reliability (2 weeks) was .83.

Validity: Correlations with other variables ranged from −.23 to .44.

Author: VanOmmeren, M. H., and Ishiyama, F. I.

Article: Development and preliminary validation of the Stereotypic Beliefs Scale.

Journal: *Psychological Reports*, August 1998, *83*(1), 395–402.

9629

Test Name: STEREOTYPING OTHERS SCALE

Purpose: To measure extent of stereotyping others.

Number of Items: 40

Format: Seven-point scales range from (1) very low likelihood to (7) very high likelihood.

Reliability: Alpha was .85.

Validity: Correlation with Individuation Scale was −.33.

Author: Humphreys, C. N., and Davidson, W. B.

Article: Individuation of self and stereotyping of others.

Journal: *Psychological Reports*, December 1997, *83*(3, Part II), 1252–1254.

Related Research: Andersen, S. M., et al. (1990). Traits and social stereotypes: Efficiency differences in social information processing. *Journal of Personality and Social Psychology*, 59, 192–201.

9630

Test Name: STRATEGY AND ATTRIBUTION QUESTIONNAIRE

Purpose: To measure reaction styles: pessimism, task-irrelevance, and avoidance.

Number of Items: 60

Format: Scales range from 1 (strongly disagree) to 4 (strongly agree). Sample items are presented.

Reliability: Alpha coefficients ranged from .72 to .83 across subscales. Test-retest reliabilities (6 months) ranged from .55 to .88.

Author: Eronen, S., et al.

Article: Planning-oriented, avoidant, and impulsive reaction styles: A person-oriented approach.

Journal: *Journal of Research in Personality*, March 1997, *31*(1), 34–57.

Related Research: Nurmi, J. E., et al. (1995). The Strategy and Attribution Questionnaire: Psychometric properties. *European Journal of Psychological Assessment*, 11, 108–121.

9631

Test Name: SUBJECTIVE PLATEAUED STATUS SCALE

Purpose: To assess one's perceived likelihood of promotion.

Number of Items: 3

Format: Responses are made on a 7-point scale ranging from 1 (strongly disagree) to 7 (strongly agree). All items are presented.

Reliability: Coefficient alpha was .90.

Validity: Correlations with other variables ranged from −.29 to .42.

Author: Ettington, D. R.

Article: Successful career plateauing.

Journal: *Journal of Vocational Behavior*, February 1998, *52*(1), 72–88.

Related Research: Milliman, J. (1992, August). *Consequences and moderators of career plateauing: An empirical investigation.* Presented at the Academy of Management Meetings, Las Vegas, NV.

9632

Test Name: SUBJECTIVE VITALITY QUESTIONNAIRE

Purpose: To measure perceptions of ethnolinguistic vitality.

Number of Items: 24

Format: Five-point scales. All

items are presented in abbreviated form.

Reliability: Alpha coefficients ranged from .74 to .88 across factors.

Validity: Correlations with other variables ranged from −.14 to .83.

Authors: Bornman, E., and Appelgryn, A. E. M.

Article: Ethnolinguistic vitality under a new political dispensation in South Africa.

Journal: *Journal of Social Psychology*, December 1997, *137*(6), 690–707.

Related Research: Bourhis, R. Y., et al. (1981). Notes on the construction of a "subjective vitality questionnaire" for ethnolinguistic groups. *Journal of Multilingual and Multicultural Development*, 2, 145–155.

9633

Test Name: TASK-SPECIFIC SELF-EFFICACY SCALE

Purpose: To measure the perceived ability to deal with the threat of sexual assault.

Number of Items: 6

Format: Scales range from 1 (not competent at all) to 10 (very competent). All items are presented.

Reliability: Coefficient alpha was .81. Test-retest reliability (6 weeks) was .86.

Validity: Correlations with other variables ranged from −.17 to .38.

Author: Weitlauf, J. C., et al.

Article: Generalization effects of coping-skills training: Influence of self-defense training on women's efficacy beliefs, assertiveness, and aggression.

Journal: *Journal of Applied Psychology*, August 2000, *85*(4), 625–633.

9634

Test Name: TEACHER EFFICACY INSTRUMENTS

Purpose: To assess teacher efficacy for student social relations.

Number of Items: 20

Format: Includes 3 factors: Teacher Efficacy, Personal Teaching Efficacy, and Teaching Efficacy for Social Relations.

Reliability: Alpha coefficients ranged from .65 to .81. Test-retest reliabilities ranged from .79 to .87 (*N* = 89).

Author: Rich, Y., et al.

Article: Extending the concept and assessment of teacher efficacy.

Journal: *Educational and Psychological Measurement*, December 1996, *56*(6), 1015–1025.

Related Research: Gibson, S., & Dembo, M. (1984). Teacher efficacy: A construct validation. *Journal of Educational Psychology*, 76, 569–582.

9635

Test Name: TEACHER EFFICACY SCALE

Purpose: To measure teacher efficacy.

Number of Items: 17

Format: Includes 2 factors: Personal Teaching Efficacy and General Teaching Efficacy. Responses are made on a 6-point scale ranging from 1 (strongly disagree) to 6 (strongly agree). All items are presented.

Reliability: Alpha coefficients were .66 and .81.

Author: Deemer, S. A., and Minke, K. M.

Article: An investigation of the factor structure of the Teacher Efficacy Scale.

Journal: *Journal of Educational Research*, September/October 1999, *93*(1), 3–10.

Related Research: Gibson, S., & Dembo, M. H. (1984). Teacher efficacy: A construct validation. *Journal of Educational Psychology*, 76, 569–582.

9636

Test Name: TEACHER EFFICACY SCALE

Purpose: To assess general efficacy and personal efficacy of teaching efficacy.

Number of Items: 30

Format: Includes two subscales: General Efficacy and Personal Efficacy. Responses are made on 6-point scales.

Reliability: Alpha coefficients ranged from .72 to .79.

Author: Warren, L. L., and Payne, B. D.

Article: Impact of middle grades' organization on teacher efficacy and environmental perceptions.

Journal: *Journal of Educational Research*, May/June 1997, *90*(5), 301–308.

Related Research: Gibson, S., & Dembo, M. H. (1984). Teacher efficacy: A construct validation. *Journal of Educational Psychology*, 76(1), 569–582.

9637

Test Name: TEACHER EFFICACY SCALE—SHORT VERSION

Purpose: To assess efficacy beliefs.

Number of Items: 16

Format: Includes two factors: Personal Efficacy and Teaching Efficacy. Responses are made on a 6-point scale ranging from 1 (strongly disagree) to 6 (strongly agree). All items are presented.

Reliability: Coefficient alpha was .79.

Author: Soodak, L. C., and Podell, D. M.

Article: Efficacy and experience: Perceptions of efficacy among pre-service and practicing teachers.

Journal: *Journal of Research and Development in Education*, Summer 1997, *30*(4), 214–221.

Related Research: Gibson, S., & Dembo, M. H. (1984). Teacher efficacy: A construct validation. *Journal of Educational Psychology*, 76, 569–582.

9638

Test Name: TEACHER REINFORCING SCALE

Purpose: To assess teacher's perceptions of the degree to which students were reinforcing in the classroom.

Number of Items: 9

Format: Responses are made on a 5-point Likert-type scale ranging from 1 (strongly agree) to 5 (strongly disagree).

Reliability: Coefficient alpha was .88.

Validity: Correlations with other variables were −.53 and .03.

Author: Cavell, T. A., and Hughes, J. N.

Article: Secondary prevention as context for assessing change processes in aggressive children.

Journal: *Journal of School Psychology*, May/June 2000, *38*(3), 199–235.

9639

Test Name: TEACHER TRAINING FUNCTIONING SCALE

Purpose: To assess the effect of a teacher training program on functioning in areas of individualized instruction.

Number of Items: 23

Format: Four-point Likert format. All items are presented.

Reliability: Alpha coefficients ranged from .76 to .86 across subscales.

Validity: GFI was .66.

Author: Newman, I., et al.

Article: Factor structure of perceived individualization of instruction: Argument for multiple perspective.

Journal: *Educational Research Quarterly*, September, 2000, *24*(1), 20–29.

9640

Test Name: TEAM AND PLAYER EFFICACY SCALES

Purpose: To measure the confidence hockey players have in their team and in their ability to outperform opponents.

Number of Items: 11

Format: Eleven-point scales are anchored by 0 (cannot do at all) and 10 (certainly can do).

Reliability: Coefficient alpha was .93 (team) and .87 (player).

Author: Feltz, D. L., and Lirgg, C. D.

Article: Perceived team and player efficacy in hockey.

Journal: *Journal of Applied Psychology*, August 1998, *83*(4), 557–564.

Related Research: Bandura, A. (1990). Perceived self-efficacy in the exercise of personal agency. *Journal of Applied Sport Psychology*, 2, 128–163.

9641

Test Name: TEST-TAKING SELF-EFFICACY SCALE

Purpose: To rate skills at taking tests.

Number of Items: 4

Format: Scales range from 0 (very inaccurate) to 4 (very accurate). A sample item is presented.

Reliability: Coefficient alpha was .80.

Author: Toray, T., and Cooley, E.

Article: Coping in women college students: The influence of experience.

Journal: *Journal of College Student Development*, May/June 1998, *39*(3), 291–295.

Related Research: Cooley, E., & Klinger, C. (1989). Academic attributions and coping with tests. *Journal of Social and Clinical Psychology*, 8, 359–367.

9642

Test Name: TEXAS SOCIAL BEHAVIOR INVENTORY (JAPANESE VERSION)

Purpose: To measure self-esteem.

Number of Items: 16

Format: Five-point rating scales range from 1 (not at all characteristic of me) to 5 (very characteristic of me).

Reliability: Alpha was .84. Test-retest (3 months) was .81.

Author: Matsui, T., et al.

Article: Long-term outcomes of early victimization by peers among Japanese male university students: Model of a vicious cycle.

Journal: *Psychological Reports*, December 1996, *79*(3) Part 1, 711–720.

Related Research: Helmreich, R., & Stapp, J. (1974). Short forms of the Texas Behavior Inventory (TSBI), an objective measure of self-esteem. *Bulletin of the Psychonomic Society*, 4 (5A), 473–475.

9643

Test Name: TEXAS SOCIAL BEHAVIOR INVENTORY— SHORT FORM

Purpose: To assess one's social self-esteem as a function of perceived social competence.

Number of Items: 16

Format: Sample items are presented.

Reliability: Coefficient alpha was .84.

Validity: Correlation with other variables ranged from −.27 to .59.

Author: Kwon, Y-H.

Article: Sex, sex-role, facial attractiveness, social self-esteem and interest in clothing.

Journal: *Perceptual and Motor Skills*, June 1997, *84*(3, Part 1), 899–907.

Related Research: Helmreich, R., & Stapp, J. (1974). Short-form of the Texas Social Behavior Inventory (TSBI), an objective measure of self-esteem. *Bulletin of the Psychometric Society*, 4 (5A), 435–475.

9644

Test Name: TIME STRUCTURE QUESTIONNAIRE

Purpose: To measure the degree to which individuals perceive their use of time to be structured and purposive.

Number of Items: 26

Format: Seven-point scales are anchored by 1 (no, never) and 7 (yes, always).

Reliability: Alpha was .86. Test-retest (15 weeks) was .76.

Validity: Correlations with procrastination ranged from −.64 to −.29.

Author: Vodanovich, S. J., and Seib, H. M.

Article: Relationship between time structure and procrastination.

Journal: *Psychological Reports*, February 1997, *80*(1), 211–215.

Related Research: Bond, M. J., and Feather, N. T. (1988). Some correlates of structure and purpose in the use of time. *Journal of Personality and Social Psychology*, 55, 321–329.

9645

Test Name: TOKEN RESISTANCE TO SEX SCALE

Purpose: To assess the extent to which token resistance to sex is a cue for sexual willingness.

Number of Items: 8

Format: Scales range from 1 (strongly disagree) to 7 (strongly agree).

Reliability: Coefficient alpha was .86.

Author: Osman, S. L., and Davis, C. M.

Article: Predicting perceptions of date rape on individual beliefs and female alcohol consumption.

Journal: *Journal of College Student Development*, November/ December 1999, *40*(6), 701–709.

Related Research: Osman, S. L. (1988). The Token Resistance to Sex Scale. In C. M. Davis et al. (Eds.), *Handbook of sexually-related measures*. Thousand Oaks, CA: Sage.

9646

Test Name: TRAIT SPORT CONFIDENCE QUESTIONNAIRE FOR CHILDREN

Purpose: To assess athletes' confidence they feel in sport competition.

Number of Items: 18

Format: Includes 3 factors: Trait General Self-Confidence, Trait Self-Confidence in Unfavorable Situations, and Trait Positive Thinking. Employs a 5-point response format.

Reliability: Test-retest reliabilities ranged from .68 to .81. Alpha coefficients ranged from .77 to .80.

Validity: Correlations with other variables ranged from −.49 to .74.

Author: Psychountaki, M., and Zervas, Y.

Article: Competitive worries, sport confidence, and performance ratings for young swimmers.

Journal: *Perceptual and Motor Skills*, August 2000, *91*(1), 87–94.

Related Research: Psychountaki, M., & Zervas, Y. (1998). Trait/ State Sport Confidence Questionnaire for Children. *Proceedings of 2nd International Congress of Sport Psychology* (pp. 234–236). Trikala, Greece: Congress.

9647

Test Name: TRANSLIMINALITY SCALE

Purpose: To assess the tendency for psychological material to move from conscious to unconscious.

Number of Items: 29

Format: True/false format. Sample items are presented.

Reliability: Alphas ranged from .85 to .90. Test-retest reliability (7 weeks) was .88.

Validity: Correlation with openness to experience was .27.

Author: Thalbourne, M. A.

Article: Relation between transliminality and openness to experience.

Journal: *Psychological Reports*, June 2000, *86*(3, Part 1), 909–910.

Related Research: Thalbourne, M. A., & Houran, J. (2000). Transliminality, the Mental Experience Inventory, and tolerance of ambiguity. *Personality and Individual Differences, 28*, 853–863.

9648

Test Name: TREATMENT EXPECTANCY AND CREDIBILITY SCALE

Purpose: To measure treatment expectancy and credibility.

Number of Items: 6

Format: Items are anchored by 1 (very weak) and 5 (very strong).

Reliability: Internal consistency was .86.

Author: Freeston, M. H., et al.

Article: Cognitive-behavioral treatment of obsessive thoughts: A controlled study.

Journal: *Journal of Consulting and Clinical Psychology*, June 1997, *65*(3), 405–413.

Related Research: Borkovec, T. D., & Nau, S. D. (1972). Credibility of analogue therapy rationales. *Journal of Behavior*

Therapy and Experimental Psychiatry, 3, 257–260.

9649

Test Name: 2X2 SENSE OF CONTROL SCALE

Purpose: To measure sense of control.

Number of Items: 8

Format: Four-point agreement scales are used. All items are presented. Scoring methods are described.

Reliability: Reliabilities ranged from .52 to .59.

Author: Sastry, J., and Ross, C. E.

Article: Asian ethnicity and the sense of personal control.

Journal: *Social Psychology Quarterly*, June 1998, *61*(2), 101–120.

Related Research: Mirowsky, J., & Ross, C. E. (1991). Eliminating defense and agreement bias from measures of the sense of control: A 2x2 index. *Social Psychology Quarterly, 54*, 127–145.

Geis, K. G., & Ross, C. E. (1998). A new look at urban alienation: The effect of neighborhood disorder on perceived powerlessness. *Social Psychology Quarterly, 61*, 232–246.

9650

Test Name: USEFULNESS OF MATHEMATICS SCALE

Purpose: To measure outcome expectations.

Number of Items: 10

Format: Responses are made on a 5-point scale ranging from 1 (strongly disagree) to 5 (strongly agree). Examples are presented.

Reliability: Alpha coefficients ranged from .91 to .93.

Validity: Correlations with other variables ranged from .11 to .51.

Author: Lopez, F. G., et al.

Article: Role of social-cognitive expectations in high school students' mathematics-related interest and performance.

Journal: *Journal of Counseling Psychology*, January 1997, *44*(1), 44–52.

Related Research: Betz, N. E. (1977, August). *Math anxiety: What is it?* Paper presented at the 85th annual convention of the American Psychological Association, San Francisco, CA.

9651

Test Name: VIVIDNESS OF VISUAL IMAGERY QUESTIONNAIRE

Purpose: To rate one's vividness of an image.

Number of Items: 16

Format: Responses are made on a 5-point scale ranging from 1 (perfectly clear) to 5 (no image at all).

Reliability: Test-retest reliability was .74. Split-half reliability was .85. Internal consistency was .94.

Author: Hill, C. E., et al.

Article: Dream interpretation sessions: Who volunteers, who benefits, and what volunteer clients view as most and least helpful.

Journal: *Journal of Counseling Psychology*, January 1997, *44*(1), 53–62.

Related Research: Marks, D. (1973). Visual imagery differences in the recall of pictures. *British Journal of Psychology, 64*, 17–24.

9652

Test Name: VOCATIONAL CHECKLIST

Purpose: To measure occupational sex role stereotypes.

Number of Items: 30

Format: Response to each item is either "male" or "female." All items are presented.

Reliability: Test-retest reliability was .58.

Author: Cook, J., and Simbayi, L. C.

Article: The effects of gender and sex role identity on occupational sex role stereotypes held by White South African high school pupils.

Journal: *Journal of Vocational Behavior*, October 1998, 53(2), 274–280.

Related Research: Taljaard, J. J., & von Mollendorf, J. W. (1987). *The South African dictionary of jobs*. Waterkloof, Pretoria: Consensus.

9653

Test Name: VOCATIONAL RATING SCALE

Purpose: To assess vocational self-concept crystallization.

Number of Items: 40

Reliability: Coefficient alpha was .94. Test-retest (2 weeks) reliability was .76.

Validity: Correlations with other variables ranged from −.35 to .55.

Author: Hamer, R. J., and Bruch, M. A.

Article: Personality factors and inhibited career development. Testing the unique contribution of shyness.

Journal: *Journal of Vocational Behavior*, June 1997, 50(3), 382–400.

Related Research: Barrett, T. C., & Tinsley, H. E. A. (1977). Measuring vocational self-concept crystallization. *Journal of Vocational Behavior, 11*, 305–313.

9654

Test Name: VOCATIONAL SKILLS SELF-EFFICACY SCALE

Purpose: To indicate the degree of confidence respondents have in completing specific tasks.

Number of Items: 37

Format: Responses are made on a 10-point scale ranging from 0 (no confidence at all) to 9 (complete confidence). Sample items are presented.

Reliability: Test-retest (9 weeks) reliability was .68 ($N = 95$). Coefficient alpha was .97.

Validity: Correlations with other variables ranged from −.43 to .91.

Author: McWhirter, E. H., et al.

Article: The effects of high school career education on social-cognitive variables.

Journal: *Journal of Counseling Psychology*, July 2000, 47(3), 330–341.

9655

Test Name: WEIGHT-LOSS EXPECTANCY SCALES

Purpose: To measure the perceived outcomes of weight-loss.

Number of Items: 23

Format: Scales range from 0 (no chance) to 6 (certain to happen). Sample items are presented.

Reliability: Alpha coefficients ranged from .71 to .93 across subscales.

Validity: Correlations with other variables ranged from −.10 to .45.

Author: Thombs, D. L., et al.

Article: Weight-loss expectancies, relative weight, and symptoms of bulimia in young women.

Journal: *Journal of College Student Development*, July/August 1996, 37(4), 405–414.

9656

Test Name: WORK–BOUND, COLLEGE-BOUND SCALE

Purpose: To assess the perceived skills important to work–bound and college-bound students.

Number of Items: 14

Format: Scales range from 1 (of little importance) to 5 (very important).

Reliability: Internal consistency ranged from .87 to .93.

Author: Barker, J., and Satcher, J.

Article: School counselors' perceptions of required workplace skills and career development competencies.

Journal: *Professional School Counseling*, December 2000, 4(2), 134–139.

Related Research: Bloch, D. P. (1996). Career development and workforce preparation: Educational policy versus school practice. *Career Development Quarterly, 45*, 20–40.

9657

Test Name: WORK ENVIRONMENT LOCUS OF CONTROL SCALES

Purpose: To measure locus of control.

Number of Items: 24

Format: Five-point Likert format.

Reliability: Coefficient alpha was .86.

Author: Riipinen, M.

Article: The relation of work involvement to occupational needs, need satisfaction, locus of control and affect.

Journal: *Journal of Social Psychology*, June 1996, *136*(3), 291–303.

Related Research: Pettersen, N. (1985). Specific versus generalized locus of control scales related to job satisfaction. *Psychological Reports, 56,* 60–62.

9658

Test Name: WORK/FAMILY AND FAMILY/WORK CONFLICT SCALES

Purpose: To measure conflict between work and family roles.

Number of Items: 18

Format: All items are presented.

Reliability: Alpha coefficients ranged from .77 to .89 across subscales.

Validity: Correlations with other variables ranged from −.24 to .25.

Authors: Eagle, B. W., et al.

Article: The importance of employee demographic profiles for understanding experiences of work-family internal conflict.

Journal: *Journal of Social Psychology*, December 1998, *138*(6), 690–709.

9659

Test Name: WORK–FAMILY CONFLICT

Purpose: To assess work–family conflict.

Number of Items: 8

Format: Includes two dimensions: Work-to-Family Conflict and Family-to-Work Conflict. Responses are made on a 5-point scale ranging from 1 (strongly disagree) to 5 (strongly agree).

Reliability: Alpha coefficients were .84 (Work-to-Family Conflict) and .81 (Family-to-Work Conflict).

Validity: Correlations with other variables ranged from −.34 to .77.

Author: Eagle, B. W., et al.

Article: Interrole conflicts and the permeability of work and family domains: Are there gender differences?

Journal: *Journal of Vocational Behavior*, April 1997, *50*(2), 168–184.

Related Research: Gutek, B. A., et al. (1991). Rational versus gender role expectations for work–family conflict. *Journal of Applied Psychology, 76,* 560–568.

9660

Test Name: WORK–FAMILY CONFLICT MEASURE

Purpose: To assess work–family conflict.

Number of Items: 12

Format: Includes two dimensions: Work-to-Family Conflict and Family-to-Work Conflict. Responses are made on a 5-point scale ranging from 1 (strongly disagree) to 5 (strongly agree).

Reliability: Alpha coefficients ranged from .81 (Work-to-Family Conflict) and .85 (Family-to-Work Conflict).

Validity: Correlations with other

variables ranged from −.36 to .80.

Author: Eagle, B. W., et al.

Article: Internal conflicts and the permeability of work and family domains: Are there gender differences?

Journal: *Journal of Vocational Behavior*, April 1997, *50*(2), 168–184.

Related Research: Wiley, D. L. (1987). The relationship between work/nonwork role conflict and job-related outcomes: Some anticipated findings. *Journal of Management, 13,* 467–472.

9661

Test Name: WORK–FAMILY CONFLICT MEASURE

Purpose: To measure work–family conflict.

Number of Items: 16

Format: Includes two dimensions: Work-to-Family Conflict and Family-to-Work Conflict. Responses are made on a 5-point scale ranging from 1 (strongly disagree) to 5 (strongly agree).

Reliability: Coefficient alpha was .89.

Validity: Correlations with other variables ranged from −.25 to .22.

Author: Hammer, L. B., et al.

Article: Work-family conflict in dual-earner couples: Within-individual and crossover effects of work and family.

Journal: *Journal of Vocational Behavior*, April 1997, *50*(2), 185–203.

Related Research: Goff, S. J., et al. (1990). Employer supported child care, work/family conflict, and absenteeism: A field study. *Personnel Psychology, 43,* 793–809.

9662

Test Name: WORK–AMILY CONFLICT SCALE

Purpose: To measure work–family conflict.

Number of Items: 4

Format: Responses are made on a scale ranging from 1 (strongly disagree) to 5 (strongly agree). Examples are presented.

Reliability: Alpha coefficients ranged from .70 to .89.

Validity: Correlations with other variables ranged from −.24 to .21.

Author: Aryee, S., and Luk, V.

Article: Work and nonwork influences on the career satisfaction of dual-earner couples.

Journal: *Journal of Vocational Behavior*, August 1996, *49*(1), 38–52.

Related Research: Kopenman, R., et al. (1983). A model of work, family and interrole conflict: A construct validation study. *Organizational Behavior and Human Performance*, 32, 198–215.

9663

Test Name: FAMILY–WORK CONFLICT SCALE

Purpose: To measure the extent to which work puts a strain on family life.

Number of Items: 5

Format: Seven-point scales ranged from "strongly disagree" to "strongly agree." All items are presented.

Reliability: Alpha coefficients ranged from .88 to .89 across samples.

Validity: Correlations with other

variables ranged from −.53 to .55.

Author: Netemeyer, R. G., et al.

Article: Development and validation of Work–Family Conflict and Family–Work Conflict scales.

Journal: *Journal of Applied Psychology*, August 1996, *81*(4), 400–410.

9664

Test Name: WORK–FAMILY CONFLICT SCALE

Purpose: To measure work–family conflict.

Number of Items: 8

Format: Responses are made on a 7-point scale.

Reliability: Coefficient alpha was .85.

Author: Boles, J. S., et al.

Article: The dimensionality of the Maslach Burnout Inventory across small business owners and educators.

Journal: *Journal of Vocational Behavior*, February 2000, *56*(1), 12–34.

Related Research: Netemeyer, R. G., et al. (1996). Development and validation of work–family conflict and family–work conflict scales. *Journal of Applied Psychology*, 81, 1–11.

9665

Test Name: WORK–FAMILY CONFLICT SCALE

Purpose: To assess work–family conflict.

Number of Items: 12

Format: Includes two dimensions: Work-to-Family Conflict and Family-to-Work Conflict.

Reliability: Alpha coefficients were

.88 (work-to-family conflict) and .80 (family-to-work conflict).

Validity: Correlations with other variables ranged from −.44 to .47.

Author: Frone, M. R., et al.

Article: Developing and testing an integrative model of the work–family interface.

Journal: *Journal of Vocational Behavior*, April 1997, *50*(2), 145–167.

Related Research: Frone, M. R., & Yardley, J. K. (1996). Workplace family-supportive programmes: Predictors of employed parents' importance ratings. *Journal of Occupational and Organizational Psychology*, 69, 351–366.

9666

Test Name: WORK–FAMILY CONFLICT SCALE

Purpose: To measure work–family conflict.

Number of Items: 30

Format: Includes 3 forms of work–family conflict: time, strain, and behavior. Responses are made on a 5-point Likert type scale ranging from 1 (strongly disagree) to 5 (strongly agree). Examples are presented.

Reliability: Alpha coefficients ranged from .85 to .90.

Validity: Correlations with other variables ranged from .02 to .55.

Author: Carlson, D. S.

Article: Personality and role variables as predictors of three forms of work–family conflict.

Journal: *Journal of Vocational Behavior*, October 1999, *55*(2), 236–253.

Related Research: Carlson, D. S., et al. (1998, August). *The development and validation of a* *multi-dimensional measure of work–family conflict.* Paper presented at the annual meeting of the Academy of Management, San Diego, CA.

9667

Test Name: WORK–HOME CONFLICT SCALE

Purpose: To assess work–home conflict.

Number of Items: 10

Format: Responses are made on a 5-point scale ranging from "strongly agree" to "strongly disagree." Sample items are presented.

Reliability: Coefficients alpha was .84.

Validity: Correlations with other variables ranged from −.18 to .62.

Author: Greenhaus, J. H., et al.

Article: Work and family influences on departure from public accounting.

Journal: *Journal of Vocational Behavior*, April 1997, *50*(2), 249–270.

9668

Test Name: WORK IDENTITY SCALE

Purpose: To measure work identity.

Number of Items: 4

Format: Responses are made on a 5-point scale ranging from 1 (strongly disagree) to 5 (strongly agree). Sample items are presented.

Reliability: Coefficient alpha was .75.

Validity: Correlations with other variables ranged from −.08 to .26.

Author: Aryee, S., and Luk, V.

Article: Work and nonwork influences on the career satisfaction of dual-earner couples.

Journal: *Journal of Vocational Behavior*, August 1996, *49*(1), 38–52.

Related Research: Lodahl, T., & Kejner, M. (1965). The definition and measurement of job involvement. *Journal of Applied Psychology*, *49*, 24–33.

9669

Test Name: WORK–LIFE CONFLICT SCALE

Purpose: To measure work–life conflicts.

Number of Items: 4

Format: Responses are made on a 5-point scale ranging from 1 (strongly disagree) to 5 (strongly agree). All items are presented.

Reliability: Alpha coefficients ranged from .80 to .83.

Validity: Correlations with other variables ranged from −.24 to .42.

Author: Bonebright, C. A., et al.

Article: The relationship of workaholism with work–life conflict, life satisfaction, and purpose in life.

Journal: *Journal of Counseling Psychology*, October 2000, *47*(4), 469–477.

Related Research: Gutek, B. A., et al. (1991). Rational versus gender role explanations for work–family conflict. *Journal of Applied Psychology, 76*, 560–568.

9670

Test Name: WORK LOCUS OF CONTROL SCALE

Purpose: To measure locus of control in work settings.

Number of Items: 16

Format: Five-point and 7-point Likert-type scales can be used and range from "strongly disagree" to "strongly agree."

Reliability: Alpha coefficients ranged from .72 to .87.

Author: Macan, T. H., et al.

Article: Spector's Work Locus of Control Scale: Dimensionality and validity evidence.

Journal: *Educational and Psychological Measurement*, April 1996, *56*(2), 349–357.

Related Research: Spector, P. E. (1988). Development of the Work Locus of Control Scale. *Journal of Occupational Psychology, 61*, 335–340.

9671

Test Name: WORK-ROLE CONFLICT SCALE

Purpose: To measure work-role conflict.

Number of Items: 8

Format: Responses are made on a 5-point scale ranging from 1 (never) to 5 (always). An example is given.

Reliability: Coefficient alpha was .83.

Validity: Correlations with other variables ranged from −.37 to .38.

Author: Duxbury, L. E., et al.

Article: Work and family environments and the adoption of computer-supported supplemental work-at-home.

Journal: *Journal of Vocational Behavior*, August 1996, *49*(1), 1–23.

Related Research: Rizzo, J., et al. (1970). Role conflict and ambiguity in complex organizations. *Administrative Science Quarterly*, *15*, 150–163.

9672

Test Name: WORK-TO-FAMILY AND FAMILY-TO-WORK CONFLICT SCALE

Purpose: To assess conflict between work and family obligations.

Number of Items: 10

Format: Five-point scales. Sample items are presented.

Reliability: Alpha was .56.

Validity: Correlations with other variables ranged from -18 to .28.

Author: Beutell, N. J., and Wittig-Berman, U.

Article: Predictors of work–family conflict and satisfaction with family, job, career and life.

Journal: *Psychological Reports*, December 1999, *85*(3, Part I), 893–903.

Related Research: Kopelman, R. G., et al. (1983). A model of work, family and interrole conflict: A construct validation study. *Organizational Behavior and Human Performance*, *32*, 198–215.

9673

Test Name: WORK-TO-FAMILY CONFLICT SCALE

Purpose: To measure work-to-family conflict.

Number of Items: 6

Format: Responses are made on a 5-point scale ranging from 1 (strongly disagree) to 5 (strongly agree). An example is presented.

Reliability: Coefficient alpha was .87.

Validity: Correlations with other

variables ranged from −.31 to .61.

Author: Parasuraman, S., et al.

Article: Work and family variables, entrepreneurial career success, and psychological well-being.

Journal: *Journal of Vocational Behavior*, June 1996, *48*(3), 275–300.

Related Research: Kopelman, R. E., et al. (1983). A model of work, family and interrole conflict: A construct validation study. *Organizational Behavior and Human Performance*, *32*, 198–215.

9674

Test Name: WORTH INDEX

Purpose: To measure the perception of the source of one's worth.

Number of Items: 24

Format: Includes 4 subscales: Basic Human Worth, Personal Security, Performance Factor, and Appearance. Responses are made on a 7-point scale ranging from 1 (very strongly disagree) to 7 (very strongly agree). All items are presented.

Reliability: Test-retest (2 weeks) reliability coefficients were .74 and .57.

Validity: Correlation with the Rosenberg scales were .82 and .83.

Author: Lockhart, B. D., and Rencher, A. C.

Article: Worth Index.

Journal: *Perceptual and Motor Skills*, December 1977, *85*(3, Part 1), 827–834.

9675

Test Name: SELF-EFFICACY SCALE

Purpose: To enable students to rate their confidence in performing writing skills.

Number of Items: 8

Format: Ratings are on a scale from 0 to 100.

Reliability: Alpha coefficients were .88 and .91.

Validity: Correlations with other variables ranged from −.52 to .56.

Author: Pajares, F., and Valiante, G.

Article: Influence of self-efficacy on elementary students' writing.

Journal: *Journal of Educational Research*, July/August 1997, *90*(6), 353–360.

Related Research: Shell, D. F., et al (1989). Self-efficacy and outcome expectancy mechanisms in reading and writing achievements. *Journal of Educational Psychology*, *81*, 91–100.

9676

Test Name: WRITING SKILLS SELF-EFFICACY SCALE

Purpose: To enable students to indicate their confidence in performing specific writing skills.

Number of Items: 9

Format: Responses are made on a scale ranging from 0 (no chance) to 100 (completely certain). Entire scale presented.

Reliability: Alpha coefficients were .85 and .88.

Author: Pajares, F., et al.

Article: Gender differences in writing self-beliefs of elementary school students.

Journal: *Journal of Educational Psychology*, March 1999, *91*(1), 50–61.

Related Research: Pajares, F., &

Valiante, G. (1997). The predictive and mediational role of the writing self-efficacy beliefs of upper elementary students. *Journal of Educational Research, 90,* 353–360.

9677

Test Name: WULFF-STEITZ CAREER SELF-EFFICACY SCALE

Purpose: To assess self-efficacy.

Number of Items: 4

Format: Responses are made on a 4-point scale ranging from 1 (strongly disagree) to 4 (strongly agree). All items are presented.

Reliability: Test-retest reliability was .85. Coefficient alpha was .75.

Author: Wulff, M. B., and Steitz, J. A.

Article: A path model of the relationship between career indecision, androgyny, self-efficacy, and self-esteem.

Journal: *Perceptual and Motor Skills,* June 1999, *88*(3) Part 1, 935–940.

Related Research: Wulff, M. B., & Steitz, J. A. (1996). A measure of career self-efficacy. *Perceptual and Motor Skills, 82,* 240–242.

CHAPTER 17
Personality

9678

Test Name: ADJECTIVE CHECKLIST—REVISED

Purpose: To measure personality.

Number of Items: 50

Format: Includes 5 subscales: Extroversion, Agreeableness, Conscientiousness, Emotional Stability, and Openness to Experience.

Reliability: Alpha coefficients ranged from .71 to .90.

Author: Barrick, M. R., et al.

Article: Accuracy of interviewer judgments of job applicant personality traits.

Journal: *Personnel Psychology*, Winter 2000, *53*(4), 925–951.

Related Research: Goldberg, L. R. (1992). The development of markers for the Big Five factor structure. *Psychological Assessment, 4,* 26–42.

9679

Test Name: AFFECTIVE INTENSITY SCALE— ADAPTED

Purpose: To rate children's emotional intensity.

Number of Items: 7

Format: Responses are made on a 7-point scale ranging from 1 (extremely untrue) to 7 (extremely true). An example is presented.

Reliability: Alpha coefficients ranged from .72 to .73.

Validity: Correlations with the

negative arousal composite ranged from .50 to .55.

Author: Eisenberg, N., et al.

Article: Parents' reactions to children's negative emotions: Relations to children's social competence and comforting behavior.

Journal: *Child Development*, October 1996, *67*(5), 2227–2247.

Related Research: Eisenberg, N., et al. (1993). The relations of emotionality and regulation to preschoolers' social skills and socioeconomic status. *Child Development, 64,* 1418–1438.

9680

Test Name: AFRICAN SELF-CONSCIOUSNESS SCALE

Purpose: To assess Black personality in terms of Baldwin's theory of Black personality.

Number of Items: 42

Format: Scales range from 1 (strongly disagree) to 8 (strongly agree). Sample items are presented.

Reliability: Alpha coefficients ranged from .78 to .82. Test-retest reliabilities ranged from .80 to .90.

Validity: A predictive validity coefficient was .70.

Author: Cokley, K.

Article: Reconceptualizing the impact of college racial composition on African American students' racial identity.

Journal: *Journal of College*

Student Development, May/June 1999, *40*(3), 235–246.

Related Research: Baldwin, J. A. (1996). An introduction to the African Self-Consciousness Scale. In R. Jones (Ed.), *Handbook of tests and measurements for Black populations* (pp. 207–215). Berkeley: Cobb & Henry.

9681

Test Name: AGGRESSION QUESTIONNAIRE

Purpose: To assess physical and verbal aggression, anger, and hostility.

Number of Items: 29

Format: Likert format.

Reliability: Alpha coefficients ranged from .72 to .85 across subscales.

Author: Gallo, L. C., and Smith, T. W.

Article: Patterns of hostility and social support: Conceptualizing psychosocial risk factors as characteristics of the person and the environment.

Journal: *Journal of Research in Personality*, September 1999, *33*(3), 281–310.

Related Research: Buss, D. M., & Perry, M. (1992). The Aggression Questionnaire. *Journal of Personality and Social Psychology, 63,* 452–459.

9682

Test Name: ALEXITHYMIA SCALE FOR CHILDREN

78905770

158571

Purpose: To assess difficulties in identifying and describing emotions in self and others.

Number of Items: 12

Format: All items are presented.

Reliability: Alphas were .84 (total), .76 (relating to others), and .87 (difficulty in describing feelings). Test-retest (2 months) ranged from .72 to .74.

Validity: Correlations with other variables ranged from −.42 to .31.

Author: Fukunishi, I., and Yoshida, H.

Article: Development of the Alexithymia Scale for Children: A preliminary study.

Journal: *Psychological Reports*, February 1998, *82*(1), 43–49.

9683

Test Name: AMBIGUITY INTOLERANCE MEASURE

Purpose: To assess discomfort in a variety of situations that are novel, equivocal, or complex.

Number of Items: 14

Reliability: Coefficient alpha was .86.

Validity: Correlations with other variables ranged from −.23 to .11.

Author: Myers, J. R., et al.

Article: Facing technological risks: The importance of individual differences.

Journal: *Journal of Research in Personality*, March 1997, *31*(1), 1–20.

Related Research: Yellen, S. B. (1992). *The Ambiguity Intolerance Measure: Development and initial construct validation.* Unpublished manuscript, Rush

Medical College, Department of Psychology and Social Sciences and Medicine, Chicago.

9684

Test Name: ANTILL TRAIT QUESTIONNAIRE

Purpose: To measure children's sex-typed personality qualities.

Number of Items: 12

Format: Responses are made on a 5-point scale. An example is presented.

Reliability: Alpha coefficients ranged from .50 to .79.

Author: McHale, S. M., et al.

Article: Family context and gender role socialization in middle childhood: Comparing girls to boys and sisters to brothers.

Journal: *Child Development*, July/August 1999, *70*(4), 990–1004.

Related Research: Antill, J., et al. (1993). Measures of children's sex-typing in middle childhood. *Australian Journal of Psychology*, *45*, 25–33.

9685

Test Name: AT-20 (AMBIGUITY TOLERANCE) SCALE

Purpose: To measure tolerance for ambiguity.

Number of Items: 20

Format: True/false format. Sample items are presented.

Reliability: KR-20 reliability was 73.

Author: Houran, J., and Williams, C.

Article: Relation of tolerance for ambiguity to global and specific paranormal experiences.

Journal: *Psychological Reports*,

December 1998, *83*(3) Part 1, 807–818.

Related Research: MacDonald, Jr., A. P. (1970). Revised Scale for Ambiguity Tolerance: Reliability and validity. *Psychological Reports*, *26*, 791–798.

9686

Test Name: AUTONOMY SCALE

Purpose: To measure autonomy.

Number of Items: 4

Format: Responses are made on a 5-point scale ranging from 1 (never) to 5 (always). An example is presented.

Reliability: Coefficient alpha was .85.

Validity: Correlations with other variables ranged from -.36 to .37.

Author: Parasuraman, S., et al.

Article: Work and family variables, entrepreneurial career success, and psychological well-being.

Journal: *Journal of Vocational Behavior*, June 1996, *48*(3), 275–300.

Related Research: Parasurman, S., & Alutto, J. A. (1984). Sources and outcomes of stress in organizational settings: Toward the development of a structured model. *Academy of Management Journal*, *27*, 330–350.

9687

Test Name: AUTONOMY SCALE —JAPANESE

Purpose: To measure autonomy in terms of reported external regulation, introjected regulation, identified regulation, and intrinsic regulation.

Number of Items: 40

Format: Sample items are presented.

Reliability: Alphas ranged from .77 to .80 across subscales.

Validity: Correlations with other variables ranged from −.37 to −.62.

Author: Yammauchi, H., and Tanaka, K.

Article: Relations of autonomy, self-referenced beliefs, and self-regulated learning among Japanese children.

Journal: *Psychological Reports*, June 1998, *82*(3) Part 1, 803–816.

9688

Test Name: BELIEF DEFENSIVENESS SCALE

Purpose: To assess openness to belief revision.

Number of Items: 17

Format: Responses are made on a 10-point scale ranging from 1 (not at all important) to 10 (extremely important). An example is given.

Reliability: Coefficient alpha was .86.

Author: Klaczynski, P. A.

Article: Motivated scientific reasoning biases, epistemological beliefs, and theory polarization: A two-process approach to adolescent cognition.

Journal: *Child Development*, September/October 2000, *71*(5), 1347–1366.

Related Research: Klaczynski, P. A., et al. (1998). Adolescent identity: The roles of rationality, critical thinking dispositions, and formal operations. *Journal of Youth and Adolescence, 27*, 185–207.

9689

Test Name: BIG FIVE INVENTORY

Purpose: To measure the components of the five-factor model of personality.

Number of Items: 44

Format: Scales range from 1 (very uncharacteristic of myself) to 7 (very characteristic of myself). Sample items are presented.

Reliability: Alpha coefficients ranged from .75 to .88.

Validity: Correlations with other variables ranged from -.23 to .47.

Author: King, L. A., et al.

Article: Creativity and the five-factor model.

Journal: *Journal of Research in Personality*, June 1996, *30*(2), 189–203.

Related Research: John, O. P., et al. (1991). *The Big Five Inventory—Versions 4A and 4B* (Technical Report). Berkeley, CA: Institute of Personality and Social Research, University of California.

9690

Test Name: BIG-FIVE PERSONALITY FACTOR SCALES

Purpose: To measure the Big-Five personality factors.

Number of Items: 50

Format: Includes 5 subscales: Extraversion, Agreeableness, Conscientiousness, Emotional Stability, and Intellect or Openness to Experience.

Reliability: Alpha coefficients ranged from .78 to .90.

Validity: Correlations with other variables ranged from −.17 to .42.

Author: Chan, K.-Y, et al.

Article: The relation between vocational interests and the motivation to lead.

Journal: *Journal of Vocational Behavior*, October 2000, *57*(2), 226–245.

Related Research: Goldberg, L. R. (1998, March 18). *International personality item pool: A scientific collaboratory for the development of advanced measures of personality and other individual differences* (p. 233). Retrieved from http://ipip.ori.org/ipip/ipip.html.

9691

Test Name: BIOGRAPHICAL INVENTORY

Purpose: To assess satisfaction, sociability, agreeableness, resistance to stress, responsibility, need for achievement, and need to make a good impression.

Number of Items: 38

Format: Various rating scales are used. All items are represented.

Reliability: Alphas ranged from .47 to .79 across subscales.

Validity: Correlations with other variables ranged from −.34 to .71.

Author: McBride, A. A., et al.

Article: Development of a biodata index to measure service orientation.

Journal: *Psychological Reports*, December 1997, *81*(3, Part II), 1395–1407.

9692

Test Name: BORDERLINE PERSONALITY INVENTORY

Purpose: To serve as a screening

instrument for borderline personality organization.

Number of Items: 53

Format: Includes 4 factors: Identity Diffusion, Primitive Defense Mechanisms, Impaired Reality Testing, and Fear of Fusion. Responses are true-false. All items are presented.

Reliability: Alpha coefficients ranged from .68 to .91. Test-retest (1 week) reliabilities ranged from .73 to .89.

Author: Leichsenring, F.

Article: Development and first results of the Borderline Personality Inventory: A self-report instrument for assessing borderline personality organization.

Journal: *Journal of Personality Assessment*, August 1999, *73*(1), 45–63.

Related Research: Kernberg, O. F. (1984). Severe *personality disorders: Psychotherapeutic strategies*. New Haven, CT: Yale University Press.

9693

Test Name: BUSS-DURKEE HOSTILITY INVENTORY

Purpose: To measure the expression of hostility.

Number of Items: 66

Format: Includes 2 factors: Neurotic Hostility and Expressive Hostility. Uses a true-false format. Includes 7 subscales: Assault, Indirect Hostility, Irritability, Nepotism, Resentment, Suspicion, and Verbal Hostility.

Validity: Correlations with other variables ranged from −.72 to .68.

Author: Felsten, G.

Article: Five-factor analysis of

Buss-Durkee Hostility Inventory neurotic hostility and expressive hostility factors: Implications for health psychology.

Journal: *Journal of Personality Assessment*, August 1996, *67*(1), 179–194.

Related Research: Buss, A. H., & Durkee, A. (1957). An inventory for assessing different kinds of hostility. *Journal of Consulting Psychology*, *21*, 343–349.

9694

Test Name: BUSS-DURKEE HOSTILITY INVENTORY

Purpose: To assess seven dimensions of hostility.

Number of Items: 75

Format: Includes 7 dimensions: Assault, Indirect Hostility, Irritability, Negativism, Resentment, Suspicion, and Verbal Hostility. Responses are true-false.

Reliability: Test-retest reliability ranged from .64 to .82.

Author: Kopper, B. A., and Epperson, D. L.

Article: The experience and expression of anger: Relationships with gender, gender role socialization, depression, and mental health functioning.

Journal: *Journal of Counseling Psychology*, April 1996, *43*(2), 158–165.

Related Research: Buss, A. H., & Durkee, A. (1957). An inventory for assessing different kinds of hostility. *Journal of Consulting Psychology*, *21*, 343–349.

9695

Test Name: BUSS-DURKEE HOSTILITY INVENTORY— REVISED

Purpose: To assess aggression.

Number of Items: 56

Format: Includes 6 subscales: Assault, Indirect Hostility, Irritability, Negativism, Resentment, and Verbal Hostility. Responses are made on a 5-point Likert-type scale ranging from 1 (strongly disagree) to 5 (strongly agree).

Reliability: Alpha coefficients ranged from .63 to .87.

Author: Wann, D. L., et al.

Article: Relationships between identification with the role of sport fan and trait aggression.

Journal: *Perceptual and Motor Skills*, June 1999, *88*(3) Part 2, 1296–1298.

Related Research: Buss, A. H., & Durkee, A. (1957). An inventory for assessing different kinds of hostility. *Journal of Consulting Psychology*, *21*, 343–349.

9696

Test Name: CHILD BEHAVIOR QUESTIONNAIRE

Purpose: To measure child temperament

Number of Items: 225

Format: Includes 15 scales composing three broad factors.

Reliability: Alpha coefficients ranged from .67 to .96.

Author: Schwebel, D. C., and Plumert, J. M.

Article: Longitudinal and concurrent relations among temperament, ability estimation, and injury proneness.

Journal: *Child Development*, May/June 1999, *70*(3), 700–712

Related Research: Rothbart, M. K., et al. (1994). Temperament and social behavior in children. *Merrill-Palmer Quarterly*, *40*, 21–39.

9697

Test Name: (COOLIDGE) PERSONALITY AND NEUROPSYCHOLOGICAL INVENTORIES

Purpose: To assess 12 personality disorders by caregiver report.

Number of Items: 200

Format: Scales range from 1 (strongly false) to 4 (strongly true).

Reliability: Median scale reliability was .72. Median test-retest reliability was .72.

Author: Coolidge, F. L., et al.

Article: Neuropsychological dysfunction in children with borderline personality disorder features: A preliminary investigation.

Journal: *Journal of Research in Personality*, December 2000, *34*(4), 554–561.

Related Research: Coolidge, F. L., et al. (2000). *The Coolidge Personality and Neuropsychological Inventory for Children (CPNI): Preliminary psychometric characteristics.* Unpublished manuscript.

9698

Test Name: DEFENSE MECHANISM RATING SCALE

Purpose: To assess defense mechanisms.

Number of Items: 30

Format: Includes 4 levels: Immature, Image-Distorting, Neurotic, and Mature.

Reliability: Reliability ranged from .04 to .80.

Author: Davidson, K., and MacGregor, M. W.

Article: Reliability of an idiographic Q-Sort measure of defense mechanisms.

Journal: *Journal of Personality Assessment*, June 1996, *66*(3), 624–639.

Related Research: Cooper, S. H. (1990). Three contemporary theories of defense and adaptation: Some clinical and theoretical considerations. *Psychoanalytic Psychology*, 7(Suppl.), 57–69.

9699

Test Name: DEFENSE-Q

Purpose: To measure defense mechanisms.

Number of Items: 25

Format: Employs a Q-Sort. All items are presented.

Reliability: Reliability ranged from .28 to .92.

Author: Davidson, K., and MacGregor, M. W.

Article: Reliability of an idiographic Q-Sort measure of defense mechanisms.

Journal: *Journal of Personality Assessment*, June 1996, *66*(3), 624–639.

Related Research: Davidson, K., et al. (1995) *Defense mechanism assessment: The Defense-Q.* Unpublished manuscript, Department of Psychology, Dalhousie University, Halifax, Nova Scotia B3H4J1, Canada.

9700

Test Name: DEFENSE STYLE QUESTIONNAIRE–40

Purpose: To provide self-ratings of defense style.

Number of Items: 40

Format: Includes 3 subscales: Mature, Neurotic, and Immature. Responses are made on a 9-point scale ranging from 1 (strongly disagree) to 9 (strongly agree).

Reliability: Alpha coefficients ranged from .58 to .80. Test-retest (4 weeks) reliability ranged from .75 to .85.

Validity: Correlations with other variables ranged from −.23 to 35.

Author: Mahalik, J. R., et al.

Article: Man's gender role conflict and use of psychological defenses.

Journal: *Journal of Counseling Psychology*, July 1998, *45*(3), 247–255.

Related Research: Bond, M., et al. (1983). Empirical study of self-rated defense styles. *Archives of General Psychiatry, 40*, 333–338.

9701

Test Name: DESIRE FOR CONTROL SCALE

Purpose: To assess how much control respondents would like to have in a variety of work areas.

Number of Items: 11

Format: Seven-point scales ranged from 1 (strongly disagree) to 7 (strongly agree).

Reliability: Coefficient alpha was .85.

Author: Ashford, S. J., and Black, J. S.

Article: Proactivity during organizational entry: The role of desire for control.

Journal: *Journal of Applied Psychology*, April 1996, *81*(2), 199–214.

Related Research: Greenberger, D. B., et al. (1988). Personal control as a mediator between perceptions of supervisory behavior and employee reactions. *Academy of Management Journal, 31*, 405–417.

9702

Test Name: DESIRED MORAL APPROBATION SCALE

Purpose: To measure individuals' desire for moral approbation.

Number of Items: 31

Format: Includes two subscales: Desired Moral Approbation from Others and Desired Moral Approbation from Self. Responses are made on a 7-point Likert-type scale ranging from 1 (strongly disagree) to 7 (strongly agree). Items are presented.

Reliability: Alpha coefficients ranged from .74 to .88.

Validity: Correlations with other variables ranged from −.40 to .57.

Author: Ryan, L. V., and Riordan, C. M.

Article: The development of a measure of desired moral approbation.

Journal: *Educational and Psychological Measurement*, June 2000, *60*(3), 448–462.

9703

Test Name: EAS TEMPERAMENT INDEX

Purpose: To measure emotionality, activity, and sociability.

Number of Items: 14

Format: Five-point scales.

Reliability: Alpha coefficients ranged from .71 to .81.

Validity: Correlations with other variables ranged from −.09 to .21.

Author: McHale, S. M., et al.

Article: Step in or stay out? Parents' roles in adolescent siblings' relationships.

Journal: *Journal of Marriage and*

the Family, August 2000, *62*(3), 746–760.

Related Research: Buss, A. H., & Plomin, R. (1984). *Temperament: Early developing personality traits.* Hillsdale, NJ: Erlbaum.

9704

Test Name: EAS TEMPERAMENT SURVEY FOR ADULTS

Purpose: To measure a person's general temperamental predisposition to experience certain emotions. Subscales include Activity, Emotionality, and Sociability.

Number of Items: 20

Format: Summated ratings format. Sample items are presented.

Validity: Correlations with the Emotional Control Questionnaire ranged from −.55 to .51.

Author: McConatha, J. T., et al.

Article: Emotional control in adulthood.

Journal: *Psychological Reports*, April 1997, *80*(2), 499–507.

Related Research: Buss, A. H., & Plomin, R. (1986). The EAS approach to temperament. In R. Plomin & J. Dunn (Eds.), *The study of temperament: Changes, continuities, and challenges* (pp. 67–79). Hillsdale, NJ: Erlbaum.

9705

Test Name: EGO CONTROL SCALE

Purpose: To provide parents' and teachers' reports of children's ego control.

Number of Items: 19

Reliability: Alpha coefficients were .80 and .84.

Validity: Correlations with other

variables ranged from −.63 to .56.

Author: Eisenberg, N., et al.

Article: Prediction of elementary school children's externalizing problem behavior from attentional and behavioral regulation and negative emotionality.

Journal: *Child Development*, September/October 2000, *71*(5), 1367–1382.

Related Research: Eisenberg, N., et al. (1996). The relations of children's dispositional empathy-related responding to their emotionality, regulation, and social functioning. *Developmental Psychology, 32,* 195–209.

9706

Test Name: EGO-PROTECTION MEASURE

Purpose: To measure ego-protection.

Number of Items: 3

Format: Responses are made on a 6-point Likert-type scale ranging from "strongly disagree" to "strongly agree." All items are presented.

Reliability: Coefficient alpha was .75.

Validity: Correlations with other variables ranged from −.50 to .42.

Author: Dai, D. Y.

Article: To be or not to be (challenged), that is the question: Task and ego orientation among high-ability, high-achieving adolescents.

Journal: *Journal of Experimental Education*, Summer 2000, *68*(4), 311–330.

Related Research: Dai, D. Y., & Feldhusen, J. F. (1996). Goal orientations of gifted students.

Gifted and Talented International, 11, 84–88.

9707

Test Name: EGO Q-SORT

Purpose: To assess level of ego functioning.

Number of Items: 60

Format: Responses are made on a 9-step distribution ranging from −4 (most uncharacteristic) through 0 (neutral) to +4 (most characteristic). Examples are presented.

Reliability: Alpha coefficients averaged .86

Author: Walker, L. J., et al.

Article: Parent and peer context for children's moral reasoning development.

Journal: *Child Development,* July/August 2000, *71*(4), 1033–1048.

Related Research: Haan, N. (1986). Systematic variability in the quality of moral action, as defined by two formulations. *Journal of Personality and Social Psychology, 50,* 1271–1284.

9708

Test Name: EGO-SUPERIORITY MEASURE

Purpose: To measure ego-superiority.

Number of Items: 4

Format: Responses are made on a 6-point Likert-type scale ranging from "strongly disagree" to "strongly agree." All items are presented.

Reliability: Coefficient alpha was .88.

Validity: Correlations with other variables ranged from −.60 to .37.

Author: Dai, D. Y.

Article: To be or not to be (challenged), that is the question: Task and ego orientation among high-ability, high-achieving adolescents.

Journal: *Journal of Experimental Education,* Summer 2000, *68*(4), 311–330.

Related Research: Nichols, J. G. (1989). *The competitive ethos and democrative education.* Cambridge, MA: Harvard University Press.

9709

Test Name: 80 BIPOLAR ADJECTIVE CHECKLIST

Purpose: To measure extraversion, agreeableness, conscientiousness, neuroticism, and openness to experience.

Number of Items: 80

Format: Nine-point scales link the bipolar adjectives.

Reliability: Reliabilities ranged from .79 to .90 across subscales.

Validity: Convergent validities ranged from .70 to .80 across subscales.

Author: Collins, J. M., and Gleaves, D. H.

Article: Race, job applicants, and the five-factor model of personality: implications for Black psychology, industrial/organizational psychology, and the five-factor theory.

Journal: *Journal of Applied Psychology,* August 1998, *83*(4), 531–544.

Related Research: McCrae, R. R., & Costa, P. T., Jr. (1985). Updating Norman's "adequate taxonomy": Intelligence and personality dimensions in natural language and in questionnaires. *Journal of Personality and Social Psychology, 49,* 710–721.

9710

Test Name: ELDERLY DRIVERS PERSONALITY QUESTIONNAIRE

Purpose: To identify the personality structure of elderly drivers.

Number of Items: 22

Format: Includes 2 factors: Competence and Emotionality. Responses are made on a 5-point scale ranging from 1 (not at all like me) to 5 (extremely like me). All items are presented.

Reliability: Alpha coefficients were .86 and .82.

Validity: Correlations with Big 5 scales ranged from −.38 to .65.

Author: Strahan, R. F., et al.

Article: Personality structure of elderly drivers.

Journal: *Perceptual and Motor Skills,* October 1997, *85*(2), 747–755.

9711

Test Name: EMOTION CONTROL QUESTIONNAIRE

Purpose: To measure the tendency to express or to inhibit emotional expression. Subscales are Emotional Inhibition, Aggression Control, Benign Control, and Health and Rehearsal.

Number of Items: 56

Format: Summated ratings format. Sample items are presented.

Reliability: Internal consistencies ranged from .77 to .86.

Validity: Correlations with the EAS Temperament Survey ranged from −.55 to .51.

Author: McConatha, J. T., et al.

Article: Emotional control in adulthood.

Journal: *Psychological Reports,* April 1997, *80*(2), 499–507.

Related Research: Roger D., & Najarian, B. (1989). The construction of a new scale for measuring emotion control. *Personality and Individual Differences, 10,* 845–853.

9712

Test Name: EMOTIONAL EXPRESSIVITY SCALE

Purpose: To measure the general disposition toward the outward display of emotion.

Number of Items: 17

Format: Responses are made on a 6-point scale ranging from 1 (never) to 6 (always true). Examples are presented.

Reliability: Alpha coefficients were .91 and .95. Test-retest (4 weeks) was .90.

Validity: Correlations with other variables were .49.

Author: Searle, B., and Meara, N. M.

Article: Affective dimensions of attachment styles: Exploring self-reported attachment style, gender, and emotional experience among college students.

Journal: *Journal of Counseling Psychology,* April 1999, *46*(2), 147–158.

Related Research: Kring, A. M., et al. (1994). Individual differences in dispositional expressiveness: Development and validation of the Emotional Expressivity Scale. *Journal of Personality and Social Psychology, 66,* 934–949.

9713

Test Name: EMOTIONAL INTENSITY SCALE

Purpose: To rate children's emotional intensity.

Number of Items: 7

Format: Responses are made on a 7-point scale ranging from 1 (extremely untrue) to 7 (extremely true). Examples are presented.

Reliability: Alpha coefficients were .72 and .73.

Validity: Correlations with a negative arousal composite score ranged from .50 to .55.

Author: Eisenberg, N., et al.

Article: The relations of children's dispositional prosocial behavior to emotionality, regulation, and social functioning.

Journal: *Child Development,* June 1996, *67*(3), 974–992.

Related Research: Larsen, R. J., & Diener, E. (1987). Affect intensity as an individual difference characteristic: A review, *Journal of Research in Personality, 21,* 1–39.

9714

Test Name: EMOTIONALITY, ACTIVITY AND SOCIABILITY TEMPERAMENT SURVEY FOR ADULTS—ADAPTED

Purpose: To measure aspects of maternal temperament.

Number of Items: 8

Format: Includes 2 subscales: Emotionality-Anger and Emotionality-Distress.

Reliability: Alpha coefficients were .56 and .82.

Validity: Correlations with other variables ranged from −.08 to .62.

Author: Curtner-Smith, M. E.

Article: Mechanisms by which family processes contribute to school-age boys' bullying.

Journal: *Child Study Journal,* 2000, *30*(3), 169–186.

Related Research: Buss, A. H., & Plomin, R. (1984). *Temperament: Early developing personality traits.* Hillsdale, NJ: Erlbaum.

9715

Test Name: EMOTIONALITY SCALE

Purpose: To assess emotionality.

Number of Items: 12

Format: Responses are made on a 6-point scale ranging from 1 (not characteristic) to 6 (not observed).

Reliability: Coefficient alpha was .72.

Validity: Correlations with global self-worth were −.20 and −.33.

Author: Feinberg, M. E., et al.

Article: Sibling comparison of differential parental treatment in adolescence: Gender, self-esteem, and emotionality as mediators of the parenting adjustment association.

Journal: *Child Development,* November/December 2000, *71*(6), 1611–1628.

Related Research: Buss, A. H., & Plomin, R. (1984). *Temperament: Early developing personality traits.* Hillsdale, NJ: Erlbaum.

9716

Test Name: EXTENDED OBJECTIVE MEASURE OF EGO-IDENTITY STATUS

Purpose: To assess four identity statuses: diffused, foreclosed, moratorium, and achieved.

Number of Items: 32

Format: Six-point Likert format.

Reliability: Alpha coefficients ranged from .57 to .79.

Author: Cramer, P.

Article: Freshman to senior year: A follow-up study of identity, narcissism, and defense mechanisms.

Journal: *Journal of Research in Personality*, March 1998, *32*(1), 156–172.

Related Research: Adams, G. R., et al. (1989). *Objective Measure of Ego Identity Status: A reference manual*. Ontario, Canada: University of Guelph.

Cramer, P. (2000). Development of identity: Gender makes a difference. *Journal of Research in Personality, 34*, 42–72.

9717

Test Name: EXTENDED OBJECTIVE MEASURE OF EGO-IDENTITY STATUS

Purpose: To measure how adolescents and young adults resolve the psychosocial task referred to as identity versus role confusion.

Number of Items: 64

Format: Includes 4 scales: Diffusion, Moratorium, Foreclosure, and Achievement. Responses are made on a 6-point Likert-type scale ranging from 1 (strongly agree) to 6 (strongly disagree).

Reliability: Alpha coefficients ranged from .64 to .90. Test-retest (2 weeks) reliabilities ranged from .82 to .90.

Author: Bartley, D. F., and Robitschek, C.

Article: Career exploration: A multivariate analysis of predictors.

Journal: *Journal of Vocational Behavior*, February 2000, *56*(1), 63–81.

Related Research: Bennion, L. D., & Adams, G. R. (1986). A revision of the extended version of the Objective Measure of Ego-Identity Status: An identity instrument for use with late adolescents. *Journal of Adolescent Research, 1,* 183–198.

9718

Test Name: FIVE-FACTORS PERSONALITY INSTRUMENTS

Purpose: To measure extraversion, agreeableness, conscientiousness, emotional stability, and openness to experience.

Number of Items: 100

Format: Nine-point scales are anchored by "extremely inaccurate" and "extremely accurate."

Reliability: Alpha coefficients ranged from .86 to .91 across subscales.

Validity: Correlations with other variables ranged from −.13 to .15.

Author: Barry, B., and Stewart, G. L.

Article: Composition, process, and performance in self-managed groups: The role of personality.

Journal: *Journal of Applied Psychology*, February 1997, *82*(1), 62–78.

Related Research: Goldberg, L. R. (1992). The development of markers of the Big Five factor structure. *Psychological Assessment, 4,* 26–42.

9719

Test Name: GENERAL CAUSALITY ORIENTATIONS SCALE

Purpose: To measure individual differences in autonomy, control, and impersonal motivation.

Number of Items: 12 vignettes.

Format: Includes 3 types of orientation: Autonomy, Control, and Impersonal. Responses are made on a 7-point scale ranging from 1 (very unlikely) to 7 (very likely).

Reliability: Test-retest (8 weeks) reliabilities ranged from .71 to .78. Alpha coefficients ranged from .68 to .79.

Author: Bartley, D. F., and Robitschek, C.

Article: Career exploration: A multivariate analysis of predictors.

Journal: *Journal of Vocational Behavior*, February 2000, *56*(1), 63–81.

Related Research: Deci, E. L., & Ryan, R. M. (1985). The General Causality Orientations Scale: Self determination in personality. *Journal of Research in Personality, 19,* 109–134.

9720

Test Name: GUDJONSSON SUGGESTIBILITY SCALE

Purpose: To measure interrogative suggestibility.

Number of Items: 20

Format: Includes a short story with two attempts at recall.

Reliability: Internal consistency coefficients were .77 and .67.

Validity: Correlations with other variables ranged from −.08 to .21.

Author: Peiffer, L. C., and Trull, T. J.

Article: Predictors of suggestibility and false-memory production in young adult women.

Journal: *Journal of Personality Assessment*, June 2000, *74*(3), 384–399.

Related Research: Gudjonsson,

G. H. (1984). A new role of interrogative suggestibility. *Personality and Individual Differences, 5*, 303–314.

9721

Test Name: GUILT INVENTORY

Purpose: To measure trait guilt, state quiet, and moral standards.

Number of Items: 45

Format: Five-point scales are anchored by 1 (strongly agree) and 5 (strongly disagree). All items are presented.

Validity: Means, standard deviations, and low and high scores are presented for females and males.

Author: Jones, W. H., et al.

Article: The Guilt Inventory.

Journal: *Psychological Reports,* December 2000, *87*(3), Part 2, 1039–1042.

Related Research: Jones, W. H., & Kugler, K. (1993). Interpersonal correlates of The Guilt Inventory. *Journal of Personality Assessment, 61*, 246–258.

9722

Test Name: HOSTILITY SCALE

Purpose: To measure cynicism, hostile affect, and aggressive responding.

Number of Items: 27

Format: Scales range from 1 (strongly disagree) to 7 (strongly agree).

Reliability: Coefficient alpha was .83.

Validity: Correlations with other variables ranged from −.39 to .55.

Author: Sinn, J. S.

Article: The predictive and

discriminant validity of masculinity ideology.

Journal: *Journal of Research in Personality,* March 1997, *31*(1), 117–135.

Related Research: Cook, W. W., & Medley, D. M. (1954). Proposed hostility and pharisaic-virtue scales for the MMPI. *Journal of Applied Psychology, 38*, 414–418.

9723

Test Name: HOSTILITY TOWARD WOMEN SCALE

Purpose: To assess hostility toward women.

Number of Items: 30

Format: True/false format. Sample items are presented.

Reliability: Coefficient alpha was .90.

Author: Christopher, F. S., et al.

Article: Premarital sexual aggressors: A multivariate analysis of social, relational, and individual variables.

Journal: *Journal of Marriage and the Family,* February 1998, *60*(1), 56–69.

Related Research: Check, J. V. P., et al. (1985, April). On hostile ground. *Psychology Today,* 56–61.

9724

Test Name: INDECISIVENESS SCALE

Purpose: To evaluate generalized indecision.

Number of Items: 15

Format: Responses are made on a 5-point Likert-type scale ranging from 1 (strongly disagree) to 5 (strongly agree).

Reliability: Alpha coefficients ranged from .80 to .90.

Author: Santos, P. J., and Coimbra, J. L.

Article: Psychological separation and dimensions of career indecision in secondary school students.

Journal: *Journal of Vocational Behavior,* June 2000, *56*(3), 346–362.

Related Research: Frost, R. O., & Shows, D. L. (1993). The nature and measurement of compulsive indecisiveness. *Behavior Research Therapy, 31*, 683–692.

9725

Test Name: INDIVIDUATION SCALE

Purpose: To measure willingness to engage in individuating behaviors such as voicing an opinion about a controversial issue.

Number of Items: 12

Format: Five-point rating scales range from (1) not at all willing to do this to (5) very much willing to do this.

Reliability: Alpha was .85.

Validity: Correlation with stereotyped thinking was −.33.

Author: Humphreys, C. N., and Davidson, W. B.

Article: Individuation of self and stereotyping of others.

Journal: *Psychological Reports,* December 1997, *81*(3, Part II), 1252–1254.

Related Research: Maslach, C., et al. (1985). Individuation: Conceptual analysis and assessment. *Journal of Personality and Social Psychology, 49*, 729–738.

9726

Test Name: INFANT BEHAVIOR QUESTIONNAIRE

Purpose: To assess infant temperament.

Number of Items: 87

Format: Responses are rated on a 7-point scale.

Reliability: Alpha coefficients ranged from .67 to .85.

Validity: Correlations with other variables ranged from −.24 to .24.

Author: Huffman, L. C., et al.

Article: Infant temperament and cardiac vagel tone: Assessments at twelve weeks of age.

Journal: *Child Development*, June 1998, *69*(3), 624–635.

Related Research: Rothbart, M. K. (1981). Measurement of temperament in infancy. *Child Development*, 52, 569–578.

9727

Test Name: INFANT BEHAVIOR QUESTIONNAIRE

Purpose: To measure children's temperament.

Number of Items: 90

Format: Includes 6 scales: Activity, Distress to Limitations, Distress to Sudden or Novel Stimuli, Duration of Orienting, Singing and Laughter, and Soothability.

Reliability: Alpha coefficients ranged from .66 to .84.

Author: Kochanska, G., et al.

Article: Individual differences in emotionality in infancy.

Journal: *Child Development*, April 1998, *64*(2), 375–390.

Related Research: Rothbart, M. K. (1981). Measurement of

temperament in infancy. *Child Development*, 52, 569–578.

9728

Test Name: INFANT BEHAVIOR QUESTIONNAIRE

Purpose: To measure infant temperament.

Number of Items: 94

Format: Includes 3 dimensions: Positive Reactivity, Negative Reactivity, and Self-Regulation.

Reliability: Alpha coefficients ranged from .77 to .88.

Author: Speltz, M. L., et al.

Article: Early predictors of attachment in infants with cleft lip and/or palate.

Journal: *Child Development*, February 1997, *68*(1), 12–25.

Related Research: Rothbart, M. K. (1986). Longitudinal observation of infant temperament. *Developmental Psychology*, 22, 356–365.

9729

Test Name: INFANT BEHAVIOR QUESTIONNAIRE—ADAPTED

Purpose: To measure infant temperament.

Format: Includes 2 scales: Activity Level and Distress to Limits.

Reliability: Alpha coefficients were .80 (Activity Level) and .83 (Distress to Limits).

Validity: Correlations with other variables ranged from −.16 to .20.

Author: Clark, R.

Article: The parent-child relational assessment: A factorial validity study.

Journal: *Educational and*

Psychological Measurement, October 1999, *59*(5), 821–846.

Related Research: Rothbart, M. K. (1981). Measurement of temperament in infancy. *Child Development*, 52, 569–578.

9730

Test Name: INFANT CHARACTERISTIC QUESTIONNAIRE—6 MONTHS VERSION

Purpose: To enable parents to rate infant temperament.

Number of Items: 27

Format: Includes 3 factors: Fussy-Difficult, Unpredictable, and Unadaptable. Responses are made on a 7-point scale ranging from 1 (very easy) to 7 (very difficult).

Reliability: Alpha coefficients ranged from .63 to .81.

Author: Andersson, H. W., and Sommerfelt, K.

Article: Infant temperamental factors as predictors of problem behavior and IQ at age 5 years: Interactional effects of biological and social risk factors.

Journal: *Child Study Journal*, 1999, *29*(3), 207–226.

Related Research: Bates, J. E., et al. (1979). Measurement of infant difficultness. *Child Development*, 50, 794–803.

9731

Test Name: INFANT CHARACTERISTIC QUESTIONNAIRE—13 MONTHS VERSION

Purpose: To enable parents to rate infant temperament.

Number of Items: 32

Format: Includes 4 factors: Fussy-Difficult, Persistent,

Unadaptable, and Unsociable. Responses are made on a 7-point scale ranging from 1 (very easy) to 7 (very difficult).

Reliability: Alpha coefficients ranged from .40 to .85.

Validity: Correlations with Problem Behavior scores ranged from .17 to .24.

Author: Andersson, H. W., and Sommerfelt, K.

Article: Infant temperamental factors as predictors of problem behavior and IQ at age 5 years: Interactional effects of biological and social risk factors.

Journal: *Child Study Journal*, 1999, *29*(3), 207–226.

Related Research: Bates, J. E., et al. (1979). Measurement of infant difficultness. *Child Development, 50*, 794–803.

9732

Test Name: INTERNALIZING NEGATIVE EMOTION SCALE

Purpose: To assess internalizing negative emotions.

Number of Items: 16

Format: Items measure Internalizing Emotion, Automatic Reactivity, Sadness, and Fear. Examples are presented.

Reliability: Alpha coefficients were .90 (teachers) and .74 (mothers).

Author: Eisenberg, N., et al.

Article: Shyness and children's emotionality, regulation and coping: Contemporaneous, longitudinal, and cross-context relations.

Journal: *Child Development*, June 1998, *69*(3), 767–790.

Related Research: Derryberry, D., & Rothbart, M. K. (1988). Arousal, affect, and attention as components of temperament.

Journal of Personality and Social Psychology, 55, 958–966.

9733

Test Name: INTERPERSONAL ADJECTIVES SCALES— REVISED

Purpose: To assess eight interpersonal types: dominant, arrogant, quarrelsome, introverted, submissive, unassuming, agreeable, and extraverted.

Number of Items: 64

Format: Eight-point scales indicate whether items (adjectives) are accurate descriptions.

Reliability: Internal consistency coefficients ranged from .83 to .91 across subscales.

Validity: Correlations with other variables ranged from −.29 to .29.

Author: Schneider, P. L., et al.

Article: Examining the relation between Holland's RIASEC model and the interpersonal circle.

Journal: *Measurement and Evaluation in Counseling and Development*, October 1996, *29*(3), 123–133.

Related Research: Wiggins, J. S., et al. (1988). Psychometric and geometric characteristics of the revised interpersonal adjectives scales (IAS-R). *Multivariate Behavioral Research, 23*, 128–143.

9734

Test Name: INTERPERSONAL POWER SCALES

Purpose: To assess need for interpersonal power.

Format: Five-point Likert and true-false formats are used.

Reliability: Alpha coefficients exceeded .74.

Validity: Correlations with other variables ranged from −.23 to .87.

Authors: Leone, C., and Burns, J. T.

Article: Assessing contingency, power, and efficacy: A psychometric investigation of social motivation.

Journal: *Journal of Social Psychology*, April 1997, *137*(2), 255–265.

Related Research: Bennet, J. B. (1988). Powers and influence as distinct personality traits: Development and validation of a psychometric measure. *Journal of Research in Personality, 22*, 361, 394.

Good, L. R., & Good, K. C. (1972). An objective measure of the motive to attain social power. *Psychological Reports, 30*, 247–251.

9735

Test Name: INTOLERANCE OF AMBIGUITY SCALE

Purpose: To measure intolerance of ambiguity.

Number of Items: 8

Format: Five-point scales.

Reliability: Coefficient alpha was .85.

Authors: Williams, S., and Narendran, S.

Article: Determinants of managerial risk: Exploring personality of cultural influences.

Journal: *Journal of Social Psychology*, February 1999, *139*(1), 102–125.

Related Research: Martin, J. G.,

& Westie, F. R. (1959). The intolerant personality. *American Sociological Review, 24,* 521–528.

9736

Test Name: INVENTORY OF SELF PSYCHOLOGY

Purpose: To measure personality functioning.

Number of Items: 80

Format: Includes 5 subscales: Healthy Grandiose Self, Healthy Idealized Parental Image, Defensive Grandiose Self—Horizontal Split, Defensive Grandiose Self—Vertical Split, and Defensive Idealized Parental Image. Responses are made on a 6-point Likert-type scale.

Reliability: Alpha coefficients ranged from .65 to .91.

Validity: Correlations with other variables range from −.52 to .49.

Author: Miville, M. L., et al.

Article: Appreciating similarities and valuing differences: The Miville-Guzman Universality–Diversity Scale.

Journal: *Journal of Counseling Psychology,* July 1999, *46*(3), 291–307.

Related Research: Goldman, G. F., & Gelso, C. J. (1997). Kohut's theory of narcissism and adolescent drug abuse treatment. *Journal of Psychoanalytic Psychology, 14,* 81–94.

9737

Test Name: JUNIOR TEMPERAMENT AND CHARACTER INVENTORY

Purpose: To assess temperament and character traits in children 9 to 13 years of age.

Number of Items: 70

Reliability: Alpha coefficients ranged from .44 to .83 across subscales.

Validity: Correlations with other variables ranged from −.24 to .31.

Author: Luby, J. L., et al.

Article: The Junior Temperament and Character Inventory: Preliminary validation of a child self-report measure.

Journal: *Psychological Reports,* June 1999, *84*(3) Part 2, 1127–1138.

Related Research: Cloninger, C. R., et al. (1994*). Manual of the Temperament and Character Inventory (TCI): A guide to its development and use.* St. Louis, MO: Center for Psychobiology of Personality, Washington University.

9738

Test Name: MASLOWIAN SCALE

Purpose: To measure physiological and safety issues, need for love and belonging, need for esteem and self-esteem, and self-actualization.

Number of Items: 12

Format: Five-point Likert format.

Reliability: Test-retest reliability was .79.

Validity: Correlations with other variables ranged from −.41 to .42.

Author: Lewis, J. D.

Article: Scores on self-actualization for gifted junior high school students.

Journal: *Psychological Reports,* August 1996, *79*(1), 59–64.

Related Research: Falk, C., et al. (1988). *Maslowian Scale.* (ERIC Document Reproduction Service ED 320 918).

9739

Test Name: (MAUDSLEY) OBSESSIONAL–COMPULSIVE INVENTORY

Purpose: To measure the presence of obsessive–compulsive behaviors (checking, cleaning, doubting, slowness).

Number of Items: 30

Format: True/false format.

Reliability: Alpha coefficients were in the .70's range.

Validity: Correlations with other variables ranged from −.04 to .21 (total score).

Author: Ferraro, F. R., et al.

Article: Relationship of Maudsley Obsessive-Compulsive Inventory subscales with negative priming.

Journal: *Journal of General Psychology,* July 1977, *124*(3), 341–349.

Related Research: Sternberger, L. G., & Burns, G. L. (1990). Maudsley Obsessional-Compulsive Inventory: Obsessions and compulsions in a nonclinical sample. *Behavior Research & Therapy, 28,* 337–340.

9740

Test Name: MULTIDIMENSIONAL ANGER INVENTORY

Purpose: To assess a person's propensity for anger.

Number of Items: 23

Format: Five-point scales are anchored by 1 (totally false) and 5 (totally true). Sample items are presented.

Reliability: Coefficient alpha was .86 (wives) and .91 (husbands).

Validity: Correlations with other variables ranged from −.33 to .33.

Author: Rogge, R. D., and Bradbury, T. N.

Article: Till violence do us part: The differing roles of communication and aggression in predicting adverse marital outcomes.

Journal: *Journal of Consulting and Clinical Psychology*, June 1999, *67*(3), 340–351.

Related Research: Siegel, J. M. (1986). The Multidimensional Anger Inventory. *Journal of Personality and Social Psychology, 51*, 191–200.

9741

Test Name: MULTIDIMENSIONAL PERSONALITY QUESTIONNAIRE

Purpose: To assess the major dimensions of personality.

Number of Items: 300

Format: Includes 11 factors: Well-Being, Social Potency, Achievement, Social Closeness, Stress Reaction, Alienation, Aggression, Control, Harm Avoidance, Traditionalism, and Absorption. Responses are true-false.

Reliability: Alpha coefficients ranged from .61 to .96.

Author: Lehman, A. K., et al.

Article: Personality and depression: A validation study of the Depressive Experiences Questionnaire.

Journal: *Journal of Personality Assessment*, February 1997, *68*(1), 197–210.

Related Research: Tellegen, A. (1982). Brief manual for the *Differential Personality Questionnaire*. Unpublished manuscript, University of Minnesota, Minneapolis.

9742

Test Name: MULTIDIMENSIONAL PERSONALITY QUESTIONNAIRE ABSORPTION SCALE

Purpose: To measure the disposition to enter into psychological states that are characterized by a marked restructuring of the phenomenal self and world.

Number of Items: 34

Format: Responses are "true" or "false". Examples are presented.

Reliability: Alpha coefficient was .88. Test-retest (30 days) reliability was .91

Author: Hill, C. E., et al.

Article: Dream interpretation sessions: Who volunteers, who benefits, and what volunteer clients view as most and least helpful.

Journal: *Journal of Counseling Psychology*, January 1997, *44*(1), 53–62.

Related Research: Telegen, A. (1992). *Note on structuring and measuring of the MPQ Absorption Scale*. Unpublished manuscript.

9743

Test Name: MULTIDIMENSIONALITY PERSONALITY QUESTIONNAIRE—ADAPTED

Purpose: To measure risk taking, impulsivity, and negative emotionality.

Number of Items: 18

Format: Includes Risk Taking, Impulsitivy, and Negative Emotionality.

Reliability: Alpha coefficients ranged from .72 to .84.

Author: Voelkl, K. E., and Frone, M. R.

Article: Predictors of substance use at school among high school students.

Journal: *Journal of Educational Psychology*, September 2000, *92*(3), 583–592.

Related Research: Tellegen, A. (1982). *Brief manual for the Multidimensional Personality Questionnaire*. Unpublished manuscript, University of Minnesota—Twin Cities Campus.

9744

Test Name: NEED FOR CLARITY SCALE

Purpose: To assess need for clarity.

Number of Items: 4

Format: Scales range from 1 (very unimportant) to 6 (very important). All items are presented.

Reliability: Coefficient alpha was .79

Validity: Correlations with other variables ranged from −.04 to .08.

Author: O'Driscoll, M. P., and Beehr, T. A.

Article: Moderating effects of perceived control and need for clarity on the relationship between role stressors and employee affective reactions.

Journal: *Journal of Social Psychology*, April 2000, *140*(2), 151–159.

Related Research: Lyons, T. (1971). Role clarity, need for clarity, satisfaction, tension and withdrawal. *Organizational Behavior and Human Performance, 6*, 99–110.

9745

Test Name: NEED FOR CLOSURE SCALE

Purpose: To measure need for closure.

Number of Items: 12

Format: Responses are made on a 6-point scale ranging from 1 (disagree strongly) to 6 (agree strongly). An example is presented.

Validity: Correlations with other variables ranged from −.19 to .36.

Author: Sá, W. C., et al.

Article: The domain specificity and generality of belief bias: Searching for a generalizable critical thinking skill.

Journal: *Journal of Educational Psychology*, September 1999, *91*(3), 497–510.

Related Research: Kruglanski, A. W., et al (1993). Motivated resistance and openness to persuasion in the presence or absence of prior information. *Journal of Personality and Social Psychology, 65*, 861–876.

9746

Test Name: NEED FOR CLOSURE SCALE

Purpose: To assess tendencies to avoid uncertain states of knowledge and to be uncomfortable with contradictory truths and ill-defined problems.

Number of Items: 42

Format: Responses are made on a 6-point scale ranging from 1 (strongly disagree) to 6 (strongly agree). Examples are presented.

Reliability: Coefficient alpha was .82.

Author: Klaczynski, P. A.

Article: Motivated scientific

reasoning biases, epistemological beliefs, and theory polarization: A two-process approach to adolescent cognition.

Journal: *Child Development*, September/October 2000, *71*(5), 1347–1366.

Related Research: Kruglanski, A. W., et al. (1993). Motivated resistance and openness to persuasion in the presence or absence of prior information. *Journal of Personality and Social Psychology, 65*, 861–876.

9747

Test Name: NEED-FOR-COGNITION—SHORT FORM

Purpose: To measure the need for cognition.

Number of Items: 18

Format: Scales range from 1 (not at all characteristic of me) to 5 (very characteristic of me). Sample items are presented.

Reliability: Coefficient alpha was .74.

Validity: Correlations with other variables ranged from −.48 to .47.

Author: Nair, K. U., and Ramnarayan, S.

Article: Individual differences in need for cognition and complex problem solving.

Journal: *Journal of Research in Personality*, September 2000, *34*(3), 305–328.

Related Research: Cacioppo, J. T., et al. (1996). Dispositional differences in cognitive motivation: The life and times of individuals varying in need for cognition. *Psychological Bulletin, 119*(2), 197–253.

9748

Test Name: NEED TO EVALUATE SCALE

Purpose: To assess stable individual differences in the tendency to engage in evaluative responding.

Number of Items: 16

Format: Responses are made on a 5-point scale ranging from 1 (extremely uncharacteristic) to 5 (extremely characteristic). An example is given.

Reliability: Internal consistency reliability estimates ranged from .82 to .87. Test-retest (10 weeks) reliability was .84.

Validity: Correlations with other variables ranged from .00 to −.12.

Author: Mohr, J. J., and Rochlen, A. B.

Article: Measuring attitudes regarding bisexuality in lesbian, gay male, and heterosexual populations.

Journal: *Journal of Counseling Psychology*, July 1999, *46*(3), 353–369.

Related Research: Jarvis, W. B. G., & Petty, R. E. (1996). The need to evaluate. *Journal of Personality and Social Psychology, 70*, 172–194.

9749

Test Name: NEGATIVE EMOTIONAL INTENSITY SCALE

Purpose: To assess children's negative emotional intensity.

Number of Items: 5

Format: Responses are made on a 7-point scale ranging from "never" to "always."

Reliability: Alpha coefficients were .85 and .72.

Author: Eisenberg, N., et al.

Article: The relations of regulation and emotionality to resiliency and competent social functioning in elementary school children.

Journal: *Child Development*, April 1997, *68*(2), 295–311.

Related Research: Eisenberg, N., et al. (1995). The role of emotionality and regulation in children's social functioning: A longitudinal study. *Child Development*, *66*, 1360–1384.

9750

Test Name: NEGATIVE EMOTIONALITY SCALE

Purpose: To assess aspects of dispositional emotionality.

Number of Items: 14

Format: A 7-point scale ranging from "extremely untrue" to "extremely true" is employed. Examples are presented.

Reliability: Alpha coefficients ranged from .68 to .73.

Author: Eisenberg, N., et al.

Article: Parents' reactions to children's negative emotions: Relations to children's social competence and comforting behavior.

Journal: *Child Development*, October 1996, *67*(5), 2227–2247.

Related Research: Eisenberg, N., et al. (1993). The relations of emotionality and regulation to preschoolers' social skills and sociometric status. *Child Development*, *64*, 1418–1438.

9751

Test Name: OBJECT RATING SCALE

Purpose: To rate the level of aggressiveness assigned to objects, as well as the qualitative assignment of the aggressive objects into groupings.

Number of Items: 126

Format: Includes Aggressive Objects, Potentially Aggressive Objects, and Neutral Words. Many items are presented.

Reliability: Test-retest reliability coefficients ranged from .95 to .99.

Author: Baity, M. R., et al.

Article: Further exploration of the Rorschach Aggressive Content (Ag C) variable.

Journal: *Journal of Personality Assessment*, April 2000, *74*(2), 231–241.

Related Research: Gacono, C. B., & Meloy, J. R. (1994). The aggression response. In C. B. Gacono & J. R. Meloy (Eds.), *The Rorschach assessment of aggressive and psychopathic personalities* (pp. 259–278). Hillsdale, NJ: Erlbaum.

9752

Test Name: OBJECTIVE MEASURE OF EGO-IDENTITY STATUS

Purpose: To assess commitment to roles.

Number of Items: 24

Format: Includes 4 subscales: Diffusion, Foreclosure, Moratorium, and Identity Achievement. Responses are made on a 6-point Likert-type scale ranging from 1 (strongly disagree) to 6 (strongly agree).

Reliability: Coefficient alpha for the Foreclosure subscale was .76.

Validity: Correlations of the Foreclosure subscale with other variables ranged from −.24 to .79.

Author: Brown, C., and Glastetter-Fender, C.

Article: Psychosocial identity and career control in college student-athletes.

Journal: *Journal of Vocational Behavior*, February 2000, *56*(1), 53–62.

Related Research: Adams, G. R., et al. (1979). Toward the development of an objective assessment of ego identity status. *Journal of Youth and Adolescence*, *8*, 223–237.

9753

Test Name: OBSESSIVE–COMPULSIVE SCALE

Purpose: To assess compulsiveness.

Number of Items: 22

Format: True/false format.

Reliability: Test-retest reliability (3 weeks) was .82.

Validity: Correlation with psychologists' ratings was .79.

Author: Ketzenberger, K. E., and Forrest, L.

Article: Compulsiveness and impulsiveness: Unidimensional or bidimensional constructs?

Journal: *Psychological Reports*, August 1998, *83*(1), 303–306.

Related Research: Gibb, G. D., et al. (1983). The measurement of the obsessive-compulsive personality. *Educational and Psychological Measurement*, *43*, 1233–1238.

9754

Test Name: OPENNESSS TO EXPERIENCE SCALE

Purpose: To measure openness to experience.

Number of Items: 3

Format: Responses are made on an 8-point bipolar response scale.

Reliability: Coefficient alpha was .62.

Author: Fried, Y., et al.

Article: Changes in job decision latitude: The influence of personality and interpersonal satisfaction.

Journal: *Journal of Vocational Behavior*, April 1999, 54(2), 233–243.

Related Research: McCrae, R. R., & Costa, P. T. (1985). Updating Norman's "Adequate Taxonomy": Intelligence and personality dimensions in natural language and in questionnaires. *Journal of Personality and Social Psychology*, 49, 710–721.

9755

Test Name: PERCEPTION OF SUCCESS QUESTIONNAIRE—CHILDREN'S VERSION

Purpose: To assess task and ego orientation.

Number of Items: 12

Format: Includes 2 subscales: Task Orientation and Ego Orientation. Responses are made on a 5-point scale ranging from 1 (strongly agree) to 5 (strongly disagree). All items are presented.

Reliability: Reliability coefficients ranged from .41 to .67.

Validity: Correlations with the Task and Ego Orientation in Sports Questionnaire were .71 and .80.

Author: Liukkonen, J., and Leskinen, E.

Article: The reliability and validity of scores from the children's version of the Perception of Success Questionnaire.

Journal: *Educational and Psychological Measurement*, August 1999, 59(4), 651–664.

Related Research: Roberts, G. C. (1998). Achievement goals in sport: The development and

validation of the Perception of Success Questionnaire. *Journal of Sports Sciences*, 16, 337–347.

9756

Test Name: PERFORMANCE ORIENTATION SCALE

Purpose: To assess the degree to which a person emphasizes doing tasks competently.

Number of Items: 8

Format: Five-point scales are anchored by 1 (strongly disagree) and 5 (strongly agree). A sample item is presented.

Reliability: Coefficient alpha was .76.

Validity: Correlations with other variables ranged from −.27 to .18.

Author: Ford, J. K., et al.

Article: Relationships of goal orientation, metacognitive activity, and practice strategies with learning outcomes and transfer.

Journal: *Journal of Applied Psychology*, April 1998, 83(2), 218–233.

Related Research: Button, S. B., et al. (1996). The development and psychometric evaluation of learning goal and performance goal orientation. *Organizational Behavior and Human Decision Processes*, 67, 26–48.

9757

Test Name: PERSONAL CHARACTERISTICS INVENTORY

Purpose: To assess five personality dimensions.

Number of Items: 120

Format: Includes 5 dimensions: Conscientiousness, Extraversion, Agreeableness, Emotional

Stability, and Openness to Experiences. Responses are made on a 3-point Likert-type scale ranging from 1 (disagree) to 3 (agree).

Reliability: Test-retest (4 months) reliability ranged from .70 to .82. Alpha coefficients ranged from .74 to .82.

Validity: Correlations with other variables ranged from −.22 to .54.

Author: Mount, M. K., et al.

Article: Incremental validity of empirically keyed biodata scales over GMA and the five factor personality constructs.

Journal: *Personnel Psychology*, Summer 2000, 53(2), 299–323.

Related Research: Mount, M. K., & Barrick, M. R. (1996). *The Revised Personal Characteristics Manual*. Unpublished manuscript.

9758

Test Name: PERSONAL NEED FOR STRUCTURE SCALE

Purpose: To measure desire for structure and reaction to lack to structure.

Number of Items: 6

Format: Scales range from 1 (strongly disagree) to 6 (strongly agree).

Reliability: Alpha coefficients were .68 (desire for structure) and .69 (reaction to lack of structure).

Authors: Kivimäki, M., et al.

Article: Effect of components of personal need for structure on occupational strain.

Journal: *Journal of Social Psychology*, December 1996, 136(6), 769–777.

Related Research: Thompson, M. M., et al. (1989). *Assessing cognitive needs: The development*

of the personal need and personal fear of invalidity scales. Paper presented at the annual meeting of the Canadian Psychological Association, Halifax, Nova Scotia.

9759

Test Name: PERSONAL PREFERENCES SELF-DESCRIPTION QUESTIONNAIRE

Purpose: To provide a measure of Jungian types.

Number of Items: 93

Format: Includes word-pair items involving semantic differential scales with a 1 to 7 response format and sentence items involving 1 (strongest disagreement) to 7 (strongest agreement) Likert-type scales.

Reliability: Alpha coefficients ranged from .88 to .90.

Validity: Correlations with the Marlowe-Crowne Social Desirability Scale—Short Form, ranged from −.14 to .16.

Author: Kier, F. J., et al.

Article: Reliability and validity of scores on the Personal Preferences Self-Description Questionnaire (PPSDQ).

Journal: *Educational and Psychological Measurement*, August 1998, 58(4), 612–622.

Related Research: Arnau, R. C., et al. (1997, April). *Measurements of Jungian personality typology.* Paper presented at the annual meeting of the Southwestern Psychological Association, Fort Worth, TX.

9760

Test Name: PERSONAL STYLE INVENTORY

Purpose: To measure sociotropy and autonomy

Number of Items: 48

Format: Six-point scales anchored by 1 (strongly disagree) and 6 (strongly agree).

Reliability: Alphas were .97 (sociotropy) and .83 (autonomy).

Validity: Correlations with other variables ranged from .10 to .76.

Author: Sato, T., and McCann, D.

Article: Vulnerability factors in depression: The facets of sociotropy and autonomy.

Journal: *Journal of Psychopathology and Behavioral Assessment*, March 1997, 19(1), 21–39.

Related Research: Robins, C. J., et al. (1994). The Personal Style Inventory: Preliminary validation studies of new measures of sociotropy and autonomy. *Journal of Psychopathology and Behavioral Assessment*, 16, 277–300.

9761

Test Name: PERSONAL VIEWS SURVEY

Purpose: To measure the hardy personality.

Number of Items: 50

Format: Four-point scales are anchored by "not at all true" and "completely true."

Reliability: Alphas ranged from .76 to .83 across subscales.

Validity: Correlations with other variables ranged from −.30 to .48.

Author: Turnipseed, D. L.

Article: An exploratory study of the hardy personality at work in the health care industry.

Journal: *Psychological Reports*, December 1999, 85(3, Part 2), 1199–1217.

Related Research: Kobasa, S. C. (1985). Type A and hardiness. *Journal of Behavioral Medicine*, 6, 41–51.

9762

Test Name: PERSONALITY ASSESSMENT QUESTIONNAIRE—CHILD VERSION

Purpose: To measure personality/psychological adjustment.

Number of Items: 36 (42)

Format: Scales range from "almost always true of me" to "almost never true of me." Sample items are presented.

Reliability: Alpha coefficients ranged from .50 to .74 across subscales. Total alpha was .88.

Author: Rohner, R. P., et al.

Article: Children's perceptions of corporal punishment, caretaker acceptance, and psychological adjustment in a poor, biracial, southern community.

Journal: *Journal of Marriage and the Family*, November 1996, 58(4), 842–852.

Related Research: Rohner, R. P. (1991). *Handbook for the study of parental acceptance and rejection.* Center for the Study of Parental Acceptance and Rejection, University of Connecticut at Storrs.

Veneziano, R. A., & Rohner, R. P. (1998). Perceived paternal acceptance, paternal involvement, and youths' psychological adjustment in a rural, biracial southern community. *Journal of Marriage and the Family, 60, 335–343.*

9763

Test Name: PERSONALITY CHARACTERISTICS SCALE

Purpose: To measure expressivity and instrumentality.

Number of Items: 12

Format: Includes 2 subscales: Expressivity and Instrumentality. Responses are made on a 5-point scale.

Reliability: Alpha coefficients ranged from .51 to .80.

Author: Updegraff, K. A., et al.

Article: Adolescents' sex-typed friendship experiences: Does having a sister versus having a brother matter?

Journal: *Child Development*, November/December 2000, *71*(6), 1597–1610.

Related Research: Antill, J., et al. (1993). Measures of children's sex typing in middle childhood. *Australian Journal of Psychology, 45,* 25–33.

9764

Test Name: PERSONALITY SCALES FOR BUSINESS CONTEXTS

Purpose: To assess three dimensions of personality: conciliatory vs. belligerent, suspicious nature vs. trusting nature, and risk-taking vs. risk-avoidance.

Number of Items: 13

Format: Seven-point Likert, yes/no, and forced distribution formats are used. All items are presented.

Reliability: Alpha coefficients ranged from .72 to .89 across subscales.

Author: Mintu-Wimsatt, A., and Lozada, H. R.

Article: Personality and negotiation revisited.

Journal: *Psychological Reports*, June 1999, *84*(3) Part 1, 1159–1170.

Related Research: Shure, G., & Meeker, R. (1967). Personality attitude schedule for use in experimental bargaining studies. *The Journal of Psychology, 65,* 233–252.

King, W., et al. (1993). A test and refinement of the equity-sensitivity construct. *Journal of Organizational Behavior, 14,* 301–317.

9765

Test Name: POSITIVE EMOTIONALITY SCALE

Purpose: To measure positive emotionality.

Number of Items: 8

Format: Responses are made on a 5-point scale ranging from 1 (very slightly or not at all) to 5 (extremely). Examples are presented.

Reliability: Alpha coefficients ranged from .80 to .93.

Author: Eisenberg, N., et al.

Article: Shyness and children's emotionality, regulation and coping: Contemporaneous, longitudinal, and cross-context relations.

Journal: *Child Development*, June 1998, *69*(3), 767–790.

Related Research: Watson, D., et al. (1988). Development and validation of brief measures of positive and negative affect: The PANAS scales. *Journal of Personality and Social Psychology, 54,* 1063–1070.

9766

Test Name: THE PREOCCUPATION SCALE

Purpose: To measure self-focused attention and its continuance.

Number of Items: 11

Format: Five-point scales are anchored by 1 (does not apply to me at all) and 5 (applies to me very much).

Reliability: Alpha was .88. Test-retest (3 weeks) reliability was .87.

Author: Sakamoto, S., et al.

Article: The relationship among major depression, depressive symptoms, and self-preoccupation.

Journal: *Journal of Psychopathology and Behavioral Assessment*, March 1999, *21*(1), 37–49.

Related Research: Sakamoto, S. (1998). The Preoccupation Scale: Its development and relationship with depression scales. *Journal of Clinical Psychology, 54,* 645–654.

9767

Test Name: PRIVATE SELF-CONSCIOUSNESS SCALE

Purpose: To assess psychological mindedness.

Number of Items: 10

Format: Responses are made on a 5-point scale ranging from 0 (extremely uncharacteristic) to 4 (extremely characteristic).

Reliability: Test-retest reliability was .79. Coefficient alpha was .72 (*n* = 59).

Author: Diemer, R. A., et al.

Article: Comparison of dream interpretation, event interpretation, and unstructured sessions in brief therapy.

Journal: *Journal of Counseling Psychology*, January 1996, *43*(1), 99–112.

Related Research: Fenigstein, A., et al. (1975). Public and private self-consciousness: Assessment theory. *Journal of Consulting and Clinical Psychology*, *43*, 522–527.

9768

Test Name: PROACTIVE PERSONALITY SCALE

Purpose: To assess a disposition toward proactive behavior.

Number of Items: 6

Format: Scales range from 1 (strongly disagree) to 5 (strongly agree). Sample items are presented.

Reliability: Coefficient alpha was .85.

Validity: Correlations with other variables ranged from −.10 to .44.

Author: Parker, S. K.

Article: Enhancing role breadth self-efficacy: The roles of job enrichment and other organizational interventions.

Journal: *Journal of Applied Psychology*, December 1998, *83*(6), 835–852.

Related Research: Bateman, T. S., & Crant, J. M. (1993). The proactive component of organizational behavior: A measure and correlates. *Journal of Organizational Behavior*, *14*, 103–118.

9769

Test Name: PROACTIVE PERSONALITY SCALE

Purpose: To measure the tendency to perceive opportunities or problems and confront them.

Number of Items: 17

Format: Scales range from 1 (strongly disagree) to 5 (strongly agree). Sample items are presented.

Reliability: Alpha coefficients ranged from .87 to .89.

Author: Chan, D., and Schmitt, N.

Article: Interindividual differences in intraindividual changes in proactivity during organizational entry: A latent growth modeling approach to understanding newcomer adaptation.

Journal: *Journal of Applied Psychology*, April 2000, *85*(2), 190–210.

Related Research: Bateman, T. S., & Crant, J. M. (1993). The proactive component of organizational behavior. *Journal of Organizational Behavior*, *14*, 103–118.

9770

Test Name: PROACTIVE PERSONALITY SCALE— SHORT VERSION

Purpose: To measure the tendency to behave and think proactively.

Number of Items: 10

Format: Scales range from 1 (strongly disagree) to 2 (strongly agree). All items are presented.

Reliability: Coefficient alpha was .86.

Validity: Correlation with the full scale was .96.

Author: Seibert, S. E., et al.

Article: Proactive personality and career success.

Journal: *Journal of Applied Psychology*, June 1999, *84*(3), 416–427.

Related Research: Bateman,

T. S., & Crant, J. M. (1993). The proactive component of organizational behavior. *Journal of Organizational Behavior, 14*, 103–118.

9771

Test Name: PSYCHOLOGICAL INVENTORY OF EGO STRENGTHS

Purpose: To assess ego strengths.

Number of Items: 64

Format: Responses are made on a 5-point scale ranging from "describes me very well" to "does not describe me well."

Reliability: Alpha coefficients ranged from .35 to .68.

Author: Markstrom, C. A., and Hunter, C. L.

Article: The roles of ethnic and ideological identity in predicting fidelity in African American and European American adolescents.

Journal: *Child Study Journal*, 1999, *29*(1), 23–38.

Related Research: Markstrom, C. A., et al. (1997). The Psychological Inventory of Ego Strengths: Development and assessment of a new Eriksonian measure. *Journal of Youth and Adolescence*, *26*, 705–732.

9772

Test Name: PSYCHOLOGICAL MINDEDNESS SCALE

Purpose: To measure client psychological mindedness.

Number of Items: 45

Format: Responses are made on a 4-point scale.

Reliability: Alpha coefficients ranged from .84 to .86.

Author: Diemer, R. A., et al.

Article: Comparison of dream

interpretation, event interpretation, and unstructured sessions in brief therapy.

Journal: *Journal of Counseling Psychology*, January 1996, *43*(1), 99–112.

Related Research: Conte, H. R., et al. (1990). Psychological mindedness as a predictor of psychotherapy outcome: A preliminary report. *Comprehensive Psychiatry, 31,* 426–431.

9773

Test Name: PSYCHOPATHIC PERSONALITY INVENTORY

Purpose: To assess personality features of psychopathy including Machiavellian Egocentricity, Social Potency, Coldheartedness, Carefree Nonplanfulness, Fearlessness, Blame Externalization, Impulsive Nonconformity, and Stress Immunity.

Number of Items: 160

Format: Four-point Likert format. Sample items are presented.

Reliability: Alphas ranged from .90 to .93 (total) and from .70 to .89 (across subscales).

Validity: Correlations with other variables ranged from −.51 to .22.

Author: Lilienfeld, S. O., et al.

Article: Psychopathic personality traits and temporal perspective: A test of the short time horizon hypothesis.

Journal: *Journal of Psycho-pathology and Behavioral Assessment*, September 1996, *18*(3), 285–314.

Related Research: Lilienfeld, S. O., & Andrews, B. P. (1996). Development and preliminary validation of a self-report

measure of psychopathic personality traits in noncriminal populations. *Journal of Personality Assessment, 66*, 488–524.

9774

Test Name: PSYCHOPATHIC PERSONALITY INVENTORY— SHORT FORM

Purpose: To measure several dimensions of the psychopathic personality.

Number of Items: 56

Format: Four-point Likert format.

Reliability: Internal consistency reliabilities ranged from .70 to .90 in the development sample. Test-retest reliabilities ranged from .82 to .94.

Author: Wilson, D. L., et al.

Article: Gender, somatization, and psychopathic traits in a college sample.

Journal: *Journal of Psychopathology and Behavioral Assessment*, December 1999, *21*(3), 221–235.

Related Research: Lilienfeld, S. O., & Andrews, B. P. (1996). Development and preliminary validation of a self-report measure of psychopathic personality traits in noncriminal populations. *Journal of Personality Assessment, 66*, 488–524.

9775

Test Name: QUESTIONNAIRE MEASURE OF EMOTIONAL EMPATHY

Purpose: To provide an index of an individual's level of emotional responsiveness to another's distress.

Number of Items: 33

Format: Responses are made on a 9-point Likert scale ranging from −4 (very strongly disagree) to 4 (very strongly agree). Sample items are presented.

Reliability: Split-half reliability was .84. Coefficient alpha was .73.

Validity: Correlations with other variables ranged from −.10 to −.52.

Author: Sandoval, A.-M. R., et al.

Article: Construct validity of the Psychopathic Personality Inventory in a correctional sample.

Journal: *Journal of Personality Assessment*, April 2000, *74*(2), 262–281.

Related Research: Mehrabian, A., & Epstein, N. (1972). A measure of emotional empathy. *Journal of Personality, 40,* 525–543.

9776

Test Name: RATIONALITY/ EMOTIONAL DEFENSIVENESS SCALE

Purpose: To assess to what extent individuals try not to express emotions.

Number of Items: 8

Format: Scales range from 1 (almost never) to 4 (almost always). A sample item is presented.

Reliability: Alpha coefficients ranged from .73 to .79.

Validity: Correlations with other variables ranged from −.31 to .29.

Author: Davidson, K. W.

Article: Self- and expert-reported emotion inhibition: On the utility of both data sources.

Journal: *Journal of Research in*

Personality, December 1996, *30*(4), 535–549.

Related Research: Swan, G. E., et al. (1991). The Rationality Emotional Defensiveness Scale—I: Internal structure and stability. *Journal of Psychometric Research, 35*, 545–554.

9777

Test Name: RESTRICTIVE EMOTIONAL EXPRESSION SUBSCALE

Purpose: To assess the latent variable of emotional inexpression.

Number of Items: 10

Format: Responses are made on a 6-point scale ranging from 1 (strongly agree) to 6 (strongly disagree).

Reliability: Average coefficient alpha was .85. Test-retest reliability was .76.

Validity: Correlations with other variables ranged from −.37 to .36.

Author: Bruch, M. A., et al.

Article: Shyness, masculine ideology, physical attractiveness, and emotional inexpressiveness: Testing a mediational model of mens' interpersonal competence.

Journal: *Journal of Counseling Psychology*, January 1998, *45*(1), 84–97.

Related Research: O'Neil, J. M., et al. (1995). Fifteen years of research on mens' gender role conflict: New paradigms for empirical research. In R. Levent & W. Pollack (Eds.), *Foundations for a new psychology of men* (pp. 164–206). New York: Basic Books.

9778

Test Name: SEATTLE PERSONALITY

QUESTIONNAIRE FOR CHILDREN—MODIFIED

Purpose: To assess the general personality characteristics of children.

Number of Items: 28

Format: Contains 2 factors: Conduct Problems and Anxiety. Examples are presented.

Reliability: Alpha coefficients were .84 and .85.

Validity: Correlations with other variables ranged from −.47 to .68.

Author: Murray, C., and Greenberg, M. T.

Article: Children's relationship with teachers and bonds with school: An investigation of patterns and correlates in middle school.

Journal: *Journal of School Psychology*, September/October 2000, *38*(5), 423–445.

Related Research: Greenberg, M. T., & Kusche, C. (1990). *Draft manual for Seattle Personality Scale for Children—R.* Unpublished manuscript, University of Washington, Seattle.

9779

Test Name: SELF-CONSCIOUSNESS SCALE

Purpose: To measure private self-consciousness, public self-consciousness, and social anxiety.

Number of Items: 30

Format: Five-point scales are anchored by 1 (extremely uncharacteristic) and 5 (extremely characteristic).

Reliability: Alphas ranged from .45 to .84.

Author: Wegner, B. S., et al.

Article: Effect of exposure to

photographs of thin models on self-consciousness in female college students.

Journal: *Psychological Reports*, June 2000, *86*(3, Part 2), 1149–1154.

Related Research: Fenigstein, A., et al. (1975). Public and private self-consciousness: Assessment and theory. *Journal of Consulting and Clinical Psychology, 43*, 522–527.

9780

Test Name: SELF-CONSCIOUSNESS SCALE—ARABIC VERSION

Purpose: To measure covert aspects of the self: private and public self-consciousness.

Number of Items: 23

Format: Five-point scales were anchored by (0) I totally disagree and (4) I totally agree.

Reliability: Item test-retest reliabilities ranged from .50 to .98. Alphas ranged from .69 to .96 across subscales. Total alphas ranged from .70 to .79.

Validity: Correlation between public and private self-consciousness was .47. Correlations with social anxiety ranged from −.13 to .01.

Author: Bendania, A., and Abeo, A. S.

Article: Reliability and factorial structure of an Arabic translation of the Self-Consciousness Scale.

Journal: *Psychological Reports*, December 1997, *81*(3, Part II), 1091–1101.

Related Research: Fenigstein, A., et al. (1975). Public and private self-consciousness: Assessment and theory. *Journal of Consulting and Clinical Psychology, 43*, 522–527.

9781

Test Name: SELF-CONTROL SCHEDULE

Purpose: To measure women's learned resourcefulness.

Number of Items: 36

Format: Responses are made on a 6-point scale ranging from −3 (least characteristic) to +3 (most characteristic). Examples are given.

Reliability: Internal consistency coefficient was .85

Validity: Correlations with other variables ranged from −.37 to .12

Author: Rosenbaum, M., and Cohen, E.

Article: Equalitarian marriage, spousal support, resourcefulness, and psychological distress among Israeli working women.

Journal: *Journal of Vocational Behavior*, February 1999, 54(1), 102–113

Related Research: Rosenbaum, M. (1990). The role of learned resourcefulness in self-control of health behavior. In M. Rosenbaum (Ed.), *Learned resourcefulness: On coping skills, self-control and adaptive behavior* (pp. 3–30). New York: Springer.

9782

Test Name: SELF-DECEPTION SCALE

Purpose: To assess the extent to which self-deceptive thoughts and feelings are true of a person.

Number of Items: 20

Format: Seven-point scales. Sample items are described.

Reliability: Coefficient alpha was .66.

Author: Johnson, E. A., et al.

Article: Self-deception vs. self-esteem in buffering the negative effects of failure.

Journal: *Journal of Research in Personality*, September 1997, 31(3), 385–405.

Related Research: Paulhus, D. L. (1984). Two-component models of socially desirable responding. *Journal of Personality and Social Psychology*, 46, 598–609.

9783

Test Name: SELF-DEFEATING PERSONALITY

Purpose: To provide a measure of the self-defeating personality.

Number of Items: 48

Format: Responses are true-false.

Validity: Correlations with other variables ranged from −.40 to .23.

Author: Schill, T., and Michels, J.

Article: Are childhood misbehavior and physical illness factors in the development of self-defeating personality?

Journal: *Perceptual and Motor Skills*, December 1996, 83(3) Part 1, 848–850.

Related Research: Schill, T. (1990). A measure of self-defeating personality. *Psychological Reports*, 66, 1343–1346.

9784

Test Name: SELF-RESPECT FOR BORDERLINE PERSONALITY

Purpose: To assess personality features across three intrapsychic dimensions.

Number of Items: 30

Format: Includes 3 subscales: Identity Diffusion, Primitive Defenses, and Reality Testing. Examples are presented.

Reliability: Alpha coefficients ranged from .75 to .92.

Validity: Correlations with other variables ranged from −.48 to .67.

Author: Sandoval, A.-M. R., et al.

Article: Construct validity of the Psychopathic Personality Inventory in a correctional sample.

Journal: *Journal of Personality Assessment*, April 2000, 74(2), 262–281.

Related Research: Oldham, J., et al. (1985). A self-report instrument for borderline personality organization. In T. H. McGlashan (Ed.), *The borderline: Current empirical research* (pp. 3–18). Washington, DC: American Psychiatric Press.

9785

Test Name: SELF/SPOUSE/INTERVIEWER-REPORTED FIVE FACTORS

Purpose: To measure the Big Five factors of personality by self, by spouse, and by interviewer.

Number of Items: 40

Format: Bipolar adjective format. Sample items are presented.

Reliability: Alpha coefficients ranged from .43 to .92 across subscales and source of support.

Author: Buss, D. M., and Shackelford, T. K.

Article: Susceptibility to infidelity in the first year of marriage.

Journal: *Journal of Research in Personality*, June 1997, 31(2), 193–221.

Related Research: Goldberg, L. R. (June, 1983). *The magical number of five, plus or minus*

two: *Some considerations on the dimensionality of personality descriptors.* Paper presented at a research seminar of the Gerontological Research Center, NIA/NIH, Baltimore, MD.

9786

Test Name: SHYNESS SCALE

Purpose: To assess self-reported interpersonal discomfort and inhibition.

Number of Items: 9

Format: Responses are made on a five-point scale of agreement–disagreement.

Reliability: Alpha coefficients were .79 and .65.

Author: Jackson, T., et al.

Article: Culture and self-presentation as predictors of shyness among Japanese and American female college students.

Journal: *Perceptual and Motor Skills*, April 2000, *90*(2), 475–482.

Related Research: Cheek, J. M., & Buss, A. (1981). Shyness and sociability. *Journal of Personality and Social Psychology, 41*, 330–339.

9787

Test Name: SMITH R-STATE INVENTORY

Purpose: To measure relaxation-related states.

Number of Items: 45

Format: Includes R-states of Disengagement, Physical Relaxation, Mental Relaxation, Strength and Awareness, Joy, Love and Thankfulness, and Transcendence. Responses are made on a 5-point scale.

Reliability: Alpha coefficients ranged from .60 to .84.

Validity: Correlations with other variables ranged from −.36 to .45.

Author: Khasky, A. D., and Smith, J. C.

Article: Stress, relaxation states, and creativity.

Journal: *Perceptual and Motor Skills*, April 1999, *88*(2), 409–416.

Related Research: Smith, J. C. (1999). *ABC relaxation theory: An evidence-based approach.* New York: Springer.

9788

Test Name: SOCIAL DOMINANCE ORIENTATION SCALE

Purpose: To measure social dominance.

Number of Items: 8

Format: Seven-point agree–disagree scales. Sample items are presented.

Reliability: Coefficient alpha was .79.

Validity: Correlations with other variables ranged from −.33 to .39.

Author: Lippa, R., and Arad, S.

Article: Gender, personality, and prejudice: The display of authoritarianism and social dominance in interviews with college men and women.

Journal: *Journal of Research in Personality*, December 1999, *33*(4), 463–493.

Related Research: Pratto, F., et al. (1994). Social dominance orientation: A personality variable predicting social and political attitudes. *Journal of Personality and Social Psychology, 67*, 741–763.

9789

Test Name: SOCIO-EMOTIONAL NEEDS SCALE

Purpose: To measure the need for approval, esteem, emotional support, and affiliation.

Number of Items: 28

Format: Seven-point scales are anchored by 1 (strongly disagree) and 7 (strongly agree). All items are presented.

Reliability: Alpha coefficients ranged from .72 to .86 across subscales.

Validity: Correlations with other variables ranged from −.19 to .20.

Author: Armeli, S., et al.

Article: Perceived organizational support and police performance: The moderating influence of socioemotional needs.

Journal: *Journal of Applied Psychology*, April 1998, *83*(2), 288–297.

Related Research: Hill, C. A. (1987). Affiliation motivation: People who need people hurt in different ways. *Journal of Personality and Social Psychology, 52*, 1008–1018.

9790

Test Name: SOCIOTROPY–AUTONOMY SCALE—REVISED

Purpose: To measure an individual's level of sociotropy and autonomy.

Number of Items: 58

Format: Five-point scales anchored by 0 (never) and 4 (all the time).

Reliability: Cronbach's alpha was .89. Alphas ranged from .73 to .78 across subscales.

Validity: Correlations with other variables ranged from .10 to .76.

Author: Sato, T., and McCann, D.

Article: Vulnerability factors in depression: The facets of sociotropy and autonomy.

Journal: *Journal of Psychopathology and Behavioral Assessment*, March 1997, *19*(1), 21–39.

Related Research: Clark, D. A., & Beck, A. T. (1991). Personality factors in dysphoria: A psychometric refinement of Beck's Sociotropy–Autonomy Scale. *Journal of Psychopathology and Behavioral Assessment, 13*, 369–388.

9791

Test Name: SPLITTING INDEX

Purpose: To assess the splitting defense mechanism.

Number of Items: 24

Format: Includes 3 factors: Splitting of the Self Image, Splitting of Family Images, and Splitting of Other Images. All items are presented.

Reliability: Alpha coefficients ranged from .84 to .92. Test-retest reliability ranged from .75 to .90.

Validity: Correlations with other variables ranged from −.77 to .68.

Author: Gould, J. R., et al.

Article: The Splitting Index: construction of a scale measuring the defense mechanism of splitting.

Journal: *Journal of Personality Assessment*, April 1996, *66*(2), 414–430.

9792

Test Name: TASK AND EGO ORIENTATION IN SPORT QUESTIONNAIRE

Purpose: To assess adolescents' ego and task orientation in school physical education.

Number of Items: 13

Format: Includes 2 subscales: Ego and Task. Responses are made on a 5-point scale ranging from 1 (strongly disagree) to 5 (strongly agree).

Reliability: Alpha coefficients were .74 and .81.

Validity: Correlations with other variables ranged from −.01 to .34.

Author: Spray, C. M.

Article: Predicting participation in noncompulsory physical education: Do goal perspectives matter?

Journal: *Perceptual and Motor Skills*, June 2000, *90*(3) Part 2, 1207–1215.

Related Research: Duda, J. L., et al. (1992). Children's achievement goals and beliefs about success in sport. *British Journal of Educational Psychology, 62*, 313–323.

9793

Test Name: TEMPERAMENT AND CHARACTER INVENTORY

Purpose: To measure temperament as Novelty Seeking, Harm Avoidance, Reward Dependence and Persistence, and to measure character as Self-Directedness, Cooperativeness, and Self-Transcendence.

Number of Items: 240

Time Required: 20–30 minutes

Format: True/false format.

Reliability: Alpha coefficients ranged from .37 to .87 across subscales and across groups (American, Swedish, and German).

Validity: Factor congruences ranged from .90 to .98.

Author: Richter, J., et al.

Article: Assessing personality: The Temperament and Character Inventory in a cross-cultural comparison between Germany, Sweden, and the USA.

Journal: *Psychological Reports*, June 1999, *84*(3) Part 2, 1315–1330.

Related Research: Cloninger, C. R., et al. (1994) *The Temperament and Character Inventory (TCI): A guide to its development and use.* St. Louis, MO: Center for Psychobiology of Personality.

9794

Test Name: TEMPERAMENT AND CHARACTER INVENTORY (JAPANESE VERSION)

Purpose: To assess temperament (Novelty-Seeking, Harm-Avoidance, Reward-Dependence, and Persistence) and character (Self-Directedness, Cooperativeness, and Self-Transcendence).

Number of Items: 125

Format: Four-point scales are anchored by 1 (strongly disagree) and 4 (strongly agree).

Reliability: Alphas ranged from .69 to .85.

Validity: Correlations with self-rated depression ranged from −.60 to .51.

Author: Tanaka, E., et al.

Article: Correlations between the Temperament and Character Inventory and the Self-Rating

Depression Scale among Japanese students.

Journal: *Psychological Reports*, February 1997, *80*(1), 251–254.

Related Research: Cloninger, C. R., et al. (1993). A psychological model of temperament and character. *Archives of General Psychiatry*, *50*, 975–990.

9795

Test Name: TEMPERAMENTAL ATTENTIONAL REGULATION SCALE

Purpose: To assess temperamental attentional regulation.

Number of Items: 8

Format: Includes attention shifting and attention focusing. Examples are presented.

Reliability: Alpha coefficients ranged from .65 to .82.

Author: Eisenberg, N., et al.

Article: The relations of children's dispositional prosocial behavior to emotionality, regulation, and social functioning.

Journal: *Child Development*, June 1996, *67*(3), 974–992.

Related Research: Derryberry, D., & Rothbart, M. K. (1988). Arousal, affect, and attention as components of temperament. *Journal of Personality and Social Psychology*, *55*, 958–966.

9796

Test Name: TEMPERAMENTAL NEGATIVE EMOTIONALITY SCALE

Purpose: To assess dispositional emotionality and regulation.

Number of Items: 14

Format: Includes sadness, fear, and autonomic reactivity. Examples are presented.

Reliability: Alpha coefficients ranged from .68 to .73.

Author: Eisenberg, N., et al.

Article: The relations of children's dispositional prosocial behavior to emotionality, regulation, and social functioning.

Journal: *Child Development*, June 1996, *67*(3), 974–992.

Related Research: Derryberry, D., & Rothbart, M. K. (1988). Arousal, affect, and attention as components of temperament. *Journal of Personality and Social Psychology*, *55*, 958–966.

9797

Test Name: TODDLER BEHAVIOR ASSESSMENT QUESTIONNAIRE

Purpose: To provide a general purpose temperament inventory.

Number of Items: 108

Format: Includes 5 subscales: Activity Level, Pleasure, Social Fearfulness, Anger Proneness, and Interest/Persistence.

Reliability: Alpha coefficients ranged from .78 to .89.

Validity: Correlations with other variables ranged from −.41 to .64.

Author: Goldsmith, H. H.

Article: Studying temperament via construction of the Toddler Behavior Assessment Questionnaire.

Journal: *Child Development*, February 1996, *67*(1), 218–235.

9798

Test Name: TOLERANCE OF AMBIGUITY SCALE

Purpose: To measure tolerance for ambiguity.

Number of Items: 16

Format: Seven-point Likert format. A sample item is presented.

Reliability: Coefficient alpha was .59.

Validity: Correlations with other variables ranged from −.19 to .32.

Author: Schaubroeck, J., et al.

Article: Organization and occupation influences in the attraction-selection-attrition process.

Journal: *Journal of Applied Psychology*, December 1998, *83*(6), 869–891.

Related Research: Budner, S. (1962). Intolerance of ambiguity as a personality variable. *Journal of Personality*, *30*, 29–50.

9799

Test Name: TOLERANCE OF AMBIGUITY SCALE

Purpose: To measure the perceived threat in ambiguous situations.

Number of Items: 20

Format: Response scales are anchored by (0) no tolerance of ambiguity and (20) highest tolerance of ambiguity.

Reliability: K-R reliability was .73.

Author: Moore, S., and Ward, M.

Article: Machiavellianism and tolerance of ambiguity.

Journal: *Psychological Reports*, April 1998, *82*(2), 415–418.

Related Research: MacDonald, A. P. (1970). Revised Scale for Ambiguity Intolerance. *Psychological Reports*, *26*, 791–798.

9800

Test Name: TORONTO ALEXITHYMIA SCALE— ITALIAN VERSION

Purpose: To measure the capacity to identify and express emotions.

Number of Items: 26

Format: Five-point scales.

Reliability: Reliability coefficients ranged from .77 to .79.

Author: Morosin, A., and Riva, G.

Article: Alexithymia in a clinical sample of obese women.

Journal: *Psychological Reports*, April 1997, *80*(2), 387–394.

Related Research: Bucca, M., et al. (1993) Una versaione italiana della Toronto Alexithymia Scale (TAS). *Bollettino di psicologia applicata*, 207, 47–54.

9801

Test Name: TORONTO ALEXITHYMIA SCALE (JAPANESE VERSION)

Purpose: To assess the cognitive–affective disturbance characteristic of persons who cannot elaborate or communicate feelings.

Number of Items: 26

Format: Five-point rating scales. All items are presented.

Reliability: Alphas ranged from .66 to .80 across subscales. Total alpha was .90. Test-retest correlations ranged from .60 to .74.

Validity: Correlations with the Beth Israel Psychosomatic Questionnaire ranged from .14 to .32.

Author: Fukunishi, I., et al.

Article: An investigation of the psychometric properties of the

26-item Toronto Alexithymia Scale in a Japanese culture.

Journal: *Psychological Reports*, October 1996, *79*(2), 555–562.

9802

Test Name: TORONTO ALEXITHYMIA SCALE— REVISED

Purpose: To assess emotional inexpressiveness.

Number of Items: 10

Format: Responses are made on a 5-point Likert scale ranging from 1 (strongly agree) to 5 (strongly disagree). Examples are presented.

Reliability: Alpha coefficients were .67 and .68.

Validity: Correlations with other variables ranged from −.08 to .32.

Author: Goodyear, R. K., et al.

Article: Predictors of Latino men's paternity in teen pregnancy: Test of a mediational model of childhood experiences, gender role attitudes, and behaviors.

Journal: *Journal of Counseling Psychology*, January 2000, *47*(1), 116–128.

Related Research: Parker, J. D. A., et al. (1993). Factorial validity of the 20-item Toronto Alexithymia Scale. *European Journal of Personality*, 7, 221–232.

9803

Test Name: TORONTO ALEXITHYMIA SCALE–20

Purpose: To provide a self-report measure of alexithymia.

Number of Items: 20

Format: Includes 3 subscales: Identifying Feelings, Describing

Feelings, and External Cognitive Orientation. Responses are made on a 5-point scale ranging from 1 (strongly disagree) to 5 (strongly agree). Examples are given.

Reliability: Test-retest (3 weeks) reliability was .77. Internal consistency reliability coefficients ranged from .66 to .78.

Validity: Correlations with other variables ranged from −.36 to .53.

Author: Mallinckrodt, B., et al.

Article: Family dysfunction, alexithymia, and client attachment to therapist.

Journal: *Journal of Counseling Psychology*, October 1998, *45*(4), 497–504.

Related Research: Bagby, R. M., et al. (1994). The twenty-item Toronto Alexithymia Scale-I: Item selection and cross-validation of the factor structure. *Journal of Psychosomatic Research*, 38, 23–32.

9804

Test Name: VEDIC PERSONALITY INVENTORY

Purpose: To assess the validity of the three guna constructs.

Number of Items: 56

Reliability: Alpha coefficients ranged from .85 to .92 across subscales.

Validity: Correlations with other variables ranged from −.51 to .65.

Author: Wolf, D. B.

Article: A psychometric analysis of the three gunas.

Journal: *Psychological Reports*, June 1999, *84*(3) Part 2, 1379–1390.

Related Research: Singh, R. (1971). An inventory from Mahabharata. *Indian Journal of Psychiatry, 13,* 149–161.

CHAPTER 18
Preference

9805

Test Name: AMBIVALENT SEXISM INVENTORY

Purpose: To measure hostile sexism/male dominance and benevolent sexism/stereotypic roles.

Number of Items: 22

Format: Scales range from 0 (disagree strongly) to 5 (agree strongly). Sample items are presented.

Reliability: Alpha coefficients ranged from .75 to .92 across samples and subscales.

Author: Wiener, R. L., and Hurt, L. E.

Article: How do people evaluate social sexual conduct at work? A psychological model.

Journal: *Journal of Applied Psychology*, February 2000, 85(1), 75–85.

Related Research: Glick, P., & Fiske, S. T. (1996). The Ambivalent Sexism Inventory: Differentiating hostile and benevolent sexism. *Journal of Personality and Social Psychology*, 70, 491–512.

9806

Test Name: APPAREL QUALITY QUESTIONNAIRE

Purpose: To evaluate apparel quality.

Number of Items: 26

Format: Includes 3 factors: Sturdiness/Durability, Style/Aesthetics, and Lasting/Care.

Responses are made on a 5-point scale ranging from 1 (strongly disagree) to 5 (strongly agree).

Reliability: Alpha coefficients ranged from .65 to .79.

Author: Forsythe, S., et al.

Article: Dimensions of apparel quality influencing consumers' perceptions.

Journal: *Perceptual and Motor Skills*, August 1996, 83(1), 299–305.

Related Research: Hines, J. D., & O'Neal, G. S. (1995). Underlying determinants of clothing quality: The consumers' perspective. *Clothing and Textiles Research Journal*, 13, 227–233.

9807

Test Name: AUSTRALIAN SEX ROLE SCALE

Purpose: To assess desirable and undesirable aspects of masculinity and femininity.

Number of Items: 40

Format: Seven-point scales.

Reliability: Alpha coefficients ranged from .62 to .81 across subscales.

Authors: Ricciardelli, L. A., et al.

Article: Relation of drinking and eating to masculinity and femininity.

Journal: *Journal of Social Psychology*, December 1998, 138(6), 744–752.

Related Research: Antill, J. K., et al. (1981). An Australian sex-role scale. *Australian Journal of Psychology, 33*, 169–183.

9808

Test Name: CHILDREN'S SEX ROLE INVENTORY

Purpose: To measure masculinity and femininity.

Number of Items: 30

Format: Scales range from 1 (not at all true of me) to 4 (very true of me).

Reliability: Coefficients ranged from .85 (femininity) to .80 (masculinity). Test-retest reliabilities ranged from .71 to .56.

Validity: Correlation with the Bem Sex Role Inventory was .86.

Author: Sellers, N., et al.

Article: Children's occupational aspirations: Comparisons by gender, gender role identity, and socioeconomic status.

Journal: *Professional School Counseling*, April 1999, 2(4), 314–317.

Related Research: Boldizar, J. P. (1991). Assessing sex typing androgyny in children: The Children's Sex Role Inventory. *Developmental Psychology*, 27, 505–515.

9809

Test Name: CLASSROOM LIFE INSTRUMENT

Purpose: To measure preferences for cooperative and competitive learning environments.

Number of Items: 15

Format: Five-point response categories. Sample items are presented.

Reliability: Alphas were .83 (cooperativeness) and .89 (competitiveness).

Author: Kline, T. J., and Spell, Y. P.

Article: Cooperativeness vs. competitiveness: Initial findings regarding effects on the performance of individual and group problem-solving.

Journal: *Psychological Reports*, October 1996, *79*(2), 355–365.

Related Research: Johnson, D. W., & Johnson, R. (1983). Social interdependence and perceived academic and personal support in the classroom. *The Journal of Social Psychology*, *120*, 77–82.

9810

Test Name: CLOTHING INTEREST QUESTIONNAIRE

Purpose: To measure interest in clothing.

Number of Items: 6

Format: Sample items are presented.

Reliability: Coefficient alpha was .86.

Validity: Correlation with other variables ranged from .10 to .34.

Author: Kwon, Y.-H.

Article: Sex, sex-role, facial attractiveness, social self-esteem, and interest in clothing.

Journal: *Perceptual and Motor Skills*, June 1997, *84*(3, Part 1), 899–907.

9811

Test Name: CONSUMER SUSCEPTIBILITY TO INTERPERSONAL INFLUENCE SCALE

Purpose: To measure multiple characteristics of undergraduate students' wardrobe purchases, with apparel color a dominant theme.

Number of Items: 11

Format: Includes two subscales: Normative and Informational. Responses are made on a 5-point scale ranging from 1 (strongly disagree) to 5 (strongly agree). All items are presented.

Reliability: Construct reliability was .70 (Informational) and .93 (Normative).

Author: Miller, N. J.

Article: Susceptibility of consumers to normative and informational influences in selecting colors for apparel.

Journal: *Perceptual and Motor Skills*, December 1998, *87*(3) Part 2, 1131–1136.

Related Research: Bearden, W. O., et al. (1989). Measurement of consumer susceptibility to personal influence. *Journal of Consumer Research*, *15*, 473–481.

9812

Test Name: COUNSELOR ETHNICITY PREFERENCE SCALE

Purpose: To assess participant preference for counselor ethnicity.

Number of Items: 4

Format: Includes 2 types of participant concerns: counselor preferences for an academic concern and for a personal concern. Responses are made on an 11-point scale ranging from 0 (do not prefer at all) to 10 (totally prefer). All items are presented.

Reliability: Alpha coefficients were .74 and .77.

Validity: Correlations with other variables ranged from −.19 to .28.

Author: Abreu, J. M., and Gabarain, G.

Article: Social desirability and Mexican American counselor preferences: Statistical control for a potential confound.

Journal: *Journal of Counseling Psychology*, April 2000, *47*(2), 165–176.

Related Research: Coleman, L. K., et al. (1995). Ethnic minorities' ratings of ethnically similar and European American counselors: A meta-analysis. *Journal of Counseling Psychology*, *42*, 55–64.

9813

Test Name: EQUALITARIAN MARRIAGE TYPE SCALE

Purpose: To assess the degree to which women perceive a clear separation of male and female roles and responsibilities along gender lines.

Number of Items: 6

Format: Responses are made on a 5-point scale ranging from 5 (strongly agree) to 1 (strongly disagree). Examples are given.

Reliability: Coefficient alpha was .70

Validity: Correlations with other variables ranged from .02 to .12.

Author: Rosenbaum, M., and Cohen, E.

Article: Equalitarian marriages, spousal support, resourcefulness, and psychological distress among Israeli working women.

Journal: *Journal of Vocational Behavior*, February 1999, *54*(1), 102–113.

Related Research: Pendleton, B. E., et al. (1980). Scales for investigation of the dual-career family. *Journal of Marriage and the Family*, 42, 269–275.

9814

Test Name: FITNESS FACILITY MEMBERSHIP QUESTIONNAIRE

Purpose: To identify reasons for joining a fitness facility.

Number of Items: 43

Format: Includes 3 factors: Socialization, Aquatic-Related Facilities, Extrinsic Motivation, Recreational Facilities, Intrinsic Motivation, Resistance Equipment, Aerobic Equipment, and Amenities. Responses are made on a 5-point scale ranging from 1 (not at all important to me) to 5 (extremely important to me).

Reliability: Alpha coefficients ranged from .72 to .89.

Author: Drummonds, J. J., and Lenes, H. S.

Article: The Fitness Facility Membership Questionnaire: A measure of reasons for joining.

Journal: *Perceptual and Motor Skills*, December 1997, *85*(3, Part 1), 907–916.

Related Research: Drummond, J. L., & Lenes, H. S. (1996). Reliability and validity of the Facility Membership Questionnaire. *Perceptual and Motor Skills*, 82, 826.

9815

Test Name: GENDER EVALUATION SCALE

Purpose: To measure gender evaluation.

Number of Items: 6

Format: Responses are made on a 5-point scale ranging from 1 (strongly disagree) to 5 (strongly agree). Sample items are presented.

Reliability: Coefficient alpha was .90.

Validity: Correlations with other variables ranged from −.24 to .25.

Author: Shaffer, M. A., et al.

Article: Gender discrimination and job-related outcomes: A cross-cultural comparison of working women in the United States and China.

Journal: *Journal of Vocational Behavior*, December 2000, *57*(3), 395–427.

Related Research: Joplin, J. R. W., & Shaffer, M. A. (1997). *Harassment, lies, theft, and other vexations: A cross-cultural companion of aggressive behaviors in the workplace.* Report presented at the National Meetings of the Academy of Management, Boston, MA.

9816

Test Name: GENDER IDENTITY MEASURE

Purpose: To measure masculinity and femininity.

Number of Items: 15

Format: All items are presented. Scoring methods are described.

Reliability: Omega reliability was .80.

Author: Burke, P. J., and Cast, A. D.

Article: Stability and change in gender identities of newly married couples.

Journal: *Social Psychology Quarterly,* December 1997, *60*(4), 277–290.

Related Research: Burke, P. J., & Tully, J. (1977). The measurement of role/identity. *Social Forces,* 55, 881–897.

9817

Test Name: GENDER IDEOLOGY SCALE

Purpose: To assess approval of traditional family values.

Number of Items: 6

Format: Five- and seven-point Likert scales. All items are presented.

Reliability: Alpha coefficients ranged from .66 to .68.

Author: Greenstein, T. N.

Article: Husbands' participation in domestic labor: Interactive effects of wives' and husbands' gender ideologies.

Journal: *Journal of Marriage and the Family,* August 1996, *58*(3), 585–595.

Related Research: Sweet, J. A., et al. (1988). *The design and content of the National Survey of Families and Households.* (Working Paper NSFH-1). Madison: University of Wisconsin, Center for Demography and Ecology.

9818

Test Name: GENDER ROLE CONFLICT SCALE

Purpose: To assess men's conflicts with their gender roles.

Number of Items: 37

Format: Includes 4 factors: Success, Power, Competition, Restrictive Emotionality, Restrictive Affectionate Behavior Between Men, and Conflict

Between Work and Family Relations. Responses are made on a 6-point scale ranging from 1 (strongly agree) to 6 (strongly disagree)

Reliability: Test-retest (4 weeks) reliability was .72 to .86.

Validity: Correlations with other variables ranged from −.23 to .50.

Author: Fischer, A. R., and Good, G. E.

Article: Perceptions of parent–child relationships and masculine role conflicts of college men.

Journal: *Journal of Counseling Psychology*, July 1998, *45*(3), 346–352.

Related Research: O'Neil, J. M., et al. (1986). Gender–Role Conflict Scale: College men's fear of femininity. *Sex Roles, 14,* 335–350.

9819

Test Name: GENDER ROLE IDEOLOGY SCALE

Purpose: To measure gender role ideology.

Number of Items: 8

Format: Scales range from 1 (totally disagree) to 7 (totally agree). Sample items are presented.

Reliability: Coefficient alpha was .71.

Validity: Correlations with other variables ranged from −.15 to .14.

Author: Kluwer, E. S., et al.

Article: The marital dynamics of conflict over the division of labor.

Journal: *Journal of Marriage and the Family*, August 1997, *59*(3), 635–653.

Related Research: Van Yperen,

N. W., & Buunk, B. P. (1991). Sex-role attitudes, social comparison, and satisfaction with relationships. *Social Psychology Quarterly, 54,* 169–180.

9820

Test Name: GOAL CHOICE SCALE

Purpose: To elicit goal preferences under a goal-conflict situation.

Number of Items: 4

Format: One item employs a 4-point scale ranging from "definitely choose good grades" to "definitely choose being challeneged." Other items employ a 6-point scale ranging from "strongly disagree" to "strongly agree." All items are presented.

Reliability: Coefficient alpha was .70.

Validity: Correlations with other variables ranged from −.60 to .62.

Author: Dai, D. Y.

Article: To be or not to be (challenged), that is the question: Task and ego orientation among high-ability, high-achieving adolescents.

Journal: *Journal of Experimental Education*, Summer 2000, *68*(4), 311–330.

Related Research: Dweck, C. S., et al. (1995). Implicit theories and their role in judgments and reactions: A world from two perspectives. *Psychological Inquiry, 6,* 267–285.

9821

Test Name: HYPERFEMININITY SCALE

Purpose: To measure adherence to extreme feminine gender roles.

Number of Items: 26

Format: Forced-choice format.

Reliability: Coefficient alpha was .80. Test-retest reliability (2-weeks) was .89.

Validity: Correlations with other variables ranged from −.27 to .60.

Author: Hamburger, M. E., et al.

Article: Assessing hypergender ideologies: Development and initial validation of a gender-neutral measure of adherence to extreme gender-role beliefs.

Journal: *Journal of Research in Personality*, June 1996, *30*(2), 157–178.

Related Research: Murnen, S. K., & Byrne, D. (1991). The Hyperfemininity scale: Measurement and initial validation of the construct. *Journal of Sex Research, 28,* 479–489.

9822

Test Name: HYPERGENDER IDEOLOGY SCALE

Purpose: To measure adherence to extreme stereotypic gender beliefs.

Number of Items: 57 (19 short form).

Format: Scales ranged from "strongly disagree" to "strongly agree." All items are presented.

Reliability: Coefficient alpha was .96 (short form alpha was .93).

Validity: Correlations with other variables ranged from −.13 to .77.

Author: Hamburger, M. E., et al.

Article: Assessing hypergender ideologies: Development and initial validation of a gender-neutral measure of adherence to extreme gender-role beliefs.

Journal: *Journal of Research in*

Personality, June 1996, *30*(2), 157–178.

9823

Test Name: HYPERMASCULINITY INVENTORY

Purpose: To measure adherence to the "macho" personality.

Number of Items: 30

Format: Forced-choice format.

Reliability: Coefficient alpha was .89.

Validity: Correlations with other variables ranged from −.19 to .61.

Author: Hamburger, M. E., et al.

Article: Assessing hypergender ideologies: Development and initial validation of a gender-neutral measure of adherence to extreme gender-role beliefs.

Journal: *Journal of Research in Personality*, June, 1996, *30*(2), 157–178.

Related Research: Mosher, D. L. (1991). Macho men, machismo and sexuality. *Annual Review of Sex Research*, *2*, 199–247.

9824

Test Name: INDEX OF MASCULINITY

Purpose: To assess to what extent individuals endorse traditional masculine characteristics of competitiveness.

Number of Items: 19

Format: Seven-point scales are anchored by 1 (extremely uncharacteristic of me) and 7 (extremely characteristic of me). All items are presented.

Reliability: Alphas ranged from .64 to .75.

Validity: Correlations with other variables ranged from .13 to .34.

Author: Lasane, T. P., et al.

Article: Hypermasculinity and academic goal-setting: An exploratory study.

Journal: *Psychological Reports*, October 1999, *85*(2), 487–496.

9825

Test Name: INSTRUCTION PREFERENCE QUESTIONNAIRE

Purpose: To identify students' preferred teaching approaches.

Number of Items: 83

Format: Includes 13 scales and 4 factors.

Reliability: Alpha coefficients ranged from .62 to .94.

Author: Hativa, N., and Birenbaum, M.

Article: Who prefers what? Disciplinary differences in students' preferred approaches to teaching and learning styles.

Journal: *Research in Higher Education*, April 2000, *41*(2), 209–236.

Related Research: Kember, D. (1997). A reconceptualisation of the research into university academics' conceptions of teaching. *Learning and Instruction*, *7*, 255–276.

9826

Test Name: INVENTORY OF DYADIC SEXUAL PREFERENCES

Purpose: To measure the sexual behavior preferences of couples.

Number of Items: 27

Format: Couples indicate their own and what they believe their partner's preferences are on 5-point Likert scales.

Reliability: Alpha was .72. Test-retest reliability was .84.

Validity: Correlations with other variables ranged from −.61 to .45.

Author: Purnine, D. M., and Carey, M. P.

Article: Interpersonal communication and sexual adjustment: The roles of understanding and agreement.

Journal: *Journal of Consulting and Clinical Psychology*, December 1997, *65*(6), 1017–1025.

9827

Test Name: INVENTORY OF OCCUPATIONAL PREFERENCES

Purpose: To identify occupational preferences.

Number of Items: 141

Format: Includes three dimensions: People/Things, Data/Ideas, and Prestige. There are 18 scales: Service, Helping, Artistic, Life Sciences, Mechanical, Technical, Business Detail, Business Contract, Business Analysis 1, Health Services, Hard Sciences, Commercial Art, Low Prestige Service, Personal Service 1, Social Sciences, Inspectors and Operators, Business Analysis 2, and Personal Service 2.

Reliability: Alpha coefficients ranged from .76 to .95.

Author: Tracey, T. J. G., & Watanabe, N.

Article: Structural invariance of vocational interests across Japanese and American tours.

Journal: *Journal of Counseling Psychology*, July 1997, *44*(3), 346–354.

Related Research: Tracey, T. J. G., & Rounds, J. (1996). The spherical representation of vocational interests. *Journal of Vocational Behavior, 48,* 3–41.

9828

Test Name: INVESTMENT CHOICE SCALE

Purpose: To assess preference for investment choice.

Number of Items: 3

Format: Responses are made on a 5-point scale ranging from "not at all important" to "crucial." An example is presented.

Reliability: Coefficient alpha was .84.

Validity: Correlations with other variables ranged from −.34 to .54.

Author: Dulebohn, J. H., et al.

Article: Selection among employer-sponsored pension plans: The role of individual differences.

Journal: *Personnel Psychology,* Summer 2000, *53*(2), 405–432.

9829

Test Name: INVOLVEMENT PREFERENCE SCALE

Purpose: To assess preference for involvement with one's retirement plan.

Number of Items: 3

Format: Responses are made on a 5-point Likert-type scale ranging from "strongly disagree" to "strongly agree." A sample item is given.

Reliability: Coefficient alpha was .69.

Validity: Correlations with other variables ranged from −.28 to .77.

Author: Dulebohn, J. H., et al.

Article: Selection among employer-sponsored pension plans: The role of individual differences.

Journal: *Personnel Psychology,* Summer 2000, *53*(2), 405–432.

Related Research: Laurent, G., & Kapferer, J. N. (1985). Measuring consumer involvement profiles. *Journal of Marketing Research, 22,* 41–53.

9830

Test Name: LEISURE INTERESTS SURVEY

Purpose: To measure leisure interests.

Number of Items: 26

Format: Feminine and masculine leisure activities are included. Responses are made on a 4-point scale ranging from "not at all interested" to "very interested."

Reliability: Alpha coefficients ranged from .62 to .84.

Author: Updegraff, K. A., et al.

Article: Adolescents' sex-typed friendship experiences: Does having a sister versus having a brother matter?

Journal: *Child Development,* November/December 2000, *71*(6), 1597–1610.

Related Research: McHale, S. M., et al. (1999). Family context and gender socialization in middle childhood: Comparing girls to boys and sisters to brothers. *Child Development, 70,* 990–1004.

9831

Test Name: LESBIAN-GAY IDENTITY SCALES

Purpose: To measure lesbian-gay identity.

Number of Items: 40

Format: Scales range from 1 (disagree strongly) to 7 (agree strongly). All items are presented.

Reliability: Alpha coefficients ranged from .65 to .97 across subscales and samples.

Validity: Correlations with other variables ranged from −.47 to .59.

Author: Mohr, J., and Fassinger, R.

Article: Measuring dimensions of lesbian and gay male experience.

Journal: *Measurement and Evaluation in Counseling and Development,* July 2000, *33*(2), 66–90.

9832

Test Name: MALE ROLE NORMS SCALE

Purpose: To assess masculine gender role ideology.

Number of Items: 26

Format: Includes 4 subscales: Rationality/Respect/Status, Antifemininity, Façade, and Physical Violence. Responses are made on a 7-point Likert-type scale ranging from 1 (strongly disagree) to 7 (strongly agree). An example is presented.

Reliability: Alpha coefficients ranged from .37 to .68.

Validity: Correlations with other variables ranged from −10 to .32.

Author: Goodyear, R. K., et al.

Article: Predictors of Latino men's paternity in teen pregnancy: Test of a mediational model of childhood experiences, gender role attitudes, and behaviors.

Journal: *Journal of Counseling*

Psychology, January 2000, *47*(1), 116–128.

Related Research: Thompson, E. H., & Pleck, J. H. (1986). The structure of male role norms. *American Behavioral Scientist, 29*, 531–543.

9833

Test Name: MATH–SCIENCE INTENTIONS SCALE

Purpose: To measure math–science intentions.

Number of Items: 6

Format: Responses are made on a 5-point scale. Examples are presented.

Reliability: Internal consistency was .81.

Validity: Validity corrected for attenuation was .66.

Author: Fouad, N. A., and Smith, P. L.

Article: A test of a social cognitive model for middle school students: Math and science.

Journal: *Journal of Counseling Psychology*, July 1996, *43*(3), 338–346.

9834

Test Name: ON-CAMPUS HOUSING QUESTIONNAIRE

Purpose: To assess reasons for living on campus.

Number of Items: 14

Format: Scales range from 1 (not an influence at all) to 5 (very influential). All items are presented.

Reliability: Coefficient alpha was .76.

Author: Luzzo, D. A., and McDonald, A.

Article: Exploring students' reasons for living on campus.

Journal: *Journal of College Student Development*, July/August 1996, *37*(4), 389–395.

Related Research: Wolfe, J. W. (1993). Institutional integration, academic success, and persistence of first-year commuter and resident students. *Journal of College Student Development, 34*, 321–326.

9835

Test Name: OPENNESS TO DIVERSITY/CHALLENGE SCALE

Purpose: To assess openness to cultural, racial, and value diversity.

Number of Items: 8

Format: Scales range from 1 (strongly disagree) to 5 (strongly agree). All items are presented.

Reliability: Alpha coefficients ranged from .83 to .84.

Validity: Correlations with other variables ranged from −.10 to .36.

Author: Flowers, L., and Pascarella, E. T.

Article: Does college racial composition influence the openness to diversity of African American students?

Journal: *Journal of College Student Development*, July/August 1999, *40*(4), 405–417.

9836

Test Name: ORGANICISM–MECHANISM PARADIGM INVENTORY

Purpose: To assess preference for one of two worldviews: organicism and mechanism.

Number of Items: 26

Format: Forced-choice format.

Reliability: Split-half reliability was .86.

Author: Chapell, M. S., and Takahashi, M.

Article: Differences in worldviews of Japanese and Americans in young, middle-aged, and older cohorts.

Journal: *Psychological Reports*, October 1998, *83*(2), 659–665.

Related Research: Germer, C. K., et al. (1982). *The Organicism–Mechanism Paradigm Inventory: Toward the measurement of metaphysical assumptions*. Paper presented at the 53rd annual meeting of the Eastern Psychological Association, Baltimore, MD.

9837

Test Name: PERSONAL ATTRIBUTES QUESTIONNAIRE

Purpose: To assess two latent variables reflecting gender identity.

Number of Items: 16

Format: Includes two indicators: lack of the latent variables masculinity and femininity. Responses are made on a 5-point scale ranging from 0 to 4.

Reliability: Alpha coefficients were .85 and .82. Test-retest (2.5 months) reliability was approximately .60

Validity: Correlations with other variables ranged from −.40 to .52

Author: Bruch, M. A., et al.

Article: Shyness, masculine ideology, physical attractiveness, and emotional inexpressiveness: Testing a mediational model of mens' interpersonal competence

Journal: *Journal of Counseling Psychology*, April 1998, *45*(1), 143–149.

Related Research: Spence, J. T., et al. (1974). Ratings of self and peers on gender-role attributes and their relation to self-esteem, and conceptions of masculinity and femininity. *Journal of Personality and Social Psychology*, 32, 29–39.

9838

Test Name: PERSONAL ATTRIBUTES QUESTIONNAIRE

Purpose: To assess masculinity and femininity.

Number of Items: 24

Format: Responses are made along a 5-point continuum. Sample items are presented.

Reliability: Internal consistency estimates were .82 and .85. Test-retest reliabilities ranged from .54 to .67.

Author: Heesacker, M., et al.

Article: Gender-based emotional stereotyping.

Journal: *Journal of Counseling Psychology*, October 1999, 46(4), 483–495.

Related Research: Spence, J. T., et al. (1974). A measure of sex, gender, and emotion: Accuracy, sex-role stereotyping, and masculinity and femininity. *JSAS Catalog of Selected Documents in Psychology*, 4, 43.

9839

Test Name: PERSONAL–VOCATIONAL PROBLEM PREFERENCE SCALE

Purpose: To measure counseling psychologists' preference for working with personal versus career problems.

Number of Items: 7

Format: Each pair of personal–vocational problems is rated on a

9-point scale ranging from 1 (very strong preference for one) to 5 (very strong preference for the other).

Reliability: Internal consistencies were .92 and .88.

Author: Spengler, P. M.

Article: Does vocational overshadowing even exist? A test of the robustness of the vocational overshadowing bias.

Journal: *Journal of Counseling Psychology*, July 2000, 47(3), 342–351.

Related Research: Spengler, P. M., et al. (1990). Diagnostic and treatment overshadowing of vocational problems by personal problems. *Journal of Counseling Psychology*, 37, 372–381.

9840

Test Name: PREFERENCE FOR NUMERICAL INFORMATION SCALE

Purpose: To measure the proclivity to use numerical information and think in numerical terms.

Number of Items: 20

Format: Seven-point scales are anchored by 1 (I totally disagree) and 7 (I totally agree). All items are presented.

Reliability: Cronbach alpha was .80.

Author: Alkhateeb, H. M., and Abed, A. S.

Article: Preference for numerical information among Arab students.

Journal: *Psychological Reports*, April 2000, 86(2), 483–486.

Related Research: Viswanathan, M. (1994). On the test-retest reliability of the Preference for Numerical Information Scale.

Psychological Reports, 75, 285–286.

9841

Test Name: PRIMARY TEACHER QUESTIONNAIRE

Purpose: To assess teachers' endorsement of developmentally appropriate practices.

Number of Items: 42

Format: Includes 2 subscales: Developmentally Appropriate Practice and Traditional Practice. Responses are made on a 4-point Likert type scale ranging from 1 (strongly disagree) to 4 (strongly agree).

Reliability: Alpha coefficients were .80 and .87.

Validity: Correlations with other variables ranged from −.34 to .58.

Author: Smith, K. E., and Croom, L.

Article: Multidimensional self-concepts of children and teacher beliefs about developmentally appropriate practices.

Journal: *Journal of Educational Research*, May/June 2000, 93(5), 312–321.

Related Research: Smith, K. (1993). Development of the Primary Teacher Questionnaire. *The Journal of Educational Research*, 87, 23–29.

9842

Test Name: PROBLEMS IN SCHOOLS QUESTIONNAIRE

Purpose: To assess control versus autonomy orientations in teachers.

Number of Items: 32

Format: Includes 8 vignettes, each followed by 4 items referred to as subscales. Responses are made on a 7-point scale.

Reliability: Alpha coefficients ranged from .73 to .80. Test-retest reliabilities ranged from .77 to .82.

Author: Moyer, P. S., and Husman, J.

Article: The development of autonomy orientations as part of teacher development: What's experience got to do with it?

Journal: *Journal of Research and Development in Education*, Fall 2000, 34(1), 40–48.

Related Research: Deci, E. L., et al. (1981). An instrument to assess adults' orientations toward control versus autonomy with children: Reflections on intrinsic motivation and perceived competence. *Journal of Educational Psychology*, 73, 642–650.

9843

Test Name: RELIANCE ON VISUAL IMAGERY SCALE

Purpose: To screen for cognitive preferences.

Number of Items: 10

Format: Responses are true-false.

Reliability: Internal consistency was .90 (N = 39). Test-retest reliability was .91 (N = 39).

Validity: Correlation with Individual Differences Questionnaire was .90.

Author: Weatherly, D. C., et al.

Article: Reliance on visual imagery and its relation to mental rotation.

Journal: *Perceptual and Motor Skills*, October 1997, 85(2), 431–434.

Related Research: Paivio, A., & Harshman, R. (1983). Factor analysis of a questionnaire on

imagery and verbal habits and skills. *Canadian Journal of Psychology*, 37, 461–483.

9844

Test Name: ROLE BALANCE SCALE

Purpose: To measure the extent to which individuals disproportionately commit themselves to selected roles or to all roles equally.

Number of Items: 8

Format: All items are presented.

Reliability: Coefficient alpha was .68.

Author: Marks, S. R., and MacDermid, S. M.

Article: Multiple roles and the self: A theory of role balance.

Journal: *Journal of Marriage and the Family*, May 1996, 58(2), 417–432.

Related Research: Marks, S. R. (1977). Multiple roles and role strain: Some notes on human energy, time, and commitment. *American Sociological Review*, 42, 921–936.

9845

Test Name: SEX ROLE BEHAVIOR SCALE—SHORT FORM

Purpose: To assess sex-role orientation.

Number of Items: 96

Format: Includes 3 subscales: Male-Valued, Female-Valued, and Sex-Specific. Responses are made on a 5-point scale ranging from 1 (not at all characteristic of me) to 5 (extremely characteristic of me).

Reliability: Internal consistency correlation coefficients ranged from .83 to .92.

Author: Johnson, M. E., et al.

Article: Concurrent validity of the MMPI-2, Feminine Gender Role (GF), and Masculine Gender Role (GM) scales.

Journal: *Journal of Personality Assessment*, February 1996, 66(1), 153–168.

Related Research: Orlofsky, J. L., & O'Heron, C. A. (1987). *Journal of Personality Assessment*, 51, 267–277.

9846

Test Name: SEX ROLE IDEOLOGY SCALE

Purpose: To measure a continuum of beliefs about sex role from traditional to feminist.

Number of Items: 30

Format: Scales range from 1 (strongly disagree) to 7 (strongly agree).

Reliability: Coefficient alpha was .79. Test-retest reliability was .87.

Author: Johnson, M. E., et al.

Article: Sex role conflict, social desirability, and eating-disorder attitudes and behaviors.

Journal: *Journal of General Psychology*, January 1996, 123(1), 75–87.

Related Research: Kalin, R., & Tilby, P. J. (1978). Sex Role Ideology Scale. *Psychological Reports*, 42, 732–737.

9847

Test Name: SEX-ROLE IDEOLOGY SCALE— PORTUGUESE SHORT FORM

Purpose: To measure prescriptive beliefs about behavior appropriate for men and women.

Number of Items: 14

Reliability: Alpha was .83.

Validity: Correlation with full form was .89.

Author: Neto, F.

Article: A Portuguese short form of the Sex-Role Ideology Scale.

Journal: *Psychological Reports*, December 1998, *83*(3) Part 1, 1104–1106.

Related Research: Kalin, R., & Tilby, P. J. (1978). Development and validation of a sex-role ideology scale. *Psychological Reports*, *42*, 731–738.

9848

Test Name: SEXUAL ORIENTATION DISCLOSURE QUESTIONNAIRE

Purpose: To assess sexual orientation disclosure.

Number of Items: 5

Format: Response to one item is on a 6-point scale ranging from 5 (to all) to 0 (out to nobody at work). Responses to the remaining four items are on a 3-point scale running from 3 (always) to 1 (never). All items are presented.

Reliability: Coefficient alpha was .52.

Validity: Correlation with climate was .41. Correlations with other variables were not significant.

Author: Driscoll, J. M., et al.

Article: Lesbian identity and disclosure in the workplace: Relation to occupational stress and satisfaction.

Journal: *Journal of Vocational Behavior*, April 1996, *48*(2), 229–242.

9849

Test Name: SOCIOSEXUAL ORIENTATION INVENTORY

Purpose: To measure sociosexual orientation.

Number of Items: 9

Format: Multiple formats are used. Items are described.

Reliability: Coefficient alpha was .88.

Validity: Correlations with other variables ranged from −.37 to .30.

Author: Reise, S. P., and Wright, T. M.

Article: Personality traits, cluster B personality disorders, and sociosexuality.

Journal: *Journal of Research in Personality*, March 1996, *30*(1), 128–136.

Related Research: Simpson, J. A., & Gangestad, S. W. (1992). Sociosexuality and romantic partner choice. *Journal of Personality*, *60*, 31–51.

Wright, T. M., & Reise, S. P. (1997). Personality and unrestricted sexual behavior: Correlations of sociosexuality in Caucasian and Asian college students. *Journal of Research in Personality*, *31*, 166–192.

9850

Test Name: TRADITIONAL ROLE IDENTIFICATION SCALES

Purpose: To assess identification with career role and parenting role.

Number of Items: 12

Format: Seven-point scales are anchored by 1 (low involvement in the role) and 7 (very high involvement).

Reliability: Alphas were .55 (career role) and .66 (parenting role).

Validity: Correlations with other variables ranged from −.11 to .05.

Author: Arnold, E. H., et al.

Article: Father involvement and self-reported parenting of children with attention deficit-hyperactivity disorder.

Journal: *Journal of Consulting and Clinical Psychology*, April 1997, *65*(2), 337–342.

Related Research: Barling, J., & MacEwen, K. E. (1988). A multitrait-multimethod analysis of four maternal employment role experiences. *Journal of Organizational Behavior*, *9*, 335–344.

9851

Test Name: UNIVERSITY NEW STUDENT CENSUS— COMPUTER AVERSION SCALE

Purpose: To assess a student's aversion towards computers.

Number of Items: 8

Format: Multiple-choice, fill-in-the-blank, and Likert items are used.

Reliability: Coefficient alpha was .82.

Author: Suthakaran, V., and Sedlacek, W. E.

Article: Computer aversion among students with and without learning disabilities.

Journal: *Journal of College Student Development*, July/August 1999, *40*(4), 428–431.

Related Research: University of Maryland Counseling Center. (1996). *University new student census*. College Park, MD: Author.

9852

Test Name: WORK-RELATED GENDER ROLE IDENTITY AND WORK ROLE IDENTITY SCALES

Purpose: To assess mothers' and daughters' gender role ideology and work role identity.

Number of Items: 14

Format: Ideology scales range from 3 (all right) to 1 (not all right). Work identity scales used several two-point scales. All items are presented.

Reliability: Alpha coefficients ranged from .48 to .76 across subscales and time of testing.

Author: Moen, P., et al.

Article: Their mothers' daughters? The intergenerational transmission of gender attitudes in a world of changing roles.

Journal: *Journal of Marriage and the Family,* May 1997, *59*(2), 281–293.

Related Research: Dean, J. P., & Williams, R. M., Jr. (1956). *Social and cultural factors affecting role-conflict and adjustment among American women: A pilot investigation.* Progress report submitted to the National Institute of Mental Health, Bethesda, MD.

• • •

CHAPTER 19
Problem Solving and Reasoning

9853

Test Name: BREAST CANCER DECISION-MAKING QUESTIONNAIRE

Purpose: To measure expectancy and value constructs regarding breast cancer treatments in terms of physician support, partner support, attractiveness to partner, consequences for self-evaluation, likelihood of cure, and likelihood of additional treatment.

Number of Items: 54

Format: Seven-point scales are anchored by various response categories.

Reliability: Alpha coefficients ranged from .82 to .91.

Author: Stanton, A. L., et al.

Article: Treatment decision making and adjustment to breast cancer: A longitudinal study.

Journal: *Journal of Consulting and Clinical Psychology*, April 1998, *66*(2), 313–322.

Related Research: Ward, S., et al. (1989). Factors women take into account when deciding upon type of surgery for breast cancer. *Cancer Nursing, 12*, 344–351.

9854

Test Name: CAREER DECISION-MAKING DIFFICULTIES QUESTIONNAIRE

Purpose: To identify career decision-making difficulties.

Number of Items: 44

Format: Responses are made on a 9-point scale.

Reliability: Interquartile ranges of alpha coefficients extended from .60 to .87. Test-retest (2 weeks) reliabilities ranged from .67 to .80.

Author: Gati, I., et al.

Article: Validity of the Career Decision-Making Difficulties Questionnaire: Counselee versus career counselor perceptions.

Journal: *Journal of Vocational Behavior,* February 2000, *56*(1), 99–113.

Related Research: Gati, I., et al. (1996). A taxonomy of difficulties in career decision making. *Journal of Counseling Psychology, 43*, 510–526.

9855

Test Name: CAREER DECISION PROFILE

Purpose: To assess how decided individuals are and how comfortable they are with their decisions and career decision needs.

Number of Items: 16

Format: Includes 6 subscales: Decidedness, Comfort, Self-Clarity, Knowledge About Occupations, Decisiveness, and Career Importance. Responses are made on an 8-point Likert scale ranging from 1 (strongly disagree) to 8 (strongly agree).

Reliability: Internal consistency estimates range from .60 to .89. Test-retest (3 weeks) reliability coefficients ranged from .66 to .80.

Validity: Correlations with other variables ranged from −.29 to .56.

Author: Heppner, M. J., et al.

Article: The relationship of trainee self-efficacy to the process and outcome of career counseling.

Journal: *Journal of Counseling Psychology*, October 1998, *45*(4), 393–402.

Related Research: Jones, L. K. (1989). Measuring a three-dimensional construct of career decision among college students: A revision of the Vocational Decision Scale—The Career Decision Profile. *Journal of Counseling Psychology, 36*, 477–486.

9856

Test Name: CATEGORICAL THINKING SUBSCALE

Purpose: To measure categorical thinking.

Number of Items: 3

Format: Responses are made on a 6-point scale ranging from 1 (disagree strongly) to 6 (agree strongly). All items are presented.

Validity: Correlations with other variables ranged from −.46 to .56.

Author: Sa, W. C., et al.

Article: The domain specificity and generality of belief bias: Searching for a generalizable critical thinking skill.

Journal: *Journal of Educational*

Psychology, September 1999, *91*(3), 497–510.

Related Research: Epstein, S., & Meier, P. (1989). Constructive thinking: A broad coping variable with specific components. *Journal of Personality and Social Psychology*, 57, 332–350.

9857

Test Name: COGNITIVE LEARNING SCALE

Purpose: To assess cognitive learning about computers.

Number of Items: 18

Format: True/false and multiple-choice formats are used. Sample items are presented.

Reliability: Coefficient alpha was .83.

Author: Simon, S. J., and Werner, J. M.

Article: Computer training through behavior modeling, self-paced, and instructional approaches: A field experiment.

Journal: *Journal of Applied Psychology*, December 1996, *81*(6), 648–659.

Related Research: Winter, S. J., et al. (1992). *Misplaced resources? Factors associated with computer literacy among end-users.* Paper presented at the 13th annual International Conference on Information Systems, Dallas, TX.

9858

Test Name: COGNITIVE RESTRUCTURING SCALE

Purpose: To assess cognitive restructuring.

Number of Items: 9

Format: Five-point scales are anchored by 1 (not at all) and 5

(very much). Sample items are presented.

Reliability: Average alpha coefficient was .84.

Author: Tix, A. P., and Frazier, P. A.

Article: The use of religious coping during stressful life events: Main effects, moderation, and mediation.

Journal: *Journal of Consulting and Clinical Psychology*, April 1998, *66*(2), 411–422.

Related Research: Tobin, D. L., et al. (1989). The hierarchical factor structure of the Coping Strategies Inventory. *Cognitive Therapy and Research*, *13*, 343–361.

9859

Test Name: COGNITIVE SPONTANEITY SCALE

Purpose: To measure cognitive spontaneity.

Number of Items: 22

Format: Items are adjectives to which responses are made on a 7-point scale ranging from 1 (strongly disagree) to 7 (strongly agree).

Reliability: Coefficient alpha was .80.

Author: Bozionelos, N.

Article: Cognitive spontaneity and learning style.

Journal: *Perceptual and Motor Skills*, August 1996, *83*(1), 43–48.

Related Research: Webster, J., & Martocchio, J. J. (1992). Microcomputer playfulness: Development of a measure with workplace implications. *MIS Quarterly*, *16*, 201–226.

9860

Test Name: COGNITIVE STRATEGIES SCALE

Purpose: To measure cognitive strategies.

Number of Items: 16

Format: Includes 2 scales: General Cognitive and Metacognitive. Responses are made on a 7-point Likert scale ranging from 1 (strongly disagree) to 7 (strongly agree). Sample items are presented.

Reliability: Alpha coefficients ranged from .64 to .88.

Author: Pintrich, P. R.

Article: Multiple goals, multiple pathways: The role of goal orientation in learning and achievement.

Journal: *Journal of Educational Psychology*, September 2000, *92*(3), 544–555.

Related Research: Pintrich, P. R., & DeGroot, E. V. (1990). Motivational and self-regulated learning components of classroom academic performance. *Journal of Educational Psychology, 82,* 33–40.

9861

Test Name: COGNITIVE STYLE INDEX

Purpose: To measure the cognitive style as an intuitive/analytical dimension.

Number of Items: 38

Time Required: 10 minutes

Format: True/false/uncertain format.

Reliability: Alphas ranged from .75 to .80.

Validity: Females scored higher than males ($p = .05$).

Author: Murphy, H. J., et al.

Article: Test-retest reliability and construct validity of the Cognitive Style Index for business undergraduates.

Journal: *Psychological Reports*, April 1998, *82*(2), 595–600.

Related Research: Allison, C. W., & Hayes, J. (1996). The Cognitive Style Index: A measure of intuition-analysis for organizational research. *Journal of Management Studies*, *33*, 119–135.

9862

Test Name: CONCEPTIONS OF LEARNING INVENTORY

Purpose: To measure secondary students' conceptions of learning.

Number of Items: 45

Format: Includes 9 categories: Increasing One's Knowledge, Memorizing and Producing, Means to an End, Understanding, Seeing Something in a Different Way, Personal Fulfillment, Duty, Process not Bound by Time or Context, and Developing Social Competence. Responses are made on a 6-point scale ranging from 6 (very strongly agree) to 1 (strongly disagree).

Reliability: Alpha coefficients ranged from .74 to .88.

Author: Dart, B. C., et al.

Article: Students' conceptions of learning, the classroom environment, and approaches to learning.

Journal: *Journal of Educational Research*, March/April 2000, *93*(4), 262–270.

Related Research: Purdie, N., & Hattie, J. (1997, August). *The development and validation of an instrument to assess students' conceptions of learning*. Paper presented at the 70th Conference of the European Association for Research in Learning and Instruction, Athens, Greece.

9863

Test Name: CONCISE NEUROPSYCHOLOGICAL SCREENING INVENTORY (CNSI)

Purpose: To assess 10 vital left- and right-hemisphere brain functions.

Number of Items: 100

Format: Items are scored 1 (correct) or 0 (incorrect).

Reliability: Alphas were .89 (Part I) and .91 (Part II). Guttman split-half reliability was .91. Test-retest reliabilities (10 days) ranged from .61 to .96 across subscales.

Validity: Overall classification efficiency was 74.4%. Correlations between subscales ranged from .38 to .84.

Author: Lecci, L., and Holler, R. E.

Article: Development and preliminary validation of the Concise Neuropsychological Screening Inventory (CNSI): A clinical tool for use in psychiatric settings.

Journal: *Journal of Psychopathology and Behavioral Assessment*, December 1996, *18*(4), 315–330.

9864

Test Name: FLEXIBLE THINKING SCALE

Purpose: To measure flexible thinking.

Number of Items: 10

Format: Responses are made on a 6-point scale ranging from 1 (disagree strongly) to 6 (agree strongly). All items are presented.

Validity: Correlation with other variables ranged from −.53 to .46.

Author: Sa, W. C., et al.

Article: The domain specificity and generality of belief bias: Searching for a generalizable critical thinking skill.

Journal: *Journal of Educational Psychology*, September 1999, *91*(3), 497–510.

Related Research: Stanovich, K. E., & West, R. F. (1997). Reasoning independently of prior belief and individual differences in actively open-minded thinking. *Journal of Educational Psychology*, *89*, 342–357.

9865

Test Name: GENERAL-DECISION MAKING STYLE SCALE

Purpose: To assess different patterns of decision-making style.

Number of Items: 25

Format: Includes 5 factors: Rational, Intuitive, Dependent, Spontaneous, and Avoidant. Responses are made on a 5-point Likert scale ranging from 1 (strongly disagree) to 5 (strongly agree). Examples are presented.

Reliability: Internal consistencies ranged from .68 to .94.

Validity: Correlations of 3 factors with other variables ranged from −.26 to .29.

Author: Rochlen, A. B., et al.

Article: Development of the Attitudes Toward Career Counseling Scale.

Journal: *Journal of Counseling Psychology*, April 1999, *46*(2), 196–206.

Related Research: Scott, S. G., & Bruce, R. A. (1995). Decision-making style: The development and assessment of a new measure. *Educational and Psychological Measurement*, *55*, 818–831.

9866

Test Name: GROUP SOCIAL PROBLEM SOLVING MEASURE

Purpose: To measure children's social problem solving.

Number of Items: 24

Format: Includes 12 possible solutions to be rated for each of two interpersonal problems. Responses are made on a 5-point scale ranging from 1 (very good) to 5 (very bad).

Reliability: Interrater reliabilities ranged from .73 to .89.

Author: Fagen, D. B., et al.

Article: Relationships between parent-child relational variables and child test variables in highly stressed urban families.

Journal: *Child Study Journal*, 1996, *26* (2), 87–108.

Related Research: Work, W. C. (1986). *The Social Problem Solving Cognitive Measure.* Unpublished manuscript, University of Rochester.

9867

Test Name: GROUPTHINK DEFECTIVE DECISION-MAKING SCALE

Purpose: To measure the symptoms of groupthink and defective decision making.

Number of Items: 12

Format: Six-point scales ranged from "strongly disagree" to "strongly agree." All items are presented.

Reliability: Alpha coefficients ranged from .45 to .85 across subscales.

Validity: Correlations with other variables ranged from −.51 to .65.

Author: Choi, J. N., and Kim, M. U.

Article: The organizational application of groupthink and its limitations in organizations.

Journal: *Journal of Applied Psychology*, April 1999, *84*(2), 297–306.

Related Research: Manz, C. C., & Sims, H. P., Jr. (1982). The potential for "groupthink" in autonomous work groups. *Human Relations, 35,* 773–784.

9868

Test Name: HEAD OVER HEART SCALE

Purpose: To measure an individual's report of relying on rationally or intuitively acquired knowledge.

Number of Items: 16

Format: Responses are made on a 5-point scale ranging from 1 (completely false) to 5 (completely true). A sample item is presented.

Reliability: Coefficient alpha was .82.

Author: Klaczynski, P. A.

Article: Motivated scientific reasoning biases, epistemological beliefs, and theory polarization: A two-process approach to adolescent cognition.

Journal: *Child Development*, September/October 2000, *71*(5), 1347–1366.

Related Research: Epstein, S., et al. (1995). *Individual differences in heuristic processing.* Unpublished manuscript, University of Massachusetts, Amherst.

9869

Test Name: INSTRUCTIONAL QUESTIONNAIRE

Purpose: To show similarities and differences in concept-oriented reading instruction and traditional instruction.

Number of Items: 75

Format: Includes 7 bipolar scales: Conceptual Theme, Real-World Observation, Self-Direction, Strategy Instruction, Collaboration, Self-Expression, and Coherence. Responses are made on a 4-point scale ranging from 1 (very true of my class) to 4 (not at all true of my class).

Reliability: Reliabilities ranged from .47 to .91.

Author: Guthrie, J. T., et al.

Article: Effects of integrated instruction on motivation and strategy use in reading.

Journal: *Journal of Educational Psychology*, June 2000, *92*(2), 331–341.

Related Research: Guthrie, J. T., et al. (1996). Growth of literacy engagement: Changes in motivations and strategies during concept-oriented reading instruction. *Reading Research Quarterly, 31,* 306–332.

9870

Test Name: INTENDED PLANNING SCALE

Purpose: To assess planning activities that could be used in product promotion.

Number of Items: 8

Format: Scales range from 1 (strongly disagree) to 5 (strongly agree). Sample items are presented.

Reliability: Alpha coefficients ranged from .74 to .80 across subscales.

Validity: Correlations with other variables ranged from .17 to .69.

Author: VandeWalle, D., et al.

Article: The influences of goal orientation and self-regulation tactics on sales performance: A longitudinal field test.

Journal: *Journal of Applied Psychology*, April 1999, *84*(2), 249–259.

Related Research: Brown, S. P., et al. (1997). Effects of goal-directed emotions on salesperson volitions, behavior and performance: A longitudinal study. *Journal of Marketing, 61,* 39–50.

9871

Test Name: KIRTON ADAPTION INNOVATION SURVEY

Purpose: To measure employee cognitive style.

Number of Items: 32

Format: Responses are made on a 6-point scale.

Reliability: Coefficient alpha was .86.

Validity: Correlations with other variables ranged from −.19 to .35.

Author: Tierney, P., et al.

Article: An examination of leadership and employee creativity: The relevance traits and relationships.

Journal: *Personnel Psychology,* Autumn 1999, *52*(3), 591–620.

Related Research: Kirton, M. J. (1976). Adaptors and innovators: A description and measure. *Journal of Applied Psychology, 61,* 622–629.

9872

Test Name: LEADERSHIP ATTITUDES AND BELIEFS SCALE

Purpose: To measure systemic thinking ánd hierarchical thinking.

Number of Items: 28

Format: Scales range from 1 (strongly agree) to 5 (strongly disagree).

Reliability: Alpha coefficients ranged from .84 to .88.

Validity: In 14 two-group comparisons, 10 produced significant *t*-test values ($p < .05$).

Author: Wielkiewicz, R. M.

Article: The Leader Attitudes and Beliefs Scale: An instrument for evaluating college students' thinking about leadership organizations.

Journal: *Journal of College Student Development*, May/June 2000, *41*(3), 335–346.

9873

Test Name: LEARNING AWARENESS QUESTIONNAIRE

Purpose: To assess learning awareness as semantic content, response strategy, processing strategy, summarization, and memory.

Number of Items: 16

Format: All items are presented.

Reliability: Split-half reliabilities ranged from .61 to .79.

Author: Kumar, S., et al.

Article: Responses of low IQ students on the Learning Awareness Questionnaire compared to students matched on mental and chronological age.

Journal: *Psychological Reports*, October 1999, *85*(2), 433–437.

Related Research: Kumar, S., & Harizuka, S. (1998). Cooperative learning-based approach and development of learning awareness and achievement in mathematics in elementary school. *Psychological Reports, 82,* 587–591.

9874

Test Name: LEARNING STRATEGIES QUESTIONNAIRE

Purpose: To identify learning strategies.

Number of Items: 17

Format: Includes the learning strategies of rehearsal, organizing, and elaboration. Responses are made on a 5-point Likert scale.

Reliability: Alpha coefficients ranged form .71 to .80.

Validity: Correlations with other variables ranged from −.20 to .36.

Author: Fisher, S. L., and Ford, J. K.

Article: Differential effects of learner effort and goal orientation on two learning outcomes.

Journal: *Personnel Psychology*, Summer 1998, *51*(2), 397–420.

Related Research: Schmeck, R. R. (1988). Individual differences and learning strategies. In Weinstein, C. E., et al. (Eds.), *Learning and study strategies: Issues in assessment, instruction and evaluation* (pp. 171–191). San Diego: Academic Press.

9875

Test Name: LEARNING STRATEGIES SCALE

Purpose: To assess awareness and regulation of general cognitive strategies.

Number of Items: 25

Format: Scales range from "not at all" to "very helpful" on knowledge and use scales.

Reliability: Reliability coefficients were .93 (knowledge) and .89 (usage).

Author: Chan, L. K. S.

Article: Motivational orientations and metacognitive abilities of intellectually gifted children.

Journal: *Gifted Child Quarterly,* Fall 1996, *40*(4), 184–193.

Related Research: Chan, L. K. S. (1994). Relationship of motivation, strategic learning and reading achievement in Grades 5, 7, and 9. *Journal of Experimental Education, 62,* 319–339.

9876

Test Name: METACOGNITION ACTIVITY SCALE

Purpose: To measure to what extent subjects engage in metacognitive activity.

Number of Items: 12

Format: Five-point scales are anchored by 1 (strongly disagree) and 5 (strongly agree). A sample item is presented.

Reliability: Coefficient alpha was .83.

Validity: Correlations with other variables ranged from −.06 to .38.

Author: Ford, J. K., et al.

Article: Relationships of goal orientation, metacognitive activity, and practice strategies with learning outcomes and transfer.

Journal: *Journal of Applied Psychology,* April 1998, *83*(2), 218–233.

9877

Test Name: OUT-OF-SCHOOL LEARNING STRATEGIES SCALE

Purpose: To measure whether students use motivational and

information-processing strategies in out-of-school endeavors.

Number of Items: 19

Format: Responses are "yes" or "no." All items are presented.

Reliability: Coefficient alpha was .86.

Validity: Correlations with other variables ranged from .02 to .48.

Author: Bergin, D. A.

Article: Adolescents' out-of-school learning strategies.

Journal: *Journal of Experimental Education,* Summer 1996, *64*(4), 309–323.

9878

Test Name: POLICE DECISION SCALE

Purpose: To measure the perceptions of the relative influence of police partners in making decisions.

Number of Items: 11

Format: Scales range from 1 (myself always) to 5 (my partner always).

Reliability: Coefficient alpha was .61.

Author: Gerber, G. L.

Article: Status in same-gender and mixed-gender police dyads: Effects on personality attributions.

Journal: *Social Psychology Quarterly,* December 1996, *59*(4), 350–363.

Related Research: Gerber, G. L., & Fortune, C. (1994). *The Police Decision Scale for police partners.* Unpublished manuscript, John Jay College of Criminal Justice, CUNY.

9879

Test Name: PROBLEM-SOLVING APPROACH SCALE

Number of Items: 4

Format: Five-point scales are anchored by opposing adjectives. All items are presented.

Reliability: Cronbach alpha was .74.

Validity: Correlations with other variables ranged from −.25 to .53.

Author: Mintu-Wimsatt, A., and Lozada, H. R.

Article: Personality and negotiation revisited.

Journal: *Psychological Reports,* June 1999, *84*(3) Part 2, 1159–1170.

Related Research: Graham, J., et al. (1994). Explorations of negotiation behaviors in ten foreign cultures using a model developed in the United States. *Management Science, 40,* 72–95.

9880

Test Name: PROBLEM SOLVING INVENTORY

Purpose: To assess self-perceptions of problem-solving behaviors and attitudes.

Number of Items: 32

Format: Scales range from 1 (strongly agree) to 6 (strongly disagree).

Reliability: Coefficient alpha was .90. Test-retest reliability (2 weeks) was .89.

Validity: Correlations with other variables ranged from −.16 (social desirability) to .61 (social control).

Author: Kahn, J. H., and Nauta, M. M.

Article: The influence of student problem-solving appraisal and nature of problem on likelihood of seeking counseling services.

Journal: *Journal of College*

Student Development, January/ February 1997, *38*(1), 32–39.

Related Research: Heppner, P. P., & Peterson, C. H. (1982). The development and implications of a personal problem-solving inventory. *Journal of Counseling Psychology, 29*, 66–75.

9881

Test Name: PROBLEM-SOLVING INVENTORY

Purpose: To assess general self-perceived problem-solving ability.

Number of Items: 36

Format: Six-point Likert format.

Reliability: Alpha coefficients ranged from .72 to .90. Test-retest reliabilities ranged from .83 to .89.

Author: Fraser, K. P., and Tucker, C. M.

Article: Individuation, stress, and problem-solving abilities of college students.

Journal: *Journal of College Student Development*, September/ October 1997, *38*(5), 461–467.

Related Research: D'Zurilla, T. J., & Goldfried, M. R. (1971). Problem-solving and behavior modification. *Journal of Abnormal Behavior, 65*, 321–327.

9882

Test Name: READING STRATEGIES SCALE

Purpose: To assess students' knowledge of and use of cognitive strategies.

Number of Items: 20

Format: Students rate each strategy for helpfulness and frequency on scales that range from "not at all" to "very helpful." A sample item is presented.

Reliability: Coefficient alpha was .86 (knowledge) and .85 (usage).

Author: Chan, L. K. S.

Article: Motivational orientations and metacognitive abilities of intellectually gifted children.

Journal: *Gifted Child Quarterly*, Fall 1996, *40*(4), 184–193.

Related Research: Chan, L. K. S. (1994). Relationship of motivation, strategic learning and reading achievement in Grades 5, 7, and 9. *Journal of Experimental Education, 62*, 319–339.

9883

Test Name: SOCIAL PROBLEM-SOLVING INVENTORY

Purpose: To measure social problem-solving that assesses problem orientation and problem-solving skills.

Number of Items: 70

Format: Five-point scales are anchored by 0 (not at all true of me) and 4 (extremely true of me).

Reliability: Alphas ranged from .92 to .94. Test-retest reliabilities (3 weeks) ranged from .83 to .88.

Validity: Correlations with other variables ranged from −.71 to .91.

Author: Clum, G. A., et al.

Article: An investigation of the validity of the SPSI and SPSI–R in differentiating high suicidal from depressed, low suicidal college students.

Journal: *Journal of Psychopathology and Behavioral Assessment*, June 1996, *18*(2), 119–132.

Related Research: D'Zurilla, T. J., & Nezu, A. M. (1990). Development and preliminary evaluation of the Social Problem-Solving Inventory. *Psychological Assessment: A Journal of*

Consulting and Clinical Psychology, 2, 156–163.

9884

Test Name: SOCIAL PROBLEM-SOLVING INVENTORY–35

Purpose: To assess self-appraised multiple dimensions of the problem-solving process.

Number of Items: 35

Format: Includes two scales: Problem-Solving Orientation and Problem-Solving Skills; and seven subscales.

Reliability: Alpha coefficients ranged from .71 to .94.

Author: Christiansen, N. D., et al.

Article: Evaluating the structural validity of measures of hierarchical models: An illustrative example using the Social Problem-Solving Inventory.

Journal: *Educational and Psychological Measurement*, August 1996, *56*(4), 600–625.

Related Research: D'Zurilla, T. J., & Nezu, A. M. (1990). Development and preliminary evaluation of the Social Problem-Solving Inventory. *Psychological Assessment: A Journal of Consulting and Clinical Psychology, 2*, 156–163.

9885

Test Name: STUDENT LEARNING STYLE SCALES

Purpose: To measure learning style.

Number of Items: 60

Format: Includes 6 scales: Independent, Avoidant, Collaborative, Dependent, Competitive, and Participative.

Reliability: Alpha coefficients ranged from .44 to .77.

Author: Ferrari, J. R., et al.

Article: Psychometric properties of the Revised Grasha–Riechmann Student Learning Style Scale.

Journal: *Educational and Psychological Measurement*, February 1996, *56*(6), 166–172.

Related Research: Riechmann, S. W., & Grasha, A. F. (1974). A rational approach to the construct validity of a Student Learning Style Scales instrument. *Journal of Psychology, 87*, 213–223.

9886

Test Name: STUDENT LEARNING SURVEY

Purpose: To identify students' learning strategies and their conceptions of learning.

Number of Items: 10

Format: A frequency scale ranging from 1 (seldom) to 4 (most of the time) is employed. All items are presented.

Reliability: k = .85 and .82.

Author: Purdie, N., et al.

Article: Student conceptions of learning and their use of self-regulated learning strategies: A cross-cultural comparison.

Journal: *Journal of Educational Psychology,* March 1996, *88*(1), 87–100.

Related Research: Zimmerman, B. J., & Martinez-Pons, M. (1986). Development of a structured interview for assessing student use of self-regulated learning strategies. *American Educational Research Journal, 73*, 614–628.

9887

Test Name: STUDY STRATEGIES QUESTIONNAIRE

Purpose: To measure students' strategies for studying their psychology course material and to measure performance expectations.

Number of Items: 16

Format: Includes 4 parts: Elaboration, Rehearsal, Lack of Strategy, and Mid-Semester Performance Expectations. All items are presented.

Validity: Correlations with other variables ranged from −.31 to .48.

Author: Harackiewicz, J. M., et al.

Article: Short-term and long-term consequences of achievement goals: Predicting interest and performance over time.

Journal: *Journal of Educational Psychology*, June 2000, *92*(2), 316–330.

Related Research: Pintrich, P. R., et al. (1993). Reliability and predictive validity of the Motivated Strategies for Learning Questionnaire (MSLQ). *Educational and Psychological Measurement, 53*, 801–813.

9888

Test Name: THINKING STYLES INVENTORY—SHORT VERSION

Purpose: To assess the thinking styles in the theory of mental self-government.

Number of Items: 65

Format: Seven-point scales are anchored by (1) statement does not characterize me at all and (7) statement characterizes me extremely well. Sample items are presented.

Reliability: Alphas ranged from .53 to .87.

Validity: Scale intercorrelations ranged from −.29 to .77. Most

were in the hypothesized direction.

Author: Zhang, L.-F. and Sachs, J.

Article: Assessing thinking styles in the theory of mental self-government: A Hong Kong validity study.

Journal: *Psychological Reports*, December 1997, *81*(3, Part I), 915–928.

Related Research: Sternberg, R. J., and Wagner, R. K. (1992). *Thinking styles inventory*. Unpublished manuscript, Yale University.

9889

Test Name: VOCATIONAL DECISION STYLE INDICATOR

Purpose: To measure individual variation along two dimensions of vocational decision-making style.

Number of Items: 40

Format: Includes 2 dimensions: Thinking versus Feeling and Internal, and Active, Decision-Making Posture versus External, Passive Posture. Responses are made on a 5-point scale ranging from 1 (always) to 5 (never).

Reliability: Alpha coefficients ranged from .77 to .89. Test-retest (2 weeks) reliabilities were .89 and .85.

Author: Bartley, D. F., and Robitschek, C.

Article: Career exploration: A multivariate analysis of predictors.

Journal: *Journal of Vocational Behavior*, February 2000, *56*(1), 63–81.

Related Research: Walsh, D. J. (1986). The construction and validation of a vocational decision-making style measure. *Dissertation Abstracts International, 46*, 2862B.

• • •

CHAPTER 20

Status

9890

Test Name: DELLAS IDENTITY STATUS INVENTORY— OCCUPATION

Purpose: To measure occupational identity.

Number of Items: 35

Format: Forced choice.

Reliability: Internal consistency coefficients ranged from .64 to .92.

Validity: Correlations with other variables ranged from .04 to .33.

Author: Munson, W. W., and Widmer, M. A.

Article: Leisure behavior and occupational identity in university students.

Journal: *Career Development Quarterly*, December 1997, *46*(2), 190–198.

Related Research: Dellas, M., & Jernigan, L. P. (1981). Development of an objective instrument to measure identity status in terms of occupation crisis and commitment. *Educational and Psychological Measurement*, 4, 1039–1050.

9891

Test Name: OCCUPATIONAL ATTAINMENT MEASURE

Purpose: To measure occupational attainment.

Number of Items: 3

Format: All items are presented.

Reliability: Coefficient alpha was .83.

Validity: Correlations with other variables ranged from −.07 to .37.

Author: Adams, G. A.

Article: Career-related variables and planned retirement age: An extension of Beehr's model.

Journal: *Journal of Vocational Behavior*, October 1999, *55*(2), 221–235.

Related Research: Tolaga, J. A., & Beehr, T. A. (1995). Are there gender differences in predicting retirement decisions? *Journal of Applied Psychology, 80,* 16–28.

9892

Test Name: TASK SIGNIFICANCE SCALE

Purpose: To measure importance of one's job.

Number of Items: 3

Format: Scales range from 1 (strongly disagree) to 5 (strongly agree). A sample item is presented.

Reliability: Coefficient alpha was .81.

Validity: Correlations with other variables ranged from −.23 to .60.

Author: Jex, S. M., and Bliese, P. D.

Article: Efficacy beliefs as a moderator of the impact of work-related stressors: A multilevel study.

Journal: *Journal of Applied Psychology*, June 1999, *84*(3), 349–361.

Related Research: Halverson, R. R., & Bliese, P. D. (1996). Determinants of soldier support for operation Uphold Democracy. *Armed Forces and Society, 23,* 81–96.

CHAPTER 21
Trait Measurement

9893

Test Name: A–B RATING SCALE (ARABIC VERSION)

Purpose: To measure Type A behavior.

Number of Items: 24

Format: Seven-point Likert format.

Reliability: Alpha was .69. Test-retest reliability was .82.

Validity: Correlations with other variables ranged from .42 to .55.

Author: Alkhadher, O.

Article: Association of Type A behavior and job performance in a sample of Kuwaiti workers.

Journal: *Psychological Reports*, August 1999, *85*(1), 189–196.

Related Research: Alnaser, H. (1996). Type A behavior and its relationship with neuroticism and extraversion. *Journal of Social Studies*, 24, 57–72.

9894

Test Name: ADAPTABILITY SCALE

Purpose: To measure adaptability.

Number of Items: 4

Format: Sample items are presented.

Reliability: Coefficient alpha was .74.

Validity: Correlation with other variables ranged from −.16 to .40.

Author: Kossek, E. E., et al.

Article: Career self-management: A quasi-experimental assessment of the effects of a training intervention.

Journal: *Personnel Psychology*, Winter 1998, *51*(4), 935–962.

Related Research: Lambert, S. (1993). *Personal communication.* Chicago: The University of Chicago.

9895

Test Name: AGGRESSION QUESTIONNAIRE—REVISED

Purpose: To measure aggression.

Number of Items: 26

Format: Includes 2 factors: Physical Aggression Anger and Verbal Aggression Hostility. Responses are made on a 5-point scale ranging from 1 (extremely uncharacteristic of me) to 5 (extremely characteristic of me).

Reliability: Alpha coefficients ranged from .86 to .93.

Validity: Correlations with other variables ranged from −.45 to .64.

Author: Sandoval, A.-M. R., et al.

Article: Construct validity of the Psychopathic Personality Inventory in a correctional sample.

Journal: *Journal of Personality Assessment*, April 2000, 74(2), 262–281.

Related Research: Buss, A. H., & Perry, M. (1992). The Aggression Questionnaire. *Journal of Personality and Social Psychology*, 63, 452–459.

9896

Test Name: ALMOST PERFECT SCALE

Purpose: To measure perfectionism.

Number of Items: 32

Format: Includes 4 subscales: Standards and Order, Anxiety, Procrastination, and Difficulty in Interpersonal Relationships. Responses are made on a 7-point scale, ranging from 1 (strongly disagree) to 7 (strongly agree).

Reliability: Internal reliability estimates ranges from .71 to .86. Test-retest (2 weeks) reliability ranged from .81 to 92. Test-retest (4 weeks) reliability ranged from .79 to .87.

Author: Rice, K. G., et al.

Article: Self-esteem as a mediator between perfectionism and depression: A structural equations analysis.

Journal: *Journal of Counseling Psychology*, July 1998, *45*(3), 304–314.

Related Research: Slaney, R. B., & Johnson, D. G.(1992). *The Almost Perfect Scale.* Unpublished manuscript, Pennsylvania State University.

9897

Test Name: ANTILL TRAIT QUESTIONNAIRE

Purpose: To provide a self-respect

measure of children's sex-type personality qualities.

Number of Items: 12

Format: Responses are made on a 5-point scale.

Reliability: Alpha coefficients were .79 (firstborns) and .74 (secondborns)

Author: Crouter, A. C., et al.

Article: Conditions underlying parents' knowledge about children's daily lives in middle childhood: Between and within family comparisons.

Journal: *Child Development*, January/February 1999, *70*(1), 246–259

Related Research: Spence, J. T., & Helmreich, R. L. (1972). The Attitudes Toward Women Scale: An objective instrument to measure attitudes toward the rights and roles of women in contemporary society. *JSAS Catalog of Selected Documents in Psychology*, 2, 153.

9898

Test Name: BATTERY OF INTERPERSONAL CAPABILITIES

Purpose: To measure interpersonal flexibility.

Number of Items: 80

Format: Includes 16 capabilities. Responses are made on a 7-point scale ranging from 1 (not at all) to 7 (very). Examples are presented.

Reliability: Alpha coefficients were .86 and .94. Test-retest (10 weeks) reliability was .86.

Author: Kivlighan, Jr., D. M., and Shaughnessy, P.

Article: Patterns of working alliance development: A typology of client's working alliance ratings.

Journal: *Journal of Counseling Psychology*, July 2000, *47*(3), 362–371.

Related Research: Paulhus, D. L., & Martin, C. L. (1987). The structure of personality capabilities. *Journal of Personality and Social Psychology*, 52, 354–365.

9899

Test Name: BORTNER RATING SCALE

Purpose: To measure Type A behavior.

Number of Items: 14

Format: Each item is a scale at the ends of which two extremes of behavior are labeled (one Type A, the other Type B).

Reliability: Reliability ranged from .53 to .68.

Validity: Agreement with structured interview data ranged from 45% to 75%.

Author: Moller, A. T., and Botha, H. C.

Article: Effects of a group-emotive behavior therapy program on the Type A behavior pattern.

Journal: *Psychological Reports*, June 1996, *78*(3) Part 1, 947–961.

Related Research: Bortner, R. W. (1969). A short rating scale as a potential measure of Pattern A behavior. *Journal of Chronic Diseases*, 22, 87–91.

9900

Test Name: BRESKIN RIGIDITY SCALE-REVISED

Purpose: To measure rigidity.

Number of Items: 13

Format: The respondent endorses a preference for one of two shapes.

Reliability: K-R Formula 20 reliability coefficients were .87 and .86.

Validity: Correlations with other variables ranged from −.06 to .25.

Author: Maltby, J., and Lewis, C. A.

Article: An examination of the reliability and validity of the Breskin Rigidity Scale.

Journal: *Perceptual and Motor Skills*, February 1996, *82*(1), 195–198.

Related Research: Breskin, S. (1968). Measurement of rigidity: A nonverbal test. *Perceptual and Motor Skills*, 27, 1203–1206.

9901

Test Name: BRIEF SCREENING INVENTORY FOR PERSONALITY TRAITS

Purpose: To screen for avoidant, borderline, and dependent personality disorders in clinic settings.

Number of Items: 54

Format: All items presented.

Reliability: Cronbach alphas ranged from .79 to .87 across subscales.

Validity: Correlations with MCM II scales ranged from .29 to .57.

Author: Clark, J. W., Jr., et al.

Article: Initial evidence for reliability and validity of a brief screening inventory for personality traits.

Journal: *Psychological Reports*, June 1998, *82*(3) Part 2, 1115–1120.

9902

Test Name: COMPETITIVENESS INDEX

Purpose: To identify interpersonal competitiveness in everyday contexts.

Number of Items: 20

Format: Responses are either "true" or "false."

Reliability: Coefficient alpha was .90.

Validity: Correlations with other variables ranged from .04 to .47.

Author: Houston, J. M., et al.

Article: Competitiveness in elite professional athletes.

Journal: *Perceptual and Motor Skills*, June 1997, *84*(3, Part 2), 1447–1454.

Related Research: Smither, R. D., & Houston, J. M. (1992). The nature of competitiveness: Construction and validation of the Competitiveness Index. *Educational and Psychological Measurement*, 52, 407–418.

9903

Test Name: CONSUMER SUSCEPTIBILITY TO INTERPERSONAL INFLUENCE SCALE

Purpose: To measure the formal and informal normative dimensions of the trait of interpersonal influence.

Number of Items: 12

Format: Seven-point response scales.

Reliability: Alphas ranged from .82 to .88.

Author: Browne, B. A., and Kaldenberg, D. O.

Article: Self-monitoring and image appeals in advertising.

Journal: *Psychological Reports*, December 1997, *81*(3, Part II), 1267–1275.

Related Research: Bearden, W. O., et al. (1990). Further

validation of the consumer susceptibility to interpersonal influence scale. In T. Srull (Ed.), *Advances in consumer research* (Vol. 17, pp. 770–776). Provo, UT: Association for Consumer Research.

9904

Test Name: EMPATHY SCALE

Purpose: To rate how genuine, empathic, and caring patients think their therapist is.

Number of Items: 10

Format: Four-point scales are anchored by 0 (weak feeling) and 3 (extremely strong feeling).

Reliability: Coefficient alpha was .76.

Author: Burns, D. D., and Spangler, D. L.

Article: Does psychotherapy homework lead to improvements in depression in cognitive–behavioral therapy or does improvement lead to increased homework compliance?

Journal: *Journal of Consulting and Clinical Psychology*, February 2000, *68*(1), 46–56.

Related Research: Burns, D. D., & Nolen-Hoeksema, S. (1992). Therapeutic empathy and recovery from depression in cognitive–behavioral therapy: A structural equation model. *Journal of Consulting and Clinical Psychology*, 60, 441–449.

9905

Test Name: GENERALIZED HYPERCOMPETITIVENESS SCALE

Purpose: To measure individual differences in generalized hypercompetitiveness.

Number of Items: 26

Format: Responses are made on a 5-point scale ranging from 1 (never true of me) to 5 (always true of me).

Reliability: Coefficient alpha was .88.

Validity: Correlations with other variables ranged from −.32 to .71.

Author: Bing, M. N.

Article: Hypercompetitiveness in academia: Achieving criterion-related validity from item context specificity.

Journal: *Journal of Personality Assessment*, August 1999, *73*(1), 80–99.

Related Research: Ryckman, R. M., et al. (1990). Construction of a hypercompetitive attitude scale. *Journal of Personality Assessment*, 55, 630–639.

9906

Test Name: GUDJONSSON SUGGESTIBILITY SCALE— FORM 2

Purpose: To measure interrogative suggestibility.

Number of Items: 20

Format: Respondents listen to a short story followed by questions presented about 40 to 50 minutes later. Negative feedback is given followed by a second administration of the 20 questions.

Reliability: Test-retest reliabilities ranged from .89 to .96.

Author: MacFarland, W. L., and Morris, S. J.

Article: Are dysphoric individuals more suggestible or less suggestible than nondisphoric individuals?

Journal: *Journal of Counseling Psychology*, April 1998, *45*(2), 225–229.

Related Research: Gudjonsson, G. (1987). A parallel form of the Gudjonsson Suggestibility Scale. *British Journal of Clinical Psychology*, 26, 215–221.

9907

Test Name: HOGAN EMPATHY SCALE

Purpose: To measure cognitive empathy.

Number of Items: 64

Format: Employs a true-false format.

Reliability: Coefficient alpha was .56.

Validity: Correlations with other variables ranged from −.06 to .31.

Author: Donavan, J. M.

Article: Reinterpreting telepathy as unusual experiences of empathy and charisma.

Journal: *Perceptual and Motor Skills*, August 1998, 87(1), 131–146.

Related Research: Hogan, R. (1969). Development of an empathy scale. *Journal of Consulting and Clinical Psychology*, 33, 307–316.

9908

Test Name: HURLBERT INDEX OF SEXUAL ASSERTIVENESS

Purpose: To measure the degree of sexual assertiveness an individual exercises with an intimate partner.

Number of Items: 25

Format: Responses are made on a 5-point scale ranging from 0 (all of the time) to 4 (never). All items are presented.

Reliability: Alpha coefficients ranged from .84 to .91. Test-

retest correlation ranged from .83 to .88.

Author: Pierre, A. P., and Hurlbert, M. K.

Article: Test-retest reliability of the Hurlbert Index of Sexual Assertiveness.

Journal: *Perceptual and Motor Skills*, February 1999, 88(1), 31–34.

Related Research: Hurlbert, D. F. (1991). The role of assertiveness in female sexuality: A comparative study between sexually assertive and sexually nonassertive women. *Journal of Sex and Marital Therapy*, 17, 183–190.

9909

Test Name: HYPERCOMPETITIVENESS IN ACADEMIA SCALE

Purpose: To measure individual differences in academic hypercompetitiveness.

Number of Items: 18

Format: Responses are made on a 7-point Likert scale ranging from 1 (strongly disagree) to 7 (strongly agree). All items are presented.

Reliability: Alpha coefficients were .82 and .86.

Validity: Correlations with other variables ranged from −.13 to .71.

Author: Bing, M. N.

Article: Hypercompetitiveness in academia: Achieving criterion-related validity from item context specificity.

Journal: *Journal of Personality Assessment*, August 1999, 73(1), 80–99.

9910

Test Name: HYPERSENSITIVE NARCISSISM SCALE

Purpose: To measure narcissism.

Number of Items: 10

Format: Scales range from 1 (very uncharacteristic or untrue; strongly disagree) to 5 (very characteristic or true; strongly agree). All items are presented.

Reliability: Coefficient alpha was .76.

Validity: Correlations with other variables ranged from −.44 to .61.

Author: Hendin, H. M., and Cheek, J. M.

Article: Assessing hypersensitive narcissism: A reexamination of Murray's narcissism scale.

Journal: *Journal of Research in Personality*, December 1997, 31(4), 588–599.

9911

Test Name: IMPULSIVITY SCALE

Purpose: To measure the speed of response initiation.

Number of Items: 13

Format: An example is presented.

Reliability: Alpha coefficients ranged from .55 to .78.

Validity: Correlations with other variables ranged from −.13 to .55.

Author: Lengua, L. J., et al.

Article: Temperament as a predictor of symptomatology in children: Addressing contamination of measures.

Journal: *Child Development*, February 1998, 69(1), 164–181.

Related Research: Goldsmith, H. H., & Rothbart, M. K. (1991). Contemporary instruments for assessing early temperament by questionnaire and in the laboratory. In J. Strelau & A. Angleitner (Eds.), *Explorations in temperament: International perspectives on theory and measurement* (pp. 249–272). New York: Plenum.

9912

Test Name: INDEX OF EMPATHY FOR CHILDREN

Purpose: To assess empathic behaviors and feelings.

Number of Items: 22

Format: Responses are either "yes" or "no." An example is presented.

Reliability: Test-retest reliability was .81 and coefficient alpha was .68.

Author: Fagen, D. B., et al.

Article: Relationships between parent-child relational variables and child test variables in highly stressed urban families.

Journal: *Child Study Journal*, 1996, *26*(2), 87–108.

Related Research: Bryant, B. K. (1982). An index of empathy for children and adolescents. *Child Development*, 53, 413–426.

9913

Test Name: INDEX OF EMPATHY FOR CHILDREN— MODIFIED

Purpose: To assess empathy of 7- to 8-year olds.

Number of Items: 10

Format: Responses to each item are "yes" or "no."

Reliability: Coefficient alpha was .72.

Author: Sutton, S. E., et al.

Article: Pathways to aggression in

young, highly stressed urban children.

Journal: *Child Study Journal*, 1999, *29*(1), 49–67.

Related Research: Bryant, B. K. (1982). An index of empathy in children and adolescents. *Child Development*, 53, 413–425.

9914

Test Name: INSTRUMENTAL SCALE

Purpose: To assess self-assertive instrumental traits.

Number of Items: 8

Format: Responses are made on a 5-point scale ranging from "not at all competitive" to "very competitive."

Reliability: Alpha coefficients ranged from .73 to .85. Test-retest reliabilities ranged from .65 to .91.

Author: Hallett, M. B., and Gilbert, L. A.

Article: Variables differentiating university women considering role-sharing and conventional dual-career marriages.

Journal: *Journal of Vocational Behavior*, April 1997, *50*(2), 308–322.

Related Research: Spence, J. T., et al. (1974). The Personal Attributes Questionnaire: A measure of sex role stereotypes and masculinity-femininity. *Journal Supplement Abstract Service Catalog of Selected Documents in Psychology*, 4, 43–44.

9915

Test Name: INTERGROUP AND INTRAGROUP DIFFERENTIATION SCALES

Purpose: To measure traits that are perceived to characterize

intra- and intergroup differentiation.

Number of Items: 11

Format: Scales range from 1 (agree) to 5 (disagree) for intergroup differentiation, and from "very similar" to "very different" for intragroup differentiation. Sample items are presented.

Reliability: Alpha coefficients ranged from .70 to .82 across subscales.

Validity: Correlations with other variables ranged from .02 to .30.

Author: Verkuyten, M., and Kwa, G. A.

Article: Ethnic self-identification, ethnic involvement, and group differentiation among Chinese youth in the Netherlands.

Journal: *Journal of Social Psychology*, February 1996, *136*(1), 35–48.

9916

Test Name: INTERPERSONAL REACTIVITY INDEX

Purpose: To measure empathy.

Number of Items: 28

Format: Includes 4 subscales: Perspective Taking, Empathetic Concern, Fantasy, and Personal distress.

Reliability: Alpha coefficient ranged from .76 to .84.

Validity: Correlations with other variables ranged from −.32 to .84.

Author: Miville, M. L., et al.

Article: Appreciating similarities and valuing differences: The Miville-Guzman Universality– Diversity Scale.

Journal: *Journal of Counseling*

Psychology, July 1999, *46*(3), 291–307.

Related Research: Davis, M. (1980). A multidimensional approach to individual differences in empathy. *JSAS Catalog of Selected Documentation in Psychology*, *10*, 85.

9917

Test Name: JUNIOR IMPULSIVENESS QUESTIONNAIRE

Purpose: To measure impulsiveness and empathy.

Number of Items: 31

Reliability: KR-20 reliability coefficients were .77 for impulsiveness and .71 for empathy.

Validity: Correlations with other variables ranged from −.16 to .54.

Author: Dykeman, C., et al.

Article: Psychological predictors of school based violence: Implications for school counselors.

Journal: *The School Counselor*, September 1996, *44*(1), 35–47.

Related Research: Eysenck, S. B., et al. (1984). Age norms for impulsiveness, venturesomeness, and empathy in children. *Personality and Individual Differences*, *5*, 315–321.

9918

Test Name: MACH IV INSTRUMENT

Purpose: To measure individual differences in Machiavellianism.

Number of Items: 20

Format: Responses are made on a 7-point Likert scale ranging from 1 (strongly disagree) to 7 (strongly agree).

Reliability: Coefficient alpha was .76.

Validity: Correlations with other variables ranged from −.28 to .48.

Author: Bing, M. N.

Article: Hypercompetitiveness in academia: Achieving criterion-related validity from item context specificity.

Journal: *Journal of Personality Assessment*, August 1999, *73*(1), 80–99.

Related Research: Christie, R., & Geis, F. L. (1970). *Studies in Machiavellianism*. New York: Academic.

9919

Test Name: MACH V SCALE

Purpose: To measure Machiavellianism.

Number of Items: 20

Format: Forced-choice format.

Reliability: Reliabilities ranged in the .60s.

Author: Moore, S., and Ward, M.

Article: Machiavellianism and tolerance of ambiguity.

Journal: *Psychological Reports*, April 1998, *82*(2), 415–418.

Related Research: Christie, R., & Geis, F. L. (1970). *Studies in Machiavellianism*. New York: Academic Press.

9920

Test Name: MMPI COVERT NARCISSISM MEASURE

Purpose: To measure narcissism.

Number of Items: 35

Format: True/false format. Sample items are presented.

Reliability: Coefficient alpha was .70.

Validity: Correlations with other variables ranged from −.34 to .61.

Author: Hendin, H. M., and Cheek, J. M.

Article: Assessing hypersensitive narcissism: A reexamination of Murray's narcissism scale.

Journal: *Journal of Research in Personality*, December, 1997, *31*(4), 588–599.

Related Research: Ashby, H. U. (1978). An MMPI scale for narcissistic personality disorder. *Dissertation Abstracts International*, *39*, 10 (University Microfilms No. 7907849, 5053-B).

9921

Test Name: MORNINGNESS–EVENINGNESS QUESTIONNAIRE

Purpose: To assess circadian rhythms.

Number of Items: 13

Format: Four- and 5-point scales.

Reliability: Coefficient alpha was .87.

Validity: Correlations with other variables ranged from −.18 to .07.

Authors: Smith, M. R., and Gordon, R. A.

Article: Personal need for structure and attitudes toward homosexuality.

Journal: *Journal of Social Psychology*, February 1998, *138*(1), 83–87.

Related Research: Smith, C. S., et al. (1989). Evaluation of three circadian rhythm questionnaires with suggestions for an improved measure of morningness. *Journal of Applied Psychology*, *74*, 728–738.

9922

Test Name:
MULTIDIMENSIONAL
PERFECTIONISM SCALE

Purpose: To measure
perfectionism.

Number of Items: 35

Format: Includes 6 subscales:
Concern over Mistakes, Personal
Standards, Parental
Expectations, Parental Criticism,
Doubts about Actions, and
Organization. Responses are
made on a 5-point Likert-type
scale ranging from 1 (strongly
disagree) to 5 (strongly agree).
Examples are presented.

Reliability: Alpha coefficients were
.91 and .92.

Validity: Correlations with other
variables ranged from −.17 to
.46.

Author: Chang, E. C.

Article: Perfectionism as a
predictor of positive and negative
psychological outcomes:
Examining a mediation model in
younger and older adults.

Journal: *Journal of Counseling
Psychology*, January 2000, 47(1),
18–26.

Related Research: Frost, R. O., et
al. (1990). The dimensions of
perfectionism. *Cognitive Therapy
and Research, 14,* 449–468.

9923

Test Name:
MULTIDIMENSIONAL
PERFECTIONISM SCALE

Purpose: To measure
perfectionism.

Number of Items: 45

Format: Includes 3 scales: Self-
Oriented Perfectionism, Other-
Oriented Perfectionism, and
Socially Prescribed
Perfectionism. Responses are

made on a 7-point scale ranging
from 1 (disagree) to 7 (agree).
Sample items are presented.

Reliability: Test-retest (3 months)
reliability ranged from .75 to .88.
Alpha coefficients ranged from
.71 to .78.

Validity: Correlations with other
variables ranged from −.13 to
.32.

Author: Chang, E. C., and Rand,
K. L.

Article: Perfectionism as a
predictor of subsequent
adjustment: Evidence for a
specific diathesis-stress
mechanism among college
students.

Journal: *Journal of Counseling
Psychology*, January 2000, 47(1),
129–137.

Related Research: Hewitt, P. L.,
& Flett, G. L. (1991).
Perfectionism in the self and
social contexts:
Conceptualization, assessment,
and association with
psychopathology. *Journal of
Personality and Social
Psychology, 60,* 456–470.

9924

Test Name:
MULTIDIMENSIONAL
PERFECTIONISM SCALES

Purpose: To assess socially
prescribed and self-oriented
perfectionism.

Number of Items: 30

Format: Includes 2 parts: Socially
Prescribed Perfectionism and
Self-Oriented Perfectionism.
Sample items are presented.

Reliability: Alpha coefficients
ranged from .84 to .88. Test-
retest reliability coefficients
ranged from .75 to .88.

Author: Dunkley, D. M., et al.

Article: The relation between

perfectionism and distress:
Hassles, coping, and perceived
social support as mediators and
moderators.

Journal: *Journal of Counseling
Psychology*, October 2000, 47(4),
437–453.

Related Research: Hewitt, P. L.,
& Flett, G. L. (1991).
Perfectionism in the self and
social contexts:
Conceptualization, assessment,
and association with
psychopathology. *Journal of
Personality and Social
Psychology, 60,* 456–470.

9925

Test Name: NARCISSISTIC
PERSONALITY INVENTORY

Purpose: To measure individual
differences in narcissistic
personality traits.

Number of Items: 40

Format: Forced-choice format.

Reliability: Reliabilities ranged
from .72 (alternate forms) to .80
(split-half).

Validity: Correlations with other
variables ranged from −.25 to
.43.

Author: Ladd, E. R., et al.

Article: Narcissism and causal
attribution.

Journal: *Psychological Reports*,
February 1997, *80*(1), 171–178.

Related Research: Raskin, R. N.,
& Hall, C. S. (1979). A
narcissistic personality inventory.
Psychological Reports, 45, 590.

9926

Test Name: NONVERBAL
PERSONALITY
QUESTIONNAIRE

Purpose: To measure personality
traits.

Number of Items: 136

Format: Includes 16 personality trait scales and 1 validity scale. Responses are made on a 7-point scale ranging from 1 (very unlikely) to 7 (very likely).

Reliability: Alpha coefficients ranged from .64 to .84.

Author: Lee, K., et al.

Article: Psychometric properties of the Nonverbal Personality Questionnaire in Korea.

Journal: *Educational and Psychological Measurement,* February 2000, *60*(1), 131–141.

Related Research: Paunonen, S. V., & Jackson, D. N. (1979). Nonverbal trait inference. *Journal of Personality and Social Psychology, 37,* 1645–1659.

9927

Test Name: O'BRIEN MULTIPHASIC NARCISSISM INVENTORY

Purpose: To measure narcissism.

Number of Items: 41

Format: Includes 3 factors.

Reliability: Coefficient alpha was .75.

Author: Hibbard, S., et al.

Article: Differential validity of the defense mechanism manual for the TAT between Asian Americans and Whites.

Journal: *Journal of Personality Assessment,* December 2000, *75*(3), 351–372.

Related Research: O'Brien, M. L. (1988). Further evidence of the validity of the O'Brien Multiphasic Narcissism Inventory. *Psychological Reports, 62,* 879–882.

9928

Test Name: PERFECTIONISM SCALE

Purpose: To measure dysfunctional attitudes related to perfectionism.

Number of Items: 10

Format: Scales range from −2 (strongly disagree) to 2 (strongly agree).

Reliability: Coefficient alpha was .76.

Validity: Correlations with other variables ranged from −.42 to .61.

Author: Johnson, D. P., and Slaney, R. B.

Article: Perfectionism: Scale development and a study of perfectionistic clients in counseling.

Journal: *Journal of College Student Development,* January/ February 1996, *37*(1), 29–41.

Related Research: Burns, D. D. (1980, November). The perfectionist's script for self-defeat. *Psychology Today,* 34–52.

9929

Test Name: PHYSICAL AGGRESSION (SUB)SCALE

Purpose: To measure trait aggressiveness.

Number of Items: 9

Format: Scales range from 1 (extremely uncharacteristic of me) to 5 (extremely characteristic of me). Sample items are presented.

Reliability: Coefficient alpha was .85.

Author: Bushman, B. J., and Wells, G. L.

Article: Trait aggressiveness in hockey penalties: Predicting hot tempers on the ice.

Journal: *Journal of Applied Psychology,* December 1998, *83*(6), 969–974.

Related Research: Buss, A. H., & Perry, M. (1992). The Aggression Questionnaire. *Journal of Personality and Social Psychology, 63,* 452–459.

9930

Test Name: PSYCHOPATHIC PERSONALITY INVENTORY

Purpose: To assess major personality traits of psychopathy in noncriminal populations.

Number of Items: 160

Format: Includes 8 factors: Machiavellian Egocentricity, Social Potency, Coldheartedness, Carefree Nonplanfulness, Fearlessness, Blame Externalization, Impulsive Nonconformity, and Stress Immunity. Examples are presented.

Reliability: Alpha coefficients ranged from .70 to .93. Test-retest reliabilities ranged from .82 to .95.

Validity: Correlations with other variables ranged from −.59 to .91.

Author: Lilienfeld, S. O., and Andrews, B. P.

Article: Development and preliminary validation of a self-report measure of psychopathic personality traits in non-criminal populations.

Journal: *Journal of Personality Assessment,* June 1996, *66*(3), 488–524.

9931

Test Name: PSYCHOPATHIC PERSONALITY INVENTORY

Purpose: To assess the core personality traits of psychopathy.

Number of Items: 187

Format: Includes 8 factors: Machiavellian Egocentricity, Social Potency, Coldheartedness, Carefree Nonplanfulness, Fearlessness, Blame Externalization, Impulsive Nonconformity, and Stress Immunity. Responses are made on a 4-point scale ranging from 1 (false) to 4 (true).

Reliability: Test-retest (1 month) reliabilities ranged from .82 to .95. Alpha coefficients ranged from .63 to .93.

Validity: Correlations with other variables ranged from −.52 to .67.

Author: Sandoval, A.-M. R., et al.

Article: Construct validity of the Psychopathic Personality Inventory in a correctional sample.

Journal: *Journal of Personality Assessment*, April 2000, *74*(2), 262–281.

Related Research: Lilienfeld, S. O., & Andrews, B. P. (1996). Development and preliminary validation of a self-report measure of psychopathic personality traits in noncriminal populations. *Journal of Personality Assessment*, *66*, 488–524.

9932

Test Name: RATHUS ASSERTIVENESS SCHEDULE

Purpose: To measure assertiveness.

Number of Items: 30

Format: Employs a Likert format. An example is presented.

Reliability: Reliability coefficient was .77.

Validity: Correlations with other variables were .38 and .02.

Author: Smith-Jentsch, K. A., et al.

Article: Training team performance-related assertiveness.

Journal: *Personnel Psychology*, Winter 1996, *49*(4), 909–936.

Related Research: Rathus, S. A. (1973). A 30 item schedule for assessing assertive behaviors. *Behavior Therapy*, *4*, 398–406.

9933

Test Name: RATING OF SELF-STATUS INTERNATIONAL

Purpose: To measure traits relevant to success in fertility regulation.

Number of Items: 50

Format: Multiple-choice format.

Reliability: Test-retest reliability (4 weeks) was .58.

Author: Quereshi, M. Y.

Article: Stability of some hypothesized psychological determinants of fertility control.

Journal: *Psychological Reports*, April 1998, *82*(2), 657–658.

Related Research: Quereshi, M. Y. (1997). Measuring behavioral, biosocial, and attitudinal correlates of fertility regulation. *Current Psychology*, *16*, 50–64.

9934

Test Name: REVISED CHEEK AND BUSS SHYNESS SCALE

Purpose: To assess the latent variable of shyness.

Number of Items: 13

Reliability: Alpha coefficients were .90 and .83. Test-retest (45 days) reliability was .88.

Validity: Correlation with other

variables ranged from −77 to .47.

Author: Bruch, M. A., et al.

Article: Shyness, masculine ideology, physical attractiveness, and emotional inexpressiveness: Testing a mediational model of men's interpersonal competence.

Journal: *Journal of Counseling Psychology*, January 1998, *45*(1), 84–97.

Related Research: Cheek, J. M. (1983). *The revised Cheek and Buss Shyness Scale*. Unpublished manuscript, Wellesley College.

9935

Test Name: RIGHT-WING AUTHORITARIANISM SCALE

Purpose: To measure authoritarianism.

Number of Items: 30

Format: Scales range from 1 (strongly disagree) to 7 (strongly agree). A sample item is presented.

Reliability: Alpha coefficients ranged from .88 to .91.

Author: Peterson, B. E., and Duncan, L. E.

Article: Authoritarianism of parents and offspring: Intergenerational politics and adjustment to college.

Journal: *Journal of Research in Personality*, December 1999, *33*(4), 494–513.

Related Research: Altemeyer, B. (1988). *Enemies of freedom: Understanding right-wing authoritarianism*. San Francisco: Jossey-Bass.

9936

Test Name: SANDLER-HAZARI SCALES

Purpose: To assess persons as

systematic and methodical (A type) versus obsessional (B type).

Number of Items: 40

Format: Yes/no format.

Reliability: Cronbach's alpha ranged from .76 to .78.

Validity: Correlations with other variables ranged from −.42 to .51.

Author: Johnson, D. P., and Slaney, R. B.

Article: Perfectionism: Scale development and a study of perfectionistic clients in counseling.

Journal: *Journal of College Student Development*, January/February 1996, *37*(1), 29–41.

Related Research: Sandler, J., & Hazari, A. (1960). The 'obsessional': On the psychological classification of obsessional character traits and symptoms. *British Journal of Medical Psychology, 33,* 113–122.

9937

Test Name: SELF-CONSCIOUSNESS SCALE

Purpose: To measure the self-consciousness trait.

Number of Items: 23

Format: Includes 3 factors: Private Self-Consciousness, Public Self-Consciousness, and Social Anxiety.

Reliability: Test-retest reliability for Private Self-Consciousness was .79 and for Public Self-Consciousness was .84.

Author: Martin, A. J., and Debus, R. L.

Article: Alternate factor structure for the revised Self-Consciousness Scale.

Journal: *Journal of Personality*

Assessment, April 1999, *72*(2), 266–281.

Related Research: Fenigstein, A., et al. (1975). Public and private self-consciousness: Assessment and theory. *Journal of Consulting and Clinical Psychology, 43,* 522–527.

9938

Test Name: SELF-RATING QUESTIONNAIRE—JAPANESE VERSION

Purpose: To measure Type A behavior.

Number of Items: 14

Reliability: Alpha was .63.

Validity: Correlations with other variables ranged from −.02 to .18.

Author: Sumi, K.

Article: Type A behavior, social support, stress, and physical and psychological well-being among Japanese women.

Journal: *Psychological Reports*, October 1998, *83*(2), 711–717.

Related Research: Bortner, R. W. (1969). A short rating scale as a potential measure of Pattern A behavior. *Journal of Chronic Disease, 22,* 83–91.

9939

Test Name: SHYNESS SCALE—REVISED

Purpose: To assess shyness.

Number of Items: 13

Reliability: Alpha coefficients ranged from .82 to .90. Test-retest (45 days) reliability was .88.

Validity: Correlations with other variables ranged from −.31 to .38.

Author: Hamer, R. J., and Bruch, M. A.

Article: Personality factors and inhibited career development: Testing the unique contribution of shyness.

Journal: *Journal of Vocational Behavior*, June 1997, *50*(3), 382–400.

Related Research: Cheek, J. M. (1983). *The revised Cheek and Buss Shyness Scale*. Unpublished manuscript, Wellesley College, Wellesley, MA.

9940

Test Name: SINO-AMERICAN PERSON PERCEPTION SCALE

Purpose: To assess imported and indigenous personality traits.

Number of Items: 32

Format: Seven-point bipolar adjective scales.

Reliability: Alpha coefficients ranged from .56 to .85 across subscales.

Author: Bond, M. H., et al.

Article: Decomposing a sense of superiority: The differential social impact of self-regard and regard for others.

Journal: *Journal of Research in Personality*, December 2000, *34*(4), 537–553.

Related Research: Yik, M. S. M., & Bond, M. H. (1993). Exploring the dimensions of Chinese person perception with indigenous and imported constructs: Creating a culturally balanced scale. *International Journal of Psychology, 28,* 79–95.

9941

Test Name: SPORT ORIENTATION QUESTIONNAIRE—FORM B

Purpose: To measure competitive orientation.

Number of Items: 25

Format: Includes 3 subscales: Competitiveness, Desire to Win in Competition, and Desire to Reach Personal Goals. Examples are presented.

Reliability: Internal consistency reliabilities ranged from .78 to .87.

Author: Page, S. J., et al.

Article: Exploring competitive orientation in a group of athletes participating in the 1996 paralympic trials.

Journal: *Perceptual and Motor Skills*, October 2000, *91*(2), 491–502.

Related Research: Gill, D. L., & Deeter, T. E. (1988). Development of the Sport Orientation Questionnaire. *Research Quarterly for Exercise and Sport, 59*, 191–202.

9942

Test Name: SPORTS COMPETITION TRAIT INVENTORY

Purpose: To measure individual differences in sport competitiveness.

Number of Items: 17

Format: Responses are made on a 7-point scale ranging from 1 (hardly ever) to 7 (almost always).

Reliability: Coefficient alpha was .98.

Validity: Correlations with other variables ranged from −.15 to .45.

Author: Bing, M. N.

Article: Hypercompetitiveness in academia: Achieving criterion-related validity from item context specificity.

Journal: *Journal of Personality Assessment*, August 1999, *73*(1), 80–99.

Related Research: Fabian, L., & Ross, M. (1984). The development of the Sports Competition Trait Inventory. *Journal of Sport Behavior, 7*, 13–27.

9943

Test Name: TRAIT GUILT SCALE

Purpose: To measure continuing nonspecific sense of guilt and regret.

Number of Items: 20

Reliability: Coefficient alpha was .89.

Validity: Correlations with other variables ranged from −.06 to −.37.

Author: Couch, L. L., and Jones, W. H.

Article: Measuring levels of trust.

Journal: *Journal of Research in Personality*, September 1997, *31*(3), 319–336.

Related Research: Kugler, K., & Jones, W. H. (1992). On conceptualizing and assessing guilt. *Journal of Personality and Social Psychology, 62*, 318–327.

9944

Test Name: TRAIT META-MOOD SCALE

Purpose: To assess the reflective experience of mood.

Number of Items: 30

Format: Scales range from 1 (strongly disagree) to 5 (strongly agree). Sample items are presented.

Reliability: Alpha coefficients ranged from .82 to .87.

Validity: Correlations with other variables ranged from .20 to .60.

Author: McCarthy, C. J., et al.

Article: The relationship of beliefs about mood to coping resource effectiveness.

Journal: *Journal of College Student Development*, March/April 1997, *38*(2), 157–165.

Related Research: Salovey, P., et al. (1995). Emotional attention, clarity, and repair: Exploring emotional intelligence using the Trait Meta-Mood Scale. In J. W. Pennebaker (Ed.), *Emotion, disclosure, and health* (pp. 125–154). Washington, DC: American Psychological Association.

9945

Test Name: TRAIT SHYNESS SCALE

Purpose: To measure shyness.

Number of Items: 16

Format: Five-point scales are anchored by 1 (never talk) and 5 (always talk). All items are presented in English.

Reliability: Alphas ranged from .88 to .89 across subscales.

Author: Matsushima, R., et al.

Article: Shyness in self-disclosure mediated by social skill.

Journal: *Psychological Reports*, February 2000, *86*(1), 333–338.

Related Research: Aikawa, A. (1991). [A study on the reliability and validity of a scale to measure shyness as a trait]. [*The Japanese Journal of Psychology*,] *62*, 149–155 [in Japanese].

9946

Test Name: TYPE A SCALE

Purpose: To measure Type A personality.

Number of Items: 20

Format: Responses are made on a 5-point Likert-type scale ranging from 1 (strongly disagree) to 5 (strongly agree). An example is presented.

Reliability: Coefficient alpha was .75.

Validity: Correlations with other variables ranged from .02 to .14.

Author: Carlson, D. S.

Article: Personality and role variables as predictors of three forms of work-family conflict.

Journal: *Journal of Vocational Behavior*, October 1999, *55*(2), 236–253.

Related Research: Thurstone, L. L. (1951). The dimensions of temperament. *Psychometrika, 16,* 11–20.

9947

Test Name: VERBAL AGGRESSIVENESS SCALE— GERMAN VERSION

Purpose: To measure the trait of verbal aggressiveness.

Number of Items: 18

Reliability: Alphas were .77 and .83.

Validity: Correlations with other variables ranged from −.34 to .22.

Author: Bickle, G., et al.

Article: Verbal aggressiveness: Conceptualization and measurement a decade later.

Journal: *Psychological Reports*, February 1998, *82*(1), 287–298

Related Research: Infante, D. A., & Wigley, C. J. (1986). Verbal aggressiveness: An interpersonal model and measure. *Communication Monographs, 53,* 61–69.

CHAPTER 22

Values

9948

Test Name: ACADEMIC ASPIRATION AND VALUATION SCALE

Purpose: To measure academic aspiration and valuation of academic pursuits.

Number of Items: 7

Format: A 5-point rating scale was employed.

Reliability: Alpha coefficients were .73 and .77.

Validity: Correlations with other variables ranged from −.33 to .60.

Author: Bandura, A., et al.

Article: Multifaceted impact of self-efficacy beliefs in academic functioning.

Journal: *Child Development*, June 1996, *67*(3), 1206–1222.

9949

Test Name: BELIEFS ABOUT ATTRACTIVENESS SCALE— REVISED

Purpose: To measure the degree to which women endorse contemporary U. S. societal values regarding attractiveness and beauty.

Number of Items: 19

Format: Includes 2 factors: Importance of Being Physically Fit and Importance of Being Attractive and Thin. Responses are made on a 7-point scale ranging from 1 (strongly disagree) to 7 (strongly agree).

Reliability: Alpha coefficient ranged from .83 to .89.

Validity: Correlations with other variables ranged from −.32 to .46.

Author: Lester, R., and Petrie, T. A.

Article: Physical, psychological, and societal correlates of bulimic symptomatology among African American college women.

Journal: *Journal of Counseling Psychology*, July 1998, *45*(3), 315–321.

Related Research: Petrie, T., et al. (1996, August). *Development and validation of the Beliefs About Attractiveness Scale— Revised.* Poster presented at the 104th annual convention of the American Psychological Association, Toronto, Ontario, Canada.

9950

Test Name: BELIEFS ABOUT WORK INVENTORY—ARABIC VERSION

Purpose: To measure humanism, work ethic, group orientation, participative and leisure ethic.

Number of Items: 44

Format: Sample items are presented.

Reliability: Alphas ranged from .54 to .81 across subscales.

Author: Abdalla, I. A. H.

Article: Work values and subjective beliefs in Arabian Gulf samples of employees and undergraduates.

Journal: *Psychological Reports*, October 1997, *81*(2), 387–400.

Related Research: Buchholz, R. A. (1978). An empirical study of contemporary beliefs about work in American society. *Journal of Applied Psychology*, *63*, 219–227.

9951

Test Name: (BELK) MATERIALISM SCALE

Purpose: To measure possessiveness, nongenerosity, and envy.

Number of Items: 24

Format: Five-point Likert format.

Reliability: Alphas ranged from .44 to .63 across subscales. Test-retest reliability (2 weeks) was .68.

Author: Sharpe, J. P., and Ramanaiah, N. V.

Article: Materialism and the five-factor model of personality.

Journal: *Psychological Reports*, August 1999, *85*(1), 327–330.

Related Research: Belk, R. W. (1984). Three scales to measure constructs related to materialism: Reliability, validity, and relationships to measures of happiness. In T. Kinnear (Ed.), *Advances in consumer research* (Vol. 11, pp. 291–297). Provo, UT: Association for Consumer Research.

9952

Test Name: BENEVOLENCE OF WORLD AND PEOPLE SCALES

Purpose: To measure benevolence.

Number of Items: 8

Format: Four-point scales are anchored by 0 (disagree strongly) and 3 (agree strongly).

Reliability: Alpha coefficients were .85 (world) and .71 (people).

Author: Herek, G. M., et al.

Article: Psychological sequels of hate crime victimization among lesbian, gay and bisexual adults.

Journal: *Journal of Consulting and Clinical Psychology*, December 1999, *67*(6), 945–951.

Related Research: Janoff-Bulman, R. (1989). Assumptive worlds and the stress of traumatic events: Applications of the schema construct. *Social Cognition*, 7, 113–136.

9953

Test Name: COLLECTIVISM SCALE

Purpose: To assess the degree to which individuals focus on interdependence on others.

Number of Items: 16

Format: Scales range from 1 (strongly disagree) to 9 (strongly agree). All items are presented.

Reliability: Coefficient alpha was .75.

Validity: Correlations with other variables ranged from −.18 to −.08.

Author: Gelfand, M. J., and Realo, A.

Article: Individualism–collectivism and accountability in intergroup negotiations.

Journal: *Journal of Applied Psychology*, October 1999, *84*(5), 721–736.

Related Research: Triandis, H. C. (1994). Unpublished research

scale on individualism and collectivism. University of Illinois, Champaign.

9954

Test Name: COMPETING VALUES FRAMEWORK SCALE

Purpose: To measure the competing values framework.

Number of Items: 16

Format: Includes 4 dimensions: Human Relations, Open Systems, Rational Goal, and Internal Process Values. Responses are made on a 7-point scale ranging from 1 (not valued at all) to 7 (highly valued).

Reliability: Alpha coefficients ranged from .77 to .90.

Author: Kalliath, T. J., et al.

Article: A confirmatory factor analysis of the competing values instrument.

Journal: *Educational and Psychological Measurement*, February 1999, *59*(1), 143–158.

Related Research: Quinn, R. E., & Spreitzer, G. M. (1991). The psychometrics of the competing values culture instrument and an analysis of the impact of organizational culture on quality of life. *Research in Organizational Change and Development*, 5, 115–142.

9955

Test Name: CROSS-CULTURAL WORLD-MINDEDNESS SCALE

Purpose: To measure world-mindedness value orientation.

Number of Items: 26

Format: Responses are made on a 6-point scale.

Reliability: Alpha coefficients were .84 and .70.

Validity: Correlations with other variables ranged from .04 to .53.

Author: Der-Karabetian, A., et al.

Article: Environmental risk perception, activism and world-mindedness among samples of British and U.S. college students.

Journal: *Perceptual and Motor Skills*, October 1996, *83*(2), 451–462.

Related Research: Der-Karabetian, A. (1972). World-mindedness and the nuclear threat: A multinational study, *Journal of Social Behavior and Personality*, 7, 293–308.

9956

Test Name: CULTURAL ORIENTATION SCALE

Purpose: To assess a cultural orientation pertaining to parental actions.

Number of Items: 13

Format: Seven-point scales are anchored by (1) not at all and (7) always. Sample items are presented.

Reliability: Alpha was .61. Split-half reliability was .61.

Author: Peltzer, K., et al.

Article: Brain fog symptoms in rural South African secondary school pupils.

Journal: *Psychological Reports*, December 1998, *83*(3) Part 1, 1187–1196.

Related Research: Bierbrauer, G., et al. (1994). Measurement of normative and evaluative aspects in individualistic and collectivistic orientations: The Cultural Orientation Scale (COS). In U. Kim et al. (Eds.), *Individualism, and collectivism: Theory, method, and applications* (pp. 189–199). London: Sage.

9957

Test Name: CULTURAL ORIENTATION SCALE (ENGLISH VERSION)

Purpose: To measure perceived norms and values of one's home country.

Number of Items: 26

Format: Seven-point scales are anchored by 1 (not at all) and 7 (always) or 1 (very bad) and 7 (very good). Sample items are presented.

Reliability: Test-retest reliability was .71. Cronbach's alpha was .61. Split-half reliability was .69.

Author: Peltzer, K., et al.

Article: Minor psychiatric morbidity in South African secondary school pupils.

Journal: *Psychological Reports,* October 1999, *85*(2), 397–402.

Related Research: Bierbauer, G., et al. (1994). Measurement of normative and evaluative aspects in individualistic and collectivistic orientations: The Cultural Orientation Scale (COS). In U. Kim et al. (Eds.). *Individualism and collectivism: Theory, method, and applications* (pp. 189–199). London: Sage.

9958

Test Name: ECONOMIC CONSERVATION SCALE

Purpose: To measure economic conservation.

Number of Items: 8

Format: Three-point responses are (3) no, (2) not sure, and (1) yes.

Reliability: Alpha was .65.

Validity: Correlates with other variables ranged from .41 to .48.

Author: Henningham, J. P.

Article: A short scale of economic conservation.

Journal: *Psychological Reports,* December 1997, *81*(3, Part I), 1014–1024.

9959

Test Name: EDUCATION VALUES SCALE

Purpose: To assess traditional educational values.

Number of Items: 29

Format: Scales range from 1 (agree with) to 5 (disagree with).

Reliability: Alpha coefficients ranged from .60 to .76.

Authors: Gari, A., and Kalantzi-Azizi, A.

Article: The influence of traditional values of education on Greek students: Real and ideal self-concepts.

Journal: *Journal of Social Psychology,* February 1998, *138*(1), 5–12.

Related Research: Gari, A. (1992). *Pupil's values and attitudes in Greece concerning educational institutions: Educational and professional decisions.* Unpublished doctoral dissertation, University of Athens: Greece.

9960

Test Name: ETHICAL JUDGMENT SCALE

Purpose: To assess ethical judgments.

Number of Items: 8

Format: Seven-point bipolar scales. All items are presented.

Reliability: Reliabilities ranged from .71 to .92.

Validity: Correlations with other variables ranged from .29 to .39.

Author: Robin, D. P., et al.

Article: The nature, measurement, and stability of ethical judgments in the workplace.

Journal: *Psychological Reports,* April 1997, *80*(2), 563–580.

Related Research: Reidenbach, R. E., et al. (1991). An application and extension of a multi-dimensional ethics scale to selected marketing practices and marketing groups. *Journal of the Academy of Marketing Science, 19*, 83–92.

9961

Test Name: ETHICS POSITION QUESTIONNAIRE

Purpose: To measure relativism and idealism.

Format: Scales range from 1 (strongly disagree) to 9 (strongly agree). Sample items are presented.

Reliability: Alphas were .73 (relativism) and .80 (idealism). Test-retest reliabilities ranged from .66 to .67.

Validity: Correlations with other variables ranged from −.69 to .44.

Authors: McHoskey, J. W.

Article: Authoritarianism and ethical ideology.

Journal: *Journal of Social Psychology,* December 1996, *136*(6), 709–717.

Related Research: Forsyth, D. R. (1980). A taxonomy of ethical ideologies. *Journal of Personality and Social Psychology, 39*, 175–184

9962

Test Name: EXTERNAL CORE VALUES SCALE

Purpose: To measure the extent to which the world is perceived as just.

Number of Items: 15

Format: Eleven-point scales are anchored by 0 (strongly disagree) and 10 (strongly agree). Sample items are presented.

Reliability: Alpha coefficients ranged from .66 to .83.

Validity: Correlations with other variables ranged from −.51 to .57.

Author: Judge, T. A., et al.

Article: Dispositional effects on job and life satisfaction: The role of core evaluations.

Journal: *Journal of Applied Psychology*, February 1998, *83*(1), 17–34.

9963

Test Name: FAMILY VALUE SCALE

Purpose: To access traditional family values and adolescent autonomy.

Number of Items: 13

Format: Sample items are presented.

Reliability: Alpha coefficients were .71 (values) and .82 (autonomy).

Validity: Correlations with other variables ranged from −.83 to .36.

Authors: Sam, D. L.

Article: Psychological adaptations of adolescents with immigrant backgrounds.

Journal: *Journal of Social Psychology*, February 2000, *140*(1), 5–25.

Related Research: Georgas, J. (1989). Changing family values in Greece: From collectivist to individualist. *Journal of Cross-Cultural Psychology, 20*, 80–91.

9964

Test Name: FUTURE-TIME ORIENTATION SCALE

Purpose: To measure future-time orientation.

Number of Items: 14

Format: Responses are made on a 4-point scale ranging from 1 (is not at all true of me) to 4 (is very true of me).

Reliability: Coefficient alpha was .67.

Validity: Correlations with other variables ranged from −.29 to .27.

Author: Thomassen, T. O., and Halvari, H.

Article: Achievement motivation and involvement in sport competitions.

Journal: *Perceptual and Motor Skills*, December 1996, *83*(3) Part 2, 1363–1372.

Related Research: Gjesine, T. (1979). Future-time orientation as a function of achievement motives, ability, delay of gratification, and sex. *Journal of Psychology, 10*, 173–188.

9965

Test Name: FUTURE TIME PERSPECTIVE INVENTORY

Purpose: To measure the extent to which the future is perceived as predictable, controllable, and structured.

Number of Items: 25

Format: Responses are made on a 7-point summated rating scale.

Reliability: Coefficient alpha was .83.

Validity: Correlations with positive health practices ranged from .20 to .52.

Author: Mahon, N. E., et al.

Article: Future time perspective and positive health practices among young adolescents: A further extension.

Journal: *Perceptual and Motor Skills*, February 2000, *90*(1), 166–168.

Related Research: Heimberg, L. K. (1963). The measurement of future time perspective (Doctoral dissertation, Vanderbilt University, 1963). *Dissertation Abstracts, 24*, 1686–1687.

9966

Test Name: GLOBAL BELIEF IN A JUST WORLD SCALE

Purpose: To measure belief in a just world.

Number of Items: 6

Format: Six-point Likert format.

Reliability: Coefficient alpha was .81.

Authors: O'Connor, W. E., et al.

Article: The reliability and factor structure of the Global Belief in a Just World scale.

Journal: *Journal of Social Psychology*, October 1996, *136*(5), 667–668.

Related Research: Lipkus, I. (1991). The construction and preliminary validation of a Global Belief in a Just World Scale and the exploratory analysis of the Multidimensional Belief in a Just World Scale. *Personality and Individual Differences, 12*, 1171–1178.

9967

Test Name: GLOBAL BELIEF IN A JUST WORLD SCALE

Purpose: To measure the extent to which individuals believe that the world is a just place.

Number of Items: 7

Format: Responses are made on a 6-point Likert-type scale ranging from 1 (strongly disagree) to 6 (strongly agree). A sample item is represented.

Reliability: Alpha coefficients were .83 and .85.

Validity: Correlations with other variables ranged from .39 to .53.

Author: Neville, H. A., et al.

Article: Construction and initial validation of the Color-Blind Racial Attitudes Scale (CoBRAS).

Journal: *Journal of Counseling Psychology*, January 2000, 47(1), 59–70.

Related Research: Lipkus, I. (1991). The construction and preliminary validation of a Global Belief in a Just World Scale and the exploratory analysis of the Multidimensional Belief in a Just World Scale. *Personality and Individual Differences*, 12, 1171–1178.

9968

Test Name: HARMONY AND SECURITY VALUE SCALES

Purpose: To measure the values of national strength and international harmony in the global system.

Number of Items: 14

Format: Scales range from 1 (I reject this) to 7 (I accept this as of the greatest importance). Sample items are presented.

Reliability: Alpha were .72 (national strength) and .86 (international harmony).

Validity: Correlations with the variables ranged from −.15 to .23.

Authors: Heaven, P. C. L.

Article: Group identities and human values.

Journal: *The Journal of Social*

Psychology, October 1999, *139*(5), 590–595.

Related Research: Braithwaite, V. (1994). Beyond Rokeach's equality-freedom model: Two-dimensional values in a one-dimensional world. *Journal of Social Issues*, *50*, 67–94.

9969

Test Name: HEALTH VALUE SCALE

Purpose: To measure the overall value of health.

Number of Items: 4

Format: Seven-point rating scales range from 1 (strongly disagree) to 7 (strongly agree).

Reliability: Alpha was .71.

Author: Buerger, J. L., et al.

Article: How the value of health moderates the link between age and depressive symptoms: Further evidence.

Journal: *Psychological Reports*, October 1996, *79*(2), 655–658.

Related Research: Lau, R. P., et al. (1986). Health as a value: Methodological and theoretical considerations. *Health Psychology*, *5*, 25–43.

9970

Test Name: IDIOCENTRISM–ALLOCENTRISM QUESTIONNAIRE

Purpose: To measure individualism–collectivism.

Number of Items: 21

Format: Seven-point agreement scales. All items are presented.

Reliability: Alphas ranged from .60 to .67 across two subscales.

Author: Freeman, M. A.

Article: Factorial structure of

individualism–collectivism in Sri Lanka.

Journal: *Psychological Reports*, June 1996, *78*(3) Part 1, 907–914.

Related Research: Hui, C. H. (1988). Measurement of individualism–collectivism. *Journal of Research in Personality*, *22*, 17–36. Triandis, H. C. (1988). Collectivism v. individualism: A reconceptualization of a basic concept in cross-cultural social psychology. In J. C. Bagley & G. K. Verma (Eds.), *Personality, cognition and values* (pp. 60–95). London: Macmillan.

9971

Test Name: IDIOCENTRISM AND ALLOCENTRISM SCALES

Purpose: To measure importance of personal identity and collective identity.

Number of Items: 16

Format: Sample items are presented.

Reliability: Coefficient alpha was .85 (idiocentrism) and .92 (allocentrism).

Validity: Correlations with other variables ranged from −.07 to .13.

Author: Schaubroeck, J., et al.

Article: Collective efficacy versus self-efficacy in coping responses to stressors and control: A cross-cultural study.

Journal: *Journal of Applied Psychology*, August 2000, *85*(4), 512–525.

Related Research: Triandis, H. C., & Gelfond, M. T. (1998). Converging measurement of horizontal and vertical collectivism. *Journal of Personality and Social Psychology*, *74*, 118–128.

9972

Test Name: IMMANENCE SCALE

Purpose: To measure the religious orientation to transcend boundaries, awareness and acceptance of experience, and emphasis on the present moment.

Number of Items: 15

Format: Nine-point response format. All items are presented.

Reliability: Coefficient alpha was .79. Split-half reliability was .59.

Validity: Correlations with other variables ranged from −.24 to .42.

Author: Burris, C. T., and Tarpley, W. R.

Article: Religion as being: Preliminary validation of the Immanence Scale.

Journal: *Journal of Research in Personality,* March 1998, *32*(1), 55–79.

9973

Test Name: INDIVIDUALISM–COLLECTIVISM MEASURE—REVISED

Purpose: To measure interpersonal values.

Number of Items: 28

Format: Includes 4 subscales: Horizontal Individualism, Vertical Individualism, Horizontal Collectivism, and Vertical Collectivism.

Reliability: Alpha coefficients ranged from .63 to .81.

Validity: Correlations with other variables ranged from −.15 to .36.

Author: Chan, K.-Y., et al.

Article: The relation between vocational interests and the motivation to lead.

Journal: *Journal of Vocational*

Behavior, October 2000, *57*(2), 226–245.

Related Research: Singelis, T. M., et al. (1995). Horizontal and vertical dimensions of individualism and collectivism: A theoretical and measurement refinement. Cross-cultural research: *The Journal of Comparative Social Science, 29,* 240–275.

9974

Test Name: INDIVIDUALISM–COLLECTIVISM SCALE

Purpose: To measure the extent to which individuals are individualistic or collectivistic in orientation.

Number of Items: 24

Format: Scales range from 1 (strongly disagree) to 7 (strongly agree). Sample items are presented.

Reliability: Alpha coefficients ranged from .34 to .81.

Author: Robert, C., et al.

Article: Empowerment and continuous improvement in the United States, Mexico, Poland, and India: Predicting fit on the basis of the dimensions of power, distance, and individualism.

Journal: *Journal of Applied Psychology,* October 2000, *85*(5), 643–658.

Related Research: Singelis, T. M., et al. (1995). Horizontal and vertical dimensions of individualism and collectivism: A theoretical and measurement refinement. *Cross-Cultural Research, 29,* 240–275.

9975

Test Name: INSTRUMENTAL VALUES SURVEY

Purpose: To assess modes of

conduct such as being responsible and honest.

Number of Items: 18

Format: Respondents rank items from 1 to 18.

Reliability: Test-retest reliabilities ranged from .65 to .70.

Author: Hodgson, A., and Bohning, G.

Article: Priorities for values of adolescents in multicultural schools.

Journal: *Psychological Reports,* December 1997, *81*(3, Part II), 1203–1209.

Related Research: Rokeach, M. (1975). *The nature of human values.* New York: Free Press.

9976

Test Name: INVENTORY OF RELIGIOUS BELIEF

Purpose: To measure religious fundamentalism.

Number of Items: 15

Format: Responses are made on a 5-point Likert-type scale. Examples are presented.

Reliability: Test-retest reliability was reported to be in the upper .70s. Spearman-Brown reliability was reported to be in the upper .80s. Coefficient alpha was .95.

Author: Rest, J. R., et al.

Article: DIT 2: Devising and testing a revised instrument of moral judgement.

Journal: *Journal of Educational Psychology,* December 1999, *91*(4), 644–659.

Related Research: Brown D. G., & Lowe, W. L. (1951). Religious beliefs and personality characteristics of college students. *Journal of Social Psychology, 33,* 103–129.

9977

Test Name: JUST WORLD BELIEF SCALE

Purpose: To assess belief in a just world.

Number of Items: 4

Format: Five-point Likert format. A sample item is presented.

Reliability: Reliability was .43.

Author: Cheung, C.-K., and Kwok, S.-T.

Article: Conservative orientation as a determinant of hopelessness.

Journal: *Journal of Social Psychology*, June 1996, *136*(3), 333–347.

Related Research: Ritter, C., et al. (1990). Belief in a just world and depression. *Sociological Perspectives, 33*, 235–252.

9978

Test Name: JUST WORLD SCALE

Purpose: To measure the extent to which people believe individuals deserve their fates.

Number of Items: 20.

Format: Scales range from 1 (completely disagree) to 6 (completely agree).

Reliability: Coefficient alpha was .70.

Authors: Tanaka, K'I.

Article: Judgments of fairness by just world believers.

Journal: *The Journal of Social Psychology*, October 1999, *139*(5), 631–638.

Related Research: Rubin, Z., & Poplau, A. (1975). Who believes in a just world? *Journal of Social Issues, 31*, 65–90.

9979

Test Name: LIFE AND WORK VALUES INVENTORY

Purpose: To measure life and work values.

Number of Items: 81

Format: Includes 2 parts. Items are rated on a 4-point scale in each part.

Reliability: Alpha coefficients ranged from .88 to .94.

Author: Glencross, M. J.

Article: Reliability of a free-format values inventory.

Journal: *Perceptual and Motor Skills*, December 1996, *83*(3) Part 1, 1056–1058.

Related Research: Munro, D. (1985). A free-format values inventory: Explorations with Zimbabwe student teachers. *South African Journal of Psychology, 15*, 33–41.

9980

Test Name: MATERIALISM SCALE

Purpose: To measure acquisition mentality, happiness from acquisition, and the importance of possessions in defining success.

Number of Items: 18

Format: Five-point scales are anchored by 1 (strongly agree) and 5 (strongly disagree). Sample items are presented.

Reliability: Alphas ranged from .70 to .83. Total alpha was .87.

Author: Zemanek, J. E., Jr., et al.

Article: Relationship of birth order and the marketing-related variable of materialism.

Journal: *Psychological Reports*, April 2000, *86*(2), 429–434.

Related Research: Richins, M. L., & Dawson, S. (1992). A consumer values orientation for materialism and its measurement: Scale development and validation. *Journal of Consumer Research, 19*, 303–316.

9981

Test Name: MEASURE OF MORAL ORIENTATION

Purpose: To measure ethics of care and justice.

Number of Items: 83

Format: Sample items are described in detail. Agreement scales range from 1 (strongly agree) to 5 (strongly disagree).

Reliability: Alpha coefficients ranged from .64 to .83 across four subscales.

Validity: Correlations with other variables ranged from −.37 to .41.

Author: Liddell, D. L., and Davis, T. L.

Article: The Measure of Moral Orientation: Reliability and validity evidence.

Journal: *Journal of College Student Development*, September/October 1996, *37*(5), 485–494.

Related Research: Liddell, D. L., et al. (1992). The Measure of Moral Orientation: Measuring the ethics of care and justice. *Journal of College Student Development, 33*(4), 325–330.
Liddell, D. L. (1998). Comparison of semistructured interviewing with a quantitative measure of moral orientation. *Journal of College Student Development, 39*, 169–178.
Jones, C. E., & Watt, J. D. (1999). Psychosocial development and moral orientation among traditional-aged college students. *Journal of College Student Development, 40*, 125–131.

9982

Test Name:
MULTIDIMENSIONAL BELIEF
IN A JUST WORLD SCALE—
SOCIOPOLITICAL SUBSCALE

Purpose: To assess belief in a just world, specifically attitudes related to sociopolitical beliefs.

Number of Items: 5

Format: Responses are made on a 7-point Likert-type scale ranging from 1 (strongly disagree) to 7 (strongly agree). A sample item is presented.

Reliability: Alpha coefficients were .43 and .66.

Validity: Correlations with other variables ranged from .34 to .61.

Author: Neville, H. A., et al.

Article: Construction and initial validation of the Color-Blind Racial Attitudes Scale (CoBRAS).

Journal: *Journal of Counseling Psychology*, January 2000, 47(1), 59–70.

Related Research: Furnham, A., & Procter, E. (1988). *The Multidimensional Just World Belief Scale*. [Mimeograph] London: London University.

9983

Test Name:
MULTIDIMENSIONAL BELIEF
IN A JUST WORLD SCALE—20
QUESTION VERSION

Purpose: To measure personal beliefs in a just world and interpersonal beliefs.

Number of Items: 20

Format: Ten "just" and 10 "unjust" statements, using 7-point scales.

Reliability: Alphas were .58 (personal) and .60 (interpersonal).

Author: Stowers, D. A., and Durm, M. W.

Article: Is belief in a just world rational?

Journal: *Psychological Reports*, October 1998, 83(2), 423–426.

Related Research: Furnham, A., & Proctor, E. (1989). Belief in a just world: Review and critique of the individual difference literature. *British Journal of Social Psychology*, 28, 365–384.

9984

Test Name: OCCUPATIONAL
WORK ETHIC INVENTORY

Purpose: To assess work ethic endorsement.

Number of Items: 50

Format: Scales range from 1 (never) to 7 (always).

Reliability: Internal consistency reliabilities ranged from .86 to .92.

Author: Hill, R. B., and Rojewski, J. W.

Article: Double jeopardy: Work ethic differences in youth at risk of school failure.

Journal: *Career Development Quarterly*, March 1999, 47(3), 267–279.

Related Research: Petty, G. C., & Hill, R. B. (1994). Are men and women different? A study of the occupational work ethic. *Journal of Vocational Education Research*, 19, 71–89.

9985

Test Name: ORGANIZATIONAL
CULTURE PROFILE

Purpose: To measure work values.

Number of Items: 40

Format: Nine response categories range from "most characteristic of my organization" to "least characteristic of my organization." All items are presented.

Reliability: Mean test-retest reliability was .87 (6 months).

Author: Cable, D. M., and Judge, T. A.

Article: Interviewers' perceptions of person–organization fit and organizational selection decisions.

Journal: *Journal of Applied Psychology* August, 1997, 82(4), 546–561.

Related Research: O'Reilly, C. A., et al. (1991). People and the organizational culture: A profile comparison approach to assessing person-organization fit. *Academy of Management Journal*,34, 487–516.

9986

Test Name: PARENTAL VALUES
SCALE

Purpose: To assess the value placed on conformity.

Number of Items: 12

Format: Five-point rating scales. Sample items are presented.

Reliability: Alpha coefficients ranged from .72 to .84.

Validity: Correlations with other variables ranged from −.19 to .22.

Author: McHale, S. M., et al.

Article: Step in or stay out? Parents' roles in adolescent siblings' relationships.

Journal: *Journal of Marriage and the Family*, August 2000, 62(3), 746–760.

Related Research: Curtner-Smith, M. E., et al. (1995). Fathers' occupational conditions, values of self-direction and conformity, and perceptions of nurturant and restrictive parenting in relation to young children's depression and aggression. *Family Relations, 44*, 299–305.

9987

Test Name: PHILOSOPHICAL ORIENTATION QUESTIONNAIRE

Purpose: To assess pragmatic, intellectual, and human operating philosophies.

Format: A sample item is presented.

Reliability: Cronbach alphas ranged from .70 to .79 across subscales.

Validity: Correlations with other variables ranged from −.25 to .29.

Author: Boyatzis, R. E., et al.

Article: Philosophy as a missing link between values and behavior.

Journal: *Psychological Reports*, February 2000, *86*(1), 47–64.

Related Research: Boyatzis, R. E. (1998). *Transforming qualitative information: Thematic analysis and code development.* Newbury Park, CA: Sage.

9988

Test Name: PROTESTANT ETHIC SCALE

Purpose: To provide a global measure of work ethic attitudes.

Number of Items: 19

Format: Responses are made on a scale ranging from −3 (I disagree strongly) to 3 (I agree strongly). Sample items are presented.

Reliability: Kuder-Richardson internal consistency was .79. Coefficient alpha was .62.

Validity: Correlations with other

variables ranged from −.15 to .17.

Author: Sandoval, A.-M. R., et al.

Article: Construct validity of the Psychopathic Personality Inventory in a correctional sample.

Journal: *Journal of Personality Assessment*, April 2000, *74*(2), 262–281.

Related Research: Mirels, H. L., & Garrett, J. B. (1971). The Protestant ethic as a personality variable. *Journal of Consulting and Clinical Psychology, 36*, 40–44.

9989

Test Name: PROTESTANT WORK ETHIC SCALE

Purpose: To measure commitment to work.

Number of Items: 4

Format: Five-point scales anchored by (1) strongly disagree and (5) strongly agree. A sample is presented.

Reliability: Alpha was .75.

Validity: Correlations with other variables ranged from −.45 to .63.

Author: Gorgievski-Duijvesteijn, M., et al.

Article: Protestant work ethic as a moderator of mental and physical well-being.

Journal: *Psychological Reports*, December 1998, *83*(3) Part 1, 1043–1050.

Related Research: Zanders, H. L. G., et al. (1977). Kwaliteit van arbeid [Quality of working life]. Den Haag: Ministerie van Sociale Zaken en Werkgelegenheid.

9990

Test Name: PROTESTANT WORK ETHIC SCALE— REVISED

Purpose: To measure the Protestant work ethic.

Number of Items: 10

Format: Responses are made on a 7-point scale ranging from 1 (strongly disagree) to 7 (strongly agree).

Reliability: Reliability was .76.

Validity: Correlations with other variables ranged from −.04 to .33.

Author: Cohen, A.

Article: On the discriminant validity of the Meyers and Allen measure of organized comment: How does it fit with the work commitment?

Journal: *Educational and Psychological Measurement*, June 1996, *56*(3), 494–503.

Related Research: Mirels, H. L., & Garrett, J. B. (1971). The Protestant work ethic as a personality variable. *Journal of Consulting and Clinical Psychology, 36*, 40–44.

9991

Test Name: RELIGIOSITY SCALE

Purpose: To measure extrinsic religiousness.

Number of Items: 2

Format: Five-point scales. Both items are presented.

Reliability: Alpha was .91.

Author: Gnaulati, E., and Heine, B. J.

Article: Parental bonding and religiosity in young adulthood.

Journal: *Psychological Reports*,

December 1997, *81*(3, Part II), 1171–1174.

Related Research: Levine, J. B., et al. (1986). The separation-individuation test of adolescence. *Journal of Personality Assessment, 50*, 123–157.

9992

Test Name: RELIGIOSITY SCALE

Purpose: To operationalize behavioral, cognitive, and affective aspects of religiosity.

Number of Items: 3

Format: Five-point scales are employed.

Reliability: Coefficient alpha was .70.

Author: Dollinger, S. J.

Article: Autophotographic identities of young adults: With special references to alcohol, athletics, achievement, religion, and work.

Journal: *Journal of Personality Assessment*, October 1996, *67*(2), 384–398.

Related Research: Dollinger, S. J., et al. (1992, August). *On the perceived incompatibility of psychology and religion.* Paper presented at the meeting of the American Psychological Association, Washington, DC

9993

Test Name: RELIGIOSITY SCALE

Purpose: To assess religiosity.

Number of Items: 6

Format: Responses are made on a 5-point Likert scale.

Reliability: Coefficient alpha was .76.

Validity: Correlation with other

variables ranged from −.06 to .17.

Author: Newcomb, M. D., et al.

Article: Acculturation, sexual risk taking, and HIV health promotion among Latinas.

Journal: *Journal of Counseling Psychology*, October 1998, *45*(4), 454–467.

9994

Test Name: RELIGIOUS BELIEFS AND BEHAVIOR SCALE

Purpose: To measure religious behavior and belief in God.

Number of Items: 6

Format: Eight-point scales range from 0 (never) to 7 (more than once a day).

Reliability: Coefficient alpha was .83.

Author: Winzelberg, A., and Humphreys, K.

Article: Should patients' religiosity influence clinicians' referral to 12-step self-help group? Evidence from a study of 3,018 male substance abuse patients.

Journal: *Journal of Consulting and Clinical Psychology*, October 1999, *67*(5), 790–794.

Related Research: Conners, G., et al. (1996). A measure of religious background and behavior for use in behavior change research. *Psychology of Addictive Behaviors, 10*, 90–96.

9995

Test Name: RELIGIOUS COMMITMENT INVENTORY

Purpose: To measure motivational and behavioral commitment to a religious value system.

Number of Items: 20

Format: Responses are made on a scale ranging from 1 (not at all true of me) to 5 (totally true of me). All items are presented.

Reliability: Alpha coefficient was .92

Validity: Correlations with other variables ranged from .64 to 71.

Author: McCullough, M. E., et al.

Article: Gender in the context of supportive and challenging religious counseling interventions.

Journal: *Journal of Counseling Psychology*, January, 1997, *44*(1), 80–88.

Related Research: Worthington, E. L., et al. (1988, November). *Preliminary texts of Worthington's (1988) theory of important values in religious counseling.* Paper presented at the First International Congress on Christian Counseling, Atlanta, GA.

9996

Test Name: RELIGIOUS WELL-BEING SCALE

Purpose: To assess religious beliefs.

Number of Items: 20

Format: Six-point scales are anchored by 1 (strongly disagree) and 6 (strongly agree).

Reliability: Coefficient alpha was .93.

Author: Murphy, P. E., et al.

Article: The relation of religious belief and practices, depression, and hopelessness in persons with clinical depression.

Journal: *Journal of Consulting and Clinical Psychology*, December 2000, *68*(6), 1102–1106.

Related Research: Paloutzian, R. F., & Ellison, C. W. (1982). Loneliness, spiritual well-being, and the quality of life. In L. A. Peplaw & D. Perlman (Eds.), *Loneliness: A sourcebook of current theory, research, and therapy* (pp. 224–236). New York: Wiley.

9997

Test Name: REVISED ENNIS VALUE ORIENTATION INVENTORY

Purpose: To measure participants' educational value orientation.

Number of Items: 90

Format: Includes 5 subscales. Responses are made on a 5-point scale ranging from 1 (least valued) to 5 (most valued).

Reliability: Alpha coefficients ranged from .65 to .82.

Author: Chen, A., et al.

Article: Universality and uniqueness of teacher educational value orientations: A cross-cultural comparison between USA and China.

Journal: *Journal of Research and Development in Education*, Spring 1997, *30*(3), 135–143.

Related Research: Ennis, C. D., & Chen, A. (1993). Domain specifications and content representativeness of the Revised Value Orientation Inventory. *Research Quarterly for Exercise and Sport*, *64*, 436–446.

9998

Test Name: REVISED MORAL AUTHORITY SCALE

Purpose: To assess how influential sources of moral authority are on moral issues.

Number of Items: 11

Format: Scales range from 0 (no influence) to 10 (a powerful

influence). A sample item is presented.

Reliability: Internal consistencies ranged from .95 to .98. Test-retest reliabilities ranged from .75 to .93.

Validity: Correlations between subscales ranged from .22 to .64.

Author: White, F. A.

Article: Relationship of family socialization processes to adolescent moral thought.

Journal: *Journal of Social Psychology*, February 2000, *140*(1), 75–91.

Related Research: White, F. A. (1997). Measuring the content of moral thought: The Revised Moral Authority Scale (MAS-R). *Social Behavior and Personality*, *25*, 321–334.

9999

Test Name: ROKEACH VALUE SURVEY—MODIFIED

Purpose: To measure to what extent a respondent's present job helped him or her to attain each of 18 values.

Number of Items: 18

Format: Five-point scales ranged from "to no extent" to "to a very large extent."

Reliability: Internal consistency was .85.

Author: George, J. M., and Jones, G. R.

Article: The experience of work and turnover intention: Interactive effects of value attainment, job satisfaction, and positive mood.

Journal: *Journal of Applied Psychology*, June 1996, *81*(3), 318–325.

Related Research: Rokeach, M. (1973). *The nature of human values*. New York: Free Press.

10000

Test Name: SCHOOL VALUE MEASURE

Purpose: To assess the extent to which respondents value academic success and the information that they learn in school.

Number of Items: 18

Format: Responses are made on a 4-point scale ranging from 1 (hardly ever) to 4 (pretty often). An example is presented.

Reliability: Coefficient alpha was .86.

Author: Rhodes, J. E., et al.

Article: Agents of change: Pathways through which mentoring relationships influence adolescents' academic adjustment.

Journal: *Child Development*, November/December 2000, *71*(6), 1662–1671.

Related Research: Berndt, T., & Miller, K. (1986). Expectancies, values, and achievement in junior high school. *Journal of Educational Psychology*, *82*, 319–326.

10001

Test Name: SOCIAL DOMINANCE ORIENTATION SCALE

Purpose: To assess the degree to which individuals endorse anti-vegetarian values.

Number of Items: 16

Format: Scales ranged from 1 (strongly disagree) to 6 (strongly agree).

Reliability: Coefficient alpha was .84.

Author: Allen, M. W., et al.

Article: Values and beliefs of vegetarians and omnivores.

Journal: *Journal of Social Psychology*, August 2000, *140*(4), 405–422.

Related Research: Pratto, F., et al. (1994). Social dominance orientation: A personality variable predicting social and political attitudes. *Journal of Personality and Social Psychology, 67*, 741–763.

10002

Test Name: SOCIAL VALUE OF WORK SCALE

Purpose: To measure social value of work.

Number of Items: 3

Format: Responses are made on a 5-point Likert scale ranging from 1 (strongly disagree) to 5 (strongly agree).

Reliability: Coefficient alpha was .76.

Validity: Correlations with other variables ranged from −.30 to .51.

Author: Wallace, J. E.

Article: It's about time: A study of hours worked and work spillover among law firm lawyers.

Journal: *Journal of Vocational Behavior*, April 1997, *50*(2), 227–248.

10003

Test Name: TIME STRUCTURE QUESTIONNAIRE

Purpose: To assess the extent to which individuals perceive the use of time to be purposive.

Number of Items: 26

Format: Scales range from 1 (no, never) to 7 (yes, always).

Reliability: Alpha coefficients

ranged from .58 to .82. Test-retest reliability (15 weeks) was .76.

Authors: Vodanovich, S. J., and Watt, J. D.

Article: The relationship between time structure and boredom proneness: An investigation within two cultures.

Journal: *Journal of Social Psychology*, April 1999, *139*(2), 143–152.

Related Research: Bond, M. J., & Feather, N. T. (1988). Some correlates of structure and purpose in the use of time. *Journal of Personality and Social Psychology, 55*, 321–329.

10004

Test Name: TRADITIONAL GENDER ROLE VALUES

Purpose: To measure traditional gender role values.

Number of Items: 7

Format: Responses are made on a Likert 5-point scale ranging from 1 (strongly disagree) to 5 (strongly agree).

Reliability: Coefficient alpha was .84.

Validity: Correlations with other variables ranged from −.17 to −.59.

Author: Werbel, J.

Article: Intent and choice regarding maternal employment following childbirth.

Journal: *Journal of Vocational Behavior*, December 1998, *53*(3), 372–385.

Related Research: Arditti, J. A., et al. (1991). Perceptions of parenting behavior and young women's gender role traits and preferences. *Sex Roles, 25*, 195–203.

10005

Test Name: TRADITIONALISM–MODERNITY SCALE

Purpose: To assess an individual's position on a traditional-to-modern values continuum.

Number of Items: 21

Format: Ten-point scales are used.

Reliability: Coefficient alpha was .67.

Authors: Williams, S., and Narendran, S.

Article: Determinants of managerial risk: Exploring personality and cultural influences.

Journal: *Journal of Social Psychology*, February 1999, *139*(1), 102–125.

Related Research: Nedd, A. N. B., & Marsh, N. R. (1970). Social traditionalism and personality: An empirical investigation of the inter-relationships between social values and personality attributes. *International Journal of Social Psychology, 14*, 73–82.

10006

Test Name: UNIVERSALITY–DIVERSITY SCALE

Purpose: To assess the universality–diversity orientation.

Number of Items: 45 (15, short form).

Format: Scales range from 1 (strongly disagree) to 6 (strongly agree). All items are presented.

Reliability: Alpha coefficients ranged from .59 to .92 across subscales.

Validity: Correlations with other variables ranged from −.41 to .45.

Author: Fuertes, J. N., et al.

Article: Factor structure of and short form of the Miville-Guzman Universality–Diversity Scale.

Journal: *Measurement and Evaluation in Counseling and Development*, October 2000, *33*(3), 157–169.

Related Research: Miville, M. L., et al. (1999). Appreciating similarities and valuing differences: The Miville-Guzman Universality–Diversity Scale. *Journal of Counseling Psychology, 46,* 291–307.

10007

Test Name: VALUE CONSCIOUSNESS SCALE

Purpose: To measure the consciousness value (utility) that consumers receive from the products they buy.

Number of Items: 7

Format: Seven-point scales are anchored by "strongly agree" and "strongly disagree." All items are presented.

Reliability: Alphas ranged from .74 to .76 across two 3-item factors.

Author: Conrad, C. A., and Williams, J. R.

Article: Examination of the factor structure for the Consumers' Responses to the Value Consciousness Scale.

Journal: *Psychological Reports,* December 2000, *87*(3), Part 2, 1133–1138.

Related Research: Lichtenstein, D. R., et al. (1990). Distinguishing coupon proneness from value-consciousness: An acquisition-transition utility theory perspective. *Journal of Marketing, 54,* 57–67.

10008

Test Name: VALUE CRISIS QUESTIONNAIRE

Purpose: To assess value crisis as the inability to organize personal values into a coherent system, loss of values, lack of integration in the valuing process, and low sense of value realization.

Number of Items: 25

Format: True-false format. Sample items are presented.

Reliability: Coefficient alpha was .90. Test-retest reliability (2 weeks) was .88.

Author: Hermans, H. J. M., and Oles, P. K.

Article: Value crisis: Affective organization of personal meanings.

Journal: *Journal of Research in Personality,* December 1996, *30*(4), 457–482.

Related Research: Oles, P. K. (1991). Value crisis: Measurement and personality correlates. *Polish Psychological Bulletin, 22,* 53–62.

10009

Test Name: VALUE ORIENTATION INVENTORY

Purpose: To measure teachers' beliefs and educational priorities when making educational decisions.

Number of Items: 90

Format: Each set of 5 items is ranked from 5 (highest priority) to 1 (lowest priority).

Reliability: Alpha coefficients ranged from .65 to .82 ($N = 495$).

Author: Ennis, C. D., et al.

Article: The influence of teachers' educational beliefs on their knowledge organization.

Journal: *Journal of Research and Development in Education,* Winter 1997, *30*(2), 73–86.

Related Research: Ennis, C. D., & Chen, A. (1995). Teachers' value orientations in urban and rural settings. *Research Quarterly for Exercise and Sport, 66,* 41–50.

10010

Test Name: VALUE SURVEY

Purpose: To assess values.

Number of Items: 48

Format: All items are presented along with scoring rules.

Reliability: Alpha coefficients ranged from .67 to .86 across subscales.

Authors: Ashkanasy, N. M., and O'Connor, C.

Article: Value congruence in leader-member exchange.

Journal: *Journal of Social Psychology,* October 1997, *137*(5), 647–662.

Related Research: Schwartz, S. H., & Bilsky, W. (1987). Towards a universal psychological structure of human values. *Journal of Personality and Social Psychology, 53,* 550–562.

10011

Test Name: VALUES QUESTIONNAIRE

Purpose: To assess the degree to which participants value certain characteristics.

Number of Items: 98

Format: Includes 18 categories.

Reliability: Alpha coefficients ranged from .60 to .88.

Author: Patel, N., et al.

Article: Socialization values and practices of Indian immigrant parents: Correlates of modernity and acculturation.

Journal: *Child Development*, April 1996, *67*(2), 302–313.

Related Research: Power, T. G., et al. (1990, March). *The assessment of adolescent values: Factor structure, reliability, and validity of a new questionnaire.* Paper presented at the Southwestern Society for Research in Human Development, Dallas.

10012

Test Name: VALUES SURVEY

Purpose: To measure self-enhancement and openness to change.

Number of Items: 18

Format: Scales range from 1 (not important) to 7 (very important). Items are described.

Reliability: Alpha coefficients ranged from .61 to .65.

Validity: Correlations with other variables ranged from −.37 to .23.

Author: Schmitt-Rodermund, E., and Silbereisen, R. K.

Article: Career maturity determinants: Individual development, social context, and historical time.

Journal: *Career Development Quarterly*, September 1998, *47*(1), 16–31.

Related Research: Schwartz, S. H. (1992). Universals in the content and structure of values: Theoretical advances and empirical tests in 20 countries. In M. Zanna (Ed.), *Advances in experimental social psychology* (Vol. 25, pp. 1–65). Orlando, FL: Academic Press.

10013

Test Name: WORK BELIEFS QUESTIONNAIRE

Purpose: To measure humanistic and Protestant work beliefs.

Number of Items: 33

Format: Five-point scales are anchored by 1 (strongly disagree) and 5 (strongly agree).

Reliability: Coefficient alpha was .72 (Protestant) and .79 (humanistic).

Validity: Correlations with other variables ranged from −.25 to .14 (Protestant) and from −.25 to .02 (humanistic).

Author: Barling, J., et al.

Article: Effects of parents' job insecurity on children's work beliefs and attitudes.

Journal: *Journal of Applied Psychology*, February 1998, *83*(1), 112–118.

Related Research: Mirels, H., & Garrett, J. (1971). The Protestant ethic as a personality variable. *Journal of Consulting and Clinical Psychology, 36*, 40–44.

10014

Test Name: WORK BELIEFS SCALE

Purpose: To measure work beliefs as worker involvement, status of the wealthy, and negative outlook.

Number of Items: 11

Format: Five-point Likert format. All items are presented.

Reliability: Alphas ranged from .71 to .79.

Validity: Correlations with other variables ranged from −.12 to .50.

Author: Pisnar-Sweeney, M.

Article: Role of normative commitment in predicting members' participation in the union.

Journal: *Psychological Reports*, June 1997, *80*(3) Part 2, 1183–1207.

Related Research: Buchholtz, R. A. (1978). An empirical study of contemporary beliefs about work in American society. *Journal of Applied Psychology, 63*(2), 219–227.

10015

Test Name: WORK ETHIC SCALE

Purpose: To measure work ethic.

Number of Items: 25

Format: Includes 4 dimensions: Hard Work, Nonleisure, Independence, and Asceticism. Responses are made on a 7-point scale ranging from 1 (strongly disagree) to 7 (strongly agree).

Reliability: Alpha coefficients ranged from .70 to .85.

Author: Blau, G., and Ryan, J.

Article: On measuring work ethic: A neglected work commitment facet.

Journal: *Journal of Vocational Behavior*, December 1997, *51*(3), 435–448.

Related Research: Furham, A. (1990). A content, correlational, and factor analytic study of seven questionnaire measures of the Protestant work ethic. *Human Relations, 43*, 383–399.

10016

Test Name: WORK VALUES SCALE

Purpose: To assess intrinsic, instrumental, and systemic work values.

Number of Items: 15

Format: Five-point scales are anchored by 1 (not important at all) and 5 (very important). All items are presented.

Reliability: Alphas ranged from .70 to .75 across subscales.

Author: Akhtar, S.

Article: Influences of cultural origin and sex on work values.

Journal: *Psychological Reports*, June 2000, *86*(3, Part 1), 1037–1049.

Related Research: Bond, M. H. (1991). Chinese values and health: A cultural-level examination. *Psychology and Health, 5,* 137–152.

10017

Test Name: WORK VALUES SCALE

Purpose: To measure work values.

Number of Items: 25

Format: Scales range from 1 (not important) to 5 (very important).

Reliability: Coefficient alpha was .90.

Authors: Abu-Saad, I., and Isralowitz, R. E.

Article: Gender as a determinant of work values among university students in Israel.

Journal: *Journal of Social Psychology*, December 1997, *137*(6), 749–763.

Related Research: Manhardt, P. J. (1972). Job orientation among male and female college graduates in business. *Personnel Psychology, 25,* 361–368.

10018

Test Name: WORLD ASSUMPTION SCALE

Purpose: To assess assumptions people entertain about the benevolence of the world.

Number of Items: 32.

Format: Six-point scales range from "strongly agree" to "strongly disagree."

Reliability: Subscale reliabilities ranged from .67 to .78.

Authors: Magwaza, A.S.

Article: Assumptive world of traumatized South African adults.

Journal: *The Journal of Social Psychology*, October 1999, *139*(5), 622–630.

Related Research: Janoff-Bulman, R. (1989). Assumptive world and the stress of traumatic events: Applications of the schema construct. *Social Cognition, 7,* 113–136.

■ ■ ■

CHAPTER 23
Vocational Evaluation

10019

Test Name: ACCOUNTING ADEQUACY SCALE

Purpose: To measure the perceived adequacy of a decision to promote an employee.

Number of Items: 2

Format: Seven-point scales are anchored by 1 (disagree strongly) and 7 (agree strongly). All items are presented.

Reliability: Correlation between the two items was .75.

Author: Bobocel, D. R., and Farrell, A. C.

Article: Sex-based promotion decisions and interactional fairness: Investigating the influence of managerial accounts.

Journal: *Journal of Applied Psychology*, February 1996, *81*(1), 22–35.

Related Research: Bies, R. J., et al. (1988). Causal accounts and managing organizational conflict: Is it enough to say it's not my fault? *Communication Research*, *15*, 381–399.

10020

Test Name: ACCURACY OF APPRAISAL SCALE

Purpose: To measure the perceived accuracy of a performance appraisal.

Number of Items: 8

Format: Scales range from "strongly disagree" to "strongly agree." A sample item is presented.

Reliability: Coefficient alpha was .96.

Validity: Correlations with other variables ranged from −.27 to .88.

Author: Keeping, L. M., and Levy, P. E.

Article: Performance appraisal reactions: Measurement, modeling and method bias.

Journal: *Journal of Applied Psychology*, October 2000, *85*(5), 708–723.

Related Research: Stone, D. L., et al. (1984). The effects of feedback sequence and expertise of the rater on perceived feedback accuracy. *Personnel Psychology*, *37*, 487–506.

10021

Test Name: ACTIVE–PASSIVE INVENTORY

Purpose: To measure the lecturer–student relationship.

Number of Items: 17

Format: Five-point scales are anchored by (1) strongly disagree and (5) strongly agree. All items are presented.

Reliability: Alpha was .93.

Author: Mji, A., and Kalashe, L.

Article: Exploring the lecturer-student relationship: Preferences of a sample of undergraduate students in business management.

Journal: *Psychological Reports*, December 1998, *83*(3) Part 2, 1297–1298.

Related Research: Williams, E.

(1992). Students attitudes towards approaches to learning and assessment. *Assessment and Evaluation in Higher Education*, *17*, 45–58.

10022

Test Name: ADHERENCE AND COMPETENCE SCALE FOR ADDICTION COUNSELING

Purpose: To assess the competence in monitoring drug use behavior, encouraging abstinence, supportively confronting negative behavior, encouraging 12-step participation, relapse prevention, and educating the client.

Number of Items: 17

Format: Seven-point scales are anchored by 1 (not present or poor quality) and 7 (highly frequent or excellent quality).

Reliability: Alpha coefficients were .84 (adherence) and .87 (competence).

Author: Crits-Christoph, P., et al.

Article: Training in cognitive, support-expressive, and drug counseling therapies for cocaine dependence.

Journal: *Journal of Consulting and Clinical Psychology*, June 1998, *66*(3), 484–492.

Related Research: Mercer, D., et al. (1994*). Adherence/ Competence Scale for Individual Drug Counseling for Cocaine Dependence.* Unpublished manuscript, Center for Psychotherapy Research, Department of Psychiatry,

University of Pennsylvania Medical Center.

10023

Test Name: ADULT ATTACHMENT SCALE

Purpose: To estimate the therapist's self-reported ability to develop healthy relationships.

Number of Items: 18

Format: Includes 3 subscales: Depend, Anxiety, and Close. Responses are made on a 5-point scale ranging from 1 (not at all characteristic of me) to 5 (very characteristic of me).

Reliability: Test-retest (2 months) reliability ranged from .52 to .71. Internal consistency reliability coefficients ranged from .69 to .88.

Validity: Correlations with other variables ranged from .71 to .73.

Author: Dunkle, J. H., and Fiedlander, M. L.

Article: Contribution of therapist experience and personal characteristics to the working alliance.

Journal: *Journal of Counseling Psychology*, October 1996, *43*(4), 456–460.

Related Research: Collins, N. L., & Read, S. J. (1990). Adult attachment, working models, and relationship quality in dating couples. *Journal of Personality and Social Psychology*, *58*, 644–663.

10024

Test Name: AGNEW RELATIONSHIP MEASURE

Purpose: To measure the client–therapist alliance in terms of bond, partnership, confidence, openness, and client initiative.

Number of Items: 28

Format: Seven-point scales.

Reliability: Alpha coefficients ranged from .55 to .87.

Author: Hardy, G. E.

Article: Therapist responsiveness to client interpersonal styles during limited-time treatments for depression.

Journal: *Journal of Consulting and Clinical Psychology*, April 1998, *66*(2), 304–312.

Related Research: Agnew-Davies, R., et al. (1998). Alliance structure assessed by the Agnew Relationship Measure (ARM). *British Journal of Clinical Psychology*, *37*, 155–172.

10025

Test Name: APPLICANT QUALIFICATIONS SOUGHT

Purpose: To identify student qualifications sought by recruiters.

Number of Items: 28

Format: Includes 5 factors: Motivation, Interpersonal Skills, Activities, Academic Record, and Experience. Responses are made on a 5-point scale ranging from "not important at all" to "extremely important."

Reliability: Alpha coefficients ranged from .72 to .89.

Validity: Correlations with other variables ranged from −.13 to .40.

Author: Barber, A. E., et al.

Article: A tale of two job markets: Organizational size and its effects on hiring practices and job search behavior.

Journal: *Personnel Psychology*, Winter 1999, *52*(4), 841–867.

Related Research: Pritchard, C. J., & Fidler, P. P. (1993). What small firms look for in new-graduate candidates. *Journal of Career Planning and Employment*, *53*, 45–50.

10026

Test Name: APPRAISAL UTILITY SCALE

Purpose: To measure the perceived utility of a performance appraisal.

Number of Items: 4

Format: Scales range from "I do not feel this way, not at all" to "I feel exactly this way, completely." A sample item is presented.

Reliability: Coefficient alpha was .91.

Validity: Correlations with other variables ranged from −.27 to .88.

Author: Keeping, L. M., and Levy, P. E.

Article: Performance appraisal reactions: Measurement, modeling and method bias.

Journal: *Journal of Applied Psychology*, October 2000, *85*(5), 708–723.

Related Research: Greller, M. M. (1978). The nature of subordinate participation in the appraisal interview. *Academy of Management Journal*, *21*, 646–658.

10027

Test Name: BARRETT-LENNARD RELATIONSHIP INVENTORY—FORM 05–64

Purpose: To reflect clients' thoughts and feelings with regard to their therapist and parental figures.

Number of Items: 64

Format: Includes 4 subscales: Level of Regard, Empathy, Unconditionality, and

Congruence. Responses are made on a 6-point scale ranging from −3 (strongly untrue) to 3 (strongly true).

Reliability: Spearman-Brown split-half reliabilities ranged from .82 to .95. Test-retest (4 weeks) reliabilities ranged from .84 to .95.

Author: Arachtingi, B. M., and Lichtenberg, J. W.

Article: The relationship between clients' perceptions of therapist-parent similarity with respect to empathy, regard, and unconditionality and therapists' ratings of client transference.

Journal: *Journal of Counseling Psychology*, April 1998, *45*(2), 143–149.

Related Research: Barrett-Lennard, G. T. (1973). *Barrett-Lennard Relationship Inventory, Form OS-64*. Unpublished manuscript.

10028

Test Name: BEHAVIOR INTERVENTION RATING SCALE—MODIFIED

Purpose: To rate behavior intervention in an adult psychotherapy situation.

Number of Items: 24

Format: Includes 3 factors; Acceptability, Effectiveness, and Time. Responses are made on a 6-point Likert-type scale.

Reliability: Alpha coefficient ranged from .87 to .97.

Validity: Correlations with other variables ranged from .29 to .58 (*N* = 91).

Author: Scheel, M. J., et al.

Article: Client implementation of therapist recommendations predicted by client perceptions of fit, difficulty of implementation, and therapist influences.

Journal: *Journal of Counseling Psychology*, July 1999, *46*(3), 303–316.

Related Research: Witt, J. C., et al. (1984). Factors affecting teachers' judgments of the acceptability of behavioral interventions: Time involvement, behavior problem severity, type of intervention. *Behavior Therapy, 15*, 204–209.

10029

Test Name: CALIFORNIA PSYCHOTHERAPY ALLIANCE SCALE

Purpose: To measure the strength of the patient–therapist therapeutic alliance.

Format: Six-point scales range from 1 (I strongly feel it is not true) to 6 (I strongly feel it is true).

Reliability: Alpha coefficients ranged from .86 to .91.

Validity: Subscale intercorrelations ranged from .55 to .70.

Author: Barber, J. P., et al.

Article: Alliance predicts patients' outcome beyond in-treatment changes in symptoms.

Journal: *Journal of Consulting and Clinical Psychology*, December 2000, *68*(6), 1027–1032.

Related Research: Gaston, L. (1990). The concept of the alliance and its role in psychotherapy: Theoretical and empirical considerations. *Psychotherapy, 27*, 143–153.

10030

Test Name: CAREER DEVELOPMENT MENTORING SCALE

Purpose: To assess career

development mentoring functions received by proteges.

Number of Items: 7

Format: Responses are made on a 5-point scale ranging from 1 (disagree strongly) to 5 (agree strongly). An example is presented.

Reliability: Coefficient alpha was .86.

Validity: Correlations with other variables ranged from −.21 to .42.

Author: Sosik, J. J., and Godshalk, V. M.

Article: The role of gender in mentoring: Implications for diversified and homogenous mentoring relationships.

Journal: *Journal of Vocational Behavior*, August 2000, *57*(1), 102–122.

Related Research: Noe, R. (1988). An investigation of the determinants of successful assigned mentoring relationships. *Personnel Psychology, 41*, 457–479.

10031

Test Name: CAREER SUCCESS SCALE

Purpose: To measure subjective career success.

Number of Items: 5

Format: Scales range from 1 (very dissatisfied) to 5 (very satisfied). A sample item is presented.

Reliability: Coefficient alpha was .83.

Author: Seibert, S. E., et al.

Article: Proactive personality and career success.

Journal: *Journal of Applied Psychology*, June 1999, *84*(3), 416–427.

Related Research: Greenhaus,

J. H., et al. (1990). Effects of race on organizational experiences, job performance evaluations, and career outcomes. *Academy of Management Journal, 33,* 64–86.

10032

Test Name: CLIENT ATTACHMENT TO THERAPIST SCALE

Purpose: To assess clients' perceptions of the client–therapist relationship from the perspective of attachment theory.

Number of Items: 36

Format: Includes 3 dimensions: Secure, Avoident-Fearful, and Preoccupied-Merger.

Reliability: Coefficient alpha and test-retest reliability coefficients were greater than .63.

Validity: Correlations with other variables ranged from −.31 to .43.

Author: Mallinckrodt, B., et al.

Article: Family dysfunction, alexithymia, and client attachment to therapist.

Journal: *Journal of Counseling Psychology,* October 1998, *45*(4), 497–504.

Related Research: Mallinckrodt, B., et al. (1995). Attachment patterns in the psychotherapy relationship: Development of the Client Attachment to Therapist Scale. *Journal of Counseling Psychology, 42,* 307–317.

10033

Test Name: CLIENT INSIGHTFULNESS SCALE

Purpose: To enable the therapist to rate client insightfulness.

Number of Items: 5

Format: Items are rated on a 7-point scale ranging from 7 (a lot) to 1 (none). All items are presented.

Reliability: Coefficient alpha was .93.

Author: Diemer, R. A., et al.

Article: Comparison of dream interpretation, event interpretation, and unstructured sessions in brief therapy.

Journal: *Journal of Counseling Psychology,* January 1996, *43*(1), 99–112.

Related Research: McCallum, M., & Piper, W. E. (1990). The psychological mindedness assessment procedure. *Psychological Assessment, 2,* 412–418.

10034

Test Name: CLIENT RATING SCALES

Purpose: To provide for clinicians' ratings of clients.

Number of Items: 6

Format: Responses are made on 6-point scales.

Reliability: Test-retest (2 weeks) reliability coefficients ranged from .59 to .81.

Author: Wisch, A. F., and Mahalik, J. R.

Article: Male therapists' clinical bias: Influences of client gender roles and therapist gender role conflict.

Journal: *Journal of Counseling Psychology,* January 1999, *46*(1), 51–60.

Related Research: Hayes, M. M. (1984). *Counselor sex-role values and effects on attitudes toward and treatment of nontraditional male clients.* (Doctoral dissertation, Ohio State University, 1984). *Dissertation Abstracts International, 45,* 3072B.

10035

Test Name: CLIENT SATISFACTION QUESTIONNAIRE

Purpose: To assess level of satisfaction with counseling.

Number of Items: 14

Format: Various 5-point scales are used. All items and response scales are presented.

Reliability: Alpha coefficients ranged from .87 to .93.

Author: Obetz, S. A., et al.

Article: Influence of actual and perceived wait for counseling services on client outcome variables.

Journal: *Journal of College Student Development,* March/April 1997, *38*(2), 173–180.

Related Research: Larsen, D. L., et al. (1979). *Client satisfaction questionnaire.* Unpublished manuscript, University of California, San Francisco.

10036

Test Name: CLIENT SATISFACTION SCALE

Purpose: To measure satisfaction with treatment.

Number of Items: 8

Format: Five-point scales are anchored by 1 (it was awful, I regretted it) and 5 (it was wonderful).

Validity: Correlations with other variables ranged from −.38 to .55.

Author: Kleinpeter, C. H., and Hohman, M. M.

Article: Surrogate motherhood:

Personality traits and satisfaction with service providers.

Journal: *Psychological Reports*, December 2000, *87*(3), Part 1, 957–970.

Related Research: Larsen, D., et al. (1979). Assessment of client/patient satisfaction: Development of a general scale. *Evaluation and Program Planning*, 2, 197–207.

10037

Test Name: COGNITIVE THERAPY SCALE

Purpose: To evaluate therapists who practice cognitive therapy and to assess session quality.

Number of Items: 7

Format: Seven-point scales are anchored by 0 (poor) and 6 (excellent).

Reliability: Coefficient alpha was .92.

Author: Crits-Christoph, P., et al.

Article: Training in cognitive, supportive-expressive, and drug counseling therapies for cocaine dependence.

Journal: *Journal of Consulting and Clinical Psychology*, June 1998, *66*(3), 484–492.

Related Research: Young, J., & Beck, A. T. (1980). *The Cognitive Therapy Scale.* Unpublished manuscript, Center for Cognitive Therapy, Philadelphia.

10038

Test Name: COMBINED ALLIANCE SHORT FORM

Purpose: To measure therapeutic alliance.

Number of Items: 20

Format: Includes 4 subscales: Confident Collaboration, Goals

and Tasks, Bond, and Idealized Therapist. Responses are made on a 7-point scale ranging from 1 (never) to 7 (always). Examples are presented.

Reliability: Alpha coefficients ranged from .84 to .93.

Author: Ackerman, S. J., et al.

Article: Interaction of therapeutic process and alliance during psychological assessments.

Journal: *Journal of Personality Assessment*, August 2000, *75*(1), 82–109.

Related Research: Hatcher, R. L., & Barends, A. W. (1996). Patient's view of the alliance in psychotherapy. Exploratory factor analysis of three alliance measures. *Journal of Consulting and Clinical Psychology, 64,* 1326–1336.

10039

Test Name: CONSULTANT EVALUATION FORM

Purpose: To measure consultees' perceptions of consultants' effectiveness.

Number of Items: 12

Format: Responses are made on a 7-point rating scale.

Reliability: Internal consistency was .94.

Validity: Correlations with other variables ranged from −.40 to .99.

Author: Busse, R. T., et al.

Article: Influences of verbal interactions during behavioral consultations on treatment outcomes.

Journal: *Journal of School Psychology*, Summer 1999, *37*(2), 117–143.

Related Research: Erchul, W. P. (1987). A relational communication analysis of

control in school consultation. *Professional School Psychology, 2,* 113–124.

10040

Test Name: COUNSELING OUTCOME MEASURE

Purpose: To enable clients to rate their amount of improvement.

Number of Items: 4

Format: Responses are made on a 7-point scale ranging from 1 (much worse) to 7 (much improved).

Reliability: Alpha coefficients ranged from .89 to .92. Test-retest (3 weeks) reliability ranged from .63 to .81.

Author: Gelso, C. J., et al.

Article: Transference, insight, and the course of time-limited therapy.

Journal: *Journal of Counseling Psychology*, April 1997, *44*(2), 209–217.

Related Research: Gelso, C. J., & Johnson, D. H. (1983). *Explorations in time-limited counseling and psychotherapy.* New York: Columbia University, Teachers College Press.

10041

Test Name: COUNSELOR EFFECTIVENESS RATING SCALE

Purpose: To measure perceptions of counselor credibility.

Number of Items: 10

Format: Includes 4 dimensions: Expertness, Trustworthiness, Attractiveness, and Utility. Responses are made on a 7-point scale ranging from 1 (bad) to 7 (good).

Reliability: Alpha coefficients ranged from .75 to .94.

Validity: Correlation with the Counselor Rating Form was .80.

Author: Ramos-Sanchez, L., et al.

Article: Mexican Americans' bilingual ability, counselor bilingualism cues, counselor ethnicity, and perceived counselor credibility.

Journal: *Journal of Counseling Psychology*, January 1999, *46*(1), 125–131.

Related Research: Atkinson, D. R., & Wampold, B. E. (1982). A comparison of the Counselor Rating Form and the Counselor Effectiveness Rating Scale. *Counselor Education and Supervision, 22,* 25–36.

10042

Test Name: COUNSELOR RATING FORM

Purpose: To assess a client's perceptions of counselor's expertness, trustworthiness, and attractiveness.

Number of Items: 36

Format: Responses are made on 7-point bipolar scales.

Reliability: Reliability coefficients ranged from .75 to .92.

Validity: Correlations with other variables ranged from .00 to .77.

Author: Hanson, W. E., et al.

Article: Differential effects of two-test-interpretation styles in counseling: A field study.

Journal: *Journal of Counseling Psychology*, October 1997, *44*(4), 400–405.

Related Research: Barak, A., & LaCrosse, M. (1975). Multidimensional perception of counselor behavior. *Journal of Counseling Psychology, 22,* 471–476.

10043

Test Name: COUNSELOR RATING FORM—SHORT VERSION

Purpose: To assess participants' perception of their counselors.

Number of Items: 12

Format: Responses were made on a 7-point scale ranging from 1 (not very) to 6 (very).

Reliability: Reliability ranged from .88 to .95.

Author: Vera, E. M., et al.

Article: Clients' perceptions and evaluations of similarities and differences from their counselors.

Journal: *Journal of Counseling Psychology*, July 1999, *46*(2), 277–283.

Related Research: Corrigan, J. D., & Schmidt, L. D. (1983). Development and validation of revisions in the Counselor Rating Form. *Journal of Counseling Psychology, 30,* 64–75.

10044

Test Name: COUNTERTRANSFERENCE FACTORS INVENTORY

Purpose: To provide supervisors' perceptions of their supervisees' ability to manage countertransference reactions.

Number of Items: 50

Format: Includes 5 factors: Self-Insight, Self-Integration, Empathy, Anxiety Management, and Conceptualizing Ability. Responses are made on a 5-point scale ranging from 1 (strongly disagree) to 5 (strongly agree).

Reliability: Internal consistency was .97.

Author: Williams, E. N., et al.

Article: Experiences of novice therapists in practicum:

Trainees', clients', and supervisors' perception of therapists' personal reactions and management strategies.

Journal: *Journal of Counseling Psychology*, October 1997, *44*(4). 390–399.

Related Research: Van Wagoner, S. L., et al. (1991). Countertransference and the reputedly excellent therapist. *Psychotherapy, 28,* 411–421.

10045

Test Name: COURSE EVALUATION INDEXES

Purpose: To assess course instruction and administration.

Number of Items: 12

Format: Scales range from 5 (much above average—top 10%) to 1 (much below average—bottom 10%). All items are presented.

Reliability: Alpha coefficients ranged from .75 (administration) to .86 (instruction).

Author: Keller, B., et al.

Article: Effects of student-centered teaching on student evaluations in calculus.

Journal: *Educational Research Quarterly*, September 2000, *24*(1), 59–73.

10046

Test Name: CROSS-CULTURAL COUNSELING INVENTORY—REVISED

Purpose: To provide a measure of perceived multicultural counseling competence.

Number of Items: 20

Format: Includes 3 categories: Awareness, Knowledge, and Skills. Responses are made on a 6-point Likert-type scale ranging

from 1 (strongly disagree) to 6 (strongly agree).

Reliability: Coefficient alpha was .88.

Validity: Correlations with other variables ranged from .12 to .73 (*N* ranged from 133 to 135).

Author: Constantine, M. G., and Ladany, N.

Article: Self-report multicultural counseling competence scales: Their relation to social desirability attitudes and multicultural case conceptualization ability.

Journal: *Journal of Counseling Psychology*, April 2000, 47(2), 155–164.

Related Research: LaFromboise, T. D., et al. (1991). Development and factor structure of the Cross-Cultural Counseling Inventory—Revised. *Professional Psychology: Research and Practice*, 22, 380–388.

10047

Test Name: DEPTH SCALE

Purpose: To evaluate the quality of counseling.

Number of Items: 5

Format: Contains 5 bipolar items. A subscale of the Session Evaluation Questionnaire—Form 4. All items are presented.

Reliability: Alpha coefficients were .87 and .91.

Author: Rochlen, A. B., et al.

Article: Effects of training in dream recall and dream interpretation skills on dream recall, attitudes, and dream interpretation outcome.

Journal: *Journal of Counseling Psychology*, January 1999, 46(1), 27–34.

Related Research: Stiles, W. B., & Snow, J. S. (1984). Dimensions

of psychotherapy session impact across sessions and across clients. *British Journal of Clinical Psychology*, 41, 175–185.

10048

Test Name: ESTIMATE OF IMPROVEMENT SCALE

Purpose: To measure improvement to date in therapy.

Number of Items: 16

Format: Nine-point scales are anchored by −4 (very much worse) and +4 (very much better). Sample items are presented.

Reliability: Subscale alphas ranged from .83 to .89.

Author: Hatcher, R. L., and Barends, A. W.

Article: Patients' view of the alliance in psychotherapy: Exploratory factor analysis of three alliance measures.

Journal: *Journal of Consulting and Clinical Psychology*, December 1996, 64(6), 1326–1336.

Related Research: Alexander, L. B., & Laborsky, L. (1986). The Penn Helping Alliance Scales. In L. S. Greenberg & W. M. Pinshoff (Eds.), *The psychotherapeutic process: A research handbook* (pp. 325–366). New York: Guilford Press.

10049

Test Name: EXPRESSIVE COMPETENCE SCALE

Purpose: To assess the expressive competence of therapists who practice cognitive therapy.

Number of Items: 15

Format: Seven-point scales are anchored by 1 (not present or poor quality) and 7 (with frequency or excellent quality).

Reliability: Cronbach's alpha was .85.

Author: Crits-Christoph, P., et al.

Article: Training in cognitive, support-expressive, and drug counseling therapies for cocaine dependence.

Journal: *Journal of Consulting and Clinical Psychology*, June 1998, 66(3), 484–492.

Related Research: Barber, J. P., & Crits-Christoph, P. (1996). Development of a therapist adherence/competence rating scale for supportive-expressive dynamic psychotherapy: A preliminary report. *Psychotherapy Research, 6*, 81–94.

10050

Test Name: GAINS FROM DREAM INTERPRETATION

Purpose: To measure specific gains from dream interpretation sessions.

Number of Items: 14

Format: Includes 3 scales: Exploration-Insight, Action, and Experiential. Responses are made on a 9-point Likert-type scale.

Reliability: Alpha coefficients ranged from .75 to .84.

Validity: Correlations with other variables ranged from −.75 to .79.

Author: Wonnell, T. L., and Hill, C. E.

Article: Effects of including the action stage in dream interpretation.

Journal: *Journal of Counseling Psychology*, July 2000, 47(3), 372–379.

Related Research: Heaton, K. J., et al. (1998). A comparison of therapist-facilitated and self-guided dream interpretation sessions. *Journal of Counseling Psychology, 45,* 115–122.

10051

Test Name: GROUP COUNSELING HELPFUL IMPACTS SCALE

Purpose: To rate group counseling helpful impacts.

Number of Items: 28

Format: Includes 4 components: Emotional Awareness-Insight, Relationship-Climate, Other-Versus Self-Focus, and Problem Definition-Change. Responses were made on a 5-point scale ranging from 0 (not at all) to 4 (very much).

Reliability: Alpha coefficients ranged from .61 to .88.

Author: Holmes, S. E., and Kivlighan, D. M., Jr.

Article: Comparison of therapeutic factors group and individual treatment processes.

Journal: *Journal of Counseling Psychology,* October 2000, *47*(4), 478–484.

Related Research: Kivlighan, D. M., Jr., et al. (1996). Helpful impacts in group counseling: Development of a multidimensional rating system. *Journal of Counseling Psychology, 43,* 347–355.

10052

Test Name: HIREE RATING FORM

Purpose: To rate hirees on hardworking/lazy, gives up easily, energetic/sluggish, strong/weak, timid/forceful, soft/tough, irresponsible/responsible, helpful/not helpful, bad co-worker, good co-worker.

Number of Items: 9

Format: Nine-point bipolar adjective scales.

Reliability: Alpha coefficients ranged from .82 to .95.

Author: Lee, J. A., et al.

Article: Sexual stereotypes and perceptions of competence and qualifications.

Journal: *Psychological Reports,* April 1997, *80*(2), 419–428.

Related Research: Heilman, M. E., et al. (1992) Presumed incompetent: Stigmatization and affirmative action efforts. *Journal of Applied Psychology, 77,* 536–544.

10053

Test Name: IMPORTANT EVENTS QUESTIONNAIRE

Purpose: To enable judges to rate counselees' insights.

Number of Items: 9

Format: Judges rate each insight on a 10-point scale ranging from 0 (no evidence present in the written report) to 9 (clearly present in the written report). All items are included.

Reliability: Interjudge reliability ranged from .75 to .90. Internal consistency was .92.

Author: Kivlighan, Jr., D. M., et al.

Article: Insight and symptom reduction in time-limited psychoanalytic counseling.

Journal: *Journal of Counseling Psychology,* January 2000, *47*(1), 50–58.

Related Research: Morgan, R. W., et al. (1982). Predicting the outcomes of therapy using the Penn Helping Alliance rating method. *Archives of General Psychiatry, 39,* 397–402.

10054

Test Name: INSTRUCTIONAL EVALUATION SCALE

Purpose: To assess student evaluations of teaching in three dimensions: Instruction, Affect, and Classroom Environment.

Number of Items: 27

Format: Five-point scales range from 1 (outstanding) to 5 (poor). All items are presented.

Validity: Three factors were identified. Kaiser-Meyer-Ohlin sampling adequacy was .95.

Author: Hahn, W., et al.

Article: Instructional evaluation and prediction of teaching effectiveness in a small private college.

Journal: *Psychological Reports,* June 1997, *80*(3) Part 2, 1091–1102.

Related Research: Benz, C., & Blatt, S. J. (1995). Factors underlying effective college teaching. *Mid-Western Educational Researcher, 8,* 27–31.

10055

Test Name: INSTRUCTOR AUTHORITY STYLE QUESTIONNAIRE

Purpose: To measure the relationship between instructors and teaching assistants.

Number of Items: 32

Format: Five-point rating scales. Sample items are presented.

Reliability: Alphas ranged from .67 to .75 across subscales.

Validity: Correlations with other variables ranged from −.31 to .52.

Author: Meyers, S. A.

Article: Consequences of interpersonal relationships

between teaching assistants and supervising faculty.

Journal: *Psychological Reports*, June 1996, *78*(3) Part 1, 755–762.

Related Research: Buri, J. R. (1989). *An instrument for the measurement of parental authority prototypes*. Paper presented at the 1991 meeting of the Midwestern Psychological Association, Chicago, IL. (ERIC Document Reproduction Service No. Ed 306 471).

10056

Test Name: INSTRUCTOR SURVEY FOR CLASSROOM EQUITY

Purpose: To evaluate instructors' tendencies to monitor their classrooms for equity.

Number of Items: 24

Format: Responses are made on a 6-point scale ranging from 1 (extremely unimportant) to 6 (extremely important). All items are presented.

Reliability: Alpha coefficients ranged from .75 to .88.

Author: Brady, K. L., and Eister, R. M.

Article: Sex and gender in the college classroom: A quantitative analysis of faculty–student interactions and perceptions.

Journal: *Journal of Educational Psychology*, March 1999, *91*(1), 127–145.

Related Research: Brady, K. L. (1995). *The effects of gender on the behaviors and perceptions of students and instructors in the college classroom*. Unpublished doctoral dissertation, Virginia Polytechnic Institute and State University.

10057

Test Name: INTERACTIONAL FAIRNESS SCALE

Purpose: To measure the fairness of a decision maker.

Number of Items: 3

Format: Seven-point scales are anchored by 1 (strongly disagree) and 7 (strongly agree). All items are presented.

Reliability: Coefficient alpha was .76.

Author: Bobocel, D. R., and Farrell, A. C.

Article: Sex-based promotion decisions and interactional fairness: Investigating the influence of managerial accounts.

Journal: *Journal of Applied Psychology*, February 1996, *81*(1), 22–35.

Related Research: Bies, R. J., & Shapiro, D. L. (1988). Voice and justification: Their influence on procedural fairness judgements. *Academy of Management Journal, 31*, 676–685.

10058

Test Name: JOB PERFORMANCE SCALE

Purpose: To enable supervisors to rate managers.

Number of Items: 5

Format: Responses are made on 5-point scales. Each type of item is presented.

Reliability: Coefficient alpha was .91.

Validity: Correlations with other variables ranged from −.29 to .22.

Author: Ettington, D. R.

Article: Successful career plateauing.

Journal: *Journal of Vocational*

Behavior, February 1998, *52*(1), 72–88.

Related Research: Denison, D. R., et al. (1995). Paradox and performance: Toward a theory of behavioral complexity in managerial leadership. *Organization Science, 6*, 524–540.

10059

Test Name: JOB PERFORMANCE SCALE

Purpose: To assess job performance.

Number of Items: 7

Format: Responses are made on a 5-point scale ranging from 1 (well below average) to 5 (well above average).

Reliability: Coefficient alpha was .87.

Validity: Correlations with other variables ranged from −.13 to .25.

Author: Shore, L. M., et al.

Article: Construct validity of measures of Becker's side bet theory.

Journal: *Journal of Vocational Behavior*, December 2000, *57*(3), 428–444.

10060

Test Name: LOYOLA CHILD PSYCHOTHERAPY PROCESS SCALES

Purpose: To assess positive and negative aspects of child and therapist behaviors.

Number of Items: 33

Format: Five-point Likert format.

Reliability: Effective reliabilities ranged from .72 to .75.

Author: Russell, R. L., et al.

Article: Confirmatory P-technique

analysis of therapist discourse: High-versus-low-quality child therapy sessions.

Journal: *Journal of Consulting and Clinical Psychology*, December 1996, *64*(6), 1366–1376.

Related Research: Estrada, A. U., & Russell, R. L. (1994*). The development of the Loyola Child Psychotherapy Process Scales.* Authors.

10061

Test Name: MASTERY–INSIGHT SCALE

Purpose: To assess the level of mastery and insight gained by clients in sessions.

Number of Items: 5

Format: Responses are made on a 3-point scale ranging from 0 (no) to 2 (a lot). An example is given.

Reliability: Alpha coefficients ranged from .78 to .84.

Validity: Correlations with the Depth Scale ranged from .54 to .74.

Author: Rochlen, A. B., et al.

Article: Effects of training in dream recall and dream interpretation skills on dream recall, attitudes, and dream interpretation outcome.

Journal: *Journal of Counseling Psychology*, January 1999, *46*(1), 27–34.

Related Research: Kolden, G. C. (1991). The generic model of psychotherapy: An empirical investigation of patterns of process and outcome relationships. *Psychotherapy Research*, *1*, 62–73.

10062

Test Name: MENTOR–FUNCTIONS SCALE

Purpose: To measure career development and psychosocial functions.

Number of Items: 19

Format: Includes 4 Career Development Functions: Career Planning, Taught Skills, Sponsorship, and Feedback; and one measure of Psychosocial Functions. Responses are made on a 5-point scale ranging from 5 (very descriptive) to 1 (not all descriptive). Examples are presented.

Reliability: Alpha coefficients ranged from .56 to .84.

Validity: Correlations with other variables ranged from −.30 to .29.

Author: Burke, R. J., and McKeen, C. A.

Article: Benefits of mentoring relationships among managerial and professional women: A cautionary tale.

Journal: *Journal of Vocational Behavior*, August 1997, *51*(1), 43–57.

Related Research: Kram, K. E. (1985). *Mentoring at work*. Glenview, IL: Scott, Foresman.

10063

Test Name: MENTOR FUNCTIONS SCALES—MODIFIED

Purpose: To assess the extent to which mentors provided psychosocial and instrumental/career support.

Number of Items: 22

Format: Includes 2 factors: Psychosocial Functions and Instrumental Functions.

Reliability: Alpha coefficients were .82 and .80.

Validity: Correlations with other variables ranged from −.04 to .47.

Author: Ensher, E. A., and Murphy, S. E.

Article: Effects of race, gender, perceived similarity, and contact on mentor relationships.

Journal: *Journal of Vocational Behavior*, June 1997, *50*(3), 460–481.

Related Research: Noe, R. A. (1988). An investigation of the determinants of successful assigned mentoring relationships. *Personal Psychology*, *41*, 457–479.

10064

Test Name: MENTOR RELATIONSHIP'S PROCESS CHARACTERISTICS SCALE

Purpose: To measure process aspects of the mentorship.

Number of Items: 4

Format: Includes two measures: Public Image and Emotional Distance. Responses are made on a 5-point scale ranging from 1 (strongly disagree) to 5 (strongly agree). Examples are presented.

Reliability: Alpha coefficients were .76 and .60.

Validity: Correlations with other variables ranged from −.19 to .26.

Author: Burke, R. J., and McKeen, C. A.

Article: Benefits of mentoring relationships among managerial and professional women: A cautionary tale.

Journal: *Journal of Vocational Behavior*, August 1997, *51*(1), 43–57.

Related Research: Clawson, J. G., & Kram, K. E. (1984). Managing cross-gender mentoring. *Business Horizons*, *27*, 22–32.

10065

Test Name: MENTOR ROLE INSTRUMENT

Purpose: To measure 11 mentor functions.

Number of Items: 33

Format: Scales range from 1 (strongly disagree) to 7 (strongly agree). All items are presented.

Reliability: Alpha coefficients ranged from .63 to .91 across subscales.

Author: Ragins, B. R., and Cotton, J. L.

Article: Mentor functions and outcomes: A comparison of men and women in formal and informal mentoring relationships.

Journal: *Journal of Applied Psychology,* August 1999, *84*(4), 529–550.

Related Research: Ragins, B. R., & McFarlin, D. (1990). Perception of mentor roles in cross-gender mentoring relationships. *Journal of Vocational Behavior, 37,* 321–339.

10066

Test Name: MENTOR-THERAPEUTIC ALLIANCE SCALE

Purpose: To assess mentors' perceptions of relationships of quality.

Number of Items: 12

Format: Responses are made on a 6-point scale ranging from 1 (not like my mentee) to 6 (very much like my mentee).

Reliability: Coefficient alpha was .90

Author: Cavell, T. A., and Hughes, J. N.

Article: Secondary prevention as context for assessing change processes in aggressive children.

Journal: *Journal of School Psychology,* May/June 2000, *38*(3), 199–235.

Related Research: Shirk, S. R., & Saiz, C. C. (1992). Clinical, empirical, and developmental perspective on the therapeutic relationship in child psychotherapy. *Development and Psychotherapy, 4,* 713–728

10067

Test Name: MENTORING FUNCTIONS SCALE

Purpose: To measure mentoring functions.

Number of Items: 18

Format: Includes 3 dimensions: Career Development, Psycho-Social Support, and Role Modeling. Responses are made on a 5-point Likert-type scale ranging from 1 (strongly disagree) to 5 (strongly agree). Examples are presented.

Reliability: Alpha coefficients ranged from .83 to .86.

Validity: Correlations with other variables ranged from .18 to .40.

Author: Scandura, T. A.

Article: Mentoring and organizational justice: An empirical investigation.

Journal: *Journal of Vocational Behavior,* August 1997, *51*(1), 58–69.

Related Research: Lankan, M. J. (1996) *An examination and comparison of mentoring and peer developmental relationships in the context of project teams.* Unpublished doctoral dissertation, University of Miami.

10068

Test Name: MENTORING SCALE

Purpose: To assess the degree to which students perceive they have a mentor within the academic setting.

Number of Items: 5

Format: Response categories ranged from "no one" to "four or more persons." All items are presented.

Reliability: Internal consistency was .76.

Validity: Correlations with other variables ranged from −.46 to .46.

Author: Gloria, A. M., et al.

Article: African American students' persistence at a predominately White university: Influences of social support, university comfort and self-beliefs.

Journal: *Journal of College Student Development,* May/June 1999, *40*(3), 257–268.

Related Research: Gloria, A. M., et al. (1993). *Psychological factors influencing the academic persistence of Chicano/a undergraduates.* Unpublished doctoral dissertation, Arizona State University.

10069

Test Name: MULTICULTURAL AWARENESS/KNOWLEDGE/ SKILLS SURVEY

Purpose: To provide a measure of perceived levels of multicultural counseling awareness, knowledge, and skills.

Number of Items: 60

Format: Includes 3 subscales: Awareness, Knowledge, and Skills. Responses are made on a 4-point rating scale.

Reliability: Alpha coefficients ranged from .75 to .96.

Validity: Correlations with other variables ranged from −.09 to .77 (*N* ranged from 133 to 135).

Author: Constantine, M. G., and Ladany, N.

Article: Self-report multicultural counseling competence scales: Their relation to social desirability attitudes and multicultural case conceptualization ability.

Journal: *Journal of Counseling Psychology*, April 2000, 47(2), 155–164.

Related Research: D'Andrea, M., et al. (1991). Evaluating the impact of multicultural counseling training. *Journal of Counseling and Development*, 70, 143–150.

10070

Test Name: MULTICULTURAL COUNSELING INVENTORY

Purpose: To operationalize some of the proposed constructs of multicultural counseling competencies.

Number of Items: 40

Format: Includes 4 subscales: Assessing Multicultural Counseling: Awareness, Knowledge, Skills and Relationships. Responses are made on a 4-point scale ranging from 1 (very inaccurate) to 4 (very accurate).

Reliability: Alpha coefficients ranged from .71 to .91.

Validity: Correlations with other variables ranged from −.12 to .73.

Author: Constantine, M. G., and Ladany, N.

Article: Self-report multicultural counseling competence scales: Their relation to social

desirability attitudes and multicultural case conceptualization ability.

Journal: *Journal of Counseling Psychology*, April 2000, 47(2), 155–164.

Related Research: Sadowsky, G. R., et al. (1994). Development of the Multicultural Counseling Inventory: A self-report measure of multicultural competencies. *Journal of Counseling Psychology*, 41, 137–148.

10071

Test Name: MULTICULTURAL COUNSELING KNOWLEDGE AND AWARENESS SCALE

Purpose: To measure perceived multicultural counseling knowledge and awareness.

Number of Items: 32

Format: Includes two factors: Knowledge and Awareness. Responses are made on a 7-point scale ranging from 1 (not at all true) to 7 (totally true).

Reliability: Alpha coefficients ranged from .75 to .90.

Validity: Correlations with other variables ranged from −.31 to .77.

Author: Constantine, M. G., and Ladany, N.

Article: Self-report multicultural counseling competence scales: Their relation to social desirability attitudes and multicultural case conceptualization ability.

Journal: *Journal of Counseling Psychology*, April 2000, 47(2), 155–164.

Related Research: Ponterotto, J. G., et al. (1999). *A construct validity study of the Multicultural Counseling Awareness Scale (MCAS) with*

suggested revisions. Unpublished manuscript.

10072

Test Name: OUTCOME QUESTIONNAIRE

Purpose: To measure patient progress in therapy.

Number of Items: 45

Format: Five-point scales are anchored by 0 (never) and 4 (almost always).

Reliability: Coefficient alpha was .93. Test-retest reliability (3-weeks) was .84.

Author: Lunnen, K. M., and Ogles, B. M.

Article: A multiperspective, multivariable evaluation of reliable change.

Journal: *Journal of Consulting and Clinical Psychology*, April 1998, *66*(2), 400–410.

Related Research: Lambert, M. J., et al. (1994). *Administration and scoring manual for the Outcome Questionnaire (OQ-45).* Salt Lake City, UT: IHC Center for Behavioral Healthcare Efficacy.

10073

Test Name: PENN ADHERENCE-COMPETENCE SCALE FOR SUPPORTIVE-EXPRESSIVE THERAPY

Purpose: To assess the extent to which Luborsky's recommended interventions have been carried out in a session.

Number of Items: 45

Format: Seven-point Likert format.

Reliability: Interjudge reliabilities ranged from .38 to .70.

Author: Barker, J. P., et al.

Article: Effects of therapist adherence and competence on patient outcome in brief dynamic therapy.

Journal: *Journal of Consulting and Clinical Psychology*, June 1996, *64*(3), 619–622.

Related Research: Barker, J. P., & Crits-Cristoph, P. (1996). Development of a therapist adherence/competence rating scale for supportive-expressive dynamic psychotherapy: A preliminary report. *Psychotherapy Research, 6*, 79–92.

10074

Test Name: PENN HELPING ALLIANCE QUESTIONNAIRE —REVISED

Purpose: To measure the strength of the patient–clinician relationship.

Number of Items: 6

Format: Responses are made on a 7-point scale ranging from 1 (never) to 7 (always). Examples are presented.

Reliability: Alpha coefficients were .88 and .90.

Author: Ackerman, S. J., et al.

Article: Interaction of therapeutic process and alliance during psychological assessments.

Journal: *Journal of Personality Assessment*, August 2000, *75*(1), 82–109.

Related Research: Barber, J. P., & Crits-Christoph, P. (1996). Development of a therapist adherence/competence rating scale for supportive/expressive dynamic psychotherapy: A preliminary report. *Psychotherapy Research, 6*, 79–90.

10075

Test Name: PERCEIVED APPLICANT FIT SCALE

Purpose: To measure recruiters' perception of applicants' fit with the organization and with the job.

Number of Items: 7

Format: Includes two scales: To measure applicants' fit with the organization and applicants' fit with the demands of the job.

Reliability: Alpha coefficients were .94 and .96.

Validity: Correlations with hiring recommendations were .79 and .86.

Author: Kristof-Brown, A. L.

Article: Perceived applicant fit: Distinguishing between recruiters' perception of person-job and person-organization fit.

Journal: *Personnel Psychology*, Autumn 2000, *53*(3), 643–671.

Related Research: Adkins, C. L., et al. (1994). Judgments of fit in the selection process: The role of work-value congruence. *Personnel Psychology, 47*, 605–623.

Cable, D. M., & Judge, T. A. (1997). Interviewers' perception of person-organization fit and organizational selection decisions. *Journal of Applied Psychology, 82*, 546–561.

10076

Test Name: PERCEIVED OVERQUALIFICATION SCALE

Purpose: To assess perceived overqualification for a job.

Number of Items: 10

Format: Scales range from 1 (strongly disagree) to 5 (strongly agree). All items are presented.

Reliability: Alpha coefficients

ranged from .73 to .80 across two subscales.

Author: Johnson, G. J., and Johnson, W. R.

Article: Perceived overqualification and psychological well-being.

Journal: *Journal of Social Psychology*, August 1996, *136*(4), 435–445.

Related Research: Khan, L. J., & Morrow, P. C. (1991). Objective and subjective underemployment relationships to job satisfaction. *Journal of Business Research, 22*, 211–218.

Johnson, G. J., & Johnson, W. R. (1999). Perceived overqualification and health: A longitudinal analysis. *Journal of Social Psychology, 139*, 14–28.

10077

Test Name: PERCEPTION OF THE SALESPERSON SCALE

Purpose: To reveal the reactions of persons toward the employee.

Number of Items: 38

Format: Includes 3 factors: Energetic, Reactive, and Reach Out.

Reliability: Alpha coefficients ranged from .67 to .79.

Author: Chebat, J.-C., and Vaillant, D.

Article: Does background music in a store enhance salespersons' persuasiveness?

Journal: *Perceptual and Motor Skills*, October 2000, *91*(2), 405–424.

Related Research: Edell, J. A., & Burke, M. C. (1987). The power of feeling in understanding advertising effects. *Journal of Consumer Research, 14*, 421–433.

10078

Test Name: PERFORMANCE RATING SCALE

Purpose: To enable supervisors to rate employee performances.

Number of Items: 3

Format: Responses are made on a 7-point scale ranging from "not at all" to "entirely." All items are presented.

Reliability: Coefficient alpha was .88.

Validity: Correlations with other variables ranged from −.42 to .72.

Author: Thacker, R. A.

Article: Perceptions of trust, upward influence tactics, and performance ratings.

Journal: *Perceptual and Motor Skills*, June 1999, *88*(3) Part 2, 1059–1070.

10079

Test Name: PERFORMANCE SCALE

Purpose: To measure employees' adherence to and completion of formal job duties.

Number of Items: 7

Format: Responses are made on a scale ranging from 1 (never or almost never) to 5 (always or almost always). Sample items are presented.

Reliability: Reliability coefficient was .92.

Validity: Correlation with other variables ranged from −.26 to .10.

Author: Vigoda, E.

Article: Organizational politics, job attitudes, work outcomes: Exploration and implications for the public sector.

Journal: *Journal of Vocational*

Behavior, December 2000, *57*(3), 326–347.

Related Research: Katz, D. (1964). The motivational basis of organizational behavior. *Behavior Science, 9*, 131–133.

10080

Test Name: PROCESS OF CHANGE QUESTIONNAIRE

Purpose: To assess the frequency with which 10 processes of change are used.

Number of Items: 40

Format: Five-point scales are anchored by 1 (never) and 5 (repeatedly).

Reliability: Alphas ranged from .57 to .90 across 10 processes.

Author: O'Connor, E. A., et al.

Article: Gender and smoking cessation: A factor structure comparison of processes of change.

Journal: *Journal of Consulting and Clinical Psychology*, February 1996, *64*(1), 130–138.

Related Research: Prochaska, J. O., et al. (1988). Measuring processes of change: Applications to the cessation of smoking. *Journal of Consulting and Clinical Psychology, 56*, 520–528.

10081

Test Name: PROCESSES OF CHANGE QUESTIONNAIRE— SHORT FORM

Purpose: To measure current use of activities resulting from psychotherapy.

Number of Items: 22

Format: Includes 8 subscales within the 2 factors of Experiential and Behavioral. Responses are made on a 5-point

Likert-type scale. Sample items are presented.

Reliability: Internal consistency ranged from .49 to .90.

Author: Koraleski, S. F., and Larson, L. M.

Article: A partial test of the transtheoretical model in therapy with adult survivors of childhood sexual abuse.

Journal: *Journal of Counseling Psychology*, July 1997, *44*(3), 302–306.

Related Research: Bellis, J. M. (1994). The transtheoretical model of change applied to psychotherapy: A psychometric assessment of related instruments. (Doctoral dissertation, University of Rhode Island, 1994). *Dissertation Abstracts International, 54*, 3845B. (University Microfilms No. AAC9332421).

10082

Test Name: PROFESSIONAL DEVELOPMENT ASSESSMENT

Purpose: To measure professional development.

Number of Items: 30

Format: Includes 10 categories: Dependability, Professional Presentation, Initiative, Empathy, Cooperation, Organization, Clinical Reasoning, Supervisory Process, Verbal Communication, and Written Communication. Responses are made on a 4-point forced-choice rating scale ranging from 1 (being rarely evidenced) to 4 (being consistently shown).

Reliability: Test-retest (1–2 years) reliability was .48.

Author: Kasar, J.

Article: Stability of the Professional Development Assessment.

Journal: *Perceptual and Motor Skills*, June 1997, *84*(3, Part 2), 1373–1374.

Related Research: Kasar, J., et al. (1994). *Professional Development Assessment*. (Unpublished manuscript, University of Scranton).

10083

Test Name: PROSPECTOR SCALE

Purpose: To rate aspiring international executives on end-state competencies and ability to learn from experience.

Number of Items: 116

Format: Sample items are presented. Seven-point scales are anchored by 1 (very strongly disagree) and 7 (very strongly agree).

Reliability: Alpha coefficients ranged from .70 to .92 across subscales.

Validity: Correlations with other variables are presented for each dimension of the Prospector Scale for two samples.

Author: Speitzer, G. M., et al.

Article: Early identification of international executive potential.

Journal: *Journal of Applied Psychology*, February 1997, *82*(1), 6–29.

10084

Test Name: PSYCHOLOGICAL REASONS FOR TERMINATION SCALE

Purpose: To assess reasons for terminating mentoring relationships.

Number of Items: 17

Format: Five-point scales range from 1 (strongly disagree) to 5

(strongly agree). All items are presented.

Reliability: Alpha coefficients ranged from .64 to .86 across subscales.

Validity: Correlations with other variables ranged from −.44 to .13.

Author: Ragins, B. R., and Scandura, T. A.

Article: The way we were: Gender and the termination of mentoring relationships.

Journal: *Journal of Applied Psychology*, December 1997, *82*(6), 945–953.

10085

Test Name: PSYCHOSOCIAL MENTORING ACTIVITIES SCALE

Purpose: To assess the extent to which proteges believe or perceive the mentors provide psychological functions.

Number of Items: 14

Format: Responses are made on a 5-point scale ranging from 1 (to a very slight extent) to 5 (to a very great extent). Sample items are presented.

Reliability: Alpha coefficients were .92 and .94.

Validity: Correlations with other variables ranged from −.04 to .28.

Author: Koberg, C. S., et al.

Article: Factors and outcomes associated with mentoring among health-care professionals.

Journal: *Journal of Vocational Behavior*, August 1998, *53*(1), 58–72.

Related Research: Noe, R. A. (1988). An investigation of the determinants of successful assigned mentoring relationships.

Personal Psychology, 41, 456–479.

10086

Test Name: PSYCHOSOCIAL SUPPORT MENTORING SCALE

Purpose: To assess career development mentoring functions received by proteges.

Number of Items: 10

Format: Responses are made on a 5-point scale ranging from 1 (disagree strongly) to 5 (agree strongly). An example is presented.

Reliability: Coefficient alpha was .87. An example is presented.

Validity: Correlations with other variables ranged from −.11 to .52.

Author: Sosik, J. J., and Godshalk, V. M.

Article: The role of gender in mentoring: Implications for diversified and homogenous mentoring relationships.

Journal: *Journal of Vocational Behavior*, August 2000, *57*(1), 102–122.

Related Research: Noe, R. (1988). An investigation of the determinants of successful assigned mentoring relationships. *Personnel Psychology, 41,* 457–479.

10087

Test Name: RATINGS OF TRAINEE SKILLS SCALE

Purpose: To evaluate counselor trainees' competence.

Number of Items: 3

Format: Supervisors rate use of therapeutic skills and strategies, openness to and awareness of personal issues interfering with treatment, and the trainee's ability to conceptualize the client's problems and dynamics. Responses are made on a 7-point scale ranging from 1 (exceptionally poor) to 7 (exceptionally skilled).

Reliability: Alpha coefficients were .82 (supervisor's ratings of trainees) and .83 (trainee's self ratings).

Author: Sells, J. N., et al.

Article: Relationship of supervisors and trainee gender to in-session verbal behavior and ratings of trainee skills.

Journal: *Journal of Counseling Psychology*, October 1997, *44*(4), 406–412.

Related Research: Bernard, J. M. (1979). Supervision training: A discrimination model. *Counselor Education and Supervision, 18,* 60–68.

10088

Test Name: RECOMMENDATION RATING SCALE

Purpose: To measure client beliefs concerning designated recommendation.

Number of Items: 27

Format: Includes 3 factors: Fit, Difficulties, and Therapist Influence. Responses are made on a 6-point Likert-type scale ranging from 1 (strongly disagree) to 6 (strongly agree). All items presented.

Reliability: Alpha coefficient ranged from .81 to .87.

Validity: Correlations with other variables ranged from .49 to .79 (*N* = 91).

Author: Scheel, M. J., et al.

Article: Client implementation of therapist recommendations predicted by client perceptions of fit, difficulty of implementation, and therapist influence.

Journal: *Journal of Counseling Psychology*, July 1999, *46*(3), 303–316.

Related Research: Conoley, C. W., et al (1994). Predictions of client implementations of counselor recommendations: Match with problem, difficulty level, and building client strengths. *Journal of Counseling Psychology, 41,* 3–7.

10089

Test Name: RECRUITERS' HIRING RECOMMENDATIONS SCALE

Purpose: To assess recruiters' hiring recommendations.

Number of Items: 4

Format: Responses are made on a 5-point scale ranging from 1 (not at all) to 5 (extremely).

Reliability: Coefficient alpha was .96.

Validity: Correlations with perceived applicant fit were .79 and .86.

Author: Kristof-Brown, A. L.

Article: Perceived applicant fit: Distinguishing between recruiters' perception of person-job and person-organization fit.

Journal: *Personnel Psychology*, Autumn 2000, *53*(3), 643–671.

Related Research: Cable, D. M., & Judge, T. A. (1997). Interviewers' perceptions of person-organization fit and organizational selection decisions. *Journal of Applied Psychology, 82,* 546–561.

10090

Test Name: SALES PERSONNEL SERVCE PERFORMANCE SCALE

Purpose: To measure customer-

perceived sales personnel service performance.

Number of Items: 4

Format: Responses are made on an 11-point scale. A sample item is presented.

Reliability: Internal consistency reliability estimate was .76.

Validity: Correlations with other variables ranged from −.19 to .78.

Author: Burke, M. J., et al.

Article: Do situational variables act as substantive causes of relationships between individual difference variables? Two large-scale tests of "common cause" models.

Journal: *Personnel Psychology*, Autumn 1996, *49*(3), 573–598.

Related Research: Borucki, C. C., & Burke, M. J. (1992, August). *Employee and customer perception of the store service practices and sales personnel performance in a national retail organization.* Paper presented at the annual meeting of the Academy of Management, Las Vegas, NV.

10091

Test Name: SELF-CONTROL SCHEDULE

Purpose: To assess tendencies to apply self-management methods in the solution of behavioral problems.

Number of Items: 36

Reliability: Internal consistency reliabilities ranged from .78 to .84. Test-retest (4 weeks) reliability was .86. Coefficient alpha was .85.

Validity: Correlations with other variables ranged from −.45 to .46.

Author: Pallant, J. F.

Article: Development and validation of a scale to measure perceived control of internal states.

Journal: *Journal of Personality Assessment*, October 2000, *75*(2), 308–337.

Related Research: Rosenbaum, M. (1980). A schedule for assessing control behavior: Preliminary findings. *Behavior Therapy, 11*, 109–121.

10092

Test Name: SALESPERSON ROLE PERFORMANCE SCALES

Purpose: To measure in-role and extra-role (citizenship) behavior of salespersons.

Number of Items: 37

Format: In-Role scales range from "very low" to "very high." Extra-Role scales range from "completely untrue" to "completely true."

Reliability: Alpha coefficients ranged from .66 to .85 across subscales.

Author: Klein, D. J., and Verbeke, W.

Article: Autonomic feedback in stressful environments: How do individual differences in autonomic feedback relate to burnout, job performance, and job attitudes in salespeople?

Journal: *Journal of Applied Psychology*, December 1999, *84*(6), 911–924.

Related Research: Behrman, D., & Perreault, W. (1982). Measuring the performance of industrial salespersons. *Journal of Business Research, 10*, 355–370.

10093

Test Name: SATISFACTION WITH TREATMENT QUESTIONNAIRE

Purpose: To assess satisfaction with treatment for addiction.

Number of Items: 11

Format: Five-point scales range from 1 (unsatisfactory) to 5 (exceptional). All items are presented.

Validity: Correlations with MMPI-2 scales ranged from −.21 to .33.

Author: Cernovsky, Z. Z., et al.

Article: Antisocial personality traits and patients' satisfaction with treatment for addiction.

Journal: *Psychological Reports*, February 1997, *80*(1), 274–282.

Related Research: Larsen, D. L., et al. (1979). Assessment of client/patient satisfaction: Development of a general scale. *Evaluation and Program Planning, 2*, 197–207.

10094

Test Name: SELF EVALUATION QUESTIONNAIRE DEPTH SCALE

Purpose: To evaluate the quality of counseling.

Number of Items: 5

Format: Bipolar, adjective-anchored self-report measure.

Reliability: Alpha coefficients ranged from .81 to .95.

Author: Hill, C. E., et al.

Article: Dream interpretation sessions: Who volunteers, who benefits, and what volunteer clients view as most and least helpful.

Journal: *Journal of Counseling Psychology*, January 1997, *44*(1), 53–62.

Related Research: Stiles, W. B., & Snow, J. S. (1984). Counseling session impact as viewed by novice counselors and their clients. *Journal of counseling Psychology, 31*, 3–12.

10095

Test Name: SESSION EVALUATION QUASTIONNAIRE

Purpose: To measure client mood before and after the session.

Number of Items: 10

Format: Includes two scales: Positivity and Arousal.

Reliability: Alpha coefficients were .90 (Positivity) and .80 (Arousal).

Author: MacKay, H. C., et al.

Article: Staying with the feeling: An anger event in psychodynamic interpersonal therapy.

Journal: *Journal of Counseling Psychology*, July 1998, *45*(3), 279–289.

Related Research: Stiles, W. B., et al. (1994). Evaluation and description of psychotherapy sessions by clients using the Session Evaluation Questionnaire and the Session Impact Scale. *Journal of Counseling Psychology, 41*, 175–185.

10096

Test Name: SESSION EVALUATION QUESTIONNAIRE

Purpose: To assess session impact in terms of two session variables (depth and smoothness) and two postsession variables (positivity and arousal).

Number of Items: 20

Format: Seven-point bipolar adjective scales.

Reliability: Internal consistency ranged from .80 to .92.

Author: Hardy, G. E., et al.

Article: Therapist responsiveness to client interpersonal styles during limited-time treatments for depression.

Journal: *Journal of Consulting and Clinical Psychology*, April 1998, *66*(2), 304–312.

Related Research: Stiles, W. B., et al. (1994). Evaluation and description of psychotherapy sessions by clients using the Session Evaluation Questionnaire and Session Impact Scale. *Journal of Counseling Psychology, 41*, 175–185.

10097

Test Name: SESSION EVALUATION QUESTIONNAIRE

Purpose: To measure in-session psychotherapy processes.

Number of Items: 24

Format: Includes 2 sections, each consisting of 12 bipolar adjective scales rated from 1 to 7.

Reliability: Alpha coefficients ranged from .78 to .93.

Author: Ackerman, S. J., et al.

Article: Interaction of therapeutic process and alliance during psychological assessments.

Journal: *Journal of Personality Assessment*, August 2000, *75*(1), 82–109.

Related Research: Stiles, W. B., & Snow, J. S. (1984). Counseling session impact as viewed by novice counselors and their clients. *Journal of Counseling Psychology, 31*, 3–12.

10098

Test Name: SESSION EVALUATION

QUESTIONNAIRE—FORM 4-DEPTH SCALE

Purpose: To measure session quality.

Number of Items: 5

Format: Items are bipolar adjectives. Responses are made on a 7-point scale. All items are presented.

Reliability: Alpha coefficients ranged from .86 to .91.

Validity: Correlations with other variables ranged from −.77 to .56.

Author: Wonnell, T. L., and Hill, C. E.

Article: Effects of including the action stage in dream interpretation.

Journal: *Journal of Counseling Psychology*, July 2000, *47*(3), 372–379.

Related Research: Stiles, W. B., & Snow, J. S. (1984). Dimensions of psychotherapy sessions impact across sessions and across clients. *British Journal of Clinical Psychology, 23*, 59–63.

10099

Test Name: SESSION IMPACTS SCALE

Purpose: To rate the experience of a session.

Number of Items: 17

Format: Five-point scales range from 1 (not at all) to 5 (very much).

Reliability: Alphas ranged from .79 to .90 across subscales.

Author: Reynolds, S., et al.

Article: Acceleration of changes in session impact during time-limited psychotherapies.

Journal: *Journal of Consulting and Clinical Psychology*, June 1996, *64*(3), 577–586.

Related Research: Elliott, R., & Wexler, M. M. (1994). Measuring the impact of sessions in process-experiential therapy of depression: The Session Impacts Scale. *Journal of Counseling Psychology, 41*, 166–174.

10100

Test Name: SESSION IMPACTS SCALE—UNDERSTANDING SUBSCALE

Purpose: To assess the amount of understanding about self or others experienced by clients in therapy sessions.

Number of Items: 3

Format: Responses are made on a 5-point scale. An example is presented.

Reliability: Coefficient alpha was .78.

Author: Heaton, K. J., et al.

Article: A comparison of therapist-facilitated and self-guided dream interpretation sessions.

Journal: *Journal of Counseling Psychology*, January 1998, *45*(1), 115–122.

Related Research: Elliott, R., & Wexler, M. M. (1994). Measuring the impact of sessions in process-experiential therapy of depression: The Session Impacts Scale. *Journal of Counseling Psychology, 41*, 166–174.

10101

Test Name: SOCIAL PROVISIONS SCALE

Purpose: To assess the quality of the therapist's social support network.

Number of Items: 24

Format: Responses are made on a 4-point scale ranging from 1

(strongly disagree) to 4 (strongly agree).

Reliability: Internal consistency was .92 and .94.

Validity: Correlations with other variables ranged from −.71 to .73 ($N = 73$).

Author: Dunkle, J. H., and Friedlander, M. L.

Article: Contribution of therapist experience and personal characteristics to the working alliance.

Journal: *Journal of Counseling Psychology*, October 1996, *43*(4), 456–460.

Related Research: Cutrona, C. E., & Russell, D. W. (1987). The provisions of social relationships and adaptation to stress. In W. H. Jones & D. Perlman (Eds.), *Advances in personal relationships* (Vol. 1, pp. 37–67). Greenwich, CT: JAI Press.

10102

Test Name: STAGES OF CHANGE QUESTIONNAIRE

Purpose: To measure stages of change in psychotherapy.

Number of Items: 22

Format: Includes 4 subscales: Precontemplation, Contemplation, Action, and Maintenance. Responses are made on a 5-point Likert-type scale. Examples are presented.

Reliability: Internal consistency ranged from .72 to .83.

Author: Koraleski, S. F., and Larson, L. M.

Article: A partial test of the transtheoretical model in therapy with adult survivors of childhood sexual abuse.

Journal: *Journal of Counseling*

Psychology, July 1997, *44*(3), 302–306.

Related Research: McConnaughy, E. A., et al. (1983). Stages of change in psychotherapy: Measurement and sample profiles. *Psychotherapy: Theory, Research, and Practice, 20*, 368–375.

10103

Test Name: STUDENT MENTOR SUPPORT SCALE

Purpose: To measure psychosocial and instrumental support provided by a peer mentor.

Number of Items: 20

Format: Scales range from 1 (strongly agree) to 5 (strongly disagree). Sample items are presented.

Reliability: Alpha coefficients ranged from .78 to .91.

Author: Grant-Vallone, E. J., and Ensher, E. A.

Article: Effects of peer mentoring on types of mentor support, program satisfaction and graduate student stress: A dyadic perspective.

Journal: *Journal of College Student Development*, November/December 2000, *41*(6), 637–642.

Related Research: Kram, K. E., & Isabella, L. A. (1985). Mentoring alternatives: The role of peer relationships in career development. *Academy of Management Journal, 28*, 110–132.

10104

Test Name: SUBJECTIVE CAREER SUCCESS SCALE

Purpose: To assess perceived career success.

Number of Items: 11

Format: Scales range from 1 (strongly disagree) to 5 (strongly agreea0. A sample item is presented.

Reliability: Estimated reliability was .78.

Author: Peluchette, J. V. E., and Jeanquart, S.

Article: Professional's use of different mentor sources at various career stages: Implications for career success.

Journal: *The Journal of Social Psychology*, October, 2000, *140*(5), 549–564.

Related Research: Gattiker, U., & Larwood, L. (1986). Subjective career success: A study of managers and support personnel. *Journal of Business and Psychology, 1*, 78–94.

10105

Test Name: SUBORDINATE PERFORMANCE SCALE

Purpose: To assess employee performance in terms of quantity and quality of production.

Number of Items: 2

Format: Scales ranged from 1 (very low or very poor) to 7 (very high or very good quality). All items are presented.

Reliability: Spearman-Brown reliability was .77.

Author: Schriesheim, C. A., et al.

Article: Investigating contingencies: An examination of the impact of span of supervision and upward controllingness on leader-member exchange using traditional and multivariate within- and between-entities analysis.

Journal: *Journal of Applied Psychology*, October 2000, *85*(5), 659–677.

Related Research: Fulk, J., &

Wendler, E. R. (1982). Dimensionality of leader-subordinate interactions: A path-goal investigation. *Organizational Behavior and Human Performance, 30,* 241–264.

10106

Test Name: SUPERVISOR-RATED PERFORMANCE INSTRUMENT

Purpose: To rate technical and managerial positions in an organization.

Number of Items: 9

Format: Responses are made on a 5-point scale ranging from 1 (poor) to 5 (outstanding). The nine areas are identified.

Reliability: Coefficient alpha was .83.

Validity: Correlations with other variables ranged from −.06 to .34.

Author: Caligiuri, P. M.

Article: The Big Five personality characteristics as predictors of expatriate's desire to terminate the assignment and supervisor-rated performance.

Journal: *Personnel Psychology,* Spring 2000, *53*(1), 67–88.

10107

Test Name: SUPERVISOR SUPPORT AND VALUE/CENTRALITY SCALE

Purpose: To measure the aspects of social support most likely to be affected by plateauing.

Number of Items: 8

Format: Includes 2 factors: Supervisor Support and Feelings of Being Valued. Examples are presented.

Reliability: Alpha coefficients were .74 and .60.

Validity: Correlations with other variables ranged from −.27 to .36.

Author: Ettington, D. R.

Article: Successful career plateauing.

Journal: *Journal of Vocational Behavior,* February 1998, *52*(1), 72–88.

Related Research: LaRocco, J. M., et al. (1980). Social support, occupational stress, and health. *Journal of Health and Social Behavior, 21,* 202–218.

10108

Test Name: SUPERVISOR SUPPORT SCALE

Purpose: To measure supervisor support.

Number of Items: 7

Format: Responses are made on a 5-point scale ranging from 1 (strongly disagree) to 5 (strongly agree). Sample items are presented.

Reliability: Alpha coefficients were .88 and .93.

Validity: Correlations with other variables ranged from −.11 to .42.

Author: Aryee, S., and Luk, V.

Article: Work and nonwork influences on the career satisfaction of dual-earner couples.

Journal: *Journal of Vocational Behavior,* August 1996, *49*(1), 38–52.

Related Research: Greenhaus, J., et al. (1990). Effects of race on organizational experience, job performance evaluation and career outcomes. *Academy of Management Journal, 33,* 64–86.

10109

Test Name: SUPERVISOR WORKING ALLIANCE INVENTORY—SUPERVISEE FORM

Purpose: To measure aspects of the relationship in counselor supervision.

Number of Items: 19

Format: Includes 2 scales: Rapport and Client Focus.

Reliability: Alpha coefficients were .90 (Rapport) and .77 (Client Focus).

Author: Patton, M. S., and Kivlighan, Jr., D. M.

Article: Relevance of the supervisory alliance to the counseling alliance and to treatment adherence in counselor training.

Journal: *Journal of Counseling Psychology,* January 1997, *44*(1), 108–115.

Related Research: Efstation, J. F., et al. (1990). Measuring the counseling alliance in counselor supervision. *Journal of Counseling Psychology, 37,* 322–329.

10110

Test Name: SUPERVISOR'S REPORT QUESTIONNAIRE

Purpose: To assess supervisees' therapeutic skills and performance.

Number of Items: 25

Format: Responses are made on a 5-point scale ranging from 1 (poorly) to 5 (outstanding).

Reliability: Reliability (Spearman-Brown corrected) ranged from .77 to .87. Alpha coefficients ranged from .90 to .92.

Author: Williams, E. N., et al.

Article: Experiences of novice

therapists in practicum: Trainees', clients' and supervisors' perception of therapists' personal reactions and management strategies.

Journal: *Journal of Counseling Psychology*, October 1997, *44*(4), 390–399.

Related Research: Jones, S. H., et al. (1992). Components of supervisors' ratings of therapists' skillfulness. *Academic Psychiatry*, *16*, 29–36.

10111

Test Name: SUPERVISORS' SUPPORT SCALE

Purpose: To measure supervisors' support.

Number of Items: 9

Format: Five-point scales are anchored by (1) strongly agree and (5) strongly disagree. A sample item is presented.

Reliability: Alpha was .94.

Author: Burke, R. J., et al.

Article: Supervisors' support received by women managers: Country and sex of supervisors.

Journal: *Psychological Reports*, August 1998, *83*(1), 12–14.

Related Research: Greenhaus, J. H., et al. (1990). Organizational experiences and career success of Black and White managers. *Academy of Management Journal*, *33*, 64–86.

10112

Test Name: SUPERVISORY SATISFACTION QUESTIONNAIRE

Purpose: To enable participants to rate their satisfaction with various aspects of their supervision.

Number of Items: 8

Format: Responses are made on a 4-point scale ranging from 1 (low) to 4 (high). Examples are presented.

Reliability: Internal consistency estimates ranged from .84 to .93.

Author: Ladwey, N., et al.

Article: Nature, extent, and importance of what psychotherapy trainees do not disclose to their supervisors.

Journal: *Journal of Counseling Psychology*, January 1996, *43*(1), 10–24.

Related Research: Larsen, D. L., et al. (1979). Assessment of client/patient satisfaction: Development of a general scale. *Evaluation and Program Planning*, *2*, 197–207.

10113

Test Name: SUPERVISORY STYLES INVENTORY— TRAINEE VERSION

Purpose: To measure aspects of the supervision relationship.

Number of Items: 33

Format: Includes 3 factors: Attractive, Interpersonally Sensitive, and Task-Oriented.

Reliability: Alpha coefficients ranged from .73 to .87. Test-retest (2 weeks) reliability coefficients ranged from .78 to .94.

Validity: Correlations with other variables ranged from −.52 to .21.

Author: Lochner, B. T., and Melchert, T. P.

Article: Relationship of cognitive style and theoretical orientation to psychology interns' preferences for supervision.

Journal: *Journal of Counseling Psychology*, April 1997, *44*(2), 256–260.

Related Research: Friedlander, M. L., & Ward, L. G. (1984). Development and validation of the Supervisory Styles Inventory, *Journal of Counseling Psychology*, *31*, 541–557.

10114

Test Name: SUPERVISORY SUPPORT SCALE

Purpose: To assess career support an employee receives from a supervisor.

Number of Items: 9

Format: Likert format.

Reliability: Coefficient alpha was .96.

Authors: Jeanquart-Barone, S., and Sekaran, U.

Article: Institutional racism.

Journal: *Journal of Social Psychology*, August 1996, *136*(4), 477–482.

Related Research: Greenhaus, J. H., et al. (1990). Effects of race on organizational experiences, job performance, evaluations and career outcomes. *Academy of Management Journal*, *33*, 64–86.

10115

Test Name: SURVEY OF PERCEIVED SUPERVISORY SUPPORT

Purpose: To measure the degree to which supervisors value the contribution of their subordinates and are concerned with the welfare of their subordinates.

Number of Items: 16

Format: Responses are made on a 7-point Likert-type response scale ranging from 1 (strongly disagree) to 7 (strongly agree). Examples are presented.

Reliability: Alpha coefficients were .97 and .98.

Validity: Correlations with other variables ranged from .57 to .66.

Author: Hutchison, S.

Article: Perceived organizational support: Further evidence of construct validity.

Journal: *Educational and Psychological Measurement*, December 1997, *57*(6), 1025–1034.

Related Research: Kottke, J. L., & Sharafinski, C. E. (1988). Measuring supervisory and organizational support. *Educational and Psychological Measurement*, *48*, 1075–1079.

10116

Test Name: SYNERGISTIC SUPERVISION SCALE

Purpose: To assess staff members' perceptions of their current supervisory relationship and activities.

Number of Items: 22

Format: Scales range from 1 (never or almost never) to 5 (always or almost always). All items are presented.

Reliability: Coefficient alpha was .94.

Validity: Correlations with other variables ranged from .64 to .91.

Author: Saunders, S. A., et al.

Article: Supervising staff in student affairs: Exploration of the synergistic approach.

Journal: *Journal of College Student Development*, March/April 2000, *41*(2), 181–192.

10117

Test Name: TASK PERFORMANCE RATING INSTRUMENT

Purpose: To evaluate task performance of Air Force mechanics.

Number of Items: 6

Format: Scales range from 1 (much below average) to 5 (much above average). All items are presented.

Reliability: Coefficient alpha was .94.

Validity: Correlations with other variables ranged from .13 to .48.

Author: Van Scotter, J. R., et al.

Article: Effects of task performance and contextual performance on systemic rewards.

Journal: *Journal of Applied Psychology*, August 2000, *85*(4), 526–535.

10118

Test Name: TASK PERFORMANCE SCALE

Purpose: To measure to what extent a person fulfills responsibilities set out in a job description.

Number of Items: 7

Format: Five-point scales are anchored by 1 (ineffective) and 5 (highly effective). A sample item is presented.

Reliability: Coefficient alpha was .95.

Validity: Correlations with other variables ranged from −.19 to .66.

Author: Allen, T. D., and Rush, M. C.

Article: The effects of organizational citizenship behavior on performance judgments: A field study and a laboratory experiment.

Journal: *Journal of Applied*

Psychology, April 1998, *83*(2), 247–260.

Related Research: Williams, L. J., & Anderson, S. E. (1991). Job satisfaction and organizational commitment as predictors of organizational citizenship and in-role behavior. *Journal of Management*, *17*, 601–617.

10119

Test Name: TEACHING EFFECTIVENESS QUESTIONNAIRE

Purpose: To measure teaching effectiveness.

Number of Items: 10

Format: Ten aspects of classroom teaching are evaluated on a 5-point scale ranging from 1 (strongly disagree) to 5 (strongly agree).

Reliability: Internal consistency reliability was .97.

Author: Renaud, R. D., and Murray, H. G.

Article: Aging, personality, and teaching effectiveness in academic psychologists.

Journal: *Research in Higher Education*, June 1996, *37*(3), 323–340.

Related Research: Horner, K. L., et al. (1989). Relation between aging and rated teaching effectiveness of academic psychologists. *Psychology and Aging*, *4*, 226–229.

10120

Test Name: THERAPEUTIC ALLIANCE SCALE

Purpose: To assess children's perception of mentor relationships.

Number of Items: 12

Format: Responses are made on a

4-point scale ranging from 1 (not like you) to 4 (very much like you).

Reliability: Coefficient alpha was .81.

Author: Cavell, T. A., and Hughes, J. N.

Article: Secondary prevention as context for assessing change processes in aggressive children.

Journal: *Journal of School Psychology*, May/June 2000, *38*(3), 199–235.

Related Research: Shirk, S. R., & Saiz, C. C. (1992). Clinical, empirical, and developmental perspectives on the therapeutic relationship in child psychotherapy. *Development and Psychotherapy*, *4*, 713–728.

10121

Test Name: THERAPEUTIC REALIZATIONS SCALE— MASTERY INSIGHT SUBSCALE

Purpose: To assess level of mastery and insight gained by client during therapy.

Number of Items: 5

Format: Responses on a 3-point scale ranging from 0 to 2. An example is presented.

Reliability: Internal consistency coefficient was .74.

Validity: Correlation with the Session Impacts Scale— Understanding subscale was .84.

Author: Heaton, K. J., et al.

Article: A comparison of therapist-facilitated and self-guided dream interpretation sessions.

Journal: *Journal of Counseling Psychology*, January 1998, *45*(1), 115–122.

Related Research: Kolden, G. C. (1991). The generic model of psychotherapy: An empirical

investigation of patterns of process and outcome relationships. *Psychotherapy Research*, *1*, 62–73.

10122

Test Name: THERAPIST SESSION INTENTIONS

Purpose: To clarify the private therapeutic intentions of therapists.

Number of Items: 19

Format: Five-point Likert scales are anchored by 0 (not at all) and 4 (very much).

Reliability: Alpha coefficients ranged from .62 to .80 across subscales.

Author: Hardy, G. E., et al.

Article: Therapist responsiveness to client interpersonal styles during time-limited treatments for depression.

Journal: *Journal of Consulting and Clinical Psychology*, April 1998, *66*(2), 304–312.

Related Research: Stiles, W. B., et al. (1996). Therapist intentions in cognitive-behavioral and psychodynamic-interpersonal psychotherapy. *Journal of Counseling Psychology*, *43*, 402–414.

10123

Test Name: TREATMENT PERCEPTION SCALE

Purpose: To assess perceived improvement and usefulness of treatment of child behavior problems.

Number of Items: 21

Format: Seven-point scales are anchored by 1 (strongly disagree) and 7 (strongly agree).

Reliability: Subscale alphas ranged from .71 to .90.

Author: Webster-Stratton, C., and Hammond, M.

Article: Treating children with early-onset conduct problems: A comparison of child and parent training interventions.

Journal: *Journal of Consulting and Clinical Psychology*, February 1997, *65*(1), 93–109.

Related Research: Forehand, R., & McMahon, R. (1981). *Helping the non-compliant child: A clinicians guide to parent training*. New York: Guilford Press.

10124

Test Name: UNDERSTANDING SCALE

Purpose: To measure the amount of understanding experienced in therapy sessions.

Number of Items: 3

Format: Responses are made on a 5-point scale.

Reliability: Coefficient alpha was .78.

Author: Rochlen, A. B., et al.

Article: Effects of training in dream recall and dream interpretation skills on dream recall, attitudes, and dream interpretation outcome.

Journal: *Journal of Counseling Psychology*, January 1999, *46*(1), 27–34.

Related Research: Stiles, W. B., et al. (1994). Evaluation and description of psychotherapy sessions by clients using the Session Evaluation Questionnaire and the Session Impacts Scale. *Journal of Counseling Psychology*, *41*, 175–185.

10125

Test Name: VANDERBILT THERAPEUTIC STRATEGIES SCALE

Purpose: To describe counselors' actions in a session.

Number of Items: 21

Format: Includes two subscales: Psychodynamic Interviewing Style and Specific Strategies. Responses are made on a 5-point scale, ranging from 1 (not at all characteristic) to 5 (extremely characteristic).

Reliability: Alpha coefficients were .93 and .87. Interrater reliability coefficients were .74 and .91.

Author: Kivlighan, D. N., Jr., et al.

Article: Counselor trainee achievement goal orientation and the acquisition of time-limited dynamic psychotherapy skills.

Journal: *Journal of Counseling Psychology*, April 1998, *45*(2), 189–195.

Related Research: Butler, S. F., et al. (1992). *Measuring adherence and skill in time-limited dynamic psychotherapy*. Unpublished manuscript, Vanderbilt University.

10126

Test Name: WORKER PERFORMANCE AND DESIRABILITY RATING SCALES

Purpose: To assess worker performance and desirability as a partner.

Number of Items: 8

Format: Seven-point Likert scales.

Reliability: Coefficient alpha was .91 (performance) and .90 (desirability).

Validity: Correlations with other variables ranged from −.17 to .78 (performance) and from −.24 to .78 (desirability).

Author: Collella, A., et al.

Article: The impact of Patee's disability on performance judgments and choice as a partner: The role of disability-job fit stereotypes and interdependence of rewards.

Journal: *Journal of Applied Psychology*, February 1998, *83*(1), 102–111.

10127

Test Name: WORKING ALLIANCE INVENTORY

Purpose: To measure the working alliance.

Number of Items: 36

Format: Includes a primary general alliance factor and three secondary specific factors. Responses are made on a 7-point scale ranging from 1 (never) to 7 (always). Examples are presented.

Reliability: Alpha coefficients ranged from .85 to .95.

Author: Kivlighan, Jr., D. M., and Shaughnessy, P.

Article: Patterns of working alliance development: A typology of client's working alliance ratings.

Journal: *Journal of Counseling Psychology*, July 2000, *47*(3), 362–371.

Related Research: Horvath, A. O., & Greenberg, L. (1989). Development and validation of the Working Alliance Inventory. *Journal of Counseling Psychology*, *36*, 223–232.

10128

Test Name: WORKING ALLIANCE INVENTORY— SHORT FORM

Purpose: To measure the working alliance.

Number of Items: 12

Format: Includes 3 subscales: Tasks, Goals, and Bond. Responses are made on a 7-point scale ranging from 1 (low) to 7 (high).

Reliability: Alpha coefficients were .95 and .98.

Author: Hill, C. E., et al.

Article: Structured brief therapy with a focus on dreams or loss for clients with troubling dreams and recent loss.

Journal: *Journal of Counseling Psychology*, January 2000, *47*(1), 90–101.

Related Research: Horvath, A. O., & Greenberg, L. S. (1989). Development and validation of the Working Alliance Inventory. *Journal of Counseling Psychology*, *36*, 223–233.

CHAPTER 24
Vocational Interest

10129

Test Name: AFFECTIVE COMMITMENT SCALE

Purpose: To measure organizational commitment.

Number of Items: 8

Format: Responses are made on a 5-point scale ranging from "strongly agree" to "strongly disagree." Sample items are presented.

Reliability: Reliability estimate was .87.

Validity: Correlations with other variables ranged from −.56 to .66.

Author: Hochwarter, W. A., et al.

Article: Commitment as an antidote to the tension and turnover consequences of organizational behavior.

Journal: *Journal of Vocational Behavior*, December 1999, 55(3), 277–297.

Related Research: Allen, N., & Meyer, J. (1990). The measurement and antecedents of affective, continuance and normative commitment to the organization. *Journal of Occupational Psychology*, 63, 1–17.

10130

Test Name: CAREER ASPIRATION SCALE

Purpose: To assess participants' higher level career aspirations.

Number of Items: 10

Format: Responses are made on a 5-point scale ranging from 1 (not at all true of me) to 5 (very true of me). Examples are presented.

Reliability: Alpha coefficients ranged from .76 to 80.

Author: Nanta, M. M., et al.

Article: A multiple-groups analysis of predictors of higher level career aspirations among women in mathematics, science, and engineering majors.

Journal: *Journal of Counseling Psychology*, October 1998, 45(4), 483–496.

Related Research: O'Brien, K. M. (1995). *The Career Aspiration Scale* (Available from K. M. O'Brien, Department of Psychology, University of Maryland, College Park, MD 20742).

10131

Test Name: CAREER CHOICE IMPORTANCE SCALE

Purpose: To assess decidedness, comfort with level of decidedness, and reasons for being undecided about career decisions.

Number of Items: 16

Format: Scales range from 1 (strongly disagree) to 5 (strongly agree).

Reliability: Alpha coefficients ranged from .70 to .79. Test-retest reliability (3 weeks) was .78.

Author: Jones, L. K., et al.

Article: Comparing the effects of the Career Key with Self-Directed Search and Job-OE among eighth grade students.

Journal: *Professional School Counseling*, April 2000, 3(4), 238–247.

Related Research: Jones, L. K., & Lohmann, R. (1998). The Career Decision Profile: Using a measure of career decision status in counseling. *Journal of Career Assessment*, 6, 209–230.

10132

Test Name: CAREER COMMITMENT MEASURE

Purpose: To measure career commitment.

Number of Items: 5

Format: A sample item is presented.

Validity: Coefficient alpha was .79.

Reliability: Correlations with other variables ranged from −.19 to .44.

Author: Adams, G. A.

Article: Career-related variables and planned retirement age: An extension of Beehr's model.

Journal: *Journal of Vocational Behavior*, October 1999, 55(2), 221–235.

Related Research: Blau, G. (1985). The measurement and prediction of career commitment. *Journal of Occupational Psychology*, 58, 277–288.

10133

Test Name: CAREER COMMITMENT SCALE

Purpose: To measure career commitment.

Number of Items: 8

Reliability: Reliability was .87.

Validity: Correlations with other variables ranged from −.36 to .57.

Author: Cohen, A.

Article: On the discriminant validity of the Meyer and Allen measure of organizational commitment: How does it fit with the work commitment construct?

Journal: *Educational and Psychological Measurement*, June 1996, *56*(3), 494–503.

Related Research: Blau, G. J. (1985). The measurement and prediction of career commitment. *Journal of Occupational Psychology*, *58*, 277–288.

10134

Test Name: CAREER COMMITMENT SCALE

Purpose: To assess the importance or salience of a long-term career.

Number of Items: 15

Format: Responses are made on a 5-point scale ranging from *strongly agree* to *strongly disagree*. Examples are presented.

Reliability: Alpha coefficients ranged from .78 to .83.

Validity: Correlation with other variables were .27 (GPA) and −.26 (a criterion item).

Author: McWhirter, E. H., et al.

Article: A causal model of the educational plan and career expectations of Mexican American high school girls.

Journal: *Journal of Counseling Psychology*, April 1998, *45*(2), 166–181.

Related Research: Farmer, H. S. (1983). Career and homemaking plans for high school youth. *Journal of Counseling Psychology*, *30*, 40–45.

10135

Test Name: CAREER EXPLORATION SCALE

Purpose: To measure exploration of the self, the environment, and the breadth of exploration.

Number of Items: 5

Format: Scales range from 1 (does not apply) to 5 (fully applies). All items are presented.

Reliability: Coefficient alpha was .70.

Validity: Correlations with other variables ranged from .07 to .31.

Author: Kracke, B.

Article: Parental behaviors and adolescents' career exploration.

Journal: *Career Development Quarterly*, June 1997, *45*(4), 341–350.

10136

Test Name: CAREER EXPLORATION SCALES

Purpose: To measure career exploration.

Number of Items: 11

Format: Includes 2 scales: Self-Exploration Scale and Environmental Exploration Scale —Revised. Responses are made on 5-point scales ranging from 1 (little) to 5 (a great deal).

Reliability: Alpha coefficients ranged from .82 to .87.

Author: Bartley, D. F., and Robitschek, C.

Article: Career exploration: A multivariate analysis of predictors.

Journal: *Journal of Vocational Behavior*, February 2000, *56*(1), 63–81.

Related Research: Blustein, D. L. (1989). The role of goal instability and career self-efficacy in the career exploration process. *Journal of Vocational Behavior*, *35*, 194–203.

10137

Test Name: CAREER EXPLORATION SURVEY

Purpose: To assess environmental exploration and self-exploration.

Number of Items: 11

Format: Includes two subscales: Environmental Exploration and Self-Exploration. Responses are made on a 5-point scale. Sample items are presented.

Reliability: Internal consistency estimates were .89 (environmental exploration) and .82 (self-exploration). Test-retest (2 weeks) reliabilit. 's were .85 (environmental) to .83 (self).

Validity: Correlations with other variables ranged from −.30 to .39.

Author: Robitschek, C., and Cook, S. W.

Article: The influence of personal growth initiative and coping style on career exploration and vocational identity.

Journal: *Journal of Vocational Behavior*, February 1999, *54*(1), 127–141

Related Research: Stumpf, S. A., et al. (1983). Development of the Career Exploration Survey (CES). *Journal of Vocational Behavior*, *22*, 191.

10138

Test Name: CAREER EXPLORATION SURVEY

Purpose: To measure career exploratory behavior.

Number of Items: 16

Format: Responses are made on a 5-point scale ranging from "little" to "a great deal."

Reliability: Coefficient alpha was .89.

Validity: Correlation with other variables ranged from −.07 to .28.

Author: Munson, W. W., and Savickas, M. L.

Article: Relation between leisure and career development of college students.

Journal: *Journal of Vocational Behavior*, October 1998, *53*(2), 243–253.

Related Research: Stumpf, S. A., et al. (1983). Development of the Career Exploration Survey (CES). *Journal of Vocational Behavior*, *22*, 191–226.

10139

Test Name: CAREER INTENTIONS SCALE

Purpose: To measure career intentions.

Number of Items: 3

Format: Responses are made on a 7-point scale ranging from 1 (strongly disagree) to 7 (strongly agree). An example is presented.

Reliability: Coefficient alpha was .82.

Validity: Correlations with other variables ranged from .08 to .47.

Author: Kraimer, M. L., et al.

Article: Psychological empowerment as a

multidimensional construct: A test of construct validity.

Journal: *Educational and Psychological Measurement*, February 1999, *59*(1), 127–142.

Related Research: Liden, R. C., & Green, S. G. (1980). *On the measurement of career orientation*. Proceedings of the Midwest Academy of Management Meetings.

10140

Test Name: CAREER INTERESTS RATING SCALE

Purpose: To assess math/science career interests.

Number of Items: 15

Format: Responses are made on a 5-point scale ranging from 1 (not interested at all) to 5 (extremely interested). Examples are presented.

Reliability: Mean coefficient alpha was .95.

Validity: Correlations with other variables ranged from .12 to .52.

Author: Luzzo, D. A., et al.

Article: Effects of self-efficacy-enhancing interventions on the math/science self-efficacy and career interests, goals, and actions of career undecided college students.

Journal: *Journal of Counseling Psychology*, April, 1999, *46*(2), 233–243.

Related Research: Hackett, G., et al. (1990). Effects of verbal and mathematics task performance on task and career self-efficacy and interest. *Journal of Counseling Psychology, 37*, 169–177.

10141

Test Name: CAREER INVOLVEMENT SCALE

Purpose: To measure the extent to which one's career is central to one's sense of personal identity.

Number of Items: 4

Format: Responses are made on a 5-point scale ranging from 1 (completely false of me) to 5 (completely true of me). All items are presented.

Reliability: Coefficient alpha was .73.

Validity: Correlations with other variables ranged from −.16 to .51.

Author: Smart, R. M.

Article: Career stages in Australian professional women: A test of Super's model.

Journal: *Journal of Vocational Behavior*, June 1998, *53*(3), 379–395.

Related Research: Gould, S. (1979). Age, job complexity, satisfaction, and performance. *Journal of Vocational Behavior, 14*, 209–223.

10142

Test Name: CAREER ORIENTATION INVENTORY

Purpose: To measure career orientations in terms of managerial processes, technical-functional expertise, entrepreneurial focus, and security concerns.

Number of Items: 18

Format: Six-point scales are anchored by (1) of no importance and (6) extremely centrally important. Sample items are presented.

Reliability: Alphas ranged from .43 to .73.

Author: Burke, R. J.

Article: Career orientations of

managers from Central and Eastern Europe.

Journal: *Psychological Reports*, June 1998, *82*(3) Part 1, 960–962.

Related Research: DeLong, T. (1982). The career orientations of MBA alumni: A multidimensional model. In R. Katz (Ed), *Career issues in human resource management* (pp. 58–64). Englewood Cliffs, NJ: Prentice Hall.

10143

Test Name: CAREER SATISFACTION SCALE

Purpose: To determine respondents' levels of satisfaction with the overall shape of their careers.

Number of Items: 4

Format: Responses are made on a 5-point scale ranging from 1 (very dissatisfied) to 5 (very satisfied). Examples are presented.

Reliability: Coefficient alpha was .85.

Validity: Correlations with other variables ranged from −.38 to .64.

Author: Smart, R., and Peterson, C.

Article: Super's career stages and the decision to change careers.

Journal: *Journal of Vocational Behavior*, December 1997, *51*(3), 358–374.

Related Research: Romezek, B. S. (1989). Personal consequences of employee commitment. *Academy of Management Quarterly, 32*, 649–661.

10144

Test Name: CAREER SATISFACTION SCALE

Purpose: To measure career satisfaction.

Number of Items: 5

Format: Responses are made on a 5-point scale ranging from 1 (strongly disagree) to 5 (strongly agree). Sample items are presented.

Reliability: Alpha coefficients were .88 and .82.

Validity: Correlations with other variables ranged from −.14 to .42.

Author: Aryee, S., and Luk, V.

Article: Work and nonwork influences on the career satisfaction of dual-earner couples.

Journal: *Journal of Vocational Behavior*, August 1996, *49*(1), 38–52.

Related Research: Greenhaus, J., et al. (1990). Effects of race on organizational experience, job performance evaluation and career outcomes. *Academy of Management Journal, 33*, 64–86.

10145

Test Name: CAREER SATISFACTION SCALE

Purpose: To measure career satisfaction.

Number of Items: 5

Format: Responses are made on a 5-point scale ranging from 1 (dissatisfied) to 5 (very satisfied). A sample item is presented.

Reliability: Coefficient alpha was .87.

Validity: Correlations with other variables ranged from −.28 to .32.

Author: Parasuraman, S., et al.

Article: Work and family variables, entrepreneurial career

success, and psychological well-being.

Journal: *Journal of Vocational Behavior*, June 1996, *48*(3), 275–300.

Related Research: Parasuraman, S., et al. (1992). Role stressors, social supports, and well-being among two-career couples. *Journal of Organizational Behavior, 13*, 339–356.

10146

Test Name: COMMITMENT TO CAREER CHOICES SCALE

Purpose: To measure one's commitment to career choices.

Number of Items: 28

Format: Includes 2 subscales: Vocational Exploration and Commitment, and Tendency to Foreclose. Responses are made on a 7-point scale ranging from 1 (never true about me) to 7 (always true about me). Examples are presented.

Reliability: Estimates of internal consistencies ranged from .71 to .92. Test-retest reliabilities ranged from .82 to .92.

Validity: Correlations with other variables ranged from −.30 to .55.

Author: Rochlen, A. B., et al.

Article: Development of the Attitude Toward Career Counseling Scale.

Journal: *Journal of Counseling Psychology*, April 1999, *46*(2), 196–206.

Related Research: Blustein, D. L., et al. (1989). The development and validation of a two-dimensional model of the commitment to career choices process. *Journal of Vocational Behavior, 35*, 342–378.

10147

Test Name: EMPLOYMENT COMMITMENT SCALE

Purpose: To assess the degree to which an individual wants to be employed.

Number of Items: 8

Format: Scales range from 1 (strongly disagree) to 5 (strongly agree). All items are presented.

Reliability: Coefficient alpha was .76.

Validity: Correlations with other variables ranged from −.14 to .32.

Author: Wanberg, C. R., et al.

Article: Unemployed individuals: Motives, job-search competencies, and job-search constraints as predictors of job seeking and reemployment.

Journal: *Journal of Applied Psychology*, December 1999, 84(6), 897–910.

Related Research: Feather, N. T. (1990). *The psychological impact of unemployment*. New York: Springer-Verlag.

10148

Test Name: ENVIRONMENTAL EXPLORATION AND SELF-EXPLORATION SCALES

Purpose: To assess internal and external search activities.

Number of Items: 11

Format: Includes two scales: Environmental Exploration and Self-Exploration. Responses are made on a 5-point scale.

Reliability: Internal consistency reliabilities were .86 (Environmental Exploration) to .83 (Self-Exploration). Test-retest (2 weeks) reliabilities were .85 (Environmental Exploration) and .83 (Self-Exploration).

Validity: Correlations with other variables ranged from −.44 to .25.

Author: Felsman, D. E., and Blustein, D. L.

Article: The role of peer relatedness in late adolescent career development.

Journal: *Journal of Vocational Behavior*, April 1999, 54(2), 279–295.

Related Research: Stumpf, S. A., et al. (1983). Development of the career exploration survey. *Journal of Vocational Behavior*, 22, 191–226.

10149

Test Name: ENVIRONMENTAL EXPLORATION SCALE

Purpose: To assess the construct of environmental exploration.

Number of Items: 5

Format: Responses are made on a 5-point scale ranging from 1 (very little extent) to 5 (very great extent). All items are presented.

Reliability: Reliability was .88.

Validity: Correlations with other variables ranged from −.01 to .51.

Author: Werbel, J. D.

Article: Relationships among career exploration, job search intensity, and job search effectiveness in graduating college students.

Journal: *Journal of Vocational Behavior*, December 2000, 57(3), 379–394.

Related Research: Stumpf, S. A., et al. (1983). Development of the career exploration mental survey (CES). *Journal of Vocational Behavior*, 22, 191–226.

10150

Test Name: ENVIRONMENTAL EXPLORATION SUBSCALE—REVISED

Purpose: To enable one to indicate one's extent of career-exploration regarding occupations, jobs, and organizations during the last 3 months.

Number of Items: 6

Format: Responses are made on a 5-point scale ranging from "little" to "a great deal."

Reliability: Test-retest (2 weeks) reliability was .85. Alpha coefficients ranged from −.83 to .88.

Validity: Correlations with other variables ranged from −.19 to .24.

Author: Ketterson, T. U., and Blustein, D. L.

Article: Attachment relationships and the career exploration process.

Journal: *Career Development Quarterly*, December 1997, 46(2), 167–178.

Related Research: Blustein, D. L. (1988). The relationship between motivational processes and career exploration. *Journal of Vocational Behavior*, 32, 345–357.

10151

Test Name: EXPLORATION BELIEFS SCALES

Purpose: To measure exploration beliefs.

Number of Items: 8

Format: Includes 2 scales: External Search Instrumentality Scale and the Obtaining Preferred Position Scale. Responses are made on a 5-point scale.

Reliability: Alpha coefficients ranged from .64 to .85. Test-retest (4 weeks) reliabilities ranged from .36 to .66.

Author: Bartley, D. F., and Robitschek, C.

Article: Career exploration: A multivariate analysis of predictors.

Journal: *Journal of Vocational Behavior*, February 2000, *56*(1), 63–81.

Related Research: Stumpf, C. A., et al. (1983). Development of the Career Exploration Survey (CES). *Journal of Vocational Behavior, 22*, 191–226.

10152

Test Name: FASHION/CLOTHING INVOLVEMENT SCALE

Purpose: To measure involvement with fashion or clothing.

Number of Items: 8

Format: Responses are made on a 5-point scale ranging from 1 (never) to 5 (always). All items are presented.

Reliability: Coefficient alpha was .90.

Author: Behling, D. U.

Article: Measuring involvement.

Journal: *Perceptual and Motor Skills*, February 1999, *88*(1), 55–64.

Related Research: Zachkowsky, J. L. (1985). Measuring the involvement construct. *Journal of Consumer Research, 12*, 340–352.

10153

Test Name: IDENTITY DEVELOPMENT SCALE

Purpose: To measure commitment

and exploration with regard to work and seeking work.

Number of Items: 13

Format: Scales range from 1 (completely untrue) to 5 (completely true).

Reliability: Alpha coefficients ranged from .81 to .94.

Author: Meeus, W., et al.

Article: Unemployment and identity in adolescence: A social comparison perspective.

Journal: *Career Development Quarterly*, June 1997, *45*(4), 369–380.

Related Research: Bosma, H. (1985). *Identity development in adolescence*. Unpublished doctoral dissertation, Groningen University, Groningen.

10154

Test Name: IDENTITY STATUS INVENTORY—OCCUPATION

Purpose: To measure occupational identity.

Number of Items: 35

Format: Forced-choice format. A sample item is presented and scoring methods are described.

Reliability: Internal consistency coefficients ranged from .64 to .92.

Validity: Correlations with other variables ranged from .04 to .33.

Author: Munson, W. W., and Widmer, M. A.

Article: Leisure behavior and occupational identity in university students.

Journal: *Career Development Quarterly*, December 1997, *46*(2), 190–198.

Related Research: Dellas, M., & Jernigan, L. P. (1981). Development of an objective instrument to measure identity

status in terms of occupation crisis and commitment. *Educational and Psychological Measurement, 4*, 1039–1050.

10155

Test Name: INFLUENCE OF ROLE MODEL SCALE

Purpose: To assess the degree to which role models influenced students' academic and career choices.

Number of Items: 14

Format: Responses are made on a 7-point scale.

Reliability: Coefficient alpha was .86.

Author: Nauta, M. M., et al.

Article: A multiple-groups analysis of prediction of higher level career aspirations among women in mathematics, science, and engineering majors.

Journal: *Journal of Counseling Psychology*, October 1998, *45*(4), 483–496.

Related Research: Basow, S. A., & Howe, K. G. (1975, April). *Effect of role models on significant life choices for male and female undergraduates*. Paper presented at the meeting of the Eastern Psychological Association, New York.

10156

Test Name: INTEREST-FINDER

Purpose: To measure RIASEC typology related activity interests.

Number of Items: 240

Format: Like/dislike format. Sample items are described for each RIASEC category.

Reliability: Alpha coefficients ranged from .93 to .96 across subscales.

Validity: Correlations with other variables ranged from .14 to .78.

Author: Wall, J. E., et al.

Article: Development of the interest-finder: A new RIASEC-based inventory.

Journal: *Measurement and Evaluation in Counseling and Development*, October 1996, *29*(3), 134–151.

10157

Test Name: INTEREST IN RESEARCH QUESTIONNAIRE

Purpose: To enable respondents to indicate their degree of interest in various research activities.

Number of Items: 16

Format: Responses are made on a 5-point scale ranging from 1 (very disinterested) to 5 (very interested).

Reliability: Alpha coefficients ranged from .89 to .91.

Validity: Correlations with other variables ranged from −.03 to .74.

Author: Bishop, R. M., and Bieschke, K. J.

Article: Applying social cognitive theory to interest in research among counseling psychology doctoral students: A path analysis.

Journal: *Journal of Counseling Psychology*, April 1998, *45*(2), 182–188.

Related Research: Bieschke, K. J., et al. (1995). Research interest among rehabilitation doctoral students. *Rehabilitation Education*, 9, 51–66.

10158

Test Name: INVENTORY OF OCCUPATIONAL PREFERENCES

Purpose: To identify occupational preferences.

Number of Items: 295

Format: Responses are made on a 7-point scale ranging from 1 (strongly dislike) to 7 (strongly like).

Reliability: Test-retest (2 weeks) reliability ranged from .32 to .92. Internal consistencies ranged from .85 to .95.

Author: Tracey, T. J. G.

Article: The structure of interests and self-efficacy expectations: An expanded examination of the spherical model of interests.

Journal: *Journal of Counseling Psychology*, January 1997, *44*(1), 32–43.

Related Research: Tracey, T. J. G., & Rounds, J. (1966). The spherical representation of vocational interests. *Journal of Vocational Behavior*, 48, 3–41.

10159

Test Name: JOB REDIRECTION SCALE

Purpose: To measure effort, initiative, persistence, and self-discipline.

Number of Items: 8

Format: Five-point scales. All items are presented.

Reliability: Coefficient alpha was .94.

Validity: Correlations with other variables ranged from .14 to .48.

Author: Van Scotter, J. R., et al.

Article: Effects of task performance and contextual performance on systemic rewards.

Journal: *Journal of Applied Psychology*, August 2000, *85*(4), 526–535.

10160

Test Name: JOB INVOLVEMENT QUESTIONNAIRE—MODIFIED

Purpose: To assess job involvement.

Number of Items: 3

Format: Responses are made on a 5-point Likert-type scale ranging from 1 (strongly disagree) to 5 (strongly agree). An example is presented.

Reliability: Coefficient alpha was .70.

Validity: Correlations with other variables ranged from −.11 to .32 (*N* = 116).

Author: Nielsen, I. K., et al.

Article: Development and validation of scores on a two-dimensional workplace friendship scale.

Journal: *Educational and Psychological Measurement*, August 2000, *60*(4), 628–643.

Related Research: Frone, M. R., et al. (1992). Antecedents and outcomes of work-family conflict: Testing a model of the work-family interface. *Journal of Applied Psychology*, 77, 65–78.

10161

Test Name: JOB INVOLVEMENT SCALE

Purpose: To measure job involvement.

Number of Items: 3

Format: Seven-point agreement scales. A sample item is presented.

Reliability: Coefficient alpha was .70.

Validity: Correlations with other variables ranged from −.11 to .38.

Authors: Rotondo, D.

Article: Individual-difference variables and career-related coping.

Journal: *The Journal of Social Psychology*, August 1999, *139*(4), 458–471.

Related Research: Lodahl, T., & Kejner, M. (1965). The definition and measurement of job involvement. *Journal of Applied Psychology, 49,* 24–33.

10162

Test Name: JOB INVOLVEMENT SCALE

Purpose: To measure job involvement.

Number of Items: 4

Format: Responses are made on a 5-point Likert scale ranging from 1 (strongly disagree) to 5 (strongly agree). Examples are presented.

Reliability: Coefficient alpha was .86.

Validity: Correlations with other variables ranged from −.27 to .36.

Author: Werbel, J.

Article: Intent and choice regarding maternal employment following childbirth.

Journal: *Journal of Vocational Behavior*, December 1998, *53*(3), 372–385.

Related Research: Lodahl, T. M., & Kejner, M. (1965). The definition and measurement of job involvement. *Journal of Applied Psychology*, 49, 24–33.

10163

Test Name: JOB INVOLVEMENT SCALE

Purpose: To measure job involvement.

Number of Items: 5

Format: Responses are made on a 5-point scale ranging from 1 (completely false of me) to 5 (completely true of me). Examples are given.

Reliability: Alpha coefficients were .63 and .73.

Validity: Correlations with other variables ranged from −.29 to .47.

Author: Smart, R. M.

Article: Career stages in Australian professional women: A test of Super's model.

Journal: *Journal of Vocational Behavior*, June 1998, *52*(3), 379–395.

Related Research: Lodahl, T. M., & Kejner, M. (1965). The definition and measurement of job involvement. *Journal of Applied Psychology*, 49, 24–33.

10164

Test Name: JOB INVOLVEMENT SCALE

Purpose: To identify the importance of work in the worth of a person.

Number of Items: 9

Format: Responses are made on a 5-point scale ranging from 1 (strongly disagree) to 5 (strongly agree). Sample items are presented.

Reliability: Spearman-Brown reliability coefficient was .73, coefficient alpha was .84.

Validity: Correlations with other variables ranged from −.46 to .37.

Author: Koberg, C. S., et al.

Article: Factors and outcomes associated with mentioning among health-care professionals.

Journal: *Journal of Vocational Behavior*, August 1998, *53*(1), 58–72.

Related Research: Lodahl, T. M., & Kejner, M. (1965). The definitions and measurements of job involvement. *Journal of Applied Psychology, 49,* 24–33.

10165

Test Name: JOB INVOLVEMENT SCALE

Purpose: To measure job involvement.

Number of Items: 10

Reliability: Reliability was .79.

Validity: Correlations with other variables ranged from −.30 to .64.

Author: Cohen, A.

Article: On the discriminant validity of the Meyers and Allen measure of organizational commitment: How does it fit with the work commitment?

Journal: *Educational and Psychological Measurement*, June 1996, *56*(3), 494–503.

Related Research: Kanungo, R. N. (1982). Measurement of job and work involvement. *Journal of Applied Psychology*, 67, 341–349.

10166

Test Name: JOB SCALES

Purpose: To assess job rewards, employee investment in a job and job alternatives.

Number of Items: 14

Format: Scales range from 1 (extremely disagree) to 5 (extremely agree). Sample items are presented.

Reliability: Alpha coefficients ranged from .60 to .70 across subscales.

Author: Chen, X.-P., et al.

Article: The role of organizational

citizenship behavior in turnover: Conceptualization and preliminary tests of key hypotheses.

Journal: *Journal of Applied Psychology,* December 1998, 83(6), 922–931.

Related Research: Rusbult, C. E., & Farrell, D. (1983). A longitudinal test of the investment model: The impact on job satisfaction, job commitment, and turnover of variations in rewards, costs, alternatives, and investments. *Journal of Applied Psychology,* 68, 429–438.

10167

Test Name: JOB SEARCH INTENSITY SCALE

Purpose: To measure job search intensity.

Number of Items: 6

Format: Responses are either "yes" or "no." All items are presented.

Reliability: Reliability was .65.

Validity: Correlations with other variables ranged from .06 to .51.

Author: Werbel, J. D.

Article: Relationships among career exploration, job search intensity, and job search effectiveness in graduating college students.

Journal: *Journal of Vocational Behavior,* December 2000, 57(3), 379–394.

Related Research: Kaufer, R., & Hulin, C. L. (1985). Individual differences in successful job searches following layoffs. *Personnel Psychology,* 38, 835–847.

Kopelman, R. E., et al. (1992). Rationale and construct validity evidence for the job search behavior index: Because intentions (and New Year's

resolutions) often come to naught. *Journal of Vocational Behavior,* 40, 269–287.

10168

Test Name: JOB-SEARCH INTENSITY SCALE

Purpose: To assess the number of job-search behaviors used by job seekers.

Number of Items: 12

Format: Scales range from 1 (never [0 times]) to 5 (very frequently [at least 10 times]). All items are presented.

Reliability: Alpha coefficients ranged from .82 to .86.

Validity: Correlations with other variables ranged from −.03 to .55.

Author: Wanberg, C. R., et al.

Article: Unemployed individuals: Motives, job-search competencies, and job-search constraints as predictors of job seeking and reemployment.

Journal: *Journal of Applied Psychology,* December 1999, 84(6), 897–910.

Related Research: Blau, G. (1994). Testing a two-dimensional measure of job search behavior. *Organizational Behavior and Human Decision Processes,* 59, 288–312.

10169

Test Name: MATH/SCIENCE INTEREST SCALE

Purpose: To assess interest in mathematics and science-related activities.

Number of Items: 17

Format: A 6-point scale is used to indicate the degree to which students liked or disliked the activity described in each

statement. A sample item is presented.

Reliability: Internal consistency was .93.

Validity: Correlations with other variables ranged from −.38 to .65.

Author: Ferry, T. R., et al.

Article: The role of family context in a social cognitive model for career-related choice behavior: A math and science perspective.

Journal: *Journal of Vocational Behavior,* December 2000, 57(3), 348–364.

10170

Test Name: MATHEMATICS-RELATED INTERESTS MEASURE

Purpose: To assess mathematics-related and science-related interests.

Number of Items: 20

Format: Responses are made on a 3-point scale ranging from 1 (dislike) to 3 (like).

Reliability: Alpha coefficients ranged from .89 to .92.

Validity: Correlations with other variables ranged from .14 to .48.

Author: Lopez, F. G., et al.

Article: Role of social-cognitive expectations in high school students' mathematics-related interest and performance.

Journal: *Journal of Counseling Psychology,* January 1997, 44(1), 44–52.

Related Research: Lopez, F. G., & Lent, R. W. (1992). Sources of mathematics self-efficacy in high school students. *Career Development Quarterly,* 41, 3–12.

10171

Test Name: MILITARY ORGANIZATIONAL COMMITMENT SCALE

Purpose: To measure commitment to the military.

Number of Items: 3

Format: Scales range from 1 (strongly disagree) to 5 (strongly agree). A sample item is presented.

Reliability: Reliability was .81.

Validity: Correlations with other variables ranged from −.27 to .53.

Author: Jex, S. M., and Bliese, P. D.

Article: Efficacy beliefs as a moderator of the impact of work-related stressors: A multilevel study.

Journal: *Journal of Applied Psychology*, June 1999, *84*(3), 349–361.

Related Research: Mowday, R., et al. (1982). *Employee-organization linkages: The psychology of commitment and turnover*. New York: Academic Press.

10172

Test Name: MOTIVATION FOR OCCUPATIONAL CHOICE SCALE

Purpose: To measure the reasons for choosing an occupation.

Number of Items: 29

Format: Five-point scales are anchored by (1) not at all and (5) to a very large extent. All items are presented.

Validity: Goodness of fit indices ranged from .80 to .88. Root mean square residuals were .08.

Author: Davis, T. J., et al.

Article: Validation study of the motivation for occupational choice scale.

Journal: *Psychological Reports*, April 1998, *82*(2), 491–494.

Related Research: Davis, T. (1987). *The development of occupational and career scales for use in identification of antecedents of job satisfaction*. Unpublished PhD dissertation, University of Georgia.

10173

Test Name: MULTIDIMENTIONAL MEASURE OF CAREER INDECISION

Purpose: To provide a multidimensional measure of career indecision.

Number of Items: 7

Format: Includes 3 scores: Decidedness, Comfort, and Self-Clarity. Responses are made on an 8-point scale ranging from 1 (strongly disagree) to 8 (strongly agree).

Reliability: Alpha coefficients ranged from .68 to .85.

Author: Lucas, M.

Article: Identity development, career development, and psychological separation from parents: Similarities and differences between men and women.

Journal: *Journal of Counseling Psychology*, April 1997, *44*(2), 123–132.

Related Research: Jones, L. K. (1989). Measuring a three dimensional construct of career indecision among college students: A revision of the Vocational Decision Scale—The Career Decision Profile. *Journal of Counseling Psychology*, *36*, 477–486.

10174

Test Name: MUTUAL PSYCHOLOGICAL DEVELOPMENT QUESTIONNAIRE

Purpose: To assess mutuality.

Number of Items: 22

Format: Responses are made on 6-point Likert-type scale.

Reliability: Alpha coefficients ranged from .89 to .92. Test-retest correlations ranged from .71 to .84.

Validity: Correlations with other variables ranged from −.07 to .47

Author: Felsman, D. E., and Blustein, D. L.

Article: The role of peer relatedness in late adolescent career development.

Journal: *Journal of Vocational Behavior*, April 1999, *54*(2), 279–295.

Related Research: Genero, N. P., et al. (1992). Measuring perceived mutuality in close relationships: Validation of the Mutual Psychological Development Questionnaire. *Journal of Family Psychology*, *6*, 36–48.

10175

Test Name: ORGANIZATIONAL COMMITMENT QUESTIONNAIRE

Purpose: To measure organizational commitment.

Number of Items: 15

Format: Responses are made on a 7-point scale.

Reliability: Coefficient alpha was .82.

Validity: Correlations with other variables ranged from −.54 to .54.

Author: Krausz, M., et al.

Article: Actual and preferred work schedules and scheduling control as determinants of job-related attitudes.

Journal: *Journal of Vocational Behavior*, February 2000, *56*(1), 1–11.

Related Research: Porter, L. W., & Smith, F. J. (1970). *The etiology of organizational commitment*. Unpublished paper, University of California, Irvine.

10176

Test Name: OCCUPATIONAL PLANS QUESTIONNAIRE

Purpose: To measure the type of work respondents think they might enter.

Number of Items: 23

Format: Multiple-choice format. Items and scoring are briefly described.

Reliability: Internal consistency reliability coefficients ranged from .68 to .73.

Author: Hartung, P. J., et al.

Article: Individualism-collectivism and the vocational behavior of majority culture college students.

Journal: *Career Development Quarterly*, September 1996, *45*(1), 87–96.

Related Research: Herschenson, D. B. (1967). Sense of identity, occupational fit, and enculturation in adolescence. *Journal of Counseling Psychology, 14*, 319–324.

10177

Test Name: ORGANIZATIONAL COMMITMENT QUESTIONNAIRE

Purpose: To measure organizational commitment.

Number of Items: 8

Format: Scales range from "strongly disagree" to "strongly agree."

Reliability: Alpha coefficients ranged from .78 to .79 across two subscales.

Validity: Correlations with other variables ranged from −.11 to .46.

Authors: Randall, D. M., and O'Driscoll, M. P.

Article: Affective versus calculative commitment: Human resource implications.

Journal: *Journal of Social Psychology*, October 1997, *137*(5), 606–617.

Related Research: Meyer, J. P., & Allen, N. J. (1984). Testing the "side-bet" theory of organizational commitment: Some methodological considerations. *Journal of Applied Psychology, 69*, 372–378.

10178

Test Name: ORGANIZATIONAL COMMITMENT QUESTIONNAIRE—ADAPTED

Purpose: To measure organizational commitment.

Number of Items: 5

Format: Responses are made on a 7-point Likert-type scale ranging from 1 (strongly disagree) to 7 (strongly agree). Sample items are presented.

Reliability: Coefficient alpha was .89.

Validity: Correlations with other variables ranged from −.71 to .77.

Author: Saks, A. M., and Ashforth, B. E.

Article: Proactive socialization and behavioral self-management.

Journal: *Journal of Vocational Behavior*, June 1996, *48*(3), 301–323.

Related Research: Mowday, R. T., et al. (1979). The measurement of organizational commitment. *Journal of Vocational Behavior, 14*, 224–247.

10179

Test Name: ORGANIZATIONAL COMMITMENT QUESTIONNAIRE—REVISED

Purpose: To measure organizational commitment.

Number of Items: 9

Format: Includes 3 dimensions: Desire to Retain Membership in the Oganization, Belief in and Acceptance of the Organization's Values and Goals, and Willingness to Exert Effort on Behalf of the Organization. Responses are made on a 5-point scale ranging from 1 (strongly disagree) to 5 (strongly agree). Examples are presented.

Reliability: Reliability coefficient was .88.

Validity: Correlations with other variables ranged from −.41 to .56.

Author: Vigoda, E.

Article: Organizational politics, job attitudes, work outcomes: Exploration and implications for the public sector.

Journal: *Journal of Vocational Behavior*, December 2000, *57*(3), 326–347.

Related Research: Porter, L. W., & Smith, F. J. (1970). *The etiology of organizational commitment*. Unpublished manuscript, University of California, Irvine.

10180

Test Name: ORGANIZATIONAL COMMITMENT SCALE

Purpose: To measure organizational commitment.

Number of Items: 8

Format: Includes two subscales: Affective Commitment and Continuance Commitment. Responses are made on a 5-point Likert-type scale ranging from 1 (strongly disagree) to 5 (strongly agree). Examples are presented.

Reliability: Alpha coefficients were .79 and .63.

Validity: Correlations with other variables ranged from −.27 to .71 (N = 116).

Author: Nielsen, I. K., et al.

Article: Development and validation of scores on a two-dimensional workplace friendship scale.

Journal: *Educational and Psychological Measurement*, August 2000, *60*(4), 628–643.

Related Research: Allen, N. J., & Meyer, J. P. (1990). The measurement and antecedents of affective, continuance, and normative commitments to the organization. *Journal of Occupational Psychology, 63*, 1–18.

10181

Test Name: ORGANIZATIONAL COMMITMENT SCALE

Purpose: To measure organizational commitment.

Number of Items: 9

Format: Includes 3 subscales: Identification, Affiliation, and Exchange. Responses are made on a 5-point Likert-type scale ranging from 1 (strongly disagree) to 5 (strongly agree). Sample items are presented.

Reliability: Internal consistency reliabilities ranged from .69 to .87.

Validity: Correlations with other variables ranged from −.61 to .77.

Author: Kacmar, K. M., et al.

Article: Antecedents and consequences of organizational commitment: A comparison of two scales.

Journal: *Educational and Psychological Measurement*, December 1999, *59*(6), 976–994.

Related Research: Balfour, D. L., & Wechsler, B. (1996). Organizational commitment: Antecedents and outcomes in public organizations. *Public Productivity and Management Review, 29*, 256–277.

10182

Test Name: ORGANIZATIONAL COMMITMENT SCALE

Purpose: To measure organizational commitment.

Number of Items: 12

Format: Includes 2 subscales: Affective and Normative Responses are made on a 5-point scale ranging from 1 (strongly disagree) to 5 (strongly agree). Sample items are presented.

Reliability: Alpha coefficients were .80 and .77.

Validity: Correlations with other variables ranged from −.43 to .18.

Author: Shaffer, M. A., et al.

Article: Gender discrimination and job-related outcomes: A cross-cultural comparison of working women in the United States and China.

Journal: *Journal of Vocational Behavior*, December 2000, *57*(3), 395–427.

Related Research: Meyer, J. P., et al. (1993). Commitment to organizations and occupations: Extension and test of a three component conceptualization. *Journal of Applied Psychology, 78*, 538–551.

10183

Test Name: ORGANIZATIONAL COMMITMENT SCALES

Purpose: To measure affective, continuance, and normative commitment to an organization.

Number of Items: 18

Format: Five-point scales are anchored by 1 (strongly agree) and 5 (strongly disagree).

Reliability: Alpha coefficients ranged from .58 to .87.

Author: Ko, J.-W., et al.

Article: Assessment of Meyer and Allen's three-component model of organizational commitment in South Korea.

Journal: *Journal of Applied Psychology*, December 1997, *82*(6), 961–973.

Related Research: Meyer, J. P., et al. (1993). Commitment to organizations and occupations: Extension and test of a three-component conceptualization. *Journal of Applied Psychology, 78*, 538–551.

10184

Test Name: ORGANIZATIONAL COMMITMENT SCALES

Purpose: To measure organizational commitment.

Number of Items: 24

Format: Includes 3 scales: Affective, Continuance, and Normative Commitment.

Reliability: Reliability coefficients ranged from .65 to .79.

Validity: Correlations with other variables ranged from −.45 to .78.

Author: Cohen, A.

Article: On the discriminant validity of the Meyer and Allen measure of organizational commitment. How does it fit with the work commitment construct?

Journal: *Educational and Psychological Measurement*, June 1996, *56*(3), 494–503.

Related Research: Allen, N. J., & Meyer, J. P. (1990). The measurement and antecedents of affective, continuance and narrative commitment to the organization. *Journal of Occupational Psychology*, *63*, 1–18.

10185

Test Name: ORGANIZATIONAL IDENTIFICATION QUESTIONNAIRE

Purpose: To assess organizational identification.

Number of Items: 25

Format: Includes 3 components: Loyalty, Similarity, and Membership. Responses are made on a 7-point scale ranging from 1 (I disagree very strongly) to 7 (I agree very strongly). All items are presented.

Validity: Correlations with other organizational commitment instruments were .86 and .82.

Author: Johnson, W. L., et al.

Article: A primary- and second-order component analysis of the Organizational Identification Questionnaire.

Journal: *Educational and Psychological Measurement*, February 1999, *59*(1), 159–170.

Related Research: Cheney, G. (1983). On the various and changing meanings of

organizational membership: A field study of organizational identification. *Communication Monographs*, *50*, 342–362.

10186

Test Name: ORGANIZATIONAL LOYALTY

Purpose: To measure organizational commitment.

Number of Items: 3

Format: Responses are made on a 5-point scale ranging from "strongly agree" to "strongly disagree." Examples are given.

Reliability: Coefficient alpha was .86.

Validity: Correlations with other variables ranged from −.47 to .49.

Author: Stroh, L. K., et al.

Article: Family structure, glass ceiling, and traditional explanations for the differential rate of turnover of female and male managers.

Journal: *Journal of Vocational Behavior*, August 1996, *49*(1), 99–118.

Related Research: Mowday, R. T., et al. (1979). The measurement of organizational commitment. *Journal of Vocational Behavior*, *14*, 224–247.

Patchen, M. (1965). *Some questionnaire measures of employee morale: A report on their reliability and validity.* Institute for Social Research Monograph No. 41. Ann Arbor, MI.

10187

Test Name: PERCEIVED AFFECTIVE COMMITMENT SCALE

Purpose: To measure organizational commitment.

Number of Items: 4

Format: Five-point scales are anchored by 1 (strongly disagree) and 5 (strongly agree). A sample item is presented.

Reliability: Coefficient alpha was .88.

Validity: Correlations with other variables ranged from −.37 to .67.

Author: Allen, T. D., and Rush, M. C.

Article: The effects of organizational citizenship behavior on performance judgments: A field study and a laboratory experiment.

Journal: *Journal of Applied Psychology*, April 1998, *83*(2), 247–260.

Related Research: Shore, L. F., et al. (1995). Managerial perceptions of employee commitment to the organization. *Academy of Management Journal*, *38*, 1593–1615.

10188

Test Name: PREFERENCES FOR ACTIVITIES

Purpose: To identify preferences for occupational activities.

Number of Items: 224

Format: Responses are made on a 7-point scale ranging from 1 (strongly dislike) to 7 (strongly like).

Reliability: Two-week reliability ranged from .29 to .90.

Author: Tracey, T. J. G.

Article: The structure of interests and self-efficacy expectations: An expanded examination of the spherical model of interests.

Journal: *Journal of Counseling Psychology*, January 1997, *44*(1), 32–43.

Related Research: U. S. Department of Labor (1977). *Dictionary of occupational titles* (4th ed.). Washington, DC: U. S. Government Printing Office.

10189

Test Name: PROFESSIONAL COMMITMENT SCALE

Purpose: To measure professional commitment.

Number of Items: 3

Format: Responses are made on a 5-point scale ranging from 1 (completely false of me) to 5 (completely true of me). All items are presented.

Reliability: Coefficient alpha was .54.

Validity: Correlations with other variables ranged from −.29 to .48.

Author: Smart, R. M.

Article: Career stages in Australian professional women: A test of Super's model.

Journal: *Journal of Vocational Behavior*, June 1998, 53(3), 379–395.

Related Research: Regoli, R. M., & Poole, E. D. (1980). Police professionalism and role conflict: Comparison of rural and urban departments. *Human Relations*, 33, 241–252.

10190

Test Name: PROFESSIONAL COMMITMENT SCALE

Purpose: To measure professional commitment.

Number of Items: 3

Format: Responses are made on a 5-point Likert scale ranging from 1 (strongly disagree) to 5 (strongly agree).

Reliability: Coefficient alpha was .61.

Validity: Correlations with other variables ranged from −.30 to .51.

Author: Wallace, J. E.

Article: It's about time: A study of hours worked and work spillover among law firms and lawyers.

Journal: *Journal of Vocational Behavior*, April 1997, 50(2), 227–248.

Related Research: Porter, L. W., et al. (1974). Organizational commitment, job satisfaction, and turnover among technicians. *Journal of Applied Psychology*, 59, 603–609.

10191

Test Name: PROFESSIONAL COMMITMENT SCALE

Purpose: To measure professional commitment.

Number of Items: 5

Format: Responses are made on a 4-point scale ranging from 1 (strongly disagree) to 4 (strongly agree). An example is presented.

Reliability: Coefficient alpha was .84.

Validity: Correlations with other variables ranged from −.09 to .27.

Author: Blau, G., and Lunz, M.

Article: Testing the incremental effect of professional commitment or intent to leave one's profession beyond effects of external, personal, and work-related variables.

Journal: *Journal of Vocational Behavior*, April 1998, 52(2), 260–269.

Related Research: Blau, G. (1985). The measurements and prediction of career commitment.

Journal of Occupational Psychology, 58, 277–288.

10192

Test Name: PROFESSIONAL CONTEXT SCALES

Purpose: To measure role orientation and professional commitment.

Number of Items: 7

Format: Includes 2 scales: Role Orientation and Professional Commitment. Responses are made on a 4-point scale ranging from 1 (strongly disagree) to 4 (strongly agree). Sample items are presented.

Reliability: Internal consistency reliabilities were .72 and .84.

Validity: Correlations with other variables ranged from −.14 to .06.

Author: Blau, G.

Article: Job, organizational, and professional context antecedents as predictors of intent for interrole work transitions.

Journal: *Journal of Vocational Behavior*, June 2000, 56(3), 330–345.

Related Research: Blau, G. (1985). The measurement and prediction of career commitment. *Journal of Occupational Psychology*, 58, 277–288.

Graen, G., & Ginsburgh, S. (1977). Job resignation as a function of role orientation and leader acceptance: A longitudinal investigation of organization assimilation. *Organizational Behavior and Human Performance*, 19, 1–17.

10193

Test Name: RAMACK AND COURSES INTEREST INVENTORIES—ENGLISH

Purpose: To assess interest in occupations and courses.

Number of Items: 72

Format: Yes/?/no format. All items are presented.

Reliability: Alpha coefficients ranged from .73 to .91.

Author: Meir, E. I., et al.

Article: Examination of interest inventories based on Roe's classification.

Journal: *Career Development Quarterly*, September 1997, *46*(1), 48–61.

Related Research: Meir, E. I. (1995). *Manual for the Ramack and Courses Interest Inventory.* Tel Aviv, Israel: Tel Aviv University, Department of Psychology.

See correction in *The Career Development Quarterly, 46*(3), 245.

10194

Test Name: SCIENTIST–PRACTITIONER INVENTORY

Purpose: To assess career specialty interests of graduate students in psychology.

Number of Items: 42

Format: Scales range from 1 (very low interest) to 5 (very high interest).

Reliability: Alpha coefficients ranged from .83 to .96.

Author: Kahn, J. H., and Miller, S. A.

Article: Measuring global perceptions of the research training environment using a short form of the RTES-R.

Journal: *Measurement and Evaluation in Counseling and Development*, July 2000, *33*(2), 103–119.

Related Research: Leong,

F. T. L., & Zachor, P. (1991). Development and validation of the Scientist–Practitioner Inventory for Psychology. *Journal of Counseling Psychology, 38*, 331–341.

10195

Test Name: SELF-EXPLORATION—REVISED SCALE

Purpose: To assess participants' career exploration behavior.

Number of Items: 9

Format: Responses are made on a 5-point Likert scale.

Reliability: Coefficient alpha was .82. Test-retest (2 weeks) reliability was .83.

Validity: Correlations with other variables ranged from .24 to .37.

Author: Luzzo, D. A., and Jenkins-Smith, A.

Article: Development and initial validation of the assessment of attributes for career decision-making.

Journal: *Journal of Vocational Behavior*, April 1998, *52*(2), 224–245.

Related Research: Stumpf, S. A., et al.(1983). Development of the Career Exploration Survey. *Journal of Vocational Behavior, 22*, 191–226.

10196

Test Name: SELF-EXPLORATION SCALE

Purpose: To measure the self-exploration component of career exploration.

Number of Items: 4

Format: Responses are made on a 5-point scale ranging from 1 (very little extent) to 5 (very

great extent). All items are presented.

Reliability: Reliability was .85.

Validity: Correlations with other variables ranged from −.07 to .51.

Author: Werbel, J. D.

Article: Relationships among career exploration, job search intensity, and job search effectiveness in graduating college students.

Journal: *Journal of Vocational Behavior*, December 2000, *57*(3), 379–394.

Related Research: Stumpf, S. A., et al. (1983). Development of the Career Exploration Survey (CES). *Journal of Vocational Behavior, 22*, 191–226.

10197

Test Name: SELF EXPLORATION SUBSCALE—REVISED

Purpose: To enable one to rate the extent of one's intrapersonally oriented career exploration involving self-assessment and retrospection during the last 3 months.

Number of Items: 5

Format: Responses are made on a 5-point scale ranging from "little" to "a great deal."

Reliability: Test-retest (2 weeks) reliability was .83.

Validity: Correlations with other variables ranged from −.16 to .31.

Author: Ketterson, T. U., and Blustein, D. L.

Article: Attachment relationships and the career exploration process.

Journal: *Career Development Quarterly*, December 1997, *46*(2), 167–178.

Related Research: Blustein, D. L. (1988). The relationship between motivational processes and career exploration. *Journal of Vocational Behavior*, *32*, 345–357.

10198

Test Name: SPORT COMMITMENT SCALE

Purpose: To assess direct and indirect commitment to sport.

Number of Items: 12

Format: Five-point Likert format. Sample items are presented.

Reliability: Alpha coefficients ranged from .52 to .96.

Validity: Correlations with other variables ranged from −.09 to .34.

Author: Martens, M. P., and Cox, R. H.

Article: Career development in college varsity athletes.

Journal: *Journal of College Student Development*, March/April 2000, *41*(2), 172–180.

Related Research: Scanlan, T. K., et al. (1993). An introduction to the sport commitment model. *Journal of Sport and Exercise Psychology*, *15*, 1–15.

10199

Test Name: SPORT SPECTATOR INVOLVEMENT SCALE

Purpose: To measure spectator involvement in sports.

Number of Items: 14

Format: Items represent emotional, cognitive, and behavioral aspects of sport spectating. Responses are made on a 7-point Likert scale ranging from 1 (strongly disagree) to 7 (strongly agree). All items are presented.

Reliability: Coefficient alpha was .96.

Validity: Correlations with other variables were .58 and .57.

Author: Bahk, C. M.

Article: Sex differences in sport spectator involvement.

Journal: *Perceptual and Motor Skills*, August 2000, *91*(1), 79–83.

10200

Test Name: SURVEY OF ORGANIZATIONAL PRACTICES

Purpose: To measure perceived participation in an organization.

Number of Items: 23

Format: Five-point scales are anchored by (1) never and (5) to a great extent. All items are presented.

Reliability: Alphas ranged from .75 to .89 across subscales.

Author: Buda, R.

Article: Perceptions of employees' participation programs in union and nonunion settings.

Journal: *Psychological Reports*, October 1998, *83*(2), 611–622.

Related Research: Ulrich, D., and Lake, D. (1990). *Organizational capability*. New York: Wiley.

10201

Test Name: TEAM COMMITMENT SCALE

Purpose: To measure identification, loyalty, and involvement with a sports team.

Number of Items: 9

Format: Scales range from 1 (strongly disagree) to 7 (strongly agree).

Reliability: Coefficient alpha was .50.

Author: Totterdell, P.

Article: Catching moods and hitting runs: Mood linkage and subjective performance in professional sports teams.

Journal: *Journal of Applied Psychology*, December 2000, *85*(6), 848–859.

Related Research: Cook, J., & Wall, T. (1980). New work attitude measures of trust, organizational commitment and personal need non-fulfillment. *Journal of Occupational Psychology*, *53*, 39–52.

10202

Test Name: UNION COMMITMENT SCALE

Purpose: To measure instrumental attachment to a union.

Number of Items: 10

Format: Five-point Likert format. All items are presented

Reliability: Alpha was .81.

Validity: Correlations with other variables ranged from −.03 to .61.

Author: Pisnar-Sweeney, M.

Article: Role of normative commitment in predicting members' participation in the union.

Journal: *Psychological Reports*, June 1997, *80*(3) Part 2, 1183–1207.

Related Research: Heshizer, B. P., et al. (1991). Normative commitment and instrumental attachment as intervening variables in the prediction of union participation. *Journal of Applied Behavioral Science*, *27*, 532–549.

10203

Test Name: VOCATIONAL EXPLORATION AND COMMITMENT SCALE

Purpose: To assess progress in committing to career choice.

Number of Items: 19

Format: Responses are made on a 7-point Likert-type scale.

Reliability: Coefficient alpha exceeded .90. Test-retest reliability was .92.

Validity: Correlations with other variables ranged from −.44 to .07.

Author: Felsman, D. E., and Blustein, D. L.

Article: The role of peer relatedness in late adolescent career development.

Journal: *Journal of Vocational Behavior*, April 1999, *54*(2), 279–295.

Related Research: Blustein, D. L., et al. (1989). The development and validation of a two-dimensional model of the commitment to career choices process. *Journal of Vocational Behavior*, *35*, 342–378.

10204

Test Name: VOCATIONAL QUESTIONNAIRE

Purpose: To measure activity preferences and vocational identity characteristics.

Number of Items: 90

Format: Liking scales range from "very much" to "not at all." Likelihood of Working scales range from "very high" to "very low." Items are described in detail.

Validity: Correlations of subscales with other variables exceeded .50.

Author: Vondracek, F. W., and Skorikov, V. B.

Article: Leisure, school, work activity preferences and their role in vocational identity development.

Journal: *Career Development Quarterly*, June 1997, *45*(4), 322–340.

Related Research: Todt, E., & Mesa, M. (1988). Die verankerung der schulfachinteressen in allgemeinen und in den freizeitinteressen von schuelern und schuelerinnen de 7. bis 10. klassenstufe. [The relationship of interests in school subjects to the general and leisure interests of students of the 7th through 10th grade]. Unpublished manuscript, University of Giessen.

10205

Test Name: WORK ATTITUDE SCALE

Purpose: To measure commitment to work.

Number of Items: 13, 18

Format: Five- or 7-point scales ranged from 1 (strongly disagree) to 5/7 (strongly agree).

Reliability: Alpha coefficients ranged from .66 to .78.

Author: Lyness, K. S., and Thompson, D. E.

Article: Above the glass ceiling? A comparison of matched samples of female and male executives.

Journal: *Journal of Applied Psychology*, June 1997, *82*(3), 359–375.

Related Research: Meyer, J. P., et al. (1993). Commitment to organizations and occupations: Extension and test of a three-component conceptualization. *Journal of Applied Pschology*, *78*, 538–551.

10206

Test Name: WORK COMMITMENT SCALE

Purpose: To measure work commitment.

Number of Items: 4

Format: Responses are made on a 5-point Likert scale ranging from 1 (strongly disagree) to 5 (strongly agree).

Reliability: Coefficient alpha was .66.

Validity: Correlations with other variables ranged from −.19 to .49.

Author: Wallace, J. E.

Article: It's about time: A study of hours worked and work spillover among law firm lawyers.

Journal: *Journal of Vocational Behavior*, April 1997, *50*(2), 227–248.

Related Research: Kanungo, R. N. (1982). Measurement of job and work involvement. *Journal of Applied Psychology*, *67*, 341–349.

10207

Test Name: WORK INVOLVEMENT SCALE

Purpose: To measure commitment to work.

Number of Items: 6

Format: Five-point Likert format. Sample items are presented.

Reliability: Coefficient alpha was .86.

Validity: Correlations with other variables ranged from −.12 to .14.

Author: Riipinen, M.

Article: The relation of work involvement to occupational needs, need satisfaction, locus of control and affect.

Journal: *Journal of Social Psychology*, June 1996, *136*(3), 291–303.

10208

Test Name: WORK INVOLVEMENT SCALE

Purpose: To measure the extent to which people devote themselves to productive projects and constructive uses of time.

Number of Items: 8

Format: Sample items are presented.

Reliability: Alpha coefficients ranged from .67 to .71.

Validity: Correlations with other variables ranged from −.20 to .24.

Author: Bonebright, C. A., et al.

Article: The relationship of workaholism with work-life conflict, life satisfaction, and purpose in life.

Journal: *Journal of Counseling Psychology*, October 2000, *47*(4), 469–477.

Related Research: Spence, J. T., & Robbins, A. S. (1992). Workaholism: Definition, measurement, and preliminary results. *Journal of Personality Assessment, 58*, 160–178.

10209

Test Name: WORK SALIENCE MEASURE

Purpose: To measure work salience.

Number of Items: 4

Format: Responses are made on a 5-point Likert scale ranging from 1 (strongly disagree) to 5 (strongly agree). Two items are presented.

Reliability: Alpha coefficients were .56 and .69.

Author: Hammer, L. B., et al.

Article: Work-family conflict in dual-earner couples: Within-individual and crossover effects of work and family.

Journal: *Journal of Vocational Behavior*, April 1997, *50*(2), 185–203.

Related Research: Quinn, R., & Staines, G. (1979). *The 1977 quality of employment survey.* Ann Arbor: University of Michigan, Survey Research Center.

Author Index

All numbers refer to test numbers for the current volume.

Abbate, C. S., 7476
Abdalla, I. A. H., 9950
Abdel-Khalek, A. M., 7594, 7718
Abed, A. S., 7468, 9840
Abel, M. H., 8277, 9405
Abeo, A. S., 9780
Aberson, C. L., 8405
Abner, J. L., 7611, 7615, 7802
Abreu, J. M., 8069, 9812
Abu-Hilal, M. M., 7521
Abu-Rabia, S., 8365, 8392
Abu-Saad, I., 10017
Achter, J. A., 7462
Ackerman, B. P., 8530
Ackerman, S. J., 7853, 10038, 10074, 10097
Adams, C. D., 8497
Adams, G. A., 8192, 9020, 9891, 10132
Adams, K. S., 8130
Ægisdóttir, S., 9392
Akey, T. M., 7810
Akhtar, S., 10016
Akimoto, M., 8386
Alden, L. E., 7652, 7992
Aldridge, J. M., 9181
Alexander, J. M., 9217, 9384
Alexitch, L. R., 8425
Alkhadher, O., 9893
Alkhateeb, M. H., 8355, 9840
Allen, F. C. L., 8711
Allen, J. P., 8887
Allen, M. W., 10001
Allen, S. M., 8912
Allen, T. D., 8143, 8224, 8248, 8257, 8626, 9014, 9318, 9514, 10118, 10187
Allison, D. G., 8141
Alnajjar, A. A., 8205
Alper, S., 7939, 9176, 9374
Alreshoud, A., 7940
Amato, P. R., 8342, 8832, 8908
Andersen, B. L., 9617
Anderson, C. A., 8348
Anderson, C. M., 9539

Anderson, K., 8389
Anderson, L. A., 8357
Anderson, N. R., 8781, 9605
Anderson, S. E., 8592
Andersson, H. W., 8812, 9730, 9731
Andrews, B. P., 9930
Andrews, K. D., 9590
Annesi, J. J., 7662, 9277
Anshel, M. H., 7637, 7860, 7866
Antonietti, A., 8777
Applegryn, A. E. M., 8083, 9632
Aquilino, W. S., 8965
Aquino, J. A., 7733
Arachtingi, B. V., 10027
Arad, S., 9788
Argov, E., 8561
Armeli, S., 9116, 9789
Arnold, E. H., 9850
Aryee, S., 7630, 7831, 7889, 8146, 8848, 9004, 9005, 9430, 9477, 9662, 9668, 10108, 10144
Asher, S. R., 8636
Ashford, S. J., 8251, 9701
Ashforth, B. E., 7572, 7793, 7878, 8186, 8236, 8529, 8611, 9212, 9228, 9436, 9492, 9593, 10178
Ashkanasy, N. M., 8752, 10010
Ashman, A. F., 9363
Aune, K. S., 7998
Aune, R. K., 8052
Avants, S. K., 8081
Ayeyemi-Bello, T., 9378

Badura, A. S., 8798, 9592
Bahk, C. M., 10199
Baity, M. R., 9751
Bajema, C., 9016, 9168
Baldo, T. D., 8734
Baldwin, D. A., 8573, 8574
Banas, J. T., 7728, 9013
Bandura, A., 8654, 9948
Banos, R. M., 9559

Banyard, V. L., 7881
Bao, W. -N., 8991
Barber, A. E., 9152, 9153, 10025
Barber, B. K., 8839, 8806, 8981, 8982
Barber, J. P., 7993, 9358, 10029
Barbuto, J. E., Jr., 9249
Barclay, D. M., III, 7960
Barends, A. W., 10048
Barker, J., 9656
Barker, J. P., 10073
Barkham, M., 7995
Barling, J., 8196, 8486, 8550, 8724, 8880, 8896, 10013
Barnes, L. L. B., 8324, 8397
Barrick, M. R., 8275, 8743, 9177, 9678
Barry, B., 7968, 9718
Bartini, M., 8687
Bartley, D. F., 7664, 9717, 9719, 9889, 10136, 10151
Basadur, M., 8383
Bass, K., 7669, 7673, 8329
Bassett, D. L., 7737
Bates, M. D., 9289
Bauer, T. N., 8335, 8751, 9138, 9511, 9543
Baugh, S. G., 9498, 9549
Baum, S. M., 8313
Bauminger, N., 7959, 8009
Bazzini, D. G., 8549
Becker, T. E., 7919
Beckham, J. C., 8809
Beckstein, B. A., 9073
Becona, E., 8588
Beehr, T. A., 8263, 9062, 9111, 9548, 9744
Behling, D. U., 10152
Belcher, L., 7908, 9224, 9373
Bell, K. N., 8354
Belsky, J., 7973, 7989
Benasich, A. A., 8787, 8793
Bendania, A., 9780
Bendas-Jacob, O., 7505
Bennett, K. J., 7772

Bennett, R. J., 9187
Bensur, B. J., 7759, 8820, 8969, 9526
Berg, D. R., 8458, 8460
Bergin, D. A., 9589, 9877
Bernal, G., 8074, 8844
Bernardi, R. A., 9448
Bernat, J. A., 8374, 8506
Berry, E. M., 8387
Berzonsky, M. D., 9417
Betz, N. E., 9347, 9349, 9476
Beutell, N. J., 7732, 8268, 9672
Bickle, G., 9946
Bidwell, C. E., 9145
Bieling, P. J., 7652, 7992
Bieschke, K. J., 8373, 8407, 9089, 9304, 9537, 9538, 10157
Bigbee, M. A., 7887, 8011, 8077, 8091
Bing, M. N., 9918, 9905, 9909, 9942
Birch, S. H., 7518
Birdi, K., 8921, 9079, 9241, 9441
Birenbaum, M., 7463, 9825
Bishop, D. I., 8521
Bishop, J. W., 8244, 8262, 8271
Bishop, M. R., 10157
Bishop, R. M., 9537, 9538
Black, J. S., 8251, 9701
Black, M. M., 8931
Blake, D. D., 8704
Blanchard, E. B., 7719
Blasko, D., 7475
Blau, G., 8189, 8216, 8219, 9173, 10015, 10191, 10192
Blickle, G., 8602, 8652
Bliese, P. D., 7790, 8229, 8304, 9383, 9892, 10171
Bluedorn, A. C., 8270, 8770
Blustein, D. L., 8890, 10148, 10150, 10174, 10197, 10203
Bobocel, D. R., 10019, 10057
Bogels, S. M., 7602
Bogenschneider, K., 8950, 8970
Bohning, G., 9975
Boles, J. S., 7597, 8210, 8252, 9553, 9664
Bond, M. H., 9940
Bonebright, C. A., 7834, 8173, 9205, 9669, 10208
Boney-McCoy, S., 7819
Booth, A., 8906, 8908
Borders, L. D., 8362
Bornman, E., 7953, 8083, 9632
Bornstein, R. F., 7980
Botha, H. C., 9899

Bourdeau, M. L., 9513
Bowen, C. W., 7487
Bowman, D., 7688
Boyatzis, R. E., 9987
Bozionelos, N., 7497, 8151, 8340, 8778, 9859
Bradbury, T. N., 8819, 8902, 9740
Bradley, J. S., 7500
Bradley, R. H., 8040, 8876, 8913, 8949, 8967
Brady, K. L., 10056
Braio, A., 8467
Bram, A. D., 7863, 7897
Brand, N., 7884
Brandt, C. J., 8286
Brandt, T. S., 9007
Brandyberry, L. J., 8401
Brasic, J. R., 8726
Braungart-Rieker, J. M., 8917
Bray, N. J., 7640
Brazelton, E., 7809, 8533
Brett, J. F., 9213, 9218
Briddick, W. C., 8509
Brigham, F. J., 9398
Brody, G. H., 7520, 7927, 8085, 8554, 8676, 8785, 8827, 8859, 8860, 9203, 9483
Broman, C. L., 8910
Brookins, C. C., 9341
Brookins, C. L., 8788
Brooks-Gunn, J., 8787, 8793
Brown, A. C., 8670
Brown, C., 9315, 9351, 9752
Brown, D. J., 8422
Brown, R., 7920, 9342
Brown, R. A., 7543
Brown, S. P., 8670, 9147, 9294
Browne, B. A., 8422, 9903
Bruch, M. A., 8076, 8756, 8767, 9598, 9653, 9777, 9837, 9934, 9939
Bryant, N. C., 8324
Buckley, M. R., 9104, 9434, 9536
Buda, R., 10200
Budd, J. L., 9012
Buehler, C., 8839, 8954
Buelow, G., 7905, 7924, 8016, 9316
Buerger, J. L., 9969
Bulger, C. A., 8731, 9109, 9402, 9574
Bumpas, M. F., 8996
Bundrick, C. M., 7727, 9339, 9340, 9596
Buras, A. R., 8817

Bures, E. M., 8339, 9221
Burgess, K. B., 7557, 8003, 8541, 8639
Burke, R. J., 8297, 8901, 8997, 9305, 9816, 10062, 10064, 10090, 10111, 10142
Burleson, B. R., 8979
Burnett, P. C., 8686
Burns, D. D., 7758, 7891, 9904
Burns, J. T., 9447, 9734
Burris, C. T., 9972
Burton, R., 8046
Bushman, B. J., 9929
Buss, D. M., 8701, 9785
Busse, R. T., 10039
Bybee, D. I., 7820, 8601

Cable, D. M., 9985
Caligiuri, P. M., 8163, 10106
Call, K. T., 8476
Cameron, J. E., 9566
Campbell, J. L., 9397, 9540
Campbell, M. E., 9334
Campbell, R., 7641
Campion, M. A., 9185
Campos, A., 7477
Caraucan, E., 7452
Carbonaro, W. J., 7529
Cardinal, B. J., 8326
Carey, M. P., 7453, 8882, 9826
Carlson, D. S., 7768, 9544, 9666, 9946
Carlson, R. E., 8717
Carmel, S., 9532
Carney, M. A., 7786, 8661
Caron, S. L., 8598, 8697, 8700
Carr, S. C., 9357
Carraher, S. M., 9012
Carraher, S. W., 9536
Carrier, C. S., 7657, 8527
Carroll, J. J., 7925
Carskadon, M. A., 7653, 8706
Carstens, J. A., 9611
Carter, D. B., 8700
Carter, R. T., 8138
Cashin, S. E., 9312
Cashwell, C. S., 8683, 8836, 8862
Cassidy, S., 9416
Cast, A. D., 8997, 9816
Cavanaugh, M. A., 8154
Cavell, T. A., 9638, 10066, 10120
Cecil, H., 9331
Cepeda-Benito, A., 7514, 8140
Cernovsky, Z. Z., 10093
Chambliss, C., 7944
Chan, D., 9044, 9769

Chan, K-Y., 9250, 9690, 9973
Chan, L. K. S., 9354, 9875, 9882
Chan, W. T., 7612, 8308
Chang, C. Y., 8344, 7449
Chang, E. C., 7635, 7636, 7665, 7895, 9922, 9923
Chang, L., 8453
Chapell, M. S., 9836
Chapman, P. L., 7576
Chebat, J-C., 10077
Cheek, J. M., 9910, 9920
Chen, A., 9997
Chen, G., 7502, 9219, 9319
Chen, X-P., 8289, 8630, 10166
Cheng, S., 9223
Cheng, S.-T., 7622
Cheng, Y. C., 8480, 8645, 9163, 9175
Cherian, L., 7553
Cherian, V. I., 7553
Cheuk, W. H., 8162, 8278
Cheung, C.-K., 7698, 9388, 9977
Cheung, S.-K., 7651, 7928, 9403
Chiachiere, F. J., 8347
Chiu, L-H., 9275
Choi, J. N., 8771, 9867
Chorpita, B. F., 7581
Chow, P., 9334
Chrisler, J. C., 8642
Christensen, A. J., 9530
Christenson, S. L., 8130
Christiansen, N. D., 9884
Christopher, F. S., 8056, 8513, 9723
Chun, Y.-J., 8829, 8885
Chung, H., 9161
Church, A. H., 9449, 9542, 9565
Chwalisz, K., 8481
Cicchetti, D., 8051
Claes, R., 8647
Clark, D. M., 9703
Clark, J. W., Jr., 9901
Clark, R., 9729
Clarke, D., 7567
Clum, G. A., 7725, 7835, 8116, 8372, 8730, 9531, 9883
Coe, G., 8941
Cohen, A., 8183, 9497, 9503, 9990, 10133, 10165, 10184
Cohen, E., 8878, 9781, 9813
Cohen, S. G., 8678
Coimbra, J. L., 9724
Cokely, K. O., 9191
Cokley, K., 8023, 9680
Cole, D. A., 7561, 7612, 7781, 8720

Coll, K. M., 9556
Collella, A., 10126
Collier, P. J., 9370
Collins, J. M., 9709
Colquitt, J. A., 9215, 9251, 9292, 9575
Comstock, J., 7998
Comunian, A. L., 7999
Conduct Problems Prevention Research Group, 7658, 8087, 8990
Connolly, M. B., 7811
Connor-Smith, J. K., 7828
Conrad, C. A., 10007
Constantine, M. G., 10046, 10069, 10070, 10071
Conway, M., 7832
Cook, J., 9652
Cook, P. F., 8483, 8648, 9442
Cook, S. W., 7632, 7633, 7806, 8795, 10137
Cooke, C. A., 8323
Coolahan, K., 8640
Cooley, E., 8582, 9641
Coolidge, F. L., 9697
Corbin, S. S., 7508, 8347
Cordery, J. L., 8213, 9232, 9501
Côté, J. E., 9091, 9285
Cotter, P. R., 8067
Cotton, J. L., 10065
Couch, L. L., 7951, 7962, 7981, 7986, 8053, 8063, 8128, 8129, 8132, 8427, 9943
Cowen, E. L., 7563
Cox, R. H., 7591, 7751, 10198
Cramer, K. M., 7695
Cramer, P., 9716
Crawford, P. M., 9398
Crick, N. R., 7887, 8011, 8077, 8091, 8546, 9421
Crits-Christoph, P., 10022, 10037, 10049
Crohan, S. E., 8903, 8905
Crook, K., 7776, 7847
Croom, L., 9841
Crouter, A. C., 8361, 9897
Crowell, J. A., 8090
Crum, M. R., 8200, 9155
Cummings, E. M., 9003
Curran, P. J., 8496, 8501, 8635
Currie, S. R., 7775
Curtis, W. J., 8874
Curtner-Smith, M. E., 8537, 8911, 8918, 9001, 9002, 9714

Dadkhah, A., 8095, 9329

Dai, D. Y., 7532, 9265, 9288, 9564, 9706, 9708, 9820
Daley, A. J., 9499
Daley, C. E., 7558, 7696, 8328
Daley, M. A., 8775, 8776
Damji, T., 7812, 8070
Damush, T. M., 7764
Daniel, L. G., 7526
Darke, P. R., 8370
Dart, B. C., 9054, 9242, 9862
Davidson, K., 9698, 9699
Davidson, K. W., 9776
Davidson, W. B., 7559, 8067, 9296, 9629, 9725
Davies, L., 8942
Davies, P. T., 9003
Davis, C., III, 7486, 8027
Davis, C. M. 9645
Davis, H., IV, 9321
Davis, J. H., 8131
Davis, M. A., 9090
Davis, T. J., 10172
Davis, T. L., 9981
De Leon, B., 7946
Dear, G. E., 8403
DeBaryshe, B., 8856
Debus, R. L., 9937
DeConinck, J. B., 8239
Deemer, S. A., 9635
Deffenbacher, J. L., 7587, 8568, 8572
DeForge, B. R., 7960
DeGarmo, D. S., 8879
DeGraaf, N. D., 8634
Delaney, A. M., 9143, 9144
Deluga, R. J., 7586
Denham, S. A., 8046
DeNisi, A. S., 9150
Dennis, M. J. B., 8029, 9485
Denton, W. H., 8979
Denzine, G. M., 9539
Der-Karabetian, A., 7970, 8733, 9303, 9389, 9955
Dickter, D. N., 8201
Diefendorff, J. M., 8491
Diekhoff, G. M., 9029
Diemer, R. A., 9767, 9772, 10033
Dijkstra, A., 8450, 8653, 9571, 9588
Dirks, K. T., 8126
Dodd, D. K., 9410
Dodge, K. A., 8546, 9421
Dollinger, S. J., 9311, 9418, 9992
Dollinger, S. M. C., 9418
Domingo, M., 7904
Donovan, M. A., 8245, 8299, 8451, 8694, 8740, 9907

Dorkin, P. L., 8575
Dorsch, M. J., 7961
Dorsey, S. D., 8966, 8960
Douglas, K. S., 9593
Doverspike, D., 7918
Dovidio, J. F., 8258, 8563
Dreger, R. M., 8503, 8547, 9170
Driscoll, J. M., 9182, 9848
Drummonds, J. J., 9814
Druskat, V. U., 8303
Duane, E. A., 7865
Dube, L., 8735
Dubner, A. E., 7613
Dubow, E. F., 8895, 8923
Dudley, B. S., 9025
Dulebohn, J. H., 9576, 9828, 9829
Dumenci, L., 9557
Duncan, L. E., 9524, 9935
Dunkle, J. H., 10023, 10101
Dunkley, D. M., 7506, 7757, 9924
Dunn, A., 9319
DuPaul, G. J., 7574
Durm, M. W., 9983
Duxbury, L. E., 8845, 8841, 8851, 8988, 9422, 9555, 9671
Dykeman, C., 8556, 9360, 9917
Dyrkacz, L., 7695

Eachus, P., 9416
Eagle, B. W., 8852, 9658, 9659, 9660
Eagstrom, C. M., 8471
East, P. L., 8691, 8919
Eby, L. T., 8295
Eccles, J. S., 8314, 8924
Eddy, E. E., 9047
Eddy, E. R., 9056
Eden, D., 8144, 8222
Edinger, J. D., 8385, 8606
Edwards, J. R., 9083, 9084
Ehrenberg, M. F., 7983, 9610
Eidelson, R. J., 7758
Eifert, G. H., 7593, 7608, 7872
Eisenberg, N., 7616, 7617, 8088, 8089, 8540, 8542, 8675, 8710, 8786, 8828, 9679, 9705, 9713, 9732, 9749, 9750, 9765, 9795, 9796
Eigenberger, M. E., 7674
Eisenberger, R., 8237, 9115
Eister, T. M., 10056
Elango, B., 8338, 8364
Elias, S. M., 9301
Eliot, J., 9319

Elkins, T. J., 9069, 9074
Ellason, J. W., 7656
Ellingson, J. E., 8274
Elliott, T. R., 7679, 7712, 7730, 7850, 7941, 8591, 9214, 9505
Embree, R. A., 8443
Ennis, C. D., 10009
Enright, R. D., 7697, 8656
Ensher, E. A., 10063, 10103
Epkins, C. C., 7623, 7779, 9367
Epperson, D. L., 9694
Epstein, J., 7681
Epstein, J. A., 8707
Erdley, C. A., 8636
Erford, B. T., 8494, 8596
Erickson, R. J., 8345, 9048, 9060
Erkis, A. J., 9325
Eronen, S., 9630
Ertmer, P. A., 8490, 9591
Eshel, Y., 7976, 7984, 7996, 7997
Espelage, D. L., 8511, 8580
Ettington, D. R., 8159, 8212, 8300, 9631, 10058, 10107
Evans, D. W., 8544
Evans, G. W., 8525
Evans, W. J., 8333

Fagen, D. B., 7489, 7822, 8440, 9361, 9866, 9912
Farrell, A. C., 10019, 10057
Farrell, A. D., 8621
Farvery, J. A. M., 8086
Fassinger, R., 8026, 9831
Fearn, W., 7482
Fedor, D. B., 8291, 9121
Feinberg, M. E., 9413, 9715
Felsman, D. E., 8890, 10148, 10174, 10203
Felsten, G., 9693
Feng, D., 8802, 8909
Fergen, D. B., 8930
Ferrari, J. R., 7537, 9885
Ferrari, R. R., 8563
Ferraro, F. R., 7685, 9739
Ferry, T. R., 9245, 9454, 9457, 10169
Fiedlander, M. L., 10023
Fields, S. A., 8489
Findley, H. M., 8632, 9010
Fine, M. A., 7913, 7935
Finkelhor, D., 7819
Finkelstein, L. M., 9305
Finkenberg, M. E., 9625
Finnegan, R. A., 8638

Fischer, A. R., 7738, 7749, 8048, 8065, 8457, 9817
Fisher, A. R., 8824
Fisher, S. L., 8228, 9258, 9874
Fiske, S. T., 7969
Fletcher, A. C., 7893, 8956
Flor, D. L., 7520
Flowers, A. L., 8674
Flowers, C., 8904
Flowers, L., 9835
Floyd, K., 8404, 8623
Fontaine, K. R., 8571
Ford, J. K., 8228, 9244, 9258, 9580, 9756, 9874, 9876
Forehand, R., 8745
Forrest, L., 9753
Forsythe, S., 9806
Fortier, M. S., 9211, 9280
Fortunato, V. J., 7864
Foster, M. D., 7692
Fouad, N. A., 9453, 9455, 9466
Foubert, J. D., 8769
Fousad, N. A., 9833
Francis, L. J., 7774, 8400
Fraser, B. J., 8662
Fraser, K. P., 9881
Frazier, P. A., 7824, 9423, 9858
Frederick, C. M., 7856, 9209, 9248
Fredrick, C. M., 8082, 9622
Freedman, J. L., 8370
Freedman, S. R., 7697, 8656
Freeman, B., 9556
Freeman, M. A., 9970
Freestom, M. H., 8900, 9648
Fried, Y., 8188, 8789, 9754
Friedlander, M. L., 9380, 10101
Friedman, I. A., 7505, 7577, 9174
Frijters, J. C., 7464, 8875
Fritz, H. L., 7708, 8136, 9512
Frone, M. R., 7510, 7568, 7767, 8181, 8184, 8193, 8301, 8302, 8597, 8657, 8600, 8715, 8737, 8843, 8854, 8855, 8973, 9112, 9171, 9184, 9186, 9665, 9743
Frosch, D. L., 8086
Fuertes, J. N., 8079, 8135, 10006
Fukada, H., 7504, 7714, 7742, 8112, 8113
Fukunishi, I., 7663, 8386, 8944, 9682, 9801
Fuligni, A. J., 8840, 8894
Fuller, A. J., 8332
Furman, W., 8032, 8101

Gabarain, G., 8069, 9812

Gadzella, B. M., 9359
Gagnier, J. J., 7647, 8519, 9597
Gaines, C., 8842, 8946, 8951
Gainor, K. A., 8311, 8456, 9458, 9506
Galanaki, E. P., 8005, 9364
Gallagher, M., 7566
Gallo, L. C., 8123, 9681
Garavalia, L. S., 9326
Garcia-Pena, M. D. C., 8203
Gardner, W. L., 8330
Gari, A., 9959
Garonzik, R., 8174, 8420, 9135, 9481
Garrett, M. T., 7890
Gasser, M. B., 7947
Gati, I., 9854
Gauze, C., 9489
Gavazzi, S. M., 7883, 8920
Gavidia-Payne, S., 8837, 8865
Gavin, L. A., 8032, 8101
Gaziel, H. H., 9117
Geis, K. J., 9087
Gelfand, M. J., 9953
Gellatly, I. R., 8246
Gelso, C. J., 8135, 10040
Gentry, M., 8474, 8475
George, D. M., 9513
George, J. M., 8230, 9999
Gerard, J. M., 8954
Gerber, G. L., 9878
Gerris, J. R. M., 8811
Ghaffarian, S., 7590
Ghose, M., 9118
Giancala, P. R., 8531
Giauakos, I., 9348
Gibbons, E. S., 9519
Gilbert, J. A., 9037
Gilbert, L. A., 8834, 9399, 9478, 9914
Gillies, R. M., 9363
Gilliland, S. W., 9073
Giordano, F. G., 9028
Giorgetti, M., 8777
Girodo, M., 8614
Gisi, S. L., 9038
Glasgow, K. L., 8968
Glastetter-Fender, C., 9315, 9351, 9752
Gleaves, D. H., 9709
Glencross, M. J., 9979
Glickman, M. M., 9410
Glomb, T. M., 7770, 7801, 8298
Gloria, A. M., 7493, 7498, 7533, 9180, 9369, 9382, 10068
Gnaulati, E., 9991

Godshalk, V. M., 10030, 10086
Goh, S. C., 8662
Goldberg, W. A., 8818
Goldsmith, E., 9601
Goldsmith, H. H., 9797
Goldsmith, R. E., 9601
Goldstein, S. B., 9306
Gomez, M. H., 8704
Goni, A., 9521
Good, G. E., 7738, 8824, 9817
Goodman, S. A., 8627, 9095
Goodyear, R. K., 7949, 8377, 8583, 9802, 9832
Gordon, R. A., 8352, 9921
Gorgievski-Duijvesteijn, M., 8247, 9070, 9989
Goster, G. D., 9220
Gottfredson, D. C., 8369, 8664
Goudas, M., 9114, 9230, 9314, 9488
Gould, J. R., 9791
Gowan, M. A., 8031, 8110, 8148, 8155, 8161, 8164, 8198
Graham, S., 9579
Graham, S. W., 7500, 9038
Granger, D. A., 8078
Granger, D. E., 8442
Grant-Vallone, E. J., 10103
Gray, F. L., 8544
Gray, M. R., 8576, 8673
Greco-Vigorito, C., 7618
Gredler, M. E., 9326, 9572
Green, K. E., 7826
Green, R. G., 8353, 8897
Green, S. G., 8751, 9511, 9543
Greenberg, M. T., 8084, 9778
Greenberger, E., 8823
Greenhaus, J. H., 7870, 8849, 9019, 9667
Greenstein, T. N., 9817
Gregersen, H. B., 7948, 9547, 9551, 9554
Gresham, F. M., 8004
Griffin, G. H., 9190
Griffith, J., 7515, 9387
Grimmell, D., 8624
Groat, H. T., 8810
Groom, K. N., 7840
Grossman, A. H., 8399, 8641, 9393
Groth-Marnat, G., 7451
Grych, J. H., 8815, 8816
Guerra, A. L., 8917
Guillen, V., 9559
Gully, S. M., 9238, 9581
Gundy, K., 8607

Gupshup, G. V., 9469
Gushue, G. V., 8138
Gustafson, R., 9266
Guth, L. J., 7455, 8316
Guthrie, J. T., 9235, 9869
Gutierrez, P. M., 7761, 7823, 8433

Habke, A. M., 7855, 8094
Hagborg, W. J., 7488, 9603
Hagstrom, A. H., 7761
Hahlweg, K., 8971
Hahn, W., 10054
Hale, J. I., 7987
Hale, J. L., 8125
Haley, W. E., 8028
Hall, C. W., 9474
Hallet, M. B., 8834, 9399, 9478
Hallett, M. B., 9914
Halvari, H., 8175, 9195, 9196, 9197, 9272, 9420, 9964
Hamburger, M. E., 8315, 8367, 8459, 9008, 9821, 9822, 9823
Hamer, R. J., 9297, 9598, 9653, 9939
Hamer, R. M., 8616
Hamid, P. N., 7612, 7622, 7807, 8308, 8768
Hammer, L. B., 8760, 9661, 10209
Hammond, M., 10123
Hanewald, G. J. F. P., 8784
Hanlon, P. J., 7626
Hannah, M. T., 8791
Hanson, K. M., 7746, 7836
Hanson, W. E., 10042
Harackiewicz, J. M., 7490, 9222, 9887
Hardy, G. E., 10024, 10096, 10122
Harizuka, S., 9440
Harmon, M. G., 7507
Harold, D. M., 8748
Harrell, J. P., 7739, 7762, 7857, 8415
Harris, A. C., 7964
Harrison, A. W., 9371
Hart, P. M., 8232, 8249, 8250
Hartung, P. J., 8346, 10176
Hassan, M. M., 7468
Hastings, T. L., 7644, 8669
Hasui, C., 9560
Hatcher, R. L., 10048
Hativa, N., 9825
Hawkins, A. J., 8912
Hayes, J. A., 9325

Heaton, K. J., 10100, 10121
Heaven, P. C. L., 9968
Heavy, C. L., 8747
Heck, R. H., 9046
Heesacker, M., 8134, 8363, 9838
Hefpner, P. P., 7632, 7633
Heimer, K., 8646
Heine, B. J., 9991
Heiss, G. E., 8825, 8935
Helgeson, V. S., 7708, 8136, 9512
Hendin, H. M., 9910, 9920
Hener, T., 7851, 8000, 8492, 9504
Heng, M. A., 7466, 7536
Henningham, J. P., 9958
Heppner, M. J., 8466, 8696, 9021, 9039, 9855
Herek, G. M., 7670, 9615, 9952
Hermans, C. A. M., 8400
Hermans, H. J. M., 10008
Hesketh, B., 8564
Heskin, K., 8030, 9260
Hess, C. W., 8663
Hibbard, S., 7795, 8118, 9927
Hickman, G. P., 8312, 8938
Higgins, H. C., 9323
Hill, C. E., 7707, 7994, 9651, 9742, 10050, 10094, 10098, 10128
Hill, E. M., 8866
Hill, R. B., 9984
Hiller, M. L., 9381
Hirai, M., 8116, 8372, 8730
Hochwarter, W. A., 8179, 8181, 8223, 8620, 9120, 9122, 9500, 10129
Hodgson, A., 9975
Hofmann, D. A., 8753, 9125, 9156
Hogan, T. L., 8417
Hoge, D. R., 8857
Hohman, M. M., 10036
Holdaway, E. A., 9160
Holder, J. C., 8102, 8235, 9027, 9128, 9189, 9451, 9550
Holland, M. L., 7575
Holler, R. E., 9863
Holmes, C. S., 7723
Holmes, S. E., 10051
Holt, C. S., 7675
Holtzer, R., 7444
Holtzworth-Munroe, A., 8566, 8744
Hood, A. B., 8799
Horan, J. J., 9431
Houran, J., 7588, 9685

Houston, J. M., 8282, 9902
Houts, R. M., 8045
Howes, C., 7535, 8813
Howes, C. E., 7556, 8538
Huang, D. B., 8668
Hubbard, M. L., 7677, 9414
Hudson, J., 9289
Huebner, E. S., 7525, 7579
Huey, S. J., 8835
Huffman, L. C., 9726
Hughes, J. N., 9638, 10066, 10120
Hui, C., 8629
Humphreys, C. N., 9629, 9725
Humphreys, K., 9994
Hunsaker, S. L., 7469
Hunter, C. L., 8025, 9771
Hunton, J. E., 9136
Hurlbert, M. K., 9908
Hurt, L. E., 9805
Husman, J., 9842
Hutchison, S., 9098, 9172, 10115
Hutzler, Y., 7481

Ickovics, J. R., 7704
Igreja, I., 7985
Ingram, K. M., 7642, 7703, 8107, 8122, 8560, 8665, 8698, 9612
Isaksen, S. G., 9167
Ishiyama, F. I., 8071, 9628
Isralowitz, R. E., 10017
Iverson, R. D., 9386

Jackson, A. P., 7922, 8543, 8871
Jackson, C. C., 7509
Jackson, T., 7977, 8068 8883, 9786
Jackson, Y., 7724, 8033
Jain, A., 7973
Jambunathan, S., 9517
Janz, B. D., 7974, 8284, 9237
Jarjoura, D., 8526
Jawahar, I. M., 8338, 8364
Jeanquart, S., 10104
Jeanquart-Barone, S., 7929, 8177, 9141, 10114
Jenkins-Smith, A., 9313, 10195
Jew, C. L., 7826, 7827
Jex, S. M., 7790, 8229, 8304, 9383, 9892, 10171
Jobes, D. A., 7702, 7804, 9479
Johns, G., 8259
Johnson, B. D., 8502
Johnson, C. E., 8018, 8371, 8578, 9520

Johnson, D. P., 9928, 9936
Johnson, E. A., 9782
Johnson, E. E., 8616
Johnson, E. M., 7538
Johnson, G. J., 10076
Johnson, J. G., 9324, 9533
Johnson, J. J., 9148
Johnson, M. E., 9614, 9845, 9846
Johnson, P. E., 8774
Johnson, R. E., 8774
Johnson, W., 8429, 9317, 9482
Johnson, W. L., 9022, 10185
Johnson, W. R., 10076
Johnsrud, L. K., 9046
Johnston, C., 7760, 8024
Johnston, J. H., 7871
Joiner, T. E., Jr., 7625, 7755, 8416
Jome, L. M., 8419
Jon, Y. H., 7504
Jones, C. H., 8327
Jones, D. C., 8846
Jones, G. R., 8230, 9999
Jones, L. K., 9157
Jones, M., 9202
Jones, W. H., 7962, 7981, 8053, 8063, 8129, 8427, 9721, 9943
Jou, Y. H., 7714, 7742, 8112, 8113
Judge, T. A., 7638, 8176, 8190, 8211, 8266, 8421, 8742, 9064, 9407, 9408, 9428, 9429, 9578, 9962, 9985
Juhasz, J. B., 9190
Jumaa, M., 8355
Jung, J., 7643, 8608
Juni, S., 7957
Juvonen, J., 7519, 8590, 9486

Kacmar, K. M., 8231, 9081, 9101, 10181
Kahil, A., 8924
Kahn, J. H., 7627, 8463, 9880, 10194
Kairouz, S., 8735
Kaiser, A., 8980
Kalantzi-Azizi, A., 8006, 9364, 9959
Kalashe, L., 10021
Kaldenberg, D. O., 9903
Kalichman, S. C., 8379, 8595, 9396
Kalil, A., 8314
Kalliath, T. J., 9954
Kamalanabhan, T. J., 9295

Kambara, M., 9432
Kammeyer-Mueller, J. D., 8276, 8604, 8763
Kao, E. M., 9322
Kapci, E. G., 7699
Karakowsky, L., 8761
Kasar, J., 10082
Kasari, C., 7959
Kashubeck, S., 8043, 8660, 9017
Kaslow, N. A., 8863
Kaslow, N. J., 7803, 8532
Katz, B., 9523
Katz, R. C., 7458, 7874, 9522
Katz, Y. J., 7774
Kaufman, D., 7713
Kawada, T., 8280
Kazdin, A. E., 9015
Kazelskis, R., 7485, 7522, 7524, 7539
Keeping, L. M., 7794, 9036, 9139, 9158, 10020, 10026
Keller, B., 10045
Keller, P. A., 7667
Kelly, A. E., 8017, 8764, 9606
Kelly, F. D., 7589
Kelly, K. T., 9397, 9540
Kemp, M. A., 7706
Kendall, P. C., 7676, 8514
Kennedy, J. H., 8993
Kenny, M. E., 8936
Keogh, E., 7756
Kerner, M. S., 8399, 8641, 9393
Keshubeck, S., 7655, 7788, 9269, 9561
Kesner, J. E., 7555, 8805
Ketner, C. S., 8449
Ketrow, S. M., 8762
Ketsetzis, M., 8790
Ketterson, T. U., 10150, 10197
Ketzenberger, K. E., 9753
Keyes, C. L. M., 8114
Khasky, A. D., 7852, 9787
Khazanovich, G., 8957
Kier, F. J., 8817, 9759
Killgore, W. D. S., 7885
Kim, E. J., 7915
Kim, J. E., 8637, 8899
Kim, M.-S., 9127
Kim, M. U., 8771, 9867
Kim, O., 7877
Kimberlin, C. L., 7609, 7680
King, D. A., 7526
King, K. A., 7472
King, L. A., 9689
Kinket, B., 7954
Kiosseoglou, G., 8984

Kirby, R. J., 9261
Kirisci, L., 9619
Kirkhaug, R., 8175
Kirkpatrick, S. A., 8375
Kitson, G. C., 8879
Kivimaki, M., 8233, 8234, 9197, 9758
Kivlighan, D. M., Jr., 7907, 7966, 7991, 8729, 9193, 9898, 10051, 10053, 10109, 10125, 10127
Kjormo, O., 9196
Klaczynski, P. A., 9257, 9688, 9746, 9868
Klein, D. J., 8214, 8741, 10092
Klein, H. J., 8001, 9103
Kleinpeter, C. H., 10036
Klewicki, L. L., 8759
Kline, T. J., 9809
Kluwer, E. S., 8877, 9819
Knee, C. R., 7649, 8677, 9401
Knudson, R. E., 8389
Ko, J-W., 10183
Koberg, C. S., 8253, 9051, 10085
Kochanska, G., 8545, 8794, 8961, 9727, 10164
Kochenderfer, B. J., 8010
Koeske, G. F., 7940
Kogan, L. R., 7937
Koledin, S., 8007
Kolko, D. J., 8803
Komiya, N., 8360
Konczak, L. J., 8612
Koper, C. S., 8369
Koper, D. S., 8664
Kopper, B. A., 9694
Korabik, K., 7784, 7815
Korabik, K., 8221, 8293, 8306, 8693, 9102
Koraleski, S. F., 10081, 10102
Korsgaard, M. A., 7938
Kosari, C., 8009
Koskinen, P. S., 9246
Kossek, E. E., 8567, 8609, 9290, 9353, 9894
Koustelios, A., 8168
Kousteliou, I., 8168
Kovacs, D. M., 9490
Kowal, J., 9211, 9280
Kracke, B., 8940, 10135
Kraimer, M. L., 8255, 9063, 10139
Kranzler, J. H., 9462
Krausz, M., 8145, 8182, 8209, 10175
Kristof-Brown, A. L., 10075, 10089

Kruger, L. J., 9515
Kulik, L., 8349
Kulinna, P. H., 8479
Kumar, S., 9440, 9873
Kumar, V. K., 8780
Kurdek, L. A., 8992
Kurman, J., 7984
Kush, J. C., 8390
Kvaal, S. A., 7740, 7783
Kwa, G. A., 9915
Kwan, K.-L. K., 7975
Kweitel, R., 8711
Kwok, S.-T., 7698, 9388
Kwon, Y-H., 9643, 9810

Ladany, N., 8139, 8381, 10046, 10069, 10070, 10071
Ladd, E. R., 9320, 9608, 9925
Ladd, G. W., 7518, 7530, 7544, 7557, 8003, 8010, 8541, 8639
Ladwey, N., 10112
Lafrancois, R., 9465
LaGreca, A. M., 7717, 7800
Lai, J. C. L., 7484, 7620
Lamborn, S. D., 9411
Lamude, K. G., 8287, 8520
Langhinrichsen-Rohling, J., 8104
Lapan, R. T., 9461, 9468
Larimer, M. E., 9094
Larsen, K. S., 8350
Larson, L. M., 10081, 10102
Larson, R., 7875, 7926
Larwood, L., 8225
Larzelere, R. E., 8728, 8807
Lasane, T. P., 8411, 9200, 9824
Latham, G. P., 9055, 9137, 9140
Lau, S., 8012
Lay, C., 7931
Lecci, L., 7550, 9863
Leclerc, G., 9463
Lee, G. R., 8870
Lee, J. A., 9487, 10052
Lee, K., 9926
Lee, M., 7875, 7926
Lee, M. Y., 8059, 8317
Lee, R. M., 7486, 8027, 8080, 8804
Lee, S.-Y., 7443, 7480
Lee, T. R., 8858
Lefcourt, H. M., 7705
Lehman, A. K., 9741
Leichsenring, F., 9692
Leigh, T. W., 9147, 9294
Leitschuh, G. A., 7629
Lemon, R. L., 8455
Lenes, H. S., 9814

Lengua, L. J., 9198, 9911
Lent, R. N., 9458
Lent, R. W., 8311, 8456, 9299, 9506
Leonard, K. E., 8097
Leonardi, A., 8984
Leone, C., 9447, 9734
Leong, F. T. L., 8202
LePine, J. A., 8396, 8773
Leskinen, E., 9755
Lester, D., 7693
Lester, R., 7909, 8535, 9335, 9949
Lev-Wiesel, R., 8867
Levine, C., 9091, 9285
Levine, T., 9023
Levy, P. E., 7794, 9036, 9139, 9158, 10020, 10026
Lewis, C. A., 7650, 9900
Lewis, J. D., 9535, 9738
Li, C., 7474
Li, F., 9366, 9426
Li, L., 7573, 9496
Li, S., 7816, 7817, 8644
Lichtenberg, J. W., 10027
Liddell, D. L., 9981
Liden, R. C., 8172, 8273, 8754, 8772
Lieberman, M. L., 8898
Liefbroer, A. C., 7736
Lilienfeld, S. O., 9773, 9930
Lim, V. K. G., 9502
Limieux, R., 7987, 8125
Lindell, M. K., 8286
Ling, W., 9365
Lippa, R., 9788
Lirgg, C. D., 9640
Liu, C-Y., 7686
Liukkonen, J., 9755
Livingston, J. A., 9247
Loadman, W. E., 9086
Lochner, B. T., 10113
Locke, E. A., 8375
Lockhart, B. D., 9674
Long, C. K., 9041
Long, J. D., 8873
Long, T. E., 7467
Lonigan, C. J., 7796
Loomis, R. J., 9301
Lopes, S. A., 7516
Lopez, F. G., 7789, 7906, 8943, 9624, 9650, 10170
Lovell, C., 9024
Lozada, H. R., 9764, 9879
Lu, T. G. C., 9621
Luby, J. L., 9737

Lucas, J. L., 9439
Lucas, M., 10173
Ludlow, L. H., 8354
Luk, V., 8146, 8848, 9005, 9477, 9662, 9668, 10108, 10144
Lundgren, D. C., 8749
Lunnen, K. M., 10072
Lunz, M., 8216, 9173, 10191
Lussier, G., 7523
Luster, T., 8952
Luzzo, D. A., 9313, 9456, 9834, 10140, 10195
Lynam, D. R., 7722
Lynch, M., 8051
Lynch, P. D., 8260, 9208
Lyness, K. S., 9013, 9033, 9045, 10205

Macan, T. H., 8149, 8215, 9231, 9446, 9670
MacDermid, S. M., 8885, 9844
MacDonald, D. A., 7647, 8519, 9597
MacFarland, W. L., 9906
MacGregor, M. W., 9698, 9699
MacIntosh, R., 7582
MacKay, H. C., 10095
MacKsoud, M. S., 7611, 7615, 7802
MacLachlin, M., 9357
MacNair, R. R., 8401
Madden-Derdich, D. A., 8808, 8962
Maes, S., 9077
Magdok, L., 8569
Magdol, L., 8504
Magwaza, A. S., 10018
Mahalik, J. R., 9700, 10034
Mahon, N. E., 7684, 7876, 8643, 9965
Mahoney, J. L., 7978
Mahoney, J. M., 7713, 7963, 8423
Mainieri, T., 8402
Makaraemi, J. A., 7624
Mallinckrodt, B., 8864, 9803, 10032
Maltby, J., 9900
Mamman, A., 8441
Man, F., 9254
Manne, S. L., 8881, 8974
Mansour-Cole, D. M., 8261, 9035, 9076, 9132, 9375
Mao, S. L., 7449, 8344
Marcoen, A., 8047, 8528
Marino, R., 7923

Marjoribanks, K., 8426, 8975, 9568, 9569
Markel, K. S., 7568, 8193, 8194, 9186
Marko, K. W., 9243
Markoi, K. W., 9192
Marks, N. F., 7799
Marks, S. R., 9844
Markstrom, C. A., 8025, 9771
Marsh, H. W., 9309
Marshall, G. N., 9107
Marsour-Cole, D. M., 7585
Marta, E., 8925
Martasian, P. J., 9306
Martens, M. P., 10198
Martin, A. J., 9937
Martin, M. W., 8746
Martin, T. R., 8649, 9585
Martinez-Pons, M., 8713, 8948
Martocchio, J. J., 8742, 9578
Martz, D. M., 8549
Marullo, S., 8503
Maslyn, J. M., 8291, 9121
Masson, S., 7586
Mathieu, J. E., 9126
Mathis, M., 7550
Matsui, T., 7846, 8265, 8689, 8995, 9642
Matsushima, R., 8064, 9945
Matthews, C., 8373, 8407, 9089, 9304
Maurer, T. J., 9590
Mayer, B., 7598
Mayer, J. D., 8002
Mayer, R. C., 8131
Mayes, B. T., 8195
Mayseless, O., 8914
Mazza, J. J., 7689
Mazzeo, S. E., 8534, 8579, 9332, 9337, 9470
Mboya, M., 8426, 8975, 9568, 9569
Mboya, M. M., 9563
McBride, A. A., 9691
McCabe, D. L., 8684
McCall, R. B., 7565, 7778, 8619, 8719, 8947, 8976, 9472
McCann, D., 9760
McCarthy, C. J., 7691, 7769, 9944
McClellan, S. A., 9082
McCollum, M. A., 7650
McConatha, J. T., 9704, 9711
McCormick, C. B., 8993
McCoy, N., 9317
McCracken, R. S., 8356

McCreary, D. R., 8428, 8507
McCrindle, A. R., 8686
McCullough, G., 7525, 7579
McCullough, M. E., 9995
McDonald, A., 9834
McDonald-Miszczak, L., 8432
McEwen, M. K., 8769
McFall, R. M., 8512
McGrath, P. B., 7495
McGuire, S., 9602
McHale, S. M., 8376, 9000, 9293, 9684, 9703, 9986
McHoskey, J. W., 9961
McIntye, C. L., 9148
McIntyre, R. P., 8557, 9130
McKay, D., 8738
McKeen, C. A., 8297, 10062, 10064
McKelvie, S. J., 7478
McLennan, J., 7982
McLenon, J., 7694
McMahon, R., 8482, 9443
McNair, L. D., 8318
McNamara, J. R., 8489
McWhirter, E. H., 7562, 8916, 9108, 9119, 9654, 10134
Meara, N. M., 7583, 7596, 9712
Mechanic, M. B., 7634, 7821, 8594
Meeus, W., 10153
Meir, E. I., 10193
Melchert, T. P., 8838, 10113
Mellor, S., 8731, 9109, 9402, 9574
Mendez, S., 7946
Merrill, J., 7879
Meston, C. M., 8587
Meyer, B., 7682, 7709, 8524
Meyer, B. B., 7967, 9282
Meyers, S. A., 10055
Meyers, S. M., 8906
Michels, J., 9783
Miles, J. A., 8115, 8156, 8285
Millar, R., 7566
Miller, D. B., 7668
Miller, J. C., 9471
Miller, K. E., 7892
Miller, K. S., 8755, 9006
Miller, N. J., 9811
Miller, S. A., 8463, 10194
Miller, T. K., 7734
Minke, K. M., 9635
Mintu-Wimsatt, A., 9764, 9879
Mintz, L. B., 7746, 7836, 8589, 8622, 8660
Mirzadeh, S. A., 8888

Miserandino, M., 9343
Miville, M. L., 8408, 9368, 9736, 9916
Miville, M. O., 8019
Mize, J., 8121
Mji, A., 9372, 10021
Moen, P., 9852
Mohr, J., 9831
Mohr, J. J., 7534, 8026, 8035, 8322, 8409, 9599, 9748
Moller, A. T., 9899
Mone, M. A., 9042, 9268, 9385, 9586
Monk, A., 9225
Montgomery, R. L., 9473
Monti, P. M., 7578
Moode, F. M., 9333, 9625
Moore, C. D., 8562
Moore, D., 7573, 9496
Moore, S., 9523, 9799, 9919
Morgan, S. B., 8120
Morgeson, F. P., 8753, 9156
Morling, B., 7969
Morosin, A., 9800
Morris, S. J., 9906
Morrison, C. S., 7856, 8082, 9209, 9622
Morrison, K. A., 9516
Morrison, T. G., 8320
Morrow, P. C., 8200, 9155
Moss, H. B., 9619
Mothersead, P. K., 7979, 8062, 8702, 8889
Motta, R. W., 7613, 7841
Mount, M. K., 8743, 9757
Moyer, P. S., 9842
Mudrak, P. E., 8723, 8725
Mueller, J. A., 8020
Muir, G., 8412
Mulford, C. L., 8317
Mulhern, F., 8398
Mullis, F., 8523, 9085
Mullis, R. L., 7576
Munson, L. J., 7639, 7666, 7731, 7744, 7813, 8272, 8279, 8309, 8692
Munson, W. W., 8498, 9587, 9890, 10138, 10154
Murdock, T. B., 9262
Muris, P., 7763, 7837, 7838, 7839, 8739
Murphy, H. J., 9861
Murphy, P. E., 9996
Murphy, S. E., 10063
Murray, C., 8084, 9778
Murray, H. G., 10119

Murray, K. T., 8961
Murrell, A. J., 8178
Murstein, B. I., 8014, 9279
Myers, J. R., 8465, 9683
Myers, S. A., 8766, 9284
Myrick, R. D., 8473

Nagin, D., 8708
Naidoo, A. V., 9356
Nair, K. U., 9747
Nakata, S., 8584, 9582
Nanta, M. M., 10130
Napoli, A. R., 7726
Narendran, S., 9735, 10005
Nash, H. C., 8642
Nasir, S. J., 7604
Nasseri, M., 8461
Nauta, M. M., 7627, 9552, 9880, 10155
Neimeyer, G. J., 7706
Netemeyer, R. G., 9395, 9663
Neto, F., 8037, 8058, 9847
Netz, Y., 8561
Neville, H. A., 7509, 7933, 9967, 9982
Newcomb, M. D., 7943, 9993
Newman, I., 9639
Niaz, M., 8310
Niaz, M., 7452
Nicholas, L., 7459
Nielsen, I. K., 8207, 8290, 9065, 9066, 9067, 9188, 10160, 10180
Niemann, Y. F., 8258
Nix, R. L., 8548, 8822, 8963
Nonis, S. A., 7496, 7531, 9493
Norlander, T., 9266
Norris, J. A., 9517
Nowicki, S., Jr., 8055, 9302
Nuovo, S. F., 7476
Nydegger, R. V., 9448

O'Andrea, M., 7896
O'Brien, K. M., 8464, 8891, 8983, 8985, 9201, 9344, 9346, 9467
O'Connell, C. E., 7784, 7815, 8221, 8293, 8306, 8693, 9102
O'Connor, C., 8752, 10010
O'Connor, E. A., 10080
O'Connor, M. E., 7840
O'Connor, W. E., 8320, 9966
O'Driscoll, M. P., 9111, 9548, 9744, 10177
O'Neil, J. M., 7915

O'Neill, B. S., 9042, 9268, 9385, 9586
Obetz, S. A., 10035
Ogles, B. M., 10072
Oles, P. K., 10008
Olivares, J., 7854
Ommundsen, R., 8350
Ommundsen, Y., 9509
Omodel, M. M., 7982
Ones, D. S., 9037
Onwuegbuzie, A. J., 7503, 7549, 7558, 7570, 7696, 8096, 8328, 8366, 8714, 9298, 9604
Orange, C., 8682
Orbach, I., 7787
Osborne, D., 7589
Oskamp, S., 8435
Osman, A., 8098
Osman, S. L., 9645
Otwell, P. S., 8523, 9085
Ozmet, J. M., 7693

Padeliadu, S., 7473
Page, S. J., 9941
Page-Voth, V., 9579
Paget, K. J., 8167
Pajares, F., 7571, 8488, 9300, 9459, 9460, 9508, 9675, 9676
Pajares, G., 9362
Paley, B., 7780
Pallant, J. F., 7729, 7785, 7791, 7898, 7899, 9406, 9424, 9450, 9491, 10091
Palmer, S. B., 7513, 7700
Paniagua, F. A., 7454, 7457, 8066
Papaioannou, A., 9075
Parasuraman, S., 7735, 8850, 8861, 9078, 9159, 9394, 9673, 9686, 10145
Parfitt, G., 9499
Parker, C. P., 9093
Parker, J. G., 8008, 8539
Parker, S. K., 9059, 9142, 9545, 9546, 9768
Pascarella, E., 8716, 9270
Pascarella, E. T., 9427, 9835
Paschall, M. J., 7677, 9414
Patares, F., 9462
Patel, N., 7901, 8484, 10011
Patodia, S., 7740, 7783
Patrick, B. C., 7886, 9233
Patton, M. J., 8119, 8667
Patton, M. S., 10109
Pavelich, B., 8721
Payne, B. D., 9636

Payne, D. L., 8413, 8414
Peacock, E. J., 7710, 9376
Pearson, Q. M., 7721, 7747
Peiffer, L. C., 9720
Pelligrini, A. D., 8687
Peltz, D. L., 9640
Peltzer, K., 7442, 7456, 7554, 7825, 8477, 9404, 9956, 9957
Peluchette, J. V. E., 10104
Peng, H., 9345
Pensgaard, A. M., 9263
Perczek, R., 7606, 9464
Perez, V., 8936
Perlini, A. H., 7631, 8703, 9577
Perosa, L. M., 8955, 8978, 9276
Perosa, S. L., 8955, 8978, 9276
Perrine, R. M., 8108
Perry, A. R., 8573, 8574
Perry, E. L., 8437
Peters, A., 7736
Peters, L. H., 9150
Peterson, B. E., 9524, 9935
Peterson, C., 10143
Peterson, R. S., 7990, 8281, 8505
Petrie, T. A., 7517, 7909, 8018, 8105, 8371, 8535, 8578, 9335, 9520, 9949
Pettit, G. S., 8121
Phares, V., 8977
Phelps, R. E., 7540, 7955
Phillips, J. M., 9238, 9581
Phillips, J. S., 9069, 9074
Phinney, J. S., 8853
Picklesimer, B. K., 7734
Pierce, J., 7545
Pierce, K. M., 8989
Pierre, A. P., 9908
Pigott, R. L., 7563
Pike, P. L., 7902
Pinto, M. D., 8341
Pintrich, P. R., 9252, 9253, 9267, 9860
Piran, N., 9328
Pisnar-Sweeney, M., 8169, 8269, 9179, 10014, 10202
Pistole, M. C., 7934
Plechaty, M., 8900
Ployhart, R. E., 9100
Plucker, J. A., 9283
Plumert, J. M., 9696
Plunkett, S. W., 8800
Podaskoff, P. M., 8631
Podell, D. M., 9637
Poindexter-Cameron, J., 8485
Pollick, M. F., 8780

Polzella, D. J., 8438
Ponterott, J. G., 7972, 8049
Ponterotto, J. G., 8454, 8478
Pope, R. L., 8020, 8137
Pope-Davis, D. B., 8436
Porrata, J. L., 8495
Post, P., 8915
Powell, F. C., 7646
Pratt, M. W., 8099
Pretorius, T. B., 8106
Prins, P. J. M., 8784
Proctor, L. J., 8036, 8093, 8585, 9030
Psychountaki, M., 7862, 7880, 9627, 9646
Puccio, G. J., 8783
Puddifoot, J. E., 8323
Pugh, D. N., 9131, 9528, 9529
Pulvers, K., 9029
Punanki, R-L., 8939
Purdie, N., 9886
Purnine, D. M., 8882, 9826
Putten, J. V., 9183

Quaglia, R. J., 9283
Quereshi, M. Y., 9933
Quick, B. G., 7963
Quinn, R. J., 7450

Rae, G., 8398
Raggioi, D. J., 7545
Ragins, B. R., 10065, 10084
Rainey, L. M., 8362
Ramanaiah, N. V., 8388, 9951
Ramnarayan, S., 9747
Ramos-Sanchez, L., 10041
Ramsay, S. G., 8393
Rand, K. L., 9923
Randall, D. M., 10177
Randhawa, B. S., 8721
Rao, V. S., 9225
Realo, A., 7932
Reed, J. S., 8895, 8923
Reidy, J., 7756
Reise, S. P., 9849
Reith, W., 7602
Renaud, R. D., 10119
Rencher, A. C., 9674
Renk, K., 8977
Rentsch, J. R., 8204, 9613
Rentz, A. L., 8417
Ressler, W. H., 7715
Rest, J. R., 9976
Reynolds, S., 10099
Reynolds, W. M., 7689

Rhodes, J. E., 7541, 8886, 9609, 10000
Ricciardelli, L. A., 8508, 8581, 9807
Rice, K. G., 7716, 8075, 8888, 9584, 9896
Rich, Y., 9634
RiCharde, R. S., 8797
Richards, H. C., 8393
Richman-Hirsch, W. L., 9011
Richter, J., 9793
Rigby, K., 8536, 8558
Riipinen, M., 8217, 9567, 9657, 10207
Riordan, C. M., 8487, 9092, 9702
Rippl, S., 8061
Riva, G., 8570, 9800
Rizzo, T., 8445
Robazza, C., 7859
Roberson, Q. M., 8283, 9124
Robert, C., 9068, 9974
Roberts, C. M., 8403
Roberts, G. C., 9509
Roberts, J. A., 8552
Roberts, L. J., 8097, 8884
Robie, C., 7942
Robin, D. P., 9960
Robinson, B. E., 8736, 8915
Robinson, L. A., 8553
Robinson, S. L., 9187
Robinson, T. L., 8485
Robitschek, C., 7655, 7664, 7788, 7806, 8043, 8795, 9269, 9561, 9717, 9719, 9889, 10136, 10137, 10151
Rocca, K. A., 9284
Roche, L. A., 9309
Rochlen, A. B., 7950, 8035, 8322, 8336, 8343, 8409, 8452, 9227, 9599, 9748, 9865, 10047, 10061, 10124, 10146
Rodgers, K. B., 8959
Rodriguez, J. R., 7460
Rodriguez, N., 8690
Rogers, J. R., 7626, 8346
Rogge, R. D., 8819, 9740
Rohner, R. P., 8933, 8953, 8972, 9762
Rojewski, J. W., 9445, 9594, 9984
Rokach, A., 8006, 8007, 8013
Romano, J. L., 9573
Ronfeldt, H. M., 8044, 8655
Roosa, M. W., 8699
Rosa, A., 8495

Rosenbaum, M., 8878, 9781, 9813
Rosenthal, R., 9009
Rosenthal-Sokolov, M., 7996, 7997
Ross, C. A., 7656
Ross, C. E., 9087, 9649
Ross, L. T., 8866
Ross, W. H., 8127, 8158, 8241
Rossello, J., 8074, 8844
Rossi, R. J., 9165
Rothbaum, B. O., 7671, 7672
Rotondo, D., 10161
Rotono, D., 8227
Rouse, K. A. G., 9312
Rousseau, D. M., 9534
Rout, U., 8218, 8220
Rowden, G. V., 8717
Roy, D. D., 9118
Royal, M. A., 9165
Rozell, E. J., 8334
Rozin, P., 8382
Rudawsky, D. J., 8749
Rudd, M. D., 7755
Rudestam, K. E., 7645, 8666, 9409
Ruelas, S. R., 7903
Ruiz, Y., 7970
Ruiz-Quintanilla, S. A., 8647
Rush, M. C., 8224, 8626, 9318, 10118, 10187
Rush, M. L., 8510
Russell, D. W., 8133
Russell, J. E. A., 8295
Russell, R. L., 10060
Ruttenberg, J., 8321
Ryan, A. M., 7471, 7942, 8391, 8847, 9058, 9099, 9100, 9236
Ryan, J., 10015
Ryan, L. V., 9702
Ryan, N. E., 8152, 8893
Ryckman, R. M., 8410, 8444, 9623
Ryska, T. A., 9264

Sá, W. C., 9745, 8368, 9856, 9864
Sabatelli, R. M., 8945, 8986
Sachau, D. A., 8157, 8658
Sacher, J. A., 7913, 7935
Sachs, J., 9888
Sahay, S., 9328
Sakamoto, S., 9432, 9766
Saks, A. M., 7572, 7793, 7878, 8186, 8235, 8529, 8611, 9212, 9228, 9436, 9492, 9593, 10178

Saliba, A. J., 8517
Sam, D. L., 9963
Sanchez, R. J., 9291
Sandler, I. N., 814
Sandler, M. E., 7512, 9226
Sandoval, A.-M. R., 9775, 9784, 9895, 9931, 9988
Sands, T., 8092, 9307, 9308, 9475
Santos, P. J., 9724
Sastry, J., 9649
Satcher, J., 8029, 9485, 9656
Sato, T., 9566, 9760
Saunders, S. A., 10116
Savickas, M. L., 9192, 9243, 9587, 10138
Sayger, T. V., 8838
Scandura, T. A., 9034, 9350, 10067, 10084
Schaefers, K. G., 9452, 9480, 9527
Schafer, R. B., 9562
Schaubroeck, J., 7592, 7845, 9061, 9412, 9438, 9525, 9798, 9971
Scheel, M. J., 10028, 10088
Scher, A., 8914
Schieman, S., 8607
Schifano, R. S., 9476
Schill, T., 9783
Schlenker, B. R., 8957
Schmalt, H.-D., 9194
Schmidt, N. B., 9338
Schminke, M., 9049, 9106, 9133
Schmitt, D. P., 8701
Schmitt, N., 9044, 9769
Schmitt-Rodermund, E., 8499, 10012
Schneider, B., 9026, 9032, 9050
Schneider, P. L., 9733
Schneider, R. A., 7765
Schnieder, K. T., 8695
Schnurr, P. P., 7818
Scholl, R. W., 9249
Schraw, G., 8462
Schriesheim, C. A., 8732, 10105
Schroeder, J. E., 8762
Schuldberg, D., 7690, 8038
Schultz, P. W., 8435
Schunk, D. H., 8490, 9591
Schwartz, D., 8036, 8093, 8585, 9030
Schwartz, L. S., 9572
Schwebel, D. C., 9696
Schwitzer, A. M., 9024
Scott, C. G., 9419

Scott, K. D., 8244, 8262, 8271
Scott, S. G., 7585, 8261, 9035, 9076, 9132, 9375
Seal, J., 8008, 8539
Searle, B., 7583, 7596, 9712
Sedlacek, W., 8471
Sedlacek, W. E., 9851
Seggar, J. F., 7595
Seib, H. M., 8651, 9644
Seibert, S. E., 9770, 10031
Seipel, C., 8061
Sekaran, U., 7929, 8177, 9141, 10114
Sellers, N., 9808
Sells, J. N., 10087
Senechal, M., 7445, 7447, 8142
Serex, C. P., 9018
Sewell, J., 8277
Shackelford, T. K., 9785
Shaffer, M. A., 8208, 8292, 9815, 10182
Shah, F., 8120
Shapiro, D. L., 9626
Share-Pour, M., 7952, 7956
Sharpe, J. P., 9951
Sharpley, C. R., 7843
Shaughnessy, P., 7991, 9898, 10127
Shaw, C. M., 7749, 8048, 8065, 8457
Shaw, D. S., 8727
Shell, R. M., 8786
Sheridan, C. L., 7711, 8041
Shiarella, A. H., 83787
Shifflet, B., 8337
Shih, S-S., 9217, 9384
Shiomi, K., 8584
Shoffner, M. F., 9057
Shokovhi-Behnam, S., 7944
Shore, L. M., 8487, 8628, 9092, 10059
Shore, T. H., 8472
Short, J. C., 8180, 8226, 8238, 8240
Short, K. H., 7760, 8024
Short, P., 7514, 8140
Short, P. M., 8613, 9162
Shultz, S. K., 8551
Shumow, L., 7528, 8872
Sidani, Y. M., 8330
Sideridis, G. D., 7473
Siegel, J. P., 8761
Siegel, K., 7681, 7748
Sightler, K. W., 8256
Sigman, M. D., 7945
Silbereisen, R. K., 8499, 8615, 8958, 10012

Silverman, S., 8479
Silverstein, M., 8873
Simbayi, L. C., 9652
Simmering, M. J., 9215, 9251, 9292, 9575
Simon, S. J., 9151, 9857
Simoni, J. M., 8351
Simons, H. D., 8516
Simons, J., 8671, 9204
Simons, R. L., 8565, 8964, 8987
Simons, T. L., 7990, 8281, 8505
Simonsen, G., 7701, 8359, 9400
Simonson, T., 8042
Sinclair, R. R., 7830, 7867
Singh, N. N., 8874
Singh, S. N., 8358
Sinn, J. S., 8418, 8468, 8765, 9722
Sitharthan, T., 8688
Sjostedt, J. P., 7687
Skarlicki, D. P., 9055, 9134, 9137, 9140
Skchminke, M., 9053
Skorikov, V. B., 10204
Skowron, E. A., 8830
Slaney, R. B., 9928, 9936
Slanger, E., 7645, 8666, 9409
Slate, J. R., 8327
Slavin, R. L., 7930
Slusher, M. P., 8348
Small, S. A., 8952
Smart, R. M., 10141, 10143, 10163, 10189
Smetana, J., 8842, 8946, 8951
Smith, B. L., 9273, 9327, 9620
Smith, D., 7798, 7858, 8111
Smith, E. V., Jr., 8502
Smith, G. E., 8469
Smith, J. C., 7852, 9787
Smith, J. T., 7619, 8625, 8712
Smith, J. W., 8039
Smith, K. E., 9841
Smith, M. R., 8352, 9921
Smith, P. L., 9453, 9455, 9833
Smith, T., 8085, 8785
Smith, T. W., 8123, 9681
Smith-Jentsch, K. A., 8722, 9932
Sodowsky, G. R., 8021, 9444, 9541
Soh, K.-C., 8559
Sohlberg, S., 9600
Solberg, V. S., 7492, 7494, 7548
Soliman, H. H., 7594
Somers, J. M., 8296
Sommerfelt, K., 9730, 9731
Sommers, R. K., 7483

Soodak, L. C., 9637
Sosik, J. J., 9210, 10030, 10086
Spangenberg, J. J., 9611
Spangler, D. L., 7891, 9904
Spector, P. E., 7546, 7678, 7792, 7861, 9096, 9149
Speitzer, F. M., 10083
Spell, Y. P., 9809
Speltz, M. L., 7743, 9728
Spengler, P. M., 9839
Sperling, M. B., 7914, 7916, 7917
Spieker, S. J., 8522, 8555
Spirito, A., 7873
Spoth, R., 8926
Sprang, G., 7882
Spratt, C. L., 9256, 9618
Spray, C. M., 7501, 9129, 9507, 9792
Sprecher, S., 7936, 8054, 8060
Sprigg, C. A., 9142, 9545
Stanley, L. S., 8446
Stanley, M. A., 7771, 7808, 9331
Stanton, A. L., 8100, 9853
Starrels, M. E., 8833
Steel, R. P., 8204, 9613
Steele-Johnson, D., 9234
Stein, C. H., 8493, 8801, 8868, 8869
Steinberg, L., 8673
Steitz, J. A., 9352, 9677
Stephens, D. E., 9287
Stephens, G. K., 8153
Stephens, R. S., 8577
Sternberg, R. L., 7470
Stets, J. E., 8901
Stetzer, A., 9125
Stevens, M., 7965, 8103
Stewart, G. L., 7968, 9718
Stewart, M. M., 9626
Stice, E., 7661, 8515, 9330
Stinson, M. S., 8073
Stoever, S., 7517, 8105
Stone-Romero, E. F., 7864, 8760
Stoneman, Z., 8837, 8865, 8922
Stout, M. L., 8589, 8622
Stowers, D. A., 9983
Strage, A., 9007
Strahan, R. F., 9710
Strein, W., 8042
Stroh, L. K., 7948, 8147, 9547, 9551, 9554, 10186
Strough, J., 9223
Strunk, D. R., 7635
Struthers, C. W., 7552
Sturman, M. C., 8180, 8226, 8238, 8240

Subich, L. M., 8199, 9379
Sugarman, A., 8514
Sullivan, C. M., 7820, 8601
Sumerlin, J. R., 7727, 9339,
  9340, 9596
Sumi, K., 9938
Summers, M., 9178
Summers, P., 8821
Sun, S. Y. K., 9403
Suthakaran, V., 9851
Sutton, S. E., 7564, 7614, 7745,
  8439, 8633, 8927, 8929, 9913
Svyantek, D. J., 8627, 9095
Swaim, R. C., 7587
Swanson, S. R., 8557
Swinford, S. P., 8500

Takahashi, M., 9836
Takai, K., 8672
Tallman, I., 7842
Tan, P. P., 8109, 8331
Tan, R. N., 7947
Tanaka, E., 7900, 9794
Tanaka, K., 8680, 9607, 9687
Tanaka, K' I., 9978
Tang, M., 8117
Tang, T. L-P., 9278
Tanner, J. F., Jr., 8552
Tarter, R. E., 7542
Tata, J., 9072
Taylor, J. A., 8325
Teal, M., 7451
Terpstra, D. E., 8334
Terry, D. J., 8150, 8185
Tesluk, P. E., 9126
Tetrick, L. E., 7830, 7867
Thacker, R. A., 8288, 8603,
  10078
Thalbourne, M. A., 7737, 8779,
  9647
Tharenou, P., 8150, 8185
Thomassen, T. O., 9197, 9964
Thombs, D. L., 8509, 9655
Thomlinson-Clarke, S., 7567
Thompson, D. E., 9013, 9033,
  9045, 10205
Thompson, R. F., 9577
Thompson-Sanders, V. L., 7910,
  7911, 7912, 8050
Thoms, P., 7475
Thorson, J. A., 7646, 7766, 7829
Thurber, C. A., 7945
Thye, S., 9040
Tibbetts, S. G., 8015, 8618
Tierney, P., 9207, 9871
Tijoriwala, S. A., 9534

Tikoo, M., 7741
Timmermin, G., 9016, 9168
Ting, S.-M. R., 9088
Tinsley, B. J., 8424
Tinzer, A., 7798, 7858, 8111
Tix, A. P., 7824, 9423, 9858
Tobias, A. K., 8473
Tokar, D. M., 8199, 8419
Tomkiewicz, J., 7669, 7673,
  8329, 9378
Toray, T., 8582, 9641
Torki, M. A., 7868
Toro, P. A., 7607, 7754
Torres, P., 8287, 8520
Totterdell, P., 7601, 7659, 10201
Townsend, B. K., 9018
Tracey, T. J. G., 9827, 10158,
  10188
Tremblay, R. E., 8708
Trevino, L. K., 8684
Tross, S. A., 7491
Trull, T. J., 9720
Truxillo, D. M., 8335
Tsai, D. C., 7902
Tschann, J. M., 8022
Tseng, V., 8840
Tuason, M. T., 9380
Tucker, C. M., 9881
Tuckman, B. W., 8650
Tuerkheimer, A., 8014, 9279
Turban, D. B., 9433
Turner, S., 8030, 9260
Turnipseed, D. L., 9761
Tylka, T. L., 93797

Ungerer, J. A., 7648
Updegraff, K. A., 7988, 8826,
  9763, 9830
Urdan, T., 9459, 9460
Uriddendorf, J., 7920
Utsey, S. O., 7971, 7972, 8049,
  8454

Vacc, N. A., 8683, 8836, 8862,
  9057
Vaicys, C., 9043
Vaillant, D., 10077
Valiantc, G., 7571, 9508, 9675
Valle, M., 9081
Valtolina, G. G., 8925
Vandell, D. L., 9009
Van Der Doef, M., 9077
Van der Sijde, P. C., 8447
Van Der Vegt, G., 8166, 9105
Van De Vliert, E., 8166, 9105

VandeWalle, D., 8605, 8750,
  9213, 9216, 9218, 9239, 9274,
  9870
van Dierendonck, D., 8243
Van Dyne, L., 8396, 8773
VanOmmeren, M. H., 9628
Van Scotter, J. R., 8187, 9154,
  10117, 10159
Van Vianen, A. E. M., 9097
VanZile-Tamsen, C., 9247
Vardi, Y., 8254
Vasilopoulos, N. J., 7660
Vaux, A., 8102, 8235, 9027,
  9128, 9189, 9451, 9550
Vazquez, F. L., 8588
Vella-Brodrick, D. A., 7750
Veneziano, R. A., 8933, 8972
Vera, E. M., 10043
Verbeke, W., 8214, 8741, 10092
Verkuyten, M., 7931, 7954, 8448,
  9915
Verlander, L. A., 8705
Vermeer, H. J., 9259
Vermeersch, D. A., 7773
Verschueren, K., 7560, 7869,
  8047, 8528, 9518
Verven, R., 7964
Vezeau, C., 8430, 9240, 9286
Vigoda, E., 8184, 8206, 9123,
  0079, 10179
Vigorito, M., 8319
Villanova, P., 9166
Viney, W., 7937
Vispoel, W. P., 9310
Vitaro, F., 8659, 8685, 8709
Vitulli, W. F., 8394
Vivona, J. M., 7782, 7921, 8792,
  8892, 8934
Vocaturo, L. C., 7934
Vodanovich, S. J., 7605, 8651,
  9644, 10003
Voelkl, K. E., 7510, 8597, 9743
Volleberch, W. A. M., 8394
Vondracek, F. W., 10204
Voyten, K. K., 9347, 9349
Vuchinich, S., 8856

Waehler, C. A., 8455
Wagner, B. T., 8663
Wagner, S. L., 8510
Waldron-Hennessey, R., 8945,
  8986
Walker, L. J., 9707
Wall, J. E., 10156
Wallace, J. E., 8305, 8307, 9146,
  9271, 10002, 10190, 10206

Waltz, J., 8586
Wan, W., 7484
Wanberg, C. R., 7683, 7728, 8034, 8160, 8165, 8170, 8171, 242, 8276, 8294, 8604, 8610, 8763, 9031, 9071, 9206, 9435, 9437, 10147, 10168
Wang, H., 8832
Wang, L., 7894, 7958
Wann, D. L., 9281, 9695
Ward, L. C., 9255
Ward, M., 9799, 9919
Warren, J. S., 7724, 8033
Warren, L. L., 9636
Waschbusch, D. A., 7446
Watanabe, N., 9827
Waterman, C. K., 8562
Waterman, J. M., 8718
Watkins, D., 8431, 9080
Watkins, M. W., 8390
Watkins, T. J., 7461, 7465, 7527, 8758, 8932
Watt, J. D., 7605, 10003
Weatherford, E. J., 9278
Weatherly, D. C., 9843
Weaver, N. A., 8001, 9103
Webster-Stratton, C., 8831, 10123
Weekley, J. A., 7448
Wegner, B. S., 9336, 9779
Wehmeyer, M. L., 7513, 7700
Weinberger, D. A., 7888
Weinfield, N. S., 8617
Weitlauf, J. C., 8518, 9570, 9583, 9633
Weitzman, L. M., 8356
Wellingham-Jones, P., 7482
Wells, B., 7866
Wells, G. L., 9929
Wenzel, A., 7675
Werbel, J., 8907, 10004, 10162
Werbel, J. D., 10149, 10167, 10196
Werner, J. M., 9151, 9857
West, M. A., 8781, 9605
Westberg, K. L., 8782
Westbrook, F. D., 8079
Westen, D., 7584
Westman, M., 8144, 8222
Weun, S., 8599

Whaley, A. L., 7777
Whatley, S. L., 7844
Whitbeck, L. B., 7610, 8470, 8796
White, C., 9272
White, F. A., 8757, 9998
White, J. D., 7547, 9495
White, K. S., 8621
White, V., 7750
Whitt, E. J., 9110
Wickrama, K. A. S., 7580
Widmer, M. A., 8498, 9890, 10154
Wieland, C., 8127, 8158, 8241
Wielkiewicz, R. M., 9872
Wiener, R. L., 9805
Wiese, B. S., 7797, 7833, 9164, 9558
Wiggins, M. S., 9333
Williams, C., 7588, 9685
Williams, D. M., 7628
Williams, E. N., 9377, 10044, 10110
Williams, J. E., 7569, 8679
Williams, J. R., 10007
Williams, L. J., 8592
Williams, L. M., 7881
Williams, S., 9735, 10005
Wilson, A., 9484
Wilson, D. L., 7805, 7848, 9774
Windecker-Nelson, E., 8928, 8937
Windle, M., 9557
Winston, R. B., 9169
Winzelberg, A., 9994
Wisch, A. F., 10034
Wise, S. L., 7499
Witherspoon, A. D., 9041
Wittig-Berman, U., 7732, 8268, 9672
Wolf, D. B., 9804
Wolfe, J., 7720, 7752
Wolff, S. B., 8303
Wolfgang, A. P., 9469
Wolfson, A. R., 7653, 8706
Wolmer, L., 7479
Wong, H-M., 7753
Wong, K. S., 8162, 8278
Wong, N. Y., 8431, 9080
Wong, P. T. P., 7710, 9376

Wonnell, T. L., 10050, 10098
Woods, D. W., 8072, 8124
Worthington, R. L., 8380, 8434, 9355, 9390
Wortman, P. M., 7726
Wright, B. M., 8213, 9232, 9501
Wright, L. W., Jr., 7739, 7762, 7857, 8406, 8415
Wright, T. A., 8225
Wright, T. M., 9849
Wulff, M. B., 9352, 9677

Xie, J. L., 8259

Yamauchi, H., 9199, 9494
Yammauchi, H., 8680, 8681, 9607, 9687
Yang, B., 9445, 9594
Yanico, B. J., 9621
Yasumoto, J. Y., 9145
Yaugn, E., 8055
Yelsma, P., 8998
Yin, Z., 9264
Yoo, J., 9113, 9229, 9510
Yoon, J., 9040
Yoshida, H., 9682
Young, M., 8999, 9415
Youngstrom, E., 7654
Yurek, D., 7849, 9616

Zagumny, M. J., 8332
Zaichkowsky, L., 9321
Zak, A. M., 8057
Zanandrea, M., 8445
Zazzaro, J. A., 8994
Zea, M. C., 7511, 7551, 7599, 7600, 9425, 9595
Zellman, G. L., 8718
Zemanek, J. E., Jr., 9130, 9980
Zenger, N., 7874
Zervas, Y., 7862, 7880, 9627, 9646
Zhang, L-F., 8799, 9888
Zhang, Y., 9366
Zhang, Z., 8797
Zohar, D., 8267, 9052
Zuckerman, M., 7649, 8677, 9401
Zulaika, L., 9521
Zuroff, D. C., 8384

Subject Index

All numbers refer to test numbers. Numbers 1 through 339 refer to entries in Volume 1, numbers 340 through 1034 refer to entries in Volume 2, numbers 1035 through 1595 refer to entries in Volume 3, numbers 1596 through 2369 refer to entries in Volume 4, numbers 2370 through 3665 refer to entries in Volume 5, numbers 3666 through 5363 refer to entries in Volume 6, and numbers 5364 through 7441 refer to entries in Volume 7.

Abasement, 1720
Aberration, perceptual, 3266
Abidingness, law, 287
Abilit(ies)(y): 6996; academic, 766, 6824, 9297; analytic, 661; cognitive, 2678; conclusions, 2217; confidence, 6018; cope, stress, 1677; coping, 5445; discrimination, 1041, 1249; general reasoning, 2220; human relation, 1714; inductive reasoning, 2209, 2221; information-transformation, 110; intuitive, 3430; letter formation, 1052; learning, 6054; lipreading, 5386; mental, 138; occupational, 305; perceptual motor, 2213; performance, 6; problem solving, 1468, 2226; reasoning, 2204; screening, 5387; self-concept, 1850; self-estimates, 305, 766, 1428, 1429; sports, perceived, 6845; supervisor(y), 1019, 2265; verbal, quantitative, 2213; visual-spatial, 6053; work, 1033
Abortion, attitude toward, 1131, 4229, 4318
Abrasiveness, self-rated, 749
Absenteeism: attitude toward, 4230; consequences of, 4118; employees; group influence, 4148; self-reported, 6302, 6303; student, 3698
Abstract(ness): conceptualization, 2216; concreteness, 2200; reasoning, 2201, 2202, 3424
Academic(ally)(s), 388, 621, 675, 2191: ability, 766, 6824, 9297; ability, confidence, 2147;

ability, self-concept, 2128; acceleration, 6104; achievement, 477, 1337; achievement accountability, 467; achievement motivation, 1987; achievement orientation, 228; achievement predictor, 2683; 2684; achievement, university residence, 704; adequacy, peer counseling, 1973; adjustment, 22; advising, 1959, 6531; advisors, undergraduates, 992; anxiety, 400, 2404; aspirations, 9948; assistant, evaluation, 992; attitudes, 1126, 6060, 7262; attribution, 3327, 5399, 5439; autonomy, 5400; barriers to women, 5894; climate, 1335; competence, 2421, 5391; constraints, 6534; course evaluation, 6532; curiosity, 1984; dishonesty, 8684; environment, attitude, 1126; factors, 527; goals, 9200; integration, 2399; locus of control, 3222, 9298; misconduct, 6188, 6189, 6190; motivation, 578, 1985, 3123, 6532, 6624, 9191, 9270, 9312; orientation, 228, 7559; performance, 471, 5430, 7531; prediction, 231, 6059; procrastination, 5401, 5402; progress assessment, 5405; self-concept, 1395, 2030, 2056, 3153, 3301, 3303, 6679, 6680, 6852, 9299–9301, 9563; self-concept, elementary school, 2147; self-efficacy, 6681, 6682, 9382; self-esteem, 2031, 3154, 3155, 3278; self-regulation,

8490; skills, 400; status, college freshmen, 904; stress, 5430, 5446; success, attributions; success, correlates, 95, 6291; success, fear of, 2410; support for achievement, 6550; talented elementary students, 1606
Acceptance, 583, 645, 655, 659, 8072: among children, 3965; of authority, 4352, 4353; blame, 907; of career stagnation, 4128; disability, 1636; father, 645; interpersonal, 5772; group, perceived, 5702; loss, 1636; of generalized other, 4065; peer, 5774; of past, 6683; perceived maternal, 759; school, 1070; self, 249, 759, 831, 1105, 1425, 4065, 4832; social, 1104, 2593
Access, social, 1452
Accidents, 6273: locus of control, 6684; pilot, 478; safety
Accountability, academic achievement, 467, 1367
Accounting: attitude toward, 4240; job satisfaction, 4146; self-efficacy, 6771
Acculturation, 1696, 5714, 5752, 5761, 7901, 7944, 7946, 8096–8070; African-Americans, 7909; Asian Indians, 7973; Asian (-American), 4100, 5880, 7915, 8116; attitudes, 5703; behavioral, 5722, 7923; Greek-Americans, 7964; Hispanics, 8079; Israeli, 7996–7997; Mexican-Americans, 2547, 3519, 3966, 790–7903, 7943; Puerto Rican, 3967; Vietnamese, 5722
Achievement, 1–21, 218, 340–

386, 949, 1035–1066, 1596–1624; 7442–7483: academic, 477, 1337; academic accountability, 467, 1367; academic, locus of control, 3196; anxiety, 23, 908, 1625, 2433, 2439; artistic and sex role, 877; athletic and sex role, 877; attitudes toward, 6175; attribution, 3157, 3253; college, 480; competitive, 989; controlled, 989; dynamics, 1631; earth science, 7449; excellence, 861; expectations, 6625; first grade, 469, 474; goals, 9192–9193; identity, 271, 628, 1286; imposter phenomenon, 6770; junior college, 1351; listening, 1043, 1063; locus of control, 3233; mathematics, 1740, 2383, 5380, 5381; mathematics and sex role, 877; Mexican-American, 5704; motivation, 1986, 1989, 1990, 1993, 2017, 2019, 2026, 3124–3126, 3141, 3142, 4694, 4697, 4714, 4717, 4724, 6522, 6627, 6628, 6629, 9194–9197, 9256, 9275; see also achievement need; motivation, academic, 1987; motivation, college, 4965; motivation, junior high, 2028; motivation, men, 1988; motivation, orientation toward success, 4963; motivation, school-age children, 4696, 4699; need, 23, 204, 210, 712, 721, 727, 744, 986, 1338, 1340, 1345, 1347, 1350, 1353, 2005, 2007, 2009, 2022, 2029, 6656, 6658; need, children, 715, 718, 737; need, college students, 726; need, disadvantaged students, 722; need, females, 728; need, high school, 729; need, males, 728; need, Mexican-Americans, 738; orientation, 713; phonics, 2398; preschool, 12; pressure for, 496, 647, 673; quantitative, 1043, 1063; reading, 350, 1035, 1036, 1043, 1063; reading, first grade, 602; reading and sex role, 877; responsibility, intellectual, 786; self criticism,

244; standards and sex role, 877; stress, 5705; striving, 716; tendency, 2006, 2274, 6626; tests, attitude, 2718; verbal, 1063; women's needs, 6652
Acquiescence, 278, 281, 296, 2244: negativism, children, 843
Acting, 568: -out, 2191
Activation, 417: -deactivation, 1839
Active: speech, 397; experimentation, 2216
Activeness, pressure for, 647, 673
Activit(y)(ies), 1339, 6274: art, 6201; class, 1380; competitive-cooperative, 5738; daily living, 8493; death-associated, avoidance of, 5465; gender stereotyping, 6857; group, 681; leisure, 198, 268, 3404, 3407; level, 1203, 1870, 6192; orientation, 6276; patterns, 400, 6256; preference, 3388, 10188; reaction, 1293; retirement, 8263; stereotypes, girls, 2032; women's attitude toward physical, 791
Actual behaviors, 601
Actualization, self, 214, 9339–9340, 9465, 9535, 9738: potential, 9463, 9465
Acuity, perceptual, 2685
Adaptability, 2285, 5448: family, 6414, 6415
Adaptation: career, 9894; college student, 3735, 5422, 5431, 7550–7551; college student, self-rated, 3700; expatriates, 7663; family, 4548–4550; individual styles, 5134; predisposition, 7118; self-reported difficulty, 4024
Adaptive regression, 606
Addiction, 8495: counseling, 10022; self-report, 6278; treatment satisfaction, 10093; to work, 6039–6041, 8736
Adequacy, college teachers, 785
Adjective(s): generation technique, 1369; prenominal, 377
Adjustment, 300, 625, 1067, 1398, 3535, 3696: academic, 22; adolescent, 3522; behavior, 1238; college life, 22, 2400, 2401, 2409, 3695, 3701, 3703,

3709, 5403, 5408, 5421, 5432, 6482; difficulties, 403; educational, 22–27, 387–402, 1067–1077, 1625–1635; 7484–7571; emotional, 5708; family, 2291, 2992; first grade, 2413; general, 1106; index, 34; kindergarten, 2422; level, 422; marriage, 1299, 2978, 2980, 3011, 3014, 3015, 3019, 4541, 4542, 4579, 6444; patient, 418; personal, 37; personal social, 397; premorbid, 421; prisoners, 1678; psychological, 28–43, 403–425, 1078–1089, 1636–1694, 5536, 5618; 7572–7900; rating, 403, 418; retarded, 1033; schizophrenia patients, 3752; school, 3728, 3729, 3740, 3741; self, 409; social, 44–70, 426–466, 1090–1116, 1695–1731, 5708, 7901–8140; teacher's perception of child, 4925; trainee, 27; vocational, 1033, 8141–8309; widowed, 1693; work, 337
Administrat(ion)(ive)(or), 662: attitudes, 1195; behavior, 1863; educational, 528; guidance, 677; image, 1307; locus of control, 818; morale, school, 1978; probation, 523; responsibilities, 657; school, 528, 1558; stereotypes, 528; stress, 8141; style, 1407, 1408; values, 979
Admission(s): college, 9088; assistance, college, 660; practices and attitudes, 553
Adolescen(ce)(ts)('), 485, 490, 605, 1751: abuse, 2964; academic stress, 5446; adjustment to alcohol use, 3160; adjustment to school, 3728, 3729; affection toward family, 4526; AIDS knowledge, 5364; alcohol use, 8496, alienation, 2549; assertiveness, 3501; attachments, 4020; 7904, attitudes, autonomy, 6992; behavior, 4354, 4426; body satisfaction, 756; boys, 848; Chicano, 1696; children behavior, 1844; cognitive functioning, 605; competence, 8707, 9602; communication,

2897; coping, 7576, 7576; creative, 133; creatively gifted, 1935; decision processes, 7577, 7577; delinquency, 1213; deviant behavior, 6194; drug use, 562,4470; egocentrism, 5167; ethical behavior, 8498; family connectedness, 8920; in family decision-making, 4639; future time perspective, 772; girls, parents of, 656; girls, social competence, 2595, 2866; goal attainment, 2898; goal setting, 4708; Hawaiian, 7015; independence attitudes, 6404; individuation, 6509, 8885; injuries, 7578; information seeking, 868; internationally mobile, 7055; interpersonal competence, 3968; knowledge of infant development, 3676; late, 498, 646; life expectancies, 5026; life events, 8800; locus control, 2072; loneliness, 4030; mentally handicapped, 4351; parent relations, 640, 760, 3001, 3030, 3040, 4532, 6388, 6501, 8923–8925; parental conflict, 6453; parental monitoring of, 6517; peer-relations, 760; perceived stress, 5450; perception of family by, 6387; perceptions, parental, 2156, 4604, 6385, 6422; personality, 854; personality priorities, 5063; physical health, 7580; planfulness, 8499; pleasant activities, 4347; pre-, 625, 644; rearing, 490; problem behaviors, 8500; problem-solving style, 5139; psychosocial maturity, 4498; rebelliousness, 8501; response to suicide supports, 3961; retarded, 1619; risky behavior, 6195; runaways, 6264; satisfaction with peer social support, 3979; school attachment, 3730; school failure, 3731; self-concept, 1430, 2102, 9341; self-description, 4964, 4965; self-disclosure, 4488; self-expectation, 1432; self-image, 4981; self-report, 8739; self-

satisfaction, 756; separation, 3909, 6509; sex-role attitudes, 4260; sex-role perception, 5080; social problem-solving, 5860; stress, 2435, 3753, 3754; structure, 760, 1070, 1378, 2175; structure needs, 1991; test anxiety, 3744; values, 974, violence exposure, 8674; 3523, 3525, 3526; vocational interest, 1591; worry, 3960
Adult(s), 485: attachment, 7906–7908, 7916–7917; biographical inventory, 840; career development, 2944; childhood behaviors of, 6334; creative, 133, 615; creatively gifted, 1935; development, 2943; interpersonal dependency, 1715; irrational ideas, 1637; locus of control, 3223, 3255, 3274; male self-esteem, 826; perception and recall, 533; self-esteem, 2046, 3312; sex-role concepts, 2132; time perspective, 758; young males, 636
Adverbial clauses, 377
Advertising beliefs, 6105
Advisers: characteristics, 994; perceived by students, 993
Advising residence hall groups, 546
Aesthetic: perception, 254; sensitivity, 2034
Affect/Affective processes, 3755, 3862, 5033, 5451–5455, 5505, 5601: alexithymia 5073; assessment, 1802; attitude toward time, 91; attitude toward school, 5426: attributed, 404; balance, 2426, 7582; behavior, 2810; behavior, student, 568; behavior changes, 572; career commitment, 5305; characteristics, 601; children, 7581, 7776, 9679; cognition, 404; commitment, 5454, 7585, 10129; communication, 4478, 8740; content, 404; depressed family, 4551; developed, 404; dimension, 404; disposition, 5456: emotional autonomy, 4000, 4001, 4544; emotional closeness, 4002; emotional

reactivity, 5042; emotional structure, 5054; empathy, 5051; expression, 121, 279, 5045; in families, 4544; food consumption and, 4444; group behavior, 596; happiness measurement, 3756; index, 3904; intensity, 3757, 5024, 5032, 7583; interaction, 1217, intimacy, 2965; judgment, 1252; labeling, 6987; negative, 3888, 5630–5632, 5679, 7027, 7767–7768, 7794–7798, 7864; parent rating of child's, 4528; parental, 7780; pet attachment, 4051; positive, 5629–5632, 7582, 7794–7798; predisposition, 7770; quality of relationships, 640; regulation, 7584; repression, 3919; response, to AIDS, 3959; response, immediate, 429; self-disclosure, 6335; self-perceived social adjustment, 4095; sensitivity, 98, 428, 429; separation, 3910; states, 1638, 5587; stress, 3894; stress response, 3852; task-associated, 3762; termination-reaction, 6329: work-related, 4143; in writing process, 3750, 5027
Affection(ate): nurturant, 652; social, 417
Affectivity, 600: assessment, 1964
Affiliation, 1720, 5710: need, 44, 745, 986, 2007; need, Mexican-American, 738; peer, 228; toward others, 1706
Affiliative tendency, 44
Affirmation action, 9093
African: children, 1740; self-consciousness, 6688; society, malaise in, 65, 301
African Americans: acculturation, 7908; attitudes toward, 4325, 4327, 5715; commitment to separatism, 3977; ethnocentrism, 3976; racial identity, 4316, 4317, 4320, 5725, 5726, 5727, 7910, 7911; racism reports, 8065; self-concept, 4929; self-consciousness, 4754, 9679; self-esteem, 9414; socialization, 7912; workplace bias, 9189

After-school programs, 9009
Agentic attributes, 9306
Aggress(ion)(iveness), 216, 397, 403, 417, 651, 920, 927, 940, 1510, 1870, 2247, 3452, 3455, 3463, 3470, 4357, 7036, 7149, 7150, 8504, 8668, 9681, 9751, 9895, 9929: anxiety, 2437; -assertiveness, 1842; attitude toward, 2706; authoritarian, 2253; behavioral, 1843, 2295, 2800, 2801, 2858; child(ren), 1840, 2277, 2878, 3453, 3464, 3498, 4364, 5179, 8541, 8545, 8546, 8548, 8619; children's outcome expectations, 4892; children's values, 5235; -conducive activities, 2190; delay, 1212; interpersonal, 1221; intragroup, 8508; job, 1033; lack of, 2251; marriage, 4625; peer relations, 946, 4078; potential, 1476; premarital sexual, 6277; self, 242; self-efficacy beliefs, 4969; sexual, 131, 8506; teacher ratings, 8619; verbal, 9947. See also Rape
Aging, 407, 415: successful, 33
Agoraphobia, 3758, 3882, 3883, 6988, 7854: behavior, 2812, 3883, 5596; cognitions, 2438
Agree(ableness)(ment), 1720: -disagreement, 483, 8000, 8287; disagreement response set, 281
Aide(s), 577: -child interactions, 577
AIDS: attitudes, 4233, 4236, 6065, 6066, 6087, 8316, 8332; attitudes toward fear of, 4293; blame, 6689; awareness, 7442; employer beliefs, 4756; fear response, 3959, 7668; HIV symptoms, 5549; knowledge, 5364, 5365, 5367, 5368, 6066, 7453, 7455–7457, 7459; legal issues, 7454; phobia, 7762; prevention, 6244; psychosocial variables, 5711; risk reduction, 7908, 8595, 9224; safe-sex behavior, 9307; traumatic stress response, 4104; victim blaming, 8317
Ailments, common, 407
Air cadets, 478

Alcohol(ic)(s), 405, 526, 1122, 1674, 3159, 3160, 4383, 4386, 4459, 6230, 6285: abuse, 2802, 2849; abstinence self-efficacy, 9308, 9619; addict, 1639; adolescents, 4470, 8496; adverse consequences, 8507, 8508; behavioral effects, 8318; biphasic effects, 8531; children of, 6395, 6396, 6399; college students, 4457; drug use, 563; expectancies, 4813, 6690, 6691; family drinking patterns, 6229; father's, 8689; intensity, 8509; mother's, 8622; motives, 9204; parents' awareness and beliefs, 8970; peer use, 8635; perceptions, 6692; positive outcomes, 6690; predication of use, 6231; screening, 8532, 8702; severity, 8660, 8688; student use, 6315; treatment behaviors, 4350; urges, 8661; use, 8576
Alexithymia, 5073, 7056, 9800–9802: children, 9682
Alienat(ed)(ing)(ion), 45, 64, 65, 430, 437, 453, 533, 809, 1090, 1093, 1699, 1701, 1709, 1725, 3969, 5712, 5713, 5758, 7963: adolescent, 2549; attitudes, 83; college student, 3747, 4111, 5443, 7567; conditions, 430; consumer, 1700; cultural, 1093; general, 442, 1091; interpersonal, 1110; job, 5941; manifest, 443, 1103; social, 1098; student(s), 64, 455, 582; university, 465, 1730, 5890; work, 2671
Aloneness, 413, 7926
Aloofness, 688
Altered states of consciousness
Alternate uses, 608
Alternatives, correct, 385
Altitude, high, 571
Altruis(m)(tic), 624, 2317, 6989, 8510: in children, 926; motivation, 3134, 9318
Alumni, follow up, 158
Alzheimer's Disease, 3666
Ambigu(ity)(ous), 2122: intolerance of, 1796; role, 2357, 2525, 3288, 3292, 4940, 4941, 6875–6880, 9543, 9544, 9547–9550, 9556; situation,

threat perceived, 2077; tolerance (for) (of), 481, 612, 646, 955, 965, 1505, 2245, 4854, 5216, 6873, 6973, 7151–7153, 7180, 7188, 9683, 9685, 9735, 9798, 9799
Ambition, teacher, 1363, 1364
Ambivalence, 2486: over emotional expression, 6990, sexism, 9805
American: Catholic priest, 1668; political behavior, 368; values, 1524
American Indian values, 3545
Anagram fluency, 1903
Analog(ies)(y), 887: figure, 2059; verbal, 1065
Analysis, 600: auditory, 1374; early childhood education, 678; schedule, 601; visual, 1041, 1441
Analytic: abilities, 661; empathy, 1370
Anaphora comprehension, 5, 2370
Anatomy test, 658
Anger, 832, 950, 1501, 2246, 2252, 2283, 3106, 3454, 3455, 3494, 5188, 5213, 7050, 7154, 7157, 7185, 7587: college student, 3759; control, 5168; discomfort with, 7155; driving, 6232; -evoking events, 6553; expression, 5169, 7156; measurement, 5170; propensity, 9740; strain, 7158
Anhedonia, 910: physical, 2507; social, 5848
Animals: attachments, 3789, 5736; attitude toward, 4337, 6067, 6068; rights attitude, 8319
Anomia, 424, 1685, 2563, 2612
Anomie, 1078, 1091, 1638, 1640, 1684: psychological, 413
Anorexia nervosa, 6235, 8511, 8512, 8580
Anthropology achievement: elementary grades, 1044; concepts, 1269
Anthropomorphism, 4051
Anti: -authoritarianism, 481; -democratic attitudes, 77; -intraception, 2253; -sexism, 1123; -social behavior, 578; -war, demonstrators, 552; -worldminded, 1795

Anticipations, personal, 2107
Antisocial behavior, 8513
Anxiety, 283, 286, 387, 405, 417, 487, 841, 860, 925, 928, 945, 947, 948, 966, 1496, 1500, 1641, 1642, 1681, 2248, 2270, 2440, 2473, 2523, 3785, 3825, 3927, 3929, 3954, 5187, 5215, 5848–5460, 5484, 5485, 7587, 7591, 7592, 7718, 7857, 7898: academic, 400; achievement, 908, 1625, 2433, 2439; adolescent worries, 3960; aggression, 2437; agoraphobia, 3758, 3882; antecedents, 5634; assessment, 3760; behavioral, 2456; cardiac, 7608; career choice, 5898, 7367; catastrophic cognitions, 5473; in children, 3921, 4075, 4468, 5652, 7196, 7763, 7781, 7837–7839; claustrophobia, 5482; cognitive-somatic, 3787, 5180, 5457, 5490; college student, 5422; competition, 3790, 5212, 7628; computer, 3705, 3774, 3792–3797, 5907–5911; concept, 1381; coping styles, 3920; criticism, 3822; dating, 3993; death, 410, 1649, 1650, 1651, 2447, 2459, 2541, 3805, 3806, 5503, 5691, 7646, 7829; debilitating, 1625, 1626, 1633, 2240; dental, 7753; depression, 773, 1686; ego, 5515; elementary children, 933; existential, 1657, 5523; facilitating, 1625, 2240; financial, 3824; first graders, 948; generalized, 3827, 3876; graduate school, test, 2427; health, 3841; heterosocial, 3987; job-induced, 1666; major choice, 1648; manifest, 1478, 2524, 3488, 5585, 7205; maternal separation, 4588, 6465; mathematics, 394, 1630, 2417, 2418, 3714–3720, 5416; motor, 5593; multidimensional measure, 3935; of negative ratings, 5521; neurotic, 749; peer nominations, 7781; Persian populations, 7590; piano, 2508; precompetition, 5491; preschool, 2509; prolonged, 3761; in psychiatric

patients, 3764; reactions, 402; science, 5427; self-rating, 911; sensitivity, 7593; separation, 3932; severity, 5466; sexual functioning, 3842; situational, 26 sixth graders, 947; social, 2604, 2605, 4072–4076, 4082, 5766, 8076–8078, 8094, 8098; somatic symptoms, 6703; sports, 7859; state, 1682; statistics, 5429, 5440; -stress, 1643; student, 3737; symptoms 1632, 2441, 7688, 7704; task-related arousal, 3762; teacher ratings, 7561; teachers, 4211; tension, 1638; test, 25, 26, 32, 209, 387, 392, 393, 395, 396, 398, 399, 401, 402, 713, 1074–1076, 1625, 1627, 1629, 1633–1635, 2428–2430, 3692–3694, 3706, 3712, 3739, 3742–3746, 3749, 5415, 5423, 5428, 5442; test, children, 32, 5441; trait, 3478; trait assessment, 5191; uncertainty, 960; vocational choice, 1648; vs. depression, 5486; writing, 3707
Anxious(ness), 5690: audience, 2551; -fearful, 1872; interaction, 2572; romantic attachment, 5461; self-talk, 8514; social, 2551
Apathy, 1103
Aphasia, 1887, 5117
Apology, -restitution, 381
Appearance: employee, 1007; physical, 593, 9327–9337
Apperception: body, 9464; pain, 2095; thematic Hispanic, 3382
Appetite suppressants, 8515
Applicant(s): job, 9433; rating, 3588
Application, 600: college, 553
Applied psychology, attitude toward, 1127
Appraisal: See Evaluation
Apprehension, 2917
Approach: withdrawal, 2285
Approval: disapproval, teacher, 659; need, 62, 450, 500, 2586; parental, 499; social, 48, 449, 5734
Aptitude, 71–75, 467–482, 1117–1121, 1732–1744, 8310–8313: community college, 75; computer, 4224, 4225;

employees, 1007; foreign language, 1733; geometry, 74; mental, 72, 4226; spatial, 479, test-taking, 5127
Arabs, negative sentiments toward, 8312
Arbitration, 1274
Argumentativeness, 3456, 7159
Arithmetic: ability, perception of, 2147; skills, 637, 1038
Arousal, 6632: children, 7581; group, 1998; level, 571, 6200; predispostion, 8517; seeking need, 2023
Art(s): activity, 6201; assessment, 1457; biographical, 2159; music, attitudes toward, 1841; self-perception, 9309, 9310
Arthritis, attitudes, 2767
Articulation, community college, 3163
Asian (Americans), 4100, 5558, 5580, 7915, 8116–8118, 8804
Aspiration(s): experiences, school related, 472; college students, reality, 740; disadvantaged, 740; educational, college students, 719; occupational, 269, 897, 3623, 9201, 10130; occupational, high school, 901; student, 2027, 9283; vocational, 204, 269
Assault, 2252, 6313
Assert(ion)(ive)(iveness), 1702, 2242, 2249, 2256, 2271, 2282, 3457–3459, 3461, 3465, 3467–3469, 3480, 3481, 3492, 3501, 3502, 5166, 5171–5173, 5181, 5182, 5201, 5203, 7162, 7168, 7170, 7176, 7195, 7209, 8518, 8642, 9932: adolescent, 7161; aggressiveness, 1842; behavior, 1873, 2803, 3451; consumers, 8557; job-hunting, 7160; non-, 408; team tasks, 8722; training, 408, 4456
Assessment: art, 1457; memory, 2384; perceptions of, 6536, 9011
Assimilation of meaning, 380
Association(s), 385: dream, 30
Associationalism, 982
Associative: responding, 264; verbal encoding, 1035
Assumptions, looking for, 2215
Assurance, self, 1101, 1427

Athlet(es)(ics): coping skills, 9314; life events, 7517; recruitment, 3413; role identification, 9315; social support, 5870; stress, 7595; success, 3215

Atmosphere: classroom, 1027; group, 2568, 3074; junior high, 700

Attachments, 6451, 5718, 8825, 9316: adolescent, 4020, 7904; adolescent-parent, 6472–6474; adults, 7905–7907, 7916, 7917, 10023; anxiety, 5461, 7914; child-mother, 6391, 6392; child-parent, 6405, 6452, 6475; history, 8805; parent, 8886–8893, 8934–8963; peer, 5813, 8886–8893; security, 8898, style, 7918; therapist, 10023, 10032

Attainment: goals, 714; occupational, 9891; satisfaction, students, 714

Attention: task focus, 9198; and temperament, 9795

Attention deficit hyperactivity disorder, 7772: adolescents, 8497; adults, 8502, school performance, 7545; symptoms, 7574, 7575; teacher ratings, 8494

Attitude(s), 23, 76–97, 481, 483–561, 1122–1202, 1745–1838, 2228, 8314–8488: abortion, 1131, 4229, 4318; academic, 4231, 6060; academic acceleration of gifted, 4261; academic cheating, 4274; accounting, 4240; acculturation, 5703; admission practices, deans, 553; adult reading, 4232; African American ethnocentrism, 3976; AIDS, 4233; alcohol, 1122; alienation, 45, 64, 65, 6065, 6066; animal research, 4337; antidemocratic, 77; Arab-American, 97; athletic competition, 4339; authoritarianism, 83; behavior, 1745; Black students, 46; bodily appearance, 4273; business, 84; career development, 5309; career/job, 4300; CEOs, 8375; changes,

9039; child rearing, 496, 1148, 3032; child's social, 4276; children, 497, 1180; children interracial, 1184; children's pictorial, 1770; church, 80; cigarettes, 1122; cockpit management, 4277; coffee, 1122; college students, 81, 743, 1530; college student patterns, 222; competitive, 6137, 8410, 8444; computers, 2724, 4237, 4278, 4280–4285, 4287, 4305, 4310, 6137, 6062, 6116; controversy, 4238; conventionality, 2734; cooperation/competition, 4286, 4371; counselor's, 4334, 8380; counsel(ing)(or), 81, 309, 560, 1173, 2788; creative, 130, 235; cross-cultural, 1153; customer service, 3066; date rape, 6077; day care providers, 6143; death, 1779; depression risk, 4289; disadvantaged adolescents, 8314; divorce, 4296; dominating, 504; drug, 1781; drug knowledge, use, 1858; drug-testing, 6074; dysfunctional, 4814, 4815, 5517, 5518, 8384; eating, 4290, 4319, 4368, 8386, 8387, 8578, 8579; educational, 2738, 2739, 8425; employee, 188, 193, 1007, 1156, 2622, 3990, 6122, 6234, 6235, 8391; fatalism, 4825; father, 645; feminist, 1767, 1834, 4239, 6075, 6076; foreign language, 6078; formation, 83; full-service restaurants, 4262; functions inventory, 4234; gender roles, 2746, 6115, 6126, 7107, 7111; grade contract, 513; guidance and counseling, 85, 189; helping, 6131; homophobia, 3843, 3855; hospice care, 4298; toward human resources management, 4263, 8334; humanitarian, 6135; hypercompetitive, 8410; illness, 8415, 8416; impunitive, 481; institutional, 82; intellectual and programmatic, 86; interpersonal, 546; interracial, 517, 1147, 1150, 1183; intimacy, 2579; language, 6141;

law-related, 1799; learning, 6648; leisure, 4301; love, 3989, 4264; managerial, 523, 1536; marijuana, 1133; marriage, 4244; masculine, 2759; mathematics, 524, 4303, 6144; mental illness, 2736; merit pay, 4304; military service, 81; modern, 3536; 4306; money, 2764; mother's, 1803; motivation, upward bound, 217; movie, 2765; multifactor racial, 482, 2766; nationalities, 1135; nonprofessional, 82; nuclear concerns, 4307; office, 3368; openness to experience, 4485, 4729, 5093; optimism, 4863, 5571–5574; parental, 504, 532, 640, 3010, 8439, 8440, 8937; parental leave, 6697; parental, research instrument, 533; peers, 1820; perceived maternal, 759; personal, 535, 593; personnel managers, 1169; policemen's, 1810; political, 536, 537, 1806; preferences for social interaction, 4017; premarital intercourse, 2237; privacy, 2751, 2752, 4272; procrastination, 2769; professional, 82, 1815, 4926; professional-self, 82; protest situational, 1817; about psychological health, 4247; psychotherapist's, 6155; pupil, 455, 540; racial, 46, 78, 79, 87, 88, 482, 520, 542, 1812, 1813, 2772, 2773, 4315, 4316, 4325, 4327, 6161, 8436; racial intermarriage, 70; rape, 4246, 4436, 6064; reading, 543, 544, 1787, 1822, 1823, 4313; referents, 555; religious, 4324; risk-taking, 8424; romantic, 2777; scholastic activities, 556; school, 66, 155, 1136, 1149, 1825, 2779, 4266, 5426; school counselor, 1826; school experience, 1820; school, general, 1820; school orientation, 534; school work, 1820, 6182; science, 2793, 4267, 4321; seat belts, 1828; secondary reading, 1824; self, 1439, 5516; self-righteous,

1170; sexual, 2781, 6165; sex-role, 1831, 2760, 2783, 4248, 4251–4258, 4260, 4270, 4322, 5083, 6164; sexual violence, 6063; social, 94, 554, 555, 1527; social acceptance in children, 3965; social mobility, 5162; social responsibility, 94, 4060; sociopolitical, 4324, 4329, 6168; speaker, 2217; of special education teacher, 6079; statistics, 4249, 4268, 4326; status obeisance, 5163; student, 859, 1163, 1188–1190, 1194; student beliefs, 556; student control, 4314; students interracial, 535; substance abuse, 4330; supervisors, 1023; teachers, 559, 1820, 8478–8480; teachers'job-related, 1827; teaching career, 4268; therapist, 96; training programs, 4335; transpersonal orientation to education, 4336; trusting, 1706; union, 1836, 1837, 3415; United States, 83; university student, 705; upward bound, 45, 217; women, 1134; women's self-concept as feminists, 4294; work, 4220, 4342; work absence, 4230; work and child care, 4265; work experience outcomes, 4217, 4219; work groups, 8487; work involvement, 2797; writing, 4343; youth, 1202

Attitude toward: aggression, 2706; AIDS, 6087, 8316, 8317, 8332; AIDS victims, 4236; animals, 6067, 6068, 8319; Arabs, 8321; art, music, 1841; arthritis, 2767; authority, 1830, 2723, 2747, 4295, 4352, 4353; aviation, 1142; banking, 156; bisexuality, 8322; Blacks, 1187, 6111, 6167; Black English, 2756; Black movement, 542; career counseling, 8336; calculators, 2721; censorship, 6088; CEOs, 8375; change, 92; cheating, 6073; children, 4271; Christianity, 4259, 6095, 7212, 7213, 8400; church, 80; classroom, 1196; collective

bargaining in education, 4292; college, 2692; college counseling, 4338; college courses, 151, 6096; community, 1312, 4279, 8378; computer, 115, 152, 2726–2729, 6082, 6125, 8338–8340, 8364; condom use, 8379; controversy, 2707, 2733; cooperation, 1371; counseling, 189, 2698, 2708; counseling Black students, 999; courses, 2735; credit card use, 8341; curriculum, 501; defense, 1197; dental health, 2725; desegregation, 1160; disabled, 2693, 2717, 6089, 6119; discrimination, 542, 8467; diversity, 8446; divorce, 8342; dreams, 2709, 2737, 8343; drug abusers, 1191; drugs, 1145, 1155, 1210; education, 529, 549, 1167; educational measurement, 8324; educational research, 2710, 6176; educational rights, 8327; elderly, 2697, 2755, 4308; employed wives, 4252; environmental issues, 1152, 8388, 8402, 8435; evangelism, 2711; family life, 8345; fat, 8320; fear of AIDS, 4293; fees, 2789; female roles, 2742; feminism, 6163, 8346; fitness, 8399; foreign language, 2744, 8347; gay men, 8348, 8351, 8352; gender roles, 8349; gifted children, teacher, 558; grievance system, 4250; group therapy, 4833; guilt, 6070; Gulf War, 6130; guns, 8323; handicapped, 2702, 2784, 4275; help-seeking, 8359, 8360; high-achievers, 6175; Hispanic people, 6132; homosexuality, 2713, 2748–2750, 4233, 4241, 4242, 4297, 6134, 6080; human resources management, 4263; human rights, 6136; illegal aliens, 8350; incest, 6091, 6138; incurably ill, 4011; interpersonal communication, 6336; interracial, 1143, 1168; Jews, 8321; job, 1346, 2754; job teachers, 557; labor unions, 6128, 6152, 6186; learning, 540, 2785, 8425,

8426; lesbians, 8351, 8352; life roles, 6142; love, 8427; mainstreaming, 2694; male nurses, 4243; male role, 8428; male social workers, 8353; marriage, family, 1161; married women's employment, 4309; masturbation, 4302; materialism, 6097; mathematics, 153, 2715, 2740, 2761, 2762, 2795, 6123, 6144–6146, 8325, 8354, 8355, 8398, 8329–8431; men, 4245; mental disorder/illness, 530, 3907; Mexican American, 2768; modernity, 1164, 1165; movies, 1166; national groups, 1180, 2798; nonmaternal care, 2967; nuclear disarmament, 2695; nuclear waste, 6084; nurses, 2696; obesity, 6090; occupations, 2700; offenders, 6157; oppressed people, 6166; pay system, 8441; peers, 541; physical activity, 791, 1171; political issues, 1172; power, 4311; problem workers, 4272; professional women, 6069; psychiatry, 6081; pupil control, 2771; psychological help, 1137, 2743; psychological reports and services, 154; questionnaires, 6100; racial diversity, 6158; rape, 8357, 8466, 8551; reading, 1175, 2741, 2763, 2775; religion, 1178; riots and demonstrations, 482; reality, 6071; recycling, 6098; research, 8358, 8453, 8463, 8464; risk, 2776; school, 540, 541, 1179, 1181, 1771, 2778; school library, 2758; school subjects, 2745; second language learning, 8392; self, 1771; self-control, 2714; sex, 3687, 4299, 4323, 4328; sex roles, 552, 2699, 2720, 2782, 2787, 8468; social issues, 1146; social studies, 1138; spouse abuse, 4521; statistics, 2701, 2786, 6083, 6169, 6174, 8366; substance use, 2790; suicide, 1192, 761, 8433, 8477; supernatural phenomena, 1139; teachers, 541, 549, 580,

1771; teaching, 1140, 2691, 2712, 2716; technology, 1162; television commercials, 2722; test(s)(ing), 1453, 2718, 2791, 2792, 4333; time, 91; tutoring, 2794; upward mobility, 1158; war, 6101, 6171; Whites, 542; witchcraft, 1139; women, 1190, 2703, 2704, 2796, 4251–4258, 4260, 4270, 6085, 6086, 6092–6094, 7210, 8328–8330, 8361–8363, 8367; women in military, 6181; women managers, 4340; women's equality, 6158; women's liberation, 1200; work, 541, 1199, 2730, 8331, 8486, 10205; working mothers, 2705, 4522; working women, 4341; writing, 6173, 6184, 6185, 7116; youth, 1141

Attraction, 426: interpersonal, 426, 1711; organizational, 6535; romantic, 5838

Attractiveness: behavior, 6249; beliefs, 7215; group, 1712: self-rated, 749, 3275; valuation, 6858

Attributed effect, 404

Attributes: personal, 561, 692, 1809, 9512; physical, 561

Attribution, 3157, 3164–3166, 3203, 3246, 3253, 3254, 3268–3270, 3327, 4760, 4761, 4762, 4881, 6850: of abused women, 6702; academic achievement, 4998, 5000, 5011, 5399, 5439, 9427; causal, 9354–9356, 9390; children, 4789, 4793; depression, 6956; dimensions, 9397, 9398; environmental-biological, 6743; heredity vs. environment, 4885; incest blame, 6776; Japanese, 9432; marital, 8902; mathematics, 4875; motivation, 9318; political, 4918; procrastination, 4802; professional success, 5895; psychological problems, 9355, 9390; responsibility, 9325; of student success by teacher, 5005; style, 6696, 6700, 9320–9324, 9432; supernatural beliefs, 5014; trait measure, 5178; for unemployed state, 5013; willingness to ascribe responsibility, 5025

Audience, anxiousness, 2551

Audio-visual, 1

Auditory: analysis, 1374; attention, 7119; blending, 1036; memory, 1066; perception, 1613; perception, first graders, 750, 1423; segmentation, 1036, 1037; selective attention, 3667; stimuli, 1233; visual perception, 765; visual rhythm, 750

Authoritarian(ism), 296, 530, 909, 912, 1500, 1807, 2250, 2253, 2258, 2263, 2264, 2293, 3460, 3507, 3509, 7163, 7197, 7199: attitudes, 83; children, 3466; family, 641, 644, 9008; legal, 7181; parental, 6435, 6477, 6478, 8938; principal, 2281; right-wing, 9935; support, 519

Authority: acceptance, 2805; adherence to, 916; attitudes toward, 1830, 2723, 2747; children's attitudes toward, 6114; decision-making, 7122; family system, 8974; hierarchy, 9053; instructors, 10055; parental, 640; personal, 6597; police, 485; rejection by, 499; relations, 400

Autocratic managerial personality, 787

Auto-driving skills, 478

Auto-kinetic, 913

Automatic thoughts, 5119, 7597, 7623: depression-associated, 5463; frequency, 3763; positive, 5464

Automaticity, word processing, 2927

Autonomous: achievement, 2298; personality, 7048, 7049

Autonomy, 214, 218, 949, 1715, 1815, 2367, 3168, 7921, 9199, 9686, 9687, 9760, 9790: academic, 5400; adolescent, 6992; career, 8146; child, 2550, 2806, 6412; emotional, 7006; family, 6426; individual differences, 9719; job, 3051, 6546; need, 2010; orientation, 7920; task, 6612; teacher, 6614, 6967, 9174, 9842

Aviation, attitude toward, 1142

Avoidance, 645, 6202: agoraphobic, 5596; claustrophobic, 5483; of death-associated activities, 5465; of failure, 8516; job, 5942; school, 7544; social, 8071, 8081; stress, 5650; success, 1362; touch, 5883

Awareness: failure, 3170; metacognitive, 6056; phonological, 6057; reinforcement, 1416; social, 1417

Babies, social responsiveness, 1235

Back pain, 3192

Bank(ing)(s): attitude toward, 156; climate, 3054; switching, 1307; teller performance, 1537

Beauty: beliefs, 8371, 9949; rating, 751

Behavior(al)(s), 562–584, 1203–1246, 1839–1886, 4355, 4848, 8489–8739: absence of goals, 4442; academic advisor, 2329, 5722; academic misconduct, 6188–6190; acculturation, 3975; activation system, 8524; actual, 601; adjustment, 1238, 8525; adjustment, school, 1628; adolescent, 4354, 4426; affective, 2810; affective group, 596; affinity-seeking, 6631; aggressive, 1843, 2800, 2801, 2858, 2875, 2878, 3453, 3470, 4357; agitated 4349; alcohol abuse, 2802, 2849; alcohol consumption, 4383, 6285; anti-social, 578; anxiety, 2456; assertive, 1873, 2803, 3451, 3481, 5166, 5171–5173, 5181, 5182; assessment, neonatal, 1849; authority, 2805; autonomy, 2806; beliefs about, 1847; bizarre, on job, 1033; blood donor, 3978; body sensations, 2812; bulimia, 2813, 2833; cancer patient locus of control, 4784, 4786; career exploration, 5312–5314, 5359; caregiver, 7242; caretakers for incurably ill, 4011; change, affective, 572; change, cognitive, 572; change, home economics, 572;

checklist, 573; child, 28, 496, 1851, 2831, 4360, 4361, 4363–4365, 4390, 4438, 4464, 4607, 6198, 6268, 7611, 8547; child abuse, 2815, 2846; child aggression, 5179; child, antisocial, 4399; child-bearing, 144; child disorders, 4346; children, 1207, 1869, 1870, 2382, 2799, 2816–2818, 2856, 2890, 2891, 6212; child's creative, 1926; child's innovative, 1926; child's social, 5811; classroom, 390, 565, 566, 574, 578, 581, 681, 718, 1108, 1209, 1211, 1227, 1237, 1854, 1855, 1878, 1885, 2820–2823, 2828, 2865, 2880, 2887, 2888, 3056, 8523; collectivism, 5225; combat, 2825; competency, 432, 8526; competitive, 2826; conformity, 3985, 4380; consumer, 4370, 4450, 4883, 5105; consumption, 2829; control, 403, 6270, 8641, 8806; coping, 2830; counselee, 427; counselor, 3565; counselor interview, 584; creative, 531; crisis, 4374; critical interview, 1864; curiosity-related, 1818; daily, 2835, 2836; dating, 253, 4034, 4378; delinquent, 1213, 2832, 2874, 6266, 6227; depression indicators, 6310; description, 388; deviant, 573, 6194; diabetes patient, 4381; diagnostic, 2838; disruptive student, 4435; dominance, 4382; drug, 569, 2819; drug use, 4384, 6187, 6191; early delinquency, 4443; early mathematics, 345; employee, 2851; environmentally-responsible, 6236; ethical violations, 971; excitability, 2852; exploratory, 1208; expressive, 4396; facilitative, 432; faculty, 2894; family roles, 4559; fantasy, 2876, 2886; feminine, 6208; frustration, 4403; gender, 1219, 1285; good, student, 578; hateful, 6290; health, 2864, 6243; heterosocial, 2885; home, 1957; hospital, 1861;

humorous, 4393; hyperactive, 2827, 2878; hypothetical, 1745; illness, 2839, 2860, 3220; impaired, 2834; impatient, 1862; impulsive, 6237; indecision, 2809; independent, 651; increase attractiveness, 6248; infant, 2840, 5052; influencing, 6248; information seeking, 2814; ingratiating, 2841, 5977, 6249; inhibition system, 8524, 8527; innovative, 432, 621, 1208; instructional, 322; instructional, by tutors, 322; instrumental, 4396; intake interview, 3988; intelligent vs. unintelligent, 4397; intentions, 6204, 6205; interaction, 585; interaction description system, 596; interpersonal, 1720, 5732; interpersonal and administrative, 1863; interpersonal advisor, 2329; intervention, 6139; interview, 4398, 6199; intimate, 2837; job, 3052; kinship restraints, 4577; leadership, 1333, 2843–2845, 2872, 2884, 2889, 2896, 4379, 4404–4410, 4417, 6261; learning, 4400; leniency, 4410; lethal, 4411; lifestyle simplicity, 4477; loving, 6290; loving-rejecting, 149; Machiavellianism, 5186, 5190; management, 4412, 4413; managers, 3560; maturity, 621, 1206, 1937; modification, 380, 1010; moodiness, 2801; moral, 981; moral-judgment, 2310; motion sickness, 2848; need for interpersonal control, 4113; negotiating, 4404; nonconforming, 4040; objectives for writing, 341; obsessive-compulsive, 3893; oppositional, 1225; organizational, 3065; organizational citizenship, 5290, 6266, 6267; orientation, 228; noise, 2850; pain, 2854, 2857, 2867; paranoid, 646; parent, 655, 2855, 3033; parent description, 643; parenting, 4615; parenting beliefs, 4569; parent's daily reports, 4602; partner's

response to quitting smoking, 4048; passive-aggressive, 6269; pathological, 1226, 1310; patient, 1205, 1870; peak performance, 4421; peer influence, 556; personal injury claimants, 4372; play, 2861, 2862; playfulness, 4362; post-lying, 4425; preschool, 1872, 4427, 6210; press, perceived environment, 2050; problems, 28, 389, 495, 2804, 2807, 2808, 2859, 2866, 6207, 8522, 8542, 8543, 8554, 8633, 8669, 8670, 10123; problem solving, 1232, 2830, 3280; procrastination, 2868, 2869, 4431, 4432; prosocial, 6281; prosocial in children, 963; prosocial, perceived benefit of, 4835; prosocial, 8654; protest, 1817, 6193; psychiatric patient, 5467; pupil, 574, 578, 6283; rating, 48, 1845, 2853, 2870, 6209; racially discriminatory, 4451; rational, 1679, 1874, 2871; reaction to threatened loss of freedom, 4433; reactivity to events, 4437; refusal, 1857, 2803; relaxation, 4356; response to criticism, 4420; rewarding, 6228; risk taking, 1234, 6195; risk taking, 4735, 7865; rule-orientation, 2158; school-related curiosity, 4673; self-assessment, 5656; self-care, 4440, 5085; self-control, 2873; self-control strategies, 4441; self-destructive, 5481, 6217; self-monitoring, 4068, 4982, 4983; sensation seeking, 4739; sex role, 4248, 5110, 5111; sexual, 1747, 6849; sexual harassment, 6251; sharing, 62; sleep, 2877; social, 388, 964, 4103, 4472, 5811; social avoidance, 4076; social skills, 4086; social support, 4023, 4401; spatial experiences and, 4389; stable dispositions, 4454; stimulus seeking, 2847; student, 601, 737, 2824, 2879, 2881, 2882; student affective, 568; student cognitive, 568; student functioning, 4388;

student withdrawal, 5444; study, 2883; style, 564, 1846, 2811; supervisory, 1241, 2842; system, client verbal, 587; task-oriented, 1854; teacher, 333, 580, 582, 811, 2892, 2893, 3406, 3604–3606, 6211, 6271, 8716, 8717; teacher knowledge of principles of, 3679; teacher rating of student social competence, 4077; test, 1242; text anxiety, 1074; theft-prone, 4455; therapeutic reactance potential, 4473; therapist's, 2197; time-management, 4474, 4475, 6256; trainee, 2863; Type A, 1886, 5164, 5165, 5174, 5185, 5193, 5218, 5220, 7165, 7208; Type A in children, 4414; verbal, 2248; vocational, 202, 426; withdrawn, 1033

Belief(s): about academic acceleration, 6104; advertising, 6104; attractiveness, 8371; about behavior, 1847; career, 6727; chance, 6733; children, 535, 2259; child-rearing, 6113; client, 3190; in conventional rules, 8369; about deafness, 6148; defensiveness, 9688; epistemological, 6361; good luck, 8370; human nature, 1522; identification of, 8368; irrational, 1516, 1665, 2505, 3226, 3228, 3284, 3287, 6767, 6870, 7713, 8423; justice, 3522, 3537, 3538; just-world, 7232, 9962, 9966, 9967, 9977, 9978, 9982, 9983; magic, 3539; mental illness, 8372; mind-body, 7240; paranormal, 3211, 6103, 6855; parenting, 6151, 8941; peers, 9485; personal, 8443; philosophical, 968; political, 1520, 2318; predicting the future, 8447; pregnancy, 6153; primary teacher, 6154; protestant work ethic, 2319, 3528, 3550, 3551, 3663; rape, 6159; reading, 6160, 8462; reality, 6106; relationship, 5835, 6870; religious, 2323, 9976, 9994; seat belt, 1829; sexual, 8374; success, 6107, 6108; systems,

8774; teacher effectiveness, 3330; teaching practice, 6177; weather, 3121; weight-loss, 5701, work, 10013, 10014

Belongingness, 4038: among Blacks, 5725; community, 5844; school, 54520

Benevolence, 530, 1807, 9952, 10018

Bereavement, pregnancy loss, 3899

Biculturalism, 5724

Biodata, 225

Biographical: factors, 1444; information, 212, 703, 1445, 1446; inventory, 213, 1120, 9691; inventory, adult, 840; inventory, student, 839; questionnaire, 229, 3349; traits, 3386

Birth control, 1748: attitudes toward, 1128; effectiveness, 8583; paternal reactions, 1958

Birth order, 5640

Bisexuality, attitudes toward, 8322

Black(s), 520, 635: alcoholic men, 1645; attitudes toward, 6111, 6167; children, locus of control, 793; counseling, 2909; cultural mistrust, 2560; disadvantaged, 342, 350; English, 1058; English attitude, 2756; ghetto diversity, 1640; history, 157; home environment, 2998; mistrust of Whites, 5739; movement, attitude toward, 542; perception of discrimination, 5817; preference toward, 1463; preschool children, 377; school beginners, 566; student attitude, 46; student attitude toward counseling, 999, 3392; students, White colleges, 180; studies, effect of, 88; -White student friendships, 452; -White student problems, 1980

Blame: acceptance of, 907; AIDS, 6689, 8317; incest, 6776

Blood donors, 3978, 4768: salience, 3174

Bloom model, 686

Blushing, 7602

Body: accessibility, tactile, 592; anxiety, 9622; appearance,

9327–9337; awareness, 6706; consciousness, 9530; -build, stereotyping, 561; cathexis, 2043, 3175; consciousness, 6696; dysphoria, 6946; esteem, 3176; image, 1417, 6806, 9327–9337; 9464, 9620; image, peer counseling, 1973; perception, 6707–6717; satisfaction, 2044, 3177, 6708, 6710, 6711, 6736, 9470; satisfaction, adolescents, 756; self-consciousness, 9336; sensations, 2812, 7603, 9338, 9530

Bonding: with companion animal, 3984, 7937; parental, 6479, 8942–8944

Borderline disorder, 5603, 9692, 9784

Boredom, 3775, 5469: driving, 3561; job, 8191; proneness, 7604, 7605; susceptibility, 2025

Boys: adolescent, personality, 858; attitudes, 77; delinquent, 24; effeminate, 119, 1219; elementary, 389; gender-deviant, 1218; junior high, 657; self-concept, curiosity, 233

Brain damage, 1469

Brainstorming, 5470

Breast cancer, 9853

Bulimia, 4358, 4359, 4369, 4385, 4783: behavior, 8534; cognitive distress, 8533; coping, 8511, 8512; symptoms, 2813, 2833, 6213, 8535, 8580

Bullying, 8536, 8537, 8687

Bureaucracy, 1309, 6112, 9016

Bureaucratic: personality, 957, 967; role, 918

Burnout, 2619, 2628, 2643, 2646, 3950, 5897, 8144, 8145: college student, 2420, 3723; marital, 6458; occupational, 5919; principal's, 5926; symptoms, 3773; teacher, 2664, 4203, 4204

Business: attitudes, 84; education, attitude toward, 84; major objectives, 661; personality, 9764; principles, 661; program, graduates, 661; social responsibility, 84

Buying, 8552, 8599

Calculators, 2721

Camps, freshmen, 774
Campus, 493: connectedness, 7486; discipline, 682; environment, 662, 1311, 9017, 9018; ethos, 7500; freedom of expression, 586; helpgiver, 993, housing, 9834, multiculturalism, 9082
Cancer patients: coping skills, 3778; decision-making, 9853; health beliefs, 4837, 7460; locus of control, 4784, 4786; perceived self-efficacy, 4785
Capital punishment, 1750
Career/job, 7369, 7379: adaptability, 9894; advancement facilitators, 9045; affective commitment, 5305; affective processes, 3862; applicant's perception of interviewer, 4853; aspirations, 9201, 10130; assertive job interview technique, 4834; attitudes, 2753, 4220, 4300, 4342; attitude toward child care and, 4265; attitude toward human resources management, 4263; attitude toward married women's employment, 4309; attitude toward merit pay, 4304; attitude toward teaching, 4265; attitude toward women, 4253, 4341; attitude toward women managers, 4340; attitude toward working mothers, 4522; attributes assessment, 4654; autonomy beliefs, 5009, 8146; barriers to management entry, 4670; beliefs, 6727; burnout, 4127; career development attitudes, 5309; career enhancement strategies, 4120; career plateauing, 4128; career stagnation, 4128; carpenter apprentice program, 4634; choice, 10131, 10146; choice anxiety, 5898, 7368; choice, influence of males on women, 710; cockpit management attitudes, 4277; college alumni, 158; commitment, 3611, 3612, 5307, 7350–7359, 7371, 10132–10134; 10146, 10203; communication of expectations, 4479; compensation

satisfaction, 4177, 4178, 4191; concerns, 5899; confidence, 9344, 9345; coping with job loss, 4125; counseling, 7272, 7346, 8336, 9346; creativity differences, 4153; decisions, 2360, 7398; decision-making, 2206, 3180, 3610, 3613, 3653, 5118, 5306, 5310, 5311, 5323, 5356, 6706–6724, 7360–7363, 7428, 9313, 9347–9349, 9854, 9855, 9889, 10131, 10172, 10173; decisiveness, 2208; dental hygienist, 4199; development, 2814, 6726, 9019; dual, 3043, 9399; education, 200; employee intentions to leave, 4184; employee perception of performance appraisal, 4192; employee perception of support, 4680–4682; employer attitudes about homosexuality, 4838; employer beliefs about AIDS, 4756; experience, 6042; expectations, 9350; exploration, 3630, 5312–5314, 5359, 7365, 7366, 7664, 10135–10138, 10148–10151, 10195–10197; family conflict with, 4555, 4631, 4632, 4944; fulfillment, 4142; goal clarity, 5348; goal directedness, 4132; growth need strength, 5324; growth opportunity, 9020; health professionals, 4134; homemaking and, 5361, 6437; ideal job, 5254; identification with, 5308; identity development and, 4509; impatience with professional progress, 4119; inappropriate behavior, 4394; indecision, 2207, 2809, 3615, 3655, 3657, 5315, 5316, 5350, 5351, 5357, 5358; information-seeking, 3616, 7380, 7427; insight, 6725; intention, 10139; intention to leave, 4141, 4184, 4212, 4215; intention to turnover, 4212; interviewer's postinterview impressions, 5284; involvement, 5325–5331, 10141; job design evaluation, 4657; job desirability, 4136; knowledge, 1040, 2379, 3614,

3678; leadership substitutes, 4678; lifelong learners, 4121; literature, 7066; locus of control, 5021, 9351; loyalty, 8147; maternal employment, beliefs about, 4523; maturity of choice in, 5333; medical, 3640; motivation to train for new technology, 4721; need for growth, 4133; nurse role conflict, 4170; nursing satisfaction, 4171; nursing stress, 4169; opportunities for advancement, 4645; orientation, 1576, 3617, 3618, 10142; outcomes, 8297; patterns, 708; perceived alternatives, 4179; perceived interest, 5360; perceived opportunity, 4140; perceptions of, 4172, 4926; perceptual measure of job characteristics, 4859; pharmacist, 4183; planning, 7365; plans, 175, 202, 3619, 5317; plateauing, 8159, 8248, 9631, 10170; preference, 625; police, 4182; police job knowledge, 3683; preferences, 5319; proactive behaviors, 8647; professional commitment, 5344–5346; psychology, 7429; readiness for vocational planning, 5347; realistic expectations, 4936; research, 7357; resident assistant satisfaction, 4135; resilience, 8148; role models, 10155; salesperson, 4139; salesperson self-evaluation, 4860; salience, 3620; 3621, 3638, 5900, 5901, 7368; satisfaction, 3173, 4131, 4137–4139, 4146, 4147, 4150–4160, 4164–4167, 4173–4175, 4216, 4221, 5902, 5903, 8149–8151, 8268, 10143–10145; satisfaction with union, 4213, 4214; search, 5332, 6728, 8152; self-efficacy, 6728–6732, 9344, 9345, 9348, 9349, 9352, 9353, 9349, 9367, 9677; self-esteem in, 4904, 4974; sense of competence, 4123; sex differences in work values, 5253; stress and strain, 4181, 4222; student-teachers, 4124;

student's exploration experiences, 5349; task satisfaction, 4204; teachers' attitudes toward teaching, 4331, 4332; transition, 5904, 9021; unemployment coping, 3952; values, 5222, 5223, 5229, 5233, 5239, 5249–5254; withdrawal, 5905, 7370; women, 1748; work experience outcomes, 4217, 4219; work experience scales, 4691; work motivation, 4743, 4744; work preferences, 5362; work-role salience, 5363; worker's family functioning, 4538. See also Job(s); Occupation(s); Vocational evaluation; Work

Caregiver: behavior, 7274; burden, 6393, 6394, 8476, 8809, 8881; conflict, 7927, 8922; depression, 4042; employment conflicts, 8833; interactions with children, 8538

Case history, 856

Categorical thinking, 9856

Categorization behavior, 623

Category width, 1271

Cathexis, body, 2043

Causal construct, 2177

Causality, 886: attributions, 9354–9356, 9390; explanations, 9608; individual responsibility, 9388; orientation, 9719; perception, 3181, 9540

Censorship, attitude toward, 1125, 6088

Cerebral palsy, 9329

Certainty, 502

Certification, counselor, 702

Chairman(ship): departmental, 657; functions, 657

Challenge, 5622, 5623: task, 1981; work, 8300

Change(s), 218, 484, 523, 624: adaptability, 5448, 7638; attitude toward, 92, 1129; dialect, 105; group processes, 5762; home economics behavior, 572; life, 2522; maintenance, university residence, 704; organizational, 9031, 9534; orientation, 1535; parenting practices, 8990;

political, 92; processes of, 2511, 7317, 10080, 10081; and psychotherapy, 10081, 10102; readiness, 8798; receptivity to, 301, 976, 6601; self-efficacy beliefs, 6110; social, 92; social, political and economic, 92; stages, 7329; teacher, 333; university policy, 3204; word meaning, 125

Character, 9793, 9794

Characteristics, college, 171

Cheating, 922, 6073, 6190, 6214: perceptions of, 6848

Checklist, symptom, 1663

Chemotherapy, 4416

Child(ren)(s), 377, 380, 402, 403, 445, 450, 451, 458, 467, 564, 577, 578, 622, 630, 633, 643, 655: abuse, 2815, 2846, 3350, 4395; academic anxiety, 2404; academic competence, 5391; academic motivation, 4738; academic performance predictors, 4223; academically gifted, 4261; achievement motivation, 4696, 4699; acquiescence-negativism, 843; action tendency, 4363, 4364; adaptive behavior, 8539; adjustment, 7614; affect, 7776, 9679; affect labeling, 6987; African, 1740; aggression, 946, 1840, 2277, 2437, 2878, 3453, 3464, 3498; aggressive behavior, 4969, 5179; of alcoholics, 6395, 6396, 6399; altruism, 962; antisocial behavior, 4399; anxiety, 3921, 5652, 7196, 7763, 7837–7839; assertive, 3464, 3465; associative response, 264; attitudinal range indicator, 497; at-risk 4-year-olds, 6052; attitude toward, 4271; attitude toward authority, 6114; attributional style, 4789, 4793; authoritarian, 3466; author recognition, 5369; autonomy, 2550, 2806; behavior, 28, 496, 1207, 1851, 1869, 1870, 2811, 2856, 4360, 4361, 4390, 4438, 4464, 4607, 6212, 6216, 7611, 8547, 10123; behaviorally difficult, 6466, 8522, 8542, 8543; behavior disorder

syndromes, 4346; beliefs, 2259; 4878; Black preschool, 377; book title recognition, 5392, 5393, 5394; causal attributions, 3205; centered, 1167; centeredness, 655; classroom adjustment, 2406; classroom behavior, 6218, 6219; classroom experience, 532; of clergy, 3937; coercive behavior, 2818; cognitive assessment, 2405, 7145; cognitive complexity, 2203; cognitive level, 2224, 2678, 7446; companion animal, 3984, 4798, 4799; competence, 2593, 3685, 3688, 3689, 9343; comprehension, 355; comprehension of print media, 4513; conceptual style, 603, 1905; conservatism, 1513; coping styles, 7616, 7617; counseling, elementary, 25, 28; creative behavior, 1926; creatively gifted, 615; creativity, 2940–2942, 4494, 6369; critical thinking strategies, 5157; curiosity, 723, 733; curriculum, 6540; daily coping, 5540; defensiveness, 5031; delay of reinforcement, 239; dependent-independent, 282; depression, 2450, 2465, 2502, 3783, 3896, 5462, 5478, 5479, 7612, 7618, 7651; development, 138, 625; development, psychosocial, 2945; development, responsibility, 762; disadvantaged, 7, 531, 621; disadvantaged, Mexican-American, 380, 384, 390; disadvantaged, Negro, 376; disadvantaged, preschool, causality, 886; disadvantaged, preschool consequential thinking, 885; disadvantaged, problem-solving, 894; disadvantaged, self-esteem, 830; disobedience, 953; disruptive, 397; disturbed, 38; divorce beliefs, 4529; drug use, 2819; echoic response, 7; egocentricism, 1443, 1485, 1503; ego strength, 3206; eight-year-old, 1771; elementary school, 101, 1043, 1136; elementary school anxiety, 933; emotional disturbance, 1082; empathy, 5221, 9912, 9913; entering school, 3; ethnic attitudes, 1184; expectations, 8813; exploratory behavior, 260; evaluation of teacher, 5294; everyday skills, 3672; expectations of aggressive behavior outcomes, 4892; fear, 2490, 3875, 5528, 7676; feelings, family, 41, 4530; feelings-judgments, 243; fifth grade, verbal absurdities, 895; fine-motor task development, 4504; first graders, anxiety, 948; first graders, vowel selection, 1045; five to ten years, 382; friendship expectancy, 5733; fourth and fifth grade, school attitudes, 155; fourth-sixth grade, cognitive style, 939; frustration, 2528; future time perspective, 772; gender attitudes, 6115; gifted, 1124, 3250; grandparent relationship, 6511; guilt, 964; handicapped peers, 4275; handwriting, 2373; health resources, 2414; helplessness, 3782, 3856; home environment, 4545, 4546, 4567, 4596; home stimulation, 1952; homework behavior, 6245; hopelessness, 2482, 3847; hospitalization behavior, 1230, 1488; hyperactive, 397, 2827, 2878; impulsive behavior, 6237; impulsive-reflective, 291; independence, 6445; innovative behavior, 1926; instrumental competence, 3677; intellectual ability, 888; intelligent vs. unintelligent behavior, 4397; intent judgment, 626; interaction aide, 577; intermediate level, science interest, 864; intermediate level, rating subjects, 871; interpersonal attraction, 55; interracial attitude, 1183; introversion-extroversion, 956; intrusive parenting, 4611; investigatory activity, 724;

judgment, 4116; knowledge of sexual abuse, 3682; language arts for, 277; learning, 17, 521, 2677; learning behavior, 4400; learning disabled, 2853; learning, teachers' perception, 2038; literacy, 3257; life satisfaction, 5684; locus of control, 754, 797, 799, 2041, 2092, 2101, 2146, 2148, 3182, 3183, 4887, 4888, 4924, 9360, 9361; loneliness, 2554, 2583, 3241, 3242, 4031, 5790, 7518, 7926, 8005, 8008, 8009, 8011; maltreatment, 5827; management confidence, 2051; manifest anxiety, 1478, 1493, 2524; maternal employment, 4523; mathematics anxiety, 3717; maturity, 621, 4510, 4511, 4516; mentally retarded, 1759; minority, 502; moral judgment, 977, 2311; moral values, 978; mother's perception of temperament, 5039; motivation to achieve, 718, 737; multitalent, 4861; name calling, 8029; negative affect, 5631, 9749, 9750; negative self-evaluation, 4886; normative beliefs, 535; obesity, 6734; one-year-old, 649; painful medical therapy, 4600; parent child communication, 640, 646, 654, 3005, 3034; parent ratings of feelings, 4528; parent relationship, 6405; parental acceptance, 4592, 4593; parental perception, 6698; parents' daily reports, 4602; parents' satisfaction with, 4598; parents, emotionally disturbed, 148; part-whole perception, 19; peer relations, 1104, 2601; perception of competence, 9489, 9490, 9517; perception of parental opinion, 6152, 6186; perception of parents, 6397; perceptions, 659, 3260; perception, auditory-visual, 1414; perception, control, 3252; perception, environment, 178; perception, mother behavior, 761; peer nominations, 4061; peer

relations, 4053; perceived competence in, 4895; perceived self-efficacy, 4917; perceived social acceptance, 4052; perceived social support, 4620; perception, 4366; perception of academic failure, 4697; perception of control, 4790; perception of parental behavior, 4536; perception of parental conflict, 4591; perception of social skills, 4792; perception of teacher behavior, 4469; performance attribution, 3268; performance orientation, 7465; persistence, 6663; personality, 842, 927, 1450; personality assumptions, 5023; personality characteristics, 5028; phonics, 2398; physical complaints, 5480; pictorial attitude, 1770; play behavior, 2861, 2862; play socialization, 61; playfulness, 4362; posttraumatic stress, 7613, 7800; preference, 1464; prejudice, 1176; preliterate, 1812; preschool, 383, 397, 425, 459, 477, 616–618, 635, 1397, 6210; preschool-aged, 2195; preschool anxiety, 2509; preschool cognitive functioning, 59; preschool disadvantaged, 403; preschool disadvantaged, problem solving, 892, 894; preschool frustration, 1229; preschool prejudice, 1174; preschool problem behavior, 4427; primary grades, 718; problem behavior, 1844, 2799, 2808, 2816, 2831, 6268; problem solving, 893, 1468, 3436, 5120; prosocial behavior, 963, 6193; provocative, 397; psychiatric pathology, 2514, 6215; rational thinking in, 5124; readiness, 1118; reading readiness, 4227; rearing, 553, 1304, 2855, 2971, 3042; rearing attitudes, 496, 1148, 3032; rearing problems, 38, 8811, 8812; reasoning, 3418, 3441; reinforcement, 1853; relatedness, 8051; reporting parental behavior, 6398;

response styles, 843; retarded, flexibility, 923; reward preference, 261; role taking, 1236; school adjustment, 7488, 7489; school age, 629; school motivation, 731; school perceptions, 4951; school-related self-concept, 4954; security, 3037; self-assessment of social skills, 3980; self-concept, 230, 807, 3186, 3213, 3221, 3232, 3254, 3279, 3297, 4791, 4956; self-concept, poverty, 798; self-concept, primary, 763; self-control, 3185, 4466, 8675, 8676; self-enhancement−self-derogation, 843; self-esteem, 458, 2039, 3197, 3206, 4975, 9518; self-regulation, 4345; self-social construct, 434; self-perception, 3187; self-regulation, 6300, 6301, 8584; self-reported social support, 3981, 5866; self-worth, 6759; sex role, 881, 3188; silent, 397; sixth grade, anxiety, 947; social acceptance, 2593, 3965; social anxiety, 4075, 8077, 8078; social attitudes, 4276; social behavior, 842, 964, 5811, 8659, 8708−8710; social class, 3189; social competence, 2567, 2606, 5707, 8084, 8086, 8120; social desirability, 251, 1708, 2557; social intelligence, 2564; social reinforcement, 725; social responsibility, 58; social situation, 2613; spatial conservation, 1061; stimulus, 1852; stress, 2536, 3184; study conflict, 1466; -teacher, interpersonal perceptions, 2076; teaching rating, 1063; teacher relationships, 5405; teacher values of disadvantaged, 990; temperament, see, temperament, child and infant; therapy, 10060; text anxiety, 32, 1076, 1635; twenty-four and thirty-six months, 641; tolerance of individual differences, 3963; Type A, 3450, 3489, 4414, 5193; unhappy, 397; verbal

absurdities, 895; word knowledge, 6363; work beliefs, 7226; work strategies, 7144; work values, 2317, 5234; working parents, 4538; young, 349, 370, 381
Child care, 4527: attitude toward work and, 4265; infant behavior, 4422
Childhood, 625: adult descriptions, 6334; early, 623; early education, 658, 678; middle, 412
Chinese, personality traits, 9940
Choice, 3390: vocational, 1574, 1587, 1594, 10172
Christianity, 4259, 7216: attitudes toward, 6095, 7212, 7213, 8400
Chronicity, 421
Church: attitudes, 80, 3062; faith-religion, 1668
Cigarettes, 1122
Circadian rhythms, 7166, 7183, 7186, 9921
Citizenship, organizational, 8628−8632
Clark-Trow subtypes, 714
Class(room): activities, 1380; activities, new, 564; adjustment, 2406; atmosphere, 1027; attendance, 3698; behavior, 390, 565, 566, 574, 578, 581, 681, 718, 1108, 1209, 1211, 1237, 1854, 1855, 1878, 1885, 2820−2823, 2828, 2865, 2880, 2882, 3056, 8523; cheating, 6214; climate, 583, 3100, 6218, 6219, 6322, 6580, 9023; college student perceptions, 6543; competition versus cooperation, 9809; environments, 680, 686, 1324, 1539, 3057, 3058, 3078, 3093, 3094, 9024, 9029, 9054, 9085, 9181; equity, 10056; experience, child's, 532; goal maintenance, 6761; integrated, 2189; interaction, 1261, 1894, 1897; involvement, 5406; life, 9025; management strategy, 880; methods, junior high school, 700; misconduct, 578; peer performance, 575; physical environment, 6592; planes and procedures, 679;

process, 681; quality, 3116; questions, 600; status, 659, 1474; structure, 1969; success, beliefs about, 6107
Classification: job, 3073, 3095; skills, 627, 2946; socioeconomic, 1471
Classifying, 2215
Claustrophobia, 5482, 5483
Clerical, 2178: family, 6516; text, 73
Client: adherence, 10088; assessment, 1080; attachment, 10032; attitude, counseling, 999; beliefs, 3190; centered counseling, 249; change, 691; expectancy, 3191, 2308, 3210; expectations about counseling, 4819−4822, 4833, 4927, 5291; growth, 646; insightfulness, 10033; perception, 227, 309; perception, problem solving, 764; reaction, 589; reaction to interview, 998; resistance, 7279; satisfaction, 182, 999, 2335, 3059, 4635−4637, 4684, 5261, 5265, 5266, 1035, 1036; self-rating, 310; therapist, 2903; verbal behavior system, 587
Climate: bank, 3054; classroom, 3100, 6580, 9023; counseling, 999; group safety, 9052; job, 1967; learning, 1323; organization, 1308, 3050, 3097−3099, 3102, 6581, 6598, 6610, 9026, 9093, 9148, 9168; perceptions, 6782; school, 3108, 9022; work, 6622
Closed-mindedness, 413, 2292
Closure; need, 9745, 9746; speed, 1612, 1617
Clothing, 7060, 7067: deprivation, perception of, 4894, 5224; interest, 9810, 10152; orientation, 875; quality, 9806; values, 5224
Cocaine, motivation, 9255
Codependency, 8403
Coding, 2215
Coffee, 1122
Cognit(ion)(ive), 3, 1255: ability, 2678, 2961, 7448; affect, 404; agoraphobic, 2438; anxiety, 7623−7625; anxiety assessment, 3787, 5457, 5485, 5486, 5490;

appraisal, 8155; assessment, children, 2405, 7145, automatic thoughts, 5119, 5463, 5464; Beck's cognitive triad, 3788; behavioral changes, 572; behavior, infant, 1287; behavior, student, 568; belief systems, 4492; career decision-making, 5118; catastrophic, 5473; child critical thinking strategies, 5157; child problem-solving skills, 5120; children, 8784, 9367; in claustrophobic situations, 5482; coherence in daily living, 3931; competence, 6835, 8785; complexity, 47, 1279, 1465, 1913, 2229, 3408, 3421; complexity, children, 2203; complexity, interpersonal, 433; complexity, simplicity, 433; complexity, vocational, 707; components, 1209; conceptual level, 4492, 4493; control, 913, 924, 1506, 2289; couple functioning, 4533; dealing with strangers, 4097; decision-making needs, 4702; in depression, 3784, 5488, 8799; development, 623, 627, 635, 4515, 5149, 6378, 8799; differentiation, 2230; difficulty, 1670, 8550; distortion avoidance, 3811; distortion in rheumatoid arthritis, 3786; educational objectives, 5138; egocentricism, 1491; emotional autonomy, 4000, 4001; error, 3192, 5028, 6735; evaluation of display formats, 285; flexibility, 923, 7167; functioning, 260, 1121, 2213; functioning, adolescents, 605; functioning, preschool, 59; future expectation, 3845–3847, 4922; hemisphere specialization, 5129, 5160; home environment, 642; hope, 3844; impairment, 2681; individual differences, 5142; information processing style, 5106, 5116, 5128, 5159; inner speech, 6250; intellectual development, 4506; intelligent vs. unintelligent behavior, 4397; intention to quit job,

4141, 4212, 4215; intrusive thoughts, 5122, 5487; irrational thinking, 5125, 5154; job outcomes appraisal, 4144; knowledge of, 3669; lapses in control, 5121; learning, 175, 5131–5133, 5135–5137, 5153; level, children, 2224; logic of confidence, 4029; logical thinking, 5158; mental states, 5590; metacognitive awareness, 6056, 9876; moral reasoning, 5126, 5140, 5232; need, 3367, 4725–4727, 7029, 7030, 9257, 9747; objectivism, 5058; obsessive-compulsive, 3893; optimism, 4863; in oral examination, 5424; pessimism, 3834; predisposition to depression, 3813; preference, 2179, 3391, 3410; problem solving styles, 5134; process, 265, 3193, 3423; processing, children, 1905; propositional logic, 5147; proverb interpretation, 5148; quick assessment in patient-care setting, 5123; rational thinking in children, 5124; reflective judgment, 5149, 5150; regulation 3669; restructuring, 9858; rigidity, 5175, 5176, 5184, 5206; schizotypal, 6220; sense of coherence, 6940; skills assessment, 5372; social studies strategies, 5151; speed, 7142; spontaneity, 8778, 9859; stimulation, children, 8818; strategies, 9860; structure, 218; student strategies, 7117; style, 1479, 1498, 3369; style, field dependence, 815; style, flexibility, 939; style, fourth-sixth graders, 939; subjectivism, 5076; suicidal ideation, 3917, 3925, 3942; during surgery, 6939; teacher decision-making, 5152; tempo, 603, 942; temporal lobe signs, 5143, 5155; testwiseness, 5127; therapy, 10037; vocational maturity, 1040, 1938

Cohabitation, off campus, 181
Coherence sense, 9611, 9612
Cohesion, 7930: gross, 1710; family, 8836, 8839, 8840;

group, 1710, 1711, 2569; social, 8275
Colleagues, evaluation, 1009
Collective: bargaining, 1773, 6542; negotiations, 538, orientation, 8156; self-esteem, 7931
Collectivism, 5525, 5765, 7228, 7932, 8883, 9953, 9970, 9971, 9973, 9974
College/University: absenteeism, 3698; achievement, 480; achievement motivation, 4695; activities, 683; adjustment, 22, 2401, 3695, 3696, 3701, 3703, 3709, 3735, 5403, 5408, 5421, 5432, 6482, 7491, 7550, 7551, 7553; adaptation, 5422, 5431; admissions, 660, 9088; alienation, 5443; application, 553; aptitude, 1120; assertiveness, 3467–3469, 5166, 7168; attendance, goals and purposes, 719; business major curriculum objectives, 661; campus dissent, 1098; characteristics, 117, 180; choice, 7068; classes, teacher effect, 333; classroom and social involvement, 3699; commitment, 206, 7512, 7548; community, sense of, 4674; counseling center effectiveness, 4638; counseling needs, 4999; courses, attitude toward, 151, 7069; course evaluation, 1024, 1540, 3064; departments, 3067; educational outcomes, 9038; environment, 165, 172, 177, 179, 184, 187, 212, 672, 675, 683, 1311, 4633, 4686; equal opportunity climate, 4675; ethnic/racial environment, 9180; expectations, 662, 6750; experience, 675; extent of sexual harassment, 4676; freshmen, 353, 364, 441, 632, 662; freshmen, academic status, 904; freshmen adjustment, 2420; freshmen, attitudes, 1135; freshmen, characteristics, 67; freshmen, commitment, 5410; freshmen, locus of control, 221; freshmen, need achievement, 726; freshmen, socioeconomic

status, 904; freshmen, university experience, 904; freshmen, values, 303, 904; freshmen year, 628; hassles, 7506; head residents, behavior, 1863; hope, 7509; importance, 3398; instructor effectiveness, 2338; Latino student, 6538; learning environment, 9091; major prestige, 896; major satisfaction, 872, 876; mathematics anxiety, 2418, 3716; mathematics efficacy, 3720; men, personal preference, 258; opinions, 231; orientation, 879; perception of academic life, 4668; performance assessment, 5407; performance expectations, 740; performance predictors, 3738; persistence, 7533; presenting problems, 3857; routine, 409; satisfaction, 212, 3704, 3727, 4647; science anxiety, 5427; sexual harassment, extent of, 4676; social support, 7495; stress, 7492, 7493, 7494, 7496, 7809; student(s), 399, 481, 527, 609, 624, 667, 698; student academic integration, 2399; student alcohol use, 4457; student alienation, 1091, 1092, 1110, 3747, 4111; student anger, 3759; student, anxious, 286, 2604, 2605, 5636; student athletes, 5566; student, attitude, 743, 1151, 1152; student, attitude, CAI, 151; student attitude change, 92; student attitude toward counseling, 4338; student attitude patterns, 222; student attributional style, 4760; student behavior, 2881; students, Black, 2909; student burnout, 2420, 3723; student career indecision, 2809; students' career planning, 2228, 3653; student distress, 5419; student dropout risk, 3702; student identity, 9311; student roles, 9370; student self-efficacy, 9369; students failing and superior, 16; students' family structure, 4563; students' fear of success,

2412, 2471; students' goal and expectations, 719, 3049; students' housing needs, 867; students' interpersonal adjustment, 2409; students, Jewish, 503, students' knowledge of occupations, 3678; student's leadership, 2682; students, level of aspiration, 740; students, life changes, 1942; students, life events, 2551; students' locus of control, 3194, 3234, 4805; student marijuana, use, 1131; students, Mexican American, 3966; students, minority, predictors of success for, 3724, 3725; student motivation, 743; student needs, 5438; student occupational choice, 719; student optimism, 2408; student parental attachments, 4594; student peer-rating, 2556; student perceptions, 706, 6543; student performance, 1856; student personality, 16; student premarriage counseling, 147; students, reading comprehension, 1615; student relationships, 2588; student response acquiescence, 930; student satisfaction, 663, 1961, 2407; students' self-concept, 2035, 3300, 3305, 3321; student self-efficacy expectations, 4797, 9369; student self-esteem, 816, 2139; student, self-interest, male, 199; student self-rated adaptation, 3700; student, self-regulation, 145; student separation from parents, 4613; student situational anxiety, 26; student social integration, 2399, 3708, 3748; student stress, 2415, 2423, 2424, 3691, 3710, 3789, 5489; student success, 1072, 1073; student, suicide, 1088, 2530; students, text anxiety, 1634, 2302, 2303; students' thoughts, 2403; student time perspective, 782, 783, 790, 805, 834; student transfer, 511; students, unassertive, 286; students' values development, 5248;

suicidal risk, 7626; teacher effectiveness, 1541, 1542, 1551, 1562–1565, 1569, 1570, 1572; teacher perceptions, 785; teaching patterns, 7312; two year, 171; two year, four year and ideal, 548; Type A behavior, 7203; women, 1303; women, equalitarianism, 1177; women, inner-outer directedness, 789

Collegial(ity): faculty, 5920; maintenance of standards, 1815

Colonialism, 512

Color meaning, 1774

Combat: behavior, 2825; experience, 6220; stress, 2454, 7720, 7752

Comfort, counselor, 999

Commitment, 214, 4105, 5622, 5623, 7373–7375, 7987, 8733: affective, 5454, 5455, 10129; career, 3611, 3612, 5307, 5308, 10132–10134, 10205–10208; college, 206, 5410, 7350–7359, 7371; community, 3983; to coworkers, 3990; cultural, 1092; employment, 3626, 10147; to goals, 4706; job, 5916: marital, 6401; military, 10171; nursing, 7396; occupational, 7399; organizational, 2014–2016, 3541, 3609, 3624, 3625, 3643–3648, 5322, 5334, 5336–5343, 10129, 10175, 10177–10187, 10205; to physical activity, 5081; professional, 5344–5346, 7422, 7423, 10190–10192; to racial separatism, 3977; romantic, 7936, 8063; sports, 10198, 10199; teacher(s), 5352; team, 10199; union, 4110, 5320, 5321, 5353, 7372, 7432–7435; vocational, 3656

Communalism, 982, 9306

Communication(s), 98–105, 523, 568, 585–601, 1060, 1247–1268, 1887–1902, 8740–8773: adolescent, 6473; affective, 8740; apprehension, 2917, 8762; competence, 2922, 2924, 6338; decision conflict and cooperation, 4480; defensive, 1250; dyads, 2905;

effectiveness, 99; expectations, 601; facilitative, 1889, 1890; in families, 4525, 8747; feedback, 2908; here-and-now/there-and-then disclosures, 6340; high school student's verbal, 3675; impression management, 4764; index, 76; in-group/out-group, 4480; interactions, 6343; interpersonal, 1900, 2914, 2920, 6336; interpersonal competence, 4483; interviewer, 2906; marital, 2972, 3017, 6459; mutual, 98; negotiation, 2918; nonverbal, 6350; between nurses, 4478; organization(al), 1898, 1901, 2919; pantomime, 6359; parent-child, 103, 640, 1295, 1297, 2897, 8745, 8755, 8757; patterns, 597; principal teacher, 688; referential, 2923; respect, 2344; satisfaction, 2904, 5842, 6344, 6354; self-disclosure, 4486–4490, 6355; self-efficacy, 8761; self-evaluation, 6356; skills, 175, 2913, 6353; spousal, 8744, 8819; suggestion, 2902; supervisors, 1023, 2915, 2916, 2926; teacher-parent, 8758; teacher-student, 2911; team, 6358; verbal-nonverbal, 2921; workplace, 4479

Community college: aptitude, 75; articulation, 3163; counselor training, 664; faculty attitudes, 1159; freshmen, 472; public, 508; sex role, 3389

Community: employee commitment, 1996; judgment, 1312; participation, 1454; satisfaction, 3060; sense of, 5844, 8067; service, 8378, 9278; violence exposure, 9030

Companion, imaginary, 1397

Comparing, 2215

Compensation, 663

Competenc(e)(y), 659, 3317, 6737: academic, 2421, 5391; adolescents, 3698, 8707, 9602; behavior, 432; children, 2593, 3260, 3685, 9343; children, young, 4052; children's self-concept, 4917; children's social skills self-assessment, 3980;

cognitive, 6825; communicative, 2922, 2924, 6338; consumer, 3681; counselor, 3571; daily living, 3672, 3681, 3791, 3926, 4367; dating, 3992, 3997, 5741; educational, 767; employees, 9487; female professional, 975, 3243; general social, 636; hockey, 6765; interpersonal, 446, 1724, 6970, 7977, 7978; language, 380, 384; leader, 1555; managerial, 3586; motor, 6805; multicultural, 8020; occupational, 4123; parenting, 4608, 8931; perceived, 6836, 9487–9490; perception of, in children, 4895; personal, 1105; physical, 6837; premorbid, 2594; presenter, 3591; problem solving, 3681; psychosocial, 7599, 7600, 8120; self-efficacy beliefs, 4986, 4989; self-perception, 6826, 6970, 6971; sense of, 2070, 6941, 9613; social, 2567, 6971; social, teacher rated, 4077; students', 2349, 6762; students' social, 5010; teacher, 7327, 7328; teaching, 1015, 1025; therapist, 5262

Competit(ion)(ive), 713, 1775, 1802, 2826, 3412, 5738: anxiety, 3790, 5212, 5491; athletic, attitude toward, 4339; attitude, 8410, 8444; attitude toward, 4286, knowledge, 2928; in sports, 6312; trait self-confidence, 5217; worries, 7862, 7880

Competitive(ness), 1720, 4700, 5183, 6219, 7169, 9914: academic, 9905, 9909; achievement, 989; classroom, 9809; hypercompetitiveness, 4711, 6318, 9905, 9909, interpersonal, 9902, mental readiness, 7751; orientation, 9941; in sports, 7866, 9627, 9941, 9942

Complexity, 614: cognitive, 1279, 3408; conceptual, 120, 1421, 1499, 1509; interpersonal, 47; perceptions, 768; sentence, 7; tolerance, 612; work, 268; vocational, 336

Compliance, 6222: employees, 8157; smoking ban, 5896; supervisors, 1005

Composition: ability, 370; evaluation, 1031; written, 370

Comprehension, 5, 15, 349, 355, 1735, 5374: age four, 134; anaphora, 5, 2370; counselors, 380, 384; humor, 2378; inferential reading, 1605; languages, 355; listening, 2688; literal reading, 1609; moral, 3556; oral, 365; reading, 14, 20, 1055, 1062, 2688; reading, college students, 1615; sentence, 5; social-moral(s) concepts, 1599, 2308; syntactic, 383; verbal, 1904, 1912, 1915; vocabulary, 365

Compulsiveness, 3493, 3497, 7025, 8544, 8552

Computer science, 2679

Computer(s): anxiety, 3705, 3774, 3792–3797, 5908–5911, 7497; aptitude, 4224, 4225; attitude toward, 115, 152, 2724, 2726–2729, 4278, 4280–4285, 4287, 5907, 6062, 6116, 8338–8340, 8364; aversion, 9851; cognitive learning, 9857; concerns, 5914; operational hassles, 3796, 3797; perceived self-efficacy, 4800, 6739, 6740; perceptions about, 4830, 4831; playfulness, 6223; self-efficacy perceptions, 9371; stress, 5912, 5913; training program reactions, 9151

Concentration, 645

Concept(s): anthropological, 1269; attainment, 2924; educational research, 1746; formation, 120, 2213; identification, 884, 2928; justice, 381; masculine-feminine, 114; meaning, 106–125, 602–605, 1269–1279, 1903–1919, 2930, 8774–8777; number, 2939; occupational, 1909; people, 502; relationships, 2936; social work, 1277; task, multiple category, 358–363; unpleasant, 35

Conceptual: complexity, 120, 1499, 1509, 2934;

development, 135;
differentiation, 1273;
flexibility, 923; set, 1068;
structure, 122, 604; style, 603,
1272, 1906; style, children,
1905; tempo, 604, 1919, 2211
Concrete(ness): abstractness,
2200; experience, 2216;
reasoning abilities, 2227
Conditions, job, 1404, 8247
Condom use, 8379, 9373
Conduct: classroom, 578;
problems, 8554
Confidence, 6018, 9317: anxiety
and, 5490; career, 9344, 9345;
child management, 2051;
examinations, 9391;
information processing, 2907;
lack of, 515; learning, 9441;
occupational perception, 4172;
reading, 3276; science and
engineering student, 3733;
social, 4103; student, 6720
Configurations, part-whole, 13
Conflict(s), 796: adolescent-
parent, 6453, 6530;
approaches to, 7939; child
study, 1466; coworkers, 8262;
couples, 6403, 6443; dating,
5742; efficacy, 9374; ethical,
3530; family 3003; group, 445;
handling, 1865, 5810; home-
career, 2228, 9394, 9395, 9430,
9658–9667, 9672, 9673;
identify, 949; interpersonal,
523, 1950, 2573, 4015, 5769;
intragroup, 5783, 8505; locus
of, 2085; management, 4003,
4480, 5091; marital, 2973,
8903; model, 616; mode of
handling, 1848; mother-
daughter, 6467; non-, 481;
parental, 6446, 6471, 6500,
8022, 8821–8824, 8894, 8895;
personal, 2208; positive choice,
2208; psychodynamic, 5621;
resolution, 1857, 9003; role,
1687, 2357, 2526, 2641, 3002,
3289, 3290, 3292, 3341, 5617,
6883–6891, 9548–9553, 9556;
spouse, 6447, 8903; tactics,
8555, 8556; 8822; work-family,
6432, 6433, 6437, 6448, 6523–
6528; 9394, 9395, 9430, 9658–
9667, 9672, 9673; workplace,
5769, 8301

Conformity, 287, 967, 2290:
types, 1731
Confucianism, 7217
Congregation, satisfaction, 3062
Congruence, 220, 227, 309, 431,
1538, 2353: cognitive, 34;
teacher-student, 175
Conscience development, 638,
8794
Consensus, semantic, 1276
Consequences of situations, 266:
anxiety, 5459
Consequential thinking, 885
Conservationism, 1776
Conservat(ism)(ive), 555, 1518,
1777, 2257, 2258, 2305, 2731,
2732, 6117: children, 1513;
dimension, mother's, 2313;
economic, 9958; hopelessness
determinant, 9388; -liberalism,
95, 280, 1527; -liberalism,
college students, 1835;
-radicalism, 1821
Consideration, 688
Constrict(ed)(ion), 408: flexibility,
924; impulsivity, counselors,
961
Constructs: personal, 1305; role,
816
Consultant: effectiveness, 10039;
reading, 1334
Consultation, 730, 2191, 7282
Consumer(s): alienation, 1700;
assertiveness; behavior, 4370,
4450, 5105; environmental
concerns, 6311; motivations,
4883; susceptibility to
influence, 9811, 9903; value
consciousness, 10007
Consumption/production, 302
Contemporary issues, 485, 498
Content, 596, 689
Contentment, 3828
Continuity, residence, 466
Contraception, 3987
Control(s), 655, 2317, 5622,
5623: action-state orientation,
849; of anger, 5168;
appraisals, 9376; behavioral,
6270, 8641, 8806; child
perception of, 4790, 7822;
cognitive, 913, 924, 1506; in
counseling, 7314; decision-
making, 6828; desire for, 7072,
9701; employee perceptions,
9111; environment, 1997;

homicide, 970; imagery, 2052,
6969; internal, 238; internal-
external, 467, 810;
interpersonal, 2075, 4113; job,
5992, 5999, 6569, 7979;
maternal, 1954; motor impulse,
386; multidimensional
assessment, 4096; organization,
1962; orientation, 9375;
parental, 145, 5743, 8946,
8981; perception, 239, 6828–
6834, 9424, 9494, 9607, 9649;
personal, 1415; problems,
behavior, 403; procrastination
attribution, 4802;
psychological, 8981, 8982;
pupil, 810, 1523, 3105; social,
52, 163, 4054; self, 6293, 6294,
7044; sense of, 6942, 6943;
social, in school, 100; student
control ideologies, 4314, 4434,
4928; teacher beliefs, 6868,
9842; teachers' self-perceived,
6026; time, 6827; workplace,
5981, 9142; in work-family
conflict, 6406. See also Locus
of control
Controlling-punitive, 652
Controvers(ial)(y): attitude, 2733;
lectures, campus, 586
Conventionalism, 2253, 2734
Cooperation, 338, 397, 1775,
1802, 3412, 5738, 8558:
attitude toward, 1371;
classroom, 9809; student, 24,
6219; subordinate-supervisor,
5917
Coordination, 575: general
dynamic, 348; general static,
348
Coparenting, 8827
Coping, 5492, 5663: ability, 5445,
7572, 7803; adequacy, 215;
adolescents, 7576; with anxiety,
3920; athletes, 9314; behavior,
2830, 7630; cancer patients,
3778; with career decision-
making, 5323; with change,
7638; child, 3697, 7616, 7617,
7717; classroom, 1211; college
students, 7552; conceptual
process approach, 3957;
control and escape dimensions,
5496; daily activities, 5538–
5540; difficult situations, 3799;
environment, 1095; family,

2984, 4535, 6416; gifted
students, 5670; with
harassment, 7639; household,
6439; humor, 3798, 5493.
7631; jealousy, 4402; job loss,
8160, 8161; in marriage, 4581;
mechanisms, 3355;
occupational, 6037; with pain,
3802; perception of others'
helpfulness, 4115; problem-
focused, 7806; self-control
behavior, 6294; self-report,
7847; situation-specific, 5497;
in sports, 7637, 7860;
strategies, 1085, 2974, 3801,
3811, 3860, 3956–3958, 5498,
5499, 5696–5700; 7633, 7634–
7636; 7710; style, 3803, 5494,
5495, 5541, 5637;
unemployment, 3952, 4125;
work-family conflict, 6410
Correctional center, 1202
Cosmopolitanism orientation,
2306
Counselee behavior, 427
Counseling, 699, 7070: addiction,
10022; appropriateness, 409,
1336; attitude toward, 2698,
2708, 2788, 6082, 6125, 8336;
attitudes of Blacks, 999;
career, 7272, 8336; center,
409, 703, 1313; client attitude,
999; client beliefs, 3190; client
expectations, 3191, 3208–3210,
6748, 6749; client reaction,
311; climate, 999, 2335; college
students, 7514; control in,
7314; cross-cultural, 10046;
disadvantaged youth, 27;
effects of, 689; elementary
children, 25, 28; elementary
school, 70, 671; evaluation,
1000, 3063, 7321–7326;
expectations, 2058, 3198, 6872,
9392; follow up, 1010; goals,
1358; group, 10051; help-
seeking behaviors, 6645, 7627,
9227; important events, 7302;
individual, 43; influence, 258;
information, 2374; interview,
student rating, 699; inventory,
689; marriage, 146, 240, 1349;
for mentally retarded, 7097;
micro, 10, 85; multicultural
awareness, 6807, 8434, 10070,
10071; need for, 1689;

outcome, 34, 500, 7277, 7284,
10040; parental, post-surgical,
5612; peer, 6823, 7313;
perceptions, 7269, 7270;
practicum evaluation, 1003;
preference, 3409; pre-marital,
147; quality, 10047, 10094;
rating of, 311; rehabilitation,
692, 1057; relationship(s),
1003, 1268, 2335; relationship,
perceptions of, 2037; religion
and, 7219; residence vs.
nonresidence, 546; satisfaction,
3564, 7287, 10035, 10036,
10094; self-evaluation, 328;
sensitivity-repression, 921;
session impact, 10095–10100;
skills, 1543, 2343, 3578;
student-student, 1000;
supervision, 10109, 10110;
termination, 5614, 6327;
underachievers, 1069;
vocational, 670; working
alliance, 10127, 10128
Counselor(s), 427, 484, 702,
2909: activity, 584; affirmative
behavior, 9304; appraisal
position, 665; attitudes, 89,
309, 560, 1173; attitudes
toward minorities, 8373;
attractiveness, 2336, 2341,
2342; behavior, 1543, 3325,
3565, 7281, 7300; career, 7346;
certification, teaching
requirement, 702; client,
2899–2901; client perception,
1372; comfort, 999, 2335;
competence, 3571, 7285;
construction-impulsivity, 961;
contracts, 665; cultural
attitudes, 8380, 10069; cultural
competence, 7297, 7311;
dogmatism, 7198; education,
255; education, graduate,
1004; effectiveness, 307, 312,
316, 325, 1001, 1002, 1057,
1559, 2335, 3566, 3567, 3569,
7286, 10041, 10042; empathy,
309, 3505, 3506; ethical
discrimination, 969; ethnicity
preferences, 9812; evaluation,
999, 1021, 7278; evaluation,
residence hall, 1006, 1019;
expectancies, 6872; experience,
1004; expertness, 2336, 2341,
2342; facilitative conditions,

2344; function, 232; high
school, 612, 660; homophobia,
6133; impulsivity-constriction,
961; interpersonal relations,
1003; interest and effort, 1003;
interview behavior, 584;
nonverbal behavior, 2351;
orientation, 2340;
paraprofessional residence
hall, 2354; perception of
counseling, 3200; perception of
residence, 1020; perceptions
of, 10042, 10043; performance,
2339, 3599, 10041, 10042;
personal characteristics, 1004;
philosophy, 968; preference,
1544, 3392, 7290; professional
responsibilities, 314, 1003;
qualification, 687; rating, 317,
3572, 3573, 3595, 7283, 7291–
7293; rehabilitation
effectiveness, 1561;
reinforcement, 1545;
restrictive-nonrestrictive, 2163;
role, 332, 820, 3195, 3199; role
concepts, 313; selection, 1004;
self-concept, 822, 1426; self-
efficacy, 9377; self-evaluation,
6741; self-rating, 769; service,
820; stress, 2620; student,
1021; tasks, 837; theory
preference, 54; therapeutic
strategies, 10125; trainee, 596,
1250, 1317, 10087; trainee's
effectiveness, 2337; training,
3568, 3570, 7289; training,
community college, 664;
trustworthiness, 2336, 2341,
2342; undergraduate residence,
2355; verbal behaviors, 2351;
verbal response, 588; viewed
by students, 993
Countertransference, 7294, 7295,
10044
Counting, 345
Couples: conflict resolution,
6403, 6443; married, 648;
partner satisfaction, 5833;
problem solving, 8819,
relationship
quality, 8992
Courage, social and existential,
1832
Course(s), 527, 667: academic
and vocational, 75; attitude,
2735; evaluation, 168, 666–

668, 698, 1546, 1547, 3064, 7296, 9170, 10045; expectation, 3158; nursing, 3639, 3641; perceived instrumentality, 9420; rating, college, 1024; satisfaction, 175; structure, 667

Courtship, 2597

Coworker(s): conflicts, 8262; esteem, 1458; satisfaction with, 8271, 8272; social integration, 8276

Creative(ly): activity, 1921, 2940; attitudes, 130; behavior, 531; behavior, child's, 1926; behavior, disadvantaged, 1922; behavior, underlying elements, 2168; gifted adolescents, 1935; gifted adults, 615, 1935; gifted children, 615; ideas, physics, 1930; inquisitiveness, 578; motivation, 607; person, 1929; personality, 620; potential, engineers, 1933; potential, scientists, 1933; predisposition, 1928; productions, 130, 613; remote associates, 2941; students, 2942; thinking, 1924; thinking, strategies, 615

Creativity, 126–133, 281, 296, 606–620, 688, 861, 1280–1283, 1885, 1920–1935, 4494, 4495, 6365, 6366, 6367, 6369, 8778–8783: differences, 132; disadvantaged, 1283; elementary children, 1927, 1932; encouragement, 487; humor and, 6368; ideational, 619; identification, 133, 1280; leadership, 1925; open elementary classroom, 1963; and organizational climate, 9167; personality, 8779; self-efficacy assessment, 4967; student, 36, 303; styles, 8780; teachers' fostering, 8559; traits, 3386; women, 840

Credibility, 1888, 4372, 4373, 6347, 6348: source manipulation, 6357; supervisor, 1556

Credit card use, attitudes, 8341

Crime: attitudes toward offenders, 6157; fear of, 3819, 7670

Criminal psychopathy, 2518

Crises, 628

Critical: evaluation, 369; differences, 981; interview behavior, 1864

Criticism: anxiety, 3822; irrational beliefs, 4804; perceptions of, 9495; response to, 4420; sensitivity to, 7547

Cross-cultural: adjustment, 7942; attitude, 1153; counseling, 8380, 10046

Cue interpretations, 1340

Cultur(al)(e): affiliation, 7944; awareness, 10069; competence, 8020; and counseling, 10070, 10071; estrangement, 1700, 1701, 7957; identity, 5891; internationally-mobile adolescents, 7055; knowledge assessment, 5373; leadership style, 6272; mistrust, 2560; novelty, 7948; organizational, 6583, 9095, 9097, 9985; orientation, 9956, 9957; tolerance, 7947; values, 516, 7498

Culturally disadvantaged: children, 531; intelligence, 72

Culture fair intelligence, 468

Curiosity, 233, 260, 716, 730, 742, 1208, 1778, 3152: academic, 1984; boys, 63; children, 723, 733; -related behavior, 1818; self-appraisal, 2021

Current issues, 498

Curriculum, 502, 527: attitude, 501; for children, 6540; choice, motivation, 720; classification by college men, 184; content, 664; development, 1314; evaluation of social welfare, 162; high school, 473; objectives, 694; people, 502; perceptions, 694; priorities, Black history, 157; ratings of, 706; use, 501

Customer service, 3066, 7071, 9130, 9032

Cynicism, 1103, 2253, 5740: freedom from, 481; police, 943; political, 537

Czechoslovakia: social stratification, 268

Daily activity, 567, 3075, 5539,

5540, 5541: chronic pain and, 3751; modern life, 4656; self-report, 8561; work experience and, 4219

Data: collecting, 2215; entry stress, 5918

Dating, 503, 593, 2603, 5744, 7913: assertiveness, 7170; behavior, 253; competence, 5741, 7949; conflict, 5742; marriage, 503; motivation, 3128, 9202; parental control, 5743, perspective-taking, 5820; rape, 6077, 8551, 8562; satisfaction, 5842, 7913

Daydreams, 7019: assessment, 3354; attitude, 2737; inventory, 858

Deactivation, 417: -activation, 1839

Deafness, 6148

Dean(s) attitudes, and admissions practice, 553

Death: acceptance, 2458; anxiety, 410, 1649–1651, 2447, 2459, 2541, 3805, 3806, 3820, 5503, 5691, 7646; attitude, 1779; concern, 411, 1652, 2460; confrontation, 2444, 5465, 5504; fear, 1081, 2453, 2467–2469, 2497; threat, 1691; transcendence, 7647

Debating, 1765

Debilitating anxiety, 1625, 1626, 1633

Decision(s): confidence, 2223; difficulty, 2180; executive, 2346; flexibility, 2223

Decision-making, 2270, 4702: adolescents, 7577; authority, 7122; career, 3180, 3610, 3613, 5118, 5306, 5310, 5311, 5323, 5356, 6721–6724, 7360–7363, 9313, 9347–9349, 9854, 9855, 9889, 10172, 10173; career indecisiveness, 5315, 5316, 5350, 5351, 5357, 5358; compulsiveness vs. decisiveness, 5036; control, 6828; dilemma, 1939; economic, 2396; effectiveness, 7123; employees, 9106; faculty, 3262; families, 8842; frontal lobe function, 5659; group, 2912; groupthink, 9867; participative, 7135; policy,

2910; sexual behavior, 5737; strategies, 2223; styles, 2205, 3425, 7124, 9865; teacher, 835, 3434, 5152; values, 2314; vocational, 1579, 3632; 7438, 7439

Decisiveness, 2265, 9724: peer counseling, 1973

Decoding, visual-social cues, 1619

Deduct(ion)(ive), 887, 3426: logic, 2202

Defense: mechanism, 850, 1653, 3355, 7000, 9698, 9699; policy, attitude toward, 1197

Defensive(ness), 255, 299, 421, 845, 1725, 9776: about beliefs, 9688; communication, 1250; coping, 7649; style, 7648, 9700

Deference, 1720

Deficiency: goal, 1994; need, 1355

Definitions: confidence in, 125; work, 354

Delay, 403: of gratification, 8564

Delinquency, 378, 656, 1213, 1221, 1244, 1245, 2832, 2874, 6226, 6227, 8565, 8566, 8683, 8685

Delinquent: boys, 24; girls, 463; girls, parents of, 656; juvenile, 519; peers, 8637; personality, 853, 855, 857

Delivery, 596

Democratic values, unmet, 2055

Demographic data, 2173

Demonstrators, anti-war, 552

Denial, 3510: of distress, 5745; of stress, 5650

Dental: anxiety, 7753; health, attitudes, 2725

Dental hygienist, 4199

Dependability: people, 2288, 7950; supervisors, 1023

Dependen(ce)(cy)(t), 281, 830, 927, 1500, 1720, 2205, 2206, 4380: emotional, 931, 5718; -independence, 400; interpersonal, 2574, 5770, 5771, 7980; job, 1034; marital, 3029, 3046; persistence, 216; political, 512; social, 434; work, 1034

Depersonalization, 7001, 8162

Depress(ion)(ive), 417, 420, 841, 1088, 1089, 1638, 1644, 1645, 1654, 1664, 1670, 1681, 2442,

2445, 2446, 2449, 2461, 2463, 2464, 2479, 2498, 2534, 2546, 3766, 3767, 3779, 3780, 3807, 3838, 3859, 3922, 3954, 5476, 5477, 5488, 5505–5513, 5561, 7587, 7609, 7650, 7652, 7716, 7899: anxiety, 773, 1663; anxiety-irritation, 1686, 2621; Arabic children, 7594; attitude, 5517, 5518, 5529; attributions, 6956; automatic thoughts, 5463; behavior, 6309, 7682, 7712; beliefs, 4815; caregiving, 4042; in children, 2450, 2465, 2502, 2503, 3783, 3784, 3896, 5462, 5478, 5479, 7612, 7618, 7651, 7781; family behavior, 4551; geriatric, 2475, 2520, 3832, 7685, 7686; high school students, 7653; hopelessness, 3770; intensity, 3768, 3769; Japanese, 7900; knowledge assessment, 5377; locus of control, 4806, 4807; marital satisfaction and, 3765; material risk, 5586; nonpsychotic, 3828; patients, 420; peer nomination, 7781; Persian populations, 7590; predisposition to, 3813, 4289; proneness, 2462, 3808; seasonal, 7840; self-assessment, 1692, 5657, 5658; self-report, 3962; sense of, 1962; severity, 3837, 3930; student, teacher report, 3949; symptomatology, 1644, 3809, 5474, 5475, 5511, 5512, 5642, 7610, 7689, 7704; therapist competence, 5262; vs. anxiety, 5486; visual analogue scale, 7885; vulnerability, 5620; work, 6047

Deprivation, 6210: environmental, 9041; foreign student, 1094; social, 466

Description: job, 1321; managers, 1447

Descriptive rating scales, 215

Desegregat(ed)(ion): attitudes, 1160; schools, 452

Desirability: responses, 8741, 8743, social, 49, 62, 251, 281, 296, 2557, 2585, 5721, 5795, 5796, 5850–5852, 8016–8018, 8021, 8041, 8088–8090

Desire to work: paid

employment, 3130; woman, 1995

Despair, sense of, 1684

Desperate love, 3995, 5746

Destructiveness, 2253

Detachment, 989, 1720

Determiners, specific, 385

Determinism, 2571, 3532

Development(al), 134–140, 621–639, 1284–1292, 1936–1944, 8784–8799: actual competence, 3685; adolescent psychosocial maturity, 4498; adult, 2943, 2944; challenges, executives, 9033; child, 137, 625; classification, 2946; cognitive, 623, 627, 635, 2961, 4515, 6378, 8799; conceptual, 135; conscience, 638; curriculum, 1314, 6372, 6373, 6383, 6384; ego, 136, 629, 1944, 2948, 2959; ego identity, 628, 2949, 2950, 4497, 4517; ego stages, 245, 2951; emotional, 637, 2952; Eriksonian stages, 632, 4496, 4503, 4514, 6379, 8788, 8791, 8792; everyday skills, 3672; fine-motor tasks, 4504; goals, 9203; grandiosity, 4519; identity achievement, 4501; infant, 625, 631, 1050, 4505, 8793; instrumental competence, 3677; intellectual, 637, 1515, 2953, 2954, 2958, 4506, 8797; kindergarten children, 1289; knowledge assessment, 5378; maturity, 4510, 4511, 4516; mental, 2956; middle-aged men, 4506; moral, 139, 638, 2957, 4518; mothers', 4589; mother's reporting of, 6377; motor, 634, 637; newborn, 1284; numbers, 2939; object representations, 4508; parents' conceptualization, 6371, 8787; parents' level, 4499; perceptual motor, 477; personality, 4520; physical, 637; Piagetian, 2960; psychosocial, 632, 1941, 2945, 2947, 2955; pupil, 637; responsibility in children, 762; sex role, 137; skills, 6381; social, 637; socioemotional, 6380; spatial ability, 3671, 3673, 3674, 3680; staff, 3112, 3113; status, 481; strategy,

880; teachers' knowledge of behavior principles in, 3679; trauma effects, 5519; verbal ability, 1300; vocational, 1291
Deviance, 1803
Deviant: behavior, 573, 8568; peers, 8569; role, 3202, in school, 8673; workplace, 9187
Devotionalism, 982
Dexterity, mental, 1738, 2689
Diabetes, 4381: eating attitudes, 8386; locus of control, 4809; quality of life, 5514; stress, 5648
Diagnosis, 421
Dialect: Black, non-standard, 1046; change, 105; training, 105
Diet and nutrition, 4444
Dieting, 8581: beliefs, 9379; cognitive behavior, 8594; concern, 8553; eating temptations, 8570; readiness, 8571
Differences, creativity, 132
Differentiation: conceptual, 1273; groups, 9915; psychological, 1417; of self, 4811, 8830, 9380
Diffusion, identity, 628
Directedness: college women, 789; inner-outer, 789
Directions and commands, comprehension, 380, 384
Directiveness, 583, 3470, 3471: primary teachers, 936
Direct object: punishment, 654; reward, 654
Disab(ility)(led), 515, 1780: acceptance, 1636, 7573; adjustment, 7850; attitude toward, 2693, 2717, 6089, 6119; functional independence, 7679; persons, 1751, 1780; perceived discrimination, 9496; physical educator attitudes, 8445; self attitude, 752; self-report, 3781; social role handicap, 7941; student facilities, 1315
Disadvantaged, 432, 1452, 1510: American Indian youth, 375; children, 7, 531, 612; children, adjustment, 27; children, creative behavior, 1922; children, delay of reinforcement, 239; children,

problem solving, 892, 894; children, self-esteem, 830; children, social responsibility, 58; children, teacher values, 990; creativity, 1283; job-conditions, 1318; job placement, 1445; job satisfaction, 1577; Mexican-American children, 380, 384, 390; Negro, 342, 350, 376; preschool children, 7, 403; preschool children, causality, 886; preschool children, consequential thinking, 885; school beginners, 434; skills, arithmetic/reading, 1038; students, 679; students, aspiration level, 740; tolerance, 1508; work attitudes, 1199, 1531; work requirements, 1246; youth, group counseling, 53
Disapproval, 659
Discipline, 625, 1748: campus, 682; formal, 880; inconsistent, 655; methods for residents, 546; mothers, 8822, 8911; parents, 8927; program, 682; self, 589–591, 593, 598, 599
Discomfort, 1725: anxiety, 5516
Discontentment, political, 1976
Discrimination, 76, 1041: ability, 1249; attitude toward, 542, 5864, 8454; complexity, 1908; gender, 6976; letter, 1051; oral, 1421; perception of, 5817, 5818; right-left, 814, 1943; self, 1431; sex, 3085; visual, 356, 357, 1412, 1442; word, 356, 357, 602
Discussion, 1295, 1297
Disengagement, 688
Disgust, 8382
Disobedience; children, 953
Disorganization, proneness, 2513
Disorientation, 1079
Dissent(ion), 484, 625; professional, 6009
Dissertations, reading, 20
Dissociative disorders, 7656, 7787
Distance, 2224: comfortable, 436; interpersonal, 436, 451, 2596; proxemic, 68; psychological, 50, 56; social, 63, 8059
Distraction, overlapping, 385

Distress, 2466, 2539, 5451, 5486, 7657: college students, 5419; psychological, 35, 2493, work, 8302
Distributive justice, 234, 9034–9036, 9072, 9074
Distrust, 1103: Black-White, 5739; cynicism, 5740; political feelings, 1975; Upward Bound Student, 45
Disturbed children, parents of, 148
Diver training, 1288
Divergent: production(s), 110, 111, 129, 1920; thinking, 608, 8383
Diversity: attitudes toward, 8446, 9835; organizational practices, 9037; universal, 8019, 8135, 10006
Divorce: adjustment, 8832; attitude toward, 4296, 8342; boundary ambiguity, 8808; children's beliefs about, 4529; propensity, 4612, 6408
Dogmatic thinking, 953, 7171: counselor, 7198
Dogmatism, 95, 227, 294, 926, 1483, 2258, 2260, 2261, 2287, 2294, 7200; client, 309; counseling client, 309
Dominance, 1720, 3472: father, 647, 673; mother, 647, 673; negative, 8030; paratelic, 9260; parental, 229, 1301; social, 5853, 5854, social, 9788, 10001; -submissiveness, 2291
Draft, 1748
Draw a: car, 846; dog, 1117
Dream(s) 2709: analyzing, 1655; associations, 30; attitudes toward, 8343; content, 5037; incident, 1655; interpretation, 10050; recall, 4796
Drinking, 1748
Driving: anger, 6232, 8572; appraisal, 8573; behavior, 8574; boredom, 3561, elderly, 9710; stress, 7719
Dropout(s), 401, 645, 651, 653: potential, 391; prediction, school, 476; risk, 3702; self-esteem, 827
Drug(s), 343: abstinence self-efficacy, 9381; abuse, 344, 505, 1042, 1220, 8575; attitude,

1145, 1155, 1191, 1781;
behavior, 569; hyperactivity,
1203; illegal use of, 1785;
issues, 506; knowledge, 343,
344, 1042, 1600; knowledge,
use, attitudes, 1858; reasons
for use, 569; sources of, 569;
testing, 6074; use, 485, 507,
569, 1130, 1204, 1210, 1214,
1215, 1228, 1698, 2223, 2819,
6187, 6233, 8576, 8577, 8621;
use, adolescent, 562; use,
alcohol, 563
Dualism, 3527, 3546
Dyad(ic): affective behavior,
2810; communication, 2905,
2911; counselor-client, 227;
feelings in, 237; marital, 2962,
2978; members perceptions,
102; parent-child, 2979; trust,
2562, 7951
Dying, fear of, 406, 1650, 1651,
2444, 2447, 2453, 2467–2469,
2497
Dynamics, 1885
Dysphoria, 416: body-image,
6946; late luteal phase, 5500

Earth science, 8344; East-West,
1782
Eating/eating disorders, 4385–
4387, 4439, 4462: attitudes,
4319, 6234, 6946, 8386, 8387,
8578, 8579; bulimia, 4358,
4359; compulsive eating, 4368,
4369; as coping mechanism,
8582; food as nurturance,
4590; locus of control, 4891;
predisposition to disorder,
4290; restraint, 1876, 8581,
symptoms, 8580
Echoic response, preschool
children, 7
Economic: change, 92;
conservatism, 9958; decision-
making, 2396; hardship,
perceived, 5520, 8165;
ideology, 3533
Education(al), 268: adjustment,
22; administrator, 528;
aspirations, college student,
719; attitude toward, 529, 549,
1167, 2738, 2739; barrier
perceptions, 9119; competence,
767; drug, 1130; early
childhood, 71, 678; flexibility,

131; forces, teacher, 2057;
goals, 511, 3068; graduates,
685; graduate counselor, 1004;
guidance effort, 687;
handicapped, 583; innovation,
receptivity toward, 1784;
parental involvement, 6490;
opinions, 529; orientation,
3393; outcomes, 9038;
preference, 200; psychology,
684; quality, 663; research,
1752, 2710, 6176; rights, 8327;
set, 1068, 1350; values, 9959,
9997; vocational, 305–339
Effectiveness: advisor, 2329;
college course, 2338; college
instructor, 2338; college
teacher(s), 1541, 1542, 2334;
college students' perception of
instructors, 2358;
communication, 99, 148;
counselor, 307, 312, 316, 325,
1001, 1002, 1559, 2335, 3566,
3567, 3569; counselor
trainee's, 2337; elementary
guidance, 316; instructor, 329;
judgment by child, 243;
managerial, 6058;
organizational practices, 1972;
peer counseling, 1973;
perceptual, 214; personal, 214;
practice teaching, 690;
psychological, 1449; speakers,
1765; teacher, 335, 1026, 1030,
3607; teaching, 2333, 2347,
7331, 7337, 7338; work
groups, 8166
Efficacy, 976, 3204, 3331:
academic, 6681, 6682; beliefs,
9383; collective, 9438; parents,
8932; teacher, 6959–6961,
6694; 9634–9637; team, 6615
Effort, 575, 9497
Ego: anxiety, 5515; -centrism,
579, 1109, 1480, 1484, 1485,
5189, 7046; -centrism,
adolescent, 5167; closeness-
distance, 913; cognitive, 1491;
control, children, 9705;
development, 135, 136, 629,
1944, 2948, 2959, 6372, 6373,
6383, 6384; functioning, 1417,
6695, 9707; identity, 949,
2241, 2949, 2950, 4497, 4517,
5040, 5046, 9716, 9717, 9752;
identity development, 628,

2951; identity status, 628;
integrity, 7005; involvement,
3359; organization, 749;
permissiveness, 3360;
protection, 9706; role-taking,
1503; strength, 2164, 3206,
9771; sufficiency, 1929
Egotism, 417
Elaboration, 861, 9039
Elderly: attitudes toward, 2697,
2755, 4308; care, 2990;
depression, 3832; drivers,
9710; functional
characteristics, 3853; health of,
5661; health concerns, 5544;
knowledge of Alzheimer's
disease, 3666; married children
of, 6529; meaningful life
experiences, 5068; mental
competence, 2385; morale,
2506, 3901; sense of
hopelessness, 5535; stress, 2531
Elementary: anaphora
comprehension, 2370; children,
attitudes, 1136; children, client
centered approach, 249;
children, creativity, 1927,
1932; children, interracial
attitudes, 1168; children,
teacher-pupil relations, 256;
first grade adjustment, 2413;
grades, 3–6, 696; grades,
anthropology, 1044; guidance,
31; reading, 1455, 1460;
school, 388, 389, 540, 595,
622, 688, 701, 1723, 1756,
1770; school, academic self-
concept, 2147; school boys,
389; school child anxiety, 933;
school children, 21, 101, 456,
491, 626, 1043; school climate,
1323; school counseling, 70,
315, 316, 671; school, English
second language, 1598; school
environment, 1316; school,
inner city, 990; school
openness, 1963; school
perceptual abilities, 2098;
school principals, 1680; school
reading attitude, 1822;
students academically talented,
1606; student teachers, 495,
701; teachers, 341, 488;
teacher evaluation, 1036;
teachers, reading beliefs, 8389,
8390; visual discrimination,
2394

Embed(ded)(ness), 1417: figures, 770, 1386

Emotion(al)(s), 404, 593, 5584, 6981: abuse, 8586, 8587, 8601, 8655; adjustment, 5708; arousal, 1231; autonomy, 6412, 7006; balance, 7797; closeness, 5709; contagion, 7659; control, 1973, 9711; dependence, 931, 1638, 5718; development, 637; differential, 7654; distance, 1103; expressiveness, 6990, 7008, 7024, 9712, 9777; factors, 138; family expression, 6418, 6419, 8844; of husbands, 6440; intensity, children, 9713; maturity, 621, 2952; negative, children, 8828, 9732, 9749, 9750; recognition, 7658; regulation, children, 8585; reliance, 1715; self assessment, 2165, 6278; self-disclosure, 5453; social climate, 583; -social state, 578; stability, 7660; state, immediate, 416; strength, 5453; support, 5748; support, university residence, 704; types, 3361; well-being, 5537; withdrawal, 405; work-related, 5509

Emotionality, 403, 944, 1641, 7010, 7022, 9703, 9704, 9712– 9715, 9749, 9750, 9765, 9796

Emotive imaging, 2063

Empath(ic)(y), 220, 227, 235, 328, 429, 757, 771, 1100, 1385, 1387, 1438, 2243, 2268, 3476, 3490, 3994, 5051, 7172, 7173, 7174, 7178, 7194, 9775, 9904, 9907, 9916, 9917: toward animals, 6067; children, 3473, 3477, 3483, 5221, 9912, 9913; counselors, 309, 3475, 3505, 3506; perception of in others, 5204; police, 781; rape, 5202; teachers, 3474; understanding, 431, 1370, 1538, 2344, 2353

Emphasis, 688

Empiricism, 301, 976

Employability, 310, 320: attitude(s), 188, 193, 1007, 1156, 2622; behavior, 2851; commitment, 1996; evaluation, 1007, 1016, 3574, 3575; motivation, 205; perceptions, 3326; personal traits, 7011;

rating, 327, 692; satisfaction, 164; self-evaluation, 1008; work relations, 1116; work values, 1532

Employee, 6545: absenteeism, 8167; advancement opportunities, 9092; appearance, 1007; aptitude, 1007; attitudes, 6122, 8391; cognitive style, 9871; compliance, 8157; decision-making participation, 9106; drug testing, 6074; indoctrination, 8177; intent to leave, 8182–8186; intrinsic motivation, 9207, 9231, 9232; perceptions, 6246, 6547, 9385, 9386; performance, 9208, 9385, 10052, 10105; retributive intent, 8264; satisfaction, 8168; supervisor ratings of, 10078; support, 9040, 9079, 9172, wariness, 8260

Employment: alternatives, 8169, 9498; commitment, 3626, 10147; desire for, 3130; fairness in hiring, 6555; hiree characteristics, 7301; immobility, 3627; intent to leave, 8182–8186; maternal 8907; outcome, 8170; physical impairment and, 5996; predictors, 8171; success, 241

Empowerment, 7810: leaders, 8612; parents, 9387; school, 6016; teachers, 9162; workplace, 8172, 8254, 8255

Encoding, associative verbal, 1035

Encopresis, 846

Encounter groups, psychological state, 841

Encouragement, parental, 713

Engaged couples, 597

Engineer(ing)(s): career interests, 3629; correlates with success, 212; creative potential, 1933; expectancies, 6818; motivation, 1366; performance, 1557; self-efficacy, 9527; self perception, 829; students, 42, 95

English: Black non-standard, 1046; invitation/ comprehension, 1046; pressures for, 647, 673; proficiency, 1732; as second

language, 7516, 8392; sound-symbol relations, 366

Enhancement, self, 1994

Enmeshment, 8839

Enrichment clusters, 8475

Enthusiasm, 679: toward learning, 540; toward school, 540

Entrepreneurs, 9078

Enuresis, 846

Environment(al): assessment, 672; attitudes, 8388, 8402, 8435; behavior, 6236; campus, 662, 9017, 9018; classroom, 1324, 1539, 3057, 3058, 3078, 3093, 3094, 9024, 9029, 9054, 9085, 9181; college, 165, 172, 184, 187, 212; community, 1060; consumer concerns, 6310; control, 1997; coping, 1095; deprivation, 9041; effects upon, 3069; exploration, 10148–10150; forces, 673; geographic, 3070; issues, attitudes, 1152; learning, 473, 673, 686, 3076, 3109, 3114; living, 3087; medical school stress, 2419; orientation, 302; perception, 179; -person fit, 6549; preserving the natural, 1776; press of, 704; psychosocial, 1960; risk perception, 9303, 9389; satisfaction, 1965; school, 1316, 9161; stress, 3071; treatment, 1310; uncertainty, 3072; university, 1440; work, 9166, 9182, 9183

Envy, interpersonal, 439

Epilepsy, 4112, 5155

Epistemology, 6361, 6362

Equalitarianism, 537, 1123, 1177, 7232, 9813

Equality, 301, 6551: ethnic, 976

Erikson(ian): ego epigenesis, 628; stages of development, 245, 632, 8788, 8791, 8792; theory, 628, 629, 949

Eroticism, 1157

Esprit, 688

Esteem: co-worker, 1458; father, 788; self, see Self-Esteem; self, adult male, 826; self, children, 458; self, college student, 816; self, high school students, 827; self, pre-adolescent, 825; self, student, 792

Estrangement: cultural, 1700, 1701, 7957; political, 1977; self, 430, 457

Ethic(al)(s), 1815, 3529, 9961: adolescents, 8498; behavior, violations, 971; conflict, 3530; discrimination, counselors, 969; judgment, 9960; norms, business, 84; organizational, 6552, 7227, 9043; Protestant, 3528, 3550, 3551, 3663, 7238, 7244–7247; reasoning, 3531

Ethlanguage, pressure for, 647, 675

Ethnic, 301: acculturation, 5752; attachments, 7952; attitudes toward, 8394; differences in development of responsibility, 762; equality, 976; identity, 5753, 7953, 7956, 7970, 7975, 8025–8027, 8137; perceived ethnicity, 5761; prejudice, 8066; pride, 7955; self-esteem, 5825; self-evaluation, 7954; stereotyping, 9628; university environment, 9180

Ethnocentrism, 1144, 8061, 8394: African American, 3976

Etiology, interpersonal, 530

Evaluat(e)(ing)(ion)(ive), 481, 600, 689, 694, 2215, 6578: academic, assistants, 992; colleagues, 1009; composition, 1031; confidence in, 6609; course, 168, 666–668, 698, 1545; courses, college, 1024, 1540, 1547, 9170, 10045; counseling, 311, 1000, 3063; counselor, 999, 3599; critical, 369; educational-vocational counseling, 311; elementary guidance, 316; elementary teacher, 1036; employee, 1016, 3574, 3575; faculty, 1548, 3576; guidance, 687; inservice, 1319; interview for teaching, 1015; job, 1016, 1027, 3061; lesson, 1027; middle school, 1326; need for, 9748; nurses, 3597; practice teaching, 690; psychotherapy, 1080; residence counselor, 1006; staff, 3112, 3113; stress, 1627; student counselors, 1021; student teachers, 3590, 3602; supervisor(s), 1007, 1017,

1023, 2332, 9010; teachers, 698, 997, 1009, 1014, 1022, 1027–1029, 1032, 1550, 1551, 3581, 3589, 3600, 3601; teaching method, 698, 3563

Evangelism, 2711

Events, 3101: life, 3111

Examination(s), 666: attitude toward, 248; coping, 7484; desire for control, 7499; oral, 5428; reaction toward, 16; self-efficacy, 9391

Excel, desire to, 713

Exchange: leader-member, 1896; orientation, 8060; social, 8122, 8123

Exercise, 4730, 4731, 6745, 7662; enjoyment, 9209; incentives for, 6664; motivation, 9273; perceived opportunities for, 4898; reasons for, 6667; social support, 8103

Exertion, physical and mental, 709

Exhaustion, 2540

Exhibition(ism), 1720, 7204

Existential(ism), 2296: anxiety, 1657, 5523; confrontation, 2443; social courage, 1832

Expatriates, 7663, 8174, 9481

Expect(ancies)(ations), 4893, 6746: adolescent, 5026, 7532; alcohol-related, 4813, 6690–6692; athletic success, 3215; career success, 8153; children, 8813; college, 662, 740, 3049, 6750; communication of, 601, 4479; course, 3158; counsel(ing)(or), 1382, 2058, 3191, 3198, 3208–3210, 4819–4822, 6748, 6749, 9392; engineering degree, 6818; family, 8845; friendship, 5733; group therapy, 4833, 6129; heterosocial interaction, 4996; hiring, 6558; interns', 4851; job, 5979, 9434; mathematics, 6794, 8311, 9480, 9650; motivation, 4704; negative, 3845; negative mood regulation, 3829, 3889; parental 1302; pay, 3258; performance, 6864; possible selves, 6862, 6863; realism of, 4935, 4936; reemployment, 6751; reinforcement, 44, 69;

role, 4942; self-efficacy, 6907; significant others, 9393; student, 6747; success, 4828, 9405; survey, 719; task success, 3207; therapist, 3336; treatment, 9648; trust, 7259; weight loss, 9655; work, 3122

Experience(s), 694: college, 675; counselor, 1004; executives, 10083; recent, 1290; religious, 1514; time, 1400, 1420

Explanation, 666

Exploratory behavior, 260

Expressing feelings, 1753

Expression(s), 1725: affective, 121, 279, 7601, 9712, 9777; feelings, 500; openness to, 481, 500; stimulus, 38; therapist, 10049

Expressive: dimensions, 594; family, 8846, 8998; style, 594, 9763; therapy, 10073 External: cognition, 2187; coping, 7666; -internal locus of control, 2049; sensation, 2187

Externalizing behavior, 8548, 8708

Extracurricular activities, 675

Extraneous clues, 385

Extrasensory perception, 8451: attitude toward, 1139, 8395

Extroversion, 841: introversion, 390, 749; children, 956; students', 2349

Eye: contact, 1257; -hand coordination, 2143

Face saving, 1352, 5794

Face validity, job measures, 9044

Facilitat(ing)(ive): anxiety, 1625; behavior, 432; communication, 1889, 1890

Facilities: disabled student, 1315; materials, junior high, 700

Factors, emotional, 138

Factually set, 1068

Faculty, 586, 595, 662: attitudes, 1159, 6577; behavior, 2894; college collegiality, 5920; classification by, 184; decision-making, 3262; evaluation, 698, 999, 1009, 1014, 1022, 1027–1029, 1032, 1548, 3576; grade beliefs, 8397; needs, 1356; orientations, 1788; policy making, 174; roles, 509;

satisfaction, 6533; stress, 5921; -student perceptions, academic advising, 1959; -student relations, roles, 675, 695; support, 6752; teaching, 2331; tenure experiences, 9046; trust, 5922, 5923, 5924; union membership, 3399

Failure: avoidance, 1833; awareness, 3170; fear of, 19, 204, 392, 1342; motivation to avoid, 209; risk, 713; student attributes, 5439; success, 526, 1373; threat, 713; tolerance, 5425

Fairness, 6556: decision makers, 10057; in hiring, 6555; perceptions of, 6546, 6608, 6820, 9047; procedural, 9132–9142; sensitivity to, 5751; smoking ban, 6623; of system, 487; workplace, 9042, 9047

Faith, 5226

Family, 141–149, 593, 640–656, 1161, 1293–1306, 1945–1958, 3047, 4547, 4561, 6427, 6495, 6498: adaptability, 4549, 4950, 6414, 6415; adjustment, 2991, 2992; adolescent perception, 6387; Asian Americans, 8804; assessment, 8915; attachments, 6451, 6452; attitudes toward, 8345; authoritarianism, 641, 644; autonomy, 6426; background, 625, 8838; child environment, 4545, 4546, 4567, 4596; childrearing behavior, 4540, 4599; children's feelings about, 4530; child's perception of parental conflict, 4591; circumplex model, 4549; clergy, 6516; cohesion, 6414, 6415, 8836, 8839, 8840; college students' parental attachments, 4594; communication, 2905, 8747; conflict, 3003, 8841; coping, 2984, 4535, 6416; decision-making, 4539, 8842; depressed normal subjects, 4551; distress, 8843; dual career, 3043, 6409, 6410; eating habits, 4891; economic stress, 4543; elderly, 2990; emotional autonomy, 4544; emotional experience, 6418, 6419, 8844; expectations,

8845; expressiveness, 8846, 8998; family-like relationships, 5788; filial responsibility, 6434; functional, 4552, 4553; functioning, 6421, 8837, 8858; with handicapped child, 4616; harmony, 466, 6424; identity, 8848; importance of, 6400; independence, 976, 2999; ideology, 9008; inappropriate interaction, 6431; integration, 8820; interaction, 597, 2986, 4630, 6491, 6518; intergenerational fusion, 4571; interparent discord, 4531, 4572, 4574, 4626; interpersonal communication, 4525; interpersonal relations, 4018; intrusive parenting, 4611; involvement, 6423, 8849–8852; job role conflict, 4944; kinship restraints, 4577; learning environment, 2985; life changes, 3863, 8800; marriage decision-making, 4573; maltreatment, 2989; maternal developmental history, 4589; maternal separation anxiety, 4588; member's perceptions, 6508; mother's parenting satisfaction, 4617; mother's perception of husband's support, 4624; needs, 6425; nurturance, 4590, 4597; obligations, 8853; organizational policies, 6588; orientation, 2302; of origin, 8838; parent-adolescent relationship, 4532; parent-child interaction, 4524, 4587, 4595, 4601, 4603; parent competence, 4608; parental, 593; parental acceptance, 4592, 4593; parental emotional stress, 3894; parental response to child medical care, 4600; parental self-efficacy, 4606; parenting beliefs, 4569; parenting style, 4609, 4615; parents' satisfaction with child, 4598; peer relations and, 6494; perceived problems, 6496; perceived support from, 4610, 4620, 4621, 6497; performance, 8855; permissiveness, 6435; personal

authority, 6597; problem-solving, 8856; process, 8857; proverbs, 4558; psychological separation, 4613; relations, 141, 142, 645, 1296, 2982, 2983, 6386; relationships, 1951; relations, peer counseling, 1973; resources, 8859; richness, 466; rituals, 6428; role, 302; role behavior, 4559; role expectations, 4578; routines, 8860; satisfaction, 4548, 4575, 6429, 8861, 8862; sibling relations, 4619; sibling support expectancies, 4565; social support, 2988, 4622, 8104, 8109–8111, 8847, 8865; step-families, 6413; strengths, 4562, 8863; stressors, 6430; structure, 4563, 4564, 4627, 4628, 8864; substance abuse intervention, 4560; system differentiation, 8829; systems maintenance, 6420; ties, 302; traditional values, 4556; union conflict, 6520; unpredictability, 8866; values, 9817, 9963; well-being, 2987; work conflicts, 4555, 4631, 4632, 6406, 6432, 6433, 6448, 6523–6528, 9394, 9395, 9422, 9430, 9658–9667, 9672, 9673; work integration, 9478; workers', 4538

Fantasy, 40, 1243, 2886: projections, 579; sexual, 2876

Fat: attitudes toward, 8320; fear of, 2477, 7687

Fatalism, 985, 4825, 9396

Father(s): acceptance, 645; alcoholism, 8589; attachment, 8891; attitudes, 645; child acceptance of touching, 5884; child relations, 6503; dominance, 647, 673; esteem, 788; identification with, 434, 830; involvement, 8867, 8972; new, 6469; non-residential, 6470; relationship with, 653, 8993, 8994; self-assessment, 6510

Fatigue, 841, 1670, 7765

Fear, 253, 3823, 3884, 6983, 6988, 7013, 7014, 7667. 7674, 7675: AIDS, 3959, 4293, 7668, 7762; bodily sensations, 3817; children, 2490, 3875, 5528,

7676; commitment, 3818; crime, 3819, 7670; death, 3820; dying, 406, 1081, 1650, 1651, 2453, 2467–2469, 2497, 7646; failure, 19, 204, 392, 1342, 3821; fat, 2477; flying, 7671, 7672; incompetence, 7669; of intimacy, 5528, 7958; litigation, 3874; negative evaluation, 3822, 5521, 5524, 5756; of pain, 5521; of powerlessness, 5525; psychotherapy, 2451; rating of, 414; success, 1658–1660, 1667, 2410–2412, 2470, 2471, 2478, 2500, 2545, 3897, 5526, 7673; suffocation, 7872; survey, 1966

Feedback, 2908: amount of, 487; analysis, 1259; consequences, 8749; interpersonal, 1899; job, 3083; perceived accuracy, 8760; propensities, 8748; seeking, 8567, 8750; teacher, 333, 1885

Feelings, 593: attention to, 7596; dysphoric, 416; expressing, 1753; expression of, 500, 773; of frustration, 5531; inadequacy, 773; inferiority, 515; negative, 5597; openness, 293; passionate love, 5812; perception, 102; personal, 804; positive-negative, 555; sensitivity to, 500; toward school, 1825; toward Whites, 2157; of vulnerability, 5695

Fees, attitudes, 2787

Felt figure replacement, 440

Female(s): career choice, 710; need achievement, 728; professional competence, 975, 3243; professors, 1754; social roles, 1755

Femin(ine)(inity)(ism)(ist), 1789, 1790, 7074, 9821, 9837, 9838: -antifeminist, 1791; attitudes, 1834, 4239, 6075, 6076, 6163, 7076, 8346; behavior, 6208; identity, 6753, 7075; ideology, 3557; liberal attitudes, 1767; -masculinity, 795, 927, 9614, 9807, 9816; orientation, 1768; rating scale, 284; women's self-concept, 4294, 7064

Fertility control, 9933

Field dependence/independence,

770, 776, 815, 3231, 4758: practice, 1317

Figure: analogies, 2059; copying, 1734; drawing, 888; human, 32; intersection, 7452, 8310

Filial responsibility, 8869, 8870

Film test, 765

Financial status, 5161: concerns, 5530; employment compensation, satisfaction with, 4177, 4178; pay disclosure effects, 4190; investment knowledge, 9601; perceived hardship, 8242; satisfaction, 215, 3923; strain, 7677, 8871; stress, 3814, 3824; stress for families, 4543

Firearms, attitude toward, 1125, 8323

Fireman: job perception, 1012; leadership, 1549

First grade(rs), 371, 374: achievement, 469, 474; anxiety, 948; auditory perception, 750; home environment, 1946; racial attitude, 1813; readiness, 1118; readiness for, 1735; reading achievement, 602

Fitness: attitude toward, 8399; facility membership, 9814

Five-year-olds, 1744

Flexibility, 15, 481, 893: conceptual, 923; cognitive, 923, 939, 7167; constricted, 924; educational, 131; interpersonal, 217, 7164, 9898; perceptual, 923; rigidity, 1486; speed, 15; spontaneous, 923; thinking, 9864

Flow, 9210, 9211

Fluency: anagram, 1903; ideational, 1911

Focus(ing), 596, 1859, 6239

Follow-up, student counseling, 1010

Food preference, 3396, 3417

Foreclosure, 628

Foreign: language, anxiety, 7503; language aptitude, 1733; language attitude, 2744, 6078; policy, 510

Foreigners, attitude toward, 2798

Foreman, perception of job, 1012: production, 1013; responsibilities, 1011

Forgiveness, 8656

Formal reasoning abilities, 2227

Formalistic, 2186

Form discrimination, 2143

Fourth, fifth, and sixth grade, 1647

Frame management, 8175

Fraternit(ies)(y): activities, 486; perceptions, 9094; social, 300, 486

Free: speech commitment, 973; time, 570

Freedom, expression, campus, 586: from cynicism, 481; students, 586

Freshmen: camp experience, 774; year, college, 628, 5410; year, transition anxiety, 7504

Friend(liness)(s)(ship), 447, 1097, 2565, 4004, 4047, 4093, 5735: identification with, 434, 830; Black-White, 452; child, 5733, 7959; social support, 5706, 8104, 8109–8111; workplace, 9067, 9188

Frustration(s), 796, 1216, 2472, 4129, 4130, 4364, 4403, 5531, 5706: delay, 1212; job, 2623, 5927, 5947, 5948, 7678; reactions to, 1675, 2528; response, 1229

Functional literacy: high school, 1611; reading skills, 1602

Functioning, 7680: and disability, 7679; facilitative, 1716

Future: goal success expectancy, 220, 9192; orientation, 207, 301, 976, 7224; time perspective, 50, 56, 9964, 9965

Gambling, 6636, 8616, 8711

Games, 1218

Gay men and lesbians: attitudes toward, 4233, 4241, 4242, 4297, 8348, 8351, 8352, 8401, 8404–8409, 8417–8419; counselor affirmative behavior, 9304; disclosure, 9848; employer attitudes, 4838; hassles, 7681; identity, 9831; jealousy, 4016; organizational climate toward, 9089; perception of homophobic environments, 5015; prejudice attributions of, 9615; social distance, 4080; stereotyping, 6754; See also Homosexuals

Gender, 1219: behavior, 1285; children's attitudes, 6115; classroom equity, 10056; evaluation, 9815; identity, 630, 3403, 7077, 9816, 9837; ideology, 9817, 9822, 9832; orientation, 7078; role, 7099, 7110; role attitude, 2746, 6126, 7109, 8352; role conflict, 7079, 9400, 9818; role ideology, 9819; role, middle childhood, 243; role, therapist bias, 10034; role, traditional, 10004; self-concept, 6853; stereotyping, 6875; work-related, 9852; workplace discrimination, 6976

General ability, perceptions, 2147

General anxiety, 1638

General health, 3826, 3830, 3831, 3833: beliefs, 4836, 4837

General information, 1738

Generations, relations, 76

Generativity, 6376

Genuineness, 328, 1438: facilitative, 2344

Geograph(ic)(y), 347, 3070: Japan, 351

Geometry, 4, 474: aptitude, 74

Geriatric: depression, 2475, 2520, 7685, 7686; hopelessness, 2476, 5535; nurses' referrals, 8624; outpatients, 2566

Gestalt completion, 1617

Gift receiving, discomfort, 7961

Gifted: academic acceleration, 6104; adults, creative, 615; children, 1124, 1387; children, creative, 615, 1283, 2940, 2942, 6370; children, self-concept, 3250, 6803, 6982; children, teacher attitude, 558; student, coping, 5670; student, school satisfaction, 5434; students, program participation, 7469; teacher, 1049

Girls: adolescent, 2866; delinquent, 463; delinquent, parents of, 656; social competence, 2595

Goal(s), 9221, 9223: academic, 9200; achievability, 9192, 9193; attainment of, 714, 5552; choice, 9820; college, 719; commitment, 6637, 6638;

content, 9213; deficiency, 1994; development, 9203; educational, 511, 3068; instability, 4132, 4500, 4709, 6639, 9214, 9276; inventory, 6641; job, 709; marital, 3021; math, 9217, 9240, 9245, Neotic, 821; orientation, 400, 6633, 6640, 6761, 9215–9219, 9267; personal, 829, 9267, 9268; pre-counseling, 1358; science, 9245; students, 9222; success, future expectancy, 2020; therapy, 1365; vocational, 511

God, 1748, 9513

Good luck, belief in, 8370

Gossip, 7053

Grad(es)(ing), 487: attitude toward, 166, 2757, 5414; contract attitude, 513; contract system, 513; faculty beliefs, 8397; high school, 700; practices, 1748; predictor, 75; systems, 487

Graduate(s): business programs, 661; education, 685; programs, 676; school, case of entry, 487; students, 528; student education, 131, 6557; students' environmental perception, 2062; student intellectual attitude, 86

Grammatical: clues, 385; structure, 380

Grandiosity, 4442, 4519, 4742, 7204

Grandparents: foster, 33; grandchildren integration, 8873

Grapheme-phoneme, 366

Graphic expression, 715

Gratification, postponement, 207, 8564

Greek Americans, 7964

Grievance, 2656, 8269

Grooming, hygiene, 1603

Group(s): activity, 681; aggression, 8505; arousal, 1998; atmosphere, 2568, 3074, 7966; attachment, 4009; attitudes about controversy, 4238; attractiveness, 1712; behavior, affective, 596; behavior, self perception, 778; career, 6766; change processes, 5762; children's perceptions,

9363; cohesion, 1710, 1711, 2569, 4008, 7967; conflict, 5783; conformity, 445, 3985; counseling, 53, 10051; decision-making, 2912; differentiation, 9915; direction by supervisor, 1005; importance, 4010; in-group/ out-group communication, 4481; individual apprehension, 6351; individual experience, 5710, 5719; individualism-collectivism, 4012; individual perception, 5759; interaction, 1722; joining, 5882; judgment, 1392; leader behavior, 6331, 8729; meetings, 8270; minority, 480; need strength, 1999; outcomes, 5778; participation, 53, 5776; perceived acceptance, 5702; positive interactions, 5760; practicum, 1259; process, 523, 880, 7990; religious, 183; solidarity, 4007, 4012; student interdependence, 5413; task conflict, 8281; task-related ideas, 8770; task strategy, 6342; trust, 7990; work, 598, 8303

Group therapy, 4650, 4651: expectations, 4833, 6129

Guidance: administrator, 677; assessment, 687; classes, elementary, 31; counseling attitudes, 85, 189; director's roles, 318; function, 325; needs, elementary, 31; practices, 185; process, 687; school evaluation, 687; state director, 318, 697

Guilt, 289, 841, 1638, 1670, 2247, 2252, 2279, 2284, 5048, 5061, 5074, 7177, 9721, 9943: attitude towards, 6070; dispositional, 2276; -innocence, 381; proneness, 5022

Gulf War, 6130, 6168

Habits, 593: study, high school, 7125; thought patterns, 7121; work, 1033, 1047

Guns, attitudes, 1125, 8323

Hair loss, 3836

Handedness, 7080, 7081, 7106

Handicapped, 1756, 2702: attitude toward, 2784;

children, 1384, 1386, 1388, 1390, 1411, 1433, 1435–1437, 3688, 4351, 4566, 4616; children, mainstreaming, 1783, 2694; children, peer attitudes, 4275; educationally, 583; preschoolers, 1597

Handwriting: children, 2373; cursive, 2375; changes, 7482; kindergarten, 1051; legibility, 2376

Happiness, 1661, 3756, 5575, 5592, 5638, 7774: marital, 3022, 8905

Harassment, 8590, 8665, 8692–8695, 9102

Harmony: control, 7969; familial, 466; within group, 1711

Hassles, 7642–7644, 7690: college students, 7506; gay men, 7681; job, 8195; police, 8249

Hawaii, 7015

Hazards: perception, 2065; workplace, 9184

Head start, 637

Health, 5532, 5533, 5543, 5588, 5624, 5671: behavior, 2864, 6243, 7691, 8591; complaints, 7884; concerns, 5544, 7874; of elderly, 5544, 5661; engenderingness, 1487; habits, 1220, 5548; job tension and, 5972; locus of control, 2066, 3217–3219, 3251, 3339, 6718, 6763, 6808; medical knowledge assessment, 5385; mental, 42; opinion, 2067; organizational, 1330; orientation, 7261; perceptions, 6764; physical, 215, 2860; resources, 2414, 8790; self-perception, 779; social support and, 5876; status, 2835, 5545, 5546, 7684, 7711; values, 9969; women, 7892

Health professionals, 4134, 5933, 5997, 7225. See also Nurses

Hebrew, visual discrimination, 2377

Help-seeking behaviors, 4247, 4303, 8592: attitudes toward, 8359, 8360; counseling, 9227

Helpfulness, of others, perceived, 4115, 8592; self-concept, 4114

Helpgivers, campus, 993

Helping: attitudes, 6131;

dispositions, 2267, 3578; perceptions of, 7269

Helplessness, 7693: child, 3856; child, teacher report, 3941; institutional, 1670; learned, 1670; psychiatric patients, 3895; women, 7692

Heterosocial: assessment, 2570; behavior, 2885

Hierarch(ical)(y), 695: of authority, 9053; influence, 1892; occupational, 269

High school, 436, 471: achievement motivation, 729; alienation, 1090; counselors, 612, 660; curriculum, 473; functional literacy, 1611; occupational aspiration, 897, 901; personality, 851; seniors, 517; sex education, 668; social studies, 601; stress, 2481; students, 401, 472, 645, 650, 653; students, self-efficacy, 9468; self-esteem, 827; social and academic integration, 7508; student barrier perceptions, 9108; study habits, 7125; vocational plans, 1590

Higher education, opportunities, 167

Higher learning, 347

Higher order need strength, 2000

Hindrance, 688

Hispanic people, 6132, 9378: acculturation, 8079

History: Black, 157; case, 856; school, 625; social, 466

HIV. See AIDS

Hmong people, 5554

Hobbies, 593, 5750

Hockey, 6765, 9640

Home, 497, 516: behavior, 1957; economics, behavioral change, 572; children's behavior, 8596; economic interest, 3631; environment, 1294, 1298, 1947, 8874; environment, cognitive, 642; environment, first graders, 1946; importance of, 6400; review, 647; learning environment, 647, 2993, 2994, 2997, 2998; observation, 1948; self-esteem, 2064; stimulation, 642; stimulations, child's, 1952, 2969, 8876; teachers, 572

Homemaker, 2995, 2996

Homicide, control, 970

Homonyms, 11

Homophobia, 514, 3843, 3855, 6072, 6133, 8401, 8404–8409, 8417–8419: internalized, 8409

Homosexuals, 514: attitude toward, 2713, 2748–2750, 6080, 6134. See also Gay men and lesbians

Honor systems, 6170

Hope, 3844, 5552, 5553, 7694–7697: college students, 7509

Hopelessness, 413, 1662, 1684, 2483, 3770, 3834, 3845, 3846, 5550, 7698, 7699; children, 2482, 3847, 5551, 7700; geriatric, 2476, 5535

Horizontality, 2224: principle, 1624

Hospice care, attitude toward, 4298

Hospital(ization): behavior, 1861; children, 1230; employee perceptions, 9118; projective test, 1488; quality, 6593; satisfaction, 6559, 6589

Hostil(e)(ity), 146, 919, 1500, 1681, 1720, 3500, 3850, 5188, 6998, 7017, 9693–9695, 9722: -aggressive, 1872, 3452, 3463; in children, 5179; cynical distrust as, 5030; indirect, 2252; mother's attributions, 8963; press, 1342; wit, 2278; towards women, 7018, 8598, 9723

Hotline facility, 4374

Household labor, discontent, 8877

Housing: issues, 319; needs, 867; on-campus, 9834

Human: figure drawing, 32; nature, philosophy, 980, 1522; relations, ability to facilitate, 1714; resources, 3078, 4263; rights attitude, 6136; values, 1529

Humor, 2278, 4393, 5562, 5669, 6368, 7589, 7705, 7766: children's preference, 1456; as coping skill, 3798, 5493, 7631; perceptiveness, 2378, 2680; response, 8703; stress, 3933

Huntington's disease, 4356

Husband, 8878, 8879

Hydrostatic principle, knowledge, 1623
Hygiene, grooming, 1603
Hyperactiv(e)(ity), 1203: adult, 6986; child, 397, 2827, 2878; -distractable, 1872
Hypersensitivity, 236
Hypnosis, 2902, 8712
Hypnotherapy, 4938
Hypochondriasis, 8415, 8416
Hypothesizing, 2215

Ideal: self, 252, 759; teacher, 679
Idealism, 2296, 9961
Ideas, 575, 3548: data, 2317
Ideational: creativity, 619; expressive style, 594; fluency, 1907, 1911
Identification, 640: athletes, 9315; concept, 884; creativity, 133; ethnic, 79753; father, 434, 830; figures, 228; high school, 7510; Jewish, 7715; letter, 12; member leader, 6802; minority, 434; mother, father, teacher and friend, 434, 830, 8880, 9600; numerical, 12; organizational, 8236; parents, 143, 8880; peer group, 100; racial, 5725–5727; religious, 988; resolution, young adults, 2166; role, 331; sex role, 1461; status, 2237, 2238; subcultural, 95, university, 7511
Identity, 5040, 6769: achievement, 271, 628, 1286, 4501; African Americans, 4754, 7910, 7911, 8023; age identity, 9305; attitude toward bodily appearance, 4273; Chickering's vector identity, 5043; cohesion, 6768; college students, 9311, conflicts, 949; cultural, 7945, 8070; diffusion, 628; ego, 949, 7003, 7004, 9716, 9717, 9752; ego development and status, 628; elements, 4759; ethnic, 4818, 5753, 5805, 5806, 7956, 7970, 7975, 8025–8027, 8137; family, 8848; feminist, 4294, 7075; gay-lesbian, 9831; gender, 630, 3403, 7077, 505, 9816, 9837; goal instability, 4500; group cohesiveness, 4008; group

identification, 4009; group importance, 4010; group solidarity, 4007; individualism-collectivism, 4012; intergenerational fusion, 4571; Jewish-American, 1403; level of, 6374; location of, 5012; maturity, 4510; nationality and, 5764; occupational, 4509, 10154, 10204; perceived, 3261; personal, 796; in prosocial action, 4768; racial, 4315–4317, 4320, 5802, 5806, 5830, 5892, 8455, 8456; sex role, 3294; shame as part of, 7021; socially desirable presentation, 4036, 4037; status, 6375, 7012; student's social, 4991; styles, 9417, 9418; White, 8138, 8138; womanist, 8485; work, 6957, 9668, 9890, 10153
Ideology: economic, 3533; feminist, 3557; mental health, 1807; pupil control, 1819, 3105
Ignoring, 504
Illegal aliens, attitudes toward, 8350
Illness, 6273: acceptance, 2432; attitude, 8415, 8416; behavior, 2839; effects, 5556; mental, 1807; perceived, 3220; satisfaction with, 5653; severity, 5664
Image(s), 1281: administrator, 1307; factor, 683; job, 9502; science, scientists, 1794
Imagery, 265, 753, 784, 794, 7475: control, 2052; endemic, 3394; preference, 3397; production, vividness, 2153; self-reported, 777; self-reported vividness, 2118; visual, 9843; vividness, 1375, 2040, 7478, 7479, 9651
Imaginary audience, 9473
Imaginative thinking, 1282, 7126
Imagining, emotive, 2063
Immanence, 9971
Immaturity, 855–857
Immediate recall, 2217
Immigration, mother's stress, 7760
Impairment, memory, 2386
Impersonal(ity)(ization), 695, 967
Implied meaning, 1278
Importance, 1318: perceived, 9499

Imposition on others, 746
Impotence, 6258
Impulse: aggression, 1638; control, motor, 386; inhibition, 386
Impulsiv(e)(eness)(ity), 481, 845, 986, 3482, 6237, 6643, 6986, 6993, 7020, 8600, 9911, 9917: buying, 8599; constriction, counselors, 961; reflection, 285, 290, 291, 1490, 1494; responding, 2262; -reflection, 2170
Impunitive attitudes, 481
Inadequacy, 515, 3861: feelings, 773, 1402
Incapability, political, 2111
Incest, 4841, 6091, 6138, 6442; blame, 6776; survivor reactions, 6407
Income, 268, 5989; -leisure trade-off, 5976; perceived hardship, 8242
Incomplete sentence(s), 400, 806
Indecision, 6225, 9724: career, 2809, 3655, 3657; vocational, 3657–3659
Independen(ce)(t), 228, 282, 301, 397, 481, 1771, 2317: adolescent, 6404; behavior, 651; child, 6445; -dependence, 400; family, 976, 2999; judgment, 612, 614; need, 1343; political, 512; pressure, 647, 673; rebellious, 481; teacher, 578; university environment, 704
Index, tension, 1667
Indian youth, disadvantaged, 375
Individual differences: acceptance of, 3963; child's social anxiety, 4075; cognition, 5142; high school students, 3675; interpersonal trust, 4019; learning processes, 5132; in objectivism, 5058; perceived locus of control, 4871
Individualism, 989, 2571, 5765, 7228, 7229, 8883, 9388: -collectivism, 9970, 9971, 9973, 9974
Individualiz(ation)(e)(ed), 681: reading instruction, 545; reinforcers, 2018; studies, 6; study in institution, 169
Individuation, 3910, 4056, 4070, 9725: adolescent, 8885

Induction, 887

Inductive: logic, 2202; reasoning ability, 2209, 3426

Industrial: problems, 150; psychology, attitude toward, 1127; rehabilitation, 515; work groups attitudes, 1127

Infan(cy)(t), 623: characteristics, 1940; development, 625, 1050, 1287, 4505, 8793; difficultness, 6247; language, 2935; psychological development, 631; temperament, see Temperament, child and infant

Inference(s), 2217: social, 114

Inferential reading comprehension, 1605

Inferiority, feelings, 515

Infertility, reactions, 8461

Inflectional performance, 17

Influence, hierarchical, 2236: in counseling, 258; leader, 1554; organizational settings, 8620, 8652; psychological, 3324; tactics, 6248, 8602, 8603, 8652, 8732; work, 2626, 2653

Information, 575: acquisition; amount, 2223; biographical, 703; community life, 1060; institutional, 150–193, 657– 706, 1307–1336, 1959–1983; job training, 709, 3079; processing, 605, 2907, 7128; processing, social, 8093; processing style, 443; seeking, adolescents, 868; seeking, 8604, 8751; seeking, careers, 3616; seeking strategies, 2223, 2814; sex, 2393; symbolic, 107; transformation abilities, 106– 108

Ingratiating behavior, 2841, 5977, 6249, 9081

Inhibition(s), 1720, 1870: behavioral, 8524, 8527; impulse, 386; motor, 59; reciprocal, 389; social, 8082

Initiative, 949, 2265, 2842, 3131: supervisors, 1023

Inmates, prison, 91

Inner-outer directedness, 789

Innocence-guilt, 381

Innovati(on)(veness), 3484, 6568, 7083: behaviors, 432, 621; educational, 1784; management teams, 9605; predisposition,

7118; university residence, 704; work situations, 8781

Inpatient behavior, mood, 1862

Inquisitiveness, creative, 578

Insecurity, 515

Inservice evaluation, 1319

Insight, 1385, 10033: therapy clients, 10053, 10061, 10121; social, 5855

Insomnia, 8606

Institution(al)(s): attitudes, 82; authority, attitudes, 2747; helplessness, 1670; information, 150–193, 657– 706, 1307–1336, 1959–1983; motivation in, 6644; political, 1806; procedures, 682

Instruction(al): attitude toward, 2712; behavior, 322; commitment, 7512, 7544; information, 9009–9190; performance, 6206; programmed, 153; television, problems, 488; threat of, 488; values, 3547

Instructor, 527, 667: behavior, 2863; communication, 8746; effectiveness, 329; evaluation, 698, 997, 1009, 1014, 1022, 1027–1029, 1032, 3581, 10054; quality, 667; student preferences, 9825; university, 680

Intake interview, 3988, 4692

Integrat(ed)(ion), 517: attitude, 79; classrooms, 2189; social, 5856

Integrative complexity, 1910, 2214, 2934

Integrity: of man, 915; of social agents, 2288

Intellectual(ity), 624, 986: ability, children, 888; achievement responsibility, 786; assessment, 7466; confidence, 9564; development, 637, 2953, 2954, 2958, 8797; efficiency, 2251; environment, 2993, 2994, 6772; feeling of phoniness, 6770; growth, university residence, 704; locus of control, 3222; pragmatism, 95, 1515; pragmatic attitudes, 86; pressure for, 647, 673; self-confidence, 2073; triarc abilities, 7470

Intelligence, 1117, 2265, 2689: children, 2677; culturally disadvantaged, 72; culture fair, 468; developmental, 1055; evaluated, 247; opinions of, 6156; social, 1096, 1099, 1100, 2555, 2564; verbal, 887

Intensity, 2285

Intent(ionality): accidental, 381; children's attributions, 9421; judgment of, 622; to leave employment, 8182–8186; retributive, 8264; therapists, 10122; to turnover, 8179– 8181, 8289–8293

Interaction, 68, 237: aide-child, 577; analysis, 427, 1049; anxiousness, 2572; behavioral, 585; behavior description, 596; classroom, 1105, 1894, 1897; counselor-client, 1253; family, 597; group, 1722, 5760; interpersonal, 448; interracial, 1143, 1745; marital, 240, 3024, 2035; mother, 1300; mother-child, 1953; parent-adolescent, 640; parent-child, 646, 1301, 1955; pupil, 1027; social, 5857, 8095; supervisor, 1248; teachers, 333, 1029; verbal, 596, 1261

Interconcept distance, 1908

Interdependence-independence, 4027, 4145: student, 5413

Interest(s), 194–203, 593, 707– 711: effort, counselors, 1003; finder, 10156; information seeking, 868; inventories, satisfaction with, 9157; job, 709; judgment of, 626; mathematics, 7084, 7095, 7096; occupations, 196, 199, 201, 3629, 3631; parental, 650; patterns, 472; political, 537; religious, 1580; in research, 10157; residence counselor, 1019; school, 391; science, intermediate, children, 864; sexual, 9279; social, 249, 8096; value, 1535; vocational, 10129–10208; work, 757; work teams, 7974

Intermarriage, racial, 90

Internal: cognition, 2187; dialogue, 4482; scanning, 1914; sensation, 2187; state, 7709, 9491; work motivation, 2001

Internal-external control, 50, 56, 238, 267, 576, 810, 1368, 1393, 1396, 1399, 1401, 1405, 1406, 1413, 1434, 2049, 2181: university freshmen, 221

Internationalism, 1795, 9968

Interorganizational relations, 1893

Interpersonal interaction, 448, 621, 625, 3998, 4018, 5733, 5773, 5803, 5828, 5893, 7976, 7984: acceptance, 4065; adequacy, peer counseling, 1973; adjustment, college student, 2409; administrative behavior, 1863; adolescent aggression, 1221; adolescent competence, 3698; adult conflict resolution, 4003; alienation, 1110; analogue measure of social skills, 3970; assumptions about persons, 4235; attitude about controversy, 4238; attitude toward cooperation/competition, 4286, 4371; attitude toward men, 4245; attitude toward power, 4311; attitudes, 546; attraction, 426, 1711, 3971; attraction to mentor, 4035; behavior, 1720; celebrity-audience, 5731; children's behavior, 465; cognitive-complexity, 433; communication, 1900, 2920, 4483; competenc(e)(y), 446, 1724, 7977, 7978; complexity, 47; concealing information, 6292; concern for others, 3986, 4012; conflict, 523, 4015; 1950, 2573; contact, 328; control, 2075, 4096, 7979; couple problem-solving, 4013; dating anxiety, 3993; dating competence, 3992, 3997, 4034; dealing with strangers, 4097; dependency, adults, 1715, 2574, 5770, 5771, 7980; development of, 5799; difficulty in maintaining, 4049; difficulty of presenting self, 4024; distanc(e)(ing), 436, 451, 2596; effectiveness, 2576; emotional closeness, 4002; emotional dependence, 5718; envy, 439; etiology, 530;

family, 4525; family-like, 5788; feedback, 1899; flexibility, 217, 7164, 9898; frequency, 4083; friendship, 4004; heterosocial, 4996, 5090; index, 447; initiating, 4101; intake behavior, 3988; intimacy, 4004; jealousy, 2575, 4016, 7981; judgment, 1717; leader-subordinate, 4379, 4404, 4405, 4417, 4428, 4458; leadership style, 4025, 5088, 5089; love concepts, 3989; need for control, 4113; orientation, 54, 67, 216; peer relationship satisfaction, 4044; perception, 428, 433, 4006, 4032; perceptions, teacher-child, 2076; positive impressions, 6275; power, 9734; preferences for social interaction, 4017; problem, 892, 5784, 7991–7995; pursuing, 2596; quality, 5767, 5801; racial mistrust, 3991; reactivity, 9916, 7983; reflexes, 448; regard, 681; relations, 51, 431, 464, 575, 1102, 1256, 1668, 2548, 2577, 2588; relations, counselors, 1003; relations, self-perceptions, 780; relations university residence, 704; relationships, 1716; relationships, locus of control, 2087; roommate rapport, 4063, 4064; self-other focus, 5843; seniority, 428, 444; sensitivity, 1663, 1681, 1718, 2269, 2288; situations, 1721; skills, 431; social desirability, 3972, 3999, 4079; social network assessment, 4484; style, 1489, 5768; support, 2578, 7985; support for quitting smoking, 4048; teacher's stages of concern, 4196; trust, 954, 1504, 2914, 4005, 4019, 4069, 7982, 7986; types, 9733; value constructs, 2304; working relationships, 4189, 5769; workplace influence, 4201, 4458, 8187, 8188, 8245

Interpretat(ing)(ion)(ive), 600, 689, 1448: data, 1607

Interracial: attitudes, 517, 1150, 1198; attitude, students, 535; interaction, 1745

Interrogative patterns, recognition, 380, 384

Intervention: acceptability, 3400; federal, 79

Interview(ing), 587, 589: assessment, 3162; behavior, 6199; behavior, counselor, 584; client reaction, 998; counseling, 699; credibility, 7303; home, 647; maternal, 927; rating, counseling, 699; reaction, 589, 998; residents, 546; schedule, 471; teaching, evaluation, 1015; techniques, medical students, 2330

Interviewer(s): knowledge of laws, 1018; rating, 803, 3594, 7267; screening, 1013; self-disclosure, 104, 2906; trustworthiness, 938

Intimacy, 688, 1257, 2580, 2592, 2837, 2965, 3004, 3998, 4004, 4105, 5775, 5777, 5798, 7987–7989, 8040, 8097: attitude, 2579; comfort with, 5709; family, 6426; fear of, 5755, 7958; mother-daughter, 6449; physical, 3039; risk, 8062; social, 2587

Intolerance: general, 1792; trait inconsistency, 2078

Intrinsic: -extrinsic job outcomes, 1786; job attributes, 8421; motivation, 481, 1994, 3127, 3136, 3138, 3140, 9207, 9229–9235, 9280, 9296; task motivation, 3137

Introspection, 481, 8607

Introversion: -extraversion, 292, 390, 749; children, 956; occupational, 292; social, 1670

Intrusiveness, 655

Intrusive thoughts, 5487, 5692

Intuitive, 2205, 2206, 9868: ability, 3430

Invasion, privacy, 1320, 2079

Inventions, evaluation, 8782

Investigatory activities, children, 724

Investments, choice, 9828

Involvement, 7100: classroom, 5406; family, 2986, 6423, 8849–8852; fathers, 8972; issue, 6140, 7231; job, 1322, 2002, 2003, 2671, 3583, 3720, 3633–3637, 7387–7391, 9068,

10160–10165, 10205–10208;
maternal, 578; parents, 7515,
8929, 8930, 8932, 8950;
positive, 655; professional,
7425; sport, 7052; student
organizations, 5409; university
residence, 704; work, 3661,
3662

Irrational beliefs, 1516, 1637,
1665, 2505, 3226, 3227, 3284,
3287, 4804, 4814, 4839, 4856–
4858, 4934, 7713, 8423

Irritability, 1638, 1670, 2552

Irritation, 2627, 3075: anxiety-
depression, 1686, 2621; work-
related, 6048

Islam, 5229

Isolated child, 397

Isolation, 1093: perceived, 453;
social, 437, 1110, 1727

Israelis, acculturation, 7996,
7997

Issues: housing, 319; individual
importance, 7256; involvement,
6140, 7231

Itching, 5562

Item distractors, 173

Italian stereotype, 3228

Japan(ese): Americans, 520;
attributional styles, 9432;
depression, 7900; geography,
351; mental-physical health,
7714; occupational strain,
5605; self-construal, 9560;
socially sensitive independence,
5787

Jealousy, 2575, 3006, 3485, 4016,
5786, 7998: interpersonal,
7981; sexual, 4016

Jewish: American identity, 1403;
college students, 503;
identification and well-being,
7715; racism toward, 5716,
8321; religiosity, 3553

Job(s), 457, 6526, 6565, 6571,
6572, 6579, 7376: aggression,
1033; alienation, 5941;
alternatives, 9500; applicants,
9433; attributes, 1040, 8421,
9058; attitude, 1346, 2754;
autonomy, 3051, 6564;
avoidance, 5942; bizarre
behavior, 1033; boredom,
8191; burnout, see Burnout;
career and, 7379; career key,

2379; characteristics, 3080–
3082, 3088, 9059, 9062–9064;
classification, 3073, 3095;
clerical, 73; climate, 1967,
3052; commitment, 7396;
competence, 9501, complexity,
3091, 6567; complexity,
perception, 2083; conditions,
1404, 9060; conditions,
clerical, 2178; control, 5992,
5999, 6569, 9142; demand,
6570, 9061; dependence, 1034;
description, 1321; design,
3092, 9083, 9084;
discrimination, 3085; distress,
5946; duties, 1040; education
required, 1040; equity, 3395;
evaluation, 1016, 3061, 6563;
expectations, 5979, 9434;
feedback, 3083; foremen
perception, 1012; foremen
responsibilities, 1011;
frustration, 2623, 5927, 5947,
5948; goals, 709; grievance,
2656; growth need, 8789,
hassles, 8195; hunting, 3458;
image, 9502; importance, 9892;
induced anxiety, 1666;
information and training, 709,
3079; intrinsic attributes,
8421; innovation, 6568;
insecurity, 8896; interference,
5947, 5948; interest, 197, 709;
interview performance, 1736,
2350; investment, 7386;
involvement, 1322, 1737, 2002,
2003, 2364, 2671, 3583, 3633–
3637, 7388–7392, 9068,
10160–10166; knowledge,
supervisors, 1005, 2380; loss,
6778, 8160, 8161, 8164, 8198;
motivation, 6566, 9237; need
fulfillment, 3143; networking,
8034; off-job interference,
5986; outcomes, 1534;
outcomes, intrinsic-extrinsic,
1786, 3136, 3138;
overqualification, 10076;
perceptions, 6596;
performance, 2647, 3584,
7304, 7305, 9126, 9208, 10058,
10059, 10079; performance,
evaluation of, 1016, 1537,
1553, 1566, 5995, 9150;
performance, perception, 3267;
physical and mental exertion,

709; physical surroundings of,
709; police, 3577, 3579;
pressure, 1687, 5948; prestige,
273; preview, 6007; problems,
1968; proficiency, 320;
propensity to leave, 8252;
quitting, 3650; quitting
intentions, 5935–5940, 6038,
8182–8186; rating, 3096, 9150;
rating of residence counselors,
1019; redirection, 10159;
relations with associates, 709;
relations with employers, 709;
recruiters, 518; rewards, 5951,
6011; richness, 9070;
robustness, 3107; satisfaction,
709, 1575, 1577, 1578, 1581,
1586, 1588, 1589, 1592, 1594,
1668, 2320, 2363, 2365, 2367,
2368, 2624, 2625, 2629–2637,
2657, 2659, 2668, 2670, 2673,
2675, 5929–5934, 5943–5945,
5952–5968, 5978, 8176, 8178,
9192–8194, 8199–8219, 8230,
8237, 8239, 8609; scope, 6573,
6574; search, 7392, 8610,
8611, 9071, 9206, 9212, 9435–
9437, 9492, 10167, 10168;
search intentions, 7384;
security, 709, 1687, 2367,
8196, 8197; selection, 1040,
3632, 9069; self-concept and,
5950; self-efficacy, 9438, 9575;
skills, 9065; status, 2645;
stress, 2621, 2641, 2642, 2649,
2650, 2654, 2658, 5970, 5971,
6779, 8143, 8154, 8220–8223,
8279, 8280; structure, 3084;
tedium, 2643, 2674; tension,
2638–2640, 2667, 5971–5974;
time demand, 2644;
transitions, 8155, 8189; values,
321; viewpoints, 546;
withdrawal intentions, 5975,
6002, 6003, 6030–6035, 7393,
8296, 8298. See also Career;
Employment

Journals in sociology, prestige,
906

Judgment, 9, 890: affect, 1252;
analysis, 2183; children's, 626;
clinical, 215; concepts, 2936;
ethical, 9960; group, 1392;
independence of, 612; interest,
622, 626; interpersonal, 1717;
moral, 139, 622, 626, 633,

638, 852, 1519, 1599, 2210, 3543; supervisors, 1023; teacher, 1059; visual, 1115
Jungian personality types, 9759
Junior high school, climate, 9022
Junior college: motivation, 1351; student ability, 766; transfers, 1311
Junior high school, 1799: abstract reasoning, 884; achievement motivation, 2028; atmosphere, 700; boys, 651; classroom methods, 700; grading, 700; knowledge of work, 711; materials and facilities, 700; need achievement, 729; skills, 700; students, 700; teachers, 700; teachers, student-centeredness, 1867
Just world belief, 9962, 9966, 9967, 9977, 9978, 9982, 9983
Justice: conceptions, 381, 3522, 3537, 3538; distributive, 234, 7222, 9034–9036, 9072, 9074; interactional, 9055; in organizations, 9101; perceptions, 9074, 9124; procedural, 9124–9142; social, 381, values, 9981
Juvenile delinquency, 519

Kidney disease, 7458
Kindergarten, 352, 356, 357, 540: adjustment, 2422; children, development, 1289; handwriting performance, 1051; learning ability, 6054; performance, 2381; racial preference, 1459; reading, 352; sex role, 874, 881, 883
Kindness, 113, 1270, 7999
Kinesthetic sensitivity, 1421
Knowledge, 6364, 7140: of accident avoidance, 1622; AIDS, 5364, 5365, 5366, 5367, 5368, 6066; of Alzheimer's disease, 3666; author recognition, 5396; baseball, 3668; 5370; of behaviorism, 5399; behavioral principles, 2382; careers, 3614; of cognition, 3669; of depression, 5377; of development, 5378; drugs, 343, 344, 1042, 1600; of infant behavior, 3676; laws,

interviewers, 1018; magazine recognition, 5379; medical, 5385; morphographic, 2387; music, 2389; newspaper recognition, 5382; occupational, 3678, 3683; organization of subject matter, 679; personal traits, 862; political, 368; product, 6839; of psychology, 5375; reproductive, 1056; rules of the road, 1622; of science, 5371; of sexual abuse, 3682; of statistics, 5390; supervisors, 1023; teachers', of behavioral principles, 3679; of technology, 5384; words, 342; work, 711
Kuder Preference Test, 10

Labor: division of, 695; gender discrimination, 6976
Labor/trade unions, 4213, 4214, 4652, 4685, 5320, 5321, 5353, 5354: attitudes toward, 6128, 6186; attitudes toward collective bargaining in education, 4292; See also Unions
Laboratory, 1182
Lack of social support, 1638
Language, 21: ability, 384; arts, 12, 637; arts, pre-first graders, 277; attitudes, 6141; competence, basic, 380, 384; comprehension, 355; infant, 2935; informal, 378; negative, 2933; oral, 1275; performance, 1035; proficiency, 376; skills, 1597; street, 378
Late adolescent(s), 498: males, 646
Latency, 585
Laterality assessment, 1881, 2681, 2687, 2690, 3422
Latinos, 5724: college climate, 6538
Law(s): abidingness, 287; enforcement personnel, 3577, 3579, 3587; jury bias, 7181; knowledge of, 1018; and order, 1797
Laxative use, 8515
Layoffs: fairness, 9134; organizational explanations, 9076; survivors, 8261
Leader(ship), 4379, 4404–4410,

4417, 5088, 5089, 6254: appraisal of members by, 6259; attitudes and beliefs, 9872; behavior, 1241, 1333, 1866, 2084, 2843, 2845, 2872, 2884, 2896, 6261, 6330; creativity, 1925; cultural style, 6272; empowerment, 8612; firemen, 1549; in groups, 8729, 8752–8754; implicit, 9365; influence, 1544; initiative, self-concept, 2056; member attitude, 5797, 6802; -member exchange, 1986, 2915, 2916, 2926, 6245, 6346, 6394; motivational style, 2184, 9250; opinion, 2104, 6265; perceptions, 6242; power, 8663; principals, 8645; qualities, 338; satisfaction, 2345; self-appraisal, 6320; self-management, 8678; students, 2349, 2684, 2844; style, 941, 8613; style, supervisors, 1023; substitutes, 4460, 4678, 6317, 6318; supportive, 6319; teacher, 1057; technical competence, 1555; trust in, 8126
Learn(er)(ing), 494, 4400, 6678, 7128: acceptance of failure, 3721; approaches, 5153; attitude toward, 540, 2785, 6648, 8425, 8426; awareness, 9440, 9873; behavior, 2829; behavior, perception of, 838; behavior in classrooms, 838; children's, 521, 2677; climate, 1323; cognitive, 175, 5131–5133; 5135–5137; conceptions of, 9862; confidence, 9441; disabled, 2853; enthusiasm for, 540; environment, 473, 647, 673, 686, 1298, 1324, 1371, 2985, 3076, 3089, 3109, 3114, 4658, 9091; format preferences, 5087; grades vs. true, 487; higher, 347; inflectional principals, 17; in kindergarten, 6054; interdependence of students, 5413; locus of control, 4843–4835; materials, 1325; memory, 8; motivation for, 4882, 6655, 9241, 9242, 9247, 9251–9253, 9259; orientation, 8425, 9238, 9239; preference, 3402;

process, 488, 3431; readiness, 2193; self-concept, 1389, 3213, 3299; self-efficacy, 9572; self-regulated, 8679, 8680, 9326; strategy selection, 7129, 9242, 9874, 9875, 9877, 9886; student perceptions, 175; style, 2216, 7130, 7131, 9885; tasks, 1868; visual arts, 5396
Learned helplessness, 3782, 4789, 6255
Learning disabled, children, phonics, 2398
Lectures, 7298, 7315: controversial, 586; quality, 3085
Legibility, 1052, 2376
Leisure, 6781: activities, 198, 268, 870, 2185, 3404, 3407, 6326, 7088, 8492; adolescents, 8615; attitudes toward, 4301; benefits, 5609; enjoyment, 7965; income trade-off, 5976; interests, 9830; satisfaction, 5564, 6780, 7089, 7721; self-efficacy, 9587
Length, 2224
Leniency, 7023
Lesson, evaluation, 1027
Lethal behavior, 4411
Letter: discrimination, 1051; formation, 1052; identification, 12; sound translation, 1062
Level of arousal, 2291
Level of aspiration, self-concept, 2056
Level of regard, 227, 309, 431, 2353
Liberal-conservative, 95, 280, 1527
Liberal dimension, mother's, 2313
Liberalism, 555, 2258
Liberalism-conservatism, college students, 1835
Libertarian democracy, 1799
Library: attitude, 2758; use, 7132
Lie scale, 499
Life: change(s), 1290, 2522, 2532, 3009; changes, college students, 1942; events, 2581, 3111, 3863–3865, 5501, 5502, 5565–5570; events, 3868, 5068, 7517, 7579, 7723–7726, 7754, 7764, 8617, 8800; experience, 1719,

3373; experiences, women's liberation, 861; history, 1288; imagined, 3193; inventory, 2836; irritants, 3075; meaningfulness in, 821, 3524, 7727; orientation, 5606, 7728, 7729; perspective, 2047; satisfaction, 33, 415, 2504, 2529, 5575–5581, 5600, 5608, 5615, 5654, 5684, 7525, 7730–7733, 7834; skills, 7734; space, 8002; statuses, perception, 2047; stress, 2533, 2543, 3866, 3867, 3885, 7735; style, 268, 1800, 8643; success, 5582; values, 9979
Lifestyle, 6256: change, 6298; orientation, 2186
Liking, 460, 2582, 7544, 8224
Line Meanings, 608
Linguistic competence, 1121
Lipreading ability, 5386
Listening, 1735, 2913: achievement, 1043; comprehension, 2688
Literacy: acquisition perceptions, 9443; basic occupational, 1038; child understanding, 3257, 3337; functional, 1611; parental initiatives, 8875
Literal reading comprehension, 1609
Locative prepositional, 377
Locus of conflict, 2085
Locus of control, 50, 221, 239, 310, 320, 1368, 1383, 1393, 1396, 1399, 1401, 1406, 1413, 1434, 1628, 2068, 2071, 2074, 2088–2091, 2093, 2094, 2102, 2150, 3166, 3171, 3178, 3222–3225, 3230, 3233–3240, 3244, 4752, 4767, 4782, 4788, 4805, 4812, 4846–4849, 4855, 4864–4870, 4947, 4963, 4992, 6685, 6705, 6772, 6773, 6774, 6775, 6783–6789, 6809–6812, 6893, 6975, 9302, 9342, 9412, 9424–9426, 9428, 9429, 9445–9448, 9474, 9514, 9525, 9657: academic, 9298; accident, 6684; administrators, 818; adolescents, 2072; adult(s), 2033, 2100, 3194, 3196, 3255, 3272, 3274; Black children, 793; cancer patient, 4784, 4786; career, 6726, 9351;

children, 754, 797, 799, 2041, 2092, 2101, 2146, 2148, 3182–3187, 3205, 3241, 3242, 3252, 4887, 4888, 4924, 9360, 9361; and chance, 9359; consumer behavior, 4883; depression, 4806, 4807; in detention, 4808; diabetes, 4809; dieting beliefs, 4810; family eating habits, 4891; fetal health, 4826; health, 2066, 3217–3219, 3251, 3339, 3340, 4837, 4887, 4888, 4862, 4924, 6718, 6763, 6808; health students, 9416; individual perceptual differences, 4871; intellectual, social physical, 2086; internal-external, 576, 2049, 2081, 3164, 6814, 6894; interpersonal relationships, 2087; learning, 4843–4845; marital, 8906; mental health, 2096; mother's perception, 4751; peer counseling, 1973; personal reaction scale, 4909; physical fitness, 4915; preschool, primary, 2113; in prisoners, 6865, 6866, 9528; and race, 9444; rehabilitation clients, 29; religious, 4937; smoking, 6948; supernatural, 5014; teacher, 3332–3334, 6963; victimization and, 6742; in workplace, 5021, 9469, 9670
Logic(al), 474, 884, 7133: ability, children, 3441; additions, 19; connectives, 123; operations, 2946
Loneliness, 1703–1705, 1729, 2552–2554, 2561, 2615, 3982, 3996, 4031, 4106–4108, 5791, 5792, 5793, 5885, 5889, 7736, 8003–8013, 8133: adolescent, 4030; children, 2583, 5790, 7518, 7926, 8005, 8008, 8009; control over, 8037; responsibility for, 8058; school setting, 7518, 7519; self-concept and, 5747
Long-term memory, 1601
Love, 3989, 3995, 4032, 4033, 4105, 4264, 8014, 8125: addiction, 2584; attitudes, 8427; desperate, 5746; loss, 5583; passionate, 5812; punishment, symbolic, 654;

reward, symbolic, 654; romantic, 2599, 2600, 5840; sickness, 3012; spousal, 8901

Loving, styles, 1871, 5841

Lower class, 349: children, test anxiety, 1076

Loyalty: career, 8147; to coworkers, 3990; organizational, 7395, 10186; supervisor, 1005; teacher, 1883; union, 4110

Lunar effects, 3172

Luteal-phase dysphoria, 5500

Lying, 4425

Machiavellianism, 1492, 1517, 1721, 3486, 3487, 3514, 5186, 5190, 7182, 9918, 9919

Magic, 3539

Majors, college, 222, 662

Maladjustment, 2492

Malaise, 5584: African society, 65

Male(s): influence on female career choice, 710; life experience, 7741; need achievement, 728; role attitudes, 8428; self-esteem, 826; sex-role attitude, 2760; social workers, 8353; young adult, 636

Mammography, 6791

Management, 388: accounting adequacy, 10019; approval of, 8158; fairness perceptions, 9047, 10057; frame, 8175, innovations, 9605; perception of, 6246; performance, 10058; strategic perceptions, 9012; strategy, classroom, 880; support by, 9079; style, 1333; trust of, 6029

Manager(ial)(s), 4412, 4413, 4461, 7093, 7098: AIDS beliefs, 4756; attitudes, 523, 1536; autocratic personality, 787; behavior, 3560; changes in practice, 1129; description, 1447; effectiveness, 6058; employee evaluation, 5264; employee perception of support, 4680–4682; employee relations, 4655; employee trust of, 6014; needs, 1348; perceived qualities for, 4874; perception of, 5925; positions, 3104; rating, 1560, 3580, 3585,

3586; self-awareness, 9449; self-monitoring, 9542; sex-role stereotypes, 1482; supervisor-employee race relations, 4765; traits, 2265; values, 5223; vocational evaluation, 5288

Manic-depression, 7737

Manifest: alienation, 443, 1102; anxiety, 29, 1478, 1493, 1647, 2524, 3488; needs, 211, 2005, 8227; rejection, 496

Marginality, 249

Marijuana, 353, 1214, 1223, 8671: attitude toward, 1133; motivation, 9204

Marital: activities, 3013; adjustment, 8900; alternatives, 3016; attributions, 8902; communication, 2972, 3017, 6459; conflict, 2973, 8903; dependency, 3029, 3046; disaffection, 8904; happiness, 8905; instability, 3023, 6461; interaction, 3024, 3025; locus of control, 8906; problems, 8980; quality, 3026, 6462, 6464, 8908, 8971; relationships, 1766, 3018, 3021; satisfaction, 2976, 3007, 3020, 3022, 3027, 3028, 3035, 6389, 6455, 8897, 8909, 8988; strain, 6458; well-being, 8910

Marketing, intrusive, 8422

Marri(age)(ed), 503, 593, 1056, 1161, 6450, 6502: adjustment, 648, 1299, 2962, 2978, 2980, 3011, 3014, 3015, 3019, 4541, 4542, 4579, 6444; aggressive behavior in, 4625; with children of previous marriage, 6413; attitude toward, 4244; attitudes toward married women's employment, 4309; commitment, 6401; complaints, 2966; conflict scale, 4580; cooperativeness in conflict, 4534; coping strategies, 4581; counseling, 146; couple cognitions, 4533; couples, 648; dating, 503; difficulties, psychiatric patients, 773; disagreement, 6460; equity in, 6463; family decision-making, 4573; husband-wife social support, 4623; husband's emotionality, 6440; influence

strategies, 4582; interaction, 240; interactional problem-solving, 4013; jealousy, 3006; motivation for, 4719; perspective-taking, 4043, 4067; premarital sexual permissiveness, 4312; provocative behavior, 4586; quality, 4583, 8986; reward, 3041; satisfaction, 648, 1305, 3765, 3923, 4576, 4584, 4585, 4618; social support from husbands, 4568, 6441; students, 1349; termination, 2963, 2968, 2977

Marxism, 7233, 7234

Masculine: attitudes, 2759, 8410; gender role ideology, 9832; gender role stress, 7738; transcendence, 1757

Masculinity-femininity, 795, 927, 2265, 7094, 9823, 9824, 9837, 9838: concepts self-reports, 7064, 7065; -femininity, 9807, 9816; self-perceptions, 9614

Maslowian Scale, 9738

Masochistic-self effacing personality, 787

Mass media, 302

Mastery, 301, 6255, 6793, 6942, 7461, 9450, 9451, 10061, 10121: orientation, 9244; physical, 6850

Masturbation, attitude toward, 4302

Materialism, 9951, 9980: attitudes toward, 6097

Materials and facilities: junior high school, 700; learning, 1325

Maternal: acceptance, perceived, 759; attitude, perceived, 759; controls, 1954; depression risk, 5586; employment, 8907; encouragement measure, 651; interview, 927; involvement, 578; perceived nurturance, 646; responsiveness, 2273; school involvement, 7520; separation anxiety, 6465; vocalization, 649; warmth, 652; See also Mothers

Mathematics, 4, 19, 21, 508, 525, 1758, 2371, 6949, 7235: achievement in, 1740, 2383, 5380; anxiety, 394, 1630, 2417,

2418, 3714–3720, 5416, 7523, 7524, 7539; attitude toward, 153, 524, 2715, 2740, 2761, 2762, 2795, 4303, 6123, 6144, 6145, 6146, 6977, 8325, 8354, 8355, 8398, 8429–8431; attribution, 3246, 4760–4762, 4875; career interests, 10140, 10169, 10170; classroom environment, 9080; conceptions, 9372; early behaviors, 345; elementary school, 7450; enjoyment, 7073; expectancies, 6794, 9453, 9454, 9650; exponent manipulation, 7463; goal orientation, 9217, 9240, 9245; intentions, 9833; interest, 7084, 7095, 7096; lecture, quality, 3086; locus of control, 3244; motivation, 9286; outcome expectations, 8311, 9480; performance assessment, 5381; problem-solving strategies, 3722, 5146; relevance, 6189; remedial, 508; self-concept, 1409, 3247, 3248, 3722, 6798; self-efficacy, 3249, 4876, 4877, 6795–6797, 6799, 9452–9462, 9506, 9624; statistics, attitude toward, 4249, 4268, 4326; stereotype, 3245; student perceptions, 3722, 6977; students' valuation of, 5245, 5246; talented student's attitude, 6099
Mattering, 7960
Maturity, 2265: adult vocational, 1936; behavior, 621, 1206, 1937; children, 621; emotional, 621; personal, 636; reading, 1053; social, 636; students', 2349; vocational, 308, 2618
Meaning: assimilation of, 380; concept, 106–125, 1269–1279; implied, 1278; unusual, 1914
Meaningful(ness): in life, 821; words, 360
Meaninglessness, 413, 424, 1700
Mechanics, word association, 119
Mechanization, attitude toward, 1162
Media therapy, 98, 307
Medical career, 3640
Medical school: learning environment, 3089; stress, 2425; students, 4879

Memorizing, 2215
Memory, 8, 11, 13, 18, 116, 117, 358–363, 382, 600, 1738, 2385: aids, 7467; assessment, 2384; auditory, 1066; beliefs about, 8432; early, 134, 848; immediate and remote, 2213; impairment, 2386; long-term, 1601; performance, 382; remote, 1601; short-term, 18; span, 1388, 1436, 1437; symbolic implications, 116; vision-spatial, 2152; visual, 2397, 5397
Mental: ability, 138; aptitude, 72; capacity, 6124; competence, 2385; development, 134, 2956; dexterity, 1738, 2689, 6055; effort, 3161, 9258; health, 42, 3848, 3879, 3906, 3908, 3911, 3947, 7683, 7742–7750, 7773, 9028; health, adolescent, 4020; health ideology, 530, 1807; health, Japanese, 7714 health, locus of control, 2096; health, locus of origin, 1801; health, psychodynamic, 880; health services, 6451; health, student, 3849; health, temperament and, 3878; health values, 7236; illness, attitude toward, 530, 2736, 6149; illness, attitudes toward, 8372; illness, care, 6575; imagery, 4880; impairment, 2834; psychopathy in criminals, 3912, 3913; readiness, 7751; rotation, 7462, 7468, 7474; workload, 8228
Mentally retarded: children, 1759; counseling, 7097; maladaptive behaviors, 6654
Mentoring, 4035, 5289, 10062–10068, 10084–10086, 10103, 10120: barriers, 9014, 10030
Merit, 502
Methods, 694: disciplining, residents, 546
Mexican Americans, 472, 549, 3966: acculturation, 2547, 3519, 5704, 7902, 7903, 7943; achievement need, 738; attitudes towards, 2768; disadvantaged children, 380, 384, 390; power need, 738; rejection need, 738; workers' status, 902

Middle school: evaluation, 1326; self-efficacy, 9466, 9468; teachers, student-centeredness, 1867
Migrant children placement, 21
Militancy, 1495, 6102
Military: commitment, 10171; experience, 518; job satisfaction, 8229; morale, 1971; reenlistment, 3652; service attitudes, 81; social support, 4099; training success, 3582; women in, 6181
Ministers, protestant, 519
Minority: children, 502; counselor attitudes, 8373; groups, 480; group rights, 79; identification, 434; student academic performance predictors, 3724, 3725; treatment of, 7148; youth, 1587
Mistrust, 2247: cultural, 2560; interpersonal, 7982
Mobility: physical, 1707; upward, 1158, 3145
Modernism, 301, 302
Modernity, 1327, 2309, 10005: attitudes, 1164, 1165, 3536
Money, 593, 2317, 2764
Monosyllabic: nonsense, 374; words, 374
Mood, 416, 1083, 2275, 2285, 2494, 3954, 5592: impatient behavior, 1862, 2801; negative, 3890, 5598, 5599, 7756–7758; disorders, 7883; negative, 7769; objective, 417, 1496; psychological, 1669; reflective experience of, 9944; regulation, 3829, 3889, 7759; sad, 1670; state, 2457; structure, 3886; thoughts about, 5589; visual analogue, 7885; in the workplace, 4143, 8306
Moonlighting, 226
Moral: approbation, 9702; authority, 9998; behavior, 981, 3529; code, 981; commitment, 3541; comprehension, 3556; development, 139, 638, 2957; evaluation, 1745; judgment, 622, 626, 633, 638, 852, 1519, 1599, 2210, 2301, 3543; -judgment, behavior, 2310; judgment, children, 2311;

orientation, 7237, 9981; reasoning, 2212, 2218, 2219, 2222, 3531, 3558; social values, 472; structure, children, 977; thought, 3542; values, 7255; values, children, 978

Morale, 415, 443, 444: elderly, 2495, 2496, 2506; military, 1871; school administrator, 1680, 1978

Moralism, 624

Moratorium, 628

Morningness, 7183, 7184

Morphographic, transfer and knowledge, 2387

Mosaic: construction, 611; test, 138

Mother(s), 578: adolescent communication, 8755; aggression rating, 8545; alcoholism, 8622; attitude, 1803; behavior problems perception, 8543; child attachment, 6390, 6391; child care, 2967; -child interaction, 649, 1300, 1953, 6503, 6507; child-rearing practices, 6411; children's perception, 761; conscience development rating, 8794; daughter, 3004, 6467, 6468; discipline, 8822, 8911; dominance, 647, 673; gatekeeping, 8912; identification with, 434, 830, 9600; immigration stress, 7760; instrumental support, 7922; marital satisfaction, 8918; monitoring of children, 8919, 9009; relations with, 419; reporting child's development, 6377; responsiveness, 8961; role of, 652, 2970, 2981; school involvement, 7520; self-efficacy, 8966; separation anxiety, 8913, 8914; temperament, 9714; working, 655

Motion picture, 1384, 1386

Motion sickness, 2848

Motivation, 204–210, 712–747, 1337–1366, 1984–2029, 3135, 4391, 4722, 4723, 6644, 6996, 9191–9296: academic, 578, 3123, 6624, 9191, 9252, 9253, 9270, 9275; achievement, 712,

721, 1338, 1340, 1347, 1350, 1353, 1986, 1987, 1989, 1990, 1993, 2017, 2019, 2026, 3124–3126, 3141, 3142, 6522, 6627, 6628, 6629; 9194–9197, 9256; achievement, children, 718, 737; achievement, men, 1988; action orientation, 4698; altruistic, 3134; attributions, 9318; to change, 4713; children's academic, 4738; college, 208, 743; competitiveness, 4700; consumer, 4883; for counseling, 4701; creative, 607; curricula choice, 720; dating, 3128; deferment of gratification, 4703; desire for challenge, 4710; effectance, 3150; employee, 205; esteem, 1360; to exercise, 4730, 9273; expectancy, 4704; face saving, 1353; factors, academic, 1985; fear of failure, 1342; gambling, 6631; goal dimensions, 4705–4709; hypercompetitiveness, 4711; inner, 9225, 9228; internal work, 2001; intrinsic, 730, 1994, 3127, 3136–3138, 3140, 9207, 9229–9235; job, 6560, 9237; job search, 9206; junior-senior high school achievement, 729, 2028; leadership, 9250; to learn, 4882, 6655, 9241, 9242, 9284, 9285; maladaptive behavior, 4718; to manage, 3148; for marriage, 4719; need for cognition, 4725, 4726; need for power, 4712; need for sensation, 4739; needs assessment, 4715–4717; novelty, 717; on-line, 9259; peer, 732; parental, 1945; perceived context, 9262; personal characteristics, 4737; physical activity, 6661, 9248; police work, 9236; power, 3129, 3132; reading, 9245; to reestablish freedom, 4733; for risk taking, 4735; safety, 1360; salespeople 6668; school, 731, 737, 2004, 3151, 6669; self-, 6670; smoking cessation, 4734; social power, 4741; sources, 9249; sports, 9113, 9114;

structure, 687, 9254; student, 4736, 6650, 6678, 9233, 9284, 9285; success avoidance, 1362; test-taking, 6179, 9291; teacher, 1029; training, 338, 3139, 6635; for training in new technology, 4721; Upward Bound, 45; upward mobility, 3145; vindication, 746; vocational choice, 720; work, 487, 1341, 1344, 1366, 4734, 4744, 6646, 9205, 9294–9296. See also Achievement motivation

Motor: activity, 397; anxiety, 5593; development, 634, 637; impulse control, 386; inhibition, 59; perceived competence, 6805; perceptual, 469; proficiency, 348, 634; speed, 1610

Motoric expressive style, 594

Mountain sickness, 571

Movement, 502: haptic, 7477; imagery, 5019

Movies, 1436: attitude toward, 1166, 2765

Multifactor social attitude, 482

Multiple sclerosis, 3887

Multiracial attitudes, 2766

Murray's needs, 211

Music and art: attitude toward, 1841; knowledge, 2389; talent identification, 8313; teaching, 7340

Mutual(ity), 10174: communication, 98

Mysticism, 3544, 4418, 6262

Name calling, 8029

Narcissism, 5192, 5194–5199, 5208, 7189–7191, 9910, 9920, 9925, 9927

Nationalities, 1135: attitude toward, 2798

Naturalism, 529

Naughtiness, 622, 626

Nausea, 4416

Navy: satisfaction, 2661; sexual harassment in, 6263

Need achievement, 204, 210, 721, 744, 986, 1340, 1345, 2005, 2007, 2009, 2022, 2029, 2265, 6656–6658: children's, 715; college students, 726;

disadvantaged students, 722;
females, 728; males, 728
Need(s): affiliation, 745, 986,
2007; affiliation, Mexican-
American, 738; approval, 450,
500; arousal seeking, 2023;
assessment, 1329; autonomy,
2010; for clarity, 9744;
cognition, 3367, 7029, 7030,
9257, 9747; college student,
5438; deficiency, 1355; desire,
2008; disposition, 601; family,
6425; financial reward, 2265;
housing, 867; independence,
1343; interpersonal, 51;
manifest, 211, 2005; power,
2265; proteges, 6653;
psychological, 1339, 6630; of
runaways, 6264; satisfaction,
1348, 1354, 1356, 1357, 2012,
1213, 3277; satisfaction, job
related, 2011, 3143; -satisfying,
leisure activities, 2185;
security, 2265; self-actualizing,
2265; for self-improvement,
6843; self-peer, 1359; social
approval, 5734; socialized
power, 6647; socio-emotional,
9789; strength, 2182; strength,
growth, 1999; strength, higher
order, 2000; for structure,
9758; vocational, 323;
workers', 6049
Negativism, 2252: -acquiescence,
children, 843
Negotiation(s): behavior, 4404;
collective, 538; groups, 324;
latitude, 2918; role force, 324
Negro-to-Black conversion model,
4317, 4320
Neighborhood: disorder
perceptions, 9087; youth
corps, 563
Neonatal behavioral assessment,
1849
Nervousness, 1683
Network: job seekers, 8034; peer,
2591; personal, 2589;
relationships, 8031–8033,
8140; support level, 8921
Neurologic status, 1284
Neuropsychology, screening, 9863
Neurotic(ism), 39, 43, 405, 853,
855–857, 3891: anxiety, 749;
manifestations, 36; symptoms,
2480

Newborn, 1284
Nicotine dependence, 8588
Ninth grade, 347, 351
Noetic goals, 821
Noise sensitivity, 2099, 2850,
3110, 3892
Nonassertive, 408
Nonconformity, 481, 4040:
orientation, 228
Nonfeminist attitudes, 1834
Nongraded school, 574
Nonsense: monosyllabic units,
374; trigrams, 363
Nonverbal, applicant rating,
3588; personality, 9926;
rigidity, 1477; verbal, 2921;
visual discrimination, 2377
Normlessness, 437, 454, 1093,
1640, 1700, 1701, 1709
Notes, student, 379
Noun(s): plural forms, 367;
possessive, 377
Novelty: -experiencing, 21, 6660;
motivation for, 717, 3133
Nuclear: disarmament, 2795;
weapons, 4419, 4889, 4890;
waste, 6084
Number(s), 345, 474, 2224:
concepts, 2939; joining, 478
Numerical, 1738: identification,
12; preferences, 9840
Nurs(es)(ing): attitude toward,
2996; career satisfaction, 4171;
commitment, 7396;
communication, 4478;
computer attitudes, 6062;
courses, 3639, 3641; geriatric
referrals, 8624; homes, quality,
9090; male, attitude toward,
4243; participative decision-
making, 9484; rating, 3596;
reformist dissent, 6009; role
conflict, 3289, 4170; school of,
694; self-efficacy beliefs, 6110;
stress, 2639, 2648, 4169, 5982;
training experience, 4660;
union, 2669
Nurses aides, 3377
Nurturance, 1720, 4590, 4597,
8807: perceived maternal, 646
Nurturant-affectionate, 652
Nutrition, self-efficacy, 9475

Obesity: attitudes, 6090, 8320;
perceptions, 6734
Obedience, four year olds, 60

Object: orientation, 2317;
permanence, 140; relations,
3772, 5602, 5603, 5834, 6995,
7853, 7924, 9316; scale, 635;
sorting, 1273
Objectives: curriculum, 694;
residence counseling, 546
Objectivism, 5058
Objectivity-subjectivity, 1769
Obligations, family, 8868, 8869
Obscene words, 1274
Observation, 574, 730
Observing and inferring, 2215
Obsessive thoughts, 5559, 5604
Obsessive compulsive, 1663,
1681, 3493, 3497, 3893, 6288,
7059, 7739, 8738, 9739, 9753
Occupation(al)(s), 1060, 2237:
ability, 305; aspiration, 269,
897, 3623; aspiration, high
school student, 897, 901;
attitude toward, 2700;
burnout, 5919; choice, 1587,
10172; choices, college
students, 719; commitment,
7399; concept, 1909, 3654;
coping, 6037; engineering,
7378; fit, 5984; identity, 9890,
10154; interest, 197, 199, 301,
10129–10209; inventory, 711;
knowledge, 2379; literacy,
basic, 1038; needs, 6903, 7399;
plans, 10176; preference, 874,
9827, 10158; prestige, 273–
275, 897, 900, 2239, 3447,
3651; prestige, psychology,
903; rating, 3096; satisfaction,
709, 5983; self-concept, 6978;
self-efficacy, 3256, 9476; sex-
role stereotypes, 9652; skills
use, 6019; status, 276, 1470,
9890, 9891; stereotypes, 270,
3642; strain, 1686, 5605;
stress, 2620, 2665, 2666, 5985,
8233–8235; student behaviors,
7382, 7384; titles, 707; values,
2315
OCS stress reaction, 1672, 1673
Off-campus cohabitation, 181
Office: opinion, open, 1805;
orderliness of, 6560
Old people, 1760
On-the-job training, 8225
Onomatopoeia, 1281
Open-mindedness, 935, 2259,
2292

Openness, 214: to diversity, 9835; elementary school, 1963; to experience, 2162, 4485, 4729, 5093, 9754

Operant conditioning, delinquent boys, 24

Operational thought, 889

Opinion(s): about education, 529; health, 2067; about intelligence, 6156; leadership, 2104, 6265; about mental illness, 6149; open office, 1805; personal, 612; pupil, 541, 1820; student, 95; about testing, 6150

Opportunities, 694: employee advancement, 9092, 9146; higher education, 167

Opposites, word, 2

Oppositional behaviors, 1225, 7772

Optimism, 2487, 3156, 5571–5574, 5633, 7620, 7665: college student, 2408

Oral: comprehension, 365; examinations, 5424; form discrimination, 1421; P/S language, 1275; traits, 934; vocabulary, 380, 384

Organicism-mechanism paradigm, 9836

Organization(al), 575, 6603: applicant attraction to, 6535; behavior, 3065, 6266, 6267; change, 9031, 9534; characteristics, 1333, 1970, 6563; choice, 2105; citizenship, 8628–8632; climate, 176, 1308, 3050, 3097–3099, 3102, 6582, 6598, 6610, 9026, 9093, 9095, 9148, 9168; climate description, 688; commitment, 2014–2016, 3541, 3609, 3624, 3625, 3643–3648, 7351–7354, 7401–7421, 10129, 10175, 10177–10187; communication, 1898, 1901, 2904, 2919; community, 1453; constraints, 9096; control, 1962; culture, 6583, 9093, 9095, 9985; dependability, 9098; deviance, 9187; diversity, 6584; employee commitment, 1996; employee perception of support, 4680–4682; ethics, 6552, 7227, 9043; family policies, 6588;

functioning, 4662–4667, 4672, 4677, 4683, 5290; health, 1330; identification, 8236; image of 9099; ingratiating behavior, 5977; interpersonal relations, 6240; justice, 9101; layoff explanations, 9076; loyalty, 7394; need satisfaction, 1354, 1357; order, university residence, 704; orientation, 6587; participation, 10200; perceived relationships, 6013; perceived support, 9115, 9116; politics, 6596; practices effectiveness, 1972; preference, 259; pride, 3649; propensity to learn, 8253; research, 1331; role overload, 6005; rule bound, 9049; satisfaction, 5988; selection procedures, 6547; socialization, 5987, 9103; structure, 1332, 6586; subject matter, 679; supervision, 1023; support, 6586, 6590, 6591, 6611; values, 7239

Organized demeanor, 1885

Organizers, advance, 8

Orientation, 2213: achievement, 248, 713; action-state, 6276; bureaucratic, 6112; career, 1576, 3617, 3618; college, 879; environmental, 302; future, 207, 301; health, 7261; humanist, 7242; goal, 400, 9215; interpersonal, 54, 67, 216; intrinsic-extrinsic, learning, 7082, 9238, 9239; lifestyle, 2186; moral, 7237; organizational, 6587, 7239, 9104; other, 989; peer group, 534; person, 1994; professional, 539, 6001; reading, 6972; research, 1816; salesperson, 7320; school, 547; science, 7105; sex role, 7087; shopping, 7112, 7113; social, 5475; sports goal, 6633, 7430, 9282, 9287; task, 9288; telic-paratelic, 9289; therapeutic progress, 5607; work, 2676

Originality, 617, 861, 1281

Outcomes: counseling, 10040; educational, 9038; instrumental, 3416; measurement, 3804, 4375, mental health, 7773;

psychotherapy, 10072; work and career, 8297

Outgroups, behavior toward, 8083

Outpatients, geriatric, 2566

Overexcitability, 3495

Overprotection, 496

Overt aggression, 1638

Pain, 7740: apperception, 2095; back, 6790; behavior, 2854, 2867; children, 7619, 8625; coping, 3955; daily living activities and, 3751; fear of, 5521; locus of control, 6810; pediatric, 2857, 7619; severity, 7775; sickle cell disease, 3802

Paintings: assessment, 1457; reactions to, 8438

Panic, 2438: body sensations, 7603; vestibular dysfunction and, 5668

Pantomime, 6359

Parachute jumpers, 406

Paragraph completion, 120, 891, 1498, 1499

Paranoid, 5610, 7777: behavior, 646; ideation, 1681

Paranormal belief, 3211, 6103, 6855, 7588

Paraplegics, 418

Paratelic-telic, 9260, 9289

Parent(al)(ing)(s), 451, 498, 1304, 3036, 6483, 6487, 6492, 6503, 6504, 6506: acceptance-rejection, 8933; adolescent attachment, 6388, 6492–6474; adolescent communication, 8745, 8755, 8757; adolescent interaction, 640, 3001, 3030, 6453, 6561, 8923–8925; adolescent monitoring, 6519; adolescent perception, 6385, 6422, 6472, 6515; affect, 7780; affection toward, 8801; approval, 499; areas of change, 8803; attachments, 6475; attitude, 144, 504, 532, 533, 640, 1148, 1193, 3010, 8439, 8440, 8917, 8937; authority, 640, 6477, 6478; behavior, 643, 655, 1295, 3033, 8939, 8940; behavior, loving-rejecting, 149; behavior problem ratings, 8633; beliefs, 8941; bonding, 6479, 8942–

8944; changes in practices, 8990; child adjustment, 7778; child anxiety; child communication, 103, 640; child depression, 7779; -child interaction, 646, 1955, 2979, 3005, 6480; child rearing, 2855, 2971, 6113, 6476; child relations, 148, 654, 3034, 6484, 6485, 6530, 8926, 8965; child-reported behavior, 6389; children's conflict perceptions, 8814–8816; competence, 8931; concepts of development, 8787; conflict, 6446, 6471, 8022, 8821–8824, 8954; control, 145, 5743, 8946, 8981; costs and rewards, 8945; cultural capital, 8634, delinquent girls, 656; developmental concepts, 6371; discipline, 8927; disturbed children, 38; dominance, 229, 1301; educational involvement, 6821; efficacy, 8932, 9483; empowerment, 9387; encouragement, 713; expectation, 1302; family, 593; frustration, 1216; identification, 143, 8880; interest, 650; investment in child, 8949; involvement, 8929, 8930, 8932; learning, 6506; leave, 6697, 6820; mental health, 7745; mother-daughter intimacy, 6449; monitoring, 8899, 8951, 8952, 9002, 9006; motivation, 1945; normal adolescent girls, 656; nurturance, 6481; overload, 8854; perceptions, 1956, 6417, 6486, 8975–8977; perception of child, 6698; performance, 8962, 8964; post-separation conflict, 6500; post-surgery coping, 5612; punishment intensity, 1949; practices, 8989, quality, 8987; questionnaire, 463; rating, 643, 1303; reading aloud, 6151; rejection, 8953, 8991; relations, adolescent, 760; responsiveness, 8956; role, 8957; role overload, 8996; school involvement, 7515, 7527, 7528, 7529, 8950, 9387;

school program concerns, 7526; satisfaction, 3008, 6454; social support from, 5706; somatic symptoms, 5611; stress, 8967; student perceptions of, 6402; as teacher, 1808; support, 640, 3038, 6519, 8958–8960; styles, 6477, 8939, 8940, 8968, 8969; temperament ratings, 9730, 9731; traditionalism-modernism, 8484; training, 6436; transition to, 3048; union participation, 6822; values, 9986; warmth, 3031
Participation, 1687: group, 53; organizational, 10200; psychological, 1419; student, 6316
Passion: 5812
Passive-aggressive behavior, 6292
Passive speech, 397
Past, remembered, 812
Paternal reactions to birth, 1958
Pathological behavior, 1226, 1310
Patient(s): adjustment, 418; behavior, 1870; depressive, 420; impairment lexicon, 8759; physician perceptions of, 9522; physician uncertainty, 9523; psychogeriatric, 2213; satisfaction, 9107; schizophrenic, 306; symptoms, 1663; terminally ill, 1656; therapist, 995; therapy, 191
Pattern(s): activity, 400; communication, 597; copying, 801; meanings, 608
Pay, 2367, 2651, 2652, 3258, 6620, 6662, 8441: cognitions, 5989; freeze, 5990; satisfaction, 5991, 8239, 8240
Peer(s), 497, 516, 523: acceptance, 1105, 5774; affiliation, 228; aggressiveness in children, 946; alcohol use, 8635; attachments, 5813, 6451; attitudes; 541, 8917; 541; behavioral assessment, 8636, 8630; beliefs, 9485; classroom performance, 575; counseling effectiveness, 1973, 6823, 7313; delinquency, 8637; deviant, 8569; evaluation, 1168, 3374; family relations and, 6494; group, 163; group orientation,

534; influence on behavior, 556; interaction self-efficacy, 9364; network, 2591; nominations, 7781, 8036, 8638; perceptions, 256; play, 8640; rating, 802, 2556, 3449; relatedness, 6840; relations, 70, 397, 472, 675, 2601, 4078, 8121; relations in adolescents, 760, 3968, 3979; relations in children, 4053, 4792; roles, 2590, 3259; self-esteem, 2064; social perceptions, 8091; victimization, 7530, 8639, 9486; teacher, 4046; tutoring, 1240
Penmanship and neatness: children, 2373; perception of, 2147
People: concepts, 502; liking, 2582; test, 535
Perceived: control, 8641; competence, 8042, 9487–9490; contingency, children, 8442; decision-making, 3262; depth of interaction, 1722; environment, behavioral press, 2050; external barriers, 2208; identity, 3261; inclusion/exclusion, 8039; interpersonal treatment, 8245; isolation, 453; lunar effects, 3172; maternal nurturance, 646; motivational context, 9262; parental behavior, 8973–8977; power, 3214; problems, Black/White somatotype, 3263; self-efficacy, 9471; social support, 5779, 5780, 8024, 8038, 8243; students, 1980; stress, 2501, 7784–7786; supervision influence, 2359; task independence, 8244; work characteristics, 2653, 8421
Perception(s), 1, 227–256, 748–838, 1367–1443, 2030–2157, 2280, 9297–9677: academic climate, 1335, 3322; adequacy by college teachers, 785; aesthetic, 254; alcohol consumption, 3159, 3160; of Alzheimer's disease, 3666; of appraisal interview and supervisor, workers, 2036, 3162; of assertive job interview techniques, 4834;

attractiveness, 3275; auditory, first graders, 750; auditory, Spanish language-oriented children, 1613; auditory and visual stimuli, 765; authentic ability, 2147; body, 3175–3177, 4769–4781, 4827; boss, 3326; campus by student, 187; causes, 3181, 3327; children, 659, 1414; of cheating, 6848; classroom, 1227; client, 227, 2336, 4803, 5265–5279; of clients by therapists, 4766; clothing deprivation, 4894; college environment, 177; college students, 706; college students of instructor effectiveness, 2358; competence, 3243; complexity of, 768; about computers, 3705, 4800, 4830; control, 239, 3168, 3252, 6828–6834; of counseling relationship, 2037; counseling session, 3200; counselor-client, 1372; counselor role, 332, 3199; counselor by students, 993; curriculum, 694; customer service, 9032; of discrimination, 5817, 5818; economic hardship, 5520; employees, 9385, 9386; environment by children, 178; environment by employee, 164; environmental, 179; equity, 5751, 9047; features, 1391; first graders, 1423; general ability, 2147; graduate students' perception, 2062; of group atmosphere, 5759; hazard, 2065; health, 6764; of helping behavior, 4114, 4115, 4835; of homophobic environments, 5015; illness, 3220; individual world views, 4950; instructor's, 2349; interpersonal, 428, 433; job, 4140, 4144, 4164, 4172, 4853, 4859, 6596; of job complexity, 2083; job control, 5992; job, by firemen, 1012; job, by foreman, 1012; job qualifications, 6022; justice, 9074; of leadership behavior, 2084, 6242; learning behavior, 838; life stresses, 2047; of love,

4032, 4033; of management, 5925, 9012; of manager qualities, 4874; marriage, 240; maternal acceptance, 759; maternal attitude, 759; mathematics, 3245, 3249; mental effort, 3161; moral vision, 4952; mother by child, 761; movement imagery assessment, 5019; noise sensitivity, 3892; of nuclear threat, 4889; of occupational competence, 4123; organizational politics, 9120–9123; of others' empathy, 5204; of others' social skills, 5832; parent, 1956, 2045; of parental reactions of birth, adolescents, 2156; part/whole, 124; part/whole, in children, 19; peer, 256, 2045; of penmanship and neatness, 2147; of people with chronic disease, 4794; performance, 3267; of personal attributes, 4908; personal control, 1415; of physical attractiveness, 4913; 3341; of power, 6847; preprofessional teacher training, 1982; principal, 1407; problem solving, 764, 3280; of professional life, 4926; psychological influence, 3324; psychologists, 3265; of reading and spelling ability, 2147; reality, 3173; recall, adults, 533; residence counselors, 1020; reversals, 813; role, 2123; of role conflict, role ambiguity, 2121; school, 700, 2045, 3055; self, 748, 2045, 3260, 3270, 3273; self-control, 3185; self-perception, children, 3187; self-report of visual functioning, 3815; sense of coherence, 4985; sex role, 2110, 3167, 3188; social, 5814; spatial ability, 3671, 3673, 3674, 3680; stereotypes, 3169, 3318, 3319; of stress, 5616; stressors, 3184; student, 175, 6539; student, of chances for success, 5417; student self-concept, 4746, 4749; student/faculty, about academic advising, 1959; of students by

teachers, 24, 4925, 4933, 5006, 5008; of success, 6021, 9263, 9264, 9755; of supervisors, 6172; teachers' of administrators, 1408; of teachers by students, 1027, 4469, 4832, 5418; team teaching, 334; of teasing, 5816; traders understanding, 3264; unmet democratic values, 2055; visual, 801, 808, 1735; work, 1404, 4161, 4179, 4180, 4188; workload, 5994; of workplace tolerance, 4795

Perceptual: aberration, 3266; ability, 1121; ability, elementary school, 2098; acuity, 2685; effectiveness, 214; flexibility, 923; handicapped, 1384, 1386, 1387, 1390, 1411, 1435, 1436; motor, 469, 1597; motor ability, 2213; motor development, 417; -motor skill, from discrimination, fine eye-hand coordination, visual motor match, 2143; rigidity, 1377; speed, 1604, 1608, 1618

Perfectionism, 5200, 7186, 7187, 7193, 9896, 9922–9924, 9928, 9936

Performance: ability, 6; appraisal, 5995, 9139, 9158, 10020–10026; attributions, 6850; child attribution, 3268; clinical, medical students, 2356; college expectation, 740; college student, 1856; contextual, 5915; employees, 1007; engineer, 1577; family, 8855; index, 636; inflectional, 17; instructor, 6206; job, 1553, 1566, 2647, 3584, 7304, 7305, 9126, 9150, 9208, 9503, 10058, 10059, 10079; job interview, 2350; kindergarten, 2381; language, 1035; leader's appraisal of, 6259; mathematics, 5381; managerial, 3585; memory, 382; orientation, 9756; parenting, 8962; perceptions, 6835; principal, 1558; ratings reactions, 9150; satisfaction, 5449; self-esteem, 6851; similes, 1054; social, 2608–2610; student, 568; teachers,

997, 1027; team norms, 9127; valence, 8246, work, 3593, 8737, 9511

Permanence, object and person, 140

Persistence/dependence, 216, 6663, 9226, 9265, 9266

Person orientation, 1994

Person permanence, 140

Personal: adjustment, 37; agency, 8521; anticipations, 2107; attributes, 561, 692, 1809, 2171, 3269–3271, 9512; attitudes, 535, 593; beliefs, 8443; characteristics, 657; characteristics, counselor, 1004; concern, 9514, 9515; constructs, 1305; control, 3272; direction, 9243; goals, 829, 9267, 9268; growth, 704, 7788, 8795, 9269; identity, 796; manager, 1169; maturity, 636; needs, 1356; opinion, 612; problem-solving, 9515; problems, 419, 7789, 9839; reactions, 9516; skills, 3320; social adjustment, 397; space, 1107, 1418; style, 8041, 9760; traits, knowledge of, 862; understanding, 175; values, 1521; worth, 2367, 2614

Personalistic, 2186

Personality, 211–226, 839–863, 1444–1452, 2158–2174, 3372, 3387, 5056, 5057, 5064, 5066, 6984, 6997, 7002, 7026, 9678–9804, 9893–9947: active-passive, 848; adolescent, 854; adolescent, boy, 848; affect intensity, 5024; aggressive-sadistic, 787; agreeing tendency, 3344; ascription of responsibility, 5025; assertiveness, 5201, 5203; assessment, 2171; assessment of temperament, 5034, 5035, 5038, 5039, 5055; authoritarian, 5177; autonomous, 7048, 7049; Big Five dimensions, 7028, 7033, 7054, 9689, 9709, 9718, 9785; borderline, 3776; bureaucratic, 957, 967; borderline, 9692; business context, 9764; children, 842, 927, 1450, 9762, 9778; children, maternal

perception of, 5039; children's understanding of, 8786; college freshmen, 223; competitive-narcissistic, 787; compulsiveness, 5036; conflict management, 5091; cooperative-overconventional, 787; creative, 620; cynical distrust, 5030; defensiveness, 5031; delinquents, 853–857; dimensions, 9741–9743, 9757; disadvantaged, 1452; disorders, 405, 9697, 9901; disorders, assessment, 5062, 6994, 7034, 7035; docile-dependent, 787; emotional reactivity, 5042; emotional structure, 5054; enuresis, 846; experiences assessment, 5044; functioning, 9736; gender traits, 5028, 5047, 5060; guilt proneness, 5022, 5061; happy-sad, 848; hardiness, 5050, 9761; high school, 851; Holland types, 3343; infant temperament, 5052, 5053, 5055, 5069; integration, 847, 849; Jungian, 3371, 9759; locus of control, see Locus of control; managerial-autocratic, 787; narcissistic, 3491, 5192, 5194–5199, 5208; objectivism, 5058; openness to new experiences, 4485, 4729, 5093; patterns, 7332; perfectionist, 5200; personal responsibility, 5065; persuasiveness, 3353; proactive, 7039, 9768–9770; process of change, 5067; psychopathology, components, 3346; rebellious-distrustful, 787; responsible-hypernormal, 787; Rorschach, 224; self-defeating, 5070; self-effacing-masochistic, 787; semantic differential, 1451; sex-typed, children, 9684; shame proneness, 5022, 5061; style, 2169; sociotropic, 7048, 7049; subjectiveness, 5076; teacher, 1027; toughness, 5077; traits, 615; trust, 5049; Type A, 7175; vocational preference, 194

Personnel: ratings of, 706; student, 859

Perspective, 2224: life, 2047

Pessimism, 1103, 1662, 1670, 2483, 2487, 7665

Pets, 5736, 5789, 7937

Pharisaic virtue, 1170

Pharmacists, 4183

Pharmacological rating, 1228

Phenomenology, 2296: of consciousness, 4911

Philosoph(ical)(y): belief, 968; counselor, 968; human nature, 980, 1522; orientation, 3552, 9987

Phobia, 3823, 7674, 7675; social, 5527, 7602, 7854, 7855; spider, 7598; symptoms, 5527

Phobic anxiety, 1681

Phoneme-grapheme, 366, 5398

Phonemic, 380: analysis, 3690, 4512, 8775; discrimination, 380, 384

Phonetic generalization, 371, 374

Phonics, 1048: achievement, 2398

Phonological: analysis, 6337; awareness, 6057; discrimination, 8776

Physical: ability, middle childhood, 244; ability, students', 2349; abuse, 8587, 8594; activity, 265, 5821, 5879, 8479, 8644, 9510; activity, attitude, 1171, 7211; activity motivation, 6661, 9248; activity, perceptions of, 6837; activity, women's attitude, 791; appearance, 593, 3275, 9327–9337; attributes, 561; competence, 6838; condition, 578, 593; contact, 649; development, 637; environment, community, 1060; intimacy, 3039; self-efficacy, 6860, 9519; self-esteem, 6861; self-perception, 9520, 9521; surroundings, job, 709; symptoms, 773, 5625–5628, 5660, 7791–7793

Physical education: adolescents' orientation, 9792; class climate, 9129; enjoyment-interests, 7501; perceptions, 9075

Physical health, 3831, 3840, 4392, 5624: adolescents, 7580; cognitive distortion in rheumatoid arthritis, 3786; employment and, 5996; illness

management, 3851;
neurological dysfunction, 3887;
parent reaction to child's,
4600; stress and, 3900;
symptoms, 7875, 7876; values,
5238; worry, 3841
Physicians: patient care
uncertainty, 9523; perception
of patients, 9522, self-esteem,
9532
Physics, creative ideas, 1930
Physiognomic reactivity, 1506
Physiological reactions, 395
Piaget(ian), 635: development,
2960
Piano anxiety, 2508
Picture: -frustration, 1675;
interpretation, 1085, 1448;
perceived competence; school,
738; stories, 113
Pilot accidents, 478
Peace group members, 510
Plan(fulness)(ning), 501, 986;
process quality, 6352
Plans: adolescents, 8499; career,
175, 202, 3619, 10176;
procedures in class, 679;
product promotion, 9870
Plateauing, career, 8159, 8248,
10107
Play, 40, 1208, 1218, 2861, 2862,
4362; playground skills, 5383;
teacher ratings, 8640
Playfulness, 6197, 6223
Pleasantness, 417
Pleasure, 2507: capacity, 3903
Plural formation patterns, 367
Police, 1666, 3577, 5259:
attitudes, 1810; authority, 485;
cynicism, 943; daily hassles,
8249; daily uplifts, 8250;
decisions, 9878; empathy, 781;
job knowledge, 3683;
motivation, 205; 9236; rating,
3577, 3579, 3587; recruits,
443, 444; stress, 4182; tasks,
257; women, 1666; work, 257
Policies and procedures, 663
Political: activity, 576; attitude,
536, 537, 1172, 1806;
behavior, American, 368;
belief, 593, 1520; change, 92;
cynicism, 537; dependence,
512; discontent, 1976; distrust,
feelings of, 1975; efficacy, sense
of, 537; estrangement, 1977;

future time perspective, 832;
incapability, 2111;
independence, 512;
institutions, 1806; interest,
537; knowledge, 368;
organizational, 9120–9123;
orientation, democratic, 1799;
orientation, superintendents,
972; preference, 873; protest,
1197; salience, 9524; sciences
skills, 369; tolerance, 537,
5823; trust, 537
Politics, 2237, 4424, 4918:
attitudes toward, 4234;
organizational, 6596; perceived
efficacy, 4919; personality
assessment, 5077
Poor, 522
Popularity, 556, 4920: self-
perceived, 458
Population control, 1811
Positive regard, 220:
unconditional, 227, 309
Positive reinforcement, 2188,
2189
Positive thoughts, 5464
Possessive nouns, 377
Possessiveness, 504, 655, 2584
Posttraumatic stress disorder:
3881, 4344, 5694, 7801, 7802,
7818, 7819: children, 7613,
7800; combat, 7720, 7752;
secondary, 7841; women, 7641
Posttreatment awareness, 1416
Potential: actualization, 9463,
9465; series learning, 1743;
success, 338
Poverty, 522: children, self-
concept, 798
Power(ful), 52, 268, 485, 659,
2253: interpersonal, 9734; in
intimate relationships, 8044;
leaders, 8663; motivation, 732;
need, Mexican-American, 738,
6847; others, 1405, 1406;
perceived, 3214, 9130; seeker,
3368; social, 460, 1112, 3129,
3132; socialized, 732, 6647;
supervisor, 1231, 6252, 6253;
sources, 6665; third world,
9357; uses of, 7207
Powerlessness, 413, 437, 809,
1093, 1700, 1701, 1709, 2112,
4054
Practical significance, 696
Practice(s): guidance, 185;

teaching, effectiveness, 690;
teacher, student evaluation of,
690
Practicum: counselor evaluation,
1003; group, 1259
Pragmatism, 2296:
intellectualism, 95, 1515
Preadolescent, 625, 644: self-
esteem, 825
Perceptual scanning, 421
Precollege testing program, 480
Precounseling training, 2374
Prediction(s): academic, 231,
232; employment, 8171; school
success, 71
Predictive index, 475
Predisposition, creative, 1928
Preference(s), 257–263, 864–883,
1453–1464, 2175–2199, 3390,
9805–9852: activity, 3388;
cognitive, 2179, 3391, 3410,
5142; competition, 3412;
conflict modes, 5091;
consumer, 5105; counselor,
1544, 3392, 3409; educational,
200; environmental stimuli,
5095; food, 3396, 3417; friend,
434; gender roles, 9823, 9824;
health treatment, 5085; humor,
1456; imagery, 3397;
information processing style,
5106, 5116; instructional
course design, 5087;
involvement assessment, 5092,
5101; job enrichment, 3405;
learning, 3402; moral, 5232;
mother, father, teacher and
others, 55; numerical
information, 7101;
occupational, 874, 9827,
10158; organizational, 259;
physical activity, 5081;
political, 873; problem solving,
5144; professor, 866; racial,
865, 1459; reading, 1460;
recreation, 3407; roommate,
262; sex role, 2181, 3314,
3389, 3411, 5080, 5082–5084,
5086, 5096–5100; sexual, 9826;
skin, 1463; social, 789;
solitude, 7102; student, 263; in
study of psychology, 5094;
task, 205, 2178; teacher, 866,
880; toys, 883; teacher
behavior, 3406; vocational,
194, 195, 213, 305; work, 692,

708, 3395, 3664, 5362; worker, 3401; workplace tolerance, 5104

Pregnancy: beliefs, 6153; loss, 3899; social support, 4085

Prejudice, 281, 296, 482, 1174, 1185, 1187, 8066, 8134, 8448: anti-Black, 2297; projective, 1176

Preliterate: children, 1812; children, racial attitude, 1814

Premarital: counseling, 147; relationships, 8045

Premenstrual: experience, 4923; syndrome, 3880

Premorbid: adjustment, 421; competence, 2594

Prenominal adjectives, 377

Preparation, 666, 8609

Prepositional phrases, locative, 377

Prereading, 352

Preschool, 578: achievement, 12; anxiety, 2509; behavior, 1872; children, 383, 397, 425, 459, 477, 616, 617, 635, 1397; children, Black, 377; children, competence, 8046; children, disadvantaged, 403; children, frustration, 1229; children, handicapped, 1597; children, prejudice, 1174; children, reflexivity, 1490; children, self-perception, 835; to primary, 390; primary locus of control, 2113; problem solving, disadvantaged children, 892, 894; program, 642; racial attitude, 1814; screener, 1714; social-emotional behavior, 1237, 8047, 8727, 8728

Presentation, self, 2558

Presenter competence, 3591

Press(ure), 487, 1666, 7804: achievement, 496, 647, 673; activeness, 647, 673; English, 647, 673; ethlanguage, 647, 673; independence, 647, 673; intellectuality, 647, 673; job, 1687

Prestige, 269, 2317: among sociology journals, 906; college major, 896; occupational, 269, 273–275, 897, 900, 3447, 3651; perception of vocational, 204

Pride, workers', 5928

Priesthood, 1668

Priests, American Catholic, 1668

Primary: children, reinforcement preferences, 739; grade, 367; grade children, 718; grades, primary and elementary, 1743; grades, reading attitude, 1775; grades, reading comprehension, 14; preschool locus of control, 2113; roles, 73; self-concept, 2114, 2115; teacher directiveness, 936

Principal(s), 484, 495: burnout, 5926; elementary school, 1680; evaluation, 1558; faculty perception, 5923, 5924, 7306; leadership, 8645; perception, 1407; role, 538; teacher, 595, 8449, 9841; teacher communication, 688

Principalization, 850

Principle(s): business, 661; centeredness, 7243; identification, 884

Print, awareness, 2390

Prison inmates: locus of control, 6865, 6866, 9528; problems, 9131; suicidal, 5471

Privacy, 4055, 5824: attitude, 2751, 2752; invasion, 1320, 2079, 9056

Proactive: personality, 9768–9770; socialization, 8251, 8763

Probability, 2224

Probation administrators, 523

Probing, 689

Problem(s): assessment, 1674; behavior, 28, 389, 495, 2807; behavior control, 403; behavior traits, children and adolescents, 1844; centeredness, 583; child-rearing, 38; client, 1080; conduct, 2251; -defining skills, 5128; educational, 131; educational-vocational, 38; elementary school, 1108; emotional, child, 1082; industrial, 150, 151; instructional television, 488; job, 1968; sexual marital, 38; social interpersonal, 38; solving, 264–267, 456, 884–895, 1465–1469, 2200–2234, 3316, 3429, 3435, 3437–3440, 5145, 6667, 7134, 9853–9889;

solving ability, 2226, 7136, 9531, 9881; solving, adequacy, 764; solving, adolescent, 5139; solving, behavior, 3280; solving, children, 893, 1468, 3433, 3436, 5120, 9866; solving, client perceptions, 764; solving, college students, 5636; solving, couples, 8819; solving, disadvantaged children, 892, 894; solving, families, 8856; solving, interactional, 4013; solving, interpersonal, 2576; solving, personal, 9515; solving, preference, 5144; solving, preschool, 892; solving, science, 7141; solving, skills, 2225; solving, social, 5860, 9866, 9883, 9884; solving, strategies, 1467, 3432, 5146; solving, students, 7536; solving, style, 5134, 7137; solving, teacher, 1232, 2804; solving, therapist perception, 764; student, 1336, 2859; supervisor, 996; wives, 1306

Procedure(s), 600, 694, 695: sampling, 161

Processing: activity, 577; cognitive, 3193; reactive, 421

Procrastination, 3281, 4431, 4432, 4802, 6196, 6241, 6279, 6280, 7537, 7538, 8648–8651: academic, 5401, 5402; attitudes, 2769, 8483; behavior, 2868, 2869; college students, 9442; decisional, 8563

Production, 676, 688: consumption, 302; foreman, 1013

Productivity, 7318: creative, 130

Profession, employee commitment, 1996

Professional(ism), 326, 327, 1816, 6000: activities, 657; attitudes, 82, 1815; commitment, 1815, 7423, 7424, 10190–10192; development, 10082; experience, 9143; identification, 1815; involvement, 7425; orientation, 539; responsibilities, counselors', 1003; role orientation, 539, 6001; self-attitudes, 82, 6001; uncertainty, 5887

Professors: female, 1754; preference for, 866
Proficiency, job, 320
Profit motive, 9271
Program: innovation, 160; planning, 694
Programmed instruction, 153
Prohibitions, 649
Project: complexity, 3103; Head Start, 637
Projection(s), 41, 850: fantasy, 579; role, 2512
Projectivity, 2253
Promotion, desire for, opportunity, 2359, 9146, 9631
Pronunciation, 371
Propensity, social, 2611; to leave job, 8252, 8253
Property, 593
Proportion, 1614
Prosocial behavior, children, 8654
Protest: behavior, 1817; situational attitude, 1817
Protestant(ism), 7238: ministers, 519, 7244–7248; work ethic, 9988–9990
Provocative child, 397
Proverbs, 1818
Pro-worldminded, 1795
Proxemic distance, 68
Psychiatric aide employees, 3592
Psychiatr(ic)(y): attitude toward, 6081; behavior, 1205, 5467; complaints, 773; evaluation, children, 2514; marital difficulties, 773; outpatients, 1681; patients, 489, 1654, 3895, 3907, 3944, 4377; progress, 2452; symptoms, 2515, 2539, 5467, 5809, 7607; treatment, 773, 3120; vocational problems, 773
Psychiatric rating, 405, 1079
Psychodynamic mental health, 880
Psychological: abuse, 8586, 8587, 8601, 8586, 8587, 8607, 8655; adjustment, 28–43, 421, 5536, 5618; androgyny, 2176; anomie, 413; balance, 8791; control, 8981, 8982; dependence, 2199; distance, 50, 56; distress, 35, 2493, 5639, 5641, 7703; functioning, 5547, 5555; health, attitude,

1137; help, attitude, 2743; influence, 3324; mindedness, 7813, 9767, 9772, moods, 1669; needs, 1339, 6630; patient communication, 6350; reactance, 6282, 6329, 8657, 8658; reports and service, attitude toward, 154; separation, 3040, 8983–8985; state, 841; stress, 2517, 7812; symptoms, 5554, 5687, 7621, 7622; testing, 1127; well-being, 2493, 5645, 5646, 7799, 7813, 7833, 7836
Psychologist: attitudes, 154; burnout, 3950; career specialization, 7430, 10194; perceived, 3265; stress, 2662
Psychology: attitude toward, 1127; knowledge assessment, 5375, 5389; misperceptions about, 6968; occupations in, 142, 903
Psychopath(ic)(y), 855–857, 7722, 7805, 7814: criminal, 2518, personality, 9773, 9774, 9930, 9931
Psychopathology, 5468, 5643: child, 6215; dimensions of, 412, 2448, 3346
Psychosexual maturity, 1668
Psychosocial: development, 632, 1941, 2945, 2947, 2955; environment, 1960; stress, 5647
Psychosomatic: complaints, 2480, 2516; health, 7815; symptoms, 3858, 7816, 7817
Psychotherapists: attitudes, 6155; and patients, 306
Psychotherapy, 1137, 10121: and change, 10081, 10102; check list, 2519; children, 10060; evaluation, 1080, 7319, 10095–10100, 10124; fear of, 2451; outcome, 10072; process, 2352, 2616; relationship, 7276, understanding of, 10124
Psychotic symptoms, 773, 853
Psychoticism, 1681
Pubertal development, 8796
Public exposure to sexual stimuli, 1761
Public policy issues, 1797
Public school(s), 687: teaching, 539

Puerto Ricans, 3967
Pun, 613
Punishment: capital, 1750; direct object, 654; parental intensity, 1949; symbolic love, 654
Punitive-controlling, 652
Punitiveness, attitudes, 2770
Pupil: affect, 1217; attitude, 455, 540; behavior, 574, 578, 6283; control, 810; control ideology, 1819, 2117, 2771, 3105, 3282, 3283; development, 637; evaluation, 3374; ideal, 1929; information acquisition, 1; interaction, 1027; interest by teacher, 1027; observation by teacher, 1027; opinion, 541, 1820; ratings, 2870; ratings by teachers, 297, 298; responses, 1267; self-esteem, 3276; social behavior, 8659; teacher, 600

Q sort, 822, 831, 1678
Qualit(ies)(y), 681: class, 3116; classroom, 6592; college departments, 3067; education, 663; hospital, 6593; leadership, 338; of life, 3914, 3915, 5608; of life, diabetes and, 5514; of life, health-related, 5532, 5556; of life, women, 7820; of life, workplace, 4187; mathematics, lecture, 3086; school life, 6599; of services, 6607; of teaching, 7280; work, 7442
Quality circles, 6284
Quantitative, achievement, 1043, 1063; aptitude, 1732
Question(ing)(s): classroom, 1266; skills, 7139

Races, tolerance of, 1792
Racial: academic predictor, 2684; attitudes, 46, 78, 79, 87, 88, 482, 520, 542, 1147, 1176, 1804, 1812, 1813, 4325, 4327, 5715, 5716, 5717, 5800, 5808, 5831, 6147, 6158, 6161, 7933, 8436; attitude, first grade, 1813; attitude, preliterate children, 1814; attitude, preschool, 1814; bias, 7925; cultural values, 5228; discriminatory behavior, 4451; evaluation, 3448; factors, 386;

identity/identification, 2772, 2773, 4315–4317, 4320, 5725–5727, 5802, 5806, 5830, 5892, 7910, 7911, 8137–8139, 8455, 8456; intermarriage attitudes, 90; mistrust, 3991; preference, 865, 1459; relations, 76, 99; self-concept, 4929; socialization, 8048, 8457; stereotype, 520, 1154, 4291, 4327; stress, 7971, 7972; subjective identification, 4818; supervisor-employee relations, 4765; workplace situations, 6007, 8258, 9027, 9189

Racism, 7929, 8049, 8050, 8065

Radicalism, 280, 529: -conservatism, 1821

Rape, 3684, 7821; attitudes, 4246, 4436, 6064, 6077, 6159, 8357, 8466, 8551; calloused beliefs, 8374; date, 8551, 8562; empathy, 5202, 8458; myth acceptance, 8412–8414, 8359, 8460; perceptions, 4931, 4932

Rapport: with students, 33; teacher, 1891

Rating: applicant, 3588; college course, 1024; counseling interviews, 699, 3594; counselor, 35, 72, 3573, 3595; curriculum, 706; managers, 3580; peer, 2556; police, 3577, 3579, 3587; sales person, 3596, 3598; scales, descriptive, 215; students, 24; teacher, 1028, 2395; work trainee, 338

Rational, 2205, 2206: behavior, 1679, 1874, 2774, 2871

Rationality, 1679, 2931, 9776, 9868

Reactance, 8657, 8658, 6282, 6329

Reaction: counseling, 311; stress, 7868; styles, 9630; to traumatic events, 5557; to unemployment, 8256

Reactiv(e)(ity): autonomic, 8741; inhibition, 399; interpersonal, 9916

Readers, retarded, 340

Readiness, for first grades: reading, 352, 356, 357, 1118; school, 469; vocational planning, 470; words, 337

Reading, 2, 12, 15, 21, 340, 516,

543, 1048, 3916: achievement, 350, 1035–1037, 1043, 1063, 1598; achievement, first-grade, 602; adult and college, 20; adult attitudes, 4232; aloud, 6151; and spelling ability, perception of, 2147; amount of, 7443; attitude, 543, 544, 1175, 1787, 1822, 1823, 2741, 2763, 2775, 4313, 8467; attitude, elementary school, 1822; beliefs, 6160; Black and White students, 2; comprehension, 14, 20, 1055, 1062, 1609, 2388, 2688, 3669; comprehension, child, 4513; comprehension, college students, 1615; concept-oriented instruction, 9869; confidence, 3726; consultant, 1334; difficulty, source of, 340; elementary school teachers, 8389, 8390; failures, 475; formal, 352; functional skills, 1602; informal, 350; input, 372; instruction, fourth grade, 544; instruction, individualizing, 545; kindergarten, 352; levels, 375; maturity, 1053; miscue, 2391; motivation, 9235, 9246, 9272; oral, 2388, 2391; orientation, 6972; parents, 8634; performance, 1744, 7473; performance predictors, 4223; phonemic analysis, 3690, 4512; pre-, 352; preference, 1455, 1460; rate, 1039; readiness, 352, 356, 357, 1121, 4227; retention, 1616; skills, 366, 1038; span, 2392; speed of, 7444; storage, 373; strategies, 9882; student perception of ability, 3736; teacher orientation, 8482; teacher survey, 545; teachers' beliefs, 6109; teaching in content classrooms, 1763; teaching of, 559

Real estate, success, 2686

Realism: color, 830; size, 434, 830, 2296

Reality: beliefs, 6106, 8332; perceptions, 3173; testing, 3772, 5602

Rearing adolescents, 490

Reasoning, 889, 1738, 9853–9889: ability, 2204; ability, formal, 2231, 3419, 3428, 3442, 7120; abilities, concrete, 2227; abstract, 2201, 2202, 3424; abstract, junior high, 884; analogical, 3418; deductive-inductive, 3426; logical, 3427, 3441; moral, 2212, 2218, 2219, 2222, 3531, 3558; proportional, 3420; scientific, 2232

Rebelliousness, 481, 8501, 8597, 8664

Recall, 4, 8, 346, 359, 360, 361, 382: perception, adults, 533

Receptivity to change, 301, 6601

Reciprocal inhibitions, 399

Recognition, 2, 363, 366, 374, 663: author name, 5369; book title, 5392, 5393, 5394; interrogative patterns, 380, 384; magazine, 5379; newspaper, 5382; word, 342

Reconstruction, 13

Recreational therapy, 6286

Recruit(ers)(ment): college graduates, 9153; hiring recommendations, 10089; job, 518, 10075; student athletes, 3413, training, 9152

Recycling attitudes, 6098

Referential communication, 2923

Referral, 2191: process, 2119

Reflection, 689: impulsivity, 285, 290, 291, 1490, 1494, 2170, 2272

Reflective observation, 2216

Reflectivity, 2262

Reflexes, interpersonal, 448

Refusal behavior, 1857, 2803

Regard: level, 1538; unconditional positive, 431

Regression, adaptive, 606

Rehabilitation, 337: clients, 29; counseling, 692, 1057; counselor effectiveness, 1561; gain, 693; industrial, 515; services, 182; vocational, 691

Reinforcement: children, 1853; contingencies, 1434; counselors, 1545; delay of, 58, 239; expectation, 69; by others, 44; positive, 2188, 2189; preferences, primary children, 739; social, 725,

2925; social, for retardates, 725

Reinforcers: effectiveness, 734; effect on children, 282; individual, 2018; survey for therapy, 735; teacher, 736

Rejection, 69, 583, 5772: by authority, 499; manifest, 496; need, Mexican-American, 738; parental, 8953, 8991; sensitivity to, 44, 1726, 8068; verbal, 585

Relatedness behavior, 432

Relations: family, 141, 142, 645; intergenerational, 99; interpersonal, 50, 51, 431, 464, 575, 1102, 2577; job, with associates, 709; job, with employees, 709; mothers, 419; other people, 593; parent-child, 148; parent-daughter, 1303; racial, 99; school community, 1827; social, 1106; students, 679; teacher-pupil, 256

Relationship(s), 431, 884: affective, quality of, 640; beliefs, 5835; central, 9358; closeness, 8055; counseling, 1003, 1268, 2899–2901; family, 1951; father, 653; interpersonal, 1256, 1716, 2548, 2588; intimate, 2580, 2592; inventory, 309, 1262, 1538; marital, 1766, 3018, 6450; mother-daughter, 6467, 6468; orientation, 8057; parent-child, 6484, 6485; peer, 397, 472, 675, 2601; perceptions, children, 8051; positive, 8043; quality of, 5720; repair strategies, 8052; residence counselor, 1019; satisfaction, 5829, 8054; self-other, 1728; sibling, 3044; skills, 6353; spouse, 3045; student-teacher, 2416; supervisors, 1023, 8257; therapeutic, 330, 2559, 7276; therapist, 995

Relative clauses, 377

Relativism, 3527, 9961: religious, 3555

Relaxation, 4356, 9787: training, 3918

Religion, 485, 593, 2237:

attitudes, 1178, 4259, 4324; commitment, 982; conventional orientation to, 2312; counseling and, 7219; dogma, 983; experiences, and activities, 675, 1514, 1580; faith scale, 5226; groups, 183; identification, 988, 5242; locus of control, 4937; orientation, 5243; parareligious beliefs, 5236; strength of beliefs, 5244

Religiosity, 2322, 3553, 3554, 5227, 5237, 5241, 7241, 7249, 7257, 9991–9993: anti-, 5230

Religious: behavior, 9994; beliefs, 2323, 3525, 3526, 9976, 9994, 9996; commitment, 9995; coping, 7824; experience, mystical dimensions, 2324; orientation, 7249–7252; relativism, 3555; science and, 7248; values, 3534

Relocation, willingness, 8295

Remedial mathematics, 508

Remembered past, 812

Reminiscence, 812, 6683

Remote: associates, 610; associational ability, 610; remote, 1601

Repatriation, beliefs, 8420

Repression, 293, 612, 840, 3919, 3920, 8666: sensitivity, 951, 1502, 3503, 3504; sensitivity in counseling, 921

Reproductive, knowledge, 1056

Research: and thinking skills, 1606; article rating, 693; attitudes toward, 8358, 8463, 8464; concept-educational, 1746; education, 1752; interests, 10157; organizational, 1331; orientation, 1816; teacher orientation, 550; outcome expectations, 9537; self-efficacy, 9538

Resentment, 1638, 2252

Residence: assistants, 1487, 4135, 4198, 5296, 5297, 9539; continuity, 466; counseling positions, candidates, 546; counselor, 1006; counselor evaluation, 1006; counselor, job rating, 1019; counselor, objectives for, 546; counselor relationships, 1019; counselor,

student perception, 1020; environment, university, 704; innovative university, 704; interest, 1019; residence vs. nonresidence counseling, 546; roommate preference, 262; viewpoints, 546

Residents: interviews with, 546; methods of discipline, 546

Resignation, 2278

Resilience, 7655, 7826, 7827: career, 8148

Resistance: in psychoanalysis, 8667; to schooling, 5433

Resolution, conflict, 1857

Resources, 575: availability, 6537; family, 8859; human, 3077

Respect, 3366

Responding, associative, 264

Response: acquiescence, college student, 930; echoic, 7; socially desirable, 5859, 8742, 8743; styles, children, 843; system, verbal, 588

Responsibilit(ies)(y), 16: attributions, 9325; counselor, 314; development in children, 58, 762; development, ethnic differences, 762; filial, 6434, 8869, 8870; intellectual achievement, 786; in OCD patients, 6288; for others, 1687; school counselors, 314; social, 58, 462, 915, 1113; task, 9173

Responsiveness, 666: maternal, 2273, 8961; parental, 8956

Restraint, 5837: eating habits, 1876

Restrictiveness, social, 530, 1807

Retail bargaining, 1762

Retail store manager, 1560

Retardates: social inference, 1114; social reinforcement, 725

Retarded, 405, 479: adolescents, 1619; children, flexibilities, 923; readers, 340; reading, 1616; work adjustment, of, 1033

Retirement, 5651: activities, 8263; plan, involvement in, 9829; reasons for early, 669

Reversals, perceptions of, 813, 850

Reward(s): by supervisor, 1005;

contingency, 2120; direct object, 654; level, 2598, 3144; marriage, 3041; perceptions of fairness, 6546; preference, 261; symbolic love, 654, work, 8265
Rheumatoid arthritis, 3786
Rhythm, auditory visual, 750
Rhythmicity, 2285
Right-left discrimination, 1943
Rigidity, 917, 1377, 1477, 1486, 1500, 2286, 9900
Riots and demonstrations, attitudes toward, 482
Risk orientations, 1786, 8266
Risk taking, 861, 1077, 1234, 2160, 2161, 2172, 2255, 2776, 7865, 8424 Rituals, family, 6428
Rod and frame, 776, 815
Role(s), 3053: ambiguity, 1687, 2357, 2525, 3288, 3289, 3292, 4940, 4941, 6875–6880, 9543, 9544, 9547–9550, 9556, ambiguity, perceptions, 2121; in alcoholic family, 6399; attitudes, 6142; balance, 9844; beliefs, 8369; breath, 9545, 9546; children's affiliation with, 8817; choice, 869; clarity, 6882; concepts, counseling, 313, 3199; conflict, 1687, 2122, 2357, 2526, 2641, 3002, 3289, 3292, 4930, 4942–4944, 5107, 5617, 6883–6891, 9548–9553, 9556; conflict, counselors, 314; conflict, gender, 5082, 7079; conflict, perceptions, 2121, 2123; conflict, sex-role, 5112, work, 9671; college graduates, 9370; consistency, 1461; constructs, 219, 816; counselor's, 332; demands, 7830; deviant, 3202; discretion, 9554; expectations, 3291; family, 302; female, attitude, 2742; force, negotiators, 324; gender, 7099; graduate student, 2426; guidance director's, 318; identification, 331, 9850; importance, 6456; men's, 7092; modeling, attitude toward, 8326; models, career choice, 10155; mother, 652, 2970; multiple, 8356; new father, 6469; orientation, 263;

orientation, professional, 539; overload, 6744, 6891, 8267, 8996, 9555; parental, 8957; peer, 2590; perception, teachers, 2038; playing, 4945, 5182; primary, 713; projection 2512; repertory, 1465; sex, 7061–7063, 7087, 7091, 7107–7111; sick, 1239; strain, 1667, 4946, 6012, 6457, 6892; stress, 2525–2527, 5522, 5395, 9557; student, 2590; taking, 579, 1096, 1236, 1503, 3259, 8997; vocational, 3660; women's, 7115; women's, perceived, 6974; work, 2672, 6050
Romantic: attachment anxiety, 5461, 7914; attitudes, 2777; attraction, 5838; commitment, 7936, 8063; feelings, 5839; love, 295, 2599, 2600, 5840, 8014, 8125; satisfaction, 8063; trust, 8053
Roommate: preference, 262; rapport, 4063, 4064, 7540
Routinization, 6604
Rule(s), 695: conformity, 967; in organizations, 9049; orientation behavior, 2158
Rumination, 7832
Runaways, 6264

Sad mood, 1670, 5592
Safety, 4038: leader commitment, 9156; in manufacturing, 9052; perceptions, 9125; practice, supervisor's, 1073; railroad industry, 9155; schools, 9057; traffic, 1622
Salesperson, 4139, 4860, 6546, 6608, 6895, 6955, 7320, 7398: goal orientation, 9274; job satisfaction, 8214; motivation, 6668; pay cognitions, 5989; perception of, 10077, 10090; performance, 10090, 10092; rating, 3596, 3598; susceptibility to, 6999; trust of sales manager, 6014; vocational evaluation, 5298
Salience, 1422: career, 3260, 3621, 3638; work, 2672; work role, 3665
Sampling procedures, 161
Satisfaction, 3923, 4147, 4175: attainment of, students, 714;

body image, 2044, 4773, 4774, 4778, 4779, 6708, 6710, 6715, 6716, 6736, 9327–9337, 9470; body in adolescents, 756; career/job, 3173, 4119, 4130, 4131, 4137–4139, 4142, 4146, 4150–4160, 4164–4167, 4173–4175, 4216, 4221, 5902, 5903, 8149–8151, 8176, 8178, 8190, 8192–8194, 8199–8219, 8237, 8238, 8268, 8273, 10143–10145; client, 182, 999, 3059; college major, 872; college student, 663, 1961, 2407, 3727, 4647; communication, 2904, 5842, 6344, 6354; community, 3060, 4279; complacency and, 6738; congregation, 3062; counseling, 3564, 7287; course, 175; dating, 5842; employee, 164, 2362, 4126, 4177, 4178, 4190, 4191, 8168; environment, 1965; faculty, 6533; family, 4548, 6429, 8861; graduate school, 6559; with grievance system, 8269; with group meetings, 8270; with hospital, 6559, 6589; with illness, 5653; job, 709, 1575, 1577, 1578, 1581–1586, 1588, 1589, 1592, 1595, 1668, 2320, 2624, 2625, 2629–2637, 2657, 2659, 2668, 2670, 2675, 5929–5834, 5943–5945, 5952–5968, 5978; leadership, 2345; leisure, 5564, 6780, 7089; life, 33, 415, 2504, 2529, 3869–3873, 3924, 3928, 5575–5581, 5600, 5615, 5654, 5684; marital, 648, 2967, 3007, 3020, 3027, 2038, 3035, 4576, 4584, 4585, 4618, 6389, 6455, 8897, 8909, 8988; with mental health services, 4635–4637, 4641, 6541; Navy, 2661; need, 1356; in nonwork settings, 4728, 8231, 8232; nursing, 4171; occupational, 709, 5983; organizational, 5988; parental, 3008; with partner, 5833, 5836; patient, 9107, 10035, 10036; pay, 2652, 5991, 8239, 8240; with peer counseling, 7313; with performance, 5449; pleasant events inventory, 3902; relationship, 4058, 5829, 8055;

with salesperson, 7398; self-, as parent, 6454; sexual, 8882, 8999, social activity, 5846; social support, 5861; with social services, 6602; with sports, 7086; student, 159, 5434; suburban life, 4649; with supervisor, 6015, 8271, 8272; task, 2663, 8282, 8283; team, 8285; training, 310, 320; with union, 4213, 6036, 7437, 7438; university student, 705; work, 178, 2673, 4122, 4744, 8273, 8274; work schedule, 2660

Scales, recommended, 666

Scanning, 612: internal, 1914, 2932

Schedul(e)(ing), 694: inflexibility, 9159; modular, 1328

Schizophreni(a)(c)(s), 526, 1084, 1085, 1224, 1504, 2491, 3776: cognitions, 6220; patients, improvement, 306; posthospitalization adjustment, 3752; socialization, 1111; vs. borderline personality, 5603

Scholastic: activities and attitude, 556; competence, 7541; potential in women, 1739; women's potential, 1119

School(s), 491, 494, 497, 516, 532, 4665, 6605: academic self-concept, 4746–4750; acceptance, 1070; achievement motivation, 9275; administrators, 528; administrator morale, 1680, 1978; adolescent adjustment, 3728, 3729, 7542; attitude toward, 66, 155, 540, 541, 1136, 1149, 1181, 1825, 2778, 2779, 4231, 4266, 5426; attitude, peer counseling, 1973; attitude toward cheating, 4274; beginners, Black and White, 655; behavior, 1238; behavior adjustment, 1628; bureaucratic structure, 695; child classroom adjustment, 3740, 3741, 7488, 7489; children, 629; classroom environment, 4658; climate, 3108; -community relations, 1827; competence, 460; connection to, 7543; cooperative attitudes, 4371; counselor attitude, 1826;

culture perceptions, 9117; decision-making process, 4176; desegregated, 452; deviant behavior, 8673; disadvantaged, 434; disruptive behavior, 4435; drop-out prediction, 476; effectiveness, 9160; elementary, 1723; elementary, inner-city, 990; enthusiasm toward, 540; environmental assessment, 4646, 9161; empowerment, 6016; failure tolerance, 3731, 5425; feelings toward, 1825; gifted children, 4261; guidance evaluation, 687; history, 625; honor system, 6120; interest, 391; last year, 494; motivation, 737, 2004, 3151, 6669; noncognitive performance organizational structure, 9163; predictors, 4228; nongraded, 574; nursing, 694; organization, 695, 4663, 4672; orientation, 547; orientation attitude, 534; perception of, 700, 3055; picture stories, 738; principal, 3107, 4429; psychologist stress, 2662; quality of life, 6599; rating, 548; readiness, 469; reading readiness, 4227; related experiences and aspirations, 472; resistance, 5433; safety, 9057; satisfaction, 2147, 5434, 7546; self-esteem, 2064; sense of belonging, 5420; sentiment, 1179; situations, 700; situations, student survey of, 700; sources of stress, 4666; students' perceived control in, 4897; subjects, attitudes, 2745; subjects, ratings intermediate grade, 871; success, prediction of, 71; teacher perceptions, 6613; unethical behavior, 4476; values, 10000; work conflicts, 7568, Science and engineering, 7377: academic achievement, 3733; activity, 6201; anxiety, 5427; aptitude, 1732; attitudes toward, 2793, 4267, 7235; career expectations, 9453, 9454; goals, 9245; interests, 10140, 10169, 10170; intentions, 9833; interest, intermediate children, 864;

knowledge assessment, 5371; laboratory, 6606; learning strategies, 3732; orientation, 7105; problem-solving, 7141; religion and, 7248; self-efficacy, 9455, 9456, 9527; teacher attitudes, 4321

Scientists, creative potential, 1933

Screening, 5387; alcohol, 8532, 8702; drug abuse, 8575; interviewee candidates, 1013

Seasonal depression, 7840

Seat belt: attitudes, 1828, 2780; beliefs, 1829

Second language, elementary school English, 1598; learning, 8392

Secondary: reading attitude, 1824; school, 1787; social studies, 600; student, 368, 369, 537, 549, 9862; students' attitudes, 93; students' political attitude, 537; teacher evaluation, 1030

Secretary, 4130

Security, 502, 2317: child, 3037; job, 709, 1687, 8196, 8197

Seeking professional psychological help, 1764

Selection: counselor, 104; job, 3632; organizational procedures, 6547, 9164; supervisors, 1017

Selective attention, auditory, 3667

Self-, 241, 250, 494, 499, 551, 6817: acceptance, 252, 759, 831, 1425, 1880, 2125, 4065, 4823, 4842, 5772, 9561; acceptance, social, 499; actualization, 214, 2367, 3285, 3286, 4953, 4990, 6944, 6945, 9339, 9340, 9535, 9738; adjustment, 409; aggression, 242; appraisal, 472, 4984; appraisal, curiosity, 2021; assessment, depression, 1692, 3962; assessment, disability, 3781; assessment of emotions, 2165; assessment, and stress, 3938; assessment, general, 5656; assurance, 1101, 1427, 2265; attitude, 1439, 5516; attitude of disabled, 752; care behavior, 4440; cathexis, 4955;

centrality, 249; concept, 219, 230, 243, 252, 255, 300, 472, 755, 759, 787, 796, 798, 823, 824, 1279, 1376, 1389, 1394, 1395, 1402, 2108, 2109, 2123, 2127, 2129, 2130, 2171, 2239, 4842, 4957, 4979–4981, 6803, 6871, 6947, 9472, 9621; concept, academic, 2030, 3153, 3301, 3303, 4907, 6679, 6680, 6695, 6719, 6852, 9299, 9301, 9312; concept, academic interest and satisfaction, 2056; concept, actual ideal, 748; concept, adolescent, 2103, 4964, 4965, 9341; concept, African Americans, 4929; concept, anxiety, 1381; concept, blood donor, 3174; concepts, children, 807, 3186, 3213, 3221, 3232, 3250, 3254, 3279, 3297, 4886, 4956; concept, college students, 2035, 3300, 3305; concept, counselor, 822; concept, crystallization, vocational, 2155; concept, disconfirmation, 9562; concept, gender, 6853; concept, global, 1398; concept, job involvement and, 5331; concept, leadership and initiative, 2056; concept, learner, 3299; concept, level of aspiration, 2056; concept, loneliness and, 5747; concept, male college students, 199; concept, math, 1409, 3247, 3248; concept, middle childhood, 243; concept of ability, 1850; concept of academic ability, 2128; concept, primary, 2114, 2115; concept, primary children, 763; concept spouse, 3298; concept, stability, 2145; concept, student, 1424, 3304, 3321, 5011, 6896; concept, vocational, 6978, 7440, 9653; concepts, general adequacy, peer, teacher-school, academic, physical, 2069, 3338; confidence, 338, 5217, 9317, 9482, 9517; confidence, intellectual, 2073; confidence, medical students, 4879; confidence, social, 1715; consciousness, 1880, 2510,

3202, 3376, 3927, 4754, 4958–4962, 5070, 6688, 6867, 6898, 6899, 7040–7043, 9565, 9680, 9767, 9779, 9780, 9937; control, 2714, 2873, 3185, 4441, 4963, 5207, 6293, 6294, 6900, 7044; construal, 9566; control, 8015, 8554, 8618, 8675, 8676, 9504, 10091; control, in children, 4466; control, women, 9781; criticism, 244, 6901; deception, 3510, 4764, 5071, 6902, 9782; defeating, 7045, 9783; defects, 6928; derogation, 2131, 7842; description, 749, 1369, 6854, 6903–6906, 9567–9570; -destructive behavior, 5481, 6217; directed classroom, 1969; directed learning readiness, 1742, 2193; disclosure, 104, 589, 590, 591, 593, 598, 599, 1254, 1258, 1263–1265, 1895, 1899, 1902, 4486–4490, 6355, 8765–8768; discrimination, 1431; efficacy, 3180, 3216, 3256, 3306–3308, 4829, 4900, 4970, 4972, 6110, 6755–6758, 6771, 6790, 6804, 6816, 6841, 6843, 6907–6917, 6937, 6951, 6958; 9402–9404; 9406–9409, 9471, 9504; 9571–9591; efficacy, academic, 6681, 6682; efficacy, career, 6728–6732, 6815,; 9344, 9345, 9348, 9349, 9352, 9353, 9439, 9467, 9654, 9677; efficacy, children, 9384; efficacy, computer, 6739, 6740, 6908; efficacy, job, 9438; efficacy, mathematics, 6795–6799, 9452–9462, 9506, 9624; efficacy, mothers, 8966; efficacy, physical, 6859; efficacy, students, 9369; enhancement, 1994; enhancement derogation, children, 843; esteem, 213, 246, 249, 272, 286, 296, 434, 499, 515, 636, 788, 800, 817, 2053, 2054, 2061, 2082, 2124, 2126, 2133, 2135–2138, 2140, 2141, 2149, 3212, 3229, 3293–3296, 3309, 3311, 3314, 3315, 4038, 4103, 4801, 4823, 4904, 4920, 4948, 4949, 4973–4978, 6686, 6687, 6719, 6721–6724,

6777, 6851, 6919–6927, 6929, 6930, 6956, 6970, 6971, 6979, 8528, 9411, 9413, 9415, 9419, 9431, 9478, 9533, 9558–9559, 9592, 9606, 9626, 9642, 9643; African Americans, 9414; collective, 7931, 9368; esteem, academic, 2031, 3154, 3155, 3278, 4749; esteem, adults, 2046; esteem, adult males, 826; esteem, children, 458, 2039, 3197, 3206, 4975, 6981, 9518; esteem, college students, 816, 2139; esteem, disadvantaged children, 830; esteem, dropouts, 827; esteem, ethnicity and, 5825; esteem, high school students, 827, 3313; esteem, low, 1670; esteem, organization-based, 9477; esteem, preadolescent, 825; esteem, pupil, 3276; esteem, school, home, peer, 2064; esteem, social, 9541, 9623; esteem, student, 792, 2134, 3310, 5010; esteem, task, 3328, 3329; esteem, work, 4904, 4974; estimate ability, 766; estrangement, 430, 457, 1701; evaluated intelligence, 247; evaluation, 828, 6120, 6694; evaluation, academic 6897; evaluation, counselors, 6741; evaluation, employee, 1008; expectations, 212, 1432; expansiveness, 9597; exploration, 9598, 10195–10197; expression, 9276; focus, 1484; future, 6862, 6863; global, 1793; -handicapping, 6295–6297; ideal, 252, 759, 8677; identity cohesion, 6985; improvement, 6843; injurious behavior, 8726; involvement, 796; justification, 746; management, 6298, 6299, 8529, 8678; mastery, 6931; monitoring, 3686, 4062, 4068, 4982, 4983, 9599; motivation, 6670, 9277; needs, 3316; non-professional attitudes, 82; other relationships, 1728, 5843; peer, 1359; perceived popularity, 458; perception, 748, 755, 819, 829, 3273, 6869, 6934–6936, 6954;

perception, adolescent, 5080; perception, children, 3187, 3260; perception, counselor, 1426; perception, engineering students, 829; perception, gifted, 1124, 6982; perception, group behavior, 778; perception, health, 779; perception, interpersonal relations, 780; perception, preschool, 835; perception, pupil, 1105; perception, retirement stress, 7843; poverty, children, 798; presentation, 2558; preoccupation, 9766; rated ability, 305; rated abrasiveness, 749; rated anxiety, 911, 7844; rated attractiveness, 749; rated depression, 7845, 7846; rated occupational interest, 196; rating, 550, 1410, 6938; rating clients, 310; rating, college students, 248; rating, counselors, 769; realization, 2317; regard, 556; regulation, children, 4345, 6300, 6301; regulation, college student, 145; rejection, 449; regulation, 8490, 8679–8682, 8713, 9326; regulation, children, 8584, 8948, 9362; reliance, 7893; report, 551; reproach, 6819; respect, loss of, 515; righteousness, 3512, 5209; satisfaction of adolescents, 756; satisfaction of parents, 6454; silencing of, 9618; social, 1728; social constructs, 830; social constructs, children, 434; subordination, 967; -talk, 6304, 8686; trauma effects, 5519; value, 400; worth, 1880, 9413, 9609; worth, children, 6759; worth, job and, 5950

Semantic: classes, 358; differential, 307, 1180, 1181, 1192; flexibility, 210; implications, 266, 359; transformations, 11, 127; units, 3360

Sensation seeking, 2023–2025, 2172, 3146, 3147, 6643, 6659, 6671–6676

Sense of: coherence, 9611, 9612;

competence, 2070, 9613; control, Asians, 9649

Sensitivity, 283, 443, 444: aesthetic, 2034; affective, 98, 428, 429, 1252; equity, 5751; interpersonal, 428, 444; noise, 2099, 2850, 3110; personal feelings, 500; repression, 951; repression in counseling, 921; to rejection, 1726, 8068; training, 186, 220

Sensitization-repression, 1875

Sensory expressive style, 594

Sentence: completion, 796, 863, 4516, 4517, 5663; complexity, 7; construction, 377; elements, elaborative, 377; imitation, 376, 377

Separation, 4056, 5644, adolescent, 3909; adult, 4070; affect, 3910; anxiety, 3932; anxiety, maternal, 4588, 6465, 8913, 8914; from parents, 8983–8985; problems, 397, 2975, 2977, 3040; student–parent, 4613

Series learning potential, 1743

Service ethic, 9278

Set: educational, 1068, 1350; size, 345

Sex, 593, 5711: coercive, 8377; discrimination, 3085; education course, high school, 668; exaggerated concern, 2253; impotence, 6258; information, 2393; -role(s), 284, 288, 552, 795, 878, 2194, 2195, 3167, 9807; -role, achievement standards, 877; -role, adolescent perception, 5080; -role adoption, 2192; -role, artistic achievement, 887; -role, athletic achievement, 877; -role attitude, 1831, 2720, 2760, 4248, 4251–4258, 4260, 4270, 4322, 5083, 6164, 7061–7063, 7107, 8468; -role, attitude toward, 552, 2699, 2782, 2783, 2787, 4255; -role, behavior, 5110, 5111, 7091; -role, beliefs, 5113; -role, children, 881, 3188, 9808, 9897; -role, concepts, adult, 2132; -role, conflict, 4193, 5082, 5112; -role development, 137; -role, female, 2303; -role

identity, 3294, 5115; -role, ideology, 9846–9848; -role, kindergarten children, 883; role, mathematics achievement, 877; -role, marriage, 9813; -role, mechanical achievement, 877; - role, occupations, 9652; -role orientation, 874, 3389, 5086, 5098, 5114, 7087, 9845; -role perceptions, 2110; -role preference, 2181, 3414, 5080, 5082–5084, 5086, 5096–5100; -role, reading achievement, 877; -role, social skills, 877; -role socialization, 2360; -role stereotypes, 1482, 2196, 3318, 3319, 5102; safe practice, 6244; token resistance, 9645

Sexual: abuse, 4447, 8690, 8699; abuse, child's knowledge of, 3682; adversarial beliefs, 8315; aggression, 131, 8506; anxiety, 3842; arousability, 4448; assault, 3684, 6307, 9633; attitudes, 2781, 3687, 4323, 4328; behavior, 485, 1747, 2875, 3998, 4376, 6257, 8691; desire, 4740, 5665, 6642; experiences, 8692–8699; fantasy, 2876; goings-on, 2253; harassment, 4676, 6251, 6263, 6305, 6306, 6309, 8665, 8692–8695; harassment, organizational sanctions, 9102; history taking, 4446, 4449; ideology, 3411; inappropriate behavior, 6849; intentions, 6674; interest, 9279; knowledge, 3687; marital problems, 38; orientation, 9848, 9849; permissiveness, 6165, 6308, 8470; preferences, 9826; premarital aggression, 6277; response cycle, 7849; role attitudes, 6063; satisfaction, 8882; self-schemas, women, 9616, 9617; sensation-seeking, 6674–6676; situation recognition, 5737; socialization, 5845; stimuli, public exposure to, 1761; symbolism, 114; tendencies, 5594; thoughts, 1260, 5666

Shame, 5061: internalized, 7021; proneness, 5022

Shop, attitude toward, 1182

Shopping, 7112, 7113
Short stories, 7090
Shyness, 3573, 5205, 5210, 5211, 7179, 7201, 7202, 8540, 9786, 9934, 9939, 9945
Siblings: negativity, 9000; relations, 4565, 4619; teaching, 6325
Sickle cell disease, 3802
Sight-sound, 1
Sight word, 2937
Silent child, 397
Similarities, 608, 619
Simil(e)(ies): appreciation, 2938; performance, 1054
Simultaneous movement, 348
Situational: confidence, 9619; motivation, 9280; response, 1462
Sixth-grade pupils, 659
Skill(s), 661: academic, 400; arithmetic, 637; auditory blending, 1036; auditory segmentation, 1037; auto-driving, 478; classification, 627; communication, 175, 2913; cognitive, 5372; confidence, 6018; counseling, 1543, 3578; development, 6382; functional reading, 1602; interpersonal, 431; job, 9065; junior high school, 700; leading process, 1860; occupational, 6019, 9065; personal, 3320; playground, 5383; problem-solving, 2225; questioning, 7139; reading, 336; reasoning, 3427, 3428; research and thinking, 1606; social, 1697, 2602, 2608–2610; supervisors, 3652; utilization of, 1687; work, 338; writing, 364
Skin cancer, knowledge, 7460
Slang, 1058
Sleep, 6332: behavior, 2877; disturbance, 1870, 7851, 8706; dysfunctional beliefs, 8385; hygiene, 8704; patterns, 8705; sleepiness, 6224
Small group, 596
Smoking, 1748, 4386, 6283: attitudes toward, 8472; cessation, 4048, 4734, 7103 8450, 8653, 9571, 9588, 10080; locus of control, 6948; workplace ban, 5896, 6623

Sociability, 1099, 1720, 1870: student, 24
Social, 624, 2173: acceptance, 1104, 8072, 8081; acceptance, children, 2593; access, 1452; achievement, 2298; activity, 5846, 5847, 8028, 8077; adjustment, 44–70, 4026, 4071, 5708; affection, 417; affiliation, 2367; alienation, 1098; anhedonia, 5848; anxiety, 2604, 2605, 4072–4076, 4082, 5766, 8076–8078, 8094, 8098; anxiousness, 2551; approval, 48, 449, 2586, 5734; attributes, 561; attitude(s), 554, 555, 1513, 1527; avoidance, 8071; behavior, 388, 3734, 4071, 4081, 4472; behavior, children, 842, 963, 964, 8659, 8708–8710, 8727, 8728; behavior, positive/negative, 390; change, 92; class, children, 3189; cognition, 7853; closeness, 1723; cohesiveness, 8275; communication, 6338; competence, 425, 459, 1719, 6971, 8075, 8084–8087, 8120; competence, adolescent girls, 2595; competence, children, 2567, 2606, 5707; competence, general, 636; constructs, children, 434; contact, intimate, 1707; control, 52, 174; dependency, 434; deprivation, 466; desirability, 49, 62, 251, 281, 296, 435, 438, 441, 449, 450, 2557, 2585, 3972, 3999, 4037, 4079, 5721, 5795, 5796, 5850, 5851, 5852, 8016–8018, 8021, 8041, 8088–8090; development, 637; diffusion, 460; distance, 63, 535, 1144, 1184, 1185, 1723, 8059; dominance, 5853, 5854, 9788, 10001; egocentricism, 1109; emotional, 1108; exchange, 8122, 8123; and existential courage, 1832; fraternities, 486; functioning, 2607; future time perspective, 832; history, 466; inadequacy, 9541; inequality, 3445, 3446; inference, 1114, 1619; influences, 8092; information

processing, 8093, inhibition, 8082; insight, 5855; institutions, 1060; integration, 2399, 5856, 8276; intelligence, 1096, 1099, 1100, 2555, 2564; interaction, 5857, 8095; interest, 249; interpersonal problem, 38; intimacy, 2587, 5858; introversion, 1670; involvement, 5826; isolation, 437, 1110, 1709, 1727; issues, 1146; justice, 381; life, 663; maturity, 636; morals concepts, comprehension, 1599, 2300; moral values, 472; networks, 8031–8033; nonconformity, 1725; orientation, 1101, 5754; orientation, university residence, 704; perception, 5814; performance, 2608–2610; personal adjustment, 397; phobia, 7047, 7602, 7854, 7855; power, 460, 1112, 3129, 3132; preference, 789; problems, 419; problem-solving, 5860; propensity, 2611; reactions, 5862; receptivity, 8100; reinforcement responsiveness, 725; relations, 456, 464, 5863; relations, middle childhood, 244; responsibility, 58, 462, 915, 1113, 4060; responsibility, attitudes, 94; responsiveness, 1235; restrictiveness, 530, 1807; roles, 461, 5849; roles, females', 1755; scenarios, 7925; schemas, 440; self-acceptance, 499; self-confidence, 1715; self-esteem, 9541, 9623; services, 5849; situations, children, 2613; skills, 1697, 2602, 3970, 4074, 4086, 5832, 8064, 8101; skills, sex role, 877; stigma, 9505; stratification, 268; studies, attitude, 1138; studies, elementary school, 1060, 1282; studies, high school, 601; studies programs, secondary school, 600; studies, student teachers, 600; support, 215, 2578, 2988, 4023, 4050, 4083, 4093, 4622, 5706, 5748; 5749, 5779, 5780, 5781, 5785, 5804, 5807, 5815, 5861, 5865–5877,

5993, 6260, 8024, 8038, 8099, 8102–8113, 8140, 8243, 8608, 10101; systems, 5878; vocabulary, 252; welfare concern, 462; welfare curriculum, 162; well-being, 8114; withdrawal, 50, 56; work concepts, 1277; work majors, 674

Socialization, 61, 236, 855–857, 3994, 4110: African Americans, 7912, children's play, 60; organizational, 5987, 9103; physical activity and, 5821; proactive, 8251, 8763; racial, 8048, 8457; schizophrenic, 1111; sexual, 5845; sport, 5879, 6312

Society, 497

Scoiocentric, 2186

Socio-economic status, 270, 277, 482, 898, 899, 1471–1473; college freshmen, 904; low, 1065; preschool children, 59

Socio-emotional: climate index, 583; problematic, 578

Sociology departments, 676, 685

Sociometric: analysis of students, 1695; measure, 214; nominations, 1713

Sociotropy, 9760, 9790

Solitude, 2317, 7102, 7926

Somatic: anxiety, 5457; concern, 405, 1079; complaints, 5480, 7858, discomfort, 571; sensation, 3934, 4769, 4770; symptoms, 5560, 5611, 5671, 5672, 7783

Somatization, 1663, 1681, 1870

Somatotype, perceived, 3263

Sons: family involvement, 9001; mother's monitoring, 9002

Sororities, 9094

Sound-symbol relationship, 366

Space, 747: personal, 1107, 1418; relations, 1738

Spanish, 380: visual discrimination, 2394

Spatial: ability, 1061, 4389, 4453, 4994, 7451; aptitude, 479; egocentricism, 1485; orientation, 1433; orientation and visualization, 2042, 2048, 2106, 2116, 2144; relations, 2060; visualization, 2097

Speakers, 1765, 2913

Speech, 388: active, 397; aphasic, 1887; forms, private, 1491; imitation, 349; passive, 397; phonological analysis, 6337

Speed, 1361: of closure, 1612, 1617; motor, 1610; perceptual, 1604, 1608, 1618

Spelling, 108, 7127: and reading ability, perception of, 2147; sound, 1062

Splitting (defense), 9791

Sports: anxiety, 7859; commitment, 10198; competence, 9507; competitiveness, 7866, 9627, 9941, 9942; confidence, 9627, 9646; coping, 7860; fans, 9281; motivation, 9113, 9114, 9229, 9261; orientation, 9282, 9287, 9941; perceptions, 9625; spectator involvement, 10199; stress, 7866; team success, 9509

Spouse: abuse, 3000, 4521; attribution for depression, 6956; affective closeness, 8802; communication, 8744; conflict, 6447, 9003; essential characteristics, 8834; perceived negative behavior, 8974; perception of other, 6521, positive feelings, 8979; relationship, 3045; response patterns, 8884; self-concept, 3298; support, 6513, 8973, 9004, 9005

Stability of self-concept, 2145

Staff, 523, 3112, 3113

State anxiety, 1682, 2440, 7861

State guidance office function, 697

Statistics: anxiety, 5429, 5440, 7549; attitude toward, 2701, 2786, 6083, 6169, 6174, 8366; basic, 2372; knowledge assessment, 5390

Status, 268–277, 896–906, 1470–1475, 2235–2239: academic, college freshmen, 904; classroom, 659; concern, 1475; developmental, 481; distance, Mexican-American migrants, 902; ego identity, 628; family, 2987; identity achievement, 271; jobs, 273, 275, 276, 2645;

occupational, 276, 1470, 9890–9892; socioeconomic, 270, 482, 898, 899, 1471–1474, 3444; socioeconomic, college freshmen, 905

Stepfamilies, 6413, 6514

Stereotype(s), 2253, 3169, 6856, 6952, 9629: banking, 156; body build, 561; ethnic groups, 9628; gay, 6754; girls, activity, 2032; Italian, 3228; mathematics, 3245; occupational, 270, 3642; political, 1186; racial, 520, 1154, 1198; sex role, 1482, 2196, 3318, 3319, 6857, 9805; vocational role, 3660

Stigmatization, 6315, 8452, 9505

Stimulation, 666: cognitive, 8818; auditory, 1233; home, 642; seeking, 741

Stimulus: child, 185; expressions, 38; seeking, 2847; varying input need, 1992

Stoicism, 7051

Strain, 5675, 7863, 7864: anxiety, 5460; financial, 7677, 8871; marital, occupational, 1686, 2627, 2638; role, 1667; work-related, 6004

Stratification, social, 268

Street language, 378

Stress: 423, 841, 1672, 1673, 1677, 1687, 2434, 2466, 2488, 2489, 2501, 2532, 2535, 2537, 2543, 3812, 3945, 3954, 5635, 5650, 5677, 5678–5683, 7764, 7852, 7870: academic, 5446; academic performance and, 5430; acculturation, 5705; administrative, 2617; adolescent, 2435, 3753, 3754, 5489, 7828; arousal and, 3936; athlete, 3868, 5566; brainstorming, 5470; children, 2536; college student, 3691, 3710, 3789, 5489, 7809; combat related, 2454; computer, 5912, 5913; conflict, 5435; coping behavior, 2830, 3958; counselor, 2620; data entry, 5918; of diabetes, 5648; disease risk and, 3900; economic, 3814, 4543; elderly, 2531; environmental, 3071; evaluative, 1627, 1694; faculty,

5921; family, 6430; foreign
student, 5558; graduate
student, 5411; health
professional, 4134; high school,
2481; humor and, 3798;
impact, 7706, 7707; job
related, 2621, 2638, 2639,
2641, 2642, 2649, 2650, 2654,
2658, 4161, 4181, 4195, 4199,
4222, 5933, 5970, 5971, 8143,
8154, 8279, 8280, 8308; life
events, 2531, 2533, 3866, 3867,
3885, 5558, 5569, 5570;
medical school, 2419, 2425;
nursing, 2639, 2648, 4169,
5982; occupational, 5985,
8233–8235; organizational,
4197; outcomes, 7867;
parental, 3894, 4566, 8967;
perception, 3898, 5616, 7784–
7786; physical response, 4452,
5673, 5674; police work, 4182;
professional, 7807;
psychological, 2517;
psychological symptoms, 3771,
3948; psychosocial, 5647; and
race, 3868; reactions, 7868;
role, 2525–2527, 4198, 5522,
5595; school, 4666; school
administrators, 8141; school
psychologist, 2662; sports,
7866; stages, 5676; student,
5435, 5436, 5437, 7554;
subjective, 1086, 2484, 7871;
suppression, 3943; of surgery,
5613; symptoms, 3939, 3940,
3946, 5688; teacher, 2655,
2665, 2666, 3117, 3810, 4186,
4203, 4204, 4207–4210, 8277;
undergraduates, 833, 2415,
2423; vulnerability, 3938;
work, 6051; work load, 4180,
4188
Striving, achievements, 716
Structure(d): bureaucratic, 1309;
cognitive, 218; conceptual,
604; family, 8864; job, 3084;
need for, 2208, 9758; need for
in adolescents, 760, 1070,
1378, 1991; organizational,
1332, 6586; situation, 656;
union, 6776
Student(s), 581, 662, 680: ability,
junior college, 766; academic
aspiration, 2027; academic
attitude, 1126; acculturation,

5714; activism, 1483, 2879;
activities, university, 705,
1293; adolescent, 1430;
affective behavior, 568; alcohol
use, 6315; alienated, 455, 582;
aspirations, 740, 9283; athlete,
3413; attainment satisfaction,
714; attitudes and beliefs, 556,
859, 1160, 1163, 1188–1190,
1193, 1194, 8393, 8473;
attitudes toward parents, 9007;
autonomy, 333; behavior, 578,
603, 737, 2824, 6321–6323;
-centered characteristics, 581;
-centered classroom, 1969;
-centeredness, junior high,
middle school teachers, 1867;
classroom perceptions, 9085
cognitive behavior, 568;
cognitive processing, 3423,
7117; confidence, 6720; course
evaluation, 9170; counselor,
1021; counselor contacts, 665;
disadvantaged, 679; drug
attitudes, 1145; effects on
White fifth-grade, 88;
engineering, 829; enrichment
cluster attitudes, 8475;
evaluation of teachers, 690,
698, 1009, 1014, 1022, 1027,
1029, 1032, 1562–1565, 1567–
1572; evaluation of instructors,
2348; efforts, 2349;
expectancies, 6747; faculty
perceptions about academic
advising, 1959; faculty
relations, 675, 694; feelings
toward Whites, 2157; foreign,
1094, 5558, 5714; freedom,
586; grade orientation, 5414;
graduate, 528, 2426; high risk,
1189; high school occupational
aspiration, 897, 901; influence,
university residence, 704;
interdependence, 5413;
interracial attitudes, 535;
junior high school, 700;
learning environment, 3114;
leaving home, 6438; male high
school occupational aspiration,
901; management of, 6792;
mathematics, 6099; motivation,
6650, 6678, 9233, 9284, 9285;
notes, 379; occupational
activity, 7381–7383; opinion,
95; organizational involvement,

5409, 9169; outcomes, 687,
5412; participation, 6317; peer
counseling, 6823; perceived
success, 5417; perceived
support, 5819; perception,
175, 3322; perception of
advisers, 993; perception of
campus, 6539; perception of
parents, 6402; perceptions of
teacher, 1027, 5418;
performance aspects, 568;
performance attribution, 3323,
5439; personal, 859;
philosophical orientation, 3552;
preference, 263; problem
behavior, 2589, 6289; relations
with, 679; roles, 2590;
satisfaction, 159, 1071, 5434;
satisfaction, university, 705;
school belonging, 5420; self-
concept, 1429, 3304, 6695;
self-efficacy, 9591; self-esteem,
2134, 3310, 3313; short story
reading, 7090; social work
majors, 674; sociometric
analysis, 1695; stress, 2415,
2423, 2424, 5411, 5430, 5435,
5436, 5437, 7554; suicide,
1087, 1088; superior, 680,
6203, 6291; survey of school
situations, 700; teacher, 701;
teacher, concerns of, 701;
teacher, elementary school,
495, 701; teacher evaluation,
3590, 3602; teacher
relationships, 2416, 2911,
6953, 7555, 10021; teachers,
social studies, 600; test
anxiety, 387, 5415; -student
counseling, 1000; tutors, 322;
university, 442, 586; White &
Black, 2; withdrawal behavior,
5444
Study: habits, 23, 1105, 2883,
7125, 7558, 8714;
individualized, 6; practices,
169; process, 7141; skills,
7471; strategy, 1072, 1073,
9887; student diligence, 6634
Style: attributional, 9320–9324;
behavioral, 564, 8530;
categorization, 1464; cognitive,
1479, 9861, 9871; ideational
expressive, 594; identity, 9417,
9418; instructional, 288;
interpersonal, 1489; leader's

motivational, 2184; learning, 9885; parental, 8939, 8940, 8968, 8969, supervisors, 3603, 8614; thinking, 9888

Sub-cultural identification, 95

Subjectivism, 5076

Submission, 2253

Submissiveness, 1720, 3464

Substance, 2224: use, 4384, 4430, 4459, 8565, 8715; use, adolescent, 4470; use, attitudes, 2790, 4330; use, family interventions, 4560; withdrawal, 4463

Substitution, symbol, 340

Success: approach orientation, 8516; athletic, 3215, 9509; attributions, 5895, 6701; avoidance, 1362, 2228; beliefs, 6107; career, 8190, 10031; computer science, 2679; employment, 241; expectancy, 9405; failure, 526, 1373; fear of, 1658–1660, 1676, 1833, 2410, 2411, 2470–2471, 2478, 2500, 2545, 5526, 7673; life, 5582; military training, 3582; negative consequences, 2455; perceptions, 6021, 9263, 9264, 9509, 9510, 9755; potential, 338; predictors for Black students, 6813; preoccupation, 9526; scholastic, 74; sports, 6108, 9509

Suffering, 417

Suffocation, fear of, 7872

Suggestibility, 279, 914, 2902, 9720, 9906

Suicid(al)(e), 1088, 2521, 2538, 5649, 7823: attitude toward, 1192, 7761, 8433, 8477; college students, 7626; cognitive processes, 3917; contemplation, 1087; counselor knowledge, 7472; ideation, 3942, 5591, 5655, 7755, 7835; ideators, 2530; intent, 1688, 3925, 7873; potential, 1671, 2485; prison inmates, 5471; youth reaction to, 3961

Summarizing, 2215

Super-ego complaints, 773

Superintendent(s): behavior, 1307; political orientation, 972

Superior(ity), 8119: students, 680

Supernatural: beliefs, 4997, 5014; phenomena, 1139

Superstition, 2253

Supervisor(s): ability, 1019, 2265; attitude, 1023; beginning, 996; behavior, 1241, 3325, 8520; clinical, 3974, 4679; communication, 1023; compliance, 1005; counselor, 1317, 10109, 10110; credibility, 1556; dependability, 1023; evaluation of, 1017, 1023, 7288, 7333; group direction, 1005; initiative, 1023; interaction, 1248; intervention characteristics, 7268; job knowledge, 1005, 1023; judgment, 1023; knowledge, 1023; leadership style, 1023, 8605; loyalty of, 1005; monitoring, 9171; organization, 1023, 6252, 6253; perceived fairness, 5925, 6955; perceptions of, 6172; power, 1231; problems of, 996; ratings of employees, 10078, 10106; relationships, 1023, 8257; rewards by, 1005, 9154; safety practice, 1023, 1073; satisfaction with, 1552, 6015, 8271, 8272, 10112; selection of, 1017; skills, 3562; style of, 183, 3603, 7226, 10113; subordinate, 2915, 2916, 5917; support, 6024, 7334, 9112, 10107, 10108, 10111, 10114, 10115; synergistic, 10116; system appraisal; teaching, 1023; trainee expectations, 4968; training needs, 1005; trainee perceptions, 6027; trust of, 6023; working alliance, 10109

Support, 689: academic 6550; for caregivers, 6393, 6394; employees, 9040, 9172; family, 8847, 8865; faculty, 6752; interpersonal, 7985; leadership, 6320; network, 8921; organizational, 6586, 6590, 6591, 9079, 9115, 9116; parental, 640, 3038, 8958–8960; social, 2578, 8024, 8038, 8099, 8102–8113, 8243, 8973; spouse, 6513, 8973, 9004, 9005; supervisor, 6024, 7334, 9112, 10107, 10108, 10111, 10115, 10115; teacher, 7341; union, 6594

Suppression, 3943

Surgery: parental coping, 5612; stress, 5613

Suspicion, 2252

Swimming skills, 7481

Symbol: recognition, 1118; substitution, 112, 340; transformations, 126

Symbolic: classes, 361; implications, 129, 362; love-punishment, 654; love-reward, 654; units, 363

Symbolism, sexual, 114

Symptom(s): anxiety, 2441; checklist, 425, 1084, 1663; depression, 5511, 5512, 5642; and loneliness, 7876, 7877; HIV, 5549; neurotic, 2480; patients', 1663; phobic, 5527; physical, 773, 5560, 5611, 5625–5628, 5660, 5671, 5672, 5687, 7875; psychiatric, 2515, 2539, 5467, 5639, 5809; psychopathology, 2448; psychotic, 773; self-reported, 5472

Synonyms, 3

Syntactic: comprehension, 383; contrasts, 383; principle, 383; structures, 349, 355

Syntax, 5

Synthesis, 600

Taboo words, 1274

Tactics, 1882

Tactile body accessibility, 592

Talent: identification, 8313; therapeutic, 3383

Target game, 618

Task(s): anxiety, 7878; arousal, 3149; autonomy, 6612; concern by teacher, 333; challenge, 1981; completion, 6649; complexity, 3115; difficulty, 6025; effectiveness, 214; group conflict, 8281; group strategy, 6342; identity, 9066; motivation, 3137; orientation, 1101, 9288, 9756; orientation, positive/negative, 390; -oriented behavior, 1854; perceived urgency, 9410; performance, 10117, 10118; preference, 205, 2178; responsibilities, 9173; satisfaction, 2317, 2663, 8282,

8283; success, 3207, teams, 8244, 8722

TAT, 204, 268, 726, 929

Teacher(s), 483, 484, 494, 566, 581, 621, 6965, 7258, 7260: accreditation, 6962; administrators' confidence, 4029; affect, 1217; aggression ratings, 8546, 8619; ambition, 1363, 1364; anxiety, 4211; anxiety ratings, 7561; approval-disapproval, 659; attitude, 557, 559, 1167, 1195, 1196; attitude toward, 541, 549, 580; attitude toward gifted children, 558; attitude toward testing, 6150, 6178; authority, 10055; autonomy, 6614, 9842; behavior, 580, 582, 811, 2887, 2888, 2892, 3406, 3604–3606, 6211, 6325, 8716, 8717, 8721; beliefs about reading, 6109; burnout, 2664, 4203, 4204, 5906; career attitude, 4331, 4332, 4629; -centered characteristics, 581; -centered, classroom, 969; characteristics, 684, 1022; -child, interpersonal perceptions, 2076; child relations, 5405, 7535, 7555–7557, 7565; college, effectiveness, 2334; commitment, 5342; competence, 7327, 7328; constellation of forces, 2057; decision making, 836, 3434; desirable, 679; directiveness, 936; education programs, 9086, 9144; effectiveness, 1026, 1030, 3331, 3607, 5292, 5304, 7316, 7337, 7338; efficacy, 6959–6961, 9634–9637, 10119; elementary, 341, 348, 2691; empowerment, 9162; evaluation, 698, 997, 1009, 1014, 1022, 1027–1029, 1032, 7275, 7342, 10054; evaluation by colleagues, 1541, 1542, 1550, 1551; evaluation by students, 1022, 1562–1565, 1567–1572, 3589, 3600, 3601; evaluation, secondary, 1030; evaluation by young students, 5294; feedback, 1885; ideal, 679; identification with, 434,

830; independence, 578; instructional media beliefs, 6177; interactions, 1029, 1251, 8662; interest in pupils, 1027; interpersonal relations, 2577; job-related attitudes, 1827, 8480; job satisfaction, 4185; junior high school, 700; knowledge of behavioral principles, 3679; knowledge, drug, 1130; language attitudes, 6141; leadership style, 1507, 2889; leisure activities, 870; locus of control, 333–3334, 6936; loyalty, 1883; of mentally retarded students, 154; militancy, 1495, 6102; moonlighting, 226; motivation by, 1029; multicultural attitudes, 8476; music, 7340; observation of pupils, 1027; organizational climate, 4672; orientation toward research, 550; parent communication, 8751; participation, 4176, 4465; pedagogical progressivism, 9145; peer support, 4046; perceived self-efficacy, 2965, 4921, 6026; perception of administration, 1408; perception of children's adjustment, 4925; perception of children's learning, 2038; perceptions of counselor role, 332; perception of parental beliefs, 4903; perception of principal, 7306; perception of school, 6613; perception of students, 24, 4736, 4933, 5006, 5008; performance, 997, 1027, 6322; personality, 1027; play ratings, 8640; practice beliefs, 6154; preference, 866, 880; presentation, 1029; primary directiveness, 936; primary school, 8449, 9841; principal, 595; professional concerns, 4205; promotion, 1364; pupil, 600; pupil control, 1523; pupil relations, 256, 1266, 1267; rapport, 1891; rating of sex role development, 136; rating of student, 24, 297, 298, 1043, 1063, 2890, 2891; ratings, 1028, 2395; ratings of composition, 1059; ratings of

students, 7560, 7563, 7564, 8121, 8708, 8718–8720; reinforcing behaviors, 736; reinforcing of, 9638; reporting student behavior, 6289; research attitudes, 6176; role perception, 2038; satisfaction, 4186; secondary school, 2347; self-assessment, 5299; self-efficacy, 6917; self-empowerment, 6918; sense of autonomy, 4445; sense of community, 9165; skills, 7339; special education, 6079; social norms, 9175; stages of concern, 4196; stimulation by, 1029; stress, 2655, 2665, 2666, 3117, 4207–4210, 8277; student control beliefs, 6868; student perceptions of, 1027, 4469, 4832, 4872, 5418, 6271, 6966; student relationships, 2416, 2911, 6953; style, 333, 1571; support, 4429, 7341; support for students, 7562, 8916; survey reading, 545; temperament, 1884; tests, 1029; thinking orientation, 7146; tolerance of classroom behavior, 3711; training, 1982; 9639; value of disadvantaged, 990; values, 10009; verbal pattern, 1255; vocational evaluation, 5260, 5280, 5302, 5304; withdrawal intentions, 5980; work autonomy beliefs, 5009, 9174

Teaching, 492: assessment, 1029; attitude toward, 1140, 2716, 7355; autonomy, 6967; college, 7312; competence, 1015, 1026; effectiveness, 335, 2333, 2347, 3330, 7331, 10119; faculty, 2331; method, 679; method, evaluation of, 698; observation, 1015; of reading, 559; practice, 690; process, 488, 3536; public school, 539; quality, 7280; rating, 1025; reading in content classrooms, 1763; reflective, 6287, 7258; of siblings, 6325; student preferences, 9825; style(s), 694, 882; by supervisors, 1023; urban school success, 1593

Team(work): cohesion, sports,

8115; commitment, 10201; communication, 6358; efficacy, 6615, 8284, 9176; functioning, 8286, 8771; interdependencies, 9105; member exchange, 8772; performance norms, 9127; satisfaction, 8285; teaching, 334, 1140, value of, 8156; viability, 9177

Teasing, 5816, 5822

Technology: attitude toward, 1162; knowledge assessment, 5384

Tedium, 2540, 2643, 2674

Telecourse evaluation, 9178

Television: commercial attitudes, 2722; instructional, 488; watching behavior, 1207

Telic-paratelic, 9260, 9289

Temperament, 1846, 2291, 3356, 7057, 9703, 9704, 9714; 9793–9797: child and infant, 2254, 2285, 2811, 2817, 2840, 3342, 3345, 3347, 3348, 3351, 3352, 3357, 3358, 3362–3365, 3370, 3375, 3378–3381, 3384, 3385, 5052, 5053, 5055, 5069, 9696, 9737, 9726–9731, 9737, 9797

Tempo, conceptual, 604

Temporal experiences, 2080

Tendenc(ies)(y): affiliative, 44; to achieve, 2006

Tendermindedness, 529

Tenseness, 1641

Tension, 1079, 1666, 1690, 2542, 2638, 2639, 4262: index, 1667; job, 2640, 2667, 5971–5974, 8223

Tenure experiences, faculty, 9046

Termination of counseling, 4471, 5614, 6328

Test(s), 6554: anxiety, 25, 26, 32, 209, 392, 393, 395, 396, 398, 399, 401, 402, 713, 1074–1076, 1625, 1627, 1629, 1633, 1635, 2428–2430, 3706, 3712, 3742, 3743, 3749, 5415, 5423, 5428, 5441, 5442, 7485, 7502, 7505, 7569: anxiety, adolescent, 3744; anxiety, children, 3745, 3746; anxiety, college students, 1634, 3739; anxious students, 387; attitude toward, 1453, 2791, 2792, 4333, 6179; behavior, 1242; clerical, 73; graduate students, 2427;

motivation, 9291; parameters, 161; perceived equity, 6616; -taking aptitude, 5127; -taking skills, 1620, 9641; wiseness, 385, 1064, 1620, 1621, 3443, 7507

Testing: practices, 190; program, pre-college, 480; teacher attitudes, 6150, 6178

Text(books), 666: appraisal, 1983; evaluation, 1325; quality, 667

Thanatophobia, 7879

Theft, 1244, 6162

Theory, preferences, 54

Therapeutic: alliance, 6360, 7347, 7348, 10024, 10029, 10038, 10048, 10120; change, 3804, 4375, 5256; change, client willingness, 4720; effectiveness, 4639–4641, 4687; outcome, 3119; progress, 5607; reactance, 4473; relationships, 330, 2559, 3953, 3973, 4491, 5282; talent, 3383

Therapist: activity, 7343; assessment of, 995; attachment, 10023, 10032; attitudes, 96; behavior, 2197; client, 2903; competence, 10073; expectancy, 3336; expressive competence, 10049; gender bias, 10034; intentions, 10122; patients' feelings toward, 10027; perception, problem solving, 764; relationship with, 995; self-disclosure, 1254; social support, 10101

Therapy, 6561, 6618: goals, 1365; rating, 3090, 6619; recreational, 6286; reinforcers for, 735; relationship, 1262; session, 191; termination, 6330

Thinking, 568, 730, 7126: categorical, 9856; complex integrative, 891; consequential, 815; creative, 1924; divergent, 608; dogmatic, 953, 7171; doing, 216; flexible, 9864; imaginative, 1282; logical, 7133; overinclusive, 1224; sexual, 1260; skills, 2215; style, 7147, 9888; teacher's, 7146

Thoughtfulness, 987

Thoughts: covert, 3201; dysfunctional, 6121; habitual, 7121; intrusive, 5487, 5692; about mood, 5589; obsessional, 5559, 5604; positive and negative, 2402, 2403; private, 7037, 7038

Threat, 299, 3951: ambiguity as, 7180; of instruction, 488; perceived in ambiguous situations, 2077, 4854; reaction to, 346

Thrust, 688

Ties, family, 302

Time: adolescents, 772; affective attitude toward, 91; experience, 1400, 1420; future perspective, 772; job demand, 2644; management, 4474, 4475, 6005; orientation, 7224; perspective, 6651; perspective, adults, 758; perspective, children, 772; perspective, college students, 782, 783, 790, 805, 834; perspective, future, 775, 806, 832, 3335, 9964, 9965; management, 8723, 8724; perceived control, 9493; perspective, political future, 832; structure, 8725, 9644, 10003; urgency, 5693; use, 8483

Time learning vs. learning for grades, 487

Tiredness, 5690, 6224

Tolerance, 3711, 3963: ambiguity, 481, 612, 646, 955, 965, 1505, 5216, 6873, 6973, 7151–7153, 7188, 9683, 9685, 9735, 9798, 9799; bureaucratic, 1508; complexity, 612; cultural, 7947; delay, 1212; for disagreement, 8287; of interpersonal violence, 3964; perception, 4795; political, 537, 5823; school failure, 5425; social, 8124; workplace, 4795, 5104

Touching, 5883, 5884, 8623

Toughness, 2253

Toy preference, 883, 3414

Tradition(al)(ism), 624, 967: family, 3047; -modernity, 10005; nontraditional values, 493, 3536; parents, 8484

Traffic safety, 1622

Trainee: adjustment, 27; counselor, 596; perceptions, 6600, 6616

Training, 661, 5395, 6027, 6617, 7288, 7299: behavior, 2863; counselor, 3568, 3570; dialect, 105; information, job, 709; judgment, 9; military, 3582; motivation, 6635, 9290; motivational, 3139; needs, supervisors, 1005; on-the-job, 8225; satisfaction, 310, 320; satisfaction, rehabilitation clients, 29; sensitivity, 186, 220

Trait(s): anxiety, 3478; children's understanding, 8786; frustration, 3517; inconsistency, intolerance, 2078; measurement, 278–299, 907–967, 1476–1510, 2240–2295, 3496, 3499, 3511, 3515, 9893–9947; oral, 934; personality, 615; rating, 2251; screening, 9901; sex-typed, children, 9684; Type A, 7206; worker, 339

Transcedence, 41

Transfer(s): student, college, 511; university, 192

Transformations, 106, 107, 111, 112, 117, 126–128, 267: word, 11

Transitions, work, 8155, 8189, 9021

Translation, 600

Transluminality, 9647

Transportation: community, 1060; concerns, 6028

Traumas, 7881: adult symptoms, 7881, 7882; early, 625, 5519; head, 5695; reactions to, 5557; social support and, 5749

Traveling, 7085

Treatment: acceptability, 7344; barriers, 9015; environment, 1310, 3120; expectancy, 9648; need of psychiatric patients, 773; seeking, 8730

Trichotillomania, 7771, 7808

Trust, 949, 958, 1497, 3366, 4005, 4373, 5049, 5078, 5775, 7950, 7962, 8126–8132, 8288: Black-White, 5739; dyadic, 2562, 7951; expectancies, 7259; faculty, 5922, 5923, 5924; interpersonal, 954, 1504; 1718,

2269, 2914, 4019, 4069, 7982, 7986, 8053; intragroup, 7990; in leader, 8126; in management, 6029, 8131; in mediators, 8127; political, 537; supervisor, 2359, 6014, 6023

Trustworthiness, 258, 2151, 5782: interviewer, 938; of human motives, 2288

Turning: against object, 850; against self, 850

Tutor(ing)(s): attitudes, 2794; observation of, 322; peer, 1240; student, 322, 2893

Type A Behavior, 1886, 3450, 3462, 3479, 3489, 3508, 3518, 7165, 7175, 7203, 7206, 7208, 9893, 9899, 9938, 9946

U-Tube, 1623

Unconditional positive regard, 227, 309, 1538

Unconditionality of regard, 2353

Underachievers, 400, 1069

Underdeveloped countries, 512

Undergraduate(s), 675, 683: as academic advisors, 993; stress, 833

Understanding, 689: empathetic, 1370; instructions, 1361; perceived, 3264; personal, 175; psychotherapy, 10124

Unemployment, 515: attributions, 5013; coping, 3952, 4125; perceived social support, 4109, psychological reactions, 8256, 8294

Union, 6152: activity, 7431, 9574; attitude, 1836, 1837, 2669, 2719, 3118, 3415; benefits, 9179; commitment, 7432–7435, 10202; faculty membership, 3399; family conflict, 6520; instrumentality, 6621, 7395; loyalty, 4110; parent's participation, 6822; participation, 8731, 9109; procedural fairness, 9137; propensity to strike, 7425; satisfaction with, 6036, 7436, 7437; structure, 6576; support, 6594

United States attitudes, 83

University, 509, 660, 704, 903: alienation, 465, 1730, 5890; counseling center, 409, 703;

entrants, 708; environment, 1440; environment, independence, 704; ethnic/racial environment, 9180; experience, college freshmen, 904; faculty needs, 1356; instructors, 680; residence, academic achievement, 704; residence, change and maintenance, 704; residence, emotional support, 704; residence, innovation, 704; residence, intellectual growth, 704; residence, interpersonal relationships, 704; residence involvement, 704; residence, order and organization, 704; residence, personal growth, 704; residence, social orientation, 704; setting, 680; student activity, 705; student attitude, 705; student influence, 704; student rigidity, 1486; transfers, 192, 218

Unusual meanings, 1914

Upward Bound Students, 45: locus of control, 238; self-esteem, 248; self-estimated intelligence, 247

Upward mobility, 3145

Vacation satisfaction, 5017, 5018

Valence, 2895, 8246, 9291, 9292

Valuelessness, 413

Values, 300–304, 968–991, 1398, 1511–1535, 2296–2328, 3535, 3540, 3549, 5232, 7104, 9948–10018: academic, 7262, 9948; acculturation, 2547, 3519; adolescents, 974, 3523; American, 1524; anti-industrial, 3521; career, 5223; children's, 66, 5235; Christian, 3525, 3526; clarification, 1511, 1533; college freshmen, 904; college students', 2308, 5248; competing, 9954; consciousness, consumers, 10007; constructs, interpersonal, 2304; crisis, 10008; core, 9962; cross-cultural, 7263; cultural, 516, 9957; decision-making, 2314; educational, 979, 9959, 9997, 10000; faith, 5226; family, 9817, 9963; gender roles,

10004; guidance practices, 185; health-related, 5238; human, 1529; individualistic, 5247; intercultural, 5228; instructional, 3547; instrumental, 2326, 7253, 9975; interest, 1535; job, 321; life goals, 5231; moral and social, 472, 7255; occupational, 2315; organizational, 7239; orientation, work, 2307; other-centered, 1526, 2327; parental, 9986; perceptions of unmet democratic, 2055; personal, 7220; prescriptive, 991; prescriptive in adolescent, 974; proscriptive, 991; Protestant, work ethic, 5239, 5240; self, 400; self-centered, 2327; social 1528; system, adolescent's, 2325; teachers, 990, 10009; terminal, 2326, 7253; traditional/nontraditional, 493; vocational, 1512; western, 976; women's role, 1530; work, 2320, 2321, 2328, 3520, 3559, 3608, 5222, 5229, 5234, 5249–5254, 7230, 7266, 9981, 9999, 10015–10017; work, intrinsic and extrinsic, 2316

Vandalism, 1245
Variety, tendency toward, 959, 1054
Vedic personality, 9804
Verbal, 1738: absurdities, children, 895; achievement, 1043, 1063; aggression, 9947; analogy, 1065; automaticity, 2927; behavior, 2248; behavior system, client, 587; behavior, teacher, 583; checklist, 561, 1198; comprehension, 1904, 1912, 1915; development, 1300; hostility, 2252; incorporation, 585; information, 373; intelligence, 887; interaction, 596, 1261; nonverbal, 2921; originality, 1281; pattern, 1255; rejection, 585; response counselor, 588; response system, 588; self-disclosure, 590; skills, 397, 7126
Verbalizer-visualizer, 1916, 8777
Victimization: children, 8594; homeless, 8560; peer, 7530, 8639; 9486; severity, 8689

Vietnam(ese), 5891: acculturation, 5722; attitude toward, 81
Vigor, 502
Vindication motivation, 746
Violence: attitudes, 6063; exposure to, 8674, 9030; individual acceptance, 3964, 6061; posttraumatic stress disorder and, 4344; risk, 8593; school, 8556
Visual: analysis, 1041, 1441; attention, 7119; -auditory memory, 1066; -auditory perception, 765, 1414; -auditory rhythm, 750; control, 6969; discrimination, 356, 357, 1412, 1442, 2377, 2394; figure-ground measure, 5388; imagery, 265, 9843; imagery, vividness of, 2154; integration, 1596; judgment, 1115; learning assessment, 5396; matching, 285; memory, 2397, 5397; -motor coordination, 1118; -motor match, 2143; perception, 801, 808, 1735; perspectives, 1443; -social cues, decoding, 1619; spatial abilities, 6053
Visualization: spatial, 2097; spatial orientation, 2042, 2048, 2106, 2116, 2144; strategies, 7476
Visualizer-verbalizer, 1916, 8777
Visuo-spatial memory, 2152
Vitality, 7886
Vividness: imagery, 2040, 7478, 7479, 9651; of imagery production, 2153; of visual imagery, 2154
Vocabulary, 3, 4, 354, 377: comprehension, 365; oral, 380, 384; sight word, 2937; social, 252
Vocalization: age four, 134; maternal, 649; recognition, 7480
Vocational, 10: adjustment, 1033; behavior, 202, 426; choice, 193, 204, 269, 1574, 1594; choice anxiety, 1648; choice motivation, 409, 707, 720; cognitive complexity, 707; commitment, 3656; complexity,

336; conflict, 2641; counseling, 670; decidedness, 2234; decision-making, 1579, 7438, 7439, 9889, 10172, 10173; development, 1291; evaluation, 305–339, 992–1034, 1536–1573, 2329–2359, 10019–10128; exploration, 10203; goals, 511; home economics, teachers, 572; identification, 212; indecision, 2233, 3657–3659; interest, 1574–1595, 2360–2369, 7421, 10129–10209; maturity, 308, 636, 639, 1040, 1291; maturity, adult, 1936, 2618, 2944; needs, 323; orientation, women, 2198; planning readiness for, 470; plans, 1590; preference, 194, 195, 2369; problems, 773, 9839; rehabilitation, 691; rehabilitation clients, 310; role orientation, 3660; self-concept, 2155, 7440, 9653; self-efficacy, 9654; training, 3139; values, 1512
Voice behavior, 8773
Volume, 2224
Voluntariness, 6333
Vowel selection, forced, 1045
Vulnerability, 7058

War, 1748: attitudes, 6101, 6171; children's trauma, 7615
Warmth, 328, 937, 1438: maternal, 652; parental, 3031; self-rated, 749; teacher, 1027
Water level, 1624
Weather beliefs, 3121
Weight: locus of control, 3340; -loss behavior, 5701; loss, expectancies, 9655; loss, goals, 9220; perception of teasing, 5816
Well-being, 2474, 2493, 2499, 2544, 2987, 5645, 5646, 7708, 7750, 7799, 7813, 7833, 7836, 7889, 7890, 8114; alcoholics, 8735, 8735; emotional, 5537; in retirement, 5651; social, 8114
Welfare, 1748
White(s), 520: identity, 8138, 8139; mistrust of Blacks, 5739; racism of, 5808, 6147; racism against, 5717; racial identity, 5892; school beginners, 566

Widowers, 1693

Widows: adjustment-depression of, 1693; coping, 2974

Wi(fe)(ves): dependency, 3029; perception of husbands, 6441; problem, 1306; separation, coping, 2975

Wilderness users, 7114

Will, strength of, 6677

Willingness, 568, 7891

Witchcraft, 1139

Withdrawal, 2191: behavior, 1033; career, 5905, 7371; children, 8541; emotional, 405; job, 5975, 6002, 6003, 6008, 6030–6035, 6038, 7393, 8296, 8298, 8299, 8309; social, 50, 56; student, 5444

Women('s), 1766, 1767, 1800, 7115: academic barriers, 5894; attitude toward, 1190, 2703, 2704, 2796, 4251–4258, 4260, 4270, 4340, 6069, 6085, 6086, 6091–6094, 7210, 8328–8330, 8361–8363, 8367, 8376; attitude, toward physical activity, 791; attitude, women's liberation, 1200; attitudes toward working mothers, 4522, 4523; attributions for abuse, 6702; career decisions, 7108; careers for, 1748; college, 1304; creativity, 840; discrimination perceptions, 9110; desire to work, 1995; equality, attitudes toward, 6158; fears of, 3884; heterosocial assessment, 2570; hostility toward, 7018, 8598, 9723; identity development, 8485; inner-outer directedness, 789; job attrition, 4168; liberation group, 1505; life course functioning, 3854; liberation members life experiences, 862; managers, attitudes toward, 1838, 4340; married, 1128, 1134; in military, 6181; movement, 8346; needs, 6652; perceived role, 6974; perceptions of discrimination against, 5818; rights, 1766; role choice, 869; scholastic personality, 1119; scholastic potential, 1739; self-control, 9781; sexual

arousability, 4448; sexual desire conflict, 5665; sexual history, 4446; sexual self schemas, 9616, 9617; significant other's attitudes toward, 7061; social situations, 1731; status of, 179; stereotyped perception, 5020; values, 1530; vocational orientation, 2198; work role identity, 9852

Word(s): association, 871; association, mechanics, 119; category recall, 7483; definitions, 354; discrimination, 356, 357, 602; fluency, 1917, 1918; knowledge of, 342; meaning, 1276; meaning changes, 225; meaningful, 360; monosyllabic, 374; obscene, 1274; opposites, 2; phoneme-deletion skills, 5398; quick test, 8312; recognition, 2, 342, 6363; representation, 602; segmentation, 602; sounds, 1374

Work, 6042, 6044: ability, 1033; absenteeism, 4118, 4230; addiction, 8736, 9205, 9669; adjustment of retarded, 1033; alienation, 2671; attitude toward, 541, 1199, 6182, 8331, 8486, 10205–10208; attrition of women, 4168; beliefs, 7226, 9950, 10013, 10014; challenge, 6043, 8300; characteristics, 9077, 9083, 9084; children's beliefs, 7226; climate, 6622, 9147; commitment, 7264, 10205–10208; company innovativeness, 4653; complexity, 268; components, 1341; conditions, 1040, 1404, 8247; conflict, 8301; context, 9050; dependence, 1034, 4145; depression related to, 6047; dimensions, 9293; distress, 8302; efficacy, 9511; effort, 9294; emotions, 5509; employee needs, 4163; employee stock ownership, 4126; enjoyment, 8173; environment, 4688, 9166, 9182, 9183; environmental interference, 6548; ethic, 2319,

3550, 3551, 7214, 7218, 7245–7247, 9984, 9988–9990, 10015; expectations, 3122; exposure to noxious elements, 4659; family conflict, 6406, 6432, 6433, 6448, 6523–6528, 9394, 9395, 9422, 9430, 9658–9667, 9672, 9673; family integration, 9478; fields of, 1040; frustration, 4129, 4130; group, 598, 8166, 8303, 8396, 8487, 9051, 9105, 9176, 9177, 9185; habits, 297, 388, 1033, 1047; hours, flexibility; 9048; identity, 6957, 9668, 9852; importance, 3622; influence, 2626, 2653; interest, 747; innovation, 6020, 8781; interpersonal conflict, 5769; interracial situations, 6006; involvement, 2361, 2797, 3628, 3661, 3662, 4148; irritation, 6048; knowledge by seventh graders, 711; load, quantitative, 1687; load, variation in, 1687; locus of control, 9469, 9670; manager-employee relations, 4655; mentoring, 4035; mood, 4143, 5563, 8306; motivation, 487, 1341, 1344, 1366, 7265, 9205, 9294–9296; motivation, internal, 2001, 6646; nonwork conflict, 3341, 6046; organizational attraction, 5335; organizational commitment, 5322, 5334, 5336–5343; orientation, 2676, 7893; outcomes, 8297; overload, 8304, 8305; perceived alternatives, 6846; perceived social support, 4117; perceived work load, 4180, 4188; perceptions, 6806; performance, 1573, 3593, 7349, 8737, 9385, 9511, 10126; performance constraints, 4149; preference, 692, 708, 3664; quality, 338, 7442; quality of work life, 4187; quantity, 338; readiness, 337; relations, 193, 1116, 4189; requirements, 1246; rewards and costs, 8265; role conflict, 6888, 9671; -role salience, 2235, 2672, 3665, 6050; salience, 10209; satisfaction, 178, 4122, 8273,

8274; schedule satisfaction, 2660; school conflicts, 7568; self-efficacy, 6908; sex-role conflict, 4193; situational constraints, 6017; situation profile, 1974; skill, 338; social support, 5993; social value, 10002; spillover, 8307; strain, 6004; strategies, children's, 7144; stress, 4161, 4197, 8308; supervisor attitude toward problem workers, 4272; supervisor/subordinate relationship, 4028; tactics of influence, 4201; tedium, 2674; tension, 2667, 4162; tolerance in the workplace, 4795, 5104; trainee rating, 338; transitions, 8176, 8189; values, 1531, 1532, 2320, 2321, 2328, 3520, 3559, 3608, 7230, 7266, 9981, 9999, 10016, 10017; value, intrinsic and extrinsic, 2316; value

orientation, 2307; withdrawal, 8296, 8298, 8299, 8309, workload, 4218, 4689
Worker('s): Marxist beliefs, 7233, 7234; needs of, 6049; older, bias, 8437; perception of appraisal interview, 2036; perception of supervisors, 2036; preference, 3401; pride, 5928; traits, 339
Working: addiction to, 6039–6041, 8376, 9205, 9669; alliance, 10127, 10128; attitude, 2730; class affinity, 2265; conditions, 663, 667, 3097; mother, 655, 2705
World minded, 1201, 6118, 9955
World view, 4950, 4985, 5255, 6183, 7254
Worry, 7192, 7569, 7782, 7896: adolescent students, 7566; domains, 7894, 7895;

emotionality, 1694, 2523, precompetitive, 7862
Writing: affective dimension, 3750, 5027; apprehension, 2431, 3707, 7570, 7571; attitude toward, 4343, 6173, 6184, 6185, 7116; outcome expectations, 8488; performance predictors, 4223; self-concept, 9300; self-efficacy, 9579, 9676; usefulness, 9508
Writing skills: basic, 364; behavioral objective, 341; cursive, 2375
Written composition, 370, 1059

Yielding, social, 1115
Youth, 531: attitude, 1201; attitude toward, 1141; vocational maturity, 1938

Zest, 7897; Zygosity, 1292

About the Editors

Bert A. Goldman, EdD, is a professor in the School of Education at the University of North Carolina at Greensboro. He has edited eight volumes of the *Directory of Unpublished Experimental Mental Measures* and has authored over 50 journal articles concerning a variety of educational and psychological topics. His latest research deals with factors in college student retention.

David F. Mitchell, PhD, is an assistant professor of sociology at the University of North Carolina at Greensboro. He is the author of several papers about attitudes toward fertility and child rearing, parent–child relationships, intraurban migration, and the empirical dimensions of ethnicity.